SEXUALITY TODAY

SEVENTH EDITION

SEXUALITY TODAY

The Human Perspective

Gary F. Kelly

Clarkson University

Boston Burr Ridge, IL Dubuque, IA Madison, WI New York San Francisco St. Louis
Bangkok Bogotá Caracas Lisbon London Madrid
Mexico City Milan New Delhi Seoul Singapore Sydney Taipei Toronto

McGraw-Hill Higher Education

*A Division of The **McGraw-Hill** Companies*

SEXUALITY TODAY: THE HUMAN PERSPECTIVE
SEVENTH EDITION

Published by McGraw-Hill, an imprint of The McGraw-Hill Companies, Inc., 1221 Avenue of the Americas, New York, NY 10020. Copyright © 2001, 1998, 1996 by The McGraw-Hill Companies, Inc. All rights reserved. No part of this publication may be reproduced or distributed in any form or by any means, or stored in a database or retrieval system, without the prior written consent of The McGraw-Hill Companies, Inc., including, but not limited to, in any network or other electronic storage or transmission, or broadcast for distance learning.

Some ancillaries, including electronic and print components, may not be available to customers outside the United States.

 This book is printed on recycled, acid-free paper containing 10% postconsumer waste.

1 2 3 4 5 6 7 8 9 0 QPD/QPD 0 9 8 7 6 5 4 3 2 1 0

ISBN   0-697-29431-5

Vice president and editor-in-chief: *Thalia Dorwick*
Editorial director: *Jane E. Vaicunas*
Senior sponsoring editor: *Rebecca H. Hope*
Senior developmental editor: *Sharon Geary*
Marketing manager: *Chris Hall*
Project managers: *Jill R. Peter/Jayne Klein*
Lead media producer: *David Edwards*
Production supervisor: *Laura Fuller*
Designer: *K. Wayne Harms*
Cover/interior designer: *Kristyn A. Kalnes*
Cover illustration: *The Stock Illustration Source/Noma*
Senior photo research coordinator: *Lori Hancock*
Photo research: *Mary Reeg Photo Research*
Supplement coordinator: *Jodi K. Banowetz*
Compositor: *GTS Graphics, Inc.*
Typeface: *10/12 Garamond Light*
Printer: *Quebecor Printing Book Group/Dubuque, IA*

The credits section for this book begins on page 599 and is considered an extension of the copyright page.

Library of Congress Cataloging-in-Publication Data

Kelly, Gary F.
    Sexuality today : the human perspective / Gary F. Kelly. — 7th ed.
        p.   cm.
    Includes bibliographical references and index.
    ISBN 0-697-29431-5
    1. Sex.   2. Sex instruction.   3. Hygiene, Sexual.   4. Sex customs—United States.
I. Title.

HQ21 .K259   2001
    306.7—dc21   00-036430
                                                                CIP

For my family—Betsy, Casey, and Chelsea—my companions in learning about life and love. There is nothing more wonderful in my life than being with each of you.

Gary F. Kelly has been a sexuality educator for 30 years. He is currently Vice President for Student Affairs at Clarkson University, where he also teaches the sexuality section of Personal Wellness course and the undergraduate psychology course in human sexuality. He is also headmaster of the Clarkson School, a special division of the University for talented high school students. He serves as chair of the Honors Council that oversees Clarkson's Honors Program. Kelly is an adjunct faculty member in the counseling and human development program at St. Lawrence University, where he teaches graduate courses in human sexuality and transpersonal counseling. He formerly maintained a practice as a counselor and sex therapist. As a person who strongly believes that young people must have solid basic information about sex and their own sexuality to make rational and responsible decisions, Kelly presents here a balanced approach to the physical as well as the psychological and sociological aspects of human sexuality. His work with students received national recognition with his election to the board of directors of the Sexuality Information and Education Council of the United States (SIECUS). Kelly served for 8 years as the editor of the *Journal of Sex Education and Therapy* and is presently a consulting editor with that journal. Kelly is a member of the American Association of Sex Educators, Counselors, and Therapists and of the Society for the Scientific Study of Human Sexuality. He is also a diplomate of the American Board of Sexology and a clinical fellow of the American Academy of Clinical Sexologists. He believes that

his work with individuals in counseling and therapy over the years has enlarged his personal and professional perspective on how people integrate their sexuality into their lives. The case studies in the book reflect that perspective.

Brief Contents

Contents

Chapter 4   Human Sexual Response   92

Chapter 5   Developmental and Social
Perspectives on Gender   115

PART 2

**Understanding Sexuality in
Ourselves and Our
Relationships   154**

Chapter 6   Sexuality through the Life
Cycle   156

PART 5

Dealing with Sexual Problems   446

Chapter 15 Sexual Coercion, Rape, and Abuse   448

Chapter 16 Sexually Transmitted Diseases   482

Preface

Approach of the Text

Robert C. Solomon in *Love, Emotion, Myth, and Metaphor* states that "Love can be understood only 'from the inside,' as a language can be understood only by someone who speaks it, as a world can be understood only by someone who lives in it." I have spent a great deal of time working to understand the nature of my own sexuality and its place in my life. Although my sexual values have shifted and changed through the years, the core of them has remained stable and forms the basis of my goals for this book.

- Sexual natures are essentially healthy and good. Decisions, however, about sexual behaviors must be made with careful thought because the potential for negative consequences also exists.
- Each individual must spend time understanding the place and importance of sexuality in his or her life.
- Each of us has a responsibility to show concern for other people who come into our lives in a romantic or sexual encounter. Sex ceases to become healthy and positive when it is exploitative or hurtful.
- People differ greatly in their sexual and gender orientations and behaviors, and it is important for all persons to find the sexual lifestyles that will yield the most happiness, satisfaction, peacefulness, and fulfillment for them.

The Field of Human Sexuality

The field of human sexuality is filled with controversy, even among the sexologists who conduct research, construct models, and develop theories. Scientific findings are not always comfortably aligned with prevailing social opinion. I believe that it is the job of a textbook author to document the various primary avenues of thought as accurately as possible, and I have attempted to stay true to that aim with each revision of the text. With each revision, I carefully weigh and consider the prevailing evidence on issues of sexuality and try to do justice to those issues as much as possible. Although some disagree, I do not feel it is my task to shape the attitudes and belief systems of others beyond what our cultural imperatives demand. It is, I believe, to enlighten with as much open-mindedness, honesty, and accuracy as possible. The controversies surrounding sexuality intrigue and fascinate me. For readers of this text, they should become the fodder for discussion, debate, and self-appraisal. As I can surely testify, it is all right to change your mind after having weighed all of the evidence on an issue conscientiously.

As with each revision, I am continually reminded of the growth of the field of sexuality both in terms of acceptability and scholarly focus in the past 25 years, attracting more and more outstanding young academics to its ranks. As I have watched sexology grow and develop over my career, it is especially exciting to be able to document the progress we are constantly making toward understanding the nuances of sexual physiology, psychology, and relational interaction. It is gratifying to have increasing numbers of students inquire about how they might enter sexology as a profession. I am also very pleased with the positive reactions I have had to past and current editions of the text from both faculty members and students. Their feedback and good suggestions help form the new template for each edition.

Goals of the Text

The charge of the seventh edition was to reinforce and strengthen the three underlying goals that have been in place throughout all editions. Those goals are to provide a text that is:

- informative and as up-to-date as possible
- readable, engaging, and interesting for the reader
- colorful, with a relevant illustration and photo program that is scientifically accurate

Improvements to the text in this edition are outlined in detail below. I am grateful to all those instructors and students who have provided feedback on their experiences using *Sexuality Today* because their comments serve as the cornerstone for this revision.

Overview of Key Changes in the Seventh Edition

- The text design has been completely revamped and is now presented in a new four-color format featuring full-color illustrations and photos that provide a more visually attractive text.
- Chapter 1 has been revised to reflect current media trends and the ever-changing general attitudes toward human sexuality.

- Chapter 2 has been split into two separate chapters (chapters 2 and 3) dividing the coverage of male and female sexual anatomy and physiology. Information on sexual disorders, formerly later in the text, has been moved up and incorporated within chapters 2 and 3 where appropriate.
- New information focusing on the fast growing relationship of media, especially the Internet, to human sexuality has been incorporated throughout the text.
- Material on same-gender sexual orientation and behavior has been integrated throughout key chapters of the text. Chapter 12 also includes focuses on special issues of sexual identity and same-gender orientation.
- The emphasis on cross-cultural coverage and examples in this edition continues to help promote understanding of the crucial role that cultural context plays in establishing attitudes and values related to human sexuality.
- Over 650 new references, providing the most up-to-date facts and research available from 1998 to 2000 are included in the seventh edition. Many older references have been deleted as a result.
- The Appendix has been thoroughly updated and placed on the text's Online Learning Center website where students can find hotlinks directly connecting them to relevant human sexuality organizations and agencies.
- A new separate Study Guide has been developed specifically to support Sexually Speaking and provides extensive study tools and activities for students.

Chapter-by-Chapter Changes in the Seventh Edition

■ Chapter 1: Historical, Research, and Cross-Cultural Perspectives on Sexuality

- The chapter has been reorganized to capture student interest early: a new section titled "The Influences of Culture on Sexuality" follows a completely revised introduction to the chapter that emphasizes popular media, the Internet, and recent political scandals.
- New photo of students viewing sex-related material online.
- Cross-cultural material therefore now leads off the content.
- The material then returns to Western cultures, and this is followed by information on how sexual attitudes continue to shift.
- The historical survey of sex research has been shortened, and "The Methods of Sexological Research" comes just before the Self-Evaluation.

- Eurocentric is a new glossary term.
- Newest perspectives on the nature-nurture debate as it relates to human sexuality.
- Updated information on increasing acceptance of same-gender sexual orientations.
- Nineteenth-century researchers have been condensed into a single subhead category.
- New section: "Sex Research in the New Millennium."
- Former boxed topic relating to explaining gender discrepancies in sex surveys has been incorporated into body of text.
- Table 1.1 has been updated with recent research trends.

■ Chapter 2: Female Sexual Anatomy and Physiology

- Chapters 2 and 3 were formerly a single chapter, and they have been reformed into two separate chapters following the suggestions of some reviewers.
- Anatomical illustrations have been changed to four-color.
- Disorders of female sex organs (moved from former chapter 15).
- Information on uterine cancer and other disorders (from former chapter 15).
- New table on breast cancer statistics that clarifies common misconceptions.
- New illustration on celebration of girl's first period in another culture.
- Material on polycystic ovary syndrome (PCOS), and a new glossary term.
- Material on premenstrual dysphoric disorder (PMDD), and a new glossary term.
- Material on perimenopause, which is also a new glossary term.
- Newest (2000) findings on risks of hormone replacement therapy.
- New Self-Evaluation ("You and Your Body"), formerly in chapter 1.

■ Chapter 3: Male Sexual Anatomy and Physiology

- Material on disorders of the testes (formerly in chapter 15)
- Material on disorders of the penis (formerly in chapter 15)
- Material on prostate problems.
- Anatomical illustrations now four-color.
- New box ("Penis Envy") that discusses penis size.
- New illustration on the cellular biochemistry of erection.
- New illustration of prostate surgical technique called transurethral needle ablation.
- New box on "manopause," or the male climacteric.

■ Chapter 4: Human Sexual Response

- Illustrations on sexual response converted to four-color.
- New illustrations of people being attracted to one another.
- Newest findings in sexual arousal theory.

■ Chapter 5: Developmental and Social Perspectives on Gender

- New illustration on progress within feminism.
- New box on transgenders.
- New material on the "Multifactorial Web" theory (Maccoby, 1998) of gender role development.
- Section on "Growing Up Female and Male" has been shortened and made more concise.
- New graphs on increase of women in law profession and owning their own businesses.
- New table on information from poll questionnaires: "Do You Consider Yourself a Feminist?"

■ Chapter 6: Sexuality through the Life Cycle

- Several new four-color photographs to illustrate various stages of the life cycle.
- Corrections in Table 6.1: Adulthood had been mistakenly omitted from Erikson's developmental stages.
- New information, graphs, and tables on "Normative Sexual Behavior in Children," taken from most recent research in *Pediatrics*. This is the best new information on childhood sexual behavior that has become available in years.
- The Cross-Cultural Perspective ("Adolescent Sexual Attitudes and Behaviors across Cultures") has been updated with new studies.
- Cites newest studies and shows graphics relating to decline in teen pregnancies, births, and abortions, showing their relation to more effective use of birth control.
- New box ("Playing the Mating Game") relating to women's attractions to male facial types.
- New box ("The Emerging Twenty-First Century American Family") with statistics from General Social Survey.

■ Chapter 7: Sexual Individuality and Sexual Values

- Table of Time/CNN 1998 poll results on attitudes toward gays and lesbians.
- New study data regarding homophobia and its effects on others.
- New Cross-Cultural Perspective: "Where There Is No Village: Teaching about Sexuality in Crisis Situations."
- Much new material on cultural diversity and sexuality education.

■ Chapter 8: Sexuality, Communication, and Relationships

- Study results on whether "nice guys finish last" in the sexual arena.
- Study on the value of using playful terms to name the genitals.
- Recent findings that bolster our knowledge concerning communication differences between women and men.
- New (1999) questionnaire to test how well the reader knows his/her partner.
- Newest research on relationships from psychologist John Gottman.
- New section on "Relating Via the Internet," including terms such as "computer-mediated communication" (CMC) and "computer-enhanced relating" (CMR).
- New photographs on relationships, including depicting computer-mediated communication.

■ Chapter 9: Reproduction, Reproductive Technology, and Birthing

- Up-to-date research information on reproductive technologies.
- Reference to first 50 years of the new millennium as the "decades of conception."
- Completion of human genome map by 2003.
- Concept of preimplantation genetic diagnosis (PGD).
- Newest information on increased likelihood of congenital abnormalities resulting from reproductive technologies.
- New summary figure of available reproductive technologies.
- New figure on sperm selection for X and Y chromosomes.
- New box on "Buying Genes"—advertising to buy ova from college women.
- Latest information on accelerated aging in mammalian clones.
- Color plates on fetal development and birth integrated into text.
- New case study: A personal perspective on pregnancy and birth.
- New section on postpartum care: postpartum depression, breast-feeding, relational adjustments.

■ Chapter 10: Decision Making about Pregnancy and Parenthood

- New graphs on world population growth.
- Updated table of contraceptive methods.
- Newest information on the leveling off of world population.

- New box on couples choosing to remain childless as a lifestyle.
- Recent information on emergency contraceptive methods and their effectiveness.
- Updated Cross-Cultural Perspective box on "Abortion around the World."

Chapter 11: Solitary Sex and Shared Sex

- New illustrations of two men and two women engaged in sexual intimacy.

Chapter 12: Same-Gender Orientation and Behavior

- New section on religious views of same-gender sexual orientation.
- New box: "Out, Proud, and Very Young."
- New box: "Two Fathers."
- Recent information about Vermont and "gay marriage."

Chapter 13: The Spectrum of Human Sexual Behavior

- Consistent use of the term "transgender" (rather than "cross-gender").
- New box: "Transgendered Scholars."
- Section on adult Internet chat lines.

Chapter 14: Sex, Art, the Media, and the Law

- Controversy over art works at Brooklyn Museum of Art.
- Reference in text to newest books and films relating to sexuality.

Chapter 15: Sexual Coercion, Rape, and Abuse

- New box showing Time/CNN poll information on sexual harassment.
- Further information about the lack of support for "sex addiction."
- New research on effects of child sexual abuse.
- New research on characteristics of sexual abusers.
- New box about the complicated matter of sexual consent.
- Newest findings regarding recovered/false memories and their value in therapy.

Chapter 16: Sexually Transmitted Diseases

- Increased use of term "sexually transmitted infections" (STI), as we make a gradual transition to this newer terminology.
- New organization of chapter into nonviral STIs and viral STIs.

- Inclusion of hepatitis C virus (HCV).
- New box on hepatitis B vaccination.

Chapter 17: The HIV/AIDS Crisis and Sexual Decisions

- Newest statistics on worldwide incidence of HIV/AIDS.
- Newest statistics on how HIV is transmitted in various regions of the world.
- Updated Cross-Cultural Perspective box: "The Global View of AIDS."
- Most recent research findings on treatment for HIV disease and HIV vaccines.

Chapter 18: Sexual Dysfunctions and Their Treatment

- Growing controversy about medicalization of treatment of sexual dysfunctions.
- Viagra: Its uses and misuses.
- New box: "Is Sex a Necessity?"
- New section on "Biomedical Engineering Devices" (for treating erectile dysfunction).
- Updated Cross-Cultural Perspective box on "Sexual Dysfunctions in Other Cultures."

A Walk Through of the Seventh Edition

Now I would like to walk you through each of the student-oriented features of the text. Each feature was selected and revised based upon feedback from instructors and students who provided key insights into their needs in both teaching and studying human sexuality.

Chapter Outline: Each chapter begins with a brief outline of its major headings to provide students with a preview of the topics covered. Students may use the Chapter Outline along with the Chapter Summary to review the chapter content more effectively.

Relevant Quotations: Each chapter also begins with a brief quotation, some of which come directly from my own counseling sessions or classes. These are carefully selected statements, opinions, and ideas intended to give students a personalized perspective on some major concept discussed in the chapter.

Case Studies: These studies illustrate in some detail a sexual problem or dilemma related to the issues of the chapter. For the most part, I have drawn these anecdotes from my own experience as a sexuality educator and sex therapist. A few have been provided by other professionals. Readers are cautioned not to draw any generalized conclusions from the case studies because they are statements about specific persons rather than about research studies on groups of people. There is at least one case study in every chapter.

Text Boxes: Each chapter contains at least one boxed feature containing material intended to give students a broad humanitarian perspective on some of the concepts being discussed. These boxes differ from case studies in that they are excerpts from various professional sexological sources or from current magazine and newspaper articles. **Cross-Cultural Perspective** boxes provide additional coverage to students and reflect sexual attitudes and behaviors that in most instances are different from the reader's.

Visual Art Program: All the photos, illustrations, tables, and graphs have all benefited from the new four-color design in this edition. Figures were selected to clarify and extend the material in the text. Charts, graphs, and tables reflect the most recent research available. Many new illustrations and four-color photos have been added to this edition. All photographs and drawings were chosen to illustrate the concepts of human sexuality in a practical yet sensitive manner.

Critical Thinking Questions: Placed strategically throughout the text, these questions can help students look more deeply at the issues, tapping their intellectual and analytical skills challenge themselves more effectively.

Self-Evaluation: Sexuality is not a topic to be considered apart from the self or separate from the nuances of human relationships. In fact, I believe that we should take the time to understand our own sexuality and its place in our personality. To this end, I have included, in selected chapters, questionnaires, self-awareness exercises, and values clarification devices, under the heading of "Self-Evaluation." By completing these activities, students may discover some things they did not know about themselves and sexuality.

Focus on Health: This feature appears at the end of each chapter and provides a list of questions pertaining to a student's personal health. Page numbers are provided for each question, and within each chapter the Focus on Health icon **FOH** appears next to each related section in the text.

Glossary: Important terms and concepts appear in boldface within the text and are set apart in a shaded area on the page where they occur for quick and easy reference. Other important terms and concepts are italicized within the text. A pronunciation guide is included in the glossary for those terms that are difficult for most students. The accent is indicated in capital letters. A complete alphabetized glossary appears at the end of the book.

Chapter Summary: Each chapter ends with a Chapter Summary, which highlights the main ideas of each chapter, and it has been expanded in this edition. As a study aid, students may coordinate the summary with the Chapter Outline at the beginning of the chapter in order to review the material effectively.

Annotated Readings: A select group of readings appears at the end of each chapter, and except for a few classic works that are cited, most of the books listed are very recent. I have briefly indicated the type of material and the approach of each book so that students can assess its usefulness. This is an excellent resource for those students seeking more information on a given topic.

Interactive Appendix: An additional resource for those students who might need to seek help for a specific problem or who want additional information on a given topic is the online Appendix. I have included, on the text's website, a list of national and international organizations and agencies, with addresses, telephone numbers, e-mail addresses, and website addresses, as available. Students can go to the text's Online Learning Center at www.mhhe.com/kelly7 and access information and hotlinks to key organizations related to his or her interests or needs. Students should also note that numerous state agencies exist that can give them information or help them with a problem. These would be too numerous to include here. A list of journals that relate to human sexuality issues is also included in the Appendix.

A Word about Accuracy and Research

One of my major concerns has been to document sex-related controversies as objectively as possible. When I served as editor of the *Journal of Sex Education and Therapy*, I often found it disconcerting to note how many authors cited statements from other authors as fact, when they were only hypotheses or generalizations based on limited personal observations, and I have taken this into account in preparing this text. It seems that there is controversy surrounding every sex-related issue. Ideas such as the biological essentialist versus the social constructionist views on gender identity and sexual orientation, the various points of view about human cloning, the differences and similarities between genders, and the issue of sexuality explicit materials on the Internet are examples of topics for which there is really not enough empirical evidence now to justify definitive conclusions. This edition contains information from 650 new references, providing the most up-to-date facts and research studies available.

Throughout the book, I have followed the American Psychological Association style, so that authors are cited and enclosed within parentheses; you will find full bibliographical details in the reference list. I have also attempted to follow the guidelines established by the Committee on Lesbian and Gay Concerns of the American Psychological Association in discussing issues relating to sexual orientation. Some readers will surely take exception to what they perceive to be another attempt at political correctness. I firmly believe that when it comes to the use of words describing various groups of people, all of us has a responsibility to choose terms that have been reasonably determined by members of those groups to be fair and nonoffensive.

I would welcome comments or suggestions for future editions from readers. I like to make contact with those who have connected with my words. If the spirit moves you, let me hear from you.

Supplements

The supplements listed here may accompany Kelly, *Sexuality Today*, Seventh Edition. Please contact your local McGraw-Hill representative for details concerning policies, prices, and availability as some restrictions may apply.

For the Instructor

Instructor's Manual/Printed Test Bank

By Christopher Ousley, North Carolina State University

New chapter features in this comprehensively revised Instructor's Manual include classroom activities, demonstrations, and the new Total Teaching Reference Package. Building on a traditional chapter outline, all the MGH resources available to the instructor have been correlated to the main concepts in each chapter. Suggested activities take particular account of class size and offer a useful time line estimate for completion. The final section offers tips on study skills, how to use the Internet in teaching, and a list of transparencies. In addition, the thoroughly expanded and revised Test Bank includes a wide range of multiple-choice, fill-in-the-blank, and critical thinking questions, as well as five short essay questions per chapter. Each item is designated as factual, conceptual, and applied as defined by Benjamin Bloom's Taxonomy of Educational Objectives. (0-07-289100-9)

Computerized Test Bank

By Christopher Ousley, North Carolina State University

This computerized Test Bank contains all of the questions in the print version and is available in both Macintosh and Windows platform. (W 0-07-289101-7, Mac 0-07-289102-5)

PowerPoint™ Lecture

Available on the Internet, these presentations cover the key points of the chapter and include charts and graphs from the text where relevant. They can be used as-is or modified to meet your personal needs. www.mhhe.com/kelly7

Sexuality Drop-In Center Supersite

The Human Sexuality Drop-In Center provides a super-structure for all of the McGraw-Hill human sexuality book sites. It acts as a place where faculty and students can access a multitude of resources to support our human sexuality titles. In addition to book-specific resources, an Activity Center contains interesting online activities and exercises, a counseling room provides links to the popular Go Ask Alice site as well as many other counseling sites, and a resource room provides still more links to useful sexuality-related resources. Visit us at www.mhhe.com/sexuality

On-Line Learning Center

This collection of student and instructor resources contains a wealth of additional materials. The password-protected instructor side of the site contains the Instructor's Manual, PowerPoint presentations, and other teaching resources. Visit us at www.mhhe.com/kelly7

PageOut—Build Your Own Course Website in Less than an Hour

You don't have to be a computer whiz to create a website. Especially with an exclusive McGraw-Hill product called **PageOut**™. It requires no prior knowledge of HTML. No long hours of coding. And no design skills on your part. www.pageout.net

The McGraw-Hill Human Sexuality Psychology Image Database, Overhead Transparencies, and CD-ROM

This set of over 160 images was developed using the best selection of our human sexuality art and tables and is available in both a print overhead transparency set as well as in a CD-ROM format with a fully functioning editing feature. Instructors can add their own lecture notes to the CD-ROM as well as organize the images to correspond to their particular classroom needs.

The AIDS Booklet

By Frank D. Cox of Santa Barbara City College

The new edition of this brief text provides a comprehensive introduction to acquired immune deficiency syndrome, which is caused by HIV (human immunodeficiency virus) and related viruses.

Annual Editions—Human Sexuality

Published by Dushkin/McGraw-Hill, this is a collection of articles on topics related to the latest research and thinking in human sexuality from over 300 public press sources. These editions are updated annually and contain helpful features including a topic guide, an annotated table of contents, unit overviews, and a topical index. An Instructor's Guide containing testing materials is also available.

Sources: Notable Selections in Human Sexuality

This is a collection of articles, books excerpts, and research studies that have shaped the study of human sexuality and our contemporary understanding of it. The selections are organized topically around major areas of study within human sexuality. Each selection is preceded by a headnote that establishes the relevance of the article or study and provides biographical information on the author.

Taking Sides: Clashing Views on Controversial Issues in Human Sexuality

This is a debate-style reader designed to introduce students to controversial viewpoints on the field's most crucial issues. Each issue is carefully framed for the student, and the pro and con essays represent the arguments of leading scholars and commentators in their fields. Instructor's Guide containing testing materials is also available.

For the Student

Student Study Guide

By Bruce D. LeBlanc, Black Hawk College

This completely new Student Study Guide features all the basics: learning objectives, key terms with definitions, self-tests, and a guided review and study. Additionally, it includes an innovative annotated outline similar to that mentioned in the Instructor's Manual. This will offer the traditional benefits of a chapter outline yet has been correlated to all the resources that McGraw-Hill makes available to the student. The Preface will offer very useful study tips including how to use the Internet effectively. (0-07-240172-9)

Making the Grade Student CD-ROM

Packaged for **FREE,** this user-friendly CD-ROM gives students an opportunity to test their comprehension of the course material in a manner that is most comfortable and beneficial to them. The CD-ROM contains with a Learning Style/Study Skills questionnaire that the student can complete to help them identify how they best study. Also included are practice tests that cover topics in the Human Sexuality course, as well as an Internet primer. (0-07-241261-5)

Online Learning Center Website

The official website for the text contains chapter outlines, practice quizzes that can be e-mailed to the professor, links to relevant Internet sites, Internet primer, career appendix, and a statistics primer. www.mhhe.com/kelly7

Sexuality Drop-In Center Supersite

The Human Sexuality Drop-In Center provides a superstructure for all of the McGraw-Hill human sexuality book sites. It acts as a place where faculty and students can access a multitude of resources to support our human sexuality titles. In addition to book-specific resources, an Activity Center contains interesting online activities and exercises, a counseling room provides links to the popular Go Ask Alice site as well as many other counseling sites, and a resource room provides still more links to useful sexuality-related resources. Visit us at www.mhhe.com/sexuality

Student and Instructor Supplements Users—We Want to Hear from You!

If you are currently using a McGraw-Hill supplement, we'd like to hear from you. In an effort to improve the quality of future supplements, we in psychology invite you to visit our text website and complete an evaluation form. This completed form will be e-mailed directly to the editors and will be considered as we develop future supplements for human sexuality. The form can be found at www.mhhe.com/sexuality

Acknowledgments

More people than I can properly recall have given me encouragement and suggestions for writing this book and revising it through its various editions. A number of them have offered specific help toward its improvement. These professionals and colleagues deserve thanks and acknowledgment. Before I began to write an earlier version, helpful suggestions were given to me by Mary S. Calderone, founder and former president of the Sexuality Information and Education Council of the United States (SIECUS); Michael Carrera, then at Hunter College, CUNY; and Patricia Schiller, founder of the American Association of Sex Educators, Counselors, and Therapists (AASECT).

I am greatly indebted to a number of my distinguished colleagues who gave their professional advice and helpful comments in reviewing the various editions of this book:

Connie C. Alexander, *Tarrant County Junior College-Northwest*
Janice and John Baldwin, *University of California, Santa Barbara*
C. Peter Bankart, *Wabash College*
Karen R. Blaisure, *Virginia Polytechnic Institute and State University*
Marilyn Blumenthal, *SUNY College of Technology at Farmingdale*
Sheila D. Brandick, *University of Regina*
Peggy Brick, *Planned Parenthood, Inc., of Bergen County*
Vern L. Bullough, *State University College of Buffalo*
T. Jean Byrne, *Kent State University*
Sandra L. Caron, *University of Maine, Orono*

Glenn Carter, *Austin Peay State University*
Carol Cassell, *Institute for Sexuality Education and Equity*
Caroline Clements, *University of North Carolina, Wilmington*
Edward E. Coates, *Judge Ely Family Healthcare*
William Collins, *West Virginia University*
Dennis Dailey, *University of Kentucky*
Donald R. Devers, *Northern Virginia Community College*
John P. Elia, *San Francisco State University*
Geri Falconer-Ferneau, *Arizona State University*
Gere B. Fulton, *The University of Toledo*
David A. Gershaw, *Arizona Western College*
Jane F. Gilgun, *University of Minnesota*
Cynthia Grace, *City College, CUNY*
Maylou Hacker, *Modesto Junior College*
Georgina Hammock, *Clarkson University*
Susan E. Hetherington, *University of Maryland*
Karen M. Hicks, *Lehigh University*
Janet I. Hirsch, *University of Rhode Island*
India Hosch, *Virginia Polytechnic and State University*
Bobby Hutchinson, *Modesto Community College*
Peter T. Knoepfler, *sex therapist in private practice*
Jennifer Krumm, *Chabot/Las Positas Community College*
Kelly Kyes, *Wake Forest University*
Molly Laflin, *Bowling Green State University*
Phillip Lau, *DeAnza College*
Bruce D. LeBlanc, *Black Hawk College*
Stuart Lisbe, *William Paterson College of New Jersey*
Teresa L. Mattson, *Keene State College*
Brian R. McNaught, *consultant to corporations and universities on the effects of homophobia; trainer, author*
Amy G. Miron, *Catonsville Community College*
Charles D. Miron, *Catonsville Community College*
Owen Morgan, *Arizona State University*
Lin Myers, *California State University, Stanislaus*
Marilyn Myerson, *University of South Florida*
Christopher Ousley, *North Carolina State University*
Nancy Parsons, *Western Illinois University*
Robert Pollack, *University of Georgia*
James Ponzetti, *Central Washington University*
Barry Poris, *Long Island University*
James H. Price, *University of Toledo*
Laurna Rubison, *University of Illinois*
Robin Sawyer, *University of Maryland*
Kay F. Schepp, *University of Vermont*
Sharon P. Shriver, *Penn State University*
Dick Skeen, *Northern Arizona University*
Stephen Southern, *The Sexual Medicine Institute of Southeast Louisiana*
Sherman Sowby, *California State University, Fresno*
Marilyn Story, *University of Northern Iowa*
Edward R. Sunshine, *Barry University*
Karen S. Tee, *Vanier College*
James E. Tucker, *Minneapolis, Minnesota*
Robert F. Valois, *University of Texas at Austin*
Paul Villas, *New Mexico State University, Main Campus*
Marti M. Weaver, *Collin County Community College, Central Park Campus*
Burton A. Weiss, *Drexel University*
Patricia Whelehan, *State University of New York, Potsdam*
Jan Widdell, *Auburn University*
Elva Winter, *York College*
William L. Yarber, *Indiana University*

My wife Betsy has been a constant source of good ideas for this text. She read each chapter and offered many suggestions for making the book more readable and interesting. My older daughter Casey efficiently coordinated the references for the sixth and seventh editions, and my younger daughter Chelsea has been learning the ropes for researching and cataloging references as well. Erin Mahoney and Chris Westcott, with the able help and supervision of my assistant Pat Thompson, entered many of the new references into the current edition.

I want to acknowledge the help of so many people within the McGraw-Hill staff who have played such an essential role in preparing the manuscript and producing the book. They include: Rebecca Hope, Senior Sponsoring Editor; Sharon Geary, Senior Developmental Editor; Jill Peter and Jayne Klein, Project Managers; Wayne Harms, designer; and Lori Hancock, Photo Research Coordinator. I would also like to thank Rita Lombard and Jodi Banowetz for their work developing the print supplements. I feel privileged to be able to keep this book available to students through the efforts of this highly motivated and professional group, and I thank them for the high quality that has been maintained in this new edition. I am also indebted to Christopher Ousley, Bruce Leblanc, Charles Verschoor, Laurie Mackensie, and Joy Wells who offered so much creative energy to the preparation of the Instructors Manual/Test Bank and the Student Study Guide.

Finally, I want to thank my clients and students for the unending learning experiences they provide for me. This willingness to share their lives and feelings is a continuing highlight of my life.

Gary F. Kelly
Clarkson University
Box 5635
Potsdam, NY 13699-5635
E-mail: Gary.Kelly@clarkson.edu

Student Walk Through

CHAPTER OUTLINE

Each chapter begins with a brief outline of its major headings, followed by a brief quotation.

CRITICAL THINKING QUESTIONS

These questions, placed strategically throughout the text, can help students look more deeply at the issues.

GLOSSARY

Important terms and concepts appear in boldface within the text and are set apart in a shaded area on the page where they occur for quick and easy reference.

Chapter 5
Developmental and Social Perspectives on Gender

Chapter Outline

How Many Sexes Are There?
Intersexuality
The Biological Levels of Sex
Gender Identity and Role

Sexual Differentiation
Prenatal Factors
What Abnormalities of Sexual Differentiation Can Tell Us
Hormones and Behavior
Factors of Infancy and Childhood
Factors at Puberty
Adult Gender Identity and Role

Interpretations of Gender
Models of Masculinity and Femininity
Lessons from Transgenderism
Gender as a Social Construction
Biological and Evolutionary Foundations of Gender Roles
Differences between Females and Males

Theories of Gender Role Development
Psychodynamic Perspectives
Social Learning Theory
Cognitive-Developmental Theory

Gender Schema Theory
Behavioral Genetics
Multifactorial "Web"

Gender in Society and Culture
Growing Up Female and Male
Gender in the Workplace
Feminism
The Men's Movement
Gender across Cultures
Gender Aware Therapy

Self-Evaluation
Masculinity and Femininity in Your Life

Chapter Summary

Note: A selection of Focus on Health questions appears at the end of each chapter. Answers to these questions are indicated within the chapter by the symbol in the margin. **F⊕H**

I consider myself to be a fairly sensitive guy, and I want to treat women with respect and a sense of equality, but I'm never sure what the rules are. Do I open doors for her, or should we take turns? Am I supposed to pay for dinner every time, or do we share the cost? Who is supposed to give the first signals about being interested in having sex?

—*Statement from a male student*

115

CASE STUDIES

These studies illustrate in some detail a sexual problem or dilemma related to the issues of the chapter.

---

116   Chapter 5   Developmental and Social Perspectives on Gender

Being a sexual human being amounts to far more than the sexual organs with which we were born and the ways in which these organs are activated by sexual arousal. There are many other dimensions of sexuality as it relates to individual people: Why is it that humans come in two sexes? Perhaps the question should be, are there really just two sexes? What factors influence the development of male and female genitals before birth? What leads to our awareness of ourselves as girl or boy, feminine or masculine, or some combination of the two? Are gender roles determined by biology, socialization, or a combination of the two? How does gender fit into contemporary social and political trends? These are some of the questions that we will explore in this chapter.

Do you think gender roles are inborn or learned? Explain your answer.

■ How Many Sexes Are There?

Our culture has generally only been willing to recognize two sexes: female and male. Those are the two categories from which we are allowed to choose when filling out most forms. Our legal systems also require that everyone be categorized as either male or female, and newborns must be identified on birth certificates as one or the other. But are things really that simple?

There are documented cases of individuals who have the physical characteristics of both the male and female. In sixteenth-century England, because succession of wealth and title often depended on an individual's gender, the courts decided that succession would be based on "the kind of sex that doth prevail," meaning which sex seemed dominant in the individual by the time of adulthood (Money, 1994). In 1843, an election for the town board of Salisbury, Connecticut, was tied, and its outcome hinged on the vote of a person named Levi Suydam, whom the local citizens considered to be more woman than man. Women were not allowed to vote, but a physician examined Suydam, found a penislike structure, and declared him a male. He was thus eligible to cast a ballot and helped elect a member of the Whig party by a single vote. However, word quickly spread that penis or not, Suydam also had a vaginal opening and menstruated regularly (Fausto-Sterling, 1993).

The concept of gender or sexes obviously has biological roots, but social constructionism holds that even biological facts become interpreted through the

screen of cultural assumptions. Thomas Laqueur (1992) argues, for example, that from the time of the ancient Greeks until the end of the seventeenth century, the Western cultural model was actually one-sexed; one sex was male, and the structures of the female anatomy were seen as inverted or underdeveloped forms of the male sex organs. In other words, "both" sexes were actually just different forms of a single sex, one more fully developed than the other. During the early eighteenth century, a clearer distinction began to emerge, recognizing female and male as two different sexes.

Intersexuality

On the larger anatomical level, some human beings do not fit the standardized male-female categories. Medical investigators have long recognized the existence of **intersexuality,** a term that refers to some mixture of male and female anatomical characteristics, often reflected in the presence of ambiguous genitalia. At least three major subgroups of intersexes exist: **true hermaphrodites,** who have one testis and one ovary; **male pseudohermaphrodites,** who have testes and some female genitals but no ovaries; and female pseudohermaphrodites, who have ovaries and some male genitals but no testes (Zucker, 2000).

If your child were born intersexed, what course of action would you consider?

In some historical periods, intersexuality was accepted as a "third sex," distinct from male and female. In many societies, alternative social statuses or gender roles are available for intersexed individuals. At least The American Plains Indians once assigned the social status of *berdache* to men who did not have the skill or interest for typically masculine, aggressive pursuits. The berdache was considered to hold special powers and sometimes served as a shaman for healing practices or in sacred ceremonies (Crapo, 1996). In India, a

intersexuality: a combination of female and male anatomical structures, so that the individual cannot be clearly defined as male or female.

true hermaphrodite: a person who has one testis and one ovary. External appearance may vary.

pseudohermaphrodite: a person who possesses either testes or ovaries in combination with some external genitals of the other sex.

---

146   Chapter 5   Developmental and Social Perspectives on Gender

CASE STUDY

Ricardo Expresses His Attitudes about "Male-Bashing"

During a discussion group following a lecture on male-female relationships on campus, Ricardo voiced his sentiments concerning what he had perceived as antimale attitudes from women. "Men today could never get away with the way some women are treating men, if the situation were reversed. I resent it that men are not supposed to say or do anything that might seem like a put-down to women, but women get away with male-bashing all the time. I don't like it when I see one of those shirts that says 'A woman without a man is like a fish without a bicycle.' I'm not saying that women are incomplete without men; it's just that things like that are deliberately mean. And when the Bobbitt woman cut off her husband's penis, a lot of women seemed to think it was just a big joke, instead of an act of violence and mutilation. Maybe she was justified to take action against him, but the result wasn't any more funny than violence toward women. I think it's time we tried to get our priorities straight."

Ricardo's remarks generated many comments and some

heated exchanges among the group members. Some of the women present said that men were only getting back what they had been dishing out for years and that they should not complain. Some women and men in the group felt Ricardo was overreacting and should try to lighten up and learn how to take a joke. Others—mostly males—agreed with his point of view and said they were tired of the building trend toward antimale messages. They emphasized that it was another example of bigotry based on stereotypes. Many men made a point of saying that they themselves did not treat women in negative or inappropriate ways and resented being lumped together with those who did.

The debate went on for nearly 2 hours and ended with little resolution between various factions that were represented. Ricardo left the group feeling at least that he had been able to express his opinions openly, and he hoped that some people who had heard them would try to be more sensitive to the issues that had been raised.

---

from being success objects, expected to provide status and security for their partners. Many male providers end up feeling powerless, meaningless, and isolated in their jobs; they work under constant fear and tension as they strive for promotion and success. Three main aspects of the traditional male role seem especially to make men uncomfortable: (1) the male as competent worker and provider; (2) the male as emotionally controlled stoic; and (3) the male as sexual aggressor and sexual educator of the female (Levant, 1996; Marsiglio, 1998).

There has been a growing men's movement in North America. Men's groups have sprung up around the country, and men are being encouraged to confront and share their feelings more openly. Many men feel able to celebrate their own masculinity in ways that would have once been considered unmanly (see Fig. 5.17). Having opportunities to talk about gender roles and reassess individual needs and goals continues to prove valuable for men in many different age groups (Good & Wood, 1995).

scapegoats for social constructs that they too were born into, and over which they have often felt little control. They do not feel that it is fair to brand all men as potential rapists or abusers; they instead insist that most men are decent individuals who want to treat women with respect and care (Kimmel, 1997). Many men have participated actively in the efforts to create a more gender-equitable and safe society for everyone.

What do you see as some of the positive and negative features of the men's movement? Explain.

Most men experience some turmoil and problems as they come to grips with what manhood will mean for them. Men must share in the constant struggle to learn how to communicate thoughts, feelings, and the degree of exclusivity they wish to maintain in relationships. Emerging out of what once seemed more like a battle between women and men has been a new spirit of cooperation. Members of both sexes have been calling for opportunities to communicate more openly,

xxii

140 Chapter 5 Developmental and Social Perspectives on Gender

FIGURE 5.12 *Changing Traditional Roles*
Both women and men may feel that the characteristics traditionally assigned to them by their society are biased and unfair. Some break away very publicly from the stereotypes. Laila Ali, youngest daughter of boxer Muhammad Ali, is shown here during the first round of her middleweight fight with opponent April Fowler. After receiving some prefight advice from her sister not to beat the other woman too badly in this traditionally male sport, Laila needed only 31 seconds to win the match.

Although some social psychologists once believed that we should work toward a gender-aschematic world, in which there would be no differentiation between male and female roles, this no longer seems as plausible or desirable as it once did to some. Instead, there is now more emphasis on the celebration of gender differences and increased understanding between the sexes (see Fig. 5.12).

Gender in Society and Culture

As a basic organizing principle of human culture, maleness and femaleness, femininity and masculinity, are central themes in all social structures. When viewed against a backdrop of variations in many aspects of human personality, gender differences may not be as dramatic or significant as we often seem to think. Nevertheless, they influence how people think, believe, and behave.

Growing Up Female and Male

The prevailing opinion in North America has been that social attitudes put females at a disadvantage in many different ways, and there is evidence to support this perception. One contention has been that our society permits a wider range of behaviors for girls, from the very frilly to the tomboy. For boys, neither the extreme of the sissy nor the too-aggressive bully is acceptable. This has been substantiated by studies indicating that among younger children, boys tend to see their gender roles and future occupational options much more narrowly than do girls (Sellers, Satcher, & Comas, 1999). For these reasons, parents and other adults are typically less disturbed by the behavior of girls than by that of boys. As a result, more demands are placed on boys to behave in the appropriate way. This may well result in boys being pressured to become more independent and self-controlled, and there are studies that show males' self-esteem arising from recognition of their individual distinguishing achievements (Major, Barr, Zubek, & Babey, 1999). Early in their lives, boys develop a sense of self-worth, relatively independent of others' responses. At the same time, female roles are devalued, and boys are criticized for stepping out of their role boundaries by being called "girls" or "sissies" in a derogatory way. As boys grow into adolescence and adulthood, they face harsher consequences for stepping outside the gender-appropriate roles established for them than do girls and women (Carlock, 1999).

Girls, on the other hand, are not as pressured to become independent and self-controlling, so they remain more dependent on others for physical comfort and a sense of self-worth, often experiencing no strong pressures until puberty. As children, girls are rewarded for their compliant good behavior by good grades, parental love, teacher acceptance, and acceptance into peer groups; this leaves them generally more passive and conformist. During adolescence, boys tend to turn their aggressions outward, whereas girls tend to turn these impulses inward, and often against themselves, resulting in lowered self-esteem (Burnett, Anderson, & Heppner, 1995).

Much of the groundwork for whatever gender discrepancies exist later in life is probably laid in the educational institutions that prepare young people for the future. Schools often seem to provide a different environment for girls than they do for boys. There is evidence that even among young children, boys interrupt teachers in their activities much more than do girls, whereas teachers tend to interrupt girls more than boys. Later on, girls in general, and especially black girls, receive significantly less attention from and interaction with their teachers than do boys. This manifests itself in the fact that in the early grades, girls tend

VISUAL ART PROGRAM

All the photos, illustrations, tables, and graphs have benefitted from the new four-color design in this edition.

FOCUS ON HEALTH

This feature appears at the end of each chapter and provides a list of questions pertaining to a student's personal health. Page numbers are provided for each question, and within each chapter the Focus on Health icon FOH appears next to each related section in the text.

128 Chapter 5 Developmental and Social Perspectives on Gender

Physical Changes during Puberty and Adolescence

FOH After the important differentiation of male or female genitals in the fetus, there is relatively little further physical differentiation between the sexes until puberty. Except for their genitals, the bodies of young girls and boys are quite similar. The pubertal hormones begin to generate the distinct physical characteristics of a man or a woman, called the **secondary sex characteristics.** Preliminary research has indicated that the hormonal influences of puberty may exert a clear effect on personalities, including some tendencies toward differences in females and males (Udry, 1990).

In boys, the onset of puberty is typically around the age of 13. The penis begins to enlarge, pubic hair starts to grow, and the growth spurt in height is initiated. The testes and scrotum have usually begun to enlarge about a year earlier. Eventually the voice becomes lower as the larynx grows, ejaculation of semen occurs, and pubic and body hair spread to some degree. A moustache and beard usually appear 3 to 5 years later. In girls, puberty typically begins around the age of 11 or 12. The first signs are usually the budding of the breasts, the growth of pubic hair, and the beginning of growth spurts. The first menstruation generally does not occur until after these initial signs have appeared.

Beginning at puberty, the sex glands of girls and boys actually produce the same hormones, with androgens such as testosterone being secreted in higher concentrations in males, and estrogen higher in females. In the normal male, the higher concentration of androgens and their resulting influences tend to override the effects of the estrogens. This effect is reversed in the normal female. Things can be temporarily disrupted with these hormone balances during puberty and adolescence, producing conditions such as slight breast enlargement in males (gynecomastia) or deepened voice and unusually enlarged clitoris in the female. The onset of hormonal puberty can sometimes be either premature or delayed. Any of these conditions can shake the stability of a young person's gender identity and lead to confusion and unhappiness (Slijper et al., 1994).

Changes in Sexual Drive and Behavior at Puberty

Of particular significance during puberty and adolescence is an increase in interest in sexual behavior. One of the important ways in which gender identity is confirmed during this period is through imagery and fantasy. Boys and girls begin to imagine sexual acts and fantasize about desirable romantic or sexual partners.

FIGURE 5.7 *Sex Drive in Adolescents*
Adolescents experience the sex drive in different degrees depending on physical as well as emotional factors. Their families, religious background, peers, and the media all influence how adolescents learn to deal with love and the sex drive.

Adolescents are sometimes upset to find themselves imagining or dreaming about sexual encounters with members of their own gender, sadistic behavior, or other behaviors they may have learned to consider "abnormal" or inconsistent with their assumed sexual orientation. Yet such fantasies may signal some of the final alterations that will be made in the achievement of an adult gender identity and sexual orientation.

Think back to when you went through puberty. Can you remember how you felt about yourself? The other gender? Explain.

There is great variation in the strength of sexual interest that develops during adolescence (see Fig. 5.7). Some youngsters experience frequent fantasies about sex and a strong drive that demands to be put

secondary sex characteristics: the physical characteristics of mature women and men that begin to develop at puberty.

TEXT BOXES

Each chapter contains at least one boxed feature containing material intended to give students a broad humanitarian perspective on some of the concepts being discussed. These boxes differ from Case Studies in that they are excerpts from various sexological sources or from current magazine and newspaper articles.

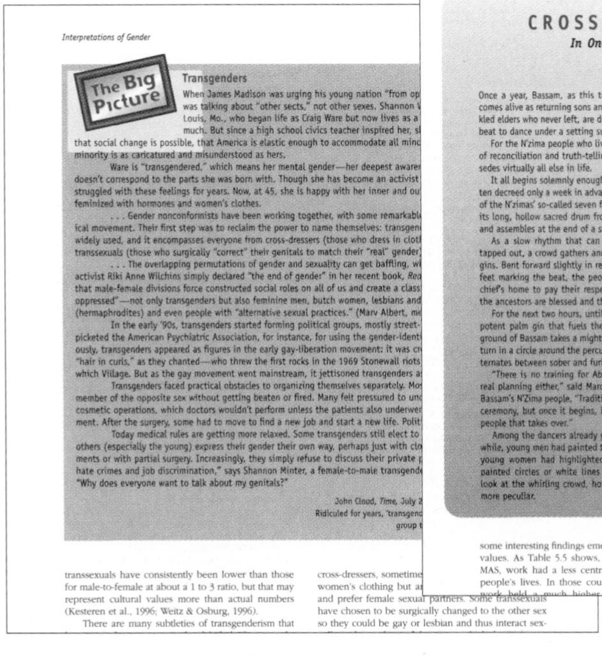

Interpretations of Gender

The Big Picture

Transgenders

When James Madison was urging his young nation "from op
was talking about "other sects," not other sexes. Shannon
Louis, Mo., who began life as Craig Ware but now lives as a
much. But since a high school civics teacher inspired her, s
that social change is possible, that America is elastic enough to accommodate all minc
minority is as caricatured and misunderstood as hers.

Ware is "transgendered," which means her mental gender—her deepest aware
doesn't correspond to the parts she was born with. Though she has become an activist
struggled with these feelings for years. Now, at 45, she is happy with her inner and ou
feminized with hormones and women's clothes.

. . . Gender nonconformists have been working together, with some remarkabl
ical movement. Their first step was to reclaim the power to name themselves: transgen
widely used, and it encompasses everyone from cross-dressers (those who dress in clot
transsexuals (those who surgically "correct" their genitals to match their "real" gender)

. . . The overlapping permutations of gender and sexuality can get baffling, w
activist Riki Anne Wilchins simply declared "the end of gender" in her recent book, *Rea*
that male-female divisions force constructed social roles on all of us and create a class
oppressed"—not only transgenders but also feminine men, butch women, lesbians and
(hermaphrodites) and even people with "alternative sexual practices." (Marv Albert, me

In the early '90s, transgenders started forming political groups, mostly street-
picketed the American Psychiatric Association, for instance, for using the gender-ident
ously, transgenders appeared as figures in the early gay-liberation movement: it was c
"hair in curls," as they chanted—who threw the first rocks in the 1969 Stonewall riots
which Village. But as the gay movement went mainstream, it jettisoned transgenders a

Transgenders faced practical obstacles to organizing themselves separately. Mo
member of the opposite sex without getting beaten or fired. Many felt pressured to un
cosmetic operations, which doctors wouldn't perform unless the patients also underwe
ment. After the surgery, some had to move to find a new job and start a new life. Polit

Today medical rules are getting more relaxed. Some transgenders still elect to
others (especially the young) express their gender their own way, perhaps just with clo
ments or with partial surgery. Increasingly, they simply refuse to discuss their private
hate crimes and job discrimination," says Shannon Minter, a female-to-male transgend
"Why does everyone want to talk about my genitals?"

John Cloud, *Time*, July
Ridiculed for years, 'transgen
group

transsexuals have consistently been lower than those for male-to-female at about a 1 to 3 ratio, but that may represent cultural values more than actual numbers (Kesteren et al., 1996; Weitz & Osburg, 1996).

There are many subtleties of transgenderism that

cross-dressers, sometime
women's clothing but a
and prefer female sexual partners. Some transsexuals
have chosen to be surgically changed to the other sex
so they could be gay or lesbian and thus interact sex-

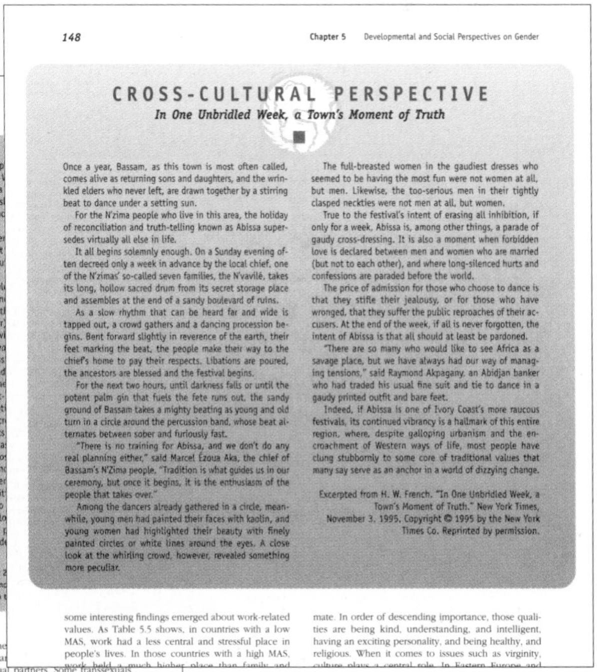

148 Chapter 5 Developmental and Social Perspectives on Gender

CROSS-CULTURAL PERSPECTIVE

In One Unbridled Week, a Town's Moment of Truth

Once a year, Bassam, as this town is most often called, comes alive as returning sons and daughters, and the wrinkled elders who never left, are drawn together by a stirring beat to dance under a setting sun.

For the N'zima people who live in this area, the holiday of reconciliation and truth-telling known as Abissa supersedes virtually all else in life.

It all begins solemnly enough. On a Sunday evening often decreed only a week in advance by the local chief, one of the N'zimas' so-called seven families, the N'vavilé, takes its long, hollow sacred drum from its secret storage place and assembles at the end of a sandy boulevard of ruins.

As a slow rhythm that can be heard far and wide is tapped out, a crowd gathers and a dancing procession begins. Bent forward slightly in reverence of the earth, their feet marking the beat, the people make their way to the chief's home to pay their respects. Libations are poured, the ancestors are blessed and the festival begins.

For the next two hours, until darkness falls or until the potent palm gin that fuels the fete runs out, the sandy ground of Bassam takes a mighty beating as young and old turn in a circle around the percussion band, whose beat alternates between sober and furiously fast.

"There is no training for Abissa, and we don't do any real planning either," said Marcel Ézoua Aka, the chief of Bassam's N'Zima people. "Tradition is what guides us in our ceremony, but once it begins, it is the enthusiasm of the people that takes over."

Among the dancers already gathered in a circle, meanwhile, young men had painted their faces with kaolin, and young women had highlighted their beauty with finely painted circles or white lines around the eyes. A close look at the whirling crowd, however, revealed something more peculiar.

The full-breasted women in the gaudiest dresses who seemed to be having the most fun were not women at all, but men. Likewise, the too-serious men in their tightly clasped neckties were not men at all, but women.

True to the festival's intent of erasing all inhibition, if only for a week, Abissa is, among other things, a parade of gaudy cross-dressing. It is also a moment when forbidden love is declared between men and women who are married (but not to each other), and where long-silenced hurts and confessions are paraded before the world.

The price of admission for those who choose to dance is that they stifle their jealousy, or for those who have wronged, that they suffer the public reproaches of their accusers. At the end of the week, if all is never forgotten, the intent of Abissa is that all should at least be pardoned.

"There are so many who would like to see Africa as a savage place, but we have always had our way of managing tensions," said Raymond Akpagany, an Abidjan banker who had traded his usual fine suit and tie to dance in a gaudy printed outfit and bare feet.

Indeed, if Abissa is one of Ivory Coast's more raucous festivals, its continued vibrancy is a hallmark of this entire region, where, despite galloping urbanism and the encroachment of Western ways of life, most people have clung stubbornly to some core of traditional values that many say serve as an anchor in a world of dizzying change.

Excerpted from H. W. French. "In One Unbridled Week, a Town's Moment of Truth." New York Times, November 3, 1995. Copyright © 1995 by the New York Times Co. Reprinted by permission.

some interesting findings emerged about work-related values. As Table 5.5 shows, in countries with a low MAS, work had a less central and stressful place in people's lives. In those countries with a high MAS,

mate. In order of descending importance, those qualities are being kind, understanding, and intelligent, having an exciting personality, and being healthy, and religious. When it comes to issues such as virginity,

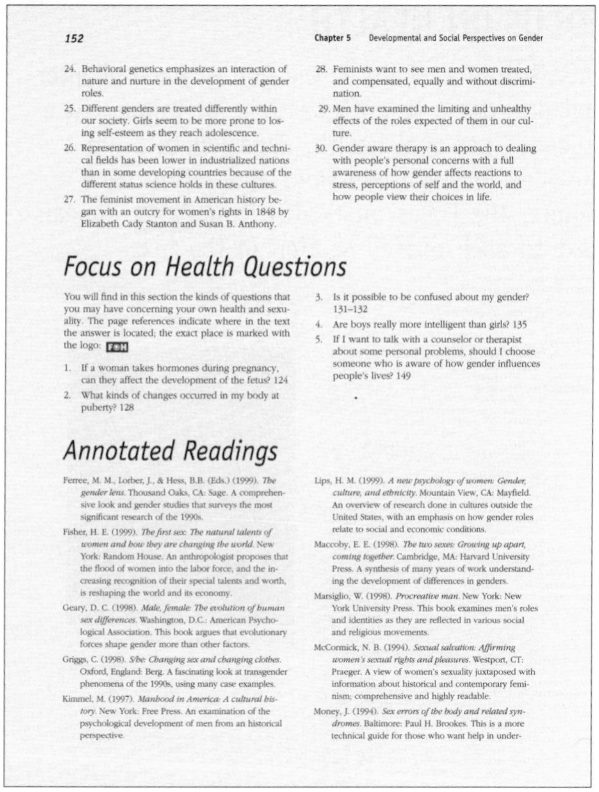

152 Chapter 5 Developmental and Social Perspectives on Gender

24. Behavioral genetics emphasizes an interaction of nature and nurture in the development of gender roles.
25. Different genders are treated differently within our society. Girls seem to be more prone to losing self-esteem as they reach adolescence.
26. Representation of women in scientific and technical fields has been lower in industrialized nations than in some developing countries because of the different status science holds in these cultures.
27. The feminist movement in American history began with an outcry for women's rights in 1848 by Elizabeth Cady Stanton and Susan B. Anthony.
28. Feminists want to see men and women treated, and compensated, equally and without discrimination.
29. Men have examined the limiting and unhealthy effects of the roles expected of them in our culture.
30. Gender aware therapy is an approach to dealing with people's personal concerns with a full awareness of how gender affects reactions to stress, perceptions of self and the world, and how people view their choices in life.

Focus on Health Questions

You will find in this section the kinds of questions that you may have concerning your own health and sexuality. The page references indicate where in the text the answer is located; the exact place is marked with the logo: F•H

1. If a woman takes hormones during pregnancy, can they affect the development of the fetus? 124
2. What kinds of changes occurred in my body at puberty? 128
3. Is it possible to be confused about my gender? 131–132
4. Are boys really more intelligent than girls? 135
5. If I want to talk with a counselor or therapist about some personal problems, should I choose someone who is aware of how gender influences people's lives? 149

Annotated Readings

Ferree, M. M., Lorber, J., & Hess, B.B. (Eds.) (1999). *The gender lens.* Thousand Oaks, CA: Sage. A comprehensive look and gender studies that surveys the most significant research of the 1990s.

Fisher, H. E. (1999). *The first sex: The natural talents of women and how they are changing the world.* New York: Random House. An anthropologist proposes that the flood of women into the labor force, and the increasing recognition of their special talents and worth, is reshaping the world and its economy.

Geary, D. C. (1998). *Male, female: The evolution of human sex differences.* Washington, D.C.: American Psychological Association. This book argues that evolutionary forces shape gender more than other factors.

Griggs, C. (1998). *S/he: Changing sex and changing clothes.* Oxford, England: Berg. A fascinating look at transgender phenomena of the 1990s, using many case examples.

Kimmel, M. (1997). *Manhood in America: A cultural history.* New York: Free Press. An examination of the psychological development of men from an historical perspective.

Lips, H. M. (1999). *A new psychology of women: Gender, culture, and ethnicity.* Mountain View, CA: Mayfield. An overview of research done in cultures outside the United States, with an emphasis on how gender roles relate to social and economic conditions.

Maccoby, E. E. (1998). *The two sexes: Growing up apart, coming together.* Cambridge, MA: Harvard University Press. A synthesis of many years of work understanding the development of differences in genders.

Marsiglio, W. (1998). *Procreative man.* New York: New York University Press. This book examines men's roles and identities as they are reflected in various social and religious movements.

McCormick, N. B. (1994). *Sexual salvation: Affirming women's sexual rights and pleasures.* Westport, CT: Praeger. A view of women's sexuality juxtaposed with information about historical and contemporary feminism; comprehensive and highly readable.

Money, J. (1994). *Sex errors of the body and related syndromes.* Baltimore: Paul H. Brookes. This is a more technical guide for those who want help in under-

ANNOTATED READINGS

A select group of recent readings appear at the end of each chapter.

CHAPTER SUMMARY

Each chapter ends with a Chapter Summary, which highlights the main ideas of each chapter.

Chapter Summary 151

Chapter Summary

1. Western culture emphasizes the existence of two sexes, while there are forms of intersexuality such as hermaphroditism or pseudohermaphroditism. In other cultures and times of history, intersexuality has been accepted.
2. There is continuing debate over the degree to which gender roles are shaped by biological and sociocultural forces.
3. Biological sex is expressed in genetics, the gonads, the body, and the brain.
4. The development of our gender identity and gender role is determined by a complex interaction of genetic, physiological, and sociocultural factors.
5. During prenatal life (before birth), the combining of chromosomes sets into motion a genetic program for producing a male, a female, or some ambivalent anatomical structure. Although the pairing of sex chromosomes is normally XX for females and XY for males, there can be abnormal combinations (for example, XXX, XXY, XYY) that produce unusual characteristics.
6. After about a month of embryonic development, an undifferentiated set of fetal gonads appears, along with Müllerian ducts (potential female organs) and Wolffian ducts (potential male organs).
7. If the Y chromosome is present, with its SRY gene, H-Y antigen is produced, transforming the gonads into testes, which in turn produce testosterone and anti-Müllerian hormone. They promote development of male organs from the Wolffian ducts and suppress further development of Müllerian ducts.
8. If the Y chromosome is absent, the fetal gonads become ovaries, and the Wolffian ducts disintegrate. The DAX-1 gene on the X chromosome may control a mechanism by which this gene inhibits the development of male genitals and promotes development of female structures.
9. Male and female genitals and inner reproductive structures then develop. The presence or absence of the male hormones affects development of the nervous system. These hormones have a masculinizing effect, while an independent process of defeminization is going on. The absence of androgens results in the processes of demasculinization and feminization.
10. Abnormal sexual differentiation patterns have offered us clues about the effects of hormones on fetal development and later behavior.
11. There may be a multiplier effect between biological and social factors that eventually leads to masculine and feminine behaviors.
12. During infancy and childhood, boys and girls are treated in particular ways, and social influences along with anatomy begin to help the child form a core gender identity.
13. At puberty, the testes or ovaries begin secreting male or female hormones, triggering the development of secondary sex characteristics. The first stage of puberty is adrenarche, and the second, more profound, stage is gonadarche. Sexual feelings and fantasies also become more pronounced.
14. Adult gender roles may be conceptualized by bipolar, orthogonal, and oblique models, each offering differing views of the relationship between femininity and masculinity.
15. People who exaggerate culturally accepted gender roles are called hypermasculine or hyperfeminine. Androgyny reflects high frequencies of both masculine and feminine traits in the same individual.
16. Transgenderism has often been interpreted as pathological and considered a gender identity disorder, but transgender individuals have been asking for increased recognition in their roles.
17. Transsexualism involves a distinct nonconformity of gender identity with physical attributes of sex. High-intensity transsexuals are more likely to desire surgical and hormonal sex reassignment.
18. Evolutionary psychologists believe that there may be biological bases for some broad categories of gender-related behaviors.
19. Masculinity and femininity are defined by the behaviors that are found in average men and women. There are some average differences between females and males in a few cognitive and motor functions.
20. There are several theoretical positions concerning gender role development. The psychodynamic approach involves complex unconscious interactions between children and their parents.
21. Social learning theory emphasizes socialization and the modeling of gender behaviors by children.
22. Cognitive-developmental theory emphasizes how human thought processes reinforce and perpetuate the gender roles learned from socialization.
23. Gender schema theory highlights the complex network of associations that people hold with regard to gender.

SELF-EVALUATIONS

Questionnaires, self-awareness exercises, and values clarification devices under the heading of "Self-Evaluation" are included in selected chapters.

150 Chapter 5 Developmental and Social Perspectives on Gender

Self-Evaluation

Masculinity and Femininity in Your Life

Attitudes toward masculinity and femininity are in a state of flux. Although some people are attempting to blur the stereotyped differences between men and women, others are trying harder than ever to establish definite, identifiable standards of masculinity and femininity. The exercises that follow may help you to clarify your present attitudes toward men and women and your view of your own gender role.

1. On a sheet of paper, list two men, by name, who for you exemplify ideal manhood; list two women, by name, who for you exemplify ideal womanhood. Then proceed with the following:
   a. Under the men's names and under the women's names, list the characteristics of these people that have made them your choices as representative of the ideal.
   b. Note which of the characteristics, if any, are listed for both the men and women.
   c. Check those characteristics from either list that you believe you exhibit.

2. Would you ever consider dressing up in clothing generally identified as being appropriate for members of the opposite sex? If not, why not? If so, consider the following:
   a. Under what circumstances would you wear clothing of the opposite sex? Only in private? In front of one other highly trusted person? In front of a small group of friends? At a masquerade party? In public places?
   b. If possible and if you are willing, go ahead and dress up in some clothes of the opposite sex, and look yourself over in a full-length mirror. (Note: In some areas, it is illegal to cross-dress and be seen in public.) As you look at yourself, how do you feel? Silly? Sexy? Curious? Happy? Sad? Why do you feel that way?

3. Examine the following list of qualities and check those that you feel are most important for you to have as a person. (Add other words of your own if you wish.)

honest	physically strong	responsible
brave		emotional
athletic	dominating	persuasive
caring	delicate	protective
competitive	intelligent	shy
gentle	successful	reliable
sensitive	submissive	flighty
aggressive	manipulative	sincere
considerate	thoughtful	sexy
	confident	

   a. Now read through the list of qualities again and pick out those that have been traditionally considered masculine and those traditionally considered feminine. Make two separate lists on a sheet of paper. Some words may appear on both lists or on neither. Include any words you have added to the list.
   b. Finally, note where the qualities you checked for yourself fall in your two lists. Think about them. This should help to show how your goals for your own femininity or masculinity relate to traditional ideas about men and women, as you view them.

4. This exercise should be done with a member of the other gender or with a group of people of both sexes. The men should make two lists on a sheet of paper: the advantages of being female and the disadvantages of being female. Likewise, the women should also make two lists: the advantages and disadvantages of being male. When the lists are complete, everyone should compare them and discuss the characteristics.

5. As you are watching television or leafing through the pages of a magazine, note how men and women are portrayed in advertisements. Note which of the men and women appeal the most to you and which are unappealing to you, asking yourself "why?" in each case. Especially note how women and men in the advertisements are shown in traditional or in nontraditional roles.

6. Think about each of the following, and attempt to get in touch with your gut reactions—how you feel. Try not to intellectualize and react in the manner in which you think you should. Instead, look carefully at how you are reacting and at what your reactions mean in terms of attitudes toward gender roles.
   a. An unmarried woman who wishes to be referred to as Ms.
   b. A married woman who insists on being referred to as Ms.
   c. An all-male organization that refuses to consider admitting women as members.
   d. An all-female organization that refuses to consider admitting men as members.
   e. A board of education that passes a school policy requiring that in all courses, "traditional family values are to be upheld, with the feminine role of wife, mother, and homemaker, and masculine role of guide, protector, and provider."
   f. In considering an equally qualified married man and unmarried woman for a position, a company personnel director hires the woman because the company needs to fulfill its affirmative action quota.
   g. After a couple has a new baby, the mother wants to continue working, so the father decides to quit his job and stay home with the child.

Part 1

*Social and Biological
Foundations of
Human Sexuality*

It may strike some of us from time to time that sex has been overrated and overexposed, especially in modern media. However, studying sexuality is one avenue to a more complete understanding of human nature. In its broadest sense, sexuality is interwoven with all aspects of being human. It was only in the last third of the twentieth century that reliable information about human sexual response emerged. As we entered the new millennium, there was still much left to be understood regarding human sexuality. To study sexuality is to dissolve disciplinary boundaries. The psychology of sex includes sexual orientations, behaviors, emotions, and interpersonal connections. The sociology and anthropology of sex mirror the many social, legal, and cultural patterns that play a role in human interactions. Communications technology is in the process of creating new forms of human relationships in cyberspace, and making the distribution of sexual images faster and easier than ever before. It has been said that sex is a biological function and love is a psychological function, but things are just not that simple. Our sexuality relates to our attitudes and feelings, our social relationships, our cultural expectations, and our history.

In terms of recorded human history, scientific inquiry and the scientific way of thinking represent relatively new approaches to perceiving the world and human nature. The first chapter deals with the diversity of cultural values relating to sexuality, how sexual attitudes have been changing, and how some of the pioneers of sex research have opened up new paths of understanding. The chapter explores the different methodologies of sex research.

Chapters 2 and 3 introduce the anatomical and physiological basics of the human body, and chapter 4 explores sexual arousal and responsiveness. There is increasing attention being given to the ways in which gender manifests itself both physically and psychologically, and these issues are explored in chapter 5. These opening chapters set the stage for the broader perspective of sex and sexuality that will emerge as you progress through this text.

Chapter 1
HISTORICAL, RESEARCH, AND CROSS-CULTURAL PERSPECTIVES ON SEXUALITY

Sexual attitudes and practices vary across the diverse cultures of the world.

Chapter 2
FEMALE SEXUAL ANATOMY AND PHYSIOLOGY

Female sex organs have sometimes been associated with reproduction more than with sexual pleasure.

Chapter 3
MALE SEXUAL ANATOMY AND PHYSIOLOGY

Male sex organs are more typically discussed within the contexts of sexual arousal and enjoyment.

Chapter 4
HUMAN SEXUAL RESPONSE

The female and the male have predictable stages of sexual response as the human body reacts physiologically to sexual arousal.

Chapter 5
DEVELOPMENTAL AND SOCIAL PERSPECTIVES ON GENDER

Our gender identity is determined by a complex interaction of genetic, physiological, and sociocultural factors.

Chapter 1

Historical, Research, and Cross-Cultural Perspectives on Sexuality

Chapter Outline

Note: A selection of Focus on Health questions appears at the end of each chapter. Answers to these questions are indicated within the chapter by the symbol in the margin. **FOH**

> The public view of sex in America bears virtually no relationship to the truth. The public image consists of myths, and they are not harmless, for they elicit at best unrealistic and at worst dangerous misconceptions of what people do sexually. The resulting false expectations can badly affect self-esteem, marriages, relationships, even physical health.
>
> —From *Sex in America: A Definitive Survey* by Robert T. Michael, John H. Gagnon, Edward O. Laumann, and Gina Kolata, 1994, Little, Brown and Company

At the beginning of the new millennium, images of sex are all around us, and people have all sorts of different reactions to them, depending on their personal values and the culture in which they live. There is now a museum of human sexuality in Berlin, Germany, displaying more than 3,000 items of erotica. The museum houses antique chastity belts, ancient Chinese scrolls depicting sexual activity, wood-carved replicas of penises from Java, and the earliest 1908 editions of *The Journal of Sexology*. Funding for the museum came from Beate Uhse, a German businesswoman who sells millions of dollars worth of pornography, sex toys, and lingerie annually and who recently began selling stock to finance the largest chain of sex shops in the world.

About 50 percent of television talk shows on the air in the United States daily deal with sexual topics, and more than 10 million Americans view these programs every day. Soap operas, with over 35 million viewers, average seven sexual incidents in an hour (Edwards, 1996). About 60 percent of 10- to 16-year-olds in the United States surveyed in a study had televisions in their bedrooms, and 65 percent had three or more televisions in their homes. Forty-four percent of these adolescents admitted that they watched different programs when they were alone than they did with their parents. Prime-time television averages 25 instances of sexual behavior for every single reference to safer sex or preventive behavior. In a recent year, television viewers spent close to $200 million ordering pay-per-view adult movies at home, and another $175 million to view such films in hotel rooms. The United States has some 25,000 stores that rent hard-core adult videos, and there are about 700,000 annual rentals of sexually explicit videos. It is now estimated that the U.S. hard-core pornography business grosses over $8 billion a year (Schlosser, 1997). The Internet is another medium that brings sex-related material directly to people's rooms. One survey of college students found that about a third of them had visited sexually explicit sites on the World Wide Web (McCollum, 1999).

Sexuality often finds its way into business and politics. Recent sex discrimination and harassment scandals among Wall Street investment firms uncovered the fact that a good many high-rolling male clients were being wined, dined, and otherwise entertained at strip clubs. The President Clinton–Monica Lewinsky affair brought debates over character, sexual morality, and sexual behavior into high-profile visibility, and many politicians became nervous about what sorts of sexual skeletons might be exposed in their own closets (Alter, 1999; Stein et al., 1999). An article published in the prestigious *Journal of the American Medical Association* at the time of the Clinton impeachment trial

Students viewing sex-related material online.

showed that nearly 60 percent of a sample of 599 college students did not consider participating in oral-genital sex to constitute having "had sex" or "sexual relations" (Sanders & Reinisch, 1999). Because of the national attention surrounding the issue at the time, officials of the American Medical Association (AMA) fired the journal's editor for focusing on sensationalism. Some observers felt that the firing was motivated by the fact that the AMA's Political Action Committee had donated nearly twice as much money to Republican candidates than it had to Democrats. Sex and politics have always constituted a volatile combination, and this scandal reminded us that we can't even agree on what it means to "have sex."

While residents of the tiny Finnish village of Kutemajarvi were vying to hold a sex fair in the summer of 1999 that would feature pleasant outdoor locations for couples to share sexual activity—and thus got their community nicknamed "Lake Lovemaking"—Chinese youth were struggling to enjoy the eroticism of disco music without being unduly criticized (Farrer, 1999). In China, where over 80 percent of college students are still virgins, a late-night call-in radio show called "Midnight Whispers" offers sexual advice and draws letters and telephone calls from as far away as Mongolia. The first of its kind in China, the program has been subjected to careful government scrutiny in order to prevent the content from becoming too explicit. The radio station's stated purpose in airing the show is to strengthen Chinese marriages, but it clearly represents a step toward a new level of sexual liberation following decades of governmental policies that perceived sex only as a biological process and denied the existence or importance of romantic love and sexual desire (Wehrfritz, 1996).

As the Chinese test out new levels of sexual openness, New York City—once known for its laissez-faire attitudes about sexuality—is touting its new zoning laws that virtually eliminated most of its adult-oriented theaters, sex shops, and live sex shows. Times Square alone once housed 120 sex shops and now has less than 10. A squad of 20 inspectors enforces the new codes, which proponents applaud for "cleaning up" the city. Critics claim that politicians are going too far with censorship and limiting free speech, while imposing their own views of what constitutes good taste. Yet, the Javits Convention Center on the other side of the same city hosted the Erotica USA convention, with its exhibits of sex toys and media, in 1999.

Human sexuality is a realm of contrasts and contradictions, social trends and cultural imperatives. The values that surround sexuality are always in flux, moved by the agendas and whims of governments, economic realities, and cultural traditions. Western cultures continue to perpetuate confusing and conflicting messages about sex. On the one hand, there are suggestions that sex is somehow "dirty." On the other hand, we are encouraged to save it for someone we really love. We are given the impression that sex is sacred and beautiful, but the less young people know about it, the better. It is no wonder that people have been anxious to pursue the study of human sexuality in as well-balanced and scientific a manner as possible. Effective sexuality education offers factual information based on research studies, as well as opportunities for people to sort through their own values and behaviors relating to their sexuality.

■ The Influences of Culture on Sexuality

When Margaret Mead conducted her groundbreaking field studies of South Seas island cultures in the 1920s and 1930s, she became one of the first anthropologists to examine sexual customs and attitudes. She concluded that the sexual attitudes and behaviors of individual human beings are shaped tremendously by the surrounding cultural imperatives (Mead, 1930). For example, it has often been assumed that passionate love and sexual desire are experienced and expressed universally. There is evidence to suggest, however, that culture profoundly affects how people perceive love; how susceptible they are to falling in love, and with whom; and why they feel sexual desire. Even within a particular region or culture, various political, economic, and social changes can also affect people's sexual attitudes and behaviors (Hatfield & Rapson, 1996; Savage & Tchombe, 1995).

North American culture has long been dominated by heritages rooted in Caucasian European ethnic groups whose people migrated to the Americas and reestablished their traditions there. The religions of these people were largely Judeo-Christian in origin. In many ways, the attitudes about human sexuality that have prevailed in North America were influenced by this backdrop of cultural and religious values. In an-

thropological terms, this perspective has sometimes been called **Eurocentric,** meaning that it grows mainly out of its European roots. The Eurocentric view of the world tends to be dualistic in nature. In other words, it tends to see things in an either-or, black-and-white way. Sexually speaking, this perspective is expressed in beliefs that people must be either masculine or feminine, heterosexual or homosexual. Sexual behaviors tend to be judged as either good or bad.

However, the population of North America is becoming increasingly diverse. The National Institutes of Health now require the inclusion of ethnic minorities in any federally funded research studies so that our understandings of human behavior and the public policies that grow out of them will include all racial and ethnic groups (Varmus, 1994). In North America there are more and more people of color and people whose heritages are African, Far Eastern, Asian, and Latino. Native Americans and the Inuit or Eskimo cultures of the North are beginning to reclaim the sexual identities that were largely replaced by the attitudes and values of Christian missionaries who taught in their boarding schools. Native Americans were originally a more gender-equitable people whose men and women shared the responsibilities for child rearing. Because European males tended to see themselves as superior to females, the sense of equality between Indian men and women was gradually subsumed by Eurocentric attitudes (Day, 1995).

Colleges are working to enhance the understanding and acceptance of cultural diversity, yet it is not unusual to find people surprised by the customs and practices of ethnic groups other than their own. On many campuses, it is not unusual to see orthodox Muslim women wearing clothing and veils that cover most of their bodies and faces. In some religious traditions, it is not permissible for men and women to worship together, or in some cases for men even to touch women prior to marriage. These are customs that relate to the culture's views of sexuality, as illustrated in Figure 1.1. In Eastern cultures, it is not at all unusual for parents to arrange marriages for their children, quite a different practice from the weight given in Western culture to marrying after a couple has "fallen in love."

Sexuality Across Cultures: A Study in Diversity

Anthropologists usually classify cultures on the basis of their subsistence patterns or on how the people produce and distribute food and other goods. Any-

Eurocentric (ur-oh-SEN-trick): a cultural attitudinal framework typical of people with western European heritages.

CROSS-CULTURAL PERSPECTIVE
The Influence of Carnival in Brazil

The practice of Carnival is a long-standing Brazilian tradition. Carnival is viewed as a liberating feast for repressed sexuality. Men dress as women; women remove their clothing; and couples indulge in public sexual activities. Anything goes, and sin is an unknown word during the days of Carnival. Class and race barriers break down as whites, blacks, mulattos, rich and poor alike, dance and parade together in the Avenida de Sapucai in Rio de Janiero. Even those who live beyond the city bounds or do not go to the great centers of Carnival (Rio, Salvador or Recife), watch on T.V. the samba-school parades, the dances, the wanton pranks, and the block parties, in which multitudes of people crowd the streets. The T.V. networks—to the vexation of the Brazilian Puritan elements—insist on broadcasting naked buttocks, breasts and bodies, groping hands in a genuine feast of the flesh which pervades the Carnival world. Indeed, it would be difficult to be a Brazilian and not be influenced by the sights, sounds, and ideology of Carnival. While in actuality these practices are limited to the days of the festival, Carnival attitudes and impact may be felt throughout the year in all the social strata of Brazil.

In other cities throughout the world where Carnival is celebrated, revelry takes the form of masks, allegorical floats, jests, and laughter. In Brazil this is also true; however, the Brazilian Carnival also launches a sexual explosion without prohibition which tends to define the particular character of Brazilian sexuality. That Brazil is synonymous with Carnival is an idea shared by foreigners and Brazilians alike. Brazilians see themselves, and are seen, as a friendly people who welcome visitors with open arms. Brazilians touch and kiss one another and freely offer spontaneous physical contact.

—Marta Suplicy, "Sexuality Education in Brazil" (Sebastian Haywood Ward, trans.), *SIECUS Report*, Vol. 22 (2), December 1993/January 1994.

FIGURE 1.1 *Cultural Standards for Appropriate Dress*
People's attitudes about their bodies and their sexuality are largely influenced by their cultures. While Americans often wear as little as they can get away with, reflecting the current focus on youthfulness and healthy bodies in the United States, these Indian women keep their heads and bodies covered as a symbol of their beauty.

thing that affects a society's subsistence pattern can influence reproduction and thus sexual behavior. Shortages of food, for example, may lead to decreased reproductive rates. Gender roles are closely tied to both reproductive patterns and other social structures within a culture. Therefore, sexuality has a place at the center of any culture (Savage & Tchombe, 1995).

In smaller, homogeneous cultures—meaning that the people are expected to be very much alike in their belief patterns and values—a great deal of effort is often spent on maintaining conformity among people. In such homogeneous cultures, individuals tend to conduct their sexual lives in accordance with accepted social roles. Larger, heterogeneous cultures, in which there is a good deal of human diversity, do not work as deliberately toward producing or stabilizing behavioral conformity. These cultures tend to have many different patterns of sexual conduct. These include not only sexual subcultures based on sexual orientation or behavioral preferences, but more highly individualistic patterns of behavior within particular people. North America is an example of a heterogeneous culture. There are many ethnic and immigrant groups, each with its own viable sexual culture. There is little direct training in "appropriate" sexual conduct and no consensus of opinion about what constitutes appropriate-

CROSS-CULTURAL PERSPECTIVE
Sexual Taboos in Africa

Due to strict cultural taboos, people in Africa do not openly discuss sexuality, a subject which is cloaked in mystery and misinformation. . . . Taboos existed against any kind of other-gender associations prior to marriage, especially heterosexual contact before initiation rites occur. Within extended families, grandparents or aunts would provide family-life education to the children. Today . . . a mixture of both traditional and western myths co-exist within African culture.

In my work in rural villages of Nigeria and beyond, I have come to better understand the myths and taboos surrounding sexuality. In Keffi, for instance, I was informed that old men are advised to have sexual contact with young virgin girls in order to cure sexually transmitted diseases. There, the Superintendent of Police shared that he had advised a friend of his to lock up his 13-year-old pregnant daughter and force her to have sex with a boy frequently, so she will stretch and better be able to give birth. He was honestly shocked when I told him that the frequent intercourse would have no impact on a young girl's ability to have an easier labor, but might possibly cause her enormous distress.

For the most part, taboos around sexuality emerge to serve a useful function in society. Often they are meant to ensure social order or maintain an ethical standard or law which exists within the community. For instance, there is a strong belief in the sexual power of the spiritual world, witchcraft, and magic in Africa. Spiritual magic in West Africa is called "Ju Ju," a practice which is related to the more commonly recognized voodoo. For example, a type of magic charm called "Mangu," is often inserted in a woman's vagina by her husband. If by some chance the woman has sexual contact with another man, it is believed that the Mangu will cause the man's penis to get stuck in the woman's vagina (penis captivus), or will cause her partner to float to the ceiling where the magic will wear off, and he will fall to his death.

—Nanette Ecker, "Culture and Sexual Scripts out of Africa," *SIECUS Report,* Vol. 22 (2), December 1993/ January 1994.

ness. There are also many conflicting messages about sex. Therefore, it is a culture in which there are high levels of sexual variability and sporadic conflicts about what should be considered proper sexual conduct.

When individuals from homogeneous cultures immigrate to heterogeneous cultures, there must often be a process of reevaluating traditional values brought from their homelands and selecting what sexual norms and options will be comfortable from the new surroundings. For example, immigrant Iranians in Canada have had to shift their views of sexuality from group norms of Iran to the greater emphasis on sexual individuality in their new country. This can create real discrepancies between behaviors that are experienced and what may be considered appropriate (Shahidian, 1999). When tribal societies migrate to urban areas, adjustments may also occur. In the African nation of Zimbabwe, tribal youth who are exposed to larger population centers experience sometimes confusing transitions. Traditional cultural values of cooperation and mutual respect are sometimes superseded by a sexual culture in which boys put more emphasis on seduction and sexual conquest, and girls expect their

sexual activities to be linked to the receipt of money and goods (Runganga & Aggleton, 1998).

It has sometimes been assumed when it comes to issues such as nonmarital sex, teenage sexual activity, and same-gender sexual contact that different societies and cultures might well be grouped into simple categories relating to the degree of permissiveness or nonpermissiveness they might show toward these general behaviors. Recent research into attitudes about nonmarital sex in 24 countries has shown this assumption to be faulty. It was discovered instead that the Western nations fit into four clear categories: those that were permissive toward teen sexuality; some that were generally sexually conservative toward nonmarital sexual behaviors (including the United States); several nations that were especially tolerant of same-gender sexual relationships (including Canada); and a fourth group that were generally quite moderate in their levels of permissiveness. Two Asian nations, Japan and the Phillipines, were part of the study as well, and their sexual values were so distinct that they constituted two separate groups. The Philippines was distinguished by its particularly conservative attitudes toward all of the nonmarital sexual behaviors, whereas Japanese were set apart by their propensity for labeling premarital sex as "only sometimes wrong," rather than expressing clear approval or disapproval for the activity (Widmer, Treas, & Newcomb, 1998).

There are wide variations in the kinds of sexual behaviors that are forbidden, tolerated, or encouraged in various cultures. There are clear differences between sexual practices in smaller, preliterate societies and the larger, more complex societies of developed countries. For example, although **voyeurism**—gaining sexual gratification from seeing others nude or involved in sexual acts—is not at all uncommon in Europe and North America, it is almost unheard of in preliterate cultures. Likewise, although exhibiting the genitals to another person may be used to solicit sexual activity in more primitive societies, exhibitionism as an end in itself is apparently absent among preliterate people. It is likely that in large, literate societies it is easier for people to avoid social sanctions through anonymity, and that this may indeed encourage them to participate in sexual activities that would be avoided in other social contexts.

Sexual behavior on the Polynesian island of Mangaia was studied in great detail several decades ago. In this society, sex was a very open topic for discussion, and children were instructed at early ages in the techniques of various sexual activities. Boys and girls began to have sexual intercourse regularly around the age of 13 or 14. Mangaian males, through the age of 30, averaged two to three orgasms nearly every day. In addition to copulating in all varieties of positions, Mangaians regularly practiced oral sex; anal intercourse; insertion of the penis between the breasts, thighs, or other body parts; and mutual genital stimulation. In any sexual activity, these people placed a great deal of emphasis on lengthy and enjoyable sexual experiences. Although orgasm was enjoyed, it was not viewed as the sole goal of sex. Interestingly, in this society where there was less emphasis on orgasm as an achievement, everyone seemed to reach orgasm easily (Marshall, 1971).

Such attitudes stand in stark contrast to what is known about Japanese, Chinese, and some African cultures today. In Japan, there is a great deal of modesty and secrecy surrounding sex, and the Japanese are reluctant to discuss sex-related matters. Japanese youth tend to wait until they are 20 years old before having sex. Birth control pills were not legalized in Japan until 1996. Even though there is a growing problem with HIV infection in the country, educational efforts have been hampered by social values that considered the word "sex" taboo until the mid-1960s (Kitamura, 1996). Although the Chinese have been exhibiting more open interest in dealing with human sexuality in the past two decades, their focus has been largely on sexually transmitted diseases and the treatment of male sexual dysfunctions. Female sexuality seems often to be ignored or subjugated to male pleasure. However, Chinese women actually report higher levels of sexual satisfaction than do the men (Renaud, Byers, & Pan, 1997; Tang, Lai, Phil, & Chung, 1997). As a large continent, Africa has many different societies and cultural influences. For the most part, however, people in Africa consider open discussion of sexuality to be taboo, and there is a great deal of misinformation and myth about sex (Ecker, 1994; Savage & Tchombe, 1995).

It is not surprising that in Europe and North America, sexual activity is most frequently a part of a context of competition—even conquest—and goal orientation. Our standards question the worth of sex without orgasm and the legitimacy of sex without the justification of love (Widmer, et al., 1998). Many societies find themselves caught between emerging attitudes of greater sexual freedom and traditional values that discourage sexual expression. Brazil is a country in which the Roman Catholic Church once exerted a strong influence. Yet, it is also a nation that is known for its sexual license and excess. It may well be the conflicting attitudes of Brazilians that have led to serious problems with violence, child prostitution, women's health issues, illegal abortions, and the spread of HIV infections. Groups in Brazil are working to increase the opportunities for sexual education among the young people there (Braiterman, 1998; Suplicy, 1994).

Same-Gender Sexual Behavior Across Cultures

Anthropologists were only able to begin studying same-gender sexuality cross-culturally when their focus changed from individual pathology to the role of culture in defining and perceiving sexual orientation (Weston, 1993). Cross-cultural generalizations about sexual behavior between members of the same gender are practically impossible, particularly when one tries to interpret or understand the sexual behaviors of other cultures using the psychological, sociological, or biological theories developed within the context of our own culture. Even applying our terminology to those behaviors makes little sense because terms carry with them the assumptions of the time and place in which they were first coined (Braiterman, 1998; Chan, 1995). The Nanshoku culture of Japan has recognized the behavior of men having sex with other men, without having a need to establish words for a separate

voyeurism (VOYE-yu-rizm): sexual gratification from viewing others who are nude or are engaging in sexual activities.

CASE STUDY

Anil: A Counselor's Preconceived Notions about Marriage Are Challenged

Anil was a graduate student from India who came to my office because he had heard that I did counseling regarding sexual matters. He explained that he was to be married in a few months, and was anxious to become better prepared to be a loving and sexually adequate husband. Upon questioning him, I learned that he had had very little sexual experience other than masturbation. We went on to discuss other aspects of marriage, including the need for good communication and being considerate of one another's needs.

Eventually, Anil began discussing his fiancée, and indicated that she was studying in China. Trying to be sensitive to what I knew of the complications of long-distance relationships, I said to Anil, "You must miss her very much." He looked at me for a moment and laughed. "Actually," he responded, "I've never met her." After recovering from having my preconceived notions

disrupted, we talked about how Anil's marriage had been arranged by his and the woman's parents when Anil and the woman were quite young. Anil had no objections to the arrangement, and in fact thought it quite acceptable and appropriate. His only hope was to prepare himself to be the best possible husband in every way.

Anil and I met several times to discuss marriage, and I loaned him several books on sexuality and relationships. By the time our counseling relationship was terminated, both of us felt that he was well prepared for his upcoming marriage. I was forced to realize that the ways of relationships in other cultures had just as much validity as those of my own culture. I also realized that in over 20 years of working with college students, I have never seen a young man give so much careful thought and preparation to being a husband.

identity, such as "gay." In India, same-gender sexual behaviors are accepted without labels that separate the people who practice them into categories of sexual identity or status (Haffner, 1995b).

Different rates of same-gender sexual behavior do not seem to bear any particular relationship to a society's climate, racial makeup, affluence, typical family structure, or state of development. Rules and social sanctions, however, seem to have some effect at least on the visibility of such behavior, because in societies where it is approved or praised, it tends to be more frequently observed, and in societies where it is condemned, sexual and romantic relationships between members of the same gender tend to be less frequently observed (Chan, 1995).

Some preindustrial societies use same-gender sexual behavior, particularly between males, in their religious rites. It is sometimes believed that an older male giving semen to a young boy orally or anally strengthens the boy and helps make him into a man. Such age-structured behavior is typically viewed as a stage of an individual's development. It occurs in 10 to 20 percent of Melanesian societies in the southwest Pacific. In these societies, the rule is that a male must engage in sexual activity with other males until he is married; then he must adopt heterosexual behavior. Most men make the transition and then remain exclusively heterosexual, but a few continue to have sexual relationships with other males. The pattern of continued same-gender behavior may reflect social codes and

taboos, or it may provide evidence that a small proportion of men seem consistently to have a same-gender sexual orientation (McConaghy, 1993). In some traditional Hindu societies, boys are married twice, first to a "blood brother" of his own gender—a tie that is considered as deep, lasting, and rewarding as marriage—and second, to a woman. Both relationships endure and are considered to offer security, a sense of belongingness, and a rootedness in relationship. Such age-structured male-male sexual relations have also been identified in Taiwan, many traditional African cultures, and Latin America, often involving a "younger brother" who is protected and sexually used by an "older brother" (Sinfield, 1998).

Discuss the various sexual standards in other cultures. Compare and contrast them with your standards.

◾ The Sexual Revolution in Western Cultures

Ideals and values about sex and love in Western cultures have seen dramatic shifts in the past two centuries. The Puritan ideal was for love between men and women to evolve within marriage, as two people began to know one another better. During the Victorian era (1837–1901), love and sex were considered to be separate human experiences, with love being the romantic and spiritual union that ideally preceded and precipitated marriage. Although sex was recognized to be a part of marriage in cautious moderation, lustful passions were not to be let out of control, lest people become slaves to their sexual emotions. Love and sex between people of the same gender were not openly discussed. Sex was certainly not linked to love, because to link the two would in fact have been considered a threat to the love that undergirded marital stability. With sex having such a conflicted place within marriage, prostitution and pornography flourished in Victorian society (Seidman, 1991).

Some of these Victorian attitudes were rooted in the eighteenth-century belief that male semen must be conserved in order to maintain strength and virility. Wasting semen through frequent or frivolous orgasms was seen as a major factor in all sorts of physical, mental, and moral degeneracy. This was a major source of antisexualism and especially of negative attitudes toward female sexuality. Women were to be avoided by men because sexual attraction to them could lead to semen wastage (Money, 1991). During this same period of history, passionate love between women was not considered in any way abnormal or dangerous, perhaps because they were not viewed as being particularly sexual, and because there was no danger of semen being wasted.

By the late 1800s, reform movements were beginning to legitimize sex within marriage, and sex and love were becoming increasingly intertwined. Throughout the early part of the twentieth century, marriage manuals were emphasizing the importance of successful sexual technique as a way to express love between partners. During the 1960s and 1970s, sex as a medium of expression began to outstrip the concept of romantic love. There were social movements that emphasized sex as a legitimate form of expression quite apart from romantic, intimate relationships. This was also a time during which sexual expression between gay men and lesbians was accepted and practiced as a right, going beyond romance and pleasure to become a tool for community building and creating a sense of identity (Seidman, 1991).

Researchers who designed and conducted the most comprehensive research survey on sexual behaviors in the United States in 50 years, the National Health and Social Life Survey, concluded that since World War II, the country had indeed experienced a sea change in regard to sexuality (Michael et al., 1994). During the 1960s, the term **sexual revolution** was in vogue, carrying with it the implication that there had been significant and relatively abrupt changes in sexual attitudes, values, and behaviors during that period. Yet there is much disagreement among professionals over the alleged revolution, whether there indeed ever

was a revolution, and if so, when it started, what its causes were, and what changes it generated.

Eminent sex researcher Volkmar Sigusch (1998) has postulated that the rapid and attention-getting sexual revolution of the 1960s and 1970s—characterized by the sexual liberation of women, gay males, and lesbians; a move toward more sexuality education; and the advent of sex therapy—may not have been nearly as significant of the dismantling of old patterns of sexuality that took place in the last two decades of the twentieth century. The earlier trends were likely spurred on by some of the startling data that were emerging from surveys of human sexual behavior being published around 1950, and they gained fuel with the counterculture movements of the sixties and seventies. Sigusch believes that the more recent "neosexual" revolution, as he calls it, has resulted in a very real reassembling of the dimensions of intimate relationships and sexual activities in whole new ways. He also believes that in this newer revolution, some of the positive mystique of sexuality has been lost, to be replaced by more conflicting and negative features relating to gender differences, sexual thrills, emphasis on self-gratification, and the substitution of sexual methods that interfere with intimacy in couples.

There remains a very real ambivalence about sex in our society. Although discussion of sexual issues is more open than in the past, the way in which people actually talk about sex is often guarded and carefully stylized. Research indicates that women and men approach discussion of sex in very different ways. What parents say to their children about sexuality and sexual values is one thing; what the kids actually listen to may be quite different. And even in the face of all this talk, there are still some aspects of people's sex lives, such as masturbation, that remain for the most part unmentionable. There seems to be a marked disparity between how openly erotic material is displayed in our society and the reticence of people to be forthcoming about private sexual practices (Laumann, Gagnon, Michael, & Michaels, 1994).

Patterns of Change

Just as the sea change we have come to call the sexual revolution has witnessed a variety of complex and interrelated changes in values and behaviors, there have been many social and cultural factors contributing to the evolution of new sexual attitudes and myths. All of these factors are themselves interwoven and complex.

sexual revolution: the changes in thinking about sexuality and sexual behavior in society that occurred in the 1960s and 1970s.

New Approaches to Morality and Personal Autonomy

One of the most striking trends of Western society in the late 1960s and 1970s was increased resistance toward centralized, institutionalized authority. A counterculture movement questioned rules, regulations, and decisions that were set forth without thorough explanation or rationale. The mobility of our society, along with the decreasing stability of the nuclear family, created conditions that demanded more independence and self-reliance. As values changed, legal restrictions on sexual activity between consenting adults gradually began to give way. Established religious restraints on sex began to shift. Academic institutions responded to the pressure by giving up their *in loco parentis* positions and liberalizing their residence hall policies on curfews, visits by members of the opposite sex, and privacy. Before long, the dominant culture began to integrate this counterculture movement into a consumption-oriented economy, and advertising picked up on the themes of sex appeal and instant gratification. Enjoyment of oneself and of one's own body was no longer condemned automatically as being immoral. New attitudes about sexuality moved into the mainstream of American life (Janus & Janus, 1993).

Changing Roles of Women and Men

Another significant factor in sexual change has been our shifting attitudes toward the roles of men and women. The traditional roles of the man as aggressive protector and provider and the woman as passive homemaker and servant have gradually been superseded by roles that are individualized to each person's needs. That is not to say that remnants of the traditional roles have not persisted or that individuals have rejected those roles completely. The changes have simply allowed both women and men more freedom to adopt ways of life that fit them more appropriately. It has been legitimized that women may have strong sexual feelings and consider sex to be important to their lives, allowing them to be the initiators of sexual activity. They may also wish to pursue their careers aggressively. Likewise, men have been freed to enjoy the more gentle and emotional aspects of their personalities, to function as homemakers in their own rights, and to be the more passive partners in sexual interactions.

Describe several beliefs about sexuality that were prevalent in the past, and explain the significance of what has been called the "sexual revolution."

Scientific Research and Technological Developments

Of special importance in recent years has been the increase in information and scientific evidence about human sexuality, resulting from the work of several researchers. Studies on human sexual behavior have helped people realize that the sexual feelings, orientations, behaviors, and concerns that they had tried so hard to ignore or hide were part of a good many other people's lives as well. Recent research has reminded us that most human beings are not as sexually energetic or adventurous as some of our social myths have led us to believe (Michael et al., 1994). These realizations continue to lead us toward a greater acceptance of the normalcy of our sexual individuality, and they have also removed much of the element of mystery from sexuality. Research into sexual behavior has helped us to grasp the fact that "sex" does not only refer to actions involving the sex organs. There are many other forms of sensual and sexual sharing that may enhance physical pleasure and expression of caring between people.

Technological advances have also helped change the terrain of human sexuality. With new advances in contraception and the legalization of abortion came reduced concerns about the risks of pregnancy, accompanied by hotly debated ethical issues. Reproductive technology is now making it possible for people who once would not have been able to have children to become pregnant and give birth. This sheds an entirely new light on the role of sex in reproduction. Medical advances have improved the treatment for some sexually transmitted diseases, even as new diseases appear, and have also resulted in the restoration of sexual functioning for some people who once would have had to give up on sexual activity altogether. However, it is never enough simply to rely on scientific or technological advances to solve immediate problems; we must also work to understand how these advances affect human lives and decisions in many different ways (Coleman, 2000).

Media and Internet Attention to Sexuality

One of the most startling developments in the last 50 years has been the place accorded to sexual images and themes in the popular media. In 1950, movies and magazines neither mentioned sex nor depicted sexual encounters in explicit ways. Nudity was never shown or even hinted at. Television was a fledgling medium that not only was inaccessible to most of the population but deliberately worked to keep its programming as sex-free as possible. The few books published that had palpable sexual themes were often banned from libraries and sold to customers from under the counter. We were not a culture that cared to be obvious about any interest in sexual matters. Today, by contrast, it is practically impossible to escape sex, nudity, provocative language, and complex sexual themes in any of the public media. Researchers who have generated what they feel are accurate data concerning the types and frequencies of human sexual behaviors believe that the media have played a substantial role in perpetuating myths and exaggerations about the levels of sexual activity among people (Laumann, Gagnon et al., 1994). This role has now been expanded even more by access to the Internet and all of the opportunities for sexual communication and exchange that it has opened. For the first time, a medium that is as yet largely unregulated brings an entirely new dimension of human sexuality into homes and institutions. Society is just beginning to grapple with the many issues and points of view that this is generating (Schnarch, 1997).

HIV and AIDS as Agents of Change

Human immunodeficiency virus (HIV) and the terminal disease to which it often leads, acquired immunodeficiency syndrome (AIDS), have been changing some of the fundamental ways in which people view sexual behavior. As awareness and fear about HIV and AIDS have increased, there has also been an increase in awareness about the need to make sexual decisions with care and to protect oneself during sexual interactions. Although the need for caution seems clear, this has not necessarily translated into marked changes in people's sexual behaviors. Although some research in progress concerning adolescent sexual activity may eventually signal other trends, recent statistics suggest that there has not been a marked increase in sexual abstinence. Anecdotal evidence with college students hints that there may be somewhat less likelihood of participation in male-female sexual intercourse, and some studies demonstrate an increase in the use of condoms during sexual activity among young people (Elliott & Brantley, 1997). However, the most recent research tells a rather alarming story about the lack of attention that individuals in North America are actually giving to safer sex. Although some people use condoms during sex very consistently, many do not. The Centers for Disease Control and Prevention have actually reported an increase from year to year in the number of people reporting that they never use a condom with a steady sex partner. Only between 30 and 60 percent of men actually use them every time they have sex. In a study of unmarried, sexually experienced women aged 17 to 44, only 30 percent reported they used condoms for disease protection every time or most times they had intercourse, although the younger women were somewhat more likely to do so (Anderson, Brackbill, & Mosher, 1996). Worldwide, AIDS had

become the fourth leading cause of death by the beginning of the new millennium, and yet sexual pleasure is consistently cited as being a more important consideration to individuals than protection from disease or unintended pregnancy (London International Group, 1998).

Like so many aspects of sexual decision making, there seem to be many factors that influence the use of condoms among college students. Those with many sexual partners and those who get drunk frequently are less likely to use condoms on a consistent basis (Mahoney, 1995). Among people who use condoms, only 1 percent follow all of the steps necessary to assure the greatest degree of protection, with another 12 to 28 percent using some of the measures that increase the likelihood of condoms successfully preventing disease transmission (Oakley & Bogue, 1995). College students report concerns about discussing or requiring condom use in their sexual relationships because they fear raising issues of trust and commitment that might be difficult to deal with (Hammer, Fisher, Fitzgerald, & Fisher, 1996). They also seem to have unrealistic ideas about the degree of risk they face in their college environments, perhaps reflective of a prevalent attitude that "it won't happen to me" (Thompson, Anderson, Freedman, & Swan, 1996).

Sexuality, Politics, and Family Values

Probably the most accurate assessment of human sexuality in contemporary Western societies is that confusion and ambivalence seem pervasive. Religious and political conservatives are anxious to make their views known about the ethics, morality, and legality of sexual behaviors and orientations. Liberals are equally intent on supporting the rights of gay males and lesbians, the freedom to use sexual words and display graphic representations of sex, and the right to make one's own individual choices about nonexploitative sexual and reproductive activities. On the one hand, we have the advocates of the "Just say no" and "Just don't do it" approaches who want sexual values to be defined rather narrowly. On the other hand, we have those who remind us that "vows of abstinence break far more easily than do condoms," and that these are times that demand more pluralism and tolerance regarding the ways in which people believe or behave sexually (Reiss, 1990). There is substantial evidence that among teens today—really the first generation to have been constantly exposed to sex-saturated media all of their lives—sexual involvement is happening at younger ages than ever before. First intercourse among teenagers is nearly twice as likely to occur prior to marriage as it was 35 years ago. The change is particularly pronounced among white young people. By age 19, over 80 percent of teens have experienced sexual intercourse (Alan Guttmacher Institute, 1994; London International Group, 1998).

Because sex-related topics can still become easily sensationalized by the media, and because they still stimulate strong opinions among people, it is inevitable that they also become intertwined with politics. Indeed, politicians have built campaigns on issues such as abortion, sexuality education, child pornography, gay rights, access to contraception, and sexual themes on television and the Internet. Human sexuality has become highly politicized, and political trends ultimately have an effect on the legislative mandates and court decisions that relate to sexual and reproductive behaviors.

Recent elections in the United States have frequently raised the issue of what is frequently called "family values." The term has been used to refer to values that emphasize abstinence from sex except within marriage, condemn anything other than male-female sexual activity, and uphold the inherent superiority of the two-parent family. In reality, the image of the American family as consisting of homemaker Mom, breadwinner Dad, and the kids is no longer representative of the average family unit. In actuality, the most common family unit is a married couple with no children living at home. Less than 40 percent of families consist of married couples with children, and increasing numbers of those are actually "blended" families in which some of the children have resulted from a former relationship. One in four babies is now born to an unmarried mother, and more than half of all mothers with preschool children now work outside the home, as compared to 20 percent in 1960. By the late 1990s, only slightly over half of all children (50.8 percent) in the United States were living with both natural parents and full brothers or sisters.

We have a long way to go before people may be assured that they will be treated fairly and considerately by others in sexual matters. There are more rapes and other violent sexual crimes in the United States than in most other countries, and yet we still often relegate discussion about sexuality to jokes and banter and are reluctant to bring sex-related topics out into the open with frankness and honesty. Political extremist groups continue to attack organizations and individuals who advocate for open and honest approaches to sexuality education (Haffner, 1996). As long as we are fettered by sexual ignorance, avoidance of sexual realities, and irresponsible sexual behavior, any sexual revolution will have been misdirected and misused. As new and more objectively reliable statistics emerge concerning human sexual behavior, we will have a more sound foundation on which to build our personal understandings and public policies relating to human sexuality.

Nature or Nurture?

One of the most enduring debates of the human sciences made its way prominently into the arena of human sexuality during the years of the sexual revolution. It is the controversy over the relative roles played by biological and social factors in determining human traits and behaviors, including sexual characteristics and activities. The two camps in this great debate have traditionally been **biological essentialism** and **social constructionism.** The biological essentialists hold that inborn genetic and physiological factors are the determinants of not only such things as physical sex, body form, and temperament, but also of the way human beings are programmed to behave in their gender roles or in their sexual attractions to other people or objects. In other words, physical, sexual, and personality characteristics are established by nature (DeLamater & Hyde, 1998; Wright, 1999).

Another variant of biological essentialism emerged in the mid-1970s with the application of evolutionary theory to humans in a new field that was called sociobiology. Evolutionary theory has been applied to sexuality in a variety of ways, and the news media have popularized research findings that claim to have found evidence that evolutionary forces have yielded genetic templates explaining such things as mating preferences in women and men, why men tend to be more prone to sexual relationships outside of primary relationships, and gender role differences between the sexes (Buss, 1998). Newspapers blare headlines about a newly discovered "gene for adultery" or a genetic explanation for thrill-seeking behavior (Nash, 1998).

On the opposite side of the debate are the social constructionists who believe that human personality traits and behaviors are mostly shaped by social influences, or "nurture." They argue against the idea that sexual behaviors and orientations are natural or inborn; instead, they believe that they are shaped by learning experiences over the years of human development. Social constructionists do not completely dismiss the role of biology in determining fundamental physical characteristics, but they hold that even biological facts become interpreted through the screen of cultural assumptions (Hogben & Byrne, 1998).

biological essentialism: a theory that human traits and behaviors are primarily formed by inborn biological determinants such as genes and hormonal secretions, rather than by environmental influences.

social constructionism: a theory that holds that human traits and behaviors are shaped more by environmental social forces than by innate biological factors.

There are staunch advocates on both sides of the nature-nurture debate, and they sometimes take their arguments to extremes. There are biological essentialists who insist that there is a gene that can determine that a person will be gay or lesbian. There are social constructionists who say that if the language of a particular culture lacked the word for orgasm, people who are part of that culture would not be able to experience an orgasm. However, a middle ground has been emerging between these two extreme camps. Most biologists no longer assume that "biology is destiny," recognizing that environmental influences clearly exert some level of effect on the expression of genetic traits. Some social scientists have had more difficulty integrating biological influences into their social constructionist models, but a new brand of evolutionary biology is emerging that incorporates social, psychological, and cultural perspectives (Buss, 1998; DeLamater & Hyde, 1998).

The most reasonable approach given our present state of knowledge would not be to reduce the debate to a decision about whether some trait is innate or learned. That is too simplistic. Rather the issue revolves around how variable a trait is and the degree to which its variability is shaped by biological and environmental factors. Genes do not act on their own, and instead their expression may be influenced to a degree by a variety of environmental factors ranging from the chemical composition of cells to cultural and social learning. It is likely that some traits are more susceptible to environmental influence than others. Likewise, society surely does not shape the characteristics of an individual human being in the absence of a genetic template that determines some degree of variability in traits. The real question to be asked in the debate over the variability of sexual traits in humans is the degree to which that variability is influenced by biology and/or by environment (Hamer & Copeland, 1998; Reiss, 2000).

The most important conclusion to be drawn here is that there is an interdependence of and interaction among human biology, consciousness, and social life. Answers to complex questions about the roots of human sexual traits are not well served by models that reduce them to an either-or status. As one researcher put it, to discuss sexuality as one-finger melodies is a disservice; human sexuality must be understood instead as a series of chords (Bermant, 1995).

■ Shifting Sexual Attitudes

There have been significant shifts in sexual attitudes spanning various periods of history and social change. Unlike Eastern cultures that until recently had a long tradition of positivity and enjoyment in relationship to sexuality, Western cultures have seen a prevalence of sexual negativity that has been rooted in social, moral, and religious belief systems. This fundamental distrust of human sexuality and its power led to the development of some fundamentally hostile attitudes toward sexuality (Bullough & Bullough, 1995).

As sex-related issues received more media exposure and research demonstrated the diversity of human sexual behavior, some of the hostilities and taboos gradually slipped away for some people. We have often been led to believe that in North America, people have become far more permissive in their sexual attitudes and behaviors since the sexual revolution took hold. Research is now beginning to suggest that although there have been some distinct changes along the way, our perceptions about sexual permissiveness may well have been exaggerated. In an annual survey of the general attitudes of college freshmen, acceptance of casual sexual relationships has been on the decline.

It is not a simple matter to study human beings' attitudes with a great degree of objectivity, especially regarding issues as complex as sexuality. One thing that attitudinal research has found is that human attitudes, particularly about sex, cannot be easily classified in any single way; there are many different factors involved in their creation and expression. The study of 24 countries cited earlier found that there were in fact six clusters of attitudes concerning nonmarital sex (Widmer et al., 1998). Likewise, there is no single set of beliefs that would easily describe the prevailing North American attitudes toward sex. Researchers have found that there are some clusters of similarity in the way groups of people view various sexual issues and behaviors that have allowed sociologists to group people into three main categories, based on what seem to be their fundamental assumptions about the purposes of sex. The *procreational* or *traditional* category includes those people who see the primary purpose of sexual activity to be reproductive. They tend to disapprove of any sex outside of marriage as well as sexual activity between members of the same gender. Beyond these attitudes, the group seems rather split on other issues such as pornography and abortion.

A second category of attitudes has been termed *relational* because people in this group tend to view sexual activity as a natural component of intimate and loving relationships. As might be expected, this group is generally accepting of sex within the context of a loving and committed relationship—marriage or otherwise—but has strong negative attitudes toward extramarital sex or "cheating" on a partner. The final attitudinal category is called *recreational,* and the people in this group consider the primary purpose of sex to be pleasure. They tend to believe that any sexual activity between consenting adults would be acceptable and tend to have mixed views on issues such as abortion and same-gender sexual activity (Laumann, Gagnon et al., 1994).

We may conclude, therefore, that we live in a time when there is no single, predominating set of social attitudes relating to human sexuality. In fact, there are several different and often quite contradictory attitudinal patterns existing alongside one another. Even more important, we are beginning to see that the sexual attitudes people hold, which are strongly influenced by the social groups to which they belong, also influence the sexual behaviors in which they engage (Michael et al., 1994).

Because we have no clearly identifiable societal or cultural sexual norm, our culture continues to send mixed messages of sexual permission and restriction. This pattern is becoming increasingly typical throughout the world. However, it is also clear that many of the old rules about sex do not seem to apply anymore (Janus & Janus, 1993). There have been some identifiable shifts in sex-related attitudes over recent decades.

In which of the three main attitudinal categories regarding sexual issues and behavior would you place yourself? Procreational or traditional? Relational? Recreational? Explain your choice.

Attitudes Toward Masturbation

Fears about masturbation among those of Judeo-Christian heritage may have stemmed originally from Old Testament references to the "sin" of Onan. Mentioned only briefly in biblical texts, Onan had been directed by God to have intercourse with the widow of his brother to produce children. Because Onan instead "spilled the semen on the ground," God slew him (Genesis 38:9). Some interpreted that as God's displeasure with an act of masturbation. As sexuality began to fall increasingly within the domain of medicine, antimasturbation campaigns developed. In 1741 the Swiss physician Tissot published *Onanism, or, A Treatise on the Disorders of Masturbation,* a book that was translated into almost every major European language. It touted the belief of the time that body fluids must be conserved and kept in balance in order to be physically and mentally healthy. Tissot extended that belief to sexual fluids, warning that if males ejaculated often or females expended the vaginal fluids produced during sexual arousal, they would become ill and debilitated.

In the late eighteenth century, two observations compounded this negative attitude. One was that individuals with many sexual partners were more likely to have diseases of the sex organs. The other was that mental patients and other institutionalized people were sometimes seen masturbating because they were afforded little privacy for any sort of sexual activity. Because the germ theory of disease had not yet been formulated and little was known either about human sexual behavior or the causes of mental illness, it was assumed that sexual activity was to blame for physical and mental disorders because it overstimulated the nervous system. From these contexts came the early idea that sexual self-stimulation was particularly immoral and unhealthy (Kay, 1992).

In Richard von Krafft-Ebing's standard medical text of the Victorian period, *Psychopathia Sexualis,* the typical 1880s European attitude toward masturbation was expressed as follows:

> Nothing is so prone to contaminate . . . the source of all noble and ideal sentiments . . . as the practice of masturbation in early years. It despoils the unfolding bud of perfume and beauty, and leaves behind only the coarse, animal desire for sexual satisfaction. . . . The glow of sensual sensibility wanes, and the inclination toward the opposite sex is weakened. This defect influences the morals, the character, fancy, feeling and instinct of the youthful masturbator, male or female, in an unfavorable manner, even causing, under certain circumstances, the desire for the opposite sex to sink to nil.

(Krafft-Ebing, 1886/1965, pp. 188–189)

Masturbation was blamed for homosexuality, insanity, sterility, and a variety of other conditions. Parents were so frightened by the possible consequences of masturbation that they purchased metal hand mitts and contraptions to cover the genitals to prevent masturbation in their children (Bullough & Bullough, 1995). Gradually, throughout the twentieth century, the attitude toward masturbation became more tolerant. Eventually it was accepted that very occasional masturbation might not have any long-lasting effects, but it was still assumed that frequent masturbation could be debilitating.

When Alfred Kinsey's (1948, 1953) statistics appeared, Americans realized that masturbation was an extremely prevalent practice. The Janus and Janus (1993) study found that about two-thirds of the American adults surveyed agreed that masturbation is a natural part of life and continues on in marriage. Another 21 to 22 percent had no opinion on the issue, and only 12 percent disagreed with the majority point of view. Prevailing professional opinion seems to be that masturbation is a very normal part of human sexual expression, common in youngsters and usually continuing to some extent well into adulthood and old age. It is often viewed as a healthy outlet for sexual tension and as a desirable way to learn about sexual responsiveness, even being recommended during some forms of sex therapy (Kay, 1992). It is now known to be a self-limiting phenomenon, and the general consensus is that, from a medical point of view, there is no such thing as too much masturbation. It seems to hold true even today, however, that masturbation is viewed more positively in relationship to males in our society than it is for females (Michael et al., 1994).

Attitudes Toward Nonmarital Sex and the Double Standard

In the late 1950s, sociologists began to study the sexual standards and attitudes of U.S. college students, focusing largely on heterosexual intercourse outside of marriage. The vast majority of students at that time indicated that they believed in sexual abstinence for both genders, and especially for women. This gender difference was rooted in Western culture's persistent double standard that presumes that men need and enjoy sexual pleasure more than do women. Additionally, men were expected to be more experienced in sexual matters and to be able to educate women. Males were once assumed to have uncontrollable sexual urges that a "good girl" would not allow to progress beyond the point where sex became inevitable. Many college women during the 1950s and 1960s chose to be technical virgins, participating in sexual acts to orgasm but not allowing intercourse to occur.

By the late 1980s and mid-1990s, the majority of young men and women no longer condemned sex without marriage, regardless of whether or not they had chosen to have sex before marriage themselves. However, there was also a growing emphasis on the importance of a loving emotional relationship between sexual partners. Younger couples who would have stopped just short of intercourse in former years, and instead reached orgasm through other means, were apparently choosing to have intercourse. At the same time, however, there has been increased legitimacy for a variety of sexual interactions that do not include intercourse but still often lead to orgasm (Alan Guttmacher Institute, 1994; Lawrance, Rubinson, & O'Rourke, 1984; Rubinson & DeRubertis, 1991; Sanders & Reinisch, 1999).

As we saw earlier in this chapter, there are distinct groupings of attitudes toward sexual activity among the U.S. population. Attitudes toward nonmarital sex are clearly more permissive than they once were among the majority of the population, and evidence from around the world suggests that women and men globally are starting to have sex at earlier ages and with greater frequency than in the recent past (London International Group, 1998). Attitudinal trends are fraught with contradictions, however, and attitudes about sexuality are no exception. Statistics from the ongoing General Social Survey in the mid-1990s indicated that the number of people in older age groups disapproving of sex without marriage has been decreasing, whereas the disapproval rate among the youngest age groups has been increasing (National Data Program for the Social Sciences, 1992).

Freshmen entering college in late 1998 and 1999, who completed the attitude questionnaire from the Cooperative Institutional Review Program, showed the lowest approval rate for casual sexual encounters since the survey was first administered in 1966. This suggests that the younger generation may be becoming somewhat more conservative in its attitudes toward sex before marriage and that the generation gap over this issue has been narrowing. Teen pregnancy rates, birthrates, and abortion rates have reached their lowest rates in two decades. Some have assumed that this was the result of decreased sexual activity before marriage, and the delay of sexual activity does indeed seem to account for about 20 percent of the decline. The other 80 percent seems to be the result of improved contraceptive use among young people who are sexually active (Saul, 1999). Studies of college students also demonstrate that those who consider themselves to be more religious are less likely to have experienced sexual intercourse and are more likely to have conservative sexual attitudes (Pluhar, Frongillo, Stycos, & Dempster-McClain, 1998).

Research consistently supports the perception that men tend to be more sexually permissive than do women. Although it is no longer assumed within some attitudinal groups that it is crucial for women to be virgins until they marry, there is still a persistent attitude that it is more acceptable for men to be sexually active with a variety of partners than it is for women. Of the people surveyed in one study, the majority of men (75 to 78 percent) and most women (87 to 96 percent) believed there is still a double standard regarding males and females being involved in sexual activities (Janus & Janus, 1993). College students continue to be in touch with a "conditional" double standard that limits the acceptable number of sexual partners for women to a very few and then only within the context of a meaningful loving relationship. Research continues to show that women's sexual and contraceptive behaviors tend to be judged more negatively than that of men (Elliott & Brantley, 1997; Hynie & Lydon, 1995).

However, there are cultural differences in such attitudes. For example, in Japan, men are not any more likely to believe that premarital sexual activity is permissible (Kitamura, 1996). This may reflect a Japanese cultural setting in which sexuality is relegated to secondary importance in comparison with academics and performance of duty. American students are generally more accepting of premarital sex than are Russian and Japanese students. College men in Russia are more likely to endorse the traditional double standard than Japanese or U.S. college men (Nardi, 1998). When it comes to sex early in a dating relationship, American men were more likely to accept and endorse the double standard (Sprecher & Hatfield, 1996).

China represents a culture in which there has been a continuing disparity between official repression of sexuality from conservative governments and relative permissiveness with regard to sexual relations among the people themselves. Sexuality in China has been closely tied to the religious traditions of the country, and sexual behavior was once seen as having great spiritual significance. Classic sex manuals, boldly depicting intercourse positions and other sexual behaviors, have survived through many centuries. The contemporary governments of China have devalued the place of sex in relationships, and this has led to an underground culture of sexual rules and activities among the Chinese people. Little has been written about the details of this sexual subculture, but it is clear that nonmarital sexual activity is becoming more commonplace there. Among Chinese university students, it was found that rates of masturbation, same-gender sexual activity, and heterosexual intercourse were much lower than those found among youth in Western cultures, and their attitudes toward premarital sex were relatively permissive. Sexual activities between men and women not involving intercourse seem to be widely practiced and accepted there (Farrer, 1999; Hong et al., 1994; Renaud, Byers, & Pan, 1997).

Attitudes Toward Sexual Orientations, Alternative Lifestyles, and Gender Identities

Heterosexual attraction and behavior, within fairly narrow boundaries of expression, have traditionally been considered the norms against which other sexual orientations and behaviors have been judged. Although we know that there is a great deal of diversity in human sexual orientations, behaviors, and expressions of gender, medical and mental health professionals have at times classified certain differing forms as sick; laws have made them criminal; religions have branded them as sinful; and the general populace have variously feared, hated, pitied, or accepted people who are open about them. It was not until the mid-1970s that the American Psychiatric Association removed "homosexuality" from its official list of mental disorders.

Sexual activity between members of the same gender provides a good example of how powerful social and historical influences may be on prevailing attitudes. Historically, there has been great ambiguity about same-gender sex (Bullough, 1990). Norms for sexual behavior were governed by political and ethical ideals rather than the gender of one's sexual partner. Records suggest that in the classical period of ancient Greece, during the fifth century B.C.E., people thought of sexuality as neutral or good, as long as it was "responsible." In those times, irresponsibility was measured by whether the behavior interfered with one's

duties to the state or whether it involved an abuse of freeborn (nonslave) children or married women. Opportunities for sex were organized more around issues of class, age, and marital status than they were around gender. A wealthy, powerful male could penetrate anyone with his penis without loss of social status, but he might be judged more harshly were he to be penetrated by another male of lower class (Boswell, 1990a).

Today, attitudes toward same-gender sex vary across the same attitudinal groups that were identified earlier. People with procreational or traditional attitudes about sex tend to have the most negative reactions toward same-gender sex, with about 95 percent of this group considering such activity to be always wrong. The relational attitudes group is more moderate in its disapproval of same-gender sex, and the people who hold recreational attitudes about sex are the most accepting (Laumann, Gagnon et al., 1994). The media have created far greater visibility for same-gender relationships and other sexual lifestyles, although that exposure does not always create positive images (Gamson, 1998). Additionally, the lives of gay people have in many ways become normalized within Western societies, and the final vestiges of discrimination because of sexual orientation seem to be slipping away (Haffner & Portelli, 1998; Seidman, Meeks, & Traschen, 1999).

Attitudes concerning the diversity of gender identities have been changing as well. As later chapters of this text will show, not all people fit neatly into female or male, masculine or feminine, categories. Transgender or cross-gender identities have been receiving increasing attention and acceptance, even as they challenge our traditional assumptions about gender (Gamson, 1998). As social attitudes have changed over time, it is clear that other sexual and transgender behaviors have gained greater social acceptance. Sadomasochism, cross-dressing, oral sex, and a variety of other sexual practices no longer shock as many people as in previous times. It is probably safe to assume that more people now believe that every person should be free to enjoy his or her sexual inclinations, providing that other people are not harmed, exploited, or forced to participate without their consent. However, there are other social factions that argue against the proposition that sexual choices are strictly a personal matter. Shifting political and religious values have tended to foster more cautious and sometimes negative attitudes about varying forms of sexual activity, orientation, and lifestyle.

Attitudes Toward the Body and Nudity

Early in twentieth-century Europe and America, the human body was thought to be rather loathsome, best kept covered to the greatest extent possible. It was also a source of shame, and nudity was frowned upon.

DOONESBURY by Garry Trudeau

Doonesbury © 1971 G. B. Trudeau. Reprinted with permission of Universal Press Syndicate. All rights reserved.

The organs that protruded from the human torso—the male genitals and the female breasts—were kept under protective support and camouflage. Today, there seem to be conflicting attitudes regarding the degree to which the human body should be exposed. Many styles of clothing and swimwear now only scantily cover the genitals and female breasts. Total frontal nudity of both women and men is accepted in some films and a variety of popular magazines. The courts generally no longer consider simple exposure of the genitals in photographs to represent obscenity or pornography. In Europe, clothing-optional beaches are commonplace. However, there are some groups that object to the amount of skin exposed in the media or in public. In Jerusalem, some Ultra-Orthodox Jewish groups have verbally and physically harassed women for wearing sleeveless blouses or skirts hemmed above the knees. Islamic fundamentalists typically require that women keep most of their bodies covered.

In the United States, nudist camps have operated for many years and are often governed by very strict codes of behavior. "Social nudists" draw a sharp distinction between nudity and sex, viewing the naked human body as natural and pure rather than as sexually arousing. Recreational nudism has been estimated by *Forbes* magazine to be a $125 million-per-year business, with the number of private campsites and beaches that permit nudity increasing. The American Association for Nude Recreation reported in the late 1900s that about 20 new nudist resorts had appeared in several states, and that the organization's membership had doubled to 50,000 in the past decade. At the same time, there have been conservative forces that are voicing their objections to the amount of skin being displayed by the media. On the Kona coast of the island of Hawaii, the native Hawaiian groups were objecting to the nude bathing that had become commonplace there, and in 1999 the National Park Service began enforcing laws against nudity at the beach.

In times when there has been more permissiveness about nudity in the United States, at least in the media, it is interesting to note that high school and college students seem to be protecting their modesty more fiercely than ever. Coaches and the leadership of the National Association for Sport and Physical Education report that very few young people now shower in locker-room facilities. Court decisions have affirmed the right of students not to shower in public situations if they so choose. Probably confirming the discomfort that most people have always felt in group showering, some schools are now eliminating their shower rooms altogether because they have fallen into disuse. Athletes often wait to shower upon returning home or to their dormitory rooms.

Attitudes Toward Sex and Romance

Philosophers since the time of the ancient Greeks have suggested that sexual desire is one type of loving and that love is fundamentally a desire for wholeness, the need to unify with the parts of ourselves we find in others. In most non-Western cultures and historical periods, infatuation and romantic love have been viewed as something quite separate from, even unrelated to, sexual longing. Whereas in our culture marriage is a social institution that springs from romance and sexual desire and appears to bond them together, in most other cultures marriage is viewed as too significant a step to be determined by such passing fancies as romantic or sexual love. We live in times that have idealized romance.

The counterculture's movement toward an instant gratification, do-it-if-it-feels-good mentality in the sixties and seventies never fit particularly well with the predominant values of the Western world. Before long, everyone realized that things could not really be that simple. Instant sex could have complicated consequences: an increase in the incidence of sexually transmitted disease, unwanted pregnancy, and shattered emotions. The final years of the century just passed saw a great deal of discussion about a return to intimacy, love, and romance. We are beginning to examine more closely the many faces of love, the intricacies of human commitment and spirituality, and the complications of intimacy. Integrating romance and sex is not as simple or "natural" as it may seem (Seidman, 1991, 1992). People's attitudes about the role of love in sexual contacts may change as they age as well, although the directions those changes take have varied with each generation. The present "older" generation seems to have become more tolerant of less connection between love and sex, and the current generation of college students seems to look less favorably on casual sex then was the case just a decade ago.

Attitudes Toward Sexuality Education

Sexuality education was first introduced into a few public schools over a century ago and has been stirring controversy ever since. Hundreds of grassroots community conflicts arose during the 1990s over the issue (Kempner, 1999). In the early 1960s, more publicity began to appear about sexuality education in public schools and colleges. Organizations were formed that encouraged and supported sexuality education programs. The most influential group was chartered in 1964 as the Sex (now Sexuality) Information and Education Council of the United States (SIECUS). One of the cofounders of SIECUS, and its first executive director, was Dr. Mary S. Calderone (1904–1998), who became one of the world's leading advocates of sexuality education. Another professional organization was formed in the late 1960s, the American Association of Sex Educators, Counselors and Therapists (AASECT). It has worked to establish standards for these fields and now certifies individuals who meet training criteria in the three different sexology fields: sexuality education, counseling, and therapy.

The state of New Jersey was one of the first to mandate sexuality education for its public schools in the mid-1980s. Nearly every state now either requires or recommends that school districts provide sexuality education, and most require HIV/AIDS education. Controversies over these programs continue to fester, often polarizing factions of people within communities. Although some groups stand in complete opposition to any form of sexuality education outside the home environment, the majority of people in North America seem to favor some sort of institutionalized effort, especially within school settings (Haffner & Wagoner, 1999). Nonetheless, most prominent sources of sexuality information for college students are peers, parents, and the media (Ballard & Morris, 1998).

The proponents of what is now called comprehensive sexuality education see the educational process as a lifelong one that encompasses not only gaining information about sexuality but also forming attitudes and learning about development, relationships, affection, gender roles, feelings, and all other aspects of being a sexual human being. It emphasizes the need to give young people the skills they will need to communicate well and make healthy, responsible choices (Nelson, 1996).

Other groups have been critical of some of the assumptions that they believe undergird comprehensive sexuality education, such as the view of individual decision making about sexual activity that young people are expected to handle. These critics also claim that the negative consequences of sexual behavior, such as unintended teen pregnancy or transmission of disease, tend not to be treated with the harder-edged negativity they deserve in such programs. They worry that the emphasis on sexual activities that are meant to provide sexual satisfaction without actually involving intercourse is unrealistic and will lead to intercourse anyway unless young people are given the skills to resist it (Whitehead, 1994). This leads them to believe that the emphasis in sexuality education should be on abstinence and learning how to resist pressures to become involved sexually. They fear that the comprehensive approach allows young people too much freedom to make up their own minds and does not emphasize clearly stated abstinence values enough (Nelson, 1996).

Sexuality education classes and programs have appeared in public schools, colleges, religious sects, and professional schools around the world (Hatfield, 1999). It is generally recognized that people of all ages want and need information about human sexuality. One study found that 90 percent of the American adults surveyed believed that sexuality education should definitely be taught in schools (Janus & Janus, 1993). However, the politics of sexuality education reflect a broader "Culture War" that is being waged between two broadly defined groups of people in North America that tend to view each other as a threat. The side that has been called the "orthodox" view fears that American society is moving too far toward governmental control, nonreligious humanistic points of view, and a moral relativism that allows too much flexibility for young people to develop their own values. The other side, sometimes called the "progressives," fears that society is sliding toward intolerance and authoritarianism, dominated by particular religious points of view (Hedgepeth, 1996). With such conflicting attitudes motivating the population, there is sure to be continuing debate about what the content and philosophy of sexuality education should be, along with heated and differing attitudes about all other aspects of human sexuality (Klein, 2000).

Think about your own attitudes toward sex and sexual behavior. What do you believe about masturbation, sexual intercourse, same-gender sexual activity, and nonmarital and marital sex? What would be your personal interpretation of the term "family values"?

◼ Milestones in Sex Research: A Brief Historical Survey

Until the mid-twentieth century, serious attempts at research in sexual behavior were seldom made. A few researchers cautiously ventured into the realm of sexuality, sometimes risking their personal and professional reputations to do so. There has been an ongoing rift between researchers who want their work to fall within the protocols of "pure" science and those who see themselves more as agents of social change. In recent decades, sex research has come of age and has become a respectable pursuit, another reflection of the interaction between cultural attitudes and scientific pursuit (Czuczka, 2000). In this section, I present a brief historical summary of some of the major advances in sex research. A summary timeline may be found in Table 1.1 on pages 28–29.

Emerging from the Nineteenth Century

The earliest sex research had to rely on historical case studies because there were almost no other data about human sexual behavior, and it was not considered permissible to ask people about such things. Early in the nineteenth century, some historical studies were published about sexuality in classical Greek and Roman times. There was a major change in methodology, however, when in 1906 a German physician, Iwan Bloch, coined the term "sexual science" and began studying the history of prostitution and what he called "strange" sexual practices. Bloch's work was the first to conceive of history as an important foundation for understanding human sexuality. It has not been until quite recently that historians have accepted sexuality as a legitimate area for historical study (Bullough, 1994). The German psychiatrist Magnus Hirschfeld was one of the first professional workers to take a stand on rights for people who were gay or lesbian. He risked personal persecution and antisemitic repercussions for saying that people with same-gender sexual orientation constituted an intermediate third sex that deserved the same rights and privileges as heterosexual people (Vyras, 1996).

In the last quarter of the nineteenth century, a period of European history when an intensely repressive moral code governed sexual behavior and attitudes, sex was thought to be a major factor in causing emotional and mental disturbances. When sexual feelings or behaviors inevitably produced guilt, fear, and self-loathing, it might be expected that they would be at the root of many disorders. Three physicians of that time significantly shaped the views of human sexuality that would set the stage for twentieth-century attitudes.

Richard von Krafft-Ebing (1840–1902)

This German-born neurologist and psychiatrist's book *Psychopathia Sexualis,* revised through 12 editions, became a widely circulated medical text that portrayed various forms of sexual behavior and arousal as disgusting and pathological. Krafft-Ebing grouped sexual deviations into four classifications of pathology: sadism, masochism, fetishism, and homosexuality.

Of special significance was his declaration that masturbation was the cause of all these sexual deviations. This is one example of how opinion and speculation, without a sound research basis, can be questionable and misleading. He illustrated his theories with case studies demonstrating the dire effects of masturbation. His case studies were highly sensational for the times, and they did call attention to the variety of human sexual orientations and activities. Unfortunately, his biased writings tainted most sexual behavior as being sick and unnatural. Even though Krafft-Ebing was not viewed as a mainstream sex researcher by his professional contemporaries, his perspective pervaded the medical and psychiatric professions well into the twentieth century.

Sigmund Freud (1856–1939)

This Viennese physician (see Fig. 1.2) focused much of his work on the study of the psychosexual development of children and how it affected adult life and mental condition. Freud's contributions had far more influence on psychology than those of Krafft-Ebing, although they also perpetuated a decidedly negative attitude toward most aspects of human sexuality. In 1895, Freud published the epochal *Studies in Hysteria,* written in collaboration with Josef Breuer. The book contained discussions of the unconscious mind, repression, and free association, concepts that became the foundation for psychoanalysis. Freud had also become convinced that neuroses were produced by unconscious conflicts of a sexual nature, an idea that alienated most scientists of his time. In 1905, his *Three Essays on the Theory of Sexuality* precipitated a storm of protest. It was in this work that Freud developed his

FIGURE 1.2 *Sigmund Freud*

Freud (1856–1939) was an Austrian neurologist who first theorized that sexuality existed throughout the life cycle and was
the basic motivating factor in human behavior. He identified
the basic stages of sexual emotional development as the oral,
the anal, and the genital.

theory of infantile sexuality and attempted to demonstrate how adult sexual perversions were distortions of
childhood sexual expressions (see chapter 6, "Sexuality through the Life Cycle").

Many of his European contemporaries considered
Freud's ideas marginal. His work was highly influential
in the United States, however, where for a time publishing in the area of human sexuality was dominated
by psychoanalysts who espoused Freudian theories of
psychosexual development. There is today much disagreement as to the value of psychoanalysis and
Freud's theories of sexuality, particularly his views
about female sexuality. Many contemporary psychologists have claimed that Freud was essentially antife-
male, and they have ventured various hypotheses
about his own problems and personal development
during adolescence. His work, nonetheless, led to an
increased interest in sex and a willingness to think and
talk about sexuality. Freud did not brand sexual behaviors as immoral, criminal, or pathological. Through
his work, sexuality became a legitimate concern of
medicine and psychology (Bullough, 1994; Leland,
1995).

Henry Havelock Ellis (1859–1939)

At the end of the nineteenth century, this English sex
researcher brought a new perspective to sexual science (see Fig. 1.3). Ellis spent several decades studying all available information on human sexuality in the
Western world and the sexual mores of other cultures.
He also studied the sex lives of his contemporaries and
carefully recorded what he learned. Eventually he began writing about his findings and published them in
six volumes between 1896 and 1910 as *Studies in the
Psychology of Sex.* A seventh volume was added in
1928 (Ellis, 1936).

Ellis played a major role in effecting the gradual
changes in sexual attitudes following Victorian times.
His *Studies* recognized that human beings exhibited
great variety in their sexual inclinations and behaviors
and that sexual mores are determined by cultural and
social influences. His conclusions were radical by Victorian standards, amazingly farsighted by present-day
standards (Bullough, 1998). Ellis noted that masturbation was a common practice in males and females at all
ages. He realized that sexual orientation toward one
gender or the other existed in degrees rather than as
an absolute. He legitimized the idea that women could
have as great a sexual desire as men, and he pointed
out that the orgasms of men and women were remarkably similar. Anticipating later trends in sex therapy, Ellis recognized that difficulties in achieving
erection or orgasm were often psychological problems
rather than physical. Ellis emphasized what most professionals today accept, that "the range of variation
within fairly normal limits is immense" when considering the sexual needs and behaviors of humans.

Sexual Studies in the Early Twentieth Century

In 1926, a Dutch physician by the name of Theodoor
van de Velde (1873–1937) published the first edition of
his book *Ideal Marriage.* Although it was not the only
sex manual available at the time, it was significant because van de Velde conveyed the allowability and validity of sexual responsiveness to a reading audience
that still had Victorian inhibitions (Bullough, 1994). Although van de Velde's suggestions for a more fulfilling
sexual relationship were described in a marriage-ori-
ented framework with some moralistic boundaries and
with an almost obsessive attention to cleanliness, he
put forth a generally positive outlook for which people
by this time were ready. His book described a variety
of coital positions, discussed the use of oral sex in
foreplay, and offered suggestions for dealing with
some sexual problems. Because of the popularity of
Ideal Marriage, his ideas played an important role in
helping thousands of couples to achieve more sexual
enjoyment.

FIGURE 1.3 *Henry Havelock Ellis*
Ellis (1859–1939), an English physician, invented the term "autoeroticism" to indicate the occurrence of masturbation in both sexes and all ages. He was farsighted in his views, particularly of the way sexuality affects women and the way mental attitude affects physical behavior.

One of the outstanding sex research efforts of the early twentieth century was a study published in 1932 by Robert Latou Dickinson called *A Thousand Marriages*. Dickinson gathered 5,200 case studies of women he treated between 1882 and 1924 while he was a gynecologist in New York City. He documented how the repressive sexual attitudes of childhood led to disastrous effects on adult sexual functioning—one of the earliest attempts at a better understanding of female sexuality. He also studied the physiological responses of the clitoris, vagina, and cervix during sexual stimulation and orgasm. Realizing that once a woman has been able to experience the pleasure of a self-induced orgasm she is more likely to have orgasm during intercourse, he introduced the use of electrical vibrators for women.

Another pioneer in the sexual liberation of women was Helena Wright, who began her gynecological medical practice in London in the 1920s. She discovered that most women found no enjoyment in sex and instead considered it to be a marital duty. Unlike other women writers, who had discussed sexuality in mostly negative terms, Wright began publishing books that in-

structed women on how to achieve orgasm, through both intercourse and masturbation (Bullough, 1996). The first of her books was *The Sex Factor in Marriage,* published in 1930. Subsequent editions of the book and Wright's other publications continued for decades to give explicit instructions to women on becoming fully acquainted with their sex organs and sexual responses.

Mid-Twentieth Century Sex Research

The preeminent sex researcher at midcentury was Alfred C. Kinsey (1894–1956), a successful zoologist who gradually moved into research on human sexual behavior (see Fig. 1.4). It was through Kinsey's work that sex research became a more legitimate scientific pursuit than it had been because he applied statistical analysis to sexual behavior instead of drawing conclusions solely from personal observations, as most of his predecessors had done. In 1937, as a conservative and highly respected biology professor at Indiana University, Kinsey had been selected to teach a new course in sexuality and marriage. In preparing lectures and attempting to answer the questions of his students, Kinsey began to realize that little reliable information about sexuality was available. He began gathering information by interviewing people about their sex lives, eventually involving associates in the interviews. By the end of 1949, he had gathered detailed histories on the sexual lives of more than 16,000 people.

Kinsey founded and directed Indiana University's Institute for Sex Research. Now called the Kinsey Institute for Research in Sex, Gender, and Reproduction (commonly known as the Kinsey Institute for Sex Research, or, more simply, the Kinsey Institute), it remains an important center for sex research. Paul Gebhard and Wardell Pomeroy became Kinsey's principal collaborators and helped design the statistical approaches and skillful interview techniques that rendered the Kinsey studies so unique. The two studies that brought Kinsey wide recognition and notoriety were *Sexual Behavior in the Human Male,* published in 1948, and *Sexual Behavior in the Human Female,* published in 1953. Both were considered milestones in this field (Bullough, 1998).

Although Kinsey's findings were long considered representative of the general population, we now know that his research had some inherent design flaws that probably skewed the statistical results. As we will see in greater detail later in this chapter (p. 33), the manner in which a researcher obtains people to be subjects for a study—the population sample—is absolutely crucial to the accuracy of the data. When Kinsey embarked on his research, he believed, probably rightfully so, that getting a standard, representative sample of the general population was a practical impossibility. He had already decided that face-to-face

FIGURE 1.4   *Alfred C. Kinsey*
Kinsey (1894–1956) was a zoologist, later a biology professor, who was instrumental in compiling face-to-face interviews with thousands of people about their sexual behavior. His work, not highly regarded in his lifetime, has come to be regarded as comprehensive, systematic, and the model upon which other studies are based.

interviewing would be the best way to obtain information from people, and it took him 6 months to persuade the first 62 people to participate. He therefore compromised in finding subjects to interview, knowing that the outcome would be less than satisfactory, but he believed that it was the best that could be done at the time (Ericksen, 1998).

Kinsey settled for what is known as a "sample of convenience," interviewing groups of people who were willing to volunteer including those from college fraternities, sororities, and college classes; other student groups; and inhabitants of rooming houses, prisons, and mental hospitals. He even interviewed hitchhikers who came through town. For increased reliability, he would attempt to interview all members of a particular group. There were two essential flaws in this approach. First, because the interviewees were recruited volunteers, the information they offered about their sexual lives could not justifiably be generalized to the larger national population. Secondly, it may be assumed that willing volunteers—especially for something such as a sex survey—may well have very different sex-related attitudes, life experiences, and sexual behaviors from those who would be reluctant to participate. The data from such volunteers may well represent an accurate portrayal of the volunteer group

but are not as likely to reflect patterns in the general population (Laumann, Gagnon, et al., 1994; Michael et al., 1994;).

There can be no argument that Kinsey's work fostered a new level of awareness about the diversity of human sexual behaviors. Until very recently, his statistics were about the most accurate and comprehensive that we had available. The surprising thing is that it took nearly 50 years for us to get more accurate information about a subject that has clearly been so much in the public eye (Nardi & Schneider, 1998). Following Kinsey's death, the Kinsey Institute staff has continued to make significant contributions to the field up to the present time.

Two researchers who contributed more to our knowledge of sexual functioning than any predecessor were William H. Masters and Virginia E. Johnson (see Fig. 1.5). Their work focused on two major areas: the physiology of human sexual response and the treatment of sexual dysfunction. Between 1855 and 1955, several studies were published that described measurements of various human physiological responses during intercourse and masturbation. During the 1940s, even Kinsey and his associates had observed intercourse and recorded the physiological responses of the participants. Yet many questions remained unanswered. William Masters launched his research study in 1954 and hired Virginia Johnson as an interviewer soon after. In the decade that followed, Masters and Johnson and their associates used sophisticated instrumentation to measure the physiological responses of 694 individuals during masturbation and coitus. In to-

FIGURE 1.5   *Virginia E. Johnson and William H. Masters*
Masters and Johnson were the first researchers to actually observe, monitor, and film the physiological responses of people engaged in coitus or masturbation. This initial research led them to develop techniques for treating sexual dysfunction effectively.

tal, they studied more than 10,000 orgasms in these laboratory conditions. The detailed account of their work is given in *Human Sexual Response* (Masters & Johnson, 1966).

Their second major research effort began in 1959, proceeding simultaneously with the studies on sexual response. For 5 years, Masters and Johnson developed and perfected clinical techniques for the treatment of male and female sexual dysfunctions. In 1965, they considered their therapy methods to be demonstrably effective and began to charge fees for the 2-week treatment that they had developed. In 1970, their revolutionary treatment format was described in *Human Sexual Inadequacy,* a book that inaugurated the age of sex therapy. Numerous other workers have now modified and enlarged upon the Masters and Johnson work, and sex therapy has become a distinct discipline of medicine and psychology. Research about sex therapy has lagged in recent years, even though demand for therapy services has been on the rise.

Surveys of the Seventies and Eighties

As information about human sexuality began to proliferate, curiosity about the sexual behaviors of others began to increase. It became obvious that there was little reliable knowledge about what people felt, wanted, did, or fantasized about sexually. The seventies became the decade of the sex survey, and books and magazines were filled with new peeks at the most private details of sex lives in the United States. The methodologies of these surveys were highly questionable, yet their results generated a great deal of attention and solidified some of the myths and misconceptions about the variety and frequency of sexual behaviors (Ericksen, 1999).

The Hunt Report

The largest survey on sexual behavior following the Kinsey studies was commissioned in the early 1970s by the Playboy Foundation. A private research foundation selected people from telephone books in 24 U.S. cities at random. Twenty percent of these individuals then agreed to complete a questionnaire, and data were gathered from 982 men and 1,044 women. The findings were reported by professional journalist Morton Hunt in the book *Sexual Behavior in the 1970s,* which was published in 1975. The questionnaire employed in the survey asked over 1,000 questions about people's sexual histories and attitudes. There have been criticisms of the statistical validity of the Hunt Report, and the results should certainly be interpreted with care. The return rate on the questionnaire was relatively low, and the fact that *Playboy* was sponsoring the study may well have skewed the sample population that was willing to respond. However, the study did provide some interesting data and was cited frequently in discussions of human sexual behavior.

The Redbook Survey

In the mid-1970s, *Redbook* magazine published a questionnaire about female sexuality to which over 100,000 women responded. Again, the results could not be considered representative of the general female population because only about 2 percent of the magazine's readers actually returned the survey. At the time, the study constituted one of the largest surveys of women's attitudes and behaviors ever attempted. The *Redbook* study conveyed a picture of U.S. women as having active sex lives and often initiating sexual activities with their partners. Most of the women expressed relative satisfaction with their marital sex, although one-third said they had experienced extramarital sexual relations. Nearly all of the women had, at one time or another, participated in oral-genital sex. The more religious the women in the study considered themselves, the more satisfied they were with their marital sex, and the less likely they were to have cohabited with a partner prior to marriage (Tavris & Sadd, 1977).

The Hite Reports

In 1976, Shere Hite's report on female sexuality, *The Hite Report,* became a best-seller and opened several issues for debate and discussion, including the degree of dissatisfaction the women who returned the questionnaire tended to express about their sexual relationships. Hite received completed surveys from 3,019 women (a very small proportion of the 100,000 questionnaires she had distributed) concerning many aspects of their sexuality. The questionnaire asked for essay-type answers and therefore provided much anecdotal information as well as data that could be quantified. Hite later surveyed 7,239 men with a similar questionnaire, the results of which became *The Hite Report on Male Sexuality* (Hite, 1981). Shere Hite would later publish two more surveys based on relatively small responses to questionnaires. Her work has been legitimately criticized for employing unrepresentative samples and for lacking hard statistical analysis. Some critics have claimed that the questions on the surveys were leading and thus biased the answers. These reports were rich with information and personal stories about the sex lives of several thousand people and therefore made interesting reading for the curious. However, like much anecdotal research of this sort, their content is often mistakenly generalized and assumed to represent prevailing attitudes or behaviors among the general population. In this way, they may create misconceptions about human sexuality that make their way into the psyche of entire generations of people.

Inherent Flaws of the Early Sex Surveys

Although the *Playboy* and *Redbook* surveys and the Hite Reports may have seemed impressive because of their sheer numbers of responses, the number of people who participate in a research study is not its most significant component. Far more important is how the researcher actually gets the participants. For example, the percentage of people responding to a widely distributed questionnaire is more important than the raw numbers. A response rate of 2 or 3 percent would yield very questionable data. Social scientists would consider a response rate of about 30 percent to be in the minimum range of acceptability in terms of accuracy. The higher the response rate, the more representative the results are of the total population that had been approached originally. Therein lies the other major flaw of these surveys. Who has actually been invited to participate? Readers of a particular magazine, such as *Redbook* or *Playboy*, may be considered to have certain characteristics in common and therefore not be representative of anything more than readers of those magazines. Readers of *The New Republic* or *Christian Century* might be expected to have very different characteristics as groups.

Another difficulty with survey questionnaires that are distributed en masse is that there is no way of really knowing who has responded. Some respondents may have filled out surveys as a joke or deliberately exaggerated their answers to bias the results. Some may have pretended to be of the other gender or may have completed more than one questionnaire. So although surveys of this sort may generate interesting results that capture our attention, there is no way of knowing what their findings really mean. It would be a serious blunder to use such studies to draw any sweeping conclusions about social trends relating to human sexuality.

Research on Childhood Sexuality

Two international studies conducted in the early eighties provided some new insights about sexuality during childhood, a much-neglected area. Ronald and Juliette Goldman (1982) interviewed 838 children in Australia, North America, England, and Sweden concerning what they thought about sex, their relationships with others, and their sexuality education. The researchers found North American children to be the least well informed about sex-related facts and issues.

The German researcher Ernest Borneman (1994) researched childhood sexuality for over 30 years, mostly through various types of interview surveys. Some of this work was longitudinal in scope, with several hundred research subjects being studied over a period of 20 years or more. His findings tended to discredit some of the widely held Freudian views of children's psychosexual development. Both the Goldman and Borneman studies concluded that there is no evidence to support the existence of the **latency period** in children, a stage in development that Freud claimed was characterized by little interest in or awareness of sexual feelings. All recent research tends to support the notion that children are sexual from birth and have a diversity of sexual feelings, behaviors, and interests as they grow.

Other Surveys

There were other important surveys after 1970. Robert Sorensen (1973) published *Adolescent Sexuality in Contemporary America,* based on answers from several hundred adolescents. Melvin Zelnik and John Kantner (1980) used sophisticated research designs and methods of statistical analysis to study the sexual and contraceptive behaviors of teenagers. Their surveys represented some of the most reliable data available for years on teenage sexual behavior.

Alan Bell, Martin Weinberg, and Sue Kiefer Hammersmith (1981) of the Kinsey Institute published the results of a unique study of sexual orientation called *Sexual Preference: Its Development in Men and Women.* From a pool of 4,639 gay males and lesbians, they conducted extensive interviews with 979, obtaining the most in-depth data of any study on same-gender sexual orientation ever conducted. Although the research focused on gay males and lesbians in only one area of the country, the San Francisco Bay area, it was considered crucial to our evolving understandings of sexual orientation and its development.

Philip Blumstein and Pepper Schwartz (1983), sociologists at the University of Washington, studied completed questionnaires from 4,314 heterosexual couples, 969 gay male couples, and 788 lesbian couples on various aspects of their relationships. Their report, titled *American Couples,* was considered to be a strong and important sociological study because of its large and diverse sample and its complicated research design. It provided a fresh perspective on the ways in which modern couples were approaching their sexual and loving relationships.

latency period: a stage in human development characterized, in Freud's theory, by little interest in or awareness of sexual feelings.

Sex Research in the Nineties

A 1990 survey from the Kinsey Institute (Reinisch & Beasley, 1990) examined the basic sexual knowledge of Americans and their sources of sex information while growing up. Eighteen questions about human sexuality were developed from the most frequently asked questions in letters to the Institute. The participants in the study were 1,974 women and men selected randomly to represent a national sample. Although there have been criticisms about the questions asked in the survey, 55 percent of the participants failed the test, calling into question just how knowledgeable about sexuality Americans really are. Men tended to be better informed about general sexual matters such as intercourse and masturbation, whereas women performed better on questions relating to sexual health and birth control. The most common sources of sex information during the respondents' formative years were friends (42 percent), mothers (29 percent), and books (22 percent). Formalized sexuality education and fathers trailed behind the other sources cited.

In 1992, the French government completed a survey of 20,055 people aged 18 to 69. The British also did an extensive study of sexual behavior in 18,876 individuals aged 16 to 59 (Johnson, Wadsworth, Wellings, & Field, 1994). Evidence from these studies suggested two things that startled a number of sexologists. One was that people were not using condoms during their sexual activities to the extent that would be advisable to protect them from HIV infection. The other controversial finding, one that has now been supported in recent U.S. research (Billy, Tanfer, Grady, & Keplinger, 1993; Michael et al., 1994), was that same-gender (homosexual) sexual activity may not be as prevalent as earlier studies, such as Kinsey's, had suggested.

Puzzled by the many variations in the way HIV may be spread, the World Health Organization (WHO) conducted a major study on sexual behavior in 15 countries. Some scientists have noted the irony of the fact that developing world countries were ready to study sexual activity in depth, while proposals for such study in the United States have become mired in political debates. One of the major methodological difficulties of the international project was designing a questionnaire that could be translated into many different languages, so that anyone might understand the sexual issues being addressed. Different research packages were designed for Africa, Europe, and the Americas (Cleland & Ferry, 1997). Cross-cultural differences had to be considered. For example, in some regions of Nigeria, polygamy (marriage to more than one spouse) is accepted as part of the culture. If a man there reports having had sex with several different women during a certain time period, it should not be assumed that the man has been promiscuous. It may instead mean that he has several wives. The WHO study gathered information on religious attitudes, educational levels, condom use, knowledge about AIDS, and premarital and extramarital sex. It represents the only coordinated international research on sexual behavior ever conducted on a major scale.

The results of one of the most comprehensive sex surveys of American college students were published in 1997. The data were gathered from an extensive questionnaire that was sent out by *Details* magazine and Random House publishers. About 20,000 survey questionnaires were distributed, and close to 2,000 usable ones were returned. Again it is clear that such techniques do not assure the accuracy of random sampling and larger return rates, but the study does provide some insights into the sexual lives and behaviors of today's students. Some of the statistics match rather closely with the results of more statistically valid samples, suggesting that they have at least some degree of accuracy. Findings from this survey will be interspersed at appropriate places within this text (Elliott & Brantley, 1997).

A general survey of sexual attitudes and behaviors in the United States was completed by Samuel and Cynthia Janus (1993), who published *The Janus Report on Sexual Behavior*. Over 4,500 people were pretested with a survey instrument, followed by the collection of data from a cross section of the U.S. adult population between 1988 and 1992. Written questionnaires were completed by all respondents, and these were supplemented by 125 in-depth interviews conducted by carefully trained professionals. Data from 1,347 men and 1,418 women were used to obtain the results of the survey. Again, however, the population sample used in the Janus survey could not be reliably used to describe the general population. Although there were respondents from every region of the 48 contiguous states, and the researchers tried to match the proportions of the population in various age groups with a comparable percentage in the survey sample, they recruited volunteers. Just because their sample reflected some characteristics of the general population does not mean that volunteers who completed their questionnaire produced results that may be generalized to that population. The Janus research did provide us with some interesting perspectives on the current sexual attitudes and activities of Americans.

Under what conditions would you respond truthfully to a survey about your sexual behavior?

The National Health and Social Life Survey

The most comprehensive study on sexual behavior in the United States to emerge since the Kinsey work was

Table 1.1	*A Timeline: Milestones for Western Culture in the Study of Sex*						
1880	**1890**	**1900**	**1910**	**1920**	**1930**	**1940**	
Richard von Krafft-Ebing publishes *Psychopathia Sexualis.*	Sigmund Freud publishes psychoanalytic interpretations of sexuality in the human personality.			Theodoor van de Velde publishes *Ideal Marriage.*	Helena Wright publishes *The Sex Factor in Marriage.*	Robert L. Dickinson publishes *A Thousand Marriages.*	

Henry Havelock Ellis publishes 7 volumes of *Studies in the Psychology of Sex.*

Early Studies Slowly Bring Human Sexuality into Focus

Sexual feelings and behaviors are feared to be physically and mentally debilitating, as well as morally questionable. Sex is considered separate from love and romance.	Sexuality begins to find a more legitimate, though still quite negative, place in human experience and early psychology.	Sexual activity is established as a potentially positive aspect of the marital relationship. Sex and love begin to be integrated.

1950	1960	1970	1980	1990	2000	2010
Alfred C. Kinsey studies at Indiana University on sexual behavior in the human male and female.	Mary J. Sherfey's study on the evolution of female sexuality. John Money's study of gender identity at Johns Hopkins Hospital. The first Presidential Commission on Obscenity and Pornography. William H. Masters and Virginia C. Johnson publish *Human Sexual Response* and *Human Sexual Inadequacy*.	The Hunt Report. The Hite Report. Robert C. Sorenson publishes *Adolescent Sexuality in Contemporary America*. *Redbook* magazine's survey.	Studies on sexual preference and sex in male-female and same-gender relationships. Studies on childhood sexuality and sex in the older years.	Out of concern for the increase in HIV infection and AIDS, several studies on human sexual behavior are undertaken: World Health Organization National AIDS Behavioral Survey Major studies in France and Great Britain Studies of male sexual behavior	The National Longitudinal Study of Adolescent Health The National AIDS Behavioral Methodology Survey *Details* magazine Survey of College Student Sexual Behavior	Studies on adolescent sexual behaviors will increase our understanding of this age group. There will be more pressure to understand HIV transmission and prevention. Greater awareness of the need to research female sexual response and behavior.

The Janus Report on Sexual Behavior

The National Health and Social Life Survey

Increased interest in cross-cultural studies of sexual behavior.

Sex Research Achieves Legitimacy as a Scientific Pursuit as Sociosexual Values Shift

Sex research becomes a tool for understanding changing sociosexual attitudes and for controlling the spread of HIV/AIDS, and theory in sex research gains a multidisciplinary perspective.

The first statistical sexual behavior studies enlighten the general population about the extent and range of sexual behavior, in and out of marriage.	Investigations of female sexuality and gender identity broaden our views of femininity and masculinity. The first studies emerge on how the body actually responds during sexual arousal and stimulation to orgasm.	Sex therapy for the treatment of sexual dysfunctions emerges as an interdisciplinary professional field. The "sexual revolution" legitimizes the right to pursue and enhance personal sexual enjoyment.	Surveys clarify the range of human sexual experience across the life span. Gay and lesbian orientation and behavior receive more attention in research.	Controversies develop over sexual values; abortion rights; gay, lesbian, and bisexual rights; and the role of sexuality education. Sex research focuses more on understanding sexual behaviors so that the worldwide spread of HIV infection may be brought under control. The government wrestles with issues of funding for sex research that some officials claim may violate personal privacy.	Sexual behavior is seen more clearly within its social contexts. More accurate data emerge to help understand human sexual behaviors, painting a less adventurous picture of sexual frequency and activity than had been previously portrayed. Attention is given to bringing greater sophistication to theory in sexual science.	The beginning of the new millennium will see more broad surveys of sexual behaviors, especially during adolescence. The feminist perspective will become clearer in sex research, and research will attempt to clarify the influences of biology and social construction in the determination of variable human traits.

FIGURE 1.6   *Robert T. Michael, John H. Gagnon, Stuart Michaels, and Edward O. Laumann*
Laumann, Gagnon, Michael, and Michaels conducted the National Health and Social Life Survey, the most comprehensive study on sexual behavior in the United States to emerge since the Kinsey work. Using scientific methodology, the study determined that most Americans are fairly content with their sexual lives.

the National Health and Social Life Survey (NHSLS). After a federal agency called for proposals for a study on the sexual practices and attitudes of American adults in 1987, three highly respected researchers entered what turned out to be a 4-year battle for federal funding that ultimately proved unsuccessful. They were Edward Laumann, provost and distinguished professor of sociology at the University of Chicago; Robert Michael, dean of the Graduate School of Public Policy Studies at Chicago, who has expertise in the study of marriage, contraception, and cohabitation; and John Gagnon, professor of sociology at the State University of New York at Stony Brook, who is widely known for his research on sexual conduct (see Fig. 1.6). Even after their proposed research had received approval in 1991, conservative members of Congress introduced legislation that effectively eliminated the funding for such research (Laumann, Michael, & Gagnon, 1994). The researchers managed to secure funding from eight private foundations and proceed with their study. Stuart Michaels, a researcher at the University of Chicago, became project manager for the study.

Although they had originally hoped to interview 20,000 people so that the data could be analyzed sep-

arately for smaller subpopulations (such as gay males and lesbians), their funding could only support a sample size of about 3,500 adults, aged 18 to 59. Their random sampling techniques are among several characteristics that have rendered this research particularly reliable and valuable. They worked through the National Opinion Research Center at the University of Chicago to generate randomly selected areas of the country. They eventually identified 4,369 households who had someone eligible to participate in the study, and then randomly selected the individual in each household to be interviewed. This is the protocol that social scientists have generally established as correct methodology (Laumann, Gagnon, et al., 1994).

The questionnaire that they employed had been carefully designed to avoid confusing people with technical language and to flow naturally from topic to topic without predicting responses. This is crucial in assuring valid results. They decided on face-to-face interviews as the best technique to ensure that respondents understood the questions. The research team selected 220 professional interviewers who were veterans of other surveys and carefully trained them. They were then dispersed to their various parts of the United States and encouraged to persuade all eligible

Source: Copyright © Gary Brookins, 1996, Richmond Times-Dispatch. Reprinted with special permission of King Features Syndicate.

individuals to participate in the survey. They sometimes returned several times in attempts to garner participant cooperation. The interviews proceeded over a 7-month period. One of the things that this research ultimately demonstrated was that people will indeed participate in sex surveys when they are convinced that there are legitimate social purposes for the research, that their answers will be considered without judgment, and that their anonymity and confidentiality will be protected (Michael et al., 1994).

Eventually, 3,432 individuals were interviewed, for a response rate of nearly 80 percent, one of the reasons why the results of this study are considered to be so accurate. Another is that the sample population was randomly selected and almost exactly mirrored many characteristics of the general American population according to numerous measures. The questionnaire itself had a number of checks and cross-checks that helped to validate the responses given. Cross-comparisons of responses with some sex-related data generated by an earlier study conducted by the highly respected General Social Survey showed remarkable similarities. In a more general sense, the results also compared well with the major studies that had been done in France and Great Britain (Giami & Schiltz, 1997; Wellings et al., 1994).

The results of the NHSLS were published in two books, one a detailed and scholarly description of the research titled *The Social Organization of Sexuality* (Laumann, Gagnon et al., 1994), and the other a popular trade book, *Sex in America: A Definitive Study* (Michael et al., 1994). Although the work had its detractors, social scientists generally accept that the NHSLS data are the best we currently have available, resulting from state-of-the-art survey techniques that yielded a high degree of validity to the data (DeLamater, 1995). The findings were in a sense counterrevolutionary because they reflected a nation that was indeed involved in a wide spectrum of sexual activi-

ties, but in general was much less sexually active than previously believed. The study also suggested that Americans were for the most part more content with their sexual lives than had been assumed. Data from the NHSLS will be used throughout this text to provide a truer picture of human sexual behavior than we have probably ever had.

Even in a time when adolescents are clearly sexually active, there is a great deal of controversy surrounding the right of researchers to question adolescents about sexual matters in order to obtain data. What are your feelings on this issue?

National Longitudinal Study of Adolescent Health

By 1994, the National Institute of Child Health and Human Development had unveiled plans for a long-term study of teenage health, which includes questioning some 20,000 teens about their sexual behavior. The first phase of this National Longitudinal Study of Adolescent Health has been completed, and it involved the collection of completed questionnaires from 90,000 students in grades 7 through 12 at 145 schools around the country. During the next phase, 500 trained interviewers visited 20,000 adolescents at their homes, gathering information from them in a confidential manner. The same teens were to be interviewed a second time at home to see how their behaviors may have changed over time. Their personal identities will not be connected with any of the data. Although there are still groups that oppose questioning young people about sexual matters, this $21.5-million study has the potential to provide a clearer perspective on sexual behavior among teens than any previous study has offered (New Adolescent Health Study, 1995).

Sex Research in the New Millennium

As we enter this new millennium, there are several trends in sex research that seem to be sorting themselves out. As the previous section demonstrates, we should begin the millennium with the most accurate data on adolescent sexual behavior that has ever been available. It is also likely that information will emerge from general surveys that examine the relationship of sexual behavior to HIV transmission more thoroughly. There needs to be an expansion of research investigating trends of sexual behaviors in the developing countries of the world. This work will also need to focus on the effectiveness of various forms of birth control to keep the global population growth under control. As the U.S. Space Program progresses, we must also work toward freeing research from its bias that has tended to see women in space as representing various sets of "problems" rather than positive challenges. Sexuality, reproduction, and space travel are on the next frontier of sex research (Casper & Moore, 1995).

Of special significance will be the emerging role of feminine and feminist perspectives in research, as increasing numbers of women make their contributions to the field (McCormick, 1996b). Just as women's issues and perceptions have long been undervalued in sex research, it will be important to evaluate data on sexual behaviors and attitudes by ethnic group. It is becoming abundantly clear that ethnicity is one factor in determining some different aspects of human sexuality, although with not any more significance than many other factors (Catania et al., 1995; Quadagno, Sly, Harrison, Eberstein, & Soler, 1998). However, defining the groups by which ethnic factors can legitimately be defined is a matter to be determined. Research often sorts out data for Hispanics, and yet the U.S. Bureau of the Census decided that data on race and Hispanic origin should be collected separately from other data. Spanish-speaking people do not represent a homogenous race, and in fact includes people who are white, indigenous Native American, black, and even some Asians (J. Diaz-Calderon, personal communication, 1997; Sabogal, Binson, & Catania, 1997).

Sex researchers in the early 2000s also face some challenges regarding sex-related theory. Theories in sexual science are often oversimplified and do not take into consideration the multidisciplinary nature of human sexuality. Specific fields often seem bound by the theoretical perspectives that grow out of those fields, while ignoring relevant theoretical frameworks from related fields. For sexology to make the progress it really needs to make in this millennium, it will need to strive for greater congruence in theory and a closer fit between theory and practice (Bancroft, 1999). Most of all, sex researchers need to adapt to being able to see beyond narrow academic disciplines to the inclusive view that a multidisciplinary perspective can yield. Additionally, they need to examine carefully the ways in which their own values may reflect the outcomes of their work (Weis, 1998). It is in these ways that sex research can truly come of age in this new century.

■ The Methods of Sexological Research

Research into the interdisciplinary realm of sexology has been increasing, and numerous professional journals are devoted exclusively to new concepts, controversies, and information relating to human sexuality. Although scientists are influenced by their own social and cultural circumstances (Ericksen, 1999), they must

always approach their subjects without preconceived notions of what the data will show and without agendas on what sexual behaviors ought to be. Theories about human sexuality represent a consensus among researchers in the field about the best ways to observe and explain things relating to sex, but researchers have a long way to go in creating solid theories about sexuality (Weis, 1998). There is a great deal of confusion between **sexology,** or the science of sex, and **sexosophy,** the ideology or philosophy of sex. Much of what is passed off without question as scientific information regarding human sexuality is actually ideological statement without real scientific merit. As a society, we need to learn how to become more astute at separating the results of valid sex research from ideological hype (Reiss, 2000).

Comprehensive scientific study requires substantial amounts of money, and more is available for work that has clearcut practical applications or product development potentials. Scientists doing research designed to yield basic scientific data about sexual attitudes, the physiology of sexual response, or the origins of human sexual orientation often find financing difficult (Bancroft, 1999). Political climates may also determine how fundable sex research can be. If an issue becomes a significant topic for political debate, government funding may suddenly emerge to support scientific research. Reliable scientific research must be carried out in an atmosphere that is as free as possible from the agendas and expectations of self-interested parties (Ericksen, 1999).

Collecting Research Data on Human Sexuality

One of the goals of scientific research is to find information that can then be generalized to the real world outside of the study. Science offers hope of being able to understand, predict, and perhaps control various phenomena. Obviously, using human beings as research subjects creates many problems because we are not as easily categorized or experimentally controlled as mice or molecules. Sex researchers have the difficult responsibility of ensuring that their own methods and assumptions do not distort the outcome of their work. There is evidence, for example, that researchers' assumptions about sexuality can influence the ways in which questions are asked (Catania, 1999; Gribble, Miller, Rogers, & Turner, 1999). Here are some of the particular methodological strategies used in conducting sex research.

---

sexology: the scientific study of human sexuality.

sexosophy: the philosophies and ideologies relating to human sexuality.

If our survey showed us anything, it was that college students see sex as part of the "big picture": just one part of what it takes to have a happy life. Long-term commitment to a partner was high on the list of life goals. Overwhelmingly, the students we surveyed affirmed that they want to get married someday: 70 percent said they love the idea of marriage, while 26 percent admitted marriage might be difficult, but definitely worth the effort.

Is sex the most important part of marriage or a long-term commitment? Not according to the students we surveyed. When asked what they would do if the frequency of sex began to decline while they were in a long-term relationship, did they opt to bail out? No! Most of them, 67 percent, realize that a relationship takes work. They favored confronting the problem and fighting to keep the fire alive. Even the lazy ones, the 31 percent who said you should just make do with a drop in sexual activity, said that there is more to a relationship than sex.

No doubt about it, though, college students are looking for great sex lives. Eighty-four percent believe that there is such a thing as "perfect sex," and they want to find it. What do they think is the most important part of great sex? Love, love, love. That's right, even in the final years of the twentieth century, love [was] the thing—54 percent listed it as the most important part of a good sex life. Believe it or not, good communication, at 19 percent, comes in second on the list of keys to good sex—five percentage points ahead of physical attraction at 14 percent.

On the downside, we learned that students are either reluctant or careless about protecting themselves from the hazardous side of sex. Less than half practice safe sex all the time. And women must still contend with partners who violently assert their sexual will: 21 percent reported being physically forced by an acquaintance to have sex. Clearly, there are some serious problems that must be resolved to make the world a better place for sex.

Overall, it looks like college students know what they want and know how to get it. And they are happy with where they are heading. Although 21 percent of the students we asked felt that their parents' generation had better romantic relationships, 36 percent felt that love and sex are better now than they used to be.

Looks like the twenty-first century is going to be one big love-in.

—Leland Elliott & Cynthia Brantley-Johnson (1997). *Sex on Campus* (pp. 235–236). Reprinted by permission of Random House, Inc.

Selecting Population Samples

When attempting to answer some questions about human sexuality, we would obviously find it impossible to get information about all human beings. Therefore, it is necessary to select a **sample** of the human population from which the results may be generalized to the larger population. The more people included in the sample and the more proportionally representative they are to the various characteristics in the total population, the more statistically reliable the study may be considered to be. The best population sample is a **random sample,** in which individuals are selected at random from the whole population. If a significant enough number of persons is selected, the sample can be assumed to be very representative of the whole. It is particularly crucial that population samples are reflective of the proportions of ethnic diversity in a particular population because ethnicity may influence sexual attitudes and behaviors to at least some degree (Catania, Binson, Peterson, & Canchola, 1997; Quadagno et al., 1998). However, such studies must also be large and expensive, so very little research of this sort has been conducted for groups as big as the population of an entire country.

There are various forms of bias that may enter human research studies and influence the results and conclusions. For example, not everyone may be willing to participate in a study on sexuality or be honest even if he or she agrees to participate. This creates volunteer bias that is bound to affect the outcome of research (Catania, 1999; Johnson & Copas, 1997). Studies have shown that people who volunteer to participate in sexuality studies tend to be more sexually experienced than nonvolunteers, more interested in sexual variety, and generally more interested in sex (Plaud, Gaither, Hegstad, Rowan, & Devitt, 1999). Beyond this participation bias is actual response bias, meaning that people may not always be accurate or truthful in self-reporting their sexual behaviors. Response bias can work in one of two ways. Some respondents may un-

sample: a representative group of a population that is the focus of a scientific poll or study.

random sample: a representative group of the larger population that is the focus of a scientific poll or study in which care is taken to select participants without a pattern that might sway research results.

derreport or conceal their sexual behaviors out of personal embarrassment, fear that their anonymity will not be guaranteed, or concerns about reprisals. Others may exaggerate or embellish their reports because it is self-enhancing for them to imagine having been more adventurous than they have actually been. Even respondents anxious to be accurate may have distorted or inaccurate memories about sexual experience (Coxon, 1999). For all of these reasons, research studies on human sexuality must be carefully designed and tested to yield the most reliable data possible.

Taking Surveys

Asking people questions about some aspect of their sexual attitudes or behaviors is one of the most common methods employed by sex researchers. This may be accomplished either in face-to-face interviews, in telephone interviews, or through completion of questionnaires or daily diaries in which behaviors are recorded. The most surveyed group in the United States has been college students. They are often asked to complete questionnaires on sexuality because they represent a population accessible to faculty working on research, a sample of convenience. Care must be taken in generalizing such data to other populations. Daily telephone calls and written diaries have both been shown to have their weaknesses (Morrison, Leigh, & Gilmore, 1999).

The Kinsey researchers and those who conducted the NHSLS used carefully structured face-to-face interviewing procedures, in which researchers were carefully trained in techniques to establish an accepting attitude and to avoid "leading" people into answers. These help to minimize dishonesty and other forms of questionnaire bias. Printed questionnaires are an efficient and economical way of gathering information from large numbers of people, but it is much more difficult to detect dishonest answers, misunderstandings, exaggeration, or frivolity than in face-to-face interviews. Nevertheless, the interviewing mode used and the training and personal characteristics of the interviewer can affect the data that are collected (Morrison et al., 1999; Turner, Millers, & Rogers 1997). In any survey technique, it is crucial that the vocabulary used in the questions be understandable to the population being tested, and that suitable statistical adjustments be made to account for individuals who have refused to participate or to answer particular questions (Stone, Catania, & Binson, 1999). Ethnic differences should also be taken into consideration and reported.

Explaining Gender Discrepancies in Sex Surveys

In surveys of sexual behavior, there has been a consistent pattern in the data that has puzzled researchers and the general public alike: Men tend to report hav-

ing had more sexual partners than women say they have had. Intuitively this does not make sense unless many men were having sex with a much smaller cohort of women, but this does not seem to be a particularly satisfactory answer either. The discrepancy has been so great that it has been difficult for anyone—from statisticians to sexologists—to explain it. Studies that have attempted to explore the reasons for this gender discrepancy have now developed a clearer picture of what is happening, and it seems to rest with the ways in which men and women tend to report their sexual histories. Men who report having had high numbers of sexual partners (i.e., more than 20) tend to round off their figures by 5s, 10s, and even 25s. This may be because of having a poorer memory as to the exact number of partners, or because men are more comfortable in exaggerating the numbers. When the data generated by people who report large numbers of partners are eliminated, the ratio of the number sex partners reported by males and females falls much closer to a one-to-one ratio, actually about 1.2 to one. It has been suggested that women are more accurate and conservative in their reporting of numbers of partners, and they may even be prone to undercounting. The bottom line, then, is that these gender discrepancies are probably not very pronounced at all, but that sex researchers must find better investigative techniques for eliminating the problem with the data (Wiederman, 1997c; 1999). It may be advisable to ask questions about shorter time frames and use questions that help people to remember more accurately. To use an analogy, people can more accurately recall how many movies they have seen in the past year if they are also asked to think about which movies they saw.

Case Studies and Clinical Research

Professional counselors, physicians, psychologists, and other clinicians often work with individuals who are experiencing some sexual concern or problem. These professionals employ various treatment strategies to help the individual and may devise new methods. They may discover that these strategies and methods are effective for large numbers of clients or patients and will sort out the characteristics that are most effective. **Case studies** may then be published, giving an in-depth look at particular individual circumstances. Although it is risky to overgeneralize from case studies, they do offer new ideas and perspectives to be considered. Some valuable and useful insights have been presented to the professional community from case study research.

case study: an in-depth look at a particular individual and how he or she might be helped to solve a sexual or other problem. Case studies may offer new and useful ideas for counselors to use with other patients.

When some sort of treatment strategy is tested with larger numbers of people, it is called **clinical research.** The study may consider the cause, treatment, and prevention of a disease or condition. For example, Masters and Johnson (1970) conducted clinical studies for several years on nearly 800 individuals who complained of various forms of sexual dysfunction, categorizing and labeling the problems, looking for possible causes, and trying out a variety of treatment methods. They then did follow-up studies with some of the individuals over a 5-year period. Although, again, generalizations to the entire population must be done with great caution in such a study, the studies offered a conceptual framework on which the new field of sex therapy was built. Clinical studies of this sort provide a foundation to which further research can add. Only too often, however, generalizations from clinical studies have been applied erroneously and broadly to larger populations. This is risky because clinical populations represent people who have problems. Until recently most of our assumptions about same-gender sexual orientation came from clinical work, and those assumptions were largely flawed because only lesbians and gay males who had sought help for problems were being considered.

Observational Research

Some researchers have chosen to observe an aspect of human sexual behavior directly, thus eliminating the biases characteristic of research in which people report on themselves. Observational studies may take place in laboratory settings or in the field. The Masters and Johnson (1966) research on human sexual response, discussed earlier in this chapter, is an example of a classic laboratory-based observational study. Various types of instrumentation were used to measure the physiological reactions of 694 people when they were aroused sexually. It was the first large-scale research in which observations were made in a systematic manner of the body's sexual responses.

Masters and Johnson were always careful to point out that their findings might not apply to the responses of all human beings. Because it is especially difficult to bring a random sample to this kind of observational research, it is often criticized for its narrowness. Correctly or not, however, physiologists have typically assumed when dealing with the processes of the human body that such activities really are very similar among different people. There is, of course, little means by which to determine how much—if at all—the laboratory setting might affect people's functioning. In subsequent studies that have recruited volunteers to measure physiological responses, significant numbers of people refuse to participate because they do not feel comfortable with the research conditions. Naturally, this biases the population sample

used (Plaud et al., 1999; Rowland, 1999). Most sexologists, nevertheless, have accepted the findings of Masters and Johnson, and many other observational researchers, as fundamental to our understandings of human sexuality.

Ethnosexual Field Studies

Anthropologists often do observational field studies of other cultures, meaning that they live among the people they are studying, observing their customs and behaviors, and attempting to collect data through communications with the members of that society. Collecting information that describes a particular culture is called **ethnography,** and when the information pertains specifically to sexual practices and beliefs, the data are sometimes called **ethnosexual.** Beginning in the 1920s, ethnographers began to show extreme reluctance to analyze the sexual aspects of other cultures (Tuzin, 1991). Anthropologist Margaret Mead was one of the first scientists to openly discuss the sexual mores of other cultures in her writings, including her famous work *Growing Up in New Guinea* (Mead, 1930). One of the earliest detailed cross-cultural surveys to appear in the field of human sexuality was a collection of field studies called *Patterns of Sexual Behavior* published by two ethnographers, Clellan Ford and Frank Beach (1951). It focused on sexual techniques, rules for mating, and the prevalence of various forms of sexual behavior in several different societies.

In recent years, anthropologists have demonstrated a high level of interest in sexuality, and cross-cultural studies concerning sexual behavior have been proliferating. As HIV and AIDS spread throughout the world, hard data concerning sexual practices in all different cultures have become even more acute. Such data help medical personnel determine the relative risks for the spread of HIV in different cultures and help develop appropriate programs of preventive education and medicine to combat the problem. Cultural values can affect the gathering of sex-related data in several ways. Certain behaviors may be stigmatized in some cultures, leading to reluctance and embarrassment when it comes to discussing or reporting the behaviors. Meaning of terms may get confused when researchers from one culture

clinical research: the study of the cause, treatment, or prevention of a disease or condition by testing large numbers of people.

ethnography (eth-NAH-gruffy): the anthropological study of other cultures.

ethnosexual: referring to data concerning the sexual beliefs and customs of other cultures.

attempt to discuss sexuality in another culture with which they are relatively unfamiliar (Herdt, 2000). Some sexual terms simply cannot be translated from one language into another. And finally, there are always subcultures within larger cultures, making it difficult to generalize about the entire population. Cross-cultural studies about sexuality demand a great deal of precision, sensitivity, and care in their design (Marin, 1997).

As the population of North America becomes increasingly multicultural, it is even more important for all of us to understand that sexual values and customs differ among various ethnic groups. It has been typical for us to view these ethnosexual differences as curiosities and peculiarities, when in fact they represent diverse ways of valuing and living out the human experience, with as much validity as our own.

Experiment Research

A keystone of science is the use of the **controlled experiment.** In this type of research, the investigator examines what happens to a particular **variable** being studied and manipulated, while an attempt is made to control all other variables and keep them constant. The researcher may then draw inferences about cause-and-effect relationships that are difficult or impossible to draw from other kinds of research.

However, well-controlled experiments are difficult to design for human subjects, whose complexity makes it nearly impossible to control all possible variables. Additionally, there is always the chance that the artificiality of a controlled experimental setting may influence the outcome of research with humans. For these reasons, experimental research evidence in human sexuality is sparse and ultimately open to the same sorts of shortcomings and criticisms found in other methods of study.

Ethical Issues in Sex Research

In recent years, a great deal of attention has focused on the need to protect and respect those people who participate as subjects in any form of human research. Because sexuality is viewed as such a private aspect of life, the ethical issues involved in sex research are particularly evident and crucial.

Human research subjects have the right of **informed consent,** meaning that they must be given complete prior information about the purpose of the study and the manner in which they will participate. It has been generally agreed that researchers do not have the right to coerce people into participation or to be dishonest in presenting information about the research. Similarly, scientists have the obligation to protect the confidentiality of their participants, making certain that personal, private facts can never be con-

nected with a particular individual. They must also protect subjects from physical and psychological harm. Researchers use a variety of methods to provide for anonymity in collecting data and to prevent inappropriate release of confidential information at some later time. Universities and governmental agencies usually have institutional review boards that must approve any research design involving human participation. These committees carefully attempt to weigh the potential value of the research to society against any inherent stresses, risks, or dangers for the participants. The decision to allow an investigator to proceed with such research is not always an easy one.

Ethical questions have been raised concerning the study of sexual behaviors and attitudes by racial group. It is quite typical for sex research to analyze data in a variety of categories, including race. However, the validity and usefulness of racial groupings have not been clearly demonstrated. The assumption is often made that people who are defined as being of the same racial group share the same heritage, and this is not necessarily accurate. Criteria for determining race are also vague, and in fact many people who are classified as black actually have multiracial ancestry. Some researchers suggest that describing human sexual behaviors and attitudes by racial grouping may in fact promote faulty assumptions and stereotypes, whereas others insist that such statistics are necessary for measuring progress in correcting injustices to some racial groups (Armstrong, 1995; Sabogal et al., 1997). This is an issue that may well receive further attention in scientific circles.

Researchers are using the Internet for many different kinds of behavioral and social science research. This medium creates a variety of ethical issues that are more difficult to monitor and control than in other venues. There have been concerns raised about how research subjects might be recruited via the Internet; how their gender and ages might be confirmed; how researchers can be assured that the subjects have offered informed consent; and how sensitive personal data can be protected and kept private. The anonymity of the Internet also raises the continuing problem of volunteer bias and how to get the most accurate data possible (Binik, Mah, & Kiesler, 1999).

---

controlled experiment: research in which the investigator examines what is happening to one variable while all other variables are kept constant.

variable: an aspect of a scientific study that is subject to change.

informed consent: the consent given by research subjects, indicating their willingness to participate in a study, after they are informed about the purpose of the study and how they will be asked to participate.

Technology versus Physiology: Penile Plethysmography

Ethical issues are being raised about one of the technologies that is being advanced within the field of sexology. Sex researchers have developed ways of measuring physiological sexual arousal by detecting the changes that occur in the vagina or the penis. In women, a probe can be placed within the vagina to detect increases or decreases in blood flow to that organ. The use of this technique in research is discussed further in chapter 4, page 97. A similar technique can be used to measure erectile responses in the male penis. A **penile strain gauge,** in the form of a cuff or wire, is placed around the penis and attached to a **plethysmograph,** which will chart change in the girth of the penis as it responds to sexual arousal or loss of arousal by gaining or losing various degrees of erection. In recent years, penile plethysmography has been increasingly employed by clinicians who want to be able to assess the tendencies of men toward particular sorts of sexual interests, or to determine if treatment to change some sort of sexual pattern is being successful.

For example, penile plethysmography has been used as an aid in determining whether a man may have a tendency to be sexually attracted to children, therefore representing a potential threat as a child molester. An individual might be referred for such an assessment by a court or social service agency because of some actual or suspected sexual offense. The man being tested will have a penile strain gauge attached to his penis and then be shown pictures of nude people of varying ages and sexes, with his erectile responses being charted on a plethysmograph.

A number of studies have claimed accuracy in being able to determine whether a particular man is sexually attracted to children. The technique is also used for men who are being treated for previous sexual offenses against children, to determine if they are lessening their degree of sexual interest in young people (Malcolm, Andrews, & Quinsey, 1993). However, questions are now being raised about the validity of such testing, and there seems to be a great deal of inconsistency in testing procedures and interpretation (Howes, 1995). One of the issues revolves around the degree of control a man might be able to exert over his own sexual responsiveness, therefore being able to "fool" the test. Studies have shown that some men are better able to exert self-control over their erectile responses and also that about 25 percent of a normal male sample tested showed some arousal in response to pictures of children. Researchers remind us that there is not necessarily any correlation between such arousal and sexual behavior involving children (Hall, Hirschman, & Oliver, 1995). Reviews of the clinical studies on penile plethysmography have pointed out that there are many methodological problems with these studies and that caution should be used in the assumptions that are made about their results (Launay, 1994; Seto & Kuban, 1996). At this point, it would clearly be risky to make too many assumptions about a person's psychological inclinations, future sexual behaviors, or degree of social unacceptability based on a technological device that measures one physiological response in the body (Plaud et al., 1999; Rowland, 1999). Penile plethysmography is certain to remain the target of ethical debate in the next few years.

penile strain gauge: a device placed on the penis to measure even subtle changes in its size due to sexual arousal.

plethysmograph (pleh-THIZ-ma-graff): a laboratory measuring device that charts physiological changes over time. Attached to a penile strain gauge, it can chart changes in penis size. This is called penile plethysmography.

Attitude Questionnaire

Rate each attitude with one of the following numbers: **0** = uncertain   **3** = relatively neutral
                                                         1 = strongly disagree   **4** = somewhat agree
                                                         2 = somewhat disagree   **5** = strongly agree

Attitude Statement	Rating for Your Parent(s)	Rating for Yourself 4–6 Years Ago	Your Present Rating
1. Masturbation is a healthy, normal mode of sexual expression.	_____	_____	_____
2. Young people should be encouraged to use masturbation as a way of exploring their sexual feelings.	_____	_____	_____
3. Sexual activity without marriage is all right for a couple who share a loving relationship.	_____	_____	_____
4. Sexual activity solely for physical pleasure is all right if both partners agree to it.	_____	_____	_____
5. In a loving partnership, having sex with others outside the primary relationship is all right if both partners agree.	_____	_____	_____
6. Gay, lesbian, and bisexual lifestyles are acceptable.	_____	_____	_____
7. Lesbians, gay men, and bisexual women or men should not be discriminated against because of their sexual orientation.	_____	_____	_____
8. Pornography depicting sexual activity between adults should be available for adults who wish to purchase and use it.	_____	_____	_____
9. Any sexual behavior is acceptable between consenting adults.	_____	_____	_____
10. At a beach, I would not be offended or made uncomfortable by having others around me in the nude.	_____	_____	_____
11. I would not be uncomfortable being nude myself with other nude people at the beach.	_____	_____	_____
12. The naked human body should be considered a source of beauty and pleasure, and not a source of shame.	_____	_____	_____
13. Women should have the same access and rights to sexual experience as men do.	_____	_____	_____
14. Women can enjoy sex and get as much pleasure from it as men do.	_____	_____	_____
15. Women should be as sexually assertive as men in initiating sexual activity.	_____	_____	_____
16. Accurate sex information should be available to all young people and adults.	_____	_____	_____
17. Birth control information and devices should be available to minors without parental consent.	_____	_____	_____
18. Physicians should be able to treat minors for sexually transmitted diseases without notification of parents.	_____	_____	_____
19. I support abortion as an alternative in cases of unplanned pregnancy.	_____	_____	_____
20. Women should have free choice about and access to abortion.	_____	_____	_____
TOTALS:	_____	_____	_____

Self-Evaluation

You and Your Sexuality

The questionnaires in this section are designed to help you take stock of your own sexual attitudes and their possible changes throughout your lifetime. They will also help you evaluate some of your sexual background and its meaning for your life today as a sexual human being. I hope that taking a closer look at your sexuality now will provide a more personal context for exploring the remainder of this book. Although there may be a variety of ways to use these questionnaires for classroom and group awareness activities, I have intended them for your own personal use.

Sexual Attitudes in Your Life

In the questionnaire on page 38, I ask you to compare your present sexual attitudes with those of your parent(s) (or the primary people who raised you) and with your own values of 4 to 6 years ago. It might be interesting to ask your parent(s) to complete the questionnaire. Otherwise, complete the column for your parent(s) with the responses that you feel accurately represent their attitudes.

Analysis: The final totals shown give a rough standard for comparison of your present attitudes with your attitudes of a few years ago and with those of the parent(s) (or others) who gave you your earliest attitudes. Generally speaking, the higher the total score, the more liberal the attitudes (highest possible score = 100). There are no right or wrong responses or good or bad scores. Examine the individual responses and totals to get a clearer picture of how your sexual attitudes compare with those of your parent(s) and how your own attitudes have or have not changed in the past few years.

Your Sexual History

The following questions are intended to provide further means of exploring where you have been as a sexual person and where you are now. It may help to write the answers down or to talk about the answers with someone you trust.

1. Nudity
   a. How often, when you were young, did you see your parent(s) in the nude? What was your family's attitude toward nudity?
   b. If you ever have children (or if you have children now), do you hope to be (or are you now) more accepting of nudity in your family than your parent(s), less accepting, or about the same?

2. Masturbation
   a. How did you first learn about or discover masturbation, and how did you feel about it at first?

   b. If you masturbated when you were younger, did you ever let anyone else know about it?
   c. If you masturbate now, how do you feel about the practice? Are you guilty? Ashamed? Happy? Proud? Disgusted? Satisfied?

3. Sex Slang—"Dirty Words"
   a. Make a list of the sex-related slang terms that you feel comfortable using, if any (such as, "screwing," "fuck," "cock," "suck," "cunt," and so forth).
   b. Which of the words on the list would your parents have been comfortable using?
   c. Which of the words on the list would be offensive to you if you heard them being spoken by a friend of the other gender? Of the same gender?

4. First Sexual Experiences (if applicable)
   a. What is the first explicit sexual experience with another person that you can remember?
   b. What were your reactions to that first erotic experience?
   c. Has that initial experience affected your feelings about yourself as a sexual person or about sex in general even until today? How?

5. Male-Female Intercourse
   a. How did you first learn about sexual intercourse between a woman and a man, and what were your reactions and feelings when you did learn about it?
   b. If you have experienced sexual intercourse with someone of the other gender, what were your feelings following the first experience?
   c. Are your attitudes toward sexuality different now from what they were when you first had intercourse? In what ways?

6. Same-Gender Activities
   a. How did you first learn about attractions and sex between members of the same gender, and what were your reactions and feelings when you did learn about it?
   b. If you have ever participated in a sexual experience (even as a youngster) with someone of the same gender, what are your feelings about the experience?

7. Sexual Behavior
   a. In thinking about sexual contact, or during sexual involvement with another person, which of the following are most exciting for you and which are turnoffs?
      1) *undressing one another*
      2) *oral sex performed on you*
      3) *oral sex performed on partner (by you)*
      4) *anal sex*
      5) *kissing and being together nude*
      6) *intercourse*

7) *touching and caressing*
8) *using some painful stimulation*
9) *acting out a sexual fantasy*
10) *mutual masturbation*

b. If you have had intense shared sexual experiences, what things about the experience(s) have pleased and satisfied you most? Which have displeased or frustrated you most?

c. What qualities do you desire in your ideal sexual partner?

8. Your Cultural Heritage

What do you see as your primary cultural heritage, and how do you think that heritage has been a basis for your sexual values, beliefs, and decisions? Have you ever felt that your attitudes about sexuality were different from others around you because of your cultural differences? If so, how has that made you feel? Has your race, religion, or ethnic background ever caused others to react to you sexually in a way that you found surprising or uncomfortable?

Chapter Summary

1. Human sexuality is an area of contradictions and complexities that crosses disciplinary boundaries. To study sexuality is a significant way of understanding many different aspects of human cultures, behaviors, and social interactions.

2. North America has a very diverse population, representing many different ethnic and cultural backgrounds. It is important to recognize that there are many cultural differences in sexual beliefs and customs globally. Understanding the cultural bases for these differences can provide a clearer perspective on the diversity within human sexuality.

3. Romance and sex were seen as separate in Victorian times. More recently, there has been an increased sexualization of romance. Now, sex is viewed as one way to express loving feelings.

4. There has been debate over the magnitude of what has been called the "sexual revolution." There have been ongoing shifts in social attitudes and values regarding sexuality and resulting changes in how people make their own decisions about sexual behavior. Although sexuality is more openly discussed now, there is still much ambivalence about sex.

5. Factors that have been part of changing attitudes about human sexuality include greater emphasis on situation ethics and personal autonomy, changing roles of men and women, greater amounts of leisure time, new knowledge about sexuality, advances in science and technology, increased media attention, and growing concern over HIV and AIDS.

6. These are times in which conservative and liberal religious and political factions hold conflicting views of sexuality. Although there has been much political debate about traditional family values, the traditional family unit of a married couple with their own children is no longer the norm in the United States. It is difficult to define what typical family values would be.

7. There is a continuing debate over the degree to which human sexual traits and orientations are determined by biological and evolutionary factors or by social factors. The variability of human traits is probably influenced by both nature and nuture.

8. North American attitudes regarding sexuality seem to fall roughly into three main categories: traditional or procreational, relational, and recreational. These often contradictory attitudinal systems exist side by side in our society, and they greatly influence people's sexual choices and behaviors.

9. Attitudes toward particular aspects of sexuality are always changing. Masturbation and premarital sex have become more accepted in recent years, and there is greater openness about sexual orientations, alternative behaviors, and gender identities, although there is still a significant degree of debate about their acceptability. Double standards concerning female and male sexual activity still exist and tend to cross cultural boundaries.

10. Nudity in the media and recreational nudity have become more acceptable in the past few decades, although students in the United States are much less likely to take locker room showers after exercising.

11. Sexual desire and behavior have become closely intertwined with romantic love in recent generations.

12. Almost all states now recommend or require sexuality education in their public schools. There is continuing debate between groups that encourage comprehensive sexuality education and those that feel sexuality education should emphasize abstinence from or postponement of sexual activity.

13. Three significant pioneers in nineteenth-century studies of human sexuality were Richard von Krafft-Ebing, Sigmund Freud, and Henry

Havelock Ellis. Their work established fundamental perspectives on sexuality that persisted well into the twentieth century.

14. The early twentieth century was heavily influenced by Victorian values about sex and romance. The Kinsey studies opened new vistas concerning the spectrum of sexual behavior, and Masters and Johnson pioneered work in understanding sexual physiology and the treatment of sexual dysfunctions.

15. Much early research on sexual behavior did not represent accurate generalizations for the entire population because only population samples of convenience were used in the studies.

16. Several surveys about sex conducted in the 1970s, 1980s, and 1990s gained worldwide attention and offered new perspectives on female and male sexuality, childhood and adolescent sexuality, sexual orientation, knowledgeability about sex, and the place of sex in relationships. However, they suffered from methodological flaws in how participants were recruited and the lack of control over completion of questionnaires.

17. Several surveys on sexual behavior have emerged in the United States and Europe, and their results are providing a new picture of sexual attitudes and behaviors.

18. The random sampling and interview techniques employed by the National Health and Social Life Survey have yielded the most statistically reliable results on sexual behaviors and attitudes in the United States. This survey has caused us to reassess many of our assumptions about the spectrum and frequency of the sexual activity.

19. A new national study on adolescent sexual behavior is in progress, and along with research on HIV transmission, inclusion of the feminist perspective, and global contraception, this represents one of the themes of sex research in the new millennium.

20. Scientific study of sex can involve various methods: population samples, surveys, case studies and clinical data, direct observation of behavior, ethnosexual field studies, and controlled experiments.

21. Scientific research raises numerous ethical issues, and informed consent is considered essential to participation in any such research. The use of penile plethysmography to determine men's sexual arousal patterns has been questioned as potentially inaccurate and therefore unethical in making clinical assessments.

22. Understanding ourselves as sexual human beings requires some introspection and self-questioning. Parental attitudes and values often influence the development of our own sexuality.

Focus on Health Questions

You will find in this section the kinds of questions that you may have concerning your own health and sexuality. The page references indicate where in the text the answer is located; the exact place is marked with the logo **FOH**.

1. Will I damage my ability to have sex with others if I masturbate too much? 16

2. If my attitudes toward sexuality are different from my parents', how will that affect my relationship with others? 20

Annotated Readings

Bancroft, J. B. (Ed.). (1997). *Researching sexual behavior.* Bloomington: Indiana University Press. A collection of papers that address some of the most current issues concerning the methods of sex research.

Brannigan, G. G., Allgeier, E. R., & Allgeier, A. R. (Eds.) (1998). *The sex scientists.* New York: Longman. A down-to-earth summary of the interviews with 15 scientists who have done sex research, explaining why they entered the field of sexology.

Bullough, B. L., Bullough, V., Fithian, M. A., Hartman, W. E., & Klein, R. S. (1997). *How I got into sex.* Amherst, NY: Prometheus Books. Personal stories of over 40 sexologists, describing their work and why they have pursued it.

Bullough, V. L. (1994). *Science in the bedroom: A history of sex research.* New York: Basic Books. A highly readable overview of sexuality research that places it in the context of social trends and issues.

Davis, C. M., Yarber, W. L., Bauserman, R., Schreer, G., & Davis, S. L. (Eds.) (1998). *Handbook of sexuality-related measures*. Thousand Oaks, CA: Sage Publications. This is a collection of more than 200 questionnaires and other instruments used in sex research.

Ericksen, J. A. (1999). *Kiss and tell: Surveying sex in the twentieth century*. Cambridge, MA: Harvard University Press. A summary of some of the significant sex research of the last century, with good insights into how researchers' preconceptions shape their results.

Francouer, R. T. (Ed.) (1997). *The international encyclopedia of sexuality*. New York: Continuum Books. Comprehensive coverage of a wide spectrum of topics in human sexuality and includes cross-cultural perspectives.

Gamson, J. (1998). *Freaks talk back: Tabloid talk shows and sexual nonconformity*. Chicago: University of Chicago Press. A fascinating look at the portrayals of sexual lifestyles on television talk shows in the United States and the United Kingdom.

Laumann, E. O., Gagnon, J. H., Michael, R. T., & Michaels, S. (1994). *The social organization of sexuality: Sexual practices in the United States*. Chicago: University of Chicago Press. This is the comprehensive, scientific description of the National Health and Social Life Survey that gave us a fresh perspective on sexual behaviors and attitudes in the United States. It summarizes the results of surveying 3,432 randomly selected women and men about their sexual practices. A landmark sociological study.

Michael, R. T., Gagnon, J. H., Laumann, E. O., & Kolata, G. (1994). *Sex in America: A definitive survey*. Boston: Little, Brown. An eminently readable, popularized summary of the National Health and Social Life Survey, this book offers an interesting and up-to-date look at our society's sexual mores and activities.

Segal, L. (Ed.). (1997). *New sexual agendas*. Basingstoke, England: Macmillan. A collection of articles about some of the more pressing political agendas of our time as they relate to human sexuality.

Chapter 2
Female Sexual Anatomy and Physiology

Chapter Outline

Note: A selection of Focus on Health questions appears at the end of each chapter. Answers to these questions are indicated within the chapter by the symbol in the margin. **FOH**

> Only two times during my childhood did my mother ever have to refer to my genitals, and both times all she could say was "down there." After I grew up, I guess she must have decided there was no need to refer to that region at all. It wasn't until I took this course that I said the word "vagina" out loud myself. It feels as though I had to take 19 years to legitimize the entire sexual part of my body enough to make it part of me.
>
> —*From a student's essay*

The basic anatomy of the sex organs, also called genitals, has been known for centuries, but reliable information on how these organs function and interact has not been available until recently. The genital organs have various functions in procreation, recreation, and as one route to intimate sharing and communication within a loving relationship.

When the female sex organs are studied in sexuality education, the emphasis clearly has tended toward the reproductive functions of the uterus, ovaries, and fallopian tubes. A study of medical texts found that illustrations of female genitalia are overrepresented in chapters on reproduction and are underrepresented in the nonreproductive chapters (Mendelsohn, Neiman, Isaacs, Lee, & Levison, 1994). The important roles of the vagina, clitoris, and other external structures in sexual pleasure have too often been neglected. This chapter and subsequent chapters of this text recognize the sex organs of both women and men (as well as babies) as potential sources of sexual pleasure and interpersonal intimacy. I cover the reproductive aspects of sex in chapter 9, "Reproduction, Reproductive Technology, and Birthing."

The Vulva

The female sex organs are not confined to the inner body (see Fig. 2.1). There are many important structures located externally that play an important role in sexual arousal, whereas the internal organs tend to be more important in regulating internal hormonal cycles and the reproductive processes.

The external female sex organs, located between the legs, below and in front of the pubic symphysis, are collectively called the **vulva** (see Fig. 2.2). A study

FIGURE 2.1   *External Female Anatomy*

The human sex organs are important for both procreation and recreation. Historically sex educators focused on the internal sex organs and reproduction, especially in women. In recent years, they have also focused on the pleasurable aspects of sexual behavior and the external sex organs.

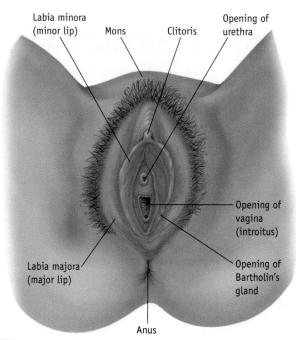

Labia minora (minor lip)   Mons   Clitoris   Opening of urethra

Opening of vagina (introitus)

Opening of Bartholin's gland

Labia majora (major lip)

Anus

FIGURE 2.2   *Vulva*

The external female sex organs consist of the mons, labia, and clitoris. They have numerous nerve endings and are, therefore, sensitive to stimulation. In shape, size, and color, the external sex organs vary greatly from woman to woman.

of 8,330 Japanese women, ranging in age from 15 to 46, showed that there is a great deal of variation in the sizes and shapes of the various external female genitalia, all perfectly normal (Kasai, 1995). Especially visible on the vulva are the **mons** and the **labia majora** (major or outer lips). The mons, sometimes termed the mons pubis or mons veneris, is a rounded pad of fatty tissue just above the other sex organs on the pubic bone. During puberty, the mons becomes covered with pubic hair, usually arranged in a roughly triangular pattern. The mons is well endowed with nerve end-

vulva: external sex organs of the female, including the mons, major and minor lips, clitoris, and opening of the vagina.

mons: cushion of fatty tissue located over the female's pubic bone.

labia majora (LAY-bee-uh mah-JOR-uh): two outer folds of skin covering the minor lips, clitoris, urinary meatus, and vaginal opening.

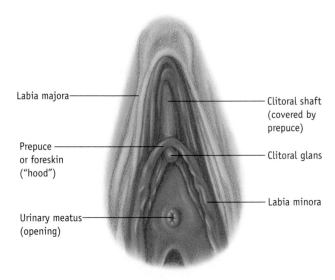

Labia majora

Prepuce or foreskin ("hood")

Urinary meatus (opening)

Clitoral shaft (covered by prepuce)

Clitoral glans

Labia minora

FIGURE 2.3 *Clitoris*
The most sensitive area of a female's genitals, the clitoris is located just beneath the point where the top of the minor lips meet. It is unique in that it is the only organ of either sex whose sole function is to provide sexual sensation and pleasure.

ings, and most women find that rubbing or exerting pressure on this area may lead to sexual arousal. The entire area of the vulva is considered to be a major erogenous zone of females because it is generally very sensitive to sexual stimulation.

The labia majora are two folds of skin that extend from the mons down between the legs. They are relatively flat and indistinct in some women and thick and bulging in others. During puberty, the skin of the major lips darkens slightly, and hair grows on their outer surfaces. These external labia cover and protect the inner, more sensitive sex organs of the woman. The inner structures cannot be seen unless the labia majora are parted, so women may find it useful to position a mirror in such a way that they are able to see the other structures.

When the major lips are separated, another pair of smaller folds of skin become visible, the **labia minora** (minor or inner lips). They are observed as pink, hairless, irregular, and asymmetrical ridges that meet at the top to form a sheath of skin covering the clitoris called the **prepuce** or clitoral hood (see Fig. 2.3). Both the major and minor lips are sensitive to stimulation and are important in sexual arousal. Just inside the minor lips are openings to ducts connected to **Bartholin's glands,** sometimes called the vulvovaginal glands. These glands produce a small amount of secretion during sexual arousal that may help moisten the entrance to the vagina and to some extent the labia. This secretion does not play a major role in lubrication of the vagina during arousal, however, and any other func-

tions these glands may have are not known. Bartholin's glands can occasionally become infected with bacteria from feces or other sources and may require medical treatment.

Often the labia minora must be separated before the two openings between them may be seen. Just below the clitoris, a tiny hole is visible, which is the **urinary meatus** or urethral opening. It is through this opening that urine leaves the body. Below the urethra a larger orifice is seen, the vaginal opening or **introitus,** which leads into the vagina. The opening of the vagina does not usually seem to be a hole, and in fact may only be recognized as an opening when something is inserted into it. In some women, particularly in younger age groups, the vaginal opening is partly covered by membranous tissue called the **hymen** (discussed later in the section on the vagina).

Clitoris

The **clitoris** is the most sexually sensitive female sex organ. Appropriate stimulation of the clitoris is usually necessary for women to reach orgasm, although the manner in which that stimulation is best applied varies from woman to woman. The most visible part of the clitoris is usually observed as a rounded tip protruding from the hood or front commissure created by the merging of the labia minora. This external, sensitive head of the clitoris is called the **glans.** For many years, it has been compared to the penis because it is sensitive to sexual stimulation and capable of erection. It

labia minora (LAY-bee-uh mih-NOR-uh): two inner folds of skin that join above the clitoris and extend along the sides of the vaginal and urethral openings.

prepuce (PREE-peus): in the female, tissue of the upper vulva that covers the clitoral shaft.

Bartholin's glands (BAR-tha-lenz): small glands located in the opening through the minor lips that produce some secretion during sexual arousal.

urinary meatus (mee-AY-tuss): opening through which urine passes from the urethra to the outside of the body.

introitus (in-TROID-us): the outer opening of the vagina.

hymen: membranous tissue that can cover part of the vaginal opening.

clitoris (KLIT-a-rus): sexually sensitive organ found in the female vulva; it becomes engorged with blood during arousal.

glans: sensitive head of the female clitoris, visible between the upper folds of the minor lips.

has also been inaccurately viewed as a poorly developed, nonfunctional penis. On the contrary, the clitoris and the entire internal clitoral system of blood vessels, nerves, and erectile tissue constitute a very functional and important sex organ.

The **shaft** of the clitoris extends back under the clitoral hood, or prepuce. The glans is the only clitoral structure that hangs free, although it is usually not particularly movable (see Fig. 2.3). The clitoral shaft is attached to the body along its entire underside. The clitoris contains two columns and two bulbs of spongy tissue, which become engorged with blood during sexual excitement, causing the entire structure to become hardened or erect. When not erect, the clitoris is rarely more than an inch in length, only the tip (glans) of which is external and visible, but during erection it enlarges considerably, especially in diameter. Typically, in earlier stages of arousal, the clitoris protrudes more than it does in an unaroused state. As arousal proceeds, it retracts again.

There are tiny glands lining the prepuce that produce oil that may mix with other secretions to form a substance called **smegma.** If this material collects around the shaft, mild infections may result. An infection could cause some pain or discomfort, especially during sexual activity. If smegma accumulations become a problem, they may be removed by a physician who inserts a small probe under the hood or prepuce. A surgical procedure is sometimes used to cut the prepuce slightly, further exposing the clitoral glans and shaft. The procedure, called **circumcision** in Western culture, is not common in females, and the medical profession has found little legitimacy for it.

Female Genital Mutilation

In other cultures and other historical periods, the clitoris and labia have been subjected to various types of surgery and mutilation. With the fears of masturbation that were rife from the mid-nineteenth century to about 1935, it was not unusual for physicians in Europe and the United States to perform female circumcision or to remove part or all of the clitoris, a surgical procedure called **clitoridectomy.** These measures were thought to "cure" masturbation and prevent insanity.

In several African and Eastern Asian cultures and religions, clitoridectomy—often inaccurately called "female circumcision"—is still practiced as a rite of passage into adulthood. The World Health Organization (WHO) estimates that millions of women each year worldwide undergo some form of what is now termed female genital mutilation (FGM). Until recently, nearly all girls in countries such as Egypt, Somalia, Ethiopia, and Sudan have been subjected to FGM. Al-

though this may take the form of a traditional circumcision, in which the hood of tissue covering the clitoris is removed, more often the clitoral glans is removed as well. Sometimes a more extensive clitoridectomy is performed, involving removal of the entire clitoris and much of the labial tissue surrounding it.

As a rite marking a girl's passage to adulthood, clitoridectomy is meant to remove any vestiges of "maleness" because the clitoris is typically viewed as a miniature penis in these cultures. Thus, to have it removed is viewed as the ultimate symbol of womanhood. Clitoridectomy, however, also reduces sexual pleasure, important in cultures where men are expected to control female sexuality. Taboos have developed in support of the practice. In Nigeria, for example, some women believe that if the head of a newborn touches the clitoris during the birth process, the baby will become insane (Ecker, 1994).

Some cultures also practice **infibulation,** in which the labia minora and sometimes the labia majora are removed and the sides of the external portion of the vagina are sewn together, or fastened with thorns or natural glues, ensuring that the woman will not have intercourse prior to marriage. The fastening materials are removed at the time of marriage, although the procedure may be repeated if the husband is going to be absent for long periods of time. Tough scar tissue often forms that can make urination, menstruation, sexual intercourse, and childbirth more difficult and painful. Infibulation is meant to protect the virginity of the woman in those cultures that place a high premium on this as a condition of marriage. Infibulated women bring high rewards for their families when they are chosen as brides, in the form of money, goods, and livestock (Ecker, 1994).

These rites are often carried out with crude instruments, without sterile conditions or anesthetic. Girls and women subjected to such procedures often get se-

shaft: in the female, the longer body of the clitoris, containing erectile tissue.

smegma: thick, oily substance that may accumulate under the prepuce of the clitoris or penis.

circumcision (SIR-cum-sizh-uhn): of clitoris—surgical procedure that cuts the prepuce, exposing the clitoral shaft.

clitoridectomy (clih-torr-ih-DECK-tah-mee): surgical removal of the clitoris; practiced routinely in some cultures.

infibulation (in-fib-you-LAY-shun): surgical procedure, performed in some cultures, that seals the opening of the vagina.

rious infections, and the unsterilized instruments have been associated with the spread of HIV. Girls sometimes die from bleeding or infection following FGM. There is also a growing body of evidence that ritualized surgical practices can create psychological trauma, with far-reaching effects on women's sexuality, marriages, and the childbirth process (Kassindja, 1998; MacFarquhar, 1996). Cultural changes have brought some modernization of traditional procedures so that in some places aseptic methods are now used, lowering the risks of infection. For a brief time, Egyptian health authorities encouraged their hospitals to do the procedure in order to prevent the medical complications from amateur practices, while providing counseling to families to discourage the practice. In 1996, the Egyptian Health Ministry decided to bar all healthcare workers in both public and private clinics from performing any FGM. However, a year later a judge struck down the ban for medical personnel, apparently again out of concern for how the procedures were being carried out by nonmedical practitioners.

There has been a growing level of condemnation toward these practices, which are considered by some groups to be barbaric and sexist. The United States has begun to examine the surrounding issues more closely because it is now becoming clear that some girls in immigrant families from 40 countries may have undergone the procedure in the United States. One study suggested that nearly 170,000 girls and women in the United States may have undergone or been at risk for FGM (Jones et al., 1997). An African woman named Fauziya Kassindja fled the country of Togo rather than submit to genital mutilation, and she eventually entered the United States illegally. After spending over a year in jail, the Board of Immigration Appeals ruled that FGM is indeed an act of persecution and constituted legitimate grounds for offering the woman asylum (Dugger, 1996; Kassindja, 1998). Although others maintain that such practices represent cultural imperatives to be respected, this ruling and other movements in the developed countries are reinforcing the notion that FGM constitutes a violation of human rights that should be condemned and halted (Rosenthal, 1996).

FGM is often deeply embedded in a particular culture's way of life, reflective of historical patriarchal traditions in which women have been considered the possessions of men, and women's sexuality has been subjugated to men. They may be seen as fundamental rites of passage to adulthood, and even looked upon with pride by the adult woman. Yet, with the increasing emphasis on women's rights even in developing countries, there is growing worldwide opposition to these procedures. Debates are raging within the countries where the practices still exist. Younger, more Westernized women, often with the support of their husbands, are calling for new symbolic rites of passage that can preserve the positive cultural meanings and traditions without subjecting girls to the actual painful and dangerous surgeries. Feminists in Western cultures have been particularly outspoken on this issue, insisting that such procedures are not only physically dangerous, but they represent attempts to emphasize the inferior status of women. The controversy represents a classic example of a clash between cultural mores and shifting values about sexuality and gender on a global level.

Discuss FGM as practiced in other cultures and historical periods. How has it been justified in these cultures? Can you think of any similar North American practices? To what degree do you think that people outside of a particular culture have the right to play activist roles in calling for an end to such practices?

◼ The Vagina

The **vagina** is a muscular tube that is important as a female organ of reproduction and sexual pleasure (see Fig. 2.4). The muscular walls of the vagina, which are very elastic, are collapsed together except when something is inserted into the cavity, so the inner cavity is best described as a "potential" space. The vagina is usually about 4 inches deep, although during sexual arousal it deepens even more. The inner lining of the vagina is fleshy and soft and is corrugated by thin ridges of tissue. Except for the outer third and the area around its opening, the vagina is not particularly sensitive. The outer area, however, has many nerve endings, and stimulation easily leads to sexual arousal.

There are two sets of muscles surrounding the vaginal opening, the *sphincter vaginae* and *levator ani* muscles. Women can exert some degree of control over these muscles, but tension, pain, or fear can lead to involuntary contraction of the outer vaginal muscles so that insertion of anything becomes difficult or painful for the woman. This condition is called **vaginismus** and is discussed in more detail in chapter 18, "Sexual Dysfunctions and Their Treatment." Women can also exert some control over the inner

vagina (vu-JI-na): muscular canal in the female that is responsive to sexual arousal; it receives semen during heterosexual intercourse for reproduction.

vaginismus (vaj-uh-NIZ-mus): involuntary spasm of the outer vaginal musculature, making penetration of the vagina difficult or impossible.

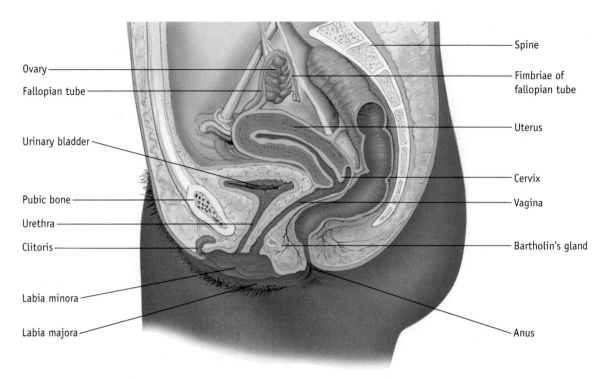

FIGURE 2.4   *Female Sexual and Reproductive Organs*

pubococcygeus (PC) muscle, much the same as the anal sphincter may be contracted or relaxed. This muscle may play a role in orgasmic response, and its tone can be improved by exercises, as is true of all voluntary muscles (see Kegel exercises in chapter 4, "Human Sexual Response").

It is important to note that the vagina cannot contract to the extent that the penis might be trapped inside (penis captivus), even though some people have heard rumors to the contrary. In Africa, there are many myths about people becoming stuck together during sex and having to be sent to the hospital for separation. Such myths seem to serve a social function in discouraging marital infidelity (Ecker, 1994). When dogs mate, the penis erects in such a way that it is caught inside the vagina until erection subsides, but this is important to successful mating in canines. Nothing similar occurs in humans. During sexual arousal in a woman, a lubricating substance is secreted through the inner lining of the vagina. This is discussed in chapter 4, "Human Sexual Response."

nal infection and odor. In a study of 8,450 women between the ages of 15 and 44, it was found that 37 percent douched as a part of their regular hygiene practices (Aral, 1992). The practice is particularly common among poor women and women of color, in which the rate may be as high as two-thirds. A representative of the National Black Women's Health Project has speculated that douching may represent a reaction of black women against negative sexual stereotypes. Studies continue to demonstrate that, contrary to popular notions, douching is actually dangerous. It can force disease organisms up into the uterus, increasing the risks for uterine and vaginal infection. Women who douche more than three times a month are almost four times more likely to get pelvic inflammatory disease than women who douche little or not at all. They also have a fourfold increase in risk for an ectopic pregnancy (Kendrick, 1997), in which the embryo becomes implanted dangerously outside of the uterus (see chapter 9, "Reproduction, Reproductive Technology,

FOH Douching

Over the years, women developed various techniques for washing out the vagina, sometimes called douching. It was believed that this would help prevent vagi-

pubococcygeus (PC) muscle (pyub-o-kox-a-JEE-us): part of the supporting musculature of the vagina that is involved in orgasmic response and over which a woman can exert some control.

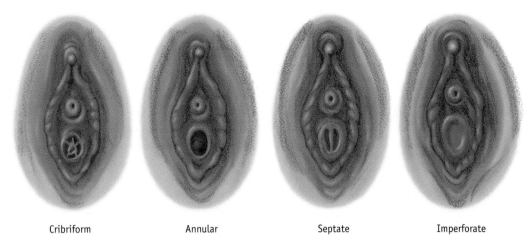

Cribriform   Annular   Septate   Imperforate

FIGURE 2.5 *Hymen*

A thin, delicate membrane, the hymen partially covers the vaginal opening in a variety of ways. It may bridge the vagina, surround it, or have several different shapes and sizes in the opening to the outside of the body. It has no known physiological function but historically has had psychological and cultural significance as a sign of virginity.

and Birthing"). In fact, the vagina has natural cleansing mechanisms that may be disrupted by douching. Unless prescribed for a specific medical condition, douching should be avoided.

Hymen

The hymen, present in the vaginal opening from birth, is a tissue usually having one or more openings in it. There are many different shapes of hymens that cover varying amounts of the introitus (see Fig. 2.5). The most common type of hymen is annular, meaning that the hymenal tissue surrounds the entire opening of the vagina, with an opening in the middle. Some hymens have tissue that extends into the introitus. The cribriform hymen has a web of tissue over the introitus, in which there may be several small openings, whereas the septate hymen has a single band of tissue that divides the introitus into two distinct apertures. In a very few girls, the hymen is imperforate, meaning that there are no openings in it. With this condition, the menstrual flow builds up in the vagina and uterus, causing pain and swelling until a physician makes an incision in the **imperforate hymen,** quickly relieving the condition. Occasionally, too, the hymen is especially thick and tough, a condition called **fibrous hymen.** This will interfere with sexual activity and must be treated surgically. Many women who experience pain during sexual activity, sometimes called dyspareunia (see ch. 18), may have problems with the hymen. Such difficulties are often not diagnosed by physicians, and the pain may be dismissed as psychosomatic. There are surgical techniques that can relieve dyspareunia caused by problems with the hymen (Brashear & Munsick, 1991).

Most hymens have a large enough opening to admit a finger or tampon. Attempting to insert anything larger, such as the erect penis, usually results in some tearing of the hymen. There are many ways other than sexual activity in which a hymen may be ruptured. Although it is often stated that some girls are born without a hymen, that claim has recently been called into question. A pediatric team at the University of Washington examined 1,131 infant girls and found every one to have an intact hymen. They concluded that the absence of a hymen at birth is an unlikely occurrence, if it occurs at all. This suggests that when hymenal tissue cannot be identified in a young girl, some sort of trauma may have been the cause (Jenny, Huhns, & Arakawa, 1987).

Some hymens are apparently flexible enough so that they can even withstand coitus, or sexual intercourse. Consequently, the presence or absence of a hymen is unreliable as an indicator of a woman's virginity or nonvirginity. Some societies place special significance on the presence of the hymen and hold rituals for the rupturing of the hymen before a girl's first intercourse.

In the United States, between 1920 and 1950, some gynecologists performed a surgical procedure on women who were about to marry but did not want their husbands to know they were not virgins. The procedure, called the "lover's knot," involved placing

imperforate hymen: lack of any openings in the hymen.

fibrous hymen: condition in which the hymen is composed of unnaturally thick, tough tissue.

several stitches in the labia, so that when intercourse happened, the stitches would be torn out and there would be some pain and bleeding (Janus & Janus, 1993). Many people in Western societies even today still believe that the presence of a hymen proves a female's virginity—a naive outlook at best. In fact, the only way to determine physically whether or not a woman has experienced sexual intercourse is by finding semen or sperm in a vaginal smear, confirmed by chemical testing or microscopic examination. This procedure must be done within a few hours after intercourse and is sometimes used in rape cases as proof that penile penetration has occurred.

If the hymen is still present the first time penetration of the vagina occurs, discomfort or pain and possibly some bleeding may occur when the hymen is torn. The degree of pain varies in different women from slight to severe. If a woman is concerned about this, she may spend some time prior to the first penetration inserting fingers into the opening of the hymen, gradually widening it. A physician may also cut the hymen or stretch its opening with dilators of gradually increasing size. During sexual intercourse, there is usually little trouble inserting the penis through the hymen if the male partner persists with careful and gentle prodding with the erect penis, using adequate lubrication. The woman may also take responsibility for guiding her partner in controlling the timing and depth of penetration.

Genital Self-Examination for Women

After acquainting themselves with their basic external anatomy, it is a good idea for women to examine their genitals monthly, checking for any unusual signs or symptoms. Using a mirror and adequate light, look through pubic hairs to the underlying skin and pull back the clitoral prepuce or hood. Then part the inner lips, exposing the area around the urethral and vaginal openings more fully. These areas should generally be free of any unusual bumps, sores, or blisters. If such lesions are present, they may be red or light-colored, or may be more easily felt than seen. Be sure to look on the inside of each major and minor lip for similar signs. It is a good idea to become aware of what your normal vaginal discharge looks like, so you will notice any changes in its color, odor, or consistency. Although such changes may occur normally over the course of the monthly menstrual cycle, some diseases cause distinct changes in vaginal discharge.

Anytime you find unusual bumps or discharges from the genitals, it is a good idea to consult a physician or other clinician specializing in women's health concerns. Often these symptoms do not even need treatment, but they may also signal the beginnings of an infection requiring medical attention. It is important to report any pain or burning upon urination, bleeding between menstrual periods, pain in the pelvic region, or an itchy rash around the vagina.

Disorders of the Female Sex Organs

The female sex and urinary organs may be the sites of infection not transmitted through sexual behavior. **Acute urethral syndrome,** an infection of the urethra, and bladder infection, or **cystitis,** are common complaints and may represent recurrent problems for some women. Urinary tract infections in younger women are associated with frequent sexual intercourse and recent use of diaphragms and spermicides (Hooton et al., 1996). The symptoms include frequent urge to urinate, burning or pain on urination, and possibly severe pain during sexual intercourse or when the urethra and bladder are placed under pressure. **Interstitial cystitis (IC)** is a relatively rare, chronic bladder condition that can be quite debilitating to some women and interfere with their sexual lives. Medical professionals frequently fail to recognize these diseases as the cause of such symptoms, and they may assume that the woman is imagining the problem. Antibiotics and other medications may be used for treatment. Because one of the most common bacteria to cause cystitis is **E. coli** (short for *Escherichia coli*), the organism that lives in the colon and is found in feces, good personal hygiene is the best preventative measure. Wiping from front to back after a bowel movement is always advisable, as is frequent washing of the vaginal and anal areas. Drinking plenty of liquids and urinating frequently is another good precaution. Washing and urinating after sexual activity is important in cleansing the urethral area of any bacteria that might cause cystitis. Of particular concern is the possibility of a bladder infection spreading to the kidneys, where the condition can be far more serious.

The vagina can be subject to several disorders. It can undergo **vaginal atrophy,** in which the inner surfaces of the vagina shrink and narrow; this occurs

acute urethral syndrome: infection or irritation of the urethra.

cystitis (sis-TITE-us): a nonsexually transmitted infection of the urinary bladder.

interstitial cystitis (IC): a chronic bladder inflammation that can cause debilitating discomfort and interfere with sexual enjoyment.

E. coli: bacteria naturally living in the human colon, which often cause urinary tract infection.

vaginal atrophy: shrinking and deterioration of vaginal lining, usually the result of low estrogen levels during aging.

more often in older women as the result of lowered estrogen levels. Sometimes during pregnancy **varicose veins** can develop in the vulva, surrounding the vagina; this leads to an aching, heavy sensation in the pelvis. Several congenital abnormalities may affect female sex organs. **Vaginal atresia** is the absence or closure of the vagina, often not discovered until puberty. In such cases, there can be a surgical construction of a vaginal passageway to permit sexual intercourse or other sexual activity, although the constructed passageway does not usually permit vaginal delivery when giving birth (Money, 1994). Sometimes two vaginas may be present at birth. There are also a number of conditions that involve a malformation or absence of the uterus, fallopian tubes, or ovaries, all variably treatable by surgery or hormones. Sometimes **vaginal fistulae**—or abnormal openings—connect the bladder, urethra, or rectum with the vagina; all of these usually require surgical treatment. Incomplete closure of the urethra and urinary tract during fetal development can occur in females, but it usually does not require surgical correction unless it is associated with an inability to retain urine or feces.

■ The Uterus and Ovaries

The neck of the **uterus** (or womb) protrudes into the deepest part of the vagina. The uterus is a thick-walled, muscular organ that provides a nourishing environment for the developing fetus during pregnancy. It is usually about 3 inches long and pear shaped, roughly 2 to 3 inches in diameter at the top, and narrowing to a 1-inch diameter at the end that extends into the vagina. During pregnancy, it gradually expands to a much larger size. When a woman is standing, her uterus is almost horizontal and at a right angle to the vagina (see Fig. 2.4).

The two main parts of the uterus are the body and the **cervix** or neck, connected by the narrower **isthmus.** The top of the uterus is called the **fundus.** Although the cervix is not especially sensitive to superficial touch, it is sensitive to pressure. The opening in the cervix is called the **os.** The inner cavity of the uterus has varying widths in different sections (see Fig. 2.6). The walls of the uterus are composed of three layers: the thin outer cover or **perimetrium;** the thick middle layer of muscular tissue called the **myometrium;** and the inner layer, which is rich in blood vessels and glands, the **endometrium.** It is the endometrium that plays a vital role in the menstrual cycle (discussed later in this chapter) and in the nourishment of a developing embryo or fetus (discussed in chapter 9, "Reproduction, Reproductive Technology, and Birthing").

Pelvic Examination

The uterus, particularly the cervix, is a common site of cancer in women. Because cancer of the uterus may present no symptoms for many years, it is especially dangerous. Women should have an internal, or pelvic, examination periodically, along with a **Pap smear** test, by a qualified gynecologist or other clinician. There is disagreement among health professionals as to the most desirable frequency for such exams, but most health experts recommend an annual examination. Pap smears have been responsible for a 70 percent decline in deaths from cervical cancer. Of the 5,000 women who die from cervical cancer in the United States each year, 80 percent had not had a Pap test in 5 or more years (Strider, 1997). A study of female university students found that more than half of the women mistakenly believed that the Pap test screened for other disorders and sexually transmitted diseases, which is not the case. About half of them did not know that a woman should prepare for the examination by avoiding sexual intercourse and the use of vaginal contraceptives for one or two days prior to having the Pap smear taken (Hasenyager, 1999).

varicose veins: overexpanded blood vessels; can occur in veins surrounding the vagina.

vaginal atresia (a-TREE-zha): birth defect in which the vagina is absent or closed.

vaginal fistulae (FISH-cha-lee *or* -lie): abnormal channels that can develop between the vagina and other internal organs.

uterus (YUTE-a-rus): muscular organ of the female reproductive system; a fertilized egg implants itself within the uterus.

cervix (SERV-ix): lower "neck" of the uterus that extends into the back part of the vagina.

isthmus: narrowed portion of the uterus just above the cervix.

fundus: the broad top portion of the uterus.

os: opening in the cervix that leads into the hollow interior of the uterus.

perimetrium: outer covering of the uterus.

myometrium: middle, muscular layer of the uterine wall.

endometrium: interior lining of the uterus, innermost of three layers.

Pap smear: medical test that examines a smear of cervical cells to detect any cellular abnormalities.

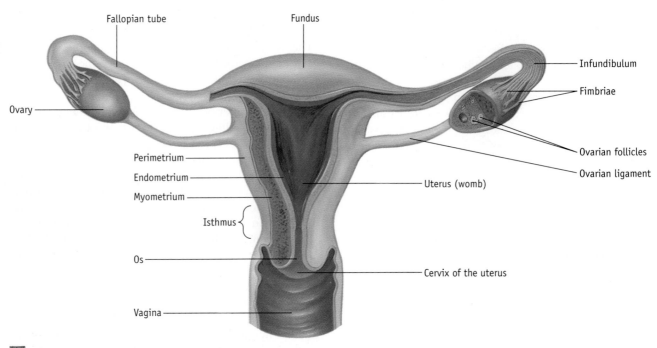

Fallopian tube   Fundus   Infundibulum

Fimbriae

Ovary

Perimetrium

Endometrium

Myometrium   Ovarian follicles

Ovarian ligament

Isthmus   Uterus (womb)

Os

Cervix of the uterus

Vagina

FIGURE 2.6 *Female Reproductive Organs*

The uterus is a hollow, muscular organ in which an embryo may grow and be nourished until it is a fully developed fetus. The walls of the uterus are of varying thickness and consist of three layers: the perimetrium, the myometrium, and the endometrium. On each side of the uterus are the almond-shaped ovaries. They have two functions: manufacturing the hormones estrogen and progesterone, and producing and releasing eggs.

For a pelvic examination, a speculum is first carefully inserted into the vagina to hold open its walls. This permits a visual inspection of the cervix. To obtain a Pap smear (named for its developer, Dr. Papanicolaou), a thin spatula or a cotton swab is used while the speculum is in place to remove some cells painlessly from the area of the cervix. A smear is made from the material and is fixed, stained, and examined under a microscope for any indications of abnormal cellular changes that might warn of cancer or precancerous conditions. In 1996, the Food and Drug Administration approved a new technique for preparing Pap smears that eliminates some of the excess mucus and blood that can sometimes make detection of abnormal cells on the slide more difficult. This has rendered the test more effective and reliable than it has ever been. Another new device is now available that may be attached to the speculum, and it projects a chemical light that produces different colors from normal and abnormal cells. This provides an extra measure of help in targeting suspicious areas of the cervix that should be carefully tested.

After the speculum has been removed, a manual examination is performed. Using a rubber glove and lubricant, two fingers are inserted into the vagina and pressed on the cervix. The other hand is placed on the abdomen. The clinician is then able to feel the basic shape and size of the uterus and associated structures.

If suspicious cells are detected in a Pap smear, then more aggressive diagnostic procedures may be recommended. There first may be a biopsy to determine if there is a malignancy present. If growth of abnormal cells proves to be advanced, another procedure may be performed called a dilation and curettage, or D&C (see also chapter 10, "Decision Making about Pregnancy and Parenthood"). The opening of the cervix is dilated or widened, so that an instrument called a curette may be inserted into the inner cavity of the uterus. Some of the uterine lining is gently scraped away and then examined for malignant cells. The D&C is occasionally used to terminate a pregnancy, as an induced abortion, and is typically used to cleanse the uterus of dead tissue following a miscarriage (spontaneous abortion).

Ovaries and Fallopian Tubes

On either side of the uterus, and attached to it, are two almond-shaped glands called the **ovaries** (see Fig. 2.6). *Ovarian ligaments* attach the ovaries to the uterus. The ovaries have two primary functions: secre-

ovaries: pair of female gonads, located in the abdominal cavity, that mature ova and produce female hormones.

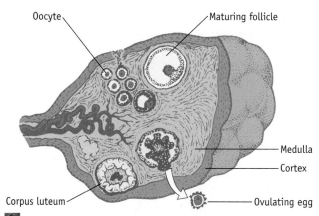

FIGURE 2.7 *Internal Structure of an Ovary*

This cross section of an ovary shows its cortex, the thick outer layer, and its central medulla, as well as the various stages of ovum development. The first cell in the process of maturation is an oocyte, which with its surrounding cells is called the follicle.

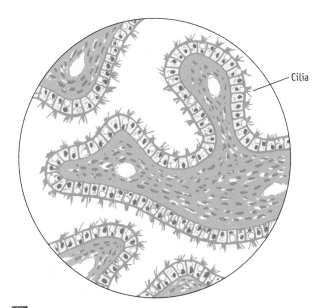

FIGURE 2.8 *Cilia of Fallopian Tubes*

This is a microscopic view of the cilia, the hairlike filaments that line the fallopian tubes. Their movement helps propel the ovum through the fallopian tube to the uterus.

tion of two female sex hormones, estrogen and progesterone, and the maturation of the egg cells or **ova** necessary for reproduction. Each ovary is about an inch long and weighs about one-fourth of an ounce. Inside each ovary at a female's birth are tens of thousands of microscopic chambers called **follicles,** each of which contains a cell that has the potential to develop into an ovum. These cells are called **oocytes.** By the time of puberty, it is believed that only a few thousand follicles remain in each ovary. Only a relatively small number of these (400 to 500) will ever mature into ova.

In a mature woman, the surface of the ovaries is irregular and pitted, evidence of the many ova that have pushed their way through the ovary walls in the process of ovulation, described on page 61. When the internal structure of an ovary is observed, follicles are seen in various stages of development. Two distinct parts of the ovary are also visible: the central *medulla* and its thick outer layer, the *cortex* (see Fig. 2.7).

Extending from one end of the ovaries to the upper portion of the uterus are the two **fallopian tubes.** The end of each fallopian tube nearest the ovary has a number of fingerlike projections called *fimbriae,* which are not attached to the ovary but rather lie loosely around it. The fimbriae lead into the thickest end of the fallopian tube, the *infundibulum.* There is a narrow, irregular cavity that extends throughout each fallopian tube. The inner cavity gets progressively smaller in the sections of the tube closest to the uterus.

The inner lining of the fallopian tubes is covered by microscopic, hairlike projections called **cilia.** It is

by movements of these cilia that an ovum is carried through the tube from the ovary to the uterus (see Fig. 2.8). If fertilization is to occur, the sperm must meet and enter the ovum while the ovum is in the fallopian tubes. In this case, the cilia in the tubes must then transport the tiny fertilized ovum to the uterus, where it will implant itself and grow into a fetus (see the section on reproduction in chapter 9).

When women experience prolonged sexual arousal without having an orgasm, their ovaries may become swollen and congested, leading to pain and feelings of fullness, although this is not a particularly common problem. The vulva may also become congested and painful by such activity. In former times, this discomfort was often called "engagement ovaries."

ova: egg cells produced in the ovary. A single cell is called an ovum; in reproduction, it is fertilized by a sperm cell.

follicles: capsules of cells in which an ovum matures.

oocytes (OH-a-sites): cells that mature to become ova.

fallopian tubes: structures that are connected to the uterus and lead the ovum from an ovary to the inner cavity of the uterus.

cilia: microscopic, hairlike projections that help move the ovum through the fallopian tube.

Uterine Cancer and Other Disorders

Cancer of the cervix is a common type of malignancy in women, second in frequency only to cancer of the breast. Uterine cancer occurs with about half the frequency of cervical malignancies. These cancers are particularly dangerous because there may be no symptoms for several years. The Pap smear test, which should be a routine part of a woman's annual physical examination, microscopically examines a smear of cervical mucus. It can detect cancerous or precancerous cells, indicating that the condition should be surgically treated or kept under observation.

There are two stages of cancer that may be detected in a Pap smear. One is **cervical intraepithelial neoplasia (CIN),** in which precancerous or early cancer cells are found. They are still confined to the cervix and can be treated easily. Pap smears of about 15 percent of teenage girls who have had sexual intercourse show evidence of CIN (Strider, 1997). The more advanced and dangerous malignancy is **invasive cancer of the cervix (ICC),** which must be treated promptly and with whatever techniques necessary to reduce the risk of its spreading to other organs. Early treatment of uterine and cervical cancer is highly successful, but if the cancer is allowed to invade other surrounding tissues, it may be far more dangerous. Studies show that there is a higher incidence of cervical cancer among women who have been sexually active with several men and/or have had children than among those who have not. The reasons for this correlation are not well understood at present. In addition, cervical cancer and other abnormalities have been found to be more common in women whose mothers were given the synthetic estrogen compound **diethylstilbestrol (DES)** during pregnancy. DES was used from the 1940s through 1971 in pregnancies where miscarriage was a high risk. Women whose mothers were administered DES during pregnancy should receive frequent pelvic examinations to detect any potential problems.

The uterus can also be the site of nonmalignant growths and numerous other disorders. Hormonal imbalances may lead to abnormal and profuse bleeding from the uterus. Often such conditions are accompanied by excessive growth of the inner uterine lining (endometrium), a condition called **endometrial hyperplasia.** It may have a variety of causes. A similar disorder is **endometriosis,** occurring in 10 to 15 percent of premenopausal women, in which the uterine lining grows outward into the organs surrounding the uterus. This typically causes pain, abnormal menstrual bleeding, and sometimes sterility. The cervix may also become irritated or infected, leading to a gradual erosion of cervical tissues (Vercellini, 1996). **Fibroid tumors** that grow on the uterus are benign, but they can interfere with uterine function and cause bleeding. Some uterine disorders require surgical removal of all or part of the uterus, a procedure called a **hysterectomy.** Over half a million women in the United States have hysterectomies each year, about half of them because of fibroid tumors (Lepine, 1997).

The uterus is sometimes displaced from its usual position in the abdomen, a condition often called "tipped uterus." Unless there is pain connected with the displacement, there is no particular need for surgical intervention. Uterine displacement apparently has no effect on the woman's ability to become pregnant or give birth naturally. Occasionally, the ligaments that support the uterus become weakened to the extent that the uterus drops down and protrudes too far into the vagina. This **prolapse of the uterus** may cause serious discomfort and require surgery.

Tumors of the ovaries—both malignant and benign—are also common in women. If the ovaries must be surgically removed, the procedure is called oophorectomy. Increasing attention is being given to a condition termed **polycystic ovary syndrome (PCOS).** It has been estimated to affect about 6 per-

cervical intraepithelial neoplasia (CIN) (ep-a-THEE-lee-al nee-a-PLAY-zhee-a): abnormal, precancerous cells sometimes identified in a Pap smear.

invasive cancer of the cervix (ICC): advanced and dangerous malignancy requiring prompt treatment.

diethylstilbestrol (DES) (dye-eth-al-stil-BES-trole): synthetic estrogen compound once given to mothers whose pregnancies were at high risk of miscarrying.

endometrial hyperplasia (hy-per-PLAY-zhee-a): excessive growth of the inner lining of the uterus (endometrium).

endometriosis (en-doe-mee-tree-O-sus): growth of the endometrium out of the uterus into surrounding organs.

fibroid tumors: nonmalignant growths that commonly grow in uterine tissues, often interfering with uterine function.

hysterectomy: surgical removal of all or part of the uterus.

prolapse of the uterus: weakening of the supportive ligaments of the uterus, causing it to protrude into the vagina.

polycystic ovary syndrome (PCOS) (PAH-lee-SIS-tick): a disorder of the ovaries that can produce a variety of unpleasant physical symptoms, often because of elevated testosterone levels.

cent of women, making it the most common female endocrine disorder and a leading cause of infertility. Although symptoms of PCOS vary a great deal among women, it can lead to abnormal production of male hormones, which in turn interfere with the menstrual cycle and can lead to diabetes, heart disease, and other long-term health problems. Surgery is sometimes required, but new medical treatments for PCOS are being developed and have been found to be quite effective in controlling symptoms.

Female Breasts

The female breast is not a sex organ, but it has taken on sexual meanings in our society. Women's breasts are often perceived as sources of sexual arousal, and many women find that stimulation of their breasts, especially the nipple, is sexually arousing. There are many individual differences in this respect. There may also be varying degrees of sensitivity depending on the woman's stage in her menstrual cycle.

Each breast (see Fig. 2.9) is composed of from 15 to 20 clusters of *milk glands,* each cluster having a *milk duct* that leads to the nipple. There are deposits of *fatty tissue* just under the skin of the breast. The darkened circular area of skin surrounding the nipple is called the **areola.** There are often a few smaller nubs of skin on the areola.

During pregnancy, the breasts go through distinct changes as they prepare for nourishing a newborn infant. Within 2 or 3 days after a woman gives birth, her breasts begin to produce milk, the process of **lactation.** The pituitary hormone **prolactin** stimulates milk production. When the baby sucks at the nipple, the pituitary is stimulated to produce another hormone, **oxytocin,** which leads to the ejection of milk from the breast.

Concern about breast size and shape seems to be one of the most common bodily worries of women. Our culture has created an exaggerated impression that large breasts are sexy and desirable, and advertisers have capitalized on the anxieties of women by offering a wide variety of questionable breast enlargement techniques and devices. They not only are ineffective in enlarging the breasts but may also be unsafe. Of course, there are a great many different sizes, shapes, and positions of the female breasts. It is typical for one of a woman's breasts to be slightly differently sized or shaped than the other. Larger breasts can be uncomfortable or even feel unattractive to some women. Smaller breasts may indeed be more sensitive to sexual stimulation because the nerve endings in the skin are less dispersed.

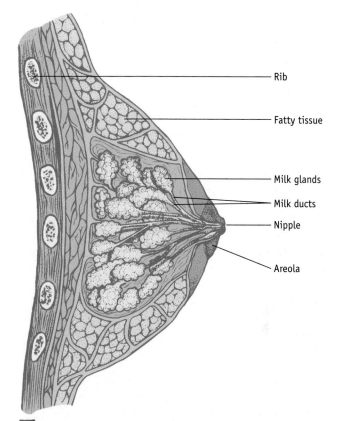

FIGURE 2.9 *Cross Section of a Female Breast*
The female breast has erotic and reproductive significance. The mammary or milk gland produces nourishment, which flows through the ducts to the nipple. The nipple is highly sensitive to stimulation, thereby playing a part in sexual arousal.

Breast Cancer

Cancer of the breast is one of the more common types of malignancy, although the risks of getting breast cancer are also often misinterpreted. It is commonly stated that women have a one in nine chance of getting breast cancer, but that figure refers to the cumulative lifetime risk for a woman who lives past the age of 85

areola (a-REE-a-la): darkened, circular area of skin surrounding the nipple of the breast.

lactation: production of milk by the milk glands of the breasts.

prolactin: pituitary hormone that stimulates the process of lactation.

oxytocin: pituitary hormone that plays a role in lactation and in uterine contractions.

CASE STUDY

Brittany: Breast Size Matters to Her

Brittany was 14 when she had begun to be concerned about the size and shape of her breasts. As she compared her own body to the bodies of other girls her age and to the photographs of women in magazines, she became convinced that her breasts were abnormally small. She was also worried that her right breast seemed somewhat smaller than the left and that the two seemed to be slightly different in the way they were positioned on her body. During high school, she avoided taking showers after physical education classes and refused to go to beaches or pools where she would be seen in a swimsuit.

Until she reached college, Brittany never discussed her worries with anyone. After becoming good friends with her roommate, she eventually shared her problem during a late-night discussion. Her roommate told her that she herself had always felt inadequate in terms of breast size and was determined eventually to have surgical breast augmentation. She passed along to Brittany some of the literature on augmentation that she had gathered. During a vacation period, Brittany told her mother that she wanted the surgery. Her mother attempted to reassure her that her body was perfectly normal and acceptable and

that surgery was wholly unnecessary. Brittany remained unconvinced.

When Brittany developed a close loving relationship during her junior year in college and became sexually involved, her partner admired her breasts during their lovemaking. She was surprised and pleased by this development but also remained committed to getting her breasts enlarged eventually. Her partner attempted to talk her out of the idea, explaining that her breasts were appealing exactly the way they were. Brittany was also encouraged to talk over her plans with a counselor and a physician. During her one session with a counselor, she explained that while she understood now that her worry was probably exaggerated beyond realistic bounds, she still believed that our society was one that placed greater value on larger breasts. Discussions with her physician convinced her that the risks associated with breast implants, although controversial, would not be worth it to her. She was a very health-conscious individual and did not care to risk her health for a procedure that was becoming clearer to her as an unnecessary acceptance of unfair societal pressures.

FOH (Phillips & Knight, 1999). As Table 2.1 indicates, the chances of getting breast cancer at younger ages are much lower. About 46,000 women die of the disease and its complications each year in the United States. As with any form of cancer, early detection greatly increases the chances of complete cure. When breast cancer is detected in its early, localized stages, the survival rate after 5 years is 91 percent. However, survival rates for breast cancer detected in all stages drop to about 75 percent after 5 years.

Researchers are attempting to find out why breast cancer seems to be on the increase, although the statistical upswing may partly be the result of techniques that allow for earlier detection of the disease. Research studies have demonstrated a link between two types of environmental pollutants (DDT pesticides and PCB industrial chemicals) and breast cancer (Hunter, 1997). Women who drink alcohol daily have an increased risk for the disease as their alcohol consumption increases (Smith-Warner, 1998). There is now evidence that about 5 percent of all breast cancers, and about one-third of the cases identified prior to age 30, result from a susceptibility caused by gene mutations that some women inherit. Breast cancer in later life is much less likely to result from genetic susceptibility (Claus, Schildkraut,

Thompson, & Risch, 1996). The faulty genes can occur on human chromosomes number 17 and 13 and have been labeled BRCA1 and BRCA2 by researchers (Marx, 1996; Scully et al., 1996). The BRCA1 gene has also been linked with a greater susceptibility to ovarian cancer. Women with the defective gene face about a 60 percent chance of developing breast cancer by age 50 and an 85 percent chance by age 65 (Miki et al., 1994; Wooster et al., 1994). It is hoped that a blood test will be developed that might easily identify those with the mutated gene (Marshall, 1997).

Women who are identified as having such a high risk sometimes choose to have their breasts surgically removed before they develop cancer. Although it was once believed that fat in the diet led to increased risk of breast cancer, it would now appear that an increased exposure to female hormones, particularly estrogen, and synthetic hormones used in contraception or other medical treatments, may play a more significant role (Marshall, 1993). It has been found that some groups of Jewish women have a higher than expected mutation in the breast cancer gene that increases their susceptibility to the disease (Egan et al., 1996).

New drugs that counteract the effects of hormones are being developed to reduce breast cancer risks. The

Table 2.1 *The Generation in Question*

Women in their 40s have a lower incidence of breast cancer, and lower mortality rates, than do older women. But their mammograms yield more false positives.

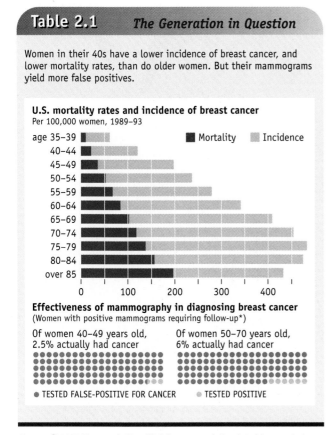

U.S. mortality rates and incidence of breast cancer
Per 100,000 women, 1989–93

■ Mortality   ▨ Incidence

age 35–39
40–44
45–49
50–54
55–59
60–64
65–69
70–74
75–79
80–84
over 85

0   100   200   300   400

Effectiveness of mammography in diagnosing breast cancer
(Women with positive mammograms requiring follow-up*)

Of women 40–49 years old, 2.5% actually had cancer

Of women 50–70 years old, 6% actually had cancer

● TESTED FALSE-POSITIVE FOR CANCER   ● TESTED POSITIVE

*Estimates based on 10,000 women, in each age group, screened annually, 5% of whom had abnormal mammograms.

drug tamoxifen has been found to be effective in preventing recurrence of breast cancer when taken following surgery, but it cannot be taken for more than 5 years because of risks of other malignancies associated with the drug. Massive clinical trials were under way with tamoxifen in the mid-1990s to test whether it could prevent first breast cancers in high-risk women, until evidence emerged that the drug was linked with the increased risks for other cancers. The consensus now is that for women shown to be at high risk for developiong breast cancer, the benefits of tamoxifen outweigh the risks (Begley, 1998a; Lemonick, 1998). There is evidence that women who breast-feed their babies may reduce the risk of developing breast cancer prior to age 50 by about 20 percent (Romieu, 1996).

Breast Self-Examination

The breasts are easily examined by oneself in order to detect changes that are large enough to be felt, and the American Cancer Society recommends that breast self-examination be done once each month. For reasons that are not completely understood, lesbian women are less likely than heterosexual women to practice breast self-examination monthly, and some believe that this places them at higher risk for mortality from the disease (Ellingson & Yarber, 1997). Women who examine their breasts regularly become familiar with the natural contours of their breast tissue. Therefore, they are likely to notice any unfamiliar lump that might develop there.

Breast self-examination should include both a visual inspection in a mirror and careful exploration of each breast by hand. It is not a good idea to do this examination just before or during menstruation because there tend to be more natural lumps during these phases. The best time for self-exam is midway through the menstrual cycle, around the time of ovulation. This would be approximately 12 to 16 days after the first day of the woman's last period. A systematic approach should be followed, as described here:

Visual Examination

Stand before a mirror with your arms at your sides and examine the appearance of both breasts. Then raise your arms high above your head and look for any changes in the contour or skin of either breast. Look for any swelling or dimpling of the skin or for any unusual signs in either nipple. Next, place your hands on your hips and flex the chest muscles, again looking for any unusual signs.

Manual Examination

The breasts may be easily examined during a bath or shower because the hands can glide easily over the wet skin. Another way is to examine them while lying down. Place a pillow under the shoulder on the same side as the breast to be examined and place that hand under your head. Use the hand from the opposite side for the actual examination. The fingers should be held together, forming a flat surface. Begin on the outer part of the breast, and move in complete, clockwise circles around the outer regions, checking for lumps, hard knots, or any unusual thickening. Then move inward toward the nipple about an inch and circle the breast again. Usually at least four concentric circles will have to be made to examine every part of the breast. It is a good idea to repeat this procedure while sitting or standing because the upright position redistributes breast tissue. Finally, squeeze each nipple to see if there is any discharge from either breast (see Fig. 2.10).

If you find any unusual features in a breast, *do not panic.* There are many nonmalignant conditions that can cause lumps, swelling, and discharge, but you

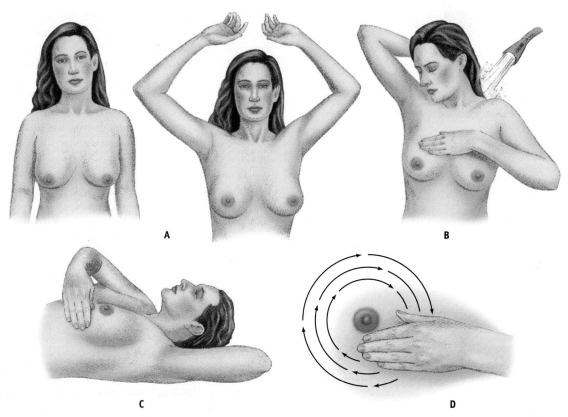

F◎H

FIGURE 2.10 *Breast Self-Examination*

It is important for a woman to examine her breasts regularly. She should look at her breasts in the mirror, first with her arms at her sides, then with them raised over her head (A). In the shower, her hands can easily move over the wet skin (B). When she is lying down, a woman can easily examine her breast tissue (C), and she should repeat the procedure when in an upright position. The fingers should be held flat and move in complete clockwise circles around the outer portion of the breast, then move progressively inward toward the nipple (D).

should not take any chances. Always consult a physician, who can then prescribe further testing to determine if the abnormality represents a malignancy.

Breast Screening Techniques

A test that is recommended on a regular basis for women over the age of 40 or 50 is **mammography.** A special X-ray picture is taken of the breast and can detect even small lumps. Only low-level radiation is used to produce the image, called a mammogram. Some women are fearful of the test, even though it is relatively painless and poses no hazards. A recent study indicated that as of 1992, nearly three-fourths of American women over 40 had had a mammogram. There has been some controversy over the age at which women should begin having mammography on a regular basis. Some research studies have reinforced the recommendations of the American Medical Association and American Cancer Society that a baseline mammogram be taken at around age 35 and then that annual

mammograms be done beginning at age 40. One study found that 15 percent of breast cancers detected by mammography were in women under the age of 50. Other research found that malignancies in this age group tend to grow faster, making early detection and treatment even more crucial. However, some other groups do not feel that annual mammograms are indicated for most women until they have reached the age of 50 (Taubes, 1997).

If a malignant tumor is discovered, modern medicine has made great strides in treatment and cure. For a woman who develops breast cancer, there is a 50 percent chance that the diagnosis will come after the age of 65, and she now has a 65 percent chance of surviving the illness and of dying ultimately from another cause (Phillips & Knight, 1999). Various combinations

mammography: sensitive X-ray technique used to discover small breast tumors.

of radiation therapy, chemotherapy, and administration of hormones can be used. It is sometimes necessary to remove the entire breast in a surgical procedure called a **mastectomy,** but current research indicates that removal of only the lump itself and some surrounding tissue, a **lumpectomy,** is often sufficient. Again, early discovery of unusual growths in the breast is a woman's best protection.

■ The Menstrual Cycle

Of special importance to the female's role in reproduction is the **menstrual cycle.** From the time of first menstruation, called **menarche,** to the period of life when her menstruation ceases, called **menopause** (or climacteric), a woman's body goes through a periodic cycle that involves hormonal, psychological, and physical changes. This menstrual cycle involves the maturation of an ovum and the periodic preparation of the uterus for pregnancy, followed by a gradual return to the "unprepared" state if pregnancy does not occur.

Today, menarche usually occurs sometime between the ages of 9 and 16, although variations from this range are normal. The onset of menopause is typically between the ages of 45 and 55. So, the years between menarche and menopause constitute a woman's potential childbearing years, although she is actually able only to conceive for a day or two usually once a month. Women in their teenage years who bear children have a greater risk of experiencing physical complications and having children with birth defects. Likewise, the older a couple is when having children, especially beyond the age of 35, the greater the possibility of the offspring having birth defects. In mature women, an average entire menstrual cycle lasts about 28 days, although it may fluctuate a great deal in individuals. In teenage girls, the length of the cycle tends to be more irregular and slightly longer, averaging closer to 31 days.

It is important for girls to be prepared for menarche through appropriate educational efforts. Only too often in the past, girls have been frightened by their first menstruation because they had not been educated about what to expect. Mothers have usually been the most significant source of information about menstruation, although many girls are learning about menarche through school health education programs. It is known that when effective education about the menstrual cycle is provided prior to menarche, girls tend to have much more positive attitudes toward the experience and toward their bodies (Kieren & Morse, 1992).

The menstrual cycle is regulated by a complex interaction of hormones secreted by the *pituitary gland,* located at the base of the brain; a portion of the brain itself called the *hypothalamus;* and the ovaries. The pituitary gland acts as a sort of relay station between the hypothalamus and ovaries. The hypothalamus produces **gonadotropin-releasing hormone (GnRH),** which stimulates the pituitary gland to produce two hormones, follicle-stimulating hormone and luteinizing hormone, which in turn regulate hormonal secretion by the ovaries. How these hormones control the reproductive organs is described in the following section. Although the menstrual cycle is continuous, it will be divided into four stages, or phases, for ease of explanation: the follicular phase, ovulation, luteal secretion, and menstruation.

Preovulatory Preparation or Follicular Phase

During the first stage of the menstrual cycle (see Fig. 2.11), two important things must take place: the maturation of an ovum in one of the ovarian follicles and the beginning preparation of the uterus for the nourishment of an embryo, in case the ovum is fertilized. These developments are initiated by the secretion of **follicle-stimulating hormone (FSH)** from the pituitary gland into the bloodstream. The FSH influences the ovaries to "ripen" one or more of the ova in a follicle and also to increase their production of **estrogen.** The estrogen works directly on the inner lining of the uterus (endometrium), causing it to thicken gradually, with enlargement of its many small glands and blood

mastectomy: surgical removal of all or part of a breast.

lumpectomy: surgical removal of a breast lump, along with a small amount of surrounding tissue.

menstrual cycle: the hormonal interactions that prepare a woman's body for possible pregnancy at roughly monthly intervals.

menarche (MEN-are-kee): onset of menstruation at puberty.

menopause (MEN-a-pawz): time in midlife when menstruation ceases.

gonadotropin-releasing hormone (GnRH) (go-nad-a-TRO-pen): hormone from the hypothalamus that stimulates the release of FSH and LH by the pituitary.

follicle-stimulating hormone (FSH): pituitary hormone that stimulates the ovaries or testes.

estrogen (ES-tro-jen): hormone produced abundantly by the ovaries; it plays an important role in the menstrual cycle.

CROSS-CULTURAL PERSPECTIVE
Celebrating Menarche across Cultures

In the larger North American culture, we have no particular puberty rites for either boys or girls. Some families will quietly celebrate when daughters have their first period, but the event is more likely passed with little discussion or fanfare. In smaller tribal societies, it is quite common for menarche to be seen as a significant passage in a girl's life, signifying that she has reached childbearing age, and —in some cultures—is available for marriage. Here is a brief look at how menarche is celebrated in a few other cultures.

When a young Japanese woman experiences her first period, friends and family are invited to a celebration but are not told why the party is being held. They are then served a food tray decorated with candied apple, a pear adorned with leaves, or red-colored rice and beans. This announces the reason for the celebration, and the girl is considered the guest of honor at the affair.

In several cultures, girls who begin menstruating are taken to a special dwelling. Among the Mbuti Pygmies in Zaire, a menstrual hut is built for a firstborn daughter. She is taken there to be taught by an older tribeswoman how to avoid pregnancy. Her feet are covered with leaves so that they will not touch the ground, and she is brought food by other girls in the village. After several days, her body is rubbed with white clay, and she emerges for a ceremony called the *elima,* characterized by dancing and singing in the forest. The celebration symbolizes her eligibility for marriage. The aboriginal people of Australia also take a girl entering puberty to a hut that has been constructed several miles from the village. The women teach her about special female powers and "love magic." The girl is then bathed in the river and decorated for the return to be given to her new husband. The hut used for her rite of passage is burned. Among the Ulithi of Micronesia, the girl is taken by her villagers to the "women's house," where she is bathed and taught about her womanly responsibilities by the elders. When it is clear that she understands her duties, she is soon allowed to live in her own hut, built near her parents', as she prepares to have a husband. In this culture, women must go to the menstrual hut every time they menstruate.

Native Americans often place great importance on a girl's first period and have traditionally viewed puberty rites as a celebration of fertility and the power of womanhood. The Mescalero Apaches have a 4-day celebration each year for all the young women who have begun menstruating in the course of that year. Boy singers recount the history of the tribe, and there is great feasting and dancing. This is followed by 4 days during which the young women celebrate privately, contemplating the changes in their bodies as they enter womanhood. The Nootka Indians of the Pacific Northwest celebrate their first "moontime" with a party, after which the girl is taken out to sea and allowed to swim back to shore. She is then cheered by the entire village for her endurance and courage.

In Sri Lanka, the mother of the menstruating girl takes information about the time of the first period to an astrologer, who makes predictions about the girl's future. She is not allowed to see males for a time. There is eventually a large celebration, during which the family's house is whitewashed, cakes are baked, and bananas are gathered. The girl stays in the smallest room of the house and is allowed to eat only certain foods. An herb preparation is prepared in a pot and poured over the girl's head, after which the pot is broken. There is then a ritual bathing, and the girl is dressed in new white clothes. Friends and families bring her money and gifts to celebrate her passage to womanhood.

—From the author's files

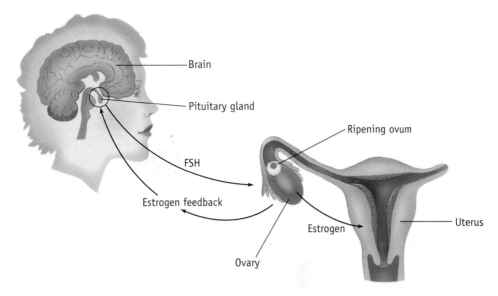

Brain

Pituitary gland

Ripening ovum

FSH

Estrogen feedback

Estrogen

Ovary

Uterus

FIGURE 2.11 *Preovulatory Preparation*

In the first stage of the menstrual cycle, the maturity of the ovum begins. The follicle-stimulating hormone from the pituitary gland influences the production of estrogen by the ovaries that causes the lining of the uterus to thicken in preparation for a fertilized ovum.

vessels. The estrogen also exerts a "feedback" effect on the pituitary gland, so that as the estrogen level in the blood increases, the production of FSH by the pituitary decreases.

Ovulation

When a high concentration of estrogen is reached (see Fig. 2.12), the hypothalamus triggers the release of **luteinizing hormone (LH)** from the pituitary. This hormone causes development of the egg to stop and is primarily responsible for the rupturing of the mature ovum through the outer wall of one ovary, the process of **ovulation.** After the ovum has left the ovary, the follicle remains as a tiny mass of cells called the **corpus luteum.** Under the influence of LH, the corpus luteum becomes a small gland. Studies of women's experience of the menstrual cycle have suggested that women tend to have higher levels of sexual arousability around the time of ovulation.

Luteal Secretion

With stimulation by LH, the corpus luteum begins secreting another essential hormone, **progesterone,** along with more estrogen (see Fig. 2.13). These hormones further thicken the uterine lining and cause it to begin secreting its own nutrient fluids that can nourish an embryo if pregnancy occurs. The progesterone also has a "feedback" effect on the hypothalamus, so that it

shuts off the production of GnRH. This in turn decreases the production of LH and FSH. While these developments are happening, the ovum is slowly being moved through one of the fallopian tubes toward the uterus, a journey of 3 or 4 days. If the ovum is fertilized by a sperm, the fertilization will occur in the fallopian tube. If the ovum is not fertilized, it disintegrates.

Menstruation

If the ovum is not fertilized, the corpus luteum degenerates, and the production of progesterone ceases. Estrogen level in the bloodstream begins to fall, and the thickened lining of the uterus begins to degenerate. Uterine cellular material, fluids, and a small amount of

luteinizing hormone (LH) (LEW-tee-in-ize-ing): pituitary hormone that triggers ovulation in the ovaries and stimulates sperm production in the testes.

ovulation: release of a mature ovum through the wall of an ovary.

corpus luteum: cell cluster of the follicle that remains after the ovum is released, secreting hormones that help regulate the menstrual cycle.

progesterone (pro-JES-ter-one): ovarian hormone that causes the uterine lining to thicken.

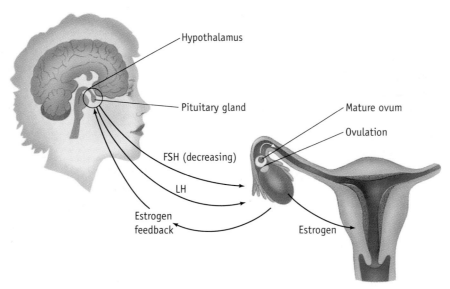

FIGURE 2.12   *Ovulation*

The pituitary gland is stimulated to release the luteinizing hormone by the presence of estrogen. This in turn causes the mature ovum to rupture through the outer wall of one ovary (the process of ovulation). The follicle that remains becomes an active gland, the corpus luteum.

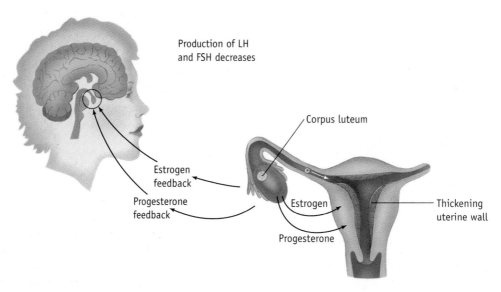

▨ **FIGURE 2.13**   *Luteal Secretion*

The corpus luteum begins secreting progesterone as well as more estrogen, which further thickens the uterine lining in preparation for the possibility that the ovum will be fertilized as it moves through the fallopian tube.

blood (usually about 2 to 5 ounces) are then lost through the vagina over a period of from 3 to 7 days. This is called **menstruation** or the menstrual period (see Fig. 2.14). The estrogen level continues to fall and eventually becomes low enough that the pituitary again begins to produce FSH. The menstrual cycle is thus initiated all over again (see Table 2.2).

A theory has been advanced concerning another possible function of menstruation. It has been pro-posed that the shedding of the uterine lining may also rid the uterus of bacteria and other microbes that might be carried into the body by sperm and semen.

> **menstruation** (men-stru-AY-shun): phase of menstrual cycle in which the inner uterine lining breaks down and sloughs off; the tissue, along with some blood, flows out through the vagina; also called the period.

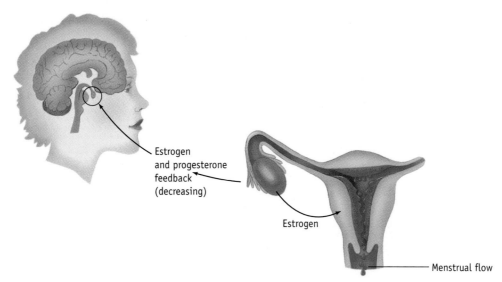

Estrogen
and progesterone
feedback
(decreasing)

Estrogen

Menstrual flow

FIGURE 2.14 *Menstruation*

If the ovum is not fertilized, the corpus luteum degenerates, and the progesterone and estrogen levels begin to fall. The portion of the uterus that had begun to thicken now begins to slough off and is lost through the vagina over a period of days.

The blood present would carry immune cells to kill the germs, and then the menstrual flow would carry the material outside the body (Angier, 1993).

Unless a woman experiences pain during menstruation, called **dysmenorrhea,** or some other medical problem, there is no need to curtail any activities during menstruation. There are a number of products that can be used to absorb the menstrual flow. These include various sizes of absorbent pads that are held over the vaginal opening by adhesive that sticks to the underpants. Tampons are cylinders of absorbent material and may be inserted directly into the vagina. Tampons do not stretch the vagina and usually cause no damage to an intact hymen, so they are favored by many women who prefer not to wear a pad externally. Because tampons may cause toxic shock syndrome, particularly if used for prolonged periods of time, care must be taken in their use (see chapter 10, p. 323).

In some Native American and Eastern cultures, the menstruating female is considered (primarily by the male hierarchy) to be unclean, and sexual intercourse is prohibited during the menstrual period. Even though men and women in these cultures may subscribe to these social imperatives publicly, they do not necessarily do so in private. Research with white, college-educated, heterosexual women in the United States indicates that they are less likely to engage in all sexual activities during menstruation, perhaps because of lowered physical interest, but also because of social and psychological factors (Hedricks, 1995). There are no particular medical risks associated with sexual activity during the period per se, although if a woman is infected with HIV, the presence of blood in the vagina

may increase the risk that a sexual partner could become infected. Use of a condom would reduce that risk. Some women experience variations in their sex drive during various stages of the menstrual cycle, but there is no general pattern that has been shown to be typical in this regard (Hedricks, 1995). Although there is less chance of pregnancy resulting from intercourse during menstruation, it should not be assumed that it is a totally "safe" time.

Premenstrual Syndrome

Many women experience some physical discomfort and psychological shifts just prior to or during menstruation. These include headaches, backaches, fatigue, fluid retention, uterine cramping, anxiety, depression, and irritability. In 5 to 10 percent of women, these symptoms may become severe enough to interfere with daily activities, and up to 30 percent have enough discomfort and unpleasant symptoms to be diagnosed with what has come to be known as **premenstrual syndrome (PMS)** (Steiner, 1997). A small number of these women have a good deal of emotional distress as part of their PMS, including depression, anxiety, and restlessness. These more severe

dysmenorrhea (dis-men-a-REE-a): painful menstruation.

premenstrual syndrome (PMS): symptoms of physical discomfort, moodiness, and emotional tensions that occur in some women for a few days prior to menstruation.

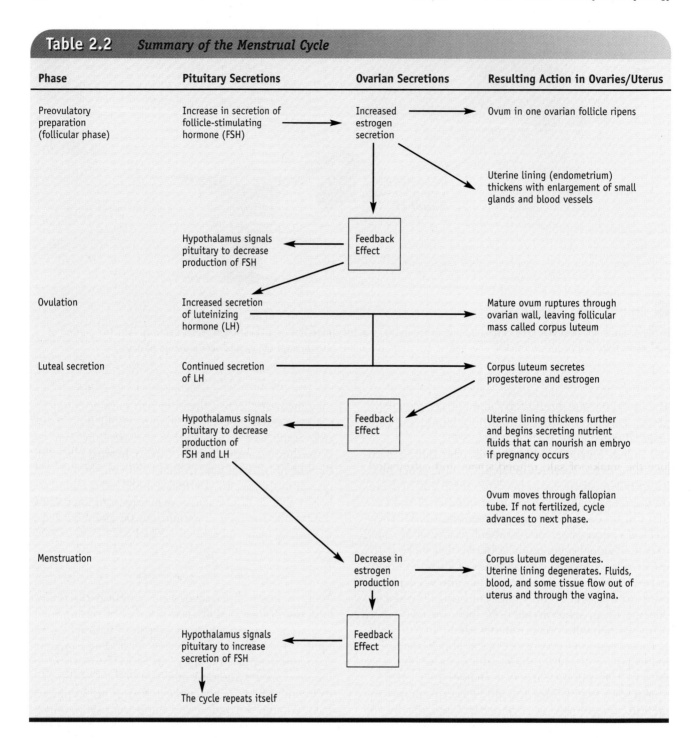

Table 2.2   *Summary of the Menstrual Cycle*

Phase	Pituitary Secretions	Ovarian Secretions	Resulting Action in Ovaries/Uterus
Preovulatory preparation (follicular phase)	Increase in secretion of follicle-stimulating hormone (FSH)	Increased estrogen secretion	Ovum in one ovarian follicle ripens
			Uterine lining (endometrium) thickens with enlargement of small glands and blood vessels
	Hypothalamus signals pituitary to decrease production of FSH	Feedback Effect	
Ovulation	Increased secretion of luteinizing hormone (LH)		Mature ovum ruptures through ovarian wall, leaving follicular mass called corpus luteum
Luteal secretion	Continued secretion of LH		Corpus luteum secretes progesterone and estrogen
	Hypothalamus signals pituitary to decrease production of FSH and LH	Feedback Effect	Uterine lining thickens further and begins secreting nutrient fluids that can nourish an embryo if pregnancy occurs
			Ovum moves through fallopian tube. If not fertilized, cycle advances to next phase.
Menstruation		Decrease in estrogen production	Corpus luteum degenerates. Uterine lining degenerates. Fluids, blood, and some tissue flow out of uterus and through the vagina.
	Hypothalamus signals pituitary to increase secretion of FSH	Feedback Effect	
	The cycle repeats itself		

psychological symptoms are sometimes classified as **premenstrual dysphoric disorder (PMDD).** However, there are many individual differences in how women experience and react to these symptoms, and the degree of their severity seems to be related to factors such as the degree of stress in their lives, their own expectations about the symptoms, and how they learned to think about menstrual symptoms (Gold, 1997; Yonkers et al., 1997). Sexual interest may vary during the menstrual cycle as well. It has been found

that women who experience PMS symptoms are more likely to have higher levels of sexual interest during the ovulatory phase of the cycle, whereas women who do not have premenstrual complaints tend to be most

premenstrual dysphoric disorder (PMDD): severe emotional symptoms such as anxiety or depression around the time of menstruation.

interested in sexual activity just prior to menstruation (Clayton, Clavet, McGarvey, Warnock, & Weiss, 1999; Van Goozen, Wiegant, Endert, Helmond, & Dan de Poll, 1997).

Two hormones are believed to be involved in producing PMS. There is a decrease in the level of progesterone prior to menstruation and an increase in the amount of the substance called **prostaglandin,** a hormonelike chemical whose source in the body is as yet unidentified. These changes may lead to physiological and resulting psychological effects because some research has confirmed that mood shifts, social frustration, and some thinking and creative skills seem to change over the menstrual cycle in some women. Some evidence suggests that psychological pressures may play a role in accentuating PMS symptoms (Ussher, 1997).

There is a great deal of controversy over how PMS should be treated. Over-the-counter drugs that are advertised for menstrual cramping are generally antiprostaglandins that interfere with that hormone's contracting effects on the uterus. Research has shown that antidepressant medications that maintain levels of the chemical serotonin in the brain may help relieve PMS symptoms in many women (Brown, 1997). Some authorities have recommended changes in diet to help with PMS. The most common suggestions are to reduce the intake of salt, refined sugar, and caffeinated foods such as coffee, colas, and chocolate. Eating more frequently during the day, taking high dosages of certain vitamins, increasing fiber intake, and drinking herbal teas have been recommended. In general, however, physicians remain skeptical over the efficacy of many remedies for PMS.

The controversy over PMS echoes a long-standing difference in our culture between women's needs and the attitudes of a male-dominated medical establishment. For decades, women had reported a spectrum of symptoms associated with the menstrual cycle. Male physicians often failed to take those symptoms seriously or were at a loss as to how to treat them. Women often ended up feeling as though they were being perceived as complainers or hypochondriacs looking for attention. Wherever the debate over PMS takes us, it is clear that the physical symptoms and mood shifts prior to menstruation are very real (Ussher, 1997).

▨ Menopause

Aging is a natural process among living things, with predictable physiological changes occurring over time at all levels from the cellular to entire organ systems. For humans, it is apparently a process that is largely genetically controlled. Various degenerative physiological aspects of aging are triggered by genes, although our bodies also experience other effects of normal wear and tear. There are wide individual differences, but each of us experiences a gradual process of slowing down and becoming physically less pliable. Although its rate may be affected by heredity, the environment, and personal health habits, the aging process is inevitable and irreversible. The sexual implications of aging stem from both psychological and biological changes. Aging bodies may be perceived as having beauty and strength if they can be approached with a positive psychological attitude.

The female body is genetically programmed to cease menstruating sometime in middle age, usually between the ages of 45 and 55. This is called menopause, and the years surrounding menopause are usually termed **perimenopause** (see Fig. 2.15). In popular usage, this is sometimes called the "change of life," simply "the change," or a more recently suggested term, "the pause." Modifications in ovarian function usually begin prior to age 30, and there is a gradual decline in the hormonal output of these glands. Structures in the brain contribute to these changes. Eventually there is increased irregularity in ovulation and menstrual periods. There are usually unpredictable sequences of scanty menstrual flow and increased flow, but a few women just stop menstruating quite abruptly, never having it happen again. Although the pituitary gland continues to produce FSH and LH that help control the woman's menstrual cycle, the ovaries apparently become increasingly insensitive to their stimulation. The hormone-producing tissues of the ovaries atrophy until their output of estrogen and progesterone becomes minimal (Wise, Krajnak, & Kashon, 1996; Brody, 1998).

As the woman's hormonal levels drop, the most noticeable result is the gradual cessation of menstruation. This results from the lack of hormonal stimulation to the inner lining of the uterus, the endometrium. This means, of course, that the woman is no longer able to conceive, although most physicians recommend using birth control for a full year after the last menstrual period. However, there are other effects on the body as well. Very gradually, the uterus and breasts decrease somewhat in size. The inner walls of the vagina become thinner, and reduction in the number of small blood vessels in the pelvic region may result in reduced vaginal lubrication. There may also be changes

prostaglandin: hormonelike chemical whose concentrations increase in a woman's body just prior to menstruation.

perimenopause: the time of a woman's life surrounding menopause, characterized by symptoms resulting from reduced estrogen levels.

Changes before "The Change"

There is no typical perimenopause. Some women experience few or no symptoms. Others are not so lucky; they suffer from a wide range. Some of the most common:

Memory lapses and loss of concentration Some women who take estrogen report an improvement in cognitive function.

Headaches May be caused by fluctuating hormone levels. Some women begin to suffer migraines.

Mood swings Changes in hormone levels may interfere with the production of the body's mood-regulator serotonin. Some women feel anxious or weepy.

Dry skin A decrease in the protein collagen —which may be linked to a decline in estrogen —means less elasticity and more wrinkles.

Bone loss Declining reproductive hormones translates to less protection for bones. The problem is at its worst after menopause.

Hot flashes Many perimenopausal women experience them, mostly around the head and upper body. They usually last several minutes. Nocturnal hot flashes, which are known as night sweats, can lead to insomnia.

Erratic menstrual cycles A classic symptom of perimenopause. Cycles vary widely from 18 days to missed periods. Excessive bleeding is common.

Vaginal dryness As estrogen levels decline, the vaginal wall thins and becomes less elastic. Intercourse may become painful.

Urinary incontinence As the vaginal wall weakens, the bladder loses support and urination is harder to control.

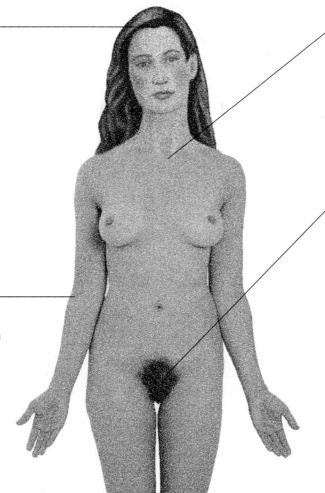

 FIGURE 2.15 *Perimenopause*

Source: © Newsweek, Inc. All rights reserved. Reprinted by permission.

in the texture and color of the skin and hair and an increased tendency to gain weight, especially on the hips. There are sometimes noticeable changes in the quality of the voice (Boulet & Oddens, 1996).

Another consequence of decreased estrogen production in some women is a weakening of bones, called **osteoporosis.** This condition most frequently strikes postmenopausal women who are slender and slight and who have led sedentary lives. Women suffering from osteoporosis are predisposed to fractures of the hip and arm, and they often suffer chronic back pain because of vertebral collapse. Although this condition cannot be completely cured, it may be treated to reduce the amount of bone weakness. The usual treatments involve the prescription of Vitamin D, calcium supplements, estrogen replacement, and/or exercise (see Table 2.3).

Menopausal changes in the body's hormonal balances may also cause mood alterations and other psychological effects. Some women complain of depression, irritability, or other emotional symptoms (Lippert, 1997). Some experience unpredictable dilation of the blood vessels in the skin, causing a flushed, sweaty feeling. This is called a **"hot flash,"** and its exact cause is unknown (Brody, 1998). However, we should not lose sight of the fact that life's major transitions are

osteoporosis (ah-stee-o-po-ROW-sus): disease caused by loss of calcium from the bones in postmenopausal women, leading to brittle bones and stooped posture.

hot flash: a flushed, sweaty feeling in the skin caused by dilated blood vessels; often associated with menopause.

Table 2.3   *The Facts about Menopause*

Factors Affecting Onset
- Smoking can bring on menopause as much as two years earlier.
- Left-handedness. Onset is about one year earlier.
- Number of pregnancies. The more pregnancies you've had, the later menopause may arrive.
- Onset of menstruation. If you began menstruating at an early age, menopause will likely be later.
- Mother's age at menopause. Although other factors come into play, heredity makes the age your mother's menopause began a good guidepost.

What Happens to Your Body?
- As early as 35, estrogen production slows, signaling peri-menopause—the beginning of the change of life.
- Premenstrual syndrome may increase or appear for the first time.
- Menstrual cycles may become erratic.
- You still can become pregnant.
- Night sweats and hot flashes may occur.
- Vaginal dryness may develop.
- Sleep may be disrupted.
- Mood swings may occur, or difficulty with concentration.
- After you have had no periods for a year, you are post-menopausal. You become susceptible to osteoporosis and have an increased risk of cardiovascular disease.

Demographics
- Menopause commonly occurs between ages 45 and 55. Average age is 51. This year, 1.3 million American women turn 50.
- 35 million American women already have reached menopause.
- Most women will live one-third of their lives after menopause.
- For every 2,000 postmenopausal women, 20 will develop severe bone loss; 6 will develop breast cancer; and 3 will develop endometrial cancer.

Estrogen Pros
- Can help prevent osteoporosis (the loss of bone mass).
- May help to prevent the onset of cardiovascular disease.

Estrogen Cons
- Can increase the risk of endometrial cancer.
- May increase the risk of breast cancer.

What Men Should Know about Menopause
- Everything women should know.
- Passage through menopause can take from one to three years.
- Some drying of the vagina occurs, so lubricants will be necessary during intercourse, and lengthened foreplay is in order.
- Lack of sleep can contribute to irritability and fatigue, making your partner more difficult to live with. She may cry easily.
- Be understanding, and do your share around the house.

Source: From Nancy McVicar, "The Facts about Menopause" in *Sun-Sentinel,* December 12, 1991. Reprinted with permission from the *Sun-Sentinel,* Fort Lauderdale, FL.

often and understandably accompanied by some degree of sadness and sense of loss, and these feelings do not have to be perceived as signs of pathology or psychological problems. It should also be emphasized that many women find very positive and freeing aspects in menopause as well. Aging, and the physiological changes it brings, need not be viewed negatively because there is still much about life to be discovered and celebrated (Lippert, 1997; Sanders, 1999).

Hormone Replacement Therapy

 Menopausal women who are treated with dosages of the progesterone and estrogen hormones experience a reversal of the physical changes that accompany menopause (Sanders, 1999). However, **hormone replacement therapy (HRT)** has at times been a controversial form of medical treatment. First popularized by Robert Wilson (1964) as a way of staying youthful and "feminine" for life, use of estrogen treatment alone eventually came under attack as a risky procedure. A number of studies in the 1970s began to demonstrate a statistical relationship between treatment with estrogen and several medical conditions, including uterine

and breast cancer. The link between estrogen replacement therapy and breast cancer has been demonstrated, particularly in women who have used estrogen for 5 years or more (Colditz et al., 1995).

When progesterone was administered with the estrogen to counteract potential risks, it was feared that it might also negate estrogen's benefits. Studies of older women who had received HRT began to suggest that its advantages outweighed the risks. One study examined questionnaires and medical records of 8,881 women, finding that those who received HRT actually tended to live longer than those who did not and they experienced less heart disease, stroke, and broken bones. Combining estrogen and progesterone over a long period of time seemed to have the most positive effects, although it has also now been shown to increase women's risks for breast cancer by 20 percent (Schairer et al., 2000).

> **hormone replacement therapy (HRT):** treatment of the physical changes of menopause by administering dosages of the hormones estrogen and progesterone.

Other studies have demonstrated that postmenopausal hormone replacement can help make the mind keener and memory sharper, reduce the risks of getting Alzheimer's disease, and significantly reduce women's risks of heart disease (Kalb, 1999). Chances of death from cardiovascular diseases are clearly reduced by HRT (Friedman et al., 1996). Combining synthetic testosterone with the other hormones improves the therapy's prevention of osteoporosis without decreasing its positive effects on heart function (Honor, Williams, & Adams, 1996; Nash, 1997b) (see Table 2.4).

The conflicting evidence about the benefits and risks of HRT have created some confusion for women and their doctors. The National Institutes of Health has undertaken a long-term study of over 57,000 women, but the final results of this research are not yet available. There is already conclusive evidence that HRT significantly reduces the risks of heart disease in women aged 45 to 65, a time of life when they are becoming more susceptible to cardiovascular problems. A carefully controlled study demonstrated that HRT did not raise blood pressure or increase the blood's tendency to form internal clots. Medical opinion has generally leaned toward recommending HRT to postmenopausal women to prevent many of the medical risks associated with aging (Healy, 1995; Sanders, 1999).

Implications for Women's Sexuality

FOH Females are typically raised to think of menstruation as a sign of being a woman, with its additional symbolic implications of fertility, femininity, and sexual readiness. Menarche is often heralded as the beginning of womanhood. Consequently, for many women, menopause represents a loss of an important facet of womanhood and femininity. They fall prey to some of the menopause-related myths: that it is the beginning of

the end of life, that sexual attractiveness and arousal deteriorate after menopause, and that one's purpose as a woman (that is, reproduction) has been lost (Lippert, 1997; Sanders, 1999).

Research studies generally confirm that menopause need not markedly affect a woman's sexual functioning, although there is research to indicate that some women experience a decrease in sexual desire during middle life. As a woman faces the physical and psychological changes of menopause, there may be a temporary shift in sexual desire. It may increase or decrease, but there are usually no major, long-lasting changes. Some women perceive menopause as a release from concern about intercourse resulting in an unwanted pregnancy, thus freeing them to be more relaxed sexually. As women approach menopause, they sometimes assume that they are no longer at risk for pregnancy. About 25 percent of women aged 40 to 44 are at risk of unwanted pregnancy, and one in five of the at-risk group uses no birth control.

Much of how a woman's sexual life is affected depends on how she views herself and menopause. It is influenced by the woman's cultural background, values about sex, social environment, overall health, and her fantasies and expectations regarding menopause. Nonetheless, even for women who expected that menopause would bring a decrease in sexual well-being, that is not necessarily the outcome (Sanders, 1999). It is therefore crucial that women get accurate information and emotional support through their menopausal experiences. There are counselors, women's centers, and trained social workers who may provide such help. Women need to be able to communicate their fears, doubts, and insecurities while being reassured that menopause is simply a natural stage of human development (Lippert, 1997). It is important for the woman's partner to receive information and counseling about her menopausal experience as well.

Table 2.4 *Weighing the Pros and Cons of Estrogen*			
Proven Benefits	**Benefits Very Likely**	**Proven Risks**	**Risks Very likely**
• Relieves hot flashes, night sweats and other menopausal symptoms • Reduces bone loss (osteoporosis) • Relieves vaginal dryness and atrophy	• Reduces risk of heart disease (improves cholesterol profile and makes blood vessels more resilient) • Reduces risk of colon cancer • Reduces mood swings, mental fogginess, and memory lapses • Keeps skin thicker, moister, and more youthful	• Increases incidence of cancer of the endometrium (the uterine lining) • Possible return of menstrual bleeding, if taken with progesterone • Premenstrual-type symptoms (fluid retention, tender breasts, irritability) • May increase growth of benign fibroid tumors in the uterus	• Higher rate of breast cancer • Abnormal blood clots • Weight gain • Increases risk of gallstones • Headaches

Source: From "The Big Pro: Estrogen and Sex" in *Time*, June 26, 1995. Copyright © 1995 Time Inc. Reprinted by permission.

Self-Evaluation

You and Your Body

When you have sufficient privacy, remove all of your clothing and stand before the largest mirror available, preferably a full-length one. Try to relax and take some time to look over your body carefully. Consider the following questions as you look at your body with as much objectivity as you can muster:

1. Do you enjoy looking at and touching your body? Why or why not?

2. What aspects of your body do you like most? Least?

3. If you are a male, how do you feel about your general body shape, your penis, and your testicles, as compared to other male bodies you have seen?

4. If you are a female, how do you feel about your general body shape, your breasts, and your external genitals, as compared to other female bodies you have seen?

5. Does your body conform to your ideas of what a (feminine or masculine) body should look like?

6. Do you think your nude body is (or would be) sexually attractive to members of the other gender? Of the same gender?

Chapter Summary

1. The female sex organs have always been recognized for their procreative (reproductive) functions, but their potentials for pleasure and intimate communication have become increasingly recognized.

2. The female vulva consists of the external sex organs known as the mons, the labia majora and minora, the clitoris, and the openings to the urethra and vagina.

3. The clitoris has a sensitive tip, or glans, and a shaft that extends back under a covering of tissue, the hood or prepuce.

4. Some cultures, religions, or social customs require surgical procedures such as clitoridectomy or infibulation to be performed as rites of passage. These forms of female genital mutilation (FGM) have created worldwide controversy.

5. The vagina is a muscular-walled organ of sexual pleasure and reproduction that extends into the woman's body. Its opening may be partially covered by tissue called a hymen.

6. Douching of the vagina is still a common practice, but it increases the risks of internal infections. The vagina has natural cleansing mechanisms.

7. The hymen may be present in the opening of the vagina and may be one of several types.

8. The hymen may cause sexual difficulties if it is imperforate (having no openings) or tough and fibrous.

9. Regular genital self-examination for women ensures early detection of infections or irritations.

10. Acute urethral syndrome and cystitis, or bladder infection, are common in women, and may be caused by the *E. coli* bacterium. Interstitial cystitis is chronic and may cause problems with sexual functioning.

11. The vagina is subject to several medical conditions, including atrophy because of lowered estrogen levels, varicose veins, and fistulae (openings between the vagina and other organs).

12. The uterus is the organ in which fetal development takes place. Its cervix extends into the posterior part of the vagina.

13. The ovaries mature eggs (ova) and produce female hormones. The fallopian tubes transport ova down toward the uterus, and it is in these tubes that fertilization of an egg by a sperm can take place.

14. Pap smears offer the possibility of early detection for cervical cancer or precancerous cells in the cervix, called cervical intraepithelial neoplasia (CIN). Untreated cervical cancer may become invasive cervical cancer (ICC).

15. The uterus may be affected by hormonal imbalances, leading to abnormal bleeding, overgrowth of its lining either in the form of endometrial hyperplasia or endometriosis, or prolapse into the vagina.

16. The female breasts are strongly connected with sexuality in our culture, and women often worry about breast size. Milk glands in the breasts produce milk after a woman gives birth.

17. Breast cancer is one of the more common types of malignancy. Regular breast self-examination is essential to the detection of potentially malignant lumps. Mammography is a form of X ray that can detect breast cancer in very early stages.

18. Between menarche and menopause, a woman's fertility is regulated by the menstrual cycle. At roughly 4-week intervals, an ovum ripens in one ovary as the result of increased levels of follicle-stimulating hormone (FSH). Estrogen thickens the uterine wall, producing a suitable location for fetal growth. The ovum breaks through the ovary wall at ovulation. If the ovum is not fertilized, extra blood and tissue are shed from the uterus in menstruation. Hormones from the pituitary,

hypothalamus, and ovaries regulate the menstrual cycle.

19. Premenstrual syndrome (PMS) consists of uncomfortable physical and emotional symptoms. Severe symptoms may be classified as premenstrual dysphoria disorder (PMDD).

20. Menopause is the time of life when menstruation ceases. The perimenopausal years may have unpleasant symptoms as hormone production decreases.

21. Hormone replacement therapy (HRT) can relieve many menopausal symptoms, but it carries some risks.

Focus on Health Questions

You will find in this section the kinds of questions that you may have concerning your own health and sexuality. The page references indicate where in the text the answer is located; the exact place is marked with the logo: **F◦H**

1. Should I douche to keep my vagina clean and odor-free? 48

2. If my hymen is missing, will my partner be convinced that I previously have had sex? 49

3. Why is it that the hymen may bleed during first sexual intercourse, and can it cause pain during sex? 50

4. What are the signs of infection or abnormality in the vulval and vaginal area? 50

5. What are the symptoms and risks of cystitis? 50

6. Can improper wiping after a bowel movement lead to vaginal infection? 50

7. What does a physician do during a pelvic examination? 51

8. What is a Pap smear for, and how is it done? 52

9. What can be done to treat endometriosis? 54

10. How much risk for breast cancer do I have? 56

11. What does a mammogram show, and at what age should I have one? 58

12. How can I examine my breasts for possible signs of cancer? 57

13. Is it all right to have sex when I'm having my period? 63

14. What causes PMS, and what can I do about it? 63

15. What will menopause be like? 65

16. Are there any medications that will relieve unpleasant symptoms of menopause? 67

17. Is hormone replacement therapy safe? 67

18. Will menopause affect my sex life? 68

Annotated Readings

Angell, M. (1996). *Science on trial: The clash of medical evidence and the law in the breast implant case.* New York: W. W. Norton. A carefully balanced treatment of the controversy and legal actions surrounding the safety of silicone breast implants, this book provides insights into the interactions of science, politics, society, and sexual attractiveness.

Barbach, L. (1993). *The pause: Positive approaches to menopause.* New York: Dutton. An up-to-date guide that offers practical suggestions for dealing with the psychological and physical transitions of menopause.

The benefits of hormone replacement therapy are discussed.

Col, N. (1997). *A woman doctor's guide to hormone therapy: How to choose what's right for you.* Boston: Tatnuck Bookseller Press. A personalized approach to understanding hormone replacement therapy, including a model that allows women to use their own health histories to assess personal risks and potential benefits.

Denniston, G. C., & Milos, M. F. (Eds.). (1997). *Sexual mutilations: A human tragedy.* New York: Plenum

Press. A cross-cultural examination of genital mutilation in both males and females.

Landau, C., Cyr, M., & Mouton, A. W. (1994). *The complete book of menopause*. New York: Perigree. A comprehensive source of information about the physiology and psychology of menopause.

Rountree, C. (1993). *On women turning fifty: Celebrating midlife discoveries*. New York: HarperCollins. A collection of personal perspectives on menopause, sexuality, and aging from several well-known women.

Sheehy, G. (1993). *The silent passage: Menopause*. New York: Pocket Books. A personal and celebrative statement of the transitions that face women during menopause.

Chapter 3
Male Sexual Anatomy and Physiology

Chapter Outline

Note: A selection of Focus on Health questions appears at the end of each chapter. Answers to these questions are indicated within the chapter by the symbol in the margin. **F⊙H**

I first came to this country as a 12-year-old boy, and in the gym showers I was almost the only boy who was not circumcised. In my country circumcision was never done, and I had never even seen a circumcised penis before. And there I was, with my penis looking different from everybody else's.... Of all my cultural adjustments here, that was the most difficult.

—From a student's essay

I n sexuality education, male sex organs have traditionally been given recognition for their capability of generating pleasant sexual feelings, whereas their role in reproduction has often been seen as a by-product of that pleasure. As in the female, the external sex organs of the male (see Fig. 3.1) are associated more with sexual arousal, whereas the internal structures are associated more with reproduction (Murray, 1997). In males, however, the lines of distinction are much more vague.

The Testes and Scrotum

The two male sex glands, the **testes** (or testicles), develop within the abdominal cavity during fetal life. A few weeks before birth, the testes gradually move downward through the *inguinal canal* into an external pouch of skin, the **scrotum.** In a small percentage of male infants, the testes do not descend into the scrotum properly, and a few of these cases require medical treatment. The testes have two major functions after puberty. One is the production of the male sex hormone **testosterone,** which plays a significant role in the development of male secondary sex characteristics and may also affect behavior to some degree. The testes also form millions of **sperm,** the sex cells necessary for human reproduction.

Each testis (see Fig. 3.2) is subdivided internally into several lobes. The lobes are filled with a tangled mass of tiny **seminiferous tubules,** inside of which the sperm cells are formed. Each of the threadlike tubules is 1 to 3 feet long if extended. Between the tubules are **interstitial cells** (or Leydig cells) that pro-

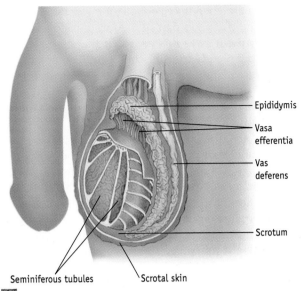

FIGURE 3.2 *Testes*

The testes are the male gonads or reproductive glands. They are paired structures located in the scrotum, and their purpose is to produce sperm and the hormone testosterone that controls male sexual development. The word "testis" is based on the root word for "witness"; the ancient custom in taking an oath was to place a hand on the genitals—to "testify."

duce testosterone. These cells are close to blood vessels, so that the hormone is secreted efficiently into the bloodstream. The seminiferous tubules combine at their ends to form larger ducts, and these empty into a series of even larger tubes, the **vasa efferentia.** Immature sperm from the seminiferous tubules are moved along by wavelike contractions into the vasa

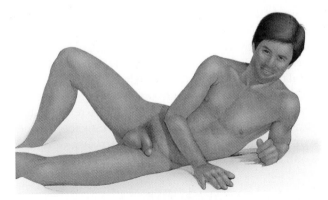

FIGURE 3.1 *External Male Anatomy*

The external male sex organs are more visible and accessible than the female's. As with the female, the external organs are the primary source of sexual pleasure, whereas the internal organs are the source of reproduction, but the distinction is not as clearly defined in males.

testes (TEST-ees): pair of male gonads that produce sperm and male hormones.

scrotum (SKROTE-um): pouch of skin in which the testes are contained.

testosterone (tes-TAHS-ter-one): major male hormone produced by the testes; it helps to produce male secondary sex characteristics.

sperm: reproductive cells produced in the testes; in fertilization, one sperm unites with an ovum.

seminiferous tubules (sem-a-NIF-a-rus): tightly coiled tubules in the testes in which sperm cells are formed.

interstitial cells (in-ter-STIH-shul): cells between the seminiferous tubules that secrete testosterone and other male hormones.

vasa efferentia: larger tubes within the testes, into which sperm move after being produced in the seminiferous tubules.

efferentia and then into a coiled tubing network folded against the back and part of the top of each testis, the **epididymis.** It is in this area that the sperm mature and become ready to leave the body. The epididymis opens into a large duct that leads up into the abdominal cavity from each testis. This duct is called the **vas deferens** and transports the sperm up to the *seminal vesicle* during sexual activity.

The scrotum of a prepubescent male is quite smooth and light in color. At puberty, the testes and scrotum grow, and hormonal influences cause the outer skin to darken and become somewhat wrinkled. The location of the testes in this external pouch is essential because sperm production can only occur at temperatures slightly below inner body temperature. One zoologist has suggested that evolution led to externally located testes in those mammals that have physically active lifestyles, rather than for reasons of temperature, but this theory has not achieved complete acceptance (Blackman, 1996). The *cremasteric muscles* suspend the testes in the scrotum and help to regulate their temperature. In cold surroundings (such as swimming in cold water) or stressful situations, these muscles and the scrotal tissue itself contract, pulling the testes up close to the body to keep them warmer and protected. In warmer surroundings (such as a hot bath), the muscles and scrotal tissue relax so the testes are lowered away from the body to keep them cooler. The adult male testes are about 1½ inches in length and 1 inch in diameter. They are slightly movable in the scrotum. One testis usually hangs slightly lower than the other, and in the majority of men, it is the left testis that is lower. In left-handed men, the right testis tends to hang lower. There seems to be no particular significance either way. The scrotal area is well supplied with nerves, and the testes are very sensitive to pressure or sharp blows. Most men find gentle stimulation of the testes and scrotum to be sexually arousing.

Tradition has held that during exercise, an athletic supporter or jockstrap should be worn by males to hold the testicles up closer to the body, providing support and a measure of protection. However, historians know that athletes in ancient times often competed in the nude. There is now some evidence that during exercise, the cremasteric muscles actually contract, providing their own natural support. However, as the body temperature rises, they tend to relax, causing the testes to lower away from the body and making them more vulnerable to injury. Younger male athletes are not wearing the traditional jockstrap as much anymore, opting instead for spandex shorts or compression pants that provide a more natural feeling of support. Some are even choosing to wear boxer shorts that do not provide much support at all. But evidence suggests that severe testicular injury, causing pain and swelling for a day or more, may be associated with later infertility. This has caused some sports health experts to recommend that a hard plastic protective cup be worn over the male genitals during contact sports.

Male Genital and Testicular Self-Examination

Men should take time at least monthly to examine their genital organs. Adequate lighting, and sometimes a mirror, can help with the self-examination process. Look through the pubic hair to the skin underneath, and examine the head and shaft of the penis carefully. If you are not circumcised, this will require pulling back the foreskin to expose the penile glans. Check for any bumps, sores, or blisters anywhere in the region. They may be reddish or light in color. It is important to lift up the penis and look underneath because this is an area that is often overlooked. Also be alert to any soreness in the genitals or to any itching or burning sensations during urination or around the urethral opening. Although many of these symptoms do not indicate serious conditions, you should have them checked by a physician or other clinician who specializes in men's health concerns.

Cancer of the testes is a relatively rare disease, with fewer than 5,000 new cases being diagnosed each year in the United States. It is primarily a disease of younger men, especially between the ages of 20 and 35. When detected and treated early, the chances of survival are excellent. However, if it is not treated within the first 3 months, the survival rate falls dramatically to only about 25 percent. Therefore it is crucial for men to get into the habit of checking their testes regularly for any lumps or other unusual symptoms.

Here is the best way to proceed with testicular self-examination. Choose a time after a hot shower or bath, so that the testes are lowered away from the body. Roll each testicle gently between the thumb and fingers, especially looking for any small hard lumps that may be found directly on the front or side surface of a testis (see Fig. 3.3). Such a lump is usually painless. Do not be alarmed at feeling the epididymis toward the top and back of each testis. Although not all lumps are malignant, any growth of this sort should be reported to a physician immediately for further investigation. Other symptoms that a man should consider suspicious and worth reporting include any "heavy" feeling in a testi-

epididymis (ep-a-DID-a-mus): tubular structure on each testis in which sperm cells mature.

vas deferens: tube that leads sperm upward from each testis to the seminal vesicles.

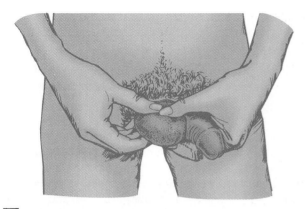

FIGURE 3.3   *Testicular Self-Examination*

The best time for a man to examine his testes is right after a hot bath or shower because the testicles descend, and the scrotal skin relaxes in the heat. He should place his index and middle fingers on the underside of each testicle and his thumbs on top. He should gently roll the testicle between his fingers and thumb. Any abnormal lump would be most likely at the front or the side of the testicle.

cle, accumulation of fluid in the scrotum, swelling of lymph nodes or other discomfort in the groin area, and any swelling or tenderness in the breasts.

If testicular cancer is diagnosed, the usual treatment involves surgical removal of the entire testis. The other testis is left in place and can easily produce enough male hormones on its own. Sexual functioning is usually not impaired in any way. An artificial, gel-filled testis can be placed in the scrotum for cosmetic reasons. Men should become comfortable with this self-examination procedure as a potentially lifesaving measure.

Disorders of the Testes

There are also several disorders of the testes. In very rare cases, both testes are completely lacking at birth, a disorder known as **anorchism.** A more common problem is **cryptorchidism,** in which the testes have not descended into the scrotum before birth. This condition usually corrects itself within a few years, but if it does not, it must be corrected by the time of puberty through hormonal or surgical treatment. If only one testis is present in the scrotum, the condition is termed **monorchidism.** However, one testis can easily handle the work of two, producing sufficient quantities of male hormones and sperm. Occasionally a male suffers from **testicular failure,** in which the testes do not produce male hormones and/or sperm. The condition usually responds to some form of hormonal therapy.

Several organic problems can affect the internal organs of the sexual and urinary systems. In men, the bladder may become infected, and various parts of the testes may occasionally become inflamed. **Epididymitis,** or inflammation of the epididymis at the top of each testis, is relatively common and can be treated with antibiotics. It can be caused by many different types of bacteria that make their way into the urethra and eventually back through the vas deferens to the epididymis. In severe cases, surgical intervention may be necessary.

If a man experiences prolonged sexual arousal without having an orgasm, the testes may become swollen, tender, and painful due to their long-term congestion with blood. The vas deferens may also become irritated, causing pain that extends up through the pubic area and lower abdomen. In slang, this condition is often called "lover's nuts," "blue balls," or "stone ache." It is not dangerous or permanently damaging—only uncomfortable. It is also much less common than usually believed.

The Penis

Just above the scrotal sac is the male sex organ called the **penis.** The sensitive smooth and rounded head of the penis is called the **glans.** The glans is filled with nerve endings and is particularly sensitive to sexual stimulation. The two most sensitive areas of the glans are the **frenulum,** a thin, tightly stretched band of skin on its underside connecting the glans with the shaft (body) of the penis; and the **corona,** which is the ridge around the edge of the glans. The urinary mea-

anorchism (a-NOR-kiz-um): rare birth defect in which both testes are lacking.

cryptorchidism (krip-TOR-ka-diz-um): condition in which the testes have not descended into the scrotum prior to birth.

monorchidism (ma-NOR-ka-dizm): presence of only one testis in the scrotum.

testicular failure: lack of sperm and/or hormone production by the testes.

epididymitis (ep-a-did-a-MITE-us): inflammation of the epididymis of the testis.

penis: male sexual organ that can become erect when stimulated; it leads urine and sperm to the outside of the body.

glans: in the male, the sensitive head of the penis.

frenulum (FREN-yu-lum): thin, tightly drawn fold of skin on the underside of the penile glans; it is highly sensitive.

corona: the ridge around the penile glans.

Penis Envy

Sigmund Freud, the founder of psychoanalysis, had a theory that girls and women were dissatisfied with their own genitals and envied men their penises. They wanted them, too. I have yet to meet a woman who wanted to have her own penis (except on camping trips), although many like to borrow one from time to time. As a woman friend once put it: "Why would I want a thing like that hanging between my legs? I'd be afraid I'd sit on it."

I think, however, that Freud was partly right about penis envy. It exists, but only in males. Almost every male seems to envy someone else's penis. He wants one that's longer, wider, harder, with more staying power, and he assumes that some other man, or lots of other men, have one just like that.

One reason we are so unhappy with our penises is the superhuman expectations we have learned. Having repeatedly read and heard about gargantuan, hard-as-steel ramrods, our own real penises don't seem like much. How can anything real seem adequate compared to the telephone poles we read about?

And most heterosexual men have never seen another erect penis, or at least not a typical one. The ones we are likely to have seen, in pornographic movies and magazines, are not representative. The producers of these films conduct broad searches for the biggest phalluses in existence. Given the absence of reasonable standards, there is good reason for us to wonder about the adequacy of our own organs. . . .

I've also talked to a number of men with very large penises. You'd think they'd be quite content, because they're the ones who measure up to the fantasies of most men. Surprisingly, many of these men are anything but happy. Most of them say they wish they had smaller organs. They complain about women gasping—not in ecstasy, but in horror—when they first lay eyes on their outsized organs. Some women have refused to have intercourse with them at all, and many have refused to do oral sex on them, fearing they would choke. And some of these men said they often have to be careful when having sex lest they do hurt their partners. Sometimes living up to a fantasy isn't all it's cracked up to be.

—B. Zilbergeld, *The New Male Sexuality*, 1992, "Penis Envy,"
p.92–93. New York: Bantam Books.

tus or urethral opening is found at the tip of the glans. When a male is born, the head of the penis is partly covered by a fold of skin called the prepuce or **foreskin.**

The longer body of the penis is called the **shaft.** The skin on the shaft is quite loose, allowing erection to occur. Inside the penile shaft are three cylinders of erectile tissue, each full of nerves and blood vessels (see Fig. 3.4). The two cylinders of tissues lying parallel along the top and sides of the penis are called the *corpora cavernosa.* The third, slightly narrower cylinder extends along the underside of the penis and is called the *corpus spongiosum.*

The penis is not only important as the male organ for sexual activity and reproduction, but it also is the organ through which urine is passed from the body. The tube that carries both sperm and urine in the penis is the **urethra,** located in the corpus spongiosum, which extends back to the urinary bladder and connects with the sperm-carrying ducts.

Erection

During sexual arousal, the three cylinders inside the penis become engorged with blood so that the penis expands in circumference, becomes longer and harder,

and stands out from the body. This is **erection,** and it is usually necessary for successful sexual intercourse. It is possible, however, for some men to have orgasm without erection. During erection, the three cylinders of erectile tissue may be felt distinctly. Penile erection occurs in several phases, involving increased blood flow into the erectile tissue and decreased flow out of the tissue. The penis elongates and expands to its maximum capacity, eventually becoming highly rigid as stimulation continues. Sometimes there is a slight curvature in the erect penis, upward, downward, or to one side. Unless the curvature is caused by some in-

foreskin: fold of skin covering the penile glans; also called the prepuce.

shaft: in the male, cylindrical base of penis that contains three columns of spongy tissue: two corpora cavernosa and a corpus spongiosum.

urethra (yu-REE-thrah): tube that passes from the urinary bladder to the outside of the body.

erection: enlargement and stiffening of the penis as internal muscles relax and blood engorges the columns of spongy tissue.

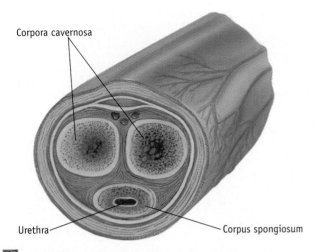

Corpora cavernosa

Urethra — Corpus spongiosum

FIGURE 3.4 *Cross Section of a Penis*

The penis is the male organ of urination and copulation. This cross section shows the three internal structures of the penis, all cylindrical in shape. The *corpus spongiosum* contains the urethra through which pass semen and urine. All three have spongelike tissue dotted with small blood vessels.

jury or disease (which is quite rare), it will not interfere with sexual performance. The angle that the penis stands out from the body varies a great deal as well, most typically ranging from 30 to 90 degrees from the upright vertical (Sparling, 1997).

Erection of the penis is controlled by a spinal reflex and is mostly an involuntary reaction (see Fig. 3.5). However, the cerebral cortex and other portions of the brain also have input and are intricately connected to the "erection center" of the spinal cord. So both reflexive and thought processes can work together to stimulate or inhibit erections (McKenna, 2000). Even in men whose spinal cords have been severed, breaking the connection between the erection center and the brain, physical stimulation of the penis generates erection, although the brain has no awareness of feeling in the penis.

The actual mechanism of erection has only recently begun to be more fully understood. Two muscles in the perineal area (below the scrotum), the *bulbocavernosus* and *ischiocavernosus muscles,* show bursts of activity just prior to erection. This activity is apparently closely related to increases in arterial blood flow into the penis, and the muscles and circulatory vessels then work together in maintaining erection. It is now known that during sexual arousal, the nervous system stimulates the linings of the penile blood vessels and the nerve endings to produce a chemical called **cyclic GMP,** a type of nitric oxide. The smooth muscles that surround the arteries inside the penis are

normally in a contracted state when the penis is nonerect. Cyclic GMP causes the muscle cells to relax, allowing the arteries to open so that blood flows into the open spaces in the erectile tissues. The rise in blood pressure within the penis squeezes the veins so that they do not drain blood out of the organ, and the penis becomes engorged with blood and erect. It is common for men to experience some loss of erection if their minds wander during sexual arousal. This happens because nerve signals from the brain are no longer reaching the penis, and the production of cyclic GMP is decreased. This causes the smooth muscle cells to begin contracting again, and arterial blood flow is therefore reduced. Erection is clearly a complex phenomenon, involving a carefully balanced interaction among the nervous system, cyclic GMP production, muscle tissue, and blood vessels (Handy, 1998b; McKenna, 2000).

Penis Size

Penis size is a nearly universal concern of men, and yet it has not been the subject of very extensive research. A survey of 112 male college students found that the men were far more likely to rate the size of their penises as average or below average than they were other bodily characteristics. None of the men indicated that their penises were much larger than average. The results suggested that men often relate feelings of self-worth to body image, and that they tend to underestimate the comparative size of their genitals in response to social pressures and expectations (Lee, 1996).

A medical text from 1949 offered some measurements but little description of how they were made. The work of Kinsey and Masters and Johnson did not give definitive results. In 1995, two urologists from the University of California at San Francisco performed standardized penile measurements on a group of men at San Francisco General Hospital. They found that the average nonerect penis was 3.5 inches in length and 3.9 inches in circumference. The average erect penis was 5.1 inches long and 4.9 inches in circumference. Using the statistical measures of a standard bell curve, the researchers concluded that the range in length for average erect penises would be between 2.8 and 7.2 inches. For the 2 percent of men whose erect penises were smaller than 2.8 inches and for the 2 percent who are larger than 7.2 inches, they would be considered smaller or larger than average (McAninch & Wessels, 1995).

cyclic GMP: a secretion within the spongy erectile tissues of the penis that facilitates erection.

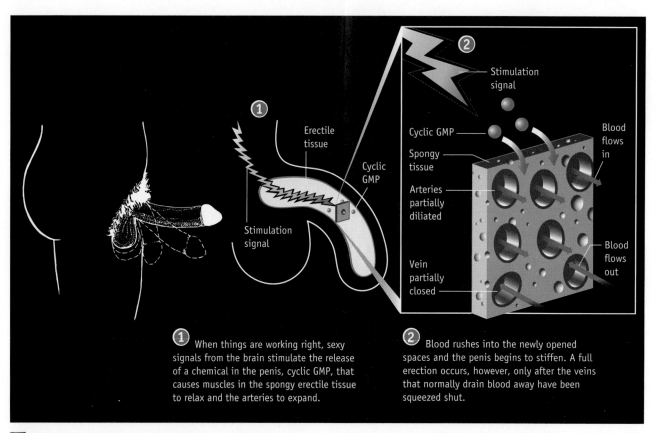

① When things are working right, sexy signals from the brain stimulate the release of a chemical in the penis, cyclic GMP, that causes muscles in the spongy erectile tissue to relax and the arteries to expand.

② Blood rushes into the newly opened spaces and the penis begins to stiffen. A full erection occurs, however, only after the veins that normally drain blood away have been squeezed shut.

FIGURE 3.5   *Penile Erection*

Penile erection is achieved primarily by the increase in blood flow through the *corpus spongiosum* and the *corpora cavernosa* during sexual arousal. Other factors, such as spinal reflex and emotion, enter into the physical act of erection.

It has been suggested that measurements of the nonerect penis do not have great meaning because the flaccid penis length of a particular man may vary a great deal depending on emotional and environmental conditions. However, it is assumed that for any particular individual, the erect length would be quite consistent from situation to situation. A recent study that used a population sample mirroring the original Kinsey study population found that erect penises tend to be somewhat shorter than what has typically been reported, especially by studies using self-measurements made by the men. The more recent study found about 40 percent of erections to be between 4.5 and 5.75 inches in length, and about 50 percent to be between 6 and 7.5 inches long. Only about 15 percent of men had erect penises longer than 6.75 inches (Sparling, 1997).

Masters and Johnson found that erection seems to have an equalizing effect because smaller penises gain proportionately more size than larger penises upon erection. This equalizing effect was confirmed by more recent researchers (Jamison & Gebhard, 1988) who divided flaccid penises into two categories: short (averaging 3.1 inches) and long (averaging 4.4 inches).

They found that shorter penises tended to gain about 85 percent in size during erection, to an average of 5.8 inches, whereas the longer penises grew only by 47 percent, to an average of 6.5 inches. Likewise, narrower penises gain more in circumference during erection.

It is clear that penises vary in length, width, and shape, all being perfectly functional and normal. Although some men and women prefer larger penises for sexual activity, there is no basis for believing that any factors of penile size affect a man's ability to be a fully satisfactory sexual partner. In heterosexual intercourse, there are some specific physiological reasons for this. The inner two-thirds of the vagina expand (balloon) during sexual arousal. The outer third (nearest to the external opening) becomes smaller, embracing the penis. It is in this outer portion of the vagina that the greater sexual sensitivity is centered. Additionally, women can contract the vaginal muscles. There is no demonstrated relationship between general body size or the size of other particular organs and penis size.

Capitalizing on men's unnecessary concerns about penile size, a variety of "penis enlargement" tech-

CASE STUDY

Jake: Concerns about the Male Body

Jake was a senior in college when he came to a counselor to talk about his current relationship, which seemed to be faltering. He seemed depressed and complained about how shy he had always been with women. After two sessions with the counselor, he began to talk more about the concerns he had with his body. He was born with an undescended testicle, and efforts to move the testis into his scrotum during childhood had failed. Prior to entering college, he had a plastic prosthetic testis surgically implanted in his scrotum, because he was concerned that his lacking testis would be noticed in shower rooms. However, he had been dissatisfied with the prosthesis because in his opinion it did not look or feel genuine.

Jake also expressed concern over the size of his penis and indicated that he had written for information on penile enlargement surgery that he had seen advertised in a men's magazine. It seemed that these bodily concerns were part of a larger pattern of insecurity in his life. The counselor answered his questions about sexuality and provided Jake with some books in which he could read more about male anatomy and functioning.

Eventually, the counselor talked with him about his reluctance in relationships with women. It was clear that part of his insecurity was based on concern that during sexual encounters, a woman might notice either his artificial testis or the penis that he believed to be too small. The reading material that Jake consulted had helped to reassure him that his penis was well within normal size ranges, and he gave up the idea of pursuing expensive, and risky, surgery. The two worked further on assertiveness in communication, and he actually practiced how he might tell a sex partner about his testicle before becoming involved with her. This seemed to help him feel more relaxed about pursuing relationships with women.

---

niques have been marketed. Most of them involve using some sort of suction device, with the penis being inserted into a plastic chamber, and then a plunger-type device being used to remove some air from the chamber. This stimulation typically creates an erection for men, therefore providing for "enlargement." Such devices have been known to cause injury to the penis, however, if too much suction is used. Television talk shows have also hosted cosmetic surgeons who offer surgical techniques to enlarge the penis. One procedure, in which some of the internal ligaments at the base of the penis were cut away so that some of the penile structure inside the body could be extended outside, has been found to be too risky. In fact, scarring may result in poor erections or pulling the penis back, making it appear even shorter. Clinical evidence has found that many men who have had penis enlargement procedures are unhappy with the results. Experts recommend that surgical interventions not be considered unless the man's *erect* penis falls in the "below average" length category of less than 2.8 inches, and he is experiencing significant functional problems with sex because of his penis size (McAninch & Wessels, 1995).

Breast size and penis size seem to preoccupy North Americans. How have the media and other factors influenced these concerns? What are your feelings about these issues?

Male Circumcision: The Debate

When a male is born, the parents may decide to have the foreskin of the baby's penis removed in a surgical procedure called **circumcision,** leaving the glans fully exposed (see Fig. 3.6). Until recently, most males in the United States were circumcised. The procedure, however, has been much less commonly used in Europe and Canada. Circumcision has sometimes been a part of a religious custom, as in the Jewish faith. The other most frequently stated reason for circumcision involves hygiene. It has been assumed that young males will find it troublesome to learn how to pull back the foreskin and wash the glans, thus permitting the buildup of a material called smegma that can then lead to infection.

There has been continuing controversy over the widespread practice of circumcising male infants (see Fig. 3.7). Some have complained that there are usually no legitimate reasons to justify circumcision, especially because there are risks in any such surgery (Potter, 1989). Because the procedure was once performed without anesthesia in infants, there was probably a fair amount of pain. Anticircumcision groups feel that this pain is an unnecessary trauma for a newborn, and they claim that it can have continuing negative psychologi-

circumcision (SIR-cum-sizh-uhn): in the male, surgical removal of the foreskin from the penis.

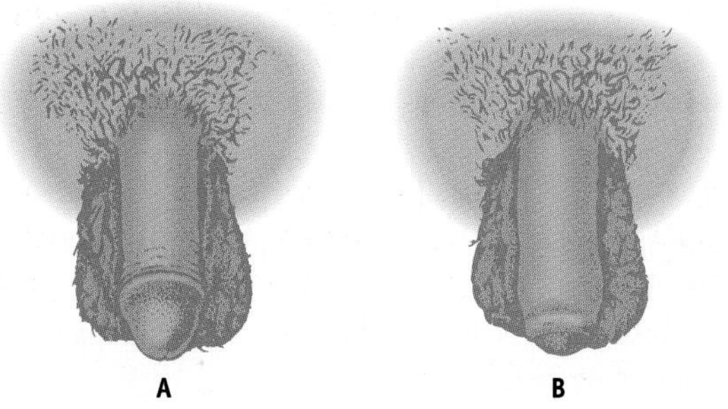

![Figure 3.6 Circumcision showing circumcised penis A and uncircumcised penis B](A) (B)

FIGURE 3.6 *Circumcision*

The circumcised penis (A) leaves the glans exposed, supposedly making it easier to keep the penis clean and prevent the possibility of cancer. The uncircumcised penis (B) in a very few instances may have a condition called *phimosis* in which the foreskin cannot be retracted over the glans.

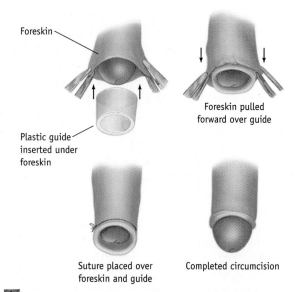

Foreskin

Plastic guide inserted under foreskin

Foreskin pulled forward over guide

Suture placed over foreskin and guide

Completed circumcision

FIGURE 3.7 *Circumcision of an Infant*

The surgical removal of the penile foreskin has a history that goes back as far as 4000 B.C.E. in Egypt. Its justification has been ritualistic, religious, and medical. The surgical procedure illustrated here is usually performed on infant males, but it is sometimes used for adult circumcision.

cal consequences. More recently, however, it has become standard procedure to use a form of anesthesia called the dorsal penile nerve block, permitting pain-free surgery.

One medical problem that has been cited as a good reason for circumcision is **phimosis,** or an unusually long and tight foreskin, making it difficult to retract (Money, 1994). Yet opponents of circumcision insist that spontaneous erections begin even before birth and gradually stretch the foreskin, so that by 6 years of age it can be retracted without difficulty in almost 100 percent of cases. If a real problem exists at some later stage in life, circumcision can then be performed. Opponents also believe that in infants the foreskin should be tight and nonretractable to protect the urethral opening from exposure to fecal material or other possible irritants. Adult males who are uncircumcised are apparently more likely to become infected with certain sexually transmitted diseases, including gonorrhea, syphilis, and HIV (Cook, Koutsky, & Holmes, 1994). However, there is no evidence that circumcision affects male sexual responsiveness in any way.

In the 1960s, 95 percent of boys in the United States were circumcised. The American Academy of Pediatrics first took a position on male circumcision in 1971, stating that there were "no valid medical indications" for routine circumcision of newborns. During the 1980s, there was a distinct decline in the procedure, so that by the end of 1986 only 59.4 percent of male infants were being circumcised. However, later in that decade, there was mounting evidence that this trend was leading to an increase in urinary tract infections in infant boys, a condition that can cause kidney complications. A review of the health records of 427,698 infants born in U.S. army hospitals over a 10-year period showed that lack of circumcision raised a boy's risk of such infection elevenfold (Wiswell, Enzenauer, Holton, Cornish, & Hankins, 1987). In 1999,

the American Academy of Pediatrics took the position that the benefits of circumcising newborns are not significant enough to recommend it as a routine procedure. They stopped short of advising against circumcision, but they did recommend that anesthesia be used for the procedure. The most recent study of 130,475 newborn circumcisions concluded that in examining the trade-offs, the procedure offers practically no medical benefit, but also causes virtually no harm. It is believed that today about 65 percent of boys in the United States are circumcised (Christakis et al., 2000).

Given the available information concerning male circumcision, if you were a physician, would you recommend to parents that they have their newborn baby boy circumcised? Justify your recommendation.

Disorders of the Penis

Disorders of the penis are relatively uncommon, but a few are worth mentioning here. Two disorders relate to the erection of the penis. One is **priapism,** a condition that involves continual, painful, undesired erec-

phimosis (fye-MOE-sus): a condition in which the penile foreskin is too long and tight to retract easily.

priapism (pry-AE-pizm): continual, undesired, and painful erection of the penis.

tion of the penis. It can be caused by circulatory disorders or abuse of certain drugs, including cocaine. If the erection cannot be relieved within an hour or two, there can be eventual destruction of the corpora cavernosa so that future erection becomes impossible. **Peyronie's disease** occurs primarily in older males and involves the development of tough, fibrous tissue around the corpora cavernosa within the penis. There may be eventual calcification of this tissue. The disease results in curvature of the penis and painful erection, both of which can make intercourse difficult or impossible (Levine, L.A., 1998).

Particularly vigorous stimulation to the penis during sexual activity can sometimes inflame lymphatic vessels, creating a swollen band around the penile shaft, just behind the glans. Although this condition may be alarming to men, it is not dangerous, and generally the swelling gradually subsides over a few weeks (Sieunarine, 1987). Use of ringlike devices to maintain erection can damage penile tissues and blood vessels, especially if they are left on too long. If damage occurs, extensive surgical treatment may be required. If the erect penis is suddenly bent or hit, the tough sheath that encloses the columns of spongy tissue may tear, and this can create permanent damage to the penis, interfering with erection and sexual function.

Cancer of the penis is quite rare, and there is a possibility that it is even less common in circumcised males. Although the hypothesis is open to debate, it has been suggested that the accumulation of secretions and impurities under the foreskin of uncircumcised males may predispose them to malignant growth on their penises. Careful attention to cleanliness and personal hygiene is, therefore, particularly important to uncircumcised males.

There are a number of congenital conditions of the penis. Occasionally, a male child is born with **agenesis (absence) of the penis,** in which the phallus is very tiny and nonfunctional. In such rare cases, it is not unusual to have the child surgically modified to have femalelike genitals and then raise him as a girl. There is little research to indicate how these individuals feel about themselves, or if they experience confusion in their gender identity. For the nonsurgically treated boy with penile agenesis, counseling may be necessary to aid in the sexual adjustments of adolescence and adulthood. There are two congenital conditions resulting from difficulties in fetal development of the penis: **hypospadias** and **epispadias.** Hypospadias is an incompletely fused penis, with an open "gutter" extending along the underside of the penis instead of an internal urethra. In the United States and some European nations, a sharp increase in the incidence of hypospadias has been noted since 1970, although the cause for the increase is not understood. There has been some suspicion that the hormone progestin,

found in some birth control pills, might be playing a role. Hypospadias occurs in about 79 of every 10,000 births of males. In epispadias, the urinary bladder empties through a large opening in the abdomen, and the penis is split open along its upper length. Both hypospadias and epispadias require surgical repair, although the penis may not be fully functional for intercourse following the surgery.

■ Internal Male Organs

The vas deferens of each testis carries sperm up into the body cavity, around to the back of the bladder, and back down to the prostate. Near the junction of the two vasa deferentia into a single ejaculatory duct, each vas deferens joins with a saclike structure called the **seminal vesicle.** Both seminal vesicles are about 2 inches long. The seminal vesicles produce secretions that help to activate the sperm and make them motile. Secretions from the vesicles, which constitute about 70 percent of the seminal fluid, join with the sperm and empty into the ejaculatory duct, which then joins the urethra within the prostate gland.

Located at the underside of the urinary bladder, and surrounding the urethra where it enters the bladder, is the **prostate** gland (see Fig. 3.8). This gland, a little larger than a walnut, has three lobes of muscular and glandular tissue. Along with the seminal vesicles, it produces secretions that help to transport the sperm through the penis. This fluid is called **semen,** or seminal fluid, and it is a milky, sticky, alkaline substance

---

Peyronie's disease (pay-ra-NEEZ): development of fibrous tissue in spongy erectile columns within the penis.

agenesis (absence) of the penis (ae-JEN-a-ses): a congenital condition in which the penis is undersized and nonfunctional.

hypospadias (hye-pa-SPADE-ee-as): birth defect caused by incomplete closure of the urethra during fetal development.

epispadias (ep-a-SPADE-ee-as): birth defect in which the urinary bladder empties through an abdominal opening, and the urethra is malformed.

seminal vesicle (SEM-un-al): gland at the end of each vas deferens that secretes a chemical that helps sperm to become motile.

prostate: gland located beneath the urinary bladder in the male; it produces some of the secretions in semen.

semen (SEE-men): mixture of fluids and sperm cells that is ejaculated through the penis.

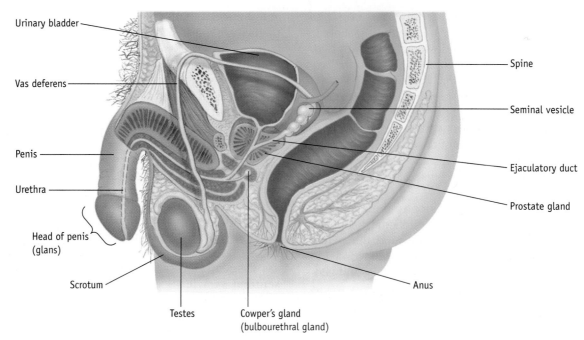

Urinary bladder

Vas deferens

Penis

Urethra

Head of penis (glans)

Scrotum

Testes

Cowper's gland (bulbourethral gland)

Spine

Seminal vesicle

Ejaculatory duct

Prostate gland

Anus

FIGURE 3.8 *Male Sexual and Reproductive Organs*

The external and internal sexual and reproductive organs of the male are shown here in longitudinal section. Although men are familiar with their more obvious external sex organs, they are often less well informed about their internal reproductive and sexual anatomy.

composed of proteins, citric acid, calcium, fats, and some enzymes. Semen may be quite thick and gelatinous when it leaves the penis, or it may be thin and watery. It usually becomes thicker soon after ejaculation, but then liquefies in 15 to 25 minutes.

Below the prostate gland, located at the base of the penis and on each side of the urethra, are two pea-sized glands called **Cowper's glands** or **bulbourethral glands.** When a male is sexually aroused, these two glands secrete a clear, sticky alkaline substance, or preejaculatory fluid, that coats the inner lining of the urethra. Some of it may appear as droplets at the tip of the penis during arousal. The secretion has often been called a lubricant, and indeed, if present in sufficient amounts it can serve as a lubricant for sexual activity. However, it is not always produced in such copious amounts and is believed instead primarily to help neutralize acids in the urethra and thus permit safe passage of sperm. Although the primary function of Cowper's gland secretion is not to carry sperm, it often does, and therefore can be responsible for pregnancy even if ejaculation does not occur within the vagina.

Prostate Problems

A large proportion of men at one time or another suffer from **prostatitis,** or inflammation of the prostate gland (see Fig. 3.9). Prostatitis may be of the *acute*

form, caused by bacterial infection, the symptoms of which include sudden onset of fever, chills, and urinary discomfort. It may also be *chronic,* typically caused by changes in the prostate other than bacterial infection. Chronic symptoms can include some thin discharge from the penis, pain in the lower abdomen and scrotum, or painful ejaculation. Antibiotics are used for acute prostatitis, but it can be difficult to cure completely in its more chronic forms.

In older men, enlargement of the prostate gland is also common and is sometimes the result of malignant tumors. There are over 200,000 new cases of prostatic cancer detected each year; if found early, the chances of complete cure are good. **Benign prostatic hyperplasia** refers to nonmalignant prostatic enlargement. Medications are now available to shrink prostate tissues. If the prostate enlarges too greatly, urination may

Cowper's glands: two small glands in the male that secrete an alkaline fluid into the urethra during sexual arousal.

bulbourethral glands: another term for Cowper's glands.

prostatitis (pras-tuh-TITE-us): inflammation of the prostate gland.

benign prostatic hyperplasia (BPH): enlargement of the prostate gland that is not caused by malignancy.

Clearing the way for blessed relief
Some 14 million American men suffer from benign swelling of the prostate.
A new procedure called TUNA could make treatment easier than ever before.

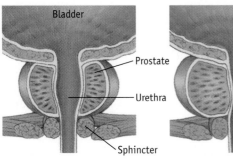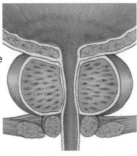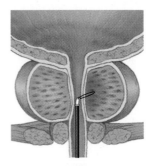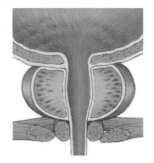

| **Healthy prostate:** | **Enlarged prostate:** | **New procedure:** | **Result:** |
| The gland fits around the urethra like a well-tailored collar. | The swelling that comes with age often blocks the free flow of urine. | Urologists can now kill excess tissue by heating it with tiny needles. | Within six weeks to three months, patients regain normal flow. |

FIGURE 3.9 *Prostate Enlargement Using Transurethral Needle Ablation (TUNA)*

become difficult, or eventually impossible, because the urethral passageway may be pinched by the swollen prostate. This increases the susceptibility to bladder and prostate infections. There are various surgical treatments available, ranging from removal of the prostate (prostatectomy), or parts of it, to less invasive treatments that can widen the urethral canal through the prostate and require only a local anesthetic (Cowley, 1997). If there is a malignancy present, surgery is often followed by radiation or chemical therapy. Newer surgical techniques reduce the risks of interfering with erectile function or ejaculation.

It is generally recommended that men over the age of 35 have regular prostate examinations to detect any possible enlargement or tumors. The physician, using a rubber glove and lubricant, inserts a finger into the rectum, where the surface of the prostate may be felt through the rectal wall. Although such an examination is not particularly pleasant, it represents an important health care measure. A blood test that can help detect prostatic cancer, the prostate-specific antigen (PSA) test, is recommended on a regular basis for men over 50. The test has led to a dramatic increase in the number of prostate surgeries, yet there is no evidence to prove that the mortality rate from the disease has been lowered. Although research has confirmed the accuracy of the PSA test and most physicians support its use, more research is needed to determine if such testing significantly reduces the number of deaths from prostate cancer (Jaroff, 1996). New tests are being developed to measure other indicators of prostate cancer presence or the risk of developing the malignancy (Chan et al., 1998).

Sperm Production and Ejaculation

From puberty to old age, the male testes produce large amounts of sperm cells. The testes are partially controlled by two pituitary hormones, two of the same hormones found in females. One is luteinizing hormone (LH), called **interstitial-cell-stimulating hormone (ICSH)** in males, and the other is follicle-stimulating hormone (FSH). The ICSH begins to be produced at puberty and stimulates the interstitial cells of the testes to produce the male hormone testosterone. The FSH helps to stimulate the sperm-producing cells—**spermatocytes**—in the linings of the seminiferous tubules to produce sperm.

Each mature sperm consists of a head and tail, separated by a short thickened area (see Fig. 3.10). The head contains the male's genetic material, and the thickened middle area contains an energy-releasing mechanism that will help move the tail. Sperm are usually about 55 microns long (0.0021 inch or 0.055 millimeter) and can be seen only through a microscope. It is believed that an adult male produces about 15 to 30 billion sperm each month.

During sexual excitement and activity, the sperm are moved from the epididymis in the testes up to the

interstitial-cell-stimulating hormone (ICSH): pituitary hormone that stimulates the testes to secrete testosterone; known as luteinizing hormone (LH) in females.

spermatocytes (sper-MAT-o-sites): cells lining the seminiferous tubules from which sperm cells are produced.

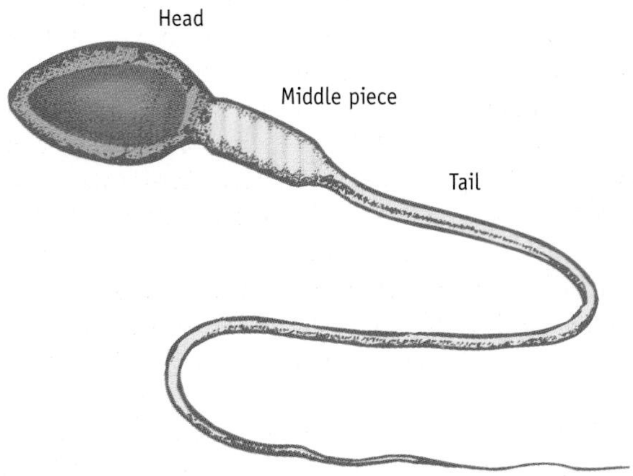

Head

Middle piece

Tail

FIGURE 3.10   *Sperm*

A mature sperm consists of a head, middle piece, and tail. The head contains the chromosomes and is the part involved in fertilization. The tail moves the sperm from the ejaculatory duct into the urethra prior to ejaculation. If all the ova needed to repopulate the world would fit into a 2-gallon container, the sperm for the same purpose would fit into an aspirin tablet.

ejaculatory duct through each vas deferens. Their tails are probably activated into a lashing movement by the secretions of the seminal vesicles. Stimulation of the erect penis sends nerve impulses to the ejaculatory center of the spinal cord. When these impulses have built to a certain threshold, the ejaculatory response is triggered. Sperm from the ejaculatory duct are moved into the urethra, along with fluids from both the seminal vesicles and the prostate that form the semen. There are then contractions in the muscles surrounding the ejaculatory duct and urethra, forcing the semen to be ejaculated through the end of the penis. This is usually accompanied by the pleasurable sensations of orgasm, or sexual climax, although the two phenomena, **ejaculation** and **orgasm,** can occur separately (see chapter 4, "Human Sexual Response").

Studies seem to indicate that average sperm counts in the male population have dropped by one-third from the mid-1970s to the mid-1990s. To what has this drop been attributed? What concerns might this trend raise for the future?

The amount of semen ejaculated depends on many factors—age, amount of sexual stimulation, general health, and interval of time since the last ejaculation—but typically there are 3 to 5 cubic centimeters of semen, about a teaspoonful or less. As much as 11 cubic centimeters of semen can be ejaculated. In the typical ejaculate, there are 150 million to 600 million sperm. Many men subjectively report that the more intense the sensation of orgasm, the more semen ejacu-

lated and the more force with which it is propelled out of the penis. Most often the semen oozes out of the penis under some pressure, but it can sometimes spurt several inches.

Although ejaculation is a reflexive phenomenon, it is possible for men to learn how to control the length of time it takes to reach orgasm and ejaculation. This usually involves learning how to modulate sexual excitement or to control inner musculature so that when ejaculation is near, stimulation to the penis is reduced until the sensation subsides. There is more about controlling ejaculation in chapter 18, "Sexual Dysfunctions and Their Treatment."

As a result of certain illnesses, some prostate surgeries, or the effects of certain tranquilizing drugs, the semen may be ejaculated into the urinary bladder. The muscles at the base of the bladder that normally close the bladder off during ejaculation apparently do not contract, so that semen is permitted to enter the bladder. There is the full sensation of orgasm, but no semen leaves the penis. This phenomenon is called **retrograde ejaculation.** There are also organic problems that simply lead to the absence of semen and a resultant dry orgasm called **anejaculation.**

Under ideal laboratory conditions, sperm may be kept alive for up to 2 weeks after ejaculation. However, after ejaculation into the vagina during sexual intercourse, it is unlikely that many sperm remain motile for more than 2 or 3 days. Once semen has been deposited in the vagina, some of it begins to seep into the uterus, and the sperm swim against mucous currents and gravitational pull. Healthy sperm can swim about 3 to 7 inches in an hour, and following ejaculation some sperm can be expected to reach the female's fallopian tubes in 1 to 2 hours. Despite the many millions of sperm deposited in the vagina, only a very few thousand actually reach the fallopian tubes, where fertilization of the ovum can take place.

Concern has been growing that sperm counts in otherwise healthy human males have been dropping in recent years, and accounts in professional journals and the popular media have gone so far as to predict that many men will become infertile by the middle of the next century. A survey of research that looked at nearly

ejaculation: muscular expulsion of semen from the penis.

orgasm: pleasurable sensations and series of contractions that release sexual tension, usually accompanied by ejaculation in men.

retrograde ejaculation: abnormal passage of semen into the urinary bladder at the time of ejaculation.

anejaculation: lack of ejaculation at the time of orgasm.

15,000 men from 1938 to 1990 found that the average sperm count had declined from 113 million sperm per milliliter of semen in the early 1940s to 66 million sperm per milliliter in 1990 (Skakkebaek, 1992). A French study that examined sperm counts of donors at a Paris sperm bank found that they had dropped by one-third from the mid-1970s to the mid-1990s (Auger, Kunstmann, Czyglik, & Jouannet, 1995). Further analysis of such data has suggested that there may be other explanations for the perceived decline. Some of the disparities reported may have been partly the result of differences in methods of analyzing sperm counts over the years. It has also been suggested that there may not have been a steady decline in sperm counts, and in fact declines might for the most part have been prior to 1970. A group of fertility researchers that convened in 1996 to study the issue concluded that rather than a worldwide decline in sperm counts, there have been declines in some geographic regions, but not in others. For example, data show that men in New York City have a higher sperm count than those in Minnesota or Los Angeles, for reasons that are still unclear. It may be that there has not been a worldwide reduction in sperm production, but instead various fluctuations in sperm count among males in various locations. Further study will be needed to understand this phenomenon more fully (Lemonick, 1996).

Men who have less than 20 million sperm per milliliter are considered to be infertile because the chances of their conceiving a child are slim with that low a sperm count. It has been proposed that chemical pollutants in the environment resembling the female hormone estrogen, fetal exposure to estrogen in the uterus, or possible changes in diet and lifestyle might be responsible for low sperm counts, but no clear link has been established (Auger et al., 1995; Stone, 1994). There is evidence from several research studies that cigarette smoking can reduce sperm production significantly, but probably not enough to impair fertility unless a man already had a low sperm count caused by other factors (Vine, 1994). There is no evidence at this point that fluctuations in sperm count have had any profound effect on male fertility (Sherins, 1995).

Male Hormones and the Male Climacteric

Men do not undergo, so far as we know, predictable cyclical changes in hormonal levels, such as the female menstrual cycle, that affect their fertility. Some medical conditions, such as epileptic seizures, seem to worsen on roughly monthly cycles, and this might be traced to subtle shifts in hormonal concentrations. Studies have shown that testosterone levels tend to be lower in the spring, when literary tradition would have it that men's sex drive is strong. About all that psychological tests have correlated with lower hormonal levels is an increase in men's spatial aptitudes (Blakeslee, 1991; Rubinow & Schmidt, 1996). There have also been suggestions that men experience periodic emotional ups and downs that seem to follow cyclical patterns, but this has been difficult to substantiate in research. Perhaps further evidence will emerge that men have cycles relating to their sexual or reproductive physiology.

Although men do not seem to have a well-defined hormonal cycle, there are changes in their bodies as they age. Men do not lose the ability to reproduce at any particular time of life. They usually continue to produce sperm cells all of their lives, even into very old age, although the risk of genetic abnormalities in the sperm also increases with age. There have been several studies of testosterone production in aging males, but their significance is debatable. There are very gradual declines in the concentrations of male hormones found in the body through the mid-40s, and by age 75, testosterone levels often drop up to 90 percent compared with levels before the age of 30. More significantly, biochemical changes in the body cause more testosterone to become chemically bound to blood proteins, or plasma, as a man ages. This results in a lower free testosterone index (FTI), and it is the free, unbound testosterone that seems to have the most important influence on the body. For 20 percent of men over the age of 60 who probably have lower-than-normal levels of testosterone, there seems to be some correlation with the presence of depression (Seidman & Walsh, 1999).

Because there is usually no marked decrease in hormonal levels in the average male, and no loss of reproductive capacity, there really is nothing in males equivalent to female menopause. Nevertheless, popular media continue to promote the idea of a "male menopause." Although it is less predictable, and its symptoms more variable, men often do experience a period of stress as they age. It is often called midlife crisis, the male climacteric, or "andropause," and is characterized by increased anxiety, depression, insomnia, hypochondria, loss of appetite, and/or chronic fatigue. These may also be the symptoms of untreated depression.

This time in a man's life is often characterized by major changes and realizations. Most professionals believe that it is these psychological stresses that constitute the male climacteric. Again, in a youth-oriented culture, men must face the fact that they are aging. Men with wives and families are sharing the menopausal changes of their spouses and having their children leave home. In more traditional family structures, in

Manopause

Just what men have been searching for over the centuries—perpetual potency—may soon be assured merely by popping a pill. This chemical machismo has special appeal to a great many boomer men, performance-conscious in every way and obsessed with remaining young. They are already overreacting to normal, age-related changes, such as hair loss, and now sex therapists note that younger and younger men are complaining of potency problems. The reason is probably not more impotence but inflated expectations. They may be tyrannized by fables of Wilt Chamberlain-esque sexual prowess. (Really, Wilt, six or seven women every day?) And the body-image ideal is now set as impossibly high for men as the Barbie-doll fantasy for women. What's a poor guy to think, now that he's married, a time-starved workadaddy who's not aroused anymore at the drop of a bra?

. . . This "MANopause" is a five- to 12-year period during which men go through hormonal fluctuations, coupled with accelerated physical and psychological changes.

MANopause is more gradual and elusive then female menopause. Common symptoms are irritability, sluggishness and mild to moderate mood swings. Physically, a man may notice a decrease in muscle mass and strength. The most familiar effect is a slump in a man's overall sense of well-being. But the greatest fear, the phobic event that may become a self-fulfilling prophecy, is intermittent problems in gaining and sustaining erections. If a man rates himself only on speed and athleticism versus his younger, friskier self, the "performer penis" will eventually fail him.

Underneath the male menopausal syndrome there may also be a man who feels he is losing control. Losing his job or being passed over for promotion in midlife, for instance, is tantamount to falling off the top of the heap in the chimpanzee hierarchy. In both humans and animals, defeat decreases testosterone. Therefore, the sudden loss of self-respect and dominance reduces male sex hormones, which may further dampen a man's sex drive.

. . . It is much easier to prevent male menopausal impotence than to correct it, and that raises another problem with the "potency pill." Men don't go to doctors nearly as often as women, and when they do go, they seldom ask questions, nor are they asked routinely about their sexual health. Women, on the other hand, have come out of their ignorance and denial about menopause and are raising hell with their physicians. One of the benefits of male midlife slowdown is that it may motivate a man to get a good physical. But if he can walk into a doctor's office and ask for a potency pill, it may never be discovered that his impotence is a result of depression, for example.

. . . Vast improvement in mid- to later-life sexual vitality can be gained by correcting an unhealthy lifestyle and cultivating more relaxed and realistic expectations of aging. That means exercise, good nutrition and finding a new level of intimacy with one's mate. No matter what bullets the drug companies try to sell men, that's where the real magic is.

—Gail Sheehy, *Newsweek,* November 17, 1997. "Beyond Virility, a New Vision: Men and their doctors need to understand that impotence is just one part of a complicated midlife passage—call it MANopause," p.69. All rights reserved. Reprinted by permission.

which the man has been a primary breadwinner, he may begin to feel weary of the years of responsibility for his family. Middle age may be a time when a career plateau has been reached, and further vocational opportunities become more limited. Physical changes and stress-generated tension may produce alterations in sexual interest and behavior, resulting in even more worry and discouragement. Psychological stress in middle-aged men has been shown to be greater when there are tensions in their marriages or in relationships with adolescent children (Sanders, 1999). The male climacteric largely seems to be a vicious cycle of middle-age stresses and gradual physiological changes that feed on one another.

Testosterone Replacement Therapy

Optimal sexual functioning in males may be dependent on the presence of a minimum amount of free testosterone in the body. For men in whom the FTI is low, administration of extra testosterone seems to improve sexual interest and potency, and it may decrease the risks of depression (Seidman & Walsh, 1999). **Testosterone replacement therapy** carries some in-

testosterone replacement therapy: administering testosterone injections to increase sexual interest or potency in older men; not considered safe for routine use.

How Age Can Change a Man's Body

The term "male menopause" drives medical experts crazy. In women, "menopause is a clearly defined biological event," says Dr. Abraham Morgenthaler of Boston's Beth Israel Hospital. "There is no equivalent for men." True enough, but middle age does bring changes, and few of them would qualify as improvements. Here's a rundown of the main ones:

Hair loss. The number of hair follicles on the scalp decreases as men age, and the hair that is left grows at a slower rate.

Vision. By age 50, lifelong thickening of the lens causes a noticeable loss of night vision and close-in focus.

Lung power. Chest wall stiffens, increasing the workload of respiratory muscles. More residual air is left in lungs after each breath.

Aerobic endurance. As the body's ability to deliver oxygen declines, the capacity for physical work falls. The work capacity of a 70-year-old is only half that of a 20-year-old.

Body fat. Between the ages of 25 and 75 the amount of fat in proportion to the body's composition doubles. Much of that growth occurs in muscles and organs.

Muscle and bone. Eventually muscles get smaller and weaker, but those changes can be offset by exercise. Bone loss, a universal aging trait, occurs at individual rates.

Brain function. Concentration and language skills don't change much with age. The ability to store and retrieve information declines slightly but steadily from the 20s on.

Hearing. Eardrums thicken and the ear canal atrophies, making pure tones and high frequencies harder to hear, especially in the late 50s.

Heart response. After 20, the heart becomes less adept at accelerating in response to exertion. Bars show maximum rate in beats per minute:

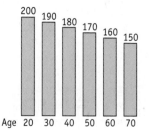

Age 20 30 40 50 60 70
200 190 180 170 160 150

Angle of erection. Many men experience a slight loss of upward mobility from 30 to 50, and a major loss from 50 to 70. Preventable vascular disease is largely to blame.

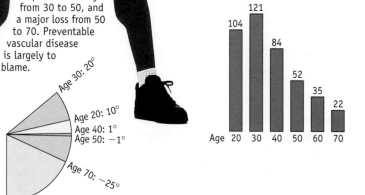

Age 30: 20°
Age 20: 10°
Age 40: 1°
Age 50: −1°
Age 70: −25°

ERECTION DEGREES ABOVE HORIZONTAL

Frequency of sex. Decline in sex drive varies from man to man, but some reduction is inevitable due to lower levels of sex hormones and loss of vitality. Orgasms per year:

Age 20 30 40 50 60 70
104 121 84 52 35 22

creased risks of prostate difficulties and cardiovascular disease, and it must be prescribed with caution (Cowley, 1996). Some researchers believe that in the next century, hormone replacement therapy for men in midlife will become as common as it now is for menopausal women.

Surviving the Male Climacteric

Because menopause has been more specifically identified, women tend to receive more support and understanding for their difficult physical and psychological symptoms. Men may need the same kind of supportive help through their midlife crises as well. Counseling can help a man express his concerns and deal with his confusing emotions, but men may be reluctant to seek this sort of help. They may need guidance to help them realize that finding appropriate support during life's various crises is a strength, not a weakness. It is

important for men to be cautioned about making major life changes during the throes of such a crisis. They may be better advised to try sticking with their present careers and relationships, while working to resolve any conflicts or tensions within those important areas of life. Then as things are brought into a more rational perspective, sensible changes in lifestyle and goals may be considered.

Both medical and psychological sciences are making great progress in understanding the changes within men's bodies and psyches as they age. It is likely that just as Viagra has offered hope to men with erection problems, other treatments will become available to help men cope with the various symptoms associated with sex and aging. Ultimately, the best help will come from within, as men draw on their own resources to accept the natural processes of aging and also the positive outcomes that these processes can yield along with the less positive.

Self-Evaluation

Your Sexuality Education: Past, Present, and Future

Sexuality education is far more than learning about the body's reproductive system. It is also an exercise in self-awareness—becoming acquainted with one's own sexual feelings, needs, and values. Sexuality education is a lifelong process that must constantly integrate new information and changing personal situations. The exercises that follow ask you to examine the process of sexuality education as it relates to your life.

1. *Looking back.* **Spend some time thinking about your answers to the following questions. They will help clarify some of the background of your sexuality education. You many want to discuss your answers with another trusted person.**
   a. Can you recall your first discussions about sexuality when you were a child with another child, a parent, or another adult? If so, can you remember any feelings or attitudes that you developed in relationship to that time and the topic of sex?
   b. How and when did you first learn what you consider to be the important information about the sex organs, reproduction, and other aspects of human sexuality? Was the information conveyed to you in a relatively positive, negative, or neutral atmosphere emotionally?

   c. Do you remember the first book or magazine you read, or the first television program or movie you saw, that had factual information about sex or that graphically depicted sexual behaviors? How did you react?
   d. In what ways have you increased your level of information and awareness about human sexuality more recently in your life?

2. **On the next page is a list of topics relating to human sexuality. You may be better informed on some of them than on others. Using the rating standards shown, rate each topic as to your level of competence, using appropriate checkmarks.**

3. **As you reexamine the checkmarks you made in question 2, pay attention to those topics you need to know more about. For each of them, indicate what your course of action, if any, will be:**
   a. Will you seek further information on the topic? Why or why not?
   b. Where will you begin the search for the information?
   c. Are there some personal implications involved in your wanting to understand the topic better?

4. **Do you expect to have children (or do you have children) for whom you will have some responsibility to**

provide effective sexuality education? If so, consider the following:

a. Have you already made some attempts at educating children about sexuality? If so, how successful do you think you were, and on what criteria do you base that evaluation?

b. Make a list of goals that you feel are important to the sexuality education of children at different age levels; choose those goals in which you may play an active part. What would you not want to be a part of your children's sexuality education?

c. What resources can you have available to assist with the sexuality education process? Consider books, films, television programs, computer software or accessible networks, other people (including professionals), and your own skills and competencies.

d. Now, either alone or with another adult, try explaining aloud some of the things you would want your child to know about human sexuality, considering the child's age and level of maturity. You might want to tape your talk so you can evaluate its effectiveness later, or you might have the other adult make comments and suggestions. This is an exercise to see how clearly and accurately you can express concepts about sexuality. Are you aware of institutional sexuality education programs that might be available in your local schools, churches, or other agencies? If none exist, you might consider becoming instrumental in working for effective sexuality education. If programs already exist, you might want to help evaluate their effectiveness. First of all, you should clarify how you feel about sexuality education and get as much information about various programs as you can.

	I know very little about this, and could use further information.	*I understand this reasonably well, but could use more information.*	*I feel comfortable with this, and do not need further information.*
Male genital anatomy and physiology	＿＿	＿＿	＿＿
Female genital anatomy and physiology	＿＿	＿＿	＿＿
Sexual intercourse	＿＿	＿＿	＿＿
The physiology of reproduction and birth	＿＿	＿＿	＿＿
Advances in reproductive technology	＿＿	＿＿	＿＿
Same-gender orientation and bisexuality	＿＿	＿＿	＿＿
Masturbation	＿＿	＿＿	＿＿
Psychosexual development of children and adolescents	＿＿	＿＿	＿＿
Sex therapy and counseling	＿＿	＿＿	＿＿
Gender identity, masculinity, and femininity	＿＿	＿＿	＿＿
Sexually transmitted diseases	＿＿	＿＿	＿＿
Transmission of HIV	＿＿	＿＿	＿＿
Sexual dysfunctions	＿＿	＿＿	＿＿
Human sexual response	＿＿	＿＿	＿＿
Improving communication in sexual relationships	＿＿	＿＿	＿＿
Sexual variations	＿＿	＿＿	＿＿

Chapter Summary

1. The male testes, located in the scrotum, produce male hormones and sperm. Sperm cells develop best at a temperature slightly lower than inner body temperature, mature in tubes called the epididymis, and will travel upward through the vas deferens.

2. Regular self-examination of the genitals and testes is an effective way to detect infections or growths that indicate the presence of testicular cancer.

3. The testes may not both descend into the scrotum before birth.

4. Epididymitis is an inflammation of the epididymis in the testes.

5. The penis has a sensitive, rounded head called the glans and a longer shaft. Three columns of

spongy tissue compose the interior of the penile shaft and become filled with blood during erection. Sperm and urine move through the penis via the urethra.

6. Penis size is quite variable among males and includes a wide range of "normal" sizes.

7. Circumcision is a surgical procedure in which the penile foreskin, or prepuce, is removed. Its advisability has been the subject of controversy.

8. Some diseases that can affect the penis are priapism (painful, continuous erection), Peyronie's disease (calcification of erectile tissue), phimosis (too-tight foreskin), and cancer.

9. The prostate gland and seminal vesicles of the male produce secretions that mix with sperm to produce the semen that is ejaculated through the penis. Cowper's glands produce a clear secretion that lines the urethra during sexual arousal.

10. Prostatitis, or prostate infection, can be either acute or chronic. A common problem in older men is prostate enlargement, which may be caused by benign prostatic hyperplasia or by malignant tumors. It must be corrected, usually by surgery. The PSA test has proved useful in detection of prostatic cancer.

11. Sperm production is controlled by the secretion of FSH. Interstitial-cell-stimulating hormone (ICSH) stimulates the testes to produce testosterone. Up to 30 billion sperm are produced by the testes each month.

12. Sexual stimulation of the penis can lead to ejaculation of semen. The ejaculate can contain between 150 million and 600 million sperm.

13. Some studies suggest that the sperm counts of human males may have been decreasing over the past few decades, although fertility has not yet been affected. Other researchers believe these changes to be geographically isolated or the result of different ways of analyzing sperm counts.

14. Men do not seem to have predictable hormonal cycles, although their emotions may follow cyclical patterns.

15. Men experience a less-well-defined male climacteric than women, involving mood changes that may be associated with reduced production of testosterone.

16. Testosterone replacement therapy may improve sexual desire and other symptoms of male midlife, but it also carries health risks.

Focus on Health Questions

You will find in this section the kinds of questions that you may have concerning your own health and sexuality. The page references indicate where in the text the answer is located; the exact place is marked with the logo: **FOH**

1. Is it normal for one of my testicles to hang lower than the other? 74

2. How much risk do I have for testicular cancer? 74

3. How do I perform the self-examination to detect testicular cancer? 74

4. Can men still have children if they have only one testicle? 75

5. What are "blue balls"? 75

6. How big is a normal-sized penis? 77

7. Are there any ways to make my penis larger? 78

8. Does the fact that I was circumcised when I was a boy change my sexual functioning? 80

9. Can the penis actually get "bent" or "broken"? 81

10. What is the fluid that comes out of my penis when I'm sexually aroused, before ejaculation? 82

11. What can be done about prostatitis or prostate cancer? 82–83

12. How many sperm do I need in order to be fertile? 85

13. Do men have anything like the menstrual cycle, controlled by hormones? 85

14. Do men go through anything like menopause? 85

Annotated Readings

Annual editions: Human sexuality. (2000). Guilford, CT: DPG/McGraw-Hill. This volume contains selected current articles by health educators, psychologists, sexologists, and sociologists, presenting their views on how and why sexual attitudes and behaviors are developed, maintained, and changed. Updated annually.

Levine, S. B. (1998). *Sexuality in mid-life*. New York: Plenum. A general guide to the effects of aging on the sexual systems and sex life, and how to adjust to these changes.

Planned Parenthood Federation of America. (1997). *All about sex: A family resource on sex and sexuality*. New York: Three Rivers Press. An encyclopedic work that covers anatomy, physiology, and the broader contexts of human sexuality.

Sachs, J. (1994). *The healing power of sex*. Englewood Cliffs, NJ: Prentice Hall. An examination of the important interactions between health and self-esteem as they relate to human sexuality.

Sheehy, G. (1998). *Passages for men*. New York: Random House. A book to help men understand and accept the various stages of their lives, with a special emphasis on midlife issues and what the author calls MANopause.

Zilbergeld, B. (1992). *The new male sexuality*. New York: Bantam Books. In addition to being a comprehensive reference on all aspects of male sexuality and sexual health, this book offers basic information on male and female sexual anatomy and functioning.

Chapter 4
Human Sexual Response

Chapter Outline

Note: A selection of Focus on Health questions appears at the end of each chapter. Answers to these questions are indicated within the chapter by the symbol in the margin. **FOH**

> My first year in high school I was having erections all the time, always unpredictable and usually without good reason. I could get a hard-on from putting a notebook in my locker or riding on the bus. Worst of all were the ones I would get during oral reports up in front of the class. Fortunately, the thing is a lot more under control now—most of the time.
>
> *—From a student's essay*

Over the centuries, the human body's sexual responses have been explained and interpreted in many different ways. They have been assigned religious significance in some cultures and shunned as unclean in others (Helminiak, 1999; Starr-Sared, 1999). Sexual arousal and responsiveness, and how they are perceived and expressed, cannot be understood outside the context of the culture in which a person lives. When Margaret Mead studied the Mundugumor of New Guinea, she remarked that lovemaking was conducted "like the first round of a prizefight," with scratching and biting as part of the foreplay. She later found that in Samoa, men preceded sexual activity by singing romantic songs and reciting poetry for their women, first preparing their minds with sensual thoughts and then their bodies with sensual touching.

Sexuality has often become intertwined with the spiritual beliefs within cultures as well. In the Jewish tradition, for example, sexuality is intimately associated with concepts of creativity and unity (Biale, 1997). In Eastern Tantric traditions of yoga, Buddhism, Hinduism, and Taoism, sexual response is perceived as an expression of spiritual energies. It is believed that the energy of life and the spirit may be focused in different ways in the body and that properly used sexual energy can help convey people to the highest levels of spiritual consciousness. The emphasis is on savoring all of the sensual and spiritual aspects of sex rather than looking toward the goal of immediate gratification or satisfaction (Dean, 1998).

Western cultural imperatives often place sexual response in a more goal-oriented context, with orgasm and satisfying release being one of its primary objectives. A view of sexual arousal and response as holistic experiences involving mind, body, emotions, and spirit may be neglected in cultures that approach such issues from a more scientific perspective. It was in 1966, in their pioneering book *Human Sexual Response,* that William Masters and Virginia Johnson provided the most thoroughly researched information on how the human body responds to sexual stimulation. Their study concentrated on careful observation and instrumental monitoring of men and women who were engaging in sexual activity. The 694 people who participated in the study were carefully interviewed and screened to obtain as "average" a sample as possible. These individuals were helped to feel comfortable with sexual activity alone in the laboratory setting before they were observed by the research team. Although Masters and Johnson saw their work as an incomplete, preliminary step to understanding human sexual response, and despite the fact that some controversies have grown out of their study, the findings quickly gained general acceptance among professionals.

Do you believe men or women have a greater interest in sex? On what do you base your assumptions?

◼ Models of Human Sexual Response

It is clear that human response to sexual arousal is not confined to reactions of the sex organs but involves marked changes throughout the body, especially in the muscular and circulatory systems. For easier understanding, the body's sexual responses have often been divided into separate phases.

The Masters and Johnson Four-Phase Model

As Masters and Johnson observed the sexual responses of men and women in their laboratory, they realized that there were many similarities in responses between the two sexes. After gathering a great deal of data, they divided the sexual response process into a four-phase cycle (see Fig. 4.1). It has been argued that the Masters and Johnson model may not represent a fair view of human sexual responsiveness because they only accepted people into their research who indicated that they reached orgasm. They built their cyclical view of sexual responsiveness on the assumptions that orgasm is a natural, built-in response, and that the response cycle is programmed to repeat itself over and over during one's lifetime, given the proper stimuli. Some sexologists believe that this may be a narrow and incomplete perspective on human sexual response. It has also been posited that our present models of sexual response are overly male-centered, still tending to create the impression that the male sex organs are more extensive, active, and explosive than those of females (Chalker, 1994; Rowland, 1999). Nevertheless, the phases that Masters and Johnson invented to describe sexual responsiveness constitute one way to understand some fundamental aspects of human sexuality.

Masters and Johnson labeled their first phase **excitement,** during which the body begins to show

excitement: the arousal phase of Masters and Johnson's four-phase model of the sexual response cycle.

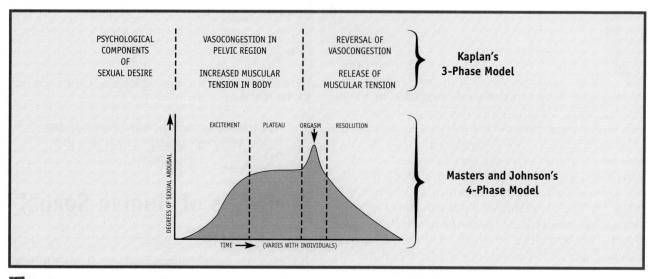

FIGURE 4.1 *Human Sexual Response*

Both Masters and Johnson and Helen Kaplan divided the human physical responses of sexual arousal into different phases. This chart compares their divisions.

signs of arousal. Blood is routed to the pelvic region, resulting in the earliest signs of arousal, such as erection of the penis and clitoris, and vaginal lubrication. A wide range of physical and psychological stimuli can initiate this excitement phase. The intensity of the body's reactions to sexual arousal gradually builds to a higher level and is maintained at that level for varying lengths of time. Masters and Johnson labeled this the **plateau phase** because of its stable, or level, state of arousal.

The plateau phase, if held for sufficient periods of time, can be a major highlight of sexual response. The intensity of plateau may ebb and flow somewhat during sustained sexual activity and thus provide some special "highs" of sensual enjoyment. In any case, the buildup of tension may eventually lead to the triggering of a pleasurable sexual release called **orgasm,** or **climax.** It is a brief phase, lasting a few seconds to slightly less than a minute, but one in which thought is momentarily suspended, and the mind becomes focused inward on a rush of pleasurable physical sensations. Almost immediately after orgasm, the body relaxes and begins to return to its unexcited state, although some people may experience more than one orgasm relatively soon. Masters and Johnson called the time of relaxation the **resolution phase.**

Although it remains only one model for describing human sexual response, the Masters and Johnson four-phase model is used in this chapter to explain the various components of responsiveness. Other researchers have raised legitimate criticisms and offered alternative models that remain open for consideration and further study. For example, research has not shown a clear de-

marcation between excitement and plateau phases in males. Instead, there tends to be a steady and continuous buildup of sexual tension that is not readily divided into stages. Some researchers have maintained that they have been unable to distinguish a measurable plateau phase at all in either men or women. It has been proposed both that the Masters and Johnson approach attempts to impose a model on male sexual response that is far more applicable to women only and, conversely, that it may actually be more applicable to men than it is to women (Chalker, 1994; Rowland, 1999).

Kaplan's Three-Phase Model

Another sex researcher and therapist, Helen Singer Kaplan (1974), first proposed that it makes more sense, from the standpoint of the body's actual neurophysiological mechanisms, to view sexual response as occurring in two phases. The first phase is characterized by vasocongestion, or buildup of blood in the pelvic area,

plateau phase: the stable, leveled-off phase of Masters and Johnson's four-phase model of the sexual response cycle.

orgasm (OR-gaz-em): a rush of pleasurable physical sensations associated with the release of sexual tension.

climax: another term for orgasm.

resolution phase: the term for the return of a body to its unexcited state following orgasm.

and an accumulation of muscular tension throughout the body, causing increases in heart rate, breathing, blood pressure, and other involuntary functions. Orgasm acts as the trigger for the second phase, **orgasmic release,** in which the vasocongestion and muscular tension are released through the sudden orgasmic bursts, and then more gradually as the body returns to less excited levels of functioning.

As Kaplan worked with people's problems in sexual arousal, often referred to generally as **sexual dysfunctions,** she realized that some people simply did not seem to have much desire to become sexually aroused. This led her to suggest that a **desire phase** precedes the body's physiological responses to arousal (Kaplan, 1979). The desire phase represents a psychological component that can lead to physical response. It was a modification of the Masters and Johnson model, focusing on the subjective, emotional aspects of sexual arousal.

Sexual desire has been one of the more elusive and interesting areas of sexuality research, and it has been closely tied to psychological studies of the human motivations behind behavior. For centuries, the assumption was made that the longing for sexual interaction was innate, and an inner drive model was used to explain it. It has been suggested that this model was much like a metaphor for a steam boiler. Internal sexual "steam" would build up until the pressure became so great that the drive to release it was very strong. This view also assumed that there was some adverse physical consequence of not releasing the pressure, which eventually was shown not to be the case. Human motivation theory eventually began to focus more on the external incentives behind sexual and other forms of motivation. Although sexual desire is still a very complex phenomenon under study, it would appear that the incentive motivation model is a more accurate one. Rather than assuming that sexual desire emanates from the physical sexual response system, this model suggests that there is a complex interaction of external stimuli that triggers certain responses; interpretations of reactions, sensations, and memories; and social rules that regulate sexual activity (Everaerd & Laan, 1995; Wright & Adams, 1999). The motivation for sexual activity seems to be rooted not only in seeking pleasurable sensations but also in the experiencing of social and emotional rewards, such as feeling valued by others and oneself (Hill, 1997; Pfaus, 2000; Plaud & Martini, 1999).

What has become known as Kaplan's three-phase model (see Fig. 4.1) has special validity when considering the various dysfunctions that can interfere with sexual responsiveness. These problems may involve inhibited sexual desire, sexual aversion, erectile dysfunction, vaginismus, or painful intercourse and are usually centered in either the desire phase, the vaso-

congestive phase, or the orgasmic-release phase of the sexual response cycle (see chapter 18, "Sexual Dysfunctions and Their Treatment").

Individual Differences in Sexual Response

It is clear that there are more physiological similarities in the sexual responses of males and females than differences. Both males and females experience pelvic vasocongestion and a general buildup of muscular tension. Orgasm is very similar in both sexes, although it may not always be experienced. Table 4.1 summarizes the sexual response cycles of females and males. It is also evident that, within certain bounds, there can be great variation in sexual response among individuals. On the average, males tend to reach orgasm more rapidly than females during intercourse, but this phenomenon may well be influenced by the kind of stimulation and by the past learning of the individual. Many women respond with orgasm more quickly during masturbation than in intercourse. In fact, it is not unusual for women to respond almost as quickly as men during masturbation. The amount of time for completion of the entire cycle varies with learning, the sexual situation, the kind and intensity of stimulation, and age. An entire cycle from excitement through resolution may take only a few minutes or last for several hours (Anderson & Cyranowski, 1995).

There seem to be subjective differences in the orgasms of males and females. Although male orgasms may vary in intensity and degree of pleasure, the experience is relatively standard among all males. Women often report experiencing different physical and psychological reactions during different orgasms. Some women even appear to have a very pleasurable feeling of sexual satisfaction but do not exhibit the usual physiological responses associated with orgasm (Basson, 2000).

Women can fake orgasm, and some women feel that faking is necessary to please their sexual partners. Research has shown that with the new emphasis on female sexual pleasure, some women experience guilt feelings if they do not reach orgasm during sexual intercourse (Davidson & Moore, 1994). Even though fak-

orgasmic release: reversal of the vasocongestion and muscular tension of sexual arousal, triggered by orgasm.

sexual dysfunctions: difficulties people have in achieving sexual arousal and in other stages of sexual response.

desire phase: Kaplan's term for the psychological interest in sex that precedes physiological sexual arousal.

Table 4.1   *Female and Male Sexual Response*

Phase	Female Responses	Male Responses
EXCITEMENT	Clitoris swells in diameter and length.	Penis becomes erect; urethral diameter begins to widen.
	Vagina lubricates, becomes expanded and lengthened, and darker in color.	Scrotal skin tenses and thickens.
	Major and minor labia thicken and may open slightly.	Testes elevate slightly within scrotum.
	Breasts increase in size and nipples become erect.	Nipples become erect in some males.
	Appearance of sex flush in some females.	
	Increase in muscular tension.	Increase in muscular tension.
	Heart rate begins to increase.	Heart rate begins to increase.
	Blood pressure begins to rise.	Blood pressure begins to rise.
PLATEAU	Clitoris retracts under prepuce.	Penis increases in diameter and becomes fully erect.
	Vagina expands and lengthens more; orgasmic platform develops.	Scrotum has no changes.
	Uterus is completely elevated.	Testes enlarge and elevate up toward body.
	Labia swell more; labia minora have deeper red coloration.	Cowper's glands secrete a few drops of fluid.
	Breasts further increase in size and nipples become turgid.	Nipples become erect and more turgid.
	Sex flush has appeared in most females, and spreads.	Sex flush appears in some males and may spread.
	Further increase in muscular tension.	Further increase in muscular tension.
	Respiration and heart rates increase.	Respiration and heart rates increase.
	Marked elevation in blood pressure.	Marked elevation in blood pressure.
ORGASM	No changes in clitoris.	Penis and urethra undergo contractions that expel semen.
	Uterus undergoes wavelike contractions.	There are no changes in the scrotum or testes.
	There are no changes in the labia.	
	Breasts and nipples show no changes during orgasm.	Nipples remain erect.
	Sex flush deepens.	Sex flush deepens.
	Loss of voluntary muscle control; spasms of some muscles.	Loss of voluntary muscle control; spasms of some muscles.
	Respiration and heart rates reach peak intensity.	Respiration and heart rates reach peak intensity.
	Blood pressure reaches its peak.	Blood pressure reaches its peak.
RESOLUTION	Clitoris returns to nonaroused position and loses its erection.	Penis erection is lost, rapidly at first, then more slowly.
	Vaginal walls relax and return to nonaroused coloration.	Scrotal skin relaxes and returns to nonaroused thickness.
	Uterus lowers to usual position and cervical opening widens for 20–30 minutes.	Testes return to nonaroused size and position in scrotum.
	Labia return to nonaroused size, position, and color.	There is a period (refractory period) during which the male cannot be restimulated to orgasm.
	Breasts and nipples return to nonaroused size, position, and color.	Nipples return to nonaroused size.
	Disappearance of sex flush.	Disappearance of sex flush.
	Rapid relaxation of muscles.	Rapid relaxation of muscles.
	Respiration, heart rate, and blood pressure return to normal.	Respiration, heart rate, and blood pressure return to normal.
	Film of perspiration may appear on skin.	Film of perspiration may appear on skin, usually confined to soles of feet and palms of hands.

Source: W. Masters and V. E. Johnson, *Human Sexual Response*, 1966, Little, Brown and Company, Boston, MA. Reprinted by permission of Masters and Johnson Institute, St. Louis, MO.

ing orgasm is less easy for men because of ejaculation, some men do fake orgasm from time to time. When such a deception enters a relationship, it can establish conditions for eventual problems. Openness and honesty about sex are a crucial part of a healthy relationship (see chapter 8, "Sexuality, Communication, and Relationships"). Individual differences in sexual response patterns make it all the more important for sexual partners to take time to learn about one another's responsiveness. This will also require developing effective lines of communication about emotions, needs, and sex.

Why was the Kaplan model so important in understanding sexual response?

◪ Activating the Response: Models of Sexual Arousal

The early models of an innate human "sex drive" presumed that the body had a preprogrammed sexual mechanism that could be activated by sufficient "sexual stimulation." However, it is now widely accepted within the field of sexology that there is no such thing as sex drive in the sense that some identifiable biological need is generated during times of sexual abstinence or that the body is physiologically harmed by lack of sex. The models never adequately defined what was meant by sexual stimulation. Thus, although the models have clarified how the human body *responds* sexually, they have not really helped us to understand how those responses are activated (Hill, 1997; Janssen & Everaerd, 1993; Laan & Everaerd, 1995).

Components of Sexual Arousal

Although various theorists have conceptualized the details in different ways, all models of sexual arousal seem to include both stimuli that are *internal,* referring to phenomena of the mind such as fantasizing about or remembering sexual activity, and stimuli that are *external,* such as direct touching of the sex organs or actually seeing someone who is considered sexy (Hill, 1997). These two aspects of activating sexual response have been divided into distinct categories: the **central arousal system,** referring to internal factors, and the **peripheral arousal system,** referring to the external. The central arousal system seems to be located largely in the emotional and pleasure centers of the brain, and the stimuli generated there form the central, fundamental template for the person's sexual response (Paredes & Baum, 1997; Stoléru et al., 1999). The peripheral arousal system refers more to the aspects of stimulation that stem from the spinal cord and its voluntary and involuntary nervous control mecha-

nisms. This system picks up cues directly from the skin, genitals, and sense organs. Sexual arousal from both the central and peripheral systems can be measured by physiological responses, verbal reports, and behavior, although studies continue to show that there can be very real discordance among various systems and reporting mechanisms (Basson, 2000; Pfaus, 2000).

We do know that some people have a greater propensity toward activation of sexual response than others, a quality that might be described as *sexual arousability.* An individual's degree of arousability seems to be influenced by the sensitivity of the entire sexual response system, including not only the genitals and other body systems but also the ways in which the mind and emotions become involved. All human responses tend to be activated by stimuli, and high arousability probably reflects a high sensitivity to both external and internal stimuli that the individual has learned to interpret as sexual. In the same way, arousability may be inhibited or "turned off" by certain negative stimuli (Bancroft, 1989; Janssen & Bancroft, 1997; Janssen & Everaerd, 1993).

Research on sexual arousal has demonstrated that people's perceptions of their own degree of arousal does not always seem to coincide with the ways their sex organs are actually responding, especially in women. Using a probe that is inserted into the vagina to measure the amount of blood flow to that organ, researchers have been able to compare the genital responses to various stimuli with women's subjective reports of their degree of sexual arousal (Laan, Everaerd, Van de Velde, & Geer, 1995). Similar studies have been made using penile plethysmography. Women are less likely than men to pick up on the physiological cues of their own sexual arousal. When shown sexually explicit films, for example, women seem to have genital responses just as quickly as do men, but they are much less likely to identify themselves as being sexually aroused. This may be partly because of socialization that discourages females from paying attention to their genital responses or feeling comfortable reporting arousal, and partly due to the fact that erection of the penis is anatomically more easily noticed than the internal vaginal changes associated with arousal (Laan & Everaerd, 1995; Wouda et al., 1998).

central arousal system: internal components of sexual arousal that come from the cognitive and emotional centers of the brain, forming the foundations for sexual response.

peripheral arousal system: external components of sexual arousal that reach the brain and spinal cord from the skin, genitals, and sense organs.

What is happening within the body's sexual response system may not always be recognized by the information-processing systems of the person's mind or be interpreted in the same way by different people.

Many contemporary theorists hold that genital response alone does not constitute sexual arousal because the genitals may respond to nonsexual stimuli. In other words, sexual arousal includes both physiological response and some inner, subjective experience that defines the response and perhaps the surrounding situation as sexual (Laan & Everaerd, 1995). All models of sexual arousal seem to recognize that psychological processes are an essential component. Emotions and the ways in which the brain processes information play a major role in activating— *or deactivating*—a person's sexual response. The various stimuli that come to the attention of the human mind must be cognitively transformed to result in emotional or sexual responses. This is obviously a very complex process, profoundly influenced by the learning processes and environments experienced by dif-

ferent people (Pfaus, 2000). Things that may seem intrinsically sexual to one individual may represent a turnoff to someone else. Then again, a stimulus that is not even perceived by the individual to be pleasurable or sexual can still cause a physical response of the genitals. Emotions that have nothing to do with sex per se—such as depression or anxiety—may still exert a strong influence on sexual arousal mechanisms, both positively and negatively (Elliott & Donohue, 1997; Mitchell et al., 1998).

Although theories of sexual arousal are still in the earlier stages of development, Figure 4.2 summarizes what is presently believed regarding the activation of sexual response. It is generally agreed that there is a sequence of events leading to sexual arousal, involving the combination of central and peripheral mechanisms, the mind and body interacting in many different ways. If the mind ascribes sexual meaning to a particular stimulus, sexual arousal can be the result. In some cases, this processing seems to be relatively *automatic,* leading to rapid physiological response such as

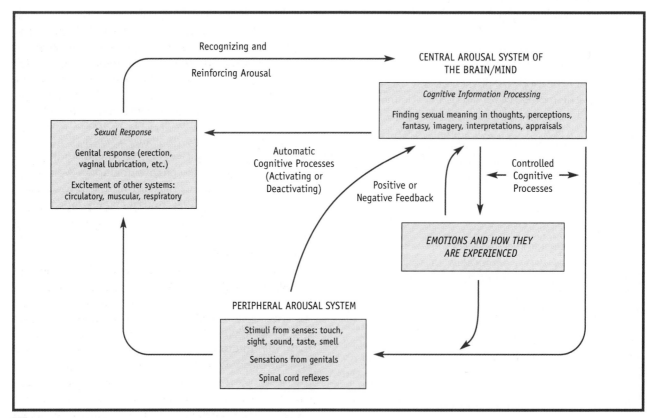

FIGURE 4.2   *Mind-Body Interactions in Sexual Arousal*

This diagram summarizes the models that explain how human sexual response is activated. The initiating mechanism is the central arousal system, mediated by the brain and its ways of processing information. The peripheral arousal system is partly influenced by input from the brain, but it also processes cues that come directly from sensory stimulation. The brain continues to participate in activation, or deactivation, of sexual response, depending on complex positive and negative feedback loops influenced by the individual's learned ways of processing potential sex cues.

Sources: Lawrence Erlbaum; and E. Janssen & W. Everaerd, "Determinants of Male Sexual Arousal," in *Annual Review of Sex Research,* Vol. 4 (1993); E. Laan & W. Everaerd, "Determinants of Female Sexual Arousal: Psychological Theory and Data," *Annual Review of Sex Research,* Vol. 4 (1995).

erection or vaginal lubrication. A *controlled* processing of stimuli may result in more complicated reactions, including the inhibition of sexual response. When human sexual response is easily activated, it is probably the result of the automatic arousal mechanisms. When people are sexually dysfunctional for psychological reasons, these automatic mechanisms are disrupted by controlling factors such as emotions and negative interpretations (Gaither & Plaud, 1997; Janssen & Bancroft, 1997; Laan & Everaerd, 1995).

Women, Men, and Sexual Arousal

Of the many purported differences between men and women, the differences in sexual arousability are among the most rigidly believed. From as far back as nineteenth-century psychology, it was believed that males spontaneously get in touch with their potentials for sexual arousal, whereas females become initiated into their sexual potentials within the context of a romantic relationship and the loving touch of a man (Laan & Everaerd, 1995). These generalizations persist today in the form of assumptions that women become sexually aroused less often and less rapidly than men. Men and women are also said to become sexually

aroused by different stimuli—whereas men are turned on by physical sex, pictures of nude people, and pictures of sexual acts, women supposedly are more aroused by the romantic aspects of loving relationships.

Although these concepts represent stereotypes that cannot be applied to all individuals, research studies do continue to confirm that women tend to "romanticize" the goals of sexual desire, seeing them as love, emotional intimacy, and commitment more than do men. Men, on the other hand, are more likely to "sexualize" these phenomena, seeing the goals of desire and arousal to be sexual activity. One study confirmed that there was a difference in the way the two genders saw the goal of sexual desire. Men were more likely to see sexual activity as a goal than women were, and much less likely than women to see love, emotional intimacy, or physical closeness as goals of arousal. When identifying the *objects* of sexual desire, women were more likely than men to indicate a loved one or a romantic partner, whereas men were more likely to specify that the object of sexual desire would be physically and sexually attractive (Regan & Berscheid, 1996).

There is general agreement now among the majority of sexologists that people *learn* to be sexual. The physiological responses of the genitals and other organ systems provide the physical template on which subjective interpretations and experiences are socially constructed. We know that social standards have generally been less permissive toward female sexual activity than toward that of males. In many laboratory settings, it has been found that men are more attuned to their bodily responses and more likely to interpret them accurately. It seems likely, then, that women's genital responses are less involved in the determination of their subjective experience of sexual arousal than are the external factors such as a relationship (Basson, 2000; Hill, 1997; Laan & Everaerd, 1995; Wouda et al., 1998).

People's methods of processing information and attaching sexual meanings to experiences and emotions seem to influence their arousal patterns. Even though an individual's automatic responses may cause some thought or fantasy to generate a genital response, that same person's controlled responses may prevent him or her from experiencing or enjoying the response as sexual. Learning probably plays an essential role in determining how sexual arousal mechanisms actually function in each individual to generate a sexual response. Some of these differences may be particularly common to males or to females, but it would be impossible to generalize them to all members of either gender.

Research on sexual arousal has sometimes been confusing and contradictory. Older evidence suggesting that males are far more easily and quickly sexually aroused than women has not been fully supported, per-

CROSS-CULTURAL PERSPECTIVE
Sexuality and Spirituality: The Relevance of Eastern Traditions

In recent years, the age-old association of sex with Adam and Eve's original sin in the Garden of Eden has lost its meaning as individuals increasingly accept sexual desire and pleasure as a natural good. Social turmoil, technological changes, increasing recognition of personal needs, and a sexual revolution have wreaked havoc with the meaning and relevance of the traditional Judeo-Christian sexual images, icons, and myths of the purpose of sex, monogamy and male primacy over female.

Because cultures draw their life blood from their myths and archetypes, human beings are searching for new myths and archetypes. At the same time, Americans in particular are increasingly fascinated by the more sex-positive images of Eastern sexual philosophies. . . .

These ancient traditions celebrate the naturalness of sexual pleasure and the spiritual potential of sexual relations, a view that may fit well with many people's sensitivities and yearnings. They also accept female sexuality and women's unlimited sexual potential, a view that is congenial with contemporary feminist awareness. Contemporary sexuality can be enriched and broadened by a reawakening of the experience of sexuality as integral to whole-person connectedness. It can also benefit from seeing sexual satisfaction as a fluctuating, non-goal-oriented continuum of responses that includes pleasuring, orgasm, and ecstasy. Can these ancient and yet very modern views be translated into the Western consciousness without being trapped by faddism? Advocates of yoga and acupuncture have succeeded in similar challenges. . . .

Eastern sexual and spiritual traditions can help Westerners break out of the prevailing reduction of sexuality to genital activity. Taoist and Tantric sexual practices highlight all the senses and involve the whole energies of both partners in slow, sensual dances that are rich variations of what Western sexologists label the "outercourse" of the Sensate Focus Exercises. In addition, Eastern thought may help refocus our understanding and appreciation of male orgasm. The obsession in sexually explicit films and videos with ejaculation as the affirmation of masculinity leaves the male with an inevitable flaccid vulnerability that requires denial in a vicious cycle of repeated "conquests" followed by inevitable detumescence. Taoist practices can help a male achieve some parity with the multiorgasmic woman by controlling his ejaculation, much to the benefit of both sexes.

—Robert T. Francoeur, *SIECUS Report*, Vol. 20 (4), April/May 1992

haps indicating some important changes in social influences on women concerning their sexual feelings. Women's self-reported feelings about sexual arousal and their evaluations of their own sexual responses tend to be consistently more negative than the self-reported feelings and evaluations of men. Males still seem to value sex and sexual stimuli more positively than do women and therefore pursue them more actively and comfortably. Men also apparently dream to the point of orgasm more frequently than do women (Janssen & Everaerd, 1993; Laan, Everaerd, & Evers, 1995).

What are your feelings about the importance or unimportance of orgasm during sexual activity?

◾ Female Sexual Response
Excitement Phase

When the female body begins to respond sexually, changes are often first noticed in the vagina. As blood begins to build up (vasocongestion) in the blood vessels of the genital region, the vaginal walls darken in color, a change that is not visible externally. This vasocongestion causes a slippery, alkaline fluid to seep through the lining of the vagina. This substance functions as a lubricant for sexual activity and may also help to create alkaline conditions in the vagina that are beneficial to sperm. The amount of lubrication in the vagina is not, however, necessarily a sign of how sexually aroused the woman is or how ready she might be for sexual activity. Particularly for females, genital responses must be supported by environmental cues and stimuli in order to create a sexual context (Laan & Everaerd, 1995; Wouda, Hartman, Bakker, et al. 1998).

Another change during the excitement phase is the lengthening and distention of the inner one-third of the vagina. The uterus is also pulled upward from its usual position (see Fig. 4.3). The vasocongestion causes changes in the labia majora and minora as they begin to enlarge and sometimes to open slightly. The clitoris begins to swell somewhat, and its shaft may elongate slightly. Some of the vaginal lubrication may flow out onto the labia and clitoris, depending on its

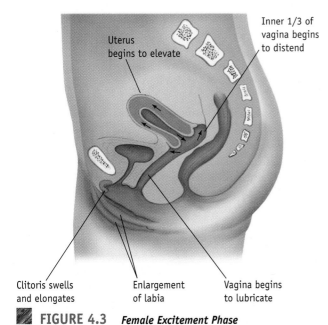

FIGURE 4.3 *Female Excitement Phase*

In the female, the first sign of sexual arousal is often the lubrication of the vagina. This is accompanied by the enlargement of the vaginal area including the clitoris and the major and minor labia, and a darkening of the color of the vaginal walls.

copiousness and on whether or not the particular sexual activity is apt to bring internal secretions to the exterior.

Other areas of the body respond to sexual excitement as well. Often the nipples become harder and erect, although this response also may result from nonsexual stimuli. Many women show a darkening of the skin through the neck, breasts, and upper abdomen during sexual excitement; this is termed the "sex flush." General muscular tension begins to build throughout the body as heart rate and blood pressure increase.

Plateau Phase

The second stage of the female sexual response cycle leads to further changes in the vagina. The outer third of the vaginal wall becomes swollen with blood, narrowing the space within the vagina slightly. The inner two-thirds of the vagina show slightly more lengthening and expansion (Shafik, 1996). The labia minora also become engorged with blood, causing thickening and a flaring outward. The swelling of the outer third of the vagina and the minor lips seems to create the tension that is an important precursor of orgasm, so together they are termed the "orgasmic platform" (see Fig. 4.4). During plateau phase, the clitoral glans retracts back under its hood or foreskin so that it no longer receives any direct stimulation.

The breasts have usually become somewhat engorged by this time, and nipple erection may be maintained. Increase in breast size is not as pronounced in

women who have breast-fed a baby. The sex flush, if present, sometimes spreads to the shoulders, back, buttocks, and thighs during the plateau phase. Muscular tension continues to increase, along with heart rate, respiration rate, and blood pressure. The heart rate usually increases to between 110 and 175 beats per minute.

Orgasm

The pleasurable release of sexual tension occurs during the sexual climax or orgasm. It is an intense experience, both physically and emotionally, and in females it is immediately preceded by a sensation of "suspension," at which time the pulse rate reaches its peak. Then there is a feeling of increased sexual awareness in the area of the clitoris, which spreads upward, and a "suffusion" of warmth that spreads from the pelvis throughout the body. Many women also experience a sensation of throbbing in the lower pelvic area.

During the pleasurable feelings of the orgasmic phase, there are muscular contractions in the outer third of the vagina and in the anal area. Following the initial contraction, which may last 2 to 4 seconds, there are three or four rhythmic contractions at intervals of about 0.8 second. There may be up to 15 such contractions, the interval between them gradually lengthening, and their intensity gradually decreasing. Two to four seconds after orgasm begins, the uterus has some

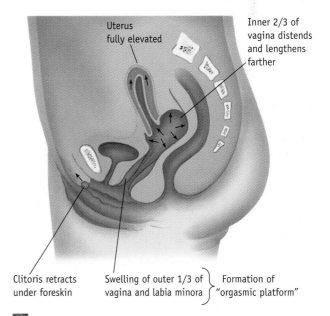

FIGURE 4.4 *Female Plateau Phase*

In the plateau phase of sexual response, high levels of arousal are maintained. In the female, the orgasmic platform is caused by swelling of tissues in the outer third of the vagina, which causes the entrance to it to narrow. The clitoris retracts under its foreskin.

mild wavelike contractions that move from its top to the cervix (see Fig. 4.5).

During orgasm, muscles throughout the body may contract involuntarily, causing pelvic thrusting and spastic movements of the neck, hands, arms, feet, and legs. The woman may scream, gasp, moan, or shout out words during the orgasmic experience. The heart and respiratory rates and blood pressure have all reached their peaks. The pulse rate may be twice as high as normal.

Resolution Phase

Following the release of sexual tension through orgasm, the body gradually returns to its unexcited state. As blood leaves the pelvic region, the vagina returns to its usual size and color, and the labia return to their prearoused state. Within 10 seconds, the glans of the clitoris emerges from the foreskin to its typical position, and within 15 to 30 minutes it has returned to its usual size. The uterus also lowers to its prearoused position.

During resolution, the other signs of sexual arousal also gradually disappear. The breasts decrease in size, and the nipples lose their erection. The sex flush leaves the body in the reverse order from which it developed, and respiration, pulse, and blood pressure soon return to their normal levels. It is quite common for the body to become wet with perspiration during resolution. As the muscles throughout the body relax, there is often a feeling of drowsiness that may lead to sleep.

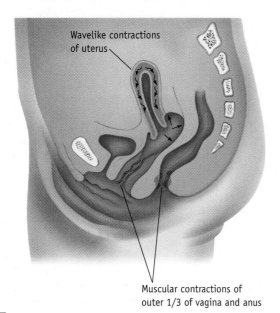

FIGURE 4.5   *Female Orgasmic Phase*
Orgasm is the release of sexual tension involving a total body response. The female physical response is marked by simultaneous rhythmic muscular contractions of the uterus, the outer third of the vagina, and the anal sphincter.

Multiple Orgasms in Women

During the resolution phase of sexual response, many females may be restimulated to orgasm. Unlike males, who go through a period when they cannot be restimulated to climax, some females are capable of experiencing numerous orgasms during a single sexual experience. Kinsey and his coworkers (1953) reported that 14 percent of the women surveyed regularly experienced sequential (or multiple) orgasms during sexual encounters, and Masters and Johnson (1966) proposed that most, if not all, women have the potential for more than one orgasm.

Research since that time has suggested that the multiorgasmic experience for women may depend a great deal on the type of sexual stimulation involved in their sexual responsiveness, and not all women report having been multiorgasmic. In one study of 720 women, about 47 percent indicated they usually had single orgasms, and 43 percent reported that they had experienced multiple orgasms. It would appear that women tend to be multiorgasmic through particular means of stimulation. In this study, for example, 26 percent of the women had experienced multiple orgasms through masturbation; 18.3 percent through stimulation by a partner; and 24.7 percent by sexual intercourse. Only 7 percent had experienced more than one orgasm by all three types of stimulation. Of those women who tended to have only single orgasms, 27 percent were interested in being able to experience multiple orgasms (Darling, Davidson, & Jennings, 1991). It has been suggested both that we should stop assuming that female sexual satisfaction rests solely on whether one or more orgasms are experienced and that we should stop undervaluing women's capacity for multiple orgasms by giving precedence to a male-centered single orgasm norm (Chalker, 1994).

Controversies about Female Sexual Response

Orgasms

For many years, there has been a controversy over the existence of two types of female orgasm: clitoral and vaginal. Masters and Johnson (1966) concluded that regardless of how it is produced, female orgasm proceeds physiologically in basically the same manner as previously described. They believed that, at least from a biological viewpoint, the clitoral-vaginal dichotomy was unfounded. However, the controversy continues as researchers report that there are distinct differences in how women experience orgasm produced by clitoral or vulval stimulation and that produced by deeper vaginal stimulation. Some women experience orgasm as the result of stimulation of the cervix. This

CASE STUDY

Angelina: Questioning Orgasmic Abilities

Angelina had been involved in a sexual relationship with her boyfriend for nearly a year when she consulted a female therapist about her sexual responsiveness. It seemed that although she regularly experienced orgasm during her sexual encounters with her partner, she had come to believe that she should be capable of having more than one orgasm when she had sex.

She explained to the therapist that she had read articles about female sexuality implying that all women had the potential for multiple orgasms during sex, and she felt as though she might have something wrong with herself. Her boyfriend also seemed to want her to try to have more orgasms and sometimes would persist in attempting to offer stimulation that might produce that result. Upon further questioning, she explained to the therapist that following orgasm, it was extremely uncomfortable for her to receive further stimulation in the clitoral area. She also explained that she felt quite satisfied with a single orgasm.

Angelina's therapist explained to her that many women seem to be sexually satiated with one orgasm, and some apparently find sexual satisfaction without any orgasm at all. She urged Angelina to invite her boyfriend to join her at their next session, so that they could talk about their sexual relationship. Although the boyfriend declined to enter counseling, Angelina was able to explain to him that she did not wish to pursue orgasms beyond the one that she typically experienced. She realized that this pattern apparently fit her best and that it was a perfectly normal one. Reporting back to the therapist 2 months later, she indicated that her relationship was going along comfortably for her and that she no longer felt pressured within herself, or by her partner, to be multiorgasmic. She also told the therapist that once she had relieved herself of the unnecessary expectation, she had felt much better about herself and her sexuality.

has been called a "uterine orgasm." It has also been suggested that some women experience a "blended orgasm," which is a combination of the clitoral-vulval experience and the uterine orgasm (Whipple, 1991). The difference in orgasmic responses could be due to the two different nerve pathways that serve the sex organs, the *pudendal nerves* and the *pelvic nerves*. The pudendal nerve system connects with the clitoris, and the *pelvic system* innervates the vagina, cervix, and uterus. It is therefore hypothesized that there may be two different neurological routes to producing orgasm (Komisaruk & Whipple, 1995).

This controversy may well represent one of those cases in which it is difficult to reconcile the objective measures of science and the subjective reports of people's experiences. It does seem clear that orgasm has both physiological and psychological components, meaning that each person will have individualized perceptions and interpretations of the experience. Regardless of what sort of orgasm a woman might experience, the most important issue is that she be able to feel that a sexual activity has been fulfilling to her personally.

The G Spot

There is a possibility that there is an area on the inner front wall of the vagina that may become particularly sexually sensitive. The existence of such an area was proposed years ago by a German physician named Gräfenberg (1950). The idea was revived in the 1980s by other researchers who claimed that there is indeed a mass of tissue in the anterior vagina that swells during sexual arousal and can lead to intense orgasmic experiences. They named it the **G spot**, after Gräfenberg (Ladas, Whipple, & Perry, 1983). Some scientists have objected, feeling that the sensitive "spot" is not found in a large percentage of women and that, when it is present, it is not in a clearly defined location (Alzate, 1990). There does seem to be evidence that stimulation of the anterior wall of the vagina usually results in more sexual arousal than stimulation of the back wall. It has been suggested that this be referred to as an "area" rather than a spot because it seems to vary in size (Ladas, 1997).

The confusion here may well result from the fact that the spongy tissue in this area may not become fully engorged with blood and sensitized until the clitoris is fully engorged. This may take up to 25 minutes in some women, and so they may never experience the sensitivity of the G spot. There has also been

G spot: a vaginal area that some researchers feel is particularly sensitive to sexual stimulation when its underlying spongy tissues are engorged with blood.

A New Vision of Women's Sexuality

While relegating women to an inferior sexual status, male-dominated cultures from ancient Greece through the Renaissance at least recognized, and celebrated, the similarities between male and female sexuality. In the eighteenth century, the definition of female sexuality narrowed dramatically. What will the twenty-first-century model be?

In her incisive critique of Masters and Johnson's model, Tiefer (1991) warns against the reduction of sexual response to mere biology, and against the exclusion of the "social realities" of relationships and "women's experiences of exploitation, harassment and abuse." She then calls for "a model of human sexuality more psychologically-minded, individually variable, interpersonally oriented, and socioculturally sophisticated," but stops short of suggesting a framework for such a model. I would suggest a model that is inclusive of both biological and psychosocial factors that would help to explain physiological sexual experience for both women and men, regardless of sexual orientation. Such a model would also illuminate the complex, contradictory, and often controversial contexts in which we experience sexuality. Given both the striking similarities and the differences between women and men, this could be neither a "one-sex" nor a "two-sex" model. Rather, it should be a bi-gender model that promotes sexual equality and at the same time acknowledges and celebrates the important differences that we are now just beginning to discover and understand.

The revised model of human sexuality should not be genitocentric, but should start from the premise that women and men have a right to complete and accurate information about how their bodies function sexually. Anatomical illustrations should be clear and complete, and the names of the clitoral and penile structures should be descriptive, rather than rendered in Latin or Greek. On a practical level, this revised model should help women see that sexuality can be as exciting and rewarding for them as it is for men. It should enable women to understand that sexuality is a vital and powerful part of who they are, and help them to feel comfortable with it, to celebrate and relish it.

This new model must also include research on and about women, with an emphasis on healthy sexuality rather than on disease and dysfunction. (An article in *Glamour* magazine reveals that in 1993, the National Institutes of Health spent $1 million on male erectile dysfunction, but not a penny on a similar category for women, or any other sex research on women.)

This new model should not be competitive with men and should not fault them for playing to their sexual strengths. Nor should it deride intercourse as a legitimate form of sexual expression. Instead, by providing information about women's sexuality that has hitherto been, for the most part, ignored or considered inconsequential, it should help women to broaden their sexual agendas, play to their own sexual strengths, and take into account their unique needs and capabilities. This reconstructed model is not aimed at overcoming penis envy. It is, instead, an effort to help women achieve penis equity. Women clearly have it. We should help them claim it.

—Rebecca Chalker, *SIECUS Report,* Vol. 22 (5), June/July 1994

speculation that this vaginal region may be activated by a different set of nerves (pelvic) than is the clitoris (pudendal), and so it has been difficult to separate the different types of orgasm that may result from their stimulation. As the media created the impression that the G spot was some sort of magic button that could be pushed to enhance female sexual enjoyment, the picture became confusing for both women and their partners (Chalker, 1994). The one thing that this controversy has confirmed is that many women are sensitive to vaginal stimulation, thus laying to rest a traditional view of the vagina as a rather insensitive organ (Ladas, 1997). It also reminds us that there are individual differences in sexual response, emphasizing the need for good patterns of communication between sexual partners.

Ejaculation

Gräfenberg also suggested in his 1950 article that some women might ejaculate a semenlike substance from their urethras at the time of orgasm. This contention has also seen a recent revival, and it has been hypothesized that **Skene's glands,** located inside the urethra, might be similar to the prostate of males (Sevely, 1987). During particularly intense orgasms, some women report that a liquid is expelled from their urethras that does not seem to be urine. A survey of 1,230 women in North America found that 40 percent of them had ex-

Skene's glands: secretory cells located inside the female urethra.

perienced such ejaculation. Those who had ejaculated were more likely to report their sexual responsiveness as above average in intensity (Darling, Davidson, & Conway-Welch, 1990). Some women seem to assume that the fluid is urine and are therefore reluctant to pursue the matter. Some of those women may even try to prevent themselves from experiencing intense orgasms in an effort to reduce the chances of emitting this fluid. Only further research will finally resolve these issues.

Social factors play an important role in how female orgasm, the G spot, and female ejaculation are perceived in our culture. There may well be male power issues involved. If the sexual focus in our society has traditionally been on what pleases men and glorifies their sexual organs, it may be difficult to shift that focus toward those places in women that are associated with intense sexual pleasure (Chalker, 1994).

Kegel Exercises and Sexual Response

FOH In the early 1950s, a surgeon by the name of Arnold Kegel developed exercises for the pubococcygeal (PC) muscle that surrounds the vagina. He originally intended the exercises for girls and women who had difficulty with urine leaking from their bladders. Eventually, Kegel found that in some of his subjects a well-toned PC muscle increased the ability to experience orgasmic satisfaction. Kegel exercises have also been recommended for pregnant women and seem to help the vagina and uterus return to normal shape and tone more quickly after the delivery of a baby. It has been suggested that men keep their PC muscles in good shape to assure

good orgasms as well. Although there is controversy over whether the PC muscle actually affects orgasmic capacity, keeping it in good shape is at least a healthy thing, and it may also enhance general sexual sensitivity.

Kegel exercises are accomplished by first locating the PC muscle. This is best accomplished by stopping and starting the flow of urine during urination because the same muscle is involved. Once the individual is familiar with its location, it is usually suggested that the muscle be contracted firmly for 2 or 3 seconds and then released. Although it has been recommended that these contractions be done in sets of tens, building up to several sets each day, some experts now believe that it is unnecessary, or even unwise, to exercise the PC muscle too much.

◾ Male Sexual Response
Excitement Phase

Vasocongestion in the pelvic area during early sexual arousal contributes to erection of the penis, the first sign of the excitement phase in males. The degree of erection during this phase depends on the intensity of sexual stimuli. Eventually the inner diameter of the urethra doubles. Vasocongestion also causes thickening of the scrotal tissue, and the scrotum pulls upward toward the body. The testes become elevated within the scrotum, although if the excitement phase continues for more than 5 or 10 minutes, the testes return to their original position for a time (see Fig. 4.6).

Nipple erection and appearance of the sex flush are less common in males than in females, but both

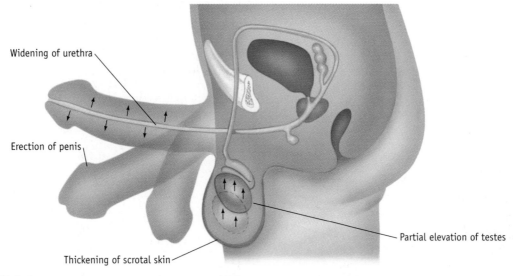

FIGURE 4.6 *Male Excitement Phase*

Vasocongestion in the male leads to erection of the penis, the first physical sign of sexual arousal. The testes are lifted up into the scrotum as a result of the shortening of the spermatic cords and contraction of the scrotal sac. The scrotal tissue itself thickens.

phenomena are usually first observed during excitement phase if they occur at all. Muscular tension increases throughout the body during late excitement phase, and heart rate and blood pressure both increase. Sometimes secretion from Cowper's (bulbourethral) glands appears during this stage or can even precede erection.

Plateau Phase

The penis does not change markedly during the second stage of sexual response, although it is less likely that a man will lose his erection if distracted during plateau phase than during excitement. As orgasm nears, the corona of the glans of the penis becomes more swollen, and the glans itself may take on a deeper, often reddish purple color. There are no further changes in the scrotum, but the testes increase in size by 50 percent or more and become elevated up toward the body. During plateau, Cowper's glands often secrete a few drops of fluid, some of which may appear at the tip of the penis. The longer plateau stimulation is maintained, the more fluid produced (see Fig. 4.7).

Muscular tension heightens considerably during plateau phase, and involuntary body movements increase as orgasm approaches. The nipples may become erect. Males often have clutching or grasping movements of the hands in late plateau. Heart rate increases to between 100 and 175 beats per minute, and blood pressure increases. Respiratory rate also increases, especially in later plateau phase. If the sex flush is present, it may spread to the neck, back, and buttocks.

Orgasm

In males, actual orgasm and ejaculation are preceded by a distinct inner sensation that orgasm is imminent. This has been called **ejaculatory inevitability.** Almost immediately after that feeling is reached, the male senses that ejaculation cannot be stopped. The most noticeable response in the penis during orgasm is the ejaculation of semen. The muscles at the base of the penis and around the anus contract rhythmically, with intervals of about 0.8 second between the first three or four contractions. This varies in different individuals. The intensity of the contractions then diminishes, and the interval between contractions lengthens. It is the first few contractions that expel the largest amount of semen. The testes are held at their maximum elevation throughout orgasm (see Fig. 4.8).

Males often have strong involuntary muscle contractions throughout the body during orgasm and usually exhibit involuntary pelvic thrusting. The hands and feet show spastic contractions, and the entire body may arch backward or contract in a clutching manner. Many men moan or yell during orgasm and have a grimacing facial expression. Breathing, heart rate, and blood pressure all reach a peak during orgasm, and some men begin perspiring during this stage.

ejaculatory inevitability: the sensation in the male that ejaculation is imminent.

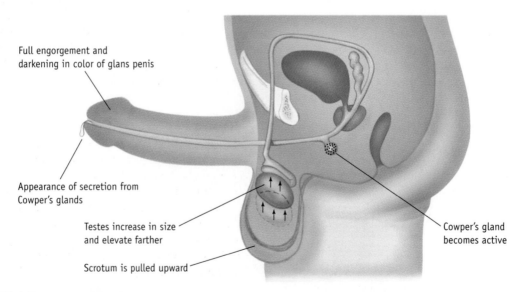

Full engorgement and darkening in color of glans penis

Appearance of secretion from Cowper's glands

Testes increase in size and elevate farther

Scrotum is pulled upward

Cowper's gland becomes active

FIGURE 4.7 *Male Plateau Phase*

A generalized increase in neuromuscular tension is experienced in both males and females in the plateau phase. In the male, the head of the penis increases slightly in size and deepens in color. The testes swell by 50 to 100 percent. The testes continue to elevate. A secretion from Cowper's glands may appear from the male urethra and may carry live sperm.

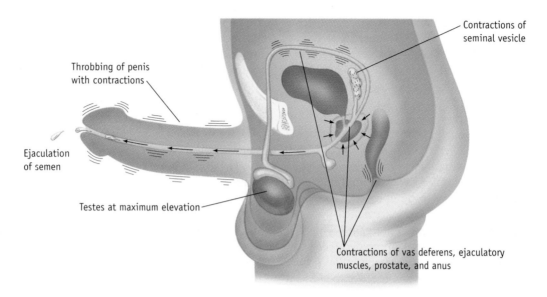

Contractions of
seminal vesicle

Throbbing of penis
with contractions

Ejaculation
of semen

Testes at maximum elevation

Contractions of vas deferens, ejaculatory
muscles, prostate, and anus

FIGURE 4.8 *Male Orgasmic Phase*

Male orgasm and ejaculation occur in two distinct phases but are perceived as occurring simultaneously. The vas deferens and prostate and seminal vesicles begin a series of contractions that force semen into the urethra. The contractions continue until the semen is ejaculated.

Men also have two different nerve pathways to different parts of their sex organs. The pudendal nerve system connects with the penile glans, whereas the pelvic nerve system serves the base of the penis and prostate gland. This could explain why orgasm is not necessarily always accompanied by ejaculation of semen. Orgasm produced from localized stimulation of the glans may be somewhat less likely to be accompanied by ejaculation. It is also known that different sets of nerves are involved, depending on whether erection is generated by direct touching of the genitals or by psychological stimuli such as erotic thoughts and fantasies, although the two systems are somewhat interactive (Janssen, Everaerd, Yan Lunsen, & Oerlemans, 1994; Stoléru et al., 1999). In any case, male orgasm and ejaculation should be viewed as two essentially separate sexual responses that most often happen at the same time.

Resolution

Immediately following ejaculation, the male body begins to return to its unexcited state. About 50 percent of the penile erection is lost right away, and the remainder of the erection is lost over a longer period of time, depending on the degree of stimulation and nonsexual activity. Urination, walking, and other distracting activities usually lead to a more rapid return of the penis to its fully flaccid state. The diameter of the urethra returns to its usual width. The scrotum begins to

relax as vasocongestion decreases, and the testes return to their prearoused size and position. Resolution in the scrotum and testes takes varying lengths of time, depending on the individual.

If nipple erection and sex flush have appeared, they gradually diminish. Muscular tension usually is fully dissipated within 5 minutes after orgasm, and the male feels relaxed and drowsy. Many men fall asleep quickly during the resolution phase. About one-third of men begin a perspiration reaction during this stage. Heart rate, respiration rate, and blood pressure rapidly return to normal. Resolution is a gradual process that may take as long as 2 hours.

Refractory Period

During resolution, most males experience a period of time during which they cannot be restimulated to ejaculation. This period of time is known as the **refractory period.** The duration of the refractory period depends on a variety of factors, including the amount of available sexual stimulation, the man's mood, and his age. On the average, men in their late thirties cannot be restimulated to orgasm for 30 minutes or more. The period gradually increases with age. Very few men

refractory period: time following orgasm during which a man cannot be restimulated to orgasm.

beyond their teenage years are capable of more than one orgasm during sexual encounters, except occasionally. Most men feel sexually satiated with one orgasm.

Multiple Orgasms in Men

There have always been tales of men who are capable of experiencing more than one orgasm during a single sexual experience, presumably without experiencing a refractory period. Some studies have reported on small numbers of men who claim to be able to experience multiple orgasms, and some laboratory measures of their responses have been taken (Hartman & Fithian, 1984; Robbins & Jensen, 1978; Whipple, Myers, & Komisaruk, 1998). These studies suggest that some men seem able to delay ejaculation but still experience some internal contractions and pleasurable sensations associated with orgasm. It has been suggested that men can learn to develop the muscle control enabling them to separate orgasm from ejaculation. However, in at least one case study (Whipple et al., 1998), the man was able to ejaculate each time while reaching six separate orgasms in 36 minutes. Evidence suggests that this is an unusual pattern, although this particular male had experienced multiple ejaculations since the age of 15. Some men, especially at younger ages, may have a brief refractory period and may experience a second ejaculation quite rapidly, sometimes without losing their erections. The best evidence at present indicates that once ejaculation has occurred, a refractory period follows for most men. For a few men (5 percent or less), there does seem to be the possibility of experiencing pleasurable orgasmic reactions two or more times prior to ejaculation. When ejaculation does not occur, the refractory period tends not to occur and so further orgasmic response is possible.

How might our general views of sexual responsiveness be unfair to women or men?

◼ Hormonal Regulation of Sexual Arousal and Response

There is a popular notion that it is sex hormones that control our levels of interest in sexual activity. This assumption would have us believe that the more "hormones" people produce in their bodies, the stronger their sex drives. The picture of how hormones affect sexual behavior is a complicated one, but we can conclude that the popular assumptions about a direct correlation between hormone levels and sexual activity may not be entirely accurate.

Although it is known that women's levels of sexual activity vary over the menstrual cycle and could therefore be associated with hormonal changes, many other factors could also play a role (Van Goozen et al., 1997). Some research studies have tended to conclude that there does not seem to be any direct or immediate correlation between sexual arousal and the concentration of sex hormones in the blood of either men or women (Heiman, Rowland, Hatch, & Gladve, 1991), although a positive correlation has been demonstrated in adolescent females (Halpern, Udry, & Suchindran, 1997).

On the other hand, there has been found to be a direct correlation between the salivary testosterone levels in adolescent males and their levels of sexual activities. It may be that testosterone simply has a more direct effect on the sexual interests and activities of young males than on adult men. However, there is also the indirect effect of testosterone creating physical changes in adolescent boys that are signs of sexual maturity, and this may have the psychological outcome of increasing sexual activity (Halpern, Udry, & Suchindran, 1998). In certain males, but not all, where low testosterone levels have been associated with difficulty achieving erections, administering testosterone as a treatment is sometimes effective in reestablishing sexual function (Rakic, Starcevic, Starcevic, & Marinkovic, 1997). All of this adds up to a picture of some sort of interaction between sexual behavior and levels of testosterone in the body, but there may be a chicken-and-egg issue here that is yet unresolved.

One study measured the amounts of testosterone in the saliva of four male-female couples on nights when they had sexual intercourse and nights when they did not. Saliva samples were taken both before and after the sexual activity. In both the men and women, the amount of testosterone present in the saliva was greater after the couples had intercourse. There was no increase in hormone levels prior to intercourse. This led the researchers to conclude that the sexual activity seemed to affect the testosterone concentration more than the hormone affected sexual activity (Dabbs & Mohammed, 1992). This is consistent with another finding that testosterone levels rise in men when they become involved in watching sporting events, especially when their teams are winning, presumably demonstrating a correlation between hormone levels and general bodily and psychological arousal (Holden, 1995).

Organizing and Activating Effects

The secretions of endocrine glands may have many different effects on an individual. Traditionally, it has been taught that hormones exert their influence in one of two ways. One is called an **organizing effect** and refers to ways in which hormones control patterns of early development in the body, playing a crucial role in the structure and function of particular organs. In chapter 5, "Developmental and Social Perspectives on Gender," for example, I will describe how certain hormones control the development of sex glands and external genitals in the fetus and how they may lead to some differences in how the nervous systems of males and females develop. However, there is growing evidence that once hormones have done their organizing, the same or other hormones may continue to alter processes of development and patterns of behavior later on.

The other effect that hormones have been thought to exert is referred to as an **activating effect.** This describes the potential some hormones can have for affecting an actual behavior, either by activating or deactivating it. In the matter of sexual response, it has been tempting to assume that levels of particular sex hormones in the bloodstream might increase or decrease a person's level of sexual desire or activity, but the evidence in support of such a model has been mixed. Recent studies demonstrate that the central arousal system, in which internal stimuli are processed by the brain, is probably more dependent on the presence of hormones for activation than is the peripheral arousal system, which is far more susceptible to localized stimuli such as touch or viewing erotic material (Halpern et al., 1998; Laan & Everaerd, 1995). There is also increasing evidence that environmental chemicals and events may disrupt the effects of some sex hormones (Hollander, 1997).

The hormone that has been shown to have the most effect on sexual desire and behavior in humans is testosterone. Although this is an **androgen,** or "male" hormone, it is produced by both males and females in the sex glands (testes or ovaries) and the adrenal glands. Men's bodies tend to produce 10 to 15 times more testosterone than do women's bodies. However, the hormone also plays a vital role in enabling women to become sexually aroused (Halpern et al., 1997):

For both men and women, testosterone apparently has an activating effect on sexual interest. It might be viewed as a "switch" for sexual desire, and human beings seem to require some minimal levels of androgen in order to have any potential for sexual desire. What that minimum must be seems to vary with different individuals. Increased levels of testosterone beyond this minimal activating level do not seem to result in increased interest in sex or amounts of sexual activity. It would be a mistake to conclude that because women produce generally lower levels of testosterone, they have a naturally lower interest in sex. It appears instead that women have a greater degree of sensitivity to testosterone, and therefore their bodies respond to

smaller quantities of the hormone (Bancroft, 1994). The "female" hormones, or estrogens, have little effect on sexual desire or activity in females. If males are given doses of estrogen, their interest in sex tends to decrease.

Before reading the section "Effects of Aging on Sexual Response," list your own perceptions of sexual activity after the age of 60. Include both the positive and negative aspects.

Effects of Aging on Sexual Response

There is a prevalent attitude in our culture that aging puts an end to responding sexually. Older people who accept this myth may allow their beliefs to become self-fulfilling prophecy. There is evidence of a gradual decrease in both sexual desire and frequency of sexual activity as people age, but this does not have to signal the loss of sexual responsiveness or pleasure altogether. Attitudes toward one's own sexual functioning can play an important role in maintaining sexual functioning into old age.

In the original Masters and Johnson (1966) study, 212 men beyond 50 years of age were interviewed concerning their sexual lives. Thirty-nine of these men, the oldest of whom was 89, agreed to have their sexual responses observed by the research team. Thirty-four women over the age of 50 were also observed, and another 118 interviews were conducted with women between 51 and 80 years of age. The following discussion is partly based on these interviews and observations. A summary of the information is found in Table 4.2.

Aging and Female Sexual Response

Two manifestations of postmenopausal hormonal imbalance can cause unpleasant sensations during sexual activity in some older women. First, because the vaginal lining has thinned and vaginal lubrication has

organizing effect: manner in which hormones control patterns of early development in the body.

activating effect: the direct influence some hormones can have on activating or deactivating sexual behavior.

androgen (ANN-dra-gin): a male hormone, such as testosterone, that affects physical development, sexual desire, and behavior. Testosterone is produced by both male and female sex glands and influences each sex in varying degrees.

possibly reduced, intercourse may produce irritation that persists as burning or itching afterward (Mansfield, Voda, & Koch, 1995). Water-soluble lubricants can relieve such problems, and estrogen-based creams may also help by increasing natural vaginal secretions. Second, some women also experience uterine cramping during and after orgasm. Masters and Johnson reported that some women beyond the age of 60 were so distressed by these sensations that they began to avoid coitus and orgasm. We know now that these unpleasant symptoms may be relieved by proper medical treatment.

As women age, there seems to be some decrease in orgasmic ability and a general tempering of the usual physiological responses to sexual arousal. This is a very gradual process of change and is somewhat dependent on how sexually active a particular woman remains. For heterosexual women over the age of 70 who have been involved in long-term relationships, their degree of sexual involvement may have a great deal to do with the availability and capability of their male partners. Their partners are generally older and thus more susceptible to medical conditions that interfere with sex. Older people of either gender whose bodies undergo regular sexual stimulation seem to maintain more intense levels of sexual response than do those who seldom participate in sex (Cross, 1993).

One effect of aging on female sexual response is a lengthening of the time for vaginal lubrication and other early signs of sexual arousal to take place. There is also less enlargement of the clitoris, labia, uterus, and breasts during sexual arousal. Orgasm takes a bit longer to occur in older women, and there are usually fewer orgasmic contractions of the vagina, uterus, and

pelvic floor. However, women who have a history of multiple orgasms apparently retain this capability even into very old age. The resolution phase of female sexual response, during which the body returns to its unexcited state, appears to be relatively unaffected by the aging process.

It is important to emphasize that how much of a decline in sexual response patterns an older woman experiences seems to depend on how sexually involved she remains. This in turn depends on factors such as the woman's health, the availability of a partner, the amount of privacy she is afforded, her attitudes and values about sexuality, and the degree of priority she has always placed on her sexual feelings and behaviors. For these reasons, some women remain sexually vital until the end of their lives, whereas others forgo sexual pleasures long before that time and gradually lose their abilities to respond sexually. Put in simple and direct language, this concept is often summarized by the phrase "use it or lose it."

Aging and Male Sexual Response

How responsive men remain in their older years seems to depend on a variety of physical, social, and psychological factors. Socially, they may lose their longstanding sexual partner or live in a setting that provides little privacy for sexual expression. Because there is a natural "slowing down" process, some men begin to feel insecure about their sexual capabilities. They may fear sexual "failure," usually meaning erection problems of various sorts, and eventually withdraw from sexual activities (Cowley, 1996). They may assume that aging is rendering them incapable of sexual performance. As a result, the amount of sexual stimulation they seek is drastically reduced, and the priority they assign to sex is lowered. This can eventually lead to at least a temporary loss of the ability to respond. Men who are in good general physical health may eventually restimulate their sexual interests and response patterns, should a change in life situation make this appropriate. This might include the availability of a new sexual partner, a renewed sense of self-worth, or sexuality education that makes the man aware of how his responses can be expected to change.

There are three aspects of male sexual response that undergo predictable changes as men age. The first is erection. For a man in his seventies, it takes two to three times longer to achieve full penile erection than it did in the man's younger years, and he usually requires direct penile stimulation. Although it is perfectly normal for men of any age to experience waxing and waning of erection during prolonged sexual arousal, it is more difficult for older men to reestablish full rigidity once erection has been partially lost. The angle of

Table 4.2 *Effects of Aging on Female and Male Sexual Response*

Changes in the Aging Female	Changes in the Aging Male
Thinning of vaginal lining	Some atrophy of testicular tissue
Reduction in vaginal lubrication	Reduction in secretion of preejaculatory fluid and amount of semen produced
Increase in uterine cramping associated with orgasm	Testes do not elevate as much during sexual arousal
Increase in amount of time needed to experience sexual arousal and vaginal lubrication	Increase in amount of time needed to achieve full penile erection
Increase in time of stimulation required to reach orgasm, and fewer muscular contractions associated with orgasm	Increase in time of stimulation required to reach orgasm, and strength of orgasmic muscular contractions is reduced
Resolution to unexcited state remains about the same	Resolution to unexcited state happens more quickly
Women who have been multiorgasmic seem to retain the capability	Refractory period lengthens, so the time before a man may be restimulated to orgasm tends to increase

Source: W. Masters and V. E. Johnson, *Human Sexual Response,* 1966, Little, Brown and Company, Boston, MA. Reprinted by permission of Masters and Johnson Institute, St. Louis, MO.

the erect penis up from the body also decreases with age (Cowley, 1996; Segraves & Segraves, 1995).

The second change relates to male orgasm and ejaculation. Older men take longer to reach orgasm than they did earlier in their lives. The strength of the orgasmic contractions is reduced, so that semen is ejaculated with less force, sometimes just seeping out of the urethra. The frequency with which men desire orgasm also seems to decline somewhat as they age. Except in rare instances, men over 60 are completely satisfied by one or, at the most, two orgasms in a week. They may enjoy participating in sexual behavior more frequently than that, experiencing full erection but no orgasm. The urge to achieve orgasm seems to be reduced with age (Segraves & Segraves, 1995). The third change is a lengthening of the male refractory period, so that by their late fifties or early sixties most men cannot achieve erections again for 12 to 24 hours

after ejaculation (Schiavi, Schreiner-Engle, Mandell, & Schanzer, 1990).

There are also decreases in other aspects of the aging male's sexual response. There is a reduction in the amount of preejaculatory secretion from the Cowper's glands and in the amount of semen produced. The testes and scrotum do not enlarge as much during sexual arousal, nor do the testes elevate so much within the scrotum. The resolution phase of men tends to occur more rapidly with age, and the penis may lose its erection after ejaculation much more rapidly (Segraves & Segraves, 1995).

These changes in female and male sexual response are not necessarily negative developments for people's sexual lives. In fact, many men and women find increased enjoyment in the moderating responses brought about by aging. There is more about sexuality and aging in chapter 6, "Sexuality through the Life Cycle."

Self-Evaluation

Sexual Arousal and Response in Your Life

This is a highly personal assessment meant for your individual use only. It can help you to evaluate and understand some of your reactions to and feelings about your own sexual arousability and responsiveness. As this chapter has emphasized, different people seem to

have different levels of arousability and different cues or sensitivities that can activate or deactivate (turn on or turn off) sexual response. There is no single "right" or "normal" way to be.

Complete the questionnaire first and then continue reading to understand what you may learn from it. This is not in any way meant to be a scientific test; it is only a simple instrument to help you further clarify some of your own reactions.

Using this scale:

5 = Strongly Agree
4 = Somewhat Agree
3 = Neutral/Uncertain
2 = Somewhat Disagree
1 = Strongly Disagree

Rate the following statements for yourself. (You may *not* want to write your responses in the book for others to see.)

1. ___ I find myself thinking about sexual things frequently.

2. ___ I think about sex more than the average person.

3. ___ My thoughts about sex often lead to sexual arousal.

4. ___ I experience sexual arousal several times a week.

5. ___ I can reach orgasm during a sexual experience anytime I wish.

6. ___ In general, I have positive feelings about my own sexual responsiveness.

7. ___ I enjoy the sensations of sexual excitement in my sex organs and in the rest of my body.

8. ___ I like experiencing orgasm (or do not mind at all if I do not reach orgasm) during sexual activity.

9. ___ I know very clearly what turns me on sexually.

10. ___ I am very comfortable with the place that sexual arousal and responsiveness have in my life.

11. ___ Sometimes I get sexually aroused at inappropriate or embarrassing times.

12. ___ I wish I could get sexually aroused more easily than I do.

13. ___ I never/rarely reach orgasm, and this concerns me.

14. ___ (If applicable now or in the past) My partner sometimes seems dissatisfied with my sexual responses.

15. ___ (If applicable) My partner wishes I would get sexually aroused more easily/often.

Evaluating Your Responses

As you examine your responses to the various items, it would be helpful to evaluate them in three different blocks:

Items 1–5: These items relate to the frequency with which you experience sexual thoughts and arousal. The higher your numbers, the more frequently you think about sexuality and experience arousal and response. As you look at the numbers, do you see any trend? What do they say to you about your sexuality?

Items 6–10: These items can help you examine your reactions to your sexual responsiveness. The higher the numbers, the greater degree of relative satisfaction you are indicating for your patterns of sexual arousal and response. The lower the numbers, the greater the likelihood that you are not particularly happy or satisfied with the ways in which you respond to sexual stimuli.

Items 11–15: These items focus on the dissatisfactions you may be experiencing with regard to your sexual responsiveness and—if applicable—with how that responsiveness fits into a relationship. Higher numbers would suggest that you have a fair amount of discomfort and negative reaction to various aspects of your sexual arousal and response.

What Does It All Mean for You?

Keep in mind that this assessment is a very rough measure of some of your own perceptions. It should help you clarify some of your own thoughts and reactions regarding your sexual responses. As you survey your responses, is there any picture that seems to emerge? Do you seem to be an individual who is quite comfortable and satisfied with his/her patterns of sexual arousal and response? Are you unsure of yourself and unable to get a very clear look at how sexual responsiveness fits into your life? Have your responses to the items suggested that you have a great deal of dissatisfaction about your sexuality?

If you are able to get some general sense of how you react to your own sexual arousal and response, it may be valuable to you as you read further chapters in this text. It may also alert you to the fact that you have some issues worth considering, some of which may be positive and some negative. If you feel that your profile is reflective of some sexual concerns and problems, you may want to seek some professional help or consultation. You may want to move ahead to the section on Preventing and Dealing with Problematic Sex (pp. 477–478) in chapter 14 and complete the Self-Evaluation on pages 480–481. It can focus your attention on what steps you might want to take.

Chapter Summary

1. Different cultures and spiritual traditions treat human sexual response in different ways.

2. Masters and Johnson were among the first researchers to study scientifically the body's physiological changes during sexual response. They developed a four-phase model involving excitement, plateau, orgasm, and resolution.

3. A three-phase model proposed by Kaplan views sexual response as beginning with psychological desire with a subsequent buildup of blood and muscular tension, followed by reversal of these states as triggered by orgasm.

4. The term "desire phase" refers to the level of interest in sexual activity an individual may experience.

5. There are many individual differences in human sexual response, and good communication is essential to developing mutual understanding in a sexual relationship.

6. Sexual response must be activated by some mechanism of sexual arousal. Several models of arousal have been proposed.

7. Penile and vaginal plethysmographs have been used in research to measure and compare the degree of sexual arousal in women and men. These studies show that people's perceptions of their own sexual response do not always match physiological measures.

8. Arousal stimuli may be internal or external, roughly corresponding to a central arousal system located in the brain, and a peripheral arousal system that picks up cues from the genitals, senses, and spinal reflexes.

9. Emotions and other psychological processes play a significant role in activating or deactivating sexual response.

10. When the mind ascribes sexual meaning to some stimulus, the genital physiological response may be quite automatic.

11. Studies reveal that there are more similarities than differences in arousal patterns of males and females.

12. In females, the vagina becomes lubricated during sexual excitement, and an orgasmic platform develops with the swelling of the clitoris and labia. The clitoral glans eventually retracts under its foreskin. Resolution refers to the return of the body to its unexcited state.

13. Some women have the potential for more than one orgasm during a single sexual experience. Women report clitoral, vaginal, uterine, and "blended" orgasms.

14. Some researchers claim that there is a particularly sensitive spot on the inner front part of the vagina that swells during female arousal. This has been called the G spot.

15. It has been proposed that some women ejaculate a substance from the urethra during intense orgasms.

16. Kegel exercises can keep the urogenital musculature in good tone and may increase the intensity or pleasure of orgasm.

17. In males, penile erection is a major sign of excitement, and there are also increases in the size of the testes and scrotum. The testes move upward in the scrotum.

18. In both women and men, sexual response involves increases in respiration, heart rate, blood pressure, and general muscular tension. A reddish "sex flush" appears on the skin of the upper body in some individuals, and nipple erection may also occur.

19. Orgasm is the pleasurable release of sexual tension, involving a series of muscular contractions in both sexes. Ejaculation usually accompanies orgasm in men.

20. During resolution, at the end of sexual response in men, there is generally a refractory period during which there can be no restimulation to orgasm.

21. It is still not completely clear what role hormones may play in regulating sexual response. Testosterone, an androgen present in both men and women, acts as an activator for sexual desire.

22. Androgens may act more directly on the central arousal system than on the peripheral arousal system.

23. In humans, sexual arousal and responsiveness seem to be controlled by both hormonal and social factors.

24. Both men and women may experience slower arousal and somewhat less intensity of response as they age. People who have been more sexually active during their younger years will tend to maintain a higher level of sexual activity.

Focus on Health Questions

You will find in this section the kinds of questions that you may have concerning your own health and sexuality. The page references indicate where in the text the answer is located; the exact place is marked with the logo: F⊕H

1. I do not seem to get sexually aroused as quickly as my partner. Does that mean there is something wrong? 95

2. Why is it that when I am turned on, the skin on my neck and shoulders gets all red? 101

3. Do all women have more than one orgasm during sex? 102

4. How can I do the exercises that help strengthen the muscles involved with orgasm? 105

5. Are men's orgasms different from women's? 106

6. Do hormones control my sex drive? 109

7. When I get old, will I still be able to function sexually? 109–111

Annotated Readings

Bonheim, J. (1997). *Aphrodite's daughters: Women's sexual stories and the journey to the soul.* New York: Simon and Schuster. Includes many anecdotal accounts of women's sexual lives, placed in a context of religion and spirituality.

Eisler, R. (1995). *Sacred pleasure: Sex, myth, and the politics of the body.* New York: HarperCollins. A book that focuses on the cultural dynamics of sexual response and all of its implications for both women and men.

Keesling, B. (1993). *Sexual pleasure: Reaching new heights of sexual arousal and intimacy.* Alameda, CA: Hunter House. One of many sexual self-help books, this is a sensible and well-written illustrated guide to sexual pleasure.

Masters, W., & Johnson, V. (1966). *Human sexual response.* Boston: Little, Brown. For any serious student wanting thorough information on the sexual response cycle, this original text describing Masters and Johnson's pioneering work is a must.

McCormick, N. B. (1994). *Sexual salvation: Affirming women's sexual rights and pleasures.* New York: Praeger Press. This book takes a new look at female sexuality and sexual response, bringing into understandable perspective many of the more controversial and confusing aspects of women's sexual pleasure.

Yaffe, M., & Fenwick, E. (1992). *Sexual happiness for men: A practical approach.* New York: Henry Holt.

Yaffe, M., & Fenwick, E. (1992). *Sexual happiness for women: A practical approach.* New York: Henry Holt. The two books above, each explicitly illustrated, provide companion guides for enhancing sexual responsiveness in either gender.

Chapter 5
Developmental and Social Perspectives on Gender

Chapter Outline

Note: A selection of Focus on Health questions appears at the end of each chapter. Answers to these questions are indicated within the chapter by the symbol in the margin.   **FOH**

I consider myself to be a fairly sensitive guy, and I want to treat women with respect and a sense of equality, but I'm never sure what the rules are. Do I open doors for her, or should we take turns? Am I supposed to pay for dinner every time, or do we share the cost? Who is supposed to give the first signals about being interested in having sex?

—Statement from a male student

Being a sexual human being amounts to far more than the sexual organs with which we were born and the ways in which these organs are activated by sexual arousal. There are many other dimensions of sexuality as it relates to individual people: Why is it that humans come in two sexes? Perhaps the question should be, are there really just two sexes? What factors influence the development of male and female genitals before birth? What leads to our awareness of ourselves as girl or boy, feminine or masculine, or some combination of the two? Are gender roles determined by biology, socialization, or a combination of the two? How does gender fit into contemporary social and political trends? These are some of the questions that we will explore in this chapter.

Do you think gender roles are inborn or learned? Explain your answer.

How Many Sexes Are There?

Our culture has generally only been willing to recognize two sexes: female and male. Those are the two categories from which we are allowed to choose when filling out most forms. Our legal systems also require that everyone be categorized as either male or female, and newborns must be identified on birth certificates as one or the other. But are things really that simple?

There are documented cases of individuals who have the physical characteristics of both the male and female. In sixteenth-century England, because succession of wealth and title often depended on an individual's gender, the courts decided that succession would be based on "the kind of sex that doth prevail," meaning which sex seemed dominant in the individual by the time of adulthood (Money, 1994). In 1843, an election for the town board of Salisbury, Connecticut, was tied, and its outcome hinged on the vote of a person named Levi Suydam, whom the local citizens considered to be more woman than man. Women were not allowed to vote, but a physician examined Suydam, found a penislike structure, and declared him a male. He was thus eligible to cast a ballot and helped elect a member of the Whig party by a single vote. However, word quickly spread that penis or not, Suydam also had a vaginal opening and menstruated regularly (Fausto-Sterling, 1993).

The concept of gender or sexes obviously has biological roots, but social constructionism holds that even biological facts become interpreted through the screen of cultural assumptions. Thomas Laqueur (1992) argues, for example, that from the time of the ancient Greeks until the end of the seventeenth century, the Western cultural model was actually one-sexed; one sex was male, and the structures of the female anatomy were seen as inverted or underdeveloped forms of the male sex organs. In other words, "both" sexes were actually just different forms of a single sex, one more fully developed than the other. During the early eighteenth century, a clearer distinction began to emerge, recognizing female and male as two different sexes.

Intersexuality

On the larger anatomical level, some human beings do not fit the standardized male-female categories. Medical investigators have long recognized the existence of **intersexuality,** a term that refers to some mixture of male and female anatomical characteristics, often reflected in the presence of ambiguous genitalia. At least three major subgroups of intersexes exist: **true hermaphrodites,** who have one testis and one ovary; male **pseudohermaphrodites,** who have testes and some female genitals but no ovaries; and female pseudohermaphrodites, who have ovaries and some male genitals but no testes (Zucker, 2000).

If your child were born intersexed, what course of action would you consider?

In some historical periods, intersexuality was accepted as a "third sex," distinct from male and female. In many societies, alternative social statuses or gender roles are available for intersexed individuals. The American Plains Indians once assigned the social status of *berdache* to men who did not have the skill or interest for typically masculine, aggressive pursuits. The berdache was considered to hold special powers and sometimes served as a shaman for healing practices or in sacred ceremonies (Crapo, 1996). In India, a

---

intersexuality: a combination of female and male anatomical structures, so that the individual cannot be clearly defined as male or female.

true hermaphrodite: a person who has one testis and one ovary. External appearance may vary.

pseudohermaphrodite: a person who possesses either testes or ovaries in combination with some external genitals of the other sex.

third gender called the *hijra* includes elements of both female and male roles, and they are considered sacred. A genetic defect within the Sambia tribe of Papua New Guinea has led to the birth of hermaphrodites who are assigned the role of *kwolu-aatmwol,* meaning an individual whose genitals appear to be female but who will eventually develop male secondary sex characteristics. Such individuals are not expected to take either male or female roles in their society, but they are allowed to become shamans or spirit doctors (Money, 1994). These are all examples of alternative gender categories that have become socially institutionalized. The Intersex Society of North America, which was recently established in the United States, was founded to offer support and information for intersexed people and their families.

In modern Western cultures that tend to accept the two-sex model, such combinations of the sexes have been viewed as biological accidents or diseases. Babies who are born with ambiguous genitalia are usually subjected to hormonal and surgical treatment to make them into either male or female. Some workers in this field have suggested that this represents a narrow-minded perspective and that intersexuality should be accepted as a legitimate position on the spectrum between female and male. Others recognize that children typically need to be raised as male or female because that is the social imperative, but they believe that sometimes their surgical alteration should be postponed until they may play a role in the decision making (Diamond, 1998; Diamond & Sigmundson, 1997).

Case histories are offered of intersexed people who adjusted to their sexuality quite comfortably (Fausto-Sterling, 1993; Laurent, 1995). However, once intersexuality began to be viewed as a mistake of nature, the only alternative was believed to be medical treatment. It was thought that the stigma of being so very different anatomically would prevent intersexed people from being well adjusted. There is evidence that intersex children ultimately tend to have later emotional and psychological problems (Dittmann, 1998; Slijper, Drop, Molenaar, & Keizer-Schrama, 1998). From this perspective, people with anatomical errors are seen as incomplete males or females and not as constituting a separate sex. It also means that they are often subjected to medical intervention as infants, a fact that some resent later in their lives (Angier, 1996; Diamond, 1998). This view holds that in the evolutionary scheme of things, humans have always been two-sexed, and to speak of other sexes simply does not make biological sense (Hunter, 1995).

These various perspectives represent salient reminders that even though our culture often attempts to define us in very polarized ways as female or male, femaleness and maleness are better understood as differing sets of traits with many variations. How these variations occur, and how they are defined, is explored further in this chapter.

The Biological Levels of Sex

Sexual development, and the expression of one's biological sex, may be seen on four major levels (Hunter, 1995; Zucker, 2000):

1. *Genetic Sex* This begins with the genetic combination that is created when sperm enters the egg at the moment of conception. A genetic map is established that will lead to the development of further expressions of maleness, femaleness, or intersexuality.
2. *Gonadal Sex* The genetic map leads to the development of **gonads** that will eventually produce hormones within the individual's body. Gonads will be either testes or ovaries, and the hormones they produce—or do not produce—have profound effects on sexual development.
3. *Body Sex* The hormones present, or lacking, during development will partly determine what sorts of internal and external sex organs become apparent in the individual. The anatomical structures with which a person is born will then play a major role in how the person is categorized and how the individual feels about himself, herself, or him-herself.
4. *Brain Sex* How the brain may be sexually differentiated is one of the most intriguing questions facing sexologists today. There is growing evidence that hormonal influences exerted by the gonads on the brain before and after birth play some role in determining certain "male-type" or "female-type" behaviors.

These biological levels of sex do not consider the more complex psychological, social, and cultural implications of being male, female, or intersexed. You will see in the next section of this chapter that as a human being develops from a fertilized egg through the various stages to adulthood, all of these different aspects of being a sexual person begin to merge and play a role.

Gender Identity and Role

Although most people do tend to fit a female or male category anatomically, the picture becomes more confusing when we examine their sense of themselves as men or women, or as masculine or feminine. Human

gonads: sex and reproductive glands, either testes or ovaries, that produce hormones and, eventually, reproductive cells (sperm or eggs).

beings have a persistent inner sense of themselves as female, male, or some cross-gendered position between the two. This private, inner experience of one's gender has been termed **gender identity.** People also outwardly demonstrate to others the degree to which they are male, female, or cross-gendered in relationship to their society through what they say, their attempts at sexual attractiveness, and their behavior. This public, outward expression of gender is called **gender role.** The qualities that individuals use to assess and understand their own gender are partly physical (such as body shape and sex organs) and partly sociocultural (such as hair length, clothing, and accepted standards of masculine and feminine behavior in a particular society).

What might be some of the effects on a person who experiences gender identity/gender role conflict?

◪ Sexual Differentiation

The process by which organisms develop into the different sexes or genders is called **sexual differentiation.** It begins with the genetic level at the moment of conception when a sperm enters an ovum. At that moment, a program is set into motion that will eventually combine with all of the hormonal, social, and psychological factors that ultimately result in an adult gender identity. The factors that can exert influences along the way are incredibly varied and complex. These factors have been well documented by Money (1977, 1994), Money and Anke Ehrhardt (1972), Gerall, Moltz, and Ward (1992), and Hunter (1995). The model that follows took shape gradually in the latter part of the twentieth century, and it is still being clarified by new research. It is useful to group the determinants of human gender identity into three categories: prenatal factors, factors of infancy and childhood, and factors at puberty.

1. *Prenatal Factors*   Before an infant is born, a variety of genetic, gonadal, and developmental factors interact with one another to set the stage for later identification as female or male. Even before a baby is born and assigned a sex, much of the groundwork for her or his gender identity has been established.
2. *Factors of Infancy and Childhood*   As soon as a baby is born, its body sex is assigned by the outward appearance of its genitals. Although that may seem to be a simple enough task, there are sometimes anomalies of fetal development that make it impossible to assign the baby's sex as clearly female or male. Ambiguous genitalia create situations in which decisions must be made about what sort of medical interventions, if any, the parents want to make so that the child may fit

into a particular category. Once these decisions and interventions are made, the infant is raised as a girl or a boy, regardless of what the genetic sex might be (Slijper et al., 1998). As stated earlier, Western cultural imperatives make it less likely that a child will be left in an intersexed state (Diamond, 1998). Eventually, every child begins to develop distinct impressions and perceptions of her or his own body and sex organs. All of these factors, in conjunction with the structure and function of the brain, determine the "core" gender identity of the child.

3. *Factors at Puberty*   Every day, children continue to receive confirmation or disconfirmation of their gender identity from other people. At puberty, new hormonal changes occur in the body that lead to further growth of the genitals and the appearance of secondary sex characteristics. There is also an increase in sexual interests around the time of puberty. These developments—if they proceed in the usual way—further confirm the individual's gender identity in the move toward adulthood. If the pubertal changes do not occur as expected—if the gender identity program has some built-in inconsistencies—and the child's gender identity is not confirmed, the result is often confusion and emotional crisis. Now we can take a closer look at some of the details in each of these categories.

Prenatal Factors
Chromosomes

The earliest factor that determines a human being's sex and initiates the program for determining gender identity happens at **conception,** when chromosomes from both parents are combined. Typically, human gametes—the ovum (egg) and sperm—each contain

---

gender identity: a person's inner experience of gender: feelings of maleness, femaleness, or some ambivalent position between the two.

gender role: the outward expression and demonstration of gender identity, through behaviors, attire, and culturally determined characteristics of femininity and masculinity.

sexual differentiation: the developmental processes—biological, social, and psychological—that lead to different sexes or genders.

conception: the process by which a sperm unites with an egg, normally joining 23 pairs of chromosomes to establish the genetic "blueprint" for a new individual. The sex chromosomes establish its sex: XX for female and XY for male.

23 chromosomes, one of which is a sex chromosome. The sex chromosome carried by the sperm may either be an X chromosome or a Y chromosome. The egg contains only an X chromosome. If an X-bearing sperm fertilizes an egg, the resulting XX combination of sex chromosomes establishes a genetic program to produce a female. If the egg is fertilized by a Y-bearing sperm, the resultant XY combination is destined to become a male. If the genetic mechanisms function normally, the program is well under way toward producing a female or male child (see Fig. 5.1).

A gene that seems to play a major role in the development of male organs has been pinpointed on the Y chromosome, a chromosome that has little other genetic activity (Lahn & Page, 1997). It has been labeled **SRY,** for sex-determining region of Y, because it is the presence or absence of this section of the chromosome that is significant in determining whether testes or ovaries will develop in the fetus (Rice, 1996). Because the more genetically active X chromosome contains many genes that are needed by both females and males, it has been suspected for decades that nature must provide some sort of regulating mechanism to prevent females with their double-X combination from getting an excess of gene products and also from preventing single-X males from having a deficiency of these same products. It has now been demonstrated that there is a *dosage compensation* mechanism that seems to equalize genetic expression from the X chromosomes for females and males (Williams, 1995).

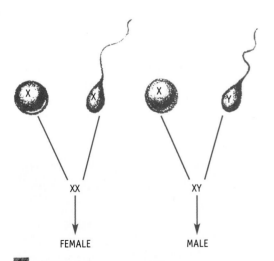

FIGURE 5.1 *Chromosomes*

Chromosomes are genetic material in the nucleus of every cell. The sex of the offspring is determined at fertilization by the type of chromosome in the sperm. All egg cells and half the sperm cells contain an X sex chromosome, and the remaining sperm have Y sex chromosomes. A zygote with two X chromosomes will become a female, and a zygote with one X and one Y will become a male.

Research involving a genetic error in dosage compensation mechanisms led to the possible discovery of a gene on the X chromosome that may also be a sex-determining gene playing some role in the development of females. Four people were identified who had an XY chromosomal pattern and yet developed some female genitalia and had been raised as girls. Researchers believed that these individuals had an abnormal, double set of the female-producing genes on the X chromosome, and that this double dose had apparently overridden the influence of the SRY gene on the Y chromosome that would have typically taken precedence over the X chromosome to produce a male. This suggested that such "sex reversal" is dosage-sensitive, depending on the dosage (number) of female-determining genes present (Bardoni et al., 1994). The gene that likely determines sex on the X chromosome has been identified as a region called **DAX-1** (Marx, 1995; Schafer, 1995). There is at least one other gene that seems to play a crucial role in sexual differentiation, and there may well be others (Ryner & Swain, 1995).

The actual mechanisms by which any of these genes may operate to develop male or female characteristics are not yet fully understood. In rare cases, a fertilized egg has only one X chromosome, or the other X chromosome is somehow damaged. The individual produced develops a female body, but the ovaries will not develop normally, and the adult woman will be unable to produce children (Turner syndrome). A fertilized egg left with only a Y sex chromosome and no X apparently cannot survive. No human being has ever been found with only a Y sex chromosome.

Other erroneous sex chromosome combinations in humans are XXX (triple-X syndrome), XXY (Klinefelter syndrome), and XYY (Supernumerary Y syndrome). In some cases, there may be a normal pairing of sex chromosomes but some defect in a gene on one of the chromosomes. Individuals born with these conditions usually show abnormal development of the sex organs, unusual body shape, behavioral disorders, or mental and emotional retardation, as summarized in Table 5.1.

Fetal Gonads

Up until the eighth week of development, it is impossible to determine the sex of a human embryo by the appearance of external genitalia (sex organs). Yet the genetic plan contained within the sex chromosomes

SRY: the sex-determining region of the Y chromosome.

DAX-1: the region on the X chromosome that seems to play a role in sexual differentiation.

Table 5.1   Human Sex Chromosome Disorders That Affect Gender

Abnormal Chromosome Combination	Medical Name	Characteristics of Individual
XXY	Klinefelter syndrome	Male genitals, but with female secondary sex characteristics. Penis, scrotum, and testes are small; enlarged breasts. Sometimes timid and withdrawn; possible learning disabilities; sterile.
XO (no Y present; only one X)	Turner syndrome	Female external genitals; ovaries lacking; lack of menstruation, pubic hair and breast development. Stunted growth, with several body abnormalities. Sense of direction and spatial relationships may be abnormal.
XO/XY	Mixed gonadal dysgenesis	May have female or male genitals, or a combination of the two. Usually no other bodily abnormalities, except may not mature sexually without treatment, and tend toward short body stature.
XYY	Supernumerary Y syndrome	Appearance of normal male. Tend to be tall in stature. May show some lack of control over impulsive behaviors. Usually average intelligence levels.
XXX	Triple-X syndrome	Appearance of normal female. Sometimes infertile. Occasional impairment of intelligence.
XX/XY	May be a true hermaphrodite	Variable. Have some combination of both ovarian and testicular tissues. Usually have uterus. External genitals may be distinctly masculine or feminine, or may be an ambiguous combination of both. At puberty, most experience breast enlargement, and the majority menstruate.

carries the necessary information to produce gonads and genital organs. At first a pair of tiny, sexless gonads form internally, having the potential of becoming testes or ovaries. There are also two pairs of duct systems present in the embryo: the **Müllerian ducts,** which represent potential female reproductive organs, and the **Wolffian ducts,** which represent potential male reproductive structures. Research has shown that it is the presence or absence of the Y chromosome, with its SRY, that determines whether the gonads differentiate into testes or ovaries. As long as at least one Y and one X chromosome are present, testes are normally produced. Any combination of sex chromosomes lacking a Y produces ovaries. The DAX-1 gene may well play some sort of role in this process, but it is not yet understood. If testes are to be formed from the fetal gonads, they appear during the sixth week of development. Ovaries develop at a later stage, but they appear by the twelfth week. Variations in these patterns are rare (see Fig. 5.2).

Fetal Hormones

Fetal gonads that are programmed by the chromosomes to produce a female will automatically develop into ovaries. However, if the gonads are programmed to produce a male, another process is required, con-

trolled by the SRY normally carried on the Y chromosome. A substance called **H-Y antigen** has been identified as the chemical agent that helps transform the fetal gonads into testes (Pennisi, 1995). When testes are produced, they also begin secreting two hormones. Testosterone promotes development of the Wolffian ducts into internal male sexual and reproductive structures. The SRY gene also activates the fetal testes to produce **anti-Müllerian hormone (AMH),** which suppresses the development of the Müllerian

Müllerian ducts (myul-EAR-ee-an): embryonic structures that develop into female sexual and reproductive organs unless inhibited by male hormones.

Wolffian ducts (WOOL-fee-an): embryonic structures that develop into male sexual and reproductive organs if male hormones are present.

H-Y antigen: a biochemical produced in an embryo when the Y chromosome is present; it plays a role in the development of fetal gonads into testes.

anti-Müllerian hormone (AMH): secretion of the fetal testes that prevents further development of female structures from the Müllerian ducts.

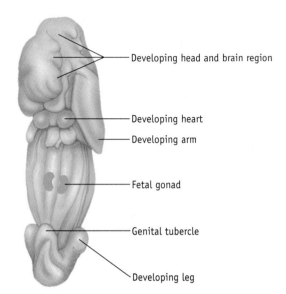

- Developing head and brain region
- Developing heart
- Developing arm
- Fetal gonad
- Genital tubercle
- Developing leg

FIGURE 5.2 *Fetal Gonads in a Developing Fetus*

During the first weeks of development, male and female embryos are anatomically identical. Two primitive gonads form during the fifth and sixth weeks of pregnancy. An H-Y antigen is necessary if the gonads are to develop into testes. Without an H-Y antigen, the gonads develop into ovaries.

ducts into the female organs (Haqq et al., 1994; Hunter, 1995).

It has been suggested that the complicated genetic and biochemical interactions that must be initiated to form a male may well make males somewhat more vulnerable to developmental problems and variations. It is known, for example, that the incidence of mental retardation, learning disabilities, certain speech pathologies, and variant sexual behaviors is higher among males than among females (Reinisch & Sanders, 1992). As far as we now know, development of female sex and reproductive organs does not depend on the production of any hormones. If the SRY gene is not present, so that male hormones are not produced, the fetal gonads become ovaries and the Müllerian ducts develop into the uterus, fallopian tubes, and part of the vagina. Without testosterone to stimulate their development, the Wolffian ducts simply disintegrate. It was once assumed that developing as a female was in a sense the "default" gender of the fetus when SRY was not present. However, the discovery of the DAX-1 gene segment on the X chromosome has called that assumption into question. In fact, there may be an entirely different mechanism, not yet discovered, by which the DAX-1 gene leads to an interruption of male genital formation and causes female genitals to form (Marx, 1995). Future research may help to clarify these mechanisms.

There are some other rare problems that can arise at these early stages of sexual differentiation. For example, if a male (XY) fetus's new testes produce testosterone but lack AMH, the external male sex organs may develop normally, but the boy will also be born with a uterus and fallopian tubes as well as internal male organs. Other developmental discrepancies may lead to hermaphroditism, in which the individual is born with both testicular and ovarian tissue. In another condition, the male fetus lacks an enzyme necessary for normal synthesis of male hormones. Affected babies usually die, but those who live have very small penises and may at birth be mistakenly identified as females. If testosterone or related androgenic hormones somehow enter the bloodstream of a developing female (XX) fetus—usually because of some medical condition such as a testosterone-producing tumor in the pregnant mother—the baby girl is born either with an enlarged clitoris or a normal-appearing penis and empty scrotum. These and related conditions can lead to the erroneous assignment of the girl as a male at birth.

Development of Body Sex: Male or Female Genitals

Until the eighth week of fetal life, the external genitals are indistinguishable as male or female. There is a tiny, sexless genital tubercle on the lower part of the fetus. By the twelfth week of development, the male or female sex organs are clearly distinguishable. Development of the testes, scrotum, and penis require the presence of **dihydrotestosterone (DHT),** which is derived from testosterone. Without DHT, the fetal genital tissue develops into the clitoris and vulval lips (see Fig. 5.3). Chromosomal and hormonal abnormalities can cause the external genitals and their inner ducts to develop abnormally, as we have already seen in the section on fetal hormones.

Brain Sex and Fetal Hormones

One of the most exciting advances in animal sex research was the discovery that fetal hormones not only control the development of the fetus's sex organs but may also affect development of parts of the brain and pituitary gland. Research with human brains is beginning to demonstrate differences between the number and location of nerve synapses in the hypothalamuses of male and female brains. There is some research evidence to support the contentions that such differences could lead to different behavior patterns later in life

dihydrotestosterone (DHT): a chemical produced by the fetal testes that promotes further development of the testes, scrotum, and penis in the fetus.

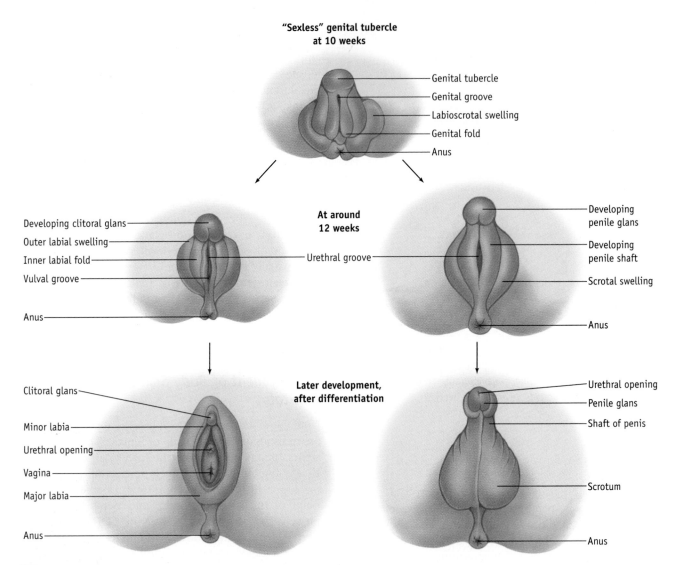

"Sexless" genital tubercle
at 10 weeks

— Genital tubercle
— Genital groove
— Labioscrotal swelling
— Genital fold
— Anus

**At around
12 weeks**

Developing clitoral glans —
Outer labial swelling —
Inner labial fold —
Vulval groove —

— Urethral groove

Anus —

Developing
penile glans —

Developing
penile shaft —

Scrotal swelling —

Anus —

**Later development,
after differentiation**

Clitoral glans —

Minor labia —

Urethral opening —

Vagina —

Major labia —

Anus —

— Urethral opening
— Penile glans
— Shaft of penis

— Scrotum

— Anus

FIGURE 5.3   *Differentiation of Male and Female Genitals*

From the tenth week of fetal development, sexual differentiation occurs at three different levels—internal sex organs, external sex structures, and the brain. The development of the male is largely controlled by the hormone testosterone. Both the ovaries and the testes first develop in the abdomen; later, the ovaries move into the pelvis, and the testes descend into the scrotum.

(Rubinow & Schmidt, 1996; Swaab & Gofman, 1995). In many lower mammals, predictably different behavior is observed in the male and female of the species. It was originally assumed that hormones had little to do with the determination of differing behavior in the sexes. The work of William Young (1961) and subsequent researchers led to the hypothesis that the presence of testosterone in the fetus of many mammals affects the structures and pathways of the central nervous system, particularly the brain, in such a way as to produce masculine behavior in the adult mammal. If testosterone is not present, the adult behavior becomes feminine. In many mammals, there seems to be a critical period at some point in development and sexual differentiation when the presence of male hor-

mones has this "masculinizing" effect. At the same time, there is a concurrent but independent process of defeminization. The absence of androgens from the testes results in reverse processes: demasculinization and feminization (Olsen, 1992; Rubinow & Schmidt, 1996).

What Abnormalities of Sexual Differentiation Can Tell Us

The actual chemical mechanisms that control these processes are slowly being pieced together, sometimes through animal studies. Because the human brain is structurally different from, and more highly developed than, animal brains, it is risky to extrapolate the find-

Table 5.2	*Summary of Abnormal Forms of Sexual Differentiation*		
Condition	**Cause**	**Typical Characteristics**	**Predominant Gender Identity**
Fetally androgenized females	Hormones administered during pregnancy	Genetic females (XX) with enlarged, penis-like clitoris. Usually surgically corrected and raised as girls.	Masculine
Exposure to DES	Administration of DES to prevent miscarriage	In boys, less separateness of brain hemisphere functioning; lowered spatial abilities; less assertiveness.	Masculine in boys, with potential for more feminine traits
		In girls, there may be some masculinizing effects, but this is controversial.	Unknown for girls
Congenital adrenal hyperplasia (CAH)	Genital disorder in which androgens accumulate in the body	Masculinization of genitals in genetic females (XX). Even after surgical correction and being raised as female, these girls tend to prefer boys' toys and behavioral patterns, and have higher spatial abilities.	Either, with a tendency toward some masculine traits
Androgen insensitivity syndrome (AIS)	Body cells of genetic males are unable to respond normally to testosterone	Genetic males (XY) are born with normal-appearing female genitals, and are usually raised as girls. At puberty, they develop breasts but cannot menstruate. Tend to behave in feminine ways.	Feminine
DHT-deficiency syndrome	Lack of enzyme necessary for normal development of male sex organs	Genetic males (XY) are born with genitals that tend to appear male. At puberty, they begin to develop masculine secondary characteristics, and may then live as males.	Masculine

ings of animal research to human beings. There may well be critical periods in human development during which the interaction of biological (for example, hormonal) and environmental (for example, learning behavior from others) factors establish some permanent characteristics of the individual (Money, 1994; Zucker, 2000). Early hormonal influences may play a significant role in permanently modifying the abilities of tissues to react to later hormonal stimulation and may form the brain template on which patterns of behavior are then formed (Hines & Collaer, 1993; Swaab & Gofman, 1995; Tchernitchin & Tchernitchin, 1992). Studying some of the genetic abnormalities of sexual differentiation in humans, and some medical treatments that have exposed fetuses to hormonal chemicals, has provided fascinating insights into this issue. Some examples follow and are summarized in Table 5.2.

In 1963, one of a set of infant twin boys had his penis damaged beyond repair during a botched circumcision procedure. Experts advised the parents to have his testes removed, his genitalia surgically modified, and estrogen administered so that he could be raised as a girl. For years, the case was cited as proof that gender identity could be largely constructed by social influences because it was reported that the former anatomical boy had adjusted well to being raised as a girl. However, the patient was tracked down by other researchers in the mid-1990s, and a very differ-

ent story emerged. In fact, he reported that during his childhood he had always felt like a boy despite constant assurances that he was a girl. By junior high school, still being forced to dress as a girl, he was standing to urinate, and girls at his school finally forced her/him to use the boys' rest room. A physician and his father told him the truth about his background when he was 14, and he actively began to pursue re-identification as a male. By the age of 25, he had a penis reconstructed, his breasts were removed, and he had married a woman and adopted children. Today, he lives and works entirely as a man. This case is a reminder of the potential innate influences on forming gender identity and the complications that the medical profession faces when making decisions about infants with ambiguous or damaged genitalia (Diamond, 1998; Diamond & Sigmundson, 1997).

Fetally Androgenized Females

A medical mistake made in the 1950s led to one of the first studies proposing the idea of biological and environmental factors interacting at a critical period in human development to influence gender-related behavior. Several pregnant women were given hormones to prevent miscarriages. Later it was discovered that the hormones had a masculinizing effect on the developing fetuses. This resulted in the birth of several **fetally androgenized females** with enlarged clitorises and a few genetic females having penises. Most of the girls considered themselves to be tomboys and showed significantly more traditional boyish traits than a control group, including a high level of energy expenditure during play, wearing practical clothing, lack of interest in dolls and infants, and a preference for a future career outside the home rather than homemaking.

Although researchers who studied these girls felt that the most likely explanation was that the male hormones present during their fetal development had created a masculinizing effect on their brains, others countered that confusion on the part of parents might instead have affected their socialization. More recently, other studies have confirmed that fetal androgen exposure during the second 3 months of pregnancy is indeed associated with a masculinizing of behavior that cannot be completely explained by social influences (Udry, Morris, & Kovenock, 1995).

Exposure to Synthetic Hormones

Other evidence demonstrates that exposure of a fetus to certain synthetic hormones that are similar to male or female hormones can lead to eventual behavioral characteristics that could be considered masculine or feminine. Large doses of certain kinds of synthetic progestins used to treat other medical conditions during pregnancy seem to affect fetuses in much the same way that testosterone does. Some females exposed to these hormones have been born with genitals that have appeared to be more malelike, with enlarged clitorises, for example. Both females and males exposed to testosteronelike hormones have been studied for later characteristics and compared with controls. On several psychological scales, these individuals tended to score higher on various "masculinity" indexes (Reinisch & Sanders, 1992).

Another synthetic hormone, which is similar to the hormone estrogen, is called diethylstilbestrol, or DES. It was widely used to prevent miscarriage for a number of years, and there was some evidence to indicate that fetuses exposed to DES may have had resulting changes in their brain development. Men who had been exposed to DES before birth have shown a reduction in the separateness of brain hemisphere functioning as well as lowered spatial abilities in comparison to their unexposed brothers. Both of these effects may represent fetal feminization or demasculinizing of the brain because males generally tend to have greater separation of hemisphere functioning and somewhat better spatial abilities than females (Reinisch & Sanders, 1992). Some studies have also suggested that DES-exposed females

might show masculinization of traits, although there is a fair amount of controversy over the effects of DES exposure on females (Hines & Collaer, 1993; Lish et al., 1992).

It is known that some anticonvulsant drugs alter hormone levels in animals, leading to disturbed sexual differentiation. A study of humans whose mothers had taken these drugs during pregnancy found that a higher proportion of them had experienced cross-gender behavior and confusion about their gender identity than those in a matched controlled group (Dessens et al., 1999).

Congenital Adrenal Hyperplasia

Congenital adrenal hyperplasia (CAH), sometimes called androgenital syndrome, is a genetic disorder that causes a buildup of androgenic hormones in the fetus or infant. Genetic females born with this condition often have masculinized genitals, and they may be surgically treated to create genitals that appear more female. There is evidence that girls with CAH tend to prefer toys and activities that are more typically considered for boys (Berenbaum & Hines, 1992), see themselves as tomboys and are more likely to have disorders with their gender identity (Slijper et al., 1992; Slijper, Drop, Molenaar, & Keizer-Schrama, 1998), and demonstrate more typically masculine traits than do their sisters (Dittman, Kappes, & Kappes, 1993). Conversely, boys who experience low levels of androgens during development seem to exhibit reduced visual-spatial abilities in comparison with other males. Research on the behavioral outcomes of such disorders has sometimes demonstrated conflicting evidence, and there is still much work to be done (Hines & Collaer, 1993; Levy & Heller, 1992; Money, 1994).

Androgen Insensitivity Syndrome

As explained earlier in this chapter, hormonal secretions from fetal gonads are necessary for the development of male genitals and the possible suppression of female structures. In a rare genetic condition called

fetally androgenized females: a condition in which hormones administered during pregnancy caused chromosomally female (XX) fetuses to have masculinization of genitals and perhaps of later behavioral patterns, even though they were raised as girls.

congenital adrenal hyperplasia (CAH): a genetic disorder that masculinizes chromosomal females and seems to lead to a masculinization of behavior as well.

androgen insensitivity syndrome (AIS), the developing body cells of genetic males (XY) are unable to respond normally to the testosterone secreted by the fetal testes. As a result, they develop normal-appearing female genitals instead of male organs, but the internal female structures develop only incompletely. Breasts develop at puberty and there may be a short vaginal canal, but because there is no uterus, menstruation never occurs. These children are raised from birth as girls because they appear anatomically to be female, and it may not be until the lack of menstruation is noted that the abnormal condition is diagnosed (Money, 1994).

Studies of some genetic males with AIS who have been raised and treated as "girls" and "women" have determined that they tend to exhibit traditional feminine traits, including a preference for being homemakers rather than having a career and having played with dolls in their younger years. They typically report desiring male sexual partners and having dreamed of raising a family. Researchers have suggested that in cases of AIS, the ineffectiveness of androgens during these genetic males' fetal development not only led to feminization of their genitals but also prevented any masculinization of their brains. This may have produced conditions that led to distinctly feminine behavior in later life (Hines & Collaer, 1993; Money, 1994). Of course, it could also be argued that the socialization process of being raised as girls developed these traditionally "feminine" characteristics. There is clinical evidence that AIS girls have difficulty adjusting to their infertility and that surgical procedures to increase vaginal size may lead to feelings of inferiority. Effective counseling for children with such disorders, and for their parents, is extremely important (Slijper et al., 1994).

DHT-Deficiency Syndrome

This is a genetic problem in which genetic males lack the enzyme, dihydrotestosterone (DHT), that is necessary for the normal development of external male sex organs in fetal life. Although his internal organs are normal, a boy with **DHT-deficiency syndrome** is born with undescended testes and an underdeveloped penis that may easily be mistaken for a clitoris. Sometimes, there is also a partially formed vagina, and the scrotum may be folded in such a way that it resembles labia. Researchers identified 18 genetic males in the Dominican Republic who had been misassigned as females at birth and then had been raised as girls (Imperato-McGinley et al., 1982). At puberty, these children suddenly began to develop male secondary sex characteristics, including increase in muscle mass, deepening of the voice, and growth of the

penis. They did not develop any breasts or other female characteristics.

These girls-becoming-boys were subjected to a great deal of ridicule and name-calling in their communities. Sixteen of them eventually adopted male gender patterns and seemed to be sexually interested in women. It has been hypothesized that because these boys apparently had testosterone secreted by their fetal gonads during prenatal life, and only the development of their external genitals had been affected by the disorder, it was easier for them to make the transition to a masculine gender identity and gender role. In other words, whatever masculinizing effects fetal testosterone might have on brain pathways would still have taken place. Others have suggested instead that social pressures may well have led to the more culturally acceptable choice of behaving as men. There was a similar case of inherited DHT-deficiency syndrome among five males in New Guinea. They, too, were raised as girls until pubertal changes masculinized them, and they began living as men. Because they lived in a male-dominant society, it meant an increase in social status to be identified as men instead of women (Herdt & Davidson, 1988).

A recent case study of a woman diagnosed with DHT-deficiency syndrome found her to be almost completely lacking in sexual desire. Subsequent treatment in which DHT was administered generated increased ability to become sexually aroused. This provides further evidence of the role testosterone may play in triggering sexual desire (Riley, 1999).

Hormones and Behavior

The effects of fetal hormones on the human brain are only beginning to be understood. There is no doubt that learning after birth is a crucial factor in determining much of what we define as masculine or feminine behavior and that society largely determines what is thought to be appropriate behavior for girls and boys

androgen insensitivity syndrome (AIS): a developmental condition in which cells do not respond to fetal androgen, so that chromosomally male (XY) fetuses develop external female genitals. There is also a feminization of later behavioral patterns.

DHT-deficiency syndrome: a condition in which chromosomally male fetuses have underdeveloped male genitals and may be identified as girls at birth. However, at puberty they begin to develop masculine secondary sex characteristics and seem to maintain masculine patterns of behavior.

(Levy & Heller, 1992). There may well be a **multiplier effect** in which biological and social-environmental factors build on one another more and more as a person grows and matures. At birth, there are relatively few detectable behavioral differences between the sexes. As individuals interact more with the environment, they learn certain roles, and then at puberty hormonal factors again cause significant changes in sexual differentiation, magnifying female-male differences even more. It remains to be shown how much prenatal chromosomal and hormonal influences may predispose an infant to a particular type of behavior and which behaviors tend to be innately a part of maleness or femaleness.

Recent attention has focused on the significance of the hypothalamus, pituitary gland, and gonads and how they interact during various stages of development. Secretions from these organs may also influence sexual orientation and behavior (Hines & Collaer, 1993; Swaab & Gofman, 1995). Except for reproductive behavior, there are no behaviors that are either absolutely male or absolutely female. Although all behaviors are found in some proportion in all humans, the threshold for eliciting a particular behavior may be lower in either females or males. This would mean that a combination of prenatal hormonal influences and environmental factors might elicit the behavior in a higher proportion of one sex than the other.

It can be seen that prenatal factors set the stage for the development of later gender identity and gender role. The relationship of those factors is summarized in Figure 5.4. Now we can consider social and environmental factors in determining how humans become mature women or men.

Factors of Infancy and Childhood

Sex Assignment at Birth

Except for the occasional baby born with ambiguous genitalia, there is usually no question about an infant's sex when it is born. A quick glance at the genitals determines whether the child is classified as a female or male. As soon as someone announces "It's a girl!" or "It's a boy!" the social mechanism that will help shape the individual's adult gender identity has been set into motion.

Rearing a Child as Girl or Boy

Most professionals believe that boys and girls are treated differently as they are raised, a phenomenon called **differential socialization.** Every society has its prescribed roles into which females and males are expected to fit, and men and women in every society tend to have fairly consistent views of what those expectations are, whether they like them or not. For ex-

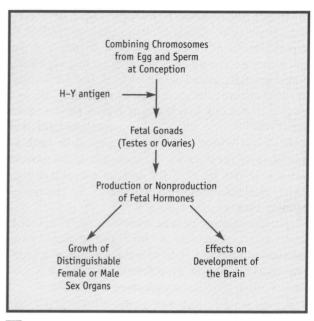

FIGURE 5.4   *Gender Identity—Prenatal Factors*

This portion of a larger figure (see Fig. 5.9) details the factors in the development of adult gender identity. Here we see the prenatal biological factors involved in determining male and female sex organs.

ample, immediately after sex assignment, there may be the distinctive use of pink or blue colors, the choosing of an appropriately sexed name, and reference to the child as "he" or "she." It has also been suggested that girls tend to be treated more gently and with greater protectiveness, whereas boys are treated more roughly and encouraged to be more independent (see Fig. 5.5). However, reviews of the scientific literature on differential socialization have reached different conclusions about the degree to which parents treat their daughters and sons differently. Some analyses point to significant differences, but others have found only minimal evidence that parents treat boys and girls differently (Jacklin & Reynolds, 1993; Lytton & Romney, 1991).

The Child's Own Body Image

As children grow older, they become further socialized into the patterns of response and behavior considered appropriate to their gender. As the child's self-aware-

---

multiplier effect: the combining of biological and socioenvironmental factors more and more with one another in the process of human development.

differential socialization: the process of treating boys and girls differently as they are growing up.

FIGURE 5.5 *Gender Characteristics*

Although some effort has been made in recent years to change society's stereotypical view of gender roles, Western culture still tends to reinforce in children the traditional differences between boys and girls.

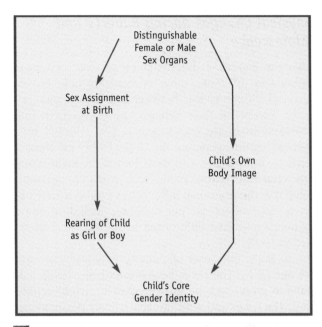

FIGURE 5.6 *Gender Identity—Factors of Infancy and Childhood*

This portion of a larger figure (see Fig. 5.9) details the environmental and cultural factors that influence the child's development of his or her gender identity.

ness increases, he or she begins to respond to the influences of other people and has a distinct self-concept that includes a sense of being a girl or a boy. The child gradually becomes aware of its body sex, its male or female sex organs, and identifies them as part of her or his sexual nature. All of these factors (summarized in Fig. 5.6) lead to the evolution of a child's **core gender identity.** In fact, gender identity becomes established so early that—with few exceptions—any attempt at sex reassignment (as in the case of a child erroneously assigned at birth) can be very difficult psychologically beyond the age of 18 or 20 months.

Factors at Puberty

There is a good deal of evidence to support the contention that even young children have romantic, sensual, and sexual feelings (see chapter 6, "Sexuality through the Life Cycle"). The individual's core gender identity is established during childhood. Puberty is the time when the gonads (testes or ovaries) begin producing large amounts of hormones, causing that gender identity to declare itself in bodily changes, deepened sexual feelings, and gender-related behaviors.

Hormones at Puberty

Following their secreting activities during fetal life, the testes largely cease their production of testosterone just before or just after birth. In both males and females, the onset of puberty is characterized by marked increases in various hormonal secretions, once a critical level of body weight and skeletal maturation has been reached (Wilson, 1992). Pubertal development

involves two distinct processes. The first stage is *adrenarche,* or the secretion of androgenic hormones by the adrenal glands. This usually happens between the ages of 6 and 8. The exact role of this stage is uncertain, and the only identifiable physical result is some early growth of a small amount of pubic hair.

Adrenarche may well set the stage for the more profound stage of puberty, characterized by *gonadarche,* occurring between the ages of 9 and 13. This stage is accompanied by a series of changes affecting the hypothalamus, the pituitary gland, and the gonads. First, the hypothalamus secretes more gonadotropin-releasing hormone (GnRH). The GnRH then stimulates an increase in gonadotropin hormone from the pituitary gland, which stimulates the gonads (testes or ovaries) to secrete sex hormones (Nottelmann, Inoff-Germain, Susman, & Chrousos, 1990). It is these hormones that result in the development of secondary sex characteristics. The renewed secretion of testosterone and DHT from the testes masculinizes boys' bodies, and the ovaries begin their secretion of estrogens that feminize girls' bodies (Wilson, 1992).

core gender identity: a child's early inner sense of its maleness, femaleness, or ambivalence, established prior to puberty.

Physical Changes during Puberty and Adolescence

FOH After the important differentiation of male or female genitals in the fetus, there is relatively little further physical differentiation between the sexes until puberty. Except for their genitals, the bodies of young girls and boys are quite similar. The pubertal hormones begin to generate the distinct physical characteristics of a man or a woman, called the **secondary sex characteristics.** Preliminary research has indicated that the hormonal influences of puberty may exert a clear effect on personalities, including some tendencies toward differences in females and males (Udry, 1990).

In boys, the onset of puberty is typically around the age of 13. The penis begins to enlarge, pubic hair starts to grow, and the growth spurt in height is initiated. The testes and scrotum have usually begun to enlarge about a year earlier. Eventually the voice becomes lower as the larynx grows, ejaculation of semen occurs, and pubic and body hair spread to some degree. A moustache and beard usually appear 3 to 5 years later. In girls, puberty typically begins around the age of 11 or 12. The first signs are usually the budding of the breasts, the growth of pubic hair, and the beginning of growth spurts. The first menstruation generally does not occur until after these initial signs have appeared.

Beginning at puberty, the sex glands of girls and boys actually produce the same hormones, with androgens such as testosterone being secreted in higher concentrations in males, and estrogen higher in females. In the normal male, the higher concentration of androgens and their resulting influences tend to override the effects of the estrogens. This effect is reversed in the normal female. Things can be temporarily disrupted with these hormone balances during puberty and adolescence, producing conditions such as slight breast enlargement in males (gynecomastia) or deepened voice and unusually enlarged clitoris in the female. The onset of hormonal puberty can sometimes be either premature or delayed. Any of these conditions can shake the stability of a young person's gender identity and lead to confusion and unhappiness (Slijper et al., 1994).

Changes in Sexual Drive and Behavior at Puberty

Of particular significance during puberty and adolescence is an increase in interest in sexual behavior. One of the important ways in which gender identity is confirmed during this period is through imagery and fantasy. Boys and girls begin to imagine sexual acts and fantasize about desirable romantic or sexual partners.

FIGURE 5.7   *Sex Drive in Adolescents*

Adolescents experience the sex drive in different degrees depending on physical as well as emotional factors. Their families, religious background, peers, and the media all influence how adolescents learn to deal with love and the sex drive.

Adolescents are sometimes upset to find themselves imagining or dreaming about sexual encounters with members of their own gender, sadistic behavior, or other behaviors they may have learned to consider "abnormal" or inconsistent with their assumed sexual orientation. Yet such fantasies may signal some of the final alterations that will be made in the achievement of an adult gender identity and sexual orientation.

Think back to when you went through puberty. Can you remember how you felt about yourself? The other gender? Explain.

There is great variation in the strength of sexual interest that develops during adolescence (see Fig. 5.7). Some youngsters experience frequent fantasies about sex and a strong drive that demands to be put

secondary sex characteristics: the physical characteristics of mature women and men that begin to develop at puberty.

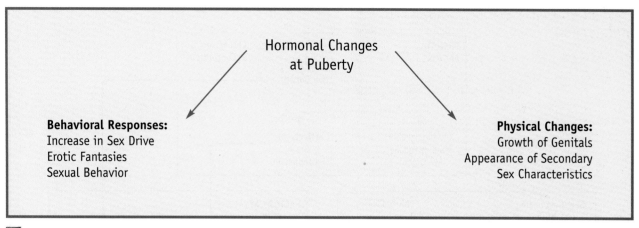

FIGURE 5.8 *Gender Identity—Factors of Puberty*

This diagram details the elements that confirm gender identity in the adolescent. The increase in hormone production produces mature male and female physical characteristics as well as heightened interest in sexual fantasies and sexual behavior.

into action. Other adolescents display little interest in sex. In either case, the level of strength of sexual interest may be subject to change in later life. The factors that determine the strength of sex drive are not known. The levels of sex hormones, particularly testosterone, in the blood may exert some effect, but research into that question is incomplete.

The amount of experience with sex and romance gained during adolescence is affected by factors such as social class, degree of interest in sex, peer group attitudes, religious background, parental influences, and exposure to the media. The new factors of puberty interact to establish firmly the core gender identity established in childhood (see Fig. 5.8). There may be a few alterations as time goes on, but the fundamental patterns are apparently unalterable.

Adult Gender Identity and Role

At this point, we can present a general outline of sequences believed to be involved in the establishment of gender identity, from conception to adulthood. An overall summary is presented in Figure 5.9. Adult gender identity and gender role usually become distinguishable as more masculine for males and more feminine for females. There may be elements of the masculine and elements of the feminine in all of us, even though our predominant identity leans more toward one or the other. Therefore, differences in behavior between males and females are largely quantitative, meaning that they differ mostly in the frequency with which a particular individual exhibits particular behaviors (Huyck, 1999). It should also be understood that many of what are considered to be appropriate masculine and feminine traits are determined by society and culture.

Interpretations of Gender

As we move from the complexities of biology to other factors involved in developing gender identity, we begin to see how many different interactions come into play. At the social and cultural levels, dividing people into two distinct groups based on their gender becomes far more complicated. Individuals must sort through the standards and scripts for behavior that their society has identified as "feminine" or "masculine," struggling to live up to the expectations of others while feeling comfortable with themselves. The expressions of masculinity and femininity come in clothing styles, ways of walking and talking, mannerisms, hobbies, and all sorts of behaviors. Subsequent parts of the chapter will examine the complex shades of gender roles and the implications they have for individual human beings and their societies.

Models of Masculinity and Femininity

The simplest model used to conceptualize gender roles is to see "totally masculine" and "totally feminine" as two extremes at opposite poles of a continuum. See Figure 5.10 for a way of visualizing this two-pole, or bipolar, model. The assumption implied by this model is that the more frequent or strong a person's masculine behaviors are, the less frequent and strong that individual's feminine behaviors will be, and vice versa. In other words, the more feminine one is, the less masculine.

Other conceptualizations of femininity and masculinity suggest, instead, that the two qualities are

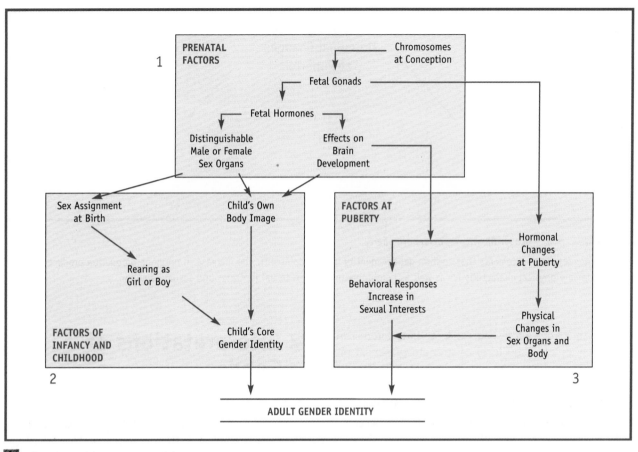

 **FIGURE 5.9**   *Gender Identity—Adult*

This figure integrates the three stages of gender identity and summarizes the prenatal factors (1), factors of infancy and childhood (2), and factors at puberty (3) that influence the development of a mature adult gender identity.

actually more independent from one another than the bipolar model suggests. These models propose that some people show high frequencies of both masculine and feminine behaviors. The presence of these high levels in a single individual is called **androgyny,** coming from the Greek roots *andro,* for "male," and *gyn,* for "female." Conversely, some people could demonstrate low levels of both behaviors, therefore being relatively undifferentiated in terms of gender. Finally, there would be what is more typical of human beings, a higher level of one set of behaviors and a lower level of the other, so that the individual would be considered either more masculine or more feminine. The *orthogonal model* assumes complete independence of masculinity and femininity. *The oblique model* assumes that at least to some degree, the more masculine people are, the less feminine they tend to be, and the more feminine, the less masculine (see Fig. 5.10). The models that conceptualize femininity and masculinity in this way differ only in the degree of independence that they demonstrate between the two factors (Reinisch & Sanders, 1992).

There have been descriptions in the research literature about people who exaggerate the culturally accepted characteristics of masculinity or femininity. **Hypermasculinity,** sometimes called *machismo,* is a tendency to exaggerate those behaviors that are perceived to be manly. It takes the form of such characteristics as aggressiveness, unemotional sexual involvement, and an emphasis on defending one's honor if it seems to have been threatened. **Hyperfemininity** is characterized by greater deference to others, particularly men, more acceptance of aggres-

androgyny (an-DROJ-a-nee): the presence of high frequencies of both masculine and feminine behaviors and traits in the same individual.

hypermasculinity: a tendency to exaggerate manly behaviors, sometimes called machismo.

hyperfemininity: a tendency to exaggerate characteristics typically associated with femininity.

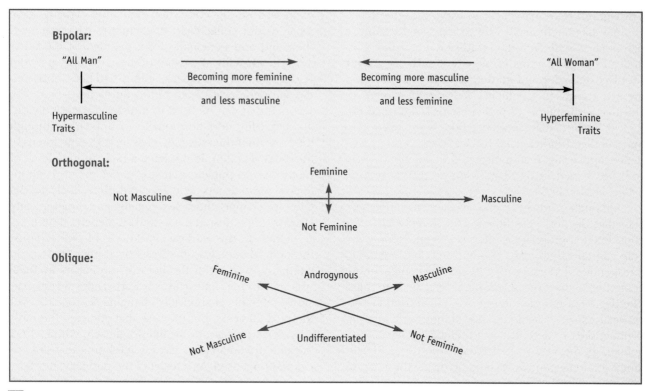

FIGURE 5.10 *Models of Masculinity and Femininity*

The definition of masculine or feminine behavior is based primarily on environmental influences and cultural expectations. The bipolar model assumes a continuum, with increased frequency of traits toward one pole resulting in a decrease in traits from the other pole. The orthogonal model assumes masculinity and femininity to be completely independent traits, and the oblique model assumes them to be semi-independent. In the orthogonal and oblique models, human beings are assumed to be able to have varying levels of both masculine and feminine traits (modified after Reinisch & Sanders, 1992).

sive sexual behavior from others, and holding traditional attitudes about the rights and roles of women in society (Murnen & Byrne, 1991; Ray & Gold, 1996). People who exaggerate the traits of masculinity or femininity are probably acting out some role that they have found to be important to them in the context of their society.

Psychologist Sandra Bem (1974, 1993) was one of the first researchers to develop a paper-and-pencil inventory to measure the degree to which people might be androgynous. She considered anyone who had both a high femininity score and a high masculinity score to be androgynous. Her study, and others since, have indicated that the term can be applied to about one-third of teenagers and college students. Research has suggested that androgynous people may be more adaptable and flexible, and have higher levels of ego development, than those who are more polarized in their feminine or masculine traits (Bursik, 1995; Vonk & Ashmore, 1993). For example, people who behave in traditionally masculine ways are more adept at aggressive behavior and less able to share feelings and be gentle. Those who behave in a traditionally femi-

nine manner are more comfortable with showing warmth, concern, and gentleness but less willing or able to demonstrate assertiveness or independence (Ray & Gold, 1996). Androgynous people may feel more at ease being independent and forceful, or warm, nurturing, and kind, depending on the situation, and are thus more flexible in adapting to a range of situations (Marsh & Byrne, 1991). Bem (1987, 1993) has emphasized that she believes there are biologically based differences in behavior between males and females and that she does not recommend societies changing in an attempt to eliminate such differences. She does want to see our cultural restrictions on behavior lifted so that men and women can be free to express the full range of individual differences that she believes biology allows for both sexes.

Lessons from Transgenderism

Some individuals cross the usual boundaries that delineate "expected" gender roles for women and men and demonstrate some level of discomfort and/or nonconformity with a traditional male or female identity.

Transgenderism may occur in varying degrees. Psychology has traditionally viewed transgenderism as a pathological state, and the professional literature continues to employ terms to identify it such as **gender identity disorder** and **gender dysphoria.** However, there is a growing sentiment even in professional circles that assumptions of pathology or lack of psychological health may not be fair with regard to transgendered individuals. In fact, there is some evidence appearing that transgendered identities may well be shaped in part by biological factors (Cloud, 1998c; Devor, 1997).

Although nearly everyone has elements of personality that do not quite fit into the stereotyped roles considered appropriate to their sex, some people devote substantial amounts of their time and energy to transgendered pursuits that seem to fit them more comfortably than the more traditional gender roles. The degree of transgenderism may range from the occasional hour or vacation period during which the individual dresses and acts as a member of the "other" gender, all the way to individuals who do so consistently for long periods of time, even establishing an identity to friends and coworkers as a member of that gender. Because these people may not fit neatly into one of our two social gender categories, they often create discomfort in others.

Transgender people provide some important lessons to us as they transcend our notions of the "two" sexes. We are reminded, for example, that an individual's genital organs no longer exclusively define gender. We also find that gender identity, social sex roles, and sexual orientation are not as closely linked as was once assumed (Bockting, 1999).

People are often reluctant to accept roles that do not fit neatly into their polarized assumptions about what is behaviorally appropriate for females and males. Unfortunately, as transgendered people are identified in real life, they may be met with harsh judgment and prejudice rather than good-humored acceptance. People are often not willing to understand those who cross the socially determined barriers that relate to gender. There are several organizations that have been formed to address the many issues relating to people who fall into sexual or gender minorities. Transgenderism may be expressed in a variety of behaviors, ranging from occasional cross-dressing to being surgically and hormonally reassigned to the other sex, both of which are explored further in chapter 13, "The Spectrum of Human Sexual Behavior."

Transsexualism

Transsexualism is the most extreme form of transgenderism. Transsexuals (sometimes spelled "transexuals") are anatomically normal males or females who express a strong conviction that they actually have what would collectively or culturally be considered the mind and personality of a member of the other sex. They usually are aware of these feelings at a very young age and often feel as if they had been born into the wrongly sexed body. Procedures have been developed that can be used to transform such individuals surgically and hormonally to appear as though they are the other sex (see chapter 13). Low-intensity transsexuals often do not have a high enough level of motivation to pursue such sex reassignment. High-intensity transsexuals, however, are quite likely to decide to change their sex legally and anatomically (Devor, 1997; Kesteren, Gooren, & Megens, 1996).

One of the earliest instances of sex change through surgery was the case of Sophia Hedwig in Germany, who, with the help of physicians in 1882, was transformed into Herman Karl. There were occasional attempts at surgically changing sex organs over the next 70 years, but the case that attracted the most attention was that of Christine Jorgensen, who in 1952 became a woman after having lived until that time as George Jorgensen. As a result of the publicity, her doctor was deluged with requests for sex changes, and the science of sex reassignment was off and running.

At this time, the origins of transsexualism are unknown, and there continues to be debate about the roles of nature and nurture. Some recent research has shown some anatomical brain differences in male transsexuals, suggesting that biology may play some role (Devor, 1997). There is agreement that transgender identity tends to be sensed by most individuals at a young age. It has been estimated that there are as many as 11,000 postoperative transsexuals in the United States, although the figures are uncertain, and they would not include those transsexuals who have not undergone sex reassignment, certainly outnumbering those who have. The total number of transsexuals in the United States and some European countries has been estimated to be 1 per 20,000 to 50,000 people over the age of 15. The estimates for female-to-male

transgenderism: a crossing of traditional gender lines because of discomfort and nonconformity with gender roles generally accepted by the society.

gender identity disorder: the expression of gender identity in a way that is socially inconsistent with one's anatomical sex.

gender dysphoria (dis-FOR-ee-a): another term sometimes used to describe a gender identity disorder.

transsexualism: a strong degree of discomfort with one's identity as male or female, characterized by feelings of being in the wrongly sexed body.

Transgenders

When James Madison was urging his young nation "from oppressing the minority," he was talking about "other sects," not other sexes. Shannon Ware, an engineer from St. Louis, Mo., who began life as Craig Ware but now lives as a woman, would grant that much. But since a high school civics teacher inspired her, she has clung to the belief that social change is possible, that America is elastic enough to accommodate all minority groups—even when the minority is as caricatured and misunderstood as hers.

Ware is "transgendered," which means her mental gender—her deepest awareness of her identity—doesn't correspond to the parts she was born with. Though she has become an activist in the past year or so, Ware struggled with these feelings for years. Now, at 45, she is happy with her inner and outward selves, the latter feminized with hormones and women's clothes.

. . . Gender nonconformists have been working together, with some remarkable successes, to build a political movement. Their first step was to reclaim the power to name themselves: transgender is now the term most widely used, and it encompasses everyone from cross-dressers (those who dress in clothes of the opposite sex) to transsexuals (those who surgically "correct" their genitals to match their "real" gender).

. . . The overlapping permutations of gender and sexuality can get baffling, which is why transgender activist Riki Anne Wilchins simply declared "the end of gender" in her recent book, *Read My Lips*. Wilchins believes that male-female divisions force constructed social roles on all of us and create a class of the "gender oppressed"—not only transgenders but also feminine men, butch women, lesbians and gays, "intersexed" people (hermaphrodites) and even people with "alternative sexual practices." (Marv Albert, meet your leader.)

In the early '90s, transgenders started forming political groups, mostly street-level organizations, which picketed the American Psychiatric Association, for instance, for using the gender-identity-disorder diagnosis. Previously, transgenders appeared as figures in the early gay-liberation movement: it was cross-dressing men—their "hair in curls," as they chanted—who threw the first rocks in the 1969 Stonewall riots in New York City's Greenwhich Village. But as the gay movement went mainstream, it jettisoned transgenders as too off-putting.

Transgenders faced practical obstacles to organizing themselves separately. Most couldn't simply dress as a member of the opposite sex without getting beaten or fired. Many felt pressured to undergo expensive genital and cosmetic operations, which doctors wouldn't perform unless the patients also underwent years of psychiatric treatment. After the surgery, some had to move to find a new job and start a new life. Political organizing was a luxury.

Today medical rules are getting more relaxed. Some transgenders still elect to have full operations, but others (especially the young) express their gender their own way, perhaps just with clothing or hormone treatments or with partial surgery. Increasingly, they simply refuse to discuss their private parts. "What's important is hate crimes and job discrimination," says Shannon Minter, a female-to-male transgender and civil rights lawyer. "Why does everyone want to talk about my genitals?"

John Cloud, *Time*, July 20, 1998. "Trans Across America: Ridiculed for years, 'transgenders' are emerging as the newest group to demand equality," pp. 48–49.

transsexuals have consistently been lower than those for male-to-female at about a 1 to 3 ratio, but that may represent cultural values more than actual numbers (Kesteren et al., 1996; Weitz & Osburg, 1996).

There are many subtleties of transgenderism that have never been categorized or labeled. The most obvious conclusion is that developing feminine and masculine traits and roles is no less complicated and no better understood than the development of the other aspects of our sexuality. Figure 5.11 shows a continuum of various forms of transgenderism as they relate to masculine traits and feminine traits. It should be noted that one's gender identity or gender role is not necessarily related to sexual orientation. Many male cross-dressers, sometimes called transvestites, dress in women's clothing but are heterosexual in orientation and prefer female sexual partners. Some transsexuals have chosen to be surgically changed to the other sex so they could be gay or lesbian and thus interact sexually with members of the sex to which they were reassigned (Bockting, 1999).

Gender as a Social Construction

The nature-nurture issue has made its way into concepts of gender roles. The question of whether gender differences are due to biology *or* environment has been recognized as too simplistic an approach. Scien-

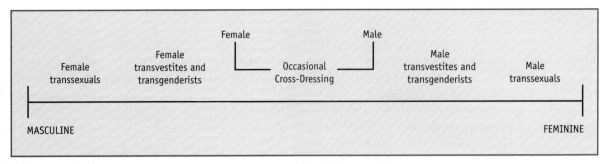

FIGURE 5.11 *Gender Identity Disorders and the Masculine-Feminine Continuum*

Transgenderism is not necessarily related to sexual orientation but rather to an emotional or psychological attitude that both men and women may have about their own sexual natures.

tists are now examining the dynamic relationships between biology and environment that seem to interact across cultures and historical periods to form gender roles (Connell, 1999). Psychology has had a long-standing interest in identifying the differences between groups, and this framework has been applied to gender roles as well. This approach in itself may have created biases that only support preconceived notions about difference rather than looking for potential similarities (Banaji, 1993).

Social psychologists, who study individuals within the contexts of their societies, generally accept the fact that biological factors may predispose females and males to certain behavioral variations. However, they also tend to believe that an elaborate system of human thought processes, fueled by social and cultural factors, heavily influences the innate variabilities and may even override them (Geis, 1993; Romaine, 1999).

The social constructionist view does not see human beings simply as passive recipients of social rules and expectations concerning gender. Instead, they are seen as active participants in the continuing process of creating a particular perspective and personal meaning for gender behavior (Yoder, 1999). Individuals build the information from their own socialization into particular sets of beliefs, feelings, attitudes, and expectations; these become the screens through which people perceive their worlds. Psychologists have known for a long time that our internal cognitive systems can influence all of our thought processes, tending to confirm only that which we believe (Glick & Fiske, 1999; Pennell & Ogilvie, 1995).

It is in this way that gender roles become self-fulfilling prophecies. We all have learned assumptions about differences between boys and girls, men and women, that affect our self-concepts and our views of others. This in turn affects how we behave, including how we treat other people as females or males. The entire system becomes self-perpetuating

because people usually want to fit into what their society expects of them and because we become more comfortable with what is familiar and predictable (Connell, 1999; Geis, 1993). There is always the danger that gender roles in any society may create an imbalance of status and power between women and men, and then those who hold the greater status and power may have a personal and political stake in perpetuating an inequitable system (Beall, 1993; Glick & Fiske, 1999).

Biological and Evolutionary Foundations of Gender Roles

During much of the twentieth century, social psychologists and anthropologists suggested that social behavior, including gender roles, are largely shaped by social and cultural influences. Evolutionary psychologists, who bring genetic and biological perspectives into the debate, believe that there may actually be some discernible behavioral differences between males and females. They cite the research that suggests that across cultures of the world, men tend to be more aggressive and competitive, whereas women are less aggressive and less concerned with establishing dominant positions in the social hierarchy. Sociobiologists have also theorized that the human animal has an innate drive to reproduce the species and that males are therefore more prone to seek sexual activity with many different partners, whereas females are more inclined to find stable partners who will provide a comfortable environment for raising children. This view hypothesizes that gender roles are part of the broad evolutionary scheme designed to promote survival of the human species (Lueptow, Garovich, & Lueptow, 1995; Wiederman & Hurst, 1998).

Naturally such views are not particularly popular with those who feel that they are being used to perpetuate unfair gender stereotypes that create negative consequences for a segment of the population. It has been suggested, for example, that gender differences in aggression do not exist in actuality—rather, they reflect the assumptions with which researchers design their studies (Fry & Gabriel, 1994). However, evolutionary psychologists claim that if their theories are accurate, they simply represent confirmation that biology and culture interact in complex ways to form gender roles. They point out that the theories do not necessarily place females at a disadvantage because a major driving force behind gender differences would be the fact that men are trying to attract women to fulfill their evolutionary imperatives (Coney & Mackey, 1998; Kenrick & Trost, 1993). Evolutionary theory should be seen as one approach to understanding how gender differences may have come about and not as a mandate for how things ought to be.

Differences between Females and Males

There are few qualitative differences between females and males, meaning that they represent the exclusive domain of one sex or the other. A few physiological male-female characteristics or functions cannot be changed on any large scale by culture: females menstruate, bear children, and produce milk from their mammary glands. Males ejaculate semen. The differences in sex organs, and their roles in reproduction, and—to a lesser degree—differences in secondary sex characteristics are usually easily distinguishable. Beyond these basic qualitative differences, there is little evidence to suggest that there are many inborn characteristics that may be identified as distinctly female or male.

In 1898, Charlotte Williams wrote, "There is no female mind. The brain is not an organ of sex. As well speak of the female liver." Nearly a hundred years later, psychiatrist and researcher Ellen Leibenluft (1996) reminded us that there are indeed differences in the ways in which male and female livers metabolize substances and that there are differences in the frequencies and effects of various mental illnesses in women and men. Until recently, women were often not included in medical research, and because they have been studied in greater numbers, it is becoming clear that the female body, its reactions to disease, and the ways in which those diseases should be treated are really quite different from the situation with males (McDonald, 1999). Gender differences should never be used to justify gender inequalities, but to deny that those differences exist or to fail to study them entails risks for everyone. There is evidence for the existence of at least some measurable differences between the sexes.

There is a growing body of scientific literature that points to a genetic basis for even complex human behaviors. It probably is not so simple as a single gene determining a particular trait, but instead a complex set of interactions among several genes. However, there also seems to be evidence that the influences of environment on this inborn genetic template are also important in determining how individual traits and behaviors emerge (Bouchard, 1994).

Research has found average differences between human males and females in a few cognitive and motor functions. It is crucial to note that any differences that have been identified are only true as statistical generalizations; they do not apply to *all* women or men. Females, on average, tend to perform at higher levels on tests of verbal fluency, spelling, writing, reading speed and comprehension, understanding social interactions and emotional information, identifying matching items (perceptual speed), fine motor skills such as placing pegs in holes on a board, arithmetic calculation, and associative memory. Males perform at higher average levels on tests of field independence (being able to perceive underlying spatial relations in an otherwise confusing context), mathematical reasoning, science, comprehension of spatial relations, and target-directed motor skills, referring to the guiding or intercepting of projectiles, and the stereotypically male vocational aptitudes such as mechanical reasoning, electronics information, and auto and shop information (Banaji, 1993; Gur et al., 1995; Hedges & Nowell, 1995; Kimura, 1992; Levy & Heller, 1992). This information is summarized in Table 5.3.

It has been generally accepted that the two cerebral hemispheres of the human brain may be responsible for different functions. There is evidence that the cerebral hemispheres of females and males may be specialized in differing ways for cognitive processing. Males are apparently more lateralized, meaning that they tend to localize particular brain functions in one cerebral hemisphere over the other. This may help explain their greater focus on mechanical aptitudes and understanding spatial relations and mathematical reasoning, for example. Females seem to be less lateralized, having more interaction between their cerebral hemispheres. This may well allow them a wider range of experience in their mental tasks and help to explain their greater abilities to understand and process emotional content and to write well (Leibenluft, 1996). Research that examined glucose metabolism in 61 healthy adults, using positron emission tomography (PET), found that there were gender differences in metabolism in different areas of men's and women's brains. Researchers felt the results supported the contention that there are gender differences in cognitive and emotional processing (Geer & Manguno-Mire, 1997; Gur et al., 1995). Other workers have insisted that the evidence for built-in differences in female and

Table 5.3	*Comparison of Average Performance of Females and Males in Tests of Various Abilities*		

Tests Exhibiting Higher Average Female Performance	*Tests Exhibiting Equal Average Performance*	*Tests Exhibiting Higher Average Male Performance*
Verbal fluency	Vocabulary	Field independence
Spelling and writing	Ability to reorganize an object from parts	Mathematical reasoning
Reading speed and comprehension	Verbal reasoning	Science
Social comprehension; understanding emotional information	Verbal IQ	Comprehension of spatial reasoning
Identifying matched items (perceptual speed)	Performance IQ	Target-directed motor skills (guiding or intercepting projectiles)
Fine motor skills		Mechanical reasoning
Arithmetic calculation		Electronics information
Associative memory		Auto and shop information

Sources: From J. Levy and W. Heller, "Gender Differences in Human Neuropsychological Functions," in A. A. Gerall, H. Moltz, and I. L. Ward, eds., *Handbook of Behavioral Neurobiology*, Vol. 11, *Sexual Differentiation*, 1992, New York: Plenum Press; D. Kimura, "Sex Differences in the Brain," *Scientific American*, Vol. 267 (3), pp. 119–25; and L. V. Hedges and A. Nowell, "Sex Differences in Mental Test Scores, Variability, and Numbers of High Scoring Individuals" in *Science*, Vol. 269, 1995, pp.41–45.

male brains is extremely thin and that the extrapolations made from available evidence have been unjustified (Tavris, 1994).

Theories of Gender Role Development

A substantial part of establishing masculine and feminine gender roles results from a learning process—our socialization as girls and boys, women and men. As children grow up, they learn to label themselves in various ways and to recognize the attributes, attitudes, and behaviors considered socially appropriate for each sex (Ferree, Lorber, & Hess 1999). In one study, 145 boys and 100 girls in kindergarten, third, sixth, and eighth grades were asked about their preferences in gifts. They tended to indicate toys that were typical for their genders. It is clear that learning gender roles takes place early in life at home, in school, and in play activities (Etaugh & Liss, 1992). Again, there are differing theoretical positions over how gender roles develop, and a summary of these theories follows.

Psychodynamic Perspectives

Psychoanalytic tradition, founded by Sigmund Freud, has gradually evolved into what is now known as the psychodynamic approach. It is largely a theoretical perspective on how the human mind works, and it has not been subject to rigorous scientific verification. Modeled after earlier Freudian thought, modern psychodynamic theory holds that there are three phases of early gender development. Children are first unaware of differences between the sexes. Then around the age of 2 years, they begin to realize that girls and boys are different. Freud suggested that children tend to attribute superior power and value to the male genitals. He also believed that girls then felt inadequate and experienced "penis envy," whereas boys feared that they would lose their genitals and had to cope with castration anxieties. Modern psychodynamic theorists have suggested that boys also experience feelings of envy and loss during this second phase, when they realize that they will not be able to give birth to children (Fast, 1993).

In the third phase of gender differentiation in this model, children must work out the implications of their gender in their relationships with the significant men and women in their lives. The contemporary psychodynamic model holds that in this stage children see their parents in terms of gender and tend to relate more with their fathers. For a time, boys are thought to be in a competitive relationship for the affection of their mothers, the Freudian concept of Oedipal wishes, but then give up and take their place as males in their society. Girls have the secret hope that their fathers will give them a penis, the Freudian concept of Electra complexes, but then let go of this hope and become more passive. It is by working through these dilemmas that children eventually find their pathways to masculinity and femininity, with both parents providing support and encouragement through the differentiation process (Buhle, 1998; Butler, 1995).

Modern psychodynamic theorists are struggling to come up with a more balanced and workable view of gender development and tend to hold that boys and girls have relatively similar tasks in learning the roles that fit their genders (Buhle, 1999). Today, the psychodynamic model of gender role development has not received wide acceptance.

Social Learning Theory

This popular model was one of the first to propose that gender roles are perpetuated by each culture, learned by children as they are socialized by their parents, peers, and others through observation, imitation, and instruction. It is assumed that this process is continuous and lifelong and that it may be affected by many particular circumstances of an individual's family and personal history. Early proponents of social learning theory tended to portray children as passive recipients of their culture's assumptions concerning genders, imitating or "modeling" the behavior of those around them of the same sex. However, modern theorists have emphasized that children themselves play active roles in this dynamic process, helping to shape it in part themselves. Research demonstrates as well that children do not simply model their gender behaviors after anyone. They respond differently to different people in their lives. Gender is recognized as not being a particularly reliable predictor of behavior because the process is so individualized for each child (Ferree et al., 1999; Lott & Maluso, 1993).

Research evidence indicates that the gender role orientation of parents seems to have some effect on their children's perceptions of themselves, and probably early interactions with parents reinforce social expectations about feminine or masculine behavior. Social learning theory was a precursor to the social constructionist model of gender that maintains that gender identity is at least partly the result of social and environmental factors. It also provides ammunition to those who feel that expectations of traditional gender roles have been detrimental to women because it demonstrates the origins of prejudice, stereotypes, and discriminatory behavior as they are passed along in the socialization process (Buhle, 1999; Lott & Maluso, 1993). This model has largely ignored potential biological influences on gender role, except to suggest

that the behaviors and values that are promoted by a culture for a particular gender might in fact be those that are most easily established from a biological standpoint. Subsequent theories have become increasingly comprehensive.

Cognitive-Developmental Theory

Cognitive-developmental theory expanded the fundamental understanding of social learning theory. This position maintains that human thought processes serve to support and reinforce the beliefs about gender that are created by the society. It recognizes gender as a basic characteristic used to understand one's social environment and interact with it (Cross & Markus, 1993). The child categorizes itself as girl or boy relatively early in its life through comparison and then develops masculine or feminine values out of the need to value things consistent with or like itself. Then the child tends to identify with the same-sexed parent and deepens its attachment to the feminine or masculine model. It also identifies gender roles by interacting with other children. A unique feature of this model is the idea that the child acquires basic male or female values on its own, and then, because of its acquired desire to be feminine or masculine, identifies with a woman or man and other girls or boys as models (Fagot, 1995).

Research does show that children tend to engage in behavior considered appropriate for their gender at relatively young ages and that by the time they are about 4 years old, they tend to regulate their own behaviors, knowing they will feel a sense of self-approval by behaving in a manner consistent with their gender and will feel self-disapproval if they do not. In a sense, children seem to develop a self-sanctioning system about their gender-linked behavior (Bussey & Bandura, 1992; Jacklin & Reynolds, 1993).

Critics of the cognitive-developmental model argue that the behavior observed in children as they interact with their peers is merely a reflection of social learning from families and the larger culture. Proponents of the theory counter that it is in the peer group that attitudes toward the opposite gender and one's own gender are forged and that these behavioral styles then carry over into adolescence and adulthood.

Gender Schema Theory

This concept of how people come to define themselves as masculine or feminine represents a more sophisticated variant of social learning theory and cognitive-developmental theory (Jacklin & Reynolds, 1993). It emphasizes the pressures inherent in social

Gender Gaps in Problem Solving

Tasks Favoring Men

Men tend to perform better than women on certain spatial tasks. They do well on tests that involve mentally rotating an object or manipulating it in some fashion, such as imagining turning this three-dimensional object:

or determining where the holes punched in a folded piece of paper will fall when the paper is unfolded:

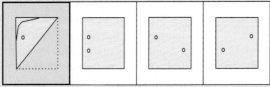

Men are also more accurate than women in target-directed motor skills, such as guiding or intercepting projectiles:

They do better on disembedding tests, in which they have to find a simple shape, such as the one on the left, once it is hidden within a more complex figure:

And men tend to do better than women on tests of mathematical reasoning:

1,100	If only 60 percent of seed-lings will survive, how many must be planted to obtain 660 trees?

Tasks Favoring Women

Women tend to perform better than men on tests of perceptual speed, in which subjects must rapidly identify matching items—for example, pairing the house on the far left with its twin:

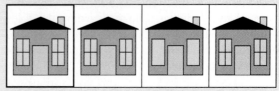

In addition, women remember whether an object, or a series of objects, has been displaced:

On some tests of ideational fluency, for example, those in which subjects must list objects that are the same color, and on tests of verbal fluency, in which participants must list words that begin with the same letter, women also outperform men:

L _ _ _	Limp, Livery, Love, Laser, Liquid, Low, Like, Lag, Live, Lug, Light, Lift, Liver, Lime, Leg, Load, Lap, Lucid ...

Women do better on precision manual tasks—that is, those involving fine-motor coordination—such as placing the pegs in holes on a board:

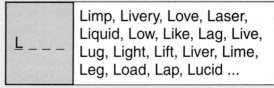

And women do better than men on mathematical calculation tests:

77	$14 \times 3 - 17 + 52$
43	$2(15 + 3) + 12 - \dfrac{15}{3}$

attitudes that assume the need for differences between females and males, even in situations where sex has no particular relevance (Bem, 1987, 1993). In most cultures, maleness and femaleness are defined by a complex network or pattern of associations, ranging from anatomical differences, to the sorts of work people engage in, to religious symbolism. This complicated set of ideas is called a **gender schema.** As people, including children, encounter their worlds, all new information and perceptions are filtered through the gender schema, and internal decisions are made concerning gender, self-concepts, and behaviors toward others (Cross & Markus, 1993). In time, everything becomes interpreted through this dualistic, male-female schema, and the individual models his or her behaviors and life choices according to those interpretations (Koivula, 1995; Signorella, 1999).

Some children and adults are very "gender schematic," meaning that they rely very heavily on their gender role associations, whereas others are more "gender aschematic," meaning that they pay less attention to these socially determined associations (Jacklin & Reynolds, 1993). Gender-schematic preschool children tend to identify toys easily as being for boys or for girls (Levy, 1994). Sandra Bem feels that many characteristics of what we have come to classify as femininity or masculinity only exist in the mind of the perceiver: "Look through the lens of gender and you perceive the world as falling into masculine and feminine categories. Put on a different pair of lenses, however, and you perceive the world as falling into other categories" (Bem, 1987, p. 309).

It has been suggested that, among children, behavioral differences between the sexes may be influenced by the ways in which the children are observed or tested in psychological studies. It has also been argued that so-called scientific pronouncements about gender are nothing more than biased statements about social and political roles. It is certainly true that as science examines questions of gender, political and cultural implications cannot be ignored.

Behavioral Genetics

More recently, another body of research has emerged that adds a biological dimension to the understanding of gender role development. Behavioral genetics attempts to examine the impact of both heredity and environment on childhood socialization. A fundamental assumption of behavioral genetics is that members of the same family are similar because of the genes and environmental factors that they have in common. Conversely, family members

are different because of the genes and environment that they do not share. Studies of twins tend to conclude that personality similarities within a family are probably more influenced by genetics than by environment. This also seems to hold true for behaviors associated with gender. People's attitudes, however, seem to be shaped more by shared genetic and environmental factors (Jacklin & Reynolds, 1993; Ryan, 1998).

Only too often, the biological models are used to justify social prejudice and inequity. However, we must be careful to weigh what research evidence means and to avoid misinterpreting or misusing it. There seems to be ample evidence that in Western culture, gender roles are often sources of power and status and that females have been disproportionately limited by their gender roles. Careful evaluation of all the knowledge we have about gender roles and how they develop can help to correct such inequities.

Multifactorial "Web"

Some of the newest theories relating to gender role have deemphasized the divide between biological, social, and learning components. Instead, they have brought these factors together into a multifactorial approach. One of the most well-known gender theorists of recent years, Eleanor Maccoby (1998), believes along with others that boys and girls grow up in what might be considered two distinct subcultures, each characterized by different sets of expectations and behaviors. Boys' playgroups are much more rough-and-tumble hierarchies, whereas girls' groups are more focused on maintaining relationships and mutuality. These groups become the foundation of gender identity and role. However, Maccoby believes that it is the biological component, built in at birth, that predisposes boys and girls to different rates of maturation and particular kinds of behavior.

Girls seem to regulate their own behavior much earlier than boys do, and this leads to all sorts of activities that please parents and other adults. Boys' greater lack of self-control lead to more disciplinary commands and directions from others. This is where the biological predispositions become influenced by socialization components. Maccoby believes this complex "explanatory web" lies at the root of gender roles, molded by the interactions of many different factors.

gender schema: a complex cognitive network of associations and ideas through which the individual perceives and interprets information about gender.

FIGURE 5.12 *Changing Traditional Roles*

Both women and men may feel that the characteristics traditionally assigned to them by their society are biased and unfair. Some break away very publicly from the stereotypes. Laila Ali, youngest daughter of boxer Muhammad Ali, is shown here during the first round of her middleweight fight with opponent April Fowler. After receiving some prefight advice from her sister not to beat the other woman too badly in this traditionally male sport, Laila needed only 31 seconds to win the match.

Although some social psychologists once believed that we should work toward a gender-aschematic world, in which there would be no differentiation between male and female roles, this no longer seems as plausible or desirable as it once did to some. Instead, there is now more emphasis on the celebration of gender differences and increased understanding between the sexes (see Fig. 5.12).

Gender in Society and Culture

As a basic organizing principle of human culture, maleness and femaleness, femininity and masculinity, are central themes in all social structures. When viewed against a backdrop of variations in many aspects of human personality, gender differences may not be as dramatic or significant as we often seem to think. Nevertheless, they influence how people think, believe, and behave.

Growing Up Female and Male

The prevailing opinion in North America has been that social attitudes put females at a disadvantage in many different ways, and there is evidence to support this perception. One contention has been that our society permits a wider range of behaviors for girls, from the very frilly to the tomboy. For boys, neither the extreme of the sissy nor the too-aggressive bully is acceptable. This has been substantiated by studies indicating that among younger children, boys tend to see their gender roles and future occupational options much more narrowly than do girls (Sellers, Satcher, & Comas, 1999). For these reasons, parents and other adults are typically less disturbed by the behavior of girls than by that of boys. As a result, more demands are placed on boys to behave in the appropriate way. This may well result in boys being pressured to become more independent and self-controlled, and there are studies that show males' self-esteem arising from recognition of their individual distinguishing achievements (Major, Barr, Zubek, & Babey, 1999). Early in their lives, boys develop a sense of self-worth, relatively independent of others' responses. At the same time, female roles are devalued, and boys are criticized for stepping out of their role boundaries by being called "girls" or "sissies" in a derogatory way. As boys grow into adolescence and adulthood, they face harsher consequences for stepping outside the gender-appropriate roles established for them than do girls and women (Carlock, 1999).

Girls, on the other hand, are not as pressured to become independent and self-controlling, so they remain more dependent on others for physical comfort and a sense of self-worth, often experiencing no strong pressures until puberty. As children, girls are rewarded for their compliant good behavior by good grades, parental love, teacher acceptance, and acceptance into peer groups; this leaves them generally more passive and conformist. During adolescence, boys tend to turn their aggressions outward, whereas girls tend to turn these impulses inward, and often against themselves, resulting in lowered self-esteem (Burnett, Anderson, & Heppner, 1995).

Much of the groundwork for whatever gender discrepancies exist later in life is probably laid in the educational institutions that prepare young people for the future. Schools often seem to provide a different environment for girls than they do for boys. There is evidence that even among young children, boys interrupt teachers in their activities much more than do girls, whereas teachers tend to interrupt girls more than boys. Later on, girls in general, and especially black girls, receive significantly less attention from and interaction with their teachers than do boys. This manifests itself in the fact that in the early grades, girls tend to be equal to, or ahead of, boys on nearly every standardized test, but by high school, they tend to fall behind boys on college entrance exams, particularly in mathematics and science (Major et al., 1999; Sadker & Sadker, 1994).

It seems that even well-meaning teachers are often susceptible to gender stereotypes, such as the one that suggests that girls should be quiet listeners in the classroom. Boys tend to be given more esteem-building encouragement than are girls. And girls are subject to far more forms of sexual harassment in schools that are apt to make them feel that school is a hostile environment for them. Clearly, there is still work to be done to ensure that young women and men have equal chances to get a wide-ranging education in a supportive environment, which will in turn offer them the levels of skill, self-esteem, and confidence to be happy and successful in the workforce (AAUW, 1992; Eccles, Barber, & Jozefowicz, 1999).

In the mid-1980s, Carol Gilligan and her research team began to study girls aged 6 through 18 over a 5-year period. They found that young girls seem to feel very good about themselves and care deeply for others. Up until about the age of 11, girls are assertive, speak about their feelings, and accept conflict as a natural part of healthy relationships. However, during adolescence they are much more hesitant to express their feelings out of fear that they will anger others. These researchers have concluded that adolescence tends to be a time of repression for girls. Some girls resist the repression by becoming rebels, whereas others become extremely cautious about what they will say publicly. Often, they resort to "I don't know" as a safe response. They typically do not want to be perceived as "brains" (Carlock, 1999).

A study sponsored by the American Association of University Women (AAUW, 1991, 1992) seems to reinforce this perception of how girls and boys grow up. Three thousand students in grades 4 through 10 were surveyed in 12 locations throughout the United States. Up to 70 percent of both the boys and girls at age 9 tended to reflect positive attitudes toward themselves and willingness to be assertive as needed. The researchers developed a self-esteem index from the questions they asked the children. By age 16, only 29 percent of high school girls indicated they were happy with themselves, whereas 46 percent of boys retained a sense of self-confidence. Interestingly, the drop in self-esteem was particularly prevalent among white and Hispanic girls. Black girls tended to be better able to maintain their self-esteem during adolescence. In the study, girls who had difficulty with particular academic subjects tended to blame themselves and assume they were not competent to do the work. Boys, on the other hand, were more likely to blame the course's subject

matter than themselves. During adolescence, there was a greater concern about appearance and body image among girls.

Did you ever fall prey to or observe gender stereotyping in the classroom? Explain the circumstance and how you reacted to it.

Gender in the Workplace

Masculinity was once the societal yardstick against which everything was measured (Burnett, Anderson, & Heppner, 1995). The characteristics traditionally attributed to men were seen as being more desirable than those attributed to women. Therefore, women sometimes internalized self-destructive, demoralizing values about their own worth in comparison to men. Female employees who exhibited more traditionally masculine characteristics were once considered more promotable than those who showed more feminine traits, depending on cultural contexts. There is growing evidence that women, and "feminine" qualities, are being perceived in more positive ways. Organizational theory is moving away from the devaluation of women's work and the emphasis on masculine organizational structure toward less gender-segregated models (Martin & Collinson, 1999).

Although many institutions and employers are trying to create equal employment opportunities for women, there are still some discrepancies in the way women and men fare in their jobs. The possibilities for promotion are sometimes greater for men than for women. Parenting and household responsibilities still often fall to women and may limit the time and energy available for their careers (Simon, 1998; Van Leeuwen, 1998). Linguistic researcher Deborah Tannen (1994) believes that the communication styles of women sometimes puts them at a disadvantage in more traditional work environments. Women tend to be consensus builders, wanting to ask for the opinions of many others. Male supervisors, who tend toward more aggressive, opinionated styles, may see this as indecisiveness. On the other hand, there is evidence that the power and influence of women in the workplace has been increasing dramatically. Many businesses seem to be recognizing the talents of women as communicators, negotiators, and networkers. With the downsizing of many corporations has come an increased reliance on consultants and freelancers, replacing the more traditional hierarchical management style that was often very masculine (Fisher, 1999).

It is often assumed that academia has been a more open environment for female success, but in fact women faculty have often felt marginalized in colleges and universities as well. Success for women in academic life may well require more concentrated effort

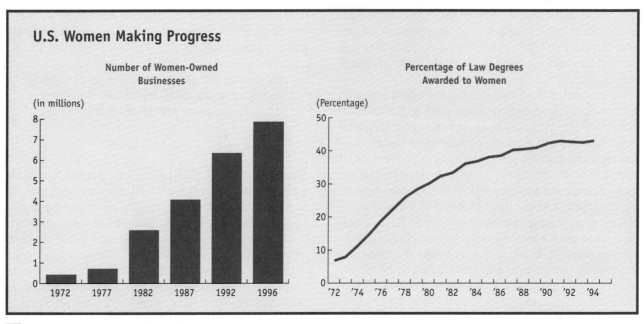

FIGURE 5.13 *U.S. Women Making Progress*

The number of female-owned businesses rose from less than a half-million in 1972 to nearly 8 million in 1996. Nearly half of all law degrees awarded in 1994 went to women, compared with less than 7 percent in 1972.

Source: Women's Figures: The Economic Progress of Women in America, *Independent Women's Forum*, 1996, based on data from U.S. Department of Education and U.S. Bureau of the Census.

on their part than it does for men (Meadow-Orlans & Wallace, 1994). In academic journals, there are significantly fewer publications by and about women (Creamer, 1994). Women are not being attracted to the quantitative science and engineering fields to the extent that men are, but the proportion of women in those fields has increased by as much as 100 percent over the past two decades. The biological and social sciences continue to attract women (Mervis, 1999). It is believed that these are fields where more traditional feminine qualities tend to be more highly valued and useful. In the social science fields, there has also been a reduction in numbers of males, a phenomenon sometimes called "male flight." Since the 1970s, the percentage of women receiving law degrees has been steadily increasing, and the number of businesses owned by women has skyrocketed from less than half a million to about 8 million (see Fig. 5.13).

Evidence also shows that in more advanced, industrialized countries, it has been difficult for women scientists to overcome entrenched systems that seem to favor men. In the developing countries, however, science and technology have emerged more recently as fields of employment concurrent with the development of women's rights. Scientific research and development have typically not been as connected to industrial economies in these countries, meaning that science is often a low-status, low-paying career there.

These conditions have made scientific careers more open to women in the developing countries (Barinaga, 1994). Figure 5.14 summarizes some of that data concerning the percentage of women in physics and astronomy across various cultures.

It was once assumed that when a "critical mass" of women in the United States succeeded in scientific careers, the field would open more to females. Current statistics would indicate that this has not necessarily been the case. As women have entered science in slightly greater numbers, they have also divided into two distinct subgroups. Senior female scientists seem to share the values and work styles of older men, a scenario that tends to discourage younger women. The other subgroup consists of those younger women scientists who have been trying to create a new scientific work ethic, with a better balance between work and family issues. They have often felt disenfranchised by the other group. The result of this situation is the perpetuation of a work environment within science and technology that is not particularly attractive or welcoming to women (Etzkowitz, Kemelgor, Neuschatz, Uzz, & Alonzo, 1994).

Feminism

Within both developing and industrialized societies, there continues to be oppression of women and

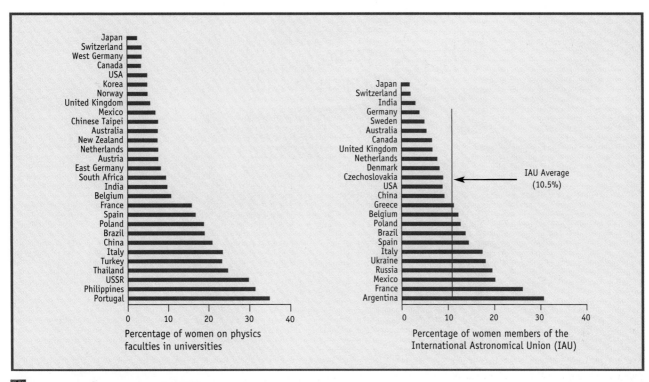

![FIGURE 5.14 icon] **FIGURE 5.14**   *Women in Science*

The graph on the left shows the percentage of women faculty members in the field of physics in various countries. The graph on the right shows the percentage of women who are members of the International Astronomical Union from several countries. These data show how women are less well represented in the sciences in some of the most industrialized countries of the world. One of the reasons for the greater representation of women in developing countries could be the lower status assigned to scientific pursuits in these cultures.

Sources: (left) Reproduced by permission of UNESCO. (right) Reprinted with permission from M. Barinaga, "Women in Science '94: Surprises Across the Cultural Divide" in *Science,* Vol. 263, 1994, pp. 1468–1472. Copyright 1994 American Association for the Advancement of Science.

marked inequality between women and men that fosters the subservience and secondary status of women. Women themselves often recognize the existence of inequality but choose not to try to correct it because they have learned to be less confrontational and more conciliatory. Instead, they often attempt to compete as individuals, playing by the rules that were often established by and for men.

Feminists are women and men who reject prejudices that imply any inferiority of either gender and are working together for equality (McCormick, 1996b). In using the word "equality," they are not implying that women and men are the same, but rather that they deserve equal opportunities and rights. The media have made much of some younger women who have been dubbed "do me feminists." They are women who do not have as much interest in social or political action and do not particularly admire strong, career-woman role models. But they are in control of their own desires, know what they want, and go after it. Sexually, they want to be able to feel free to make their own choices. Some commentators insist that such women

are not feminists but simply have been caught in stereotyped roles and want to justify them. Others say that feminists want to avoid compartmentalizing people by narrowly defined characteristics, instead encouraging members of both sexes to be comfortable in whatever roles they choose (Bellafante, 1998).

There have been several waves of feminist activity throughout American history (see Fig. 5.15). The first major public outcry for women's rights came in 1848 when Elizabeth Cady Stanton, Susan B. Anthony, and several other women wrote their "Declaration of Sentiments" and presented it at the first U.S. women's rights convention in Seneca Falls, New York. As the move to abolish slavery grew in the nineteenth century, women began to liken their position to that of slaves and began to fight for their own rights. After women gained the right to vote in 1920, the movement subsided somewhat until the mid-1960s. Then, partly due to the atmosphere of protest occasioned by the Vietnam War, and partly due to a new awareness of inequality in society that was fueled by mass media communication, the modern feminist movement gained momentum

FIGURE 5.15 *Active Feminists*

Early feminists campaigning for suffrage were in for a hard fight, but in 1920 they won the right to vote with the passage of the Nineteenth Amendment. The size of the eligible voting population nearly doubled. But it was not until the latter half of the 1900s that the turnout of women at the polls reached the level of male turnout.

(Horowitz, 1998). Terms such as "women's liberation" and "sexism" became part of everyone's vocabulary.

Some people have developed an inaccurate image of feminists as bra-burning women who picket against sexist issues and hate men. In fact, feminists are working to reduce inequality between the sexes. In a 1998 TIME/CNN telephone poll, it became clear that over the decade from the late 1980s to late 1990s, the proportion of women willing to call themselves "feminists" had declined significantly, and the proportion of women who did not consider themselves to be feminists had risen. Yet, it also seems clear that most women recognize and appreciate the many advances toward equality that the most recent feminist movement has created for them (Bellafante, 1998) (see Table 5.4).

Contemporary feminist thought has created a renewed awareness that women can be equal participants in sexual activity, as well as other aspects of human life. Traditional stereotypes held that women were less interested in sex and less easily aroused than men. This also meant that men were expected to be the primary initiators of sex, wooing and seducing their female partners until they finally gave in. Modern feminism has raised our consciousness about female sexuality, showing that women want to enjoy and be full participants in sex. It has become clear that women can desire sexual intimacy in all of its dimensions, and it is now more socially permissible for them to initiate sexual encounters. Sex is no longer something to which women are expected to submit as an obligation to a male partner. Instead, it is part of the human experience that can be negotiated, discussed, and actively enjoyed by both women and men if and when they choose to do so (Sonnet, 1999; S.D. Walters, 1999).

Do you consider yourself a feminist? Are you uncomfortable with the term? Explain.

Table 5.4 *Do You Consider Yourself a Feminist?*

Is feminism today relevant to most women?

Women who answered yes	48%
Feminists who answered yes	64%
Nonfeminists who answered yes	42%

Is feminism relevant to you personally?

Women who answered yes	28%
Feminists who answered yes	58%
Nonfeminists who answered yes	16%

Do feminists share your values?

Women	Yes	No
18–34	50%	39%
35–49	41%	44%
50–64	42%	45%
65+	27%	49%

What is your impression of feminists?

	1989	1998
Favorable	44%	32%
Unfavorable	29%	43%

What is the main problem today facing women that men don't face?

Inequality in the workplace	34%
Difficulties balancing work/family	12%
Lack of quality child care	7%

Do the following describe feminists?

	Work for equal rights	Work for equal pay	Work against sexual harassment	Support abortion rights	Work for affordable day care	Don't respect married stay-at-home moms	Don't like most men
Women who answered yes	85%	85%	81%	72%	65%	44%	37%
Feminists who answered yes	93%	93%	92%	71%	83%	28%	23%
Nonfeminists who answered yes	83%	84%	78%	75%	60%	50%	44%

From a telephone poll of 721 adult American women taken for TIME/CNN on May 18–19, 1998 by Yankelovich Partners Inc. Sampling error is 63.6%, for feminists is 66.8% and for nonfeminists is 64.6%. Copyright © 1998 Time, Inc. Reprinted by permission.

FIGURE 5.16 *Then and Now Feminism*

Some observers believe that feminist influence on popular culture has evolved in the past thirty years from being intellectually provocative, as personified by Gloria Stienem's activism of the 1970s, to today's emphasis on stylish fluff and sexy game-playing, typical of television's "Ally McBeal" cast.

The Men's Movement

The women's movement raised consciousness about the ways in which women in our society have often been victims of injustice and discrimination. Yet it also brought into focus the fact that men have been trapped by certain roles and stereotypes as well. Men have been caught in a vicious circle of proving their strength, invulnerability, and effectiveness as providers; yet, because of social attitudes, they are also taught to be dependent on women—first their mothers, then often their romantic partners. Although women have felt resentment about being treated as sex objects, men sometimes have suffered

CASE STUDY

Ricardo Expresses His Attitudes about "Male—Bashing"

During a discussion group following a lecture on male-female relationships on campus, Ricardo voiced his sentiments concerning what he had perceived as antimale attitudes from women. "Men today could never get away with the way some women are treating men, if the situation were reversed. I resent it that men are not supposed to say or do anything that might seem like a put-down to women, but women get away with male-bashing all the time. I don't like it when I see one of those shirts that says 'A woman without a man is like a fish without a bicycle.' I'm not saying that women are incomplete without men; it's just that things like that are deliberately mean. And when the Bobbitt woman cut off her husband's penis, a lot of women seemed to think it was just a big joke, instead of an act of violence and mutilation. Maybe she was justified to take action against him, but the result wasn't any more funny than violence toward women. I think it's time we tried to get our priorities straight."

Ricardo's remarks generated many comments and some heated exchanges among the group members. Some of the women present said that men were only getting back what they had been dishing out for years and that they should not complain. Some women and men in the group felt Ricardo was overreacting and should try to lighten up and learn how to take a joke. Others—mostly males—agreed with his point of view and said they were tired of the building trend toward antimale messages. They emphasized that it was another example of bigotry based on stereotypes. Many men made a point of saying that they themselves did not treat women in negative or inappropriate ways and resented being lumped together with those who did.

The debate went on for nearly 2 hours and ended with little resolution between various factions that were represented. Ricardo left the group feeling at least that he had been able to express his opinions openly, and he hoped that some people who had heard them would try to be more sensitive to the issues that had been raised.

from being success objects, expected to provide status and security for their partners. Many male providers end up feeling powerless, meaningless, and isolated in their jobs; they work under constant fear and tension as they strive for promotion and success. Three main aspects of the traditional male role seem especially to make men uncomfortable: (1) the male as competent worker and provider; (2) the male as emotionally controlled stoic; and (3) the male as sexual aggressor and sexual educator of the female (Levant, 1996; Marsiglio, 1998).

There has been a growing men's movement in North America. Men's groups have sprung up around the country, and men are being encouraged to confront and share their feelings more openly. Many men feel able to celebrate their own masculinity in ways that would have once been considered unmanly (see Fig. 5.17). Having opportunities to talk about gender roles and reassess individual needs and goals continues to prove valuable for men in many different age groups (Good & Wood, 1995).

There has been a good share of finger-pointing between members of the women's and men's movements. Increasingly, men are resisting being blamed individually for the inequities between the genders and are calling for a more balanced view of the social picture (Levant, 1996). They are tired of being the

scapegoats for social constructs that they too were born into, and over which they have often felt little control. They do not feel that it is fair to brand all men as potential rapists or abusers; they instead insist that most men are decent individuals who want to treat women with respect and care (Kimmel, 1997). Many men have participated actively in the efforts to create a more gender-equitable and safe society for everyone.

What do you see as some of the positive and negative features of the men's movement? Explain.

Most men experience some turmoil and problems as they come to grips with what manhood will mean for them. Men must share in the constant struggle to learn how to communicate thoughts, feelings, and the degree of exclusivity they wish to maintain in relationships. Emerging out of what once seemed more like a battle between women and men has been a new spirit of cooperation. Members of both sexes have been calling for opportunities to communicate more openly about differences and to make recommendations for more equitable partnerships between men and women. Professionals have been working on new approaches to help everyone feel more empowered and to create a sense of reconciliation between the genders. It seems likely that the next step for both femi-

FIGURE 5.17 *Changing Masculine Roles*
The feminist movement, in fighting for equal rights for women, has at the same time given men the right to change their expected roles as well. As we enter this new millennium, many men are more comfortable than they ever have been in caring for their children, sharing the role of wage earner, and expressing a full range of emotions.

Table 5.5	Summary of Connotations of Masculinity Index (MAS) Differences across Cultures
Countries with Low MAS	**Countries with High MAS**
Managers relatively less interested in leadership, independence, and self-realization.	Managers have leadership, independence, and self-realization ideal.
Belief in group decisions.	Belief in the independent decision maker.
Weaker achievement motivation.	Stronger achievement motivation.
Achievement defined in terms of human contacts and living environment.	Achievement defined in terms of recognition and wealth.
Work less central in people's lives.	Greater work centrality.
People prefer shorter working hours to more salary.	People prefer more salary to shorter working hours.
Company's interference in private life rejected.	Company's interference in private life accepted.
Greater social role attributed to other institutions than corporation.	Greater social role attributed to corporation.
Lower job stress.	Higher job stress.
Less skepticism as to factors leading to getting ahead.	Skepticism as to factors leading to getting ahead.
Managers have more of a service ideal.	Managers relatively less attracted by service role.
Smaller or no value differences between men and women in the same jobs.	Greater value differences between men and women in the same jobs.
Sex-role equity in children's books.	More sex-role differentiation in children's books.

Source: From G. Hofstede, *Culture's Consequences: International Differences in Work-Related Values*, pp. 228–229. Copyright © 1980 by Sage Publications. Reprinted by permission of Sage Publications, Inc.

nism and the men's movement will be to find a common ground for communicating and relating (Herron, 1994; Marsiglio, 1998).

Gender across Cultures

Gender roles are an integral part of any society. They reflect attitudes and values of the population toward women and men and often affect individual behaviors and relationships. Ethnographic data from 93 nonindustrial societies show that the gender roles associated with raising children and control of property are closely associated with the degree to which men display dominance in each society. In societies in which men maintain close relationships with children, and women have a significant amount of control over property, the men are much less likely to affirm their masculinity through boastfulness, aggressiveness, or high levels of sexual activity. Women in such societies tend to be less deferential to the men, and husbands are less likely to dominate their wives. Conversely, in those societies where men are less involved with children and have more control over property, there is a greater likelihood of demonstrations of strength, aggression, sexual prowess, and male dominance in relationships (Lips, 1999; Peplau, Veniegas, Taylor, & De Bro, 1999).

In reviewing the literature on perceptions of gender across various cultures, it becomes clear that gender roles can be heavily influenced by cultural values. In the early 1980s, a study was published that com-

pared how various countries valued traditional masculine qualities in the workplace (Hofstede, 1980). This research used various scales of work-related values to assign a masculinity index (MAS) to 40 countries that were being studied. This index measured the degree to which people of both sexes tended to endorse goals that were usually more popular among males. Some countries emerged with a high MAS including Japan, Austria, Venezuela, Italy, and Switzerland. Others had a low MAS, such as Sweden, Norway, Netherlands, Denmark, and Finland. When these results were compared with other research findings concerning attitudes, beliefs, and social roles,

CROSS-CULTURAL PERSPECTIVE
In One Unbridled Week, a Town's Moment of Truth

Once a year, Bassam, as this town is most often called, comes alive as returning sons and daughters, and the wrinkled elders who never left, are drawn together by a stirring beat to dance under a setting sun.

For the N'zima people who live in this area, the holiday of reconciliation and truth-telling known as Abissa supersedes virtually all else in life.

It all begins solemnly enough. On a Sunday evening often decreed only a week in advance by the local chief, one of the N'zimas' so-called seven families, the N'vavilé, takes its long, hollow sacred drum from its secret storage place and assembles at the end of a sandy boulevard of ruins.

As a slow rhythm that can be heard far and wide is tapped out, a crowd gathers and a dancing procession begins. Bent forward slightly in reverence of the earth, their feet marking the beat, the people make their way to the chief's home to pay their respects. Libations are poured, the ancestors are blessed and the festival begins.

For the next two hours, until darkness falls or until the potent palm gin that fuels the fete runs out, the sandy ground of Bassam takes a mighty beating as young and old turn in a circle around the percussion band, whose beat alternates between sober and furiously fast.

"There is no training for Abissa, and we don't do any real planning either," said Marcel Ézoua Aka, the chief of Bassam's N'Zima people. "Tradition is what guides us in our ceremony, but once it begins, it is the enthusiasm of the people that takes over."

Among the dancers already gathered in a circle, meanwhile, young men had painted their faces with kaolin, and young women had highlighted their beauty with finely painted circles or white lines around the eyes. A close look at the whirling crowd, however, revealed something more peculiar.

The full-breasted women in the gaudiest dresses who seemed to be having the most fun were not women at all, but men. Likewise, the too-serious men in their tightly clasped neckties were not men at all, but women.

True to the festival's intent of erasing all inhibition, if only for a week, Abissa is, among other things, a parade of gaudy cross-dressing. It is also a moment when forbidden love is declared between men and women who are married (but not to each other), and where long-silenced hurts and confessions are paraded before the world.

The price of admission for those who choose to dance is that they stifle their jealousy, or for those who have wronged, that they suffer the public reproaches of their accusers. At the end of the week, if all is never forgotten, the intent of Abissa is that all should at least be pardoned.

"There are so many who would like to see Africa as a savage place, but we have always had our way of managing tensions," said Raymond Akpagany, an Abidjan banker who had traded his usual fine suit and tie to dance in a gaudy printed outfit and bare feet.

Indeed, if Abissa is one of Ivory Coast's more raucous festivals, its continued vibrancy is a hallmark of this entire region, where, despite galloping urbanism and the encroachment of Western ways of life, most people have clung stubbornly to some core of traditional values that many say serve as an anchor in a world of dizzying change.

some interesting findings emerged about work-related values. As Table 5.5 shows, in countries with a low MAS, work had a less central and stressful place in people's lives. In those countries with a high MAS, work held a much higher place than family and seemed more directly connected with perceptions of personal success and power (Best & Williams, 1993; Peplau et al., 1999).

Cross-cultural studies have demonstrated that there is a fair amount of agreement across cultures as to what characteristics are preferable in selecting a mate. In order of descending importance, those qualities are being kind, understanding, and intelligent, having an exciting personality, and being healthy, and religious. When it comes to issues such as virginity, culture plays a central role. In Eastern Europe and Southeast Asia, selecting a virgin as a wife is of great importance. In Northern European countries, this is seen as irrelevant or unimportant (Williams & Best, 1990). There is also a fair amount of agreement in various cultures about the traits associated with women and men. In examining gender stereotypes across 25 countries, men were generally seen as more active, strong, aggressive, and dominating, whereas women were seen as more passive, weak, nurturing, and self-abasing (Williams & Best, 1990).

A small island society near Papua New Guinea is thought to be one of the only gender-egalitarian cultures in the world. A study of the 2,300 inhabitants of Sudest Island has found that there is truly equal participation by women and men in decision making, ritual practices, and ownership of property. Both women and men seem to have the same degree of sexual freedom, and both sexes care for younger children. Their language contains no words for masculine or feminine pronouns, reflecting a much less genderized perception of the world than most other languages traditionally demonstrate. Kinship lines are traced through the mother's family. It has been suggested that Sudest Island, known by its inhabitants as "the motherland" may well represent a model of what a gender-egalitarian culture can be (Lepowsky, 1994).

Gender Aware Therapy

Gender is one of the central organizing principles in society and in interpersonal relationships. Many cultural regulations and expectations are systematically related to gender. The stresses and problems that men and women encounter during their lifetimes are often the result of these social and cultural requirements and demands. It has been found that certain types of psychological and behavioral problems are more typical of one gender than of the other. For example, although men are more likely to have difficulties with alcohol and illicit drug abuse, antisocial behaviors, and suicide, women exhibit a higher incidence of phobias, anxiety disorders, prescription drug abuse, eating disorders, and depression. In fact, depressive syndromes are more than twice as common in females than in males (McDonald, 1999).

FOH

The fact that women and men may manifest psychological distress in different ways is one of the reasons why some mental health professionals have called for *gender aware therapy*, once called feminist therapy, an approach to counseling and psychotherapy that takes into consideration and legitimizes these differences. Gender aware therapy adheres to the following principles to raise consciousness about gender-related issues for counselors and therapists (Good, Gilbert, & Scher, 1990; Wisch & Mahalik, 1999):

1. Gender should be regarded as an integral aspect of counseling and mental health because of the important role it plays in people's lives.
2. Personal problems must be considered within their social and political contexts.
3. Gender injustices experienced by women and men should be actively changed, and counselors can actively encourage clients to look at options that might involve such changes.
4. In therapy, there should be an egalitarian, collaborative relationship between therapist and client, in which the client is free to explore and discover optimal solutions, rather than a traditional paternalistic approach of therapist "helping" client.
5. People have the right and freedom to *choose* attitudes, feelings, and behaviors that are most congruent for them, despite the gender scripts that have been prescribed for them.

Gender aware therapists may be either women or men who work with either women or men. However, there is evidence that the dynamics of the counseling process vary with the type of gender pairing between counselor and client. People's willingness to disclose information about their intimate relationships seems to depend on their own gender and the gender of the counselor, and a client's sexual orientation and modes of emotional expression affect how the counselor interacts with and perceives clients (Wisch & Mahalik, 1999). However, the gender of the counselor picked by a client seems to be a very individual matter, and sometimes it is simply a matter of chance. It remains to be seen whether gender aware therapy is all that much different from any form of effective counseling and therapy, but it is at least now possible for clients of either sex to find professional counselors who consider the issues of gender to be a significant part of individuality and the counseling process.

Self-Evaluation

Masculinity and Femininity in Your Life

Attitudes toward masculinity and femininity are in a state of flux. Although some people are attempting to blur the stereotyped differences between men and women, others are trying harder than ever to establish definite, identifiable standards of masculinity and femininity. The exercises that follow may help you to clarify your present attitudes toward men and women and your view of your own gender role.

1. **On a sheet of paper, list two men, by name, who for you exemplify ideal manhood; list two women, by name, who for you exemplify ideal womanhood. Then proceed with the following:**
   a. Under the men's names and under the women's names, list the characteristics of these people that have made them your choices as representative of the ideal.
   b. Note which of the characteristics, if any, are listed for both the men and women.
   c. Check those characteristics from either list that you believe you exhibit.

2. **Would you ever consider dressing up in clothing generally identified as being appropriate for members of the opposite sex? If not, why not? If so, consider the following:**
   a. Under what circumstances would you wear clothing of the opposite sex? Only in private? In front of one other highly trusted person? In front of a small group of friends? At a masquerade party? In public places?
   b. If possible and if you are willing, go ahead and dress up in some clothes of the opposite sex, and look yourself over in a full-length mirror. (Note: In some areas, it is illegal to cross-dress and be seen in public.) As you look at yourself, how do you feel? Silly? Sexy? Curious? Happy? Sad? Why do you feel that way?

3. **Examine the following list of qualities and check those that you feel are most important for you to have as a person. (Add other words of your own if you wish.)**

honest	physically	responsible
brave	strong	emotional
athletic	dominating	persuasive
caring	delicate	protective
competitive	intelligent	shy
gentle	successful	reliable
sensitive	submissive	flighty
aggressive	manipulative	sincere
considerate	thoughtful	sexy
	confident	

   a. Now read through the list of qualities again and pick out those that have been traditionally considered masculine and those traditionally considered feminine. Make two separate lists on a sheet of paper. Some words may appear on both lists or on neither. Include any words you have added to the list.
   b. Finally, note where the qualities you checked for yourself fall in your two lists. Think about them. This should help to show how your goals for your own femininity or masculinity relate to traditional ideas about men and women, as you view them.

4. **This exercise should be done with a member of the other gender or with a group of people of both sexes. The men should make two lists on a sheet of paper: the advantages of being female and the disadvantages of being female. Likewise, the women should also make two lists: the advantages and disadvantages of being male. When the lists are complete, everyone should compare them and discuss the characteristics.**

5. **As you are watching television or leafing through the pages of a magazine, note how men and women are portrayed in advertisements. Note which of the men and women appeal the most to you and which are unappealing to you, asking yourself "why?" in each case. Especially note how women and men in the advertisements are shown in traditional or in nontraditional roles.**

6. **Think about each of the following, and attempt to get in touch with your gut reactions—how you feel. Try not to intellectualize and react in the manner in which you think you should. Instead, look carefully at how you are reacting and at what your reactions mean in terms of attitudes toward gender roles.**
   a. An unmarried woman who wishes to be referred to as Ms.
   b. A married woman who insists on being referred to as Ms.
   c. An all-male organization that refuses to consider admitting women as members.
   d. An all-female organization that refuses to consider admitting men as members.
   e. A board of education that passes a school policy requiring that in all courses, "traditional family values are to be upheld, with the feminine role of wife, mother, and homemaker, and masculine role of guide, protector, and provider."
   f. In considering an equally qualified married man and unmarried woman for a position, a company personnel director hires the woman because the company needs to fulfill its affirmative action quota.
   g. After a couple has a new baby, the mother wants to continue working, so the father decides to quit his job and stay home with the child.

Chapter Summary

1. Western culture emphasizes the existence of two sexes, while there are forms of intersexuality such as hermaphroditism or pseudohermaphroditism. In other cultures and times of history, intersexuality has been accepted.

2. There is continuing debate over the degree to which gender roles are shaped by biological and sociocultural forces.

3. Biological sex is expressed in genetics, the gonads, the body, and the brain.

4. The development of our gender identity and gender role is determined by a complex interaction of genetic, physiological, and sociocultural factors.

5. During prenatal life (before birth), the combining of chromosomes sets into motion a genetic program for producing a male, a female, or some ambivalent anatomical structure. Although the pairing of sex chromosomes is normally XX for females and XY for males, there can be abnormal combinations (for example, XXX, XXY, XYY) that produce unusual characteristics.

6. After about a month of embryonic development, an undifferentiated set of fetal gonads appears, along with Müllerian ducts (potential female organs) and Wolffian ducts (potential male organs).

7. If the Y chromosome is present, with its SRY gene, H-Y antigen is produced, transforming the gonads into testes, which in turn produce testosterone and anti-Müllerian hormone. They promote development of male organs from the Wolffian ducts and suppress further development of Müllerian ducts.

8. If the Y chromosome is absent, the fetal gonads become ovaries, and the Wolffian ducts disintegrate. The DAX-1 gene on the X chromosome may control a mechanism by which this gene inhibits the development of male genitals and promotes development of female structures.

9. Male and female genitals and inner reproductive structures then develop. The presence or absence of the male hormones affects development of the nervous system. These hormones have a masculinizing effect, while an independent process of defeminization is going on. The absence of androgens results in the processes of demasculinization and feminization.

10. Abnormal sexual differentiation patterns have offered us clues about the effects of hormones on fetal development and later behavior.

11. There may be a multiplier effect between biological and social factors that eventually leads to masculine and feminine behaviors.

12. During infancy and childhood, boys and girls are treated in particular ways, and social influences along with anatomy begin to help the child form a core gender identity.

13. At puberty, the testes or ovaries begin secreting male or female hormones, triggering the development of secondary sex characteristics. The first stage of puberty is adrenarche, and the second, more profound, stage is gonadarche. Sexual feelings and fantasies also become more pronounced.

14. Adult gender roles may be conceptualized by bipolar, orthogonal, and oblique models, each offering differing views of the relationship between femininity and masculinity.

15. People who exaggerate culturally accepted gender roles are called hypermasculine or hyperfeminine. Androgyny reflects high frequencies of both masculine and feminine traits in the same individual.

16. Transgenderism has often been interpreted as pathological and considered a gender identity disorder, but transgender individuals have been asking for increased recognition in their roles.

17. Transsexualism involves a distinct nonconformity of gender identity with physical attributes of sex. High-intensity transsexuals are more likely to desire surgical and hormonal sex reassignment.

18. Evolutionary psychologists believe that there may be biological bases for some broad categories of gender-related behaviors.

19. Masculinity and femininity are defined by the behaviors that are found in average men and women. There are some average differences between females and males in a few cognitive and motor functions.

20. There are several theoretical positions concerning gender role development. The psychodynamic approach involves complex unconscious interactions between children and their parents.

21. Social learning theory emphasizes socialization and the modeling of gender behaviors by children.

22. Cognitive-developmental theory emphasizes how human thought processes reinforce and perpetuate the gender roles learned from socialization.

23. Gender schema theory highlights the complex network of associations that people hold with regard to gender.

24. Behavioral genetics emphasizes an interaction of nature and nurture in the development of gender roles.

25. Different genders are treated differently within our society. Girls seem to be more prone to losing self-esteem as they reach adolescence.

26. Representation of women in scientific and technical fields has been lower in industrialized nations than in some developing countries because of the different status science holds in these cultures.

27. The feminist movement in American history began with an outcry for women's rights in 1848 by Elizabeth Cady Stanton and Susan B. Anthony.

28. Feminists want to see men and women treated, and compensated, equally and without discrimination.

29. Men have examined the limiting and unhealthy effects of the roles expected of them in our culture.

30. Gender aware therapy is an approach to dealing with people's personal concerns with a full awareness of how gender affects reactions to stress, perceptions of self and the world, and how people view their choices in life.

Focus on Health Questions

You will find in this section the kinds of questions that you may have concerning your own health and sexuality. The page references indicate where in the text the answer is located; the exact place is marked with the logo: **F◆H**

1. If a woman takes hormones during pregnancy, can they affect the development of the fetus? 124

2. What kinds of changes occurred in my body at puberty? 128

3. Is it possible to be confused about my gender? 131–132

4. Are boys really more intelligent than girls? 135

5. If I want to talk with a counselor or therapist about some personal problems, should I choose someone who is aware of how gender influences people's lives? 149

Annotated Readings

Ferree, M. M., Lorber, J., & Hess, B.B. (Eds.) (1999). *The gender lens.* Thousand Oaks, CA: Sage. A comprehensive look and gender studies that surveys the most significant research of the 1990s.

Fisher, H. E. (1999). *The first sex: The natural talents of women and how they are changing the world.* New York: Random House. An anthropologist proposes that the flood of women into the labor force, and the increasing recognition of their special talents and worth, is reshaping the world and its economy.

Geary, D. C. (1998). *Male, female: The evolution of human sex differences.* Washington, D.C.: American Psychological Association. This book argues that evolutionary forces shape gender more than other factors.

Griggs, C. (1998). *S/he: Changing sex and changing clothes.* Oxford, England: Berg. A fascinating look at transgender phenomena of the 1990s, using many case examples.

Kimmel, M. (1997). *Manhood in America: A cultural history.* New York: Free Press. An examination of the psychological development of men from an historical perspective.

Lips, H. M. (1999). *A new psychology of women: Gender, culture, and ethnicity.* Mountain View, CA: Mayfield. An overview of research done in cultures outside the United States, with an emphasis on how gender roles relate to social and economic conditions.

Maccoby, E. E. (1998). *The two sexes: Growing up apart, coming together.* Cambridge, MA: Harvard University Press. A synthesis of many years of work understanding the development of differences in genders.

Marsiglio, W. (1998). *Procreative man.* New York: New York University Press. This book examines men's roles and identities as they are reflected in various social and religious movements.

McCormick, N. B. (1994). *Sexual salvation: Affirming women's sexual rights and pleasures.* Westport, CT: Praeger. A view of women's sexuality juxtaposed with information about historical and contemporary feminism; comprehensive and highly readable.

Money, J. (1994). *Sex errors of the body and related syndromes.* Baltimore: Paul H. Brookes. This is a more technical guide for those who want help in understanding how to work with people who have various gender-related abnormalities. There is good general coverage of each condition.

Peplau, L. A., Veniegas, R. C., Taylor, P. L., & DeBro, S. C. (1999). *Sociocultural perspectives on the lives of women and men*. Mountain View, CA: Mayfield. An examination of how the meanings associated with being a woman or a man depend on the person's sociocultural context.

Pollack, W. (1998). *Real boys: Rescuing our sons from the myths of manhood*. New York: Random House. A book that looks beyond political rhetoric to what studies reveal is best for boys during the child-rearing process.

Yoder, J. D. (1999). *Women and gender: Transforming psychology*. Upper Saddle River, NJ: Prentice Hall. Explores issues within feminist psychology relating to gender.

Part 2

*Understanding Sexuality in
Ourselves and Our Relationships*

■

No one has been able to completely delineate the many complex roles sexuality plays in the human personality. Chapter 6 focuses on the stages of human development and the unfolding of one's sexual nature as one makes the passages through these life stages, each with its own particular hurdles to be faced. Adult sexuality often involves selecting a partner, relating to another person intimately, and establishing long-term bonds such as marriage. Relating sexually within the context of lasting relationships carries its own set of complications and needs, but research is showing that people who are married seem to be relatively satisfied with their sexual lives.

The ways in which human beings are either programmed to behave or taught to behave sexually are matters of conjecture and debate. Certainly the choices we make are based partly on our sexual attitudes and values. As chapter 7 explains, we develop a very individualized set of sexual needs, orientations, fantasies, turn-ons, turnoffs, and behaviors, influenced by social networks and other factors. Developing sexual values is a crucial part of our development as people and of understanding our sexuality. Sexuality education can play a role in shaping attitudes, but it has been met with much controversy. Another controversial area explored in chapter 7 involves the sexual expression of persons with disabilities. Our values and attitudes regarding these issues shape our worldview.

Experts agree that intimacy between people is based on the ability to communicate about a whole range of feelings and issues, including the hurtful and difficult ones. Involvement in a loving relationship may take on many different dimensions. Chapter 8 looks at sexuality and loving and how people need to learn the ground rules for communicating about them. There is no such thing as *not* communicating, because the avoidance of talking or other sharing represents a message in itself. The most important thing is the quality of the communication, and whether it fosters a more positive interchange and lessening of tension, or instead creates new impasses and stresses that drive people further apart. This chapter includes guidelines for improving patterns of communication.

Chapter 6
SEXUALITY THROUGH THE LIFE CYCLE

Our development as sexual beings continues throughout our lives. Several different theories attempt to describe the patterns of psychosexual development. Children move from a generalized awareness of their sensual natures to more specific experiences. Adolescents explore their sexuality through relationships with others. Adult sexuality involves mate selection and establishing intimacy with others.

Chapter 7
SEXUAL INDIVIDUALITY AND SEXUAL VALUES

The factors that lead to the development of sexual individuality are highly complex. Social networks play a role in reinforcing sexual attitudes, which in turn influence people's sexual behaviors. Sexuality education can help people understand sexuality and decision making in their lives. People with disabilities may challenge our concept of sexual individuality.

Chapter 8
SEXUALITY, COMMUNICATION, AND RELATIONSHIPS

A healthy relationship requires open lines of communication. Only too often, couples assume that the best way to stay happy together is to avoid conflict. Good communication includes an openness to dealing with hurtful and difficult issues as well as the joyful ones. Theories of love help us understand the coupling process. Building sexual intimacy depends on effective communication as well.

Chapter 6
Sexuality through the Life Cycle

Chapter Outline

Note: A selection of Focus on Health questions appears at the end of each chapter. Answers to these questions are indicated within the chapter by the symbol in the margin. **FOH**

The thing that scared me the most about getting older was the thought of my sexual powers declining. While I have noticed some degree of moderation in my sexual needs, the frequencies of my sexual activities are really not that much different from when I was in my twenties. I guess the "use it or lose it" principle may be operative here, since I've always believed in using it.

—From a letter to the author

This chapter focuses on the ways in which we develop sexually and express our sexual natures in different stages of the life span. How do our sexual feelings and behaviors become part of our personalities and social interactions? What are the important ways in which children, adolescents, and adults become acquainted with their sexual needs and make decisions about acting on them? How does sexuality fit with different types of human relationships? What effects does the aging process have on our sexual behaviors and interactions? As we look at some answers to these questions, you will again see that there are many unanswered questions and areas of controversy.

Issues of sexuality in relation to human development take on special significance as the characteristics of our population shift. Although the number of people under the age of 18 outnumber the elderly by two to one, the average age of the population is changing dramatically. The number of Americans aged 65 or older has doubled since 1960, and it is expected to double again by the year 2030. By that time, it is predicted that children will outnumber the elderly by only 18 percent. Demographic changes of this sort have a profound effect on social attitudes, including our views of sexuality at various stages of human life.

■ Psychosexual Development

One way or another, we all gradually develop our own individualized ways of thinking and feeling about sexuality, along with our own patterns of sexual orientation and behavior. This complex process is called **psychosexual development,** and it seems to entail interactions of biological factors and learning from the social environment. For the most part, experts seem to agree that human infants are essentially sexually nonspecific. In other words, although they have the capacity to experience physiological sexual response, the specifics of how they exercise that capacity—or even *if* they exercise it—are probably heavily influenced by a whole range of factors. Controversy remains over the relative significance of these various aspects of development.

There may well be critical periods in human development during which a person's stage of biological development interacts with the various processes of socialization present in the environment to establish particular characteristics of the individual's sexuality. Such critical periods would mean that necessary growth has occurred for learning to be optimal, all capacities are at a maximum, and conditions are ideal for a particular kind of learning to take place. It has been speculated that these are times in human development when sexual attitudes and preferences are formed, although there is still little research in this area.

The origins of sexual behavior in the individual have been a source of curiosity and investigation for a long time. In the remainder of this section, I discuss the various theories of psychosexual development that evolved during the last century. These theories seem gradually to be leading toward a more comprehensive understanding of how we become sexual human beings.

Biopsychological Drive/Instinct Theory

Among the earlier attempts to explain psychosexual development was the idea that humans have an inborn "sexual instinct." Human beings are born with sex organs that become increasingly functional during their early years, and these organs are necessary for the propagation of the species. A logical presumption would be that nature had also built into each of us instincts for putting those sex organs into operation. This viewpoint assumes that there is a sexual "drive" that causes people to experience a buildup of sexual "tension" or "need" during times of sexual deprivation or when the environment is sexually stimulating. When sexual activity is experienced, the drive is temporarily satisfied and reduced, eventually to build up again so that the cycle continues. Because this theory squared intuitively well with what many people seem to experience in their own lives, it received much support.

Sex researchers have begun to believe, however, that the concept of a biopsychological sex drive is probably simplistic and inaccurate. Although genetic and hormonal factors obviously give us the potentials for sexual arousal and response, they do not go very far in explaining how individual human beings learn to perceive—or *not* perceive—various stimuli to be sexually arousing. There is a growing consensus that social and cultural environment is extremely important in shaping sexual behavior, including the encouragements and constraints that social sanctions offer, as well as interaction with actual sex partners (Everaerd & Laan, 1995).

> **psychosexual development:** factors that form a person's sexual feelings, orientations, and patterns of behavior.

Theories about inborn sexual drives or instincts led to other assumptions about the "naturalness" or "unnaturalness" of particular sexual behaviors. For example, whatever sexual behavior led to potential propagation of the species (male-female intercourse) could easily be classified as natural, whereas other forms of behavior (such as masturbation or same-gender interactions) could be considered unnatural by default. This concept has been carried even further into value judgments of good and bad or healthy and sick. Behind it all was the idea that as children grew and developed, their sexual instincts gradually emerged and unfolded according to nature's plan. As sexual drive theory has been called into question, we have had to look to other explanations for psychosexual development.

Psychodynamic Theory

Psychodynamic theory, as the name implies, focuses on the working dynamics of the mind. The background of this theory was discussed on page 136. Relying heavily on the concept of instincts, Sigmund Freud postulated the existence of the **libido,** a word used to describe the sexual longing or sex drive that he believed was built into the human psyche. He realized that in addition to this psychological aspect of the sexual instinct there was the physical aspect, involving bodily responses and behaviors. He also introduced the concept of the unconscious mind, purported to control much of human development and behavior even though its thought processes are outside conscious awareness. The libido and unconscious thought processes are essential elements in the psychodynamic theory of psychosexual development, although there have been modifications made since Freud's early formulations (Buhle, 1999; Fisher & Greenberg, 1996).

The major assumption of this theory is that infants are born with a store of sexual energy in the form of the libido. At first, the energy is completely undifferentiated and indiscriminate. It can be directed at anything. For this reason, Freud said that infants were "polymorphously perverse." This energy gradually becomes associated with different pleasurable areas of the body until it finally localizes in the sex organs. Freud believed that it was variations in this process that molded not only the individual's sexual nature but the entire personality.

Psychodynamic theory sees the libido becoming invested in bodily parts that are important in a child's physical development. During infancy, when there is no particular awareness of differences between the sexes, sexual energies of the infant become centered in the mouth, important to gratification of the young child. This is referred to as the oral stage (see Fig. 6.1). As a child then begins to be toilet trained and learns

FIGURE 6.1 *Freud's Oral Stage*

The Freudian theory of sexual development states that in the first year of life, the libido, or sex drive, is located in the mouth. This is the reason, according to Freud, that infants enjoy sucking and putting things into their mouths.

how to control pleasurably the retention and elimination of the bowels, her or his libido moves to the anus, a transition to the anal stage. It is then believed that by the age of about 3 years, children begin to be aware of their genitals, and the libido becomes centered in the penis or clitoris. By this time, children have begun to become aware of the anatomical differences between the sexes (Schalin, 1995).

Freud believed that there is then a **latency period,** during which the sexual energies are said to lie dormant while intellectual and social growth continues. Not all proponents of psychodynamic theory accept the existence of the latency period because there is evidence that children remain in touch with their sexual and romantic feelings throughout childhood. The final stage, when the libido becomes focused in

libido (la-BEED-o or LIB-a-do): a term first used by Freud to define human sexual longing, or sex drive.

latency period: Freudian concept that during middle childhood, sexual energies are dormant; recent research tends to suggest that latency does not exist.

the sex organs, begins at puberty and is called the genital stage (Fisher & Greenberg, 1996).

Psychodynamic theory includes the idea that there are many things that can go wrong as the libido gradually moves to various parts of the body. It holds that adult emotional and mental problems are the result of difficulties during some stage of psychosexual development. Ideally, according to this theory, young women and men should integrate genital orgasm with loving heterosexual relationships, leading toward healthy lifestyles of satisfying sex, reproduction, and work. Needless to say, the emphasis on orgasm in this theory often created undue concern for many people. Others have taken issue with psychodynamic theory because they perceive it to be male-centered, discriminatory toward females, and irrelevant to contemporary knowledge of human sexuality (Buhle, 1999).

Conditioning and Social Learning Theory

Early psychology concerned itself with the mechanisms by which animals learned patterns of behavior. Simple conditioning mechanisms were thought to be applicable to some human behaviors as well, including human sexual arousal. It was assumed, for example, that if particular erotic words were heard repeatedly during sexual arousal, eventually the words themselves could become a conditional stimulus that could elicit some degree of sexual arousal, the conditioned response. Later work in psychology clarified more complex principles of operant conditioning. According to these principles, when behavior is **reinforced**—either through pleasure, reward, or removal of some unpleasant stimulus—it is likely to be repeated. Negative consequences of a behavior through unpleasant results, pain, or the loss of rewarding stimuli tend to decrease the frequency of the behavior. Hypothetically applied to sexual development in humans, this perspective emphasizes the influences of positive and negative consequences on sexual behaviors.

Conditioning theorists emphasized that the development of modes of sexual functioning is a complex phenomenon, influenced by many different sources. They also used the concept of **generalization** to explain how specific, learned sexual responses might be generalized to other, similar circumstances. For example, an individual who was conditioned to become sexually aroused by seeing female breasts might generalize that experience to other things associated with breasts (bras, other underwear, blouses, other parts of a woman's body, perfume, and so on). The generalization process would be kept in check by **discrimination,** which enabled the individual to avoid responding to one stimulus while responding to similar stimuli.

Conditioning theory, then, held that we learn our sexual preferences and behaviors through observational learning, a complex pattern of reinforcement, and the pairing of stimuli with sexual response. As human beings grew up, social cues would be picked up that helped determine what would be considered "acceptable" sexual behavior. Gradually the set of stimuli to which the individual responds sexually was narrowed. If sexual behaviors or needs that the person did not consider socially acceptable remain, then conflicts and emotional disturbances might develop.

An extension of conditioning theory emerged in the 1960s with the model called social learning theory. This model suggested that the learning process was influenced by cumulative observation of and identification with other people. This cumulative learning process was seen as a crucial one, as people's perceptions were shaped by the impressions and attitudes they formed in their early development. For example, children and adolescents would be prone to imitating (modeling) and adopting the behaviors they see in other people whom they admire and identify with (see Fig. 6.2). This theory emphasized the potential power of television and movies, as well as of parents, friends, and others in the modeling of sexual behaviors.

Although there is ample scientific literature devoted to the roles of conditioning and social learning in establishing patterns of sexual arousal, there really is very little evidence that they represent particularly valid explanations (O'Donohue & Plaud, 1994). Their value in understanding psychosexual development lies more in having opened the possibility that sexual behaviors are influenced by environmental factors.

Developmental Theory

Other theories began to focus more clearly on the influence of social forces on child development that could be applied to psychosexual development as well. Piaget (1932) considered the importance of cognition, intellect, and reasoning in children, and Kohlberg (1981) examined the many facets of moral development. Erik Erikson (1968) made significant strides toward devising a model of *developmental psychology* that clearly showed the tasks that had to be

reinforcement: in conditioning theory, any influence that helps shape future behavior as a punishment or reward stimulus.

generalization: application of specific learned responses to other, similar situations or experiences.

discrimination: the process by which an individual extinguishes a response to one stimulus while preserving it for other stimuli.

FIGURE 6.3   *Erikson's Psychosocial Development*

In Erikson's life-span theory of psychosocial development, young children learn skills as well as identity and values from those around them. Positive values about themselves and their sexuality will aid children in developing intimacy with others.

FIGURE 6.2   *Social Learning Theory*

According to this theory, children learn attitudes and values by observing and imitating the behavior of others. What they learn depends partly on the power and prestige of the person observed. Television, movies, and music can be powerful influences on the sexual values and behavior of children and adolescents.

accomplished at various stages of human growth and development (see Fig. 6.3). He considered the tasks so crucial that he called them crises. Erikson conceptualized an eight-stage life span of **psychosocial development** that extended from birth to old age. Because of his psychoanalytic training, Erikson believed that there was a powerful libido built into all of us, but he also realized that cultural and social influences help to shape our sexual identities, including our sexual behaviors. He maintained that at each of the eight stages of life, there is a crisis of psychosocial development that must be resolved (see Table 6.1). Each crisis can take the individual either in a direction of adjustment, health, and positive self-concept, or in a direction of maladaptation, unrest, and low self-esteem (Lippert, 1997).

According to Erikson, during adolescence and young adulthood each individual has the task of achieving a clear understanding of herself or himself as a sexual person and of achieving a sense of inti-

macy with other human beings. Failure to reach these goals may result in role confusion and isolation that can generate unhealthy methods of sexual functioning for a lifetime. Success in achieving a healthy sexual identity partially hinges on how successfully the earlier tasks of the life span have been resolved. Erikson also emphasized the importance of other people and how they respond to the individual—social factors—in this model of psychosexual development.

A Unified Theoretical Model of Psychosexual Development

Researcher John Bancroft (1990) proposed a unified theory of how sexual development takes place. It considers the various stages of physical and psychological development through which human beings pass, and it identifies three principal "strands" that are part of each person's developmental framework. These three strands tend to develop in parallel during the childhood years but relatively independent of one another. Then, during adolescence, the strands come together and become more integrated as they form the foundations of a sexually mature adult. These strands have been identified as the following:

1. *Gender identity.* The inner experience of one's gender plays a crucial role in sexual development. During childhood, the basic identity is established, and during adolescence, sexual

psychosocial development: the cultural and social influences that help shape human sexual identity.

Table 6.1	The Crises to Be Resolved during Erikson's Stages of Psychosocial Development
Stage in Life Cycle	**Crisis**
Infancy	Gaining trust in self and environment vs. Feeling mistrust and wariness of others
Ages 1½–3	Achieving a sense of autonomy vs. Shame and doubt over one's ability to be independent
Ages 3–5½	Learning how to take initiative comfortably vs. Feeling guilty over motivations and needs
Ages 5½–12	(The time when school and other external influences gain more significance) Gaining a sense of industry and competence vs. Feeling inferior and inept
Adolescence	Forming a sense of one's own identity vs. Role confusion and self-questioning
Young Adulthood	Achieving intimacy and connection with others vs. Feeling alone and isolated
Adulthood	Realizing generativity and positive interpersonal relationships vs. Feeling stagnant and unfulfilled
Maturity	Achieving ego integrity and relative peace with one's life vs. A sense of despair and wastedness

Source: Data from E. Erikson, *Identity: Youth and Crisis,* 1968. W. W. Norton, New York, NY.

behaviors serve an important function in reorganizing the specifics of one's gender identity. This begins to establish the sense of oneself as man, woman, or transgendered.

2. *Sexual response and understanding one's sexual orientation.* Puberty triggers a variety of physical and emotional changes within the individual, and it usually leads to a greater awareness of and urge toward sexual arousal. The coming to terms with these needs and responses plays an important part in figuring out who one really is sexually.

3. *Capacity for intimate dyadic relationships.* In later adolescence and early adulthood, people begin exploring their sexuality within the context of partnerships or dyads (pairs). How effective the individual is in handling the complexities of dyadic relationships is significant in later sexual development.

Part of sexual development is gaining a deeper understanding of one's own sexual orientation, a process that unfolds as people negotiate the various stages of their physical and psychological development (Bancroft, 1990; Sanders, 1999). Children first go through a *prelabeling* process, and they begin to identify what is expected of them sexually. Adolescents then begin to categorize their own sexual orientations according to the labels that their social groups provide. This is the *self-labeling* stage of identifying sexual orientation. The adolescent privately compares her or his own feelings and responses to those that are prescribed in the prevailing social scripts. If self-labels are out of step with what the adolescent has learned is expected and desired by the society and culture, a great deal of personal conflict and confusion may result. Finally, sexual orientation is defined through *social labeling*. The person's perceptions of self are subject to validation by what is known about the society's labels for various sexual orientations and preferences.

Contemporary Social Process Theory

When the researchers who conducted the National Health and Social Life Survey (NHSLS) designed their comprehensive study of sexual behavior, they realized that would have to go beyond the study of individual human beings because we do not develop sexually in a social vacuum. To help interpret the meaning of their statistics on sexual behavior, researchers drew on some of the most respected theories of social psychology, sociology, and economics. The following three theoretical perspectives proved to be the most useful to their work (Laumann, Gagnon et al., 1994).

Sexual Script Theory: Social Foundations

John Gagnon and William Simon (1973) were among the first sociologists to take issue with theories that relied on the presumption of an intense, biologically generated sex drive. They believed that internal sexual energy might not be very intense at all, at least in many individuals. They also proposed that too much emphasis had been placed on the effects of childhood sexual patterns on later development. Many novel factors come into play at the beginning of adolescence that can exert significant influence on sexual development, quite independent of childhood experience. They developed what came to be known as *scripting theory*. This theoretical stance was one of the first attempts to explain how sexual behavior was socially constructed. In addition to minimizing the effects of sex drive, it holds that patterns of sexual conduct are derived from the social and cultural contexts that are filled with messages or **social scripts** that regulate most human behavior. Through a lifelong acculturation process, people acquire the sexual scripts—or patterns of sexual conduct—that suit their own needs. This sometimes means that people adopt sexual scripts that deviate from cultural norms (Gagnon, 1999; Simon, 1999).

In terms of sexual behavior, this would mean that although particular social situations are not sexually oriented in themselves, we organize the elements of a situation—for example, an available partner, privacy, sexual desire—in such a way that they become sexual. Because sexual scripts are learned, new learning experiences during each emergent stage of an individual's physical development help to contribute to that individual's sexual development.

There are three different types of sexual scripts, reflective of different levels of functioning for the individual. In the broadest context, scripts have *cultural scenarios,* referring to the messages and instructional guidance about sexual behavior offered by one's culture. It is almost as if every possible message about sex within a culture is part of the picture. One of the reasons the process is so complex and individualized is because there are so many combinations and permutations. The social constructionist view holds that social and cultural imperatives play a significant role in determining what sexual choices people will make within their society or culture. On a more intermediate level, there are the *interpersonal scripts* determined by the expectations of other people about conduct within interpersonal relationships. Then, at the level of the individual's own mind, are the *intrapsychic scripts.* The person takes all of the information from the cultural and interpersonal contexts and then processes it internally. As individual men and women make sense of what the surrounding sexual messages mean for them, they begin to develop their own sets of sexual scripts. These three levels of scripting are constantly interacting with one another, and they may be modified over the course of a person's life span (Gagnon, 1999; Laumann, Gagnon et al., 1994).

Choice Theory: Sexual Decision Making

Although sexual scripts provide people with codes of sexual conduct from their cultures, they do not fully explain how individuals choose from the varieties of sexual behavior available to them. *Choice theory,* borrowed from economics, assumes that human beings make choices out of the need to apportion their "resources"—in this case, sexual and relational—in order to reach certain goals. Some typical goals of sexual behavior are sexual pleasure, the emotional satisfaction derived from intimacy, having children, and building a positive reputation among one's peers. In order to

reach such goals, various human resources must be managed because there is a "cost" involved in securing a sexual partner; it takes time, emotional energy, social skills, and sometimes money to do so. So like economic outcomes, there is always a limit to the number of sexual partners an individual can "afford" to choose. For most people, that number is really quite small (Laumann, Gagnon et al., 1994).

There are two other components of choice theory that have been applied to the sexual arena: risk management and the market. Sexual choices are usually made with a degree of uncertainty, and they involve weighing a degree of risk. There are both positive and negative consequences to be considered, and these can affect people's sexual choices markedly. Some people are better than others at assessing and managing sexual and relational risks. All of these elements affect how individuals approach the "market" for sex partners. How well one fares in the social marketplace depends on all sorts of variables, including physical attributes, attractiveness, personality, intelligence, and age. It is the components of this social-sexual economy that influence the choices of sexual behavior that individual human beings make (Sprecher, 1998).

Social Network Theory: Sexual Relationships

Although scripting and choice theories can help us comprehend how patterns of sexual conduct are determined by the individual's experiences, circumstances, and decisions, they have less to say about the actual social connections that can influence sexual activities. *Social network theory* recognizes that most sexual activity is negotiated within the context of social relationships, and it is the characteristics of those relationships that become significant in determining what sexual activities, if any, will occur. Two-person partnerships, or sexual dyads, do not exist in a vacuum; they are part of a larger network of social relationships that also influences the sexual activities of the individuals who are part of them (Sprecher, 1998).

The social composition of a sexual relationship affects the type of sexual behavior that will be experienced in the relationship. For example, whether or not people share oral sex is clearly affected by their age, educational level, and race (Michael et al., 1994). We also label partnerships in different ways: "lovers," "girlfriend-boyfriend," "one-night stand," "married couple." The way in which a relationship has been labeled and socially defined affects how

social script: a complex set of learned responses to a particular situation that is formed by social influences.

the individuals within that relationship view it and also affects how the larger social network defines what is appropriate sexual conduct for it. Social network theory looks at the principles of relationships, but it must rely on scripting theory and choice theory to explain what happens within specific relationships. At the same time, sexual scripts and choices are influenced by the qualities of the relationship, and the relationship helps to shape the scripts and choices of its members. This complex interaction of factors constitutes the *social process* of psychosexual development.

Which of the six theories that attempt to explain psychosexual development seem most convincing to you? Why? Are there any aspects of different theories you would combine to create a more viable theory?

■ Sexuality in Infancy and Childhood

At least in Western cultures, there seems to be enough evidence to conclude that infancy and childhood are periods of human development that include a continuing emergence of sexuality that began prior to birth (see Fig. 6.4). There is not sufficient cross-cultural data to determine whether the patterns of sexual development observed in Western societies apply universally. Most of the anthropological information on childhood sexuality that we do have has been a byproduct of broader studies, and anthropologists in general have been reluctant to focus on the sexual development of

infants and children. So in a global sense, we really do not yet have a reliable picture of what constitutes "normal" childhood sexuality (Frayser, 1995).

Ultrasound images of fetuses still in the uterus show that a male fetus can experience erection of the penis even before birth. Very early in development, infants seem to show interest in exploring their own bodies and seeking whatever pleasure they can gain from that exploration. There is ample evidence to suggest that baby boys experience genital responses. Erection has even been observed within the first few minutes after birth. A number of male infants seem to have orgasms, as evidenced by sequences of tension-building, rhythmic muscular contractions, and pelvic thrusting, culminating in what appears to be pleasurable sensations and relaxation. In baby girls, the labia may be quite prominent and the vaginal lining pinkish in color for several weeks after birth, the result of maternal hormones still present in the bloodstream. There is also evidence of vaginal lubrication that occurs spontaneously in regular cycles from the time a female is born (Blake, 1994; Martinson, 1994).

Although these early patterns of physical arousal and sensual enjoyment do not represent the socialized patterns of eroticism that form later in human development, they do demonstrate the extreme sensitivity of infants. Austrian researcher Ernest Borneman (1994) has suggested that the entire surface of the skin in a newborn infant is a single **erogenous zone,** meaning that it is sensitive to sensual stimulation that can lead to arousal.

The foundations for sensuality, intimacy, and relationship to other people are established during infancy. Bonding between infants and their parents is an important part of this process. Infancy may also be a time when small children begin to notice how they are treated by their fathers and mothers and begin to form early concepts of their relationships with others (Casper, Hawkins, & O'Connell, 1994).

There are several significant developmental tasks accomplished during infancy. Immediately after birth, there is a period when babies seem very alert, and a bonding process occurs between them and their parent(s). The holding, touching, and cuddling given to an infant are part of the evolution of its ability to relate to and be intimate with others. Between 6 months and 1 year of age, babies begin to touch their genitals, if they are not prohibited from doing so. As we have seen in the preceding chapter, infancy is also the time when the baby begins to be socialized concerning the cultural expectations of gender roles.

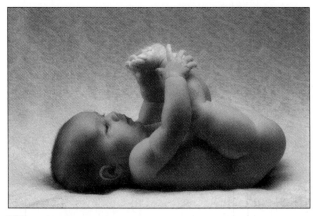

FIGURE 6.4 *Infant Sexuality*

Infants develop an awareness of their bodies and their sexuality, first, through a bonding with the parents and the sensuous contact involved in cuddling and holding, and, second, by exploring their own bodies, including their genitals.

erogenous zone (a-RAJ-a-nus): any area of the body that is sensitive to sexual arousal.

Sexual Curiosity Grows in Childhood

Very young children are often observed fondling their genitals, sometimes seeming to produce sexual excitement and orgasm. Children begin to gain a sense of what their bodies are and of the capacities for pleasure that their bodies have. This can be seen as a beginning period of potentiation, when vague awareness of sexual feelings and early ranges of sexual responsiveness are established. Only a few children seem to have particularly specific sexual preferences, whereas most are apparently "multisexual," or able to respond to many different forms of sexual stimulation (Frayser, 1995). Children also learn more and more about sex and reproduction as they progress through childhood and as their verbal capabilities grow, with a spurt of knowledge and understanding occurring around the age of 11 (Goldman, 1994; Goldman & Goldman, 1982).

Two recent studies have provided new insights into what might be considered "normative" patterns of sexual development during childhood. For the most part, these studies have relied on the reports of parents, especially mothers, concerning the behaviors of their children. The UCLA Family Lifestyles Project (FLS) has followed over 200 children from birth until adulthood, and it has been the source of a wealth of longitudinal data (Okami, Olmstead, & Abramson, 1997). An even more comprehensive examination of childhood sexual behavior has been conducted by a group of psychologists at the Mayo Clinic, using questionnaires that were administered to the primary female caregivers of 1,114 children aged 2 to 12 years (Friedrich, Fisher, Broughton, Houston, & Shafran, 1998). This research has confirmed that children exhibit a broad range of sexual behaviors, many of which are common enough to be considered "normal" for various developmental stages.

The UCLA study found 77 percent of parents reporting that their children had engaged in sex play prior to the age of 6, including masturbation. Nearly 47 percent of those parents indicated that their children had engaged in some sort of interactive sex play with another child during the same period of life. By the age of 2 or 3, many children begin to explore the bodies of their playmates, ranging from simple embraces, to stroking, caressing, kissing, and touching the genitals. They also continue to have an interest in their own genitals (see Fig. 6.5). Some become involved in games that permit mutual body exploration, such as "doctor" or "nurse." From the ages of 3 to 5, awareness of being a boy or girl seems to make itself known, although many children cannot really explain how they know they are a girl or a boy. They most often make their identification based on social markers such as clothing, rather than by anatomical differences, such as genitals (Frayser, 1995; Okami et al., 1997). Knowledge

FIGURE 6.5 *Sexual Curiosity*

Most children around the age of 2 or 3 are curious about their own bodies as well as the bodies of others. Any sexual activity usually involves a fondling of the genitals. Because children tend to respond to each other affectionately at these ages, touching, hugging, and kissing may extend to the genital area.

about where babies come from and how they are born seems to become more refined as children grow and develop, and this may be enhanced by parents who make a point of providing this information to their children (Berends & Caron, 1994).

The Mayo Clinic research found that the most frequently observed behaviors among children aged 2 to 12 were self-stimulation, exposing body parts to another child, and behaviors relating to the personal boundaries of others, such as rubbing against another person. More intrusive behaviors, such as oral-genital contact or insertion of things into the vagina or rectum, were less frequently observed. Although the amount of sexual behavior observed among children declines quite steadily during the childhood years (see Fig. 6.6), the researchers have cautioned that this does not mean the behaviors are decreasing, only that as children become older, they become more private with their sexual behaviors (Friedrich et al., 1998).

Based on their study and the findings of other research, a tentative outline of sexual behaviors was formulated for boys and girls at various stages in their development (see Table 6.2). Although the table again confirms much of what has always been assumed about children, it also reflects the greater level of privacy they achieve as they reach adolescence

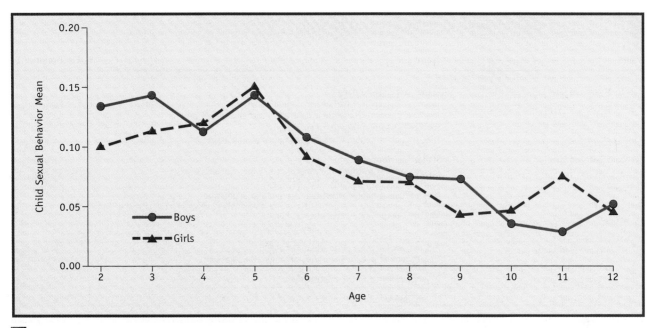

FIGURE 6.6 *Observed Sexual Behavior in Children*

The sexual behaviors of children between the ages of 2 and 12, as observed and reported by their primary caregivers, tend to decrease with age. It is believed that this does not represent a decrease in actual sexual behavior but in a greater awareness of social appropriateness and seeking more privacy.

Source: From W. N. Friedrich et al., "Normative Sexual Behavior in Children: A Contemporary Sample." *Pediatrics,* 101 (4), p. e9, 1998. Used with permission of the American Academy of Pediatrics.

(Friedrich et al., 1998). Exposure to sex play in childhood does not seem to be associated with the level of adjustment in the late teen years (Okami, Olmstead, & Abramson, 1997).

Masturbation and exhibiting genitals to other children are common forms of childhood sex play. In later childhood, some youngsters experiment with other forms of behavior, including oral-genital contact and attempts at anal or vaginal intercourse. These activities may be with a same-gender partner or one of the other gender. Repeated aggressive sexual behavior in younger children toward other children, such as coercive oral sex, insertion of objects into the rectum, or attempted rape, may well represent signs of previous sexual abuse of the child. This is discussed in greater detail in chapter 15 "Sexual Coercion, Rape, and Abuse"

Parental attitudes and lifestyles seem to play a role in determining how children will behave sexually, or at least how observable their sex play will be. More "relaxed" or liberal approaches to such things as family nudity, co-bathing, and co-sleeping were correlated with higher levels of observed sexual behaviors among children, although this might again be more related to the degree of privacy a child will seek. Ethnicity did not seem to be related to reported sexual behaviors in childhood (Friedrich et al., 1998; Okami et al., 1997).

How parents and others respond to sex play in children begins to set the stage for later sex-related values. If a parent constantly punishes a child's attempts at genital exploration or sex play, the child may rapidly learn that her or his sex organs and exploratory behaviors are bad. At times, the reactions of anxious adults can transform an innocent, natural phase of sexual exploration and development into a traumatic event. If parents accept sexual exploration as a natural, positive part of growing up and help children to understand what will be socially acceptable in later life, they may contribute enormously to the development of a healthy sexuality in their children. Professionals often recommend that parents be involved in teaching their children the names of their sex organs, as part of a broader sexuality education effort that will include awareness of sexual abuse and personal safety.

One of the concerns that parents sometimes have is the degree to which nudity should be allowed or encouraged within the family's setting. Most professionals agree that when nudity within the home is permitted and that there is no sexual abuse, there do not seem to be negative consequences. This is also true of situations in which children have accidentally viewed their parents engaging in sexual behavior. Neither does allowing younger children to sleep at times in the parental bed seem to create any adverse consequences. Children themselves may well reach stages in

Table 6.2	Developmentally Related Sexual Behaviors	
Age	**Item**	**% Endorsement**
2- to 5-year-old boys	Stands too close to people	29.3
	Touches sex (private) parts when in public places	26.5
	Touches or tries to touch their mother's or other women's breasts	42.4
	Touches sex (private) parts when at home	60.2
	Tries to look at people when they are nude or undressing	26.8
2- to 5-year-old girls	Stands too close to people	25.8
	Touches or tries to touch their mother's or other women's breasts	43.7
	Touches sex (private) parts when at home	43.8
	Tries to look at people when they are nude or undressing	26.9
6- to 9-year-old boys	Touches sex (private) parts when at home	39.8
	Tries to look at people when they are nude or undressing	20.2
6- to 9-year-old girls	Touches sex (private) parts when at home	20.7
	Tries to look at people when they are nude or undressing	20.5
10- to 12-year-old boys	Is very interested in the opposite sex	24.1
10- to 12-year-old girls	Is very interested in the opposite sex	28.7

Source: From W. N. Friedrich et al., "Normative Sexual Behavior in Children: A Contemporary Sample." *Pediatrics,* 101 (4), p. e9, 1998. Used with permission of the American Academy of Pediatrics.

their development when they signal some discomfort with being seen naked by other family members or with seeing their parents nude. It is important for parents to respect these needs, making as little fuss as possible, and avoiding inflicting any embarrassment on the child. Nonetheless, studies confirm that childhood exposure to nudity in the home does not adversely affect adult sexual adjustment or functioning; in fact, boys with such backgrounds may actually have more positive developmental outcomes such as increased comfort with physical contact and expressions of affection in adult life and lowered risk for contracting sexually transmitted disease (Okami, Olmstead, Abramson, & Pendleton, 1998).

Love and Romance in Childhood

Largely because of the Freudian concept of latency, it was once assumed that children between the ages of roughly 6 and 12 have little interest in sexual feelings or relationships with the opposite gender. Instead, it was believed that the sexual energies were dormant and that children tended to reject members of the other sex in favor of same-gendered friends. Researchers who have studied children and their sexual development have generally expressed skepticism about the existence of a latency phase. They have found evidence that children can develop romantic and even sexual attractions to others as their brains become more fully grown and their bodies begin to reach reproductive maturity (Borneman, 1994; Frayser, 1995; Goldman, 1994). These romantic and sexual attachments eventually become defined as "love."

Around the ages of 11 or 12, girls and boys begin to show a distinct increase in levels of interest toward the other gender, and they begin to develop more intimate relationships when the opportunity is available (Friedrich et al., 1998). Children appear to take their love very seriously and begin to move toward more concrete wishing and planning. A final step is arranging a "date" with the loved one, among those 10- to 12-year-olds who have the courage to do so.

In some cases, the preadolescent romantic attachments are with a member of the child's own gender, but because of social pressures, children are less inclined to label these attachments "love" and instead describe them as friendships. Such same-gender attachments in earlier years may represent a preliminary awareness of later same-gender orientations and sexual attractions. Other times, even very intense same-gender relationships in childhood appear to have no particular bearing on an individual's future romantic and sexual proclivities.

■ Sexuality in Adolescence

Adolescence is that period of social, emotional, and cognitive development that moves young people toward adulthood. It is a time during which individuals become biologically mature and develop a greater sense of independence, autonomy, and personal

adolescence: period of emotional, social, and physical transition from childhood to adulthood.

CROSS-CULTURAL PERSPECTIVE
Adolescent Sexual Attitudes and Behaviors across Cultures

Adolescents develop their sexual identities, attitudes, and behaviors within their cultural contexts, and these differ markedly from society to society. Distinct changes in the sexual values of adolescents have been occurring in most areas of the globe in recent decades, reflective of increased urbanization, industrialization, and influence by Western media. It appears that all over the world, young people are starting to have sex earlier and they are valuing their sexual pleasure more than they are safer sexual practices. In 14 developed and developing countries, the average age for first sex was 17.4 years (London International Group, 1997).

Surveys of young people in Great Britain and Ireland have shown marked differences. The level of sexual activity among British adolescents is much higher than that of the Irish, and there is more risky, unprotected sexual activity in Great Britain as well. Even though Ireland is a highly religious country, with much more conservative values regarding love, sex, and marriage, Roman Catholic adolescents have a relatively positive attitude toward the use of contraceptives (Breakwell & Fife-Schaw, 1992).

In Mexico and Latin America, adolescents have also been caught in the ambivalence of traditional religious values that seem to be conflicting with changing patterns of sexual behavior. The *machismo* tradition often creates conflicts surrounding power imbalances in relationships and the degree of comfort males have with their gender identities (Kulick, 1998; Prieur, 1998). In general, Mexican adolescents receive information about contraception too late, and they tend to receive sexuality education that emphasizes biological facts over decision-making skills. This mirrors problems that are plaguing the youth of Latin America, where there is a high rate of adolescent pregnancy, and yet information about and access to contraception are very limited.

Scandinavian countries, by contrast, have often been considered progressive for their efforts in the area of sexuality and contraception education. In the developed world, adolescent pregnancy rates have been consistently lower in this part of Europe than in the United States. In Norway, the median age of first intercourse for girls is 17.3 years, and for boys it is 18 years, about the same for most other European countries (Traaen & Kvalem, 1996). The age for first intercourse in Switzerland is essentially the same, and yet this country has the lowest adolescent fertility rate in western Europe, with a rate of 4.6 births per 1,000 15- to 19-year-olds per year. This seems to be the result of widespread Swiss school sexuality education programs and a nationwide AIDS campaign that has stressed the use of condoms in sexual activities (Narring, Michaud, & Sharma, 1996; Widmer et al., 1998). In Russia and in India, the situation is considerably different. Sexuality education is largely lacking, and young people often have unprotected sex. The rate of unintended pregnancies is much higher in these two countries, and there is a great deal of misinformation about HIV and condom use. Indian youth seem to have relatively little awareness of the sexual behaviors of their peers (Nardi, 1998; Tikoo, 1996).

Asian and African cultures have been experiencing marked contrasts between traditional sexual values and more permissive sexual attitudes in adolescents today. With its strict Confucian history, Korean society always severely restricted adolescent sexual activity, traditionally separating girls from boys at the age of around 7. Rapid modernization in Korea has led to a marked increase in youthful sexual activity and also to resulting guilt and confusion on the part of its youth (Youn, 1996). In Japan, sexuality has been minimized and regulated as being tangential to the performance of responsible duty. Although typical European adolescents do not place a high value on sexual abstinence, Japanese youth consider chastity to be very important. There is less teenage sexual activity and far less single motherhood there than in the United States, although abortion is quite accessible. Japanese youth often rush into sexual activity during late adolescence, as if catching up for their more chaste earlier years (Kitamura, 1996; WuDunn, 1996). China has been seeing marked increases in adolescent sexual activity even in the face of official government condemnation, but there is little evidence that these changes have much to do with Western influences. Instead, they may well reflect fundamental cultural shifts in China (Tang et al., 1997).

African adolescents continue to face mixed signals regarding their sexual behaviors. In some societies, there is encouragement to postpone sexual activity. In others, virginity is not seen as a virtue, and in fact it may be considered a sign of unsociableness or ill-health. Even so, many families still want their daughters to be virgins when they marry. In African countries, Western influences do seem to be playing a role in exposing youth to sexual themes in the media, and this has led to the breakdown of some traditional restrictions on adolescent sexual behavior (Runganga & Aggleton, 1998; Savage & Tchombe, 1995). Satellite dishes have brought Western television to places such as Morocco, and this has led to the need for redefinition of gender roles and sexual attitudes while the people struggle to maintain some core traditional values (Davis & Davis, 1995).

identity. The capacity for abstract thinking increases, and planning for the future is balanced with a recognition of the potential impacts of current actions. During adolescence, young people strengthen their gender identities and begin clarifying their sexual orientations and identities as they experience more adultlike erotic feelings and experiment further with sexual behaviors (Haffner, 1995).

The boundaries of adolescence are poorly defined in Western societies. In many cultures other than our own, there are rites of passage in which a youthful individual participates, declaring that she or he is no longer a child. Along with that passage into young adulthood come carefully prescribed (and proscribed) modes of sexual behavior. Youngsters in Western culture usually must deal with growth into adulthood in a much more vague and gradual way. In their sexual development, as in many other aspects of their growth, adolescents often experience confusion, fear, and misunderstandings about their bodies and emotions. Girls typically experience puberty sooner than boys, so there is often an awkward period around ages 11 to 13 when boys' physical maturation lags behind that of girls. Although most adolescents experience an increased level of interest in sex, this phenomenon occurs in varying degrees. There are young people who experience an insistent sexual interest and the need for frequent sexual gratification, but there are others who experience very little in the way of sexual needs.

Adolescents today experiment with sexual activities at younger ages than once was the case, and in fact 80 percent of people in the United States have intercourse by the time they reach the age of 20. There was an increase in sexual activity among teens that began in the 1970s and continued through the 1980s. During the 1990s, however, there was a decline in the number of high school students who experienced sexual intercourse. In 1997, the percentage of high school students indicating they had experienced intercourse dropped to 48.4 percent, as compared to 54 percent the prior year (Warren et al., 1998). Among urban males aged 17 to 19, the percentage who had ever had sex increased from 66 percent in 1979 to 76 percent in 1988. By 1995, the figure had decreased to 68 percent (Ku et al., 1998). Since the 1980s, differences in teen sexual behavior patterns across socioeconomic, racial, and ethnic groups have narrowed considerably. It is now clearly established that the initiation of sexual intercourse during adolescence is a typical pattern of behavior in the United States and a significant characteristic of the transition to adulthood. Whether the reported frequencies of sexual intercourse among teens have stabilized or represent the beginning of a decline is not yet clear (Singh & Darroch, 1999).

Among those teenagers who refrain from engaging in sexual intercourse, the most common reasons cited relate to fears of pregnancy, disease, or parental disapproval. The second level of reasons relate to conservative values that mitigate against sexual involvement. The least common reasons for abstaining from sex revolve around embarrassment or concern about peer or partner disapproval. Researchers have found that remaining sexually abstinent is a great challenge to contemporary teens and that no single message, value stance, or approach will help all adolescents who wish to abstain from sex actually achieve that goal (Blinn-Pike, 1999).

There have been persistent claims that sexual activity during the adolescent years leads to negative self-concepts, when in fact the evidence would suggest that sexually experienced adolescents over the age of 15 actually tend to have higher levels of self-esteem than those who are inexperienced (Haffner, 1995). NHSLS data showed that 71 percent of women and 92 percent of men who experienced heterosexual intercourse during their teen years report that they wanted it to happen and were not pressured into it (Laumann, Gagnon et al., 1994). Two studies involving over 2,500 high school students in tenth grade or beyond found that significant numbers of those who had had first sexual intercourse actually felt better about themselves after their most recent sexual encounters. However, it was also found that girls are at somewhat higher risk of negative reactions such as guilt or feeling used (Donald, Lucke, Dunne, & Raphael, 1995; Langer, Zimmerman, & Katz, 1995). Among a sample of 71 sexually experienced teenage girls aged 13 to 15, 60 of them felt they should have waited until they were more ready (Rosenthal et al., 1997).

Our society continues to send very powerful and contradictory messages to young people regarding sexuality. Although the media are saturated with messages encouraging sex, educational efforts directed at teenagers are increasingly emphasizing the ideal of refraining from sexual activity. For some time, experts have focused on the dangers and risks of adolescent sexual activity, often overlooking the fact that many adolescents feel a desire for sexual pleasure and are planning to act on that desire when circumstances make it possible. Adolescents may also approach their sexual activities unrealistically and without careful consideration to the risks involved. They typically do not have access to the kinds of sexuality education that will inform them accurately, aid them in developing the necessary skills and understandings to manage their own sexual decisions, and help them to recognize the responsibilities that go along with sexual behavior (Haffner, 1995).

The primary sources of sex information for the majority of young persons are friends of the same sex and independent reading. There is an increasing body of research data indicating that mothers' attitudes about dating sexuality have significant effects on the attitudes and behaviors of their children. When their mothers disapprove of premarital sex, are willing to discuss sexuality and birth control, and have clear rules about dating, adolescents tend to postpone sexual activity longer and have sex less frequently (Jaccard, Dittus, & Gordon, 1996). Conversely, when mothers themselves began having sex at an early age, their adolescent children are far more likely to engage in sexual intercourse before age 14 (Manlove, 1997). The mass media and the Internet are becoming increasingly important to adolescents in learning about issues such as sexual biology, sexually transmitted diseases, abortion, and same-gender orientation, but there is less evidence to suggest that this information actually leads to attitudinal or behavioral change.

Aside from family and peer influences, there is some interesting research suggesting that age of first intercourse may also be somehow associated with some genetic factors, especially among white males (Miller et al., 1999; Rodgers, Rowen, & Buster, 1999). These studies draw attention to the nature-nurture issues in an entirely new context: the potential influences of genes on the initiation of sexual behavior. Further study may clarify these issues more fully.

Early Adolescent Sexuality

As the physical changes of puberty occur, the adolescent must begin to integrate new awareness into her or his core gender identity. Boys experience their first ejaculations of semen, and girls begin menstruating. New attention is therefore called to their sex organs. At the same time, parents and others begin to attach new meanings to behaviors and emotions. The adolescent must build these developments into an awareness as a young man or woman. The ages between 12 and 16 often see the beginning of more overt sexual behavior. Increased testosterone levels in teen males is associated with increased levels of sexual activity (Halpern et al., 1998).

The earlier research evidence suggested that most boys experience their first ejaculation during masturbation, although they may have previously experienced orgasm without emission of semen. The first ejaculation usually occurs between the ages of 11 and 15, although Kinsey reported cases of the earliest remembered ejaculation occurring as young as 8 years and as old as 21 years. In about 12 percent of boys, first ejaculation happened as a nocturnal emission ("wet dream"), and in about 5 percent it occurred during some sexual activity with another male (Kinsey et al., 1948). Some boys, after puberty, report having "spontaneous" ejaculations from time to time, produced by nonsexual physical activity or psychological influences (for example, viewing pictures, watching an

attractive person). By late adolescence, the capacity to have "spontaneous" orgasms is apparently lost in nearly all males. The capacity for "spontaneous" orgasm, without physical stimulation, apparently exists in some girls and even persists in a few women. They can experience orgasm by viewing sexually arousing material or just by thinking about sex.

Research would suggest that boys still become sexually active somewhat earlier than girls do. As adolescence progresses, girls clearly become more involved in sexual activity and better acquainted with their sexual responsiveness, a trend that often continues for another 10 to 20 years of their lives, when involvement in sexual activity tends to level off. Throughout adolescence, females exhibit a somewhat lower incidence of masturbation, same-gender sexual activity, and heterosexual experimentation (Janus & Janus, 1993; Kinsey et al., 1953; Laumann, Gagnon et al., 1994).

The early adolescent may also experience an increase in erotic fantasies and dreams. As the body matures and new sexual feelings emerge, an awareness develops of the social significance of sex, and young people begin to daydream about sex. Adolescents may fantasize about loving relationships that involve sexual activity with a particular person or about a wide array of sexual practices with nonspecific partners. The fantasies that accompany masturbation are often quite vivid and add to the pleasure of the masturbatory experience, also helping young people to become more fully acquainted with their sexual preferences. Many adolescents use their fantasy experiences to plan for real sexual and relational encounters later in life (East, 1998). The new awareness that comes with experiencing sexual feelings, orgasm, and erotic fantasies is an important step in learning to be sexual.

Recall some of your earliest sexual thoughts and feelings. Describe your reaction to them.

Masturbation in Adolescence

The most prevalent form of sexual activity in adolescence is masturbation. Most males and many females begin to learn about their bodies' sexual responses through masturbation. Adolescent boys have tended to discuss masturbation among themselves—often in a joking way—more than adolescent girls. Consequently, more slang terms have evolved to describe male masturbation (jerk off, jack off, whack off, beat off, beat the meat) than for female masturbation (rubbing off, rolling the pill, fingering). Although we do not really have reliable statistics on adolescent masturbation, what data we do have indicate that at all age levels, masturbation is more common among males than among females. Retrospective studies, in which adults offer information about their behaviors as adolescents, suggest that the majority of adolescent males masturbate at least occasionally, but that less than half of adolescent females do so.

The data also indicate that of those adolescents who do masturbate, boys do so about three times more frequently than girls (Leitenberg, Detzer, & Srebnik, 1993; I.M. Schwartz, 1999). An older study of over 1,100 high school youth (Gagnon, Simon, & Berger, 1970) showed that 77 percent of high school males and 17 percent of high school females reported masturbating twice a week or more. Another 12 percent of the boys and 23 percent of the girls admitted to masturbating at least once, to as often as once per month. A smaller percentage of the boys (11 percent) and the majority of girls (60 percent) said they had never masturbated. There may be a slight decline in frequency of masturbation during the years when young people are in college. A study of over 300 college students found that 85 percent of the males indicated they masturbated, 70 percent of them with moderate to high frequency. The women in the study were far more likely to indicate that they had never masturbated (63 percent), with 24 percent responding that it was with moderate to high frequency (I.M. Schwartz, 1999). Among adults, frequency of masturbation is affected by factors such as education, religion, and ethnicity, and we can probably assume that these same factors exert influences over masturbatory behavior during adolescence (Laumann, Gagnon et al., 1994). There is more information on masturbation in chapter 11, "Solitary Sex and Shared Sex."

Social Development

Most adolescents become involved in social relationships with members of both sexes. Self-concept can play a major role in how comfortable the person is with these relationships as the individual's identity takes form. Developing the skills to be emotionally intimate is important, because the long-term consequences of emotional intimacy are as great as the consequences of sexual intimacy. Different adolescents place differing degrees of emphasis on identity-formation goals and intimacy goals, and this can affect the likelihood that they will engage in various forms of sexual behavior (Sanderson & Cantor, 1995). In their early relationships, adolescents begin to learn about the ground rules of relating to other people and about commitments and expectations that are part of those relationships. There is growing experience with how relationships can cause emotional hurt and with the limits of one's responsibility toward another person in a relationship (Hillier, Harrison, & Bowditch, 1999).

Important steps in personal development occur within the context of teenage romances and relationships. One phase in the formation of affectionate partnerships is what social psychologists call **dyadic withdrawal,** a period of time during which the couple pulls away from other social responsibilities with parents, peers, and other significant persons in their lives. The potential for sexual involvement increases during this time (Laumann, Gagnon et al., 1994). With the privacy available to most adolescents, a close relationship can easily progress to sexual exploration if they want it to. Learning how to deal with the new intimacy is essential to becoming comfortable with sharing one's sexuality.

How far sexual intimacy proceeds can be important in defining the boundaries of adolescent relationships. Many sexual activities may be viewed as part of sex play behavior. Intensive sexual sharing takes on extra meaning for most individuals, however. For one thing, to manage intense sexual activity successfully, the two people usually have to cooperate in a number of ways. For another, the two are opening themselves to each other more fully—and with more vulnerability—than ever before. These factors, along with the emotional reactions of intense physical intimacy, often lead to a deepening of the relationship. If this is desired and expected, things may go well, but if it is a surprise or undesirable, conflicts may develop between the partners. Whatever the consequences of intensive sex, after their initial experiences many adolescents begin to clarify the place sex will have in their adult relationships (Gilmore, DeLamater, & Wagstaff, 1996).

Adolescent Same-Gender Sexual Activity

Early adolescence is a period when girls and boys tend to associate more with members of their own gender. Sexual preferences are also relatively nonspecific at these ages. Consequently, it is not surprising that as youngsters experience pronounced physical changes in their sex organs and begin to become more aware of their sexual feelings, they may experiment with sex in encounters with same-gender peers. Again, the statistics on same-gender sexual activity are inconclusive and have not been based on random samples of the population. The incidence of adolescent same-gender sexual behavior has ranged from 5 percent of 13- to 18-year-olds in one study, to another study in which 11 to 14 percent of adolescent boys

> **dyadic withdrawal** (die-ADD-ik): the tendency of two people involved in an intimate relationship to withdraw socially for a time from other significant people in their lives.

CASE STUDY

Ernest: A College Student Questions His Sexuality

As a second-year college student, Ernest took the human sexuality course that was offered in the Psychology department. He made an appointment with the instructor to talk about some personal matters, and the instructor then referred him to the counseling center. Ernest seemed nervous during his first counseling session, as he told the counselor that he was very uncomfortable talking about the sexual issues that were troubling him. After some reassurance from the counselor, he discussed his concerns. His two major worries were masturbation and the fantasies that he had when he masturbated.

With the counselor's help, Ernest described the background of his sexual behavior, explaining that he had started masturbating with some frequency when he was about 14 years old. During masturbation, he would fantasize about girls taking off their clothes. Sometimes, he admitted with some embarrassment, he would fantasize about his two older sisters, although he had never actually seen either of them in the nude. He was more concerned that his masturbation was unusual for his age than he was about the fantasies because he was not interested in sexual activity with his sisters.

The counselor provided Ernest with reading materials relating to masturbation and other sexual behaviors and also encouraged him to read the text that was being used in the human sexuality course. Ernest had not realized that it was quite typical for adults to masturbate with some regularity. Further discussions with the counselor led to exploration of his feelings of inadequacy within relationships and his desire to find a girlfriend. The counseling contacts continued occasionally over a period of about a year, and during that time Ernest did begin a relationship in which he eventually became sexually involved with his partner.

and 6 to 11 percent of adolescent girls reported having participated in some sort of sexual act with someone of the same gender. Boys tend to report more frequent same-gender experiences in later adolescence (ages 16 to 19), whereas girls reported less frequent experiences in this later age level (Haffner, 1995; Sorensen, 1973). The reasons for this disparity are not well understood.

Some adolescents begin to get in touch with their same-gender sexual orientations during adolescence. Adult gay men report that their first same-gender experience generally occurred by the age of 14, whereas adult lesbians report that their first experiences tended to occur in the late teenage years. In a questionnaire administered to 89 gay males and 31 lesbians aged 14 to 21 years old, about one-third indicated they were aware of their sexual orientation between the ages of 4 and 10. Most of the rest were aware by the age of 17. Forty-two percent of the females in this study and 30 percent of the males indicated that their families had responded negatively toward their sexual orientations (Telljohann & Price, 1993).

Cite several reasons why some lesbian and gay adolescents and young adults might refuse to acknowledge their same-gender attractions.

For adolescents who have clearly identified themselves as having a primarily same-gender orientation, there are some very real social obstacles to their sexual development. Society expects heterosexual behavior, pays far less attention to same-gender orientations, and discourages positive role modeling for gay and lesbian adolescents. As a result, these adolescents have to achieve self-acceptance of their sexual orientation in the face of pressures not to accept or act upon that orientation (Savin-Williams & Diamond, 1999). They may experience conflict with their social environment, especially in school, and may find that counselors do not take their concerns particularly seriously (Seem, 1997). They also face the task of developing intimate emotional attachments with members of their own sex, when there are many social prohibitions against doing so. These pressures take their toll because gay, lesbian, and bisexual adolescents seem to have higher risks of psychological distress, running away, dropping out of school, and suicide. Nevertheless, attitudes in recent years toward differing sexual orientations have been changing, and there is more information and support available for people with same-gender orientations (Nesmith, Burton, & Cosgrove, 1999). Some lesbian, gay, and bisexual teenagers have been able to surmount the extra measure of social difficulty with resilience and self-acceptance, whereas others have continued to wrestle with their sexual identity issues into adulthood (Remafedi, 1994). (See also chapter 12, "Same-Gender Orientation and Behavior.")

Adolescent Heterosexual Activity

Sexual experimentation between males and females is an important step in the development of many adolescents. Young people frequently believe that their friends are more sexually knowledgeable and experienced than they actually are (Whitley, 1998), and they may fear that their own lack of experience will be exposed by their initial awkwardness (see Fig. 6.7). Additionally, some young people have guilt feelings about their new sexual feelings and desires. Eventually, most adolescents find someone with whom they try some form of heterosexual experimentation, and they soon become more comfortable with their sexuality. For others, the initial sexual experiences do not lead immediately to other sexual activities, and they share sex only sporadically or not at all for the time being (I.M. Schwartz, 1999).

Heterosexual contact usually seems to proceed through stages of progressive intimacy or what have been called levels of sharing (Kelly, 1993). How rapidly a particular couple progresses through the stages depends, of course, on many factors, including the type of relationship involved. There is evidence that young people today progress through the stages more rapidly, and perhaps in a different order, than in former years (Haffner, 1995). In any case, the first level of intimacy is kissing and tongue ("French") kissing. Bodily contact below the neck usually begins with hand-holding and the male touching the female's breasts, first through the clothing and then inside the clothing. Both partners begin to touch one another's genitals through the clothing and then directly. It is quite common during this level of intimacy for the two individuals to bring their genitals close together while clothed. It is not uncommon for males to have the experience of ejaculating with their clothes on at some time in this process.

What social forces could be playing a role in the dramatic shifts in adolescent sexual behavior that have been observed since the 1950s?

These latter stages of sexual exploration can lead to intercourse, although there seem to be many factors that play a role in determining when first intercourse will actually occur. Patterns of family socialization, stage of biological development, and the ability to exercise social controls all seem to interact in this process (Crockett, Bingham, Chopak, & Vicary, 1996; Resnick, 1997). There may also be some oral-genital contact either preceding intercourse or instead of it. Oral sex has become more common among adolescents in the past two decades. One survey showed that 41 percent of 17- to 18-year-old women and 33 percent of males in that age group had performed oral sex on a member

FIGURE 6.7   *Adolescent Sexuality*

Adolescents in contemporary industrial societies acquire adult status much later than they acquire biological maturity. This accounts for some of the confusion in adolescent sexual behavior. Adolescence is a time of awkward experimentation in sexual behavior and the acquisition of adult sexual attitudes involving commitment, intimacy, and fidelity.

of the other gender (Haffner, 1995). There are clear indications that as adolescents age, the likelihood of their having heterosexual intercourse gradually rises, although the age for first intercourse increased during the 1990s. Figure 6.8 summarizes some of the data on sexual experience among adolescents. Nevertheless, some adolescents seem very comfortable with their decisions to remain virgins. Not unexpectedly, females feel more pressure to abstain from sexual intercourse and are more likely to feel proud and unembarrassed about their virginity than males, who are more likely to report that they expect to become sexually active in the near future (Edwards, 1998; Trends in sexual risk behaviors, 1998).

In the United States, nonwhite teenagers once consistently showed a consistently higher incidence of

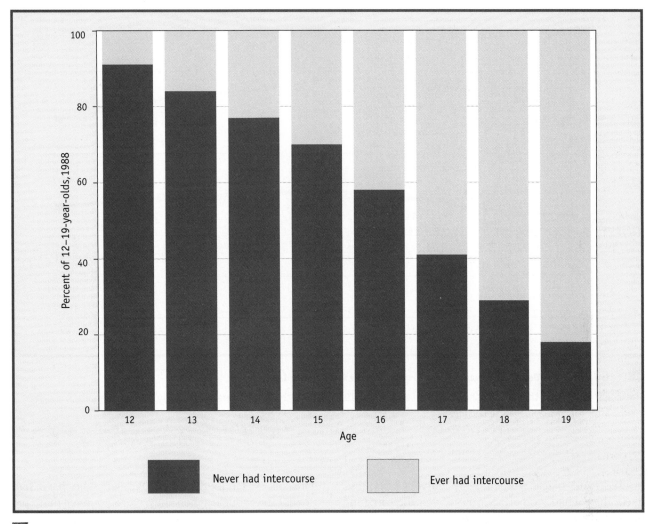

FIGURE 6.8 *Intercourse and Age among U.S. Teenagers*

Sexual intercourse is rare among young teenagers in the United States, but more than four-fifths have experienced intercourse by the end of their teenage years.

Source: Reproduced with permission of the Alan Guttmacher Institute, from: The Alan Guttmacher Institute, *Sex and America's Teenagers*, New York and Washington, The Alan Guttmacher Institute, 1994, p. 19, Figure 9.

From: **Women and men:** AGI tabulations of data from the 1990 Youth Risk Behavior Survey. **Women:** AGI tabulations of data from the 1988 National Survey of Family Growth. **Men:** F. L. Sonenstein, J. H. Pleck, and L. C. Ku, "Sexual Activity, Condom Use and AIDS Awareness among Adolescent Males," *Family Planning Perspectives*, 21:152–158, 1989, Table 1, p. 153. **Total population:** F. W. Hollmann, "Estimates of the Population of the United States by Age, Sex, and Race," *Current Population Reports*, Series P-25, No. 1095, 1993, Table 1, p. 10.

Note: The National Survey of Family Growth (NSFG) and the NSAM (National Survey of Adolescent Males) do not survey youth under age 15. Estimates of age at first intercourse for 12- to 14-year-olds are based on data from the Youth Risk Behavior Survey (YRBS).

sexual intercourse than white adolescents. However, during the 1980s those ethnic statistical differences diminished and became much less significant (Alan Guttmacher Institute, 1994; Wyatt, 1990). Data suggest now that sexual experience for white teens leveled off at new higher levels between 1979 and 1982. For nonwhite adolescents, however, the incidence of sexual experience leveled off between 1976 and 1979 and then declined somewhat during the early 1980s. The 1990s saw declining rates of adolescent sexual experience in both white and nonwhite teens, but the decline was far more pronounced among black teenagers (Edwards, 1998; Saul, 1999).

Although the NHSLS surveyed only people aged 18 to 59, it did ask retrospective questions about first intercourse, and there is now some evidence that adult responses are not always consistent with what they reported as adolescents (Lauritsen & Swicegood, 1997). Of the adult individuals surveyed who were adolescents in the 1970s and 1980s, 48 percent of the males and 37 percent of the females had experienced intercourse by age 16. Eighty-five percent of the males and 83 percent of the females had had intercourse by age 19. Gender differences in sexual experience close with age. Among all age groups studied, it was clear that not everyone's first sexual intercourse was necessarily

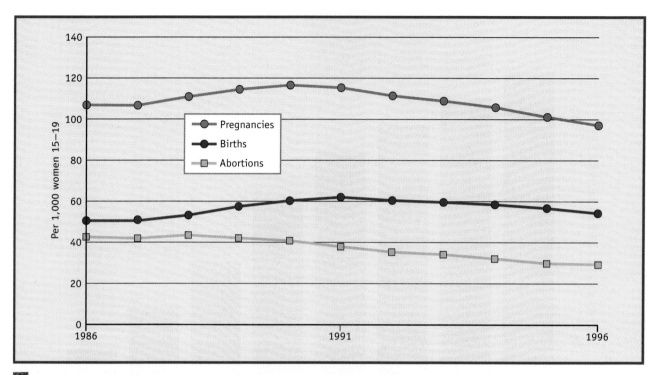

FIGURE 6.9   *Decline in Pregnancy, Birth, and Abortion Rates in the 1990s*

This graph shows that the rates among all women aged 15 to 19, including those who were not sexually active, rose until the early 1990s, after which they began to decline.

Source: Reproduced with the permission of The Alan Guttmacher Institute from: Rebekah Saul, "Teen Pregnancy: Progress Meets Politics," *The Guttmacher Report* (p. 6), June, 1999, Figure 1.

desired, and black women were considerably less likely than white women to indicate that their first intercourse was wanted (Laumann, Gagnon et al., 1994). Younger adolescent girls, under age 14, are highly likely to have been coerced into intercourse and most often by males who are older (Abma, Driscoll, & Moore, 1998; Miller, Clark, & Moore, 1997).

A great deal of research has been devoted to the life factors that may influence when adolescents have their first sexual experiences. Although a correlation has been found among a great many factors, it would be difficult to prove that there is a clear cause-and-effect relationship. For example, adolescents who use illegal drugs, tobacco, or alcohol, who get into fights, who tend to be generally unconventional in their behaviors, who have divorced parents, or who have moved frequently are more likely to have intercourse sooner, without protection, and with greater numbers of partners than others (Kiernan & Hobcraft, 1997; Kowaleski-Jones & Mott, 1998; Valois, Kammermann, & Drane, 1997). Relationships with family and peers and the amount of supervision provided to a teenager also seem to play a significant role (Resnick, 1997).

Research indicates that once adolescents have had intercourse, it is relatively likely they will participate more than once, although comparatively few have multiple sexual partners within a year's time (Moore,

Driscoll, & Lindberg, 1998). Women who have had sexual intercourse when they were younger than age 17 also seem to be more likely to have multiple sexual partners later on (Santelli, Brener, Lowry, Bhatt, & Zabin, 1998). Again, however, we must be cautious not to assume that there is a cause-and-effect relationship here. Some people seem to have a higher level of interest in sex than others, and there is a general tendency to have an increase in the number of partners as one moves into later adolescence. Data from the NHSLS revealed that of adults born between 1963 and 1974 (the youngest group studied), 38.7 percent of the males and 41.8 percent of the females reported not having had intercourse before the age of 18. Another 37.3 percent of the males had one to three sex partners before that age, and 19.3 percent had five or more partners. Among the females, 42.5 percent reported having had one to three sex partners prior to age 18, and 9.6 percent indicated they had sex with five or more partners (Laumann, Gagnon et al., 1994).

Teenage Pregnancy

Teenage pregnancy continues to be a very real public health problem, and its rate in the United States tends to be much higher than in most other developed countries (Singh & Darroch, 2000). Young women who

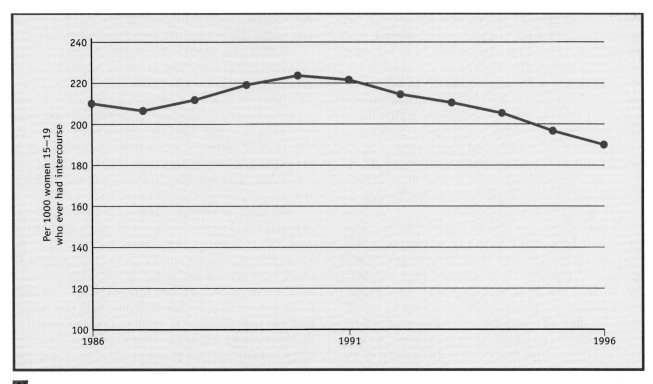

![FIGURE 6.10] **FIGURE 6.10** *Decline in Pregnancy Rate among Sexually Active Teenaged Women*

The steep decline in pregnancy among sexually active women aged 15 to 19 is believed to be related more to effective use of contraception than it is to sexual abstinence or lowered frequency of sex.

Source: Reproduced with the permission of The Alan Guttmacher Institute from: Rebekah Saul, "Teen Pregnancy: Progress Meets Politics," *The Guttmacher Report* (p. 8), June, 1999, Figure 3.

have had one baby are at special risk of a second pregnancy, and those whose older siblings have been sexually active as teenagers also have elevated levels of pregnancy risk (Widmer, 1997). The degree of risk depends on factors such as whether they return to school following their first pregnancy and their level of motivation to use contraception (Stevens-Simon et al., 1998). Assessments of programs designed to prevent teenage pregnancy have found that only those providing access to contraception significantly decrease the proportion of adolescents who become pregnant (Frost & Forrest, 1995).

Teen pregnancy and childbearing have demonstrated social consequences, both for the girl and the father of the child. Adolescent girls who give birth to a child are much less likely than other girls to complete high school or go on to higher educational attainment (Klepinger, Lundberg, & Plotnick, 1995). Youthful unwed fathers are more likely to have problems with delinquency and economic hardship (Nock, 1998; Stouthamer-Loeber & Wei, 1998). These are scenarios that then create longer-term social and health problems for the entire society, including strains on the social welfare and healthcare systems because of poor socioeconomic conditions. Analysis of the data also demonstrates that there is no single effect of teenage

childbearing and that it is not necessarily the catastrophe it has been portrayed to be. Some of the conditions surrounding teen parents may well have been part of their lives *before* the pregnancy, and therefore they may have played a role as a cause rather than as an effect (Hoffman, 1998).

There are some encouraging signs, as Figure 6.9 shows. The rates of pregnancy, births, and abortions among all 15- to 19-year-old women began to decrease in the early and mid-1990s. If we examine the rate of pregnancy only among women who are sexually active, we find that it has declined even more (see Figure 6.10). Although some groups claim that these declines are due to increased levels of sexual abstinence, the evidence suggests that the trends are more likely due to more effective use of birth control among sexually active teens (Saul, 1999; Ventura, Curtin, & Mathews, 1998). The decline in adolescent pregnancy rates seems to be occurring across the industrialized world (Singh & Darroch, 2000).

Adolescent Sexual Health

Ours is a culture that continues to demonstrate great ambivalence toward sexual activity among the young. We tend to confuse the sex-related public health issues with issues of morality and punishment, even as we see the negative consequences of not dealing with these problems head-on. The statistics have led some experts to conclude that we may be at a point in human history where we must accept the fact that adolescent sexual activity is inevitable and that adults can no longer fool themselves into thinking that many teenagers can be convinced not to have sex. When it comes to the risks of adolescent sex, it is crucial to remember that adolescent egocentrism tends to yield attitudes of invulnerability, which make them believe that the negative consequences will not happen to them (Curtin, 1996).

If our society is to help adolescents develop into sexually healthy adults, there are several steps that must be taken. We must begin educating children openly and honestly about sexuality from the time they are born and promote in them a healthy and positive self-concept. Young people also need to understand the range of values and experiences that will be open to them as they grow up in a pluralistic society such as ours and be prepared for the realistic work that must go into maintaining long-term relationships. We must also better train professionals who work with young people to be proactive in their sexual health interventions and make certain that funding for teen health care is available (Haffner, 1995; Schoen et al., 1998; Thrall et al., 1998).

We must also address issues of poverty and political obstacles that prevent some of the population from having equal opportunity for education and a hopeful future. These issues affect self-esteem and therefore the sex-related decisions that young people make. As a society, we must also identify those adolescents who are at high risk of negative sexual consequences. High-risk youth include those who are pregnant or are already parents; have a history of substance abuse; get low grades in school; have been emotionally or physically abused; are homeless or have run away from home; are gay, lesbian, or bisexual; and are institutionalized for any reason. They tend to have a greater likelihood of participating in high-risk sexual activities without protections such as condoms. These are young people who have special needs for sexuality education, support services, and counseling interventions (Erickson, 1999; Lock & Steiner, 1999; Rosario, Mahler, Hunter, & Gwadz, 1999).

At a time when the incidence of shared sexual activity among teenagers is on the rise, evidence continues to mount that their age group is at greater risk for contracting sexually transmitted diseases, including HIV. A screening at an urban clinic found that 1 in 10 of the adolescent women tested over a period of time had recurrent sexually transmitted diseases (Oh, 1996). Even with reports showing increased use of condoms, studies also continue to show that many teenagers do not adequately assess the risks of HIV infection and in fact participate in high-risk sexual activities.

Longer-term studies of condom use among adolescents tend to show that as young men become increasingly sexually active, their use of condoms declines. Condom use is likely to be highest at the beginning of a sexual relationship, and then it diminishes over time. It would seem that males eventually begin to rely more on the woman's method of birth control for protection from unintended pregnancy, but this makes both partners more vulnerable to the transmission of disease (Ku, Sonenstein, & Pleck, 1994).

Because our society continues to treat adolescent sexuality in negative and often unrealistic ways, American teenagers are not being encouraged to develop sexual attitudes and behaviors that could help them grow into sexually happy and healthy adults. Educational efforts need to find ways that can help foster perspectives on sexuality among young people that will help them to be healthy. Teenagers need to be able to make decisions about their sexual behavior that will help them set personal limits, understand alternatives to penetrative sex, say no and mean it when they do not wish to participate in any form of sexual involvement, and have convenient access to condoms and contraception. Table 6.3 summarizes the characteristics of sexually healthy adolescents as outlined by the National Commission on Adolescent Sexual Health (1995).

◼ Adult Sexuality and Relationships

As the culture that invented the term "adolescence," we have attempted to prolong the youthful period of the life span, often to provide time for advanced education. The lifestyles, expectations, and responsibilities of adult life tend to be approached gradually in North America. As a result, our society often asks sexually mature young adults to fit their sexual interests and behaviors into lifestyles more appropriate to people much younger.

The college years represent a transitional phase for young adults. They are often still bound to home and parents financially and as a permanent address, and yet they have a great deal of freedom to choose their own relationships and sexual activities. During the 1970s and 1980s, the ***in loco parentis*** role of American colleges and universities faded, and dormitory curfews and visitation rules for the most part dis-

---

in loco parentis: a Latin phrase meaning "in the place of the parent."

Table 6.3   *Characteristics of a Sexually Healthy Adolescent*

Self

Appreciates Own Body

- Understands pubertal change.
- Views pubertal changes as normal.
- Practices health-promoting behaviors, such as abstinence from alcohol and other drugs and undergoing regular check-ups.

Takes Responsibility for Own Behaviors

- Identifies own values.
- Decides what is personally "right" and acts on these values.
- Understands consequences of actions.
- Understands that media messages can create unrealistic expectations related to sexuality and intimate relationships.
- Is able to distinguish personal desires from that of the peer group.
- Recognizes behavior that may be self-destructive and can seek help.

Is Knowledgeable about Sexuality Issues

- Enjoys sexual feelings without necessarily acting upon them.
- Understands the consequences of sexual behaviors.
- Makes personal decisions about masturbation consistent with personal values.
- Makes personal decisions about sexual behaviors with a partner consistent with personal values.
- Understands own gender identity.
- Understands effect of gender role stereotypes and makes choices about appropriate roles for oneself.
- Understands own sexual orientation.
- Seeks further information about sexuality as needed.
- Understands peer and cultural pressure to become sexually involved.
- Accepts people with different values and experiences.

Relationships with Parents and Family Members

Communicates Effectively with Family about Issues, Including Sexuality

- Maintains appropriate balance between family roles and responsibilities and growing need for independence.
- Is able to negotiate with family on boundaries.

- Respects rights of others.
- Demonstrates respect for adults.

Understands and Seeks Information about Parents' and Family's Values, and Considers Them in Developing One's Own Values

- Asks questions of parents and other trusted adults about sexual issues.
- Can accept trusted adults' guidance about sexuality issues.
- Tries to understand parental point of view.

Peers

Interacts with Both Genders in Appropriate and Respectful Ways

- Communicates effectively with friends.
- Has friendships with males and females.
- Is able to form empathetic relationships.
- Is able to identify and avoid exploitative relationships.
- Understands and rejects sexual harassing behaviors.
- Understands pressures to be popular and accepted and makes decisions consistent with own values.

Romantic Partners

Expresses Love and Intimacy in Developmentally Appropriate Ways

- Believes that boys and girls have equal rights and responsibilities for love and sexual relationships.
- Communicates desire not to engage in sexual behaviors and accepts refusals to engage in sexual behaviors.
- Is able to distinguish between love and sexual attraction.
- Seeks to understand and empathize with partner.

Has the Skills to Evaluate Readiness for Mature Sexual Relationships

- Talks with a partner about sexual behaviors before they occur.
- Is able to communicate and negotiate sexual limits.
- Differentiates between low- and high-risk sexual behaviors.
- If having intercourse, protects self and partner from unintended pregnancy and diseases through effective use of contraception and condoms and other safer sex practices.
- Knows how to use and access the health care system, community agencies, religious institutions, and schools; and seeks advice, information, and services as needed.

Source: From Debra W. Haffner, M. P. H., "Facing Facts: Sexual Health for America's Adolescents," in *SIECUS Report,* Volume 23, Number 6, August/September, 1995. Reprinted with permission of SIECUS, 130 W. 42nd St., Suite 380, New York, NY 10036–1802.

appeared. Studies have indicated that 89 percent of college males surveyed and 70 percent of college women engage in sexual intercourse (Elliott & Brantley, 1997; Rubinson & DeRubertis, 1991) and that over 60 percent of freshmen men and women are currently sexually active.

The young adult years provide a transition to adulthood, but it would be a mistake to view adulthood as a time when all of the loose ends are tied up, all spontaneity and fun are left behind, and lifestyle patterns are established that will take people through the rest of their lives. Rather, like all other stages of human life, it is a dynamic time filled with transitions,

new decisions, inner journeys to be undertaken, and problems to be resolved. One's sexuality weaves its way through all of these twists and turns of adult life.

Intimacy, Sexuality, and Coupling

One of the major tasks of early adulthood is to achieve intimacy with others. Intimacy is the ability to open oneself to others in a way that permits mutual sharing and caring, and it represents an essential quality in the deeper forms of human relationships (see Fig. 6.11). Most people long for intimacy and look for opportunities to build the sort of trust with another human being

FIGURE 6.11   *Adult Intimacy*

Early adulthood is a time of establishing sexual identity and acquiring sexual intimacy. The cultural freedom to enjoy premarital sex and cohabitation, however, presents its own set of problems, not the least of which is the transmission of sexual diseases.

that allows for openness and sharing. The desire for intimacy is also a primary basis for relating to another person sexually.

What are some behaviors that get in the way of developing intimacy with another person?

When people have difficulty establishing intimate relationships, they may well display behaviors that make it difficult for others to relate to them on more than a superficial level: shyness, hostility, self-centeredness, or insensitivity. Sexual sharing, in such a nonintimate context, may be physically satisfying, but in time it often loses the deeper feelings of fulfillment and commitment that help a relationship to flourish and endure. There is evidence that women and men sometimes view intimacy in different contexts. Men often interpret intimacy within the contexts of genital sexual activity. Such differences may mean that couples will need to negotiate levels of intimacy that are acceptable to each partner (Ridley, 1993; Sprecher, Regan, McKinney, Maxwell, & Wazienski, 1997). There is more about intimacy and the role of effective communication in chapter 8, "Sexuality, Communication, and Relationships."

At some point in their lives, most individuals build an intimate relationship with someone else. There are many different kinds of couples: cohabiting couples, married partners, gay and lesbian couples, couples with and without children, and so on. Although there is much variety in how partners negotiate their particular partnership, there are also cultural expectations and social scripts that guide the process of human coupling. A survey of attitudes toward sexual health found that sexual satisfaction in a relationship was rated fourth in importance, behind family relationships, financial security, and religious or spiritual life (National Institutes of Health, 1999). Couples today can see how easily and frequently partnerships seem to break up, so they are always aware of their potential demise as a couple. This can create pressures that ultimately become harmful for the relationship.

Coupling seems to be a process that does not progress in a straight line, but instead it continues through endless cycles of advancing and retreating; of increasing and decreasing intimacy. In the beginning *expansive stage* of coupling, there is a burst of romance, sexual attraction, and exploration. It is in this stage that the individual identities of the partners become secondary to the characteristics of the couple. The two "I"s become a "We." The relationship seems full of promise. Eventually, this is followed by a stage of *contraction and betrayal,* during which old fears, insecurities, and personal realities of the individuals resurface. This is a time of bewilderment, as things no longer seem as they were, and the partners pull back into themselves in disillusionment. Not all couples survive this stage, and many partnerships end at this point. However, if they are able to find ways of confronting their differences openly, facing conflicts and working out compromises and accommodations for one another, they can move to the next stage of *resolution.* As much as couples like to believe that they can stabilize their relationships indefinitely, coupling really is a continuing process, during which they will be cycled through these stages again and again. Yet this is exactly the process that can keep relationships healthy, growing, and filled with renewal (Dym & Glenn, 1993).

Mate Selection

In recent years, a great deal of attention has been given to trying to understand human mate selection. What are the qualities that actually attract two people to one another? So far, this work has focused mostly on opposite-sex, or heterosexual, partnerships, although there is some research indicating that those with same-gender sexual orientations seem to be motivated by very similar mate selection criteria. Theories of mate selection have fallen into three main categories:

Psychological Theory

Psychological theories of mate selection assume that the process is essentially the same for both women and men and that people search for mates that remind them of their opposite-sexed parent, or who at some deeper psychological level represent qualities they long to attain within themselves. It is sometimes assumed that people want mates who have qualities and characteristics similar to their own, or, conversely, that opposites attract. Unfortunately, such hypotheses have not lent themselves particularly well to testing and verification.

Social Network Theory

There are some aspects of social network theory as defined on page 162 that have been supported by research. For example, there seems to be a tendency toward what social psychologists call *equal status contact,* meaning that people initiate and maintain relationships with others who have similar social characteristics. These include factors such as age bracket, race, education, religion, and the ways in which one perceives oneself in terms of social class.

These factors seem to be especially influential in more committed, longer-term relationships. People do indeed tend to meet their partners through their most immediate social networks, involving friends, families, classmates, and coworkers. This offers plenty of time to evaluate whether a potential partner will fit in well with family and friends (Michael et al., 1994). In general, sexual relationships also tend to occur between partners who share similar characteristics. There are exceptions, of course, and some sexual contacts such as extramarital sex or sex with a prostitute are actually more likely to occur among those of dissimilar social status. But these are forms of sex that tend to take place with little commitment and little likelihood that the two partners will be living together (Laumann, Gagnon et al., 1994).

People who ultimately enter into long-term commitments such as marriage tend to know their partners longer before having sex with them than do couples who have short-term relationships. Therefore, they are really choosing a mate from a relatively limited group of potential partners within their social networks. Well before adolescents become sexually active, they tend to associate with one another in social circles where the members are quite similar to one another. When a potential sexual partner is chosen from within that social network, one tends to be more cautious about moving too quickly toward sexual activity because there may well be a social price to pay for making a mistake (Michael et al., 1994).

Evolutionary or Sociobiological Theory

This theoretical stance assumes that human beings use sexual *strategies* in selecting a mate that are advantageous from an evolutionary perspective because they contribute to the survival and perpetuation of the human species. Two other assumptions in evolutionary mate selection theory are that actual selection behavior will differ in short-term and long-term couplings and that males and females have different mating goals (Buss, 1998). A team of scientists surveyed the mating preferences of over 10,000 women and men in 37 countries over a 6-year period. The data from this extensive cross-cultural survey have shown that there do seem to be some common sexual strategies that supersede cultural influences. One interesting pattern shows that men and women generally differ in their willingness to have sexual intercourse, depending on the length of the relationship. After a couple has been together for 5 years, both partners are almost equally willing to have sex. Prior to that time, men tend to be more willing than women.

This is one of the cross-cultural findings that has supported the evolutionary assumption that male and female sexual strategies differ. There are several hypotheses about these strategies for which the studies of David Buss (1994) and his colleagues have lent some validity. All of them require further support from continued research, and all of them may well be judged as controversial (Knodel, Low, Saengtienchai, & Lucas, 1997).

Evolutionary theory has often been accused of attempting to find a basis for legitimizing behaviors that many deem to be sexist and inappropriate. This is not the intent of sociobiologists, who instead see their role as clarifying patterns of behavior that may indeed differ between men and women as they choose their sexual partners. Here are some of the hypotheses that studies in 37 countries have made more credible:

1. Short-term sex partners are more important to men than to women, and men will identify sexually accessible women. This may well be one of the reasons that men tend to have more sex part-

ners than women, and they tend to find sexual promiscuity more desirable in a short-term partner than do women (Walsh, 1993).

2. When seeking a short-term partner, men tend to want to minimize commitment and therefore find it undesirable when a short-term mate tries to extract signs of commitment (Knodel et al., 1997).

3. In terms of evolutionary success, which translates into success in reproducing, men want to find mates who will likely bear children, and women have more interest in male partners who will be able to provide adequate resources for their offspring, as identified by social status. Studies continue to show that men place a higher value on attractiveness and a younger partner, whereas women place a higher value on partners who are older and therefore likely to have more resources (Hayes, 1995; Johnston & Oliver-Rodriguez, 1997; Townsend, 1993). Figures 6.12 and 6.13 on page 182, show some of the cross-cultural variations in this theme.

4. Women are more selective than men in choosing a short-term mate, because they are more likely to be evaluating them as potential long-term mates. Therefore, even in short-term couplings, women seek mates who are willing to impart immediate resources. Women appreciate qualities in males such as their likelihood of succeeding in a profession and having a reliable career (Lampert, 1997).

Evolutionary psychology theorists, then, believe that traditional assumptions about mate selection being arbitrary or culture-bound are incorrect. They feel that cross-cultural evidence suggests that the complex decision-making processes involved in choosing a mate are patterned and universal themes built into human psyches and societies by evolutionary imperatives. This does not mean that men look solely upon women as sex objects, or that women view men only as success objects. They will also be looking for personality characteristics that would suggest the other person will be cooperative and make a good parent. Both sexes clearly place tremendous importance on factors such as mutual love and kindness when seeking a long-term mate (Buss, 1994, 1998).

Which factors of the various theories of mate selection seem most plausible to you? Why?

Marriage, Cohabitation, Singles, and Sex

In Western culture, romantic love and sexual attraction have become bases for marriage, along with the expectation that they will be continuing parts of any

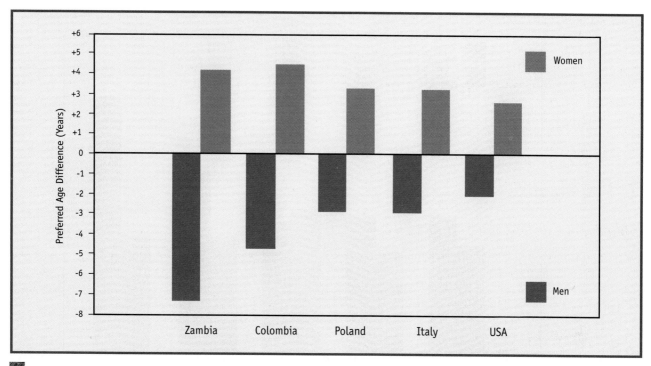

![figure icon] **FIGURE 6.12** *Age Preferences for Males and Females*

Preferences for an age difference between oneself and one's spouse differ for men and women. Men in each of the 37 cultures examined prefer to mate with younger women, whereas women generally prefer to mate with older men. Here the disparities between the mating preferences of men and women in five countries show some of the cultural variation across the sample.

Source: David M. Buss, "The Strategies of Human Mating," *American Scientist* (p. 247), May/June 1994.

marriage. This is not quite so true for other cultures and other periods of the world's history in which marriage has been seen as too serious a step to be left to individual decision making and passions. In some cultures, marriages are arranged by the parents on the basis of age and social status. The partners are expected to build their relationships and learn how to love and care for one another after they are married.

To maintain a loving relationship over a long period of time takes attention, work, and commitment. Married couples must invest their relationships with sharing, energy, and communication if a healthy and growing marriage is to continue. As with any sort of coupling, marital intimacy is maintained best when there is a sense of equality between the partners, an attempt to understand one another's points of view, and a willingness to work on the relationship (Monaghan, 1999a).

The vast majority of people intend to marry eventually, and U.S. Bureau of the Census figures show that 90 percent of all people in the United States have tended to marry by their late thirties, with another 5 percent marrying by the time they are 55. There are indications that younger people are marrying less, however, and the Census Bureau is predicting that up to 10 percent of people now may never marry.

Sexual activity is one of the expected parts of a marital relationship in Western cultures, although in those cultures where marriages are arranged by family members, sex often does not have such a prominent place in the expectations of the partners. Research studies on marriage in North America indicate that a wide variety of sexual behaviors are shared by married people. The majority of couples apparently include oral-genital sexual activity in their sexual repertoires, and about one-quarter have at least tried anal intercourse. Couples also seem relatively adventurous with the positions they are using for sexual intercourse (Janus & Janus, 1993; Laumann, Gagnon et al., 1994). It is believed that approximately 20 percent of married couples may have sex infrequently enough to essentially be considered nonsexual (McCarthy, 1997b).

More than ever before, women and men are also choosing to be single or to live together in loving and sexual relationships without marrying, a pattern called **cohabitation.** Over 4 million people in the United States were cohabiting in 1997, up from 2.9 million in

cohabitation: living together and sharing sex without marrying.

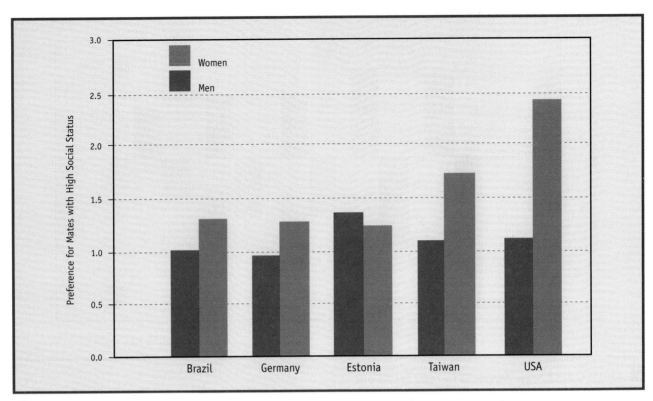

FIGURE 6.13   *Social Status and Human Mating*

Mate's high social status (ranging from 3, *indispensible,* to 0, *unimportant*) is typically greater for women than for men. Of the 37 cultures examined, only males in Estonia valued the social status of their spouses more than did their female counterparts. (Only a sample of five countries is shown here.) Women generally prefer men with a high social standing because a man's ability to provide resources for her offspring is related to his social status.

Source: David M. Buss, "The Strategies of Human Mating," *American Scientist* (p. 246), May/June 1994.

1990. About half of these people had been previously married, and close to half were college students. Because of increased acceptance of cohabitation as a lifestyle, there has been a corresponding increase in the arrangement among younger age groups. The majority of young people believe that living together prior to marriage is a good idea, although those who do cohabit do not see the relationship necessarily as a long-term commitment. About half of cohabitations end within the first year, and the younger the male partner the more likely the relationship will terminate (Michael et al., 1994). About another 40 percent of cohabiting couples eventually marry, but research is indicating that cohabitation is certainly no guarantee of a successful marriage. One study has shown that less than 25 percent of people ultimately marry the partner with whom they are cohabiting. There is evidence from a 23-year study that couples who lived together prior to marriage have a substantially higher divorce rate (50 to 100 percent higher) than those who did not live together and have a lower level of marital satisfaction in general (Axinn & Thornton, 1992).

The frequency of sexual activity tends to be higher in the first 2 years of a relationship, as partners explore one another sexually, gradually decreasing with the length of the relationship and the age of the partners (Rao & Demaris, 1995). However, popular myths have led us to believe that people are far more sexually active than studies tend to show. The most recent data show that people in the United States fall into three groups with regard to their frequency of having sex with a partner. About a third have sex with a partner a few times a year or do not have a partner at all. Another third have partnered sex a few times a month, and a final third have sex with a partner two times per week or more. Younger and older people have sex the least often, with people in their twenties having sex most frequently. Married and cohabiting people have the most sex. Forty percent of married people and over half of cohabiting people have sex two or more times per week. Single people have less sex than other groups. Table 6.4 summarizes the data on frequency of sex with a partner by various characteristics. Race, religion, and education do not seem to be particularly

Table 6.4   Frequency of Sex in the Past 12 Months by Age, Marital Status, and Gender

Social Characteristics	Not at All	A Few Times per Year	A Few Times per Month	2 or 3 Times a Week	4 or More Times a Week
Gender					
Men	14%	16%	37%	26%	8%
Women	10	18	36	30	7
Age					
Men					
18–24	15	21	24	28	12
25–29	7	15	31	36	11
30–39	8	15	37	33	6
40–49	9	18	40	27	6
50–59	11	22	43	20	3
Women					
18–24	11	16	32	29	12
25–29	5	10	38	37	10
30–39	9	16	36	33	6
40–49	15	16	44	20	5
50–59	30	22	35	12	2
Marital/Residential Status					
Men					
Noncohabiting	23	25	26	19	7
Cohabiting	0	8	36	40	16
Married	1	13	43	36	7
Women					
Noncohabiting	32	23	24	15	5
Cohabiting	1	8	35	42	14
Married	3	12	47	32	7

Source: From *Sex in America*. Copyright © 1994 by C.S.G. Enterprises, Inc., Edward O. Laumann, Robert T. Michael, and Gina Kolata. By permission of Little, Brown and Company, Inc.

influential on frequency of sex (Laumann, Gagnon et al., 1994).

However, frequency of intercourse should not be construed as a measure of happiness in marriage or cohabitation. Different couples find different levels of sexual interaction appropriate and pleasing for them. Some older research that did not study random samples of the population suggested that sexual satisfaction was directly correlated with sexual frequency, but the newest data paint a different picture. Even those people whose frequency of sexual interaction is relatively low often report a high degree of satisfaction with their sexual lives. Even as people age and the frequency of sexual activity decreases, they tend to be quite satisfied. Even though popular opinion might imply that swinging singles are the most happy with their sex lives, married couples are in fact the most physically satisfied. Eighty-eight percent of married people report that they receive great physical pleasure from their sexual lives, and 85 percent said they receive great emotional satisfaction. People who have more than one sexual partner available in their lives report less sexual satisfaction than those with one partner (Michael et al., 1994).

Monogamy versus Nonmonogamy

Not all married or cohabiting individuals remain **monogamous,** sharing sexual relations only with their primary partner. The prevailing social attitude in the United States is that couples, particularly those who are married, should maintain sexual exclusivity. Ninety percent of adults believe extramarital sexual activity is always or almost always wrong. Less than 2 percent believe that having sex with someone other than a spouse is "not wrong at all" (Laumann, Gagnon et al., 1994). In social network theory, third parties may be stakeholders in preserving exclusivity within sexual partnerships. For example, friends and family members may want the relationship to remain stable because they want to maintain and legitimize their own relationships. If they do not stray, they do not want others to do so either. This may be one of the reasons that extramarital activity often occurs outside the social network.

Although there have been some studies of limited validity that suggested a high degree of sexual infidelity among couples, recent research with valid population samples indicates that this is not the case. In fact, the evidence demonstrates that regardless of how sexually active with different partners people may be prior to marriage or between marriages, the vast majority tend to be sexually faithful to their spouses while the marriage is intact. Statistics from the General Social Survey and from the NHSLS indicate that about 90 percent of married women and over 75 percent of married men have been sexually exclusive during their marriages. Unmarried, cohabiting couples have a higher rate of extrarelational sex, but not dramatically so. Of people who had never married but were living together, 75 percent had one partner in the previous year. Ninety-four percent of married adults indicate having had only one sex partner during the previous year (Laumann, Gagnon et al., 1994). The General Social Survey has also found that between the late 1980s and mid-1990s, there was actually a decline in the number of married individuals reporting having had extramarital sex during the previous year (Smith, 1994).

Explain some reasons why sexual fidelity could or could not be important in a relationship.

There has been almost no research to suggest why people turn to extramarital sex. The Janus and Janus (1993) survey found that extramarital sexual activity did not seem to be related in any clear-cut way to the degree of happiness in the marriage or to attitudes about religion. Sometimes the activity represents a search for sexual variety, excitement, and a need to feel attractive and desirable. More often it seems to be motivated by a need for stronger emotional involve-

ment and intimacy than what is being achieved with a spouse (Levine, 1998).

During the 1960s and 1970s, when attitudes toward human sexuality were seeing some major shifts, there was a fair amount of debate about the viability of monogamous relationships. There was talk then of **consensual adultery,** in which couples would allow their partners greater sexual freedom. However, these were not trends that ever translated into behavioral change for the majority of married or cohabiting couples. The general maintenance of monogamy has also been shown in major European studies of sexual behavior. There may be some "swinging" or mate-swapping couples who indulge in recreational sex consensually, but they are apparently a very tiny part of the population.

Men have a somewhat greater likelihood of having sexual affairs outside of committed relationships, and evolutionary psychologists have attempted to offer explanations for this. Again making the assumption that one evolutionary imperative is reproductive success, evolutionary theory holds that males have a built-in need to distribute their sperm to as many different females as possible because females have far fewer eggs available than males have sperm (Buss, 1998). As we have seen in previous sections of this chapter, there is some evidence from human mating patterns that supports these differences. There are far more cultures in the world that permit **polygamy,** the practice that permits men to have more than one wife, than there are examples of systematic **polyandry,** in which women take more than one husband. Nevertheless, evolutionary psychology represents mostly hypothetical explanations for a phenomenon that is reflected in statistics but has not yet been adequately explained.

We do know that extramarital affairs can take their emotional toll on all who are involved. Secrecy and dishonesty often create tension within the various relationships. When one partner suspects the other of infidelity, it may not be confronted for a time because of uncertainty or fear of the outcome. Once the truth

monogamous: sharing sexual relations with only one person.

consensual adultery: permission given to at least one partner within the marital relationship to participate in extramarital sexual activity.

polygamy (pah-LIG-a-mee): practice, in some cultures, of being married to more than one spouse, usually referring to a man having more than one wife.

polyandry (PAH-lee-ann-dree): also referring to being married to more than one spouse, usually refers to a woman having more than one husband. Cross-culturally, it is less common than polygamy.

Table 6.5 — *The Emerging Twenty-First Century American Family*

% of Children in Various Types of Families					
	One Single Parent	Two Parent, Continuing	Two Parent, Remarried	Two Adults, Ex-married	Adults, Never Married
1972	4.7	73.0	9.9	3.8	8.6
1978	10.2	65.3	13.6	4.0	6.9
1982	14.3	59.3	13.7	5.2	7.3
1988	18.6	54.7	13.0	5.0	8.7
1990	14.9	56.1	17.9	5.1	6.0
1994	18.4	52.8	14.7	7.1	7.0
1998	18.2	51.7	12.3	8.6	9.2

Source: From GSS News, Number 13, August 1999. Reprinted with permission.

Single Parent—only one adult in household

Two Parents, Continuing—married couple, never divorced

Two Parents, Remarried—married couple, at least one remarried (unknown if remarriage came before or after children born)

Two Adults, Ex-Married—two or more adults; previously but not currently married

Adults, Never Married— two or more adults; never married (This category also includes some other family structures.)

is known, there may be intense feelings of betrayal and loss. If the extramarital affair is still going on, decisions must be made by all parties as to how they plan to proceed. Sometimes, the marriage ends, and the other relationship goes on. The tensions and bad feelings that develop may also destroy both relationships. There may also be fears of what risks may be present if the affair involved unprotected sexual activity (Buunk & Bakker, 1997) However, if the affair ends, and both partners want to preserve the marriage, confronting all feelings with honesty and appropriate counseling can sometimes lead to an even stronger relationship. However, the limited data available suggest that affairs lead to the termination or worsening of the marital relationship in the majority of cases (Levine, 1998).

Trends in Marriage

There has been a trend toward delaying marriage until somewhat later in life than in the past, and younger professional women and men sometimes want to establish themselves in careers before they pursue committed relationships. Census Bureau statistics show the extent of this trend. Nearly 35 percent of 25- to 34-year-olds have never married. For people ages 30 to 44, the proportion of never-married individuals has more than doubled since 1970. People are getting married later now than at any time in the past century. In 1997, the median age for women to first get married was 25

years, and the median age for men marrying for the first time was 26.8 years, the highest these figures had been in that century. Having a child before marriage reduces the likelihood that women will marry (Bennett, Bloom, & Miller, 1995). There may also be increased apprehension about divorce rates and economic pressures. The availability of sexual relations outside of marriage may be contributing somewhat to the trend. Table 6.5 shows the emerging trends of the American family. Both family structure and family values are moving in congruence away from traditional families with two married parents with an employed father and a stay-at-home mother toward modern family types with either only one parent or two parents both of whom are employed outside the home. For example, the table shows how the family situation of children has changed over the last quarter century, In 1973, 72 percent of children under 18 were living in an intact family with two parents. This fell to about 50 percent by the mid-1990s. In contrast, single-parent families rose from less than 5 percent in 1972 to 18 to 20 percent in the 1990s. For other family-related changes, see Tom W. Smith, 1999, "The Emerging 21st Century American Family." GSS Social Change Report No. 41. Chicago: NORC, 65pp.

Although no official statistics are kept on the topic, there are indications that there has been an increase in what have been termed "starter marriages." They are marriages between relatively young people, who do not have children and amass very little joint

Table 6.6   *Divorce Rates in the United States, 1900–1990*

	Divorces			Divorces	
Year	Number	Number per 1,000 Population	Year	Number	Number per 1,000 Population
1900	56,000	0.5	1970	708,000	3.5
1910	83,000	0.9	1975	1,036,000	4.8
1920	171,000	1.6	1980	1,189,000	5.2
1930	196,000	1.6	1985	1,190,000	5.0
1940	264,000	2.0	1986	1,178,000	4.9
1950	385,000	2.6	1988	1,167,000	4.7
1960	393,000	2.2	1990	1,175,000	4.7

Source: Based on statistics from *Advance Report of Final Divorce Statistics,* Vol. 39, No.12 (Suppl. 2), May 21, 1991. Washington, DC: National Center for Health Statistics. Adapted from S. S. Janus & C. L. Janus, *The Janus Report on Sexual Behavior.* Copyright © 1993, John Wiley & Sons, Inc. Reprinted by permission of John Wiley & Sons, Inc.

property. After a few years, and usually prior to age 30, they are divorced. Their uncoupling process is less complicated than in marriages of longer standing. In many ways, these brief marriages are similar to cohabitive relationships, except they have taken the step of legalizing the commitment. Starter marriages are reminiscent of anthropologist Margaret Mead's suggestion in the 1960s that young couples have the opportunity to join in legally sanctioned, childless trial marriages (Schupack, 1994).

There is no longer the stigma attached to remaining single that once existed. If we include the numbers of never-married single people with those who have been divorced and have not remarried, we find that single adults make up about 25 percent of American households. Single people, however, often find it difficult to meet with others outside a social network such as college, where dating is widely accepted and encouraged. Singlehood, though not the ultimate choice of a major portion of our population, has become an accepted lifestyle in Western culture.

Divorce

Based on recent statistics, it has been predicted that 20 percent of those who marry today will be divorced within 5 years; one-third may be divorced within 10 years; and 40 percent will be divorced before they might have celebrated their 15th anniversary. Ultimately, half of U.S. marriages end in divorce. The number of annual divorces per 1,000 population rose significantly during the twentieth century (see Table 6.6), although by 1990, there was a leveling off in the national divorce rate. There is apparently an underre-

porting of divorce and a lack of statistics about marriages that end in separation without a legal divorce. There is a possibility that close to two-thirds of first marriages eventually break up. About 70 percent of divorced people try marriage again, hoping that things will be better the second time around. However, close to half of these second marriages also end in divorce, 37 percent of them within the first 10 years.

There has been some research on predicting the likelihood of divorce, finding that the husband's dissatisfaction with the relationship is one of the most potent predictors that divorce is a likely possibility. Premarital counselors may eventually be able to use tests to make predictions about the long-term stability of a couple's relationship (Gottman, 1999). Because divorce rates continue to be so high, many religious groups and social agencies are placing greater emphasis on divorce prevention. Premarital counseling, coupled with compatibility-rating tests, is becoming more popular. There has also been an increase in the availability of couples' workshops and therapy opportunities designed to teach conflict-resolution techniques that could head off divorce (Silliman & Schumm, 1999).

Some state governments have begun to make premarital counseling a prerequisite for obtaining a marriage license, but it remains to be seen if these programs actually prevent divorce. There is at least some evidence that they may delay the break-up of some marriages. In the most complete study done to date, the divorce rate after 5 years of marriage of those who had participated in a premarital preparation program was about a third of that of a control group without the preparation. After 12 years, however, the gap had narrowed to a statistically insignificant margin (Russo, 1997).

Relatively Speaking

Our daughter will be getting married soon. My husband and I recently met our future son-in-law, Ed, who seems to be a great guy. He has a good job providing a comfortable income. He's a spiritual man, with many talents, well thought of in the community, and, more important, he's head over heels in love with our daughter—as she is with him.

We especially pray for their happiness because they're not your average twentysomething couple starting their marital journey with all the idealism of youth. They're in their late 30s, each bringing to this union the baggage of failed prior marriages. They wish to recommit—to try again, in Samuel Johnson's words, "the triumph of hope over experience." As all parents do, we want this marriage not only to succeed but to flourish.

Like many other couples starting over, they have children—his daughter, her two girls. Their honeymoon will be brief. Then it's instant family. Mothering and fathering children they've known a short time. Two last names on the mailbox. Two girls in the house, a third there every other weekend. Child-support payments going out and coming in. One child's mother across town, a father a state away. Children confused over loyalties to the parents they live with and those they visit. The couple pulled in opposite directions by the wants and needs of their kids and their own need to form a successful, intimate marital relationship.

Their situation is pretty complex, but, these days, quite common. Some "step" families are more complicated than the word implies. Ours is one such family. I began by saying that our daughter will be getting married. Technically this is not true. My husband and I are in a second marriage ourselves, and the bride is my husband's child.

He was a widowed father of nine and I the divorced mother of four when we met at Parents Without Partners 16 years ago. Of the 13 children between us, only his four oldest were out of the house and on their own. The other nine children ranged in age from 4 to 19. Even though he and I were crazy about each other, we knew that combining our two households was not a good idea. Too many kids reared with different parenting styles. Two religions. Two income levels. Too much age difference (he is nearly a generation older than I). Yet we loved each other, so we became a weekend family of sorts, courting one another while surrounded by kids. Eventually the kids grew up, and six years ago we married. Our long courtship helped solidify the mutual affection all of us now enjoy. We are a family. But still the bonds are fragile.

Questions arise as to who is family. Will our daughter's new family be a family of four, made up of those who live in the house? Or a family of five—the four plus the child who visits on weekends? In their home, who is the real parent? Who sets the rules? When does the mother relinquish some of her parenting role to her husband? When does the stepparent step in; when does he or she back off? How much time should the visiting child spend alone with her father and how much time with her new family?

Then there's the question of what they call one another. If a child called her stepfather "Dad," does this take something away from her real father? When children speak about parents, whom are they referring to? When parents say "our children," should they explain the relationship?

Yet whatever we choose to call this relationship created through two remarriages, Amy will be part of our family. She will likely spend some Christmases at our home. She may join our granddaughters when they come to Kansas for their vacation. We've already begun sending her birthday cards and the same holiday treats and trinkets grandmothers (even stepgrandmothers) send grandchildren throughout the year. We will remember her in our thoughts and prayers as we do the other kids in the family.

All this has not escaped Amy, 11 years old going on 35. At our last meeting she asked me, "What shall I call you? You're like a grandmother, but not really my grandmother. I have two grandmothers already, you know." (What she didn't say was that should her mother remarry, she will have one more.)

"I know," I said with a sigh, "it is pretty complicated." We talked a bit, trying to make sense of this convoluted, many-branched, pruned and grafted family tree. We discussed some of the choices, tried out some of the step-this, step-that options, even suggested a step/step or double-step something or other. Each sounded more ridiculous than the last. Finally we decided it would be "Amy and Jan, Jan and Amy." That would have to do.

— Jan Borst. *Newsweek,* July 29, 1996, p. 16.
Borst is an instructor in family sociology at
Emporia State University, Kansas.

It is unclear to what extent sexual incompatibility and dissatisfaction with sex are factors in divorce. Couples who are having marital difficulties often experience sexual problems, yet these problems are just as frequently the effect as they are the cause. There is some evidence that sexual problems present in a first marriage reappear in a second marriage. Adjusting to divorce can be a traumatic experience and it involves the grieving experiences typical of any major loss. Divorced people often experience upheavals in their lifestyles that create new stresses and pressures. They may feel depressed or anxious and loss of self-esteem. Children whose parents have divorced often experience stresses that affect their lives into their college years (Johnson & Nelson, 1998).

Sexuality and Aging

The sharing of sex is usually viewed as something for lustful and passionate youth and for the earlier years of marriage, with old age finding us politely asexual. There are anecdotes and jokes about the occasional "dirty old man," an object of ridicule and disgust. In a youth-oriented culture such as ours, being old is equated with giving up sex. Yet studies have revealed that the elderly are indeed sexual beings. Older people not only retain sexual desires but enjoy the pleasures of the same sexual activities they knew as younger people. In fact, sometimes they apparently even enjoy them more (Deacon, Minichiello, & Plummer, 1995; Jacoby, 1999; National Council on Aging, 1998).

One cross-cultural study examined data relating to sexual activity in 106 traditional societies. In 70 percent of those societies, continuation of sexual activity was expected among the aging. Men were not expected to have much, if any, loss of their sexual capabilities until they were very old. In the majority of these societies, women were also expected to maintain their sexual interests and activities. In fact, women frequently reported signs of stronger sexual interests and fewer inhibitions toward discussing sex after they had passed their childbearing years. A significant finding of this and related research is that whether expressions of sexuality among the aged are encouraged or discouraged seems to depend on the cultural attitudes of a particular society (Greer, Herkov, & Hill, 1994; Winn & Newton, 1982).

Larger proportions of our population than ever before are now in middle and older age groups as post-World War II baby boomers age (see Fig. 6.14). In this sense, we are becoming an older society. People are also retiring earlier, extending the amount of time between retirement and old age. Improved medical care and increased emphasis on good health habits are helping many of us to have a longer life span than we might have once expected. All of these factors have

FIGURE 6.14   *Midlife Transitions and Commitments*
Middle age is often a period of transition and re-evaluation. As couples commit and recommit themselves to relationships, their sense of shared intimacy and sexual enjoyment may be deepened. In this photograph, the founder of Kwanza performs a marriage ceremony ritual for a couple approaching midlife.

created a considerable interest and awareness about aging. Nonetheless, there are many persistent misconceptions about sexuality and the older population.

Myths and Attitudes about Sex and Aging

I mentioned some of the physiological effects of aging on sexual functions in chapter 4, "Human Sexual Response." Here are some myths and attitudes that lead to misunderstandings about the sexuality of older people:

Loving and Sexual Feelings Are Experienced Only during Youth

In fact, human beings retain a full range of emotions—including romantic and sexual ones—throughout the life span (see Fig. 6.15). A major reason behind the suppression of these feelings in many older people is the societal attitude that such reactions are indeed lost with age. To the contrary, a survey of 1,604 people aged 65 to 97 found that 52 percent of the males and 30 percent of the females indicated they were still sexually active. They engaged in sexual activity on the average of 2.5 times per month, although they would have preferred to have sex about twice that amount. During their previous 10 sexual experiences, the men reached orgasm an average of 80 percent of the times, and the women about 50 percent (Mark Clements Research, 1996). Another study of people over the age of 45 found that about two-thirds were extremely or very

FIGURE 6.15 *Old Age and Sexuality*

Patterns of sexual activity vary greatly among the elderly. Cultural and social expectations of sexual behavior as well as the state of health of both partners may play a part in the frequency and type of sexual activity engaged in by elderly couples.

satisfied with their sexual relationships (Jacoby, 1999). A survey conducted with 1,292 people in their 60s, 70s, and 80s by the National Council on Aging (1998) confirmed that about half had sexual activity at least once a month, and 70 percent of those who were sexually active indicated that their sex lives were at least as satisfying as it had been when they were in their forties.

Sex Is Primarily for Reproduction

This is an attitude that negates a spectrum of nonprocreative sexual experiences and obviously sets aside those who are past the age of reproductive capability or interest. Yet for older people who have held this value during their lifetimes, it may become a factor in discouraging sexual expression. Nevertheless, an analysis of national poll data of 6,000 people in the United States has shown that 37 percent of married people over 60 have sexual intercourse once a week, whereas another 16 percent do so even more frequently. Nine out of 10 couples who had sex at least once a week found their spouses "very attractive," and 55 percent said their spouses were skilled lovers. Two-thirds of the sexually active older couples indicated that they still experimented sexually (Calamidas, 1997; Greeley, 1992; Sbrocco, Weisberg, & Barlow, 1995).

Older Men Remain More Sexually Interesting to Younger Partners than Do Older Women

There is a distinct double standard when it comes to the sexual desirability and attractiveness of older people. Although the graying hair and bodily changes of

an aging man are often perceived as being distinguished, women are more likely to be viewed as becoming less attractive with aging. Such attitudes only foster further negative attitudes in aging women about their own sexuality. The pairing of older men with younger women happens relatively frequently; whereas the reverse situation is still not as common, it seems to be gaining increased acceptance (Deacon et al., 1995).

Institutional Prohibitions on Sexual Expression

All of these sex-negative myths and attitudes add up to policies or attitudes that prohibit sexual expression among the aged. Nowhere is this more evident than in nursing homes and other institutions that provide care for older men and women. Not only are outward expressions of sexual interest seen as inappropriate and therefore discouraged, there is often a lack of privacy for any sort of personal or shared sexual activity (Spector & Fremeth, 1996). Studies have shown, however, that many elderly nursing home residents remain sexually active and interested in sex. Even when nursing home personnel are aware of the facts about the sexuality of the aged, their own attitudes may be negative, and appropriate policy changes may be hindered by lack of support from administrative personnel, physicians, and the families of older patients (Hillman & Stricker, 1994).

Changing such conditions can meet with positive results. Increased opportunity for physical and emotional interaction often results in a healthier and more cheerful atmosphere and leads to significant improvements in the social behavior of the residents. Only too often, institutional staffs forget that their clients are adults with rights to privacy and social interaction. Providing older people with opportunities for choice and a sense of personal autonomy can enhance sexual identity and adjustment (Goldstein-Lohman & Aitken, 1995).

Special Sexual Problems and Patterns of Aging

In addition to the psychological stresses that may inhibit sexual activities, there are a number of illnesses and physical infirmities that interfere with sexual abilities (see Table 6.7). Fifty percent of the sexual dysfunctions of individuals over 40 may well be due to physiological changes and illnesses (Sbrocco et al., 1995). It is sometimes the treatment of such problems that produces negative sexual consequences. In one study, 43 percent of older people indicated that medications had affected their sexual functioning, with

Table 6.7	*Suggestions for Coping with Sexual Difficulties of Aging*

Problems	Solutions	
Decreased desire	• Use mood enhancers (candlelight, music, romantic thoughts). • Hormone replacement therapy (estrogen or testosterone).	• Treatment for depression. • Treatment for drug abuse (alcohol). • Behavioral counseling.
Vaginal dryness; vagina expands less in length and width	• Use a lubricant. • Consider hormone replacement therapy.	• Have intercourse regularly. • Pelvic exercises prescribed by your doctor.
Softer erections; more physical and mental stimulation to get and maintain erection	• Use a position that makes it easy to insert the penis into the vagina. • Accept softer erections as a normal part of aging.	• Don't use a condom if disease transmission is not possible. • Tell your partner what is most stimulating to you.
Erection lost more quickly; takes longer to get another	• Have intercourse less frequently. • Emphasize quality, not quantity.	• Emphasize comfortable sexual activities that don't require an erection.

Source: Reprinted from February 1993 Medical Essay of *Mayo Clinic Health Letter* with permission of Mayo Foundation for Medical Education and Research, Rochester, MN 55905.

diminished desire being the most common side effect (Mark Clements Research, 1996). Because the elderly are usually not recognized as being sexual, medications for conditions such as arthritis or high blood pressure and other cardiovascular disorders may be prescribed without any explanation of potential sexual side effects. The older person may simply assume that the change in sexual function is a natural outcome of aging, perpetuating a downward spiral in sexual activity (Pope, 1999).

Likewise, certain surgeries can have effects on sexual behavior that should be thoroughly explained to the elderly patient. Prostate surgery, for example, is very common in older men and may in a few cases inhibit the capability to have an erection and ejaculate. However, with reassurance, encouragement, and education, many men who have had prostatic surgery can resume satisfactory sexual activity (Sbrocco et al., 1995).

Similarly, hysterectomy (removal of the uterus and cervix) need not adversely affect the sex lives of women. For some women, there are many psychological stresses to be faced following hysterectomy, but with appropriate education and adjustment counseling, the majority of women can emerge feeling healthier, sexier, and more self-confident than before. Because of hormonal and other physiological changes of older age, many women report decreased interest in sexual activity and orgasm as they get older. Although there is a distinct decline in levels of sexual interest and behavior as people age, many elderly people remain active—or at least capable of sexual activity—until very old age. There are several life factors that influence sexual potentials in old age:

The Individual's or Couple's Sexual History

A very significant factor is the degree of importance and priority that the individual or couple has placed on sex throughout the life cycle. There is a high correlation between the amount of sexual interest shown in the young adult years and that shown in older adult years. Those who have tended to see sex as an important part of their lives and who have sought frequent sexual outlets tend to continue these patterns into old age. Likewise, letting it become a low priority of life may well lead to an absence of sexual interest as one ages (Deacon et al., 1995).

Partner Availability

How much shared sexual activity is pursued by an older individual depends a great deal on the availability of a sexual partner. Evidence shows that as women age, they become far less likely to have a sexual partner than men (see Fig. 6.16 on p. 192). By age 50 to 59, 30 percent of women report having had no partnered sexual activity within the previous year, and by ages 55 to 59, that figure rises to more than 40 percent. Figures from the General Social Survey indicate that 70 percent of women in their seventies no longer have partnered sex, and by the time they are over 80 years old, 90 percent no longer do. This contrasts with figures for men over 80 that indicate that less than 60 percent report having no partnered sex. Researchers believe that these figures reflect a disproportionate availability of partners rather than different levels of sexual interest. Men in their forties begin to die in higher numbers than women of the same age. In the 60 to 64 age

A Kind of Sexual Revolution

They met last New Year's Eve. He was tall with an easy manner. She was petite with a girlish smile. He asked her to dance and held her close. "I didn't push him away," she said. "I've been around awhile. I've pushed a lot of men away."

It was a modern romance, at once pure and complicated. First, there was his wife. He was still married, although separated. Then, there was his walker.

Fritzie Heilbron's prince came to her not astride a white horse, but in black orthopedic shoes, shuffling along with the help of a walker. He is 76 years old.

This is not a case of geriatrics going clubbing. It is a scene from a nursing home, where those who care for the elderly and infirm report a kind of sexual revolution. The revolution is not among the elderly, who experts say have always demonstrated an enduring urge for intimacy, but in the attitude of those who provide care. They are beginning to recognize that sexual activity is normal and beneficial for patients—even for those with Alzheimer's disease.

"It's not just a matter of dirty old men and disgusting old women," said Robert N. Butler, the director of the International Longevity Center at Mount Sinai Hospital. "The importance of tenderness, touching, being together in bed is an expression that remains vital to the end of life."

At the Hebrew Home for the Aged, a 1,200-bed nursing home and Alzheimer's research center in the Riverdale section of the Bronx where Mrs. Heilbron and her companion found each other, a new policy gives patients the right to privacy so they can carry on intimate relationships. In confronting the issue directly, the Hebrew Home is in the vanguard of the shift away from seeing sex in nursing homes as a behavior problem.

The policy states that "residents have the right to seek out and engage in sexual expression" and the right to obtain "materials with sexually explicit content," including books, magazines and videos.

The home is training its staff to recognize and respect intimate relationships, and officials there say they will try to assist budding romances by moving one member of a couple to a single room to provide privacy. (None have asked to live together.) In the case of Alzheimer's patients or other cognitively impaired residents, the nursing home officials consult with social workers, nurses and families to determine if both residents are willing participants and decide whether the relations should continue.

Because most nursing home residents share rooms, some homes around the country have set aside rooms that couples can use for privacy, and others have formalized policies for addressing sexual activity, like the one at the Hebrew Home.

Janet Lowe, a nurse's aide at the Hebrew Home, said that the first time she realized two unwed residents were having a relationship, "I was shocked. You don't think of your grandparents having sex."

Ms. Lowe said other members of the staff had stronger objections. "Some people thought it should be stopped because they weren't married."

At the Hebrew Home, Mrs. Meltzer, who lives on a different floor than her husband because he suffers from dementia, said even in his confused state his need for closeness emerges.

"I think intimate sex is the farthest thing from his mind," she said. "He reaches for my hand and kisses me. And he says why don't you just get undressed and get into bed. I think he just wants intimacy."

Mrs. Meltzer said the need for companionship doesn't fade with age. She said that when she first moved to the home she was told about a man who was found naked and dead in the bed of a woman who lives there. Mrs. Meltzer said she still remembered her reaction: "I said, 'Well, anyway, he died happy.'"

From: M. Purdy. *The New York Times,* November 6, 1995, pp. B1, 6. Reprinted by permission.

bracket, there are 88 men per 100 women. Above age 75, there are only 55 men per 100 women. Clearly, it is more difficult for older women to find potential sexual partners than it is for older men (Jacoby, 1999; Laumann, Gagnon et al., 1994).

Sexual Values and Attitudes

Throughout the life span, sexual behaviors are influenced by attitudes and values. People who are old today grew up in times during which negative and repressive sexual codes were taught, and many have carried these values with them into old age, where they may become self-fulfilling prophecies. Research confirms that among older people, negative attitudes toward sex correlate with relative sexual inactivity (Purifoy, Grodsky, & Giambra, 1992). Unfortunately, opportunities for older people to discuss, explore, or even change their value systems are often neglected, because it is assumed that their values are too entrenched.

Knowledge about Sexuality

Ignorance about sex is rampant; this is no less true among seniors than it is among the young. Older people often labor with myths and misinformation about

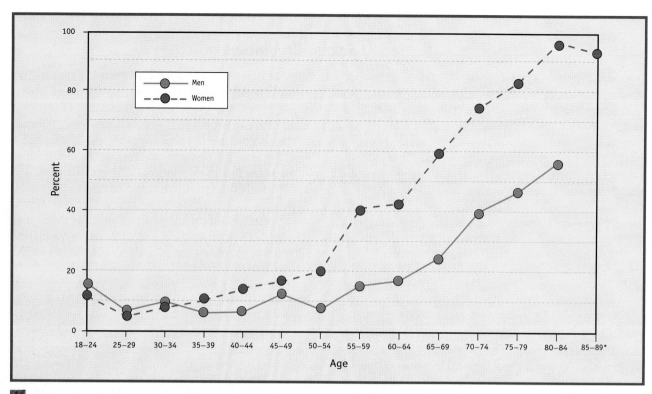

FIGURE 6.16   *U.S. Adults with No Sexual Partner in the Past 12 Months*

As women age, they become far less likely than men to have a sexual partner.

Source: From *Sex in America*. Copyright © 1994 by C.S.G. Enterprises, Inc., Edward O. Laumann, Robert T. Michael, and Gina Kolata. By permission of Little, Brown and Company.

*Note: Insufficient data available for men aged 85 to 89.

sex and sexual behaviors, leading them to further conflicting attitudes and values about their own sexual lives. At the same time, older people often want more information about sexuality.

Maintenance of Self-Esteem and a Sense of Identity

Seniors must adapt to many physical, emotional, social, and economic changes in their lives. There may be loss of companionship, loss of role status after retirement, and some losses of physical and cognitive functioning. The individual's perception of her or his sexuality is a crucial part of her or his adjustment to a new stage of life. Dissatisfaction with sexual activity relates to depression and feelings of worthlessness, which in turn can discourage further activity (Calamidas, 1997).

Masturbation and Heterosexual Intercourse in Old Age

For many older people who have lost their sexual partners, masturbation becomes their sole means of sexual gratification. There are few statistical data concerning

masturbation among the aged, although there are indications from the NHSLS that the frequency of masturbation declines in the 54- to 59-year-old age brackets (Laumann, Gagnon et al., 1994). In their first study on human sexual response, Masters and Johnson (1966) reported that most of the older people in their study had tended to continue masturbating into old age if they had masturbated previously. The frequency of reported masturbation among seniors is largely determined by sexual attitudes and knowledge. In one study, people over the age of 65 reported masturbating an average of once per month, and those under 65 reported doing so about four times per month (Mark Clements Research, 1996).

Research on the sexual behavior of older people has usually concentrated on heterosexual intercourse. Every study suggests that the frequency of intercourse steadily declines with age and that availability of a healthy partner plays a major role in determining the frequency (Keil et al., 1992; Laumann, Gagnon et al., 1994). However, our preoccupation with intercourse as a standard of measurement does not do justice to the sexuality of the aging. When we broaden our definition of "sexually active" to mean a spectrum of sexual and sensual behaviors, older people fare quite well. This may signal the maturation of older people away from the narrow, limiting genital focus of intercourse, toward a fuller and more complete sense of what it means to be a sexual human being. In this sense, younger generations may well have lessons to learn from older generations (Calamidas, 1997).

Stereotypes about Aging and Same-Gender Orientation

The research on gay men, lesbians, and bisexuals in midlife and older age is very limited. For the most part, it is expected that they face the same sorts of passages and adjustments as heterosexual persons. However, it is also true that of those lesbians and gay males who are presently in their older years, few were exposed to very much information or many positive attitudes about same-gender sexual orientation when they were young. This may have made some of their life adjustments more difficult, and many older gay, lesbian, or bisexual adults have never disclosed their sexual orientations (Altman, 1999). As in society at large, it has often been believed that the gay and lesbian culture values youth, rendering aging particularly difficult for gay men and lesbians. In actuality, lesbians, gays, and bisexuals do not exhibit any significant decrease in self-acceptance or increase in depression or loneliness as they get older. In fact, there is evidence that, because they recognize and manage role conflicts earlier in their lives because their lifestyles are unconventional and socially less accepted, older gay men and lesbians actually have better self-concepts and tend to be more stable than those who are younger (Reid, 1995; Van de Ven, Rodden, Crawford, & Kippax, 1997).

Gay men and lesbians face essentially the same adjustment problems of aging as heterosexuals. There is evidence to suggest that gays and lesbians who are in midlife are beginning to become more open about their sexual orientations and to want medical, legal, and social services appropriate to their needs (Kimmel & Sang, 1995). In general, studies of aging in lesbians and gay males have focused on urban populations with relative affluence. A great deal more research

needs to be done to understand thoroughly any special needs and concerns that aging presents for those with same-gender sexual orientation.

Maximizing Sexual Expression during the Later Years

It is clear that while the aging process makes an indelible mark on the ways in which the human body responds sexually, older people can remain in touch with the sexual part of their lives if they wish. Table 6.6 summarizes some of the ways of maximizing sexual pleasure as one ages. Some nursing homes and healthcare clinics have offered sexual education and enhancement programs for the elderly that have helped them understand their own sexuality more completely. Appropriate counseling services for elderly people can also lead to greater sexual satisfaction, and with increased proportions of older adults in the population, these services are more crucial than ever (Spector & Fremeth, 1996).

Ernest Borneman (1994) believes that infants find sexual and sensual pleasure over the entire surface of their bodies, only focusing those pleasures on the sex organs later in their development. Borneman also suggests that as adult human beings age and become less genitally oriented once again, they have the potential of rediscovering the sensuousness of their entire bodies. Older people consistently report the sexual satisfaction they gain from kissing, caressing, holding, cuddling, and other types of lovemaking that involve both spiritual and physical intimacy. In a sense, elderly people can be freed from many of the concerns that interfere with sexual intimacy in younger age groups: risks of pregnancy, the need to "prove" oneself with sex, obsessions with performance and orgasms, balancing work and personal time, and having children to care for. All of us could stand to learn from those older people who have come to value sexual intimacy in its holistic sense and have come to realize that sex is far more than only what genitals do together. They know the meaning of a cherished touch and the sense of intimacy that shared bodies can enjoy.

Self-Evaluation

Looking Ahead: Sex in Later Years

Some of the strongest misconceptions and prejudices about older people relate to their sexuality. It is assumed that older people lose their sexual feelings, needs, and behaviors. Actually, as this chapter has

demonstrated, many elderly people are still aware of sexual feelings and still seek physical sexual gratification. This questionnaire is designed with two primary goals: to evaluate your attitudes about sex and the aged and to clarify what you hope your sexual life will be when you are older.

1. **Read each of the following statements and rate your level of approval or disapproval for each, using the following scale:**

   5 = **Strongly Approve**
   4 = **Approve Somewhat**
   3 = **Neutral**
   2 = **Disapprove Somewhat**
   1 = **Strongly Disapprove**

   a. A widowed man of 73 confided to his physician that he enjoyed masturbating occasionally but wondered if this practice might cause any ill effects. The physician encouraged him to masturbate as frequently as he wished—the more the better. ___

   b. A man and woman whose spouses have died, both in their late seventies, have decided to live and sleep together. For reasons of finances and distribution of estates, they have decided against marrying. ___

   c. A 67-year-old woman announces that she is in love with a 40-year-old man and that they are planning to marry. ___

   d. A 70-year-old widower announces that he is planning to marry a 37-year-old woman. They have been dating for several months, and he has bragged about how the relationship has restored his sexual potency. ___

   e. An elderly man and woman meet in the recreation room of the nursing home where they both reside. The staff at the home will not allow them to spend time together in privacy, even though the older couple has asked for this privilege. ___

2. **Now go back to all of the preceding situations and imagine how you would feel if the older person in each instance were your father or mother. Also consider how you would feel if the older person were you.**

3. **Are you frightened of how aging will affect your sex life? Or doesn't it really matter that much how sexually active you remain in your later years?**

4. **Ideally, how would you like to see yourself functioning as a sexual human being at the age of 60? 70? 80? 90? Do you have any plan in mind for working toward these ideals?**

Chapter Summary

1. Individual patterns of sexual orientation and behavior probably develop through the interaction of biological, social, cultural, and psychological factors. The process is called psychosexual development.

2. Biopsychological drive or instinct theories of psychosexual development state there is a natural, instinctual drive toward sexual behavior.

3. Psychodynamic theory has taught that the sexual instinct, or libido, becomes invested in different bodily areas through stages in human development: oral, anal, latency, and genital. It is believed that boys and girls must resolve unconscious sexual issues with their parents during their development. This theory has seen much revision in recent years.

4. Conditioning theorists believe that positive and negative reinforcement play a role in how people learn to behave sexually. Social learning theory is an extension of conditioning theory that emphasizes the importance of identification with other people and modeling behavior after them.

5. Developmental theory expresses the importance of stages in the emergence of behavior patterns, including those relating to sexuality. Erik Erikson described eight stages, each of which has particular tasks to be completed and crises to be resolved.

6. A unified model of psychosexual development considers three crucial strands that eventually integrate to form adult sexuality: gender identity, sexual response and orientation, and the capacity for dyadic intimacy.

7. In shaping sexuality, contemporary social process theory focuses less on individual persons as the unit of analysis and more on the social processes in which the individual is immersed.

8. Social script theory teaches that human behavior is controlled by complex social scripts. Sexual scripts have cultural, interpersonal, and intrapsychic dimensions that shape people's patterns of sexual behavior.

9. Choice theory explains how individuals decide which sexual behaviors to participate in, factoring in the resources, risk management, and the "market" of accessible partners.

10. Social network theory focuses on how sexual connections and relationships are negotiated within a social context.

11. In infancy and childhood, the sex organs respond to many stimuli. Babies are sensitive over the entire surface of their bodies. Children become more curious about their bodies and sex-related matters.

12. Children's sexual preferences are vague or multisexual at first. Sex play with other children,

masturbatory behavior, and educational efforts by parents can play a significant role in how children feel about sexuality and their own bodies.

13. Children are capable of strong romantic attachments and varying levels of sexual interaction.

14. Adolescence is the period of life between childhood and adulthood. At puberty, the body becomes capable of reproduction and develops its secondary sex characteristics. It is a time for exploring masturbation and relationships.

15. Adolescents learn more about sex and develop their sexual values and attitudes through interaction with peers, by contact with the media, and in their sexual experimentation. There have been social pressures for adolescents to become sexually active at earlier ages.

16. Masturbation is particularly prevalent among adolescents, more so among males than females. The frequency of masturbation varies a great deal among individuals.

17. Understanding and coping with emotional intimacy is important during the adolescent years and is crucial to the establishment of effective social relationships.

18. Same-gender sexual activity among adolescents may be experimental, or it may reflect later sexual orientation. A significant proportion of adolescents have at least one same-gender sexual experience.

19. Heterosexual contact among adolescents often proceeds through levels of increased intimacy, with the likelihood of sexual intercourse increasing with age.

20. Many different factors seem to influence the likelihood of intercourse and the use of condoms, including social dominance, appearance, and testosterone levels in males.

21. Teenage pregnancy continues to be a problem in the United States, creating consequences for teen parents and for the larger society, although rates of teen pregnancy have been decreasing.

22. Adolescent sexual health has become a more pressing concern with the risk of HIV infection, increases in sexually transmitted diseases, and the high rate of unintended pregnancy. The National Commission on Adolescent Sexual Health has established clearer guidelines on the subject.

23. Age, length of time a male has been sexually active, and social factors influence the likelihood of condom use during sex.

24. Adult sexuality involves establishing intimacy with others and the exploration of the place of sex in intimate relationships.

25. When people form couples today, they face the conflicts of high expectations versus reality and limited resources; individual fulfillment versus maintenance of the partnership; and the hope of a lifetime relationship versus the awareness of how frequently relationships break up.

26. Coupling goes through continuing cycles of three stages: the expansive stage, contraction and betrayal, and resolution.

27. There are three main theoretical approaches to understanding how people select a mate or sexual partner. Psychological theory assumes some inner mechanism of attraction; social network theory demonstrates the significance of social groups in finding a partner; and evolutionary or sociobiological theory holds that there are certain innate tendencies of males and females that shape their mate selection processes.

28. Although some 4 million people are cohabiting, or living together, most people in the United States eventually marry. Cohabiting couples who marry are more likely to divorce than couples who did not live together before marriage.

29. Sexual activity tends to be highest in the earlier years of a relationship, gradually decreasing in frequency. Sexual satisfaction does not seem to be correlated with frequency, and married couples express more satisfaction than other groups.

30. Although monogamy is still accepted as the most socially appropriate type of relationship, some level of extramarital sexual activity has been reported. Sexual infidelity seems to occur with less frequency than was once thought.

31. At least half of marriages in the United States end in divorce or separation, with 70 percent of divorced people going on to subsequent marriages, half of which also end in divorce.

32. Even though older people retain their interests and physical capacities for sexual expression, our youth-oriented culture often fails to recognize it.

33. In nursing homes and institutions for elderly people, lack of privacy and policies of sex segregation may prevent expression of sexual needs.

34. The concerns of gay, lesbian, and bisexual persons as they age seem to be essentially the same as for heterosexual persons. Gays do not face a greater likelihood of lowered self-esteem or depression as they age.

35. How sexually active an older person is depends on past activity, partner availability, physical health, and knowledge of sexuality.

Focus on Health Questions

You will find in this section the kinds of questions that you may have concerning your own health and sexuality. The page references indicate where in the text the answer is located; the exact place is marked with the logo: **FOH**

1. Does everybody start having sex when they are in high school? 172–173

2. I feel extremely awkward when I attempt to have sexual intercourse. Is there anything I can do to make myself more comfortable? 178

3. If we live together for a while, won't that give us a better edge on a happier marriage? 182

4. How can I prepare for remaining sexually interested and active when I am older? 193

Annotated Readings

Alan Guttmacher Institute. (1994). *Sex and American teenagers*. New York: Author. One of the most comprehensive surveys of available information on adolescent sexuality, this volume provides graphic representations of the current state of our knowledge.

Borneman, E. (1994). *Childhood phases of maturity: Sexual developmental psychology*. Amherst, NY: Prometheus Books. A survey of the author's 20 years of research with some 4,000 European children, this work presents perspectives that differ from mainstream findings on childhood sexuality.

Buss, D. M. (1994). *The evolution of desire: Strategies of human mating*. New York: Basic Books. An excellent discussion of evolutionary theory concerning mate selection, summarizing the wealth of cross-cultural data presently available.

Chudacoff, H. P. (1999). *The age of the bachelor: Creating an American subculture*. Princeton, NJ: Princeton University Press. Presents an historical and social perspective on the single life for men.

Daniluk, J. C. (1998). *Women's sexuality across the life span*. New York: Guilford Publications. A comprehensive examination of sexual awareness and behavior from childhood through the aging process among women.

Gottman, J. M. (1999). *Seven principles for making marriage work*. New York: Crown. Based on years of work in his famous "marriage lab," Gottman offers sound advice on ways of improving marriage and keeping relationships strong.

Harris, J. R. (1998). *The nurture assumption: Why children turn out the way they do*. New York: Free Press. This book puts forth a controversial claim that genes have far more to do with shaping children's personalities and behaviors than parents do.

Irvine, J. M. (Ed.). (1994). *Sexual cultures and the construction of adolescent identities*. Philadelphia: Temple University Press. Examines the role of various social and cultural factors on the development of adolescent sexual identities.

Lampert, A. (1997). *The evolution of love*. Westport, CT: Praeger. An evolutionary perspective on love, relationships, and sexuality.

Levine, S. B. (1998). *Sexuality in mid-life*. New York: Plenum. A perceptive and insightful examination of sexuality and relationships during midlife, especially beyond the age of 50.

Maurer, H. (1994). *Sex: An oral history*. New York: Viking Penguin. Presents the personal sexual histories of numerous individuals at varying stages of their life-span development.

Rossi, A. S. (Ed.). (1994). *Sexuality across the life course*. Chicago: University of Chicago Press. A collection of papers that surveys human sexuality at several different stages of the life span, with special emphasis on midlife development.

Wallerstein, J. S., & Blakeslee, S. (1995). *The good marriage: How and why love lasts*. Boston: Houghton Mifflin. Sound guidelines for a healthy marriage based on interviews with 50 couples who consider themselves successfully married.

Chapter 7

Sexual Individuality and Sexual Values

Chapter Outline

Note: A selection of Focus on Health questions appears at the end of each chapter. Answers to these questions are indicated within the chapter by the symbol in the margin. **FOH**

Until I came to college, I thought of myself as a very normal person sexually—a little on the conservative side, maybe, but normal. As I watch my peers' sexual exploits, I'm not so sure anymore. I am doing a lot of questioning about who I really am, or ought to be, sexually.

—*From a college student's essay*

Humans have the potential to participate in, and find physically pleasurable, a wide spectrum of sexual activities at every stage of the life cycle. As we have begun to see, there seems to be a complex interaction of innate and social factors that determines which of these activities are ultimately chosen by a particular individual. Cultural and social mores and values also determine the extent and types of sexual behaviors to be found in any human society at any particular time in history. Social networks seem to play the most significant role in the formation of sexual relationships and the shaping of personal sexual attitudes and conduct (Laumann, Gagnon et al., 1994). Sexuality education provides one forum for discussing, examining, and understanding these issues.

List several sexual activities you believe are considered normal in our society. List several sexual activities you believe are considered abnormal.

■ Labeling Sex: Establishing Standards

The predominating assumption in Western culture regarding human sexuality has been as follows: to be **normal** is to be attracted sexually to members of the opposite sex and to desire penis-in-vagina intercourse as the ultimate expression of that attraction; everything else, in varying degrees and at various times, has been considered **abnormal.** Yet there is ample historical, anthropological, and psychological evidence that human beings are—and have always been—extremely diverse and variable in their sexual attractions and behaviors (see Fig. 7.1).

Literature and art have portrayed all sexual activities through the ages, but the extent to which they have been expressed and permitted in various societies and times in history is only known in bits and pieces (see Fig. 7.2). For some past cultures, we know what sexual behaviors were considered unlawful or the codes of sexual activity that were established by religion. For others, we know what the practitioners of medicine thought about specific behaviors. However, the extent to which information about a sexual activity was recorded in a society may have depended on the extent to which the activity was tolerated and accepted (Bullough & Bullough, 1995). Consider the examples of prostitution and same-gender sexual behavior. Because prostitution has generally been more accepted over the span of human history than has same-gender

FIGURE 7.1   *Erotic scene from Attic cup, Pompeii, Italy, 5th century, B.C.E.*

For centuries, depictions of human sexual behaviors have reflected various standards of acceptability.

behavior, we have far more historical records about it than we do about sexual activity between members of the same sex.

One of the jobs of science is to categorize, classify, and label. To organize and name things and phenomena are the only ways for us to continue being able to communicate about them intelligently. The same has been true for human sexuality, as science has attempted to explain, understand, and classify sexual attractions and activities.

However, it is important to remember that scientists are products of their sociocultural environments too. Their conclusions and labels may reflect the agendas of their society (Braiterman, 1998). Labels can have great power, both positive and negative. You

normal: a highly subjective term used to describe sexual behaviors and orientations. Standards of normalcy are determined by social, cultural, and historical standards.

abnormal: anything considered not to be normal (that is, not conforming to the subjective standards a social group has established as the norm).

FIGURE 7.2 *The painter of this red-figured Attic kylix portrayed a variety of sexual activities.*

may recall that, during the latter part of the nineteenth century, Richard von Krafft-Ebing condemned masturbation as depraved and identified it as a source of mental contamination, weakened sexual desire, and all manner of physical and sexual problems. His attitudes were promulgated throughout the medical profession, thus promoting the view that masturbation was one of the most damaging of sexual acts. Hence, it was given labels such as secret sin, self-abuse, and self-pollution. Generations of young people grew up viewing masturbation with fear and frustration.

Krafft-Ebing reflected, reinforced, and perpetuated the values of his place, time, and social network. It was not a time when science could see the description of behavior as being unrelated to moral implications and teachings. As we know, the twentieth century saw a shift in attitudes toward masturbation. Medical science has yielded accurate information about its effects and its frequency. Although some religious prohibitions against masturbation remain, the general opinion in the professions of medicine and psychology is that the practice is a widespread and generally harmless form of sexual expression (Sanford, 1994). It is interesting that books about sex have now shifted to using labels such as **self-gratification** and **self-pleasuring** to describe masturbation. It has become one of the norms against which other behaviors are compared and standardized.

For years, sexologists have been struggling to come up with general terms to describe more atypical

behaviors such as sadomasochism or cross-dressing. They continue to face the issue of how to judge whether or not some sexual activity truly is atypical or socially inappropriate. Psychoanalysis first gave us the term **deviation,** which of course implies that one has strayed from some defined, normal pathway. It may be a pathway determined by statistics, so the deviant is one who is located on one of the ends of a bell curve. Or it may be established simply by prevailing values. In any case, the label "deviation" has taken on so much emotional content and vagueness that it is no longer widely used to describe sexual behaviors.

A more recent label has been **variation** or variance, also implying that an individual is somehow different or aberrant sexually. The question remains of how the standard for determining the norm is established. One might ask, "A variation on what?" or "Different from what?" These terms have come to have negative connotations, even though originally they were not meant to have any particular value implications. A somewhat more scientific label has emerged within the last decade. The term **paraphilia,** loosely meaning "a love beside," is considered to be sexual attachment or dependency on some unusual or typically unacceptable stimulus. These behaviors do not necessarily have any pathological implications, and there is still much cross-cultural comparison to be done to understand the degree to which paraphilic behavior is defined by culture (McConhagy, 1993).

Sociocultural Standards for Sexual Arousal and Behavior

It is easy to see that labels such as deviation, variation, and paraphilia all imply some degree of aberration from an accepted sexual standard. There are several standards that permeate the values of Western culture

self-gratification: giving oneself pleasure, as in masturbation; a term typically used today instead of more negative descriptors.

self-pleasuring: self-gratification; masturbation.

deviation: term applied to behaviors or orientations that do not conform to a society's accepted norms; it often has negative connotations.

variation: a less pejorative term to describe nonconformity to accepted norms.

paraphilia (pair-a-FIL-ee-a): a newer term used to describe sexual orientations and behaviors that vary from the norm; it means "a love beside."

today. In informal—and sometimes quite formalized—ways, they tell us how we are supposed to feel and act sexually (Braiterman, 1998). They are as follows:

The Heterosexual Standard

We are supposed to be sexually attracted to members of the other gender and desire therefore to be sexually involved with them (see Fig. 7.3).

The Coital Standard

We are supposed to view sexual intercourse between woman and man, or **coitus,** as the ultimate sexual act. Most other forms of shared male-female sexual activity have come to be labeled as **foreplay,** with the implication that rather than being enjoyed for their own sake or as sexual goals and ends in their own right, they represent steps toward intercourse. They prepare the couple for coitus.

The Orgasmic Standard

We are supposed to experience orgasm as the climax of any sexual interaction. This standard has been particularly prevalent among males in Western culture, although in recent years it has been predominating among women as well.

The Two-Person Standard

We are supposed to view sex as an activity for two. Although masturbation has gained in legitimacy as an acceptable behavior, it is still typically viewed as a substitute for shared sexual activity, especially intercourse. It is still better, according to the standard, to experience sex as a duo. And any sexual activity involving more than two is considered distinctly kinky.

The Romantic Standard

We are supposed to relate sex to love. Romance and sex have become inseparably intertwined, and it is certainly true that the intimacy generated by one may enhance the other. But it is also true that love and sex can be subject to very different interpretations and values. In Victorian times, healthy and positive loving relationships were supposed to be unspoiled by the desires of the flesh. Today, according to the new standard, it would seem that romantic love without sex would be incomplete and that sex without love would be emotionally shallow and exploitative (Seidman, 1992).

The Safe Sex Standard

This is the most recently developed standard for our culture, and it holds that when people make the choice to share sex, they should take appropriate precautions to prevent unwanted consequences such as unintended pregnancy or transmission of disease. It has evolved out of an increased awareness of the threat of HIV and AIDS and has expressed itself in a new level of emphasis on abstinence from risky sexual behaviors and on the use of condoms during shared sexual activity.

These standards are reinforced by prevailing cultural values and mores and by the social networks in which we live. That is not to imply that they are inconsequential or should not be respected because we are all products of and integral parts of our society and culture. Yet, at the same time, we cannot ignore the fact that such standards shift and alter with time. Neither can we deny the fact that significant proportions of the human population simply do not live their sexual lives according to these standards.

Which sociocultural standards for sexual arousal and behavior do you believe are most commonly held within your social network: the heterosexual standard, the coital standard, the orgasmic standard, the romantic standard, or the safe sex standard? Explain your choices.

FIGURE 7.3   *Heterosexual Standard*

The form and meaning of behavior are influenced by the culture and the time in which one lives. Thus, in North American society as we begin the twenty-first century, heterosexuality is the standard form of sexual behavior. The cultural standard, however, should not be confused with a moral and ethical standard that is individualistic and flexible.

coitus (KO-at-us or ko-EET-us): heterosexual, penis-in-vagina intercourse.

foreplay: sexual activities shared in early stages of sexual arousal, with the term implying that they are leading to a more intense, orgasm-oriented form of activity such as intercourse.

Sexual attitudes and values seem to be associated with, and may be determined by, many factors in people's lives, including ethnic background, socioeconomic status, and whether one grows up in a rural, suburban, or urban setting. These are factors that help to determine our social networks. There are also pressures at times to buy into social values that may be unrealistic for the individual. For example, even with the growing emphasis on sexual abstinence as the safest course of action for unmarried people, statistics are continuing to demonstrate that significant numbers of young people are not choosing to abstain from sex. Some of them are apparently making this choice even though they may believe the prevailing social standard that it would be safer for them to abstain. This may reflect an internal conflict for some people that will prevent them from preparing for safer sex through the use of condoms, choosing alternatives to penetrative sex, or using contraception.

The United States and Canada are clearly pluralistic nations, in that they approach such things as politics, religion, education, and occupational choice with an acceptance of a wide range of differences and cultural diversity. However, both countries have been slower to accept the possibility that a spectrum of sexual orientations and behaviors might also be legitimate.

Who Is Normal?

Anthropologists speak of **ethnocentricity,** the quality of assuming that one's own culture is the right one, superior to all others. Our ethnocentricity finds us surprised, amused, and shocked by the beliefs and customs of others, who of course are just as taken aback by ours. In their classic anthropological study, *Patterns of Sexual Behavior,* Ford and Beach (1951) concluded that there is such a wide variation in sexual behaviors across cultures that no one society can even be regarded as representative. Yet a type of ethnocentricity that might be called **erotocentricity** causes us to assume that our own—either cultural or individual—sexual values, standards, and activities are right and best.

Ours is a culture of dichotomies and categories. Everything must fit into some classification. If something is not right, it must be wrong. If some behavior is not bad, it must be good (Braiterman, 1998). The normal/not-normal dichotomy is often strongly held, and people constantly worry about whether their feelings and behaviors are indeed normal. Every society sets sexual standards and regulates sexual behaviors. These standards are adopted by social networks in varying degrees and are then passed from one generation to the next, sometimes being modified as they go along. Boundaries therefore arise, distinguishing the

good from the bad, the acceptable from the unacceptable. They become the criteria that are used to establish the concepts of normal and not normal. Here are the most widely accepted methods of defining normalcy in Western culture today:

Statistical Normalcy

One of the most common ways of deciding the relative normalcy of some sexual behavior is based on how widespread and frequent it is in a particular population. If most people do it, then it is considered normal. If it is practiced by only a small minority, it is not considered normal. Some behaviors, such as masturbation and oral sex, began to be considered more "normal" when major sex surveys showed how widespread they were (Pomeroy, 1997).

Normalcy by Expert Opinion

Every society has its experts, either by choice or by default. Our society venerates educational and professional credentials and listens to the opinions of those who possess what are perceived to be expert credentials. For example, members of the psychiatric profession's associations may decide, by vote, to consider a certain sexual orientation healthy or unhealthy, normal or abnormal. In 1974, the American Psychiatric Association decided, by polling their members, that same-gender sexual orientation and behavior would no longer be considered an illness (see Fig. 7.4). For the purposes of diagnosing and classifying various mental illnesses, including certain sexual behaviors, professionals often refer to a major psychiatric handbook called the *Diagnostic and Statistical Manual of Mental Disorders.* Now in its fourth edition, this manual is usually referred to as the *DSM-IV.* Questions have been raised about the basis for deciding what is to be considered abnormal and therefore listed in the *DSM-IV* as such. It has been claimed that the process for making such decisions is sometimes arbitrary and scientifically inadequate. Yet it is often expert opinion that will determine what is normal or abnormal, and expert opinion may vary depending on the input available (Caplan, 1991; Socarides, 1995).

ethnocentricity (eth-no-sen-TRIS-ih-tee): the tendency of the members of one culture to assume that their values and norms of behavior are the "right" ones in comparison to other cultures.

erotocentricity (ee-ROT-oh-sen-TRIS-ih-tee): the application of ethnocentriclike judgments to sexual values and behaviors, creating the assumption that our own ways of approaching sexuality are the only "right" ways.

FIGURE 7.4   *What Is Normal?*

Labels such as "homosexual" are sometimes employed to construct rigid boundaries between "normal" and "not-normal" behavior. In fact, same-gender orientation and behavior are part of a continuum of sexual behavior that encompasses numerous individual factors.

Moral Normalcy

Religions usually have standards regarding sexual morality. The predominant religions in a particular society therefore establish the norms for morality. These standards are perpetuated in laws and social sanctions. In most societies, behaviors and values that are seen as morally acceptable are also defined as normal.

A Continuum of Normalcy

In Western societies, there has recently been increased acceptance of concepts such as situation morality, reality as a matter of perception, and nonjudgmentalness. As a result, there has been an increased willingness to view sexual attraction and activities in relative terms, by asking such questions as: Is a behavior healthy and fulfilling for a particular person? Is it safe? Does it lead to exploitation of others? Does it take place between responsible, consenting adults? In this manner, normal and abnormal are seen as part of a continuum that considers numerous individual factors. Nevertheless, societies must establish sexual norms and make decisions about what is to be done with people who violate them. They may be treated by healing practitioners with anything from witch doctor spells to modern drugs, depending on the culture. They may be banished from the society or forced to live in a kind of special sexual exile. Or they may be subject to legal sanctions and even imprisoned. They may also be ignored or tolerated.

Limits and Misuses of Labels: The Language of Sexual Orientation

Labels for various forms of sexual behavior can really only provide a very general category of definition. The *DSM-IV* provides diagnostic categories to facilitate communication among clinicians in the psychological and psychiatric professions. However, whatever defines groups of people can separate them as well.

FoH Consider, for example, the term **homosexual.** Most people believe that they understand what is meant by the term. Closer examination might call the use of such a label into question (Sell, 1997). Here are some of the issues to be clarified in deciding who once might have been labeled a homosexual:

1. Must the person participate in actual sexual activity with another of the same gender, or is it enough to just want it?
2. If a person has had just one sexual experience with a same-gendered partner, should he or she be considered homosexual? If not, how many same-gender sexual acts should lead to such classification?
3. Should only those who have been sexually involved exclusively with members of their own gender be called homosexual? Or what percentage of same-gender experience is required?
4. Should people who have been attracted sexually to members of their gender all of their lives, but have married and engaged exclusively in heterosexual activity, be considered homosexual?

With heterosexual orientation and behavior perceived as the norm in contemporary society, heterosexuals as a group tend to be relatively unnoticed. The term "heterosexual" is not likely to be used to define a person, behavior, or lifestyle because a great deal of diversity is accepted among those people considered to be heterosexual. The term "homosexual", on the other hand, is quite a different story. It has usually represented a distinct and permanent category, a defining characteristic of the person who has been labeled that implies a great deal beyond some occasional sexual behavior. As a consequence, people who have any degree of same-gender sexual orientation are seen as constituting a separate minority, often provoking disapproval, fear, or loathing because of their perceived "abnormalcy" or "unhealthiness" (Boswell, 1990a).

There has been a tendency to categorize sexual activities by the gender of the people involved and then draw inferences about those who fit into the categories. Knowing about a person's same-gender sexual behaviors actually reveals nothing about her or his psychological adjustment, hormone balances, masculinity or femininity, childhood development, or any other characteristic that would distinguish the person from one whose sexual behaviors have been exclusively heterosexual. Research data continue to indicate that people who have sex with members of their own gender are remarkably similar to people who do not. Perhaps science has been trying to invent categories and commonalities where none exist (Sell, 1997).

Definitions of the term "homosexual" have tended to focus only on sexual activity and thus have sometimes ignored the individual's **affectional** preferences.

One's sexual behavior does not necessarily reflect inner orientations and inclinations. It is quite possible that individuals who find themselves sexually attracted to members of their own gender never participate in sexual acts with them. Instead these individuals apparently function effectively in relationships with the other gender. It is also possible for those with a primarily heterosexual orientation to participate in same-gender sexual behavior.

Current models of sexual orientation take into consideration many different variables, including behavior, attraction, self-identification, lifestyle, frequency of sex with different partners, and changes over time. The present state of knowledge about human sexuality no longer allows us to identify the term "homosexual" as anything very specific (Laumann, Gagnon et al., 1994). It is for these reasons that some psychologists have recommended that the term "homosexual" no longer be applied to people. It is laden with negative stereotypes, is often applied only to males, and is generally ambiguous. A special committee of the American Psychological Association developed new guidelines for the use of terms that are considered to be more precise and less pejorative (Committee on Lesbian and Gay Concerns, 1991). This text will employ this terminology in an effort to avoid these unnecessary and unfair connotations or stereotypes.

The terms "gay male" and "lesbian" are used primarily to describe people's sexual and affectional identities and the communities of individuals that have developed among people who share those identities. Although the term **gay** is sometimes used to describe either men or women, it will be used in this book mostly in reference to males; the word **lesbian** is used in reference to females. Although there is growing use of the term "queer" by professionals who are gay, bisexual, or transgendered themselves, the term often describes a particular set of political values relating to sexual orientation (Humphrey, 1999). The word has not been widely embraced by those in the gay and

homosexual: term traditionally applied to affectional and sexual attractions and activities between members of the same gender.

affectional: relating to feelings or emotions, such as romantic attachments.

gay: refers to persons who have a predominantly same-gender sexual orientation and identity. More often applied to males.

lesbian (LEZ-bee-un): refers to females who have a predominantly same-gender sexual orientation and identity.

lesbian community yet, and I have chosen not to use it because it is still so often employed by others with a negative connotation. The term **heterosexual** can be used to refer to opposite-gender (male-female) orientation, identity, or behavior. The slang term **straight** is often applied to primarily heterosexual persons, although it also implies the negative connotation that nonheterosexuals are somehow "crooked," perpetuating a stereotype of deviance from the norm.

The term **bisexual** is used in reference to people who relate sexually and affectionally to both females and males. It may be used to describe both sexual identity and behavior. One of the complex aspects of bisexuality is that there are so many different ways in which it may be manifested. Some bisexual people are simultaneously attracted to both men and women, whereas others have sequential relationships with members of both genders. In other words, some bisexual persons spend some time in a gay male or lesbian relationship, followed by involvement in a heterosexual relationship, or vice versa. Bisexual people often feel as though they do not have a clear place in society that their identity fits. Heterosexual people, lesbians, and gay males may not be accepting of bisexual orientations and behaviors, assuming instead that the bisexual person should make a decision to go one way or the other, choosing up sides as it were. On the one hand, bisexuals may be accused by gay males or lesbians of trying to preserve heterosexual privileges, but on the other hand they are perceived by both heterosexual people and gay males and lesbians as being gay or lesbian but afraid to admit it. These conflicting messages perpetuate the confusion and misunderstanding that often face people who consider themselves bisexual (Pope & Reynolds, 1991; Weinberg, Williams, & Pryor, 1994).

Confusing questions may also arise with other sex-related labels. A man who dresses in women's clothing is often labeled a **transvestite,** and yet there are all sorts of different motivations for such behavior (Braiterman, 1998). Terms such as "sadism" and "masochism" are so general and ill-defined that they have little meaning at all in talking about the behavior of individuals (see chapter 13, "The Spectrum of Human Sexual Behavior"). Of special concern is the use of specific sexual labels to define the entire person. Only too often an individual's entire identity seems to be summarized in a single descriptor of his or her sexual orientation. We say, "Isn't she a lesbian?" or "There goes a transvestite," instead of recognizing these orientations and behaviors as only one small part of an individual's personality. Yet we never label anyone a heterosexual or with other terms for what we consider normal behavior. Such misuses of terminology are a disservice to individual human beings.

◾ Sexual Individuality

Personal sexuality is far more complex than gender roles and sexual attraction to a particular gender. There are certain characteristics about other people we may find sexually attracting and arousing: facial features, body types and builds, hairstyles, age, certain parts of their bodies (for example, legs, buttocks, genitals, breasts), styles of clothing, or complete lack of clothing. When we interact with others sexually, there are usually specific sexual acts that we prefer. We may have our own particular frequencies and techniques for masturbation, and there are activities and things that some people find sexually exciting that have little to do with other people.

Most people have a sexual life of the mind, too, consisting of sexual fantasies and dreams, as well as sensations of sexual need, desire, and attraction (see Fig. 7.5). Only some of the time are these inner experiences expressed in physical responses or overt sexual behaviors. Because performing sexual acts involves a degree of decision making, our inner sexual reactions and needs are not always consistent with our outward expressions of sexual behavior (Byers, Purdon, & Clark, 1998).

All of these aspects of a person's sexuality are intimately intertwined with all other aspects of the personality. Like classifying fingerprints by loops, whorls, and other configurations, it is possible to find general categories for some parts of everyone's sexual nature. But, taken together, the aspects of our personal sexualities are as individualized and specific as our fingerprints. They constitute our **sexual individuality.**

How Does Sexual Individuality Develop?

One of the most common questions asked of sexologists is, what causes a person to be gay or lesbian? The classic answer is that we will not know how one gets

---

heterosexual: attractions or activities between males and females.

straight: slang term for "heterosexual."

bisexual: refers to some degree of sexual activity with or attraction to members of both sexes.

transvestite: an individual who dresses in clothing and adopts mannerisms considered appropriate for the opposite sex.

sexual individuality: the unique set of sexual needs, orientations, fantasies, feelings, and activities that develops in each human being.

FIGURE 7.5 *Sexual Curiosity and Fantasy*

People are curious about the human body and sexuality most of their lives. Our inner sexual lives often help us develop and explore our sexual needs and interests. Sexual fantasy gives people the opportunity to experience sexual interests in a safe environment and release inner tensions. Sexual fantasies may mirror developing sexual desires, or in some case promote sexual desires.

to be attracted to people of the same gender until we understand how one gets to be attracted to those of the other gender. If we examine all aspects of one's collective sexual individuality, the picture becomes even more complex. Sex research into the origins of sexual attractions, orientations, preferences, and behaviors is still in a very primitive state. At this point, the most honest statement would be that we really do not know how human beings take on the specific characteristics of their sexuality. However, we do have some hypotheses that may form a foundation for eventual understanding. Research in the late twentieth century offered the following generalizations about sexual orientation and sexual activity (Bell et al., 1981; Laumann, Gagnon et al., 1994):

1. The importance of the relationship with parents and identifying with a parent in determining a

child's sexual orientation has probably been overestimated. Parents may influence the development of sexual attractions to some extent, but these influences are likely not very profound.

2. An individual's basic sexual orientation is largely determined by adolescence, even though the person has not been particularly sexually active. Adult expressions of sexual orientation and preference tend to be a continuation and confirmation of earlier sexual feelings, although some of those expressions may not actually be realized behaviorally until later in life.

3. Developing patterns of sexual feelings and responses within children and young people cannot be traced to a single social or psychological root. They are instead the result of many factors that are a part of any human being's life—too numerous, complex, and poorly understood at this time to be predictable or controllable.

4. There seem to be some biological bases for the development of sexual orientation and preference for certain sexual activities. These inborn factors most likely establish sexual predispositions that may then be influenced in various ways by psychological and social factors. Thus, it is likely that the *interaction* between nature and experience, rather than one or the other, influences our sexual development, along with most other facets of human development.

5. Social networks, those groups of people with whom we associate on a regular basis, are extremely significant in shaping and perpetuating an individual's sexual attitudes and behaviors.

6. There does not seem to be a "natural" sexual way for human beings to be, or an inborn sexual instinct to guide sexual behaviors. The diversity of sexual individuality provides ample evidence that there is no single, representative human sexuality.

Klein (1990) was one of the first researchers to develop a model showing many different components of sexual identity, all relating to one another but having a degree of independence from each other at the same time. He initially developed a list of seven variables that needed to be considered when describing a person's sexual orientation or identity: sexual attraction, sexual behavior, sexual fantasies, emotional preference, social preference, self-identification, and actual lifestyle. He soon realized, however, that these dimensions of a person's life often change with time (Sell, 1997). Where people are today in terms of their sexual identities is not necessarily where they were in the past or where they will be or would like to be in the future. Therefore, he developed a matrix, the Klein

Sexual Orientation Grid (KSOG), that considers this time factor along with each of the seven variables (see Fig. 7.6).

Other researchers have reinforced the concept that sexual individuality is a combination of many life dimensions and includes many facets of the personality and patterns of behavior. It reflects an evolution of one's own perception of self through the development of a sexual identity (Schensul, 1999). It would be too narrow to define a person's sexual orientation on the basis of any one activity or fantasy. To label a whole person with the name given to one sexual category cannot do justice to the complexity of human sexual identity or orientation. The development of sexual individuality takes place over a lifetime and includes many different components.

Sexual Attitudes and Sexual Choices

Regardless of how we develop sexually, and regardless of the sexual fantasies, needs, attractions, and orientations that become part of every human being, each of us must make choices about his or her sexual behaviors. It is through these choices that we may fulfill some of the other expectations of being civilized human beings: to be responsible, to develop self-respect, and to be nonexploitative toward others.

In North America, social forces encompass a very mixed set of attitudes and beliefs about sex-related matters (Meston, Trapnell, & Gorzalka, 1998). Research

has continued to confirm that sexual attitudes represent predictors of sexual behavior (Clements-Schreiber, Rempel, & Desmarais, 1998; Hynie & Lydon, 1996). There is also evidence that there are complex combinations of attitudes when they are examined cross-culturally (Widmer, Treas, & Newcomb, 1998). Little has been known about what groups of people might be more likely to have particular sexual attitudes. The National Health and Social Life Survey (NHSLS) asked the participants questions about both their attitudes and behaviors.

NHSLS researchers assessed attitudes on premarital sex, teenage sex, extramarital sex, same-gender sex, pornography, sex and love, religious beliefs, and abortion. They then examined the data using cluster analysis, a statistical technique used when social scientists are searching for patterns in masses of data, but they do not have a strong theory to guide them or a clearly defined hypothesis to be tested. As discussed in chapter 1, three broad categories of attitudes emerged, but there were some clear differences among groups within each category that led to the formation of a few subcategories as well (Laumann, Gagnon et al., 1994). Table 7.1 summarizes these findings.

About one-third of the population indicated that their religious beliefs always guide their sexual behaviors; this group was called *traditional*. People in this group tended to believe that premarital sex, teenage sex, extramarital sex, and same-gender sex are wrong and that legal abortion should be restricted to some

Variable	Past	Present	Ideal
Sexual attraction			
Sexual behavior			
Sexual fantasies			
Emotional preference			
Social preference			
Self-identification			
Lifestyle			

FIGURE 7.6 *Klein Sexual Orientation Grid (KSOG)*

Where people are today in terms of their sexual identities is not necessarily where they were in the past or where they will be or would like to be in the future. Klein developed this chart, which, when filled out, helps the researcher determine a person's sexual identity.

Source: From Fritz Klein, *Bisexualities: Theory and Research,* 1985. Copyright © 1985 The Haworth Press, Binghamton, NY. Reprinted by permission.

	Traditional		Relational			Recreational		
	Conserva-tive	Pro-Choice	Religious	Conven-tional	Contem-porary Religious	Pro-Life	Libertarian	Total Sample
1. Premarital sex is always wrong	100.0*	23.6	0.0	0.4	0.8	6.5	0.0	19.7
2. Premarital sex among teenagers is always wrong	99.5	90.3	78.6	29.1	33.6	65.7	19.7	60.8
3. Extramarital sex is always wrong	98.2	91.0	92.1	94.2	52.1	59.3	32.0	76.7
4. Same-gender sex is always wrong	96.4	94.4	81.9	65.4	6.4	85.9	9.0	64.8
5. There should be laws against the sale of pornography to adults	70.6	47.2	53.1	12.2	11.7	14.9	6.4	33.6
6. I would not have sex with someone unless I was in love with them	87.5	66.0	98.0	83.8	65.3	10.1	19.5	65.7
7. My religious beliefs have guided my sexual behavior	91.3	72.9	74.7	8.7	100.0	25.0	0.0	52.3
8. A woman should be able to obtain a legal abortion if she was raped	56.3	98.6	82.3	99.1	99.3	84.3	99.8	88.0
9. A woman should be able to obtain a legal abortion if she wants it for any reason	0.5	100.0	0.0	87.4	84.9	9.3	88.6	52.4
N = 2,843	15.4%	15.2%	19.1%	15.9%	9.3%	8.7%	16.4%	100.0%

Table 7.1 *Description of Seven Normative Attitudinal Orientations toward Sexuality*

Source: From *Sex in America.* Copyright © 1994 by C.S.G. Enterprises, Inc., Edward O. Laumann, Robert T. Michael, and Gina Kolata. By permission of Little, Brown and Company.
*Indicates the percentage of persons in the "Conservative Traditional" cluster who believe that premarital sex is always wrong.

degree. They were divided in their opinions about the availability of abortion, so the group was subdivided into *conservative* and *pro-choice* types. The conservative traditionalists were more conservative in all of their sexual attitudes than were the pro-choice subgroup.

The largest of the attitudinal groups was the *relational* category, consisting of close to half the population. They believed that sex should be part of a loving relationship but not necessarily reserved exclusively for marriage. Therefore, they did not see premarital sex as wrong but did tend to rate extramarital sex or casual sex as wrong. These people were then subgrouped into three types. The *religious* subgroup, whose religious beliefs shaped their sexual behaviors, was the most conservative, opposing same-gender sex, teenage sex, and abortion. The *conventional* category was less influenced by religious beliefs and tended to

be more tolerant than the religious group toward teenage sex, pornography, and abortion, but this group was still opposed to same-gender sex. A third subgroup was called *contemporary religious.* Although they were also guided by their religious beliefs in their own behaviors, they were more tolerant of same-gender sex than the previous subgroup.

About one-fourth of the population fit into a category that was labeled *recreational* because they did not feel that sex and love needed to be connected. Most people in this category also opposed laws that would prohibit the sale of pornography to adults. They were subdivided into a *pro-life* group that opposed both same-gender sex and abortion but was more accepting of teenage sex and premarital sex. The other subdivision constituted the most liberal of all groups, the *libertarians,* who were not guided by any religious beliefs and were most accepting on all the attitudinal items.

Table 7.2   *Distribution of Attitudinal Orientations within Certain Demographic Groups*

| | Normative Orientation | | |
Social Characteristics	Traditional	Relational	Recreational
Gender			
Men	26.9%	40.1%	33.0%
Women	33.7	47.6	18.7
Age			
Men			
18–24	17.4	46.9	35.7
25–29	21.0	46.2	32.9
30–39	26.2	38.6	35.2
40–49	31.2	38.2	30.5
50–59	40.1	31.3	28.6
Women			
18–24	23.0	51.8	25.3
25–29	27.5	54.6	17.9
30–39	34.6	46.6	18.8
40–49	34.5	44.9	20.6
50–59	47.0	43.4	9.6
Education			
Men			
Less than high school	31.6	39.5	28.8
High school graduate or equivalent	28.3	40.9	30.8
Any college	25.0	39.8	35.2
Women			
Less than high school	36.6	47.6	15.9
High school graduate or equivalent	38.3	46.0	15.7
Any college	30.4	48.7	20.9
Religion			
Men			
None	11.7	39.1	49.2
Mainline Protestant	24.2	43.8	32.0
Conservative Protestant	44.5	30.1	25.3
Catholic	17.8	49.6	32.6
Women			
None	10.4	44.4	45.2
Mainline Protestant	30.9	51.4	17.7
Conservative Protestant	50.5	38.4	11.2
Catholic	22.2	58.0	19.8

Source: From *Sex in America.* Copyright © 1994 by C.S.G. Enterprises, Inc., Edward O. Laumann, Robert T. Michael, and Gina Kolata. By permission of Little, Brown and Company.

Which group do your sexual attitudes and beliefs most closely align with: traditional, relational, recreational, or some combination of the three? Defend your choice.

These findings showed that there is no clear-cut system of "American attitudes" when it comes to human sexuality. There is instead a wide distribution of beliefs across the population. There were some other interesting conclusions the researchers were able to draw, as summarized in Table 7.2. For example, women were somewhat more likely than men to fit into the traditional category and less likely to fit into the recreational. Older people were also more likely to

be traditional. More women than men indicated they believed strongly in love and commitment as part of sexual relationships. Educational level did not seem to be associated with any clear attitudinal pattern, although there was a slight trend away from conservative sexual attitudes and toward liberal attitudes with an increase in educational attainment. Religious affiliation, on the other hand, showed some correlations with attitudes. Nonreligious people were unlikely to fall into the traditional category and were more likely to be recreational. Conservative Protestants were much more likely to be in the traditional category (Michael et al., 1994).

One of the more salient findings of the NHSLS research was the clear link between people's attitudes

Table 7.3   *Attitudes toward Same-Gender Sexual Orientation*

How do you feel about homosexual relationships?

	1998	1978
Acceptable for others, but not self	52%	35%
Acceptable for others and self	12%	6%
Not acccepatable at all	33%	59%

Are homosexual relationships between consenting adults morally wrong or not a moral issue?

	1998	1978
Yes, morally wrong	48%	53%
Not a moral issue	45%	38%

Do you have a family member or close friend who is gay or lesbian?

	1998	1994
Yes	41%	32%
No	57%	66%

Is homosexuality something that some people are born with, or is it due to factors such as how they were raised or their environment?

Born with	33%
How raised or environment	40%
Both	11%

Can people who are homosexual change their sexual orientation if they choose to do so?

Yes	51%	No	36%

Do you favor or oppose permitting people who are openly gay or lesbian to serve in the military?

Favor	52%	Oppose	39%

Do you favor or oppose permitting people who are openly gay or lesbian to teach in schools in your community?

Favor	51%	Oppose	42%

Source: Copyright © 1998 Time, Inc. Reprinted by permission.

From a telephone poll of 1,036 adult Americans taken for TIME/CNN on Oct. 14–15, 1998 by Yankelovich Partners Inc. Margin of error is ±3%. "Not sures" omitted.

and their sexual behaviors. Although it is beyond the scope of this text to analyze these correlations in detail, it was shown that an attitudinal group was closely associated with particular sexual practices and frequency of sexual thoughts. Traditional people tended to have fewer sexual partners and thought about sex less than the other two groups. Conversely, those with recreational attitudes had more sexual partners and more frequently thought about sex. Masturbation, oral sex, anal sex, and same-gender sex all were more common among the recreational group than the traditional group. Frequency of sexual activity did not seem to be linked with an attitudinal group (Laumann, Gagnon, et al., 1994).

Sexual attitudes are very firmly held in most people. Family members, friends, and other members of our social networks tend to be like-minded in their attitudes and therefore provide constant reinforcement for shared beliefs. This is one reason why people's behaviors tend to be consistent with their belief systems. It may also help to explain why people find it difficult to understand and accept other attitudinal viewpoints and have no desire to change their own. This provides us with some understanding of why there are so many conflicts in our society regarding sexual matters, and why discrimination can be one of the unfortunate results (Meston et al., 1998).

Sexual Attitudes and Discrimination: Homophobia and Biphobia

Irrational fears of lesbians and gay men, and strongly held negative attitudes about them, have been labeled **homophobia,** although it has been argued that this is not an accurate term because a true "phobia" is not usually involved (Adam, 1998; White, 1999). Public attitudes toward people with same-gender sexual orientations have tended to become somewhat less negative in recent years. A 1998 TIME/CNN poll of 1,036 adults, slightly over 40 percent of whom had a close friend or family member who was gay or lesbian (see Table 7.3), showed that 64 percent considered same-gender sexual relationships to be acceptable, as compared to 41 percent a decade earlier. Nonetheless, close to half of those surveyed believed such relationships between consenting adults to be morally wrong. Slightly more than half believed that gay people could change their sexual orientation if they chose to do so.

homophobia (ho-mo-FO-bee-a): strongly held negative attitudes and irrational fears relating to gay men and/or lesbians and their lifestyles.

Some negative attitudes were evident about gay and lesbian people in some specific occupations. Only about half of the respondents in the poll wanted openly gay people to be allowed to teach in their community's schools. Apparently there is a common misconception that gay or lesbian teachers might somehow represent an inappropriate role model for students (see Fig. 7.7). The attitude may also be based on the common misconception that gay men and lesbians are more likely to molest children, a belief that is not supported by statistics (Schneider, 1993). People who believe that innate, biological factors are involved in the formation of same-gender sexual orientation often have fewer homophobic attitudes than those who see it as being shaped solely by environmental influences (Oldham & Kasser, 1999).

Why do you think that people who believe sexual orientation to be biologically determined are less likely to have homophobic attitudes than others?

Gay and lesbian students are frequently subjected to harassment, misunderstanding, and discrimination. Attitudes toward gay men tend to be more negative among other students than they are toward lesbian women. Faculty members tend to be more homophobic than those who work with students as student affairs administrators (Engstrom & Sedlacek, 1997; Hogan & Rentz, 1996; Schellenberg, Hirt, & Sears, 1999). The justice department has reported that lesbians and gays are subjected to proportionately more physical violence than any other minority community, and there are indications that antigay violence has

been increasing, both on college campuses and elsewhere. It may be for these reasons that some gay men and lesbian women have been found to have negative attitudes toward heterosexual people (White & Franzini, 1999).

Sexuality education classes and textbooks have often employed an underlying set of assumed heterosexual norms, leading to the claim that they are unfairly biased in heterosexist directions. Cultural **heterosexism** fosters antigay and antilesbian attitudes by providing a system of values and stereotypes that seem to justify prejudice and discrimination (Waldo, 1999). Homophobic attitudes found on college campuses may be one of the reasons why gay men and lesbians sometimes find their college environments less emotionally supportive and less tolerant of change and innovation than the environment they would find in the larger society (Louderback & Whitley, 1997). Campus diversity efforts have begun to challenge heterosexism and offer active acceptance and nurturance of those with differing sexual orientations, and students with same-gender sexual orientations have become increasingly visible. Those institutions that have been successful in creating a supportive environment for gay males, lesbians, and bisexuals have found that these students can feel very comfortable and safe there and are less prone to self-destructive attitudes and behaviors than those in less supportive environments (Swan, 1997).

Misunderstanding and prejudice toward bisexual people, which is sometimes called **biphobia,** has been on the rise, and it may well be more prevalent than homophobia on college campuses (Eliason, 1997). One proposed reason for this increase is the misconception that bisexual males have been primarily responsible for spreading HIV to the heterosexual population. Probably the most blatant form of biphobia, however, is the common belief that bisexuality does not exist at all. The assumption is made that people must naturally fit into either a heterosexual identity or a gay or lesbian identity, and that all others simply have not been able to make up their minds where they fit (Pope & Reynolds, 1991).

Both homophobia and biphobia may be *externalized* or *internalized*. When externalized, they manifest themselves in name-calling, discrimination, or prejudice toward others. It has frequently been suggested that the homophobic or biphobic reactions

FIGURE 7.7 *Coming Out*

Gay, lesbian, and bisexual people sometimes fear that being open about their sexual orientations will have negative consequences. National Coming Out Day provides an opportunity for some individuals to challenge negative stereotypes and find acceptance.

heterosexism: the biased and discriminatory assumption that people are or should be attracted to members of the other gender.

biphobia: prejudice, negative attitudes, and misconceptions relating to bisexual people and their lifestyles.

of some may arise from confusion or uncertainty about their own sexual identity, although there is no empirical evidence to support such a contention. When people are uncomfortable about their own same-gender attractions, feelings, desires, or behaviors, their homophobia or biphobia is said to be internalized. This may lead to high-risk sexual behaviors, depression, and other personal problems (Friedman, 1998).

▨ Sex and Values

Consider your reactions to the following situations: Susan, a sophomore in college, goes with some friends to a favorite bar just off campus. She meets Alan for the first time and they spend 2 hours together, sharing drinks and conversation. He invites her back to his dorm room, and after some kissing and mutual fondling, he asks her to have intercourse. Susan agrees, with the understanding that they will use a condom, and she spends the night in Alan's room. The next morning, they agree that neither is looking for a heavy relationship, although both would enjoy remaining friends.

***

Mike has just entered college and has agreed to maintain an exclusive relationship with his girlfriend at home, some 600 miles away. He feels strongly about their commitment and is determined to make it last. He decides that he will not date at all and that his only sexual outlet will be masturbation.

***

Worried about his grades in English, Derek pays a visit to the office of his instructor, a woman in her late twenties. They discuss his recent papers and examinations, with Derek admitting that English has never been his strongest subject. To Derek's surprise, the professor hints that one sure way to earn an A would be to spend some time alone with her at her apartment. At first he thinks she is joking, but she touches his hand and makes it clear that she is being very serious.

***

Lucy returns to her dorm room following a shower and begins to dress. Her roommate Karen seems to be watching her rather intently, and Lucy is trying to hide her discomfort. Karen asks her to sit down for a moment and is soon telling her about how attracted she has been to her. She expresses fear of Lucy's rejection but explains that she just could not hide her feelings any longer. Lucy is somewhat surprised but not at all angry. In fact, she finds the idea of sex with Karen a bit intriguing.

***

Now try to think about why you had the reactions and thoughts you did in relation to these sex-related situations. What were the specific aspects that made you feel positively or negatively about the people? Would there be any difference in your reaction if Susan and Alan had been dating for several months before having sex? If they were engaged? If they had failed to use a condom? What if Mike had decided that what his girlfriend does not know will not hurt her? What if he had decided not to masturbate either? What if Derek's instructor had been a man? What if the instructor were a man and the student a woman? What if Lucy and Karen had been two men instead? What if Lucy had been disgusted by Karen and immediately sought to change rooms?

How you as an individual view these and other sex-related situations is determined by your **values.** It is not simply based on your sexual values but also your values about relationships, coercion, responsibility, and a long list of other issues. Our sexual values are weighed in our sexual decision making, along with other related values. When people decide to participate in sexual activities that are inconsistent with their values, they may feel some conflict and guilt.

Dealing with Sex as a Moral Issue

Moral values deal with the ethics, or rights and wrongs, of life situations. Theories of morality generally assume that humans are capable of making choices based on rational thought, thus making them responsible for their decisions and actions. The nature-nurture debate has also been represented in two schools of thought regarding the origins of moral values. The *essentialist* perspective holds that there may well be some intrinsic or built-in meanings relating to sexuality in human life. Some believe that energy for sexual connection may be divinely given. The *social constructionist* view is that moral values relating to sexuality are formed by social forces and thus are subject to change as societies go through various transitions (Nelson & Longfellow, 1994; Wilson, 1998). Because sexuality is such a pervasive and powerful aspect of human nature, all societies have sought to control and regulate it. Religion is the social institution usually concerned with ethics, so moral values related to sex have often been rooted in religious teachings. Sexual morality today tends to be founded in one of the following ethical traditions:

values: system of beliefs with which people view life and make decisions, including their sexual decisions.

moral values: beliefs associated with ethical issues, or rights and wrongs; they are often a part of sexual decision making.

Adherence to Divinely Established Natural Laws

Those with an essentialist view of sexual ethics believe that sexual meanings are divinely ordained, establishing clear and unwavering boundaries between right and wrong. They may further assert that there is a singular interpretation of holy books such as the Bible or Koran and that there are clearly defined prescriptions and proscriptions for sexual behavior. This essentialist approach to sexual morality is found in many orthodox or fundamentalist religious traditions, whose teachings tend to fall into traditionalist categories (Wilson, 1998).

The Existence of a Religious Covenant between Humankind and a God

Jesus, Moses, Mohammed, and some of the other prophets spoke of a covenant of love and hope between human beings and their God. Some religions have interpreted this to mean that moral principles can change as societies and human behavior patterns change. Within this more social constructionist approach to sexual ethics, there is a belief that social values may change with time, rather than being bound to rigid traditional standards. New information from science, medicine, psychology, and sociology may be incorporated into new moral perspectives.

This more flexible approach to morality still calls for establishment of moral codes of behavior, often by delegations of people in the governing body of some religious group. They may still decide that adultery or sexual activity between members of the same gender is unacceptable, but they allow the issues to be discussed, debated, and then decided upon.

Situation Ethics

This is a system of morality that sees every situation as a unique collection of considerations and conditions. Therefore, moral decisions must be made only in the context of a particular situation, with a view toward all of the people involved. Situation ethics does not attach moral judgments to any sexual orientations or acts per se. The key to whether some form of sex is right or wrong lies in the human motivations behind it and the foreseeable consequences it might have. From this ethical perspective, a particular sexual behavior might be considered wrong in one context but acceptable in another. Obviously, it gives much more responsibility to the individual for making such judgments in arriving at sexual decisions.

Hedonistic and Ascetic Traditions

These moral perspectives represent opposite ends of the ethical spectrum. **Hedonists** have recreational attitudes, holding that pleasure is the highest good, out-

weighing religious dogma or situational context. This point of view can be crystallized by the phrase, "If it feels good, do it." The sex drive is viewed as an appetite to be satisfied with a maximum amount of physical and emotional pleasure. There are few people who manage a purely hedonistic lifestyle because the complications of relationships can easily get in the way.

Asceticism has been a part of some religious and spiritual traditions and is characterized by celibacy. The goal is to rise above base physical pleasures and instead emphasize self-denial, self-discipline, and the life of the mind or spirit. Asceticism is often characterized by the teaching that denial of sexual pleasure helps one be closer to spiritual needs and to God, and it is part of the celibate lifestyle expected of some priests, nuns, and monks.

Holistic Belief Systems

Some contemporary philosophers have suggested that we are coming into a time of human social evolution when we no longer have to view the ascetic and hedonistic pursuits as mutually exclusive. Holistic perspectives suggest that we should place sexuality in a broader context that considers many different levels of the human experience: physical, emotional, rational, social, and spiritual. It has been suggested that we need both the lofty side of things that at times asks us to rise above self-centered bodily pleasure, *and* the earthier, fleshy side that offers sensual delights. Rather than advocating for choosing one direction or the other, it is suggested that we seek a more united and whole pursuit of balancing these different but valuable parts of our sexuality in healthful, responsible ways (Wilber, 1995).

Spirituality, Religion, and Sex

Understanding and developing spirituality are important to many people, and fitting sexuality into the picture is often a significant part of that search. Organized religions are the social institutions that attempt to help people find a place for the spiritual in their lives, although many also seek spiritual development outside its contexts.

In the earliest religious traditions that archeologists have been able to trace, the emphasis was on feminine power, fertility, and earth-centeredness as expressed through various great goddesses. It is believed that

hedonists (HEE-don-ists): people who believe that pleasure is the highest good.

asceticism (a-SET-a-siz-um): usually characterized by celibacy, this philosophy emphasizes spiritual purity through self-denial and self-discipline.

CASE STUDY

Jonathan: A Man with a Disability Searches for a Relationship

Jonathan was first diagnosed with schizophrenia when he was in college. He had been hospitalized briefly, and his symptoms had been brought under control through the use of various medications. He subsequently finished his undergraduate work and then completed a master's degree in a technical field. He got a job in a small company that developed computer software. Jonathan was a highly intellectual individual, and partly because of his illness was not always able to read other people's reactions well. From time to time, he also had difficulty keeping his thought patterns clear, although he was always aware that this was a result of his chronic mental illness.

After three failed relationships, he talked with his psychiatrist about his frustrations. He explained that he knew he was not the easiest person to get along with and that his illness sometimes made people uncomfortable, but he deeply wanted an intimate relationship and longed for sexual involvement. The psychiatrist helped him to sort through some of the behavior patterns that women might find unsettling or hard to understand. She also recommended that Jonathan begin attending a support group for people who were recovering from mental illness.

The group setting proved to be particularly useful for Jonathan. The other members were honest with him about his behaviors, and they offered suggestions for how he might increase his level of self-awareness and avoid repeating actions that might bewilder potential partners. He soon developed a relationship with a woman who was part of the group and was herself recovering successfully from manic-depressive illness. At first, Jonathan expressed some negative feelings to his psychiatrist about having a relationship with someone who had also been ill, but eventually he became very comfortable with the new partnership. He and the woman shared a sexual relationship that they both valued positively. At last report, they were considering marriage.

---

sexuality and fertility were intimately connected to the practices of these traditions. Sometime between 1800 and 1500 B.C.E., there was a significant transformation in human conceptualizations of God(s), and throughout China, India, the Middle East, and Greece, the female goddess principle gave way to a more phallic (penis-centered) power of male God figures. College students still tend to conceptualize the idea of God with male images (Foster & Keating, 1992).

Judeo-Christian-Muslim religious values have traditionally constituted the moral backbone for various prohibitions against sexual behaviors in Western culture. In ancient Israel, for example, sexual intercourse was tantamount to marriage, and there was no such thing as a casual, obligation-free sexual relationship. In Christian theology, Augustine (354–430 C.E.) decided that sexual desire represented the ultimate clash between desire and reason, thus establishing sex as the culprit that passed sin from one generation to the next (Steinberg, 1994). It was not until the Middle Ages that marriage became a religious event in Christianity and therefore a religious sanctioning of sexual activity (see Fig. 7.8). Western religious traditions have typically taken a rather sex-negative position in which the emphasis is on the repression of sexual desire (Beck, 1999; Bullough & Bullough, 1995). Some Muslim traditions have placed a great deal of importance on the separation of male and female roles, sometimes expressed in the sexual mores that have called for women to keep much of their bodies covered. Behaviors that might encourage sexual attraction or arousal are also sometimes forbidden.

In contrast to this perspective, the Eastern traditions—Hindu, Buddhist, Tantric, and Taoist—have tended to view sexuality in terms of its creative potential and its power in spiritual development. Eastern thought places more emphasis on the harmony of body and spirit than on the opposition of the two. The combination of desire and a sense of duty have made both ascetic, celibate lifestyles and the religious celebration of sexual pleasure possible in Hinduism. In Buddhist, Tantric, and Taoist religions, sexual union is often viewed as a mystical and spiritually uplifting experience.

Within all major religious traditions, there are two basic ways in which the world tends to be perceived. One is a fixed worldview, in which it is assumed that the universe was created by a deity and is now completely finished. This is the fundamentalist perspective that finds followers within every tradition. The other point of view is more process-oriented, seeing the world and human nature as constantly changing and evolving. These two viewpoints are usually associated with differing attitudes toward sexuality as well. The fundamentalist view is that there is a constant battle between good and evil and that sex is a major source of temptation and sin (Kennedy & Whitlock, 1997). Those with a more evolutionary worldview tend to see the essential goodness of the human body and sexual desire, and they place the emphasis on people choosing

FIGURE 7.8 *Religious Attitudes toward Sexuality*

Religion may play an important role in establishing the sexual standards of a society. People may face conflicts if their personal values contradict the established morality.

sexual behaviors that are healthy, responsible, and considerate of others (Runkel, 1998; Speas, 1990).

Several studies have demonstrated correlations between people's religious belief systems and their sexual attitudes and behaviors (see Table 7.4). The more religious people consider themselves to be, the more likely they are to feel that it is important to have sexual practices that are in harmony with their religious beliefs, and the less likely they are to have sex prior to marriage. (Laumann, Gagnon et al., 1994). Men who are not members of an organized religion tend to engage in risky sexual activities (Billy et al., 1993), and yet men who are religiously active tend to have sex more frequently and are somewhat more likely to be aggressive in their pursuit of sexual goals (Runkel, 1998). People who have stronger intrinsic religious orientations are often more conservative in their sexual attitudes (Welch, Leege, & Cavendish, 1995). It has also been noted that when a person seeks help for sexual problems, it is crucial that professionals understand the client's religious orientation, which may well influence how sexual concerns should be discussed and treated (Kennedy & Whitlock, 1997).

Within some religious denominations, attitudes toward sex have undergone significant transitions in recent decades. Many religious groups have been debating and changing their official positions regarding sexual activity. One of the most significant areas of impact on religion in recent years has been feminism. There has been a reshaping of some religious symbolism to recognize the feminine images of God that are a part of religious history. Some religious groups have attempted to eliminate what they have come to see as sexist language within their texts—including the

Bible—and hymns. Women are taking stronger leadership roles in many religious groups, moving away from the patriarchal structures that have dominated Western religion for centuries (Stackhouse, 1990).

Aligning Yourself with Social and Cultural Values

There is now a fair amount of evidence that moral and ethical development proceeds in predictable stages as a child grows and develops. The two primary theorists on the moral development of children have been Jean Piaget and Lawrence Kohlberg. There are enough similarities in their theories to summarize some of their major points together. They believed that children essentially lack any sense of right or wrong when they are born.

In their first few years of life, children gradually pick up the rules of behavior expected of them, learning to some degree that they must obey parents or other adult authorities or else risk disapproval and punishment. Their basic approach to life, however, is to satisfy their own needs. They react to their environment reflexively. By the time children are 8 to 10 years old, they are beginning to adapt to the moral codes required of them by their environment. They realize that they are expected to behave in particular ways and often conform in order to be seen as good boys and girls. As adolescence and young adulthood progress, they become increasingly aware of the attitudes and values espoused by their social networks and gradually define the standards of morality and the ethical principles they want to guide their own lives.

In a pluralistic society such as our own, it is impossible to find general agreement with any particular approach to sexual morality and values. However, several widely accepted moral principles seem to be in effect today, and they would be supported by most religious teachings as well (Reiss, 1991):

1. *The principle of noncoercion:* People should not be forced to engage in sexual expression. Sexual expression should occur only when there is voluntary consent to do so.
2. *The principle of nondeceit:* People are not to be enticed into sexual expression based on fraud or deception.
3. *The principle of treatment of people as ends:* People are not to be treated as a means only; they must be treated as ends. In the sexual realm, this means that another person should never be viewed solely as a means to one's own sexual satisfaction.
4. *The principle of respect for beliefs:* People must show respect for the sexual values and beliefs of others. This means that one person should not

Table 7.4	Influence of Religion on Attitudes toward Sexual Behavior			
	Very Religious	**Religious**	**Slightly Religious**	**Not Religious**
That My Sex Practices Are in Harmony with My Religion Is:				
Very important	45%	18%	2%	3%
Important	36	38	24	8
Not sure	7	24	26	15
Unimportant	5	17	37	37
Very unimportant	7	3	11	37
Very important + Important	81%	56%	26%	11%
Unimportant + Very unimportant	12%	20%	48%	74%
N =	262	857	976	611

Source: From S. S. Janus and C. L. Janus, *The Janus Report on Sexual Behavior.* Copyright © 1993 John Wiley & Sons, Inc. Reprinted by permission of John Wiley & Sons, Inc.

pressure another to act in a way not in accord with his or her sexual values and beliefs. However, this does not preclude someone from attempting to persuade others rationally that they are mistaken in their beliefs.

For people in their late teens, the transition from home to college or some other environment away from home can be filled with new stimuli and new choices. There is often greater freedom to experiment with sexual activities and values with the possibility of making mistakes. But even mistakes can provide a useful purpose in clarifying the individual's personal code of sexual morality. However, the balancing act between satisfying one's own sexual needs and living up to the moral principles that are demanded by one's social networks and oneself may actually last a lifetime. Every stage of life offers new sets of sexual decisions and questions to be resolved, and society's values are always shifting.

Finding Healthy Sexual Values

Achieving a healthy sexuality must involve a level of consistency between a person's behaviors and values (see Fig. 7.9). In recent years, several different social factions and political groups have claimed to have values that represent the "moral high ground." Because their positions are often quite divergent, it can be even more confusing for someone to arrive at a personal set of values. One unfortunate consequence of this confusion for many people is choosing not to choose. Instead of thinking through their values and deciding in advance how they will want to behave in

FIGURE 7.9   *Loving Relationships*

An important part of finding healthy sexual values is determining the place of loving relationships in your life. Although loving and sex are often linked within relationships, they do not necessarily need to be.

certain sexual situations, they wait until they are swept away by passion or a persuasive partner. This may then become an excuse for denying responsibility for sex or its consequences.

In order to establish your own set of values regarding sex, there are several steps that you can take:

1. Know yourself and work toward acceptance of your sexual needs and orientations. Basic to the success of any code of values is feeling good about yourself. Even if you find some aspects of your sexuality that you would not feel comfortable acting on, it is important that they be accepted as part of you. Whether you ever act on them or not is up to you. That is what choice and personal decision making are all about.

2. Try not to let yourself be bound by popular sexual standards with which you are personally uncomfortable. Popular songs, television programs, advertising, computer bulletin boards, and other media presentations often promulgate specific values about sex and sexual attractiveness. You may receive pressure from peers at times about what is currently in vogue sexually. Weigh all this information carefully, decide how much you want and need to fit in with a particular group, and then choose how you want to become involved sexually. Be cautious about going along with any aspects of sex that do not seem quite right to you. Give yourself as much time as you need to think; after all, your goal is to feel good about yourself.

3. Examine your feelings about religion and find out what your religion has to say about sexual matters. You may be surprised. Many religious groups have given careful consideration to human sexuality and have devised written guides to help with personal decision making. You will need to consider just how important your religious background and your current feelings about religion are to you. Even if you do not consider yourself "religious," you may want to explore your spiritual dimensions and how they relate to your sexuality. Agnostics and atheists also develop their own codes of moral behavior that emphasize responsibility to others.

4. Think ahead. It is a good idea to think carefully about various sexual situations and issues and anticipate how you might react to them. This is an excellent way to clarify your personal values about sex. For example, when do you think it is all right for two people to share a sexual relationship? If heterosexual intercourse will be involved, how should decisions about contraception be made? What are some of the possible consequences of various sexual activities, and how would you deal with those consequences?

How will you ensure that anyone involved in a sexual encounter will be protected from disease?

5. Consider what level of responsibility you have toward other people. Most forms of sex involve interaction between people. Whenever interpersonal relationships are involved, the issue of responsibility to others comes up. How do you think you should treat others? What degree of responsibility do you have to not put others in exploitative or potentially hurtful situations?

6. Remember that you are not a mind reader. This is where good communication comes in. Part of sexual values must be to know how a potential sexual partner thinks and feels about sex before you get involved. It is dangerous to make assumptions about the values and feelings of others. You will need to spend time and energy communicating in order to find out what they are.

7. Decide what role you want loving relationships to play in your life. Loving and sex are often intertwined in relationships, though not necessarily so. An important part of establishing your own sex-related values is to know how you feel about the place of loving relationships in your life.

8. Take opportunities to clarify your sexual values on an ongoing basis. Sexuality education books, classes, and discussion groups provide opportunities for understanding your own sexual values more fully. The Internet has some fine websites with good information about sexuality, along with its more explicit sites. Using opportunities to clarify values can keep your personal code of moral behavior clear and workable for everyday life.

Where did you get most of your sexuality education? In what ways was it accurate or inaccurate?

■ Sexuality Education

In a survey conducted with over 500 U.S. high school students by Roper Starch Worldwide, the average age of first intercourse was just under 15 years. About three-quarters of those who had experienced sex reported feeling positive about their sexual activities, although more than half also reported they should have waited until they were older. The majority of all teenagers had apparently talked with their parents about sex, and 60 percent of the sexually active teens believed that their parents knew about their sexual behavior. Over half of them said they wished they could talk further with their parents about sex. Despite this sexual behavior on the part of teens, only 58 percent took sexuality education courses in junior high school, and 56 percent took them at the senior high level ("Executive summary," 1994).

Studies continue to demonstrate that one of the major barriers to effective parent-teenager communication regarding sexuality is the parents' lack of comfort with the subject and that the other is the teens' own uneasiness. However, young people also continue to indicate that they wish they could hear from their parents about such issues as dating, relationships, having sex and how to say no to it, sexually transmitted diseases, and preventing pregnancy. Only too often, parents are not well prepared to deal openly with these topics in ways that do not turn their children away from the communications (Miller, Miller, Kenney, & Clark, 1998; National Campaign to Prevent Teen Pregnancy, 1998).

The American Public Health Association (APHA) has adopted a resolution endorsing the right of children and youth to receive broad-based sexuality education. The group recommended that facts, information, and data be taught within a context that appreciates racial, ethnic, and cultural diversity. In addition, they advocated the teaching of skills that would help young people communicate effectively with others and make responsible decisions about sex (see Fig. 7.10). The APHA resolution urged schools to develop kindergarten through twelfth grade curricula that would not impose religious, ethical, or moral values on students (APHA, 1994).

Although few disagree about the need for children and adolescents to learn about human sexuality, there are divergent views about what they should be taught, where the learning should take place, and whether information should be accompanied by clearly defined value standards. The controversies surrounding sexuality education have been simmering for over 40 years, and they have often become the focal point of localized political campaigns and national public policy debates (Kempner, 1998, 1999).

The Development of Sexuality Education

Only limited and sporadic attention was given to formalized sexuality education until the 1960s, when attention began to focus on the sexual behavior of youth. It was during that decade that two professional groups, the Sex (now Sexuality) Information and Education Council of the United States (SIECUS) and the American Association of Sex Educators, Counselors and Therapists (AASECT) began to highlight the need for improved sexuality education efforts and to work toward the establishment of sexuality education programs.

The first generation of sexuality education efforts arose out of a desire to reduce rates of unwanted pregnancy and the incidence of sexually transmitted disease among the young. They were built on the assumption that if young people had more knowledge about sexuality, pregnancy, and birth control, they would avoid unprotected sexual intercourse. As it eventually became clear that knowledge in itself was insufficient to prevent unprotected intercourse or pregnancy, a second generation of curricula emerged. They placed increased emphasis on the need for young people to understand and clarify their own values and learn the decision-making and communication skills that would lead toward more responsible sexual behavior and relationships. The more inclusive term **comprehensive sexuality education** has gained in popularity over the term "sex education" as the content and goals of these courses have broadened (Maddock, 1997). Evaluations of such programs produced mixed results, but again they did not seem to lead to significant reductions in sexual risk-taking behaviors (Kirby, 1993).

The next wave of sexuality education programs emerged in the late 1980s and constituted a reaction to what was perceived as a lack of success on the part of the earlier attempts. Some conservative religious and political groups felt that openness about sexuality had gone too far, and they developed programs that

FIGURE 7.10 *Sexuality Education Class*

To dispel sexual ignorance and the problems that ignorance can cause, attention is being given to sexuality education in some of our nation's schools. Discussing contraceptive methods, however, can cause controversy.

comprehensive sexuality education: an approach to educating young people about human sexuality that includes information about sexuality but also encourages clarifying values and developing decision-making skills.

CROSS-CULTURAL PERSPECTIVE
Survival Sex

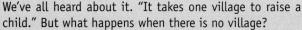

We've all heard about it. "It takes one village to raise a child." But what happens when there is no village?

As a sexuality education and reproductive health trainer working in Africa, I witnessed a country's destruction from tribal wars while I was managing projects in Liberia, a small, ruggedly beautiful nation formed by freed American slaves. . . .

The district and regional medical officers, doctors, nurses, and family planning workers spoke of how displaced youth are sexually victimized in exchange for food, shelter, and protection. Many of these youths grow up in an artificial culture created by the tribal war forces that have torn apart the social fabric of the countries they have fled. They live in a nether world where "survival sex" ensures another day. Exploitative sex is inextricably linked to survival. Rape and sexual abuse sadly become the badges of courage worn as a rite of passage to adulthood.

Many of the relief workers shared with me their experiences with refugee youth. Story after story unfolded to reveal an almost universal, collective pattern of experiences. They told of girls who were sent by their guardians or families to collect food and provision at distribution sites. These girls could accept a man's offer for sexual intercourse if he promised to buy her oranges. He would often pay her all the oranges and "then some" if she allowed him to perform sexual acts with her. When she returned home to her family with food and money in hand, they rarely questioned her. . . .

Action must be swift and widespread and should promote the agent of change in the refugee community to mobilize in support for adolescent sexuality education initiatives within their ongoing job responsibilities. . . .

Yet the cries of the young still go unheard. Many refuse to pay adequate attention to the adolescent refugee crisis. This is not surprising in a world where the majority of cultures are uncomfortable dealing with sexuality, in general, and adolescent sexuality, in particular. . . .

We as sexuality educators cannot continue to overlook the needs of adolescents in refugee camps, when, in fact, they are in the most precarious situations—with no adults to protect them, no access to contraceptives or condoms, no feelings of control, no set cultural scripts, no knowledge of the dangers of unprotected sexual intercourse, and no way to refuse acts that may lead to their death from the very real threats of AIDS and complications from adolescent pregnancy and childbirth.

Whether or not there is a village need not matter. There can still be love. There can still be hope. People who care can make all the difference in the world. We must raise children to be happy, healthy, and informed. We are, after all, a global village, and the future must be made bright for all our children.

—Nanette Ecker, M. A., *SIECUS Report*, June/July 1998, Vol. 26, No. 5. "Where There Is no Village: Teaching about Sexuality in Crisis Situations," pp. 7–10. Reprinted with permission of *SIECUS*.

emphasized sexual abstinence until marriage. These curricula avoided discussion of protection during sexual activity, because the groups felt that it implied a message condoning such behavior. They represented what became known as the "just say no" or "just don't do it" approach to sexuality education. Proponents of abstinence-only education have also been concerned that comprehensive sexuality education is not appropriate for some nonurban settings, where they believe there is less sexual activity than in cities (Jensen, Gaston, & Weed, 1994). Although evaluative research concerning these programs suggests that they may result in students having more conservative attitudes toward premarital sex in the short term (Eisenman,

1994; Weed & Jensen, 1993), there is no particular evidence that the students delayed intercourse or participated in sexual activity any less frequently (Donovan, 1998; Kirby, 1993, 1995).

Another generation of sexuality education curricula emerged in reaction to the HIV/AIDS crisis. Often without examining what had worked and not worked in the past, these programs urgently tried to alert young people to the very real dangers of unprotected sex, in an effort to persuade them to avoid such behaviors. Like early sexuality education efforts, these programs were based largely on the apparently faulty assumption that knowledge about consequences translates to immediate changes in behavior. Officials of the

Centers for Disease Control and Prevention recognized that careful study must be given to what approaches actually led to behavioral change and that long-term efforts to mold generational changes in social norms were ultimately needed. "Quick-fix" approaches seem to have little value (CDC Advisory Committee, 1995).

The history of sexuality education has some lessons to teach. Although education in general has been dominated by the concept of adults imparting their wisdom and truth to the young, in an age of radically changing communication technologies, it may be more helpful for young people to learn how to find their way in a complex and always-changing world (Edwards, 1998; Roffman, Shannon, & Dwyer, 1997). It is also crucial that as ethnic and cultural values mix in our populations, the very real differences among groups with regard to sexual attitudes and customs be validated (Edwards, 1999; Juzang, 1999; Maddock, 1997). Sexuality education will always have an element of controversy, because it deals with fundamental issues about which complete consensus is unlikely. It also deals with issues that parents often consider matters for the family, even if families do not seem always to take much responsibility for facing them. Educating parents may be as crucial as educating their children (Donovan, 1998; Kyman, 1995). Finally, sexuality education will have to come to grips with the emerging technological potentials and risks of the Internet and its role as a transmitter and exchanger of sex information. It holds potentials for revolutionizing educational approaches, but it also raises the spectre of people who no longer communicate face-to-face or skin-to-skin (Gotlib & Fagan, 1997).

The Need for Sexuality Education

Public opinion polls consistently demonstrate that over 85 percent of adult Americans favor the teaching of sexuality education in schools and that most teenagers favor such courses (Haffner & Wagoner, 1999). Studies continue to show that teens often lack the knowledge they need to protect themselves from unintended pregnancy or disease (Winn, Roker, & Coleman, 1995). Nearly all states either mandate or encourage sexuality education and teaching about HIV/AIDS and other sexually transmitted diseases. Beyond these facts, there is a great deal of controversy over what appropriate sexuality education should be all about. Most sexuality education instructors are teaching their students about intercourse and abstinence, use of condoms, sexual decision making, and transmission of AIDS. The fact remains, however, that young people still report that they learn the most about sexuality from their peers or from entertainment media (Ballard & Morris, 1998; "Executive summary," 1994). There is a strong likelihood that much of this

peer and media education is laden with misinformation and exaggeration.

As states have mandated sexuality and HIV education programs, it has also become clear that many sexuality educators lack professional training in those fields. Experts are concerned that not only are many teachers underprepared, they are also being forced to teach material with which they do not feel personally comfortable (Donovan, 1998). It has been suggested that compulsory teacher training be part of any legislation mandating sexuality education (Haffner, 1998). There is also a need for some specialization in sexuality education efforts. Special groups in our society—the developmentally disabled, the aged, adolescents, and young people living out of their homes, for example—need sexuality education that addresses their special concerns (Mayden, 1995). This will continue to be part of the trend toward helping each individual live the most comfortable, problem-free sexual life possible.

To expect all parents to be able to handle the long and complicated job of sexuality education by themselves is simply unrealistic today. There has been a resurgence of interest in strengthening school-based sexuality education, although there is always controversy about what fits in such curricula (Kyman, 1998). There may be times when involvement of other people in a child's life can be the most valuable direction to take. We also know that over a half million young people in the United States live in foster care, group care, or residential living settings (Mayden, 1995). The best sexuality education is represented by a concerted effort on the part of many different people: parents or other primary caregivers, teachers, religious leaders, counselors, youth organizations, and the media. In this way, young people receive messages and skills from a variety of individuals and are helped to integrate sexual feelings and decisions into their lives more realistically (Brick, 1999).

The Current Sexuality Education Debate

Comprehensive sexuality education has usually emphasized a positive view of human sexual behavior, balanced with factual information about its potential risks and consequences. Sexuality educators who espouse the comprehensive model believe that in order for young people to make responsible sexual decisions, they must have a healthy and positive view of themselves as sexual human beings.

Comprehensive Sexuality Education

Sexuality educators do not assume that all teenagers are sexually active, but they see in the statistics the

Branch—© 1994 *San Antonio Express News*

prediction that many teens will likely be eventually. Even though they may encourage abstinence or postponement of sexual activity, they also want to see young people prepared to protect themselves as much as possible if they choose to engage in sex with others.

It is the sex-positive view and the emphasis on being prepared for sexual activity that has offended and concerned many of those who oppose comprehensive sexuality education, because they fear it has led to, or at the very least not countered, sexual permissiveness. They feel that permissiveness is exactly what sexuality education should be combating. They cite what they believe to be the failure of comprehensive sexuality education, basing that judgment on statistics about the rates of teen sexual activity and pregnancy (Whitehead, 1994). Proponents of the comprehensive approach argue that in fact the kind of comprehensive sexuality education they would like to see has been available to fewer than 5 percent of youngsters, and so considering it a "failure" at this point is unreasonable. They also cite figures that show how rates of pregnancy among sexually active teenagers have actually declined since the 1970s, even as the actual numbers of adolescents having sex increased. This seems to be in large part because of more effective use of birth control by sexually active teens. Nevertheless, it is indeed the frequency of sexual activity among the young that has many people concerned, and they believe that it is the place of sexuality education to strongly encourage young people not to have sex. They fear that information about contraception and safer sex, and the accessibility of such methods, will only encourage more sexual experimentation.

Abstinence

Aside from fears of promiscuity, pregnancy, or disease, proponents of the abstinence approach feel that chastity is a value to be promoted. Numerous sexuality education curricula now teach the "abstinence until marriage" philosophy. The central theme behind these curricula is that if we can persuade young people to practice sexual abstinence until they marry, many social problems would be solved. Opponents of this approach maintain that it is not realistic, given how prevalent sexual activity has become in recent years. These opponents remind us that even when chastity was taught as the highest virtue, there were still many sexual problems. People simply suffered them in private. Nevertheless, the U.S. Congress approved a plan for distributing $50 million per year from 1998 through 2002 to states for abstinence-only education as part of welfare reform legislation. Some observers reported that the availability of this funding actually reduced the effectiveness of some programs that had helped young people at least postpone sexual activity (Kirby, Korpi, Barth, & Cagampang, 1997; Lamstein & Haffner, 1998).

An aspect of the abstinence-based sexuality education approach that disturbs many observers is its reliance on scare tactics, fear, and shame as ways of discouraging students from engaging in sexual activity. Review of numerous such curricula have revealed the following educational and philosophical strategies that most of them employ (Haffner & Goldfarb, 1997; Ross & Kantor, 1995; Whatley & Trudell, 1993):

1. The use of simplified slogans and scare tactics to encourage abstinence.
2. Omission of information about contraception, or an emphasis on the unreliability of birth control.
3. Strong emphasis on the negative consequences of sex, and the substitution of biased opinion for fact, while only presenting one side of controversial issues such as abortion, condom use, and the teaching of contraception.
4. Misinformation and inaccuracies concerning the medical aspects of abortion, sexually transmitted diseases, and human sexual response.
5. Lack of discussion about same-gender sexual orientation, or the judgment that such orientations represent an unhealthy "choice."
6. An emphasis on and reinforcement of traditional stereotypes of male and female gender roles.
7. Lack of recognition of the sexual nature of people with disabilities, and lack of respect for cultural and economic differences among people.
8. A strong religious bias that advocates only one set of values concerning sexual behavior.
9. A limitation on the number of family structures presented, with nontraditional families depicted as being troubled.
10. Failure to adequately involve parents, and marketing the programs with inadequate evaluative data to back up their effectiveness.

Because most of the popular abstinence-based programs are produced by organizations or individuals that represent particular religious moral frameworks, state departments of education and the courts have begun to restrict their use in public school settings (Kempner, 1999). This is not to say that consideration of abstinence or the postponement of sex should not have a place in sexuality education. Given the current risks of sexual behavior, they represent very reasonable and rational choices. The middle ground in the sexuality education controversy is represented by programs that place an emphasis on abstinence without relying on scare tactics, misrepresentation of medical facts, or the teachings of any one particular religious doctrine. They share the goal that most sexuality educators feel is legitimate: that young people should indeed postpone sexual sharing until they are ready for mature, well-informed, and safe sexual relationships (Cagampang, Barth, Korpi, & Kirby, 1997; Kirby et al., 1997).

Some programs have become very proactive in teaching young people skills for avoiding peer pressures and being assertive about postponing sex until they are ready. At the same time, they teach young people how to protect themselves from unwanted pregnancy and disease should they ultimately choose to engage in sexual activities (Denny, Young, & Spear, 1999; Frost & Forrest, 1995; Kassirer & Griffiths, 1997). For many observers of the sexuality education debate, these approaches may ultimately represent the compromising ground.

> *Which approach to sexuality education do you support: comprehensive sexuality education, sexuality education that focuses on abstinence, or something in between?*

Research to date would seem to support the contentions that current sexuality education programs do not hasten the onset of intercourse, and they may even increase the use of contraception and safer sex techniques somewhat (Feigenbaum, Weinstein, & Rosen, 1995; Schuster et al., 1998). There are also several studies that demonstrate how sexuality education can delay participation in intercourse, reduce the numbers of sexual partners, and reduce the frequency of intercourse without contraception or protection from disease. Some programs have significantly reduced unprotected sexual activity.

Again, there are some particular characteristics associated with sexuality education approaches that have been successful in changing sexual behaviors. They provide accurate information in a variety of ways that students are able to personalize and retain, often using interactive methods rather than lecturing to students. They also address the social pressures to have sex and help young people to know how to respond to those pressures. They model ways for young people

to decline sexual activity or unprotected sex. They encourage younger, inexperienced youth to wait until they are older, and they advise experienced, high-risk youth always to use a condom (Kirby, 1995). The programs that have been most successful in increasing the use of contraceptives and reducing teenage pregnancy are those that provide access to contraception (Schuster et al., 1998).

Sexuality Education and Cultural Diversity

One of the greatest challenges to sexuality education programs is the need to develop approaches that will be sensitive to cultural differences. This not only applies to North America, where the population continues to become increasingly diverse, but to countries around the world that are attempting to develop their own forms of sexuality education (McCaffree, 1998a). Although they often model their approaches after programs developed in the United States, it is crucial that they remain aware of the differences in attitudes, behaviors, expectations, and needs that are created by differences in social and cultural environment (Atkinson, 1998; Edwards, 1997). The perspectives of a Eurocentric heterosexual culture in sexuality education settings often fail to address the needs of youth of color and those who are gay, lesbian, or bisexual (Advocates for Youth, 1995).

Sexuality educators have to sort through the impact of demographics on people's attitudes and behaviors and move beyond cultural awareness or sensitivity to what has been termed "cultural competence" (Edwards, 1999). This is a long-term process by which educators expand their horizons, think critically about issues of power and oppression in societies with diverse populations, and then act appropriately. They learn the attitudes, knowledge, and skills that will help them develop positive communication and trust with people of varying cultural backgrounds. This is one way in which barriers of culture, language, and attitude may be minimized so that sexuality education can become available for and relevant to a wider spectrum of the population (Cunningham, 1998; Irvine, 1995).

It has been pointed out, for example, that much sexuality education in the United States has been based on assumptions taken from Eurocentric social norms. These include the concept that changing people's attitudes can motivate them to make rational decisions and modify behaviors. Such assumptions often presume that they feel they have personal control over traditional resources such as money, education, and mobility. In fact, many blacks, Native Americans, and Latinos often do not feel much sense of control over such resources, although they may well see their sexuality as a positive source of power over which they do have control. For some groups, sexuality education approaches that place an emphasis on a sense of personal control and individual change may not be as effective as programs that focus on social norms and commitment to broader social responsibilities or group empowerment (Goodman, 1998; Okwumabua, Okwumabua, & Elliott, 1998).

There are millions of young people in the United States who have been identified as being at high risk for sexual activity that may lead to pregnancy or infection with HIV and other diseases (Juzang, 1999; Martinez, 1999). Some of these youth live on urban streets. Others are substance abusers or have been sexually abused. Many juveniles live in foster homes or end up being incarcerated for at least short periods of time and are thus considered at high risk. These youth represent another example of populations for whom sexuality education must go beyond the traditional programs found in middle-class schools, and it must be offered by people especially trained to deal with the problems and concerns these young people face (Mayden, 1995). There have been crises in Africa and Eastern Europe as the result of tribal wars and ethnic cleansing campaigns that have left children and teenagers without parents or have rendered them refugees in strange surroundings. It is crucial that the sexuality education needs of these young people be addressed for their own protection (Ecker, 1998).

> *Do you have confidence that the following professionals would be able to advise you correctly on matters of sexuality: your family physician, a school counselor, a private therapist, a nurse in your health center?*

Other countries of the world are also struggling with issues relating to sexuality education as global media become increasingly saturated with sex-related material. Russia's official policy was once to approach education in an atmosphere of sexual nonstimulation, focusing solely on biological information and medical terms. Recent studies have shown that over 80 percent of Russians favor more comprehensive approaches to sexuality education, and attempts are under way to develop better programs (Chervyakov, 1997; Popova, 1996).

Nigeria has been working with American experts in designing clear guidelines for nationwide sexuality education and has begun implementing efforts to provide comprehensive sexuality education to the nation's youth. They are placing a great deal of emphasis on preparation and training of the professionals who will offer the education to young people (Shortridge, 1997).

Brazil is a nation that has a population representing diverse heritages. Because most parents there do not discuss sexuality with their children, there has been growing support for school-based sexuality education. City and national governmental agencies have been working toward the implementation of comprehensive sexuality education, and it is being tested and developed in numerous schools (Egypto, Pinto, & Bock, 1996). A national project for sexuality education has been inaugurated in Colombia, and attempts are being made to solicit input and direction from youth, even though this has traditionally been a paternalistic culture that pays little attention to the opinions of the young (Mendez, 1996). Bolivia has launched a massive media campaign about sexuality and reproductive health that encourages people to take responsibility for their own health (Valente & Saba, 1997). Puerto Rico has launched a comprehensive program for teens, based on alarming figures relating to sexual risktaking in that country (Cunningham, 1998).

The Japanese Ministry of Education has begun to include some rudimentary sexuality education in its public school curriculum, but the traditional values of Japan make the teaching of such material difficult indeed. Western ideas that value individual sexual choices are generally in opposition to the Japanese tradition of adherence to the norms of the group. Although private Japanese groups continue to urge sexuality education, most educators there resist the idea (Shimazaki, 1994). Quite recently, China seems to be changing its focus of sex from its procreational aspects toward its pleasurable aspects. Overpopulation in China has long fostered accessibility to birth control education and methods, as well as abortion, but the emphasis on sexual fulfillment is a whole new trend. Books, movies, and videotapes about human sexuality are becoming increasingly available to Chinese citizens, and there is governmental awareness of the need to educate young people about their changing bodies and sexual desires.

Education for Sexuality Professionals

Sexuality professionals are those who promote the importance of sexuality knowledge, attitudes, skills, and behaviors in the work that they do. Most such professionals have advanced degrees, but few have specialized in the field of human sexuality. Sexuality professionals are found in education, medicine, social work, psychotherapy, counseling, and any other area that deals with the special concerns of people's lives (McCaffree, 1998b). Unfortunately, the presence of sexuality education and HIV/AIDS prevention in schools has not translated into adequate preparation of those teachers who may ultimately be expected to conduct the classes, and many of them have never had any formal academic preparation in sexuality. In fact, almost no public school preparation and certification programs require any courses on sexuality (Haffner, 1998b).

Seminaries and theological schools have begun to prepare their students for working with sexual issues because it is often suggested that people talk to their religious leaders when troubled by problems with their sexuality. There is little standardization of this training, however, and experts have recommended a better balance in training between the positive aspects of sexuality and the problematic issues (Conklin, 1997; Conklin & Goodson, 1998).

There has been significant headway made in training those individuals who are preparing for work within the clinical health and psychology professions. An extensive survey of U.S. and Canadian medical schools revealed that about a third of these schools have gradually increased the number of curriculum hours devoted to studying human sexuality, with 92 percent of medical schools requiring core curriculum preparation in sexuality (Dunn & Alarie, 1997). However, the goals in sexuality education for professionals are not always clearly defined, and the courses either may not be required or may neglect the broad range of sexual issues that could eventually be encountered in work settings, including the impact of illness and disability on sex. In addition, clinical supervision of professionals as they learn how to offer treatment for sexual problems is often lacking in professional training programs (Weerakoon & Stiernborg, 1997).

The ability of educators, health and counseling professionals, and clergy to perceive sexual problems in their students, patients, or clients, and then pursue these problems once they have been noticed, depends on the degree of comfort the professionals feel toward sexuality. The more anxious professionals are about dealing with sexual issues, the less apt they will be to pursue a patient's sexual history. Medical students often have levels of homophobia that interfere with certain aspects of treating gay male and lesbian patients (Klamen, Grossman, & Kopacz, 1999). Some health professionals will also avoid discussing sex because they are uncertain of how to alleviate patient anxiety about the topic. Training programs that involve mentoring with professionals who already have experience dealing with sexual concerns can be of particular value in overcoming such reluctance (Keeling, 1998). Fortunately, a number of sexuality education programs for professionals now help them see and understand their own sexual values, detect sexual concerns in their patients or clients, and develop the skills that will be needed to treat these sex-related problems.

◾ Sex and Disability Groups

Physical and mental disabilities may influence a person's sexuality in many different ways. They can affect self-perception and social relationships. Only too often, persons with disabilities are assumed to be asexual or too impaired to have functional sexual responses. These assumptions rarely have any basis in fact. Public consciousness about the needs and rights of individuals with disabilities has been leading to greater levels of understanding and acceptance, but there are still many barriers and complications for such people in finding a fulfilling and meaningful place for their sexuality in their lives (Gordon & Benishek, 1998). Adults with disabilities are likely to find acceptance in their roles as fellow employees or casual friends but are much less likely to find themselves perceived as potential dating or sexual partners. Myths and misconceptions about the needs of children with disabilities may lead to impediments in their development as healthy sexual individuals. Parents, educators, counselors, and caregivers for people with disabilities have a special responsibility not to ignore or deny the sexual natures of these individuals. Sexuality needs to be a part of a holistic approach in dealing with the special needs and concerns of people with particular disabilities (Burling, Tarvydas, & Maki, 1994).

Most disabling conditions do not directly affect the sex organs or their ability to function, nor do they affect the individual's sexual feelings, need for sex, or the desire to be physically and emotionally intimate with others (see Fig. 7.11). However, they may have a great effect on how people with disabilities view their own attractiveness and the degree to which they seek

◾ **FIGURE 7.11** *Sexuality and People with Disabilities*

People with physical and mental disabilities have as much right to intimacy and sexual pleasure as anyone else. The quality of the sexual relationship will depend, as in any relationship, on the quality of the total care and respect each partner has for the other.

Sexuality of Persons with Disabilities

Persons with physical, cognitive, or emotional disabilities have a right to sexuality education, sexual health care, and opportunities for socializing and for sexual expression. Family, healthcare workers, and other caregivers should receive training in understanding and supporting sexual development and behavior, comprehensive sexuality education, and related health care for individuals with disabilities. The policies and procedures of social agencies and health-care delivery systems should ensure that services and benefits are provided to all persons without discrimination because of disability. Individuals with disabilities and their caregivers should have information and education about how to minimize the risk of sexual abuse and exploitation.

—From "SIECUS Position Statements on Human Sexuality, Sexual Health and Sexuality Education and Information 1995–96" in *SIECUS Report,* Volume 24, Number 3, February/March, 1996. Reprinted with permission of SIECUS, 130 W. 42nd St., Suite 350, New York, NY 10036-7802.

sexual relationships (Kupper, 1995). Consider a man with a serious skin disease that causes unsightly blotches all over his body, or the woman born with cerebral palsy who has difficulty controlling her arm movements and speech. Although these individuals have the same sexual drives and interests as anyone else, they may find themselves limited by their own perceptions and by the prejudice and misunderstanding of others. We now have a wider acceptance of the notion that sexual pleasuring need not be viewed solely as an act of sex organs but rather as an intimate emotional and physical connection between two human beings that may involve a variety of behaviors. This perspective on sexual interaction is particularly valuable for people with disabilities, who may have to make special accommodations for their sexual practices.

Intellectual or Developmental Disability

One of the most sexually oppressed groups of people with disabilities are those with mental retardation, now more commonly called an intellectual or developmental disability. One of the historical roots of this problem has been the fear that sexual activity among those who are intellectually disabled would lead to pregnancies and risk passing on genetic defects to children (Patti, 1995). The trend has been to integrate individuals with intellectual disabilities into the community as much as possible, giving them training in the kinds of skills that will help them interact in socially acceptable ways (Shepperdson, 1995). There is evidence that people with such disabilities often lack crucial knowledge about their sexuality and that educational efforts can lead to both cognitive and behavioral change that will help them

understand and manage their sexual needs (McDermott, Martin, Weinrich, & Kelly, 1999). Institutional caregivers are now more accepting of the sexual natures of their clients than previously, although they may still have ambivalent feelings about sexual expression among people with disabilities (Heyman & Huckle, 1995).

Gradually, those with mental disabilities have been helped to articulate their sexual rights, and educational efforts have been improving. The principle of **normalization** came to the United States in the 1960s from Scandinavia and has led to the development of simplified programs in social skills and sexuality education for use with those who have intellectual disabilities, designed to help them adapt to the norms and patterns of mainstream social life (see Fig. 7.12). Some couples with developmental disabilities have been able to marry and learn how to manage their social and sexual lives very effectively as the result of these new efforts (Yohalem, 1995).

What guidelines do you feel should be in place regarding sexual activity between intellectually impaired people?

Issues relating to reproduction by people with intellectual disabilities continue to be debated. In the early 1900s, when there was a strong eugenics movement that advocated careful genetic selection in human reproduction, people with developmental disabilities were usually considered unfit to reproduce and were often involuntarily sterilized in institutions. Now it is clear that

normalization: integration of mentally retarded persons into the social mainstream as much as possible.

FIGURE 7.12 *Sexuality and Developmental Disability*

With the proper instruction in meeting their own sexual needs and following the rules and ethics of a given society's sexual behavior, some people with developmental disabilities can lead fulfilling lives in a mutually supportive relationship.

many such individuals are able to learn enough about birth control methods to choose and use them effectively. The issue of informed consent for sterilization continues to be a difficult one because developmentally disabled individuals may not fully understand the procedure and its outcome. Influenced by authority figures, they may too easily give their consent to sterilization. Surveys of attitudes of professionals toward the sterilization of people with developmental disabilities indicate that there is still little consensus as to how this complicated issue should be handled (Patti, 1995).

Visual and Auditory Disabilities

Individuals with visual or hearing impairments face two major challenges in developing sexual awareness. The first is gaining an understanding of sex and sexuality. People with impaired sight cannot see diagrams that could help them understand anatomy and physiology. People who are hearing impaired are limited in how some information can be presented to them. Both groups may experience delays in the total education process, including learning to read, because of their respective disabilities. A second major difficulty lies in the socialization process. Those who are visually or hearing impaired are often hindered in their social contacts because others are uncomfortable with their disabilities and may feel afraid or embarrassed about their own attempts to communicate. In addition, some

of the usual routes for interpersonal communication are blocked. People who are severely visually impaired cannot read the subtleties of facial expressions and body language. People with hearing impairments may miss words in lipreading or might risk being misunderstood when using sign language with someone who is unfamiliar with it.

Sexuality educators for the sensorially impaired have challenged some of these problems. Life-size plastic models of human sexual anatomy are now available, as are visual materials such as models, charts, photographs, slides, and transparencies. Captioning services for much of television programming and for visual sexuality education aids provide another opportunity for the hearing impaired to understand the material.

Spinal Cord Injuries

The spinal cord, running through the vertebrae that make up the backbone, is the nervous system's major link between the brain and the body's various organs. Injuries to the back or neck can cause damage, or even complete severing, of the spinal cord. If an injury does not prove fatal, there may still be interruption of nerve messages to the parts of the body below the injury. This results in partial or total paralysis of those organs and muscles. There is little or no sensation, and the muscles can no longer be directed by the brain to contract. Typically, the spinal cord does not heal and repair itself, so the paralysis is permanent. If only the legs are paralyzed, the person is said to be **paraplegic;** if the arms are involved as well, the term used is **quadriplegic.**

It is often assumed that paraplegics and quadriplegics are incapable of sexual sensations or response, but this is not necessarily the case. In a study of 140 males and 46 females with spinal cord injury (SCI), about 25 percent of the males and up to 50 percent of the females reported having sensations in the genital area. By the third year after their injuries, nearly all of the females and 90 percent of the males had resumed having sexual intercourse and other sexual activities (Donohue & Gebhard, 1995). The degree of interference with sexual functions depends on the exact location and extent of the SCI. When paralysis of the pelvic region exists, thinking sexy thoughts or having sexual needs no longer has any effect on the

FOH

---

paraplegic: a person paralyzed in the legs, and sometimes pelvic areas, as the result of injury to the spinal cord.

quadriplegic: a person paralyzed in the upper body, including the arms, and lower body as the result of spinal cord injury.

Sexual Consent and Developmental Disability

Sexual expression takes many forms; for some individuals, certain forms of sexual expression may be appropriate, while others may not be. An individual should be capable of giving consent—either verbally or by gesturing—to sexual behavior involving another person. To be judged capable of giving consent to sexual contact, an individual must meet the state's minimum age requirement; be able to indicate yes or no, behaviorally or verbally, to a sexual overture by another person; be free of coercion or intimidation; and demonstrate an understanding of the potential risks and consequences of sexual behavior. Individuals with severe and moderate mental retardation, however, typically fail to meet the last criterion and therefore are judged not capable to give consent to sexual contact. Until the consent issue can be modified in some manner to address the limitations of individuals with severe and moderate mental retardation (for instance, third-party consent or situational determination by an individual's treatment team or service agency), ensuring these individuals' right to sexual expression will invariably give way to the principle of protection. This will only restrict sexual expression without allowing any "approved" sexual contact. The primary goal of any management plan that addresses mutual sexual behaviors should be to ensure, to the degree possible, the health and safety of the individual while still allowing for the occurrence of the behavior, even if this presents an element of risk.

Evaluating and determining the capability of persons with mild mental retardation to consent to sexual activity does not pose a significant problem for most service providers. Although some agencies may formally or informally oppose and limit sexual activity among the people they serve on the basis of religious convictions, parental pressures or staff philosophies, this opposition is gradually receding with the increasing emphasis on "consumer empowerment" and self-advocacy. Difficulty almost certainly arises when individuals not capable of giving consent engage in sexual activity with each other.

Service providers continue to have the fundamental obligation to safeguard the welfare of the people placed in their trust, to promote their health and well-being, and to protect them from harm to the degree necessary and reasonable while still maintaining their right to self-expression. The professionals given the task to evaluate individuals with developmental disabilities for the purposes of determining consent should include in their assessments each person's nonverbal behavior and interpersonal interactions, as well as communicative abilities. This is especially true for individuals with diminished intellectual capacities who are sexually active. As it exists now, the consent determining issue will continue to represent a major challenge for service providers and the individuals they serve.

—Paul J. Patti, "Sexuality and Sexual Expression in Persons with Mental Retardation," *SIECUS Report,* Vol. 23 (4), 1995

genitals, because the connection with the brain has been lost. However, erection of the penis and lubrication of the vagina are also partially controlled by a localized spinal reflex. Many paralyzed men and women can experience arousal of their sex organs, and sometimes even orgasm, through direct stimulation. There may also be small areas of skin in the pelvic area where feeling remains intact. Up to 40 percent of quadriplegic males are able to have an orgasm accompanied by ejaculation (Ducharme & Gill, 1997).

Each case of SCI is unique, but any patient and his or her partner can learn new forms of sexual expression. Often, intercourse is still possible, with adjustments in position. Some paraplegics and quadriplegics have a bladder catheter (tube) in place to carry urine out of the body to a storage bag. Although the catheter may be an inconvenience during sex, a couple committed to maintaining their sexual relationship can learn how to accommodate it. Some suc-

cess has also been achieved with the implantation of electrodes on localized nerves that can be stimulated by the individual to increase bladder control or even produce increased blood flow to the genitals (Sipski & Alexander, 1995).

Often, the partners of people with SCI are left out of the adjustment and rehabilitation process. They too have many emotional issues to resolve as they face a very stressful time in adjusting to the changes that occur in the relationship, including its sexual dimensions. When one partner in a couple suffers injury, the relational difficulties frequently lead to disharmony or a breakup of the relationship. The majority of couples facing SCI experience relational difficulties, but fewer than a quarter of them receive counseling. With appropriate and skilled professional help, couples may be helped to learn how to recapture a viable emotional and physical relationship following the devastating effects of SCI. Increasingly, institutions involved in the rehabilitation of

SCI patients are dealing with their sexual concerns and providing techniques to assist with their sexual readjustments (Sipski, Alexander, & Rosen, 1999).

Other Physical and Mental Disabilities

Many chronic physical conditions or injuries and mental illnesses can affect sexual functioning and the place of sexuality in relationships. These may be diseased or damaged sex organs, general physical debilitation that lowers interest and energy for sex, difficulty in socializing, or lowered feelings of self-worth.

Cerebral palsy can cause spastic conditions in various parts of the body. Victims of heart attacks or strokes may be physically debilitated and may worry about how much physical exertion they can withstand during and after their recovery. Traumatic brain injury may necessitate the relearning of roles and appropriate sexual behaviors within the contexts of a family and other social contexts (Medlar, 1993). A variety of neuromuscular conditions, such as multiple sclerosis and muscular dystrophy, can result in gradual loss of bodily control. Chronic lung disease makes exertion during sex difficult and uncomfortable. Cancer can affect sexual organs and/or general body fitness. Mental and emotional illnesses, ranging from depression to schizophrenia, can rob patients of a sense of security and well-being basic to fulfilling sex. The medications used to treat these conditions may also have sexual side effects, and only too often patients are not informed about these possibilities (Rowlands, 1995; Winship, 1995).

Terminally ill patients often experience sexual disruption because of internal stress, which, in turn, affects relationships. They may feel guilty about experiencing sexual arousal, and their lovers may find it difficult to desire intimacy when experiencing anticipatory grief or fear of their partner's fatal illness. However, open communication and, when available, counseling and the opportunity for privacy in hospital settings can all help with the sexual adjustments of long-term illness.

When people approach the special sexual problems associated with their disabilities and illnesses honestly, they can make new adaptive approaches to sex. It is important to recognize that sexual needs remain even when there is a health crisis, disability, or in the aftermath of a serious injury or illness. Maintaining one's involvement in sexual activities can also help maintain one's sense of integrity and personal self-worth (Sipski & Alexander, 1997).

Institutions

Some people with disabilities and chronic illnesses require long-term institutional care, in which sexual problems may multiply. Where the sexes are segregated, institutional residents may be limited to same-gender sexual contact. There may be little privacy for masturbation or shared sex. The keys to preventing desexualization in institutions are the attitude of the staff, and their understanding of the different levels of need that different people may have. Some institutions have provided condoms for patient use along with educational efforts, finding that these actions did not cause an increase in patient sexual activity (Winship, 1995). Often, in-service training on sex-related issues, along with establishment of humane administrative policies regarding sex, can help. The first step in preventing sexual problems relating to those who are disabled, ill, or institutionalized is admitting that all human beings are sexual and that they have a right to find the best ways for them, as individuals, to express that sexuality. Then steps may be taken to categorize people according to the types of help they may require to realize and take charge of their own sexual identities and needs (Buttenschon, 1994).

Self-Evaluation

1. Human beings have the potential for participating in a range of sexual activities.

2. Definitions of normalcy and abnormalcy are influenced by prevailing social norms.

3. General labels such as deviation, variation, and paraphilia have been applied to sexual activities and preferences that fall outside of the accepted norm.

4. In present-day Western culture, sex is still judged by several fundamental standards: two-person heterosexuality, a focus on coitus, expectation of orgasm and romantic feelings, and degree of safety.

5. Ethnocentric attitudes that one's own culture has the right standards toward sexuality can be called erotocentricity.

6. The concept of normalcy can be determined by statistical norms, by prevailing expert opinion (such as the *DSM-IV*), by moral standards perpetuated by religion and law, or as part of a more flexible continuum. Normalcy is a relative concept.

7. Labels represent generalities and are inadequate to a full understanding of a particular person's sexuality.

8. The term "homosexual" often has negative connotations. The terms "gay" and "lesbian" are used in reference to people when describing same-gender orientation. The term "bisexual" is used to describe some level of attraction to, or activity with, members of both sexes.

9. The factors that lead to the development of sexual individuality are highly complex. Patterns seem to be established by adolescence and probably develop through a combination of learning experiences, superimposed on some biological predispositions.

10. Social networks rather than relationships with parents seem to be important in shaping sexual attitudes and behaviors.

11. The Klein Sexual Orientation Grid demonstrates seven different variables that play a role in determining sexual orientation or identity. Sexual individuality includes many different life dimensions.

12. Sexual choices are affected by sexual attitudes. The National Health and Social Life Survey has identified three broad categories of sex-related attitudes in the United States: traditional, relational, and recreational. There is no single system of "American values" regarding sex.

13. Clear links have been observed between sexual attitudes and sexual practices, numbers of partners, and how often one thinks about sex. Frequency of sex does not seem to be related to attitudinal group.

14. Large portions of people in the United States have negative feelings and discriminatory attitudes about gay, lesbian, and bisexual people. These fears and misconceptions are called homophobia or biphobia. Leading professional organizations no longer view same-gender orientation within the framework of pathology.

15. Decisions about sexuality are often made after weighing moral values, religious teachings, and ethical beliefs. Some believe that moral values are built-in, whereas others believe that they are socially constructed.

16. Different ethical traditions influence sexual morality: adherence to divine laws, the idea of a religious covenant that allows for changing social circumstances, situation ethics, and the extremes of the hedonistic and ascetic traditions.

17. Many believe spirituality is connected to sexuality. In recent years, religions have been debating and changing their positions with regard to sexuality.

18. Research has demonstrated several ways in which religious belief systems influence sexual behavior.

19. Noncoercion, nondeceit, treating people as ends, and respect for the beliefs of others are moral principles that guide sexual decisions today.

20. In developing sexual values that are right for you, it is necessary to see how you will align yourself with the values of your society and culture. Self-examination and introspection are necessary to making decisions that will be healthy and nonhurtful for yourself and others.

21. Sexuality education has evolved since the early 1960s, when its aims were largely to prevent unwanted pregnancy and disease by giving young people knowledge. The next stage emphasized the need for values clarification and communication skills. We now have to evaluate the role of the Internet.

22. The attitude among the general public has tended to be favorable toward sexuality education in schools, although studies show that young people still get most of their sex information from peers or the media. Parents usually cannot provide all of the education that young people need.

23. There is a debate going on between groups who advocate comprehensive sexuality education, emphasizing sex-positive concepts and preparing young people for possible sexual activity, and those who want abstinence-only sexuality education, often based on fear tactics or particular religious biases. Other programs are focusing on postponing sex but still being prepared with information on contraception, protection, and the need to prevent transmission of HIV.

24. To be successful, sexuality education must recognize cultural differences. Cultural competence on the part of sexuality educators can help them communicate effectively with people from cultural traditions that differ from their own. Other countries of the world are attempting to shape sexuality education programs.

25. Sexuality education can change attitudes, but there is less research on behavioral change. Programs that devote adequate time to issues, are frank, make their goals clear, and discuss contraception and safer sex do seem to change sexual behaviors and prevent pregnancies and disease transmission. There is no evidence that sexuality education hastens the onset of intercourse.

26. Some professional groups, such as medical students, nurses, social workers, seminarians, theologians, and counselors in training, have been

receiving education to assist them in dealing with sexual concerns of future patients/clients.

27. People with disabilities have the right to recognition and expression of their sexuality.

28. Intellectually or developmentally disabled people need special approaches to sexuality education, including how to express their sexuality in private and how to employ appropriate methods of birth control. They are particularly vulnerable to

sexual abuse. There is still no ethical consensus about how sterilization of the developmentally disabled should be handled.

29. Spinal cord injuries may affect physical aspects of sexual response. Most paraplegics and quadriplegics can find levels of sexual functioning that will be satisfying to themselves and their partners. Many couples experience relational problems after one partner has had such an injury.

Focus on Health Questions

You will find in this section the kinds of questions that you may have concerning your own health and sexuality. The page references indicate where in the text the answer is located; the exact place is marked with the logo: **F◦H**

1. How do I know if my sexual feelings and behaviors are normal? 198

2. Where do people get their values and moral standards about sex? 201

3. If I had sexual feelings for both men and women when I was a teenager but have had intercourse

only with my opposite gender so far, does that mean I have a same-gender orientation? 203

4. Is homophobia all that bad? What negative effects does it actually produce? 210

5. My parents and my church tell me it is safer to avoid sexual intercourse until I get married. But most of my friends think that attitude is ridiculous. Whom should I believe? 211

6. If a person becomes paralyzed below the waist, can he or she still engage in and enjoy sex? 225

Annotated Readings

Drolet, J. C., & Clark, K. (Eds.). (1994). *The sexuality education challenge: Promoting healthy sexuality in young people*. Santa Cruz, CA: ETR Associates. A compendium of chapters on many different aspects of sexuality education, ranging from historical perspectives to classroom approaches.

Ducharme, S. H., & Gill, K. M. (1997). *Sexuality after spinal cord injury: Answers to your questions*. Baltimore: Paul H. Brookes. A sensitive and realistic guide for people with spinal cord injuries as they pursue their sexual lives.

Feuerstein, G. (1992). *Sacred sexuality: Living the vision of the erotic spirit*. East Rutherford, NJ: Putnam. Examines core teachings about human sexual expression from a diversity of religious and spiritual traditions.

Hollins, S., Perez, W., Abdelnoor, A., & Webb, B. (1999). *Falling in love*. London: St. George's Medical School. A book that takes parents and caregivers of young people with developmental disabilities through issues to be addressed when these youth want to develop close, intimate relationships.

Irvine, J. M. (1995). *Sexuality education across cultures*. San Francisco: Jossey-Bass. Examines how cultural differences affect sexuality education and offers guidelines for considering these effects in educational programs.

Kantor, M. (1998). *Homophobia: Description, development, and dynamic of gay bashing*. New York: Praeger. A controversial treatment of homophobia from a psychodynamic perspective.

Knoll, K., & Klein, E. L. (1995). *Enabling romance: A guide to love, sex, and relationships for the disabled (and the people who care about them)*. Bethesda, MD: Woodbine House. A practical resource regarding the special sexual concerns and issues of people with a spectrum of developmental and physical disabilities.

Krotoski, D. M., Nosek, M. A., & Turk, M. A. (1996). *Women with physical disabilities: Achieving and maintaining health and well-being*. Baltimore: Paul H. Brookes. A comprehensive book on the issues facing women with various disabilities, including concerns about sexual and reproductive health.

Maddock, J. W. (Ed.). (1997). *Sexuality education in postsecondary and professional settings*. New York: Haworth Press. A strong collection of papers regarding sexuality education in higher education and for professionals in training.

Nelson, J. B., & Longfellow, S. P. (Eds.). (1994). *Sexuality and the sacred: Sources for theological reflection.* Louisville, KY: Westminster/John Knox. A collection of scholarly articles that explore the wide range of issues associated with sexual ethics.

Rothbaum, E. D., & Bond, L. A. (Eds.). (1996). *Preventing heterosexism and homophobia.* Thousand Oaks, CA: Sage. A collection of chapters that deals with the complexities of these attitudes.

Sipski, M. L., & Alexander, C. (1997). *Sexual function in people with disability and chronic illness: A health professional's guide.* Gaithersburg, MD: Aspen. A guide for health care providers to talking with patients about their special sexual concerns.

Note: Most religious denominations publish books and guides concerning human sexuality, written from the perspectives of their specific religious beliefs and teachings. Copies of two bibliographies of these materials, *Current Religious Perspectives on Sexuality* and *Sexuality Education Resources for Religious Denominations,* may be purchased by sending $3.00 to SIECUS, 130 West 42nd St., Suite 350, New York, NY 10036.

Chapter 8

Sexuality, Communication, and Relationships

Chapter Outline

Note: A selection of Focus on Health questions appears at the end of each chapter. Answers to these questions are indicated within the chapter by the symbol in the margin. **F●H**

He was my first real love, and my first sexual partner. I honestly thought it would last forever. We certainly made each other enough promises that it would. Obviously we were wrong. For about a week, I thought I would never get over it, but I did. I think we're both pretty happy now, and I really wish only the best for him.

—Written by a student following the breakup of a relationship

Most people long for close relationships with others. One survey found that 96 percent of the men and 98 percent of the women who responded indicated that love was important in their lives. They long for the intimacy, companionship, sharing, and contentment that we associate with friendship and loving relationships. Sometimes, sexual sharing is also part of what a relationship brings, although 69 percent of men and 75 percent of women in the same study saw sex and intimacy as two different aspects of a relationship (Janus & Janus, 1993). Data from the National Health and Social Life Survey (NHSLS) indicated that of those individuals who wanted their first sexual intercourse, women were nearly twice as likely to say they loved their first sex partner than were the men. For those who said that their first intercourse was not particularly wanted but they went along with it anyway, 10 percent of the men and 38 percent of the women said they loved the partner (Michael et al., 1994). These statistics would indicate that at least in their initial heterosexual experiences, females are more likely to feel romantically involved with a partner than males are (Taris & Semin, 1997).

Men sometimes wonder if "nice guys finish last" in the sexual arena, and the question has actually been researched. Although definitions of "nice guy" characteristics certainly vary, the majority of women report a preference for nice guys, whom they assume to have had fewer sexual partners. In fact, nice guys who respect women and are sensitive communicators are preferred for friendships and committed, intimate relationships (Herold & Milhausen, 1999).

Keeping any relationship on an even keel can be complicated enough; bringing sexual feelings or activities into the picture often only makes things more complex and confusing. One of the major foundations for a healthy, lasting relationship is effective communication between people who feel relatively comfortable and confident with themselves. As any counselor can testify, relationships typically experience tension and crisis when the communication process has become blocked or muddled (Markowitz, 1997). This chapter deals with that process, its role in relationships, and how to keep lines of communication open.

▧ Communicating about Sex

Communication is an ongoing, dynamic process. It has been said that "one cannot *not* communicate." Even silence and avoiding another person convey certain messages, often very powerful ones. Unfortunately, many people do not realize the importance of communication in building a healthy sexual relationship. As a male student once stated to me, "Sex is something you *do* with each other; you shouldn't have to *talk* about it." That philosophy might work fine if people were just walking sex organs who slipped in and out of sexual encounters. Instead, we human beings have a range of thoughts, feelings, fantasies, and needs that must be shared with one another if we are to maintain relationships within and beyond the bedroom. A great many sexual problems could be prevented or resolved through open, honest communication. Yet people often seem reluctant to pursue such communication.

Although information about sexuality has certainly increased in the media, individuals are still insecure about discussing their private concerns regarding their own sexual lives and relationships with others. They may be afraid of seeming inappropriately bold or of betraying some ignorance about sexual matters. Joking about sex is easier for many people than asking about a potential partner's sexual history or explaining to a partner how they feel or what they might like to do sexually. Knowing about a partner's past sexual behaviors can be particularly important when considering the potentials for contracting sexually transmitted diseases (Buysse & Ickes, 1999). Our culture delivers a great many mixed messages about sexuality—on the one hand saturating our senses with sexy messages, and on the other hand hinting that sex is still a dangerous and dirty thing.

The Communication Process

Just about anything can be communicated: ideas, feelings, attitudes and values, needs and desires. From culture to culture, there is great diversity in the way people communicate (Markowitz, 1997). What may seem friendly and intimate in one society may be perceived as overly aggressive and offensive in another. Our eyes, facial expressions, and body language convey a great many messages for us. The tone and intonation of voice we use in speaking are crucial in communicating subtle aspects of our message. And of course, words are an important ingredient in any communicative interaction between people. However, words are also imperfect and often imprecise, and in our society when we talk about sex we tend to be caught between terms that are either too scientific or too vulgar to be appropriate in all circumstances. Their meanings may be interpreted differently by different people. One party to the communication process may not be paying as close attention as the other or may be swayed by internal moods or mind-sets.

The process of communication is filled with subtleties and opportunities for misinterpretation. It is not surprising, then, that human communication may sometimes be fraught with complications and misunderstandings. Figure 8.1 illustrates the basics of any process of communication. Someone, the sender, has some thought that she or he wishes to convey to someone else, who will become the receiver. However, there are many factors that influence the way in which the sender's message is formed. It is made up of specific understandings of certain words and is also filled with beliefs, attitudes and values, cultural expectations, and emotions (Purnine & Carey, 1999).

The sender may well hope to fulfill a particular agenda or accomplish some objective. As the thought to be conveyed is filtered through this interpretive system, the message takes shape and is "sent" to the receiver. At this point, it must be filtered through the receiver's own very individualized interpretive system, from which that person then draws his or her own understanding of the message. Obviously, the process is complicated enough that the message intended by the sender may not at all be the message understood by the receiver. Figure 8.2 shows how misunderstandings can take place. Communication works best when there is a well-developed feedback system through which the receiver may ask for clarification and check out the assumptions that have been made in understanding the message. As with most shared human processes, good communication takes a committed effort from everyone involved so that misinterpretations and misunderstandings are kept to a minimum.

The Words We Use to Talk about Sex

The sex-related words that people use reflect a great deal about the concerns and preoccupations of their society and their time in history (Plaud, Gaither, & Weller, 1998). The appropriateness of particular words can change over time, sometimes relatively rapidly. In early twentieth-century America, the words "leg," "bull," and "pregnant" were considered taboo for mixed company, because of their presumed sexual connotations. Even in reference to fowl, the terms "drumstick" and "dark meat" were substituted for "leg." Bulls were referred to as "he-animals," and pregnant women were said to be "expecting" or "in confinement." A generation ago, the term "suck" had clearly sexual connotations not expressed in public, and the slang word "dork" meant penis. Today "suck" has become a commonplace term used to describe almost anything in a negative way, and "dork" is used like the word "jerk." These and many other terms have gradu-

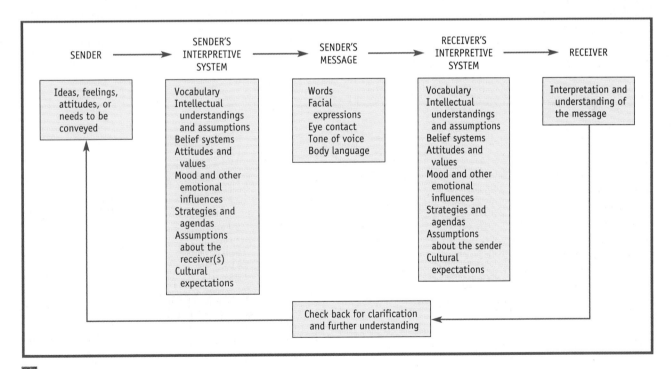

FIGURE 8.1 *The Process of Communication*

Whatever is to be conveyed from one person to another is filtered through each person's individualized interpretive system. Therefore, the message intended by the sender may be quite different from the message that is picked up and understood by the receiver. An active feedback system is one of the best ways to keep communication on track.

ally found their way into common usage, reflecting changing social values (Shrieves, 1994).

For some people and in some contexts, the "proper" scientific terminology about sex may seem more inappropriate or embarrassing than slang terms. This is probably one of the reasons why so many slang terms exist for the description of sex-related body parts and sexual activities. I have asked students to make lists of slang terms for sexual words in classrooms. When it comes to some things such as masturbation, there are far more slang terms used to describe male masturbation than female masturbation. When it comes to talking about sex in private, there seem to be rather predictable norms for the terms that women and men use with each other. For college students, these norms are shaped by the students' social networks.

There is some research that demonstrates the changing nature of sexual slang among college students. Two decades ago, a study (Sanders, 1978) showed that men were most likely to refer to their own sex organ as a "dick" (26 percent) or "penis" (25 percent) when talking with a lover or to avoid using any term at all (17 percent). However, only 8 percent of women used the term "dick." Nearly half of the women would say "penis," and 18.5 percent used no term for the male organ. In data gathered a decade later with another sample of college students, these trends again become clear, but with a significantly greater number of men and women reporting that they would use no term at all in reference to the penis (Fischer, 1989).

In 1978, women were even less likely than men to name their own sex organs in intimate conversations, with nearly 25 percent avoiding the use of any term. Those who did use some term were most likely to say "vagina" (32 percent). Men were more likely to use the term "pussy" (22 percent) to describe the partner's genitals than they were the term "vagina" (19.4 percent). The term "cunt" was more frequently used by men (14 percent) than by women (1 percent), who are more apt to find the term offensive.

In the follow-up study, women were still much less likely to use slang terms to describe the vagina than were men. Again, both sexes showed a much higher number of individuals who would use no term at all to describe the female genitals. The term "sexual intercourse" was used by over 10 percent of both men and women in 1978, although the term "make love" was far more popular for both women (56 percent) and men (32 percent). Men used the term "fuck" in their intimate conversations more than women did, although men were more likely to use this word in the presence of other men than they were with women. The term "having sex" has become more popular in recent years, with "intercourse" being used much less frequently. Students in the more recent study were less likely to use terms such as "fuck" or "screw" and again more likely to use no term at all to describe sexual intercourse (Fischer, 1989).

Sanders (1978) found that in describing the penis, men were more likely to use what she called "power slang," with such labels as "rod," "womp," and "pistol." Women tended toward "cute" euphemisms such as "penie," "oscar," or "baby-maker." Gender differences were also noted for the female genital terminology. Whereas males tended to use very specific terms,

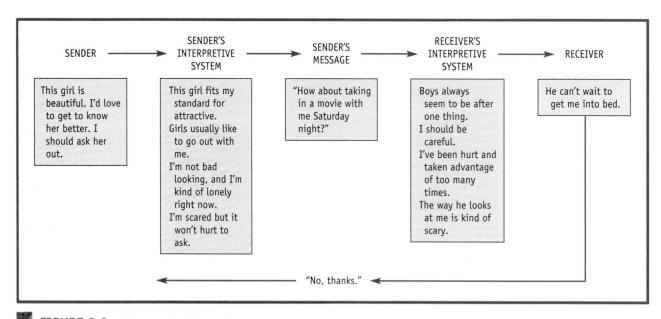

FIGURE 8.2   *Misunderstood Communication*

The process of communication may yield a misunderstanding between sender and receiver.

women tended more toward nonspecific personal terms such as "me," "mine," "she," or "my body." Women have been shown to be somewhat more reluctant to use sexual terms than men are (Geer & Melton, 1997; Plaud, Gaither, & Weller, 1998). Men tend to be more comfortable today using terms such as "fucking," "cunt," or "cock" than women are, although words such as "lovemaking," "vagina," and "penis" are generally more acceptable to both genders (Geer, 1996).

What makes communicating about relationships and sexual issues difficult?

Every relationship will evolve its own vocabulary for the intimate discussions of sex. Fifty-seven percent of the women in one study and 58 percent of the men considered "talking dirty" to be acceptable within their relationships (Janus & Janus, 1993). Using playful terms to name their genitals has been found to be therapeutic for couples experiencing sexual problems (Godow, 1999). The important thing is that both partners feel comfortable with the terms used. Neither should employ words that seem offensive, insensitive, or insulting to the other. Working out the details of acceptable terminology may itself require some careful communication and negotiation.

Contemporary Myths about Communication

Different societies and different times in history have always had their mythology surrounding communication and relationships. Unwritten rules evolve from that mythology and make their way into most human interactions. Our society is no exception. There are several myths that have governed how we communicate in our society. Consider how many of them have played a role in your own interactions with others.

Myth 1: You should have a confident opinion on every issue. We live in opinionated times. Media news focuses its attention on gathering people's opinions. If you listen carefully to the disagreements that people have with one another in everyday life, you will also notice that many individuals argue their points without much solid information to back them up. Even when it comes to sex, many people feel they must have all the answers, never appearing uncertain or insecure. The truth of the matter is that nearly everyone feels somewhat shy and scared in new situations, meeting new people, and forming new relationships. Whenever we come face-to-face with a stranger and need to communicate, there is usually an initial, tense period during which we begin evaluating what we will have to offer each other. And when we find ourselves in a position where we think we have to offer an opinion about some subject about which we know very little, it

can be perfectly acceptable to say "I'd really have to think that through and learn more about it before I could have much of an opinion about it."

Myth 2: An impressive conversationalist never permits any dead air. The most uncomfortable part of any conversation can be silence. People's eyes search around trying to avoid the other person's gaze. They begin to fidget or shift their weight from one foot to the other. They vainly hunt in their minds for some fresh topic to talk about.

It is this fear of silence that can force people to fill the air with words. Silence forces a kind of intimacy when two people have to look at one another momentarily, simply and quietly sharing each other. That intimacy can often make us feel vulnerable, and so we search for topics that will help us keep each other at "words' length." However, when we want to become closer to someone and develop a deeper relationship, being able to be quiet—and being able to listen carefully—can be important elements of communication.

Myth 3: Mapping out strategies ahead of time makes for better communication. A young man who was once a counseling client of mine told me about the advice a friend had given him before a date at a fraternity party. It went something like this: "Stay loose. Keep three or four things in mind to talk about, but only use them when the conversation lags. Don't look too interested. Smile a lot to yourself and look a little bored. When you look hard to get, women chase even harder. When you're ready to get things really moving, tell her you're sick of the party but she's welcome to come back to your room with you. But don't look too anxious." My client tried to carry out this strategy at the party, only to end up feeling foolish and having his date indicate that she preferred to stay at the party and go home alone. As popular and common as they may be, planned communication strategies set up games to which only one person knows the rules. Sometimes they work, but then a relationship has been established on the basis of manipulation, or even dishonesty. Usually the best "strategy" is to work at being yourself.

Myth 4: Using the right line will convince a partner to have sex. Rarely are relationships that simple. While one partner is rehearsing the line to carry out a seduction, the other partner may well be rehearsing the best way to turn down the proposition. Sexual relationships that grow out of invented lines can rarely be effective or lasting, and enticing someone into sex in this manner is ethically objectionable.

Myth 5: The rational mind is the only basis for effective communication. People often make the mistake of assuming that logical, rational thought processes constitute the only basis of good communication. There is a common misconception that "feelings only get in the way." In fact, emotional reactions are a legitimate part of what human beings need to communicate, especially in close relationships. To work only with one aspect of human nature during communication is to ignore crucial parts of oneself that need to be shared.

These myths can form the basis for a surefire prescription to stifle good communication. They stimulate the development of games, phony conversation, manipulative sexual seduction, and shallow relationships. When effective communication is lacking, even minor sexual problems are more likely to turn into major ones.

The Sexual Games We Play

When it comes to romantic and sexual relationships, there can be a dynamic tension between two people that results in posturing and attempts at "reverse psychology" to achieve certain ends. We live with the illusion that if we always do X and Y, we will automatically get Z as the result. However, human relationships are simply more complicated than mathematical equations or generalized scientific predictions. They must be approached in very individualized ways. Nevertheless, people are forever playing games with one another when it comes to sex and relationships. Here are some of the most common ones:

Operating by "The Rules"

The once best-selling book *The Rules* (Fein & Schneider, 1995) suggested that women resort to various playing-hard-to-get games in order to win the heart of some "Mr. Right." Rule number 4 suggested that women should not call men and should only rarely return their calls. Rule 13 cautioned women not to see men more than once or twice a week. Some have insisted that such rules are indeed necessary and that they do work. Critics of these approaches argue that they represent a serious setback in honest interaction and good communication.

The Power Games

Sex is a common place for people to express their struggles for power over one another. Most relationships have their share of such struggles. An individual who is fearful of appearing vulnerable may always want to be in a dominant position during sexual activity, quite literally needing always to be "on top." Someone who resents something about a partner might show little interest in sex to punish the other person through the withholding of sexual activity.

Some men and women use power games to spoil sex by being unavailable at the "right" time. Being drunk may sometimes be a handy way either to avoid sex or to justify a sexual failure. Some people play

"hard to get" by being too busy, too tired, or emotionally detached. Power games can turn into a sort of sexual sabotage, in which one partner manages to ruin a sexual encounter without looking like the "guilty party." Dropping some subtle criticisms about the other person's sexual performance may sometimes lower that individual's level of sexual interest considerably. As long as these power struggles proceed, sexual sharing will have its difficulties.

The Relationship Games

There are many different ways in which partners play games within their relationships. For example, some men and women bring unresolved conflicts and emotional problems with them to their sexual relationships. A stormy relationship with a parent that has resulted in certain patterns of reaction may affect one's present relationship if some of the old feelings are lingering inside. Mutual trust is a crucial factor in building intimacy and a satisfying sex life. When trust is lacking, the inner barriers stay up, holding a partner away. People who feel as though significant others in their lives have always left them may test how much a partner will put up with. The partner is in a sense being called upon to prove his or her love and devotion by sticking by the other person no matter what. Such games can create great strain in relationships and are often the cause of their destruction.

The Communication Games

One of the most common communication games is to push for the resolution of a conflict as quickly as possible. One partner, wanting the problem to be over, comes up with what seems the most logical solution to her or him then tries to impose the solution on the other. Statements may be made such as "You shouldn't feel that way," or "Come on, cheer up," or "You're blowing this all out of proportion." In the face of such seemingly logical suggestions, the other person may end up feeling guilty for having some reaction and then pretend that all is resolved. Many communication games are designed to avoid confronting potentially hurtful feelings or situations. Yet when truly effective communication happens, both partners feel that they have permission to feel and express whatever they need to. Sexual and relational difficulties often grow out of situations where two people fool themselves into thinking that some rough spots have been logically resolved, but in actuality, their differences are still simmering under the surface.

One key to a full and satisfying sexual relationship is knowing how to communicate effectively with a partner. That does not mean that you have to be an extravert or well versed in the social graces. Neither does

CROSS-CULTURAL PERSPECTIVE
Sex Is All the Talk in China, along with Banking

A sexual revolution of sorts is under way in China, not because the world's largest population has just discovered sex but because it is discovering how to talk about it.

In newspaper columns, on radio talk shows and over dinner, the Chinese are discussing sex, how to enjoy it and how to deal with its consequences more than at any time in this century.

And what they are discovering is that even though millions of Chinese have already thrown off the sexual constraints of the orthodox Communist era, China is still struggling against huge pockets of ignorance as it tries to normalize the role of sex in society.

Some Chinese "are still very shy about sex," said Wen Jingfang, the proprietor of Beijing's only shop for sexual aids, called the Adam and Eve Health Care Center.

"With so much shyness, scientific knowledge about sex cannot spread widely," Mr. Wen said.

The Chinese couple that everyone seems to be talking about this fall may be most famous not for what they did but for what they failed to do during more than a year of marriage: have sex. Their story has been publicized on the front pages of official newspapers, and has been tittered about on late-night radio shows.

The official *Legal Daily*, which reported their amorous ineptitude this year, spared them the mortification of public identification. But their loss of face occurred when the newspaper reported that after months of trying to conceive a child, the couple sought the advice of a doctor, who discovered that the wife had remained a virgin.

Both highly educated university lecturers, they thought that sleeping together, literally just sleeping together in the same bed, was a reproductive act.

"It's no joke," the official *Guangming Daily* reiterated this week in retelling the story.

A 22-year-old female university graduate, who like most of her classmates giggled through mandatory sex education videos as a freshman and decided by her third year that having sex with her boyfriend was O.K., said, "Maybe this couple is the only one that could make such a mistake."

Maybe, maybe not, say Chinese officials who want to reinforce sex education programs that began in the mid-1980's.

In Guangdong Province, one magazine devoted to sexual topics gave out 16 essay awards for the best version of "My Story of Contraception." The winner was a man in his 50s whose contraceptive bunglings had brought him "psychological trauma" through two marriages.

The popular *Southern Weekend* newspaper now carries a regular column on sex, which this month posed the question, "What do women need from sex?"

In Mandarin, the answer is a "high tide," or orgasm. The newspaper said that women reach high tide 40 percent of the time and that one-sixth of the women surveyed had never experienced a high tide.

"Husbands should understand women's needs about sex," the article said. "Sexual high tide not only benefits women's health, but also benefits women's spirit."

Such openness was not only unheard of a decade ago but it might also have been illegal.

For decades under Mao, prudery was the ideological fashion, at least out in the open. But in Deng Xiaoping's era of reform, sex—like capitalism—has enjoyed a huge resurgence. Not only is there enormous public interest in sex, but the old icons of Communist restraint have been toppled as well, most recently in the account of Mao's prolific private sex life, as revealed by his personal physician, Li Zhisui. . . .

One recent survey of 100,000 callers to Shanghai's information radio line showed that "sex" and "banking" were the two topics most often asked about.

[A] landmark sex survey of 23,000 respondents in 1990 revealed what many Chinese instinctively understood about their country: More people were having sex and were also enjoying it. Although only 60 percent of the respondents said they were "often or sometimes" naked during sex, nearly 75 percent of them said sex was necessary for both emotional and physical health.

—Patrick E. Tyler, "Sex Is All the Talk in China, along with Banking," *New York Times International*, November 27, 1994. Copyright © 1994 by the New York Times Co. Reprinted by permission.

it mean that you have to be a great conversationalist or even talk a great deal. What it does mean is that you care enough about yourself, your partner, and the relationship you share to put some effort and energy into communicating.

Before reading the section "Effective Communication," assume the role of counselor and list several strategies that you might suggest to a client seeking to improve her or his communication with a partner.

Effective Communication

For the most part, people do not find it easy to communicate about the more intimate aspects of their lives, such as their sexuality. The opinion or "idea" topics may be discussed with some ease—issues such as how society should deal with gays in the military, values concerning sex and marriage, or which form of birth control is most effective. But when it comes right down to talking about one's own sexual orientation, a preferred sexual activity, or the form of birth control the individual wants to use, the conversation may not flow quite so smoothly. This section of the chapter presents some basic guidelines for facilitating good lines of communication.

The Ground Rules

There are some preliminary steps to opening up channels for effective communication between two people about sex or any other sensitive topic. Here are some ground rules for getting started:

1. *Think about the degree of commitment you hold for each other and the relationship.* Not much will happen with two-way communication unless *both* partners really want it to happen. This may well depend on the quality of the relationship you are sharing. Communicating honestly about sex takes energy. You may begin to feel tired, frustrated, or hopeless at times, and it will take a solid commitment from both people to see you through the more difficult steps. Relationships in which sex is discussed may exist on many different levels. On one end of the scale is the casual encounter in which two people barely know one another. On the other end is the long-term loving involvement where discussing sex is continually necessary to ensure mutual satisfaction.

2. *Know your own values.* Before you try communicating about sex, it is a good idea to have thought through where you stand on some of the value issues that may be involved. Know your own beliefs, while letting yourself be open to the attitudes and values of the other individual.

3. *Keep yourselves on equal ground.* A sense of equality between two people is usually essential to their communicating well. If someone is always feeling in the "one-down" inferior position, it is not likely that he or she will be able to communicate very openly or confidently. Power inequalities are dangerous to relationships (Gottman, 1999).

4. *Build trust for one another.* When there is a lack of trust between two partners, there is likely to be not only a strain in their sexual interactions but also a tendency toward reserved and uncomfortable communication. A sense of trust is fundamental to honest, genuine dialogue. Lack of trust can lead to "stonewalling" the other person during communication, a practice that can create serious obstacles in relationships (Kantrowitz & Wingert, 1999).

5. *Pick the right location and time for talking.* Where and when you talk may be very important. You will both want to feel as relaxed and comfortable as possible and have adequate privacy. Sometimes bed is the ideal place to talk, but it may also produce an emotionally charged situation for some kinds of communication. Beware of atmospheres that encourage superficial conversations and games. Ask your partner where she or he would feel most comfortable talking, and be certain you feel all right there as well.

Making It Happen

A central message of this chapter is that the process of making good communication happen takes some deliberate effort. There are several qualities that have repeatedly been shown through research to facilitate open and honest communication between people:

Demonstrate an Attitude of Warmth, Caring, and Respect

In order to feel enough trust to open up to another person and share on more than a superficial level, there has to be some sense of mutual positive regard. However, it is not enough to feel a sense of caring for another person; the feelings need to be demonstrated or communicated in some way (see Fig. 8.3). Sometimes it may be a simple willingness to be quiet and listen attentively; other times, it will require overt expressions of love or kindness. Patterns of criticism and contempt are extremely harmful in building positive communication (Gottman, 1999).

Avoid Making Snap Judgments and "All-ness" Statements

One of the greatest problems in human communication is the tendency of some to jump to premature conclusions and make snap judgments about others. Most people open up best to those who are not judgmental. Because sex is one of those areas of life about which people have strong opinions, intimate communication would be improved if we set assumptions aside and allowed other points of view to be expressed openly. In a more technical sense, it is also valuable to avoid using "all-ness" words such as "always" or "never." When referring to another person, use of statements including these words is rarely fair or accurate.

Listen Carefully and Really Hear

Often when people appear to be listening, they are actually thinking ahead, formulating their response to what the other person is saying. It is all too easy for ideas and concepts to become garbled and misunderstood unless one listens carefully. Let yourself hear the other person out, then think through your reactions and responses.

Listening is not just a passive state of resting the senses; it is an active process of being attuned to the words and nonverbal messages someone else is conveying to us.

Empathize and Understand That Feelings Need to Be Felt

Empathy is the ability to identify with what another person is feeling and to experience, in a sense, "walking a mile in their shoes." All of us have experienced

a full range of emotions, although for different reasons. When listening to another, listen for their feelings too, and try to recall the experience of your own emotions so you can better understand where they are coming from. Two people who want to communicate about personal things must be willing to share emotions, even hurtful ones, and empathize with each other. Empathy can help ward off our natural tendencies to become defensive when we are facing disagreements. Constant defensiveness in a relationship can be a source of very real problems (Kantrowitz & Wingert, 1999).

It is also important to allow one another to express feelings. Sensing that your feelings are being heard and understood is one of the most crucial aspects of good communication.

Be Genuine

Hidden agendas make communication more difficult and problems harder to resolve. Most people can sense superficiality and deceptiveness and respond much more positively to genuineness and honesty. Effective communication about sexual matters must be based on such openness. However, sometimes the issues are subtle and difficult. Shades of meaning may cloud the truth. No lasting relationship can escape the need to communicate about difficulties and misunderstandings. Otherwise, they accumulate under the surface and create problems later. For these reasons, you must work at being honest and being yourself in personal communications. Some level of self-disclosure about one's sexual feelings and needs seems to enhance the sexual satisfaction within relationships (Byers & Demmons, 1999).

Make Sense and Ask for Clarification

It is all too easy for words or mannerisms to be misunderstood in the communication process. We often make assumptions about what the other person means, without ever bothering to check out those assumptions with that individual. It takes work to listen carefully, understand what is being said, and then clarify if your understanding is correct.

In order to do this, it is a good idea occasionally to feed back your understanding to your partner by saying, "So what I hear you saying is. . . ." or "Do you mean . . . ?" You have clarified your interpretation of their words, and they are then able to correct any misconceptions. When formulating a reply to any message, take the time you need to think it through, choose your words carefully, and give a focused response. The response may not always be verbal but may be made through expressions of the face, eyes, or body.

FIGURE 8.3 *Warmth, Caring, Respect*

Loving relationships depend on attitudes of warmth, caring, and a genuine respect for each other.

Do Not Let Silence Scare You

As pointed out earlier in this chapter, gaps in conversation often make people feel uneasy and vulnerable. People may rush to fill the gap with words. Instead, it is more important to take your time, allowing silence to be a part of communication at times. It can be intimate and calming as well.

Beware of the "I Do Not Want to Hurt You" Cop-Out

FOH In relationships, hurtful things must be shared. That sort of confrontation is not always easy, but in the long run it will help get tension-producing conflicts resolved. It is not unusual for counselors to hear one partner explain that they avoided dealing with painful topics because they were afraid of hurting someone's feelings. Of course, they were also avoiding their own discomfort that comes from having to talk about hurtful issues.

Use Self-Talk Effectively

How we talk to ourselves can have a profound effect on the ways we relate to other people. The things we say inside our own minds can color our emotions and our reactions both positively and negatively. For example, if during sex you are worrying about how you look or sound, or are thinking negatively about your own body, sex is not likely to be a very positive experience. However, if you work at positive self-talk, emphasizing how good the experience seems, and how much you are enjoying being with your partner, it is much more likely the experience will be enjoyable and fulfilling.

Sex is deeply personal to most of us and to discuss it with someone else represents a special degree of vulnerability. Yet in a partnership where sex is shared, words and feelings must also be shared. There are always decisions to be made, signals to be checked, worries to be resolved, and feelings to be discussed. Communication about sex takes effort and practice, but the results can be worth it.

Different Personality Types Communicate Differently

Two things remain quite clear as we study personality: (1) It may be demonstrated that people really are different in the ways they perceive and approach life; and (2) most people tend to view their own perceptions and approaches as the "right" ones. It is no wonder, then, that when people attempt to establish an intimate partnership, their differences sometimes create tensions, disagreements, and arguments. It can

help if you have a clearer picture of your own personality and its characteristics.

One of the most popular tests to be used for evaluating personality traits has been the Myers-Briggs Type Indicator (MBTI) (Myers & McCaulley, 1985) and its modified version, the Kiersey Temperament Sorter (Kiersey & Bates, 1984). These tests are based on a model that portrays the human personality as a combination of varying balances between four main pairs of traits. Although any such model is bound to oversimplify the complexities of being human, tests can also offer some general insights into one's personality. Most counseling centers have such tests available and are willing to interpret and explain their results.

Everyone is familiar with the pair of personality traits known as extraversion and introversion, although these terms are frequently misused and misunderstood. Extraverted individuals tend to be energized by other people and the external environment. They connect with others easily and enjoy group situations. Introverted people prefer being their own company, but being introverted does not necessarily imply that they are shy or antisocial. They simply tend to draw their energy more from inside themselves. They need more time and privacy for processing their inner experience, and they often prefer one-to-one interactions with others.

The Myers-Briggs typology also makes a distinction between people who are specific and concrete in their approach to life and those who rely on their abstract, intuitive natures. It suggests too, that whereas some individuals make their judgments through logical, step-by-step analysis and reasoning, others are influenced more by their feelings and the desire to maintain harmonious relationships. In the final pair of MBTI characteristics, people are viewed either as punctual, decisive, scheduled, and orderly, or as unstructured, open-ended, and spontaneous.

It is these various combinations of personality traits that must come together in any relationship between two people, sometimes creating difficulty in understanding one another (Kiersey & Bates, 1984). The extravert may be miffed that an introverted friend is more content to stay at home and avoid large parties. The individual who pays attention to feelings and wants to preserve harmony between people may be frustrated by a partner who prefers approaching problems in a highly rational manner, only wanting to arrive at the most logical conclusion.

Personality differences in relationships only underscore the need for good communication skills and a commitment to using them. The differences may also be expressed through an individual's sexual preferences and styles. Although it is certainly not always true that opposites attract or that it is easy for them to get along well, human differences—

sexual and otherwise—can be managed and even enjoyed. They sometimes provide the spice of a loving relationship.

Communication Differences between Women and Men

FOH

Women and men sometimes express frustration with their shared communications. Deborah Tannen (1990, 1994), a sociolinguist, and Lillian Glass (1992), a speech pathologist, studied the intricacies of communication patterns in males and females. Their work has revealed some fascinating differences in the ways the two sexes are taught to communicate. Tannen began by studying the videotapes of people in different age groups having conversations with best friends of the same gender. She noticed that girls tended to face each other squarely, look directly at each other, and enjoy talking together.

Boys seem to grow up in a much more hierarchical social order than do girls, and their groups usually have a leader who tells others what to do. An elaborate system of rules filters down through the group, and there is a struggle to maintain one's status within the group. Boys must often vie for attention and deflect the challenges of other boys to maintain "center stage."

Girls are more apt to play in small groups or in pairs, and they focus on maintaining intimacy and a sense of community. They want to get along with their friends so that everyone can have a turn, and there often are no "winners" or "losers." When they encounter conflict, both boys and girls want to get their own way, but they will try to achieve that in different ways. Boys resort to insistence and threats of physical violence, whereas girls usually try to mediate the situation and preserve harmony through compromise and avoidance of confrontation.

Differences in communication style between adult men and women are rooted in the fact that they have practically grown up in different cultures when it comes to communicating (Maccoby, 1998). Women place a premium on being agreeable and congenial. Men react much more personally to verbal rejection and have a tendency to resist doing what they are told because they do not want to feel dominated or in a one-down position in their social interactions. These differences may cause confusion and turmoil in male-female relationships. Keep in mind that the patterns discussed represent generalizations and certainly do not apply to every individual woman or man (Kerr, 1999; Potts, 1998).

Talking over Problems

A man is much less likely to tell a woman about his difficult feelings or life problems because he does not want to worry her or seem helpless. Men also feel more obligated to offer solutions when someone tells them about a problem, even if the other person is just looking for an empathetic ear. They tend to be more brusque, forceful, loud, and demanding in their communications. For women, not being told about something such as personal feelings or troubles seems like a rejection from a partner. Women are gentler, softer, and more emotional in their communications. They value the intimacy in telling secrets and worries, whereas men are more likely to feel too vulnerable in doing so. In fact, men do live in a social milieu where other men may indeed be trying to put them down, and they therefore have to be somewhat self-protective (Taris & Semin, 1997). The social atmosphere for women is very different, and so misunderstandings develop.

Asking for Directions

In the same way, men are more resistant to asking for directions when they are trying to find or do something. For them, it is putting yourself one down with someone else. Women welcome the chance to connect with another person and are not bothered by seeming to need help.

Expressing Needs

One of the areas of communication that often causes trouble for women and men is how they express various needs. For example, Tannen (1990) cites a typical situation in which a woman asks her husband if he would like to stop in somewhere for a drink. He truthfully answers "No," and nothing more is said for the moment. It eventually becomes evident that the wife was hurt and angered by his response. Although he had seen the interaction as a simple statement of fact—he did not want to stop for a drink—she had felt that her wishes had not been considered. The wife had not realized that he would have been open to further negotiation, and in fact could have been easily persuaded to follow her lead had she made it clear that it was an important issue for her. Tannen theorizes that because of how they learn to communicate, men are more likely to start any sort of negotiation with a clear statement of where they stand, but they understand that there will be further discussion. Women, on the other hand, are likely to accept any such statement as a clear indication of a man's position and see it as immovable unless she presses the communication into some form of unpleasantness.

Another variation on this theme is that when women are trying to focus on intimacy and connection by expressing needs, men tend to view such expression as a demand and feel that they must resist it. Male socialization causes them to be cautious about one-

The Big Picture

Four Keys to a Happy Relationship

Despite all his sophisticated analysis of how relationships work (and don't work), researcher John Gottman's advice to the lovelorn and fight-torn is really quite simple.

Learn to Calm Down

This will cut down on the flooding response that makes further communication so difficult. The most brilliant and philosophically subtle therapy in the world will have no impact on a couple not grounded in their own bodies to hear it, he says. Once couples are calm enough, suggests Gottman, they can work on three other basic "keys" to improving their relationship.

Learn to Speak and Listen Nondefensively

This is tough, Gottman admits, but defensiveness is a very dangerous response, and it needs to be interrupted. One of the most powerful things you can do—in addition to working toward the ideal of listening with empathy and speaking without blame—is to "reintroduce praise and admiration into your relationship." A little appreciation goes a long way toward changing the chemistry between people.

Validate Your Partner

Validation involves "putting yourself in your partner's shoes and imagining his or her emotional state." Let your partner know that you understand how he or she feels, and why, even if you don't agree. You can also show validation by acknowledging your partner's point of view, accepting appropriate responsibility, and apologizing when you're clearly wrong. If this still seems too much of a stretch, at least let your partner know that you're trying to understand, even if you're finding it hard.

Practice, Practice, Practice

Gottman calls this "overlearning," doing something so many times that it becomes second nature. The goal is to be able to calm yourself down, communicate nondefensively, and validate your partner automatically—even in the heat of an argument.

—Alan Atkisson, "What Makes Love Last?" *New Age Journal,*
September/October 1994

down positions. So when a woman suggests to her male partner that she would like to know when he is going to be late because otherwise she feels upset, he may see it as a challenge to his freedom and rebel against the suggestion.

Talking and Listening

Research shows that, contrary to popular opinion, men tend to talk more than women in public situations such as meetings, group discussion, or classrooms. When questions are asked in a group meeting, men tend to ask the first question, more questions, and longer questions. They tend to speak in lengthy monologues and interrupt people more than do women (Campbell, Kleim, & Olson, 1992). Not unexpectedly, in the listening process women tend to show frequently that they are listening to another person, whereas men focus more on the literal content and react only when they agree or disagree.

At home, however, the talking roles seem reversed. Women see talking as a way to foster intimacy with their partners at home. Men view talking as a way to negotiate status, and therefore they do not fit it into the private home context as much as do women. When women talk about their feelings and problems and see that as a way to work on them, men tend to perceive the communication as wallowing in complaints. They tend to be more solution-oriented and want to resolve the difficulty with definitive action.

Communicating in the Workplace

Differences in communication patterns may also create misunderstandings and differing perceptions of women and men in the workplace. In their interactions with other employees, even those subordinate to them, women are often deferential in their communications, seeming more tentative and polite than their male colleagues when asking to have tasks completed or offering suggestions and new ideas. Men tend to be more assertive and direct in their workplace communications. Because they are more

CASE STUDY

Jennifer and Ted: Failed Communication

By the time Jennifer and Ted made contact with the Counseling Center to work on their problems together, their relationship had become very precarious. They had already discussed going their separate ways, and they both viewed counseling as a last-ditch effort to make things work again. Jennifer explained to the counselor that she felt Ted was becoming increasingly detached and that she could never get him to talk about what he was feeling. Expressing his frustration, Ted countered that Jennifer always seemed to be wanting something from him, but he was never quite sure what. "No matter what I do," he said, "I can't seem to please her. After a while, it doesn't seem worth bothering anymore." Jennifer responded by saying, "A relationship has to be more than sleeping together, or going out for a drink, or talking about what happened that day. I want to know more about what's going on inside you."

They continued to share their differing points of view. Ted maintained that Jennifer was looking for something in him that he didn't think was there: "I just don't have that many deep feelings, and I don't want to make them up for you. I was satisfied the way things were." Jennifer felt that there was a missing dimension in their relationship because Ted seemed unwilling or unable to deal with things on an emotional level. The counselor suggested that they both take some personality tests, and the

results of these tests suggested that Ted and Jennifer really did have very different approaches to dealing with their reactions to life. Ted was a very practical and decisive person, dependable in his pursuits and thorough in paying attention to details. He got along well with other males and did not like "fanciness" in speech or manner. He placed a high value on loyalty and faithfulness, but he did not deal very much with the affective levels of his personality.

In contrast, Jennifer's tests confirmed that she was an outgoing and emotionally passionate individual who tended to form her views of the world impulsively. She liked romance and frivolity and had little patience for sorting through all of the rational and practical aspects of situations. She observed other people carefully, and she often speculated about their hidden motivations. As the counselor discussed their personality profiles and differences with the couple, both Ted and Jennifer agreed that the summaries were quite accurate. The counselor went on to explain that when people's personalities differ to such a degree, it takes an extra measure of effort to make mutual communication work. Indicating that they were hoping to find ways of preserving and improving their relationship, the couple agreed to try some communication exercises and to continue for several weeks in the counseling relationship.

used to vying for attention, men may also be less threatened by public-speaking necessities, an essential skill of the business culture. In occupational settings that are still male-oriented in their power structures, these differences may lead to women being perceived as less decisive or competent than their male counterparts, which may put them at a disadvantage for advancement in their careers (Kerr, 1999; Tannen, 1994).

Even though men have more difficulty with it, intimate talking seems to be a healthier mode of communication. The sooner people talk out problems, the sooner they tend to get over them and feel better. Talking in the manner described earlier in this chapter is a learnable skill, even for men. What the work of researchers such as Tannen and Glass has demonstrated, however, is that when communication behavior frustrates a partner of the other sex, it may represent a normal expression of gender rather than some individual failing. To understand the gender differences in communication is the first step toward changing one's behavior or learning how to live with some of the

differences. It is possible instead to learn and recognize and celebrate differences for what they truly are: opportunities to find openings to new levels of mutuality (Kerr, 1999).

Quarreling and Relational Impasses

Even the happiest of couples are bound to have disagreements, some of which will become arguments. These conflicts may be complicated by differences in communication styles resulting from personality factors or gender. Conventional wisdom has held that quarreling is a sign of dissatisfaction and unhappiness in the relationship and that it ultimately is destructive for the partnership. However, recent research has shown that things are not that clear-cut. In fact, certain kinds of quarreling can actually improve relationships (Markman et al., 1993). Even couples who describe themselves as unhappy but who are able to express their anger and resentment in constructive ways have been shown to be much happier 3 years later than they previously had been (Gottman, 1999).

Internal/External Consistency in Communication

Using assertive communication skills can reduce misunderstandings and conflicts in relationships. The more consistency there is between the thoughts and feelings going on internally and what is expressed externally, the more likely that minor concerns may be resolved before they become major problems. Note these hypothetical interactions between a couple: how things were said, and how they could have been expressed more effectively.

As this example shows, effective and assertive communication may not always change the ultimate outcome of people's behavior. However, it can change how people end up feeling about the interaction, themselves, and each other.

The Setting: Afterplay

	What Was Said:	**What Was Being Thought and Felt:**	**What Could Have Been Said:**
Man	"You haven't seemed very into sex lately. Is there something wrong?"	Something is wrong. She just lies there. I guess I'm not much of a lover.	"I'm embarrassed to bring this up, but I've been worried lately that I'm not pleasing you much during sex."
Woman	"No, I'm fine."	Oh my God, he doesn't think I'm much good in bed.	"I've been worrying that you would think I'm not much good in bed."
Man	"Was it good for you this time?"	Maybe she doesn't love me anymore. Or maybe I'm just not doing something right.	"I really love you a lot, and I've been scared that either you don't feel the same about me or that my sex techniques just aren't working for you."
Woman	"Yes, it was fine, I said."	He must know that I'm not reaching orgasm. This is so embarrassing.	"It's not you. I love you so much. I haven't wanted to admit this to anybody, but I've never been able to have an orgasm. I'm really embarrassed."
Man	"Come on, are you sure? You just don't seem very turned on."	She just doesn't want to admit that she doesn't feel the same about me anymore. I've never been able to hold on to a relationship.	"I was afraid that things were falling apart between us. It must be a real letdown not to be able to come. Maybe we can work on it together."
Woman	"Do we really need to talk about this? I don't really like analyzing our sex life. I've told you everything is okay. Okay?"	I'm going to lose him if I don't find a way to fake having an orgasm. I love him so much.	"It's not easy for me to talk about this, but I would sure like to do something about it."

The key here is whether the mode of arguing is constructive or destructive (see Fig. 8.4). In the most destructive kinds of fights, anger is expressed in vicious and attacking ways, with blaming and character assassination. The two people are defensive, accusatory, and stubborn, while resorting to insults, contemptuous remarks, and whining complaints (Arellano & Markman, 1995). A more constructive and hopeful pattern is found in couples who feel free to express their anger to one another but without allowing the anger to escalate until it gets out of control. They make a concerted effort to acknowledge their differences, be open to one another's points of view, and listen to each other. Eventually, they work toward arriving at some resolution to their differences, often involving negotiation and compromise (Atkisson, 1994).

The Setting: After Class

	What Was Said:	What Was Being Thought and Felt:	What Could Have Been Said:
Chris	"How about joining me at the snack bar so we could go over these notes? I'm getting confused."	I'm really attracted to him/her. If there was only a way to strike up a relationship.	"I've been noticing you in class, and I was wondering if you might be interested in going to the snack bar to talk."
Jan	"I'm pretty busy right now. Maybe another time."	What's going on here? S/He has been watching me in class for weeks.	"I've noticed you watching me. You just want to talk?"
Chris	"How about this afternoon? We could meet around 4:30 and then catch a bite to eat."	If I let him/her get away now, there'll never be another chance. Maybe if I press it a little further.	"I'd like a chance to get to know you better. How about it?"
Jan	"I've got another commitment for dinnertime, okay?"	This person doesn't know when to give up. I wish I knew what he/she was really looking for. I've got enough problems.	"I don't know. I'm feeling a little uncomfortable. My life is kind of complicated right now, and I'm hesitant to make any new commitments."
Chris	"Well, how about Friday after class?"	I think I'm making a jerk of myself. S/He thinks s/he's pretty hot stuff, apparently. What's so wrong with me?	"I don't want to look like a jerk, but I really hope you'll consider it. We'll just talk; I'm not so bad."
Jan	"Look, I may not be here Friday. Maybe you could find someone else to go over the notes with you."	I just want to get out of here. Won't this person take no for an answer?	"I appreciate the invitation, but this just isn't a good time for me. I don't mean to hurt your feelings."
Chris	[sarcastically] "Sorry I asked. I won't trouble you again. See you around."	I really blew it. I always have to push too hard.	"Well, if you ever change your mind, I'll be sitting in the same seat in this class. Keep me in mind."
Jan	"Fine."	Maybe I was too hard on him/her. But he/she wouldn't let up. I feel like a heel.	"Look, it was really nice of you to ask. I just don't want any more complications right now. But I will keep you in mind. Thanks for understanding."

Women and men who are involved in relationships with each other typically play different roles in fights. It is more common for males to want to avoid conflict with their partners, and they may at first withdraw or become defensive. Women, on the other hand, are often the "emotional managers" of relationships. They are more likely to bring up some issue about which there is disagreement, wanting to confront the problem with their partners. However, anger may be presented in such a way as to lead to positive outcomes. Likewise, men can work at listening to the other point of view and recognizing that there is a problem in need of resolution (Gottman, 1999).

Couples sometimes reach a *relational impasse*, meaning that the process of two people relating has become stuck and unmoving. This is a frustrating

FIGURE 8.4   *Quarreling*

Quarreling in a relationship can be constructive or destructive. Anger expressed in a violent or accusatory manner is destructive. Rather, couples should make an effort to express their views openly, listen to the other person, and learn to compromise.

predicament, because nothing seems to be happening between the partners, and both of them have retreated into themselves. Research with groups of women and men has identified three general types of impasse that can shut down relational processes at least for a time. It seems likely that these impasses occur in individual male-female relationships as well (Bergman & Surrey, 1992):

1. *Dread/Anger Impasse* results when men begin to feel that they are being criticized or that difficult emotional issues are being raised. They get a sense of dread about what is developing and become uncomfortable about dealing with emotions; they then withdraw into themselves and become silent. Women react to this by getting angry and feeling abandoned or misunderstood. With this, men either withdraw even further or begin to become angry at the women. It is at this point that impasse may easily occur.

2. *Product/Process Impasse* reflects some other typical differences in the way men and women approach tasks. When there is a problem to be resolved or a task to be done, women tend to be process-oriented. They want to keep the process open, examining it and understanding all of the feelings associated with it. Men, on the other hand, tend to be much more product-oriented, with the clearly defined goal of getting the job done and over with. They get impatient with feeling stalled in the process, whereas women feel hurried along by men toward a goal that is much less important to them. Again, they may end up feeling misunderstood and stymied. Many couples get stuck here.

3. *Power-over/Power-with Impasse* typically emerges when there is some sort of conflict being faced. Men tend to see conflict as a competitive contest, in which the other person is attempting to gain control of, or power over, them. Women tend to be more concerned that everyone's voice be heard, and they favor the distribution of power between people so that it is shared. They are put off by definitive stands and may make the mistaken assumption that any room for negotiation or compromise has been lost.

Impasses represent a difficult place for any relationship to be, because things simply are not going anywhere. Both partners are nursing negative feelings and have withdrawn from relating. However, these problems are not insurmountable. Knowing how to carry on effective relationships involves knowing how to move beyond relational impasses.

Resolving Impasses Effectively

People have different responses to interpersonal conflict (Arellano & Markman, 1995). Some prefer the obliging style, giving in quickly to satisfy the other, or avoiding unpleasant encounters altogether by withdrawing from the situation or the relationship, or ignoring the conflict. Those with a dominating style jump in with full force, ignoring the needs of the other and using coercion or power to get their own way. A greater sense of mutuality may be achieved through the integrating style that involves discussion of differences and collaboration to find a solution that will be acceptable to both people. Similarly, compromising uses a give-and-take approach in which both people sacrifice some of their own needs in order to have other needs met. Although some people place more significance on principles, others place more value on maintaining relationships. One person may want to confront conflicts, and another may want to smooth over ruffled feelings as quickly as possible.

The best way to resolve relational impasses is to press into the conflict with a sense of mutuality and feel that the problem is being faced by a "we" instead of a "you" and "me" (Atkisson, 1994; Bergman & Surrey, 1992). An important beginning step to working out solutions to conflicts is realizing and admitting that people and their points of view are indeed different. Everyone has his or her own perceptions of any situation, and all of us tend to see ourselves as more correct in our perspectives than others. Once couples begin to approach a conflict with a greater sense of mutuality, it is crucial for each partner to explain in clear terms what her or his perception of the problem is. One of the most effective ways of doing this is to work at formulating "I" messages. That means taking

Table 8.1   *Useful Strategies for Improving Communication in a Loving Relationship*

Here are some ways of keeping your relationship open, honest, and caring:

1. If you must criticize, focus on specific behavior rather than criticizing the person. For example, say something like *"That* irritates me," rather than *"You* irritate me." Your partner will feel less "attacked."

2. Don't make assumptions and judgments about your partner, so you end up telling him or her what he or she is thinking or feeling. We cannot be mind readers.

3. Avoid using "all-ness" words such as "always" and "never." They typically represent unfair generalizations. Again, try to be more specific.

4. Try to see gray areas in issues, rather than strictly black-and-white, good-bad dichotomies. Remember that our own "truths" often depend on our individual perceptions.

5. Use "I feel . . . " messages rather than "You are . . . " statements. No one can dispute what you feel. However, your partner may well be offended by judgments about his or her character that are perceived as being unfair or untrue.

6. Be direct and honest, avoiding games, power plays, and attempts at using reverse psychology.

7. Work toward a sense of equality. An "I'm OK—You're OK" feeling is fundamental to good communication.

8. Positive reinforcement is preferable to negative reinforcement. Compliment and thank the other person when she or he pleases you. When she or he does something that displeases you, try making a positive suggestion for a change ("Could you try doing . . . ") rather than a negative prohibition ("Stop doing that . . . ").

And remember:

Whether the issue is pleasant or hurtful, don't put it off. Communicate about it as soon as possible.

---

responsibility for communicating about the problem to a partner. For example:

Instead of attacking: "You are such a bastard for doing that."

Use an "I" message: "I feel really hurt whenever this happens."

Instead of making assumptions about another's motives: "You deliberately set out to make a fool of me."

Use an "I" message: "I am really angry and embarrassed about how this situation makes me look."

Instead of dwelling on past offenses: "This is another example of the way in which you show no consideration for me. Last week, you. . . ."

Use an "I" message: "I often feel demoralized and frustrated by the way you treat me."

Typically, when couples struggle with an impasse for a while, there comes a point at which they begin to feel that they are really working together, the *shift to mutuality.* Even though the conflict is not fully resolved, there is at least the sense that progress is being made and all is not lost. Women and men may come to this shift to mutuality in different ways. These days, many women are feeling tired of doing what they perceive to be much of the work in male-female relationships. They no longer want to be the emotional caretakers. Therefore, they often need to feel that men have some willingness to work on an impasse. Women are often also looking for new models for their relationships and want to have a better balance between the partners in working at communication.

Men may reach their shift to mutuality in some-

what different ways, one of which involves becoming aware of the relationship as an entity and an experience in itself. Labeling relational experience with names such as "our conflict" or "our misunderstanding" is important for men in understanding this experience in a context of mutuality. It is also important for men to learn about the differences in how relationships work for them and for women. They have often come to perceive different communication styles as types of conflict rather than simply *differences* in how people respond, and so they often react with defensiveness at first. Finally, it is crucial for men to learn how to empathize with the feelings of others, so that they may begin to understand the feelings that are being experienced (Bergman & Surrey, 1992).

The communication strategies discussed in this chapter may assist in resolving many conflicts. A fundamental principle is to be assertive, stating clearly and in a personalized way how *you* feel. This is in contrast to aggressive behavior, in which you attack, blame, and accuse others, making assumptions and judgments about their motives. Some useful suggestions for improving communication are given in Table 8.1.

Loving Relationships and Sexuality

When they enter into a loving relationship, couples want that relationship to last. Researcher John Gottman (1994, 1999) of the Family Research Laboratory at the University of Washington is one of the first scientists to study systematically the qualities that might make or break relationships. In his laboratories, psychologists conduct extensive interviews with couples and take an array of physiological measurements. They have developed an emotion-identification coding system that has helped them analyze masses of data about relationships. Although their conclusions have been largely limited to heterosexual marriages, their findings may well hold worthwhile advice for all couples of any gender who want to maintain their loving relationships. Here are some of the main findings:

1. *Couples who have more positive moments than negative moments have a better chance of lasting together.* In fact, the ratio of positive behaviors needed to offset negative behaviors with some weight in order to create a strong bond is about five to one.
2. *Volatile relationships, with heated arguments and passionate reconciliations, can be very lasting.* It seems that such relationships may be as happy as those that are more reserved, so long as conflicts really get resolved.
3. *Emotionally inexpressive relationships can be very successful,* if the five-to-one ratio of positive and negative things they do share with one another is maintained.
4. *Confronting complaints and differences early in the relationship seems to help.* Avoiding tensions and fights early on leads to a greater likelihood of trouble later. Expressing anger openly seems also to be a continuing factor in keeping relationships vital.
5. *In happy relationships, there is no discernible difference between how women and men express themselves emotionally.* Men may even be more likely to reveal intimate information about themselves in a happy relationship.
6. *Positive feelings about the beginning of the relationship are correlated with a higher likelihood of remaining together.* When partners have warm memories about the unfolding of their relationship, psychologists have been able to predict with great accuracy the likelihood that the couple will still be together in 3 years.

Have you ever experienced a communication problem with someone of the other sex based on what might be considered typical communication differences between men and women? Describe this personal experience.

Building any worthwhile relationship takes effort and commitment. When sexual sharing is part of the relationship, it becomes that much more sensitive and complicated. To share sex is to share a deep level of intimacy and the strong feelings that usually accompany such intimacy. Although sex may be important in many relationships, the closeness of another person who is willing to listen, understand, and talk is often just as significant (Atkisson, 1994; DeVillers, 1997). Positive sexual relationships do not just fall into place from one encounter in bed; they evolve from a deliberate process of communicating together and working to be responsive to one another.

The "Other" Risks of Sex

There have always been highly publicized risks of indiscriminate sexual activity, such as unplanned pregnancy, sexually transmitted disease, or, more recently, HIV and AIDS. However, there are other risks of sex too—risks that are associated with the relational aspects of human interaction. Here are some examples:

Risk: Modeling Your Sexuality Only after External Standards Rather than Your Own

Each of us must find ways of bringing our own unique blend of sexual needs, orientations, fantasies, attractions, and behaviors into some sort of balance and harmony with our society, which is always circumscribed by its cultural, political, and historical boundaries. Not to achieve that harmony is to be alienated from ourselves, perhaps playing some sexual role that is inconsistent with the core of our being. That can create a remarkable degree of personal pain and confusion.

Risk: Confusing Romantic Attachments and Sexual Attractions

Many people find it difficult to distinguish between romantic attachment and sexual attraction. There may be a tendency to rush toward saying "I love you" in order to justify sex. Or sexual interaction may mistakenly be construed as evidence of love (Hillier, Harrison, & Bowditch, 1999). In many cultures other than our own, especially in Eastern countries, there has been far less confusion over these matters. There, love is not allowed to become an excuse for sex. Sexual passion and infatuation are not considered legitimate bases from which to embark on major life adventures such as marriage.

Risk: Not Allowing Yourself to Be Vulnerable Enough to Accept the Risks Inherent in Loving Relationships

Eventually, every relationship has some pain. Fear of dealing with hurt—in oneself or in a partner—is one of the leading causes of broken relationships. People must be willing to be vulnerable to the fears of being hurt or of hurting someone else. Without vulnerability, relationships and their sexual components eventually become sterile, brittle, and empty. Before we can deal

The Big Picture

What Goes into Sex Appeal?

Studies suggest that male attractiveness hinges on outward signs of maturity, robust health and, above all, dominance. Most of the features associated with feminine beauty signal youthfulness and an abundance of female reproductive hormones.

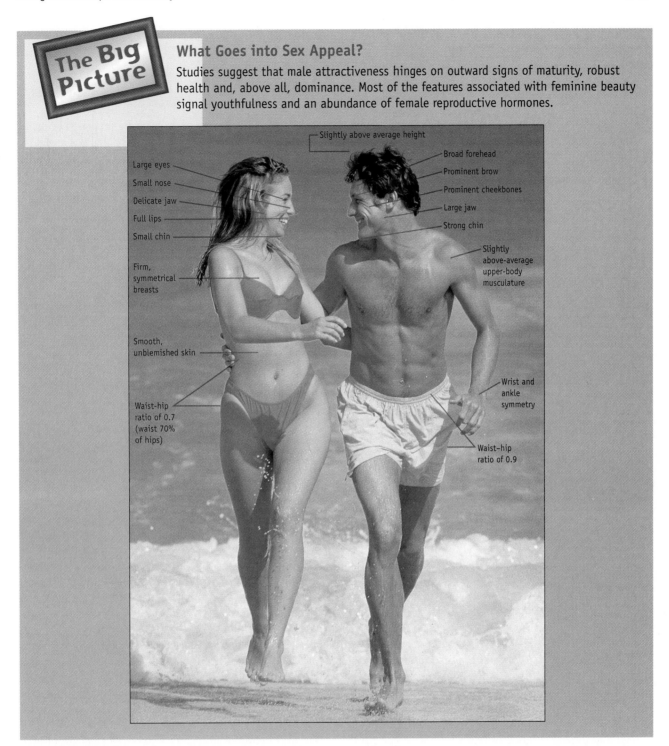

Slightly above average height

Large eyes
Small nose
Delicate jaw
Full lips
Small chin

Firm, symmetrical breasts

Smooth, unblemished skin

Waist-hip ratio of 0.7 (waist 70% of hips)

Broad forehead
Prominent brow
Prominent cheekbones
Large jaw
Strong chin

Slightly above-average upper-body musculature

Wrist and ankle symmetry

Waist-hip ratio of 0.9

with vulnerability in a healthy, positive manner, we must also know and accept ourselves. We have to develop a level of self-esteem and self-confidence that will help us to feel worthwhile and validated as individuals. When we depend too heavily on others to make us feel good, we give up a great deal of personal power in the relationship. This can exaggerate the risks of vulnerability, as well as robbing ourselves of the right to accept ourselves as we are and feel good about who we are.

Risk: Being in a Situation in Which You Feel Bound to Do Something Sexual That Just Does Not Feel Quite Right to You

Our society does not encourage much sense of "ownership" over our genitals until we reach some arbitrary age of passage when we are suddenly expected to become sexually responsible. This results in a good deal of confusion about sexual values and behaviors, and it often leads us to engage in sexual activities out of a

Know Your Partner

Test the strength of your relationship in this relationship quiz prepared especially for *Newsweek* by John Gottman.

1 I can name my partner's best friends. TRUE □ FALSE □

2 I can tell you what stresses my partner is currently facing. TRUE □ FALSE □

3 I know the names of some of the people who have been irritating my partner lately. □ □

4 I can tell you some of my partner's life dreams. □ □

5 I can tell you about my partner's basic philosophy of life. □ □

6 I can list the relatives my partner likes the least. □ □

7 I feel that my partner knows me pretty well. □ □

8 When we are apart, I often think fondly of my partner. TRUE □ FALSE □

9 I often touch or kiss my partner affectionately. □ □

10 My partner really respects me. □ □

11 There is fire and passion in this relationship. □ □

12 Romance is definitely still a part of our relationship. □ □

13 My partner appreciates the things I do in this relationship. □ □

14 My partner generally likes my personality. □ □

15 Our sex life is mostly satisfying. □ □

16 At the end of the day, my partner is glad to see me. TRUE □ FALSE □

17 My partner is one of my best friends. □ □

18 We just love talking to each other. □ □

19 There is lots of give and take (both people have influence) in our discussions. □ □

20 My partner listens respectfully, even when we disagree. □ □

21 My partner is usually a great help as a problem solver. □ □

22 We generally mesh well on basic values and goals in life. □ □

Scoring: Give yourself one point for each "true" answer. Above 12: you have a lot of strength in your relationship. Congratulations. Below 12: your relationship could stand some improvement and could probably benefit from some work on the basics, such as improving communication.

sense of obligation rather than a conviction that they are right for us. We need to be open to our sexuality so that we can think and plan ahead. We never have to be at the mercy of whims or urges, whether our own or those of others. It takes introspection, time, and even some experimentation to know where we stand with sexual values and what we want for our lives sexually.

What Is Love?

Love, intimacy, and sex seem to be parts of a singular, confusing package that writers, poets, priests, and scientists have been trying to understand and explain for centuries. Love is a quality and an experience that until recently has seemed more comfortable in the hands of artists than in the hands of scientists, but there is evidence that the experience of passionate love is found in all cultures (Jankowiak, 1995).

Studies on romantic love and sexual desire worldwide have shown three global transformations that seem to be occurring, all of which are affecting loving relationships. There is an increasing belief in the equality of genders and ethnic groups that is eroding long-standing double standards and prejudices, thus freeing people to love without as many social constrictions. The pursuit of happiness has been becoming a more acceptable and worthwhile goal, leading to a more positive view of passionate love and sexual desire. And there is a growing belief that life can be

changed for the better, with the pleasures of love and sex being seen as a legitimate part of life improvement (Hatfield & Rapson, 1996). Love and sex seem to be primary ingredients that bring people together in intimate relationships. Every loving partnership also has its own unique history and configuration. Each relationship has its own identity, just as do the two individuals who make it up (Love & Robinson, 1994).

Love represents a challenge to go beyond the single-minded pursuit of personal gratification and to break down some of the habitual patterns of behavior that have been a part of being nonpartnered. It has been said that love and relationship have a transformative power; they bring two people together who then have to sort through the many complications of being together. We live in a mobile, more disconnected culture and in a time in history when the rules about love and relating are sometimes vague and confusing. In many ways, love is an ideal toward which people strive, often with some level of internal conflict (Levine, 1995a). The external pressures and reasons for people to come together and form a partnership are far less convincing than they once were. Now it is internal reactions and the intrinsic qualities of two individuals' personal connection that will keep a relationship going (Hatfield & Rapson, 1996). It has been suggested that creating and sustaining a relationship constitute a whole new frontier in the human journey. Whenever we enter into a loving connection with another person, it is largely unexplored territory, with all sorts of new things to discover—within ourselves and within the dynamics of what we are sharing as a couple (Andrews, 1991).

Theories of Love

Love is not something that just happens; it is something to be practiced, perfected, and worked at with the foundation of one's cultural imperatives and belief systems. Some close relationships begin with a process of "falling in love" or *infatuation*. This kind of loving involves an intense desire to be close to another person, and strong emotions may surface as well as intense sexual attraction (see Fig. 8.5). Infatuation can be exciting and exhilarating, but it can have its difficult side because such strong emotions are involved, and it may be particularly painful when the other person is unable to feel mutually attracted and loving. On the other hand, when two people fall in love, they typically want to spend a great deal of time together, gradually let down their usual barriers, and become more and more vulnerable to one another. Their sense of shared intimacy deepens, and they may eventually progress to sexual sharing. Often there is a sense of never wanting things to change, never wanting to be apart. It is typical at this point for partners to make promises to each other such as "I'll always love you," or "I'll never leave you," or "I'll never hurt you" (Levine, 1996).

However, the process of falling in love must always come to an end. It is often at this point that relationships end too, largely because people in our society have been led to believe that infatuation is the only kind of loving worth having. This intense phase may also evolve into the more stable and deeply committed stage of *being* in love. This involves a conscious choice on the part of both partners to be together. They care about one another and trust each other enough to commit themselves to working at the relationship. They recognize that their love is more than just a passionate emotion. They see it as a process of communicating, negotiating, compromising when differences get in the way, and agreeing to struggle through the more difficult times together. Being in love also means that two people are struggling to accept and love each other, even in the face of their individual differences and idiosyncrasies. They may eventually find ways of celebrating their mutual differences instead of finding them to be obstacles.

Concepts of love based on research have gradually taken shape. Some scientists insist that love is not so much a built-in tendency as it is a socialized response, whereas others believe it to be a basic human emotion. Comparisons of ethnographic data have shown a good deal of similarity among cross-cultural views of love, sex, and intimacy, and yet they have

FIGURE 8.5 *Infatuation*

Infatuation, the process of falling in love, is emotionally and physically exhilarating but must inevitably end. A couple may decide either to end the relationship or to commit more fully to each other.

also suggested that individual differences may well be more powerful than cultural influences in shaping particular people's attitudes and behaviors that constitute their styles of loving (Frey & Hojjat, 1998; Hatfield & Rapson, 1996). This has been supported by research in behavioral genetics. Although human behavioral traits such as shyness often seem to be at least partially genetically determined, no such connection has been found in styles of loving. They seem more likely to be determined by life experiences than by genes.

One of the most widely researched typologies of love identified six attitudes toward loving that were labeled with Greek terms (Hendrick & Hendrick, 1986). *Eros* is a style of loving characterized by passion, commitment, and physical attraction ("My lover and I were meant for each other"). *Ludus* is a much less committed style, in which love is treated more as a game to be played with numerous partners ("I love the game of love with as many as possible"). The *mania* style of loving is characterized by obsessiveness, possessiveness, and jealousy ("I feel terrible when my lover does not pay attention to me"). *Pragma* is a very practical style of loving in which a lover is chosen by following a carefully established set of criteria ("I will choose a lover carefully, so that we will have the best possible chance for success").

Agape is an altruistic loving style, in which the needs of the lover are put before one's own needs ("I would rather suffer than see my lover suffer"). *Storge* is a style of loving based on strong and enduring friendship ("My lover is my best friend"). Further research with this model has found that eros and agape are associated with higher levels of satisfaction in loving relationships, whereas ludic attitudes lead toward more dissatisfaction, short-term relationships, and less intimate engagement with partners (Frey & Hojjat, 1998). As might be expected, mania does not make for very satisfactory relationships, and pragmatic approaches are associated with long-lasting relationships.

Sternberg's Triangular Theory of Love

Yale researcher Robert Sternberg (1986) studied the dynamics of loving relationships for several years and developed an interesting model that accounts for three distinct components of love. These components may be viewed as the three sides of a triangle, with the area of the triangle representing the amount and style of loving.

1. *Intimacy* is the emotional component and involves closeness, mutual support, and sharing. In relationships, intimacy tends to increase gradually but steadily at first, naturally leveling off as two persons become more comfortably knowledgeable about each other. In well-established, healthy relationships, intimacy may not even be particularly noticeable on the surface, but it will quickly become evident during some crisis that the couple must face together (see Fig. 8.6).
2. *Passion* provides a motivational component to love. It is manifested in a desire to be united with the loved one, leading to sexual arousal and sharing. It is the aspect of some loving that tends to increase most rapidly at first. Sternberg has likened passion to an addictive substance because people are so drawn to its stimulation and pleasure. If one person abruptly ends the relationship, suddenly withdrawing the outlet for passion, the other person may have to suffer all of the depression, irritability, and emotional pain of the withdrawal process. In time, even in a lasting relationship, passion levels off, simply not providing the stimulation and arousal it did at first. That does not mean that passion necessarily becomes unimportant or lacking. It simply loses some of its importance as a motivating force in the relationship (see Fig. 8.6).
3. *Commitment* represents the cognitive side of love, in both its short- and long-term senses. The devel-

opment of commitment in a relationship is easy to understand, as Figure 8.6 demonstrates. When you first meet another person, there is no particular commitment to a loving process. As you get to know each other better, however, the commitment begins to grow and develop. As with all other components of love, commitment eventually levels off, and if the relationship fails, it will then decline even further.

Sternberg's research has also shown that the best predictor of happiness in a loving relationship is the degree of similarity between how an individual wants the other person to feel about him or her and how the individual thinks the partner actually feels. If one person believes that the other does not feel enough love, there can be disappointment and conflict.

The Brain Chemistry of Love

Everyone recognizes that love is one of the more complex human emotions and that it cannot be adequately explained by any single research model. It has been suggested that love has powerful disease-prevention and healing influences within the body (Cowley & Underwood, 1998). Researchers are just beginning to piece together the even greater puzzle of biochemicals in the brain that are associated with human loving emotions. From this perspective, the process of loving is thought to be founded on a complex process of *imprinting* that results from the interaction of genetics, hormonal influences, and psychological experiences during our early lives (Crenshaw, 1996). This results in a built-in, subliminal guide to the characteristics of potential partners to whom we are likely to be attracted. This inner set of guidelines has been called a lovemap (Money, 1989).

Various chemical stimuli may activate a romantic reaction toward others. There is increasing evidence that the scents of chemical sex attractants or **pheromones** may play an influential role in this process (Cutler, 1999). A chemical called androstenol is found in male sweat, and its dry musky smell is appealing to women. When it oxidizes to form androstenone, women tend to react more negatively to its odor *unless they are ovulating*. Copulines are chemicals found in women's vaginal secretions, and controlled experiments in which males inhaled these substances found that the exposure tended to upgrade men's attractions to women and assessments of their beauty. In this study as well, men were even more positively affected by the copulines from ovulating

pheromones (FAIR-oh-moans): human chemicals, the scent of which may cause an attraction or behavioral change in other individuals.

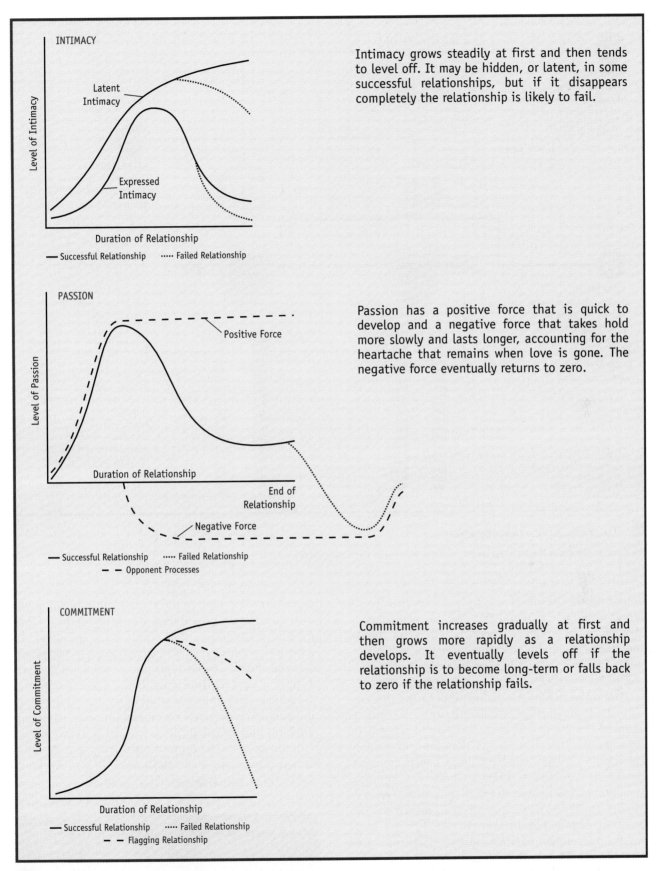

Intimacy grows steadily at first and then tends to level off. It may be hidden, or latent, in some successful relationships, but if it disappears completely the relationship is likely to fail.

Passion has a positive force that is quick to develop and a negative force that takes hold more slowly and lasts longer, accounting for the heartache that remains when love is gone. The negative force eventually returns to zero.

Commitment increases gradually at first and then grows more rapidly as a relationship develops. It eventually levels off if the relationship is to become long-term or falls back to zero if the relationship fails.

FIGURE 8.6 *Sternberg's Triangular Theory of Love*

Yale researcher Robert Sternberg has developed one model for the complicated emotion of love. In the model, he describes intimacy, passion, and commitment as love's basic components.

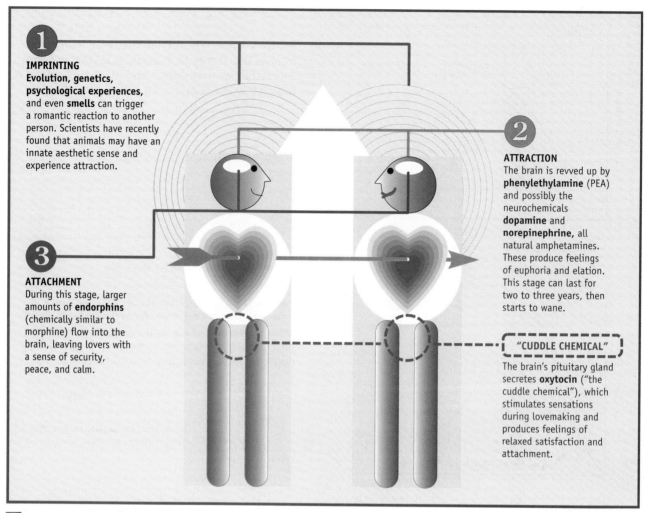

1

IMPRINTING
Evolution, genetics,
psychological experiences,
and even **smells** can trigger
a romantic reaction to another
person. Scientists have recently
found that animals may have an
innate aesthetic sense and
experience attraction.

2

ATTRACTION
The brain is revved up by
phenylethylamine (PEA)
and possibly the
neurochemicals
dopamine and
norepinephrine, all
natural amphetamines.
These produce feelings
of euphoria and elation.
This stage can last for
two to three years, then
starts to wane.

3

ATTACHMENT
During this stage, larger
amounts of **endorphins**
(chemically similar to
morphine) flow into the
brain, leaving lovers with
a sense of security,
peace, and calm.

"CUDDLE CHEMICAL"

The brain's pituitary gland
secretes **oxytocin** ("the
cuddle chemical"), which
stimulates sensations
during lovemaking and
produces feelings of
relaxed satisfaction and
attachment.

FIGURE 8.7   *The Chemistry of Love*
The various stages of loving correspond with chemical changes in the brain.

women, with a resultant rise in levels of their testosterone levels (Grammer, 1996). We are beginning to
have empirical evidence about the effects of human
pheromones, with one study demonstrating that pheromones increased the tendency of males to have shared
sexual activity (Cutler, Friedmann, & McCoy, 1998).

During *attraction,* or the phase of loving that cor-
responds to infatuation or falling in love, the brain is
stimulated by phenylethylamine (PEA) and possibly by
dopamine and norepinephrine. These are close chemical relatives to the stimulant drugs called amphetamines, and they tend to produce elation and euphoria.
Attraction makes people feel very swept away and energized. However, there are chemical reasons why infatuation cannot last forever. Eventually, the body
builds up a certain tolerance to these biochemicals, so
that their profound effects begin to wear off. Some
people seem to become "attraction junkies," constantly
craving the intoxicating highs of falling in love. They
therefore must move from one relationship to the next,

as the attraction high in the brain begins to run down
each time (Botting & Botting, 1996).

The relationships that endure beyond attraction
settle into a longer period of *attachment.* In this phase
of loving, being around a loved one stimulates the production of **endorphins** in the brain. These are natural
painkillers that produce a sense of security, tranquility,
and calm. The chemical **oxytocin** is produced during
cuddling and physical intimacy, and it is associated
with the powerful feelings of orgasm and sexual satisfaction (Crenshaw, 1996; McDonald, 1998). The brain
chemistry of love is illustrated in Figure 8.7.

endorphins (en-DORE-fins): brain secretions that act as
natural tranquilizers and pain relievers.

oxytocin (ox-ee-TOH-sin): a chemical produced by the
brain in response to physical intimacy and sexual satisfaction.

Establishing Sensual and Sexual Intimacy

We hear a great deal about intimacy in relationships, and the term seems to mean different things to different people. Intimacy usually describes a special kind of closeness between people, a deep connection that feels more special than the superficial interactions that tend to dominate our lives (see Fig. 8.8). But how do people go about building the kind of intimacy that they seem to crave at some deeper level within themselves?

1. *Touching* can establish a crucial foundation for intimacy. Skin sensitivity is apparently the first of the senses to develop in fetal life. We feel with the nerve endings of our skin before we make use of any other sense organs. The sensations of touch then remain at the forefront of our conscious experience. Sensual touching is gratifying to the senses but does not necessarily lead to sexual interaction. Only too often, people's sensual needs are ignored or starved. The need to be touched in caring, loving ways—to be taken care

of through touching—is an important one for both women and men. Only too often, if such touching leads to sexual arousal, the sensual aspects are hurried along so that genital sexual activity may be initiated (Love & Robinson, 1994). Like being in love, touching is an art, to be developed, worked at, and perfected through time and practice (DeVillers, 1997).

2. *Relaxation* is another important factor in intimacy. People need to be able to feel relaxed together in order to be open to one another. Physiologically, the term "relaxation" refers to a relatively low level of tension in the muscles. Although it is possible to use relaxation techniques and other stress-control methods to reduce tension, psychological factors are often an important part of the picture. Anxiety, depression, anger, hostility, or even subtle disagreements between people can create tension. Even subtle tension may block intimacy and interfere with sexual enjoyment. Although sexual arousal involves a buildup of body tensions, it paradoxically is most effective within the context of a relaxed atmosphere between the partners. The more people have to work at sex, the more tension may destroy the sense of intimacy (Louden, 1994).

3. *Being a participant* in a relationship is necessary to intimacy. Only too often, people allow themselves to become spectators, in a sense standing outside themselves and watching what is going on. Or they may escape into the withdrawal of daydreams and inattention. It is far better to be fully in touch with one's own inner reactions and with one's partner at the moment (Levine, 1996). To be preoccupied only with future goals, or how sex is going to go, is a distraction from experiencing and dealing with how things are actually going *right now*. That is what participating in an intimate relationship is all about—being fully aware of what is going on and taking responsibility to communicate or act as necessary.

Confusion about Love and Sex in Relationships

Issues of love and sex have become blurred in our culture. In fact, romantic love is a fairly recent development historically, and a century ago it was not necessarily associated with sexual feelings. Love was meant to be a pure feeling, expressed through the idealization of the loved one. In the modern period, romantic love has been associated with sex (S. Seidman, 1992), but this change in attitude has not occurred without confusion. One of the complications of this perspective is that we have come to expect the intense feelings of love and the passion of sex to

FIGURE 8.8 *Intimacy*

Developing intimacy in a relationship involves touching in a caring, loving manner, learning to reduce tension by physically and psychologically relaxing, and being fully aware of the need to communicate.

be a continuing part of lasting relationships such as marriage, when in fact these emotions change with time. Individuals sometimes use sex to hold on to their partners, or they pretend that having sex must mean that you are in love (Hillier, Harrison, & Bowditch, 1999).

People may assume that if they have chosen a partner well, the love and the relationship should last forever, and the love will never change. In fact, loving feelings and levels of interest in sex change over time. The important thing is how well the couple keeps up with the process of change (Levine, 1996; Love & Robinson, 1994). It is also assumed that when people love each other, sex will just happen. However, most couples have busy lives; as they spend time together, their priorities may change. Sometimes, they will have to create the opportunity for sex to happen but without making it seem too contrived (Louden, 1994).

Love may be abused in relationships as well. It may be used as a justification for controlling others: "I only did it because I love you." Or it may be cited as the reason for some imperative being imposed on a partner: "If you really loved me, you would ___." The blank in this imperative could be completed in any number of ways, including:

. . . want sex as often as I do

. . . have eyes for no one else but me

. . . trust me without question

. . . have sex with me now

. . . know how to turn me on

. . . never hurt me

Such imperatives can place the receiver in a situation sometimes called the "double bind." In other words, you are "damned if you do and damned if you don't." The sender of the message has created a no-win situation in which if you resist the entreaty, you are only demonstrating your lack of caring. On the other hand, if you follow through as dictated by the imperative, you may be accused of only trying to please the person but not really meaning it (DeVillers, 1997).

Have you ever been "head over heels" in love with someone? Describe the experience.

The confusions over love and sex are best resolved through effective communication methods, based on a real commitment to work together on having a dynamic and caring relationship. In many relationships, partners care as much about their partners' sexual satisfaction as they do about their own. In one study, over half of the men surveyed and one-third of the women stated that their partners' pleasure in sex was more important than their own (Janus & Janus, 1993).

Same-Gender Intimate Relationships

In conceptualizing same-gender intimate relationships, it has been typical to single out shared sexual activity between the partners as the primary distinguishing factor. However, there are nonsexual loving relationships between members of the same sex, too. There are also situations in which two individuals of the same gender share a lengthy sexual affair but do not consider themselves to be lesbian or gay. They simply have chosen to have sex with this one particular partner. Therefore, in examining some relationships, we must also take into consideration how the partners identify themselves (Heaphy, Weeks, & Donovan, 1998; Kurdek, 1995).

Theorists have suggested that same-sexed partners are sometimes attracted to one another because of differences other than gender. Many lesbian couples seem to form a bond because one woman is exclusively attracted to women and the other has had a more bisexual orientation (Burch, 1993). Several studies have pointed to the possibility that males are drawn into romantic attachments because of their long-standing sense of being different from other males as they are growing up. The hypothesis suggests that this leads them to an interest in forming a relationship with other males as a way of achieving a sense of self-completion and mergence (Johnston & Bell, 1995). There is often an element of competition in male-male relationships that can interfere with intimacy (George, 1997).

In the nineteenth century, romantic friendships were apparently common among upper-middle-class women, who were often single, childless, and career-oriented. They would sometimes live together, although the scarce evidence available would suggest that their relationships, sometimes called "Boston marriages," may not have included genital sexual activity. Around the turn of the century in America, some women dressed as men, adopted male names, and "passed" for men. Sometimes they established marriagelike relationships with other women. Women in this time and culture had fewer life options than men did, and it may be that these relationships represented ways of escaping from the limited social roles available to them (Nichols, 1990).

There are three primary patterns of intimate relationships that develop between gay men and between lesbians. One pattern employs the heterosexual model for dating and marriage as the prototype for determining roles within the relationship, with one partner adopting more of the traditional masculine functions and the other adopting more of the feminine roles. Another common pattern involves a marked age difference between the partners, with an older individual paired with a younger person of the same gender. A third pattern seems to be modeled after friendships,

Love Rules Redux?

Authors Ellen Fein and Sherrie Schneider are the first to admit that their controversial best-seller *The Rules: Time-Tested Secrets for Capturing the Heart of Mr. Right* would seem "to send women back 25 years." So we went back a bit farther. Using the list of sources below, guess the origins of the words of romantic wisdom that follow.

A. *The Rules* (1995)
B. *Amy Vanderbilt's Everyday Etiquette* (New Revised Edition, 1967)
C. *Emily Post's Etiquette* (revised by Elizabeth L. Post, 1965)
D. *Eleanor Roosevelt's Book of Common Sense Etiquette* (1962)
E. *The Girl That You Marry*, by Dr. James H.S. Bossard and Dr. Eleanor Stoker Boll (1960)

1. "The male is supposed to be the overt pursuer. The 'nice girl' is supposed to find some way in which to make the boys want to pursue. . . ."
2. "Men are different from women. Women who call men, ask them out, . . . or offer sex on the first date destroy male ambition and animal drive."
3. "A woman would like to have at least four or five days ahead for an invitation to an informal evening on a weekend, two or three days ahead for a weekday date, and a week or two ahead for a formal dance or dinner or a house party."
4. "Don't accept a Saturday-night date after Wednesday."
5. "If you don't get jewelry or some other romantic gift on your birthday or other significant occasion, you might as well call it quits. . . . "
6. "Convention decrees that he may give her flowers, books, knickknacks for her room, candy, and similar things, but not wearing apparel—especially not lingerie, stockings, or jewelry."
7. "It is the man's responsibility to plan and pay for everything they do that evening. . . ."
8. "It's just chivalrous . . . for men to pick up their dates and pick up the checks."
9. "The girl [indicates when to leave]. She places her napkin unfolded at the left of her plate, looks questioningly at her escort, and then prepares to rise."
10. "[Women should] always end the date first. . . . A good way to end the date is to nonchalantly glance at your watch and say something like, '. . . I have such a busy day tomorrow.'"

ANSWERS: 1. E, 2. A, 3. C, 4. A, 5. A, 6. D, 7. C, 8. A, 9. B, 10. A

with emphasis on sharing and equality between partners who are similar in age and social status (Kurdek, 1995). One survey of 95 gay, 61 lesbian, and 145 heterosexual couples found that the lesbian partners were more likely to share household tasks. Gay male partners and married heterosexual partners were more likely to have a division of labor in which one partner did more household work than the other (usually the woman of a heterosexual couple).

Friendship and Sexuality

Many people would say they love their friends, but they would not be referring to a romantic or sexual attachment. Studies on friendship show that, in general, people tend to prefer friendships with members of their own sex and that individuals who have close friendships tend to be less anxious and depressed than those who do not.

Friendships can sometimes become confusing sexually. Single men and women are far more likely than married people to have friends of the other gender. For people who are part of a committed relationship, it may be threatening to know that a partner has a close friendship with someone else. There may be a fear that the friendship will lead to deeper intimacy or sexual sharing. Therefore, friendships outside the primary relationship are often considered acceptable only to a point that clearly distinguishes them as auxiliary and secondary to that primary relationship.

Close, intimate friendships are a domain where there seem to be few clear social rules. The sexual aspect of friendships may well exist and have to be sorted out. To deny sexual attraction within the relationship may prove unhealthy and unproductive to open communication. Another largely unexplored territory is the friendship that does include sex. An obvious risk here is that one partner's expectations and emotions will shift, and more will be wanted than what is being called friendship. It is sometimes difficult to make clear distinctions between friendship and love. It may be that "friendship" is simply a safer word that allows couples to remain comfortable with a relationship that has actually become loving, but the term "love" will represent more of a dilemma for their lives (Ellin, 1994).

Relating via the Internet

Our ability to communicate through computer terminals over the Internet has created an entirely new virtual community in which people interact. People are falling in love and sharing online sexual activity through this medium. Computer-mediated communication (CMC) and computer-mediated relating (CMR) have been feared as enemies to human intimacy, and yet some studies are indicating that they often lead to very positive interpersonal relationships (Cooper & Sportolari, 1997; Plaut, 1997).

There are various forms of "chat" modes and rooms that can bring people together either in delayed communication modes or in real-time communications over the Internet. Typically, one is drawn to these sites by some indication of common interest with others at the site. Sometimes these expressions of interest may be romantic or overtly sexual. The motivations behind seeking out this contact generally seem to fit into five basic categories: anonymity, time constraints that interfere with the pursuit of fact-to-face (FTF) relationships, the desire to share sexual fantasies, the opportunity to share online sexual behavior (often accompanied by masturbation), and the hope of eventually meeting the person with whom one has developed a meaningful connection (Wysocki, 1998).

Some interesting findings are beginning to emerge about romantic relationships in cyberspace that explain how CMR may actually enhance FTF relationships rather than completely replacing them. We know, for example, that attraction is fostered through the proximity and familiarity that two people share. Electronic communication can actually create greater feelings of closeness and familiarity because of the frequency of contact that is possible. Because of the vast network available, it is also more likely that people will find others who share similar characteristics and attitudes. CMC surely provides opportunities for self-disclosure and interpersonal intimacy relatively quickly because of the degree of anonymity present at the beginning of the relationship. Finally, the significance of the erotic connection that can develop between people through the Internet should not be underestimated. All of these characteristics have the potential for moving relationships into intimate territory quite rapidly (Cooper & Sportolari, 1997; Schnarch, 1997).

This is not to say that CMR does not have its share of risks. There are certainly frightening tales of how cyberrelationships have ended in harassment, abuse, or violence. One of the risks of online relating lies in its advantages: the tendency for the relationship to develop very rapidly into an intimate connection. The intensity can also mean that the relationship becomes quickly eroticized but then cannot be sustained be-

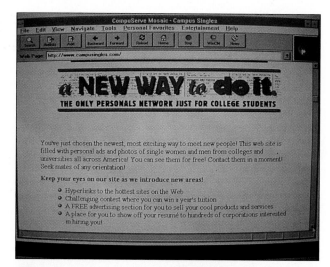

FIGURE 8.9   *Computer-Mediated Relating*

The Internet has opened entirely new ways of establishing relationships, with both positive and negative consequences. Only time will tell how successful such relating may be. Cyberspace yields anonymity that may embolden some, while making others more vulnerable.

cause there is not sufficient underlying trust and knowledge to support it. If an individual is having an online relationship at the same time as a FTF relationship, the same stresses and strains can develop whenever the boundaries of relationships are crossed (Wysocki, 1998).

All in all, romance and sex via the Internet is a developing phenomenon that will require further careful study (see Figure 8.9). The pervasive impression created by the media is that the Net promotes superficial, destructive relationships, but the realities are far more complex, and positive, than this. The virtual community into which the Internet can lead us is simply a new and evolving kind of community that must develop clearer ethical guidelines for its users. Like any human community, it will have its share of untrustworthy, abusive, and even dangerous individuals. It will also have many people who are genuinely interested in good relationships, founded on courtesy, honesty, integrity, and respect (Cooper & Sportolari, 1997; Plaut, 1997).

Attachment Theory: Jealousy and Possessiveness

When we become highly attached to something—whether it be a material object we have paid dearly to own or another person whom we dearly love—there is often a growing fear that we could end up losing what we long to possess. Attachment theory has clari-

© 1993 by Andrew Lehman
He loved her more than words could say. She left him because he didn't talk.

fied three main styles of emotional bonding with another person. The *secure* attachment style is characterized by increased self-confidence and self-esteem and a growing sense of satisfaction with the loving relationship. Those who show a *preoccupied* style of attachment are anxious and ambivalent about their relationships and tend to have a negative view of themselves and a positive view of their partners. They are quite dependent on their partners for nurturance. Other people fall into *avoidant* patterns of attachment, meaning that at some level they are managing to hold themselves back from effective emotional attachment with the partner. This may well represent a way of avoiding the vulnerability that could eventually open the individual to hurt. There are two subsets of the avoidant style. Some people are *dismissing avoidant*. They view themselves more positively and as more worthwhile than the partner, tending to ignore and diminish their partners. *Fearful avoidant* people hold negative views of both themselves and their partners and seem fearful of intimacy. They often worry that their partners do not care about them as much as they care about their partners (Shaver & Hazen, 1993; Stephan & Bachman, 1999).

Loving relationships can have elements of territoriality and fear. We want the object of our affection to love us in return and, frequently, to love only us. We fear rejection by that person and especially fear the loss of his or her love to someone else. If there is some inkling, even an imagined one, that a partner's interests might be straying, it is quite natural to feel jealous. A reasonable amount of jealousy can be expected in any relationship. It is one of those issues about which couples need to communicate openly. It is important to remember that even those individuals who are happy and comfortable in a loving and sexual relationship will still occasionally find themselves attracted to others. This does not have to threaten the relationship, nor does it signal that there is some sort of difficulty between the partners (Buss et al., 1999; Simpson et al., 1999).

Sometimes, jealousy gets out of control and becomes possessiveness. This is particularly common in people who have a preoccupied style of attachment. Such an individual seems always worried about losing the other and may even imagine that there is something more going on in other relationships. There may be an unreasonable degree of anger over the partner's casual and innocent social interactions. Such possessiveness can have many roots. Feelings of inferiority often play a role and may be accompanied by some basic insecurity and immaturity in the individual (Pistole, 1995; Stephan, 1999). Some people who become overly possessive expect complete and utter devotion from a partner and have difficulty seeing that individuals always need room for personal growth, even within a committed relationship. Possessiveness usually signals some fundamental insecurities in the person's personality that may well deserve some attention. Professional counseling can be a viable option for consideration (Wiederman & Hurd, 1999).

It is also often true that overly jealous people are not willing to take much responsibility for changing their behavior. They may even assume that their obsession with their partner is perfectly justified. There are several ways for dealing with a situation in which your partner is being unreasonably jealous (Forward & Buck, 1992; Shaver & Hazen, 1993):

1. *Do not fall into the trap of trying to answer unreasonable questions.* A jealous lover may be convinced of your unfaithfulness and grill you with questions. As rules for good communication suggest, focus on how the questions are making you feel and stick with the truth.

2. *Encourage your partner to work on the jealousy with you.* You may want to suggest seeking out a counselor together. In any case, act with assertiveness. Do not simply give in to keep the peace for the time being. The jealousy may be signs of trouble in the relationship that should not be ignored.

3. *Do not be ruled by pity for the other person.* Even if you feel that you understand the unfortunate reasons why your partner is so desperately jealous, do not feel that he or she should justify unfair accusations or suspicions. It is your partner's responsibility to find a way to work on her or his problems. When you hear threats of suicide or violence, you are being subjected to the most extreme forms of relational coercion and manipulation. They represent serious problems for which you should seek professional advice.

4. *Take a close look at whether this is a relationship that is healthy for you.* If the jealousy and possessiveness begin to seem hopeless, it may simply be that you will be unable to find much relaxed fulfillment in the relationship. Even if you love the other person, it may be important to sort through whether it is wise to remain in the relationship. Again, talking the situation over with a trained counselor can represent a significant step toward maintaining your own psychological balance.

Dealing with the Loss of a Loving Relationship

FOH As you look around at loving relationships, it is clear that many of them ultimately fail. Does that mean that people are picking out the wrong partners for loving? Not necessarily. Relationships typically begin with attention being given to what matters to the partners in the short run. Like all things, people and their relationships change. The long-range issues may be quite different. Therefore, as relationships grow, it becomes increasingly important for partners to be willing to change in their response patterns toward one another. What first seemed to be a charming idiosyncrasy may in time become a grating nuisance. What once was sexual turn-on may become boring and humdrum. Couples must be open to these changing patterns in relationships and learn how to tolerate the changes (Cutter, 1994).

Have you ever had to recover from a broken heart? Describe the process. What suggestions might you offer to others going through a similar experience?

With time and change, it may also become evident that there are too many differences between two people to allow for a comfortable and fulfilling loving relationship and that it no longer makes sense for them to remain together. The uncoupling process is almost always a painful one, but it may also represent a viable choice for a failing relationship in which one or both of the partners lacks the desire and motivation to move to a new level of commitment (Gottman, 1999).

The bottom line here is that love holds no guarantees. No matter how much lovers promise to be true to each other forever, there really are no guarantees against the possibility of one or both eventually choosing to end the relationship. Loving leaves one vulnerable, so to choose to enter a loving relationship is to choose the risk of being hurt. This is one reason why knowing, understanding, and feeling good about oneself can be so crucial before entering a relationship.

The initial reactions that follow the breakup of a relationship may be quite varied. If the final days of the relationship have been troubled and full of turmoil, there may even be a sense of relief. There are often intense feelings of loneliness and grief, accompanied by the sense of having been rejected or by guilt at having initiated the breakup. Anger is also a common emotional reaction and can represent a very healthy response. If anger is expressed in ways that are not harmful, it is prevented from turning inward, where it can become depression and self-deprecation. Crying may also be a healthy release of emotion. Studies with college students have found that those whose attachment style has been secure experience a less negative grief experience than those who have preoccupied or fearful avoidant styles. This may well reflect their more positive feelings about themselves and the relationship. Dismissing avoidant types do not have as much difficulty with separation either, probably because they have not held their partners in particularly high esteem (Pistole, 1995).

Some people rush to put the pain of their loss behind them. They may even hurry into a "rebound" relationship to soothe their wounds. However, like any grieving process, the aftermath of a broken relationship must be given its time, and the painful reactions are best resolved by allowing them to be experienced. If you hurry them, or try to escape from them so that the breaking-up process remains incomplete, the reactions will eventually find new outlets in your life (Forward & Buck, 1992). They may make it difficult for you to be trusting and intimate in new relationships that eventually develop for you.

Therefore, recognize that losing a love is as much a part of life and loving as the joyful experience of falling in love. If you allow yourself to have that process fully, and seek whatever help and support you may need to get through it, you will eventually be able to put the painful aspects behind you eventually and get on with your life and new relationships.

Self-Evaluation

Communicating about Sex

One of the most necessary human processes, and yet one of the most complex and difficult, is communication. Many difficulties in relationships—including many sexual problems—are at least partly the result of lack of, or misunderstood, communications.

Thoughts, ideas, feelings, values, attitudes, opinions, needs, and desires are not only communicated verbally but also through eye contact, facial expressions, and body language. The questions and exercises in this section are designed to help you evaluate and facilitate your communication about sex with someone who is important to your life and therefore worth the effort. You may find some of the suggestions difficult to carry out, but good communication does take work.

Working on Communication: An Exercise for Two

The following exercise can help you and your partner improve your patterns of communication. Start by rating each other, using the rating scale of 1–4 on the following qualities listed below. Write your answers on separate sheets of paper without first discussing the rating scale or qualities with each other.

Rating Scale:
4 = Tops. He/she does a great job of showing this quality to me.
3 = Okay. Most of the time I feel this from him/her.
2 = Fair. I could really stand to have more of this quality from her/him.
1 = Poor. I rarely, if ever, feel this from her/him.

Rating of Your Partner	Qualities in Your Partner
_____	Caring and consideration toward me.
_____	Ability to show warmth and love.
_____	Sensitivity and understanding toward my emotions.
_____	Lets me feel whatever I need to feel, without trying to talk me out of it.
_____	Seems to listen and really hear what I mean.
_____	Acts real and honest with me so that I can feel that he/she is being genuine.
_____	Treats me as an equal.
_____	Does not jump to conclusions or make snap judgments about me or others.
_____	Treats me with respect.
_____	Is trustworthy.
_____	Seems to trust me and shares inner feelings and thoughts with me.

When you have both finished your ratings, exchange them so that you each may take a look at how you were rated by the other. However, you both should agree to the following:

1. **Do not talk about your reactions to the ratings for 15 minutes, during which time you should:**
   a. Think about why your partner might have rated you as he or she did. Assume that the ratings represent honest reactions.
   b. Think about which ratings made you feel best and which made you feel worst.
   c. Ask yourself if you were surprised by any of the ratings. Why or why not?
   d. Look beneath any anger you might feel or any need to "defend" yourself against a rating. If you are hurt, be ready to admit it. Keep in mind that your partner had a right to rate you in any manner that seemed honest to her or him. It can lead to a deeper understanding.

2. **When you are ready to start talking together about your mutual ratings:**
   a. You should agree on the most comfortable location.
   b. Share only your own feelings and reactions, being careful not to make assumptions and judgments about your partner's feelings or motivations. Use "I" messages.
   c. After one of you has had a chance to make a point, the other should spend some time summarizing what was heard, so you can be sure that you are hearing each other accurately. Clear up any misunderstandings that your partner has about anything you have said. Give each other time to do this. Now, where do you go from here? If this exercise has shown you ways to improve your ability to communicate, are you ready to work toward this goal? Decide whether or not you think the two of you could work on particular areas.

Working on the Fundamentals

There are certain basic qualities that underscore good communication. Here are some ways to evaluate them:

1. *Lack of manipulation.* In healthy, two-way communication, there is no need for games or manipulations. Before proceeding any further, answer the following questions. Write down your answers.
   a. Why are you working on this section concerning communication?
   b. What are your short-term and long-term goals for improving communication with your partner?
   c. Do you have any ulterior or exploitative motives in pursuing communication about sex? If so, what are they?
   d. Do you really think you can face the vulnerability that comes with honest, two-way communication? Before answering, you may want to look through the

remainder of this section. When you answer in the affirmative, proceed.

2. *A desire to involve your partner in communication.* There is no point in waiting. Communication takes at least two people. Now allow your partner to read this section, and share with him or her your answers to the previous questions. If your partner is willing, have him or her answer those same questions and share the answers with you. If you are both willing, proceed with the remainder of this section. It is designed for use by two people who together want to improve their communication about sex.

3. *Sense of equality.* Both of you should write your own answers to the following questions on separate sheets of paper. Do not compare any answers until both of you are finished answering all questions.
   a. Do you feel there is any difference in the general common sense possessed by you and your partner? If so, which one of you do you think has more of this quality?
   b. Does one of you tend to give in more to the other when there are disagreements? If so, who?
   c. Generally in your relationship, does one of you seem to emerge as the dominant partner and the other as the submissive partner? Which of you is which?
   d. Which one of you tends to initiate sexual contact most often?
   e. Are there any other factors that seem to lead to continuing feelings of inequality between the two of you?

After each of you has written answers to all questions, exchange papers and read them. Make the following agreement: Do not make any comments for 10 minutes. Read one another's answers and silently think about them and how you feel about them.

Both of you should also read the following two paragraphs:

As you are thinking about your partner's responses and comparing them to your own, can you detect that one or both of you see certain inequalities in your common sense, willingness to stick by points of view, degree of dominance, and/or willingness to initiate sex?

Two-way communication seems to work best when there is a sense of equality between both partners. Otherwise, there is the danger of one person feeling inadequate to deal with conflicts and disagreements in communication. With this in mind proceed with part 4.

4. *Working at it.* Your answers to the questions in part 3 can provide some beginning topics for discussion.
   a. If both of you answered questions in such a way that reflects nearly complete equality, perhaps you will want to move on to the next section of this communication questionnaire. If not, try part b.
   b. Go through the answers to your questions one by one, following these rules:

1. State only what you feel or think, without making any judgments or assumptions about what the other person is feeling or thinking or about the other person's accuracy.
2. After one of you has made "I feel . . ." and "I think . . ." statements about the answers to one question, the other person should take time to summarize what has been heard. Then the first partner should clarify any misunderstandings. Do this with each of the questions. If anger or hostility develops, consider the following:
3. If you are feeling angry or resentful, try to pause, look beneath your negative feelings, and see what is at their roots. Perhaps you are really feeling some hurt or sense of threat. Look honestly at what you are feeling and share it with your partner.
4. Persist with this process until you both feel some real sense of resolution about the differences of opinion that have arisen. If you feel stumped by this, you may even want to consider consulting an outside person to talk over some of these issues.
5. When you both feel ready, go on with the remaining parts of this communication exercise.

Sharing Sexual Attitudes and Values

An important part of communication is letting your partner know your personal attitudes and values about sex. The following exercises may help you get started:

1. **Turn back to the sexual attitude questionnaire in chapter 1, "Historical, Research, and Cross-Cultural Perspectives on Sexuality."** If you have not already done so, both of you should complete your ratings on separate sheets of paper for each of the attitude statements. Go through the questionnaire item by item, and compare your present ratings. On those items where you show a difference of opinion, talk about those differences. If either of you begins to feel anger or tension during the discussion, you may want to try using the approaches in exercise 4b. Remember, it is perfectly all right to have different attitudes. The essential thing is to be able to accept these differences in one another. The key to acceptance is full understanding of one another.

2. **Now continue going through the sexual history section of the questionnaire in chapter 1.** Share as many of your answers with your partner as you feel comfortable with. If both of you already feel very well acquainted with one another's backgrounds, you might try going through the questions one at a time, answering for your partner in the ways you feel are most accurate. Your partner can then clear up any inaccuracies or misconceptions you seem to have concerning his or her sexual history. When you are finished with this process, summarize any new understandings that you have gained about your partner.

3. **Here are some other issues that might be worth discussing with one another. You may skip any questions you prefer not to answer. Again, you may either share your answers with one another or try answering each question in the way you think your partner would.**
   a. What is your opinion on abortion? Should it be legal and available to those women who wish to have an abortion? To what degree should the man be allowed to participate in the decision-making process about abortion?
   b. What sexual activities do you like the best? Why?
   c. What are some of your wildest sexual fantasies? How do you feel about them?
   d. How do you feel about your partner's nude body? What parts of his or her body do you like most? least?
   e. Have you ever participated in sexual activity that was in some way risky or that you have regretted? How do you feel about that now?
   f. What precautions do you consider essential in reducing the risk of contracting HIV?

Nonverbal Communication

Very often more can be communicated without words than with them. The following is a list of suggestions for nonverbal communication between you and your partner, each step becoming progressively more intimate. At any step, some verbal communication may be necessary to sort through difficult feelings that may surface. Before proceeding with each new stage of intimacy, there should be complete mutual agreement and willingness between the two of you. Each step should continue until one of you feels ready to stop. Even if you both feel that your relationship has already reached deep levels of intimacy, it would be best to spend at least some time with even the earliest steps of the nonverbal communication process.

Activity 1. In comfortable positions, sit facing one another and look at each other's faces. Spend plenty of time looking into one another's eyes and attempting to express positive feelings to each other. You may feel a little foolish and feel like laughing; go ahead and get it out of your system.

Activity 2. Take turns touching and caressing each other's faces. The person being touched should close his or her eyes and fully enjoy the sensations. The person doing the touching should make an effort to convey warm, caring messages with the touches.

Activity 3. Take turns feeding one another a piece of fruit or some other food.

Chapter Summary

1. Women are more likely than men to have loved their first sexual partners.
2. Communication is a key to healthy sexual relationships.
3. Any communicated message is filtered through the interpretive systems of both the sender and the receiver. There is a strong likelihood of misinterpretation and misunderstanding unless a feedback system is part of the process.
4. People often use slang terms, or no words at all, when making sexual references.
5. Communication can be hindered by the myths people believe and the sexual "games" they have learned to play out in relationships.
6. Effective communication grows out of mutual commitment, shared understanding, mutual regard, avoidance of snap judgments, careful listening, empathy, genuineness, clear expression, viewing oneself positively, and appropriate confrontation.
7. As the Myers-Briggs Type Indicator demonstrates, there are very real personality differences among people that can have important implications for how they get along with one another.

8. Males and females are taught different patterns for communicating as they grow up, and these differences show up in adult communication.
9. There are three main types of relational impasses: dread/anger, product/process, and power-over/power-with.
10. Effective conflict resolution involves approaching it as a couple, clear ownership of the problem, and the use of "I" messages to communicate about it.
11. Research has elucidated some of the main characteristics that are correlated with lasting relationships, with one factor being nice behavior to one another outweighing negative behavior by a five-to-one ratio.
12. Healthy sexual sharing in a relationship involves being comfortable with one's own sexual needs, not confusing romance and sex, knowing how to risk vulnerability, having a clear sense of one's own identity, and avoiding sexual coercion.
13. Cross-cultural studies suggest that love attitudes and behaviors may be more affected by individual differences than by genetics or social imperatives.

14. Infatuation or "falling in love" eventually ends; being in love involves a choice and commitment to the process of being together.

15. Love has recently become a legitimate area for scientific study, and several theories have emerged. One theory has identified six styles of loving: eros, ludus, mania, pragma, agape, and storge.

16. Sternberg's theory holds that love is a dynamic interaction of three components: intimacy, passion, and commitment.

17. Pheromones are chemicals that give off odors that may act as subliminal attractants to potential sexual partners.

18. Brain chemicals are related to the emotional experience of love following initial imprinting in earlier life: PEA, dopamine, and norepinephrine produce the high of attraction; endorphins produce the peacefulness of attachment; and oxytocin is associated with physical intimacy.

19. Sexual intimacy involves touching, relaxation, involved participation, and a realistic view of how romantic love and sex fit into relationships.

20. Same-gender relationships do not necessarily follow the heterosexual model. Most gay men and lesbians want long-term close relationships, and there are three main patterns of relating.

21. Sometimes, friends must work out the place that sexual attraction will have in the friendship.

22. The Internet is providing a new medium for intimate, and sometimes sexual, relationships to develop. Although some of these relationships seem very positive, there are risks associated with this form of connection.

23. Three main styles of attachment to others have been identified: secure, preoccupied, and avoidant, the latter of which may be either dismissing or fearful.

24. Although a degree of jealousy and possessiveness is expected in any loving relationship, these qualities may become destructive if they are rooted in serious insecurities.

25. Loss of a loving relationship can be painful and often needs to be followed by a process of grieving.

Focus on Health Questions

You will find in this section the kinds of questions that you may have concerning your own health and sexuality. The page references indicate where in the text the answer is located; the exact place is marked with the logo: **FOH**

1. Most of the time I just avoid telling my partner something I think will hurt him or her. Isn't that better than causing emotional pain? 240

2. My boyfriend never wants to tell me what's bothering him./My girlfriend just bores me with all

that talk about intimacy./I just want to get on with it. How can we learn to understand each other better? 241

3. Are sex and love the same thing? 250, 255

4. My partner seems unnecessarily jealous most of the time. What can I do to change the situation? 259

5. How can I get over the end of my most important loving relationship ever? 260

Annotated Readings

Botting, D., & Botting, K. (1996). *Sex appeal*. New York: St. Martin's Press. A thorough and interesting look at the various elements that are part of human romantic and sexual attraction.

Crenshaw, T. (1996). *The alchemy of love and lust: Guide to the ingredients in our sex soup*. A look at the hormonal and chemical regulation of human attraction, with suggestions for potential medical intervention.

DeVillers, L. (1997). *Love skills: More fun than you've ever had with sex, intimacy and communication*. San Luis Obispo, CA: Impact. A down-to-earth, readable how-to

book for the improvement of loving and sexual relationships, with an emphasis on effective communication skills.

Forward, S., & Buck, C. (1992). *Obsessive love: When it hurts too much to let go*. New York: Bantam Books. A down-to-earth guide for people who are attempting to let go of a relationship, or who are trying to extricate themselves from a possessive relationship.

Gottman, J. (1999). *Marriage clinic: A scientifically based marital therapy*. New York: W.W. Norton. A more scientific treatment of Gottman's "marriage lab" work, with implications for treating couples who have relational difficulties.

Hatfield, E., & Rapson, R. L. (1996). *Love and sex: Cross-cultural perspectives*. New York: Allyn & Bacon. A study of the global transformations that are establishing new standards for loving partnerships around the world.

Illouz, E. (1997). *Consuming the romantic utopia: Love and the cultural contradictions of capitalism*. This book has a cross-cultural political slant on loving and intimate relationships.

Louden, J. (1994). *The couple's comfort book: A creative guide for renewing passion, pleasure, and commitment*. San Francisco: HarperSanFrancisco. A collection of creative and practical approaches for nurturing and renewing loving relationships.

Moore, T. (1994). *Soul mates: Honoring the mysteries of love and relationships*. New York: HarperCollins. Taking an often spiritual orientation to the subject, this book focuses on how to make relationships better.

Ornish, D. (1998). *Love and survival: The scientific basis for the healing power of intimacy*. New York: Harper-Collins. Presents convincing evidence of how powerful loving, intimate relating can be for disease prevention and healing.

Richter, A. (1995). *The dictionary of sexual slang*. New York: HarperCollins. This book takes an insightful look at the sexual slang terms used from Elizabethan times to the street language of present-day America and England.

Schnarch, D. (1997). *Passionate marriage: Love, sex, and intimacy in emotionally committed relationships*. New York: W. W. Norton. A practical book of suggestions for increasing intimacy and sex in longer term relationships.

Winstead, B. A., Derlega, V. J., & Rose, S. (1997). *Gender and close relationships*. Thousand Oaks, CA: Sage. Examines the different types of relationships and how they are influenced by gender issues and politics.

Part 3

*Human Reproduction,
Contraception, and Abortion:
Sexuality Confronts Social Policy*

Sexuality has always been clearly linked to the process of reproduction. Human biology gives most people the capability of producing offspring. However, reproductive technology has made it a far more complex issue than propagation of the species. Chapter 9 first deals with the mechanisms of fertilization and development of the fetus. For individuals who choose to have children but experience difficulty doing so, medical specialists now offer many forms of technological assistance, some of which have raised serious and complicated ethical questions. It has been suggestd that the first 50 years of the new millennium will be the age of assisted reproductive technology.

Society continues to weigh and set precedents about the complicated ethical and legal issues of reproduction, contraception, and abortion. Guidelines for research are beginning to emerge. For most individuals, heterosexual intercourse will carry with it the risks and choices relating to pregnancy. As chapter 10 describes, there are many ways in which the probability of pregnancy may be reduced. Yet we are hardly living in the golden age of contraception. Development of new, more effective, and safer methods of birth control has lagged markedly in recent years, largely because research funding has been unavailable.

There is still a high rate of unintended pregnancy in our society. People fail to use contraception, or they use it incorrectly, or it fails, and people are left with some difficult choices. This chapter also deals with the options available to those facing an unintended pregnancy. The issue becomes how much responsibility for the decision making the individual is willing to take.

The reproductive aspects of human sexuality are an important part of sexuality's complex role in society and should not be taken lightly. The issues surrounding reproduction, contraception, and termination of pregnancy have become highly politicized as social policy takes shape. There is much polarization and political struggle about abortion. Human sexual reproduction is far more than a biological phenomenon; it is a social and cultural controversy closely associated with the cutting edge of biotechnology.

■ *Chapter 9*
REPRODUCTION, REPRODUCTIVE TECHNOLOGY, AND BIRTHING

Modern technology has revolutionized reproduction for childless couples and for couples at high risk for a difficult pregnancy and/or delivery. Genetic engineering and gene therapy are opening whole new possibilities for the prevention and treatment of genetic disorders. Artificial insemination, frozen storage of gametes and embryos, the cloning of mammals, in vitro fertilization in all of its variations, and surrogate motherhood give childless couples more options for having a child than they previously had. Amniocentesis, ultrasound, and new ways of examining the fetus in the womb help identify difficulties earlier than ever before. The diagnosis and treatment of disease during fetal life have become possible with modern technology. Yet, the biological processes of conception, fetal development, and birth continue to occur much as they have for millions of years.

■ *Chapter 10*
DECISION MAKING ABOUT PREGNANCY AND PARENTHOOD

Ethical, moral, and religious factors affect people's decisions about the use of contraceptives. The type of contraceptive used varies in effectiveness, and a couple should consider together which method is best for them. Decisions about how to handle an unintended pregnancy are complex. Terminating an unwanted pregnancy is difficult for most couples, and yet placing a child for adoption has become a less attractive option in recent years. Physical as well as moral issues must be considered, and counseling can help both the woman and the man deal with guilt, a sense of loss, or other conflicts they may experience if they opt either for abortion or adoption.

Chapter 9

Reproduction, Reproductive Technology, and Birthing

Chapter Outline

Note: A selection of Focus on Health questions appears at the end of each chapter. Answers to these questions are indicated within the chapter by the symbol in the margin. **FOH**

It looks as though our only chance to have a baby of our own will be by using in vitro methods. I feel like I am going to end up spending the kid's college education funds before he or she is even conceived. Sometimes the "investment" of time, emotion, and money seems strange, and rather scary.

—From a personal essay given to the author

Human sexuality and reproduction are obviously linked closely together, biologically and socially. The combining of genetic material, in a way that produces another human being with characteristics of both parents, is nothing short of a miracle. New understandings of reproduction, coupled with new scientific technologies, have also permitted these processes to be manipulated and transformed in ways that not long ago were considered nothing more than tales of science fiction (Fischman & Ray, 1994).

Although reproduction of the human species once could not have taken place without sexual contact, reproductive technology can now intervene to bring sperm and egg together in a variety of ways. It is no longer even necessary for the genetic mother—the contributor of the egg—to be pregnant with the child that is eventually born. Indeed, reproduction and the prevention of reproduction have gone far beyond the realms of human sexuality and biology. Social policy, politics, legislation, court precedents, and ethical debate are now as much a part of understanding reproduction as is the age-old question asked by every child: "Where do babies come from?" This chapter addresses all of these issues.

Fertilization and Fetal Development

During the menstrual cycle, an ovum matures and is released from one of the female's ovaries. The most recent research indicates that fertilization of the ovum is most likely to occur when sperm are present during any of the 6 consecutive days of the cycle that end with the day of ovulation (Wilcox, Weinberg, & Baird, 1996). This is in contrast to the old assumption that the most likely time for fertilization was during the 2 days following ovulation. As soon as semen is ejaculated from the penis into the vagina, the sperm begin their journey into the uterus, and they may remain viable for up to 5 days. A few thousand usually reach the fallopian tubes. The more sperm present, the greater the probability that fertilization, or conception, will occur. Sperm apparently have receptor molecules that are attracted to a sperm-attracting chemical that is released by the egg, and the membrane of the sperm cell contains a chemical called **fertilin** that seems to play a role in helping the sperm to adhere to the egg and eventually penetrate its outer layer (Cho et al., 1998).

When a sperm cell comes into contact with the ovum, a very specific cell recognition process is triggered that binds the sperm tightly to the outer mem-

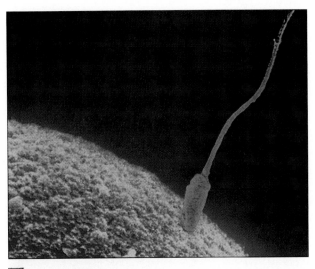

FIGURE 9.1 *Sperm Penetrating Egg*

A sperm, with its oval head and long tail, approaches the egg, or ovum. Having been capacitated during its journey through the female reproductive tract, the sperm will secrete an enzyme that will help it penetrate the outer membrane of the ovum.

brane of the ovum, the **zona pellucida.** The sperm then secretes enzymes that help it pass through the zona and its underlying membranes to penetrate into the ovum (Aitken, 1995). Usually only one sperm manages to burrow its way into the interior of the ovum (see Fig. 9.1) because a hard protein surface develops that prevents further sperm from entering. The actual mechanisms of sperm penetration and exclusion of other sperm are still only partially understood. If an extra sperm enters an ovum, it may well destroy the ovum, or its own genetic material may be destroyed. As the sperm passes through the outer layers of the ovum, it is probably primed by the hormone progesterone for the actual fertilization process. Contact with the zona pellucida seems to be essential to causing **exocytosis,** in which the sperm cell opens to allow its chromosomes to be released into the ovum (Roldam,

fertilin (fer-TILL-in): a chemical in the outer membrane of a sperm that assists in attachment to the egg cell and penetration of the egg's outer membrane.

zona pellucida (ZO-nah pe-LOO-sa-da): the transparent, outer membrane of an ovum.

exocytosis (ex-oh-sye-TOH-sis): the release of genetic material by the sperm cell, permitting fertilization to occur.

Murase, & Shi, 1994). The combining and pairing of chromosomes from both the sperm and egg allow fertilization, or conception, to occur. A fertilized ovum is called a **zygote.**

Fertilization not only initiates the growth of a new human being, but inherited traits are determined at the moment of conception. Both the ovum and the sperm contain 23 chromosomes, each bearing genes that contain hereditary information stored in the form of **deoxyribonucleic acid (DNA)** (see Fig. 9.2). In the combining and pairing of these 46 chromosomes, essential programs for the individual's heredity are initiated. It is the pairing of sex chromosomes at fertilization that determines the sex of the developing embryo—XX for female and XY for male. The process of sexual differentiation and its implications

for later development were discussed in more detail in chapter 5, "Developmental and Social Perspectives on Gender."

Twinning and Other Multiples

Giving birth to twins, triplets, and other multiples always creates attention and excitement: the more babies born, the more excitement. In the last two decades of the twentieth century, the number of twin births rose by about half, and the number of higher-order multiple births almost quadrupled. Twins now occur in about 30 out of every 1,000 births in the United States, and triplets occur about once in 1,341 births. As Figure 9.3 demonstrates, the rates of multiple births have been increasing markedly in recent years, in small part because children are being born to older mothers, who are more prone to multiples, but largely because of the increased use of fertility drugs (Martin & Park, 1999). These drugs stimulate the ovaries to release more than one ovum in order to enhance the chances of conception taking place, and they have been shown to be highly successful in yielding pregnancy for infertile couples (Guzick, Carson et al., 1999). However, because the risks to both the babies and the mother increase with the number of fetuses, physicians are beginning to use fertility drugs with greater care (Velde & Cohlen, 1999). Nevertheless, the number of births of quadruplets (four babies) or more increased from 269 in the United States in 1989 to 361 in 1994. In 1997, septuplets (seven babies) were born to a couple in the United States who had been using a fertility drug.

Twins may be either **fraternal,** formed from two separate ova being fertilized by two separate sperm, or **identical,** formed by a single ovum and sperm. Fraternal twins may also be called *dizygotic* because they are produced from two zygotes, whereas identical twins are sometimes called *monozygotic* because they have come from a single zygote. In fraternal twins, the two zygotes develop separately, and the twins look no more alike than any other siblings in the family. They may be of the same or different

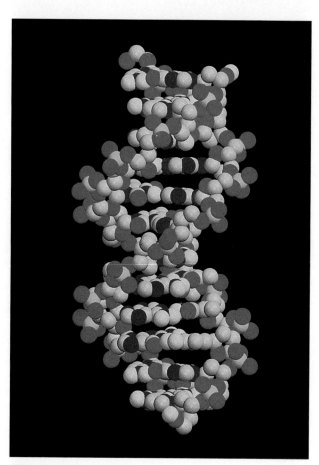

FIGURE 9.2 *DNA*

This model of a molecule of deoxyribonucleic acid (DNA) clearly shows its double helix shape. DNA is the building block of heredity, containing within it the genetic code that produces a specific type of offspring. Scientists hope that by learning more about DNA they will be able to prevent genetic diseases and control some aspects of the reproductive process. On the other hand, skeptics point to some of the risks involved in manipulating the structure of genes.

zygote: an ovum that has been fertilized by a sperm.

deoxyribonucleic acid (DNA) (dee-AK-see-rye-bow-new-KLEE-ik): the chemical in each cell that carries the genetic code.

fraternal twins: twins formed from two separate ova that were fertilized by two separate sperm.

identical twins: twins formed by a single ovum that was fertilized by a single sperm before the cell divided in two.

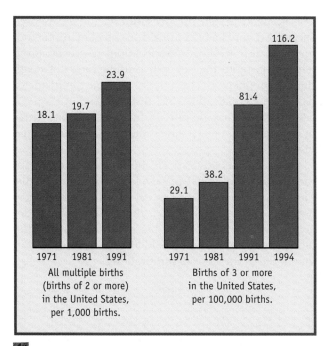

FIGURE 9.3 *Multiple Births in the United States*

As statistics from the National Center for Health Statistics demonstrate, the number of multiple births in the United States has been increasing over recent decades. The use of fertility drugs probably constitutes the most significant reason for the increase, although the older ages of mothers may also be a factor because older women are most likely to have multiple births.

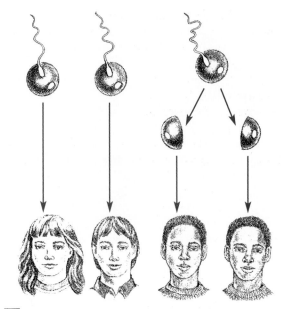

FIGURE 9.4 *Twins*

Fraternal or dizygotic twins are formed from the fertilization of two ova by two separate sperm. Identical or monozygotic twins are formed from the same fertilized ovum that divides before implantation in the uterus.

FOH sexes. In identical twins, when the first division of the zygote occurs, the two cells separate and develop as two individuals. Because they have exactly the same chromosomes, however, they are of the same sex and identical in appearance (see Fig. 9.4). Triplets, quadruplets, and other multiple fetuses may all be fraternal or may include one or more sets of identical twins. Identical triplets and higher-order multiples are extremely rare.

The development of multiple fetuses increases the risk of premature birth and birth defects for the baby and may cause other problems for the pregnant woman. The higher the number of fetuses, the greater the likelihood of premature birth, low birth weight, birth defects, or death of an infant before birth or within the first year after birth. When one of the fetuses has some sort of defect, the likelihood of problems in the pregnancy increase even more. Compared to 10 percent for single births, the rate of premature birth for twins is nearly 50 percent, and it is about 90 percent for multiple births of more than two. For the mother, there is an increased risk of serious bleeding, high blood pressure, and metabolic disturbances (Cowley & Springen, 1997).

With the tendency of fertility drugs to increase the rate of multiple births, a controversial new procedure became available in medical practice. **Selective reduction** involves selectively aborting one or more of the fetuses in large-multiple pregnancies so that a lower-risk number of two or three remains. In the past, when multiple fetuses were discovered, the couple had the option of either doing nothing and taking their chances on a successful outcome or else terminating the entire pregnancy. They now have this third option available, although it obviously represents a difficult choice. Nonetheless, the selective reduction technique has succeeded in reducing the number of premature multiple births and their accompanying complications (Malone et al., 1996).

Implantation of the Embryo

After fertilization has occurred, the zygote begins a process of cell division as it continues to move through the fallopian tube toward the uterus (see Fig. 9.5). The

selective reduction: the use of abortion techniques to reduce the number of fetuses when there are more than three in a pregnancy, thus increasing the chances of survival for the remaining fetuses. Also called selective termination.

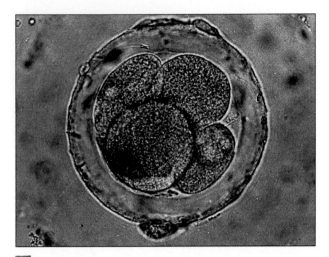

FIGURE 9.5 *Cell Division*

Four new cells of the forming embryo. Following fertilization of the ovum by the sperm, their chromosomes join, and the genetic plan to produce an embryo is set into motion. The zygote, or fertilized ovum, begins to undergo cell division, first producing two cells, then four, and so on. Each new cell receives a complete set of 46 human chromosomes, programmed to produce an entirely new human being.

first division produces two cells; these both divide to form four, and so on. With each cell division, the chromosomes are replicated so that every new cell has a full complement of hereditary material. Within 3 days, a spherical, solid mass of cells has been formed, called the **morula.** By the end of the fifth day after fertilization, the sphere has developed a fluid-filled cavity in its interior and is termed the **blastocyst.** By this time, the mass of dividing cells has left the fallopian tube and entered the uterine cavity. Because there is no rich source of nourishment, the cells are not growing, and the blastocyst is not appreciably larger than the original ovum.

Around a week after fertilization, the blastocyst comes into contact with the uterine lining, the endometrium. The blastocyst has by this time developed specialized cells that secrete enzymes, helping it to burrow into the lining. The specialized cells of the blastocyst also form blood vessels that grow toward the blood vessels of the uterus (Cross, Werb, & Fisher, 1994). The blastocyst becomes implanted in the uterine wall and is now considered an **embryo,** about to undergo a series of dramatic changes in growth and development (see Fig. 9.6). Occasionally a blastocyst becomes implanted in a fallopian tube or strays into the abdominal cavity and attaches itself to some other tissue where it continues to develop as an embryo.

This is called an **ectopic pregnancy,** and the embryo should be surgically removed to prevent rupture of the tube and bleeding. Complications of ectopic pregnancy constitute the seventh leading cause of death during pregnancy. The rate of ectopic pregnancies has risen dramatically, and researchers have speculated that this may be due to the use of fertility drugs or increases in societal stress and sexually transmitted disease.

Typically, a baby is born after about 266 days (approximately 9 months) of development in the uterus. There are wide variations in the length of pregnancy, however. During that period, the fertilized ovum develops into an infant capable of living outside the uterus and weighing about 6 billion times more at birth than it did at the time of fertilization.

Extraembryonic Membranes and the Placenta

Early in embryonic development, several extraembryonic membranes essential to the embryo's survival are formed from some of its specialized cells (Cross, Werb, & Fisher, 1994). The membrane that creates a sac to enclose the embryo is called the **amnion.** The sac is filled with fluid, which keeps the embryonic tissues moist and protectively cushions the embryo. The amniotic sac is called the bag of waters, and just before birth it breaks, releasing its clear watery fluid through the vagina. There are two membranes, the *yolk sac* and the *allantois,* that seem to function only in early embryonic development and gradually become partly incorporated into the umbilical cord. The outermost extraembryonic membrane is the **chorion.**

morula (MOR-yuh-la): a spherical, solid mass of cells formed after 3 days of embryonic cell division.

blastocyst: the ball of cells, after 5 days of cell division, that has developed a fluid-filled cavity in its interior; it has entered the uterine cavity.

embryo (EM-bree-o): the term applied to the developing cells when, about a week after fertilization, the blastocyst implants itself in the uterine wall.

ectopic pregnancy (ek-TOP-ik): the implantation of a blastocyst somwhere other than in the uterus, usually in the fallopian tube.

amnion (AM-nee-on): a thin membrane that forms a closed sac around the embryo; the sac is filled with amniotic fluid, which protects and cushions the embryo.

chorion (KOR-ee-on): the outermost extraembryonic membrane, essential in the formation of the placenta.

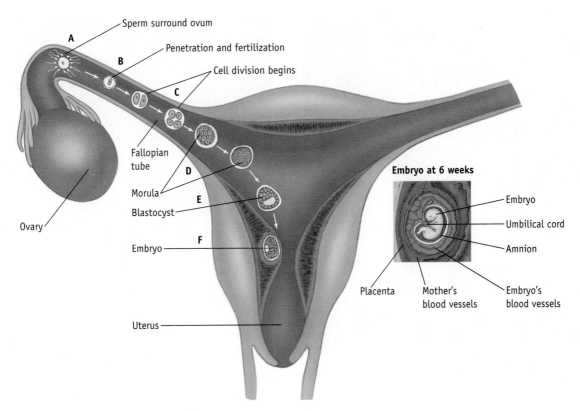

Embryo at 6 weeks

FIGURE 9.6 *Blastocyst Implantation and Placental Function within the Uterus*

After hundreds of sperm surround the ovum (A), one penetrates and fertilizes it (B). Cell division begins (C), and after 3 days produces a spherical mass called a morula (D). The fifth day after fertilization, the mass develops into a hollow sphere of cells called a blastocyst (E) and within a week implants in the uterine lining; it is now considered an embryo (F). The developing embryo receives nourishment and oxygen from the mother's blood through the placenta and returns his or her waste products back through it. This exchange takes place through the umbilical cord, which connects the fetal and maternal circulatory systems.

It plays an essential role in the formation of the **placenta,** the structure that provides nourishment for the embryo. The chorion produces small fingerlike projections, called **villi,** that grow into the uterine tissue and form a major part of the placenta. It is within the placenta that blood vessels from the embryo come into close contact with blood vessels from the mother, although there is no actual intermingling of the two bloodstreams. While the blood vessels are in close proximity, however, food molecules and oxygen from the maternal blood diffuse into the embryo's blood. Carbon dioxide and other metabolic wastes diffuse from the embryo's blood into the mother's blood, and her body then disposes of them through the lungs and kidneys. The embryo is connected to the placenta by the **umbilical cord,** which forms during the fifth week of pregnancy. It is through the umbilical cord that the embryo's blood vessels pass into and out of the placenta (see Fig. 9.4).

Usually after 2 months of development, the embryo is called the **fetus.** It is beyond the scope of this book to detail embryonic and fetal development.

However, from the moment of conception to the time a baby is born, remarkable changes occur. An entire human body develops, with internal systems that can function to support life and enable the fetus to move and react to stimuli (see Figs. 9.7–9.10). Figure 9.11 summarizes some of the important stages of fetal development.

placenta (pla-SEN-ta): the organ that unites the fetus to the mother by bringing their blood vessels closer together; it provides nourishment and removes waste for the developing baby.

villi: finger-like projections of the chorion; they form a major part of the placenta.

umbilical cord: the tubelike tissues and blood vessels originating at the embryo's navel that connect it to the placenta.

fetus: the term given to the embryo after 2 months of development in the womb.

FIGURE 9.7 *Spine of Embryo at 6 weeks*

At 6 weeks of development, the embryo floats in the fluid of its amnion. In this rear view of the embryo, its developing spinal cord may be clearly seen, flanked by its two red vertebral arteries. The yolk sack, seen at the lower left of the photograph, will eventually become incorporated into the umbilical cord.

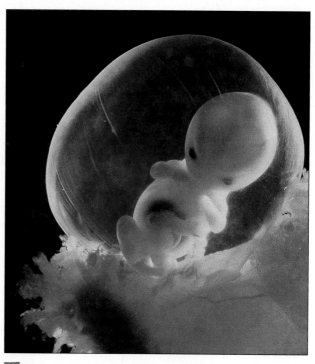

FIGURE 9.8 *Embryo at 7 Weeks*

At 7 weeks, the embryo is nearly an inch long, and both its internal and external organs are rapidly forming. Facial features are beginning to take shape, and the skeleton is developing internally. The fontanel, or soft area in the center of the developing skull, is clearly visible in this picture.

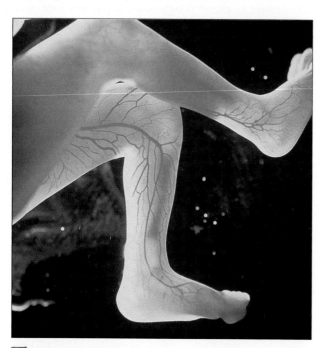

FIGURE 9.9 *Legs of Fetus at 4 Months*

The blood vessels and developing bones are visible in the legs of this 4-month (6.4-inch) fetus. The skeleton is first formed from cartilage. Bone tissue then begins to grow out from the middle of the cartilage toward both ends. Bone development is not fully completed until an individual reaches the age of about 25 years.

FIGURE 9.10 *Fetus Sucking Thumb at 4 1/2 Months*

At 4 1/2 months, the fetus has formed its human features and proportions. Survival reflexes, such as the sucking reflex, are already able to function. This photograph provides a startling demonstration of the potential for thumb-sucking in a fetus that is only halfway to being full-term.

Reproduction and Fetal Technology

In recent years, many important social, legal, religious, personal, and ethical questions have been raised by biotechnological advances in the areas of genetic manipulation, gamete retrieval and storage, fertilization, implantation, and medical manipulation of the embryo and fetus. The first "test-tube baby" was born in England in 1978. In the United States today, over 75,000 babies are born each year as the result of fertility drugs and various other assisted reproductive technology techniques (ISLAT Working Group, 1998). They have called into question some of the fundamental assumptions about sex, reproduction, and family structure. In cases where one woman contributes an egg and another woman carries the baby, which one is the biological mother? It is even possible now for a woman to give birth to her own grandchild. The new ability to become pregnant following menopause challenges age-old concepts of human development. Reproductively, it is already a brave new world, and it has been suggested that the first 50 years of the new millennium may well be considered the "decades of conception." Yet social policies have been slow to adjust to the many new ethical and moral issues and decisions that have emerged (Djerassi, 1999; Kolata, 1996; Monaghan, 1999).

Discuss the moral and ethical implications of genetic engineering.

We have moved beyond the time when we have to rely exclusively on chance in reproductive sex. Scientists are developing means by which we can manipulate genes and reproductive processes so that many options are now available. Yet the new technologies are controversial because of their medical and ethical implications. There are often as many risks as there are advantages both to the mother and the fetus. There is, as well, the continuing concern that women are being viewed as reproductive vessels to be manipulated by science rather than as human beings (Lemonick, 1997; Monaghan, 1999). The bypassing of the natural processes of reproduction raises new doubts and concerns about the roles that men and women will play in the future of human procreation.

Genetic Engineering and Gene Therapy

Research has yielded significant information on how genes function. The types of offspring produced by sexual reproduction depend on the gene combinations made during the fertilization of a random sperm and egg. Genes give chemical messages to cells, causing them to carry on particular functions for which the cells are responsible. The genetic code that determines the traits of the offspring is contained in strands of DNA. The heritable traits of human beings are essentially the result of that random combination and indeed have been at the mercy of the process. However, molecular geneticists are continuing to learn more about how genes work and how they may be modified. Scientists are perfecting techniques for removing genetic material from one cell, combining it with genes from another, and implanting the recombinant DNA into a host cell. This results in cells that have a new genetic makeup and therefore new characteristics. Sometimes, whole new species of microorganisms have been produced in this manner.

Controlling cellular functioning through the manipulation of genetic material is called **genetic engineering,** and it has the potential for producing tremendous benefits. It has already been put to a number of agricultural uses. Research is also under way to develop **gene therapy** techniques for the treatment of the more than 4,000 human disorders that have genetic causes such as hemophilia, sickle-cell anemia, some disorders of the immune system, certain types of diabetes and heritable developmental disabilities, diseases of the liver and lung, cystic fibrosis, and Alzheimer's disease. Gene therapy is still too inefficient to be helpful in most cases today, but improved techniques are expected to create a medical revolution within the next three to four decades (Anderson, 2000). Amidst growing concerns about lack of monitoring in gene therapy research, the National Institutes of Health are calling for closer regulation of the work (Wheeler, 1999).

Scientists are making good progress on a multibillion dollar project to create a complete map of the human genome, the DNA structure that makes a human being. At the end of the 1990s, virtually all of human chromosome number 22 had been decoded (Kiernan, 1999). International efforts are adding thousands of new genetic markers to the map each year, and it is now projected that the 3 billion bits of human DNA sequences will be fully mapped by the year 2003 (Collins et al., 1999). This map will lead to further types of genetic testing and therapy to diagnose and treat various genetic conditions. Therefore, the Human Genome Project, as it is called, carries with it tremendous implications for the future of medical science. Countries

genetic engineering: the modification of the gene structure of cells to change cellular functioning.

gene therapy: treatment of genetically caused disorders by substitution of healthy genes.

		Prenatal Development	*Changes in Mother*
1 Month		Fertilization occurs. Zygote implants itself in the lining of the uterus. Rapid cell division occurs. Embryonic state lasts from 2 weeks to 8 weeks. Cells differentiate into 3 distinct layers: The ectoderm, the mesoderm, and the endoderm. Nervous system begins to develop. Embryo is ½ inch long.	Possible morning sickness, or nausea, and fatigue. Breasts may begin to feel tender. No weight gain.
2 Months	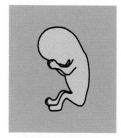	Heart and blood vessels form. Head area develops rapidly. Eyes begin to form detail. Internal organs grow, especially the digestive system. Sex organs develop and gender can be distinguished. Arms and legs form and grow. Heart begins to beat faintly. Embryo is 1 inch long and weighs ¹⁄₁₀ ounce.	Increased frequency of urination. Possible nausea and tiredness. Constipation, heartburn, and indigestion may begin in the second month and last throughout the pregnancy. Breast tenderness. No noticeable weight gain.
3 Months	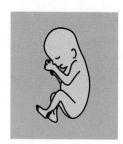	Head growth occurs rapidly. Bone formation begins. The digestive organs begin to function. Arms, legs, and fingers make spontaneous movements. Fetus is 3 inches long and weighs 1 ounce.	Perspiration may be increased. Possible nausea. Continued need to urinate more frequently than usual. Breast heaviness and tenderness. Small weight gain (2–3 pounds).
4 Months		Lower parts of the body show rapid growth. Bones are distinct in X rays. Reflex movement becomes more active. Heartbeat can be detected. Sex organs are fully formed. Fetus is 7 inches long and weighs 5 ounces.	Belly begins to show. Faint movement of the fetus may be felt. Fatigue. Decrease in frequency of urination. Increase in appetite. Morning sickness may diminish or end. Weight gain in month 4: 3–4 pounds.
5 Months		A fine, downy fuzz covers the entire body. Vernix (a waxy coating) collects over the body. Ears and nose begin to develop cartilage. Fingernails and toenails begin to appear. Fetus may suck thumb, hiccup, and kick. Fetus is 12 inches long and weighs 14 ounces.	Possible shortness of breath. Possible fluttering movements as fetus stretches. Possible food cravings. Pelvic joints begin to relax. Weight gain in month 5: 3–4 pounds.

FIGURE 9.11   *Embryonic and Fetal Development and Changes in the Mother's Body*

Source: From Terry F. Pettijohn, *Psychology: A Concise Introduction*, 3rd edition, 1992, Dushkin Publishing Company, Guilford, CT, The March of Dimes, and Earth Surface Graphics.

	Prenatal Development	Changes in Mother
6 Months	Eyes and eyelids fully formed. Fat is developing under the skin. Fetus is 14 inches long and weighs 2 pounds.	Possible backache. Fetus's movements now usually felt. Weight gain in month 6: 3–4 pounds.
7 Months	Cerebral cortex of brain develops rapidly. Fetus is 16 inches long and weighs 3 pounds.	Fetus is very active. Possible blotchy skin, which will clear up after the baby is born. Ankles may swell from standing. Possible backache. Weight gain in month 7: 3–4 pounds.
8 Months	Subcutaneous fat is deposited for later use. Fingernails reach beyond the fingertips. Fetus is 17 inches long and weighs 5 pounds.	Occasional headaches, backache, difficulty sleeping. Weight gain in month 8: 3–5 pounds.
9 Months	Hair covering the entire body is shed. Organ systems function actively. Vernix is present over the entire body. Fetus settles into position for birth. Neonate is 21 inches long and weighs 7 pounds.	Uterus has now moved a few inches lower. Feeling of heaviness in lower abdomen. Ankle swelling. Shortness of breath. Weight gain in month 9: 3–5 pounds. Total weight gain: 20–29 pounds.

around the world have been debating the ethical consequences of this work, reaching a degree of consensus in several different areas. It is agreed, for example, that information gained through genetic testing should be utilized with great caution and with the individual's full knowledge. Because this information will make predictions of future medical conditions more accurate, many people may ultimately want to preserve their right *not* to know. Similarly, the need for privacy is clear because knowledge about an individual's genetic makeup might be used in making decisions about employment, parenthood, and health insurance coverage (Koonin, 1998; Wheeler, 1999).

The international community has also expressed concern over the rights of vulnerable populations, such as those with intellectual disabilities, minors, and even future generations. It is generally agreed that we must be cautious about misuse of genetic technology toward eugenic ends in an attempt to create "more perfect" populations of human beings. As with any emerging technology, there must also be a way of ensuring that it is made available in a fair and equitable manner and not just for an elite group who might be able to afford its benefits. There is a desire to ensure that certain principles of fundamental human dignity are respected (Drlica, 1996).

FOH

Mapping and testing for the genetics of complex human traits still have a long way to go, but progress is being made. Various forms of genetic testing are already allowing for early detection of certain genetic disorders. Using technology described later in this chapter to obtain fetal cells, scientists can now analyze them for possible chromosomal abnormalities. Couples who are concerned about the possibility of transmitting a genetic disorder to their offspring may be tested to determine the likelihood of such an event. People who fear a genetic disorder common in their families may also want to be tested to see if they carry the gene that might predispose them to the disease (Couzin, 1998; Reiss & Straughan, 1996). For genetic disorders that do irreversible damage to the fetus before birth, techniques are being developed through which gene therapy could be administered to the fetus while it is still developing in the uterus (Zanjani & Anderson, 1999).

Genetic testing has raised certain ethical and social issues already. For example, if a fetus is found to have a defective gene, should it be aborted? Who should be allowed access to information concerning potential risks of inherited diseases? In some cases, insurance companies have refused health insurance to couples who have a greater likelihood of giving birth to a child with some genetic disorder. Some states have passed legislation prohibiting discrimination by employers on the basis of genetic traits, and there are still no clear guidelines as to who should have access to genetic testing information. Federal and state legislation will need to continue addressing the many issues of privacy and protection that are created by genetic engineering. Although some factions argue that gene manipulation should be prohibited as an undesirable tampering with nature, others counter that, in a sense, all medical science represents a tampering with nature (Collins et al., 1998; Drlica, 1996).

Artificial Insemination

Artificial insemination, or the placing of donated semen in the woman's vagina or uterus without intercourse, has been available for over 200 years, although it was not considered standard medical practice until the 1930s. During the following decade, it was discovered that human semen could be frozen quickly in liquid nitrogen without damaging sperm cells. The first baby conceived from frozen semen was born in 1954.

This method of impregnation is most typically used with couples in which the man's sperm count is low (less than 40 million sperm per milliliter of semen) or, in extreme cases, zero, rendering it difficult or impossible for him to impregnate his partner. Although concentrating the sperm count from several of the man's own semen specimens has been one approach,

it has not proven especially successful. A more common method is to use semen contributed by an anonymous donor, chosen for characteristics of good health, intelligence, and physical traits similar to those of the intended "father." The semen may be frozen or used fresh, after the donor has been tested for possible HIV infection. For males who are infected with HIV, techniques are being developed by which the virus may be removed from the semen, so that it may be used for reproduction (Marina, 1998).

The semen is inserted by a physician into the back of the woman's vagina, near the cervix. The pregnancy rate in artificial insemination ranges from 60 percent to 75 percent. The procedure is sometimes used by couples without medical assistance as well. The artificial insemination can be carried out with common kitchen devices such as a basting syringe. Lesbian couples and gay male couples with a cooperative female friend have been using artificial insemination in order to have children.

Reproductive technology of this sort has led toward legal clarifications relating to the meaning and rights of parenthood, as courts must make decisions about complicated cases. In a California court case, a man fought to keep the children that his wife had borne after being impregnated by another man's semen. The wife had sued him for custody when she wanted to leave with the children, but the judge ruled that because the man had raised the children as his own, he had no less right to retain custody than an actual biological father. There have also been two cases in which the U.S. Social Security Commissioner has awarded benefits to a child whose father has died, even though the child was conceived from the man's frozen semen after his death. The commissioner has indicated that technological developments have necessitated a review of existing Social Security laws.

Storage of Gametes and Embryos

The preservation of sperm by quick-freezing techniques was a major advance in artificial insemination because men could donate semen for storage in sperm banks, to be used later as needed. This added efficiency and convenience to the procedure for all involved. Techniques continue to be developed for the freezing of human eggs, to be fertilized at a later time. In 1997, the first babies were born from eggs that were fertilized after having been frozen and stored (Kluger, 1997).

artificial insemination: injection of the sperm cells of a male into a woman's vagina, with the intention of conceiving a child.

In the early 1980s, Australian scientists began experimenting with freezing human embryos resulting from in vitro fertilization (IVF) (described on this page) for possible later uterine implantation. This was for the sake of convenience and efficiency as well because several eggs could be withdrawn in a single surgical procedure, fertilized, and then saved for future use. If one IVF failed, another embryo could then be tried, bypassing all of the earlier stages of the technique. The first baby from a previously frozen embryo implant was born in 1987.

Numerous ethical issues have arisen surrounding the storage of gametes (sperm and eggs) and embryos. A few years ago, a man proposed starting a sperm bank intended to "strengthen the human gene pool." He wanted to freeze semen from Nobel Prize winners, to be used in the insemination of particularly bright women. Classified advertisements occasionally appear in college newspapers, offering to pay thousands of dollars for the eggs of women who meet certain physical and intellectual criteria. The question of eugenics, or selecting human traits for improvement of the species, is one that has always created controversy (Rothman, 1999). On the most basic level, it becomes a question of who has the right to determine which characteristics should be preserved and fostered and which should be eliminated.

Couples who participate in fertility technology in order to enhance the chance of having children often have several embryos stored for possible future use. The American Fertility Society has reported that at the over 300 fertility clinics in the United States, there are probably tens of thousands of stored embryos. Couples are usually asked ahead of time what they want done with any leftover frozen embryos, which can be destroyed, offered to infertile couples, or used for research. Although many want them donated to other couples, there is actually very little demand for them. Some ethicists feel they should not be destroyed, whereas others have suggested that they might even be saved for use by future generations. Although early animal research raised some concern that freezing embryos might increase the risks for later difficulties, most research with infants who developed from frozen embryos has not yet shown any greater risk for birth defects or developmental abnormalities (Wennerholm, 1998). There are reports of abnormalities in few cases, but it is not fully understood whether the technologies used actually led to the problems (Strain et al., 1998).

Society continues to grapple with the complex ethical and legal ramifications of storage banks for gametes and embryos. Ethical guidelines are beginning to be established that will help decisionmakers of the future. It has been suggested that the biotechnical revolution in reproduction has implications as profound as those of the Industrial Revolution and that we are just as unprepared for it.

In Vitro Fertilization

There are two fundamental steps to be taken in technologically assisted fertilization. One is to secure viable sperm and ova in the most efficient manner possible, and the other is to bring them together in a way that will maximize the chances of conception occurring. In the late 1960s, a team of English scientists began working with **in vitro fertilization (IVF),** a technique in which ova are fertilized by sperm in laboratory glassware. The first "test-tube baby" produced by IVF was Louise Brown, born in Oldham, England, in 1978, and this is still the simplest and most frequently used procedure. Since then, over 300,000 babies have been born as the result of IVF (Djeassi, 1999). Many infertile women have blockages in the fallopian tubes that prevent the sperm and egg from meeting. IVF permits a woman who would otherwise be unable to conceive to have her own child. In the original technique, ova are removed, or harvested, from one of her ovaries by a simple microsurgical technique and are then mixed with sperm cells from her partner, usually obtained through masturbation. Fertilization can be confirmed by microscopic examination, and the fertilized egg is then placed in the woman's uterus, which has been appropriately readied by hormonal treatment. If the process is successful, the embryo will implant in the uterine wall as would happen under natural conditions, and development of the fetus continues.

In one variation on this theme, zygotes resulting from IVF are inserted directly into the woman's fallopian tubes, where they will then move naturally down into the uterus and possibly implant. This procedure is called **zygote intrafallopian transfer (ZIFT).** It seems to increase the chances of success to about 24 percent.

There are now numerous clinics in the United States that offer this process to infertile couples. Over 2,000 babies resulting from the IVF method are now born each year. IVF has generated many controversies, one of which is the use of **preimplantation genetic diagnosis (PGD)** to detect any possible defects. One or more cells may be removed from the blastocyst and then analyzed for chromosomal abnormalities. Presumably, if

in vitro fertilization (IVF): a process whereby the union of the sperm and egg occurs outside the mother's body.

zygote intrafallopian transfer (ZIFT): zygotes resulting from IVF are inserted directly into the fallopian tubes.

preimplantation genetic diagnosis (PGD): examining the chromosomes of an embryo conceived by IVF, prior to implantation in the uterus.

Table 9.1	Scientific Methods for Human Conception			
Procedure	Method	First Successful Outcome with Humans	Cost	Success Rate
In vitro fertilization (IVF)	Dosing a woman with hormones to trigger superovulation, harvesting the eggs and then uniting them with the father's sperm in the laboratory. The resulting embryo is implanted in the mother's womb.	1978 (England)	About $7,800 for each attempt	18%
Gamete intrafallopian transfer (GIFT)	Using a laparoscope, a doctor inserts eggs and sperm directly into the woman's fallopian tube. Any resulting embryos travel naturally into her uterus.	1984 (U.S.)	$6,000 to $10,000 for each attempt	28%
Zygote intrafallopian transfer (ZIFT)	Eggs and sperm are combined in the laboratory. If fertilization occurs, the resulting zygotes are inserted into the woman's fallopian tube.	1989 (Belgium)	$8,000 to $10,000 for each attempt	24%
Intracytoplasmic sperm injection (ICSI)	Injecting a single sperm cell into an egg.	1992 (Belgium)	$10,000 to $12,000	24%
Immature oocyte collection	In a twist on conventional IVF, immature eggs are harvested from the ovaries, cultured in the lab, fertilized and transferred back into the woman's womb.	1991 (South Korea)	Not available	Not available

From "Helping Mother Nature" in *Time,* Fall 1996. Copyright © 1996 Time Inc. Reprinted by permission.

some disorder is detected by PGD, the embryo is then destroyed, raising ethical concerns on the part of people who feel that an embryo is a viable stage of human life that should not be terminated.

In the United States, the success rate of births from IVF averages about 20 percent. Patients who have special risk factors, such as being older or having a history of repeated miscarriages, are less likely to be successful. The actual sperm-ovum fertilization is achieved about 60 percent of the time, but the chances of clinical pregnancy occurring with transplants of single embryos are only about one in six. Beyond that, there is still a one-third risk that the pregnancy will be ectopic or end in miscarriage. Success rates are improved when more than one embryo is transferred to a woman's uterus during a single try. The chances of pregnancy increase to 25 percent when four embryos are transferred and increase to 26 percent with five or six embryos. However, use of multiple embryos then increases the potential for multiple pregnancy, with subsequent risks of miscarriage, premature delivery, and infant mortality at the time of birth.

Some fertility clinics have advertised inaccurately high IVF success rates of 25 to 50 percent, apparently referring to the estimated number of pregnancies achieved, rather than the number of actual live births. It is therefore crucial that couples investigate any IVF clinic's length of service, success rates, costs, and manner of producing statistics on "success." It is important to know whether all attempts to achieve IVF are included in the statistics or only those that result in actual fertilization and transfer of the embryo to the uterus. The financial stakes can also be high. Although a single treatment cycle averages $8,000, the chances are not that good that it will yield a viable pregnancy. Extrapolating from current data, it has been estimated that the average couple will spend between $67,000 and $114,000 to have a child through IVF (Neumann, Gharib, & Weinstein, 1994). Because there is no guarantee of success, there may also be a significant emotional toll in continuing disappointment. See Table 9.1 for a summary of various procedures and their costs.

Other Fertilization Technologies

One of the more complex and costly technological problems with IVF has been assuring that enough viable sperm and eggs are available for the fertilization process. Alternative techniques have been developed to optimize the chances of conception, depending on

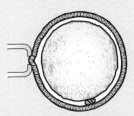

1. A micropipette 60 microns wide uses gentle suction to hold the egg.

2. A single healthy sperm is taken up by an even smaller pipette 7 microns wide.

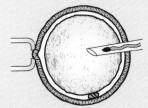

3. The pipette with the sperm is carefully inserted into the egg and the sperm is pumped out.

4. The pipette is withdrawn, allowing the egg to fertilize. The fertilized egg is then implanted in the woman's uterus.

FIGURE 9.12 *Intracytoplasmic Sperm Injection*

Intracytoplasmic sperm injection, unlike conventional IVF, involves placing the sperm within the egg, using a micropipette. About 60 percent of eggs fertilized this way are carried to term.

Source: From "New Method Aids Infertile Men" in *New Haven Connecticut Register,* November 14, 1995, New Haven, CT.

the fertility problem involved. In about half of infertile couples, the man has a low enough sperm count to make conception impossible. In one technique designed to increase the likelihood of fertilization for such couples, eggs are removed from the ovary and injected through a catheter into the woman's fallopian tube. Sperm cells that have been separated from the partner's semen, thus concentrating them, are then injected directly into the same area, making fertilization a more likely result. This procedure is called **gamete intrafallopian transfer (GIFT)** and increases the chances of success to about 28 percent.

Another technique is called **intracytoplasmic sperm injection (ICSI).** A single sperm cell is isolated in a microscopic pipette and then is injected directly into an ovum that is being held in place by a slightly larger pipette (see Figs. 9.12 and 9.13). Although this technique was originally developed in Belgium, it is being used with a 24 percent success rate in the United States. Research has indicated that infants conceived in this manner are about twice as likely to have major abnormalities as compared to infants conceived naturally (ISLAT Working Group, 1998).

There are two ways in which the most viable sperm may be selected for use in ICSI. **Computerized sperm selection** makes use of a computerized scanning method that identifies the most motile sperm in a

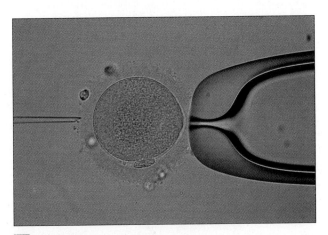

FIGURE 9.13 *Moment of Truth*

Injection of egg with sperm.

gamete intrafallopian transfer (GIFT): direct placement of ovum and concentrated sperm cells into the woman's fallopian tube to increase the chances of fertilization.

intracytoplasmic sperm injection (ICSI): a technique involving the injection of a single sperm cell directly into an ovum. It is useful in cases where the male has a low sperm count.

computerized sperm selection: use of computer scanning to identify the most viable sperm, which are then extracted to be used for fertilization of an ovum in the laboratory.

What Not to Say to an Infertile Couple

When a couple is having trouble getting pregnant, it's painful for them to constantly field questions such as "Are you pregnant yet?"

Here are the 10 worst things to say to an infertile couple, according to a member of the support group RESOLVE.

1) "Relax." Tops in the blame-the-victim category.
2) "No children? Then you must have a big career." What about aging baby boomers with no big careers or children?
3) "I know two women who adopted and then got pregnant." The rate at which adoptive parents spontaneously conceive is about 5 percent, the same as for infertile couples who have not adopted.
4) "You're not taking drugs, are you?" Chances are she is and, of course, she's concerned about multiple births.
5) "Maybe you've created it." Another tacky version of blame-the-victim.
6) "Well, you must be having fun trying." Not with regimented sex dominated by thermometers, charts, medical tests and the clock.
7) "You want kids? Take mine." You don't really mean this, and the infertile person doesn't want your kids.
8) "It's better not to bring a baby into this world anyway." Age-old advice that has been considered and discarded for life affirmation.
9) "I have the opposite problem. He looks at me and I'm pregnant." You do not have a problem.
10) "Your work is your contribution to society." Infertile people feel robbed when they hear this and resigned to childlessness.

Source: "1 in 6 couples has problem of infertility." *Watertown (NY) Daily Times,* April 6, 1996, p. 14.

semen sample. These sperm are then individually removed by a microscopically fine pipette. For men who have anatomical abnormalities that interfere with transport of sperm out of the testes or whose sperm tend to have low motility, sperm may be suctioned directly out of the epididymis of the testes through a tiny pipette. This is called **microscopic epididymal sperm aspiration (MESA)** (Katz, 1995). The technique has even been used to obtain sperm from men who have just died, when their wives wish to reserve the possibility of having their children. In 1998, a woman was impregnated with sperm from her dead husband. One of the controversial issues surrounding ICSI and related technologies for infertile men is the recent finding that males produced by such fertilization technologies are likely to perpetuate the genetic glitches that originally caused their fathers' infertility (Pryor et al., 1997).

There is other hope for males who have impaired sperm production. Experimentation with other mammals has succeeded in transplanting sperm-producing cells from the testes of one male into the testes of an infertile male. In 70 percent of the transplanted animals, viable sperm have been produced after the transplants. There is now evidence that the sperm-producing cells could be frozen and stored for later use, and then sperm might even be able to be cultivated in the testes of a different mammal species. Naturally, this work

raises even further ethical issues (Brinster & Zimmerman, 1994; Kolata, 1996).

The most common technique presently used to obtain eggs from the woman involves daily fertility injections for a period of 2 weeks. These cause several ova to mature in the ovaries but may also have uncomfortable physical and emotional side effects such as bloating, pain, and mood swings. The ovaries are carefully monitored through daily blood tests and ultrasound techniques, so that the mature eggs may be surgically removed at exactly the right time. IVF researchers in Australia are developing a new approach that may save a great deal of time and money and eliminate the need for fertility drugs. Called **immature oocyte collection,** this technique makes use of a specially designed needle to enter small, immature follicles in the ovary, removing immature egg cells, or oocytes. Cell-culturing processes

microscopic epididymal sperm aspiration (MESA): a procedure in which sperm are removed directly from the epididymis of the male testes.

immature oocyte collection: extraction of immature eggs from undeveloped follicles in an ovary, after which the oocytes are matured through cell culturing methods to be prepared for fertilization.

What's Available Now

 Fertility Drugs
A woman usually produces one egg a month. These drugs can cause multiple eggs to ripen.

 In Vitro Fertilization
Eggs are harvested from the ovary and fertilized in a petri dish. After embryos begin to develop, they are placed in the uterus.

 Sperm Injection
Using an ultrafine needle, a single sperm is injected into an egg to achieve fertilization.

 Donor Egg
Eggs are taken from one woman and fertilized in a petri dish. The resulting embryos are implanted in another woman.

 Frozen Embryo
Extra embryos created during the in vitro process can be frozen and stored for future use.

What's On The Horizon

 Frozen Eggs
A woman's eggs are harvested and frozen for thawing and fertilization at a later date. The procedure is still experimental and not widely available.

 Frozen Ovaries
Sections of the ovaries containing immature eggs can be removed and frozen. When the eggs are needed, they may be thawed and matured.

 DNA Transfer
To bypass an older egg's less reliable cellular machinery, the nucleus of the older egg is swapped with that of a younger one.

 Cytoplasmic Donation
Cytoplasm from a younger egg can be added to an older one, improving chances that the receiving egg will develop properly.

 Improved Growth Media
New chemical solutions that mimic those in the female reproductive tract will make it possible to implant hardier, more mature embryos.

 FIGURE 9.14 *Infertility Treatment—Now and in the Future*

Source: Copyright © 1997 Time, Inc. Reprinted by permission.

are then used to ripen the immature eggs in the laboratory, readying them for IVF. Because much of the cost of IVF is associated with the treatment of ovaries to produce mature eggs, this new process could trim the costs of IVF by as much as 80 percent.

What sorts of ethical controls do you feel should be exerted over the reproductive technologies?

There is also a procedure that allows one woman to donate eggs to another woman, whose mate's sperm may then be used for fertilization. This is used in women who have already reached menopause or have some ovarian condition that prevents them from producing healthy ova. Following IVF, the embryo is then implanted into the uterus of the woman unable to produce eggs of her own. This is called **ovum donation.** Some fertility clinics have established "egg banks," so that eggs can be made available to sterile women. In another procedure, called **artificial embryonation,** a developing embryo is flushed from the uterus of the donor woman 5 days after fertilization and transferred to another woman's uterus. This technique has the potential for allowing otherwise infertile couples to go through a pregnancy and birth, even though the child would not genetically be their own.

Ovum donation and artificial embryonation have helped some women defy their biological clocks, enabling them to become pregnant even after menopause (see Fig. 9.14). Although menopause causes a cessation in the production of viable eggs, the uterus of postmenopausal women can sometimes still

support a pregnancy. Techniques have been developed that have actually enabled a number of postmenopausal women to bear children. In 1997, there was controversy surrounding the case of a 63-year-old woman who had told physicians that she was 50 and then was treated over a 3-year period before becoming pregnant with an IVF embryo formed from a donated ovum fertilized by her husband's sperm. Typically, such procedures are limited to women no older than 55, and this case raised ethical issues about the advisability of defying nature in such a way that allows older parents to bear children because they will be relatively old as the child develops and matures (Kolata, 1996). A few postmenopausal women have given birth to their own grandchildren, produced by IVF from their daughters' ova and sons-in-law's sperm. Some countries have considered legislation banning postmenopausal women from becoming pregnant through such techniques, although social commentators have pointed out that older men have never been prohibited from fathering children.

ovum donation: use of an egg from another woman for conception, with the fertilized ovum then being implanted in the uterus of the woman wanting to become pregnant.

artificial embryonation: a process in which the developing embryo is flushed from the uterus of the donor woman 5 days after fertilization and placed in another woman's uterus.

The Big Picture

Buying Genes

Brown eggs cost more than white at my supermarket. From large through extra-large to jumbo, there's an orderly progression of prices, with a premium for color.

There is a market in human eggs, too, although we judge them by different criteria.

The latest story about human eggs comes from early March, when a couple advertised in newspapers on the campuses of such universities as Harvard, Princeton, and Stanford, offering to pay $50,000 for the eggs of a woman who is 5'10" or taller and who had scored at least 1400 on her SATS. It's the height thing that pulled the story forward. The money isn't out of line, actually: $35,000 to $50,000 has been the going rate for Ivy League eggs for months now. But people have been wondering, "Why so tall?" Not, I notice, "Why so smart?"

Adoption, too, operates like a market, but the hierarchy for human children is the opposite of that for hen's eggs. With children, the younger (smaller) and lighter are more expensive than the older and darker. Big enough or dark enough, and you can't give the kids away: Our foster-care system is overflowing with unplaced children, too dark or too long on the shelf.

The marker has long affected sperm banks, too, with ads for sperm donors aimed at medical students through the 1970s, but shifting to business students in the 1980s. Surely that change reflected the increasing status of business executives in our culture.

In a system of "donating" gametes in which banking is the dominant metaphor, sperm and eggs naturally are sorted by "worth." That forces us to confront the question of what makes for "worth" in human beings. We don't like to speak of eugenics anymore, but it is hard not to think of eugenics when people are actively seeking the very best genes money can buy. . . .

If we cannot ban the sale of human eggs and sperm, what can we do? When we discuss the implications of new reproductive technologies, we usually focus on ways to protect the children who result. However, we must not ignore what the technologies mean for potential mothers and fathers, and for the way we define family. Children are not consumer good, and parenting is more about nurturing relationship than about biology and genetics.

Nor must we forget the third parties. It is college women who are being targeted in college-newspaper ads for egg donors. They are our students. In the days of the eugenics movement, elite college women were told to go home and breed, to prevent the "elite stock" from dying out. Eugenics courses are no longer, as they once were, a regular and respectable part of the college curriculum. But does it absolve us of responsibility if the class session that a woman misses for her appointment at the egg-donation clinic is in bioethics, instead of eugenics?

—Barbara Katz Rothman, "The Potential Cost of the Best Genes Money Can Buy," *The Chronicle of Higher Education,* June 11, 1999, p. A52. Adapted from *Genetic Maps and Human Imaginations,* by Barbara Katz Rothman. Reprinted with permission.

For the time being, these procedures are expensive, unreliable, or still in development. It is not likely that the expense and inconvenience would persuade anyone to use the procedure as a substitute for procreative sexual intercourse. Yet as the techniques are perfected and made more affordable, it is conceivable that they could be used by women who want their own genetic babies but are unwilling to become pregnant. Their embryos could be transferred to another woman for gestation. An even more startling step would be the complete in vitro gestation of a fetus in a laboratory, until it could be removed and be self-sustaining. Some scientists believe that it will only be a matter of time and continued experimentation before someone produces a full-term, living baby outside of the human body—a real test-tube baby.

Choosing the Sex of a Fetus

People are usually curious about the sex of a child before it is born. In fact, some would like to be able to choose the sex of their child ahead of time. There have been many folk methods purported to predetermine a child's sex described in various cultures, but reproductive technology has not yet been able to offer simple and reliable techniques for assuring the outcome. There has been some evidence over the years that social and psychological factors might affect the sex determination of human offspring. For example, during and after major wars, more males than females are born, sometimes called the "returning soldier effect." The older the father is and the younger the mother, the more likely the baby will be a boy. When the mother is older, the more likely a baby will be a girl (Manning, Anderton, & Shutt, 1997).

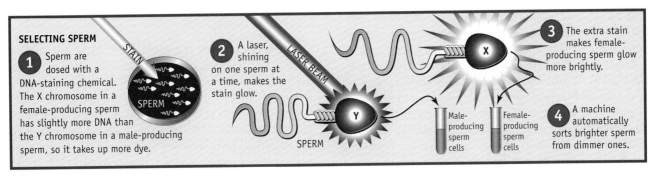

What are your opinions about being able to choose the sex of your child? Would you make use of technology to make such a choice?

FOH   A few approaches to selecting an infant's sex have emerged in modern technology. There are techniques by which either the X-bearing or Y-bearing sperm may be sorted out before artificial insemination or IVF to increase the chances of the baby's being a girl or a boy. Though complicated and expensive, these techniques may increase the chances of having a girl to about 80 percent and the chances of having a boy to about 65 percent (see Figure 9.15) (Golden, 1998). Other techniques have been suggested as well, including changing the diet prior to conception, timing of intercourse to be slightly before or slightly after ovulation in the menstrual cycle, and modifying the pH of the vagina. Research has tended to indicate that such procedures do not produce statistically valid results and are probably worthless (Wilcox, Weinberg, & Baird, 1996).

A prevalent view in the medical community is that patients should have the right to make choices about issues that they feel are in their best interests, and more than half of U.S. geneticists have indicated a willingness either to perform prenatal tests to determine the sex of the fetus or to refer a patient to someone who would perform such a test. However, the ability to choose the sex of a child raises some troublesome ethical issues for the parents and for society. Studies in the United States consistently demonstrate that couples tend to have preferences for sons, especially as their first child (Unger & Molina, 1997). When parents have had two children of the same sex, either female or male, there is a greater likelihood that they will have another child (Yamaguchi & Ferguson, 1995). The preference for male children is, in fact, found in many cultures and can translate into prejudice and sexism. This has raised fears that predetermination of gender could create a population overweighted by males, whereas others feel that couples should be free to use available

technology for choosing the sex of their children and that the genders will ultimately balance out anyway (Layne, 1999).

Techniques such as chorionic villi sampling or amniocentesis (see p. 289) can identify the sex of a fetus within a few weeks after conception by identifying the sex chromosomes in fetal cells. Beyond simply knowing the sex of the expected child, parents then have the option of early abortion if the sex of the child is not what they had hoped for. This has become a common, though

CLOSE TO HOME   JOHN McPHERSON

"What? Oh, geez, no. The baby's not due until September. We just got our sonogram results today."

still illegal, practice in China, where couples are generally allowed only one child (Gillis, 1995). The ratio of males to females among live births in China has increased overall to 114 to 100 and in some rural areas to as high as 140 to 100. Concern is now growing that by the year 2010, there will be an estimated "excess" of about 1 million males in the first-marriage market. Similar trends are developing in India, Bangladesh, Pakistan, and South Korea. Such an outcome may have profound social implications and may eventually require some new partnering patterns to accommodate the imbalance (Gillis, 1995; Tuljapurkar, Li, & Feldman, 1995).

Ethical questions have also been raised about the use of costly medical resources and procedures for what might be seen as rather frivolous, nonmedical reasons, when some women could not afford the procedures as valid medical treatment. It has been argued that if precedents are set in favor of gender selection, parents may then begin selecting for other characteristics such as height, weight, skin color, and so on. At this point, the techniques for sex selection are not frequently used in North America as such because they are unreliable and costly.

Human Cloning

Cloning is a process of reproductive technology that allows for duplication of genetic material so that the offspring are genetically identical. The original cloning process bypassed even the fertilization stage. In 1968, Oxford University scientist J. B. Gurdon succeeded in replacing the nucleus of a frog's egg with the nucleus of an intestinal cell from another frog. The egg divided normally and eventually formed a tadpole that became an adult frog. Because the new frog's cells contained exactly the same set of chromosomes as the frog that donated the intestinal cell, the two frogs were genetically identical; the exact-copy offspring is called a **clone.** A

> **cloning:** a process by which genetic duplicate of an organism is made either by substituting the chromosomes of a body cell into a donated ovum or by separation of cells in early embryonic development.
>
> **clone:** the genetic-duplicate organism produced by the cloning process.

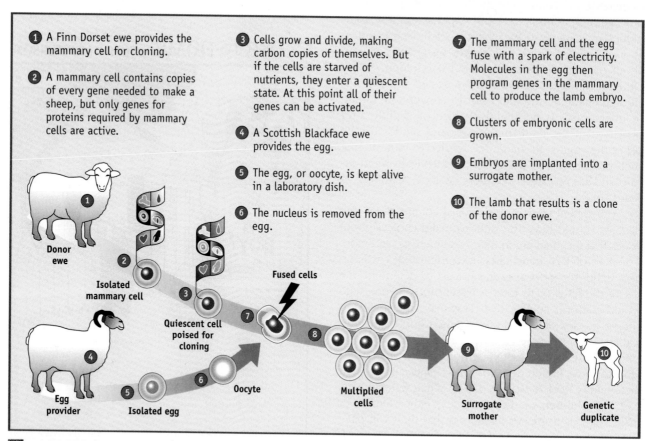

1. A Finn Dorset ewe provides the mammary cell for cloning.
2. A mammary cell contains copies of every gene needed to make a sheep, but only genes for proteins required by mammary cells are active.
3. Cells grow and divide, making carbon copies of themselves. But if the cells are starved of nutrients, they enter a quiescent state. At this point all of their genes can be activated.
4. A Scottish Blackface ewe provides the egg.
5. The egg, or oocyte, is kept alive in a laboratory dish.
6. The nucleus is removed from the egg.
7. The mammary cell and the egg fuse with a spark of electricity. Molecules in the egg then program genes in the mammary cell to produce the lamb embryo.
8. Clusters of embryonic cells are grown.
9. Embryos are implanted into a surrogate mother.
10. The lamb that results is a clone of the donor ewe.

Donor ewe · Isolated mammary cell · Egg provider · Isolated egg · Quiescent cell poised for cloning · Oocyte · Fused cells · Multiplied cells · Surrogate mother · Genetic duplicate

FIGURE 9.16   *Send in the Clones*

Scientists once thought that cloning an animal from an adult cell was impossible. Although every cell contains the complete genetic blueprint for making a new animal, those instructions cannot be read in adult cells; they have become specialists, producing cells only for a single body part. The Scottish team figured out how to turn on all the genes needed to make a lamb from a single adult sheep cell.

great public stir was created in 1997 when Scottish researcher Ian Wilmut introduced to the world a 7-month-old sheep clone named Dolly. She had been cloned from an udder cell of another sheep, and she represented the first known successful cloning of a mammal (see Fig. 9.16). Subsequently, mice, cows, monkeys, and pigs have also been successfully cloned (Cibelli et al., 1998). Concerns continue to be raised about the potentials for human cloning, and legislatures around the world have proposed laws to ban such work. Given the pace of scientific inquiry, the laws quickly become obsolete (Andrews, 1998). Scientists are equally concerned that haphazard enactment of laws may well interfere with other forms of research that advance the techniques of medicine (Berg & Singer, 1998; Kiernan, 1998).

A variation of the cloning technique has already been tried at the human embryonic level, using a technique to separate embryo cells at a very early stage of development. This "cloning" of embryos is of great interest because of the desire to produce embryos more easily for IVF. Scientists were successful in using an ex-

perimental technique for this purpose in 1993, although the clones were not used for IVF, and there was no attempt to gestate the embryos to maturity. The researchers worked with human ova that had been fertilized by more than one sperm, so that they constituted abnormal embryos. After the fertilized ovum had divided to form two cells, the protective zona pellucida was removed with an enzyme preparation so that the two identical cells could be completely separated. A new artificial protective coating, created from a gel derived from seaweed, was then placed around each cell, and the cells continued to divide for 6 more days. The development process apparently stopped because the embryos were genetically abnormal from the time of fertilization (see Fig. 9.17). Forty-eight embryo clones were created in all. The purpose of this research was to investigate ways of producing extra embryos to be used for IVF that would avoid the complicated process of removing individual eggs from the ovary and fertilizing each of them with sperm. Using this variant cloning process, multiple embryos could be produced from a

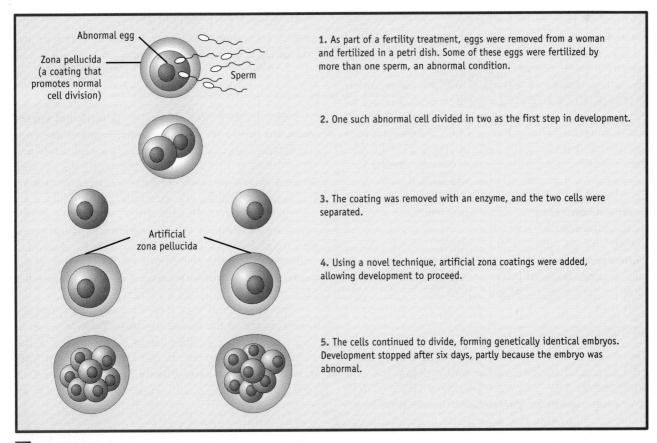

Abnormal egg

Zona pellucida (a coating that promotes normal cell division)

Sperm

Artificial zona pellucida

1. As part of a fertility treatment, eggs were removed from a woman and fertilized in a petri dish. Some of these eggs were fertilized by more than one sperm, an abnormal condition.

2. One such abnormal cell divided in two as the first step in development.

3. The coating was removed with an enzyme, and the two cells were separated.

4. Using a novel technique, artificial zona coatings were added, allowing development to proceed.

5. The cells continued to divide, forming genetically identical embryos. Development stopped after six days, partly because the embryo was abnormal.

FIGURE 9.17 *How Human Embryos Were Genetically Duplicated*

Duplicate human embryos, "clones" in the sense that their genetic material was exactly the same, were created in 1993. Although it would be primarily intended to help infertile couples become pregnant, this "cloning" technique has raised serious ethical questions around the world and has now been generally considered unethical. This figure describes a process used to effect the separation of two fertilized cells.

single fertilized egg and then stored for possible implantation at a later time. In essence, the researchers created identical twins, or other multiples, that could hypothetically be gestated and born at different times. Public furor over such research, coupled with ethical doubts in the scientific community, has put much embryo cloning research on hold (Andrews, 1998).

Cloning raises some of the most fascinating ethical questions concerning the future of reproductive technology. For example, cloning techniques could be used to reproduce a child with exceptional characteristics and achievement for the same or different parents. Or parents might set aside genetic duplicates of each of their children, so that if one died, they could in theory produce another child who would look exactly the same. Another scenario predicts the possibility of using cloned embryos to produce a genetic duplicate if a child needed a bone marrow or kidney transplant, therefore eliminating problems of immune system rejection. It is even possible that someday a woman could give birth to her own twin. Naturally, these are controversial possibilities that have raised the ire of many observers. Public opinion polls reflect a predominantly negative stance concerning cloning, although in one poll, 7 percent of respondents said they would clone themselves if they had the chance (Kluger, 1997).

By 1999, studies on the development of cloned mammals were beginning to raise serious concerns about the technique. It was found that the cells of clones tend to be accelerated in their aging process, seeming to catch up with the age of the genes in the original animal that donated the cell for cloning. Dolly, the sheep clone, has genetic material that is aging at about twice the rate that would be typical for her age. Several mammalian clones have either suffered from serious birth defects or have developed fatal conditions after seeming to be healthy at birth. These studies suggest that there is much more to be learned about the action of genes within cloned animals. Like other reproductive technologies, cloning techniques will surely continue to be developed, and we must begin to prepare for the impact they will have for human sexuality and human life.

Guidelines for Embryo Research

The complex ethical issues surrounding human embryo research have entered the public policy and political arenas. The National Institutes of Health (NIH) have promulgated recommendations from an advisory committee indicating that it would be in the public interest to fund experimentation with human embryos in the early stages of development. Recognizing that there were moral issues at stake as well, the NIH also imposed restrictions on such research. One of the most significant guidelines was that research should not proceed past the 14th day of development, when

tissues of a rudimentary nervous system begin to appear, although some work up to the 18th day was considered worthy of further consideration. However, in 1996, Congress voted to ban the use of federal funds for any human embryo research. At least one embryologist has lost all NIH funding because officials said he violated the Congressional ban (Marshall, 1997), and a number of lawsuits are in process against fertility clinics that have used embryos conceived by IVF for purposes that were not approved by their donors.

The embryo research guidelines specifically prohibit the transfer of human embryos to animals for gestation, cloning of twins for actual gestation, sex selection of embryos, cross-species fertilization, and the use of gametes or embryos from donors who have not given explicit consent to have them used for research. The guidelines call for further consideration of embryo cloning for research purposes only and the use of fetal oocytes to create embryos for research (Marshall, 1997). Because there are potentially significant financial gains that will eventually emerge from such research, it is likely that private funding will continue to be used in support of embryo research in the United States. Some other countries, including France, have banned most forms of embryo research altogether. The controversies are bound to continue and will surely generate heated debate.

Surrogate Motherhood

Surrogate motherhood, also called **gestational surrogacy,** has been a feasible reproductive procedure since the 1980s. Typically in these cases, a couple in which the woman is unable to bear children pays another woman several thousand dollars to carry a pregnancy for them. Sometimes the surrogate is inseminated by the infertile woman's husband, and sometimes an embryo formed from IVF of the couple's sperm and egg is implanted in the surrogate's uterus. A legal agreement is drawn up among the parties involved in which the woman who is to be impregnated promises to give the child to the couple when it is born.

The ethical and legal issues surrounding surrogacy were first put to the test in the 1987 "Baby M" case, in which a surrogate mother asked for the return of the child she had borne for another couple. The surrogate mother claimed in court that the intended mother had paid her to have the child because of a desire not to let

gestational surrogacy: implantation of an embryo created by the sperm and ovum of one set of parents into the uterus of another woman who agrees to gestate the fetus and give birth to the child, which is then given to the original parents.

pregnancy interfere with her own career. The woman and her husband, who had contributed the sperm for the child, argued that they had opted for surrogate motherhood because the woman suffered from multiple sclerosis. Eventually the court allowed the couple to keep the child but also granted the surrogate mother some visitation rights because she had contributed the egg for conception. In 1993, building on previous state precedents, California's supreme court denied any rights to a surrogate mother who had given birth to a child who was the product of the egg and sperm of the couple that had contracted with her. In this case, the surrogate had no genetic relationship to the child. The court ruled that the surrogacy agreement was as valid as any other voluntary contract and that it did not exploit the surrogate mother. Given the complicated issues that have been arising, numerous state legislatures have developed statutes to regulate gestational surrogacy.

Although some have hailed gestational surrogacy as a significant advance for childless couples, others have argued that it is nothing more than reproductive prostitution. It has been suggested that gestational surrogacy, which today may cost well over $25,000, including medical procedures, legal costs, and the fee paid to the surrogate, could represent the first step toward creating a caste of poor female breeders who would bear genetically improved children for upper-class couples. Opponents feel there is little difference between this procedure and the long-prohibited practice of selling babies for private adoption. It has also been claimed that the legal protections for the surrogate mother are slim compared with those for the couple, further escalating the argument that surrogate motherhood represents a form of exploitation for women (Layne, 1999).

Fetal Technology

Problems can occur during fetal development. Great strides are being made in diagnosing, and even treating, medical difficulties in the fetus. When techniques such as IVF are used, embryos may be genetically tested prior to implantation in the uterus. Beyond that point, there are other procedures that may be used to monitor the health and genetic makeup of the fetus.

Amniocentesis

FoH A well-known technique is **amniocentesis,** used to detect certain genetic disorders such as Down syndrome, an increasing risk in the children of women who become pregnant after age 35, and muscular dystrophy, as well as to monitor fetal development (Rapp, 1999). In this procedure, a needle is inserted through the abdominal wall, into the uterus and the amniotic sac, so that amniotic fluid may be withdrawn (see Fig. 9.18). Cells from the developing fetus may be found in this fluid and their chromosomes studied for possible abnormali-

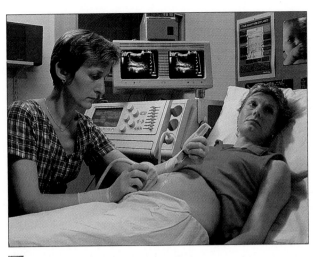

FIGURE 9.18   *Amniocentesis*

A woman, 16 weeks pregnant, undergoes the procedure of amniocentesis. The amniotic fluid is extracted from the uterus and analyzed. It will indicate the gender of the child as well as possible birth defects.

ties. If some birth defect is identified, the parents can make a decision about whether to continue or terminate the pregnancy. Analysis of chromosomes also can determine whether the fetus is female or male. Because there are some risks associated with the procedure, including possible miscarriage, amniocentesis is not used routinely for sex determination. Pregnancy complications are significantly less common when amniocentesis is performed 16 to 19 weeks into pregnancy, as opposed to 11 to 14 weeks (Blumfield et al., 1996). A new way of examining fetal blood cells that carries none of the risks associated with amniocentesis is now being tested. It involves the sifting out of fetal blood cells from the mother's bloodstream, so there is no need to penetrate the amnion (Durrant et al., 1996).

Chorionic Villi Sampling

Whereas amniocentesis cannot be used until the end of the fourth month of pregnancy, there is another diagnostic technique called **chorionic villi sampling (CVS),** which can be used as early as the

---

amniocentesis (am-nee-oh-sen-TEE-sis): a process whereby medical problems with a fetus can be determined while it is still in the womb; a needle is inserted into the amniotic sac, amniotic fluid is withdrawn, and fetal cells are examined.

chorionic villi sampling (CVS): a technique for diagnosing medical problems in the fetus as early as the eighth week of pregnancy; a sample of the chorionic membrane is removed through the cervix and studied.

eighth week. A thin catheter is inserted through the cervix, and a small sample of tissue from the chorionic membrane is withdrawn. The chromosomes in these cells may then be analyzed. Although it was once suspected that CVS was associated with a higher incidence of limb defects in infants, research has now demonstrated that the procedure is actually correlated with a decreased likelihood of such problems (Froster & Jackson, 1996).

Ultrasound Images

One of the techniques that has made amniocentesis and other fetal diagnostic methods possible is the use of ultrasound images or **sonograms.** It is dangerous to expose a mother and fetus to X rays, and so ultrasonic waves are used instead to produce a computer-generated picture of internal structures. This assists in the positioning of the needle for amniocentesis and may also be used for finding certain birth defects, determining the position of a fetus, or checking to see if more than one fetus is present. Ultrasound may produce a slight rise in temperature and jarring vibrations in the surrounding tissues, so the Food and Drug Administration (FDA) has recommended that the technique be used as sparingly as possible. Many clinicians in the United States are using at least one ultrasound as a routine procedure during pregnancy, as is standard in Germany and France, but several studies have indicated that the outcomes for both the fetus and mother do not seem to be improved by its routine use (R. Turner, 1994). Frequent ultrasound examinations seem to be associated with a lower birth weight for the infant (Macdonald, 1996). "Keepsake" sonograms—lengthy videos of ultrasound images of the fetus made by nonmedical personnel solely for the enjoyment of the parents—are considered unnecessary and potentially damaging by the FDA. There is general agreement that ultrasound should be considered unnecessary unless there is a specific medical reason such as internal bleeding, indications the fetus is not growing properly, the possibility of multiple fetuses, or a family history of birth defects.

Embryoscopy, Fetoscopy, and Imaging

Technology now permits visual examination of embryos and fetuses. An endoscope is inserted through a hollow needle that is used to penetrate the uterus and amnion. The embryoscope or fetoscope may then be used to look for possible developmental abnormalities. It is expected that variations on this technique may be used to offer surgery or treatment during the first 12 weeks of pregnancy. Magnetic resonance imaging (MRI) and other noninvasive imaging techniques continue to be developed in ways that they could be used to examine embryos and fetuses as well.

Fetal Surgery

Ultrasound images are also crucial in one of the newest technological advances, **fetal surgery.** At a few major medical centers, techniques are being used to perform actual surgical procedures on a fetus while it is still in the uterus. This has been most successful with urinary tract problems that can be diagnosed during pregnancy. There have also been several successful surgeries on fetuses that have actually been removed from the uterus and then replaced following surgery. They were then born normally. This technique has been used to repair diaphragmatic hernia and fetal heart defects. Fetal surgery represents one of the frontiers of reproductive and fetal technology that is seeing rapid and dramatic developments on a regular basis, although many fetuses do not survive the surgical procedures (Casper, 1998).

> *Even though we have the technology to examine all fetuses for birth defects, should we? Explain your position.*

Infertility and Sexuality

Not all couples who want to have children are able to do so. If successful pregnancy has not occurred after a period of a year or more of intercourse without contraception, there may be an **infertility** problem (Velde & Cohlen, 1999). There is evidence that the rate of fertility difficulties is on the increase, and there has been some concern that environmental pollutants may be leading to the increase. About 15 percent of nonsterilized, sexually experienced women, or about 10 percent of all women of reproductive age, report having problems with conception or carrying a pregnancy to term. Women with histories of pelvic inflammatory disease, endometriosis, diabetes, or hypertension seem to be particularly prone to infertility (Chandra & Stephen, 1998), and women who smoke tobacco seem to take a longer time to conceive (Bolumar, 1996). It may be that half or more of infertile women can eventually become pregnant without any medical intervention, but the problem may be more persistent for the others.

Male infertility is usually caused by a low sperm count, which is less than 40 million sperm per cubic

---

sonograms: ultrasonic rays used to project a picture of internal structures such as the fetus; often used in conjunction with amniocentesis or fetal surgery.

fetal surgery: a surgical procedure performed on the fetus while it is still in the uterus or during a temporary period of removal from the uterus.

infertility: the inability to produce offspring.

CASE STUDY

Pregnancy and Birth: A Personal Experience

"The distinct moments of giving birth to my two children were the most powerful and profound acts I have ever performed. At no other time in life does the planning, waiting, physical exertion, and time devoted to a task pay off with such magnificent results—the beginning of life for a whole new person. Both times, Gary and I were rendered speechless when our daughters emerged. You always know intellectually that the processes of reproduction and birth are supposed to result in the birth of a child. But not until you see that little body with eyes wide and searching with a powerful intensity are you struck with a miracle that has become reality.

"The physical aspects of pregnancy and birth are the most obvious, but the psychological and relational aspects have the most profound effect. During the pregnancies, there were times when I very deeply needed to feel loved and protected by my husband. There were times

before and after the birth that I needed some proof of autonomy from the child that was a physical part of me for 9 months. Gary and I both vacillated between periods of wanting to escape the whole thing and feeling certain that this experience would bind us together forever. The most crucial thing about facing all of our conflicting emotions was that each of us allowed the other to feel whatever was surfacing and offered support.

"Each time, when I gave that final draining, straining push, and my husband seemed so proud of me and what we had created together, it was a moment like no other in my life. Every rich detail will be forever woven into my memory. To be part of the life-giving forces of the universe is truly an awesome experience."

—Betsy A. Kelly

centimeter of semen, or by sluggish motility of the sperm. Although low sperm counts do not make conception impossible, they do reduce the chances of its occurring. There are several infections and injuries of the testes that may damage the sperm-producing tubules and lead to this problem. Certain drugs, alcohol, and tobacco have also been implicated. Although some medical and surgical treatments have been tried with male infertility, the results have been poor. One recommended method is to avoid ejaculation for 48 hours prior to intercourse in an attempt to raise the number of sperm in the ejaculate. It is also typically suggested that men with low sperm counts avoid lengthy submersion in very warm water, which may temporarily interfere with sperm production. Sperm are produced at a temperature slightly below internal body temperature, due to the external location of the testes.

For couples who have been planning on having children, infertility can represent a very real disappointment, accompanied by a sense of deprivation and a range of difficult emotions such as guilt, anger, and frustration. The reproductive technologies described earlier in this chapter may sometimes help, but they are generally expensive and may have limited success rates that may even increase the levels of frustration and disappointment (Keye, 1999). However, the effects of infertility may not be as devastating as popular myths have suggested. In a survey of the literature on the relational effects of infertility, it was clear that it creates stress and anxiety for both partners, and in particular the woman. Males are more distressed

when the problem is found to be theirs. Infertility may also create feelings of personal inadequacy and interfere with sexual spontaneity. Nevertheless, it does not seem to have a pervasively negative effect on either marital or sexual satisfaction. In fact, for many couples, working together on infertility often brings a deepened sense of commitment and intimacy to the relationship (Burns, 1999).

Pregnancy and Birthing

Prompt diagnosis of pregnancy is crucial, so that prenatal care may be sought in a timely manner. Women who have more comprehensive prenatal care from the early stages of pregnancy are more likely to prevent birth defects in their babies and to have infants with higher birth weights (Elam-Evans, 1996). Children with low birth weights are at significantly higher risk for developmental disabilities, visual impairments, and cerebral palsy, and are less likely to perform well in school (Hessol, Fuentes-Afflick, & Bacchetti, 1998; Paz, 1995). There is abundant evidence that prenatal care is highly cost effective, eventually reducing the costs associated with delivery, especially in high-risk pregnancies (Piper, Mitchel, & Ray, 1996). Choosing a clinician with whom the woman can feel comfortable is always helpful. Physicians who provide prenatal care and delivery of babies are usually obstetrician-gynecologists, although many prenatal clinics use nurse practitioners or other health care providers. In addition, nurse-midwives who can also provide care during pregnancy and the birthing process are in private practice in some areas, with physician backup for complicated cases.

The cause for the majority of birth defects is not known. However, there is growing evidence that toxins and radiation in the environment may damage sperm cells, leading to possible damage to the developing fetus. Pregnant women who are exposed to organic solvents have a sharply elevated risk of having an infant with serious birth defects (Khattak et al., 1999). The chance of birth defects involving development of the brain and spinal cord is increased by exposure to heat during early pregnancy, such as through immersion in hot tubs. The likelihood of neurological defects seems to be reduced in women who use supplements of folic acid, one of the B vitamins, before becoming pregnant. Women who become pregnant in their late thirties or forties may face some special risk factors that should be explained carefully to them. However, it should be noted that women who become pregnant at age 35 or over for the first time seem to adjust emotionally quite well in general. Alcohol use and stress during pregnancy are associated with increased risks for problems with the pregnancy and later health problems for the baby (Nordentoft, 1996; Shu, 1996).

Both women and men can have a wide range of reactions to pregnancy. There are often periods of elation and excitement alternating with feelings of apprehension and concern. It is a stressful time for everyone, with many unknowns. Fathers-to-be often have difficulty sorting out their reactions to pregnancy and feel some shifting in the relationship to the woman. Mothers-to-be may feel somewhat trapped in the "pregnant woman" role and resent that their former individual sense of identity seems to slip away at times. Both parents wonder what it will be like to have a new child in the family and worry about potential problems with the pregnancy, birth, or the baby itself. They may vacillate between being irritable with each other and feeling the special closeness of sharing the pregnancy.

The Biology of Pregnancy

There are many initial signs of pregnancy, although all of them may be caused by other factors. One of the first symptoms is usually the missing of a menstrual period; however, this can have a variety of other causes—including illness, emotional upsets, or changes in living conditions. Also, about 20 percent of women continue having some menstrual flow even during the early stages of pregnancy. Other typical early signs of pregnancy are enlargement and tenderness of the breasts, increased frequency of urination, fatigue, and the experiencing of nausea and vomiting,

especially upon waking in the morning. If most or all of these symptoms are present, pregnancy should be at least suspected. There are other signs for which a clinician can look, such as softening of the lower uterine segment, color changes in the cervical tissues, and enlargement of the uterus.

Pregnancy Tests

Tests for pregnancy involve analysis of the woman's urine or blood to detect the presence of the hormone **human chorionic gonadotropin (HCG),** produced by the embryo and the placenta. There are now many brands of home pregnancy tests available in stores. Directions should be read and followed very carefully. Research indicates that the accuracy of home-test prediction varies a great deal, depending on how carefully the directions have been followed. Women often perform the tests too early in pregnancy, yielding a false positive result. Some women may be misled by the results of home-pregnancy testing (Hatcher et al., 1994). Therefore, even if a home test is positive, most clinics or physicians will still do a repeat test to confirm the pregnancy. Highly sensitive laboratory diagnostic procedures are considered to be 95 to 98 percent accurate 2 weeks after a missed period. There are also laboratory blood tests for HCG that can be almost 100 percent accurate within 7 days after conception.

Pregnant women are usually given advice on diet, proper vitamin supplements (not self-prescribed megadoses), proper rest, clothing, and moderation of activities. Exercise during pregnancy seems to produce healthful results for both mother and infant. Good nutrition is essential to healthy fetal development, and research is indicating that smoking, alcohol, and drugs play a role in creating birth defects and endangering the fetus's life.

Alcohol, Drugs, and Smoking

Heavy alcohol consumption can lead to **fetal alcohol syndrome (FAS),** characterized by abnormal fetal growth, neurological damage, and facial distortion. FAS is the leading cause of birth defects in the United States. It can also cause miscarriage, stillbirth, and premature birth. In infants, FAS can be manifested as brain damage, heart problems, and behavioral difficulties

human chorionic gonadotropin (HCG): a hormone detectable in the urine of a pregnant woman.

fetal alcohol syndrome (FAS): a condition in a fetus characterized by abnormal growth, neurological damage, and facial distortion caused by the mother's heavy alcohol consumption.

such as hyperactivity. Pregnant women are generally advised to avoid drinking alcohol because of these risks. Smoking has also been associated with complications in pregnancy, lower birth weights in babies, lowered intellectual abilities, and later behavior disorders in children.

Use of other drugs—whether prescription, over-the-counter, or illegal—is also ill-advised during pregnancy, although is has been found that the newer antidepressant medications are safe for the fetus (Kulin et al., 1998). Mothers who are addicted to drugs such as cocaine, heroin, amphetamines, or barbiturates give birth to babies who are already addicted themselves and actually experience dangerous withdrawal symptoms. Although the research has been inconclusive, it may be that marijuana use affects fetal development and that heavy, frequent marijuana use can cause defects similar to those in FAS.

Sex during and after Pregnancy

Many clinicians neglect to discuss sexual activity with their patients, and many myths have evolved concerning sex during pregnancy. Research shows that unless there is a medical problem, there is no particular reason to prohibit sexual intercourse at any time during pregnancy, up until the birth process has begun. Clearly, sexual activity that could risk exposure to sexually transmitted diseases should be avoided during pregnancy. In the final months of pregnancy, the woman's abdomen is often distended enough to require modification of the couple's usual intercourse positions. Studies have shown that many pregnant women experience a gradual decline in their sexual drive and frequency of intercourse, which become even more marked in the final 3 months. Some women experience some degree of discomfort or pain during intercourse in the third trimester (Hyde et al., 1996). If coitus is uncomfortable or impossible for either partner, other forms of sexual activity may be engaged in.

After the baby has been born, there seems to be no medical reason to prohibit intercourse after vaginal bleeding has stopped and any tears in the vaginal opening have healed. Most couples have the lowest frequency of sexual activity during the four weeks immediately following giving birth. Research shows that most women resume sexual intercourse within a few weeks, and after 12 months levels of sexual activity typically tend to have returned to the levels experienced prior to pregnancy. Breast-feeding women tend to have less sexual activity and lower levels of sexual satisfaction, possibly the result of both hormonal and psychological factors (Hyde et al., 1996). The new responsibilities and activities of parenthood usually absorb much time and energy for new parents, and this sometimes reduces the opportunities for sex. Using

birth control will be crucial to preventing pregnancy too soon after the birth of a baby. The most recent evidence would suggest that it is best to space pregnancies at least 1 to 2 years apart, in order to give the woman's body a chance to build up nutritional reserves needed to nourish a developing fetus. There is a greater risk of fetal death in pregnancies that occur too soon after another pregnancy (Klebanoff, 1999; Zhu et al., 1999).

The Birth Process

The birth process (see Figs. 9.19 and 9.20) is complex, and its controlling mechanisms are not fully understood. The hormone **oxytocin,** manufactured by the pituitary gland, is believed to play some part in the process. About a month before birth, the fetus shifts to a lower position in the abdomen. By this time, it is normally in its head-downward position. The most common signal that the birth process is beginning is the initiation of uterine contractions experienced as **labor.** The mucus plug that blocked the opening of the cervix is usually expelled just before birth begins and is sometimes seen as a small amount of bloody discharge. At some point in the process, the amniotic sac ruptures, and its fluid pours or dribbles out of the vagina. The labor contractions are relatively mild at first, occurring at intervals of 15 to 20 minutes. Although most couples might find it difficult to relax enough or find the privacy to participate, lovemaking, including intercourse, during the early stages of labor has been shown to facilitate the process of labor and delivery (Moran, 1993). The uterine contractions gradually increase in strength and frequency as the fetus moves downward in the uterus and the cervix is dilated to a diameter of about 10 centimeters. This process of cervical opening or **dilation** and thinning or **effacement** begins before labor and then continues until the cervix is fully open and thinned, permitting delivery of the fetus. This first stage of labor typically takes 10 to 14 hours for a woman experiencing her first delivery. In subsequent deliveries, the time for labor may be somewhat shorter.

oxytocin (ox-ee-TOH-sin): a pituitary hormone believed to play a role in initiating the birth process.

labor: uterine contractions in a pregnant woman; an indication that the birth process is beginning.

dilation: the gradual opening of the cervical opening of the uterus prior to and during labor.

effacement: the thinning of cervical tissue of the uterus prior to and during labor.

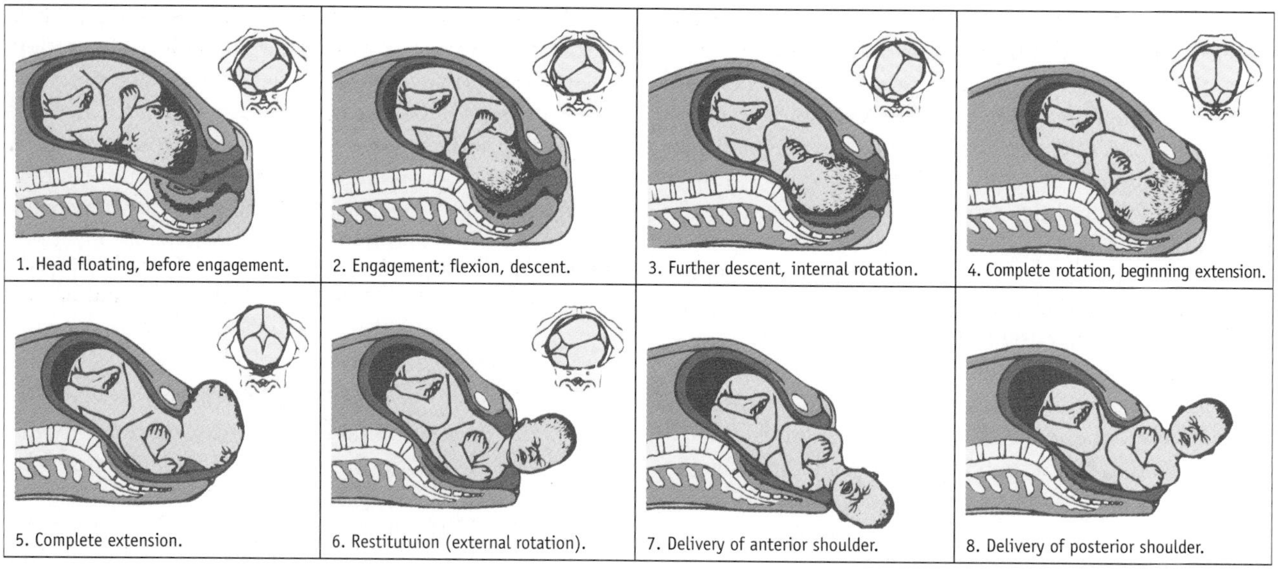

294   Chapter 9   Reproduction, Reproductive Technology, and Birthing

FIGURE 9.19 *Major Stages in the Birth Process*
The fetus is shown in the uterus as labor contractions begin, and the fetus progresses through the stages of birth.

The second stage involves the movement of the fetus through the vagina, now called the **birth canal.** This stage takes an hour or two for a first delivery but may happen more rapidly in subsequent births. The mother can help with this stage of labor by pushing with her abdominal muscles. Eventually the fetus's head appears at the vaginal opening, followed by one shoulder, then the other shoulder, and the rest of the body. The clinician assisting with the birth generally does not pull on the baby but gently guides it out of the birth canal. In the majority of deliveries in North America, it has been typical for a procedure called an **episiotomy** to be performed in order to prevent the tearing of the vaginal opening. It involves cutting the outer part of the vaginal tissue. The incision is later sutured and usually heals without problems. However, it sometimes becomes infected and may take up to 4 weeks to heal completely. About one-sixth of women experience pain or discomfort in the episiotomy scar up to a year after giving birth. Some consider episiotomy to be nearly always unnecessary and recommend against its routine use because it may slow the recovery process. The procedure should only be used when the fetus is in distress or because some instrument must be used to assist in delivery.

When serious problems affect the birth process, the fetus seems too large for the woman's pelvis, or the fetus is experiencing some other form of distress, a surgical procedure can be performed in which the child is removed through an incision in the abdominal wall and uterus. This is called a **cesarian section,** and

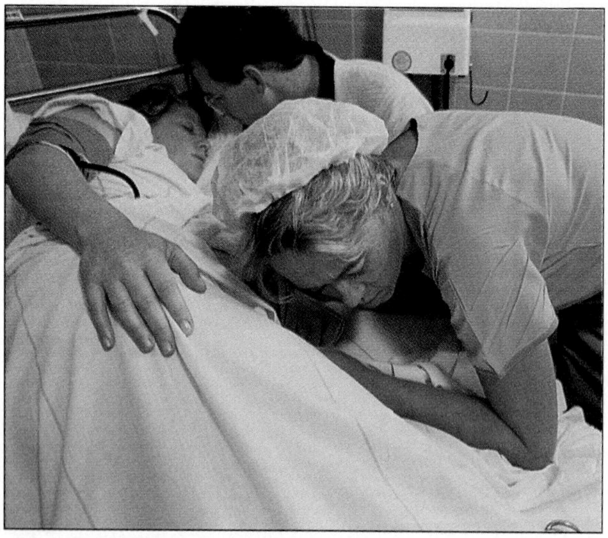

FIGURE 9.20 *Fetal Heartbeat*
As the fetus nears the time for its birth, its heartbeat is monitored.

birth canal: term applied to the vagina during the birth process.

episiotomy (ee-piz-ee-OTT-a-mee): a surgical incision in the vaginal opening made by the clinician or obstetrician to prevent the baby from tearing the opening in the process of being born.

cesarian section: a surgical method of childbirth in which delivery occurs through an incision in the abdominal wall and uterus.

the method has been used increasingly in recent years to lower the risks of complications for the mother and baby. Some authorities believe that a substantial proportion of cesarian births are unnecessary, and since the mid-1990s there has been a decline in use of the procedure. The Department of Health and Human Services wanted to reduce the rate of cesarian deliveries from 21 percent to 15 percent by the year 2000. However, some experts believe that the availability of cesarian delivery has markedly increased the safety of childbearing and that care should be exercised in reducing its incidence just to meet an artificial goal. It was once standard practice to perform cesarian sections on women who had given birth to an earlier child in this manner, but it has now been demonstrated that vaginal delivery can be successful in about 75 percent of women who have previously had cesarian delivery. Again, however, some experts believe that these statistics are not based on solid research and are calling for a reexamination of the potential risks (Sachs et al., 1999).

Very soon after the baby has been born, the third stage of the birth process occurs. The placenta, now a disk of tissue about 8 inches in diameter and 2 inches thick, pulls away from the uterine wall. The uterus expels the placenta, along with the remaining section of umbilical cord and the fetal membranes, through the birth canal. The expelled tissues are collectively called the **afterbirth.**

Birthing Alternatives

In many cultures, giving birth to a baby is viewed as a natural phenomenon not requiring any particular degree of special attention. Over the past century, in more developed countries, medical intervention increasingly became a part of the birthing process. For a time, the whole process was perceived in an illness context, and physicians emphasized using drugs and anesthetics to reduce pain and prescribed a prolonged period of complete bed rest as "convalescence." Delivery of a baby became a mysterious event, best left to doctors and nurses in a hospital setting. Proponents of several other approaches have gradually changed this perspective, restoring more power over birthing to the mother, and often the father.

Natural Childbirth

In 1932, a British physician named Grantly Dick-Read published a book called *Childbirth without Fear*. He believed that the fear of the birthing process generated by medical intervention only created more tension and pain. He educated women thoroughly about labor and delivery and developed relaxation techniques to reduce their tension, calling his method **natural child-**

birth. He instituted the trend toward returning control of the birth process to women and their partners that continues today.

The Lamaze Method

In the 1950s, a similar approach was introduced by a French obstetrician, Fernand Lamaze. The **Lamaze method** of "prepared" childbirth, and methods patterned after it, are very popular today and make use of the baby's father or some other willing participant as a coach for the woman. In prenatal classes, the couple is taught how to use different relaxation and breathing techniques through increasing levels of intensity during labor. Although the Lamaze approach does not prohibit the use of pain medication during labor, it usually reduces the need for it. The woman is able to remain an alert and active participant in giving birth to her baby, a process that her body is well equipped to accomplish.

Pain-Relieving Medication during Birth

As general anesthesia came into common usage for surgical procedures, it also became widely used during delivery of babies so that women would not have to endure any of the pain associated with the latter stages of labor. However, as fetal technology began to demonstrate the potentially harmful effects that general anesthetics could have on a newborn baby, alternative methods were explored. In the earlier years, proponents of the natural and prepared childbirth movements discouraged the use of any pain-relieving medications during birthing, arguing that they represented an abdication of control over the process. Some women who eventually resorted to some form of anesthetic when giving birth were left with feelings of guilt and failure. Although the debate over the use of such medications continues, recent statistics indicate that much of the stigma has been lost surrounding the use of certain methods of pain control. More women are now using epidural blocks, anesthetics that are injected at the base of the spinal cord to lessen painful sensations. These medications do not seem to have

afterbirth: the tissues expelled after childbirth, including the placenta, the remains of the umbilical cord, and fetal membranes.

natural childbirth: a birthing process that encourages the mother to take control, thus minimizing medical intervention.

Lamaze method (la-MAHZ): a birthing process based on relaxation techniques practiced by the expectant mother; her partner coaches her throughout the birth.

CROSS-CULTURAL PERSPECTIVE
New Tally of World Tragedy: Women Who Die Giving Life

In the first comprehensive survey in a decade to look at maternal deaths worldwide, UNICEF reported today that about 585,000 women die each year in pregnancy and childbirth, many needlessly. Millions more, perhaps as many as 18 million women, suffer debilitating illnesses or injuries that often disable them.

The figures are nearly one-fifth higher than previous estimates of about 500,000 deaths, according to the report by UNICEF, the United Nations Childrens Fund, which compiled the new data with the World Health Organization and Johns Hopkins University. Much of the tragedy is preventable, the study says.

"For the most part, these are the deaths not of the ill, or the very old, or the very young, but of healthy women in the prime of their lives," says the report, The Progress of Nations 1996.

Data from the report indicate that 1 in 13 women in sub-Saharan Africa and 1 in 35 in South Asia dies of causes related to pregnancy and childbirth, according to UNICEF officials, compared with 1 in 3,200 in Europe, 1 in 3,300 in the United States and 1 in 7,300 in Canada.

The survey faults the shortage of obstetric care in many nations. It calls for the proper medical training of more midwives who would be better qualified than traditional birth attendants to assist mothers before, during and after delivery.

About 75,000 women die annually of botched abortions and another 75,000 of brain and kidney damage in eclampsia, a disorder that can cause high blood pressure and convulsions late in pregnancy. At least 100,000 die of blood poisoning and 40,000 of obstructed labor.

The report on maternal risks was prepared under UNICEF's director, Carol Bellamy, a former New York City Council president and director of the Peace Corps who took over the agency last year. It is stronger in its language and imagery than many United Nations publications. Of the preventable deaths of women in their teens, 20's or 30's, the report says: "Over 140,000 die of hemorrhaging, violently pumping blood onto the floor of bus or bullock cart or blood-soaked stretcher as their families and friends search in vain for help."

The new figures produced in the UNICEF report raised some questions among experts, who say that getting accurate information on maternal mortality is notoriously difficult. At Harvard University, Dr. Lincoln Chen, professor of international health and head of the Center for Population and Development Studies, said that the difference between 500,000 maternal deaths, the previously accepted figure, and 585,000 or 600,000 may fall within a margin of error, since all such numbers were "insecure."

He said, "But we do know that maternal deaths are only the tip of the iceberg of a whole range of women's health problems that have until now been comparatively underrecognized and certainly underserved."

A separate chapter in the UNICEF report examined malnutrition in South Asia—India and its neighbors drawing comparisons with sub-Saharan Africa, where children are often as poor or poorer than South Asians but are far less likely to suffer malnutrition and stunting.

But the authors of the South Asia chapter conclude that while poverty, overcrowding and low levels of hygiene may be factors in South Asia, a more important underlying cause of poor nutrition is poor treatment of women. When women have low status in the family and in society, mothers and children both suffer and are less likely to be able to help themselves, the report says.

"The women of sub-Saharan Africa, and particularly poor women, have greater opportunities and freedoms than the women of South Asia," the report says. "Women are subordinated in both continents, as indeed they are in most regions of the world, but in kind and in degree the subordination of South Asia's women is of a different order."

Elsewhere in the world, UNICEF finds many encouraging signs, particularly in the growing use of vaccinations, covering 80 percent of children in the developing world. Twenty developing nations, most in Latin America and the Caribbean, now produce their vaccines or buy them with their own money and no longer rely on aid.

While the condition of children in the United States is generally good by many measures, there is cause for concern about poor children, according to UNICEF. Drawing on the Luxembourg Income Study, the report shows that half the children living with a single mother in the United States, Canada and Australia are living in poverty.

"In other countries, government policies mitigate the effects" of single motherhood, the report says. "Denmark, Finland and Sweden also have a high percentage of children in solo-mother families, yet fewer than 10 percent live below the poverty line."

Among 44 industrialized nations—including former Soviet republics and Balkan nations like Bosnia and Croatia—the United States has the highest number of births to teenage mothers, 64 per 1,000 young women between the ages of 15 and 19, United Nations population figures show. Japan ranks lowest, with 4 births per 1,000 young women.

—Barbara Crossette, *New York Times,* June 11, 1996, pp. A1, A12 Copyright © 1996 by the New York Times Co. Reprinted by permission.

any effect on the infant being born. Others insist that pain can be easily managed by the breathing and positioning techniques that can be learned by women prior to giving birth.

Home Birth

Although most professionals still recommend hospital delivery, so that appropriate care can be available in case of complications, some couples choose to have a baby born at home. Trained and licensed **midwives** or certified nurse-midwives may assist, and it is usually recommended that a cooperative physician at least be on call in case of emergency. Sometimes, other children, family members, and friends are invited to be present for the home birthing event. For low-risk pregnancies, planned home birth can be as safe as hospital delivery (Remez, 1997; Stewart, 1998).

Birthing Rooms

Responding to the new trend to make birthing a cooperative process, many hospitals have established **birthing rooms.** These are usually decorated and furnished in nonhospital fashion, and sometimes other children or family members are allowed to be present for the birth. When a birthing room is used, the woman remains in the same room and bed for labor and delivery, rather than being taken to a special delivery room for the actual delivery.

Additional Birthing Techniques

Some women have given birth in tubs of warm water because the warmth is relaxing. The baby is lifted out of the water immediately after birth and before the umbilical cord is cut. There are also advantages of giving birth in a squatting position rather than lying down because gravity works with the uterine contractions.

French physician Frederick Leboyer advocated several methods for reducing the shock a baby feels when coming into a bright, noisy delivery area. He recommended that birth take place in a quiet, dimly lit, and warm setting and that time be taken for the baby to lie on the mother's abdomen before the umbilical cord is cut. He also suggested giving a newborn baby a gentle, warm bath.

Do you know which method of childbirth your mother used in delivering you? Which method of childbirth do you find most appealing?

The Newborn

After delivery, a baby is checked for any signs of distress, measured, and kept very warm. Drops of dilute silver nitrate or antibiotics are placed in the eyes to pre-

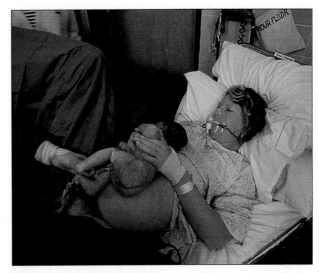

FIGURE 9.21 *Birth*
The newborn is placed on its mother's stomach.

vent infections from bacteria that may have entered the eyes during the birth process. In developing countries, these medications are often too costly, and so physicians are now recommending that less expensive antiseptics such as Betadine be used as eyedrops in these areas of the world. It is believed that this treatment could prevent thousands of cases of infant blindness and hundreds of thousands of severe eye infections worldwide each year. It is widely believed that newborn babies are quite alert for the first hour or two immediately following birth and that time should be given for the parents to form a **bond** with their new infants (see Figs. 9.21–9.23). This early bonding may well provide more security and comfort for the baby's adjustment and growth processes, although research evidence to confirm this contention is presently incomplete.

Problems during Pregnancy

About one out of four pregnancies experiences some potentially serious complication. Each year in the United States, about 31,000 fetuses die prior to delivery,

midwives: medical professionals, both women and men, trained to assist with the birthing process.

birthing rooms: special areas in the hospital, decorated and furnished in a nonhospital way, set aside for giving birth; the woman remains here to give birth rather than being taken to a separate delivery room.

bond: the emotional link between parent and child created by cuddling, cooing, and physical and eye contact early in the newborn's life.

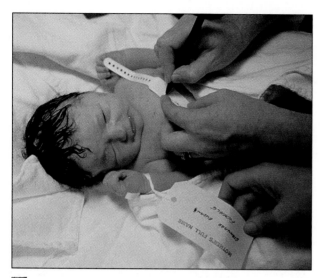

FIGURE 9.22   *Identifying the Newborn*
Each newborn is given an identifying bracelet, which the nurse fills in with the name of the baby and the baby's parents.

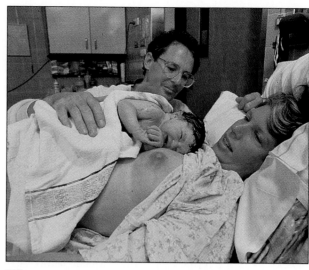

FIGURE 9.23   *The New Family*
The father, as a part of the natural birthing process, greets his newborn and comforts his wife.

FOH and another 22,000 newborns die within a month of being born. The U.S. infant mortality rate is presently higher than that of 21 other industrialized nations (Wilcox et al., 1995), and it rose in the early 1990s. Rates of death of pregnant women and of their fetuses is especially high among black women (Koonin et al., 1997; Raab, 1998). Worldwide, childbearing takes its toll on mothers as well. The United Nations has reported that about 585,000 women die each year around the globe in pregnancy and childbirth (see Fig. 9.24), often as the result of inadequate medical care (Crossette, 1996). All the possible problems of pregnancy will not be explored in detail here, but a few common ones will be at least mentioned.

Pregnancy-Induced Hypertension

One disorder that occurs in women in less than 10 percent of pregnancies is **pregnancy-induced hypertension,** formerly called toxemia or eclampsia. This begins with a rise in blood pressure, swelling in the ankles and other parts of the body, and protein appearing in the urine. Usually this can be treated by bed rest, diet, and medication, but it sometimes progresses to serious or life-threatening conditions for the mother such as blindness, convulsions, or coma. A large international study has shown that low daily doses of aspirin can be helpful in preventing this condition without harming fetal development (CLASP Collaborative Group, 1995). Pregnancy-induced hypertension increases the risk of stroke during the first few weeks following giving birth (Kittner, 1996).

Premature Birth

Any birth that takes place prior to the 37th week of pregnancy is considered a **premature birth.** It is more common in fetuses who are growing more slowly than they should be (Piper et al., 1996), and it more frequently involves male fetuses (Cooperstock & Campbell, 1996). About three-quarters of infant deaths in the United States are associated with premature delivery. The more prematurely a baby is born, the lower its chances of survival. More than 60 percent of infants born at 22 to 25 weeks of gestation die prior to or during birth or within 6 months of delivery. Respiratory problems, cranial abnormalities, and their complications are particularly common among these early "preemies." The survival rate steadily rises the later in pregnancy an infant is born.

Often, care in an isolette (formerly called an incubator) is necessary for a time. Although the cause of a premature birth is not always known, it is particularly common among teenage mothers, among women who smoke or have a genitourinary tract infection

pregnancy-induced hypertension: a disorder that can occur in the latter half of pregnancy, marked by a swelling in the ankles and other parts of the body, high blood pressure, and protein in the urine; can progress to coma and death if not treated.

premature birth: a birth that takes place prior to the 36th week of pregnancy.

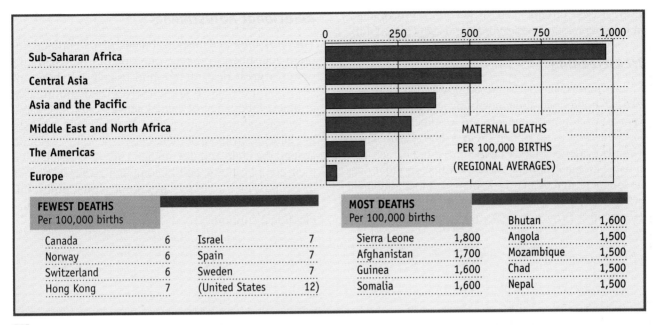

FIGURE 9.24 *Childbearing's Toll*

A UNICEF study has found that 585,000 women die each year during pregnancy and childbirth, nearly 20 percent more than previously estimated.

during their pregnancies, and in those who have experienced high stress, inadequate nutrition, or lack of proper prenatal medical care. In some cases, the fetal membranes rupture too soon, leading to premature delivery (Kost, Landry, & Darroch, 1998; Reichman & Kenney, 1998).

Rh Incompatibility

A major risk for pregnancies in former times was **Rh incompatibility.** The Rh factor is a blood protein; blood may be either Rh positive if it contains this factor or Rh negative if it does not. A baby has its own blood type as the result of a genetic combination from its mother and father, and so it often will not have the same blood type as the mother. If a mother has Rh negative blood and her baby is Rh positive, the mother's body will begin producing antibodies that destroy red blood cells in the fetus, especially in second and subsequent pregnancies. Administering a medication called **RhoGAM** to the mother prevents the formation of these antibodies and has effectively eliminated many of the risks of Rh incompatibility. However, the potential for the problem must be noted in prenatal blood tests, another reason why good prenatal care is so crucial to a pregnant woman and her child-to-be. It is also important for women to take RhoGAM after a miscarriage or abortion, if it is known that there was an Rh incompatibility with the fetus.

Postpartum Care

Following the birth of a baby, the postpartum time, there are many physical and psychological adjustments to be made by both the mother and child. Proper medical follow-up for both is essential. As the mother's body returns to its prepregnancy state, the reproductive organs must recover, and the internal hormonal balances must be reestablished. It can be a very emotional time, during which support and help from others can be extremely important. Many women experience at least a brief period of **postpartum depression,** characterized by low energy levels, feelings of being overwhelmed by new responsibilities, and sleep disturbances. In more

Rh incompatibility: condition in which a blood protein of the infant is not the same as the mother's; antibodies formed in the mother can destroy red blood cells in the fetus.

RhoGAM: medication administered to a mother to prevent formation of antibodies when the baby is Rh positive and its mother Rh negative.

postpartum depression: a period of low energy and discouragement that is common for mothers following childbearing. Longer-lasting or severe symptoms should receive medical treatment.

severe cases, prompt medical attention is warranted, and antidepressant medications are usually successful.

Breastfeeding

Women must make decisions about whether to breast-feed or bottle-feed their newborns. Those who will soon go back to full-time jobs are less likely to choose breast-feeding as an option (Fein & Roe, 1998). There is ample evidence to indicate the breast-fed babies tend to have stronger immune systems at first and that over the longer term they may be somewhat more intelligent and less likely to get certain diseases such as diabetes (Horwood & Fergusson, 1998; Pettitt et al., 1997).

Relational Adjustments

The pressures and responsibilities of parenthood require adjustments on everyone's part. A new baby requires a great deal of care and usually lost hours of sleep. Couples may find themselves tired and irritable at times. Frequency of sexual activity often decreases at least for a time. Some fathers become fully engaged in childcare, whereas others begin spending less time around the child and the mother. Life passages all have their complications, and becoming a parent is one of those passages that requires good communication, willingness to adapt and compromise, and mutual emotional support.

Chapter Summary

1. As science has gained new understanding of reproductive processes and developed new technologies to facilitate them, reproduction has become more closely scrutinized by social policy, legislation, and court actions.

2. A sperm must penetrate the zona pellucida of the ovum for conception to occur. Progesterone and contact with the zona cause exocytosis of the sperm, allowing fertilization to occur.

3. When a sperm fertilizes an ovum to form a zygote within the fallopian tube, 23 chromosomes from both the sperm and the egg combine to form a total of 46. The DNA in these chromosomes establishes the genetic instructions for developing the new organism.

4. The rate of multiple births has been increasing, largely because of increased use of fertility drugs. Multiple births are associated with greater risks of birth defects and premature birth.

5. Fraternal (dizygotic) twins result from the fertilization of two separate ova by two sperm. Identical (monozygotic) twins are formed when a single zygote divides into two cells that separate and develop into individual embryos. Because they have exactly the same chromosomes, they are identical in appearance.

6. Selective reduction is sometimes used to reduce the number of fetuses when a multiple pregnancy is diagnosed.

7. The zygote divides into increasing numbers of cells, eventually forming a spherical blastocyst. A few days after fertilization, the blastocyst implants itself in the inner lining (endometrium) of the uterus, where embryonic and fetal development will continue.

8. The embryo forms several extraembryonic membranes for its protection and nourishment. The amnion is a fluid-filled sac to keep the embryo moist and cushioned. The yolk sac and allantois become partly incorporated into the umbilical cord that connects the fetus with the placenta. The chorion is the outside membrane that helps form the placenta, through which the blood systems of the fetus and the mother come close enough to permit exchange (by diffusion) of nutrients and wastes.

9. Advances in reproductive technology are revolutionizing the processes of conception and gestation. Genetic engineering and gene therapy are opening the possibilities of early diagnosis and treatment of human genetic disorders, although they have yet to prove their worth.

10. The human genome is being mapped, and gene therapy technology raises issues of privacy and consent regarding information about genetic makeup. International guidelines are being developed to regulate genetic engineering.

11. In cases where one man has a low or nonexistent sperm count, artificial insemination permits sperm from another man to be used for fertilization.

12. Gametes (sperm and eggs) and embryos may now be frozen and kept for long periods for later

use in various reproductive technologies. There are growing concerns about the ethics involved with frozen embryos and about possible links of freezing with later problems of pregnancy and birth defects.

13. In vitro fertilization (IVF) allows for fertilization outside a woman's body with the developing embryo then being implanted into the uterus afterward. The success rate of IVF is still limited, and its associated costs are high.

14. Gamete intrafallopian transfer (GIFT), in which sperm and eggs are placed directly into the fallopian tube, increases the likelihood of fertilization in the tube.

15. Zygote intrafallopian transfer (ZIFT) allows for zygotes produced by IVF to be placed directly into fallopian tubes.

16. Intracytoplasmic sperm injection (ICSI), computerized sperm selection, and the transplantation of sperm-producing cells to infertile males all offer hope of increasing the likelihood of having viable sperm for reproduction.

17. Immature oocyte collection permits immature eggs to be obtained, after which they are matured by cell-culturing methods. This technique could reduce the costs of IVF significantly.

18. There has been debate over the possible use of immature egg cells from fetal ovaries.

19. Ovum donation and artificial embryonation may be used for women who no longer can produce eggs, and they have enabled postmenopausal women to become pregnant.

20. Choosing the sex of a fetus ahead of time has raised many ethical concerns. Sex selection is causing an imbalance in the number of males in China and some other countries.

21. Cloning involves the creation of genetically identical organisms. New techniques have allowed the separation of early embryonic cells and thus the creation of genetic duplicates of an early human embryo. The prospect of human cloning raises ethical, social, and legal complications, and clones may be more at risk for eventual defects.

22. Regulations and guidelines have been developed to control the types of embryo research that can be conducted with federal funds. Some countries have completely banned such research.

23. Surrogate motherhood, or gestational surrogacy, is a controversial approach in which one woman agrees for a fee to carry a pregnancy and give the baby to another couple. Sometimes the surrogate is impregnated by the sperm of a man whose partner cannot become pregnant, and sometimes

IVF is used to transfer an embryo produced from the egg and sperm of one couple into the surrogate's uterus.

24. There are several methods used to diagnose potential medical problems in a fetus. Amniocentesis withdraws fetal cells from the amniotic sac so that possible chromosome abnormalities may be discovered. Chorionic villi sampling (CVS) also examines chromosomes but may be used as early as the eighth week in the pregnancy. Ultrasound pictures, or sonograms, are an alternative to X rays for examining the features of the developing fetus. Ultrasound is not recommended for routine use.

25. Embryoscopy and fetoscopy allow for visual examination of embryos and fetuses. Fetal surgery is a developing technology that can be used to treat some medical difficulties.

26. Infertility can have many causes and often creates stress for couples who are anxious to have children. New reproductive technologies are offering more hope for infertile couples.

27. Prenatal care is cost effective and important in preventing problems with pregnancy and birth defects.

28. Pregnancy may be signaled by many symptoms. Pregnancy tests detect a hormone produced by the embryo and placenta called human chorionic gonadotropin (HCG).

29. Fetal alcohol syndrome (FAS) results from excessive alcohol use during pregnancy.

30. Unless there is a problem with a pregnancy, there is no need to avoid sexual contact during pregnancy. To assure healthy pregnancies, it is best that they be spaced one to two years apart.

31. The birth process begins with contractions of the uterus, or labor. Gradually the baby is moved through the birth canal and is born. The placenta, umbilical cord, and fetal membranes follow as the afterbirth.

32. There are many approaches to birthing, including those that emphasize full awareness and participation on the mother's part, such as the Lamaze method. Many women use some pain-relieving medications or anesthesia during labor and delivery.

33. Home delivery and hospital birthing rooms represent two options that are available to pregnant women.

34. Leboyer has advocated a quiet, warm, and comfortable area for the baby's delivery.

35. Newborns must be kept very warm, and eyedrops are placed in their eyes to prevent infection by bacteria.

36. Pregnancy-induced hypertension is a complication of pregnancy. It involves a rise in the mother's blood pressure and a buildup of fluids in her body, sometimes with life-threatening consequences.

37. Births that take place prior to the 37th week are premature.

38. Prenatal blood tests are crucial, so any dangers of Rh incompatibility may be eliminated with medical treatment. RhoGAM is administered to the mother when Rh incompatibility exists.

39. The postpartum period requires many adjustments and may be characterized by some level of postpartum depression for the new mother.

Focus on Health Questions

You will find in this section the kinds of questions that you may have concerning your own health and sexuality. The page references indicate where in the text the answer is located; the exact place is marked with the logo: **FOH**

1. Why are identical twins identical? 271

2. Are there any practical applications of genetic engineering to cure human diseases? 275

3. Members of my family are prone to a certain genetic disorder. Is there any way to determine the risks of my children inheriting the disease? 277

4. What are the chances that artificial insemination will work? 278

5. My spouse and I are interested in trying in vitro fertilization. What are the chances that it will produce a pregnancy? 280

6. If a man has a low sperm count, is there any way to increase the chances of fertilization using his own sperm? 281

7. We're anxious to have a girl. Is there any way to influence the probabilities in that direction? 285

8. Is there a way to tell if a baby has some genetic problem before it is born? 289

9. We've been trying to get pregnant for 2 years, without success. What can we do? 291

10. How can I find out if I'm pregnant? 292

11. Should I avoid smoking and drinking if I am pregnant? What are the risks if I don't? 292

12. Should we avoid sex during pregnancy? 293

13. When I go into labor, what is actually happening? 293

14. When I deliver my baby, is it advisable to have an episiotomy? 294

15. If I use the Lamaze method of childbirth, does that mean I'll have less pain? 295

16. Can I have my baby at home? 297

17. What are some of the common physical problems of pregnancy? 298

Annotated Readings

Colman, A. D., & Colman, L. L. (1991). *Pregnancy: The psychological experience*. New York: Noonday Press. Examines the many psychological experiences and adjustments of pregnancy that are faced by the pregnant woman and her partner.

Davis-Floyd, R., & Dumit, J. (Eds.). (1998). *Cyborg babies: From techno-sex to techno-tots*. New York: Routledge. The authors in this collection examine the effects of reproductive and fetal technologies on our view of babies.

Lay, M.M., Gurak, L.J., Gravon, C., & Myntti, C. (Eds.). (1999). *Body talk: Rhetoric, technology, reproduction*. Madison: University of Wisconsin Press. A fascinating collection of essays focusing on the ways in which our social and medical rhetoric about childbirth affects women's perceptions of their bodies and birthing.

Marsiglio, W. (1998). *Procreative man*. New York: New York University Press. An excellent look at how men are affected by pregnancy and birthing and fatherhood. Birth control for males is also examined.

Morgan, L. M., & Michaels, M. W. (1999). *Fetal subjects, feminist positions*. Philadelphia: University of Pennsylvania Press. An examination of how modern technology has affected our view of the human fetus and its status.

Rapp, R. (1999). *Testing women, testing the fetus: The social impact of amniocentesis in America*. New York: Routledge. Looks at the profound effects that reproductive technologies such as amniocentesis have on our views and policies regarding human reproduction.

Reiss, M. J., & Straughan, R. (1996). *Improving nature? The science and ethics of genetic engineering*. New York: Cambridge University Press. A careful look at the history of gene manipulation and its current trends, with an emphasis on the positive and negative potentials inherent in such work and the ethical issues that must be considered.

Chapter 10

Decision Making about Pregnancy and Parenthood

Chapter Outline

Note: A selection of Focus on Health questions appears at the end of each chapter. Answers to these questions are indicated within the chapter by the symbol in the margin. **F◆H**

> We have tried several forms of birth control, and none of them has proven completely satisfactory. I don't think I need to use something like the pill, and I don't like using a diaphragm. He uses condoms sometimes, but we don't seem to be very consistent. That leaves us with withdrawal more often than not, which we both know carries lots of risks.
>
> —*From a student's essay*

*B*ringing children into the world carries important responsibilities—not only to the child but to a planet that many believe is being overpopulated. Throughout the world, there is evidence that as people's sense of well-being increases, whether because of technological advances or the availability of money and other resources, people tend to have more children. Although there are often family and social pressures to procreate, especially for married couples, there is not a particularly close association between sex and fertility among humans. The primary reason for this is that throughout history, people have deliberately sought to weaken that association through the types of sexual activities they chose and through the use of birth control. They have deliberately tried to avoid pregnancy while continuing to enjoy sexual intercourse. Even when conception occurs, abortion, miscarriage, and stillbirth may interrupt the connection between conception and live birth (Trussell, 1998b).

After World War II, the birthrate in the United States went up dramatically. Annual birthrates jumped more than 30 percent between 1945 and 1947 and reached their peak during the 1950s, when women of childbearing age were having an average of 3.7 children each. This period has been called the "baby boom." The birthrate then tapered off to a low point in the mid-1970s, when women were averaging about two children each. Although there were some brief increases, the birthrate among U.S. women had fallen to one of its lowest levels ever by the end of the twentieth century (Population Reference Bureau, 1998). Fertility rates seem to be declining worldwide. Coupled with improvements in health care, this is leading to an increase in the proportion of older people in the global population, a trend that has taken demographers somewhat by surprise and has many significant social implications (Wattenberg, 1997).

◼ Historical Perspectives

Throughout history, people have found that the practicalities of life sometimes necessitate the limiting of family size. Folk methods of contraception, often spiced with liberal doses of superstition, have been developed. Insertion of substances (such as crocodile dung) into the vagina was frequently used in some ancient cultures and may have been the first "barrier" method of contraception. There is evidence that women in antiquity may actually have had significant control over their reproductive lives. As early as the seventh century B.C.E., it is known that sap from the now extinct silphium plant was widely used for its contraceptive effects. The plant was so popular that it was overharvested and apparently disappeared completely by the third or fourth century C.E. Several other botanical preparations were also used with varying degrees of effectiveness. Ingesting the seeds of the Queen Anne's lace plant were long known to reduce fertility by blocking preparation of the uterus for implantation, and this method is still employed in rural areas of India and North Carolina's Appalachian Mountains (Riddle, Estes, & Russell, 1994). Folklore has also fostered myths about being able to prevent pregnancy by having intercourse standing up, by jumping up and down following intercourse, or immersing oneself in a hot bath afterward (Henken & Whatley, 1995).

During ancient and medieval times, it is also likely that people engaged in sexual activities that would not result in pregnancy. By the Middle Ages, medical training no longer included information on contraceptive methods, and the knowledge about contraceptive preparations and techniques from ancient times gradually disappeared. In the seventeenth century, condoms made from internal sheep membranes had been developed in Europe to contain the ejaculate during intercourse. It is worth noting that condoms were originally designed to protect against syphilis, not pregnancy. Historically, birth control has sometimes been discouraged by sociocultural values and religious teaching. Sexual intercourse was viewed as a procreative act, and so to employ contraception was an indication that sex was being used for the gratification of nonprocreative desires. In many periods of history, pleasures of the flesh were considered at the very least improper and at the most evil.

As the mores of Victorian England filtered through to the United States in the 1860s, a great deal of attention was focused on sexual vices. A New York grocery clerk by the name of Anthony Comstock was incensed by the distribution of information about birth control methods and set out to suppress it. He became secretary of the New York Society for the Suppression of Vice and lobbied in Washington to have the Federal Mail Act prohibit the mailing of contraceptive information, placing it in the same category as obscene materials. In the 1870s, these federal regulations became known as the **Comstock Laws.** They represented

---

Comstock Laws: enacted in the 1870s, this federal legislation prohibited the mailing of information about contraception.

governmental sanction of the idea that abstinence is the only permissible form of birth control.

The birth control movement in the United States was spurred on by an activist named Margaret Sanger, who was a nurse and worked in a section of Brooklyn where poor people lived (see Fig. 10.1). She saw women who were almost constantly pregnant, often resulting in serious consequences to their health, and women who had so many children they could not effectively raise them. Many of these women resorted to self-induced abortions or abortions performed in unsanitary conditions by illegal abortionists, frequently resulting in the women's deaths. Sanger became determined to remedy this problem and in 1914 founded the **National Birth Control League.** In her protests, she deliberately violated the Comstock Laws and fought against attitudes that discouraged advertising about the use of contraceptive devices, eventually opening her own birth control clinic in Brooklyn. She was arrested numerous times. After a number of court battles, physicians were finally given the right to give contraceptive information to women. In time, contraception became more socially acceptable, and new methods were developed. In 1965, the last major law forbidding the sale of contraceptives to married people was repealed, following the U.S. Supreme Court's historic *Griswold v. Connecticut* decision. This ruling invalidated a state law that had been used to prosecute a physician for providing contraceptive information to

a married couple. It was not until 1972 that the Supreme Court's ruling in *Eisenstadt v. Baird* removed a final state barrier to providing contraceptive information to unmarried individuals.

World Population and the Status of Children

Observers of the global population continue to be concerned about the implications of the world's expanding numbers of people. It took a million years for the global population to reach a billion people; it took only 12 years to add the most recent billion to the planet (Cohen, 1996). In the four decades between 1950 and 1990, the global population more than doubled, from 2.5 billion to 5.3 billion people. By 2000, it had surpassed 6 billion (Foster, 1999). Worldwide efforts during the 1970s to curb the rate of population growth began to produce some results, and there was a gradual decline in the growth rate. If the growth rate had continued to fall, the world population would have reached what is called **zero population growth** in the year 2030 with 6.7 billion people. Although it is unlikely that this state will be realized soon worldwide, and it may not even be desirable for sociological reasons, there is now evidence that population growth is leveling off.

Industrialized nations doubled their populations during the twentieth century, but with improved birth control methods and new financial pressures on families, they are likely to see population growth leveling off or even declining over the next century. Europe could actually see its population reduced by about one-quarter over the next half century or so (Mosher, 1998). Population growth will tend to be limited to the less-developed countries of the world, although as these nations modernize, their fertility rates seem to be dropping as well. It seems likely that it will take a few years longer to add the next billion people to the global population than it did the last billion (Foster, 1999). As Figure 10.2 demonstrates, the balance of the world population has been changing in such a way that industrial countries have a decreasing proportion of that population (Feeney, 1994). There is still concern that the earth's ecosystems and resources simply will not support population growth, especially in less-

FIGURE 10.1   *Margaret Sanger*

Sanger (1883–1966) was instrumental in causing changes in the availability of birth control information and contraceptive devices in the United States. She believed that every woman has the right to control her own fertility and was the first president of the International Planned Parenthood Federation.

National Birth Control League: an organization founded in 1914 by Margaret Sanger to promote use of contraceptives.

zero population growth: the point at which the world's population would stabilize, and there would be no further increase in the number of people on earth. Birthrate and death rate become essentially equal.

Margaret Sanger

In her autobiography, Margaret Sanger told of an incident during her nursing career that convinced her of the direction her life would have to take. In July 1912, she tended a 28-year-old woman who had nearly died from the effects of a self-induced abortion. The woman and her husband, Jake Sachs, already had three children for whom she was barely able to care on her husband's truck-driver wages. Sanger nursed Mrs. Sachs back to health, although the patient often seemed lost in thought. Finally the woman was able to deal openly with her concerns:

At the end of three weeks, as I was preparing to leave and the fragile patient [preparing] to take up her difficult life once more, she finally voiced her fears, "Another baby will finish me, I suppose?"

"It's too early to talk about that," I temporized.

But when the doctor came to make his last call, I drew him aside. "Mrs. Sachs is worried about having another baby."

"She may well be," replied the doctor, and then he stood before her and said, "Any more such capers, young woman, and there'll be no need to send for me."

"I know, doctor," she replied timidly, "but," and she hesitated as though it took all her courage to say it, "what can I do to prevent it?"

The doctor was a kindly man, and he had worked hard to save her, but such incidents had become so familiar to him that he had long since lost whatever delicacy he might once have had. He laughed good-naturedly, "You want to have your cake and eat it too, do you? Well, it can't be done."

Then picking up his hat to depart, he said, "Tell Jake to sleep on the roof."

I glanced quickly at Mrs. Sachs. Even through my sudden tears I could see stamped on her face an expression of absolute despair. We simply looked at each other, saying no word until the door had closed behind the doctor. Then she lifted her thin, blue-veined hands and clasped them beseechingly, "He can't understand. He's only a man. But you do, don't you? Please tell me the secret, and I'll never breathe it to a soul. *Please!*"

What was I to do? I could not speak the conventionally comforting phrases which would be of no comfort. . . . A little later, when she slept, I tiptoed away.

Night after night the wistful image of Mrs. Sachs appeared before me. I made all sorts of excuses to myself for not going back. I was busy on other cases; I really did not know what to say to her or how to convince her of my own ignorance; I was helpless to avert such monstrous atrocities. Time rolled by and I did nothing.

The telephone rang one evening three months later, and Jake Sachs's agitated voice begged me to come at once; his wife was sick again and from the same cause. . . . I turned into the dingy doorway and climbed the familiar stairs once more. The children were there, young little things.

Mrs. Sachs was in a coma and died within ten minutes. I drew a sheet over her pallid face. Jake was sobbing, running his hands through his hair and pulling it out like an insane person. Over and over again he wailed, "My God! My God! My God!"

I left him pacing desperately back and forth, and for hours I myself walked and walked and walked through the hushed streets. . . . [The city's] pains and griefs crowded in upon me: women writhing in travail to bring forth little babies; the babies themselves naked and hungry, wrapped in newspapers to keep them from the cold; six-year-old children with pinched, pale, wrinkled faces, old in concentrated wretchedness, pushed into gray and fetid cellars, crouching on stone floors, their small scrawny hands scuttling through rags, making lamp shades, artificial flowers; white coffins, black coffins, coffins, coffins interminably passing in never-ending succession. The scenes piled one upon another on another. I could bear it no longer.

As I stood there the darkness faded. It was the dawn of a new day in my life also. The doubt and questioning, the experimenting and trying, were now to be put behind me. I knew I could not go back merely to keeping people alive.

I went to bed, knowing that no matter what it might cost, I was finished with palliatives and superficial cures; I was resolved to seek out the root of evil, to change the destiny of mothers whose miseries were vast as the sky.

—Margaret Sanger, *Margaret Sanger: An Autobiography,*
1938, New York: W. W. Norton

developed regions. With 90 percent of the people added to the global population each year living in economically and ecologically impoverished areas, the situation continues to worsen.

The continuing expansion of the population is particularly distressing given the fact that even in countries such as the United States, the status of children has been declining. By the beginning of the new millenium, 25 percent of children were living in poverty. Nine out of every 1,000 babies in the United States die before their first birthdays, one of the highest rates of infant mortality in the industrialized world.

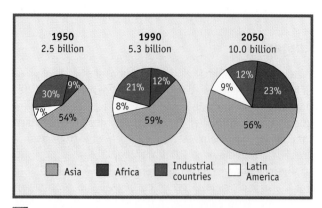

1950	1990	2050
2.5 billion	5.3 billion	10.0 billion

Asia   Africa   Industrial countries   Latin America

FIGURE 10.2   *The Shifting of World Population by Region*

As the world population grows over the century-long period shown, it is expected that developed nations will have a proportionately lower share of people than nonindustrialized, often poor nations.

Source: UN Medium Projection. Reprinted with permission from *Science,* "Population: The View from Cairo," Volume 265, August 26, 1994. Copyright 1994 American Association for the Advancement of Science.

About 40 percent of 2-year-olds have not been immunized against childhood diseases. Prenatal care for poor pregnant women has become even less available than before, leading to more health and developmental problems for their children. Nearly two-thirds of women with low incomes do not breast-feed, a practice that is believed to bolster immunity and nutrition in children. One-third of American children are not ready to start school because of health and developmental problems.

There are conflicting views about how we as a world community should address the needs of a burgeoning population. Do you support the promotion of contraception, a redistribution of global wealth, or some other method? Support your position.

Choosing to Become a Parent

Bringing a child into the world and caring for it through its years of growing up represent major life responsibilities. Experts agree that it is best for any couple to choose to become pregnant through a process of discussion and mutual agreement, carefully weighing all of the new obligations that parenthood will entail. These are complicated times in which to become parents. Raising a child is not only filled with social requirements, it is very expensive. It is estimated that the average cost of raising a child to the age of 18 in the midwestern United States, including housing, clothes, food, medical care, public education, and transportation, is well over $100,000. With the number of fami-

lies requiring child care increasing because of parental occupations, less than half of preschoolers are watched by relatives while parents are working. It is also significant that the costs of day care continue to rise. Child-care costs continue to escalate, averaging around $75 per week.

There are many *wrong* reasons to become a parent. For example, the desires to give your parents grandchildren or to give your first child a sibling do not represent good reasons in themselves. Neither is it appropriate to have a child in order to save or refresh a shaky relationship. Sometimes a person is anxious to have a baby in order to have something to love or possess, but this may be reflective of other issues in the person's life that need work and resolution; it is not fair to ask a new baby to fill all of those emotional gaps. It is known that babies who were unwanted or resulted from mistimed pregnancies tend not to develop their skills as quickly as wanted babies; they also tend to be more fearful and subject to other psychological difficulties (Baydar, 1995).

The choice to become a parent should be made with careful consideration given to all of the positive *and* negative aspects of parenthood (see Fig. 10.3). Every stage of child development places demands on

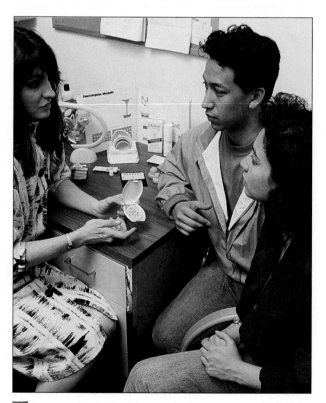

FIGURE 10.3   *Pregnancy or Birth Control?*

Deciding to have a child is a complicated issue for most people. Consideration must be given to health. Pregnancy itself may have greater risks than any particular method of birth control.

The Bright Side of Overpopulation

But there's a bright side to overpopulation, if we take the long long-term point of view. Until about 10,000 years ago, the human population was probably less than 25 million, mostly scattered in bands of 30 to 40 members each. Mates were probably hard to find—especially if you weren't interested in mating with a sibling or a parent—and extinction was only an Ice Age or epidemic away.

So the fact that there are 5.7 billion of us today, many living in cities that could house half the entire Paleolithic population, doesn't have to be seen as a disaster. Overpopulation also represents an enormous biological victory, if that's how we choose to see it. In either case, of course, we're going to have to start contracepting and curbing births far more vigorously than ever before. But the spirit is entirely different, depending on how we interpret our numerical strength: if the current population is an achievement rather than a "bomb," then we should be patting ourselves on the back and heaving a deep sigh of relief. Population control should be seen as a regard for a job well done rather than as a new form of discipline and self-denial.

And from a maternal way of thinking, our current numbers are indeed a stunning achievement. Over the millenniums, millions of women gave their lives to "overpopulate" the earth. They died in childbirth, as did three of my own great-grandmothers, each by the age of 31. Or they squandered their health on pregnancy after pregnancy, with as many as half ending in miscarriage or dead babies. Even within this century, medical wisdom held that "maternity is another word for eternity" and that women really were the weaker, sicker sex. . . .

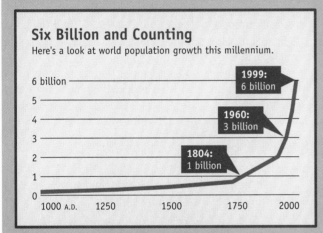

Six Billion and Counting

Here's a look at world population growth this millennium.

1999: 6 billion

1960: 3 billion

1804: 1 billion

Source: United Nations Population Division

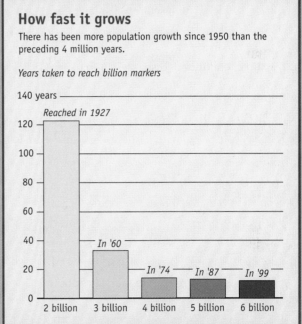

How fast it grows

There has been more population growth since 1950 than the preceding 4 million years.

Years taken to reach billion markers

Reached in 1927

In '60

In '74   In '87   In '99

2 billion   3 billion   4 billion   5 billion   6 billion

Source: U. S. Department of Commerce; U. S. Census Bureau; United Nations, Worldwatch Institute

But the happiest consequence of overpopulation, which no one at Cairo dared say and probably few have even ventured to think, is that sex can finally, after all these centuries, be separated from the all-too-serious business of reproduction. Technology has made it possible to uncouple sex and babymaking; ecology has made it necessary. Now all that remains is for us to make the cultural leap to an ecologically responsible sexual ethic. This means, at a minimum, guaranteeing contraception, with abortion as a backup, to all who might need it. But it also means telling our teenagers the hard ecological truth—which is probably also the best news they could get—that sex, in our overpopulated world, is best seen as a source of fun.

If, after all, the essence of morality is respect for each life, and if furthermore, all future life is threatened by rampant reproduction, then what could be more moral than teaching teenagers that homosexuality is a viable lifestyle? Or that masturbation is harmless and normal? Or that petting, under most circumstances, makes far more sense than begetting? The only ethic that can work in an overcrowded world is one that insists that women are free, children are loved, and sex—preferably among affectionate and consenting adults—belongs squarely in the realm of play.

—Barbara Ehrenreich, "The Bright Side of Overpopulation,"
Time, September 26, 1994 Copyright © 1994 Time, Inc.
Reprinted by permission.

Childless Couples

First comes love, then comes marriage. Then comes the pressure to have children.

It comes from family, from friends, even from coworkers. They want grandchildren. They want nieces and nephews. They want another smiling face at the neighborhood play group.

What happens if a couple says no? Not because they can't have a baby, but because they don't want one.

It's happening with increasing frequency, but men and women who make that decision say it is still a touchy subject.

And, they say, it's most often the woman who is expected to justify the unconventional choice to friends and family.

"The woman herself hears the silent question all around her, because there is an assumption that you'll have children," said poet Molly Peacock, who wrote "Paradise, Piece by Piece," a memoir explaining her decision to remain childless. . . .

"Women start thinking of themselves and their own motherhood at an extraordinarily early age," she said. "Think of how young little girls are when they are asked how many children they want. Little boys are never asked how many kids they want when they grow up."

Married women with no children say they are often called selfish, are asked if they hate kids, and warned that, one day, they'll deeply regret their decision.

Yet the number of childless married, divorced or widowed women who are without children by choice has more than doubled in the United States since the 1970s, hovering in 1990 at about 25 percent, according to a study by the National Center For Health Statistics.

That means one out of four women who have ever been married, and are childless, rejected motherhood by choice. But that doesn't mean the issue is not still a topic of emotional debate.

"Early on in my marriage, my mother was certainly hoping to have grandchildren," said Ellen Peskin, who has been married to her husband, Jan Harrison, for 11 years.

"We basically told her that we probably were not going to have any kids, and pressure was not going to do anything to change that," Peskin said.

Harrison agreed that it's easier for a man to say that he doesn't want to have children than it is for a married woman.

"I've had many men say to me that if they could do it over again, they wouldn't have kids," he said.

"And, while I know that Ellen has a good circle of friends who are also childless, I also know that being cut out of the conversation, or the group, because we don't have kids is more of a factor in her life."

Peskin, a health-information researcher at the University of Pennsylvania, recalled that her mother quickly stopped pressuring them, but "she has said that she thinks I'm missing out on a great experience."

Maybe, said Harrison.

"We both understood, you know, that some people will not be fulfilled in their lives unless they have children," he said. "We are acutely aware of what we have given up. . . .But, overall, I don't think we'd make a different choice."

Peacock said she has learned to separate sadness from regret.

"I can be sad that I don't have children. I can hold sadness in my life, like I hold happiness," she said. "But I do not regret it, not at all."

—Knight Ridder Newspapers, "More Couples Today Remain Childless as Lifestyle Choice," *Watertown (NY) Daily Times*, June 6, 1998, p. 9. Reprinted with permission of Knight Ridder/Tribune Information Services.

parents and requires the exercise of appropriate parenting skills. None of us is born knowing those skills, and they take time to develop. Although it may be a thrill to anticipate the arrival of a baby, any parent can testify that the realities are at times exhausting, nerve-wracking, and confusing. To be a parent requires maturity and a commitment to long-term efforts. Having children also changes the relationship between the two parents, creating new pressures and complications. Most parents have found that their sexual lives, for example, change markedly with pregnancy and the presence of a child in their lives. It takes real work and communication to maintain a happy and healthy relationship in the face of the new pressures of parenthood.

Of course, being a parent carries great satisfactions and rewards as well. It not only can help individuals to become more mature and responsible, but it may strengthen the bonds between the child's parents. That is especially true of couples who make their decision to have children carefully and with thorough information about the implications of parenthood. Choosing if and when to have a child means that contraception must be part of planning for heterosexual intercourse. Any couple that shares intercourse must also give some thought and planning to the possibility that birth control might fail. The information in this chapter is basic to thinking and deciding about these issues.

Birth Control Today

The risk of unintended pregnancy has always been one of the major arguments used by those who wished to discourage premarital sex. Although coitus always carries some risk of pregnancy, modern methods of birth control have at least reduced this risk to the point where many couples pursue their sexual activities with relatively little concern for unintended pregnancy. The World Health Organization estimates that 25 percent of all pregnancies worldwide are unwanted and that about 50 million of them are terminated by abortion each year. Among developed countries, rates of unintended pregnancy vary widely. They tend to be especially prevalent in the United States, where the proportion of pregnancies that are unplanned is about 50 percent (Hatcher et al., 1998). This is in contrast to countries such as Canada and the Netherlands, where the rates are 39 percent and 6 percent, respectively. Although adults in all three of these countries are relatively well informed about contraceptives, Americans tend to be more skeptical about the effectiveness of birth control methods and more likely to blame the incidence of unwanted pregnancies on societal problems (Delbanco, Lundy, Hoff, Parker, & Smith, 1997). Research and development of new and more effective contraceptives has lagged far behind other areas of biomedical research, partly because of a decline in the availability of research fund for these pursuits (Gabelnick, 1998).

Even when birth control techniques are available, people do not necessarily make use of them. Data from various studies indicate that among sexually active individuals, some do not use contraception with any regularity or at all. We can assume that some of them may be attempting to get pregnant, but when data were examined from only those individuals who were unmarried and not cohabiting, 13 percent of the women and 12 percent of the men never used birth control (Laumann, Gagnon et al., 1994; Piccinino & Mosher, 1998). Slightly more than 60 percent of college students report always using birth control, with another 27 percent indicating that they do so most of the time or sometimes (Elliott & Brantley, 1997).

■ Deciding about Contraceptives

FOH Individuals who do not wish to be parents should either avoid intercourse or employ an adequate means of birth control. Different methods of birth control are best suited to different people and situations. It is often wise to consult a gynecologist or family planning specialist to determine which method(s) will be most effective for a particular couple's lifestyle and sexual choices. The information that follows is meant to be a brief guide to various methods of birth control. It is a summary, and for those seeking more detailed information, a number of excellent resources are listed at the end of the chapter. Making decisions about whether or not to use a means of birth control, and which method to use, can be very complicated. There are several methods of contraception that, if used consistently and properly, will mean that less than 5 women in 100 will conceive over the course of a year.

Research has shown that women's attitudes toward sexuality can affect their decision making about contraception. Those who have more positive attitudes about sex tend to use more effective methods of birth control and to do so with greater consistency than women with negative attitudes (Hynie & Lydon, 1996). It is typical for women to select their first method on the basis of its effectiveness, but second and third selections are more likely to be made on the basis of health concerns and potential effects on the body. For example, it is common for women to choose the birth control pill at first because of its effectiveness. There are many different factors to be weighed and considered in making a decision about contraception, but sorting through the complexities is preferable to having sex without considering the risks of pregnancy or its potential consequences.

Ethical and Religious Influences

For many people, contraception is an ethical issue, rooted in the issue of the "purpose" of sex. Some insist that sexual intercourse is meant to be a biological function, the primary objective of which is reproduction. Others believe that it is their ethical responsibility to prevent unintended pregnancies, or overpopulation, even while choosing to share sex. Those individuals who hold more recreational attitudes toward sexual activity perceive sex as an act of shared pleasure and communication within a loving relationship, with procreation representing an additional aspect to be chosen only when the time is right.

There has been continued recognition of the need for comprehensive reproductive health care and reproductive rights, empowerment of women, and wider access to educational and health services. These steps are crucial in achieving any decline in fertility (Dailard, 1999; Johnson & Turnbull, 1995). Some of the world's major religious groups are opposed to efforts that encourage use of birth control or abortion, especially Roman Catholic and Muslim groups. In making any sex-related decision, we must examine the ethical and religious values that we hold to be important in our lives. Sometimes decisions require an internal balancing act to sort out how much weight we will give to our various beliefs, opinions, emotions, practical difficulties, and inner drives. Nevertheless, contraception is never an issue that can be ignored.

Political Factors

Political and social forces can play a significant role in determining the availability of various contraceptive methods. In Japan, for example, historical factors led to almost total dependence on condoms, the traditional "rhythm method" (see p. 326), and abortion for fertility control. Concern among those in political power about Japanese sexual morals prevented the approval of birth control pills and other medical contraceptives in that country until just recently (Kitamura, 1999). In the United States, funding for reproductive health care is always a sensitive political issue and prone to influence by whatever political party happens to wield the most power at any particular time. There are thousands of family planning clinics in the United States that receive funding from federal programs such as Medicaid or Title X, and these—along with managed health care plans—often place restrictions on contraceptive services (Frost, 1998; Haas-Wilson, 1997). Another volatile area politically has been that of pregnancy and family planning services for teenagers, where there seem to be two distinct kinds of sexual activity. One takes place in middle or late teenage years, among young people who are mature enough to make choices and perhaps use contraception. The other occurs among very young teens, for whom it is unlikely that the issue of choice is very relevant. There continues to be abundant evidence that most adolescent women do not want to bear children. However, there is also a continuing debate about how available contraceptives should be for teenagers and whether parental consent should be required before they are offered such services (Trussell, Koenig, Stewart, & Darroch, 1997).

Health Considerations

Anytime various methods of birth control are considered, possible effects on one's health should be an integral part of the decision-making process. Although several methods (such as condoms or diaphragms) have minimal effects, others, such as hormonal methods or the IUD, can have potentially greater effects on a woman's health. Even women who use reliable contraceptive methods may still harbor fears about the health risks they may be incurring (Hynie & Lydon, 1996).

It is sometimes difficult to obtain fully accurate information on potential health effects. Pharmaceutical companies anxious to market a particular method may popularize research studies that have not fully met rigorous evaluative standards. Myths develop as well that may take time to sort through. Many people, for example, still have misconceptions and fears about the possible dangers of birth control pills. In fact, recent research tends to show that, when properly prescribed, the pill is actually quite safe for nonsmokers and may even provide some health advantages. Research on the health implications of the pill and other contraceptive methods is ongoing. Prior to making a decision about birth control, one should become updated on the most accurate medical knowledge available.

Any potential risks of a method of contraception must be balanced against the risks inherent in pregnancy, which are consistently higher than any method of birth control. The key issue is making sure that the chosen contraceptive method is fully understood by the user and properly prescribed if it requires a medical professional's approval. When methods such as the pill, hormonal implants or injections, or IUD are possibilities, a thorough medical history must be taken and a careful evaluation made of any potential health risks. Women and men should take the responsibility for becoming fully informed about all health considerations, so that they can make the most careful and safe decisions possible.

Psychological and Social Factors

How people feel about contraception themselves, and how they believe others in their social networks would view their choices, are also a part of the decision-making process. We live in a culture that often sends conflicting messages about sexual expression. Although intellectually most people acknowledge that they must practice safe sex, both women and men are often placed in the position of feeling that sexual activity is acceptable only if it is spontaneous and unplanned. Therefore, to plan ahead—to choose and have available a method of contraception "just in case"—can still be a difficult step to take. It may call into question their views of personal morality, and this has important implications for how they feel about themselves. Although the majority of men believe that both partners should share equal responsibility for decisions about contraception, some see it primarily as the woman's responsibility (Grady, Tanfer, Billy, & Lincoln-Hansen, 1996).

Research on the psychological and social factors that determine contraceptive behavior continues to show that negative emotional responses toward sex such as guilt, fear, or anxiety tend to inhibit sexual intercourse. However, when those same feelings are not sufficiently strong to inhibit a person from having intercourse, they often interfere with the ability to plan for potential consequences of sex. Therefore, people who have such negative responses tend to have less accurate information about contraception, to select more ineffective contraceptive methods, and to use them much less consistently (Hynie & Lydon, 1996). To avoid pregnancy requires the successful completion of numerous steps. There must be an acceptance on the part of both partners that their sexual activity places them at risk of pregnancy. Then they must obtain appropriate information about birth control methods and decide which method to acquire and use. Ultimately they must then use the contraceptive method consistently and properly. Negative attitudes about the relationship, love, sex, and one's own sexual feelings can cause difficulty in negotiating any or all of these steps.

Preparing the Way for Effective Contraception

As the evidence shows, sexual responsibility can entail some personal work to ensure that you are ready to approach sexual intercourse with effective contraception, providing you are not ready to be a parent. Here are some of the necessary factors to consider and steps to take in becoming an effective user of birth control:

1. Consider your ethical and moral values about sex, pregnancy, and contraception. What sorts of social, family, and religious influences do you have to take into consideration in your decision-making process?
2. What are the health concerns that you might have regarding contraception? What resources will you use to become more fully informed about available facts? How will you check the reliability of your information?
3. Weigh carefully your attitude about your own sexual feelings and potential sexual activities. If you find a good deal of guilt or anxiety, you may want to rethink the decisions you have made. In particular, consider how you may have been ignoring or neglecting the whole issue of birth control.
4. Can you give yourself permission to be sexual? (This does not have to mean intercourse.) If not, consider how your inner reluctance may interfere with your sexual life.
5. Be prepared to talk with your partner about contraception and the possibility of pregnancy before engaging in sexual intercourse. Sharing mutual concerns, hesitations, and values is the best way to prepare for effective contraception.

Choosing the "Right" Contraceptive

The goal of people who use some method of birth control is to prevent pregnancy. They have decided they do not want to be parents, at least for the time be-

ing. On the surface of things, then, it might seem most reasonable to look at a chart, find the method that shows the lowest rate of failure, and use it. However, choosing a contraceptive is just not that simple. Several other issues should be discussed by both partners, preferably with a family planning counselor.

In choosing a contraceptive method, you should know the risks involved—the risks that pregnancy may still occur and the risks of any possible side effects to your health. Some methods are definitely more effective or safer than others. Although you should have as much accurate information as possible when choosing a method, there are many other factors to consider when choosing a contraceptive that go beyond statistics:

1. *Age and amount of protection needed.* Age relates to fertility. Younger women may need a higher degree of contraceptive reliability than older women. For example, vaginal barrier methods (diaphragm, cervical cap) are less effective for women under the age of 25. The progestin-only pill (discussed on p. 320) is particularly effective for older women and women who are breast-feeding (Hatcher et al., 1998). Similarly, a person who has sexual intercourse frequently may want to consider different forms of contraception than someone who has intercourse only occasionally. Also to be weighed are the potential side effects of a particular method versus the complication or crisis a pregnancy would provide.
2. *Safety.* Some birth control methods are not recommended for women with histories of particular medical conditions in themselves or their families. Therefore, suitability for a contraceptive method should be evaluated in cooperation with a trained professional.
3. *Factors that might inhibit use.* In choosing a contraceptive method, you should know yourself and any influences that might hinder regular use of the method. Are there any fears or hesitancies about side effects that create reluctance on your part about its use? Do you find it difficult to remember daily routines, which are necessary in taking birth control pills? Would you be embarrassed to buy supplies in a store or to interrupt sexual activity to put a condom or diaphragm in place? Will your religious values make use uncomfortable for you? Are you reluctant to touch your sex organs or, if you are a woman, to insert something into your vagina? Would you avoid a method for which a visit to a physician or family planning clinic was necessary, possibly with follow-up visits?
4. *Cost.* You will need to choose a method that you know you will be able to afford on a consistent basis. Research indicates that a large percentage

CASE STUDY

Joanne and Arthur Settle on a Contraceptive Method

Joanne and Arthur had been involved in a relationship for 7 months, and they had been using male condoms during sexual intercourse. Arthur continued to be dissatisfied with condoms, saying that he found it difficult to maintain his erection with a condom on. They both agreed that they wanted an effective means of preventing pregnancy, and they also realized that the condom was providing protection from possible disease transmission. Both had been sexually active with other partners prior to this relationship. After some discussion, they agreed that because they had both been sexually exclusive with each other, they would get tested for HIV and other sexually transmitted diseases and then make a decision about a contraceptive. Their medical tests were all negative, and they then made an appointment at a local family planning clinic to talk about contraception.

After hearing about the various methods of birth control available to them, Joanne and Arthur decided to consider the diaphragm or female condom. Joanne's med-

ical history ruled out the hormonal methods such as the pill or injections. They wanted to use a method that had as few side effects as possible and that could be discontinued with ease. The clinic worker scheduled an appointment for Joanne to be fitted with a diaphragm, but they also received some female condoms to try in the meantime. As it turned out, they liked the female pouches because they provided better sexual sensations for both of them. Joanne decided not to proceed with getting a diaphragm because she was not satisfied that it provided the degree of contraceptive protection she wanted. The couple chose to continue using the female condom because they both found it to be comfortable and easy to use. The clinician had explained that statistics on the effectiveness of the female device were still incomplete, but Joanne and Arthur felt that they could use it correctly and carefully and would have more control over its effectiveness than they would a diaphragm.

---

of pregnancies are unplanned—and it is safe to extrapolate that a substantial number of those unintended pregnancies are unwanted. Sexual intercourse in which the partners do not regularly make use of some form of contraception runs an extremely high risk (about a 90 percent chance) over a year's time of incurring pregnancy, and this can lead to extensive costs of one sort or another. Therefore, birth control is typically very cost-effective when considered over time (Trussell et al., 1997).

The most common methods of birth control are summarized in the sections that follow. Their effectiveness, advantages, causes of failure, and potential side effects are listed in Table 10.1. The Self-Evaluation activity on page 337 may help you sort through some of your own personal issues and concerns.

■ Methods of Birth Control

No method of contraception is foolproof or without both positive and negative aspects (see Fig. 10.4). Every method sometimes fails. Over half of unintended pregnancies occur in women who were using some form of birth control (Fu, Darroch, Haas, & Ranjit, 1999). This section focuses on the various methods of birth control currently available and evaluates their effectiveness, advantages, and risks.

Understanding Contraceptive Effectiveness

It is important to understand that there is a difference between the **theoretical failure rate** and the **typical use failure rate** of any contraceptive method. The theoretical, sometimes called "perfect" or "lowest observed," failure rate refers to the percentage of times a method might be expected to fail when used exactly according to directions and without error or technical failures. Typical use failure rate takes into account human error and carelessness as well as technical failure. Contraception can only reduce the risk of pregnancy, not eliminate that risk completely. Clinical trials of contraceptive methods tend to generate lower failure rates, probably because the participants are carefully chosen and well-educated about the method. In real life, methods are often not used correctly or consistently (Trussell & Vaughan, 1999). Studies show that

theoretical failure rate: a measure of how often a birth control method can be expected to fail when used without error or technical problems, sometimes called perfect use failure rate.

typical use failure rate: a measure of how often a birth control method can be expected to fail when human error and technical failure are considered.

certain groups of women seem more likely to experience contraceptive failure. Those aged 15 to 19 are less likely to use a birth control method consistently (Glei, 1999). Failure rates are also high among cohabiting and other unmarried women, especially those who are well below the poverty income level, and among black and Hispanic women. The sociological reasons for these statistics are not entirely understood (Fu et al., 1999).

Contraceptive failure rates are measurable, whereas actual rates of *effectiveness* are somewhat more elusive. In other words, it is not so simple to predict in percentages how likely it will be that a method of birth control will work because no studies can ascertain the proportion of women who would have become pregnant had they not used the method. Pregnancy is always a matter of chance, and so even when contraception is not used, pregnancy does not necessarily occur. So the best way to express contraceptive "effectiveness" is in terms of how likely it is to fail. Failure rates are typically given as percentages. The failure rates used in this book reflect the percentage of times that pregnancy could be expected to occur when 100 couples are using the method during a 1-year period of average frequency intercourse; this takes into consideration the total number of times the women were susceptible to pregnancy (Trussell, 1998a). The rates given are based on research studies considered to be the best designed and most statistically valid by the widely respected resource *Contraceptive Technology* (Hatcher et al., 1998). The chances of any contraceptive method being effective are increased when the method is used correctly and consistently.

Some forms of birth control cause unpleasant or unhealthy side effects in a few individuals. As with any kind of medical treatment, there is even a very small risk of fatal side effects in the use of hormonal contraceptives, intrauterine devices (IUDs), and surgical sterilization of the female. Medical professionals agree, however, that the risks are minimal enough that these methods should be made fully available to those who wish to use them. Research has also demonstrated repeatedly that the risks inherent in all methods of birth control are markedly lower than the risks associated with pregnancy and childbirth. Nevertheless, methods such as the diaphragm or condom have fewer health-related side effects than some other methods, such as the pill or IUD.

Sharing the Responsibility for Birth Control

Although women bear children, overpopulation of the world will not be brought under control until men share fully in the family planning responsibilities. It is

FIGURE 10.4 *Methods of Birth Control*
The goal of people who use some method of birth control is to prevent pregnancy. However, choosing a contraceptive is just not that easy. No method is foolproof or without both positive or negative aspects.

clear that decision making about the type of birth control to be used, and then the responsibility for using it, can be shared by the woman and man. For now, only a few methods of birth control are available for use exclusively by males: withdrawal, abstinence, the male condom, and vasectomy. The latter choice, because it is not always a reversible form of sterilization, is not usually considered an option until later in life when a man has either fathered all the children he might want or has decided with certainty that he never will want to have children.

In choosing a contraceptive method, women tend to place the highest priority on pregnancy prevention, whereas men are more likely to consider disease prevention for themselves. Women and men also have differing perceptions about the effectiveness of various methods. Women, for example, are more likely to see the pill as a very good method than are men (Grady, Klepinger, & Nelson-Wally, 1999). Couples in which the male partner has primary responsibility for selecting contraception are 40 percent more likely to

Table 10.1		*Contraceptive Methods: Failure Rates, Advantages, Causes of Failure, and Side Effects*			
Method	Theoretical or Perfect Use Failure Rate*	Typical Use Failure Rate in Typical Users*	Potential Advantages to Users	Possible Causes of Failure That Could Result in Pregnancy	Potential Negative Side Effects
Abstinence	0%	?	No cost or health risks. Freedom from worry about pregnancy. Prevents infections.	Inability to continue abstaining.	Sexual frustration. Avoiding planning for eventual use of contraception.
Withdrawal (coitus interruptus)	4%	19%	No cost or preparation involved. No risks to health (if sexually transmitted diseases are absent). Available even if no other methods are.	Sperm present in preejaculatory fluid from the penis (even more likely if intercourse is repeated within a few hours). Lack of ejaculatory control, causing ejaculation in vagina. Ejaculating semen too close to vaginal opening after withdrawal.	Inability to fully relax during sexual intercourse and not be on guard. Frustration created by inability to ejaculate in the vagina.
Natural family planning/ fertility awareness	1–9%	20%	Accepted by Roman Catholic Church. May be used to increase chances of pregnancy if that choice is made. No health risks.	Inadequate time devoted to charting female's menstrual cycle or misunderstanding of method. Ovulation at an unexpected time in the cycle. Deciding to have intercourse during the unsafe period of the cycle, without other contraception.	Sexual frustration during periods of abstinence.
Combined oral contraceptive (birth control pill containing estrogen and progestin)	0.1%	3%	Reliable; offers protection all the time. Brings increased regularity to menstrual cycle. Tends to reduce menstrual cramping, PMS. Associated with lower incidence of breast and ovarian cysts, pelvic inflammatory disease, and ovarian cancer.	Not taking pills as directed or skipping a pill. Improper supervision by clinician. Ceasing taking the pills for any reason.	Nausea, weight gain, fluid retention, breast tenderness, headaches, missed menstrual periods, acne. Mood changes, depression, anxiety, fatigue, decreased sex drive. Circulatory diseases.

use a method that will prevent transmission of disease (Forste & Morgan, 1998).

Even though most available methods are used by women, there are still many ways in which couples may share in birth control. For example, male partners can participate in the decision about which method to use, and couples can go together for clinical counseling and care. Clinics must be certain that they evaluate

males' sexual and contraceptive histories if they are going to be fully effective in prescribing a useful method (Brindis et al., 1998).

Couples can purchase the contraceptives together and share in their actual use. The man can help insert spermicidal foam or a female condom into his partner's vagina, or he can prepare the diaphragm with spermicidal jelly prior to insertion. Men can play a role

Method	Theoretical or Perfect Use Failure Rate*	Typical Use Failure Rate in Typical Users*	Potential Advantages to Users	Possible Causes of Failure That Could Result in Pregnancy	Potential Negative Side Effects
Minipill (progestin only)	0.5%	3%	Safer for older women. Reliable; offers protection all the time. Brings increased regularity to menstrual cycle. Tends to reduce menstrual cramping, PMS. Associated with lower incidence of breast cysts, pelvic inflammatory disease, and ovarian cancer.	Not taking pills as directed or skipping a pill. Improper supervision by clinician. Ceasing taking the pills for any reason.	Irregular menstrual periods are a common side effect. Bleeding between menstrual periods. Appearance of ovarian cysts.
Hormonal implants	0.05%	0.05%	Long-term protection. Extremely reliable. Requires no attention after initial treatment. Easily reversible. May have some benefits as pills.	Use beyond a 5-year period. Gaining a significant amount of weight (less effective in women over 155 lbs.)	Slight visibility of implants. Menstrual cycle irregularities, depression. Improper insertion or difficult removal. May have risks similar to pills, but research is incomplete.
Depo-Provera injections	0.3%	0.3%	3-month protection. Extremely reliable. May protect against endometrial cancer. Convenient, requiring only occasional injection. Easily reversible.	Neglecting to get reinjected after 3 months.	Weight gain. Excessive bleeding. Menstrual cycle irregularities. Increased depression. Decrease in sex drive. May be associated with slight increase in breast cancer risk for younger women, but research is incomplete.
Sponge (contains spermicide)	9–20%	20–40%	Ease of use. Relatively inexpensive. Protection over 24 hours, several acts of intercourse. No odor or taste.	Difficulty in proper insertion and placement. Internal anatomical abnormalities that interfere with placement or retention.	Increased risk of toxic shock syndrome. Allergic reaction to polyurethane or spermicide. Vaginal dryness. Increased risk of vaginal yeast infections.
Cervical cap with spermicide	6%	18%	Can be left in place for long periods of time.	Improper fitting or insertion/placement. Deterioration by oil-based lubricants or vaginal medications.	Possible risk of toxic shock syndrome. Allergic reaction to rubber or spermicide. Abrasions or irritation to vagina or cervix.

in reminding their partners to take a birth control pill each day. A woman can put her partner's condom on him as a part of sexual foreplay. Studies indicate that for this type of shared responsibility to be effective, couples need to develop good communication skills and both genders need to play a role in getting the contraceptive that will be best for them (Van den Bossche & Rubinson, 1998).

Good communication between partners should include discussion of what avenues could be pursued should contraception fail. Each partner should be ready to discuss how he or she would want to deal with an unintended pregnancy. If serious conflicts develop over this issue, it may call into question the advisability of sharing sexual intercourse at all.

Method	Theoretical or Perfect Use Failure Rate*	Typical Use Failure Rate in Typical Users*	Potential Advantages to Users	Possible Causes of Failure That Could Result in Pregnancy	Potential Negative Side Effects
Spermicidal foam, cream, jelly, suppositories, or film	6%	26%	Available without prescription. Minimal health risks. Easy to carry and use. Does not require partner involvement. Provides lubrication for intercourse.	Not using enough spermicide or running out of a supply. Failure to use spermicide out of desire not to interrupt the sexual act. Placing spermicide in vagina too long before intercourse begins. Douching within 6–8 hours after intercourse. Failure of suppositories or film to melt or foam properly.	Allergic reactions to the chemical. Unpleasant taste of chemical during oral-genital sex.
Male condom	3%	14%	Available without prescription. Offers protection from sexually transmitted diseases. A method for which the man can take full responsibility. Easy to carry and use.	Breakage of condom. Not leaving space at tip of condom to collect semen. Lubrication with petroleum jelly, or presence of some vaginal medications, weakening rubber condom. Seepage of semen around opening of condom or condom slipping off in the vagina after coitus. Storing of condom for more than 2 years or in temperature extremes. Not placing condom on penis at beginning of intercourse.	Allergic reactions to latex (natural "skin" condoms and polyurethane condoms are also available). Some reduction in sensation on the penis.
Female condom (vaginal pouch)	5%	21%	Allows woman to choose protection from disease, along with contraception. Easy to carry and use. Polyurethane is strong, conducts body heat easily, and rarely breaks.	Slippage of outer rim into vagina during intercourse. Twisting of pouch during intercourse.	Some reduction in sensations of intercourse. Relatively high rate of contraceptive failure. Sometimes makes noises.

Abstinence, Sex without Intercourse, and Withdrawal

One obvious approach to birth control is to avoid the depositing of semen in the vagina. Some couples, especially unmarried teenagers, choose abstinence—usually defined as refraining from sexual intercourse—for this reason. Abstinence is sometimes defined as the avoidance of any form of sexual behavior, but more often means that intercourse is avoided. There are varieties of sexual behaviors that couples may find pleasurable and satisfying without having intercourse. These include massage, mutual masturbation, oral sex, and all sorts of physical intimacy not involving penetration. The alternatives to intercourse have been called "outercourse," which has been praised as a form of birth control that is

Method	Theoretical or Perfect Use Failure Rate*	Typical Use Failure Rate in Typical Users*	Potential Advantages to Users	Possible Causes of Failure That Could Result in Pregnancy	Potential Negative Side Effects
Diaphragm	6%	20%	Negative side effects are rare. Inexpensive; can be reused.	Improper fitting or insertion of the diaphragm. Removal of diaphragm too soon (within 6–8 hours after coitus). Not using sufficient amount of spermicidal jelly with the diaphragm. Leakage in or around diaphragm or slippage of diaphragm. Deterioration by oil-based lubricants or vaginal medications.	Allergic reaction to the rubber (plastic diaphragms are also available) or spermicide. Increased risk of toxic shock syndrome. Bladder infection or vaginal soreness because of pressure from rim.
Intrauterine device (IUD): Progesterone T (Progestasert)	1.5%	2%	Reliable. Can be left in place, so that nothing must be remembered or prepared immediately prior to intercourse.	Failure to notice that IUD has been expelled by uterus.	Uterine cramping, abnormal bleeding, and heavy menstrual flow. Pelvic inflammatory disease following insertion or perforation of the uterus during insertion of the IUD; infection of the ovaries.
Copper T 380A	0.6%	0.8%			
levonorgestrel	0.1%	0.1%			
Vasectomy	0.1%	0.15%	Permanent; no other preparations. Very reliable. Minimal health risks.	Having unprotected intercourse before reproductive tract is fully cleared of sperm following vasectomy (may be several months). Healing together of the two cut ends of the vas.	Psychological implications of being infertile can sometimes lead to some sexual problems.
Tubal sterilization	0.5%	0.5%	Permanent; no other preparations. Very reliable. Minimal health risks.	The procedure not being properly done by the physician.	Rarely, postsurgical infection or other complications. Psychological implications of being infertile.

From Richard A. Hatcher, et al., *Contraceptive Technology*, 17th edition, 1998, Ardent Media. Reprinted by permission of Contraceptive Technology Communications, Inc. Decatur, GA.

*See explanation of failure rates in text.

simple to use and free of side effects and that may reduce the risks of giving or getting sexually transmitted diseases. A study of 2,206 high school students found that 47 percent reported they were "virgins." Of this group, 30 percent had engaged in mutual masturbation, and about 10 percent engaged in some form of oral sex (Schuster, Bell, & Kanouse, 1996).

Withdrawal, also known as **coitus interruptus,** is a method that is sometimes used among couples who

coitus interruptus (ko-EET-us *or* KO-ut-us): a method of birth control in which the penis is withdrawn from the vagina prior to ejaculation.

have not yet obtained some safer method. It is used by about 20 percent of college students in their sexual interactions (Elliott & Brantley, 1997). The risk of pregnancy with the withdrawal method is high. The penis is withdrawn from the vagina prior to ejaculation, and it is crucial that ejaculation not take place near the opening of the vagina. Withdrawal can prove frustrating for couples who use it frequently. There are a number of reasons why its failure rate is high. One complication is the possibility that sperm may be present in fluids that are sometimes secreted from the penis during intercourse well before ejaculation. There is a greater likelihood of sperm being present in these secretions if the man has experienced ejaculation within the previous few hours. Of course, not all men have the ejaculatory control to withdraw in time, and some may simply choose not to do so after all. Nevertheless, when intercourse has been chosen and no other contraceptive method is available, withdrawal is preferable to using no birth control at all.

Oral Contraceptives: The Pill

Birth control pills were introduced in 1960 and rapidly gained in popularity. After concerns developed over potential side effects of some of the earlier types of oral contraception, many women decided to use other methods. Public opinion about the safety of "the pill" has now become markedly more positive, and tens of millions of women around the world now use this method. The pill is available in many countries without prescription, and some believe that its safety and efficacy warrant that accessibility in North America.

The most widely used birth control pill is the *combined oral contraceptive* that contains a combination of two hormones, estrogen and progestin, taken for 21 days during the menstrual cycle. Most manufacturers provide seven "inert" pills to be taken on the remaining days of the 28-day cycle. There are also *progestin-only pills,* sometimes called *minipills,* containing only a low dosage of progestin. It is crucial that birth control pills be taken each day at about the same time, or their effectiveness will be compromised. Studies indicate that about half of women taking the pill may inadvertently miss one or more of the pills in any given month (Peterson, Oakley, Potter, & Darroch, 1998; Rosenberg, Waugh, & Burnhill, 1998). If an entire day goes by without taking the skipped pill, however, it is advisable to use an alternative method of birth control for the remainder of the cycle, while continuing to take the rest of the pills. The missed pill should be taken as soon as possible. Indications are that a delay in taking the first three pills of a single cycle does not lead to ovulation during that cycle, providing pill use is resumed. However, taking the pills on schedule during the next cycle is essential, or a back-up method should be used (Elomaa, 1998).

Oral contraceptives create changes in the menstrual cycle that interrupt normal patterns of ovulation and implantation, thus preventing pregnancy. Combined oral contraceptives maintain estrogen at artificially high levels, thus inhibiting the release of FSH and LH, two hormones that control ovulation (see chapter 2, "Female Anatomy and Physiology"). Progestin changes the consistency of the cervical mucus so that sperm cannot pass as easily into the uterus and also makes the uterine lining less receptive to implantation by an embryo. Progestin-only pills apparently work in this latter manner, as well as occasionally preventing ovulation. The progestin-only pills are not widely used because they sometimes produce unpleasant side effects, but they are particularly useful for women who are breast-feeding babies and choose to take oral contraception. Combined pills sometimes interfere with lactation, whereas the progestin-only pills do not. Neither pill seems to have any negative effects on the babies of women who breast-feed (Erwin, 1994).

The amounts of synthetic hormones contained in oral contraceptives have been markedly reduced since the earlier days of their use, and this has also reduced the frequency and intensity of their side effects. More recently, a number of noncontraceptive benefits of the pill have been identified. It usually makes menstrual periods lighter and more regular, with less cramping. It has reduced the incidence of breast cysts, ovarian cysts, endometriosis, ectopic pregnancy, and pelvic inflammatory disease as well as cancers of the ovary and endometrium. Use of the pill has also been associated with increases in bone mass among women in their twenties, perhaps lowering their risk for bone-weakening osteoporosis in later years. It used to be thought that pill users were more likely to develop gallbladder disease, but research now tends to discount this risk (Hatcher et al., 1998). Pill use may very slightly elevate the risks of stroke, heart disease, or breast cancer, although newer pills and progestin-only pills have minimized these risks (Moore, 1999a; Suisa, 1997; WHO Collaborative Study, 1998). After discontinuation of the pill for 10 years, all risks are the same as for women who have never used the pill (Beral, 1999; Remez, 1997b).

Current research seems to indicate that for healthy women under the age of 35 who do not smoke, the benefits of the pill outweigh the risks. Although smoking increases the risk of heart attack and stroke for anyone, using the pill seems to compound the risk of these disorders even more. Therefore, it is usually inadvisable for a woman who smokes to take birth control pills.

A very important consideration before obtaining oral contraceptives is to receive a good physical examination and have a complete health history taken. There are certain conditions, such as a history of blood-clotting disorders or high blood pressure, that indicate to family planning specialists that the pill should not be prescribed (Heinemann, 1998; WHO Collaborative Study, 1997). Follow-up checks that include blood pressure readings and an annual Pap test should also be required of anyone taking birth control pills.

There are a few symptoms that a pill user should consider to be warning signs. Pain in the abdomen or gastrointestinal disorders may signal the development of liver disease, Crohn's disease, or ulcerative colitis, all conditions that are occasionally associated with oral contraceptive use. Pain in the chest, accompanied by coughing or difficulty breathing, may be a sign of a blood clot in the lungs or of a heart condition. Pain in the legs may result from blood clots in the veins there. Severe headaches or marked changes in vision may indicate high blood pressure or other conditions that can increase the risk of stroke and cardiovascular disease. Although these complications are not widespread among women who use oral contraceptives, symptoms or concerns should be reported to a medical clinician immediately (Hatcher et al., 1998).

There can be other troublesome side effects of contraceptive pills, although they are not usually dangerous. These include depression, acne, fluid retention and associated weight gain, abnormal bleeding, or absence of menstrual periods. Research with the pill has shown mixed results in terms of possible effects on mood or sexual interest. Some studies have shown that combined pills may lower the user's sense of well-being and sexual interest, whereas others tend to show that combined pill users actually have greater sexual interest than users of the progestin-only pills (McCoy & Matyas, 1996). Cautionary notes have been sounded with regard to effectiveness of the pill. Certain antibiotics, including ampicillin and tetracycline, interfere with internal absorption of the pill. Tranquilizers, barbiturates, sleeping

pills, some anti-inflammatory medications, and some sulfa drugs may also reduce its contraceptive effectiveness. Nevertheless, oral contraceptives continue to represent a particularly effective and relatively safe form of birth control for many women.

Hormonal Implants

Contraceptive implants consist of six slender silicone rubber capsules, each about the size of a matchstick. The capsules contain a contraceptive steroid called levonorgestrel, a form of progestin. They are placed under the skin on the inside of the woman's upper arm, in a fan-shaped configuration, and the drug very slowly diffuses through the walls of the capsules into the body (see Fig. 10.5). Like other forms of progestin-only contraception, the implant hormone prevents ovulation and causes cervical mucus to thicken so that sperm may not easily penetrate into the uterus.

Contraceptive implants represent a particularly reliable means of birth control because they essentially cannot be used incorrectly. The effectiveness of this method very gradually decreases over a 5-year period, so that the highest rate of failure tends to be toward the end of that period, but the implants are considered reliable for use during an entire 5 years. Implants are slightly less effective in women who weigh more than 155 pounds. They do require careful insertion and removal by a trained clinician. Six tiny incisions are made in the skin, after a local anesthetic has been used to numb the area. The tubes are then slipped into place, and the incisions are covered by small bandages for a few days. No stitches are required because the openings in the skin are so tiny. The implants are slightly visible as six raised lines under the skin. At the end of 5 years, they must be replaced. If at any time a pregnancy is desired, they may be removed by a clinician, and fertility returns right away. The implants themselves cost about $400. Therefore, the total one-time cost of $600 or more may be prohibitive for some people. They do not require other costs over the 5-year period of their effectiveness. Removal of the implants costs between $50 and $150. If used over the entire 5-year span, the method is ultimately less expensive than oral contraceptives or hormonal injections, but the up-front costs may represent a stumbling block for some women.

The most common side effect of hormonal implants is irregularity in the menstrual cycle, including prolonged bleeding or spotting between periods. Slightly more than 10 percent of users have the implant removed

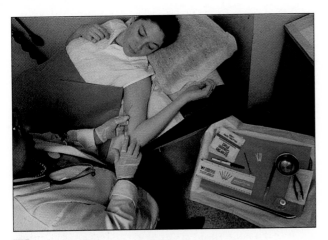

FIGURE 10.5 *Contraceptive Implants*
Contraceptive implants are inserted under the skin of the upper arm. The hormone that they release will prevent ovulation for 5 years.

contraceptive implants: contraceptive method in which hormone-releasing rubber cylinders are surgically inserted under the skin.

within the first year because of these irregularities. There may also be mood changes, weight fluctuations, headaches, acne, or other symptoms associated with the hormonal methods of birth control. The side effects vary with women's individual body chemistry. However, they generally subside after the first year of use.

Hormonal implants have generated some controversy because some clinicians who work with poor women and teenagers at high risk for pregnancy have strongly urged their use. For teenagers, they are nearly 20 times more effective than the pill. Studies indicate that the attitude of clinicians toward implants can have a strong impact on whether a patient will be interested in using them as a method (Stevens-Simon, Kelly, & Singer, 1999), and so concern has developed about women being coerced into using a contraceptive method because of the social or political agendas of others. Proponents of the implants argue that providing such contraceptive choices gives high-risk women a better chance to plan for the future. They insist that it is less a moral issue than one of facing reality. Opponents counter that such a long-term method of birth control constitutes inappropriate social engineering.

Injectables

Injections of long-acting progestin have also been used for contraception in many countries, and one form, **Depo-Provera,** the brand name for depot medroxyprogesterone acetate (DMPA), acts by creating conditions in the uterus that are inhospitable for embryo implantation. A single injection is effective for 3 months. The drug can have a number of side effects, including weight gain, hair loss, heavy menstrual bleeding, disruption of periods, emotional reactions, and fatigue. Only about 57 percent of women who have received an injection return for a second, and the 1-year continuation rate was about 23 percent in one study (Westfall, Main, & Barnard, 1996). Side effects seem to be the main reason why some women discontinue use of the contraceptive, especially following a second injection, although it has also been suggested that the definitions of discontinuing injectable use are confusing and need to be refined (Potter, 1999; Sangi-Haghpeykar, Poindexter, Bateman, & Ditmore, 1996). Tests on Depo-Provera have generally indicated that it is not associated with increased risks of liver cancer, and it may protect against cancer of the endometrium, although it may slightly elevate the risks for cervical cancer (Thomas, 1995).

Spermicides, Sponges, and Suppositories

Spermicides, or chemicals that kill sperm, are available without prescription as foams, creams, or jellies, or are placed in a sponge or suppository. There is also a spermicidal film, a paper-thin sheet that may be placed near the cervix and allowed to melt. The two spermicidal chemicals usually used are nonoxynol-9 or octoxynol. They are generally not considered to be a highly effective method of contraception when used alone, but they are very effective when used with other methods such as condoms or diaphragms. Used alone, they must be inserted deeply into the vagina so they will cover the cervical opening. Some spermicides have an unpleasant taste that can limit the pleasure of oral sexual contact with the woman following their insertion, although some companies are marketing brands that are flavored and scented. Nonoxynol-9 has the added advantage of providing some protection against sexually transmitted diseases, especially gonorrhea and chlamydia. On the other hand, it may also be associated with a greater incidence of certain types of urinary tract infection in young women (Fihn, 1996). Its effectiveness in preventing HIV infection is still being debated.

The contraceptive **sponge** is a round, thick, polyurethane disk with a dimple that fits over the cervix. Its manufacture was discontinued for a few years in the mid-1990s, but it is now back on the market. The sponge contains nonoxynol-9 and also acts as a barrier to sperm. It may be left in place for up to 24 hours, representing a significant advantage, although its rate of effectiveness is somewhat lower than that of several other methods (Springen, 1999).

Contraceptive **suppositories** are designed to melt or foam in the vagina to distribute the spermicide contained in them. However, this takes between 10 and 30 minutes, necessitating the postponement of intercourse. Some suppositories do not always liquefy completely. Their effectiveness is the same as that of other forms of spermicide.

Barrier Methods

The barrier methods are those contraceptives that block sperm from entering the uterus, thus preventing conception. Their effectiveness is enhanced when used in conjunction with a spermicide, although directions should always be followed carefully so that the proper

Depo-Provera: an injectable form of progestin that can prevent pregnancy for 3 months.

spermicides: chemicals that kill sperm; available as foams, creams, jellies, or suppositories.

sponge: a thick, polyurethane disk that holds a spermicide and fits over the cervix to prevent conception.

suppositories: contraceptive devices designed to distribute their spermicide by melting or foaming in the vagina.

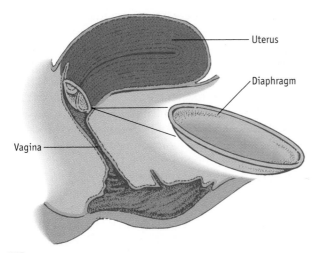

FIGURE 10.6 *Diaphragm*

The diaphragm is a mechanical barrier to sperm that comes in different sizes and must therefore be fitted to a woman by a clinician or physician. Because it may be dislodged during love-making, it is best to combine its use with a condom. Its reliability rate is fairly high when used properly and with a spermicide.

spermicide is chosen and so that it is used correctly with the barrier. Additional use of a condom also increases the effectiveness of the other barrier methods and helps prevent the spread of sexually transmitted diseases.

Diaphragms and Cervical Caps

A **diaphragm** is a latex rubber cup with a flexible rim that is placed in the vagina in such a way as to cover the cervix (see Fig. 10.6). **Spermicidal jelly** or cream is placed inside the diaphragm and around its rim to help hold it in place and kill sperm (Bounds, 1995). A clinician must fit the diaphragm to the woman, and the woman must learn how to insert it properly (Scott, 1996). Once this is learned, insertion of a diaphragm becomes a quick and simple matter. It should not be inserted more than 2 hours prior to intercourse. After this time period, if intercourse has not yet occurred, a diaphragm should be removed and more spermicide added before intercourse takes place. The diaphragm is left in place for at least 6 to 8 hours, but not more than 24 hours, following intercourse, after which it is removed and washed. It can be used for many months, although it should be checked by a doctor from time to time to ensure that it still fits over the cervix properly and is not damaged. Because the diaphragm is comparatively inexpensive, can be used for years, and presents few risks to health, it has been increasing in popularity in recent years. Some research is now focusing on the development of disposable diaphragms. The diaphragm is not, however, an ideal contraceptive for a woman who might feel uncomfortable touching her own genitals or inserting something into her vagina.

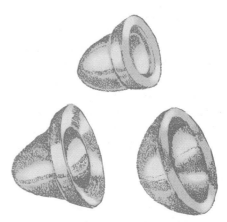

FIGURE 10.7 *Cervical Caps*

Similar to the diaphragm, the cervical cap must be fitted by a clinician. It stays in place by suction and can be worn for several weeks at a time. It may be uncomfortable for some males during intercourse and can be easily dislodged.

The **cervical cap** looks like a large thimble with a tall dome (see Fig. 10.7). As its name implies, it is designed to fit over the cervix. Because relatively few companies are manufacturing them, they are not as easily obtained in the United States as some other methods. Like the diaphragm, caps must be fitted by a clinician, inserted properly, and used with a spermicide. They can dislodge fairly easily during intercourse, and they have been implicated in some scratching of the vagina and cervix. Researchers are working to develop a cervical cap out of a material that will automatically release spermicide when semen is present.

Diaphragms and cervical caps may increase the risk of a woman developing **toxic shock syndrome (TSS).** This is an infection caused by *Staphylococcus aureus*

diaphragm (DY-a-fram): a latex rubber cup, filled with spermicide, that is fitted to the cervix by a clinician; the woman must learn to insert it properly for full contraceptive effectiveness.

spermicidal jelly (cream): sperm-killing chemical in a gel-base or cream, used with other contraceptives such as diaphragms.

cervical cap: a device that is shaped like a large thimble and fits over the cervix; not a particularly effective contraceptive because it can dislodge easily during intercourse.

toxic shock syndrome (TSS): an acute disease characterized by fever and sore throat; caused by normal bacteria in the vagina that are activated if tampons or contraceptive devices such as diaphragms are left in for long periods of time.

bacteria that are normally present in the body, which multiply if something is left in the vagina for long periods of time. For that reason, TSS has been associated with tampons as well. It is not a common disease, and resulting deaths are rare. Nevertheless, when using a diaphragm or cervical cap, it is advisable not to leave the device in place for more than 24 hours. Use should be avoided during menstruation, for a few months following the birth of a baby, or if a vaginal infection is present.

Male Condoms

The **male condom** is a sheath worn over the penis during intercourse that collects the semen when the male ejaculates (see Fig. 10.8). Most condoms today are made of latex rubber (hence the name rubbers) and are available inexpensively in drugstores, supermarkets, convenience stores, vending machines, and some college bookstores. Rubber condoms may be purchased dry or lubricated, and some have a small nipple at the tip, providing a semen-collection area. Some condoms are lubricated with a spermicide that has been shown to be effective in killing sperm within a minute or two after ejaculation, thus providing more contraceptive effectiveness. The spermicide is also effective in counteracting disease germs, including HIV. Condoms made of animal membrane are also available and cost slightly more than rubber condoms. These

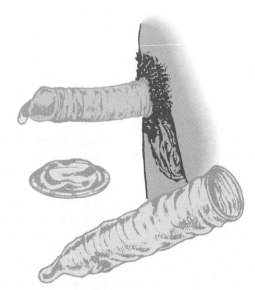

FIGURE 10.8 *Male Condoms*

A birth control device for men, the condom is made of latex rubber or animal skin. It is unrolled onto the erect penis before intercourse begins and collects the semen ejaculated. Care must be taken so that the penis does not lose its erect state while in the vagina. Latex rubber condoms are also important in preventing many sexually transmitted diseases, including HIV disease.

skin condoms purportedly allow for more sensation on the penis, although they fit more loosely than rubber condoms and should be checked from time to time during intercourse to make certain that slipping has not occurred. Skin condoms are *not* acceptable as a preventive against transmitting HIV, whereas latex rubber condoms offer substantial protection.

Rubber condoms should never be stored in wallets or automobile glove compartments because warm temperatures deteriorate rubber. Petroleum jelly (such as Vaseline), mineral and vegetable oils, and some moisturizing lotions or creams will also weaken rubber and cause tearing. Polyurethane condoms are also available. Polyurethane is thinner and stronger than latex and is especially valuable for people who are allergic to latex, and they may be used with oil-based lubricants. Polyurethane condoms provide protection from HIV as well as other sexually transmitted diseases. More specific directions and suggestions for condom use are found in chapter 17, "The HIV/AIDS Crisis and Sexual Decisions."

Among the possible reasons for condom failure are breakage or slippage of the condom. Several studies have placed the rate of latex condom breakage or slippage at under 7 percent of the times they are used. Although polyurethane condoms are preferred over latex by about half of the couples who use them, the frequency with which they break or slip off seems to be significantly higher, making them somewhat riskier for both pregnancy and disease prevention (Frezieres, Walsh, Nelson, Clark, & Coulson, 1998, 1999). Both breakage and slippage are more likely with inexperienced condom users.

Even though it is widely known that condom use is one of the best ways to prevent the spread of sexually transmitted diseases, many couples do not use condoms as long as they have an alternate method of birth control (Lindsay, Smith, & Rosenthal, 1999; Santelli et al., 1997). There are indications that young women and men are becoming more conscientious about using condoms specifically for disease prevention in recent years (Cushman et al., 1998; Murphy & Boggess, 1998). Although condom use seems to have increased because of awareness of HIV, all studies of condom use tend to suggest that couples are not using them on a consistent basis (Althaus, 1999; Bankole, Darroch, & Singh, 1999). Women tend not to use condoms when they perceive their sexual activity to be at low risk, whereas men are more likely not to use condoms because of perceived lack of availability or inconvenience of the method (Carter, McNair,

male condom: a sheath worn over the penis during intercourse that collects semen and helps prevent disease transmission.

Corbin, & Williams, 1999). In one survey of college students, less than half of the respondents reported having used a condom every time they had sex (Elliott & Brantley, 1997).

There has been controversy about the distribution of free condoms in school systems or clinics. Research evidence indicates that condom availability in high schools actually does not increase rates of sexual activity, but it does increase the use of condoms during sex. Such availability particularly increases the likelihood of condom use among people who have multiple sex partners, partly because cost of condoms is sometimes prohibitive (D. Cohen, 1999; Raab, 1998). Among young people, the likelihood of using a condom during sexual activity is increased when there has been parent-teenager discussion about sexuality and condoms (Whitaker, Miller, May, & Levin, 1999).

Female Condom or Vaginal Pouch

The **female condom** is a lubricated polyurethane pouch that may be inserted into the vagina. It is sometimes called the *vaginal pouch,* and it is marketed in the United States under the brand name Reality. In Europe, it is called Femidom. The female condom design (Fig. 10.9) consists of a ring at both ends, one of which is sealed closed. The closed ring is inserted into the back of the vagina and over the cervix, much as a diaphragm would be fitted into place. The open-ended ring then rests outside on the vulva, providing an extra measure of protection against skin-to-skin contact.

In research on the device, over half of women had initial positive reactions to the female condom, with 75 percent eventually preferring it over the male condom. Women tended not to be aware of it during intercourse, and in some cases it increased their sexual pleasure. Apparently using extra lubricant during intercourse is key to reducing each partner's awareness of the presence of the device. Women who have had negative reactions to the vaginal pouch object to its feel and sound when it was inserted, and they feel the lubricant made it messy. Some object to its appearance on the outside of the vulva. Many women endorse the female condom because it allows them a greater degree of control over maintaining safer sexual practices (Hatcher et al., 1998; Stockbridge, 1996). Men who have not tried the female condom have mixed attitudes about it, indicating that more educational efforts should be directed at men (Seal & Ehrhardt, 1999).

The obvious advantage of the female condom is that women may take full responsibility for its use as a protection from pregnancy and disease. The device almost never breaks or leaks. It also conducts body heat well, enhancing the sensation for both partners. So far, the failure rates have been moderate to high and may range up to slightly more than 20 percent, considerably higher than for male condoms. However, it is likely that in typical use, the failure rate of the female condom is not significantly different from that of the diaphragm and cervical cap (Trussell, Sturgeon, Strickler, & Dominik, 1994). Apparently, the outer edges of the female condom can get pushed down into the vagina during intercourse, permitting spillage of semen. This may well be something that regular checking during intercourse could help detect and avoid.

The barrier methods must all be inserted or put on sometime prior to sex. Although some people find this inconvenient, there is also the possibility of integrating the use of a contraceptive into sexual activities. For example, if a couple is using condoms and foam, the man can insert the foam into the woman's vagina, and the woman can unroll the condom onto the man's penis. A man could help insert the female condom into his partner's vagina. Birth control methods, like any other aspect of a responsible sexual relationship, require communication and cooperative effort. Effectiveness of the vaginal barrier methods is heavily influenced by the age of the user. Younger women are apparently more fertile and may have a greater frequency of intercourse. The failure rate for women under 30 is approximately twice the failure rate of women over 30 when using barrier methods (Hatcher et al., 1998).

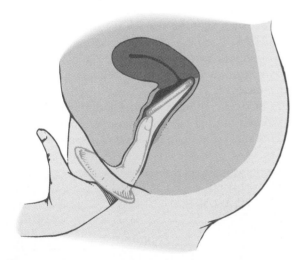

FIGURE 10.9   *Female Condom*

This diagram shows one "female condom" design that is now available. The ring at the bottom is closed and is inserted into the vagina to cover the cervix. The top open ring covers the vulva.

female condom: a lubricated polyurethane pouch that is inserted into the vagina for intercourse to collect semen and help prevent disease transmission.

Intrauterine Devices (IUDs)

Intrauterine devices (IUDs) have been used for over a century and were particularly popular in the 1960s and 1970s. Three types of IUDs are currently marketed in the United States. One is called the Progesterone T or Progestasert and includes the progestin, a progesteronelike synthetic hormone, which is gradually released from the device. Another is the Cu T 380A, which contains copper; because of its shape it is sometimes called the Copper T. A third type of IUD, the LNg 20 IUD, releases the hormone levonorgestrel into the uterus for up to 5 years, and studies indicate that it will be the most effective of all IUDs. It also tends to have fewer side effects (Hatcher et al., 1998). IUDs are made of plastic and have a nylon thread attached to one end. The contraceptive is inserted into the uterus by a clinician, with the thread left protruding into the vagina so that the woman can check regularly to make certain the IUD is still in place (see Fig. 10.10). If pregnancy is desired, the device must be removed by a clinician. Threadless IUDs are being tested and may help prevent the uterine infections that are sometimes associated with IUD use (Gardosi, 1996).

The most current evidence indicates that the IUD prevents fertilization of the egg through its effects on sperm and the egg. The chemicals and copper ions present in the uterus and fallopian tubes also alter the transport of sperm. It was once believed that IUDs interfered with implantation of a fertilized egg in the uterus, but that does not seem to be the case (Hatcher et al., 1998).

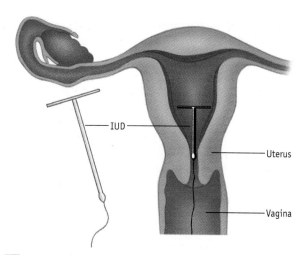

FIGURE 10.10 *IUD*

The IUD, or intrauterine device, is a small plastic object inserted into the uterus by a trained physician or clinician and left in place for long periods of time. It can be a highly effective form of birth control, but there have been serious side effects caused by some types of IUD. Only three types of IUDs remain available in the United States.

For the first three weeks after insertion of an IUD, the woman has a slightly greater risk of an infection called **pelvic inflammatory disease (PID).** If untreated for a long enough time, PID can cause damage to the fallopian tubes, resulting in sterility. It was once believed that IUDs were associated with a higher risk for ectopic pregnancy, but that has not been supported by recent studies. In fact, the IUD represents a very effective form of contraception, and it may well become more popular in the years to come as some of the myths and misperceptions about its use disappear (Hatcher et al., 1998).

Natural Family Planning/Fertility Awareness

Natural family planning/fertility awareness, once known as the rhythm method, relies on awareness of a woman's menstrual/fertility cycle so that intercourse can be avoided when it is likely that the ovum might be available for fertilization. Because it does not require any chemical or manufactured device, it is considered more "natural"; in another sense, it certainly is not natural if a couple must avoid intercourse just when they naturally want to have it. Because it requires a great deal of planning and daily attention, it is associated with a high rate of failure as a contraceptive method. On the other hand, because fertility awareness allows a couple to know when the ovum is most likely to be present for fertilization, it may also be used by couples who are attempting to get pregnant.

There are actually three fertility awareness methods. To use it effectively, the woman or couple should receive careful and complete instruction from a trained specialist in any of these methods, which may be used in combination with one another. Various charts must be made for 6 or more successive months before the method should actually be tried as a contraceptive. The *calendar method* charts the beginning and length of the menstrual cycle. The *basal body temperature (BBT) method* charts the resting body temperature of the woman throughout the menstrual cycle (see Fig. 10.11). Usually the temperature drops slightly just be-

intrauterine devices (IUDs): birth control method involving the insertion of a small plastic device into the uterus.

pelvic inflammatory disease (PID): a chronic internal infection of the uterus and other organs.

natural family planning/fertility awareness: a natural method of birth control that depends on an awareness of the woman's menstrual/fertility cycle.

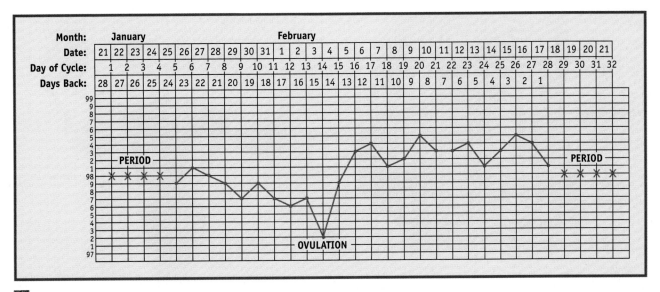

FIGURE 10.11 *Basal Body Temperature Record*

The woman's resting body temperature is taken each morning immediately upon waking. Just prior to ovulation, there is a noticeable drop in the temperature. Then, for up to 3 days after, the temperature rises. It is usually recommended that the basal body temperature be charted for 3 or 4 successive months so that any peculiarities in the woman's cycle may be noted. After it has become obviously predictable, the information may be used as part of the natural family planning method of birth control or for determining the best time for conception to occur.

fore ovulation and rises thereafter. A special oral thermometer must be used to take these readings. Finally the *mucus method* keeps track of the appearance and consistency of the woman's cervical mucus during the menstrual cycle. Women can learn to recognize that cervical mucus becomes clearer and more slippery during ovulation.

By combining information from these methods, the woman should be able to predict with accuracy about when ovulation will take place. During several days prior to ovulation, and up until 4 days after, either intercourse should be avoided or alternative birth control used. As a whole, fertility awareness requires a great deal of cooperation and communication between the partners. The most recent research has shown that pregnancy is most likely to occur during the 6 consecutive days that end in ovulation. This is different from what has previously been believed and may help to explain the rather high failure rates associated with this method of birth control (Wilcox et al., 1996).

There are some over-the-counter tests available that can help a woman determine when ovulation is most likely to occur. The tests involve measuring the amount of luteinizing hormone (LH) in the urine once a day for about a week during the middle part of the menstrual cycle. Like other predictive techniques, these tests may be used either to avoid pregnancy or to increase the likelihood of becoming pregnant. When used consistently, these tests can predict ovulation within a 48-hour period (Miller & Soules, 1996).

Continued development of accurate, easy-to-use indicators of ovulation may well improve the effectiveness of natural family planning significantly.

Voluntary Surgical Contraception (Sterilization)

Voluntary surgical contraception (VSC), or sterilization, usually renders a person permanently infertile and has become the most common method of contraception. Two-fifths of ever-married women or their husbands in the United States aged 15–44 have been sterilized. Fewer than 25 percent of them desire to have the procedure reversed (Moore, 1999a). VSC is accomplished either by cutting the vas deferens in the male, the tube through which sperm travel, or by tying or clamping off the fallopian tubes in the woman so an ovum can no longer travel through them. Of course, surgical procedures that remove the uterus or ovaries will also cause sterility.

Under what circumstances might you consider having a tubal ligation or vasectomy?

voluntary surgical contraception: sterilization; rendering a person incapable of conceiving with surgical procedures that interrupt the passage of the egg or sperm.

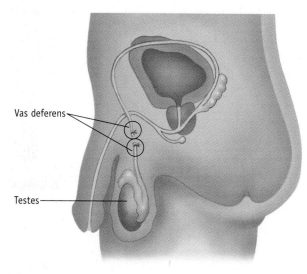

FIGURE 10.12   *Vasectomy*

A permanent form of male contraception, vasectomy is a surgical procedure in which the vas deferens is cut and tied. This blocks the passage of sperm from the testes to the upper part of the vas deferens. It is a simple and safe form of birth control and does not interfere with erection or ejaculation.

Male sterilization, called **vasectomy,** is a simple procedure in which a small incision is made in each side of the scrotum, and each vas deferens is cut and tied (see Fig. 10.12). It is one of the most frequently chosen methods of birth control in the United States. The operation is usually an office procedure that requires less than 30 minutes (Hans, McKenzie, Mehta, & Pollack, 1997). It does not affect sexual functioning or ejaculation. There simply are no more sperm cells in the semen. There are a few rare instances in which men have again ejaculated sperm and impregnated a partner even after an apparently successful vasectomy, so there is a tiny possibility of failure (Smith et al., 1994).

Tubal sterilization is the method of sterilization most often used for women. It may be performed through an operation called a **laparotomy,** which requires a hospital stay, or the more simple **laparoscopy,** in which a small fiber-optic scope is inserted into the abdomen through a tiny incision, enabling the physician to see the fallopian tubes clearly. Through either method, the fallopian tubes are located, a small portion of each tube is removed, and then the ends are tied and sealed, a procedure called **tubal ligation** (see Fig. 10.13). There is evidence that women who undergo tubal sterilization have a reduced risk of ovarian cancer but have a slightly greater chance of eventually having their uteruses removed because of menstrual disturbances or pelvic pain (Hillis, 1998; Miracle-McMahill, 1997). Although failure of this method is not common, the possibility of failure may persist for many years after the procedure.

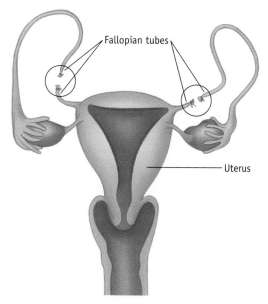

FIGURE 10.13   *Tubal Sterilization*

A permanent form of female sterilization, this surgical procedure is somewhat more complicated than a vasectomy. The fallopian tubes are cut and tied, usually with a small portion of each tube being removed. This prevents the egg from traveling into the uterus and joining with sperm.

Tubal ligations and vasectomies can sometimes be reversed, restoring fertility. However, attempts at reversal are complicated, expensive, and only 40 to 70 percent effective, so sterilization should be chosen as a contraceptive method only when a decision has been made that a permanent method is desired. Some physicians require the consent of a spouse before performing sterilization, or they refuse to sterilize individuals who do not have any children, but there are no laws requiring that either condition be met prior to sterilization. Newer, more reversible methods of sterilization are under study.

vasectomy (va-SEK-ta-mee *or* vay-ZEK-ta-mee): a surgical cutting and tying of the vas deferens to induce permanent male sterilization.

laparotomy (lap-ar-OTT-uh-mee): operation to perform a tubal ligation, or female sterilization, involving an abdominal incision.

laparoscopy (lap-ar-OSK-uh-pee): simpler procedure for tubal ligation, involving the insertion of a small fiber-optic scope into the abdomen, through which the surgeon can see the fallopian tubes and close them off.

tubal ligation (lie-GAY-shun): a surgical cutting and tying of the fallopian tubes to induce permanent female sterilization.

Postcoital or Emergency Contraception

Because contraceptive technology is imperfect, and people continue to experience sexual intercourse, or coitus, without birth control, there continues to be a demand for "morning-after" or emergency birth control. Women who have experienced unprotected intercourse have traditionally used a variety of methods to avoid pregnancy, such as douching (washing out) the vagina, wiping out the vagina with their fingers, or moving their bodies in an attempt to expel the semen. There are folk remedies that recommend insertion of objects or special concoctions into the vagina. However, there is no evidence that such techniques in any way reduce the likelihood of conception. Sperm cells will still make their way into the woman's reproductive system, and if an ovum is present, fertilization may well occur.

It is not completely clear how the emergency contraceptive methods now available actually work. They most often probably delay or prevent ovulation, so that the ovum is not available for fertilization. They may sometimes act as "interceptors," preventing implantation of a blastocyst in the uterine wall, although this seems less likely. It is for this reason, however, that emergency contraception is a controversial issue. If these methods prevent implantation of the embryo, some would consider them to be **abortifacients,** substances that cause termination of pregnancy. The American College of Obstetricians and Gynecologists technically defines pregnancy as implantation, and interceptors do not allow this process to occur. Therefore, proponents of emergency contraception claim instead that it prevents abortions because there is no need for terminating a pregnancy.

FOH The FDA has approved the use of extra doses of birth control pills for emergency contraceptive use, even though many physicians have been prescribing them as such for some time. The method has proven to be quite effective (American College of Obstetrics and Gynecology, 1999; Glasier & Baird, 1998). There is also an emergency contraception kit that can be available by prescription, although some drugstores and Catholic hospitals have not made it available to patients (Bucar, 1999). In recent years, the general public has become increasingly aware of emergency contraceptive availability, and clinicians have been making increased use of these methods (Delbanco, Mauldon, & Smith, 1997). Studies indicate that women are highly accepting of and satisfied with these emergency methods (Harvey, Beckman, Sherman, & Petitti, 1999).

There are several emergency methods that are used routinely today. The hormonal method involves taking two doses of oral contraceptive pills containing ethinyl estradiol and dl-norgestrel within 72 hours of coitus. This is followed by two more pills 12 hours later. The birth control pill marketed under the name Ovral is most often used for this purpose. Levonorgestrel-only pills may offer even more protection than combination pills (Olenick, 1999). Lower-dose minipills may also work if more than two are taken, but there is little research to demonstrate their effectiveness. Studies have indicated that the Ovral treatment may work in one of several ways, including delaying release of the ovum, causing it to be less penetrable by sperm, or interfering with implantation of a blastocyst. It has been estimated that this postcoital method averts at least 75 percent of pregnancies that might otherwise have occurred. About half of the women who use the method experience side effects such as headache, nausea, or vomiting. Women should use the procedure only under medical supervision and should also be alert to the other danger signs (see p. 321) of contraceptive pill use. A second method involves the insertion of a copper IUD into the uterus within 7 to 10 days following coitus. This is an even more effective method of preventing an unwanted pregnancy, with a failure rate of about 1 in 1,000 (Hertzen & VanLook, 1996; Trussell, Ellertson, & Rodriguez, 1996).

The drug **mifepristone (RU 486),** a progesterone **FOH** antagonist, has also proved effective in preventing pregnancy postcoitally (Task Force on Postovulatory Methods, 1999). It blocks the hormone progesterone from preparing the uterine lining for pregnancy, causing earlier menstruation. Implantation is therefore prevented, or if it has already occurred, the fertilized egg is sloughed off with the uterine lining. Mifepristone may be administered within 6 weeks after unprotected intercourse, although after the first 3 days it would clearly be acting as an abortifacient. Studies have continued to conclude that mifepristone has fewer side effects and risks than other emergency contraceptive approaches, and this may well eventually become one of its more common uses (Hatcher et al., 1994). There is more about this and other drugs starting on page 333.

New Methods of Contraception

Development of new contraceptives has proceeded very slowly. Drug companies are often reluctant to invest in researching new birth control methods because the costs are high, profit potentials are often low, and there are always fears of lawsuits because of possible

abortifacients: substances that cause termination of pregnancy.

mifepristone (RU 486): a progesterone antagonist used as a postcoital contraceptive.

side effects. Although there has been continued discussion among family planning specialists about making more methods available for males, marketing studies conducted by pharmaceutical companies have suggested that men are reluctant to use methods that might alter their internal chemistry in some way (Gabelnick, 1998).

FOH   One avenue of research has involved the suppression of sperm production in males. The World Health Organization (WHO) has been studying the contraceptive effectiveness of weekly injections of a synthetic testosterone. For many years, it has been known that elevated levels of this substance in men causes a reversible and pronounced reduction in sperm production. Taking the drug by mouth carries an unacceptable risk of liver damage, but weekly injections have been shown to be very effective. Sperm counts are greatly lowered, and only a few pregnancies have resulted. Preliminary research has found a higher degree of acceptance of the method among male users than had originally been anticipated. Research and development of testosterone injections for males will continue, and a new product may eventually be available to the general public (Ringheim, 1995; WHO Task Force, 1996).

Vaccinations that would block various hormones involved in the production of sperm are also under investigation. Clinical trials have begun on a vaccine that would interfere with gonadotropin-releasing hormone (GnRH), which regulates the production of sperm cells. Another vaccine is under development that would block follicle-stimulating hormone (FSH), a hormone also essential to sperm production, but this vaccine would not interfere with sexual interest. Other possibilities include chemicals that would either interfere with the maturation of sperm cells in the testes or in some way destroy the sperm or render them immobile. One of these chemicals is gossypol, derived from cottonseed oil. It has been used in China and has been shown to cause reversible infertility in men but has the unfortunate side effect of depleting potassium in the body, a condition that can lead to rhythm problems in the heart and other medical difficulties (Harrison & Rosenfield, 1996).

Contraceptive vaccines are also a possibility for women. One that is under development in India involves immunizing women against human chorionic gonadotropin, so that implantation of the blastocyst in the uterus would be prevented. These injections would have to be followed by booster shots every few months to continue protection. One of the newest avenues for contraceptive research and development involves various ways of blocking the union of sperm and egg. As cellular chemists elucidate the various protein structures of the outer coverings of the sperm and egg, it may well become possible to develop contraceptive chemicals that could interfere with the sperm binding to the zona pellucida of the egg or prevent it

from burrowing through the zona, thus preventing fertilization. Such contraceptive methods are not likely to be available for at least another decade, but they do provide hope for the future of contraceptive technology (Gabelnick, 1998).

◼ Unintended Pregnancy: The Options

There is evidence that the rate of unintended pregnancies among adults in North America has been declining (Henshaw, 1998b). It has been established that 12 percent (or about 1 million) women aged 15 to 19 in the United States become pregnant each year. Of those teenage women who are unmarried, only about 7 percent actually want to give birth to a child. Among married teenagers, that figure increases to about 33 percent. Among women of all age groups, about 57 percent of births are actually intended. These statistics vary greatly among countries. In Canada, for example, about 39 percent of pregnancies are unintended (Delbanco et al., 1997; Kost & Forrest, 1995). Some teenage women have dropped out of school prior to becoming pregnant, whereas many others drop out after becoming pregnant or having their babies. Many young mothers are poor even before they become pregnant. For others, however, pregnancy and young motherhood render them less likely to complete their education and less able to compete in the job market. Some 60 percent continue living with their own parent(s) after giving birth to a child (Mosher & Bachrach, 1996). Regardless of age or circumstances, an unintended pregnancy can create emotional anguish and the necessity for careful decision making.

Public perceptions about unintended pregnancy also vary among nations. People in the United States tend to see it as a "very big problem" (60 percent), whereas in Canada about 36 percent of the population rates it in this manner, and in The Netherlands, only 6 percent perceive it as such. In the United States, the most commonly cited reasons for the problem of unintended pregnancy are a decline in moral standards, lack of education, and barriers to contraceptive use (Delbanco et al., 1997; Mauldon & Delbanco, 1997). U.S. women who experience unintended pregnancies because of contraceptive failure do not necessarily react negatively to their situation. In only 59 percent of these cases do women report feeling unhappy about pregnancies, a fact which has raised some confusion regarding the meaning of "unintended" (Trussell, Vaughn, & Stanford, 1999).

What method of birth control would you favor and why?

CASE STUDY

Rebecca, Christine, and Beth Make Decisions about Their Pregnancies

The group of pregnant teens numbered 10 when a social worker first met with them. The girls ranged in age from 13 to 17 and came from a variety of backgrounds. They used the group as a supportive network for one another and as a way to sort through their own decision making. Rebecca made it clear that she had wanted to be pregnant. Her parents had not approved of her boyfriend, who was 5 years older than she. He had wanted Rebecca to live with him, and she was anxious to have children. Now that she was pregnant, her boyfriend had been paying less attention to her, and she was beginning to think that the relationship would end. Her parents had agreed to help her finish high school and raise the child until she was able to leave home. She was firm in her conviction that having a child would be exciting, even though some of the other group members warned her that being a parent would not be as simple as she seemed to believe.

Christine was equally convinced that she did not want to be pregnant at all. She was 16, wanted to attend college, and had no more contact with the boy who was the father. She indicated that her parents had wanted her to attend the group in order to think through her decision carefully. The family did not believe in abortion, but

Christine had decided that abortion was the right option for her. Because she was already 2 months pregnant, the social worker emphasized the importance of making her decision as soon as possible. After 2 weeks in the group, Christine did not return, sending word that she had chosen abortion for her pregnancy.

Beth was already 7 months pregnant and had considered abortion earlier. She had decided that it was not the best choice for her, and instead felt that she would like to have the child placed for adoption. She was also planning on pursuing her education and did not want to stay with the baby's father. She lived with her mother, herself a single parent who worked all day. The mother was not interested in caring for a new baby. Beth explained to the group that she had been wrestling with guilt feelings about her choice, but she felt certain that it was the best option for the baby. "I'm just not ready to be a mother," she said. "And I think the best thing I could do for this baby is to make sure it has a good home." She worked closely with an adoption agency that allowed her to arrange an open adoption with a childless couple, so that she could continue to stay in contact with the child if she wished. The group helped her to talk about her feelings and concerns.

It should not be forgotten that the fathers involved in unintended pregnancies often experience a great deal of conflict and psychological distress. Contrary to popular belief, most young men do not see impregnating a partner as enhancing to their masculinity. Fathers in unintended pregnancies sometimes feel resentful that they have little or no part to play in deciding what to do about the pregnancy and yet can be held financially responsible for the baby. They may experience resentment, guilt, and eventual distress if they have little access to their babies or if the woman chooses abortion (Kiselica, 1995). Fathers are typically older than mothers, especially when the mothers are teenagers (Landry & Forrest, 1995).

There are basically three alternatives from which to choose (see Fig. 10.14): keeping the baby, adoption, or termination of the pregnancy. The choice that is ultimately made apparently depends on several different factors, with attitudes toward childbearing and abortion playing a significant role. Teenagers tend to have more conservative attitudes toward abortion than adults, and yet because of life circumstances they are more likely to decide to have an abortion (Miller,

1994). It is known that whether a baby is wanted or not can have long-lasting implications for its health and well-being (Sable et al., 1997).

Keeping the Baby

This is a more typical option for married couples or those who are cohabiting than it is for single individuals (Manning & Landale, 1996). For unmarried young people, there may be a decision about whether or not to enter into marriage. Some teenaged parents allow their children to be cared for by other relatives until they have completed their educations or are otherwise more ready to assume parenting responsibility themselves.

In cases of unintended pregnancy, one of the first issues to be considered is if the mother can accept all of the emotional and physical implications of the pregnancy and birth process. Depending on his degree of involvement in the situation, the father's reactions and needs may also need to be considered with care (Kiselica, 1995). If other family members will in any way be involved in caring for the child, their feelings about the situation must be weighed. For any in-

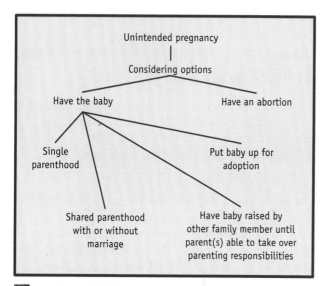

Unintended pregnancy
|
Considering options

Have the baby   Have an abortion

Single
parenthood   Put baby up for
                         adoption

Shared parenthood   Have baby raised by
with or without   other family member until
marriage   parent(s) able to take over
                         parenting responsibilities

FIGURE 10.14   *The Options for Unintended Pregnancy*
This chart reminds us that whenever an unintended pregnancy
occurs, some decision must be made. There is no such thing as
not making a decision. To avoid considering abortions as an
option constitutes a decision to have the baby. The choices
may not be comfortable or easy, but in one way or another they
must be faced and made.

dividual who is intending to keep a baby, there should
be a clear commitment to and adequate preparations
for effective prenatal care, the learning of appropriate
parenting skills, and planning for the financial requirements of child rearing.

Adoption

Up until about 1970, the majority of young women
who had unintended pregnancies placed their babies
for adoption. Today the situation is very different, in
that less than 5 percent of mothers relinquish babies
for adoption. Presently, agencies that handle adoptions are finding it difficult to provide newborn babies
for the many childless couples who hope to adopt.
This reflects a generally negative attitude toward placing children for adoption that is prevalent today. Many
young women have learned to think of this option as
"giving up your child," the connotations of which are
mostly negative. In fact, adoption can represent a viable alternative, and, in some cases, the mother is allowed to have contact with the child and its adoptive
parents. Young women who place babies for adoption
tend to be more affluent, more motivated to pursue
education, and more positively disposed toward adoption than those who keep their babies.

Most adoptions are handled through social agencies, but private arrangements involving physicians
and/or lawyers are sometimes made. Close to 15,000
children from foreign countries are adopted by Ameri-

can parents each year. It is helpful to talk with adoptive parents and adults who were adopted as children,
to get a realistic and complete perspective on the situation. The degree to which adopted children should
be allowed to find or contact their birth parents, and
vice versa, continues to be a matter of controversy.
The most recent studies on children who were
adopted as infants have concluded that adopted children and adolescents tend to be happy and well adjusted. Parents of adopted children are more likely
than other couples to stay together, and adopted teens
are less likely to engage in high-risk health behaviors.
It seems that one factor in the positive adjustment of
children to the fact of having been adopted is parents
who have accepted adoption in a matter-of-fact way,
not dwelling on it (Benson et al., 1994).

*Do you think adopted children/adolescents/adults
should be in touch with their birth parents? Defend
your position.*

Adoption represents a reasonable option for unintended pregnancies when the mother chooses to continue the pregnancy—or it is too late to do
otherwise—and yet she does not feel ready for the responsibilities of parenthood. Mothers and fathers who
choose to have their child adopted often feel that the
child will have a chance for a better life with another
family. As with any choice that is made in cases of unintended pregnancy, there are emotional consequences to be weighed. Yet most people realize that
the option of becoming pregnant will be available
again at a later time in life when circumstances lend
themselves more fully to acceptance of the responsibility for parenting.

Termination of Pregnancy

If a pregnancy terminates naturally, it is called a **miscarriage** or **spontaneous abortion.** Some women
who experience an unintended pregnancy choose to
seek ways of terminating it, also known as **induced
abortion.** There are about 1.4 million abortions performed in the United States each year, representing
about one-third of all pregnancies, although it is also
believed that there is an underreporting of abortions
(Fu et al., 1998; Henshaw, 1998a). The ratio of abortions to live births has been falling in recent years, primarily because young women under the age of 15 are

miscarriage: a natural termination of pregnancy.

spontaneous abortion: another term for miscarriage.

induced abortion: a termination of pregnancy by
artificial means.

opting to have abortions less than they did a few years ago and because fewer clinics and health care providers are offering abortion (O'Connor, 1998). Recent polls indicate that between 80 and 90 percent of people believe that abortion should be available under certain circumstances, and 32 percent believe that abortion should be legally available for any reason. About 22 percent of Americans believe that abortion should be illegal under all circumstances. There has been a trend toward conditional acceptance for abortion, with the majority of people favoring the procedure in cases of rape, when the health of the mother is endangered, or when there is a strong chance of a defect in the baby. Nevertheless, about three-fifths of voters indicate they are more likely to support pro-choice candidates (Center for Reproductive Law and Policy, 1998).

The many moral and political conflicts regarding abortion hinge on an essential difference in the beliefs of pro-life antiabortion forces and pro-choice supporters concerning when human life begins. Abortion foes often believe that life begins at the moment of conception and that abortion is tantamount to murder because it involves the ending of another human life. Some extremist factions have even felt that the burning or bombing of abortion facilities, or murdering of abortionists, are justified by these views. Although most proponents of the availability of abortion feel that it should not be a decision made lightly, they see it as a right for women to choose in an overpopulated world where many families cannot adequately care for the children they have. They tend not to hold to the idea that life begins at conception and instead see the potential quality of life for the unborn child and its parents as a primary issue. Advocates insist that women should have the right to determine what happens to their own bodies, including whether or not to proceed with a pregnancy.

FOH

The Supreme Court has itself struggled with the continuing debate. The historic *Roe v. Wade* decision in 1973 legalized a woman's right to obtain an abortion from a qualified physician. In subsequent rulings, the Court has upheld the right to abortion established by *Roe v. Wade,* while giving states the right to legislate various kinds of restrictions on abortion in order to accommodate the beliefs of their citizens. For example, state laws have been enacted that prohibit certain health care personnel from providing information about abortion; require notification of husbands, or, in the case of minors, a parent; require a waiting period of up to 24 hours before the abortion may take place; and/or prohibit the use of public facilities for abortions. As might be expected, such laws have placed added burdens of time and cost on women seeking abortions and on the facilities that serve them (Lichter, McLaughlin, & Ribar, 1998).

Methods of Abortion

There are several procedures that can be employed to terminate pregnancy (see Table 10.2). The particular method chosen usually depends on the stage of pregnancy. An abortion can be legally performed in the United States by a doctor through the 24th week of pregnancy (measured from the first day of the last menstrual period). The earlier it is performed, the simpler the procedure and the lower the risks to the woman. **FOH**

Vacuum Curettage

About 90 percent of abortions in the United States are performed within the first trimester, the first 12 weeks of pregnancy. The method most often used during this stage is **vacuum curettage,** sometimes called vacuum aspiration or the suction method. First, the cervical opening is dilated through the use of graduated metal dilators. Another more gentle approach to cervical dilation involves the earlier insertion of a cylinder made from a dried seaweed called **laminaria.** The laminaria insert slowly absorbs moisture from the cervix, and as it expands, the cervical os opens wider. Maximum dilation can take from 12 to 24 hours. This procedure is more comfortable for the woman and reduces the risk of injury to the cervix. After the cervical opening is dilated, a thin plastic tube is inserted into the uterus and is connected to a suction pump. The uterine lining, along with fetal and placental tissue, is then suctioned out. This part of the procedure usually takes 10 to 15 minutes.

Medical Induction

As mentioned earlier in this chapter, the drug mifepristone, or RU 486, has been widely used in Europe for early abortions and is now used routinely in the United States. The earlier it is used during the pregnancy, the higher its rate of effectiveness. It is typically used within 7 weeks of the woman's first day of her last menstrual period. The drug is administered in tablet form under a physician's supervision, and it causes the embryo to break away from the uterine wall. Two days later, a prostaglandin, a hormonelike chemical, is administered orally or by injection or suppository, causing the uterus to contract and expel the embryo. Studies have shown that use of mifepristone is less painful and carries less danger of infection than surgical methods of abortion. **FOH**

vacuum curettage (kyur-a-TAZH): a method of induced abortion performed with a suction pump.

laminaria (lam-a-NER-ee-a): a dried seaweed sometimes used in dilating the cervical opening prior to vacuum curettage.

Table 10.2   *Means to an End: Three Abortion Techniques*

Though their results are the same—the termination of a pregnancy—medical and early-stage surgical abortion work in different ways. The benefits and disadvantages of three methods:

Procedure	Side Effects, Risks	Cost, Timing, Status
RU 486 Mifepristone (RU 486) pills block hormone sustaining pregnancy; misoprostol pills two days later induce contractions.	Intense cramping and bleeding can last more than a week. Four percent failure rate.	About $300. Effective until the 9th week of pregnancy. FDA has given provisional approval.
Methotrexate and Misoprostol A shot stops fetal cells from dividing. A vaginal suppository 5 to 7 days later induces contractions.	Nausea and diarrhea in rare cases. Four percent failure rate.	Drugs are $10, M.D. visits bring tab to $300. Effective up to 9th week. Approved in 1998.
Surgery Usually vacuum aspiration of the fetus through the vagina. Performed under a local anesthetic.	Slight chance of perforation of the uterus or injury to the cervix.	About $300. Used from 6th to (in rare cases) 24th week. Legal, but 85% of U.S. counties have no practitioners.

From Debra Rosenberg, Michele Ingrassia, and Sharon Begley, "Blood and Tears" in *Newsweek,* September 18, 1995. Copyright © 1995 Newsweek, Inc. All rights reserved. Reprinted by permission.

Injection of methotrexate, a drug that is already on the U.S. market for other purposes, has also proved to be 96 percent effective for inducing abortion when combined with misoprostol, another approved drug. This method requires less medical monitoring than mifepristone (Joffe, 1999; Schaff, 1999).

Aside from the objections of antiabortion groups, concerns have been raised about drug-induced abortion for other reasons. Some experts on women's health feel that focusing attention on drugs will detract from the need to provide safe conventional abortion facilities. They also fear that if drugs become too readily available, they will be used too often without proper medical supervision, jeopardizing women's health and safety. If drugs gain general acceptance as abortifacients, it is certainly possible that early-term abortions will become a simpler and more private procedure, over which women will be able to have somewhat greater personal control.

The WHO sees mifepristone as an important option to be offered to developing world countries. There are indications that it not only is safer than surgical abortion, but that it may be useful in the treatment of breast and ovarian cancer, tumors of the brain and spinal cord, a disease of the adrenal glands, and endometriosis, a disease of the uterine lining (Ewart & Winikoff, 1998).

Dilation and Evacuation or Dilation and Curettage

Beyond the first trimester, the uterus has enlarged, and its walls have as a result become thinner. The contents of the uterus cannot be as easily removed by suction or by injections of drugs such as mifepristone. Therefore, vacuum curettage is no longer considered as safe and suitable for abortions in the second trimester of pregnancy.

During the 13- to 16-week period, the usual method employed is **dilation and evacuation (D & E).** After cervical dilation, a suction tube is still used, but this procedure is followed by the scraping of the inner wall of the uterus with a metal curette to ensure that all fetal tissue is removed. This is a variation of **dilation and curettage (D & C),** which omits the initial

dilation and evacuation (D & E): a method of induced abortion in the second trimester of pregnancy; it combines suction with a scraping of the inner wall of the uterus.

dilation and curettage (D & C): a method of induced abortion in the second trimester of pregnancy that involves a scraping of the uterine wall.

CROSS-CULTURAL PERSPECTIVE
Abortion around the World

EGYPT   Illegal unless the woman's life is in danger. Government hospitals strictly enforce the rule, but abortion is quietly available in private clinics and hospitals throughout Cairo.

FRANCE   Legal for any reason until 10th week of pregnancy. Parental consent required for unmarried minors. Cost covered by national health system.

GREAT BRITAIN   Legalized in 1967; the abortion law requires approval from two physicians before a woman can have an abortion. This has medicalized the procedure and taken it more out of the political arena.

IRELAND   Although abortion is outlawed, thousands of women go to other countries each year for the procedure. There is a growing campaign to change the country's abortion laws.

JAPAN   Generally legal up to 22 weeks but can be performed after that point to protect the life of the mother. Husband's or partner's consent is usually required. National health system does not pay. Mourning ritual often follows the procedure.

LATIN AMERICA   Outlawed everywhere except in Cuba and Barbados, but there is increasing consideration of whether abortion should be legalized in other countries.

POLAND   In 1994, the Polish Parliament attempted to reverse a 1993 ban on abortion in cases of economic or personal hardship. Although legal abortions all but disappeared under the new noncommunist government, illegal and self-induced abortions were rampant. Women's groups are fighting to have abortion legalized again.

RUSSIA   Abortions are legal and used as a form of birth control, and about two-thirds of pregnancies are terminated. The average Russian woman will have several abortions during her childbearing years. There is a small antiabortion movement in the country, and abortion rates have been decreasing slightly.

---

vacuum aspiration of the uterus and is sometimes used to terminate pregnancy.

Procedures Used Later in Pregnancy

For abortions later in pregnancy (16–24 weeks), procedures must usually be employed that render the fetus nonviable and induce its delivery through the vagina. These approaches are more physically uncomfortable and often more emotionally upsetting for the woman because she experiences uterine contractions for several hours and then expels a lifeless fetus. The two most commonly used procedures at this stage of pregnancy are **prostaglandin-induced** or **saline-induced abortions.**

Prostaglandins are injected directly into the amniotic sac through the abdominal wall, administered intravenously to the woman, or inserted into the vagina in suppository form. Prostaglandins stimulate uterine contractions leading to delivery. Saline (salt) solution is injected into the amniotic fluid and has a similar effect. Some clinicians have also substituted a substance called urea for saline. Sometimes, various combinations of prostaglandins, saline, and urea are used to terminate later pregnancies (Hatcher et al., 1998). Late-term abortions, sometimes called partial-birth abortions, have created a great deal of controversy.

Use of Fetal Tissue

An issue related to abortion has surfaced among the other controversies. It is the use of fetal tissue in research and medical treatment. By the late 1980s, several researchers were transplanting tissues from aborted fetuses into humans in an attempt to cure certain diseases. These tissues are particularly valuable because they grow faster, are more adaptable to a variety of environments, and are less likely to be rejected by the recipient's immune system than tissues

prostaglandin- or saline-induced abortion: used in the 16th to 24th weeks of pregnancy, prostaglandins, salt solutions, or urea are injected into the amniotic sac, administered intravenously, or inserted into the vagina in suppository form, to induce contractions and fetal delivery.

transplanted from other adults. Work has been done to investigate the value of fetal tissue transplants in treating Parkinson's disease, Alzheimer's disease, spinal cord damage, diabetes, epilepsy, and a variety of neuromuscular disorders. The outcomes of the research have been encouraging (Begley & Glick, 1998).

FOH Use of fetal tissue has of course been fraught with controversy, and for a time there were governmentally imposed bans on federal funding for any research involving their use. Those in favor of permitting such research argue that as long as abortion is legal, it makes no sense to destroy fetal tissue that could be put to use in ways that might save lives. Because of ethical and political pressures, some researchers are looking for ways of reducing their dependency on fetal tissues for certain disease treatments (Begley, 1998b; Kiernan, 1999a).

Safety of Abortion for Women

FOH All studies have indicated that legal medical abortions have fewer risks to the woman than carrying a pregnancy to full term and giving birth. Although in both cases the risk of the woman's death is extremely low, the chance of a relatively healthy woman dying from a legal abortion in the United States is about 1 in 100,000 in abortions performed up to 12 weeks of pregnancy. The rate rises somewhat as the length of pregnancy increases. That compares to nearly 20 deaths per 100,000 in continued pregnancies and births (Hatcher et al., 1994).

Do you believe that abortion should be continued as a legal option? Under what circumstances?

First-trimester abortions are simplest and safest and have few complications other than some excessive bleeding or subsequent infection that can be treated with antibiotics. If all of the fetal tissue is not removed, this can cause infection and require further scraping of the uterine wall, usually through a D & C procedure. Later abortions have somewhat higher risks of bleeding or infection because labor is induced, but the risk of fatal complications is still minimal. Although having two or more abortions has been linked with a higher incidence of miscarriage in later pregnancies, and it also increases the likelihood of later ectopic pregnancy, abortion does not reduce fertility or the ability to conceive (Tharaux-Deneux, 1998). Some studies suggested that young women who have an induced abortion might have a slightly higher risk of breast cancer in later life, but the most recent conclusion is that there is no link between abortion and increased risk for breast cancer (Brind, 1996; Melbye et al., 1997).

Psychological Considerations

The psychological effects of abortion for a woman depend a great deal on her own beliefs and values and the degree of care with which she has made the decision. She needs to consider her own feelings and the reactions of others close to her. Few people see abortion as an easy option, but many view it as a necessary choice given their personal circumstances. **FOH**

Although serious emotional complications following abortion are quite rare, some women and their male partners experience some degree of depression, grieving, regret, or sense of loss (Janus & Janus, 1993). These reactions tend to be even more likely in second or third abortions. Support and counseling from friends, family members, or professionals following an abortion often help to lighten this distress, and it typically fades within several weeks after the procedure. Counseling often helps in cases where the distress does not become alleviated in a reasonable time. A review of the wealth of data gathered in studies conducted for the American Psychological Association suggested that most women will not suffer lasting psychological trauma following an abortion. There does not seem to be any evidence to support the existence of what has been termed a "postabortion syndrome," and severe negative reactions following abortions are apparently rare (Russo & Dabul, 1997).

Self-Evaluation

Contraceptive Comfort and Confidence Scale

Method of birth control you are considering using: _____

Length of time you used this method in the past: _____

Answer YES or NO to the following questions:

		YES	NO
1.	Have I had problems using this method before?	❑	❑
2.	Have I ever become pregnant while using this method?	❑	❑
3.	Am I afraid of using this method?	❑	❑
4.	Would I really rather not use this method?	❑	❑
5.	Will I have trouble remembering to use this method?	❑	❑
6.	Will I have trouble using this method correctly?	❑	❑
7.	Do I still have unanswered questions about this method?	❑	❑
8.	Does this method make menstrual periods longer or more painful?	❑	❑
9.	Does this method cost more than I can afford?	❑	❑
10.	Could this method cause me to have serious complications?	❑	❑
11.	Am I opposed to this method because of any religious or moral beliefs?	❑	❑
12.	Is my partner opposed to this method?	❑	❑
13.	Am I using this method without my partner's knowledge?	❑	❑
14.	Will using this method embarrass my partner?	❑	❑
15.	Will using this method embarrass me?	❑	❑
16.	Will I enjoy intercourse less because of this method?	❑	❑
17.	If this method interrupts lovemaking, will I avoid using it?	❑	❑
18.	Has a nurse or doctor ever told me NOT to use this method?	❑	❑
19.	Is there anything about my personality that could lead me to use this method incorrectly?	❑	❑
20.	Am I at any risk of being exposed to HIV (the AIDS virus) or other sexually transmitted infections if I use this method?	❑	❑

TOTAL NUMBER OF YES ANSWERS: ___ ___

Most individuals will have a few "yes" answers. "Yes" answers mean that potential problems may arise. If you have more than a few "yes" responses, you may want to talk to your physician, counselor, partner, or friend to help you decide whether to use this method or how to use it so that it will really be effective for you. In general, the more "yes" answers you have, the less likely you are to use this method consistently and correctly at every act of intercourse.

Source: R. A. Hatcher et al., *Contraceptive Technology* (17th edition), 1998, New York: Ardent Media. Reprinted by permission of Contraceptive Technology Communications, Inc. Decatur, GA.

Chapter Summary

1. People's sense of well-being contributes to their choices about having children. Human beings have sought to minimize the connections between sex and childbirth.

2. In ancient times, botanical preparations may have provided contraceptive protection.

3. Distribution of information about birth control was limited in the United States by the Comstock Laws, passed in the 1870s. Activist Margaret Sanger was influential in broadening the rights of women to learn about and use contraception in the early part of this century,

although laws prohibiting the sale of contraceptives existed until the 1960s.

4. Because of the earth's burgeoning population, some believe that increased efforts to develop and promote contraception are necessary; others look toward redistribution of global wealth. Many children live in substandard conditions.

5. The decision to have children is an important one, involving significant costs and personal responsibilities.

6. It is believed that many global pregnancies are unwanted. Political and social factors may determine what kinds of birth control are accessible.

7. In making decisions about contraceptive use, people are influenced by several factors. These include ethical/moral and religious beliefs, possible effects on the woman's health, and psychological and social factors. Guilt, fear, or anxiety may not always inhibit sexual behavior but may inhibit preparing for it.

8. Each person must sort through his or her personal values and concerns about birth control, understand his or her personal reactions to sexual feelings and activities, and learn how to communicate with a partner effectively in order to prepare fully for contraceptive decision making.

9. There is no "best" method of birth control for all individuals. Each couple must consider several factors in making a choice: age and amount of protection required, how long the method will be used, what might hinder the method's use, and cost.

10. The theoretical or perfect use failure rate assumes the birth control method is being used correctly and without technical failure. The typical use failure rate is the more realistic rating of the method, taking into account human error, carelessness, and technical failure.

11. Even though most methods of contraception are designed for women, there are many ways for the responsibility to be shared by both partners: cooperating in applying the method, communicating openly about birth control, and sharing the cost. Cultural imperatives sometimes interfere with the sharing of this responsibility.

12. For summary information on methods of contraception, their rates of effectiveness, potential advantages, possible causes of failure, and possible negative side effects, see Table 10.1.

13. For couples who choose abstinence from intercourse for birth control, there are many alternatives for sexual and nonsexual intimacy. Although withdrawal is better than no method at all, it is not one of the more reliable forms of contraception.

14. Hormones that prevent ovulation and change the consistency of cervical mucus can be administered in the form of combined oral contraceptive pills or progestin-only minipills. The pill provides protection against ovarian and endometrial cancers but may also have some side effects.

15. Hormonal implants consist of six capsules that are implanted under the skin, releasing a synthetic hormone that prevents ovulation for up to 5 years. The up-front costs are prohibitive for some women, and there is sometimes difficulty in removing the implants.

16. Depo-Provera injections create a hostile uterine environment for sperm and for implantation, and they last for 90 days.

17. Spermicides kill sperm and are available without prescription as foams, film, jellies, creams, vaginal suppositories, and implanted on the contraceptive sponge.

18. Barrier methods of contraception prevent sperm from entering the uterus and are most effective when used with a spermicide. They include the diaphragm, cervical cap, and condom.

19. Condoms provide protection against disease as well as pregnancy. Male condoms fit over the penis and are made of latex, natural membranes, or polyurethane. Female condoms consist of a polyurethane pouch that is inserted into the vagina. Female condoms do not have as high a rate of effectiveness as male condoms.

20. The intrauterine device (IUD) is inserted into the uterus and may work by preventing fertilization or implantation by the embryo. It was once implicated in a high risk of pelvic inflammatory disease (PID), and its use declined.

21. Natural family planning/fertility awareness allows the woman to become more aware of her fertile period during the menstrual cycle by charting the length of her cycle, basal body temperature, and consistency of cervical mucus.

22. Vasectomy involves cutting and tying the male vas deferens. Tubal sterilization seals off the fallopian tubes. Studies are being done on more reversible forms of sterilization.

23. The most accessible means of emergency contraception at present is to take extra doses of certain birth control pills. IUD insertion is also effective, and the drug mifepristone may become a form of postcoital birth control.

24. New forms of contraception are being researched. For males, these include vaccines

with GnRH or FSH inhibitors, testosterone injections, and other chemicals that suppress sperm production. For women, a vaccine that would immunize against gonadotropin could prevent implantation. Research is also investigating possible ways of preventing fertilization by altering the chemistry of the sperm or egg.

25. When an unintended pregnancy occurs, one of several options must be chosen: keeping the baby, placing it up for adoption, or abortion.

26. When an unintended pregnancy occurs, couples in established relationships are more likely to keep the baby. Less than 5 percent of mothers now place their babies for adoption. Adopted children are as well adjusted, or better so, than other children.

27. Some pregnancies terminate naturally, and this is called miscarriage or spontaneous abortion.

28. Induced abortion has been legal in the United States since 1973, but Supreme Court decisions have gradually allowed states to restrict its availability. There are still conflicts between right-to-life and pro-choice groups about whether abortion should be continued as a legal option.

29. First-trimester abortions are usually done by vacuum curettage. Mifepristone (RU 486) in combination with prostaglandins offers a nonsurgical alternative. Later abortions may be done by dilation and evacuation (D & E) or dilation and curettage (D & C) or induced by injection of prostaglandins, saline, or urea.

30. The use of fetal tissue transplants in medical research has become part of the abortion controversy. The U.S. federal government currently allows fetal tissue to be used for research.

31. Abortion is statistically safer for the woman than pregnancy and giving birth. Some women experience a degree of guilt, loss, or other psychological reactions. The availability of supportive counseling before and after an abortion is important.

Focus on Health Questions

You will find in this section the kinds of questions that you may have concerning your own health and sexuality. The page references indicate where in the text the answer is located; the exact place is marked with the logo: **F◦H**

Annotated Readings

Alan Guttmacher Institute. (1996). *Readings on emergency contraception*. New York: Author. A selection of wide-ranging articles relating to postcoital birth control methods.

Claire, M. (1995). *The abortion dilemma: Personal views on a public issue*. New York: Insight Books/Plenum. Provides up-to-date information and a balanced treatment of the various sides of the abortion debate.

Harrison, P. F., & Rosenfield, A. (1996). *Contraceptive research and development*. Washington, DC: National Academy Press. Explores the politics and pharmaceutical issues relating to the development of new birth control methods.

Hatcher, R. A., Trussell, J., Stewart, F., Cates, W., Stewart, G. K., Guest, F., & Kowal, D. (1998). *Contraceptive technology* (17th ed.). New York: Irvington Publishers. Updated regularly, it is the most comprehensive and reliable book on contraception available. Reasonably technical, but easy to use in finding information about specific methods.

Joffe, C. (1995). *Doctors of conscience: The struggle to provide abortion before and after Roe v. Wade*. Boston: Beacon Press. An analysis of the historical roots of American laws and philosophies regarding abortion that helps to explain why doctors and others seem to support abortion rights more than they do the abortion providers.

Luker, K. (1996). *Dubious conceptions: The politics of teenage pregnancy*. Cambridge, MA: Harvard University Press. A fresh and realistic look at how poverty and other social ills lead to problems such as teen pregnancy.

Tsui, A. O., Wasserheit, J., & Haaga, J. (Eds.). (1997). *Reproductive health in developing countries*. Washington, D.C.: National Academy Press. A comprehensive look at issues affecting reproductive health throughout the world.

Wattleton, F. (1996). *Life on the line*. New York: Ballantine Books. A personal account of the struggle for reproductive rights, written by a former head of Planned Parenthood.

Winikoff, B., & Wymelenberg, S. (1997). *The whole truth about contraception*. Washington, DC: Joseph Henry Press. A guide to birth control methods written for teenagers.

Part 4

Sexual Behavior and Contemporary Society

The two most common forms of sexual activity are masturbation and heterosexual intercourse. Although masturbation is usually a solitary activity and may involve both positive and negative feelings on the part of the person doing it, there are many other behaviors that bridge the gap into shared sexual encounters. The dynamics of the interaction, whether they relate to technique or how personalities are connecting, become crucial to determining whether a sexual interaction is pleasurable or exploitative. Chapter 11 deals with both solitary and shared sexual activity.

It seems clear from research that a substantial percentage of human beings have been predominantly sexually attracted to members of their own gender. Although many people espouse a live-and-let-live attitude toward gay males, lesbians, and bisexual persons and their sexual behaviors, ours is essentially a heterosexist culture. Many view same-gender orientation as being reflective of abnormalcy, illness, or immorality. Chapter 12 takes a close look at what we know about sexual orientation and tries to dispel the idea that it is an either-or phenomenon.

The kinds of sexual activities in which people have chosen to participate seems limited only by the imagination. Chapter 13 focuses on the range of sexual behaviors exhibited by humans. Only in recent years has scientific research begun to give us a clearer picture of human sexual diversity.

Chapter 14 concentrates on several issues of sociosexual significance. What are the effects of sexually explicit materials? How have sexual themes become a part of art, literature, films, television, and computer technology? To what extent should laws regulate erotic themes in the media and the sexual activities of human beings? These are major issues facing society today, and courts and legislative bodies are struggling to grapple with their complicated natures.

Chapter 11
SOLITARY SEX AND SHARED SEX

Masturbation can occur at all stages of life. There is a wide range of shared sexual behavior, and understanding their techniques can make them more comfortable and pleasurable.

Chapter 12
SAME-GENDER ORIENTATION AND BEHAVIOR

Several conceptual models attempt to describe the origin of same-gender attractions, behaviors, and identities. Same-gender behavior exists in all cultures and is treated and valued according to each society's attitudes. Sexual orientation is an issue that has social and political implications.

Chapter 13
THE SPECTRUM OF HUMAN SEXUAL BEHAVIOR

Sexual interests and gender identity may be expressed in many different ways. There is a wide range of sexual activities that may be considered unusual and may be exploitative.

Chapter 14
SEX, ART, THE MEDIA, AND THE LAW

Erotica is sexually explicit material that is portrayed in an artistic manner, and pornography portrays raw lust with aspects of violence or aggression. Research into the effects of sexually explicit materials is beginning to be analyzed.

Chapter 11
Solitary Sex and Shared Sex

Chapter Outline

Note: A selection of Focus on Health questions appears at the end of each chapter. Answers to these questions are indicated within the chapter by the symbol in the margin. **FOH**

I think about sex a lot, and I enjoy experiencing sex, whether by myself or with a partner. I've managed to be careful about the partners I have chosen, and I always am careful to protect both of us. These days though, sex alone seems much less complicated, but sometimes you just long to be with somebody too.

—From a student's essay

This chapter examines some of the most common sexual behaviors in which human beings participate. Although masturbation and heterosexual or vaginal intercourse constitute primary parts of the discussion, many other forms of sexual experiences that can be shared by partners of the same or different genders are also examined. There seems to be a fair amount of evidence to suggest that, generally speaking, males demonstrate higher levels of sexual interest and activity than do females. This is probably due to an interaction of both biological and social factors (Baldwin & Baldwin, 1997; Laan & Everaerd, 1995).

Although Kinsey (1948, 1953) emphasized that the statistics on sexual behavior gained from his sample of about 16,000 individuals could not be generalized to the total population, they did allow us to glimpse the many variations of human sexual experience. With the data from the National Health and Social Life Survey (NHSLS), we now have more reliable statistics on the types and frequencies of sexual behaviors among people in the United States, and they seem to be relatively consistent with data coming from European research. For the first time, we can make some generalizations from the random population sample surveyed in the NHSLS to the general population. We can also see that sexual behaviors are influenced by factors such as age, race, religious beliefs, and educational background (Laumann, Gagnon et al., 1994).

List several factors that might influence the acceptability and frequency of various sexual behaviors.

Statistics should be considered approximations of what people are doing and only that. Although they can give us interesting information and establish certain statistical norms for sexual behavior in particular groups of people, we must not assume that such data necessarily represent standards for behavior. Just because most males masturbate does not mean that males should masturbate or that nonmasturbating males are abnormal. Just because the majority of females have not experienced intercourse by the age of 17 does not mean that 15-year-old females who have intercourse are immoral.

Each of us possesses his or her own specific sexual interests, values, preferences, needs, and behaviors. These aspects of our sexuality may change many times during our lifetimes because sexual individuality is more of a dynamic process than it is a fixed state of being. I hope the information in the chapters concerning sexual behavior can help you gain a clearer understanding of your own sexuality as it is now and

inform you of the spectrum of sexual behaviors that are part of the human experience.

There are two distinct worlds of human sexual experience. One is the social world in which sex is shared with others that necessitates all sorts of negotiable processes between people and involves expectations, judgments, performances, and consequences that can be both positive and negative. The other is the private world that in many ways may even be more active and consuming than the partnered world. In this domain, personal pleasure is paramount, and social constraints may intrude in less demanding ways, although private sex is often not without its guilt or fear of discovery.

■ Solitary Sex: The Private World

The private world of sex involves the solitary pursuit of sexual thoughts and fantasies, erotic materials and toys, and masturbation, often in combination with one another. The NHSLS data showed that men report thinking about sex more frequently than women. Over half of men (54 percent) said that they think about sex every day or even several times a day, with another 43 percent reporting that they think about sex a few times a month or a week. Only 19 percent of women indicated they think about sex every day, whereas 33 percent said they think about sex a few times per week or month. Four percent of men and 14 percent of women reported thinking about sex less than once a month or never. As Table 11.1 shows, men are also considerably more likely than women to purchase and seek out materials and activities that are associated with private sexual arousal and pleasure.

Conventional wisdom holds that people who engage in solitary sexual pleasures probably do so because of the unavailability of sexual partners. In fact, research has demonstrated that this assumption is incorrect. NHSLS data showed that people who are the most likely to think about sex the most, to pursue erotic materials for their own use, and to masturbate, actually tend to have the most active sexual lives with partners as well. The more private sexual experience an individual has, the more shared sexual experience he or she is likely to have (Michael et al., 1994).

Masturbation

Masturbation is one of the most common ways human beings seek sexual pleasure. I will use the term "masturbation" to refer to deliberate, rhythmic stimulation

Table 11.1   *Percentage Purchasing Autoerotic Materials in the Past 12 Months*

Materials	Men	Women
X-rated movies or videos	23%	11%
Visit to a club with nude or seminude dancers	22	4
Sexually explicit books or magazines	16	4
Vibrators or dildos	2	2
Other sex toys	1	2
Sex phone numbers	1	1
Any of the above	41	16

Source: From *Sex in America* by Robert Michael. Copyright © 1994 by C.S.G. Enterprises, Inc., Edward O. Laumann, Robert T. Michael, and Gina Kolata. By permission of Little, Brown and Company, Inc.

Note: Percentages are separate for each cell.

of the sex organs—often along with other parts of the body—to produce pleasurable sexual sensations and (usually) orgasm. Masturbation is not confined to the human species; it is common among many mammals, especially the primates. It is a form of sexual behavior that has been subject to much misunderstanding, folklore, religious attention, moral analysis, and ignorance.

Because of its decidedly private nature, masturbation continues to be a sexual practice that is infrequently discussed. As sexuality was being brought into the domain of medicine during the eighteenth century, negative attitudes about masturbation made their way into the perceptions of the medical profession. A Swiss physician by the name of Tissot published a book in 1741 that perpetuated the popular belief of the time that body fluids had to be kept in perfect balance for the person to be healthy. It was further believed that expending the sexual fluids of the body would deplete it of essential fluids and lead to illness. Physicians of this time also believed that the stimulation of the nervous system that took place during sexual arousal and orgasm was damaging. Tissot's theories were perpetuated by medical writers throughout the nineteenth century, as the claims of physical and mental deterioration that would result from masturbation became even more extreme. Although the medical perspective on the practice has now been almost completely reversed, masturbation still remains cloaked in a somewhat negative, and often inaccurate, shroud of secrecy.

Although statistics from previous research samples have not been representative of the total population, it is reasonable to conclude from the data we have that masturbation is a very common practice among adolescents and that the vast majority of people masturbate at some time in their lives. The *Details* magazine survey of college students found that 88 percent of the men and 60 percent of the women indicated that they presently masturbated at least occasionally. Seventeen percent of the males masturbated every day, and another 44 percent did so at least once a week. Among the women, 4 percent masturbated every day, and 23 percent at least once per week (Elliott & Brantley, 1997).

The NHSLS data studied masturbatory behavior of adults and again have provided the most reliable statistics presently available. Of Americans aged 18 to 59, 60 percent of the men and 40 percent of the women had masturbated in the previous 12 months. About 25 percent of the males and 10 percent of the females indicated that they masturbated once a week or more. Interestingly, the survey found that the younger people in the study, aged 18 to 24, actually masturbated less than any other age group except those over the age of 54. Researchers speculated that the younger group might feel that they should leave masturbation behind as they enter into partnered sexual relationships, and that in the older group, it probably represented the general decline in their overall rates of sexual activity (Laumann, Gagnon et al., 1994).

Do you feel that masturbation is a behavior deserving of moral judgment or prohibition? What is the basis for your answer?

Eighty-five percent of men and 45 percent of women who were living with a sexual partner indicated that they had masturbated during the previous year, although frequency of masturbation does not seem to be particularly correlated with how often they have sex with a partner. White, educated liberals are apparently more likely to masturbate. Most people reported that they masturbate in order to "relieve sexual tension." About one-third of men and women said they did so because they did not have a sexual partner. One-third of men and one-fourth of women indicated that masturbation was used to help them relax. Very few of the people surveyed—5 percent of the women and 7 percent of the men—said they masturbated in order to avoid HIV infection or other sexually transmitted diseases (Michael et al., 1994). Everyone who chooses to masturbate must find her or his own way of masturbating—ranging from the guilt-ridden, hurriedly finished, hidden act to the fully enjoyed, unhurried, luxuriously sensual experience that can even be shared with someone else (Geer & Manguno-Mire, 1997; Sank, 1998).

How Girls and Women Masturbate

Masturbation is one way in which many women become acquainted with their own sexual responsiveness and learn how to have an orgasm (see Fig. 11.1).

FIGURE 11.1   *Female Masturbation*

This may serve them well as they develop their responsiveness with a partner. Masters and Johnson (1966) reported in a study in which they observed women masturbating that although no two women out of a sample of several hundred masturbated in exactly the same way, very few of them seemed to use direct stimulation of the glans clitoris. The tissues of the clitoral glans are apparently too sensitive for any prolonged direct stimulation, just as the glans of the penis is. Women who stimulate the clitoris tend to stroke gently only the shaft. Right-handed women usually manipulate the right side of the shaft and left-handed women the left side. A more common way for females to masturbate is by manipulation of the entire mons area, and this exerts less direct stimulation to the clitoris. The minor lips or other areas surrounding the clitoris are also frequently stimulated. It is important to note that immediately following orgasm, the clitoral glans is especially sensitive to touch or pressure, and most women avoid touching it at that time.

Although use of the hands is the most common method of masturbation, many girls and women find other means of stimulating their genitals. Rubbing the mons or other parts of the vulva against a pillow, bed, doorknob, or some other object is quite typical. It is also not unusual for a female to insert a finger or some suitably shaped long object into the vagina during masturbation. Cylindrical electric vibrators or flexible plastic devices (often called dildos) may also be used during masturbation. Some women are able to produce sexual arousal and orgasm by creating muscular tension in the pelvic region through the tightening of leg and abdominal muscles. Others may cross their legs and apply rhythmic stimulation to the vulva by contracting and relaxing the thigh muscles. Women sometimes find that running a stream of warm water over the vulva, and especially the clitoris, or sitting in a whirlpool bath can create sexual stimulation. Many women stimulate other parts of their bodies while masturbating. Stimulation of the breasts and nipples is very common, and some women enjoy stroking the anal region. There are many individual differences in the ways people stimulate themselves for sexual pleasure. No one pattern needs to be considered the only right way of doing so. Common sense dictates that cleanliness should be observed during masturbation and that women should not insert sharp, pointed, or rasping objects into their vaginas. It is also important not to introduce bacteria from the anal region into the genital area because infection may result.

How Boys and Men Masturbate

Masters and Johnson (1966) also found highly individualized methods of masturbating in the hundreds of men they observed. Some type of stimulation of the penis almost always occurs in male masturbation. Typically, the penis is grasped by the hand and stroked until orgasm takes place (see Fig. 11.2). How the penis is grasped and stroked varies with different males. The most common method is for the man to stroke the shaft of the penis, just touching the top edge of the corona around the glans and the frenulum on the underside where the glans and shaft join. The amount of pressure used, number of fingers employed on the penis, how rapidly the stroking proceeds, and how far up and down the hand moves all vary from man to man. Some men—particularly those with circumcised penises—stimulate just the glans by pulling at it or rubbing its entire surface. As men get closer to orgasm, the stroking or rubbing of the penis tends to become more rapid, then usually slowing or stopping during actual ejaculation. This is in direct contrast to most women, who continue stroking the clitoris during orgasm.

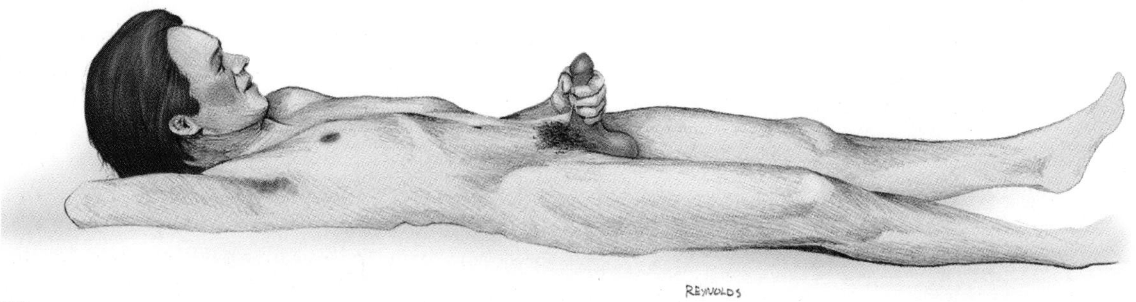

FIGURE 11.2   *Male Masturbation*

During manual masturbation, many men enjoy occasionally using both hands to stroke the penis, or using their free hand to fondle the scrotum or anal region. Some men insert a finger or object into the anus during masturbation. It is also not unusual for a male to use some sort of lubricating jelly or liquid on his hand during masturbation to create intense sexual sensations. It seems safe to assume that most boys and men experiment with a variety of ways of producing orgasm. Many males enjoy rubbing their penises on blankets, pillows, beds, and other suitable objects. Kinsey (1948) reported that a significant proportion of men attempt **autofellatio** at one time or another; that is, they try to put their penises into their own mouths, a feat that very few have the acrobatic dexterity to achieve.

There are also masturbation aids that are marketed for men. These include rubber pouches into which the penis can be inserted, artificial vaginas made of flesh-simulating plastics that often show the external organs of the vulva, and full-sized inflatable dolls that have built-in pouches at the location of the vagina, mouth, and/or anus (Elliott & Brantley, 1997). A few boys and men enjoy inserting objects into the urethra at the end of the penis, especially those who find pain sexually arousing. There are obvious dangers to this practice because injury or infection in the urethra could result. Physicians occasionally see boys or men who have inserted some small object into their urethras, only to have it become lodged there. Again, it is common sense that masturbation should be done with attention to basic cleanliness and safety, so that genitourinary injury or infection will not result.

Fantasy and Pictures in Masturbation

As noted earlier, many people fantasize about sex or employ pornography and sex toys as part of their autoerotic activities, with males doing so more frequently than females (Geer & Manguno-Mire, 1997). In a survey of college students, over 60 percent of the males reported they had used pornographic magazines or videos to enhance masturbation, whereas about 12 percent of the females reported doing so. Males were also more likely to use nonpornographic magazines or advertisements during masturbation. The most common fantasies seem to be about sexual activity with a loved partner, although fantasies about sexual involvement with acquaintances, celebrities, and strangers are also very typical (Elliott & Brantley, 1997). Additionally, there is the whole gamut of fantasies about group sex, being forced to have sex, forcing another person to have sex, and every other imaginable form of behavior. It is probably safe to assume that erotic pictures, videos, and literature help to generate fantasies in many individuals during masturbation and that people often project themselves into the subject matter of the erotic material.

Facts and Fallacies about Masturbation

It is surprising how many myths and misconceptions about masturbation persist. The next few paragraphs attempt to separate the fallacies from the facts. Each of the following italicized statements is a fact.

Fact: Masturbation is not confined to childhood and adolescence or to single persons. Many adult men and women—including married individuals—continue to masturbate throughout their lives. There is solid evidence to indicate that the majority of adult males and close to half of adult females masturbate from time to time. Their frequency of masturbation actually seems to be highest between the ages of 24 and 50. Married people, particularly married men, tend to masturbate somewhat less than single people. There is a wide range among those who masturbate very seldom (once or twice a year) and those who masturbate more frequently (once a day or more). All

autofellatio (aw-toh-fe-LAY-she-o): a male providing oral stimulation to his own penis, an act most males do not have the physical agility to perform.

of these patterns are found in normal, healthy, happy individuals.

Fact: Masturbation is not necessarily a substitute for sex with a partner. It is certainly true that masturbation is sometimes used as a substitute for sexual activity with a partner. However, masturbation also represents a form of sexual expression in itself, regardless of what other sexual activities the individual has available. Many people who have very fulfilling sexual lives and have access to shared sexual activity whenever they wish still enjoy masturbating. The NHSLS research showed that an active masturbatory and private sexual life seems to be one component of a generally sexually active life that includes shared sex as well. People who masturbate frequently are more likely to participate in partnered sex frequently as well (Michael et al., 1994). Some people may actually prefer masturbation to other forms of sexual behavior; this should not be considered a sign of immaturity or sexual dissatisfaction.

Fact: Masturbation can be shared. In my counseling and sex therapy practice, I never cease to be surprised by the number of couples who share sex but who never even discuss masturbation. Even though both partners may be masturbating regularly, it is often impossible for them to admit that fact to one another. Masturbation is apparently one of the secrets that partners most often keep from one another. Being able to surmount this communication barrier and talk about masturbation can be an important step toward better sexual communication. Some couples find that masturbating together or watching one another masturbate can be an enjoyable form of sexual sharing.

Fact: There is no such thing as excessive masturbation. For years, books on sex for young people implied that there is nothing wrong with masturbation, so long as it was not practiced to excess. The fact is that there is no medical definition of what excessive masturbation might be. Frequent masturbation does not cause physical harm. For the most part, it seems to be a self-limiting practice, and when the individual is sexually satiated, he or she loses interest in being sexually aroused. The number of orgasms necessary to reach satiation will vary among individuals and their circumstances. Of course, if a person has masturbated to satiation, she or he may not be interested in other forms of sex for a while. Masters and Johnson (1966) reported that most men they questioned expressed vague concerns over excessive masturbation but consistently established the frequency that they considered excessive to be greater than their own masturbatory frequency. A man who masturbated once a month stated that once or twice a week would be excessive, whereas a man who masturbated two or three times a day thought that five or six times a day might be excessive.

Fact: Masturbation can be as physically sexually satisfying as shared sex. From a purely physical standpoint, masturbation can offer full sexual satisfaction for some people. Of course, if physical and emotional intimacy with another person is important to an individual's fully experiencing sexual feelings, masturbation will leave some gaps. Particularly in women, however, masturbation often provides the opportunity for the kind of self-regulated stimulation that produces a more intense orgasm than can be obtained with coitus. Some of that effective stimulation can be transferred to shared sex when the partners have good communication about sex. Although about a third of college students consider masturbation a poor substitute for shared sex, over half indicated that they either found it to be always enjoyable or the best way to relieve anxiety and frustration (Elliott & Brantley, 1997).

Fact: Masturbation is a good way to learn about sexual feelings and responsiveness. Among sex therapists and sexuality educators today, the attitude is quite prevalent that masturbation is not only healthy and normal but that it can be a very useful learning experience. In males, it is likely that patterns of sexual functioning may be influenced by early patterns of masturbation. For the boy who learns to masturbate to orgasm in the shortest possible time, the pattern may well carry over into later intercourse as premature ejaculation. Men who have learned to prolong the time it takes to ejaculate during masturbation often can transfer that control into their shared sexual activities. There is one caveat here. A few men develop patterns of masturbation that require unusual amounts of penile pressure or stimulation. Some of these men have difficulty replicating these sensations in shared sexual experiences (Sank, 1998).

For women, masturbation is recognized as an important way to learn first what orgasm feels like and how to produce it. Various masturbation exercises are commonly used as a preliminary step toward orgasmic response and full enjoyment in shared sexual activity. Research has shown that when compared to married women who have never experienced an orgasm through masturbation, those married women who have masturbated to orgasm had significantly more orgasms in shared sex, greater sexual desire, higher self-esteem, a greater level of marital and sexual satisfaction, and a tendency to require less time to become sexually aroused with a partner (Hurlbert & Whittaker, 1991).

Fact: Masturbation does not lead to weakness, mental illness, or physical debilitation. As the myths about masturbation's connection with all sorts of mental and physical maladies have faded, it is now clear that there are no medical conditions caused by masturbation, regardless of frequency. Coaches once warned athletes to avoid masturbation, or other forms of sex, especially the night before the big game, because they saw it as an energy-sapping practice. Although orgasm may indeed release tension and lead to relaxation, many athletes claim that this can be a real boost to their performance. Masturbation does not drain the body of energy.

Fact: Males do not eventually run out of semen if they masturbate frequently. It has been a common misconception that the male body is granted the potential of producing only a certain amount of semen and that each ejaculation leads a man closer to the bottom of the barrel. In actuality, the glands that produce sperm and semen tend to be active from puberty into old age. They do not cease production after a certain number of orgasms. In fact, evidence shows that the more sexually active an individual is in earlier life, the more active he or she will be in later years. The more semen a male ejaculates, the more his body produces.

Fact: Masturbation does not lead to same-gender orientation and behavior. In many people's minds, masturbation is associated with sexual attraction to one's own gender. Apparently, the idea of a person seeking pleasure from her or his own genitals is interpreted as sexual attraction to same-sexed genitals. This is not true. Heterosexual people masturbate and so do gay, lesbian, and bisexual people. The practice does not change their sexual orientations.

Fact: Masturbation is not physically essential. Some people—particularly men—believe that it may be harmful to abstain from having orgasms. They fear that storing sperm and semen, or experiencing erection without orgasm, may eventually be harmful to the body. Actually, the body adjusts its production of semen to the amount of sexual activity. Although masturbation can be a pleasurable learning experience and important to a person's sexual life, it is not essential for physical or mental well-being.

Masturbation, Guilt, and Morality

Perhaps because of the long-standing negative attitudes toward masturbation, it is not always a guilt-free sexual practice. About half of women and men report some degree of guilt in association with their masturbatory activities. Guilt does not seem to affect the frequency of masturbation in males, but it is somewhat associated with less frequent masturbation in females (Laumann, Gagnon et al., 1994). Women who feel guilty about their self-stimulation are less likely to have positive physical and psychological reactions to masturbation and are less likely to report being sexually adjusted or satisfied (Baldwin & Baldwin, 1997; Davidson & Darling, 1993).

Adolescent males seem to talk together more about masturbation than adolescent females. Why might this be?

As with all other forms of sexual behavior, various cultures and religions have attached many different moral implications to masturbation. The Judeo-Christian-Muslim position was once predominantly antimasturbation, although their attitude as well as that of most religious groups has largely changed with the new findings of medicine and psychology. The story of Onan has often been cited as evidence of the sinfulness of masturbation. The Old Testament tells that while having sexual intercourse with the wife of his deceased brother, Onan withdrew before ejaculation and "spilled his seed on the ground." God was angered and struck him dead. Actually, of course, Onan was not masturbating but practicing what we now call coitus interruptus or withdrawal as a means of birth control. In any case, masturbation has also been called **onanism.** It is clear that each individual—considering his or her religious, parental, and peer values—must decide whether or not masturbation will be part of an acceptable personal repertoire of sexual behaviors.

Shared Sexual Behavior

The kinds of physical contact described in this section are usually sexually arousing, may in themselves lead to orgasm, or may serve as a prelude to other behaviors that may or may not include orgasm. As figures from the NHSLS research in Table 11.2 demonstrate, vaginal intercourse is clearly the most popular of all shared sexual behaviors among all age groups of both women and men. The researchers were somewhat surprised to find that the second most appealing activity was to watch a partner undress. This was even more appealing to men than to women (Michael et al., 1994).

Although vaginal intercourse is still often assumed to be the definitive heterosexual act, there is growing evidence that other forms of shared sexual activity have gained in popularity and are practiced for the pleasure they provide in themselves, rather than as a preparation for intercourse (I. M. Schwartz, 1999; Weinberg, Lottes, & Gordon, 1997). Instead of assuming that these noncoital behaviors necessarily represent "foreplay" that will ultimately lead to intercourse, it has been suggested that they constitute a system for negotiating the

onanism (O-na-niz-um): a term sometimes used to describe masturbation, it comes from the biblical story of Onan, who practiced coitus interruptus and "spilled his seed on the ground."

America Keeps Onan in the Closet

To students of sexual politics, it was perhaps no surprise that the remark that finally prompted President Clinton to jettison Surgeon General Joycelyn Elders involved masturbation. No other sexual practice indulged in by a majority of adults has an image so dark and dirty, so controversial and forbidding that it is seldom mentioned even in today's world of say-anything, show-anything sexuality. . . .

Dr. John Gagnon, a professor of sociology at the State University of New York at Stony Brook, argued that Americans are in part still burdened by a long history of proscriptions against masturbation. The Old Testament warns against the sin of Onan—the spilling of seed on barren ground.

But real zealotry in the battle against masturbation emerged in the 18th century when sex became medicalized.

The anti-masturbation wave began with a Swiss doctor, S. A. D. Tissot, and his wildly popular pamphlet, published in 1741, called "Onanism, or a Treatise on the Disorders of Masturbation." Dr. Tissot proclaimed that the act drained the body of vital fluids, causing wasting illnesses like tuberculosis. Too much sexual excitement, masturbation in particular, he said, caused neuroses and could damage the nervous system.

"Onanism," reprinted dozens of times and translated into all of the major European languages, sounded the first alarm in what was to become a wave of dire warnings that masturbation was not only immoral but also dangerous. Benjamin Rush, a signer of the Declaration of Independence and a physician keen on bleeding and purging patients, wrote that masturbation caused poor eyesight, epilepsy, memory loss and tuberculosis. Doctors argued that masturbators were easy to spot because they looked sickly and repugnant.

In the 19th century industrious entrepreneurs produced and peddled cures. J. H. Kellogg invented corn flakes and Sylvester Graham, the graham cracker. Both wrote best-selling books detailing the terrible ills that befell masturbators. In his 1888 book, "Plain Facts for Young and Old Embracing the Natural History and Hygiene of Organic Life," Mr. Kellogg informed parents that there were no fewer than 39 signs of masturbation, including acne, bashfulness, boldness, nail biting, use of tobacco and bed wetting. He advised parents to bandage their child's genitals, to enclose them in a cage or, simply, to tie the child's hands. He also suggested circumcising boys without an anesthetic. For girls (by now at risk), the cure was carbolic acid on the clitoris. And yes, corn flakes eaten daily would prevent masturbation.

Mr. Graham's 1834 book, "A Lecture to a Young Man," warned that a teenage boy who masturbated turned into "a confirmed and degraded idiot, whose deeply sunken and vacant, glossy eye and livid shriveled countenance . . . denote a premature old age! a blighted body—and a ruined soul!" He prescribed as a preventive a healthy lifestyle founded on vigorous exercise, sleep on a hard wooden bed and a diet that shunned meats and emphasized grains.

The attributes of masturbators became so well known that Charles Dickens had only to describe Uriah Heep as a pale creature who lacked eyebrows and had red eyes and clammy hands which he chafed together constantly, and "everyone knew he was a masturbator," Dr. Gagnon said. Heep, the villain of "David Copperfield," was "the salutary lesson to everyone," he added.

Some 19th century inventors patented devices to stop masturbation, including a genital cage that held a boy's penis and scrotum with springs, an alarm sounding when an erection occurred. Though later reformers like Sigmund Freud later denounced these remedies, they believed that the act could cause impotence, premature ejaculation and a dislike of intercourse.

Today, Americans presumably know better. But the grim, unenlightened history of self-pleasuring may be dogging them still.

Gina Kolata, *New York Times*, December 18, 1994. Copyright © 1994 by the New York Times Co. Reprinted with permission.

level of intimacy the couple wants to share (Schnarch, 1998). Because of the higher risks associated with intercourse, couples are beginning to recognize that it does not have to constitute the inevitable goal and that other forms of sexual sharing can be highly satisfying (Gavey, McPhillips, & Braun, 1999).

In a continuing sexual relationship, there is a gradual learning process between the partners concerning their own individual preferences for various activities. Conflicts may arise when one partner finds a particular activity to be appealing and desirable, but the other partner finds it to be offensive or unappealing. Such conflicts

Table 11.2	*The Appeal of Selected Sexual Practices*

Panel A: Women

Selected Sexual Practices	Ages 18–44				Ages 45–59			
	Very Appealing	Somewhat Appealing	Not Appealing	Not at All Appealing	Very Appealing	Somewhat Appealing	Not Appealing	Not at All Appealing
Vaginal intercourse	78%	18%	1%	3%	74%	19%	2%	6%
Watching partner undress	30	51	11	9	18	49	16	17
Receiving oral sex	33	35	11	21	16	24	14	45
Giving oral sex	19	38	15	28	11	20	17	52
Group sex	1	8	14	78	1	4	9	87
Anus stimulated by partner's fingers	4	14	18	65	6	12	14	68
Stimulate partner's anus with your fingers	2	11	16	70	4	12	12	73
Using dildo/vibrator	3	13	23	61	4	14	17	65
Watching others do sexual things	2	18	15	66	2	11	13	74
Same-gender sex partner	3	3	9	85	2	2	6	90
Sex with stranger	1	9	11	80	1	4	6	89
Passive anal intercourse	1	4	9	87	1	3	8	88
Forcing someone to do something sexual	0	2	7	91	0	0	5	95
Being forced to do something sexual	0	2	6	92	0	1	5	95

may have to be accepted as a part of the relationship and appropriate compromises made, but it is also quite typical for people to experiment with new activities as a relationship progresses, sometimes even learning to enjoy them more than before (DeVillers, 1997).

Nongenital Oral Stimulation

The lips, tongue, and oral cavity are often associated with intimate, sexually arousing activity (see Fig. 11.3). The oral areas are replete with nerve endings, moist, and associated with pleasurable sensations of taste and food consumption. The mobility of the tongue and lips affords them versatility and allows them to be voluntarily controlled by the individual. All of these factors are involved in the various uses of the mouth in pleasurable sexual sharing.

Although there exist a few small societies where it is not practiced at all, and a few where it is frowned upon, kissing is used to express affection in most parts of the world. Kissing usually carries with it important

messages concerning the depth of intimacy in a relationship. The least intimate is the simple peck on the cheek. Lengthy lip contact, gentle rubbing of another person's lips, and insertion of the tongue into the partner's mouth (French kissing or soul kissing) are considered to be more deeply intimate and sexually arousing. Kissing, licking, or nibbling at other parts of the body—such as the abdomen, breasts, ears, or genitals—is also considered to be particularly intimate by many.

Stimulation of Erogenous Zones

There are certain areas of the body that almost always generate sexual arousal when they are touched. The penis and the clitoris are two examples of particularly sexually sensitive organs. However, it seems that almost any area of the body can become conditioned to respond erotically to tactile stimulation in particular individuals. If touching a particular part of a person's body leads to sexual arousal, the area is called an erogenous zone for that person. Typical nongenital erogenous

Panel B: Men

Selected Sexual Practices	Ages 18–44				Ages 45–59			
	Very Appealing	Somewhat Appealing	Not Appealing	Not at All Appealing	Very Appealing	Somewhat Appealing	Not Appealing	Not at All Appealing
Vaginal intercourse	83%	12%	1%	4%	85%	10%	1%	4%
Watching partner undress	50	43	3	4	40	47	7	5
Receiving oral sex	50	33	5	12	29	32	11	28
Giving oral sex	37	39	9	15	22	33	13	32
Group sex	14	32	20	33	10	18	22	50
Anus stimulated by partner's fingers	6	16	24	54	4	12	23	60
Stimulate partner's anus with your fingers	7	19	22	52	4	16	20	60
Active anal intercourse	5	9	13	73	1	7	9	83
Using dildo/vibrator	5	18	27	50	3	17	24	57
Watching others do sexual things	6	34	21	39	4	25	21	50
Same-gender sex partner	4	2	5	89	2	1	5	92
Sex with stranger	5	29	25	42	2	23	23	52
Passive anal intercourse	3	8	15	75	2	5	10	84
Forcing someone to do something sexual	0	2	14	84	1	2	12	86
Being forced to do something sexual	0	3	13	84	0	2	10	89

Source: From *Sex in America* by Robert Michael. Copyright © 1994 by C.S.G. Enterprises, Inc., Edward O. Laumann, Robert T. Michael, and Gina Kolata. By permission of Little, Brown and Company, Inc.

Note: Row percentages total 100 percent

zones are the mouth, earlobes, breasts, buttocks, lower abdomen, inner thighs, and the anal-perineal area. In a fulfilling sexual relationship, it is important for both partners to learn about the most pleasurable kinds of stimulation to exert on these zones.

In treating sexual dysfunctions (see chapter 18), sex therapists have long recognized that touch is a vital part of the experience that gives meaning to sexual responsiveness for women and men. Therapy programs typically encourage couples to spend time together in the nude, gently massaging, fondling, and tracing one another's bodies in pleasurable ways. Both partners are encouraged to accept and enjoy being stimulated to the fullest possible extent. Most people in our culture find some degree of sexual arousal in having their bodies close to another naked body and having the opportunity to share touching experiences. The sense of touch is usually an essential part of sexual arousal (DeVillers, 1997).

Some people find an element of sexual arousal in more aggressive forms of touch. Sexual contact can have its aggressive, even violent, sides. Light scratching, pinching, and biting are considered enjoyable by some. It is not unusual for one partner to bite and suck the other during strong sexual passion, even to the extent of producing a bruise. Such a bruise on the neck is commonly called a hickey, and it seems to represent a badge of experience for some individuals.

Oral-Genital and Oral-Anal Sex

Many individuals derive intense genital pleasure from being orally stimulated, partly because they can relax and enjoy it, and partly because the partner can provide intense, localized stimulation. Although using the mouth to stimulate the genitals of a sexual partner can be highly exciting for some people, it can be distinctly

FIGURE 11.3 *Kissing*

In most parts of the world, kissing is a sign of affection. This young American couple shares a warm and loving moment.

disgusting for others. The term **fellatio** refers to kissing, licking, sucking on the penis, or allowing the penis to move in and out of the mouth. Some men particularly enjoy oral stimulation of the frenulum on the underside of the penile head, one of their most sensitive genital areas. **Cunnilingus** involves kissing, licking, or sucking the clitoris, labia, and vaginal opening or inserting the tongue into the vagina. Sometimes partners perform oral sex on one another simultaneously, the position called, in slang, "sixty-nine," due to the relative positions of the bodies.

The NHSLS provided the most reliable statistics on oral sex ever made available. There has been a fair amount of evidence indicating that oral sex became an increasingly acceptable and desirable form of sexual behavior on college campuses during the 1960s and 1970s, and the NHSLS data make it clear that the practice is still especially popular among young, better-educated, and white persons. It is much less common among people with less education and among blacks. According to the survey, 68 percent of women and 77 percent of men had performed oral sex on a partner during their lifetimes, with 19 percent of women and 27 percent of men having done so in their last sexual interaction. Similar proportions of both genders had been recipients of oral sex: 73 percent of women and 79 percent of men during their lifetimes; and 20 percent and 28 percent, re-

spectively, during their last sexual experience. A willingness to perform oral sex and/or have it performed on them is twice as common among women who have gone to college as compared with those who did not finish high school. People over 50 and those who have a conservative Protestant religious background are much less likely to engage in oral sexual practices (Anderson & Pollack, 1994; Laumann, Gagnon et al., 1994). As Table 11.2 shows, oral sex ranks third on the list of people's favorite shared sexual activities, with most every other behavior trailing rather distantly behind. In the *Details* magazine survey of college students, just over 80 percent of both sexes reported they had performed and received oral sex (Elliott & Brantley, 1997).

Why do you think oral sex and some other forms of sexual behavior are more common among women who have gone to college than among those who did not finish high school?

With the important proviso that oral-genital sex [FOH] can be responsible for spreading sexually transmitted diseases, it is generally considered a relatively safe practice so long as the rules of basic hygiene are followed. Some partners fear the ejaculation of semen into their mouths during fellatio because of the mistaken notion that the substance is, in itself, dangerous to ingest. If the male is known to be free of sexually transmitted diseases, HIV, and prostate infection, and the partner wishes to do so, there is no particular danger in swallowing semen. It is simply digested.

There are now some documented cases of HIV being transmitted through oral sex, although the actual degree of risk remains unclear. Therefore, unless there is absolute certainty about a partner's lack of exposure to HIV, the safest practice is for a condom to be worn during fellatio or a **rubber dam** placed over the vulva during cunnilingus. Rubber dams may be of the type used in dental work or may be a nonlubricated latex condom or a rubber surgical glove cut to form a sheet of rubber. As yet, there have not been any studies concerning the actual effectiveness of such rubber dams in preventing transmission of HIV, but experts have reasoned that any barrier to the mixing of body fluids certainly reduces the risks. How practical the rubber dam can be in even acting as such a barrier is particularly debatable. Other infections can also be transmitted through oral-genital contact, including throat infections from genital bacteria, and urethral or vaginal infections

fellatio: oral stimulation of the penis.

cunnilingus (kun-a-LEAN-gus): oral stimulation of the clitoris, vaginal opening, or other parts of the vulva.

rubber dam: a piece of rubber material, such as used in dental work, placed over the vulva during cunnilingus.

355

CROSS-CULTURAL PERSPECTIVE
A Simple Smooch, a Blissful Buss: All about Kisses

The young do it. The old do it. Even the butterflies—well, they probably don't do it. But chimpanzees and orangutans do.

The Egyptians, Romans and Greeks did it. The Puritans did it (although they probably didn't enjoy it). The Romantics perfected it. The Victorians dreamed about it—and then did it discreetly.

They all kissed. Romantically. Passionately. Longingly. And, most likely, often.

"It's logical to conclude it's very ancient, very primitive and very common," said Helen Fisher, an anthropologist at Rutgers University. . . .

Kissing is older than humanity. Well-acquainted chimpanzees and orangutans kissed before humans arrived. They still do. There is evidence they even French kiss because some of the bolder ones have tried their luck with anthropologists, Fisher said.

Our ancestors came down out of the trees and began roaming the grasslands of Africa about 4 million years ago, and they surely spent some of their time kissing, hugging, stroking and feeding each other bits of fruit, Fisher said.

And apparently humans haven't stopped. Kissing is a lovely, luscious, lusty legacy.

Fisher estimates more than 90 percent of all peoples on record kiss. Until Western contact, kissing was reportedly unknown among the Somali, the Lepcha of Sikkum and the Sirionon of South America. The Thonga of South Africa and a few other peoples traditionally found kissing to be disgusting, she said. But even in those societies lovers patted, licked, rubbed, sucked, nipped or blew on each other's faces before sex.

Asian cultures regard kissing as a much more private activity than Western cultures do. In November [1994], *The Washington Post* reported that the Japanese media had been castigating young people who were defying the unwritten social rule against kissing in public. The Japanese have been raised to greet friends, spouses and lovers with a polite bow. Even soldiers returning home from months overseas are welcomed by their wives at the airport with a smile and a bow, the *Post* found.

Diane Ackerman, staff writer for *The New Yorker*, explored the allure of kissing in her newest book, "A Natural History of Love." . . .

She described Finnish tribes who bathe together completely nude but regard kissing as indecent. She also mentioned certain African tribal people whose lips are decorated, mutilated, stretched or in other ways deformed and who don't kiss.

But they are unusual. Most cultures engage in kissing and enjoy it. . . .

There is one myth you can kiss goodbye. Eskimos do kiss; they don't rub noses, according to anthropologist Bill Jankowiak, an associate professor at the University of Nevada, Las Vegas.

The rubbing-noses myth probably developed out of the method of kissing practiced by societies from the South Sea islands, up through Alaska and the Siberian side of the former Soviet Union, he said. A man in one of those cultures kisses by putting his mouth over his beloved's mouth and moving his mouth back and forth, which might give the appearance they are rubbing noses, Jankowiak said.

—*Watertown (N.Y.) Daily Times*, February 27, 1995
(originally published in the *Hartford Courant*)

transmitted from the mouth. It is unsafe to blow on the penis during fellatio (even though a common slang term is "blow job") or to blow into the vagina during cunnilingus because bacteria may be forced in or actual injury can result. There are some indications that blowing air into the vagina, particularly during pregnancy, can lead to the formation of air embolisms in a woman's blood vessels that could potentially be fatal.

Sometimes the anal region is stimulated orally, but strict hygienic measures are crucial to prevent transmission of bacteria. Even with thorough washing, there is a chance of some rectal bacteria being ingested. This practice would again be considered dangerous if there were any chance that HIV were present in the person being stimulated anally. A rubber dam can be placed over the anal region to protect against transmission of HIV, other sexually transmitted diseases, and bacteria.

Mutual Manual Stimulation and Masturbation

Most sexually active couples use some form of mutual manual stimulation of the genitals. The clitoris may be manipulated with a finger, although direct stimulation of the glans can be uncomfortable for some. One or more fingers may be inserted into the vagina and moved. The penis may be grasped and stroked and the scrotum fondled. These techniques are often used by sexual partners to stimulate each other to orgasm. About 70 percent of college students in one study reported having manually stimulated another person to orgasm or having been stimulated in this manner by someone else (Elliott & Brantley, 1997). Mutual manual stimulation of genitals and the anal region is also one of the most common forms of sexual sharing.

Although some couples find it difficult to discuss their masturbatory practices and even more difficult to masturbate in each other's presence, others report that they find enjoyment in watching one another masturbate and in being so observed. Slightly more than one-third of college students reported having masturbated while another person watched (Elliott & Brantley, 1997). Masturbation is usually a very private experience, and sharing it often represents a level of intimacy even deeper than some other forms of sexual sharing. Many couples at least occasionally incorporate manual stimulation of the partner or masturbation into their sexual activities.

Interfemoral and Anal Intercourse

Many sexual partnerships that include at least one male make use of various forms of nonvaginal penile intercourse. The penis is versatile and may be inserted into the partner's hand, between female breasts, between the buttocks, or between the thighs (interfemoral intercourse), or it may be rubbed on the partner's abdomen or any other body area. These forms of sexual activity are often accompanied by pelvic thrusting. It is wise for heterosexual couples who practice interfemoral intercourse to know that if semen is ejaculated near or at the vaginal opening, there is some risk of pregnancy. Even a small amount of semen entering the vagina will carry sperm, and though the chances are minimal, it is possible for some of those sperm to travel into the fallopian tubes and fertilize an ovum.

A type of sexual sharing that seems to wax and wane in popularity is **anal intercourse,** insertion of the penis into the partner's rectum. In most countries, the prevalence of anal intercourse is quite high (Powis, Griffiths, Gossop, & Strang, 1995). NHSLS data showed the activity to be somewhat more prevalent than might be expected, and there was a slightly greater tendency for white and better educated people to have experienced anal sex. For the total study population, 26 percent of men had engaged in anal intercourse during their lifetimes, and 10 percent had done so in the previous year. Twenty percent of women had had anal sex during their lives, 9 percent during the prior year (Lau-

mann, Gagnon et al., 1994). About 20 percent of college students reported that they had engaged in anal sex (Elliott & Brantley, 1997) As Table 11.2 demonstrates, anal intercourse is somewhat more appealing to males than to females. It is interesting to note that 11 percent of males indicated they found being the passive partner in anal intercourse, presumably a male-male activity, to be somewhat or very appealing.

The anal sphincter muscles tend to resist penile entry, and it usually takes appropriate lubrication (such as K-Y lubricant), gentle prodding by the penis, and concentrated relaxation of the anus by the partner to permit penetration. Physicians occasionally see rectal or anal injuries resulting from anal sex, and they can even be quite serious (Orr et al., 1995). There is a danger that the tissue damage that can occur with anal intercourse may increase the chances of transmitting HIV if the inserting male is infected. Again, unless there is absolute certainty that the man is not infected, a condom should be worn, which affords substantial—but not absolute—protection. Condoms are somewhat more likely to break during anal intercourse. It is unsafe to insert the penis into the mouth or vagina following anal intercourse because bacteria are easily transferred and may cause infection.

Vibrators, Pornography, and Fantasies

Any aids used for sexual stimulation by individuals can be shared and probably often are. Electric vibrators that are typically used in masturbation may be used by couples to provide intense sexual pleasuring for one another (Davis, Blank, Lin, & Bonillas, 1996). NHSLS data show that 16 percent of women and 23 percent of men find such devices appealing. Some couples enjoy viewing pornographic materials together, such as magazine photographs or movies showing a variety of sexual acts. Others enjoy reading books that portray sexual scenes in explicit language. One study found that men achieved sexual arousal fastest through use of a vibrator and erotic video, as compared to using the vibrator alone or the video alone (Rowland & Slob, 1992).

It has long been recognized that fantasy can be an integral part of sexual experiences and that it can induce sexual arousal (Tokatlidis & Over, 1995). Some books have dealt with the sexual fantasies of individuals, and many people seem more willing to talk about their own fantasies than once was the case. Some couples enjoy acting out their sexual fantasies together and find them sexually stimulating. Fantasies

anal intercourse: insertion of the penis into the rectum of a partner.

that involve the inflicting of pain or humiliation on a partner are stimulating to some people (Plaud & Bigwood, 1997). Behavior that leads to sexual stimulation through pain or humiliation is termed sadomasochistic and is discussed in more detail in chapter 13, "The Spectrum of Human Sexual Behavior."

Aphrodisiacs

FOH Some foods and chemicals have been purported to act as sexual stimulants for those who consume them. Substances that create erotic stimulation are called **aphrodisiacs.** A wide variety of exotic substances have been labeled aphrodisiacs, including powdered rhinoceros horn, powdered stag's horn, dried salamanders, and dried beetles, along with some common foods, such as eggs, olives, peanuts, oysters, venison, and bananas.

Some individuals report increased interest in sex under the influence of alcohol or marijuana. Both of these drugs lead to relaxation and lowered inhibitions and therefore when used in moderation enhance sexual activities. Used in larger amounts, however, they may inhibit sexual desire and arousal. Even though cocaine has been purported to act as an aphrodisiac in women, a study of heavy users of crack cocaine showed in fact that they had lower levels of interest in sex and a greater likelihood of problems with sexual functioning (Henderson, Boyd, & Whitmarsh, 1995). In some individuals, another group of chemicals, the volatile nitrites, are reported to enhance response to sexual stimulation and orgasm. These chemicals, especially amyl nitrite and isobutyl nitrite, have been marketed as room deodorizers. They are volatile and are absorbed quickly by inhalation, causing immediate dilation of blood vessels, with a resulting rush. They are also highly flammable. Although most users have suffered no ill effects other than headache and temporary pounding pulse, these chemicals have been implicated in some fatal cerebral hemorrhages. NHSLS data showed that drug use in association with sexual activity is actually quite rare, with only about 1 percent of males and 0.5 percent of females having used drugs before sex in the previous year. Alcohol use was far more common, with 9 percent of males and 6 percent of females saying that they frequently drank alcohol before or during sexual activity.

Workers in the field of sex therapy have been experimenting with various medications that might increase sexual desire or enhance sexual performance. This has led to the use of some prescribed drugs to improve sexual functioning. They include yohimbine, opioid receptor blockers, and dopamines. These drugs seem to act in the brain or central nervous system in ways that can stimulate sexual response, and they have been used primarily to help males who are ex-

periencing erectile difficulties. Research in this area is still in its infancy.

A widely touted aphrodisiac is "Spanish fly," the slang name for **cantharides,** a chemical extracted from a certain species of southern European beetle. Taken internally, the drug produces inflammation of the urinary tract and dilation of blood vessels in the genital area. This can lead to prolonged, often painful, erection of the penis. Cantharides is considered to be a dangerous chemical that can cause serious illness and even death. An aphrodisiac for men consisting of dried toad skin secretions and herbs, marketed as an erectile aid, killed four men in New York City during early 1996.

Have you ever heard of anyone using an aphrodisiac? Describe his or her experience.

Available research would suggest that there are no surefire aphrodisiacs available. It is probably true that so-called aphrodisiacs work because their user believes in their effectiveness. Whenever an individual desires sexual stimulation, looks for it, and expects it, it is not surprising that it may be generated.

After Sharing Sex

Many couples find that the period during which they are together following shared sexual activity is significant to their relationship. If the sexual experience has been satisfying to both partners, and they both are feeling relaxed or even drowsy, this may be a time for communicating quiet, gentle, loving feelings. Women in general seem to take longer than men in the resolution phase of the sexual response cycle, although this phenomenon may be the result of lack of satiation because of an inadequate number of orgasms.

However, satisfaction with sexual activity seems to depend on a variety of factors, orgasm representing only one of them. About 29 percent of women and 75 percent of men report always having an orgasm in their sexual activities, and yet the proportion of both sexes who report being extremely emotionally satisfied is about 40 percent. It is clear that there is more to a good sex life than being able to have an orgasm, and not everyone who has an orgasm is necessarily satisfied with sex in other respects. Thirty percent of

aphrodisiacs (af-ro-DEE-zee-aks): foods or chemicals purported to foster sexual arousal; they are believed to be more myth than fact.

cantharides (kan-THAR-a-deez): a chemical extracted from a beetle that, when taken internally, creates irritation of blood vessels in the genital region; it can cause physical harm.

women and 5 percent of men report having orgasms sometimes or never, although married women are much more likely than unmarried women to reach orgasm more frequently in their shared sexual activities. NHSLS research showed that people who report being happy with their lives in general are also more likely to be happy with their sex lives. The more satisfied people are sexually, the more they tend to remain married and faithful to their spouses (Laumann, Gagnon et al., 1994).

When sex has been unsuccessful in any way or has generated some negative feelings, the period following sexual contact may be especially valuable for two-way communication. Many couples store up fears, resentments, and feelings of inadequacy because of sexual problems, only to find that these tensions eventually catch up with the relationship and place strains on it. Talking out the negative feelings while they are fresh—in an atmosphere of mutual warmth, caring, and reassurance—can often be a strengthening influence on any relationship.

After a suitable length of time (see chapter 4, "Human Sexual Response," on the male's refractory period), some couples proceed to orgasm for a second time. Whether or not a second orgasmic experience takes place depends on many factors, such as age, level of sexual arousal, arousing aspects of the surroundings, newness of the relationship, and desire for further sex on the part of both partners.

■ Same-Gender Sexual Sharing

To approach an understanding of different persons' lifestyles solely from the perspective of their shared sexual orientation is constraining and limiting because sexuality represents only one aspect of people's sharing. Partners of any gender combination can share a full range of sexual activity and can find great joy and satisfaction in this sharing. Some men fondle one another's genitals or masturbate each other. There are often gentle, loving gestures such as kisses, embraces, and body stroking (see Fig. 11.4). Oral-genital contact is common, and many gay males practice fellatio. Anal intercourse is practiced by some male couples, although not as frequently as fellatio (Elliott & Brantley, 1997; Innala & Ernulf, 1992; Laumann, Gagnon et al., 1994). Gay men now approach both fellatio and anal intercourse with increased caution and are more likely to wear condoms because there is concern about transmission of HIV. Men who share sex have definite preferences, and there are some who are not at all interested in oral-genital sex or anal intercourse. Many gay males apparently have a strong preference for

FIGURE 11.4   *Male-Male Sexual Expression*

manual manipulation of one another's genitals or lying together in such a way that the genitals may be rubbed together. It is also common for one partner to practice interfemoral intercourse or to rub his penis on the other's abdomen. There have been some reports of **brachioproctic activity,** commonly called fisting or handballing, in which the hand of one partner is inserted into the rectum of the other, producing an intense sexual experience. There are risks of damage to the anal or rectal tissue with such practices (Driggs & Finn, 1990; Orr, Clark, Hawley, & Pless, 1995).

Lesbians have a wide range of intimate activities to share, and research indicates that even though lesbian couples share sex less frequently than heterosexual or gay male couples, they tend to be more satisfied with their sexual lives and feel a greater sense of intimacy (Hurlbert & Apt, 1993; Schreurs, 1993). Many women almost exclusively use techniques such as kissing and general body contact with one another, especially those women who are less experienced with female-

brachioproctic activity: a sexual activity, sometimes called "fisting" in slang, involving insertion of the hand into a partner's rectum.

FIGURE 11.5 *Female-Female Sexual Expression*

female sexual activity (see Fig. 11.5). Manual manipulation of one another's genitals and finger penetration is one of the most frequently used forms of stimulation among lesbian couples, with oral-genital contact (cunnilingus) being the preferred technique for reaching orgasm (Schreurs, 1993). The use of dildos or other objects to be used in vaginal insertion is less common. Women involved in a sexual encounter usually spend a longer period than male couples in gentle and affectionate foreplay, also giving more attention to caressing and nongenital stimulation. Single lesbians have sex less frequently than single gay men, and lesbians have relatively low levels of sexual activity when they are involved in a long-term committed relationship. They often seem to prefer hugging and cuddling to more genitalized forms of sexual sharing (Nichols, 1990).

◼ Heterosexual Intercourse

In most cultures, the act of vaginal sexual intercourse, or coitus, is surrounded by a variety of moral and social values. Most societies and religions have sought to place some restrictions on coital behavior in order to regulate which heterosexual couples have babies, to prevent people from enjoying bodily pleasures that some may consider sinful, and to regulate sexual forces that may be considered too powerful to be indulged in casually. NHSLS statistics demonstrate that vaginal intercourse is the most prevalent of shared sexual activities. Eighty percent of survey respondents said they had vaginal sex every time they shared a sexual experience in the previous year. An additional 15 percent indicated they usually had vaginal sex during that time period (Michael et al., 1994).

Sexual intercourse takes on different meanings for different couples and in different circumstances, as do all forms of sex. It may be a perfunctory, hurried experience with little communication or a lengthy, sensual experience involving the exchange of love and other warm emotions between the partners. The personal needs and characteristics that each partner brings to coitus help to determine the depth and degree of pleasure that results. Factual knowledge about sex, the capacity to accept differences in needs and responses, and personal attitudes all play a part in determining the enjoyment and meaning of coitus for each individual and each couple.

Sexual Intercourse and HIV

Vaginal intercourse is one of the ways in which HIV is transmitted because it is carried in semen and vaginal fluids. If a partner has ever had sex with someone else, there is at least some risk that he or she carries the virus. It is always safest for a male partner to wear a condom containing the spermicide nonoxynol-9 during intercourse or for the female to wear a vaginal pouch (female condom) unless there is absolute certainty that neither person could ever have been exposed to HIV. See chapter 17 for additional information on HIV, its transmission, and how infection may be prevented.

Intromission

Male-female sexual intercourse, by definition, involves the insertion of the penis into the vagina. Comfortable intromission requires a suitable degree of penile erection, lubrication, relaxation of the vaginal opening, and cooperation between the two partners. Erection of the penis is a natural part of male sexual arousal, and the vagina usually produces enough lubricant to permit easy movement of the penis in the vagina. If there is insufficient vaginal lubrication, artificial lubricants may be applied to the penis and the vaginal opening. Water-soluble silica-based lubricants, such as K-Y jelly, or saliva are generally satisfactory. Petroleum-based jellies are not recommended, because they are less healthful for tissues and are less easily cleansed away.

The vaginal opening is sometimes tense, and gentle patience is necessary to give time for it to relax. If the outer vaginal muscles cannot relax to the point where intromission can take place comfortably, the woman may be experiencing vaginismus. If there is some difficulty with intromission, the male may begin to lose some of his erection. Both of these prob-

CASE STUDY

Carlos and Sarah Find Privacy for Sex

Carlos and Sarah met during their college's first-year orientation program. Their residence halls were in close proximity, and they spent a great deal of time in one another's rooms. Over a period of weeks, their relationship became increasingly intimate. They dated frequently and eventually began to discuss a sexual relationship. Sarah lived in a suite with three other women, and Carlos shared a dormitory room with another freshman. His roommate had already made it clear to him that he did not appreciate having Carlos's friends in the room very often because he spent much time studying and liked to go to bed early. Sarah's suitemates had agreed as a group at the beginning of the year that boyfriends would not be allowed to spend the night.

The couple had their first sexual encounter at a time when Sarah's suitemates were out. When one of them returned to her room, finding Sarah and Carlos in bed with each other, the woman was angry and embarrassed. She reported her discomfort to their resident advisor, who brought the complaint to Sarah's attention. Sarah explained to the R.A. that she and her boyfriend were trying to be considerate of the others, but they also felt frus-

trated by their lack of privacy. The R.A. made it clear that it would be their responsibility to work out arrangements that would not inconvenience their roommates. Carlos and Sarah both felt some resentment that they had indeed tried to be considerate, but there did not seem to be much room for negotiation.

As the semester progressed, they occasionally managed to have one of their rooms to themselves for brief periods of time. They would plan ahead for weekends or evenings when their roommates were going to be away. The following year, Sarah was able to arrange for a single room, and this provided them with the privacy for which they had been hoping. As they looked back on the first year of their relationship, they remarked that they had often felt as though their sexual life had lacked spontaneity and fun. "Whenever you have to make an appointment for sex, it loses something. It almost doesn't feel worth it sometimes. I'm just glad we had good communication to get us through what was a stressful year. I don't blame our roommates for wanting their rights and privacy, but I also feel that they could have been more understanding of us. Sometimes I think they were just jealous."

lems are discussed in chapter 18. Actual insertion of the penis can represent an awkward time for both partners, and active cooperation is helpful. Either partner may part the minor lips to expose the vaginal opening and then guide the penis into the vagina. The position of the couple also helps to determine the ease of intromission. The first few coital thrusts of the male may be progressively more forceful as the penis is pushed gradually deeper into the vagina. Depth of penetration depends on the size of the penis and vagina, the coital position, and the relative comfort for both partners.

As discussed in chapter 2, "Female Sexual Anatomy and Physiology," if the hymen is still present at the opening of the vagina, prodding by the penis may be necessary to rupture it, and the female should expect some discomfort or pain. Cooperation and understanding on the part of both partners can lead to easy, unembarrassing intromission. Some males feel awkward in attempting to find the opening and the best angle for inserting the penis; the female partner may be able to help reduce such difficulties. Frequently, difficulties or discomfort in intromission during early coital experiences generate performance fears in both males and females. These fears can lead

to problems in later experiences, such as lack of erection or lack of vaginal lubrication. After several sexual contacts, intromission is usually accomplished with more ease.

Intercourse

Intercourse usually involves movement of the penis in and out of the vagina, resulting from pelvic movements of both partners. Different coital positions afford different amounts of control over these movements to both partners. The rate and vigor of thrusting depend to a large degree on the mood of the couple and how long they wish to prolong coitus. The factor that usually determines duration of intercourse is the length of time required for the male to reach orgasm. Because erection of the penis almost always subsides following orgasm, intercourse then can rarely continue. Rapid, forceful movements of the penis generally bring males to orgasm quite quickly, and the amount of precoital stimulation also plays an important role. Because intercourse itself may not be effective in generating orgasm for women, additional clitoral stimulation may be necessary for orgasm to occur. There is evidence that some women pretend to

FOH

reach orgasm during intercourse and that this relates to their views of themselves as being "good" sexual partners (Wiederman, 1997b).

It is very possible for couples to learn how to modulate the amount of stimulation required for both of them to obtain maximum enjoyment. By occasionally slowing his pelvic thrusting, making shallow thrusts of the penis, and even temporarily ceasing coital movements, the male may exert a great deal of control over the amount of time required to reach orgasm. Certain positions also enhance this control. Data from the NHSLS found that about 70 percent of people said they spent from 15 minutes to an hour during their last shared sexual event. That time would typically include more than just the experience of intercourse. Roughly 15 percent of people indicated they took 15 minutes or less in their last shared sex, and another 15 percent said they took an hour or more (Laumann, Gagnon et al., 1994). It is up to each couple to work on developing the duration of sexual activity most suitable for them. Open and specific communication can be an important help in this process.

The movements used by both partners during intercourse may be varied a great deal, and finding the most pleasurable movements can be an exciting learning process in a growing sexual relationship. Alternating shallow and deep thrusts of the penis is often recommended, and the penis may also be rotated or moved from side to side in the vagina. According to most research, including that reported in this textbook, penis size has no bearing on the amount of sexual pleasure derived by the female during intercourse. Although some women do contend that size of the penis makes a difference to them in terms of physical pleasure, it is more typical for them to report that this is not a crucial factor in their pleasure. Clitoral stimulation by some means is often important for women during intercourse. Many couples caress one another and use their hands to give added pleasure to each other. Some couples strive for the simultaneous orgasm of both partners. Although some couples enjoy having orgasm at the same time and can accomplish this with relative ease, others find that trying for orgasm at the same time detracts from their sexual pleasure. Some people enjoy experiencing their partner's orgasm without being preoccupied with their own. If one partner has not reached orgasm during coitus and wishes to do so, it is very appropriate for the other to employ suitable techniques to help the partner to achieve orgasm.

Do you believe that orgasm is essential for both partners during shared sexual activity? Why or why not?

Couples usually have intercourse in bed, but many at least occasionally experiment with other locations, including the out-of-doors. Although some people pre-

fer coitus in the dark or in dim lighting, others enjoy bright light. Finding ways to enhance the pleasure of sexual intercourse continues to be a human pursuit.

Positions for Intercourse

There are various body positions in which the penis FOH may be comfortably inserted into the vagina. Many couples enjoy experimenting with different positions, and they find that sex can be made more interesting by changing positions during intercourse, often several times. Some changes of position can be accomplished by rolling over or other slight movements, without any interruption of coitus. Other changes require that the penis be withdrawn until the new position is assumed. Which positions a couple finds the most enjoyable, comfortable, and manageable will depend on their own individual characteristics such as body size and weight, degree of physical fitness, length and diameter of the erect penis, personal attitudes about particular positions, and their moods during the sexual encounter. Different positions may place more physical strain on one or the other and afford one of them more ability to control the rate and vigor of coital movements. For each of the following 10 basic positions, there are myriad variations.

Reclining Face-to-Face

Positions in which the two partners face each other are most commonly used because the two are more free to look at one another, kiss, and communicate in these positions. Reclining positions are preferred because they usually require less physical energy than supporting the body in some upright posture.

Man on Top, Woman Supine

This position is the most common one used in European and American societies and is erroneously considered by some couples to be the only normal way to have intercourse (See Fig. 11.6). Recent studies show that most people now at least experiment with a variety of positions. The position seems particularly compatible from an anatomical standpoint, considering the usual angles of the erect penis and the vagina in a reclining position. The male often supports part of his weight on his arms and knees, although this may place real strain on some men. Women sometimes find it suitable in this position to hold their legs up somewhat or to wrap them around the male's waist or even over his shoulders, the latter variation requiring more of a kneeling position from the man. Some couples insert a pillow under the woman's buttocks for greater ease. These positions give the male partner maximum control over the coital thrusting,

FIGURE 11.6   *Man on Top, Woman Supine*

because the female's pelvis is relatively immobile, and they allow deep penetration by the penis. Conversely, they may also make it somewhat more difficult for the woman to have the sort of stimulation necessary to achieve orgasm. Women, or their partners, may want to increase manual stimulation of the clitoris during intercourse to assist in producing the orgasmic response.

Woman on Top, Man Supine

This is the second most commonly used coital position (See Fig. 11.7). There are many variations because the woman may lie on the man with her legs fully extended or may straddle him in a sitting, crouching, or kneeling position. The position provides the woman more opportunity to control the coital movements and leaves the male's hands more free to caress her body. Some men experience some difficulty keeping the penis in the vagina in this position, and some women experience discomfort with the deep penile penetration

that is possible. However, this position reportedly is more likely to result in orgasm for the female partner, due to the fact that she can exert more control over the movements, leading to better stimulation for her.

Side-by-Side

There are many advantages to coital positions in which both partners are lying on their sides, and the lateral position is often recommended in the treatment of several sexual dysfunctions (See Fig. 11.8). Many couples use a side-by-side position more frequently than other positions. Because both partners are lying down and need to worry less about supporting their bodies, there is less strain on both of them. They are able to share in controlling their thrusting motions, and both are free to use their hands for touching and caressing. Deep penetration by the penis is sometimes more difficult in the side-by-side positions, and some couples find it less comfortable than do others.

FIGURE 11.7 *Woman on Top, Man Supine*

Other Variations on Face-to-Face
Woman on Edge of Bed or Chair

When the woman positions herself on the edge of a bed or chair, her back reclining and her feet resting on the floor, the man may either stand or kneel on the floor in a manner that enables him to enter her (See Fig. 11.9). The male is in control in these positions. The male's position on the floor gives him a good deal of leverage for controlling movements and giving powerful thrusts. He is also easily able to vary the angle at which the penis enters the vagina.

Both Partners Seated

Seated intercourse with the partners facing each other is easier for some couples to achieve than it is for others (See Fig. 11.10). The typical manner is for the male to sit, sometimes in a chair or on the edge of the bed; a reasonably solid support is usually

more desirable. The female then lowers herself onto his erect penis, either keeping her feet on the floor or placing her legs around his waist. The woman usually has greater control over the coital movements in this position, although the degree of control varies with the positioning of her legs and feet. The man's hands are relatively free, and he may help to move the female's body up and down on his penis. Usually, deep penile penetration is possible in seated positions.

Both Partners Standing

Coital positions in which both partners stand are generally the most difficult to manage and sustain (See Fig. 11.11). Attention must be given to maintaining balance and stability, along with keeping the penis comfortably inside the vagina. Although many couples experiment with standing intercourse and some use the position occasionally, it is not a popular one. Deep

FIGURE 11.8 *Side-by-Side*

FIGURE 11.9 *Woman on Edge of Bed or Chair*

penile penetration is difficult while standing because the angles of the penis and the vagina are not particularly complementary. For couples who find standing intercourse positions comfortable, this option is apparently exciting for occasional variation.

Rear Vaginal Entry

Most mammals use a rear entry position for copulation. It may be for precisely this reason that many people do not choose such positions. Yet those who do employ these variations often find them comfortable and exciting, and they are employed regularly in many cultures around the world. Although some intimacy

may be lost without face-to-face contact, natural body contours afford especially close body contact during many rear-entry positions.

Both Partners Kneeling, Rear Entry

In this position, the woman may hold the upper part of her body up on her arms while kneeling or lower her shoulders and head downward (See Fig. 11.12). The man kneels behind her and inserts his penis into the vagina from behind. He may also assume a higher crouched position. Deep penile penetration is usually achieved in this position. The man's hands are generally free to offer stimulating contact for the woman, includ-

FIGURE 11.10   *Both Partners Seated*

FIGURE 11.11   *Both Partners Standing*

ing contact with the clitoris. Another variation is the wheelbarrow position, in which the male stands behind the female and holds her legs while having intercourse.

Man on Top, Woman Lying on Her Abdomen, Rear Entry

This position is difficult for some couples to manage but can be enjoyable (See Fig. 11.13). The man may lie on top of the woman with his legs fully extended or straddle her body in a crouched or seated position. If

FIGURE 11.12   *Both Partners Kneeling, Rear Entry*

the woman arches her back somewhat, pushing her vulva backward, penile entry is usually easily accomplished. This can be a relatively comfortable position, although deep penetration may be difficult.

Side-by-Side, Rear Entry

In the side-by-side position, intromission is quite easily accomplished, and this position is often recommended during pregnancy (See Fig. 11.14). Both partners are lying down, and neither is placed under any strain. Their hands are generally quite free to touch one another, although because the man is behind, his hands have easier access to his partner (for example, her breasts and clitoris).

Both Partners Seated or Standing, Rear Entry

Rear entry is also possible when both partners are seated or standing (See Fig. 11.15). The seated position is the easiest and is a comfortable way for the woman to sit on the man's lap while participating in intercourse. She can exercise a good deal of control over coital movements. Standing rear entry is not as easily managed, although it is generally easier than face-to-face standing intercourse.

It should be reemphasized that sexual intercourse need not be a series of acrobatics to be pleasurable for

← screech

FIGURE 11.13   *Man on Top, Woman on Abdomen, Rear Entry*

both partners. Yet if both partners are willing and able, varying coital position from time to time can be an exciting part of an ongoing sexual relationship.

Intercourse and Marriage

The social mores related to sexual intercourse are often intimately associated with a particular society's marriage customs. In many societies, including most Western societies, marriage represents a social and/or religious legitimation of coitus and childbearing. Hence sex, with its risk of pregnancy, has often been discouraged outside the context of marriage. Social institutions, such as religion, school, family, and social networks, are typically charged with the enforcement of these rules. Premarital and extramarital sex are more permissible in some societies than in others. In Western cultures, as definitions of what constitutes a family have changed a great deal, the relationship between sex and marriage has become less clearly defined than it once was.

In other cultures, sexual relationships fit differently into the varying structures of marriage. In societies where people are permitted to have more than one spouse, or in which married couples are encouraged to forge close working bonds with one another, sexual intercourse may be permitted among many different combinations of persons. There are also nonsexual marriages, arrangements based on political or economic benefits to the partners or their relatives, with no expectation of sexual interaction (Crapo, 1996).

There can be no doubt that in North America sex is perceived as a significant part of marriage. Sexual problems can lead to severe marital difficulties and even divorce, and all sorts of publications are available to spice up and renew sex within marriage. It is also true that communication problems in marriage are often reflected in sexual difficulties between the partners. Sex is a potential source of marriage enrichment, reinforcing the interdependence of husband and wife, unifying them through shared enjoyment, symbolizing their shared life,

FIGURE 11.14   *Side-by-Side, Rear Entry*

FIGURE 11.15 *Both Partners Seated or Standing, Rear Entry*

and helping to resolve episodes of alienation. Sexual activity can exert these same positive factors on relationships other than those involving marriage.

> *If and when you received your formal sexuality education, did your source address masturbation, or was sex discussed simply as a penis-in-vagina act? Was intercourse presented merely as a procreative act? Were the emotional aspects as well as the biological aspects discussed? Were other forms of sexual sharing also presented?*

For most married individuals, vaginal sexual intercourse with the spouse constitutes the major and preferred, though not the only, form of sexual outlet. Oral-genital sex seems to be second in preference as a sexual outlet in marriage (Janus & Janus, 1993; Laumann, Gagnon et al., 1994). The frequency of shared sexual activity seems to vary a great deal. The average frequency of sex for women is six times per month, and the average frequency for men is seven times per month. Of course, individual couples show wide variations away from the median, and the frequency of intercourse can be affected by many factors.

Our society has a mixture of values concerning premarital and extramarital sexual activity. On the basis of present evidence, it seems safe to state that not only have more people been experiencing coitus before marriage and at a younger age, they have been doing so more often and with fewer inhibitions than in the past.

Chapter Summary

1. NHSLS statistics are the most reliable data we have on human sexual behavior in the United States.

2. The social world of sex involves negotiative processes among people and has different consequences than the private world of sex.

3. Solitary sex includes thoughts and fantasies, erotic materials and toys, and masturbation. Males think about sex and seek out erotic materials more frequently than do females.

4. The frequency with which people experience private sexual pleasure seems to be positively correlated with how frequently they seek shared sex. Solitary sex does not seem to be a compensation for lack of availability of a sexual partner.

5. Masturbation, or self-stimulation of the genitals, is a sexual activity in which most people participate at one time or another.

6. There is a variety of ways in which people masturbate, although most commonly women stimulate their clitoral area and men stimulate the penis.

7. Masturbation can occur at all stages of life. Medically speaking, there is no such thing as excessive masturbation; it does not produce physical weakness or illness.

8. Negative attitudes persist concerning masturbation, and some people feel guilty about the practice. Guilt does not affect frequency of masturbation in males, but it does to some extent in females.

9. Vaginal intercourse is the most popular of shared sexual behaviors, followed by watching a partner undress and oral sex. Partners must learn about their mutual sexual preferences.

10. There are many forms of shared nongenital stimulation that are considered intimate and arousing. Kissing and massaging of erogenous zones may be highly erotic.

11. Fellatio is oral stimulation of the penis, and cunnilingus is oral stimulation of the clitoris and other areas of the vulva. Oral sex has become more acceptable in recent years, but it is more common among young, better-educated white people.

12. The penis may be inserted between a partner's legs, breasts, or buttocks, or into the anus. Anal intercourse is somewhat more appealing to males than females, and it is one of the high-risk behaviors for transmission of HIV.

13. Vibrators, erotic pictures and films, and personal sexual fantasies may be integrated into sexual sharing.

14. There are many myths about foods or chemicals leading to sexual arousal. Substances that create erotic stimulation are labeled aphrodisiacs, although they are believed to operate largely on suggestion and imagination.

15. Following the end of shared sexual activity may be a quiet, warm, and comfortable time for communication between partners, or it may become a time of tension and further misunderstanding.

16. Couples of the same gender share a whole range of sexual activities, depending on individual preferences and tastes. Male-male oral sex is more common than anal sex; female couples often prefer nonpenetrative activities.

17. Heterosexual intercourse is often subject to strict moral, social, and relational codes of behavior. It is also one possible mode of transmitting HIV.

18. The techniques and timing of intercourse are variable, as are the positions in which a woman and man can share penile-vaginal penetration.

19. Happier people seem more satisfied with their sexual lives. Satisfaction is not necessarily correlated with having orgasms.

20. Intercourse is closely associated with marriage customs in most cultures. In North America, sex is considered to be a significant part of the marital relationship, with vaginal intercourse being the most preferred activity.

Focus on Health Questions

You will find in this section the kinds of questions that you may have concerning your own health and sexuality. The page references indicate where in the text the answer is located; the exact place is marked with the logo: **FOH**

1. Do both males and females masturbate? 346

2. When do most people stop masturbating during their lives? 348

3. If people who are involved in a sexual relationship masturbate, does that mean there is something wrong with their sex life? 349

4. How much is too much masturbation? 349

5. Are there any dangers to masturbating? 349–350

6. Does masturbation interfere with athletic prowess? 349–350

7. Are there any health risks associated with oral sex? 354

8. What are the dangers of anal intercourse? 356

9. Are there any foods or drugs that turn people on sexually? 357

10. How may the risks of contracting HIV be reduced in heterosexual intercourse? 359 (See also pp. 527–528, chapter 17.)

11. How long should intercourse last? 361

12. How do different positions for intercourse affect sexual pleasure? 361

Annotated Readings

Ackerman, D. (1995). *A natural history of love.* New York: Random House. A fascinating look at the place of intimate interactions in human life.

Barbour, J. R. (1993). *Becoming a sexually intimate person.* Saratoga, CA: R & E. A particularly valuable guide for college students, focusing on masturbation and shared sexual activities, with an emphasis on intimacy and communication strategies. Its honest and personal tone makes this book particularly useful.

Bechtel, S., & Stains, L. R. (1996). *Sex: A man's guide*. Erasmus, PA: Men's Health Books. A guide to sexual health and techniques written especially for men.

Birch, R. W. (1996). *Oral caress: The loving guide to exciting a woman*. Columbus, OH: PEC. An illustrated guide and collection of trivia relating to cunnilingus.

Comfort, A. (1995). *The new joy of sex* (rev. edition). New York: Random House. This updated version of a best-selling classic is aimed mostly at heterosexual couples, and it offers a wide range of suggestions for understanding and enhancing a couple's sexual relationship.

DeVillers, L. (1997). *Love skills: More fun than you've ever had with sex, intimacy, and communication*. San Luis Obispo, CA: Impact. A highly readable and useful guide to the skills of communication, intimate touch, and shared sexual behavior.

Elliott, L., & Brantley, C. (1997). *Sex on campus: The naked truth about the real sex lives of college students*. New York: Random House. In addition to the statistics from the *Details* magazine survey of college students, this book includes guidelines and information concerning a wide variety of sexual activities.

McCarthy, B., & McCarthy, E. (1993). *Sexual awareness*. New York: Carroll & Graf. Written for individuals and couples who want to enhance their sexual pleasure. There are chapters on overcoming specific sexual dysfunctions and problems.

Resnick, S. (1997). *The pleasure zone: Why we resist good feelings and how to let go and be happy*. New York: Conari Press. A groundbreaking book that examines how we deny ourselves physical and emotional pleasure, and it offers suggestions for surrendering to our pleasurable potentials.

Chapter 12

Same-Gender Orientation and Behavior

Chapter Outline

Note: A selection of Focus on Health questions appears at the end of each chapter. Answers to these questions are indicated within the chapter by the symbol in the margin. **FOH**

I somewhat resent the pressure that I feel to define myself as straight, gay, or bisexual. I am who I am. I have had romantic and sexual involvement with both men and women, and eventually got married. That doesn't mean I have lost my attraction to or interest for others of my sex, or the other sex for that matter. I have simply made a commitment to monogamy.

—From a letter to the author

his chapter offers a survey of research and theory on same-gender sexual orientation, identity formation, and social issues. Because this is an area of research that is often surrounded by cultural expectations and political agendas, it should be remembered that scientists are products of their cultures and that their perceptions and values are sometimes reflected in the conclusions they draw from their research (Sell, 1997).

Only recently has the focus of the research begun to move away from sexual behaviors and toward the dynamics and implications of loving relationships between members of the same gender. Although heterosexual behavior is often viewed as psychologically and emotionally connected to romance and love, same-gender relationships have too often been viewed in terms of sexual behavior alone. This is a distorted view because strong loving relationships develop between people of the same gender as well, and nonsexual intimacy is as important to same-gender couples as it is to heterosexual couples (Seidman et al., 1999). As later discussion in this chapter will show, there has been a continuing debate between the biological essentialist and social constructionist perspectives regarding sexual orientation. This has been a particularly active area of sex research in recent years, and the debate is likely to continue for some time to come.

Do you believe that sexual orientation is biologically or socially mandated? On what do you base your opinion?

■ Understanding Same-Gender Sexual Orientation

Concepts of sexual orientation and identity have been evolving much as our views of masculinity and femininity did when these traits came under scientific scrutiny. Instead of conceptualizing masculinity and femininity as polarized entities in themselves, we now see them as representing clusters of relatively independent traits that may coexist within the same individual, regardless of whether that individual is male or female. Masculinity and femininity are now viewed as multidimensional sets of characteristics, existing to varying degrees within both men and women. We have begun to suspect that sexual orientation is also a multidimensional phenomenon rather than an either-or (Sell, 1997).

The Kinsey Scale and Its Limitations

When Alfred Kinsey began his research on sexual behavior in the 1930s and 1940s, he faced the same confusion we do today about what constitutes homosexuality. At that time, sexual acts between women were often ignored altogether, and no consideration was given to the frequency with which same-gender sexual acts took place. One sexual experience with a member of the same gender might be sufficient to define one as a "homosexual." Social scientists of that day had not given much consideration to making distinctions among behaviors, orientations, and identities. What one did sexually was assumed to reflect what he or she wanted most to do sexually.

Kinsey recognized early on in his research that substantial numbers of people had experienced both same-gender and other-gender sexual activity. He devised a seven-category sexual behavior rating scale for use in his studies. It was designed to classify individuals based on their behavior (see Fig. 12.1). On the scale he used the numbers 0 to 6, with 0 representing exclusively heterosexual behavior, and 6 representing exclusively homosexual, or same-gender, behavior. Those individuals who showed some combination of both behaviors were classified somewhere between these two extremes, in categories 1 through 5. Categories 1 and 5 were for those who showed predominantly heterosexual or same-gender sexual behavior, respectively, but had experienced at least some of the other type of behavior. Category 2 included people who had experienced more than incidental same-gender behavior but still leaned more toward the heterosexual; category 4 was for those who leaned more toward same-gender behavior but had experienced more than incidental heterosexual behavior. Category 3 included people with approximately equal amounts of sexual experience with both men and women (Kinsey et al., 1953).

Kinsey's scale has been called a "stroke of political genius," because it seemed to resolve issues that had been troubling researchers for many years, and it opened up a whole new way of understanding human sexual behavior (Bullough, 1990). The scale and the behavioral statistics that accompanied it demonstrated that sexual behavior between people of the same gender was more common in the U.S. population than had been formerly believed. This was comforting not only to persons who perceived themselves as gay, lesbian, or bisexual, but also to people who considered themselves heterosexual and yet had experienced some same-gender activity. Because there was now a continuum of

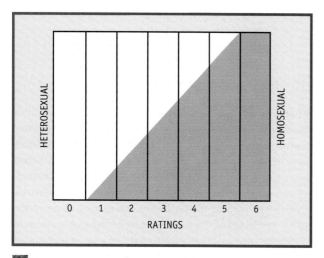

FIGURE 12.1 *Heterosexual-Homosexual Rating Scale*

Based on both psychologic reactions and overt experience, individuals rate as follows:

0 Exclusively heterosexual with no homosexual

1 Predominantly heterosexual, only incidentally homosexual

2 Predominantly heterosexual, but more than incidentally homosexual

3 Equally heterosexual and homosexual

4 Predominantly homosexual, but more than incidentally heterosexual

5 Predominantly homosexual, but incidentally heterosexual

6 Exclusively homosexual

Kinsey recognized that for some people the strict dichotomy between same-gender and heterosexual behavior did not exist. In order to classify his clients into appropriate categories for study, Kinsey devised this rating scale.

sexual behavior, people no longer had to see themselves at one pole of experience or the other. The middle ground of the scale clarified the idea that there is a range of sexual behavior that does not fall neatly into dualistic categories. Kinsey's approach is believed to have played a major role in allowing American society to begin coming to terms with same-gender sexual orientation.

Research since the time of Kinsey's work has shown that the more we know about the complexities of human sexuality, the less valuable his bipolar scale is in offering a thorough understanding of sexual orientation as part of the human personality. One of the problems with the scale is its implication that the more same-gender oriented one is, the less heterosexual one can be, and vice versa. It has been proposed instead that these characteristics are relatively independent. Some people may exhibit high levels of both same-gender eroticism and heteroeroticism, low levels of both, or differing levels of each. Across people's life spans, there may be changes and discontinuities in sexual behavior patterns and identities. For example,

in a Kinsey Institute study of 262 self-identified lesbians, 75 percent had had sex with men at least once since the age of 18 (Wallen & Parsons, 1997).

Incidence of Same-Gender Sexual Behavior and Attraction

There has been considerable controversy about the prevalence of same-gender sexual behavior. The average figures most frequently cited from Kinsey (1948, 1953), often without much explanation, were that 37 percent of the men and 13 percent of the women surveyed in his research population of over 16,000 people had had at least one same-gender sexual experience to the point of orgasm since adolescence. The Kinsey data have also been cited as evidence that 13.95 percent of males and 4.25 percent of females, or a combined average of 9.13 percent of the total population, have had either extensive same-gender experiences (21 or more partners or 52 or more experiences) or more than incidental same-gender experiences (5–20 partners or 21–50 experiences) (Gebhard, 1977). This figure was often rounded off and said to mean that about 10 percent of the population is gay or lesbian. More recent evidence suggests that these figures are probably not representative of the total population. This may be partly due to the fact that Kinsey researchers did not employ a random sample of the population and may also be partly due to the rather broad definitions that they employed in analyzing their data.

In 1973, there was a reanalysis of the cases of 2,900 college-educated men who had been interviewed by the Kinsey team that indicated that in their same-gender experiences, *either* the interviewee or his male partner, but not necessarily *both*, had reached orgasm—a description different from what Kinsey had implied. The retabulation also showed that in 25 percent of all males interviewed, the same-gender experience had been confined mainly to adolescence or isolated experiences before the age of 20 (Gagnon & Simon, 1973). Several other studies have indicated a lower incidence of same-gender behavior than the widely quoted Kinsey figures suggested. A Louis Harris poll of 739 men found that 4.4 percent reported having had sex with another man during the previous 5 years. In one survey of 3,321 men aged 20 to 39, only 2 percent reported having had any same-gender oral or anal sexual activity during the last 10 years, and only 1 percent reported being exclusively gay (Billy et al., 1993). Data from the General Social Survey in the United States indicated that in 1994, 2.6 percent of sexually active men and 2.5 percent of sexually active women reported having had a same-gender sexual partner in the previous 12 months.

The researchers who conducted the National Health and Social Life Survey (NHSLS) found that there were many subtleties and gray areas in attempting to identify the incidence of same-gender orientations and behaviors (see Fig. 12.2). They found that people often change their patterns of sexual behavior over their life-times, making it difficult to generalize about orientation in any definitive manner. They also realized that there is no single set of desires that uniquely defines an individual as lesbian, gay, or bisexual. Does sexual desire for someone of your same gender define you as gay, even if you have never acted on that desire? Does identifying yourself as a lesbian make you so if you have never had sex with another woman? Finally, researchers recognized that because of the stigma and discrimination associated with same-gender sexual orientation, some people might be reluctant to say much about such attractions or behaviors. The survey was designed to encourage honest answers as much as possible, and it focused on same-gender behaviors and attractions in several different ways, using the term "homosexual" in only one question (Michael et al., 1994).

The NHSLS sought data about three aspects of same-gender orientation, recognizing that it is a multi-dimensional aspect of human sexuality (Laumann, Gagnon et al., 1994). The researchers asked questions about *desire*, focusing on attractions to others of the same gender and the appeal of various sex acts; sexual *behavior* with same-gender partners; and *self-identification,* or the sexual orientation one associates with oneself. Figure 12.3 summarizes the findings of these aspects of the study. The results of the survey showed that more people find others of their gender sexually attractive than actually act on that attraction.

Desire issues were measured by two questions, indicated by the "attraction" and "appeal" scales on the graph. One question asked, "In general are you sexually attracted to . . ." and offered five choices as answers: only women, mostly women, both men and women, mostly men, or only men. About 4 percent of the women and close to 6 percent of the men in the study responded that they were attracted to others of their own gender. When asked about the degree of appeal they found in the thought of having sex with someone of their own gender, 5.5 percent of the women and slightly more than 4 percent of the men

FIGURE 12.2 *Intimate Relationships*

It is erroneous to view gay and lesbian relationships strictly in terms of sexual behavior. As with heterosexual relationships, same-gender intimacy is based primarily on warmth and caring.

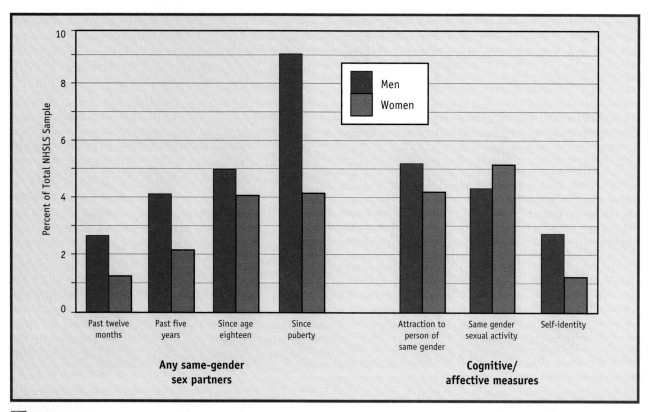

FIGURE 12.3   *Aspects of Same-Gender Sexuality*

The NHSLS reveals that more men and women find others of their gender sexually attractive or appealing than identify themselves as gay, lesbian, or bisexual. In addition, many of those who have not recently had any same-gender sex partners report having had same-gender partners at some time in their lives.

Source: From *Sex in America*, by Robert Michael. Copyright © 1994 by C.S.G. Enterprises, Inc., Edward O. Laumann, Robert T. Michael, and Gina Kolata. By permission of Little, Brown and Company, Inc.

Note: Attraction measured by the following question: "In general, are you sexually attracted to . . . only women, mostly women, both men and women, mostly men, only men?" (order of answer
  categories reversed for women). Appeal measured by the following question: "How would you rate this activity: having sex with someone of the same sex . . . very appealing, somewhat appealing,
  not appealing, not at all appealing?" Self-identification was derived from the following question: "Do you think of yourself as . . . heterosexual, homosexual, bisexual, something else?"

indicated they found the idea very appealing or appealing. When asked about having had sexual behavior with another person of the same gender, less than 2 percent of women had done so in the previous year, and about 4 percent had done so since the age of 18. Nine percent of the men surveyed indicated they had had sex with another male since puberty, but 40 percent of them (5 percent of all the men surveyed) indicated the behavior had occurred prior to the age of 18. Somewhat more than 2 percent of all men said they had had sex with another man in the previous year. One of the clear differences between males and females that emerged in the survey data was that much of the same-gender sexual contact of males happens during the earlier teenage years, whereas women are more likely to have sex with another woman after turning 18.

Regardless of the rates of same-gender sexual activity or attraction, the lowest rates of response were found with the question of self-identification. About 2.8 percent of the men indicated they identified them-

selves as "homosexual" or "bisexual," and about 1.4 percent of the women identified themselves as such. NHSLS researchers also analyzed all of the relevant data from the 150 women (8.6 percent of the total 1,749) and 143 men (10.1 percent of the total 1,410) who indicated any degree of same-gender desire, behavior, or self-identification, to see how the various factors overlapped or were independent. As Figure 12.4 shows, 59 percent of these women and 44 percent of the men indicated some level of attraction to others of their gender or appeal of same-gender sexual acts but did not report any same-gender actual behavior or self-identification. Thirteen percent of the women and 22 percent of the men had had some kind of same-gender sexual behavior but did not report any desire or self-identification as such. All three dimensions of same-gender sexual orientation were reported by only 15 percent of the 150 women and 24 percent of the 143 men (Laumann, Gagnon et al., 1994). In the *Details* magazine survey of college students, 3 percent of men and 1 percent of women self-identified as gay or

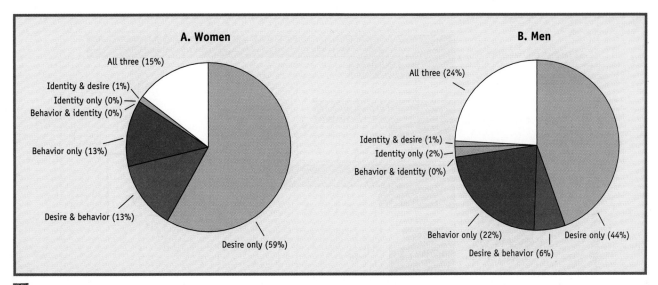

lesbian, with an additional 4 percent of men and 6 percent of women labeling themselves as bisexual. Ninety-two percent of both genders considered themselves to be heterosexual (Elliott & Brantley, 1997).

The NHSLS analysis has again confirmed that the incidence or prevalence of same-gender sexuality cannot be accurately characterized by any single number. It is a multidimensional phenomenon that may be perceived and interpreted in a variety of ways, depending on various contexts. Of the people who find same-gender sex desirable in some way, only about half of the men and slightly over 40 percent of the women ever act on those desires. Men who desire other men and have had sex with them are more likely than women with same-gender desire and behavior to identify themselves as gay ("homosexual" in the survey) or bisexual. The research data also show that people who identify themselves as lesbian, gay, or bisexual tend to be more highly educated and of middle- or high-class socioeconomic status. This may only indicate, however, that middle-class, college-educated people are more willing than others to report a same-gender sexual orientation.

The NHSLS research also demonstrated that the incidence of same-gender sexuality can be influenced by factors such as age and geographic location. For example, the proportion of people who identify themselves as gay, lesbian, or bisexual is much higher in cities than in suburban or rural locations, although this trend is more pronounced among gay men than it is among lesbians. As Figure 12.5 indicates, more than 9 percent of the men identify themselves as gay or bisexual, and close to 3 percent of the women identify themselves as lesbian or bisexual in the 12 largest cities of the United States. One obvious conclusion to be reached from these data would be that city life provides a concentration of people sufficient to allow identifiable sexual cultures and communities to become visible, thus increasing the likelihood of relationships developing. Although it is true that people with same-gender interests do tend to move away from suburban and rural locations to cities, another intriguing finding is that people raised in cities are actually more likely to be gay or lesbian than people raised in the suburbs or rural areas. We may only speculate as to the reason for this finding, but it may be because it is easier to notice, realize, and explore same-gender lifestyles in urban areas where they are more noticeable (Seidman et al., 1999).

Cross-Cultural Comparisons

Examples of differing cultural standards regarding same-gender sexual behavior were introduced in chapter 1, page 10. It has been suggested that the proportion of persons with same-gender orientation in the population is relatively consistent among different cultures, and contemporary research demonstrates at least some similarities. European studies have found rates of same-gender sexual behavior just slightly lower than those of the NHSLS. A major study in France surveyed the sexual behaviors of 20,055 people aged 18 to 69.

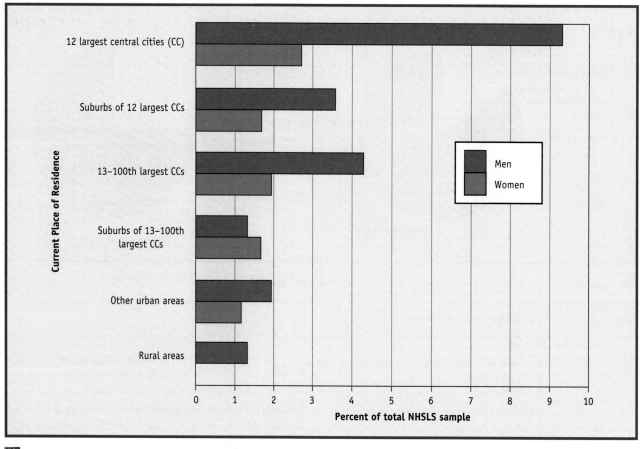

FIGURE 12.5 *Percent of NHSLS Subjects Identifying Themselves as Homosexual or Bisexual*

NHSLS research demonstrates that the incidence of same-gender sexuality can be influenced by geographic location. We can only speculate as to the reason people raised in cities are more likely to be gay or lesbian.

Source: From *Sex in America*, by Robert Michael. Copyright © 1994 by C.S.G. Enterprises, Inc., Edward O. Laumann, Robert T. Michael, and Gina Kolata. By permission of Little, Brown and Company, Inc.

Four percent of the men and 3 percent of the women said they had experienced same-gender sex during their lifetimes. Of these persons, 82 percent of the men and 78 percent of the women had had sex with members of both genders. The proportions of people reporting same-gender sex were lower during the previous year (1.1 percent of men and 0.3 percent of women) and the previous 5 years (1.4 percent of men and 0.4 percent of women). Same-gender and bisexual activity was considerably higher among residents of Paris than in rural areas (Analyse des Comportements Sexuels en France Investigators, 1992).

A British study of 18,876 people aged 16 to 59 reported similar statistics on male-male sexual activity; female same-gender sexual activity was not studied. Of the male respondents, 6 percent reported having had "some homosexual" experience as defined by themselves. Four percent indicated that they had had oral, anal, or other genital contact with another male at some time, and 1.4 percent reported they had experienced such contact within the previous 5 years. Men younger

than 35 were the most likely to have had same-gender sexual activity within the past 5 years, whereas those aged 35 to 44 were most likely to have had same-gender sex at some point during their lifetimes. The highest percentage of same-gender sexual activity was reported among men who lived in the greater London area, where 9 percent reported they had had a same-gender sexual partner, 5 percent within the previous 5 years (Johnson et al., 1992). In a sample of 2,460 Danish citizens aged 18 to 88, 0.9 percent identified themselves as homosexual, and 1.2 percent indicated they considered themselves bisexual (Ventegodt, 1998).

In some cultures, same-gender sexual behavior is accompanied by reversals in gender roles. Not only does the individual interact sexually with members of the same gender, but he or she dresses and acts as someone of the other gender is expected to in that society. This may reflect one way in which discontinuities in gender identity are adapted to in these cultures. The *berdache* tradition among American Plains Indians is an example of this gender-reversed sexual orientation (see chapter 5,

CROSS-CULTURAL PERSPECTIVE

Gay Zimbabweans Win Fight for Book-Fair Booth

HARARE, Zimbabwe, Aug. 1—Despite threats of violence and intense Government opposition, a Zimbabwean gay organization opened a stand today at an international book fair being held here after winning a court ruling granting it the right to take part in the exhibition.

President Robert Mugabe, who has described homosexuals as "worse than dogs and pigs," denied that the group, the Gays and Lesbians of Zimbabwe, had the right to take part in the book fair. Last year, the group was refused permission to have a stand at the annual exhibition.

The group took the Government to court and won its case on Tuesday. Zimbabwe's Attorney General immediately filed an appeal with the Supreme Court, charging that a gay booth at the book fair would bring a "breach of peace and disorder and immoral behavior."

In addition, Mr. Mugabe's supporters vowed to tear down the stand. Undaunted, the group opened its booth today.

There were no posters and no pamphlets, only flowers at the stand. But it immediately became the most popular of the nearly 300 booths at the fair. Scores of Zimbabweans crowded around the booth to talk with representatives about homosexuality. Some questioners were antagonistic and taunting, while others seemed merely curious.

"When the Zimbabwean public can see that we are ordinary people, then they will realize they don't need to be afraid of us," said Keith Goddard, a representative of the group.

"This may not look like much," said Mr. Goddard, gesturing toward the bare stand. "But for us this is a great step forward. This public education is good for everybody."

Gerald Chibwanya, a member of the group, said, "This has been difficult for us, but now people realize that we have rights, too."

Some fear anti-gay violence before the book fair ends on Saturday. Threats have come from Mr. Mugabe's ruling party, the Zimbabwe African National Union-Patriotic Front, and from Sangano Munhumutapa, a university group claiming to be Zimbabwe's "cultural police."

The controversy over gay rights in Zimbabwe was joined a year ago when the book fair bowed to Government pressure and refused the gay group the right to have a booth at the fair.

In a series of speeches last year, President Mugabe denounced homosexuals as "un-African" and denied that gay Zimbabweans have any legal rights.

Despite Mr. Mugabe's bitter words, no arrests or prosecutions have so far taken place.

The gay group had planned to display pamphlets about its counseling service, homosexuality and the Zimbabwean law, a statement from the Roman Catholic Church and an anthology of writing by gay Zimbabweans about winning acceptance in their society. All of the material had previously been cleared by the Zimbabwe police.

But because of the impending Supreme Court ruling over its right to have a stand at the book fair, the organization decided not to hand out any publications and to simply answer questions from the public.

Mr. Mugabe's anti-gay stance has galvanized Zimbabwe's gay minority and has won the organization significant international support. After Mr. Mugabe made an anti-homosexual speech while on a visit to the Netherlands, a Dutch organization pledged $120,000 to the Zimbabwean gay group. The organization, which previously operated on a shoestring budget from membership fees and proceeds from parties, suddenly finds itself with enough money to open an office and hire staff.

—*Source: New York Times*, August 2, 1996, p. A4. Reprinted by permisson.

"Developmental and Social Perspectives on Gender," p. 116). There are also societies in which same-gender sexual activity is recognized as legitimate only for people who hold a certain status role. If an Indian shaman were told in a vision to engage in sexual activity with someone of the same gender, it might well be considered acceptable because of the individual's status. In societies where men take more than one wife, it is quite common for the wives of one man to form permanent sexual and affectional bonds with each other.

Cultures around the globe display their own complex attitudes and mores related to same-gender sexual orientation and relationships. Brazil seems to have ambiguous values relating to same-gender sexual orientation. The gay subculture in Brazilian cities seems to flourish and be highly public, even attracting tourists from other countries. Yet some males with a machismo mentality have reacted against gays with violence and murder, and many gay males in Brazil apparently fear for their safety (Mendes-Leite, 1993).

Similar conflicts and political struggles exist in machismo countries such as Mexico and Cuba (Carrier, 1995; Leiner, 1994). Traditional Russian laws have imposed strong sanctions on male-male sexual activity, including years of imprisonment. Russian statutes have gradually decriminalized same-gender sexual activity between males, and gay men have begun to emerge slightly from years of secretiveness. They still fear social ostracism, however, and negative attitudes toward gays persist among the general population (Barshay, 1993).

Same-gender sexual orientations and relationships apparently exist to varying degrees in all cultures. They are sometimes accepted or tolerated, sometimes condemned or punished. Nevertheless, subcultures of people with same-gender orientations seem to appear in all societies, and social norms apparently have little effect on whether these orientations emerge (Rind, 1998).

The Effects of Homophobia and Biphobia

FOH Homophobia, biphobia, and their resultant prejudices take their toll on people's lives and attitudes toward themselves. The murder of college student Matthew Sheppard in 1998 focused public attention on the very real dangers of homophobia. For example, even among boys who are not attracted to other males, there is a fear of behaving in any way that might give an appearance of being gay. A report from the federal Task Force on Youth Suicide pointed out that gay and lesbian youth are at a higher risk of suicide and that this is the leading cause of death among young people who see themselves as part of some sexual minority. They are also more prone to self-destructive behaviors such as abusing alcohol and drugs. A study of 121 lesbian and gay college students found that 77 percent had been verbally insulted (49 percent more than once), and 27 percent had either experienced or been threatened with physical violence (Hershberger & D'Augelli, 1995; Nelson, 1994).

Several professional organizations have taken public stands with regard to same-gender sexual orientation and behavior. In 1973, the American Psychiatric Association's board of trustees voted unanimously to remove homosexuality from its list of mental illnesses, declaring that it does not constitute a psychiatric disorder. Individuals who are either disturbed by or are in conflict about their same-gender inclinations have since then been considered to have a sexual orientation disturbance. The American Psychological Association has taken a similar stand. The Association of Gay Psychologists and the Gay Caucus of the American Psychiatric Association provide gays, lesbians, and bisexuals in these professions a forum for their views.

There is a growing recognition among American corporations that homophobia is bad for business. More companies are now advertising their products in publications directed specifically at gay males, and to a lesser degree lesbians, because they realize that there is a substantial market in this segment of the population. Because gay and lesbian workers cannot function optimally if they have to be constantly concerned about the attitudes and behaviors of their colleagues, some businesses have begun to offer workshops to their employees, with the aim of reducing homophobic attitudes. In the corporate environment, as well as on college campuses, homophobic attitudes will not change until a serious effort is made to educate people about sexual orientation, dispelling some of the stereotypical beliefs about gay, lesbian, and bisexual persons (Croteau, 1996; Tyler, Jackman-Wheitner, Strader, & Lenox, 1997).

How accepting do you think students on your campus are of same-gender relationships and sexual behavior?

Religious Views

The attitudes and teachings of some religions toward **FOH** same-gender sexual behavior have traditionally played an important role in the formation of public opinion. Sex not intended for the purpose of reproduction may be viewed by some as lustful and therefore sinful. Furthermore, sexual behavior that cannot be conducted within the bond of heterosexual marriage is sometimes viewed as sinful. Many Judeo-Christian-Muslim denominations have sought to judge and regulate various forms of sexual behavior, including same-gender behavior (Chua-Eoan, 1997).

In the ancient world, no religions apart from Judaism categorically prohibited same-gender sexual behavior (the Torah's prohibition applied only to male-male sexual behavior), although some religions did advocate celibacy. Around 400 C.E., Christianity began to introduce a new sexual code that focused on maintaining "purity" and equated some sexual behaviors with the "fallen" state of the human soul (Boswell, 1990a). Over the centuries, same-gender sexual behavior has been variously accepted and condemned within religious traditions. In recent times, many theologians have called for increased understanding and acceptance of gays, lesbians, and bisexuals (Hartman, 1996).

All of the major Judeo-Christian-Muslim religious denominations have theologians who argue that the Torah, the Christian Bible, or the Koran do not condemn same-gender behavior as we know it. Scholars have debated the meanings of various passages in religious texts, some insisting that they admonish people for same-gender behavior, and others claiming that such meanings have been misinterpreted (Siker, 1994). There are a number of religious groups studying the moral implications of same-gender orientation and behavior. Gay men and lesbians have called for a new religious and moral ethic that would allow for human diversity, acknowledge variant sexual orientations, honor the concept of mutual sharing by consent, and affirm the freedom to grow and change (Chua-Eoan, 1997; Frontain, 1997). Many religiously oriented counselors help people sort out these issues in relationship to their own lives.

▧ Conceptualizing Same-Gender Sexual Orientation

The origins of sexual orientation have been the subject of much conjecture, research, and debate in recent years. Sexual orientation concerns are frequently brought to physicians, psychiatrists, psychologists, and counselors. The manner in which professionals deal with these issues may differ according to the theoretical framework with which they work. It is worth noting that same-gender sexual orientation was "medicalized" and defined as a "disease" between 1880 and 1900, at first being called "sexual inversion," and later, "homosexuality" (Wallen & Parsons, 1997). One of the medical assumptions was that people with a same-gender sexual orientation were fundamentally different from those with a heterosexual orientation. This is a classic example of social constructionism, in which social beliefs create whole new perceptions of phenomena that have always existed, thus constructing a concept that is then perpetuated as a scientific or medical truth (Blumstein & Schwartz, 1999; Kitzinger, 1995).

Theories and models about the origins of sexual orientation have focused on psychodynamic, biological, and socioenvironmental factors. In weighing the issues, it is crucial to keep in mind that there is a great deal of diversity among individuals who identify themselves as bisexual, lesbian, or gay. It is very possible that same-gender behavior and attraction may be about the only thing these individuals have in common. The possibility exists that there are many different pathways to a common sexual orientation—whether same-gender, bisexual, or heterosexual (Berger, Suematsu, & Ono, 1994). Several different conceptual models concerning same-gender sexual orientation follow.

Psychodynamic Models

Freud believed that same-gender sexual inclinations could result from a variety of difficulties in passing through the various stages of development—oral,

anal, latent, and genital. Late in his life, Freud stated that he did not consider homosexuality to be an illness but instead a sexual function produced by arrested sexual development. Nevertheless, many psychoanalysts advanced numerous hypotheses on the psychodynamics behind the development of same-gender sexual orientation, viewing it as a type of neurosis that should receive psychiatric treatment. One of the traditional psychodynamic perspectives, popularized in the 1960s, was that family interactions caused same-gender orientation in males—the most typical background consisting of a close-binding, overprotective mother and a detached, absent, or openly hostile father. It is now known that this theory has no basis in fact, although some professionals still espouse it (Schwartz, 1999; Socarides, 1995). Psychodynamic theory relating to women's sexual orientation has tended to perpetuate the presumption that heterosexuality is the normal, healthy way to develop sexually (Peraldi, 1992). Many recent psychodynamic theorists have begun to integrate some of the newer findings about possible biological and social influences on sexual orientation, modifying classical assumptions. Same-gender sexual orientation is now generally accepted as a normal, mature, developmental state rather than as a pathological one requiring treatment (Isay, 1993). Psychoanalysts are beginning to conceptualize gay males and lesbians from a new and more positive perspective that rejects notions of problematic psychosexual development or "arrested" psychological development.

Normal Variant Model

Beginning in the 1960s, an increasingly large and powerful group of theorists and researchers began to conceptualize same-gender sexual orientation as a normal variation within the continuum of human sexual behavior (see Fig. 12.6). They recognized that same-gender sexual behavior was less common than heterosexual behavior, but they did not see any grounds for classifying it as pathological, deviant, perverse, or abnormal. Instead, they viewed same-gender behavior as a natural, but less prevalent, form of sexual expression (Sell, 1997).

One of the first studies to support a nonpathological view of same-gender orientation emerged in England during the late 1950s. A special legislative committee was formed to study homosexual offenses and prostitution and concluded that most gay males and lesbians were well-adjusted individuals. The committee's report drew wide attention because of its recommendations for repeal of British laws prohibiting homosexual acts between consenting adults (Wolfenden, 1963). Another important British study compared lesbians and heterosexual women who had been matched by age, education, and intelligence.

FIGURE 12.6   *Same-Gender Orientation*

Many researchers believe that same-gender sexual behavior is simply a variant on the continuum of human sexual activity. The psychological health of both heterosexuals and gay men or lesbians appears to be, statistically, about the same.

Both groups were administered a series of personality tests, and the lesbians and heterosexual women were found to be equally healthy psychologically (Hopkins, 1969).

In the United States, Evelyn Hooker was one of the most influential researchers to propose that same-gender sexual orientation and behavior are normal variants. As a young psychologist in Chicago in the 1950s, she had been taught that homosexuality was a pathological condition. However, she had befriended a group of young gay men, and her real-life observations seemed to suggest that they were quite healthy and well-adjusted. One of the men said to her one day, "Now, Evelyn, it is your scientific duty to study men like me," and she was struck with the realization that very little scientific information was available about same-gender orientation (Hooker, 1993). Hooker received a grant from the National Institute of Mental Health, and she began to study gay men living in the gay community, eventually expanding her research to include lesbians. Her findings confirmed that in terms of psychological health, people with same-gender and heterosexual orientations were indistinguishable. She reported that many gay men and lesbians were living

happy, productive lives. She was critical of earlier studies that had focused on people who were either patients in psychoanalysis or prisoners, and she suggested that same-gender orientation could not scientifically be defined as pathological (Hooker, 1993). More recent studies have continued to confirm that there are no significant psychological differences between heterosexuals and people with a same-gender orientation (Crowden & Koch, 1995).

The Bell, Weinberg, and Hammersmith Study on Sexual Orientation

This groundbreaking study on the development of sexual orientation focused on a research population of lesbians and gay men in ways that attempted to identify possible "causes" of same-gender orientation. Representing the Kinsey Institute, Alan Bell, Martin Weinberg, and Sue Kiefer Hammersmith (1981) carried out a controlled study, involving interviews with 979 gay men and lesbians and a comparison sample of 477 heterosexual men and women. In examining any difference found between the two population samples, the researchers controlled for the possible effects of age, education, and social status to make sure any differences between the two groups were not due to such factors.

A tremendous amount of data was gathered in the 3- to 5-hour, face-to-face interviews conducted with each person. The questions in the interview were drawn from a variety of theoretical stances concerning the development of same-gender sexual orientations. The data were then subjected to a statistical technique known as path analysis. The researchers then drew the following conclusions concerning sexual orientation:

1. Sexual orientation appears to be largely determined prior to adolescence, even when youngsters have not been particularly sexually active.
2. Same-gender attractions are typically experienced for about 3 years prior to any overt same-gender sexual behavior. Such feelings play more of a role in eventually identifying oneself as gay or lesbian than any particular activities with others.
3. Lesbians and gay men tend to have a history of heterosexual experiences during childhood and adolescence. Unlike the control group heterosexuals, however, they report these experiences as being relatively unsatisfying.
4. Identification with a parent of either gender appears to play no significant role in the development of sexual orientation.
5. There is no support for the hypothesis that any particular type of mother produces children with a same-gender orientation. In the study, there

was a slightly higher proportion of lesbians and gay men that had poor relationships with their fathers. However, it was impossible to determine if this was a causative factor in their sexual orientation or simply a reflection of the difficulty that sexually different sons or daughters might have in relating with their fathers.

These findings provided little support for the models that emphasized psychoanalytic or early learning theories as determinants of same-gender sexual orientation. Although these researchers did not study genetic or hormonal characteristics, they did state that their findings were "not inconsistent with what one would expect to find if, indeed, there were a biological basis for sexual [orientation]." They further speculated that such a biological mechanism would probably account for gender identity as well as sexual orientation (see chapter 5) and that it might well be operative in varying degrees. That is to say, it would operate more powerfully in individuals who are exclusively same-gender-oriented or heterosexual than it would for bisexual people. This crucial study shed new light on the development of sexual orientation. Most importantly, it demonstrated the complexity of this issue and the research that attempts to study it.

Biological Determinants Model

In one of the last revisions of his famous work, *Three Essays on the Theory of Sexuality,* Sigmund Freud speculated that the roots of homosexuality might eventually be found in the effects of hormones on mind and body. Since that suggestion was made in 1920, theories emphasizing a biological basis for same-gender orientation—either hormonal, genetic, or anatomical—have waxed and waned. Research studies have approached the question from three different angles: (1) examining possible hormonal influences during prenatal development or during postnatal development; (2) attempting to detect genetic factors that might be involved in the determination of later sexual orientations and activities; and (3) examining anatomical differences between the brain structures of gay and heterosexual men.

Hormonal Influences

Because research with animals had demonstrated the crucial role that hormones could play in regulating the sexual behaviors of nonhuman animals, it was not surprising that endocrinologists speculated that hormonal levels might well play a role in the development of same-gender orientation (Wallen & Parson, 1997). This direction was further fueled by findings that prenatal hormonal factors might exert some influence over later gender identity or gender role, as elucidated in chapter 5. The evidence suggests that certain brain structures may be masculinized and defeminized by male hormones produced in the fetal testes. It is believed that these influences on the brain lead to a predisposition toward masculine-identified behavior after birth. Conversely, if the fetus is female and no male hormones are produced, the brain pathways are not masculinized, and the behavior of the child is feminine-identified.

So far, there has been no clearly demonstrated relationship between such prenatal factors and the development of sexual orientation in humans (Doell, 1995). On the other hand, genetic females who suffer from congenital adrenal hyperplasia (CAH) at birth are believed to have had some masculinizing hormonal influences on their central nervous systems (see chapter 5, p. 124), and there is evidence that close to 40 percent of women with CAH identify themselves as lesbian or bisexual, a much higher proportion than in the general population (Burr, 1996; Hines & Collaer, 1993). Conversely, in those individuals who have androgen insensitivity, there is no evidence that lowered levels of androgen have any effect on sexual orientation in later life (Macke et al., 1993). However, there is no solid evidence as yet concerning the possible role played by prenatal hormones in influencing later sex partner preferences in humans (Byne, 1995).

Some researchers have hypothesized that hormone levels might differ between adult gay men or lesbians and heterosexual men and women or that administering hormones to these groups might lead to differing biochemical responses because of differing sexual orientations. Another line of speculation has been that imbalances of hormones in adolescents or adults might lead to changes in sexual orientation. Although studies have sometimes yielded mixed results when investigating such hypotheses, the most widely accepted position at present is that hormone levels in adolescence or adulthood are not a factor in determining sexual orientation and that hormone metabolism is not affected by sexual orientation (Burr, 1996).

Genetic Influences

There is building evidence that genes can exert influences over human behavior, but it would also appear that pinning down which genes influence which behaviors is a frustrating task for researchers. Behavioral geneticists are increasingly coming to the conclusion that several genes may actually be involved in the expression of particular human behaviors (Hamer & Copeland, 1998). Recent research has begun to suggest some interesting genetic links to sexual orientation, and in fact these studies provide the strongest support for possible biological roots of sexual orientation. Some suggestive data first emerged indicating that same-gender orientation tends to run in families. Gay males have a significantly higher likelihood of having a brother, uncle, or male cousin who is gay. Lesbian women also have a greater likelihood of having a lesbian or bisexual sister, although this tendency is less pronounced than is the trend among males. It is not yet clear whether gay males are more likely to have lesbian sisters, or if lesbians are more likely to have gay brothers. These findings could indicate some sort of familial connection in the development of sexual orientation, especially in male or female lineages (Bailey & Pillard, 1995; Pattatucci & Hamer, 1995).

It has been speculated for a long time that studying twins might also provide some clues to the development of sexual orientation, but researchers have only recently begun to demonstrate the usefulness of this approach. One study compared 56 identical male twins, 54 fraternal male twins, and 57 genetically unrelated adopted brothers. At least one in each pair of brothers was gay or bisexual and had a twin or an adopted brother with whom he had started living at least by age 2. The assumption of the researchers was that if same-gender sexual orientation is at least partly genetic in origin, the more closely related people are, the more likely their sexual orientation is to be the same. What they found tended to support that assumption. Among the pairs of adoptive brothers, only 11 percent were both gay. That rate rose to 22 percent for the fraternal twins, and 52 percent for the identical twins. The results suggest that same-gender sexual orientation is highly attributable to genetics (Bailey & Pillard, 1995).

Another study found that among 38 pairs of identical twins (34 male and 4 female), both twins were gay or lesbian in almost two-thirds of the pairs. In 23 pairs of fraternal twins (14 male and 9 male-female), both twins had a same-gender sexual orientation in over 30 percent of the pairs. Also included in this study were two sets of triplets. In one case, there was one set of identical twins among the three, and those two were both gay whereas the third sibling was not. In the other triplet set, all three were monozygotic, or identical, and all three had a same-gender sexual orientation. The researchers felt that these findings supported a supposition that there was a biological basis for sexual orientation (Whitam, Diamond, & Martin, 1993).

Another study was conducted with 147 lesbians and their sisters. Of the 71 lesbians who had identical twins, 48 percent of the twins were also lesbians. Of those whose sisters were fraternal twins, 16 percent of the sisters were lesbians, and only 6 percent of adopted sisters had a same-gender orientation. These statistics were consistent with lower incidences of same-gender orientation typically reported for women as compared to men. Some other studies by the same researchers also found that lesbians were four times more likely to have a lesbian sister than a control group of heterosexual women but were only slightly

more likely to have a gay brother (Bailey & Pillard, 1995). Gay males are more likely to have a later birth order in their families, and the more older brothers present, the greater the likelihood that the youngest brother will be gay. Gay males are also more likely to have a lower body weight than brothers and an earlier onset of puberty (Blancard, 1997; Blanchard & Bogaert, 1996; Bogaert, 1998).

These studies do not mean that same-gender sexual orientation is 100 percent dependent on genetics, as are characteristics such as eye color. They suggest instead that there is some degree of *heritability,* meaning that sexual orientation is at least partially dependent on genes passed along from generation to generation. For example, a person's height is about 90 percent genetically determined, but it can also be affected slightly by such factors as nutrition. It is therefore said to be multifactorial, meaning that many factors—including genetics—play a role in its expression. It may be that same-gender sexual orientation is 50 to 70 percent attributable to genetics, but its expression would also be multifactorial and probably quite complex (Hamer & Copeland, 1998; LeVay, 1996).

One of the biggest supports for proponents of a genetic basis for same-gender sexual orientation came from research done by a team of geneticists at the National Cancer Institute. The researchers first traced family backgrounds for 76 gay men, identifying as many family members as they could who had a same-gender orientation. Confirming the findings of earlier studies, they discovered that gay men were more likely to have a gay brother than were men in the general population. However, they also found that there was a greater likelihood that these men would have gay male relatives on the maternal side of the family, suggesting that the sexual orientation might be linked in some way to the X chromosome that males inherit from their mothers. The researchers then took DNA samples from 40 pairs of gay brothers and analyzed them for genetic markers. Of the 40 pairs of brothers, 33 pairs shared a set of five genetic markers on one end of their X chromosomes. This was the first time that sexual orientation had ever been linked to a specific part of a chromosome (Hamer, Hu, Magnuson, Hu, & Pattatucci, 1993; Turner, 1995). There has continued to be debate about whether genetic markers for male same-gender sexual orientation actually exist (Hamer, 1999; Rice, Anderson, Risch, & Ebers, 1999), but there is now evidence that sexual orientation could actually be more heritable in women than in men (Hershberger, 1997).

Differences in Brain Anatomy

Anatomical differences have also been found between the brains of gay and heterosexual men. Although the findings are preliminary and based on a relatively small number of subjects, they have opened up a new area of research into the possible biological foundations of sexual orientation (Wegesin, 1998). The first such study found that a part of the brain that governs daily rhythms, the suprachiasmatic nucleus, is twice as large in gay men as it is in heterosexual men. Because that part of the brain has not been associated with sexual behavior, brain researchers went on to study the hypothalamus, again finding some measurable differences (Swaab & Gofman, 1995).

The development of the brain's hypothalamus does seem to be influenced by hormones, and it is known to play a role in determining sexual behavior in some mammalian groups. It is also known that the anterior part of the human hypothalamus plays some role in human sexuality. Highly compelling research has determined that a particular collection of cells typically found in the anterior hypothalamus is much smaller in gay men and in women than it is in heterosexual men (LeVay, 1996). Another study found that the anterior commissure, a band of fibers that connects the two hemispheres of the brain, was 34 percent larger in the gay men studied than it was in heterosexual men, and 18 percent larger than it is in women. Although this brain structure is not known to have any direct bearing on sexual inclinations, the finding again suggests that sexual orientation may be part of a larger package of brain characteristics. These findings still need further confirmation, and their implications are still being debated (Bailey & Pillard, 1995).

Studies on certain motor tasks that are determined by the brain's cerebral hemispheres have found that gay males sometimes function more similarly to heterosexual women than to heterosexual men (Sanders & Wright, 1997). It has also been determined that the inner ears of lesbian and bisexual women function more like the inner ears of men than they do like those of heterosexual women (McFadden & Pasanen, 1999).

Even though no single study can tell us definitively that sexual orientation is at least partly biologically determined, proponents of the biological model insist that there is now enough evidence from a variety of different researchers, using different methodologies, to make a strong case for this point of view. They also argue that the evidence for a purely social constructionist perspective does not hold up particularly well to close scrutiny (Hamer & Copeland, 1998). As specific biological differences have been discovered, they have increased the danger that homophobic people may react by claiming that these differences are clearly "defects." On the other end of the spectrum are those who would see these differences as evidence that same-gender orientation is as natural a human variation as left-handedness. More work remains to be done before we can offer final conclusions about any biological correlates of same-gender sexual orientation.

Multifactorial Model

As proponents of a social constructionist model of sexual orientation continue to claim that the biological evidence is weak (Byne & Parsons, 1994; Looy, 1995), there has been a tendency for the debate to be based on assumptions about either nature *or* nurture. Theorists are now broadening that view in favor of a more *multifactorial model,* or one that incorporates a biopsychosocial perspective, taking into account a range of biological, psychological, and socioenvironmental factors (Haumann, 1995). It seems increasingly likely that sexual orientation develops through a complex interaction of innate and external influences. It might be that there are different subpopulations of people with same-gender sexual orientations, representing different combinations of causative factors (Berger et al., 1994). Some of the "programming" that results in an individual's sexual orientation may take place during "critical periods" of development when biology and environment interact with each other, possibly both during prenatal life and after birth (Bancroft, 1994; Bem, 1996).

A view is emerging of the brain as a mosaic of different areas that may respond to sex hormones at various stages of fetal and childhood development. Average or usual levels of female or male hormones would produce the typical female or male brain. However, unusual hormone levels present at some critical period in brain growth may affect the development of susceptible areas. This could mean that different regions of the same brain might undergo various kinds of sexual differentiation. Depending on hormone levels and the timing of their exposure to the developing brain, there could be influences on a wide range of characteristics, including handedness and sexual orientation (Hamer & Copeland, 1998). It has also been proposed that these influences could produce different childhood temperaments that then might lead to varying erotic attractions during development (Bem, 1996).

There is a growing realization that biologists and social psychologists may simply be looking at and interpreting the same phenomena from different perspectives. Biologists tend to view things from the standpoint of molecular influences and neurological mechanisms. Social psychologists are looking at the broader behavioral implications that stem from cultural influences. The most recent theorists suggest that sexual orientation is in fact the result of complex interactions of all these factors: biological processes and predispositions, life experiences, the structure of the nervous system, genetics, and brain development (LeVay, 1996; Looy, 1995).

If the genetic component in determining sexual orientation is further confirmed, the early research would suggest that it is not 100 percent heritable and that other factors play a role. When one of the gay men involved in the twin genetic study informed his identical twin brother that he was gay, the brother was surprised. He had been living a distinctly heterosexual lifestyle and yet had also been aware of some level of attraction to other men. It had never occurred to him to define his feelings as gay. Following his brother's revelation, he decided to try sex with men and indeed found these experiences to be more fulfilling than his heterosexual encounters. A year later, both twins told their parents they were gay. This is a clear reminder that there can be powerful social influences on how individuals define themselves sexually, even when some traits may be inborn. Some theorists have suggested that people pick and choose from a wide variety of environmental stimuli, based on their genetic makeup. In doing so, they actually *create their own environments* in a sense. This perspective sees human beings as dynamic, creative organisms whose learning and experiencing amplifies and modifies the effects of genetics (Bem, 1996; Bouchard, 1994). It has been suggested that human beings might be "flavored" by genetics rather than "programmed" by them. Our genes may thus provide the foundation for a range of outcomes.

The multifactorial model suggests that there could be many shades of sexual orientation, the origins of which are more complex and subtle than the either-or approach could accommodate. Human beings are filled with individual quirks and ambiguities that defy simple classification (Bancroft, 1994; Burr, 1996; Kitzinger, 1995). It seems likely that as research into the origins of sexual orientation continues, further support will emerge for a concept that considers a wide range of factors. Because same-gender and bisexual sexual orientations have been viewed as variants from the heterosexual norm, studies have tended to focus on their origins. In fact, we know little about the origins of heterosexual orientation. It may well be that the research into same-gender sexual orientation will provide valuable clues concerning the development of all orientations.

Perspectives on Therapy

Among those professionals who traditionally viewed same-gender orientation as a disorder, a great deal of attention was given to therapy and cure. The psychodynamic models usually recommended that people with a same-gender orientation face the conflicts and problems left over from childhood, resolve them in some manner, and thereby free themselves to pursue heterosexuality. However, the new information about possible biological determinants of sexual orientation has begun to force a reexamination of such points of view (Chandler, 1995; Isay, 1996).

Some psychotherapists claim to have "cured" or changed gay or lesbian people into heterosexuals. This usually seems to mean that the patient has stopped participating in same-gender sexual behavior and has begun functioning sexually with members of the opposite sex. However, the people who have made this change have apparently been unhappy with and felt guilty over their same-gender activities and have wished very much to give them up. Other professionals assert that a behavioral shift simply represents a conscious choice to act in a way that both the patient and the therapist consider more appropriate and thus does not constitute a change in sexual orientation. Behavioral therapy methods that were popular for a brief time in the 1960s made use of aversive techniques, in which attempts were made to extinguish same-gender sexual arousal by using electrical shocks or other negative stimuli. These techniques quickly lost favor because of their methods and lack of measurable success in accomplishing their goals. "Conversion therapies," now often rooted in religious values, raise many ethical concerns because they operate with a presumption that sexual orientation can and should be changed, both of which are debatable points (Leland & Miller, 1998).

It is clear that some counselors and therapists have homophobic or biphobic attitudes that may be detrimental to bisexual, lesbian, or gay clients. Of particular concern are those professionals who are not aware of their own prejudices but bring their negative sentiments in subtle ways to the counseling process (Bieschke & Matthews, 1996; Bux, 1996). Recent surveys have shown gay men, lesbians, and bisexuals to be quite satisfied with their experiences in counseling and psychotherapy, although they sometimes face negative messages from professionals (Jones & Gabriel, 1999). They sometimes prefer to select a professional who also has a same-gender sexual orientation, avoiding those who might hold homophobic attitudes. However, many heterosexual counselors have often been able to offer effective, unbiased support and counsel as well (Milton & Coyle, 1999). It is worth noting that even a gay, lesbian, or bisexual counselor may have some homophobic or biphobic attitudes of his or her own (Klitzman, Bodkin, & Pope, 1998).

◼ Forming an Identity as a Gay Male, Lesbian, or Bisexual

Although categories and labels represent generalizations and are often used as excuses for bigotry or oppression, they also provide a way of making sense out of an immense array of information. Sometimes people need a label or category into which they can fit themselves and thus have a greater sense of who they are. This inner sense of personal identity can have important implications for the way an individual experiences herself or himself. It is also true, however, that we have many different identities to integrate into our sense of self: gender, occupation, marital status, and parenthood, among others. The formalized, theoretical concept of sexual identity has emerged rather recently in European and North American sociopsychology (Gonsiorek, 1995; Weeks, 1998).

For a long time, gay, lesbian, and bisexual people in North America had little more than myths and stereotypes with which to identify. Even now, it is often assumed that gay males are always effeminate and lesbians are mannish. Although there are individuals who fit such stereotypes, people with a same-gender sexual orientation are generally indistinguishable from heterosexual people, and there are no characteristics that clearly distinguish either group (Gonsiorek, 1995). There are men with effeminate mannerisms and women with masculine mannerisms who are exclusively heterosexual; there are macho gay men and delicate lesbian women. The majority of gay men dislike effeminacy and are not sexually aroused by it. Only about 5 percent of gay males exhibit an effeminate walk, clothing style, or speech with any consistency, and probably less than 3 percent of lesbians show masculine behavior and style consistently (Atkins, 1998; Ludwig & Brownell, 1999). However, there is some evidence to indicate that among children and adolescents who show gender nonconformity in appearance and mannerisms, there is indeed a somewhat greater likelihood of same-gender attractions and behaviors later in life (Bailey, Nothnagel, & Wolfe, 1995).

It was in the late 1960s and early 1970s that the notion of "homosexual identity" began to emerge. It was an important transition time socially because it began to draw attention away from specific sexual behaviors and toward an understanding of sexual orientation as it becomes integrated into the personality. Becoming able to identify oneself as gay or lesbian and disclosing that orientation to selected others seem to be important in the formation of a comfortable sexual identity and in promoting the person's psychological adjustment (Weeks, 1998).

Because people who have a same-gender orientation function in a society with mostly heterosexist assumptions, at some point in their lives they begin to perceive themselves as members of a minority. This also involves changes in values and redefinitions of acceptable behavior and is largely an internal, psychological

CASE STUDY

Martha: Reexamining Sexual Orientation

Martha and her husband had married when Martha was 23. Now 38, Martha had two children, aged 10 and 12. In discussing her situation with a counselor, Martha explained that she had grown up dating boys and looking forward to raising a family. She was successful in her career as a supervising social worker, and she valued her relationship with her husband. However, she had recently found herself falling in love with another woman, whom she had known as a friend and confidant for years. The woman was unmarried, and she eventually told Martha that she was a lesbian and very attracted to Martha both physically and emotionally. She also explained her hesitancy in bringing the subject up, because she was concerned about complicating Martha's life.

Although Martha too had no particular wish to disrupt the life of her family, she had increasingly realized her own interest in pursuing the relationship with her female friend. Eventually, the two had shared sex, and Martha realized that she had tapped into some long-unrealized desires. She later wrote to the counselor: "Even though I always was attracted to other women, I was never in a context that allowed me to connect my feelings with my own identity as a sexual person. I grew up in a heterosexual world, and never questioned the assumption that I was heterosexual. I do enjoy my relationships with men, but I now know that I have never been all that drawn to them romantically or sexually. Having to draw away from my husband was one of the most painful experiences of my life. Drawing closer to my female lover has been one of the most wonderful experiences of my life. Perhaps if I had understood my sexuality earlier, I could have saved everyone a lot of turmoil, but I guess that's not always the way life works."

After several months of counseling, Martha and her husband agreed to a divorce and to shared custody of their two children. The husband was confused and hurt by their situation but was also able to understand that Martha had never deliberately deceived him. They maintained a cordial relationship following the breakup of their marriage, and they worked cooperatively in the raising of the children. The children also saw counselors as they made the difficult adjustments to a very new family structure.

process that seems to involve various stages. Although different theories have emerged with respect to sexual orientation and identity formation, there are some things most models have in common. There is almost always a predictable progression from some sort of first awareness of same-gender attractions and feelings; to a stage of self-labeling as being gay, lesbian, or bisexual; through stages of becoming more accepting of the new identity and sharing it with others; to a final stage of incorporating the identity into the total sense of self (Rhoads, 1995; Savin-Williams, & Diamond, 1999).

Australian psychologist Vivienne Cass (1983–1984, 1990) emphasized the need to pay attention to people's self-perceptions in understanding the experience of same-gender sexual orientation. This perspective assumes that sexual orientation is not so rigidly fixed that it cannot be modified. Rather, it assumes that people's perceptions of their sexuality may shift with time, even during the adult years, and such shifts may result in new patterns of sexual behavior or relationships. In other words, sexual identity is not something that is necessarily permanently fixed, even though it may be long-lasting and relatively unswerving for many people. This model of sexual orientation assumes that individuals may consciously alter their sexual behaviors to a degree, depending on the ways in which they have come to see themselves (Stokes, Damon, & McKirnan, 1997).

Stages of Sexual Identity Formation

Cass's theory holds that in order for the process of same-gender sexual identity formation to begin, the individual must experience some degree of sexual interest in, or attraction for, someone of the same gender. This does not necessarily have to be expressed through any overt sexual behavior but may instead take the form of fantasies or daydreams. Cass has elucidated six stages in the process of sexual identity formation and maintains that there may be many individual variations in how different people progress through these stages. She believes that movement through the stages is motivated by the persistent need to maintain some sort of consistent image of oneself in relationship to sexual orientation and by the need to maintain a sense of self-esteem—or positive feelings about oneself—relevant to one's sexual orientation.

The concept of navigating through various stages in order to clarify a sexual identity may apply more aptly to dominant North American and European cultures and be much less applicable to other ethnic groups. Sexual identity may be somewhat public and even have political overtones, both of which may not suit some populations. For example, many African Americans, Latino men and Latina women, and Asian Americans do not seem to want or need a gay, lesbian, or bisexual identity as such, and instead tend to integrate the same-gender sexual behaviors into other,

nonsexual identities. Asians and Asian Americans often see sexual behavior as a strictly private matter, not one that needs to fit into any larger social scheme (Chung & Katayama, 1999; Savin-Williams, 1999). Nevertheless, Cass's model seems to have found relevance for many people in Western culture, and a summary of her six stages of sexual identity formation follows (Cass, 1990):

Stage I: Identity Confusion

This stage occurs when people begin to realize that information about same-gender sexual orientation somehow relates to them and their reactions. As they realize that the personal relevance of this information cannot be ignored, they begin to experience a sense of inconsistency and incongruence in their view of their sexual selves. This period of confusion may go on for some time, during which there may be an attempt to avoid sexual activities with members of the same gender, even in the face of persistent dreams and fantasies about them (Savin-Williams & Diamond, 1999). Individuals may attempt to find more information about same-gender orientation as the question "Am I gay/lesbian/bisexual?" is addressed. This moves them along toward the second stage of identity formation.

Stage II: Identity Comparison

It is during this stage that people begin to examine the broader implications of being lesbian, gay, or bisexual, as they begin to feel different from family members and peers. Nearly everyone grows up with certain heterosexual expectations and behavioral guidelines. As people's same-gender identities develop, those expectations and guidelines are gradually given up, and there may be a profound sense of loss and grieving. Individuals who are experiencing this sense of social alienation may react in a variety of ways. They may react positively to being different and begin devaluing the importance of heterosexuality in their lives. However, they may still need to "pass," or pretend heterosexuality, in order to avoid negative confrontations about their sexual orientation that they are not prepared to deal with. Many people react by rejecting a same-gender identity at this point, even though they may recognize their behaviors and inclinations toward members of their own gender (Stokes, Damon, & McKirnan, 1997). They may define their same-gender behavior as the result of a particular relationship, of having been innocently seduced, or as only a temporary state. Another possible reaction is to devalue same-gender identity because of fear of negative reactions from others. Some people at this stage undoubtedly turn their own confusion and "internalized homophobia" over personal identity into antigay and antilesbian attitudes and exaggerated heterosexual behavior, even though they may be covertly indulging in same-gender activities or fantasies (Isay, 1996).

Stage III: Identity Tolerance

When individuals come to accept their same-gender sexual orientation and begin to recognize the sexual, social, and emotional needs that accompany it, an increased commitment to and tolerance for the identity emerge. Typically, there is increased involvement with others in the gay or lesbian community, offering a support group that understands the person's concerns, more opportunity to meet partners and see positive role models, and a chance to begin feeling more at ease with the identity. This stage may be more difficult for people who are shy and lacking in social skills or who have low self-esteem and fears of having their sexual identity known by others. People whose experiences are largely negative during this stage may never progress any further in the development of a same-gender sexual identity. However, those who perceive their experiences as more positive will eventually develop enough commitment to their identity to be able to say, "I am lesbian/gay/bisexual" (Isay, 1996; Savin-Williams, 1999).

Because there are still many forms of discrimination and homophobic sentiment, decisions must be faced about how open one wishes to be about sexual orientation. Being secretive about one's same-gender orientation has been called "being in the closet." The process of allowing oneself to acknowledge same-gender attractions and then express them to others has been called "**coming out** of the closet." How far a gay man, lesbian, or bisexual individual will come out, and to whom, depends on a variety of factors, one of the most crucial being her or his degree of self-acceptance. Some feel that it is crucial to share sexual orientation with friends and family members, whereas others feel that it is more a personal matter that is irrelevant to others. Decisions about coming out must be weighed with care, and the possibility of negative or hurtful consequences considered. Many people have found, however, that others can accept their same-gender sexual orientation comfortably (Bhugra, 1997; Rhoads, 1995).

Stage IV: Identity Acceptance

This stage occurs when people accept a self-image as lesbian, gay, or bisexual rather than simply tolerating it and when they have continuing and increased contact with gay and lesbian culture. There is a positive identification with others who have a same-gender orientation. The attitudes and lifestyles of these other people can play a significant role in determining how comfortable individuals are in expressing their own identity. If they associate with others who feel that a same-gender orientation is fully legitimate, then this is the attitude that will most likely be adopted. As self-acceptance increases, people move toward Stage V.

Stage V: Identity Pride

By this point in their identity formation, people with a same-gender sexual identity are not as likely to be using heterosexuality as the standard by which they judge themselves and the behavior of others. As they identify more with the gay and lesbian community, pride in the accomplishments of that community deepens. Sometimes people in this stage become activists in political movements to fight discrimination and homophobia, and there may be more confrontations with the heterosexual establishment. For many, this is an angry stage. Efforts to conceal one's sexual orientation are increasingly abandoned, and selected family members and coworkers may be informed.

Because of prevailing social attitudes, people may be alarmed to discover that a spouse, parent, child, sibling, or friend is bisexual, gay, or lesbian. Some people react to such a discovery with fear and loathing, others with blame and guilt, still others with tolerance, understanding, sensitivity, and acceptance. It is quite typical for parents, upon discovering that a son or daughter is gay or lesbian, to blame themselves and wonder "what we did wrong." Yet, as earlier sections of this chapter have demonstrated, there is no solid evidence to support the belief that parental behavioral influences are important in the formation of sexual orientation. Coming out to parents and other family members remains one of the greatest challenges to gay men and lesbian women as they consolidate their personal identity (Rhoads, 1995; Savin-Williams, 1999). There is an organization called Parents and Friends of Lesbians and Gays (PFLAG), through which parents and others can learn more about same-gender sexual orientation and deal with their feelings. Eventually, many parents come to accept the sexual identity of their child. There are other unfortunate cases, however, in which the lesbian daughter or gay son is excluded from the family. This reaction usually only intensifies feelings of guilt and rejection.

What do you believe are the most powerful determinants of sexual orientation?

Whether individuals move to the final stage of sexual identity formation is often determined by the reaction of significant others to the disclosure of their orientation. If there are mostly negative reactions, the person may only feel more confirmed in her or his belief that heterosexuals represent the opposition and are not to be trusted. If the reactions tend toward the positive and accepting, individuals may well be able to move on (Isay, 1996; Stokes et al., 1997).

coming out: to acknowledge to oneself and others that one is lesbian, gay, or bisexual.

Stage VI: Identity Synthesis

In this final stage of identity formation, people realize that the world is not divided into us (gays, lesbians, and bisexuals) and them (heterosexuals). Not all heterosexuals need to be viewed negatively, and not all people with same-gender orientation positively. The anger that is so often experienced in Stage V is reduced, and the gay, lesbian, or bisexual aspects of one's identity may be fully integrated with other aspects of the self and personality. The identity formation process is complete.

Male-Female Differences in Sexual Identity Formation

Different patterns of socialization between women and men lead to a few differences in the ways that same-gender sexual identity is acquired by the two sexes. For example, the evidence suggests that on average, more gay males seek contact from a variety of sexual partners than do lesbians or heterosexual males (Laumann, Gagnon et al., 1994). They may also be more willing to participate in anonymous, casual sexual encounters, a practice that is almost unknown among lesbians. Several research studies have indicated that gay males may tend to become aware of their same-gender orientation earlier than do lesbians and in a somewhat more abrupt manner, often during childhood or adolescence (Gonsiorek, 1995; Rosario et al., 1996). Because of their earlier awareness of same-gender sexual feelings and attractions, males are more likely to enter the identity formation process earlier than is typical for females. They often fantasize sexually about other males relatively early in their lives. Males are also more likely than females to enter the process of sexual identity formation on the basis of sexual stimulation, while at the same time adjusting to male stereotypical roles by dressing and acting in the traditional male manner. This is probably because there is less incentive for gay men to reject male gender roles because these roles are more highly valued in our culture than traditional female gender roles, which tend to be given a lower status (Cass, 1990).

Achieving a lesbian identity seems to be a somewhat more ambiguous and fluid process (Brown, 1995). Most lesbians fully embrace their same-gender identity only after involvement in an intense romantic relationship with another woman. Most have also had previous sexual involvements with men, which have proven to be less fulfilling than what they discover with other women (Rosario et al., 1996; Whitman, Daskalos, Sobolewski, & Padilla, 1998). There is a common myth that if gay men or lesbians were exposed to a happy heterosexual encounter with a good lover, they would realize "what they are missing."

However, same-gender sexual orientation is not caused by traumatic heterosexual experiences, nor is it changed by a pleasant heterosexual experience (Hall, 1999; Peters & Cantrell, 1991).

Lesbians are less likely to use sexual stimulation as a route into the same-gender sexual identity formation process. Instead, that process is more typically initiated when a woman falls in love with another woman. Again, because this often occurs later in life for women than for men, it is not uncommon for a woman in midlife to experience same-gender love for the first time. In the earlier stages of sexual identity formation, women are more likely to reject the passive, nurturing aspects of the traditional female sex role (Peplau, Spalding, Conley, & Veniegas, 2000). Sometimes, women begin adopting a lesbian identity as the result of their association with feminist groups and philosophies, which may have also put them in touch with loving feelings for other women that have previously been unrealized or unexplored (Whitam et al., 1998). Other times, a woman may first begin to have fantasies and feelings for other women only after having first experienced pleasurable sex with a woman. For these reasons, it may also be that the lesbian experience of sexual orientation may not fit the more sexual behavior-oriented Kinsey scale particularly well. Women generally seem to show less consistency than men over time in their sexual fantasies, emotional attractions, and behaviors (Nichols, 1990; Rosario et al., 1996).

Bisexual Identity Formation

All studies of human sexual behavior have indicated that substantial numbers of people have had at least some sexual experience with both females and males (Laumann, Gagnon et al., 1994). Slang terms such as "AC/DC" and "switch-hitter" have been applied to these individuals. It is likely that they are often identified as being gay or lesbian, although data from the NHSLS indicated that among people who had experienced sex with someone of their own gender, many did not consider themselves to be bisexual, gay, or lesbian.

Even people who have experienced a great deal of same-gender behavior, or who have had a fairly even mix of same-gender and opposite-gender sexual activity, tend not to define themselves as bisexual. They are more likely to see themselves as either gay or heterosexual, sometimes behaving bisexually because of social expectations or for other reasons. This may well reflect the difficulties that people face in forming a bisexual identity, which can be exacerbated by being tacitly told by both heterosexuals and gays or lesbians to make up their minds and make a choice (Garber, 1996). Because they often do not conform to a heterosexist culture, many bisexual people align themselves with the gay and lesbian communities for

Out, Proud, and Very Young

Cabot, a charming village of 1,000 in the heart of northern Vermont's dairy country, is known for its world-famous cheese, not is gay activists. That's one reason why Palmer Legare is so unusual. Earlier this year, he founded Cabot's first and only lesbian and gay group and circulated a petition supporting gay rights. Two weeks ago, he discussed gay issues with the state's Governor, Democrat Howard Dean. The other unusual thing about Legare is that he's just 17, and his group meets at Cabot High School.

Gina De Vries is only 14 and lives a continent away from Legare, in San Francisco, but perhaps not quite a world apart. Having come out to her parents and schoolmates at age 12, she now calls herself "a queer youth activist"—an identification she uses effortlessly, as though she were saying "ninth grader" or "aspiring poet," other terms that describe her. Articulate beyond her years, De Vries' work with a gay youth group led to her appointment to an advisory committee of the city's Human Rights Commission. She is, by more than a decade, the committee's youngest member. Jarringly precocious, she scheduled an interview with TIME for a Saturday morning, sparing enough time to attend a "transgender film festival" later that day. . . .

There is, of course, some evidence that homosexuality is something of a fad among young people. On a few college campuses, the term "gay until graduation" is used derisively to describe those who experiment with gay sex. Gay equality has nonetheless become a '90s version of Birkenstock environmentalism for many youths. Even in certain parts of suburbia, gay is becoming more than O.K.; it's cool.

But for most students taking baby steps from the closet, the decision to broadcast homosexual feelings is fraught with the possibility of negative, even violent reaction. The students often dislike lying to classmates but know the consequences of coming out can be dire. After Legare circulated a petition last spring urging Cabot to combat antigay bigotry, some students yelled "faggot" at him. An athlete in four sports, Legare didn't suffer the worst abuse because, he says, "I'm not stereotypically gay." But he was once shoved and kicked. For De Vries, harassment came in the form of vulgarities whispered behind her back.

Once Legare and De Vries spoke up, however, administrators responded. Legare persuaded 34 of Cabot High's 100 students to sign his petition, which led to faculty meetings and his discussion with Governor Dean in a gathering with other gay youths. Since school started, Legare says, he has heard "faggot" just once. Similarly, even at the Catholic school De Vries used to attend, several teachers applauded her for fighting anti-gay attitudes. She's now enrolled at a private school where everyone knows she's a lesbian.

Others aren't so lucky. According to a 1995 Massachusetts study, 62% of students identifying themselves as gay, lesbian or bisexual said they had been in a fight in the previous year, in contrast to 37% of all students. According to the Gay-Lesbian-Straight Networks' Jennings, administrators often do little to stop the violence. Some of the stories are harrowing. Jamie Nabozny, who in the early '90s attended high school in Ashland, Wis., says he was kicked in the stomach so many times he required surgery. A group of boys also urinated on him. Robert McDonald, 20, a former student at Jefferson Township High School in southern New Jersey, claims he was spat upon while he rode the bus and beaten up after track practice one day.

Gay bashing is nothing new, but what's unusual is that these students are holding their schools accountable. In 1996 Nabozny brought a groundbreaking federal lawsuit alleging that administrators hadn't done enough to protect him. A jury agreed and the school district settled for $900,000. Four similar lawsuits have followed—McDonald filed one in October [1997]—and the U.S. Department of Education issued guidelines in March [1997] barring certain kinds of antigay harassment. . . .

For the students themselves, coming out is as personal as it is political. After Christopher Humphreys, 18, came out at West Valley High in Hemet [California], he received death threats. But he held his ground and in May took a friend named Dan to the prom. His date forgot his boutonniere, and other guests hurled dirty looks, but in the end, he and Dan slow-danced to *The Lady in Red,* one of Humphreys' favorites.

John Cloud, "Out, Proud, and Very Young: Gay teenagers are emerging as never before. But these new activists still face the old prejudices," *Time,* December 8, 1997, pp. 82–83. Reprinted by permission.

support. Yet they may find a level of biphobia there, as they do in the heterosexual community, and are sometimes considered to be fence-sitters, traitors, and cop-outs politically. For these reasons, bisexuals may be less willing to disclose their sexual identities than lesbians or gays (Storr, 1999).

Some professionals have maintained that some individuals go through a period of bisexuality when they are in transition from heterosexual behavior and identity to same-gender sexual behavior and identity. There is evidence that many people define themselves as bisexual before eventually defining themselves as lesbian or gay (Rosario et al., 1996; Stokes et al., 1997). Arriving at a bisexual identity in this way is often associated with confusion, conflict, and ambivalence about sexual orientation. This has been called the *conflict model* of bisexual identity formation. In contrast, the *flexibility model* associates bisexual identity with personal growth, a wider range of possibilities for fulfillment, and flexibility in personal lifestyle. It may be that bisexual people respond emotionally and erotically to particular human qualities that are not exclusive to either females or males (Pope & Reynolds, 1991). The identity formation process for bisexuals may not follow a linear, stage-by-stage progression. Bisexual identity may well be more of an ongoing process, emerging from either a formerly heterosexual identity or a gay or lesbian identity. The process may include both self-acknowledgment and disclosure to others. However, bisexual identity formation reminds us again of how changeable people may be over time in their sexual inclinations, depending on many different factors in their lives. Because our society has been more reluctant to affirm bisexuality than gay or lesbian orientation either scientifically or socially, to take on a bisexual identity requires a higher tolerance for ambiguity than does acceptance of a gay or lesbian identity (Stokes et al., 1997; Storr, 1999).

■ Sexual Orientation and Society

Same-gender sexual behavior has always received attention from our social institutions. Judaism, Christianity, and Islam have each to some extent forbidden same-gender sexual activities as a matter of religious law (Murray & Roscoe, 1997). There are also some civil laws that prohibit or restrict sexual behavior between people of the same gender. Families frequently face crises when they discover that one of their members is lesbian, gay, or bisexual. Openly gay, lesbian, and bisexual persons have at times not been allowed to hold positions with the CIA, FBI, or U.S. military. Nevertheless, people with same-gender sexual orientation have

achieved a much more visible presence in North American society in recent years (Laumann, Gagnon et al., 1994). This section will deal briefly with the relationship between same-gender orientation and society.

Gay and Lesbian Culture

Data from the NHSLS showed that gay, lesbian, and bisexual persons are not evenly distributed geographically; in fact, they tend to live in large cities. Among the 12 largest cities in the United States, more than 9 percent of the males identified themselves as being gay. This is in comparison to between 3 and 4 percent of males in suburban locations, and about 1 percent in rural areas. Lesbians also seem somewhat more clustered in cities, but not to the same extent as gay males. Researchers believe that cities offer an environment where critical masses of same-gender-oriented individuals are likely to develop, providing more well-developed social networks and greater economic opportunity. It is clear that many lesbians, gays, and bisexuals move to cities in order to find a greater sense of community, although it may also be that people who grow up in cities are somewhat more able to identify same-gender tendencies in themselves and then ultimately self-identify as such (Michael et al., 1994).

Wherever the social atmosphere permits, and this is sometimes in suburban or rural areas as well as in cities, it is quite typical for some lesbians and gay males to group together as a community. The size and structure of such a community vary with many circumstances. Colleges and universities often have gay, lesbian, and bisexual organizations or course offerings (Croteau & Lark, 1995; Reisberg, 1998); cities and even some smaller communities have gay and lesbian organizations, meeting centers, bookstores, newspapers and magazines, political groups, health and counseling services, housing cooperatives, restaurants, and bars, sometimes located in specific sections or streets. Many people with a same-gender orientation, on the other hand, may never associate themselves with a gay/lesbian community. Even in cities with well-developed lesbian communities, many lesbians do not participate, preferring instead to associate with smaller groups of friends (Laumann, Gagnon et al., 1994). There has always been controversy about whether certain professions tend to be populated by more gay persons than others. One study has indicated that male professional dancers are more likely to be gay, whereas only a small percentage of female dancers were lesbians (Bailey & Oberschneider, 1997).

The gay and lesbian community has come to serve several important functions, one of which is bringing people together socially. The community also provides a supportive atmosphere in which they can share mutual concerns and experiences and be met with understanding. Another important function of the community is to provide a culture of language and ideology that accepts same-gender orientations and behaviors as valid lifestyles, identities, and forms of romantic and sexual expression (Bech, 1999; D'Augelli & Garnets, 1995). The concept of a village has emerged among some gay men and lesbian women, in which groups of people pool their resources, time, and energy to provide volunteer meals, home care, transportation, and emotional support to other gays, lesbians, and bisexuals who are suffering from chronic illness or life tragedies (Logan, 1997).

> *What are the existing policies on your campus regarding gay and lesbian couples living together in residence halls?*

On some college campuses, there has been controversy about the cohabitation of same-gender couples in residence halls. Opponents claim that having special living areas for gay or lesbian partners would create a kind of segregation that might aggravate tensions between campus groups, leading to possible harassment of, or violence against, same-gender couples. On the other side of the debate are those who feel that these residences permit people who have certain commonalities, such as sexual orientation, to share other important aspects of their culture more easily as well (Gose, 1997).

There is evidence that gay male relationships have their share of domestic violence, with one source estimating that between 330,000 and 650,000 gay men in the United States are battered or physically abused by their partners each year (Kurdek, 1995). Power imbalances within male-male relationships ultimately determine which partner is the victim and which the batterer. On the more positive side, researchers have reported that the income of same-gender households tends to be considerably higher than heterosexual households. The average annual income of gay male couples is over $50,000, and the average income for lesbian couples is over $45,000, as compared to an average income of just over $36,000 for heterosexual households.

One of the controversies in a society that has an increasing number of same-gender families is whether the schools should educate children about alternative lifestyles. Some schools have faced heated debates about the use of books in elementary school that portrayed households headed by two adults of the same gender. Proponents insist that children should understand the many alternative lifestyles and partnership arrangements that they may encounter, whereas others argue that such materials promote a lifestyle that they consider inappropriate or immoral (Patterson, 1995).

HIV/AIDS and the Gay Community

The disease that can result from sexual transmission of HIV, called acquired immunodeficiency syndrome or AIDS (see chapter 17), was first recognized in the United States among gay males who had shared sex with numerous partners. HIV infection is now clearly a problem for all populations, but because it was initially associated with gay men, that stigma has been difficult to shake (see Fig. 12.7). Early education efforts about safer sex were directed at helping gay men to change some sexual practices. In fact, these efforts proved to be effective because there has been a decline in unsafe sexual encounters among gay males. As with all populations, however, it is also true that even though gay men are aware of the risks of unprotected sex, they do not always protect themselves adequately (Carballo-Dieguez,

FIGURE 12.7 *HIV/AIDS and the Gay and Lesbian Community*

Although not exclusively a disease of gay men, HIV and AIDS have visibly affected the gay community in the United States. To call attention to the need for more research to combat AIDS, the Names Project sponsored the creation of the AIDS Quilt, a 150- by 450-foot memorial consisting of individual squares of cloth, each one representing someone who has died of AIDS.

Remien, Dolezal, & Wagner, 1999; Elwood & Williams, 1999). Alcohol and drug use seems to increase the likelihood of unsafe sexual practices among all groups of people, and various personality disorders can also play a role (Barrett, Bolan, & Douglas, 1998). Some gay males actually knowingly have unprotected anal sex with HIV-positive men, apparently in an attempt to become infected themselves (Gauthier & Forsyth, 1999). With an absence of continuing, positive reinforcement of safer sex practices, some gay and bisexual males may revert to more high-risk sexual activities (Appleby, Miller, & Rothspan, 1999).

HIV/AIDS education efforts have been burdened with homophobia and biphobia and with blaming, hostility, and misinformation about same-gender sexual behavior and AIDS (Miller, 1995). People have mistakenly feared that even casual social interaction with an infected person could be dangerous. In fact, it is those sexual activities in which bodily fluids are exchanged that are dangerous and should be avoided. This applies particularly to activities involving the exchange of semen. Anal intercourse has been shown to be a primary means of transmitting HIV. Wearing a condom can substantially reduce, but not eliminate, the risks. Many gay males are using condoms more consistently or choosing sexual activities that are less risky, such as mutual masturbation. In an apparent search for connectedness and sexual affirmation, others seem to be paying less attention to health and safety issues (Diaz, 1999).

Although the risks of woman-to-woman transfer of the virus are less certain, experts warn about the exchange of vaginal fluids. Probably the likelihood of transmission of HIV between women is less than between men, but women should also guard against contact involving internal bodily fluids until more is known about the phenomenon. There is evidence that substantial numbers of lesbian and bisexual women do take risks in having unprotected sex with potentially infected males (Norman, 1996). Rubber dental dams or sheets of latex cut from condoms or rubber gloves can be used to cover the vulva and vaginal opening during oral sexual contact, and rubber gloves or finger cots can be worn when inserting a finger into the vagina or anus.

HIV and AIDS have taken an emotional toll in the gay community. Many gay men have lost large numbers of friends to the disease and know others who are infected with HIV. For some, it has led to clinical depression, hypochondria, sexual dysfunction, or a profound sense of personal loss. The realization that there will be more losses to face, as well as fears for personal health, create a great deal of stress. For gay men who are not infected with HIV, there is sometimes a feeling of guilt about being able to enjoy jobs, relationships, and other aspects of life while witnessing the suffering and stresses of other gays who are infected (Goodkin et al., 1999). In the gay communities where HIV and AIDS have had a high impact, there is often a realiza-

tion that there is now and will continue to be much personal tragedy to be faced and accepted (see chapter 17, "The HIV/AIDS Crisis and Sexual Decisions").

Sexual Orientation and the Military

For many years, there was a ban on lesbians and gays serving in the U.S. military, and the enlistment forms asked about sexual orientation. During the 1990s, a "Don't ask, Don't tell" policy was put into effect. This ended the long-standing practice of questioning recruits about their sexual orientation. All forms of sexual behavior on military bases continued to be prohibited, except between married couples in their living quarters. However, people who openly declared themselves to be gay or lesbian could still be discharged from the military because their sexual orientation was still officially considered "incompatible with military service," whether or not they were known to be sexually active.

The U.S. armed forces continue to discharge over 1,000 people a year for reasons of same-gender sexual orientation or behavior, and in some cases there seems to have been a fairly active investigatory process to uncover people's sexual orientations. Even though the policy has been challenged in federal court as being discriminatory and declared unconstitutional for equating sexual orientation with misconduct, there still seems to be a degree of confusion about the relationship between the U.S. military and gay and lesbian individuals. In 1999, new training policies were initiated to prevent the harassment of individuals in the military who are thought to be gay, and politicians began claiming that the "Don't ask, Don't tell" policy was simply not working. The armed services in numerous other countries allow gay men and lesbians to serve, in spite of the homophobic attitudes and abuse these servicemen and women have sometimes encountered. Studies have tended to demonstrate that notions about the incompatibility of same-gender orientation and the military are simply unfounded (Herek, Jobe, & Carney, 1997).

Do you think your attitudes and feelings about same-gender orientation differ from those of your parents? Grandparents? Explain.

Marriage and Legalized Same-Gender Partnerships

Many people with a bisexual or sometimes even predominantly same-gender sexual orientation marry members of the other gender. In choosing heterosexual marriage, the individual may have decided to live as an exclusive heterosexual or may still expect to maintain some level of sexual activity with members of the same gender.

What are some social pressures exerted on same-gender couples with which heterosexual couples do not have to cope?

Bisexuals, lesbians, and gay men enter into heterosexual marriages for a variety of reasons, although it is clear that some do not become fully aware of their sexual inclinations until after they have married. Some see marriage as a way to achieve social respectability, as an escape from their sexual tendencies, or as a way to avoid the loneliness they may stereotypically associate with gay or lesbian lifestyles. Others want children and feel strong loving feelings toward their spouses. Yet these marriages often face sexual conflicts of various sorts. There are some couples who can deal with such conflicts honestly and with sensitivity, thus enriching their marriage. There are others who cannot handle such conflicts and can no longer continue their marriage.

Legalized partnerships between members of the same gender have received increasing attention in recent years, but despite the legal hurdles, many couples of the same gender have found ways of formalizing their partnerships (see Fig. 12.8). Some members of the clergy have sanctioned same-gender partnerships. The Metropolitan Community Church has branches in numerous cities, especially aimed at members of the gay and lesbian community. Unitarian-Universalist ministers, and some other members of the clergy, will also conduct unions of lesbian and gay male couples. Although holy union ceremonies are performed in these churches and in some others, they are still not legally binding in the United States.

Some governments have begun to reconsider the regulations with regard to same-gender couples. New York State's Court of Appeals has ruled that a long-term gay relationship could qualify as a family and could therefore be eligible for rent-control assistance in New York City. New York City, San Francisco, and some other cities maintain a registry of "lawfully recognized domestic partners" to allow couples of any gender to receive some of the same rights as married couples. Partners who register are given a certificate similar to a marriage certificate. Being registered as domestic partners entitles couples to such things as discounts on health club memberships and airline tickets, visitation rights in hospitals or prisons, and rent-control housing. A number of states have passed legislation that will allow them not to recognize the legality of marriages between members of the same gender, and the U.S. Congress passed the Defense of Marriage Act that permits states to do this. Conversely, the Vermont Supreme Court issued a ruling in 1999 that gay and lesbian couples in that state should enjoy all benefits and privileges afforded heterosexual couples who can marry. The Vermont

FIGURE 12.8 *Intimate Relationships*

It is erroneous to view gay and lesbian relationships strictly in terms of sexual behavior. A lesbian couple in Boston is shown here exchanging vows in a union ceremony to symbolize their shared relational commitment to one another.

FIGURE 12.9 *Parents of the Same Gender Raising Children*

Most children adapt readily to families that have parents of same-gender orientation. But not all communities accept their lifestyle, and some families struggle to be accepted. This lesbian couple is shown with their daughter.

Two Fathers

The Holden-Galluccio household in suburban Maywood, N.J., is unremarkable in most respects. There's oatmeal with bananas for breakfast, then preschool for Adam, 2, regular feedings for his one-year-old foster sister and bedtime stories when Dad returns from a long day at his telecommunications job. Dad No. 1, that is: John Holden and Michael Galluccio are a Ward and June Cleaver for the '90s, gay partners whose yearning for a traditional family of sorts—Dad, Dad and the kids—may have just transformed the battle for gay equality.

New Jersey became the first state to explicitly allow lesbian and gay couples to adopt children jointly, just as married couples do. The state agreed to change its policy after Holden, Galluccio and a group of 200 other gay couples brought a lawsuit arguing that New Jersey's no-gay-couples rule violated both state law and their right to equal protection. Previously, gays in the state could adopt only as individuals, forcing couples to undertake the lengthy and expensive adoption process twice. Now, all married couples, gay and straight, can adopt.

The new court-affirmed agreement, which resulted from settlement talks between state officials and the American Civil Liberties Union, contains some of the strongest gay-rights language ever approved by a state. While most pro-gay legislation has banned job and housing discrimination against gays, the adoption agreement enters more fraught territory. It not only says gay couples must be treated as full equals with straight couples but does so in the delicate arena of child rearing. . . .

To be sure, Holden and Galluccio aren't the first American gay partners to adopt jointly. Judges in other states, including California, have quietly allowed such adoptions in the past, according to the A.C.L.U.'s Michael Adams, the point man on the New Jersey case. And according to a 1996 report by the Lambda Legal Defense and Education Fund, a gay legal-rights group, courts in 21 states have approved so-called second-parent adoptions, or adoptions by the partners of individuals who have given birth to or who have already adopted a child. (This was the lengthy double-adoption procedure that Holden and Galluccio rejected.) Courts in Colorado and Wisconsin have disallowed such adoptions; New Hampshire and Florida prohibit any adoptions by gays, even individuals. There have been on rulings in the other states. . . .

The New Jersey case, says Arne Owens, a spokesman for the Christian Coalition, "will serve as a wake-up call to people, because what we see is another effort by the homosexual lobby to advance their agenda, and here they're doing it on the backs of children. Traditional family arrangements are proven to work." Gay groups countered with an American Psychological Association study concluding that children of gay parents turn out no better or worse than children of heterosexuals.

Last week's bickering meant little to Adam, the two-year-old who started it all. Born addicted to cocaine and suffering from a respiratory virus and a weak liver, his chief concern last week was trying to open some of the Christmas presents crammed under the tree. Having finalized his adoption . . ., Holden, 34, and Galluccio, 35, plan to adopt their foster daughter as well. Of Adam, Holden said last week, "he has two physical parents, two psychological parents, two emotional parents. The only things we weren't were his two legal parents." Now Adam has those as well.

John Cloud with reporting by Elizabeth Rudulph, New York, "A Different Fathers' Day: New Jersey gay couples can now adopt jointly. But will one state's move trigger a backlash in others?" *Time*, December 29, 1997–January 5, 1998, p. 106. Reprinted by permission.

legislature subsequently passed a law in 2000 confirming these civil rights, without actually providing for same-gender marriage.

Many major U.S. corporations and colleges have extended employee health and insurance benefits to the partners of gay and lesbian workers, including IBM, Walt Disney Co., American Express, Time Warner, and Apple Computer. Gay rights activists consider these to be major steps toward recognition of the legal rights of couples who are not heterosexual (R. Wilson, 1999). Most gay and lesbian rights organizations have been focusing their efforts less on changing the marriage laws and more toward the legal changes to ensure that all couples who have formed committed relationships—same-gender or heterosexual—have the same rights and privileges as those who have chosen to formalize their commitment in marriage.

Gay and Lesbian Families

Many gay, lesbian, and bisexual persons have children, either from heterosexual marriages or through deliberate efforts to conceive or adopt (see Fig. 12.9).

Research on lesbian mothers, gay fathers, and their children has only been taking place rather recently, and then usually because courts have been attempting to decide if lesbians and gay males could be considered fit parents. The research that is available confirms that lesbian and gay families can indeed provide as healthy an environment as any family structure and that the parenting skills of gays and lesbians are as adequate as those of heterosexuals (Buxton, 1999; Patterson, 1995). Studies have also confirmed that children raised by gay parents are no more likely to have a same-gender orientation themselves than are children raised by straight parents. The children also seem to have no greater likelihood of social or emotional difficulties (Golombok & Tasker, 1995). Legal precedents are still being set with regard to custody of children by gay and lesbian parents.

More and more same-gender couples are intentionally planning their own families. Lesbian couples have the options of artificial insemination or choosing a male partner for reproductive purposes. Gay male couples must either depend on adoption or surrogate motherhood (Cloud, 1998a). Because this type of family structure is a relatively recent origin, there is less research studies on the children. The studies that have been done would again suggest that there are really no particular differences between the children of lesbian and gay parents and other children raised in mixed-gender households (Golombok & Tasker, 1995). As society increasingly accepts same-gender partnerships, there has been an increasing visibility of gay and lesbian families with children who have made their way into the mainstream of social life (Kantrowitz, 1996).

Chapter Summary

1. Same-gender orientation and behavior have been viewed differently in various societies and historical periods.

2. The behavioral emphasis of much research into same-gender orientation has caused the affectional and relational aspects to be neglected.

3. There continues to be controversy between the biological essentialist point of view that same-gender orientation is somehow inborn, and the social constructionist perspective that its origins lie more in socioenvironmental factors.

4. Kinsey developed a scale demonstrating that there is no single pattern of same-gender sexual behavior but instead different degrees between the heterosexual (opposite-gender) and same-gender orientations. His bipolar scale is less useful today.

5. The incidence of same-gender orientation among humans has been an issue of controversy, and different studies have reached their conclusions in different ways. Some people may identify themselves as gay, lesbian, or bisexual even though their behaviors do not seem consistent with the labels, and vice versa.

6. The NHSLS data examined desire, behavior, and self-identification with regard to same-gender sexuality, finding differences in the incidence of each, with some overlap among the three factors. More people indicated having felt attraction to members of their own gender than had experienced same-gender sex.

7. People in urban areas are more likely to identify themselves as gay, lesbian, or bisexual.

8. Same-gender orientation and behavior are found across all cultures, typically in similar proportions.

9. Homophobia and biphobia can have negative effects on individuals with same-gender orientations and behaviors. Leading professional organizations no longer view same-gender sexual orientation within the framework of pathology, and many businesses are attempting to reach gay and lesbian markets.

10. Religions take various morally based positions regarding sexual orientation and behavior. Some religious groups have taken an accepting and positive view of same-gender orientation.

11. About a century ago, same-gender sexual orientation was medicalized as an illness or pathology, and that has determined many perceptions of gay men and lesbians since.

12. Psychodynamic theories focus on the different stages of psychosexual development in creating sexual orientation. The normal variant model has been evolving since the 1960s, and it sees same-gender orientation and behavior as one form of expression within a range of sexual orientations and behaviors. This represents a shift away from an illness-oriented model.

13. The Bell, Weinberg, and Hammersmith research represented one of the most thorough studies on the development of sexual orientation, and it

established a foundation on which more biologically based models could be built.

14. There is much speculation about the possible biological determinants of sexual orientation. Some researchers believe that hormonal factors during prenatal life may predispose people to particular sexual orientations.

15. Twin studies have suggested that same-gender orientation may be genetically linked and partly heritable. Researchers have identified a portion of the X chromosome that tends to show up in gay males. Studies of brain anatomy have demonstrated some measurable differences in brain structure among gay men, heterosexual men, and women.

16. The multifactorial model holds that there are shades of difference in sexual orientation, determined partly by biological factors that interact with socioenvironmental factors.

17. Among professionals who have viewed same-gender orientation and behavior within a model suggesting illness or abnormalcy, attempts have been made to change people to be more heterosexual. Current professional opinion is more oriented toward seeing this as one of several orientations that need no particular intervention or cure. Gay and lesbian people have no more psychological problems than heterosexual people.

18. Several theories have been advanced concerning the development of a lesbian, gay, or bisexual identity. Cass's theory proposes that sexual identity forms through a series of up to six stages. People proceed through these stages differently, and a person's perceptions of his or her sexual orientation may shift over time. This model may apply only to North American and European cultures because other cultures may not need a sense of sexual "identity" per se.

19. There are some differences in the ways gay males and lesbians progress through the stages of sexual identity formation. Gay males tend to enter the process earlier in life than lesbians. Lesbians are more likely to realize their identity after having an intense same-gender relationship.

20. Most cities have well-developed, same-gender communities that permit communication and support for lesbians, gay men, and bisexual people. This may be one reason why city populations have a higher proportion of people with same-gender sexual orientation.

21. AIDS was first identified in the United States among gay men, and HIV spread rapidly among the gay male population. This has led to increased homophobia and biphobia. Loss of friends and partners to AIDS has had a strong impact on the gay community.

22. The U.S. military continues to judge same-gender sexual orientation as incompatible with military service. The "Don't ask, Don't tell" policy has not markedly changed the fact that gays and lesbians are frequently discharged from the armed forces.

23. Many bisexuals, gays, and lesbians marry heterosexual partners and raise families. Their same-gender orientation may or may not be known by their partners. Gays and lesbians have been fighting for the right to have legalized partnerships with members of the same gender because they have financial and legal implications. Although same-gender marriage is not yet sanctioned by law, some churches will perform holy union ceremonies, and some cities register domestic partnerships.

24. Children raised by gay or lesbian parents do not seem to differ particularly from children raised by mixed-gender parents, nor are they more likely to develop same-gender sexual orientations themselves.

Focus on Health Questions

You will find in this section the kinds of questions that you may have concerning your own health and sexuality. The page references indicate where in the text the answer is located; the exact place is marked with the logo: **F⊕H**

1. Do gay and lesbian people actually love members of their own gender? 371

2. Are some people really bisexual, or are they just pretending to be so they won't have to think of themselves as lesbian or gay? 375, 388

3. Is homophobia all that bad? What negative effects does it actually produce? 378

4. If I acknowledge my same-gender orientation, will my church condemn me? 378

5. Do gay males come from families where the mother dominates the father? 379

6. Isn't same-gender sexual orientation a sign of psychological problems? 380

7. Is sexual orientation the result of hormones or genes? 381

8. Can therapy help people of same-gender orientation become heterosexual? 384

9. How can I know if I am gay? (or lesbian?) (or bisexual?) 386

10. Will it be easier for me to "come out" as a bisexual than it would be if I were gay? 388–390

11. Isn't HIV primarily a gay male infection? (See also chapter 17.) 391

12. Do scare tactics help gay males change their unsafe sex practices? 392

Annotated Readings

Adam, B.D., Duyvendak, J.W., & Krouwel, A. (Eds.). (1999). *The global emergence of gay and lesbian politics*. Philadelphia: Temple University Press. A collection of essays on gay rights movements in many different nations.

Alyson, S. (Ed.). (1995). *Young, gay, and proud*. Los Angeles: Alyson Publications. A personal and practical guide for young people who are facing issues of coming out and finding sources of support.

Atkins, D. (Ed.). (1998). *Looking queer: Body image and identity in lesbian, bisexual, gay and transgender communities*. Binghamton, NY: Haworth Press. Discusses the special body image issues faced by those in sexual minorities.

Berzon, B. (1996). *Setting them straight: You can do something about bigotry and homophobia*. New York: Penguin Books. Realistic and clear guidelines for responding to insensitivity and hostility regarding same-gender sexual orientation.

Faderman, L. (1999). *To believe in women: What lesbians have done for America—A history*. New York: Houghton Mifflin. Describes some of the most influential women in American history who happened to be lesbians.

Goss, R., & Strongheart, A. (1997). *Our families, our values*. Binghamton, NY: Haworth Press. An exploration of lesbian and gay relationships, marriage, and families with children.

Haeberle, E. J., & Gindorf, R. (Eds.). (1998). *Bisexualities: The ideology and practice of sexual contact with both men and women*. Dulles, VA: Cassell & Continuum. A collection of papers on the meanings of bisexuality.

Hamer, D., & Copeland, P. (1998). *Living with our genes: Why they matter more than you think*. New York: Doubleday. Two researchers offer a wide-ranging perspective on the influence of genetics.

Herek, G. M., Jobe, J. B., & Carney, R. M. (Eds.). (1997). *Out in force: Sexual orientation in the military*. Chicago: University of Chicago Press. A collection of essays by social scientists who believe that same-gender sexual orientation could be compatible with military life if the military would adapt to social change.

Isensee, R. (1997). *Reclaiming your life: A gay man's guide to love, self-acceptance, and trust*. Los Angeles: Alyson Books. A first-person account of how one can regain his footing after coming out.

LeVay, S. (1996). *Queer science: The use and abuse of research into homosexuality*. Cambridge, MA: MIT Press. A broad survey of various concepts and models of same-gender sexual orientation, including the most recent biological studies.

Murray, S. O. (1996). *American gay*. Chicago: University of Chicago Press. Traces the emergence and growth of openly lesbian and gay communities in North America.

Murray, S. O., & Roscoe, W. (1998). *Boy-wives and female husbands: Studies of African Homosexualities*. New York: St. Martin's Press. A perceptive cross-cultural study that focuses on the wide range of attitudes and behaviors in African societies.

Perez, R., DeBord, K. A., & Bieschke, K. J. (Eds.). (1999). *Handbook of counseling and psychotherapy with lesbian, gay, and bisexual clients*. Washington, DC: American Psychological Association. A helpful resource for professionals.

Rayside, D. (1998). *On the fringe: Gays and lesbians in politics*. Ithaca, NY: Cornell University Press. Examines typical controversies in the politics of gay rights in Britain, Canada, and the United States.

Swan, W. (1997). *Gay/lesbian/bisexual/transgender public policy issues*. Binghamton, NY: Haworth Press. Explores the political and cultural issues within education, the workplace, relationships, and the courts that relate to various sexual orientations and gender states.

Tasker, F. L., & Golombok, S. (1997). *Growing up in a lesbian family*. New York: Guilford Press. The most complete examination available of how children develop with same-gender couples as parents.

West, D.J., & Green, R. (Eds.). (1997). *Sociolegal control of homosexuality: A multi-nation comparison*. New York: Plenum. An examination of worldwide governmental and religious reactions to same-gender sexual orientation and behavior.

Windmeyer, S. L. (Ed.). (1998). *Out on fraternity row: Personal accounts of being gay in a college fraternity*. Los Angeles: Alyson Publications. A collection of first-person essays by 30 gay men who joined traditional fraternities while in college.

Chapter 13

The Spectrum of Human Sexual Behavior

Chapter Outline

Note: A selection of Focus on Health questions appears at the end of each chapter. Answers to these questions are indicated within the chapter by the symbol in the margin. **FOH**

> I never realized how diverse human beings are in their sexual interests and needs until I finished reading this chapter. I can hardly say that very many of these options interest me, but on the other hand, I do not necessarily condemn them either. Human sexuality can be a mysterious thing!
>
> —From a student's essay

We are living in a time unmatched for its diversity of sexual values and the openness with which various sexual lifestyles and behaviors may be expressed (Gamson, 1998). This also means that it is a period of confusion for many individuals and for society as a whole. Our culture has attempted to reconcile a plurality of value systems and sexual interests within a democratic political framework. A continuing fundamental question for such a society is how wide a latitude of sexual values and expressions can be permitted. Never has there been such freedom to accept and live out nearly any aspect of one's sexual individuality. At the same time, debate will continue over which behaviors will be accepted and tolerated and to what degree (Laws & O'Donohue, 1997; Skeen, 1999).

In the earlier days of sex research, Kinsey based his understandings of sexual expression on a concept of *total sexual outlet,* or what has been termed the "hydraulic theory" of sex. Kinsey saw orgasm as the outlet for people's sexual tensions, and he assumed that varying levels of sex drive in different individuals could be expressed through a range of sexual outlets. In this way, sexual expression was seen as following the principles of hydraulics, or movement of liquids. If one sexual outlet were blocked or unavailable, another outlet would simply be used. It was usually assumed, for example, that autoerotic activity, such as masturbation, compensated for a lack of partnered sex (Laumann, Gagnon et al., 1994).

This concept was closely related to the assumption that the sexual impulse was biologically driven, a need that required periodic satisfaction. Although there are sexual conditions that are innately pleasurable, such as genital stimulation or orgasm, there really does not seem to be an innate sex drive (Everaerd & Laan, 1995; Janssen & Everaerd, 1993). The most recent findings in sex research concerning the types of sexual behaviors in which people participate suggest that the specific content of any person's sexual conduct depends a great deal on the cultural meanings that have been attributed to various sexual behaviors as the result of social interactions (Gagnon, 1999; Simon, 1999). Also see chapter 6, p. 162.

Cross-cultural studies demonstrate that cultures impose many guidelines for how people should feel and act about sex. There is also increasing evidence that sexuality can be quite situational and changeable and that people's sexual needs and behaviors may be modified by day-to-day life circumstances. The research so far has not clarified how individualized preferences for seeking sexual arousal and orgasm are

formed or how they may be modified over time. As the previous chapter suggested, sexual orientation seems to develop from many influences, with environmental and learning factors being superimposed on whatever biological templates may be inborn (Hogben & Byrne, 1998; Sell, 1997).

Sex research has tended to ignore the distinction between *sexual performance,* which might be measured objectively by things such as numbers of orgasms or types of behavior, and the more *subjective erotic experience* going on in a person's mind and emotions. This latter experience includes *desire,* or the ways in which one might be emotionally drawn to people and things. Simply stated, sexual desire refers to interest in sexual activity, and that interest may be either for solitary or shared activity (Hill, 1997; Spector, Carey, & Steinberg, 1996). Studies have shown that desire and behavior are not necessarily connected. Sexual desire does not always lead to sexual activity, and people sometimes engage in sexual behavior even though they are not experiencing a sense of desire (Meston et al., 1998). Subjective eroticism also includes what has been termed *sensuosity* or *sensuality,* referring to the inner enjoyment of the whole sensual experience of sex, not just orgasm.

We know that the spectrum of human sexual preferences and behaviors is broad indeed, and the varieties of these activities have been subject to many medical, legal, and moral judgments. There are both personal and public political expressions that are made with our sexuality as well, as a symbol of power or control. Sexual behavior may also represent a form of self-expression or a means of asserting one's identity. Some researchers have reminded us that definitions of sexual "deviance" should always be seen as relative to social norms and in a constant state of flux because today's deviance may well be tomorrow's norm (Laws & O'Donohue, 1997).

Although some professionals still use words such as "aberrant," "deviant," "abnormal," and "perverse" to describe some sexual preferences and acts, two other terms have gained acceptance recently. The term "variant" implies that a particular sexual phenomenon varies from what is considered typical or that it exists in addition to those more mainstream sexual behaviors. The term "paraphilia" carries with it the same connotations, but it is more often used to describe sexual preferences and behaviors that are viewed within a framework that considers them to be pathological or antisocial. This chapter deals with sexual preferences and behaviors that are not as common as masturbation or heterosexual and same-gender sexual activity. We will look at variations that are part of the extensive mix of feelings, expressions, and activities from which components of any person's sexual individuality can be drawn. Studies of sexual behavior continue to demonstrate that even among what would be considered "normal" samples of people, there is a wide range of sexual stimuli and sexual experiences, some of which would even be considered illegal (Laws & O'Donohue, 1997; Skeen, 1999).

Sexologists who have studied paraphilias, or unconventional sexual variations, have established several criteria for determining when an attraction or behavior may represent a problem for the individual. For example, the sexual attraction must be a long-standing, highly arousing preoccupation. The person must feel a need to act on the sexual fantasy and be unable to have a "conventional" sexual or loving relationship. To a degree, there must be a problem with self-regulation of behavior; in other words, there must be a gap between how the individual wishes to behave and how he or she actually chooses to behave. It has been suggested that the paraphilias are frequently confused with compulsive behavior or the acting-out of inner conflicts (Cooper, 1998; Krivacska & Money, 1994; McDougall, 1995).

Varying Degrees of Sexual Interest and Activity

It is evident that different people have different degrees of interest in sex, pursue sexual activity with different amounts of energy, and participate in sex with varying frequencies. Some people report thinking about sex and being interested in sexual matters several times each day, whereas others report that they seldom or never think about sex (Michael et al., 1994). It is logical to conclude that the more interested one is in sex, the more one becomes sexually aroused and seeks sexual gratification. Yet there are some individuals who feel guilty or anxious about their sexual preferences and interests; therefore, they tend to engage in sexual activity as seldom as possible. Others are influenced by social networks to behave in certain ways. There are still others who have relatively low interest levels in sex but feel obligated by social or personal pressures to participate in a great deal of sexual behavior. Therefore, levels of sexual activity do not necessarily correlate with levels of sexual desire (Hendrick & Hendrick, 1999; Sprecher, 1998).

Consistently responding positively to sexual cues has been called **erotophilia,** whereas responding negatively has been termed **erotophobia** (Fisher, Byrne, White, & Kelley, 1988). The degree to which

any individual is erotophilic or erotophobic obviously depends on a great many factors, including learning during childhood and adolescence (Hogben & Byrne, 1998). Erotophilia-erotophobia affects many dimensions of a person's sexual responses. Erotophobic individuals tend to react negatively to sexual images, to have little interest in sexual activities, to be less likely to use contraceptives during intercourse, and to experience more guilt about sexual behaviors and fantasies.

Some individuals possess a very high level of sexual desire, **hypersexuality,** whereas others have an abnormally low level of sexual interest, **hyposexuality.** These might also be considered the extremes on the bipolar scale of erotophilia and erotophobia. And although there are physical and emotional factors that can cause a drop in sexual interest and activities, some people appear to have been fundamentally asexual throughout their lives. Most people, of course, tend to fall somewhere in the middle of the spectrum. Hypersexuality once seemed to generate more attention than hyposexuality; it was the extremely sexually active person whom society seemed to have the most trouble understanding and accepting (Kafka, 1997b). However, media attention has now focused more on low sexual desire and how it might be overcome. In a society that has placed such a high premium on sexual performance and a high level of interest in sex, such a shift in attitudes is not surprising (Hill & Preston, 1996).

Define promiscuity as you perceive it, and then describe any social or personal biases that you may bring to your definition.

Promiscuity is a term that is applied to the behavior of those who have sexual contact with several different partners on a relatively emotionally uninvolved, casual basis. It is an emotionally and morally loaded label that has also been applied to those who have had more than one sexual partner. Because of the double standard of our society, it is more often ap-

---

erotophilia (air-aht-oh-FEEL-i-ah): consistent positive responding to sexual cues.

erotophobia (air-aht-oh-FOBE-i-ah): consistent negative responding to sexual cues.

hypersexuality: unusually high level of interest in and drive for sex.

hyposexuality: an especially low level of sexual interest and drive.

promiscuity (prah-mis-KIU-i-tee): sharing casual sexual activity with many different partners.

plied negatively to women than to men. Although promiscuous men are often praised and admired for their impressive "records," promiscuous women tend to suffer more guilt, self-abasement, and social ostracism. It seems likely from clinical evidence that some people simply enjoy sex with a variety of partners, perhaps for a limited period during their lives, and prefer to avoid emotional involvements for various reasons. If the individual approaches these encounters in a responsible, nonexploitative manner, taking appropriate steps to reduce the risks of transmitting disease, and emerges from them without negative feelings or inner conflict, there is no particular reason to judge the behavior problematic (Anderson & Struckman-Johnson, 1998).

Sometimes, however, having multiple sex partners may be motivated by more unhealthy factors. These include unsatisfactory personal relationships, antagonism toward members of the opposite sex, or lack of self-respect. Individuals may feel a need to prove themselves—men who must live up to the macho ideal of having a long list of sexual "conquests," women who use sex to experience a sense of power or control in their lives. A high level of sexual activity may become compulsive in some people. Compulsive sexual behavior sometimes represents a response to some stressful situation such as separation from parents upon entering college, the onset of early menopause, the experience of a significant loss, or some other traumatic event. Multiple sexual contacts may also represent a means of escape, compensation, or retaliation for a troubled partnership or unhappy family. Obviously, these motivations have the potential for creating serious stresses and further problems for the individual and his or her partners (Cooper, 1998; Kafka, 1997b).

The more compulsive form of hypersexuality, purportedly characterized by uncontrollable sexual drives as part of various mental illnesses, is known as **erotomania.** This condition has sometimes been called **nymphomania** in females and **satyriasis** in males. Again, the double standard seems to generate a far greater interest in women's compulsive sexual needs than in men's. "Nymphomaniac" is often used rather lightly and applied mistakenly to women who show any level of interest in sex. Yet "nymphomania" is actually difficult to define and has been subjected to a great deal of interpretation rooted in prejudice, double standards, and male chauvinism (Groneman, 1994, 1995). The term is so vague and outmoded, it should be dropped altogether. Erotomania and other conditions of uncontrollable sexual desire (discussed in chapter 15, "Sexual Coercion, Rape, and Abuse,") are extremely rare; erotomania is probably most often a misdiagnosed form of compulsive sexual behavior (Nesca, Dalby, & Baskerville, 1999). Very few people seek help for excessive sexual desire, and even for

those who do, it is doubtful if many of those cases could truly be classified as erotomania.

People often worry about having too much or too little sexual desire and activity, especially if their degree of interest or activity differs significantly from that of a continuing sexual partner. The individual with low levels of sexual desire and behavior is often made to feel dull and uninteresting, or as if there must be something wrong with him or her. Available evidence would suggest that wide variations in sexual desire and activity are a part of the normal human sexual continuum. There is nothing inherently dangerous or harmful in thinking about sex and having sexual activity very often, and there is no harm or danger, per se, in a lack of sexual interest or activity (Hogben & Byrne, 1998; Kafka, 1997b).

Celibacy as a Choice

In a culture that places such a high premium on sexual gratification and enjoyment, **celibacy,** or not engaging in any kind of partnership sex, might be viewed with suspicion and surprise. Celibacy can be the result of life circumstances, such as imprisonment or the death of a partner; it may represent normal **asexuality,** characterized by a very low interest in sex; or it may be a conscious choice.

Erotophobic individuals may be celibate because of guilt or fear about sexual issues. The term "asexuality" is sometimes used in reference to celibate individuals, although it can be misconstrued as suggesting that they have no sexual interest or arousal, which is usually not the case. The National Health and Social Life Survey (NHSLS) did find that 4 percent of men and 14 percent of women reported rarely or never thinking about sex. Fourteen percent of the men and 10 percent of the women in the survey reported that they had not had a sexual partner in the previous year (Laumann, Gagnon et al., 1994). A survey of college students found that 20 percent of them indicated they were still virgins (Elliott & Brantley, 1997).

---

erotomania (air-aht-oh-MAY-nee-ah): a very rare form of mental illness characterized by a highly compulsive need for sex.

nymphomania (nim-fa-MAY-nee-a): a term sometimes used to describe erotomania in women.

satyriasis (sate-a-RYE-a-sus): a term sometimes used to describe erotomania in men.

celibacy (SELL-a-ba-see): choosing not to share sexual activity with others.

asexuality: a condition characterized by a low interest in sex.

Some priests and nuns vow to be celibate because their church requires it. Other people make such a choice because of their personal values. An increasing number of young to middle-aged adults in Western culture are choosing to be celibate. Some of these individuals are reacting to having tried various sexual lifestyles that turned out to be unfulfilling or destructive or are looking for alternatives to the pressures brought about by the sexual revolution. They have sometimes found that the intensity of sex created tensions in their relationships. Concern over the spread of HIV has also made celibacy seem to be a less risky, healthier, and more acceptable choice of lifestyle for some individuals (Sprecher & Regan, 1996).

Celibacy is not necessarily a symptom of a problem or of feelings of inadequacy. Some marriages become sexless eventually, but this is not necessarily a difficulty. Often a deep affection and respect between the partners provide adequate fulfillment for the couple, and sex is not a necessary component. It is important to be reminded that sexuality is far more than an interaction of sex organs. Caressing, kissing, and other forms of physical sharing that are not overtly sexual may be deeply satisfying to some couples.

The Variability of Sexual Individuality

Statistical evidence highlights an interesting fact about human sexuality: Men seem more prone to participating in atypical sexual activities and straying more from established societal sexual norms and standards than do women. All available statistics on the frequency of various nonstandard forms of sexual orientation and behavior show them to be more common in men than in women.

Attempts have been made to explain this by both social and biological theories. It has been proposed that our culture has traditionally been more discouraging of female sexual expression and therefore has tended to discourage women from getting in touch with their sexuality. For whatever social or political reason, a double standard with regard to sexual behavior has persisted in our culture. It has been permissible, even expected, for men to be more sexually active than women. Such an attitude offers one explanation for less involvement on the part of women in varied sexual practices, but it may not be the only one (Sprecher & Regan, 1996). Research shows that although women very much believe that a double standard still exists in North American culture, they tend personally not to support double standard beliefs (Milhausen & Herold, 1999).

It has also been suggested that there may be some inborn biological propensities that cause male sexual behavior to exhibit greater diversity, and biologically

based hypotheses have begun to receive higher levels of acceptance and scientific verification. It has been proposed that because of prenatal developmental differences, males become more responsive than females to visual stimuli in learning sexual cues. Men may establish images of erotic arousal in response to early life experiences at certain critical periods of development. If the visual image does indeed play a larger role in sexual arousal in males, they would be far more easily influenced by diverse and variable kinds of visual learning than females. Only further research will provide the explanation for this sexually differentiated phenomenon (Hogben & Byrne, 1998).

■ Transgender Behaviors

In chapter 5, theories concerning the development of gender identity and gender role were discussed, and transgender, sometimes called cross-gender, identities were introduced. In this section, various transgender behaviors and lifestyles are presented, demonstrating the many ways in which humans express their transgenderism.

Before reading the section on transvestism, describe what you would consider a "typical" transvestite.

Cross-Dressing: Transvestism

The definitions of cross-dressing behavior are variable. The term "transvestite" has been applied to anyone who cross-dresses, or wears clothes of the opposite sex, for any reason. It has also been applied to individuals who feel driven to cross-dress, sometimes in association with sexual arousal. Many cross-dressers feel a greater sense of relaxation in escaping their usual gender roles. Cross-dressing is certainly not a new phenomenon; it has been identified in most cultures from earliest recorded history through the Greco-Roman, Judeo-Christian-Muslim, and Renaissance periods (Bullough & Bullough, 1997a). Cross-dressing is found in heterosexual people, but it is also found in people with a same-gender sexual orientation, bisexuals, and people with low levels of any sexual attraction or desire, which together represent a very diverse group (Docter & Prince, 1997). Cross-dressed males are sometimes said to be "in drag." (Refer to chapter 5, p. 116, for discussion of examples of cross-dressing from various cultures.) Transvestites are generally productive citizens whose preferences for gender identity expression do not harm others. Although personal concerns and relational problems associated with the practice may lead transvestites to therapy, many professionals feel that transvestism, per se, does not require any intervention or treatment.

CROSS-CULTURAL PERSPECTIVE
Temple Ceremony Briefly Frees Eunuchs from Rejection and Persecution in India

Koovagam, India—For a brief moment, 10,000 eunuchs were transformed from outcasts to exuberant newlyweds.

Under a full moon, dressed in their finest saris and jewelry, the eunuchs entered a temple to marry Aravan, their mythological demigod.

On Wednesday morning, they pulled a wooden cart bearing a 20-foot effigy of their new husband down dirt roads, singing, dancing and smashing open coconuts. At the end of the ceremony, when Aravan was decapitated, they beat their chests in mourning.

About 50,000 people, including 10,000 eunuchs, attended the annual festival, according to police estimates.

The word "eunuch" refers in India not only to castrated men, but also to transvestites and transsexuals.

According to the Indian epic Mahabharata, Aravan is sacrificed to increase his family's chance of a victory in battle. Before being decapitated, he wants to marry. When no woman accepts him, the Hindu god Krishna turns himself into a woman, marries Aravan and has sex with him.

For the last 10 years, thousands of eunuchs have flocked to Koovagam in the southern state of Tamil Nadu for the ceremony. Many come from distant cities such as Bombay and New Delhi, where they fled years ago from villages that rejected them.

In this male-dominated nation where homosexuality is taboo, many gay men join urban eunuch clans, get themselves castrated, and live as women. There are an estimated 200,000 eunuchs in India.

None live in Koovagam, a rural village that allows the festival to cash in on the crowds and, more important, to win good luck from Aravan.

"This is a great festival for us," said Banu, a 28-year-old man with long black hair, who wore an orange sari, dark make-up, silver ear rings, a pink necklace and nail polish.

"We can dress up as eunuchs without any inhibitions or criticism."

Banu said he was rejected by his parents at age 12 and lives in a clan in a small town. When he earns enough money, he plans to join a bigger clan in Bombay.

Hundreds of years ago, eunuchs guarded the harems and sacred relics of India's Muslim rulers, or served as court entertainers.

While they were once common across Europe and Asia, their heyday was in India during the Mogul empire from 1550 to 1750, where some became chamberlains, governors and generals.

That system collapsed when the British colonized India and dismissed eunuchs as freaks. Most survive in cities by selling good luck or working as prostitutes.

—Watertown (N.Y.) Daily Times, April 28, 1994

One form of transvestism represents a kind of fetishism in which a person is sexually attracted to some object of clothing usually worn by the opposite sex (see p. 412) (Ekins, 1997). For example, a male may become sexually aroused by viewing and touching various objects of women's underwear. He may find that it is even more exciting to actually wear the garments, usually as an accompaniment to masturbation or other sexual activity. The heterosexual male transvestite may become aroused by completely dressing up in women's attire and makeup and adopting feminine mannerisms (see Fig. 13.1). Sometimes, there is only minimal sexual arousal connected with the activity, or the sexual arousal eventually fades. Individuals often continue to cross-dress because it makes them feel more relaxed and emotionally open. Usually these behaviors begin in childhood and become well established by adolescence. Sometimes they disappear by adulthood, but most often they do not (Docter & Prince, 1997; Zucker, Bradley, & Sullivan, 1993).

There are no reliable statistics on the incidence of cross-dressing phenomena, but they are probably more common than generally believed. A survey of sexual behavior indicated that 6 percent of men and 3 percent of women had personal experience with cross-dressing (Janus & Janus, 1993). The *Details* magazine survey of U.S. college students found that 5 percent of the males and 3 percent of the females indicated that they had cross-dressed (Elliott & Brantley, 1997). Although the evidence suggests that cross-dressing is more common in males, there are studies of women who have an erotic attachment to men's garments (Bullough & Bullough, 1997). At least for the limited number of female examples available, the drive toward cross-dressing seems less demanding than it typically is for male transvestites. Again, there are

FIGURE 13.1 *Transvestism*

Those who dress in clothes of the opposite sex seem to derive sexual pleasure from doing so. Anthropologist Robert Monroe has noted that transvestism occurs more frequently in cultures where the male assumes more of the economic burden than does the female.

plausible sociological explanations for a lower incidence of transvestism in women. Western society permits a wider range of fashion for women than for men. There are few, if any, male outfits that now would be deemed inappropriate for a woman. Conversely, men are quite specifically restricted from wearing most articles of female attire unless they are willing to risk ostracization and name-calling. This establishes a very different social context for male cross-dressing, one demanding privacy and often subterfuge (Wysocki, 1993).

Some male transvestites participate in an underground subculture. There are organizations and magazines designed for men who experience a need to wear women's clothing to relieve tension and anxiety, and there are occasional regional gatherings for such individuals, with meetings on fashion and makeup techniques. The majority of the participants are heterosexuals, although there may be a higher proportion of gay and bisexual transvestites than has generally been believed (Bullough & Bullough, 1997). A study of 1,032 male cross-dressers found that 87 percent described themselves as heterosexual. All but 17 percent had been married, and 60 percent were married at the time of the study (Docter & Prince, 1997). Some hide their transvestism from their wives and cross-dress away from home; some inform their wives of the practice. The limited clinical evidence available indicates that some wives are able to accept and integrate their husbands' cross-dressing behaviors into their lives. One organization for transvestite males indicates that about 50 percent of the participants' wives are quite accepting and understanding (Beecroft, 1992).

There have been ongoing studies of boys ranging in age from 4 years through adolescence who have shown a preference for dressing in girls' clothing. When denied access to such garments, these boys will even fashion their own dresses from blankets, T-shirts, and other materials. They have also tended to assume female roles during play and exhibit distinctly feminine mannerisms. It is as yet impossible to predict which of these behaviors represent simple play activity and which are expressions of gender identity disorders (Zucker, Bradley, & Sullivan, 1993).

Transgender Lifestyles

Some people remain in their cross-dressed roles for days or even months at a time, depending on their life situations, often becoming comfortable with sustaining this identity. Transgendered individuals may also maintain separate lives that are more consistent with their anatomical gender for varying periods of time (Denny, 1999).

An interesting historical example is found in the English writer William Sharp, who lived from 1855 to 1905. Over a period of some years, he created for himself the personality of a woman whom he called Fiona MacLeod. He spent increasing proportions of time as Fiona, who emerged as a leading writer in the Scottish Celtic literary movement. In his later years, very little of the male William Sharp identity was left (Bullough & Bullough, 1997).

There is a spectrum of intensities among transgender persons that often reflects the degree of dissatisfaction they may experience with regard to their anatomy. Some transgenderists are very comfortable with their bodies and are content to cross-dress and adopt mannerisms of the other gender. However, high-intensity transsexuals feel a strong enough level of discomfort or disgust with their bodies to lead them to prefer not to have the sexual anatomy with which they were born (Devor, 1997).

Sex Reassignment for Transsexuals

Transsexuals, because of feeling trapped in the wrongly sexed body and wishing for a different anatomy, may be troubled and unhappy. Psychotherapy alone has not proven to be especially effective with transsexuals, but they need opportunities to explore their personal conflicts and options for dealing with their gender identity (Money, 1994; Rehman, Lazer, Benet, Schaefer, & Melman, 1999). One recognized form of rehabilitative therapy has been the hormonal and surgical transformation of the individual's external features into a form resembling the anatomy of the other sex. As one might expect, this process of sex reassignment has been fraught with clinical and ethical complications (see Fig. 13.2). First has been the

CASE STUDY

Vincent: Living a Transgender Identity

Thinking that one of the students on his floor "had problems," a residence hall adviser (RA) referred the student to the counseling center. Vincent arrived for his appointment expressing skepticism about the need for him to be there, but he was happy to explain the lifestyle issues that had led the RA to refer him. He explained that he considered himself to be a transgenderist and resented having to be categorized as one sex or the other. He knew that anatomically he was fully male, and he had no intentions of changing that. In fact, he said that he was very satisfied with his male body most of the time.

However, Vincent said that since he had been quite young, he had also come to value what he called his "feminine side." To him, this was made up of the soft, gentle, and sensitive aspects of his personality that felt very comfortable to him. The counselor discussed the fact that many men considered these qualities to be an integral part of their masculinity, and Vincent responded by saying that although he understood this for others, the masculine and feminine sides that he experienced seemed quite distinct. He told the counselor that he sometimes

preferred to dress in women's clothes and use a female name. He said that he had tried to do this as discreetly as possible, but that others on his floor may have once noticed some women's clothes in his closet. Although he was not anxious to incur the wrath of anyone who might consider him somehow odd, he also seemed to have a rather strong resolve not to hide his transgenderism with undue vigor. As he put it: "It's time for people to wake up to the fact that not everybody fits the same mold."

Vincent remained at the college, and he would occasionally surprise or shock people by wearing some article of female attire in a public setting. Some people on the campus openly expressed their distaste for these practices, feeling that he was being too flagrant with his propensities. He occasionally heard himself being called names, but he persisted in what he felt were valid educational efforts. He also continued to talk with the counselor from time to time, but he basically seemed comfortable with the lifestyle that apparently fit him best. He also made many friends and was an active participant in campus activities.

difficulty of diagnosing the high-intensity transsexual, as distinguished from a frustrated gay male or lesbian, from a lower-intensity transgenderist whose desire to change sex will eventually wane, or from the schizophrenic who has deeper personality disturbances (Bodlund & Kullgren, 1996). A study of transsexuals in the process of sex reassignment has found that they are generally not prone to other major psychiatric disorders (Cole, O'Boyle, Emory, & Meyer, 1997).

Once diagnosed as a transsexual, the individual must face the huge medical expenses of reassignment, possibly reaching $35,000 or more. Most health insurance companies consider such processes elective and cosmetic and do not cover them. Sometimes if a physician such as a psychiatrist is willing to indicate that reassignment is necessary to the person's future well-being, health insurance will cover part of the costs.

Some unethical physicians will agree to treat anyone desiring reassignment, so long as the money is paid up front. But anyone who desires advice about these matters should go to a medical center that specializes in such treatments. In North America, most gender clinics are designed to diagnose and treat gender identity disorders, as well as to offer sex reassignment procedures. Typically, an individual is given a psychiatric evaluation, a series of psychological tests,

and counseling. Then, if sex reassignment emerges as the most reasonable course of treatment, it begins with a trial period, a real-life test lasting up to 2 years. Usually, it is during this time that the person dresses and lives as a member of the desired sex, receiving adjustment counseling and appropriate legal advice concerning a name change, a new birth certificate, and a new driver's license (Weitz & Osburg, 1996).

It is also during the real-life test that hormonal treatment begins. The changes brought about by hormone therapy, with the exception of a deepened voice in the female-to-male transsexual, are reversible should a decision be made not to continue the reassignment process. Female hormones administered to men cause breast enlargement and a feminine redistribution of fat. Although the growth of facial and body hair may be somewhat retarded, it is necessary to remove permanently unwanted beard and body hairs by electrolysis. Hormonal masculinization of the female, in addition to deepening the voice, suppresses menstruation and promotes growth of some facial and body hair. If the real-life test continues to confirm the individual's resolve to change sex, the surgical procedures are begun. As low dosages of hormones as possible are recommended because there can be longer term complications of hormonal therapy (Futterweit, 1998; Schlatterer et al., 1998).

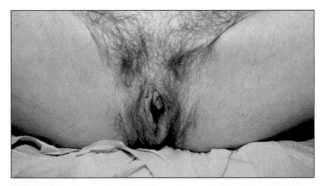

🖎 **FIGURE 13.3**   *Post-surgical male-to-female transsexual*

Following surgical procedures to construct a vulva and vagina from sensitive penile and scrotal tissues, this individual's external genitals are hardly distinguishable from those of any woman.

called *phalloplasty.* An artificial penis is created over several operations with skin taken from other parts of the body. A scrotum is also constructed, using tissue from the labia that is stretched by inserting increasingly larger silicon balls (see Fig. 13.5). The clitoris is usually left intact beneath the new penis and is still sensitive to sexual arousal. Most female-to-male transsexuals report an increase in orgasmic capacity following surgery (Lief & Hubschman, 1993). There are several techniques being tried to simulate penile erection, ranging from the insertion of a plastic rod into a special canal within the constructed penis to surgical implantation of a special hydraulic system. Sometimes a canal is created through the middle of the penis so that it may be used for urination. Of course, postsurgical transsexuals cannot reproduce, ejaculate, or menstruate (Devor, 1997).

🖎 **FIGURE 13.2**   *Transsexualism*

Transsexuals are people who are one sex biologically but who feel an identity with the opposite sex. Renée Richards faced many legal battles when she attempted to compete as a female tennis player after male-to-female surgery in the 1970s.

Although a detailed description of sex-change surgery is beyond the scope of this text, a summary follows. In male-to-female surgery, the testes are removed, and an artificial vagina and labia are constructed from the sensitive skin of the penis and scrotum (see Fig. 13.3). Breasts are fashioned through the use of mammary implants (see Fig. 13.4). Following reassignment, male-to-female transsexuals usually report some decline in their orgasmic capacities, but they still enjoy their sexual activities (Kesteren et al., 1996; Lief & Hubschman, 1993).

In female-to-male surgery, the breasts, uterus, and ovaries are first removed. There are two options for genital surgery. *Metoidioplasty* is a simpler and less expensive one-step surgery. The clitoris, which has been enlarged somewhat by testosterone therapy, is formed into a small penis, and the labia are formed to look like a small scrotum. Because the penis resulting from metoidioplasty is too small for penetrative sexual activity, most high-intensity female-to-male transsexuals choose the more complex and expensive procedure

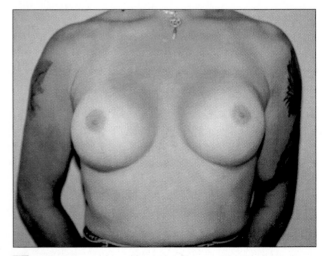

🖎 **FIGURE 13.4**   *Surgically Constructed Breasts*

In male-to-female transsexual surgery, the breasts may respond to hormone treatment, but, if not, they are generally augmented with implants.

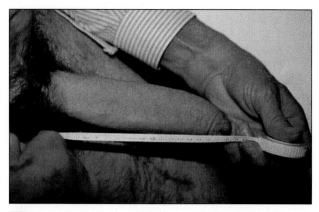

FIGURE 13.5 *Surgically Constructed Penis*

In female-to-male phalloplasty, the penis is constructed from forearm tissue or from labial and perineal tissue. The penis is not capable of erection in response to sexual arousal, but several inflatable devices are available that produce an erection, as shown in this photograph.

Because not all people are fully satisfied with the results of their sex reassignment, there has been controversy at times over such expensive and risky medical procedures. The standard medical protocol has been that surgical intervention should be restricted to high-intensity transsexuals meeting highly selective criteria. There is clinical evidence and research suggesting that sex reassignment can indeed lead to improved psychological and social adjustment for many individuals. Reviews of the world literature on this surgery indicated only a 10 to 15 percent failure rate with patients. In general, people seem subjectively satisfied with their sex reassignments. Dissatisfaction with the results was more common as the age of patients increased, and in cases where the person was not a carefully diagnosed, highly motivated transsexual (Bodlund & Kullgren, 1996; Rakic, Starcevic, Maric, & Kelin, 1996; Rehman et al., 1999). As with many newer medical treatments, issues of prognosis, cost effectiveness, and ethics continue to be debated.

Transgender Identity and Sexual Orientation

One of the most interesting factors relating to transgenderism is the fact that some transsexuals, after changing their anatomical sex, are sexually attracted to members of their "new" gender. Studies of postsurgical female-to-male transsexuals have found that significant proportions of them are attracted to other men (Devor, 1997). This information is often confusing because conventional wisdom assumes that people who would go through the trouble of changing their sex would

CASE STUDY

Marilyn: Exploring Sex Reassignment

At 17, Marilyn had talked with her high school counselor about wanting to change her sex. The counselor referred her to a therapist who specialized in sexual matters. Marilyn explained to the therapist that she had always felt more like a boy inside than a girl. In fact, she came dressed to the session in a manner that made her appear quite masculine. She wore jeans, a loose-fitting flannel shirt, and an athletic jacket, with a hat covering her short hair. After seeing a television talk show when she was 13 that featured transsexuals, she had begun to believe that this label indeed fitted her too.

The history that she described supported that self-diagnosis. She had always been interested in traditionally male activities and presently had a girlfriend with whom she was sexually involved. However, she also expressed frustration with the assumption that she was a lesbian, because she said she would much prefer to be a male in her sexual interactions. She had adopted her initials M.J. as her nickname, and preferred that her friends call her "Mike." She had negative feelings about her breasts and genitals, and she indicated a preference for having a penis. She had done some reading about the sex reassignment processes and was aware that they would require a fair amount of money. She already had a job and was attempting to save funds for the future. Her mother, a single parent, had been relatively uninvolved in her upbringing and expressed support for whatever direction M.J. wished to take.

The therapist put her in touch with some organizations and clinics that specialized in supportive help for transsexuals and that carried out sex reassignment procedures. It was explained to her that she would have to be carefully tested to confirm that she was a good candidate for reassignment and that the entire process might well take several years. Her resolve to pursue this direction seemed strong, and she continued to see the therapist over a period of months as she began to establish preliminary contacts with the nearest gender identity clinic. About a year after her initial session with the therapist, M.J. was beginning the evaluative process that would determine if this particular clinic would consider initiating the legal and medical procedures that would lead to her reassignment as a male.

surely want to be able to have sex with members of what has become the other gender. In fact, this information serves as a significant reminder that gender identity and sexual orientation may well be independent aspects of human sexuality (Ekins, 1997). Transsexuals who have changed their sex may be heterosexual, gay, lesbian, or bisexual in their transformed bodies (Bockting, 1999; Denny, 1999). There are cases in which sexual orientation seems to have changed following sex reassignment. Some male-to-female transsexuals who considered themselves to be heterosexual (i.e., attracted to women) prior to their reassignments report having become more interested in and sexually active with men after their hormonal and surgical treatments (Daskalos, 1998).

Nevertheless, an analysis of 41 studies that included 1,729 lesbians, 5,734 gay men, and several thousand heterosexual women and men has suggested there may be some correlation between childhood gender behavior and eventual sexual orientation. The study found that 89 percent of gay men and 81 percent of lesbians had a history as children of engaging in cross-dressing and cross-gendered games and of preferring playmates of the other gender. This was in comparison to 2 percent of the heterosexual men and 12 percent of the heterosexual women who had been studied (Zucker & Bailey, 1995). Yet it has been estimated that only about one in seven of the gay males and lesbians would actually have been formally diagnosed as having a gender identity disorder as children (Goleman, 1994). Information of this sort suggests that there may indeed be some interaction of factors in the formation of gender identity and sexual orientation, although the mechanisms of such interaction are completely unknown. The data also confirm that childhood gender behaviors are not wholly accurate predictors of eventual sexual orientation or identity.

Implications of Treating and Diagnosing Gender Identity Disorders

When terms such as "treatment" are used in conjunction with a label such as "gender identity disorder," there obviously are implied assumptions that something is wrong, that indeed something requires therapy. This is a situation that many transgendered people resent. They believe that because their gender-related expressions and preferences do not harm or exploit others, the decision over whether any kind of therapy is indicated, and what type, should be left to them. Because sex reassignment is a complicated medical process, the medical profession has assumed the right and responsibility of deciding who will receive various alternatives of treatment. Our society has not

as yet questioned this mode of decision making to any great degree, but transsexuals do not always believe that the present system is fair to them (Devor, 1997).

Another complicated issue involves the diagnosis of gender identity disorder during childhood or adolescence. The 1994 edition of the American Psychiatric Association's *Diagnostic and Statistical Manual,* usually called the *DSM-IV,* has for the first time included guidelines for determining if a child has a gender identity disorder. They include a strong, persistent identification with the opposite sex, including desires to cross-dress, behaving in transgender roles, and preferring playmates of that gender. Other criteria include expressed discomfort and dissatisfaction with their own sex and significant distress, self-hatred, or impairment of their lives because of the condition. There is some evidence that transsexuals may be somewhat more prone to certain psychiatric disorders that would also need to be carefully evaluated (Walling, Goodwin, & Cole, 1998).

One of the difficulties in diagnosing children is that there are not clearly defined lines of "appropriate" gender behavior, and we must be cautious not to stigmatize children who simply do not fit the gender expectations that someone has created for them (Goleman, 1994). There is evidence that boys and girls with gender identity disorders do indeed display behaviors that are less characteristic of their physical sex than same-sexed controls (McDermid, Zucker, Bradley, & Maing, 1998). Such findings, and the diagnosis of gender identity disorders in childhood in general, raise questions about how they should be treated. There is some evidence that children who are treated prior to the age of about 8 years old may be helped through therapy to become more comfortable with roles that are consistent with their anatomy. Older children do not respond to therapy as well (Goleman, 1994).

Several studies have examined men who as children stated that they wanted to be girls and who acted out their wishes through dress and play activities. Often these men have not carried their desire to be female into adulthood, leading the researchers to conclude that the likelihood of adult transsexualism or transvestism cannot yet be reliably predicted in childhood (Zucker, Bradley, & Sullivan, 1993).

What treatment do you think should be made available to children who have been diagnosed with a gender identity disorder?

Because most parents do not recognize or seek help for gender identity disorders in their children, the issues of treating children and adolescents remain controversial. How early should hormonal or surgical treatment be used, especially with the knowledge that not all transgendered young people grow up to be

The Big Picture

Transgendered Scholars

Before he delivers a lecture on gender identity to his philosophy class this semester, Michael A. Gilbert must decide what to wear. Most likely, he will put on a knee-length skirt, a long-sleeved blouse, and low pumps. Standing before a mirror at home, he'll fix his wig and apply some makeup before heading out the door.

Professor Gilbert is a cross-dresser who teaches philosophy at York University, in Ontario. When he appears in drag this semester, it will be the second time that he has introduced students in his "Gender and Sexuality" course to a side of himself that he had kept hidden for nearly 50 years. "Having tenure is a two-edged sword," he says. "It means I can't be fired. But when it's appropriate, it's also incumbent upon me to take a risk and stick my neck out. My main goal is to provide an openness for transgendered people."

Preventing Discrimination

Dr. Gilbert is among a growing cadre of "trans" people on campuses who are going public. Organizations for gay, lesbian, and bisexual students have already begun taking a "T" on the end of their names to embrace "transgendered" or "transsexual" students. In the past year, students and professors have also pushed universities to extend protection to transgendered people under policies that prevent discrimination against minorities. . . .

Despite its growing visibility, most people still need help in navigating the world of transgenderism. The label "transsexual" typically is reserved for people who have had at least some sex-change surgery and who take hormones to further change. "Transgendered" is a catchall term that is used to refer to people who live as the opposite sex, whether or not they have had sex-change surgery. The description encompasses cross-dressers, also known as transvestites, and is used by some lesbians and gay men to describe themselves. . . .

A Personal Choice

Having a sex change is a deeply personal matter, but several transsexual academics spoke freely about the experience for this article. Most of them told of being well received on their campuses after they changed gender.

C. Jacob Hale chose to become a man and sought tenure on California State University's Northridge campus in the same year. The timing was risky. But Dr. Hale, a professor of philosophy, didn't want to wait.

"I could not imagine going through my tenure review and then telling my colleagues, 'Guess what? There's something I forgot to tell you,' " says Dr. Hale, who made the decision to change sex in 1995. But the professor did feel vulnerable. "I was very afraid of losing my academic career," he says. "What else do philosophers do?"

The first thing Dr. Hale did after announcing that she would become a man was to buzz-cut her bleached-blond hair. Dr. Hale also began taking male hormones and had her breasts removed, but has stopped short of genital surgery. . . .

Robin Wilson, "Transgendered Scholars Defy Convention, Seeking to Be Heard and Seen in Academe," *The Chronicle of Higher Education*, February 6, 1998, pp. A10–A12. Excerpted with permission.

---

high-intensity transsexuals? If transsexualism could be identified prior to puberty, and hormonal and surgical intervention occurred prior to the development of secondary sex characteristics, the process would be far simpler and more effective. The ethical issues and objections surrounding these questions are obviously complicated and far from being resolved.

◼ The Need to Enhance Sexual Arousal

Being a sexual human being, expressing that sexuality, and experiencing sexual responsiveness involve far more than our sex organs. Human senses, especially sight and touch, play a major role in sexual individuality. Our sensory input, emotions, and thought processes blend in our brains to promote or inhibit sexual desire and arousal in ways that are only poorly understood at this point. We do know that the sensations of sexual stimulation and orgasm are controlled by the pleasure centers in the limbic system of the brain.

Human beings whose personalities are on the erotophilic side of the spectrum may spend a great deal of time and energy perfecting and enhancing their sexual experiences. Just as some people become good cooks and connoisseurs of great food, so do some take pride in learning the sexual techniques that will provide the optimal levels of enjoyment and satisfaction for them and their partners. As men and women learn the very individualized triggers and enhancers for their own sexual arousal, they find many different avenues to explore.

Use of Erotica and Pornography

Nudity and a variety of sexual acts have been depicted in statuary, pottery, and paintings since ancient times. It is estimated that in the United States today, the sale of sexually explicit media—magazines, videotapes, and material that may be accessed via the Internet—is a $5- to $8-billion-a-year business. Such materials are often associated with sexual arousal. Researchers for the NHSLS reported that 23 percent of the males and 11 percent of the females surveyed had watched an X-rated movie or video within the previous year. Twenty-two percent of the men and 4 percent of the women had visited a club that had nude or seminude dancers within the same time period (Laumann, Gagnon et al., 1994). There is also evidence that at least in males, continued exposure to the same pornographic material results in habituation, meaning that their sexual arousal in response to the same material decreases over time (Over & Koukounas, 1995). Therefore, one of the reasons erotica and pornography are such strong businesses is that customers continually seek new material to view. Sexually explicit media continue to be an extremely controversial topic, as we will explore further in chapter 14, "Sex, Art, the Media, and the Law."

Sexual Devices and Toys

Although sexual-enhancement toys are nothing new, their availability to the general public has been increasing since the 1960s. Sex shops sell a variety of devices designed to heighten sexual arousal and pleasure. Mail-order catalogs and Internet sites are easily found. The devices vary in their effectiveness, and each one will have advocates who have found it satisfies their tastes and needs. Most individuals who give sex toys a try use them only occasionally or as an experiment. A few people come to rely on them as constant aids to sexual satisfaction.

Vibrators are probably the most common of the sexual aids, providing an intense vibration to the genitals or other sensitive body parts. There are battery-operated and plug-in models. Some are cylindrical or penis-shaped, in a variety of lengths and widths. Others come with several attachments to be used for stimulating different sex organs. Vibrators are sometimes recommended for people who have trouble reaching orgasm, especially women. The rapid, localized vibration is often helpful in triggering the orgasmic reflex. Vibrators can, of course, be used for masturbation or integrated into shared activities.

Cylindrical dildos, made of everything from ivory to clay, have existed for at least 2,500 years. Today they are usually made of soft flexible plastics. Although they may be used for solitary masturbation, for vaginal or anal insertion, dildos are also used in some partnership sex. Plastic penis extenders are designed to fit over the head of a man's penis, supposedly to make it seem longer during sex. Actually such devices rarely yield much extra pleasure for either partner and may even reduce sexual sensations for the man. NHSLS data reported that during the previous year, 2 percent of both women and men had used a vibrator or dildo, and 1 percent of the men and 2 percent of the women reported having used "other sex toys" (Laumann, Gagnon et al., 1994). Another survey of 7,700 people aged 18 to 90 found that 10.2 percent said they had used sex toys with partners, although it is believed that even more people tend to use such devices during masturbation. Sex toys use was most common among persons aged 30 to 49 (Catania, 1997).

Some men enjoy wearing various bondage or pressure devices, including metal, leather, or rubber rings that fit around the base of the penis and scrotum. Although these "cock rings" are advertised as being helpful in maintaining erection, there is no particular evidence that they do so, and in fact if they are too tight they can cause some damage. A variation on this theme is the clitoral or French tickler, worn at the base of the penis and having projections on the top surface. The projections are supposed to press on the female's clitoris during vaginal intercourse, providing extra stimulation.

Sexual Fantasy

The NHSLS found that 19 percent of women and 54 percent of men fantasize about sex at least once a day (Laumann, Gagnon et al., 1994). Mental images, daydreams, and fantasies seem to be a significant part of most people's sexual individuality. Such imagery may be fleeting and incomplete or lengthy and detailed. Sexual fantasy is not necessarily connected with one's sexual behavior. For example, most men who fantasize about forcing a partner to have sex with them would never carry out such an action. Studies indicate that human beings fantasize about many sexual practices in which they would actually never participate in real life, and sometimes they experience these fantasies negatively. Fantasies may also reflect areas of sexual longing and frustration in a person's life (Byers, Purdon, & Clark, 1998).

Studies find some gender differences in the typical fantasy lives of males and females. Sexual fantasies tend to begin between the ages of 11 and 13, with males usually having their first fantasies at earlier ages than females (Leitenberg & Henning, 1995) and feeling more positive and guilt-free about them (Byers et al., 1998).

CASE STUDY

Craig: A Harmless Fetish Worries a Young Groom

Following a class in human sexuality, a male graduate student named Craig asked for an appointment for counseling, explaining that he had a sexual problem to talk over. During the counseling session, he nervously described his plans for marriage in 2 months and said that there was an aspect of his sexuality that bothered him. He went on to explain that he became sexually aroused by touching soft blankets and often enjoyed lying on a blanket during masturbation or intercourse. He was also quite certain that his partiality to blankets resulted from his earliest masturbatory experiences, in which he would rub his penis against a blanket.

Craig was told that the fetish did not seem particularly troublesome, and some further questioning elicited other important facts about his preference. Basically he had very open and positive attitudes toward his sexuality and felt concern only about his mild blanket fetish. Of

special importance was the fact that he did not feel compelled or driven to become sexually aroused by blankets, and they were instead employed only when convenient. His fiancée not only had been told about his inclinations but found the whole situation humorous. She had assured Craig that she would be happy to cooperate in the use of blankets in their sexual experiences whenever he wished. They were both highly satisfied with their present sexual relationship. On the basis of this information, it was concluded that if Craig could come to accept his blanket fetish as a desirable, harmless part of his sexual responsiveness, there was no reason to see it as a problem or sign of sexual disturbance. Before leaving the counseling session, he sighed with great relief and said that he felt confident he could feel very positively about the fetish as long as he did not have to view it as sick or abnormal.

Men's fantasies tend to be more active, impersonal, and visually oriented, whereas women's fantasy themes are generally more passive and romantic. Women who have fantasies of forced sex tend to be more erotophilic, interested in a range of sexual activities, and more sexually experienced (Strassberg & Lockerd, 1998).

Sexual fantasies have been categorized into four main groups: exploratory, including themes such as group sex, mate swapping, and same-gender behavior; intimate, with the themes of passionate kissing, oral sex, making love outdoors, and mutual masturbation; impersonal, which includes sex with strangers, looking at pornography, watching others engage in sex, and fetishism; and sadomasochistic, including themes such as whipping, spanking, and forceful sex. Men tended to have more fantasies in all four of these categories, but the greatest proportion for both sexes was in the intimate category (Meuwissen & Over, 1991). The most common sexual fantasies involve having sex with a past, new, or imaginary partner, or having sex in various settings and positions (Elliott & Brantley, 1997; Leitenberg & Henning, 1995). Both men and women had the fewest number of fantasies reflecting impersonal or sadomasochistic themes.

The kinds of sexual fantasies people experience—their length and degree of explicitness—seem to be determined to a large degree by the amount of guilt they experience about sex. As might be expected, the less guilt people experience, and the more liberal their attitudes about sex, the longer and more explicit their fantasies tend to be (Meuwissen & Over, 1991). In gen-

eral, sexual fantasies do not seem to be indications of an inactive sex life or dissatisfaction with sex. Fantasies occur more often in people who have high rates of sexual activity and are relatively happy with their sexual lives. Sexual fantasies do sometimes produce guilt or other unpleasant reactions (Byer et al., 1998; Leitenberg & Henning, 1995).

Why do you think sexual fantasies occur more often in people who have high rates of sexual activity and are relatively happy with their sex lives?

Different people have different levels of imaginative ability and use it in very individualized ways to enhance sexual arousal and gratification. Sexual fantasies can be one of the most powerful avenues to sexual arousal (Dekker & Everaerd, 1993). Sex therapists often encourage people to make use of their "inner erotica."

Fetishism

Fetishism is usually defined as finding sexual excitement in objects, articles of clothing, or the textures of particular materials that are not usually considered to be sex-related per se. Sometimes parts of the body not usually considered sexually arousing are included in

---

fetishism (FEH-tish-i-zum): sexual arousal triggered by objects or materials not usually considered to be sexual.

the definition. There are many degrees of fetishism, ranging from these mild preferences that accompany most sexual relations, to an intense drive and complete substitution of the fetish for any other forms of sexual gratification (McConaghy, 1993). In one study, 11 percent of men and 6 percent of women surveyed reported having had personal experience with sexual fetishism (Janus & Janus, 1993).

There are certain things that are very commonly held as fetishes, including underwear, soft and silky clothing, rubber, and leather. Women's breasts can have an almost fetishistic attachment for some men, and occasionally feet are found to be sexually arousing. The inner mechanisms by which sexual fetishism develop are unknown, but it is typical for the fetishist to have experienced sexual arousal in association with the fetished object at some point in her or his life. Use of the fetish during masturbation is most typical, in which the object is fondled, rubbed on the genitals, viewed, or used for direct stimulation of sex organs. Some males ejaculate in or on the fetished object. Sometimes fetishes are integrated into shared activities as well, but this may create some emotional discomfort for the fetishist's partner.

Most fetishes are harmless and inoffensive to others. However, they sometimes are carried to extremes that may have negative implications for others. It is not uncommon to read newspaper accounts of an adolescent male who has entered someone's home to touch the feet of a sleeping girl or to steal some of her undergarments. True **kleptomania,** involving sexual excitement when stealing, and **pyromania,** in which the individual derives sexual arousal from setting fires, are considered to be forms of fetishism.

Fetishes are a poorly understood facet of sexual individuality. Because they are usually socially innocuous, they have not generated much attention among sex researchers. It is possible that someone who is inordinately sexually attached to a fetish, to the exclusion of other forms of sex, may be exhibiting some signs of emotional insecurity or stress worthy of professional consultation. This level of fetishism would be considered a paraphilia.

Varying the Numbers

Partly because of the social standards that place sex within the context of an intimate and romantic one-to-one relationship, sex for more than two has generally been considered inappropriate in Western culture. In other cultures, large orgies are sometimes a part of rites or religious ceremonies. In our culture, sexual involvement for more than two is more typically done as an experiment that develops unplanned out of some other social activity. It may be seen as a way to enhance the usual arousal patterns. Of the

people interviewed in the NHSLS, 1 percent of the women and 13 percent of the men indicated that they found group sex very appealing, although they had not necessarily participated in such activities (Laumann, Gagnon et al., 1994).

Group sex can apply to a variety of situations, ranging from threesomes (**troilism** or **ménage à trois**) to large groups. Among college students surveyed, 13 percent of the men and 10 percent of the women reported having participated in a sexual threesome (Elliott & Brantley, 1997). The activity may involve one or more persons simply observing a couple engage in sex or actual physical interaction among all present. Probably the most common form of group sex occurs when more than one couple engage in sexual activity, but each couple remains quite separate from the other(s). A group in which everyone participates with one another may be called an **orgy,** although this is a somewhat outmoded term. The incidence of such behavior is still uncertain. Available evidence suggests that it is not commonly a continuing or regular form of sexual behavior and instead usually represents an occasional episode (Wiederman, 1997c).

There are, of course, other implications to group sex. There are the elements of exhibitionism, voyeurism, and same-gender sexual interaction that are natural byproducts of group activities, sought by some participants and upsetting to others. There is always the risk of generating discord among participants because it is difficult to devise shared activities that will help everyone feel involved, cared for, and satisfied. Feelings of possessiveness and jealousy may easily arise, or feelings of spontaneity may be destroyed by the individual who becomes too autocratic or ritualized. As with any kind of shared intimacy, later nonsexual social contacts between the people involved may feel awkward and strained (Levine, 1998). Group sex may also accompany mate swapping, also called swinging, and other variations on extrarelational sex. By the end of the twentieth century, swing clubs had become even more popular, perhaps through Internet contacts, and were believed to number about 400 in the United States. However, the swinging phenomenon has not been studied in many years (Jenks, 1998).

kleptomania: extreme form of fetishism in which sexual arousal is generated by stealing.

pyromania: sexual arousal generated by setting fires.

troilism (TROY-i-liz-um): sexual activity shared by three people.

ménage à trois (may-NAZH-ah-TRWAH): troilism.

orgy (OR-jee): group sex.

Atypical and Potentially Problematic Sexual Connections

As earlier sections of this book have demonstrated, human sexual desire and behavior are extremely variable and may become associated with a wide range of relational circumstances and objects of attraction. Sometimes sexual practices fall enough outside societal norms that they are considered paraphilias, or at the very least, atypical. In some cases, they may become problematic because of the potential consequences they have for the individual participant or others who may be affected by the behavior. This section deals with some of those sexual interests.

The Sex Worker Industry

Like anything that can provide people with pleasure, sex has often become a commodity. Both male and female prostitutes, now often called sex workers, participate in sexual activity for money. Often called the world's oldest profession, it has been suggested by recent observers that prostitution has often represented the only way some women in a male-dominated world have been able to survive (Bullough & Bullough, 1997). Prostitution has met with varying degrees of tolerance throughout history and in various societies. In recent years, there has been a prevalent attitude that prostitution represents an exploitation and victimization primarily of women. However, there is also a countering set of opinions suggesting that sex workers should have a right to make their living in this manner, free from harassment or interference by various authorities (Rickard, 1998).

Male sex workers who serve women have been known as gigolos, or, more recently, as escorts. However, sometimes escorts are just that—companions to some social event. Almost no empirical data have been gathered on gigolos or male companions. More typically, male sex workers engage in sexual activity with other males. Some young male prostitutes consider themselves heterosexual and view their same-gender involvement purely as a business venture. The longer they work as prostitutes, however, the more likely they are to think of themselves, and be identified by their peers, as gay (Pleak & Meyer-Bahlburg, 1990). Male **hustlers** tend to work full-time as street sex workers or in other locations. Some of the particularly good-looking and well-mannered male prostitutes may eventually become attached to an older affluent man or become more highly paid **call boys.** Research suggests that male sex workers do not always engage in safe sex practices (Joffe & Dockrell, 1995).

Although female prostitutes are usually hired to give their clients an orgasm, male prostitutes are typically hired to have an orgasm themselves through stimulation by their clients, often older men who wish to perform fellatio (oral sex) on the prostitute. Given the realities of male sexual response, particularly the refractory period, this limits the numbers of clients a male may serve in one day. Female prostitutes, by contrast, are not limited by this physiology and typically do not experience orgasm in their paid encounters. Studies of female street sex workers have found that many of them do in fact enjoy intercourse and oral sex with their customers and that these women enjoy sex with their boyfriends or husbands as well.

The most common street name given to female sex workers is **hookers.** Although **brothels,** or houses of prostitution, can still be found, they have largely been replaced by **streetwalkers** who work for **pimps** and in **massage parlors** (see Fig. 13.6). **Call girls** tend to be more highly paid prostitutes who cater to a more exclusive clientele.

There is controversy over whether the sex worker industry actually constitutes a victimless line of business. Research continues to demonstrate that many sex workers have a background of alcohol and drug abuse and of sexual and physical abuse that presumably played a role in leading them to prostitution (Potterat, Rothenberg, Muth, Darrow, & Phillips-Plummer, 1998; Schissel & Fedec, 1999). Prostitution can also be a dangerous job in which women may be raped, beaten, robbed, and forced to perform various sexual acts against their will. Another increasingly serious concern is the spread of HIV or other sexually transmitted diseases through prostitution (Kanouse et al., 1999). However, it has also been claimed that a relatively small amount of disease transmission actually comes from prostitution and that this would be reduced if prostitution were decriminalized and regulated. Although absolute protection cannot be

hustlers: male street prostitutes.

call boys: highly paid male prostitutes.

hookers: street name for female prostitutes.

brothels: houses of prostitution.

streetwalkers: female prostitutes who work on the streets.

pimps: men who have female prostitutes working for them.

massage parlors: places where women can be hired to perform sexual acts under the guise of giving a massage.

call girls: highly paid female prostitutes who work by appointment with an exclusive clientele.

FIGURE 13.6 *Streetwise*

Young girls are particularly vulnerable to becoming prostitutes if they have a poor self-image, have run away from home, have friends who are already prostitutes, or are seeking an adult to care for them.

guaranteed for the prostitute or the client, any man seeking sex with a prostitute should wear a condom throughout the sexual activity. Clients of male sex workers should insist that they wear a condom in order to somewhat reduce the risks of HIV transmission.

Of increasing concern among professionals is the number of prostitutes who are adolescents, ranging in age from 13 to 18. Girls are particularly susceptible to becoming prostitutes if they have a poor self-image, have run away from home, have friends who are already prostitutes, or are seeking an adult on whom to depend (Schissel & Fedec, 1999). Pimps quite often fill this need by showering a girl with attention and gifts, developing a romantic attachment with her, then using the relationship to entice the girl into prostitution. Most experts in this area believe that one way to reduce or eliminate adolescent female prostitution would be to address social problems such as poverty and sexual abuse that sometimes lead girls to the activity in the first place.

Close Encounters

There are several forms of sexual connection that involve some form of contact with a typically unknown and often unwilling participant. The unknowing person who is sought out for such a sexual connection may be a victim to the degree that she or he has been an unwilling participant in someone else's sexual activity. The degree of victimization may range from feeling some petty annoyance to being seriously traumatized by the experience.

Obscene Telephone Calls

Men who have strong feelings of insecurity and inadequacy have a tendency to engage in obscene telephone calls, sometimes called *telephone scatologia.* Their phone calls to women, or occasionally other men, represent ways of anonymously asserting their sexuality without having to face a frightening social contact. Because their calls are usually spiced with sexual obscenities, designed to shock or surprise women particularly, the behavior may also reflect some negative attitudes toward women. Sometimes such calls surely represent a prank, but they may also become a continuing form of sexual release, often accompanied by masturbation (McConaghy, 1993). It is very rare for an obscene telephone caller to follow up the call with any sort of actual contact with the victim. The best way to react to such a call is to hang up immediately, without comment, and then using call-tracing methods while reporting the call to the telephone company or police.

Consensual Telephone Sex

Another form of sexual encounter involving a professional sex worker is represented by the "900," and sometimes "800," telephone numbers by which people can reach those who are willing to talk in a sexually provocative way over the phone, or where they can listen to someone else talking in this manner (see Fig. 13.7). Most callers to dial-for-sex services are apparently men who typically are masturbating during their phone call. In a survey of college students, 13 percent of the men and 7 percent of the women said they had made use of phone-sex lines (Elliott & Brantley, 1997). There is very little research on telephone sex at this point, but it may well represent a relatively harmless, and certainly safe, form of sexual encounter. Sometimes the need to make such a call may indicate problems within a relationship, but this is not always the case (Flowers, 1998).

There have been many concerns about "dial-a-porn" because it is so easily accessed by minors. In 1989, the U.S. Supreme Court ruled that telephone sex could not be outlawed, although stricter controls were

FIGURE 13.7 *Consensual Telephone Sex*

Dial-for-sex services allow callers to reach women or men who will talk in a sexually provocative manner. Because of concerns about the easy access of minors to "dial-a-porn," some telephone companies have imposed stricter controls to prevent calls from minors.

imposed to prevent calls from minors. Nevertheless, such regulations are difficult to enforce. The general public and state legislatures have placed pressure on telephone companies to eliminate these services, but they continue to proliferate. Some smaller countries around the world have leased their excess telephone lines to companies in North America or Europe for telephone sex services.

Adult Internet Chat Lines

The Internet has also provided ways for people to carry on sexually suggestive or explicit communications with relative anonymity. Although it is sometimes suggested that such contact represents a way of replacing face-to-face relationships, it may also enhance relationships (Wysocki, 1998). Chat lines are preferred by women over the more explicit erotic sites (Cooper, 2000). For a small proportion of regular chat line visitors, the behavior becomes compulsive and is associated with difficulties within their personal relationships (Cooper, Scherer, Boies, & Gordon, 1999).

Frotteurism and Toucherism

A term that applies to gaining sexual enjoyment from pressing or rubbing one's genitals against another, unknown person in some anonymous setting is **frot-**teurism. Crowded places, such as elevators, subways, or theaters, are common locations in which the **frotteur** may operate because the close contact will usually go unnoticed. **Toucherism** refers to the intimate touching of an unknown person's body, typically on the buttocks or breasts (Freund, 1990). It is sometimes considered to be a subcategory of frotteurism. Little is known about frotteurism or toucherism, but professionals assume again that they represent a way for insecure people to seek out minimal physical contact with someone who is sexually appealing to them. The act is probably often followed by masturbation in private.

Exhibitionism

Exposing the genitals to someone else for sexual pleasure is called **exhibitionism.** Usually the one who commits this act is a man who exposes his penis to children or to an adult woman, although women sometimes gain sexual pleasure from exposing their breasts. The exhibitionist may go to great pains to make it seem as though he was caught undressing or urinating, so that the victim will be less prone to reporting it as a crime. People who are arrested for such behavior are charged with indecent exposure or public lewdness. The repeating male exhibitionist usually gains pleasure from shocking others with the sight of his penis, thereby gaining some sort of confirmation of his male power.

What might motivate a man to expose his penis to others? Or a woman to expose her breasts?

It is apparent that many people display some degree of exhibitionism in their attempts to appear and feel sexy. Bikinis for women and men, see-through clothing, and tight trousers and blouses all attest to that fact. Some women add extra padding to their bras to emphasize their breasts, and some males admit to adding extra padding to their genital areas occasionally. These are subtle forms of exhibitionism. Nudity is obviously a form of exhibitionism, although it may have few, if any, sexual connotations. People shower

---

frotteurism (frah-TOUR-izm): gaining sexual gratification from anonymously pressing or rubbing one's genitals against others, usually in crowded settings.

frotteur: one who practices frotteurism.

toucherism: gaining sexual gratification from the touching of an unknown person's body, such as on the buttocks or breasts.

exhibitionism: exposing the genitals to others for sexual pleasure.

© *Punch/Rothco Cartoons.*
"You don't often see a real silk lining, these days . . ."

together in gym locker rooms, and at least some of them report a feeling of enjoyment in being nude together with other people. There seem to be few sexual implications of nudity in actual nudist camps and on nude beaches, and in fact, attaching sexual meanings to nudism in these settings is generally frowned upon. It can be expected, however, that in a society that typically requires the sex organs to be covered, a real sense of liberation and sexual pleasure might sometimes accompany the uncovering of these organs in the presence of other people.

Because such behaviors are generally considered antisocial, exhibitionism is one of the more common sexual offenses for which men are arrested in Europe, the United States, and Canada. There are various treatment programs designed to help these individuals channel their sexual energies into more acceptable directions, and even some medications have proven successful in treating compulsive behaviors (Abouesh & Clayton, 1999).

The motivations behind exhibitionism vary among individuals. Although exhibitionism is often found in the criminal and sexual histories of rapists and abusers of children, it typically stems from the exhibitionist's feelings of inadequacy and inferiority. In exposing his penis, a man seeks reassurance of his maleness and masculinity. There are probably some aggressive motives as well, because the victim may react so strongly to the situation that the exhibitionist creates a degree of emotional distress. If a victim does not react with any particular surprise or fear upon being confronted

by an exhibitionist, his primary source of gratification is destroyed. Public exhibitionism can be offensive to the individual who, without consenting to do so, is confronted with having to see someone else's sex organs. This is not necessarily a seriously harmful event, but it still can be emotionally exploitative. A study of 846 women found that 18 percent of those who had encountered exhibitionists found the experience severely distressing. An additional 25 percent had their attitudes about men, sex, or themselves affected in some way by the experience (Cox, 1988). In a survey of sexual activities in which a group of male college students had participated, 21 percent admitted to having exhibited themselves in public (Person, Terestman, Myers, Goldberg, & Salvadori, 1989). Whenever possible, the best response to an exhibitionist is probably to ignore him. The police or other authorities may also be contacted and asked to take action.

Voyeurism

The gaining of sexual pleasure from observing nudity or disrobing in others or by watching others engage in sexual acts is **voyeurism.** There is certainly an element of voyeurism in most of us, and it is quite natural to be interested in other people's genitals and body form. The NHSLS found that watching a partner undress was the second most appealing of all sexual practices, after vaginal intercourse. The survey also reported that 16 percent of the women interviewed and about 33 percent of the men found the idea of "watching others do sexual things" at least somewhat appealing (Laumann, Gagnon et al., 1994). In a survey of American college students, 13 percent of both the women and men said they had taken photographs of nudity or sexual acts, and 5 percent indicated they had used a video camera during sex (Elliott & Brantley, 1997).

The prevalence of sexually explicit media materials provides ample evidence of the voyeuristic needs of the public. In a survey of university students, 58 percent of the males and 37 percent of the females reported having watched or read pornographic materials in the preceding 3 months (Person et al., 1989). Voyeuristic behavior becomes more offensive when the voyeur, or "peeper," goes out of his or her way to peer in windows of bedrooms or spy on people in public bathrooms to satisfy his or her needs. Voyeurs tend to be younger males in their early twenties, usually unmarried or separated, but about 25 percent are married. Very few seem to have any serious mental disorders but

voyeurism (VOYE-yur-i-zum): sexual gratification from viewing others who are nude or who are engaging in sexual activities.

most have had unsatisfactory sexual relationships. Voyeurs are usually interested in viewing strangers and usually do not interact physically with their victims. Nonetheless, the act is an obvious violation of another's right to privacy. Again, it may not harm the victim, and in fact the voyeur's presence may never be known, but it is an exploitative act. Because voyeurism is less easily detected than other sexual proclivities, it is not reported to authorities as frequently as behaviors such as exhibitionism (McConaghy, 1993).

It is certainly true that men are implicated in these forms of sexual connection far more often than women, and the scanty statistics available seem to confirm that males do indeed find such behaviors sexually arousing, more so than females. However, social attitudes and values may also be operating here. It has been suggested, for example, that if a man is standing outside an open window watching a woman undress, he will be arrested for being a voyeur. However, if the situation were reversed, with the woman watching the man undress beyond the open window, it would still be the man who would be arrested—for exhibitionism.

Sadomasochism

Sadomasochism is probably the least understood of the relatively common routes to sexual arousal and connection. The term includes a whole range of sexual behaviors involving discomfort, pain, humiliation, excretion or excrement, dominance and submission, and bondage (tying up all or part of the body). It has been traditional to define the **sadist** as the partner who derives sexual pleasure from being in a dominant role, perhaps inflicting, or threatening to inflict, some usually negative stimulus on another person, the **masochist** being the individual who is aroused by being in the submissive, receiving role. These are surely simplistic definitions because many people seem to be able to enjoy either role. Sadism and masochism are opposite sides of the same coin and tend to accompany one another, even though one may dominate the other at any given time (Sandnabba, Santtila, & Nordling, 1999; Weinberg, 1995).

Sadomasochism is always a matter of degree. For most people, shared sexual activity has its share of urgency and rapid movements, with tightly gripping hands, hard sucking movements, and the possibility of mild pinching, scratching, and biting. Between 25 and 30 percent of college students surveyed indicated that they have engaged in spanking or some sort of bondage during sexual activities (Elliott & Brantley, 1997). Such behaviors are part of the intensity of sex. For the sadomasochist, variants of such stimuli have become an important part of sexual arousal and gratification. The intensity of the stimulation desired may vary from scratching or biting through spanking, whip-

ping, and severe beating. Occasionally, cutting to draw blood or to mutilate may be involved. People who pair up for sadomasochistic sex usually make careful agreements ahead of time concerning how far the activities should go. There are always risks of such contracts being broken, of course. It is also true, ironically, that the person in the submissive or masochistic role often wields more power and control over the interaction because it will be his or her reactions that largely determine the eventual direction of the encounter (Weinberg, 1995).

The acting-out of fantasies or rituals in which one individual plays a dominant role is probably the most common sadomasochistic activity. Often the dominant person plays the role of a severe parent, teacher, or police officer who demands compliance from the submissive partner. The scenario often ends with some mock forced sexual activity. Urination and defecation sometimes are included in the sexual acts, and some individuals find sexual interest and arousal in urine (**urophilia**) or feces (**coprophilia**) (Wise & Goldberg, 1995). In the Janus and Janus (1993) survey of sexual behavior, 4 percent of women and 6 percent of men reported experience with "golden showers," or urophilic behavior, and about the same percentages found the behavior acceptable. In the recent college student survey, nearly 10 percent of respondents indicated they had been involved with golden showers (Elliott & Brantley, 1997).

Bondage, the tying or restraining of parts of the body, seems to be a variant of sadomasochism. Wearing a hood is often a part of such shared activities. Adult sex shops sell all sorts of devices for binding the body or genitals. Most common are rings, straps, and other pressure devices used by males to bind the penis and/or testicles to generate or heighten sexual pleasure. Eleven percent of both women and men report having had sexual experience involving dominance or bondage (Janus & Janus, 1993).

---

sadomasochism (sade-o-MASS-o-kiz-um): refers to sexual themes or activities involving bondage, pain, domination, or humiliation of one partner by the other.

sadist: the individual in a sadomasochistic sexual relationship who takes the dominant role.

masochist: the individual in a sadomasochistic sexual relationship who takes the submissive role.

urophilia: sexual arousal connected with urine or urination.

coprophilia: sexual arousal connected with feces.

bondage: tying, restraining, or applying pressure to body parts as part of sexual arousal.

A very dangerous variation on the bondage theme is **hypoxphilia,** which may lead to **auto-erotic asphyxiation.** Some people, usually boys or men, have found that wearing a noose around the neck, which induces a state of *hypoxia,* or reduced oxygen to the brain, can enhance erotic pleasure and orgasm. They often devise various hanging techniques from which they can cut themselves loose prior to losing consciousness (Johnstone & Huws, 1997). What these individuals do not realize is how easy it is to lose consciousness when pressure is placed on the carotid artery in the neck. The Federal Bureau of Investigation estimates that between 500 and 1,000 people die accidentally each year from this sort of sexual activity. Given these statistics, it is believed that the practice must be more widespread than commonly assumed. Families of victims are often confused about the sexual nature of the death and are embarrassed about reporting it as such. Partly for the same reason, the dangers of this kind of bondage have not been widely publicized to young people (Cooper, 1996; Garos, 1994).

There are few statistics on the frequency of sadomasochistic preferences and activities. The Janus and Janus (1993) statistics indicated that 14 percent of men and 11 percent of women had had some personal experience with sadomasochism. In a survey done on over 2,000 students in the United States, Canada, and European countries, 8 percent of males and 5 percent of females in the United States reported that they had engaged in "whipping or spanking before petting or other intimacy." These percentages were markedly higher among British students (17 percent of males; 33 percent of females), where spanking is a prevalent form of childhood punishment, and this may well take on sexual meanings (Butt & Hearn, 1998). There is a well-developed network of gay male and lesbian sadomasochists within the gay/lesbian subculture as well (Blau, 1994; Sandnabba et al., 1999).

In sex-oriented tabloids available in some cities, sadomasochists advertise for sexual partners, making it clear which role is preferred. Some typical advertisements follow:

DISCRIMINATING MASTER, 32, Caucasian, very controlled but strict, desires applications from obedient, attentive slaves. T.J.M., Box 172.

FEMALES AND FEMININE MALES only. Have you had a good cry lately, or are you too grown up for that? Have you disciplined yourself so much that you mask your real feelings? Well, if you wear that mask in front of me, I'll slap you right out of it! I'm an attractive, imaginative black female, late 20s, and will give you highly private teachings in freeing your emotions. Send phone and fantasies to: Josa, P.O. Box 82.

One theory suggests that masochistic behavior may represent an escape from the usual burdens and responsibilities of one's normal identity. In a masochistic role, the individual is spared the anxiety of making decisions, asserting control, or maintaining a favorable image. The role may also deter feelings of guilt and insecurity (Bader, 1993). It is also true that practitioners of S&M are generally socially well-adjusted and that these behaviors simply facilitate their sexual lives. They tend to be flexible in their role-taking, although those who prefer the dominant role tend to be younger and more sexually active than those who prefer passive roles (Sandnabba et al., 1999).

A survey of research on S&M has suggested that these behaviors constitute a social phenomenon that occurs in cultures with certain characteristics. For example, dominance and submission are usually embedded in the culture, and aggression is socially valued. There is also a clear and unequal distribution of power among social groups, creating a situation in which the temporary illusion of power reversals could become erotically stimulating. Two additional social characteristics are sufficient affluence to provide the leisure and opportunity for such involved sexual practices and the positive valuing of creativity and imagination (Weinberg, 1995). There is far more that we do not understand about sadomasochism, and future research needs to focus on S&M relationships and the role of symbolism in such sexual practices.

Sex with Animals

Since before recorded history, humans have lived in close association with a variety of domesticated animals. Folklore and the literature of mythology contain many examples of humans having sex with animals, often portraying a woman who has become enamored of the large genitals and sexual prowess of some animal. The half-bull, half-human Minotaur of Greek mythology was the offspring of Pasiphae, wife of the King of Crete, and a bull whom she purportedly seduced.

Cross-cultural studies have reported many cases of humans having sex with animals, such as dogs, cattle, sheep, burros, horses, and chickens. This activity is called **bestiality** or **zoophilia.** There was even the sug-

hypoxphilia: creating pressure around the neck during sexual activity to enhance sexual pleasure.

autoerotic asphyxiation: accidental death from pressure placed around the neck during masturbatory behavior.

bestiality (beest-ee-AL-i-tee): a human being's having sexual contact with an animal.

zoophilia: (zoo-a-FILL-ee-a): bestiality.

gestion that some animals may make sexual advances toward humans (Ford & Beach, 1951). The Alfred Kinsey studies reported that in his research sample, 8 percent of the adult males and 3 percent of the adult females admitted having had at least some sexual contact with animals. In a study that compared a group of psychiatric patients with a control group of nonpsychiatric hospital patients and psychiatric staff members, it was found that over half of the psychiatric patients had experienced bestiality at some point in their lives. However, 10 to 15 percent of the control groups had also experienced zoophilic behaviors (Alvarez & Freinhar, 1991). In the Kinsey research, among men raised on farms 17 percent reported having had at least one orgasm after puberty through contact with an animal. The greater likelihood of zoophilia in rural populations has been confirmed more recently (Cerrone, 1991). One percent of college students in a survey admitted to having had sex with an animal (Elliott & Brantley, 1997).

It appears likely that sex with animals usually represents sexual experimentation and/or arises from the frustration of lacking an available sexual partner. It does not necessarily reflect serious psychological disturbance and seldom becomes a continuing pattern of sexual activity. What humans actually do with animals is as varied as any other aspect of human sexuality. Kinsey found masturbation of the animal and actual intercourse to be more common among men. General body contact with the animal is more common among women. Oral-genital contacts with animals were reported by both women and men.

Sex with animals is a concept usually met with abhorrence and disgust for several reasons. First, Judeo-Christian-Muslim tradition carries strong prohibitions about humans having sex with animals, which may have grown out of fears that monstrous hybrids might be formed by such unions. In fact, no offspring can be formed by sexual intercourse between humans and animals because of the genetic differences between species. Second, possible injury or pain may be inflicted on the animal, especially if restraints have been used to keep it from moving during the sexual activity. The behavior is illegal in most areas today, covered by various types of laws concerning sodomy and lewd behavior.

Sex with the Dead

Probably no form of sexual behavior stirs negative reactions in quite the same way as **necrophilia,** or sexual relations with a corpse. It has been said that in ancient Egypt women of high rank and women of particular beauty were not given to embalmers until they had been dead for 3 or 4 days, to prevent the embalmers from having intercourse with them.

There are no statistics concerning the incidence of necrophilia, and almost nothing has been written about people who participate in sex with the dead. It is believed to be a rare phenomenon because few people have access to cadavers. It is likely that necrophilic sex acts are committed primarily by people who work with corpses, as in mortuaries or morgues, and have therefore become desensitized to them. Case studies of necrophiles published decades ago showed that they took jobs where they would be able to have such contact (Klaf & Brown, 1958). This behavior is prohibited under laws regarding the handling of bodies in most states, although Iowa just passed such a law in 1996 after a man was discovered fondling a woman's body at a funeral home, and there was no law at the time that could be invoked against the behavior.

Casual Sex and Pansexualism

Changes in sexual values during the latter half of the twentieth century seem to have led to a wider acceptance of casual sex. Proponents of recreational sex claim that shared sexual emotion can be a creative human force. Those who advocate casual sex go even further, claiming that sex can be fun even when shared without any depth or structure in the relationship, as long as no one is hurt. As an even more expansive sexual concept, the term **pansexual** has been used to describe individuals who see their sexual capacities as transcending particular human objects of attraction. They find a variety of behaviors and inanimate objects, or even concepts, sexually exciting.

Which sexual behaviors, as described in this chapter, do you believe should be condemned or regulated by law?

Trends have also been developing that may tend to mitigate against casual approaches to sex, and the statistics from the NHSLS indicate that most people do not have particularly adventurous sexual lives anyway. There are those times, such as college spring breaks, when people are more likely to participate in casual sexual encounters, but these seem to be relatively isolated periods for the average individual (Maticka-Tyndale, Herold, & Mewhinney, 1998). There has been a gradual shift toward more conservative values about sexual behavior. Even more significantly, growing concerns over HIV/AIDS may have discouraged casual sexual encounters.

necrophilia (nek-ro-FILL-ee-a): having sexual activity with a dead body.

pansexual: lacking highly specific sexual orientations or preferences; open to a range of sexual activities.

Self-Evaluation

Your Sexual Fantasies

It seems that nearly everyone experiences a rich sexual life in his or her imagination. Yet we react to our sexual fantasies in different ways. We may feel aroused, amused, frightened, ashamed, proud, or guilty, depending on how we have learned to think of our sexual fantasies. They may give us clues to what we like and dislike about sex, help us plan future sexual encounters, put us in touch with the richness of our imaginations, and provide interesting accompaniments to our sexual activities. Sexual fantasies are just that—fantasies. There is no particular need to fight or deny them. In fact, sometimes the more we try not to think about something, the more it plagues us. Keep in mind that it is our sexual actions for which we must accept responsibility; our fantasies need only be accepted as very personal parts of our minds. The following questions and exercises may help you take a closer look at your fantasy life and its meaning.

1. **Take some time to think in some detail about your most common sexual fantasies. It may help to close your eyes and relax. Write down each fantasy if you wish.**
   a. What are the predominant feelings generated in you by each fantasy? Start by deciding whether it gives you mostly positive feelings that make you glad to indulge in it, or whether it generates negative feelings that make you wish the fantasy would go away.
   b. More specifically, what feelings does each fantasy generate? Write down a list of all feelings that you experience during each fantasy.
   c. Have you ever told another person about any or all of your sexual fantasies? Why or why not? If so, what conditions helped you to feel able to share such a personal aspect of your life?

2. **Here is a list of some typical topics of sexual fantasies. They may be simply fleeting thoughts or rich in detail. For each fantasy you can remember experiencing, assign it a number, using the following scale as a way of noting the relative intensities of your fantasies.**

   0 = I have not experienced this fantasy.
   1 = An appealing, arousing, enjoyable fantasy.
   2 = Most aspects of the fantasy were enjoyable and positive.
   3 = A mixture of positive and negative aspects.
   4 = Most aspects of the fantasy were unenjoyable and negative.
   5 = A disgusting, guilt-producing, unenjoyable fantasy.

   a. Having sex with someone to whom you are attracted but who is unavailable to you or uninterested in you. ___
   b. Kissing or hugging someone of your own gender or admiring his or her nude body. ___
   c. Having quick, uninvolved sex with a stranger whom you will never see again. ___
   d. Having sex with someone of your own gender. ___
   e. Watching a couple you know having sex with one another. ___
   f. Forcing another person to have sex with you. ___
   g. Being forced to have sex with someone against your will. ___
   h. Seeing the nude body and genitals of someone you judge to be attractive. ___
   i. Being watched while you masturbate. ___
   j. Being watched while engaging in some sexual activity with a partner. ___
   k. Inflicting or being subjected to pain or humiliation during sexual activity. ___
   l. Paying a female or male prostitute to have sex with you. ___
   m. Having sex with someone under the legal age of consent. ___
   n. Being tied up during sex or tying up someone else during sex. ___
   o. Participating in oral-genital sex with a desirable partner. ___
   p. Being part of a group sexual experience or an orgy. ___

3. **Are there any sexual fantasies that you enjoy using as an accompaniment to masturbation? If so, try to sort out the unique features of each fantasy that contribute to your sexual enjoyment.**

4. **Do you sometimes find yourself fantasizing while engaging in masturbation or sexual activity with a partner?**
   a. If so, how does this make you feel?
   b. Do you consider such fantasizing unusual? (It's not.)
   c. Have you ever discussed these fantasies with your sexual partner? If so, did your partner share any of his or her sexual fantasies with you?
   d. Have you ever acted out a sexual fantasy with a partner or considered doing so? (Some couples find this to be an occasional source of enjoyment and mutual arousal.)

5. **Have you been able to give yourself permission to experience, accept, and enjoy your sexual fantasies? If not, is this a goal toward which you would like to work? If your fantasies are giving you problems, perhaps you would like to consider talking with a qualified professional about your concerns.**

Chapter Summary

1. The total sexual outlet concept (hydraulic theory) of sexuality has been modified by data from the newest sex research.

2. Contemporary sex research has emphasized the physical, orgasmic aspects of sex. The subjective erotic experience that includes sensuosity and desire is also important.

3. Preferences for various sexual behaviors and objects of sexual desire may change with circumstances and time.

4. Human beings are diverse in their sexual orientations and activities. Behaviors that differ from whatever is considered the norm may be classified by terms such as deviance, variance, or paraphilia.

5. There is a wide range of levels of interest in sex and amounts of actual sexual activity among people, ranging from the erotophilic to the erotophobic. An unusually high level of sexual interest or drive is called hypersexuality, whereas an especially low level is called hyposexuality. Although either may reflect a normal pattern for a particular person, they may also signal deeper emotional distress.

6. Compulsive sexual behavior can result from traumatic life experiences. Erotomania is an apparently rare form of mental illness characterized by extreme sexual compulsivity. It has been called nymphomania in females and satyriasis in males.

7. Celibacy refers to the choice not to share sexual activity with other people. It can represent a response to ethical or religious values.

8. Diverse sexual behaviors are more common among men than among women.

9. People with transgender identities may sometimes cross-dress or live for periods of time as if they were members of the other sex.

10. There are specific surgical procedures for male-to-female and female-to-male transsexuals.

11. Although transgender identity and sexual orientation are largely separate phenomena, there is some evidence that they interact to some degree.

12. Now that there are diagnostic guidelines for gender identity disorder in children, there is controversy over what treatments or counseling should be made available to them.

13. People sometimes enhance sexual experiences through the use of various sexual media and toys and through sexual fantasy.

14. Fetishism is the term used to describe sexual arousal by objects, parts of the body, or materials not usually considered sexual.

15. There are several forms of sexual interaction for more than two persons.

16. There are both female and male sex workers. Legal debates over prostitution continue, and the HIV/AIDS issue has raised new concerns for this kind of casual sex.

17. Among the sex-related behaviors that have unwilling or unwitting victims are obscene telephone calls, frotteurism, and toucherism.

18. Consensual telephone sex and Internet chat lines offer opportunity for sex-related communication on a relatively anonymous basis.

19. Frotteurism and toucherism involve sexual arousal through close contact with other people.

20. Exhibitionism refers to exposing the genitals or breasts to others, usually for sexual arousal.

21. Voyeurism refers to finding sexual arousal in viewing others in the nude, disrobing, or engaged in sexual activity.

22. Sadomasochism encompasses a range of behavior involving inflicting pain or humiliation, tying parts of the body (bondage), or acting out of dominant-submissive fantasies, all for sexual arousal. Hypoxphilia is the practice of using devices to reduce oxygen to the brain for sexual enhancement.

23. Sex with animals has been reported in a small percentage of humans.

24. Sex with the dead (necrophilia) is a rare phenomenon, typically prohibited by law.

25. The term "pansexual" refers to people who are open to a wide range of sexual activities.

Focus on Health Questions

You will find in this section the kinds of questions that you may have concerning your own health and sexuality. The page references indicate where in the text the answer is located; the exact place is marked with the logo: **F⊙H**

1. Are some people "oversexed" or "undersexed"? 400

2. How do I know if I'm promiscuous or just normally enjoying sex with several partners? 401

3. Isn't there something wrong with someone who doesn't want to have sex? 401

4. Is it abnormal for a man to enjoy dressing in women's clothes? 402

5. What actually happens when a person gets a sex change? 404

6. Is it normal to fantasize about sex a lot? 410

7. What exactly is a foot fetish? 412

8. What is wrong with those who expose their genitals to other people? 415

9. Isn't sadomasochism painful and dangerous? 417

Annotated Readings

Avna, J., & Waltz, D. (1994). *Celibate wives: Breaking the silence*. Los Angeles: Lowell House. A book that explores the reasons behind and consequences of celibacy among married women.

Califia, P. (1997). *Sex changes: The politics of transgenderism*. San Francisco: Cleis Press. Thought-provoking look at the social and political ramifications of transgender lifestyles.

Chapkis, W. (1997). *Live sex acts: Women performing erotic labor*. New York: Routledge. A comprehensive examination of the sex worker industry and its social implications.

Devor, H. (1997). *FTM: Female-to-male transsexuals in society*. Bloomington: University of Indiana Press. A wide-ranging book on the history and theory of transsexual women who desire to become men.

Ettner, R. (1996). *Confessions of a gender defender*. Evanston, IL: Chicago Spectrum Press. A personal and sometimes touching perspective from a clinical psychologist who is an advocate for transgendered people.

Flowers, A. (1998). *The fantasy factory: An insider's view of the phone sex industry*. Philadelphia: University of Pennsylvania Press. A down-to-earth treatment of the author's doctoral research on telephone sex.

Laws, D. R., & O'Donohue, W. (Eds.). (1997). *Sexual deviance: Theory, assessment and treatment*. New York: Guilford Press. A collection of papers that examine the spectrum of sexually variant behaviors.

Moser, C., & Madeson, J. (1996). *Bound to be free: The SM experience*. New York: Continuum. A collaborative work between a sexologist and a practitioner of S&M that gives a somewhat more personalized view of a complex subject matter.

Prosser, J. (1998). *Second skins: The body narratives of transsexuality*. New York: Columbia University Press. A scholarly view of the meanings of transgendered states.

Skeen, D. (1999). *Different sexual worlds: Contemporary case studies of sexuality*. Lanham, MD: Lexington Books. Sensitively presented case studies of the various sexual lifestyles of several individuals that offer a real-life view of the spectrum of human sexual behaviors.

Chapter 14
Sex, Art, the Media, and the Law

Chapter Outline

Note: A selection of Focus on Health questions appears at the end of each chapter. Answers to these questions are indicated within the chapter by the symbol in the margin. **F⊙H**

When I was about 12, my mother found some porno magazines that I had hidden in my bedroom closet. She turned them over to my father, who gave me the biggest lecture of my lifetime about what kinds of material would be permitted in our house. I was really embarrassed, but I also hated losing those magazines.

—From a student's essay

Depictions of human sexuality have been abundant in most cultures and periods of history, from the figures on a Greek urn to the billboards on Times Square; from the couples on a television soap opera to the advertisements for Gap clothes; from frontal nudity on the big screen to the lyrics of the most current raunchy musical group. These images and words, implicitly or explicitly, reflect the attitudinal trends of the society in which they appear. However, the more tolerant a society becomes in its representation of sexuality, the more it invites criticisms from certain factions within it.

The terms **pornography** and **obscenity** are often used interchangeably. Both terms are subject to multiple definitions and interpretations, and both have become emotionally charged. Typically, however, pornography refers to any visual or literary portrayal that may be sexually arousing to some people. Obscenity usually includes that which may be offensive to public taste and morals. The term "sexually explicit material" is sometimes used to describe pornography.

In erotically realistic art or fiction, sometimes called **erotica,** sex is portrayed as part of the broad spectrum of human emotions present in intimate relationships. The people involved are shown to be complex human beings with a variety of nonsexual feelings in addition to sexual ones. The sex may be depicted in just as graphic a way as in pornography; it is the overall context that differs. It has also been suggested that pornography has aspects of violence, aggression, or the degradation of another human being, whereas erotica reflects a balance of mutual respect, affection, and pleasure.

Nudity and Sex in Art

In recent times in Western culture, art has been a relatively uncensored means of expression, in which nudity at least has been considered quite permissible. That is not to say, however, that paintings or sculptures of nudes have not incurred the ire of some viewers. Erotic art has a long history, as do the cultural and social reactions to it.

Historical Foundations of Erotic Art

The prehistoric representations of the human body and sexual activities were very likely fertility symbols with magical and religious significance. Representations of the sex organs themselves probably became objects of worship with great symbolic meaning. Pe-

nis-shaped monuments and adornments have been found in the ruins of many ancient cultures. Religious erotic art tended to portray the aspects of sex that were seen as important and necessary to the survival and well-being of the human species (intercourse for procreation, for example). Other forms of erotic art, mostly three-dimensional, were used to ward off evil spirits or improve the harvest of crops.

Every culture has seen its share of erotic art that departs from such religious intent. Artists, sometimes by definition, are those who test the limits of moral values and sexual tolerance. It is this form of erotic art that is sometimes treated with greater secrecy, used for sexual titillation, or strictly limited to a select group of privileged viewers. Many Greek and Etruscan paintings show sexual intercourse, fellatio, orgies, pedophilic behavior, and a variety of other sexual activities. There are examples of pre-Columbian pottery from Mexico and Peru that represent male masturbation and fellatio, often with great exaggeration of phallic size (see Fig. 14.1).

Some erotic art has been used for special educational functions. In Japan, there was a tradition of "bride scrolls" and "position pictures," or **shunga,** which were passed on from mother to daughter upon the daughter's betrothal. Their dual purpose apparently was to instruct and to encourage the daughter's erotic interest in her husband-to-be. This reflects the double purpose of most erotic art—to make us think as well as to respond with feeling, including sexual arousal. Erotic art is also of great use in fostering an understanding of the sexual values and mores of both historic and present-day cultures other than our own.

Do you think public funding should be available for the creation of art with sexual themes? Defend your position.

pornography: photographs, films, or literature intended to be sexually arousing through explicit depictions of sexual activity.

obscenity: depiction of sexual activity in a repulsive or disgusting manner.

erotica: artistic representations of nudity or sexual activity.

shunga: ancient scrolls used in Japan to instruct couples in sexual practices through the use of paintings.

FIGURE 14.1 *Pre-Columbian Pottery*

The ancient Peruvians from the southern coast of Mochica were famous for their stirrup-spout jars. They were molded without the aid of a potter's wheel and featured a large flat bottom with a dominant sculptured form. This jar shows an act of fellatio.

FIGURE 14.2 *Renaissance Painting*

Peter Paul Rubens's painting *The Rape of the Daughters of Leucippus* (1617) depicts the abduction of two young mortals by the gods Castor and Pollux, who have fallen in love with them. The content of the painting was less interesting historically than its composition and the artist's technique of using paint and light. However, some accuse art historians of glorifying what most people today would find objectionable subject matter for any type of art.

Nudity in art is often directly affected by cultural attitudes. Ancient Greek artists portrayed the nude male and female figures without hesitation. Gradually, however, as their attitude toward nakedness changed, they began to include gestures of modesty, with the genitals at least partially covered.

Probably the roots of modern, commercial sexually explicit material can be found in the sixteenth century, when engraving, etching, and woodcutting made reproduction of erotic scenes simpler and much less expensive. Eventually, there was a resurgence of a more puritan attitude that discouraged artistic representations of nudity and sex. In this repressive movement, we probably find the roots of modern censorship and suppression of erotic images. However, there have also been claims that art historians sometimes glorify and eroticize acts that we would today judge in a negative light (see Fig. 14.2), such as the rapes portrayed in many Renaissance paintings (Wolfthal, 1999).

Erotic Art Today

The first two or three decades of the twentieth century saw some new approaches to erotic art (see Fig. 14.3). Surrealism, for instance, often relied on sexual fantasy and free association borrowed from psychoanalysis. Although contemporary art has created some fresh erotic themes in Western culture, it seems that photography, video, films, and computer images now provide the erotic stimuli that painting, drawing, etching, and sculpture once did. These have elicited their share of controversy as well.

It has been the custom of many governments to subsidize artists, but when the work produced from such support offends the tastes of some individuals, debates erupt over the use of public funds for products that push the envelope of sexual values. The photographic themes of Robert Mapplethorpe, containing homoerotic and sadomasochistic themes, have come under fire because of the artist's support from the National Endowment for the Arts (NEA). Galleries that display such works are also subject to criticism. One of the most recent examples was when the Mayor of New York City threatened to withhold funds from the Brooklyn Museum of Art in 1999 when the museum displayed a series of controversial work in its "Sensational" exhibit. Federal courts in the United States have tended to rule that funding of the arts should not be limited by controversy or based on the artist's social or political messages.

FIGURE 14.3 *Life Model*

One basic area of study for art students continues to be the depiction of the nude human body. Students frequently work with life models, men or women who often pose in the nude.

Controversies of this sort highlight the difficult balance every society must struggle to find between freedom of expression, which might include rather explicit images that may even be offensive to some, and the never-ending interest on the part of others to have such images available. The George Pompidou Center in Paris exhibited 500 works of twentieth-century art for several months that explored sexual themes ranging from transgenderism to voyeurism to sadomasochism. This served as a reminder of the many ways in which eroticism and sexuality make their way into the artworks of all eras and how they may well be at the roots of artistic creativity (Litt, 1995).

Sex and the Printed Page

Just as erotic themes have universally found their way into visual art, so have they always been a part of literature. The explicitness of sexual descriptions varies with the cultural and sexual mores of the times. In some societies and periods of history, little more than a romantic embrace is described, with participants fully clothed. The rest is left to the reader's imagination. In other societies and times, minute and graphic details of a sexual encounter are discussed; the reader needs no flight of imaginative fancy (McCormick, 1994). Like other erotic art forms, sexually explicit literature has often been available only as costly contraband.

The Evolution of Sexuality in Literature

It seems that because sex was viewed as joyous and pleasurable in ancient times, authors were permitted to write about it openly and unashamedly. In most lan-

guages, including English, some of the oldest writings are the most ribald. Sumerian love songs written about 4,000 years ago contain verses that are more explicit than love songs of today.

Ancient Greek writers drew much of their eroticism from the fertility rites of Dionysian festivals, which were dramatic orgies in honor of certain Greek gods of pleasure and intoxication. These rites developed into wild orgies in some communities, occasionally to the dismay of Greeks, who preferred more staid and formal ceremonies. The plays and songs that emerged were the mass media of the times, often glorifying the phallus and retelling stories about the sexual activities of the Gods. Many of the masters of Greek tragic and comedic writing created plays with central sexual themes. The erotic literature of the ancient Romans was more lighthearted than that of the Greeks, although there is evidence to indicate that their sexual behaviors surpassed whatever excesses the Greeks may have displayed. One of the most famous Roman "pornographers" was Ovid, whose *Art of Love* and *Heroides* are erotic classics. Another Roman, Caius Petronius, wrote the *Satyricon,* a work that is filled with sexual themes.

It has been suggested that prior to the early nineteenth century, there was not really a separate or distinct genre of literature meant to arouse sexual feelings. Sexually explicit materials were instead used as vehicles to criticize political and religious authorities. Sexual literary themes have often been associated with freethinkers and political activists and have often proliferated prior to major political revolutions against restrictive or oppressive regimes. Pornography seems to have begun taking on its more distinctively sexually titillating role during the late eighteenth century, as a more materialistic view of the world began to emerge in philosophy and science (Boone, 1998; Hunt, 1993).

The nineteenth century brought a rise in prudery, and during this period ladies could be offended not only by explicit sexual references but by any sort of indelicate statement made in writing. Sexual feelings were increasingly repressed, and sexual attitudes, at least superficially, became models of propriety. Nevertheless, erotic literature flourished; by 1834, 57 pornography shops had opened on one London street (Mason, 1994).

Themes in Contemporary Literature

Although sexuality has never been totally repressed in literature, the kind of exuberance and acceptance of erotic themes that was prevalent in Greek and Roman literature did not fully manifest itself again until the twentieth century. In the early years of this century, some writers rebelled against the notion that sex must be accompanied by feelings of shame and guilt.

Undoubtedly, the writings of Sigmund Freud, Havelock Ellis, Kinsey, Masters and Johnson, and others have influenced the emergence of new sexual attitudes.

D. H. Lawrence's *Lady Chatterley's Lover* (1929) stirred controversy with its sexual explicitness for decades. Lawrence is now recognized as a literary genius who was a pioneer in the sensitive treatment of erotic themes. James Joyce's *Ulysses* was not allowed into the United States for years after it was published. In 1933 John Woolsey, a district judge for New York, wrote a landmark decision that redefined the limits of pornography and allowed *Ulysses* to be admitted into the United States. Woolsey's basic principle was that the redeeming artistic value of an entire book needed to be considered before it would be banned as obscene because of any given passage. This decision set a precedent that has persisted to this day, and *Ulysses* became recognized as a modern masterpiece.

All sexual themes have now found their way into literature. Since the early 1970s, there have been tens of thousands of books published on many different levels of literary quality that treat sex openly and frankly. Sometimes the erotic themes are interwoven with other themes of literary importance. In other cases, the author's intent seems to be to crowd as many sexually explicit scenes onto the pages as possible. There has also been a resurgence in the popularity of romantic themes. Books and ensuing films such as *The Bridges of Madison County* demonstrate this trend. Currently, 46 percent of all mass-market paperbacks are romance novels, read by both women and men (Bartley, 1994). In addition, some experts believe that economic and sexual pressures are making monogamous, romantic relationships more appealing both in real life and in literature. Another recent trend in romance novels has been the portrayal of men who are interested and involved in fatherhood and family life.

With the beginning of the new millennium, the sale of erotic books, collections of short stories, and poetry has actually been booming. Women are dominating the erotic literature scene both as the writers of such materials and as buyers and readers. This seems to reflect a new trend in eroticism, in which sexual themes are intertwined with good literary style and well-developed characters who have an emotional side as well.

Although there have been no widespread recent attempts to censor erotic themes in literature, local libraries and school systems are frequently subjected to pressure by special-interest groups to remove books these groups judge to be too sexually suggestive. The number of challenges concerning materials used in public schools has been escalating dramatically during the 1990s, and in close to half of these cases, books or other materials have been removed or given some restricted status (Spindel & Duby, 1994). Some of the most challenged titles include classics and award-winning books such as Judy Blume's *Forever,* Mark Twain's *Huckleberry Finn,* and Maya Angelou's *I Know Why the Caged Bird Sings.*

Can you think of any books that should not be allowed in your college library? In a high school library? In a public library?

Magazines, Tabloids, and Comics

Magazines with stories about sex have been available for more than a century. It has been only within recent times that they have been so readily available and openly displayed. When *Esquire: The Magazine for Men* appeared in 1933, a new precedent was set for sophistication in erotic magazines. Twenty years after *Esquire*'s beginnings, *Playboy* appeared on the newsstands. This magazine attempted to strike a balance among offerings on sex information, advice on male attire, an open philosophy toward sex, and photographs of nude women and titillating fiction. The *Playboy* approach was adopted by a large number of other magazines for men. As women began to ask for a more balanced view of sex, magazines such as *Cosmopolitan* and *Playgirl* began printing photographs of nude men and stories with special erotic appeal for women.

By the late 1960s, other magazines began to appear that were more blatantly sex-oriented and included hard-core pornography. *Penthouse, Hustler,* and *Oui* were among the first to deal explicitly with sex. In 1968, *Screw* scored a resounding commercial success for a time and was followed by a number of other sex tabloids with provocative titles such as *Smut, Ball, Stud, Hot Stuff,* and *Sex.* Not only did the sex tabloids publish photographs of male and female nudes showing genitals, but they usually also published pictures of people engaged in a variety of sexual activities, as well as fiction, articles relating to new developments in the study of sex, and a classified section in which people advertised their sexual services or requested sexual partners for all sorts of activities.

Over the past decade, there has been a marked increase in magazines dealing with sexuality. In a typical year, close to 1,000 new magazines appear, about 15 percent of which are sex publications. Only about a third of new magazines survive for a few years, but among the more popular ones, the trend has been toward more coverage of sex-related articles and news. The popular women's magazines such as *Glamour* and *Cosmopolitan* have generally forsaken feminist themes in favor of articles about sexuality (Kuczynski, 1999). Several new men's magazines have appeared that seem to be emphasizing some of the traditional gender stereotypes regarding men's interests in explicit sexual themes and photographs (Turner, 1999). Even the popular magazine for teen girls, *Seventeen*, has been publishing more articles about sexuality, although the publishers also tend to stick to more traditional scripts of what is socially acceptable sexually (Carpenter, 1998).

Until recently, comic books and comic strips in newspapers did not venture into gender- or sex-related themes, but that has been changing. Women have become superheroes in some comics. A character in Marvel Comics' "Alpha Flight" declared he was gay, and another gay character appeared in DC Publications' "Flash" series. In the comic book series "Icon," the 15-year-old girl who tells the story becomes pregnant. The newspaper comic strip "For Better or For Worse" featured the character of a gay teenage boy who came out to his parents and best friend. The issue was carried through several days of the strip but was blended into the story line in such a way as not to appear startlingly unusual. In Japan, sexually explicit comics for women are quite popular, and they often seem to feature rape themes or other depictions of forced sexual submission. Those published for younger girls often portray relationships between gay males. It is believed that such themes in the women's comics may help play out the subconscious mind within the contexts of a sexually conservative culture (Kristof, 1995).

■ Sex in the Media

Film, television, video, and the Internet represent modern mass media. They have undergone—and continue to undergo—an evolutionary process that parallels, reflects, and often stimulates the evolution of social attitudes. The integration of nudity and sex into films and television has been gradual and careful, yet because of their mass audiences, reaction to nudity and sex in these media has been more visible than any responses to erotic art or literature ever were. Research studies confirm that sexually explicit films and videos produce higher levels of arousal response in viewers than do still pictures (Davis & Bauserman, 1993).

Films

From the earliest days of film, there were some moviemakers who made use of the medium to photograph sexual activity. At first, such films were available only through the underground market. The movies that were offered to the public for the first 50 years were almost totally lacking in anything that would today be judged as sexually explicit. There were innuendos and seductive women even in silent films; Greta Garbo's first talking picture, *Anna Christie* (1930), was

about a prostitute. But whatever people did together sexually was left strictly to the viewer's imagination. Movie actors were never seen wearing less than a bathing suit considered appropriate at the time; a man and woman were never shown in bed together; kisses rarely betrayed any sense of real passion. This was partially due to the producers' code established by the movie industry itself as a response to several sexual themes that appeared in a few movies in the 1920s.

The Roman Catholic Church instituted the Legion of Decency in 1934, and its standards were soon adopted by Hollywood producers (Walsh, 1996). Conservative attitudes in the early twentieth century influenced the depiction of alcohol, drug abuse, equality for blacks, women's rights, prostitution, communism, and other themes that did not fit into the prevailing mode of behavior or thought. That is not to say that "sex symbols" did not emerge from among the movie stars. Actors such as Mae West, Jean Harlow, Clark Gable, Humphrey Bogart, James Dean, and Marilyn Monroe undoubtedly drew theatergoers who were romantically attracted to their filmed images. Every year, new media sex symbols emerge.

In 1965, *The Pawnbroker* became the first American film to show bare female breasts. Today they are a standard part of a great many movies, and overtly erotic themes and explicitly sexual scenes have begun to emerge in films. *Midnight Cowboy* (1969) dramatized the story of a male prostitute, and *Klute* (1971) dealt with some intimate details of a female prostitute's life. One of the most popular films of its day, *The Graduate* (1967) portrayed a brief sexual encounter between a young man and an older woman. *Myra Breckinridge* (1970) and *The Christine Jorgensen Story* (1970) dealt with sex-change operations.

Every sexual theme has found its way into the movies. The film *Boogie Nights* (1997) followed the life of a physically well-endowed young man into the underworld of pornographic film production. Director Stanley Kubrick's last film was the well-publicized *Eyes Wide Shut* (1999) that presented the surrealistic sexual adventures of a married, but sexually bored, couple.

As sexual explicitness and nudity have increased in films, the industry continues to struggle with the question of ratings. The X rating for films, which had proved to be a box office liability for movies, was replaced with the NC-17 classification, meaning no children under the age of 17 were permitted in the theater. However, the new rating seems to carry the same stigma as the old X rating, and many theaters will not show NC-17 movies. Polls have found that R-rated films are the most popular, particularly among the 18- to 34-year-old group, followed by films with PG-13 ratings, and then with the PG rating. Films with NC-17 and G ratings trail behind the others in their popularity. Producers face decisions of whether to cut explicit

CROSS-CULTURAL PERSPECTIVE
Objects of Desire: What Do Women Want? Sexy Underwear.

History does not record whether Confucius ever considered the WonderBra. But today there's bad news from the world of lingerie for Asian leaders who hope that Confucianism's stress on propriety will ward off the West's obsession with sex. Asia's growing class of affluent urban women is eager to flaunt their sexuality. And that has created a boom market for the raciest of G-strings and skimpy push-up bras. The hottest market of all: stuffy Singapore, where graffiti artists are caned and the country's government has outlawed chewing gum. "It's nanny land, with the government always telling you what to do," says Madelyn Lip, who promotes underwear in the region. "But they can't tell you what to do underneath. Under it all, women are rebellious."

It was not always thus. Even in cosmopolitan Hong Kong, women wanted only padded polyester bras and quilted dressing gowns when beauty expert Marguerite Lee opened the city's first boutique for fancy lingerie in 1973. But Western pop culture has transformed Asian women's idea of beauty. Today the chain Lee founded sells $75 thong panties and $150 push-up bras. The trend is so clear that WonderBra, the brand that popularized the super-push-up brassiere, next month will launch a special product line sized for the slim Asian body. "There's a strong desire to be sexy," says Dorothy Lau, a Hong Kong accountant. "People want to marry a good husband, and a push-up bra is part of the package to achieve that goal."

This is still a limited market. Most Asian women remain shy about their bodies. In Seoul, according to a study by Japanese underwear manufacturer Wacoal, 82 percent of women sleep with underpants and a bra under their nighties. But advertising evidently can erode such conservatism. The study also suggests a direct relationship between the amount of racy ads and the dissatisfaction that can lead women to try to improve on nature. In Tokyo, where 84 percent of women said they are unhappy with their bodies, 48 percent of those polled said they own more than four girdles. In Beijing, exposed to Western advertising for only a few years, 74 percent of the women said they're happy with their bodies.

It may not be long, though, before the world's biggest consumer market embraces Victoria's Secret. Already there are flashy lingerie departments in Shanghai and Beijing stores, selling daring underwear to Chinese women newly made rich by capitalism. And Valentino, an upscale underwear brand, is promoted on Star TV, seen all over China. Where undergarments are concerned, a philosopher of the sixth century B.C. may prove no match for the blandishments of Seventh Avenue.

—Dorinda Elliott. *Newsweek*, February 12, 1996, p. 41. All rights reserved. Reprinted by permission.

sexual scenes from their films in order to win the safer, and more lucrative, R rating. There has been a recent trend toward sexy films that are clearly aimed at teenagers, who can often manage to see R-rated films even if they are under 17. The films *American Pie* (1999) and *Cruel Intentions* (1999) represent examples of such movies (Chambers & Chang, 1999).

Educators, philosophers, and psychologists have engaged in a good deal of debate concerning the significance of sex-related themes in films. As a society evolves, does its art reflect its changing values, or do artists and filmmakers form the avant-garde in effecting these changes? As a society becomes more tolerant and breaks down the barriers of its stereotypical attitudes toward groups of people and sexual behaviors, how does the art of that society reflect these changes? There are no definitive answers to these questions, but perhaps a discussion of some cinematic themes will provide a clue.

Women in Films

There has been controversy, for example, over how women have been depicted in American films. One study compared male and female roles from 1927 through the late 1980s, finding that women's roles were generally rather rigidly stereotyped (Levy, 1990). Women have been frequently portrayed as self-destructive, manipulative, and sexually seductive (see Fig. 14.4). A common cinematic scene over the years has involved an aggressive man pulling a woman into his arms and forcing kisses on her. At first, the woman pushes and fights against him with clenched fists, but eventually her body softens, her hands open and slide around his neck, and she surrenders herself to him passionately. This "rape myth" is believed to be perpetuated by such cinematic themes. Nonetheless, there are also films that offer more positive and strong images of women, often demonstrating strong bonds of friendship between women.

Tuning in to Teenagers

Like the weather, everyone talks about teenage sex, but no one seems able to do anything about it. One million pregnant teens a year? Hey, just say no. Several million sexually transmitted diseases a year? Let teens go to a Planned Parenthood clinic somewhere (as long as it hasn't been bombed out by pro-life extremists). HIV infection and AIDS? That's what sex-education classes in school are supposed to deal with (even though many aren't even allowed to mention condoms).

Teenagers watch an average of 3 hours of TV per day, listen to the radio for an additional one to two hours and often have access to R-rated movies and even pornography long before they are adults. According to the best study from the late 1980s, the average American teenager views almost 15,000 sexual jokes, innuendoes and other references on TV each year.

Given the voluminous amount of research implicating media violence as one cause of real-life violence, we wanted to see whether a similar connection existed between inappropriate sexual depictions in the media and inappropriate adolescent sexual behavior.

First we carefully designed a questionnaire that asked teens about every medium they would ordinarily come into contact with—television, movies, radio, print magazines, the Internet, you name it. Next, we adapted many questions from the Centers for Disease Control's Youth Risk Behavior Survey that asked teens not just about their sexual activity but their drug history and their tendencies toward violence—all so-called risk-taking behaviors that, in teens, tend to go together. Finally, we added some questions about sexual knowledge and attitudes: simple things like when is a female most likely to become pregnant, and should only married people have sex?

We tested the survey on a very diverse group of 74 kids (mostly 12-year-olds) at a special summer-school program at a prestigious private school. The director of the program had no problem with our asking the kids such questions, nor did their parents. Unfortunately, 74 students do not make a study.

Since we did our pilot study, not one school system or foundation has shown any interest in our work. First we approached the local public schools. Too controversial, said the administrators. I spoke with two school-board members. They might approve it if the State Department of Education would endorse it. The State Department of Education said no sex questions, please. Next we approached one of the more liberal school districts in the state, one in which the school-based clinics are actually allowed to have condoms available on site. No way, the administrators said. Too controversial. "We have our priorities," they said.

Next, we contacted research colleagues in two other states. They said such research would be impossible in their states because only abstinence-based sex education and research were now being allowed. Meanwhile, we applied to the foundation that is the leading funder of sexuality research in the United States. No way, an administrator said. "We don't fund 'effects research'," she explained. "We just want to work to get the entertainment industry to change." What's wrong with this picture?

I am convinced that parents are mad as hell about the amount of sexual material that their kids are exposed to, and they don't want to put up with it anymore. They would welcome a study that showed that the more media their teens consume, the more medialike their behavior becomes. But school administrators are running scared of anything that might be even slightly controversial.

—Victor C. Strasburger. *Newsweek*, May 19, 1997, pp. 18–19.

List two recent films in which women are portrayed in positive roles. Explain your definition of "positive role."

Same-Gender Relationships

Prior to 1960, gay and lesbian relationships were avoided as a cinematic theme. Some European films were frank about same-gender relationships, but American films tended to obscure even suggestions of same-gender attractions. When plays such as *Streetcar*

Named Desire (1952), *Tea and Sympathy* (1957), and *Cat on a Hot Tin Roof* (1958) were made into movies, their significant allusions to same-gender sexuality were lost. In the early 1960s, however, Hollywood became less hesitant about using gay themes. Tennessee Williams's 1960 film *Suddenly Last Summer* was reasonably straightforward about the topic (Waugh, 1996).

As society has become tolerant of lesbian and gay relationships, these themes have been depicted in a variety of ways (see Fig. 14.5). *The Boys in the Band* emerged in 1972 as the first film to explore the problems of the gay male subculture, although some peo-

FIGURE 14.4 *The Depiction of Women in Films*

Despite strong female characters, many American films still portray women as manipulative and sexually seductive.

FIGURE 14.5 *Same-Gender Sexual Orientation in Films*

In the 2000 film "If These Walls Could Talk," Sharon Stone and Ellen Degeneres portray a lesbian couple trying to have a baby.

ple have objected to the stereotyped image that is presented. In the 1980s, the film *Making Love* (1982) dealt frankly with a married man who eventually left his wife to establish a gay relationship with another man. *Kiss of the Spider Woman* (1985) focused on the touching relationship of two male political prisoners, one openly gay and one heterosexual. *The Crying Game* (1993) delighted critics and viewers with its intriguing story of a man who falls in love with a woman, only to learn later that "she" is actually a man. The film poses complex questions of romantic and sexual attraction. More stereotypical and sometimes comical roles were evident in films such as *Birdcage* (1996), *To Wong Foo, Thanks for Everything! Julie Newmar* (1996), and *In & Out* (1997), but they also represented very popular movies in which gay characters had the lead roles.

Gender Identity

Questions of romantic sexual attraction are complicated by issues of self-identity and social perceptions of gender in three recent films. In *The Ballad of Little Jo* (1993), Josephine masquerades as a young male in the American frontier simply as a means of survival. As a woman, she is too vulnerable to male violence, but as a male, she realizes that she has lost her own identity. In *Farewell My Concubine* (1993), a male character prepares to play the female lead in a Chinese opera. Offstage, he sexually desires his male counterpart in the opera, thus confusing his own nature. This film at the same time becomes a metaphor for the identity crisis of China itself from the time of the warlords to the end of Mao's Cultural Revolution. *M. Butterfly,* also set in the world of Chinese opera, tells the true story of a French diplomat who had a long affair with an opera star while never having known, by his own account, that she was really a man. The diplomat

is depicted as being unable to see beyond the artifice of femininity, and thus his perception of his lover becomes his reality (James, 1993).

Romantic Themes

As discussed earlier, romantic themes are finding their way back into the media, and cinematic fare has been no exception. From period romances such as *Circle of Friends* (1995), *Sense and Sensibility* (1996), and *Titanic* (1998) to contemporary stories such as *Reality Bites* (1995), *Up Close and Personal* (1996), and *You've Got Mail* (1999), romance has overtaken explicit sex. There continues to be evidence that women particularly enjoy romantic themes in movies, tending to see sex as part of an organic whole, whereas men tend to be more focused on sexual behaviors (Sarris, 1994).

Pornographic Films and Videos

Films whose main purpose is to show lengthy scenes of genitals and/or persons engaged in any form of sexual activity are considered **hard-core pornography.** The earliest "adult films" were made before 1925, mostly by professionals who had access to 35mm movie camera equipment. As 16mm and 8mm film became available, amateurs began producing hard-core films for private use and sale. Popular from the 1950s through the early 1980s, these movies were 10 to 20 minutes in length and were sold for amounts that far exceeded the costs of production. In Great Britain, they were called blue movies, and in the United States,

hard-core pornography: pornography that makes use of highly explicit depictions of sexual activity or shows lengthy scenes of genitals.

they were often labeled as stag films. The latter term reflects the fact that such films were generally used at all-male (stag) parties.

As explicit sex began to become permissible in theaters, the underground pornographic film business suffered. Their picture quality was often poor, and they were expensive, so many viewers chose to pay less for what could be seen more clearly. As home video cassette recorders (VCRs) and video cameras proliferated, the adult movie business in theaters was reduced to almost nothing, and the video business has been booming. Video shops often have sections devoted exclusively to full-length adult films that show explicit sexual acts. In 1978, about 100 hard-core films were produced, often at a cost of $300,000 or more each. Thousands of new hard-core videos are now released every year, some costing only a few thousand dollars to produce. In the United States, there are some 25,000 stores that rent or sell these videos, often deriving as much as a third of their incomes from them. There are over 600 million annual rentals of sexually explicit videos, with the entire hard-core pornography industry estimated to gross more than $8 billion a year (Schlosser, 1997).

Although men are the largest consumers of pornography, evidence suggests that a good share of adult videos are rented by women. They often rent explicit videos to watch with their husbands after the kids have watched their PG films and gone to bed. Adult videos are rented most frequently on weekend nights. Some chains of video stores have asked sexologists for guidelines in choosing sexually explicit materials for their outlets. These experts discourage use of films in which children are portrayed sexually in any way, and they seek to avoid scenes in which sex is associated with violence or blood. Some believe that explicit videos represent a significant source of sexuality education to many people and therefore should be regulated to provide as positive a sexual message as possible. The viewing public now seems to react more negatively to adult film themes that seem degrading to women (Cowan & Dunn, 1994), and in fact more recent videos portray women in more equal and sex-initiating roles than was once the case (Schlosser, 1997).

Research into the content of sexually explicit videos has yielded some interesting findings. Over time, there has been a decrease in the number and proportion of sexually aggressive scenes in such videos (Davis & Bauserman, 1993). One study compared R-rated films with highly explicit videos and found that the videos had the higher proportion of sexual behaviors and the lower proportion of violent behaviors. Violent behavior was particularly high in R-rated films, which contained comparatively little sexual behavior. Sexually violent behaviors were relatively consistent at 3 to 5 percent of the content in both media. Women tended to be the initiators of sexual activity in both, but they were also the more typical recipients of both violent and sexually violent behaviors (Yang & Linz, 1990). Four common themes have been noted in sexually explicit videos: high levels of sexual desire, diverse sexual activity, many sexual partners readily available, and pleasure as the purpose of sexual activity (Schlosser, 1997).

There are some sexual-enhancement videos that have been produced by sexologists specifically for use by couples in their homes for educational purposes. These videos offer explicit graphic instruction for the improvement of sexual relationships and sometimes for the treatment of particular sexual dysfunctions. Clearly, there is a fine line between the sexual arousal people enjoy from pornography and what they experience while watching educational videos.

One of the newest pornographic video phenomena is the homemade, amateur sex video, taped by couples in their own homes. Apparently, some of the people who make such videos derive sexual excitement from knowing that others will be viewing their sexual acts. There are numerous companies who pay modest sums for these videos and then distribute them via mail-order to others. It is believed that from one-fifth to one-third of the hard-core videos being sold in the United States today are at least partly amateur, and one company offers a selection of 500 such videos to its customers, with new submissions being sent to their offices every week (Schlosser, 1997).

CD-ROMs and the Internet

The computer represents the newest medium for transmitting information, and it has been adapted for a variety of sex-related uses ranging from computer dating services and sexuality education to the transmission of sexually explicit materials. The interconnection of computers through the Internet has opened new vistas for sexual communications and raised new concerns about how cyberspace interactions should be controlled and regulated. Not only can people at some distance from one another carry on sensual conversations on their keyboards or play X-rated computer games with each other, there are services that can provide the most recent information on a variety of sexual topics. Computer bulletin boards, available through some networks, allow people to leave sexual messages for one another. There are bulletin boards and forums for every imaginable sexual interest and fetish, easily accessible to people of all ages from the privacy of their own computers (Wysocki, 1998). In a single year, nearly 10 million people logged on to the 10 most popular cybersex sites (Cooper, 2000).

On some of the multimedia portions of the Internet that constitute the World Wide Web, pictures showing frontal nudity and all manner of sexual acts are stored and may be downloaded for viewing or printing by individual computer users. Some researchers have suggested that sexually explicit pictures or descriptions available on the Internet may number in the hundreds of thousands. The majority of the consumers of on-line computer porn are male (Kim & Bailey, 1997; Leland, 1999a). For those who are predisposed to compulsive behavior, use of the Net for access to sexual material may also become compulsive. The combination of easy access, affordability, and anonymity often conspire to cause some individuals to become involved with sexually explicit materials for hours at a time, sometimes interfering with daily life and work (Cooper et al., 1999, 2000). The Internet has also provided links among people who share a common sexual orientation or paraphilia (Leiblum, 1997).

Software in the form of CD-ROMs offers self-help for understanding and enhancing sexual relationships and for treating sexual dysfunctions and other problems. These media have received high ratings from users in comparison to other modes of seeking help because they are relatively inexpensive, easily available, and very private (Schlosser, 1997).

Like any medium, computers have potential for abuse in sex-related matters. Some people have been subjected to sexual harassment or stalking by anonymous participants in computer networks (Foote, 1999). Computer bulletin boards that serve child pornographers by transmitting explicit sexual photos of children have been shut down by the government. Concern still exists about uncontrolled access to cybersex by underage individuals, and some pedophiles have used computer networks to make contact with young people. A

recent survey found that 25 percent of teens reported they had visited sexually explicit sites with the aid of their computers (Leland, 1999b). Even though there are a number of controls that may be used to prevent access by minors to sexual material via the Net, the U.S. Congress has tried to take steps that would essentially eliminate expressions of sexuality from the Internet altogether. The Supreme Court has tended to block such efforts on Constitutional grounds, and its decisions have set the pace for sexuality in cyberspace for the beginning of the new millennium (Levy, 1997).

Interactive adult CD-ROMs and the sale of sexually explicit materials via the Internet have yet to generate profits that make them lucrative prospects for potential marketers. However, it does seem to be a market that is expected to grow. The *Playboy* website, featuring free glimpses of its Playmates along with advertisements for other services that require payment, averages about 5 million contacts, or hits, every day. There are many other sites on the Web that offer all sorts of explicit images and interactions for a price (Schlosser, 1997).

Television

For several decades, television has represented one of the most powerful forms of mass communication, and it has increasingly emphasized sexual themes. The Telecommunications Reform Act of 1996 required the television industry to develop a ratings system for viewers. The original system was based on motion picture ratings relating to sex and violence. The general public and Congress did not feel that the TV ratings system was having much of an impact, and so additional rating letters were proposed to designate sexual content, violence, and explicit language.

Producers of soap operas have been attempting to become more educative about safe sex and other issues such as date rape and unintended pregnancy. At the same time, in their attempts to appeal to youthful audiences, the sexual activity is extending to younger characters in the stories (Greenberg & Buselle, 1996). The soaps tend to reflect sexual content that is true to society's current sex-related themes, and although it is not yet known with any real accuracy how they affect viewers' attitudes and values, it is generally believed that they do have some effect on their perceptions of sexuality (Greenberg & Woods, 1999). Movies originally made for theaters are popular television offerings, although there are standards that determine what dialogue and scenes will have to be cut before airing on television. Some of the nudity, sexual scenes, and sexual language are usually eliminated, although the guidelines have been clearly loosening up in recent years.

There is conflicting research evidence about the effects of television on the sexual activities of teenagers.

Reprinted with special permission of King Features Syndicate.

Talk about sex is extremely frequent on television, as are depictions of flirting and kissing. Intercourse is either depicted or strongly implied in roughly one out of every eight shows on television (Kunkel, Cope, & Biely, 1999). There is certainly evidence that adolescents are somewhat affected by such content. The more teens are exposed to these themes on TV, the stronger their endorsement of recreational sexual activity and the higher their expectations of the amount of sex their peers are experiencing (Ward & Rivadeneyra, 1999). However, there is also evidence that there is more to the relationship between teenagers and the media than simple "exposure." Teens' own sense of themselves—their identities—determine not only what they will seek out to view in the media, but also how they will interact with and be affected by what they see (Steele, 1999).

There have also been studies on the portrayals of women and men on television. It has been reported that men on TV frequently comment on women's bodies and physical appearance and that masculinity is often equated with being sexual. Feminist issues and themes tend to be trivialized and undervalued (Ward, 1995). Experts have warned that television needs to offer images of sexuality that emphasize planning, honesty, pleasurability, and protection.

The police drama *NYPD Blue* was one of the most sexually explicit shows to first appear on American network TV, and it has been followed by others. *Melrose Place* and *Baywatch* have also featured sex-related themes and partial nudity. It is increasingly common for sexuality to become part of the scripts for TV dramas and situation comedies. The popular comedy show *Seinfeld* was the first prime-time network television program to deal with masturbation as a theme, and allusions to masturbation have now made their way into most situation comedies, along with frequent references to penises and breasts. Such programs have tackled other sexual themes as well, including impotence and gay relationships. Television talk shows have a reputation for dealing with every conceivable sexual variation and relationship, even during daytime hours (Gamson, 1998). Today's television viewing public is arguably the most widely sexuality-exposed public in history. How much of an impact that exposure to sexual themes has on the lives of people in all age brackets is yet to be fully understood.

Advertising

More than any other medium in American society today, advertising uses and exploits sex to sell products. Calvin Klein advertisements for underwear have been highly popular, although they have also come under fire for using models that appear to be underage. Print advertisements for Obsession perfume often make use

of naked bodies in rather subdued romantic lighting. It is the young, attractive male and the beautiful female who predominate in advertisements for alcoholic beverages, perfume, jewelry, cars, and clothing, because the basic idea behind using sex to sell a product is something advertisers call "identification." If the consumer uses a certain perfume, wears a certain pair of jeans, or drives a certain car, he or she will be as glamorous and attractive as the model and will have the kind of excitement and romance in her or his life that is implied in the advertisement (see Fig. 14.6).

If the advertisement is not blatantly sexual, then it may be subliminally so. Advertisers may use a technique called embedding, in which they deliberately hide emotionally or sexually charged words or pictures in the background of an advertisement. More frequently, women and men in advertising tend to be portrayed in rather specific and stereotypical ways, generating criticism that they are perpetuating outmoded and unfair images. On the other hand, it has been argued that such images are simply reflections of

FIGURE 14.6 *HIV-Positive Model*

Stereotypes may be perpetuated by advertising—or they may be undermined. Chris Crays was the first member of Proof Positive, a division of the Morgan Agency that includes only HIV-positive models. Crays has been HIV positive for 7 years.

the prevailing attitudes about gender that seem to help sell products on the basis of sex appeal (Jensen, 1996). Precisely because of these facts, advertising causes consternation among critics because some of them view these advertising messages as a type of mind control.

One might ask why the sexual message is such a powerful one. Why does everyone want to identify with a symbol of sex? One possible answer is that in our culture, sex is synonymous with youth, attractiveness, and desirability, and implies wealth and power. However, whether the media have created that image identification or simply mirror it is still a debatable point.

Child Pornography

One of the most secretive, most lucrative, and most damaging types of pornography is that involving children. Children are emotionally unable to give true consent to sexual behavior and thus are the innocent victims of adult greed. **Kiddie porn,** as it is more popularly known, involves everything from children simply posing in the nude, to suggestive movement, to sexual activity with others their own age and with adults. Although statistics on child pornography can be only estimates, U.S. customs officials believe that up to 20,000 pieces of such material are smuggled into this country each week, primarily from Scandinavia. Although they are often monitored by authorities, child pornography sites are still available through the Internet.

Courts in the United States continue to support the contention that child pornography lies outside First Amendment protection. The Child Protection and Obscenity Enforcement Act of 1988 supports stiff penalties for those who involve children in sexual exploitation through the making and distribution of pornography. The penalties for causing a child to engage in explicit sexual behavior before a camera or for distributing child pornography have escalated. Rings of people engaged in transmission of child sex images over the Internet have been prosecuted and given stiff sentences. Some photographers, book distributors, and librarians believe that parts of the law are too restrictive and counter to constitutional guarantees of freedom of speech. There has also been controversy over what constitutes child pornography. In one case, a man was convicted because he had videotapes of teenaged and preteen girls in bathing suits who were dancing, and he had zoomed in on the clothed genital area. Another court overturned the conviction because there was no nudity or discernible "lascivious exhibitions." The Barnes & Noble book chain came under fire for selling an art and photo book called *The Age of Innocence,* which showed prepubescent girls in nude poses (Handy, 1998a). Such controversies will certainly persist, but the message condemning the use of underage individuals in pornography seems clear.

◼ Effects of Sexually Explicit Materials

Many people have conflicting attitudes about sexually explicit material. They may be reluctant to admit that they are aroused by reading or seeing pornographic material, or they have some degree of guilt about their reactions. And perhaps because pornography makes very private acts very public, various groups in society have been concerned with the effect pornographic material is likely to have on those who read and see it. Early research into the effects of pornography tended to concentrate on the immediate and the short-term effects, especially on males. Results were mixed and hardly representative of the general population. However, it has seemed clear that exposure to sexually explicit materials can lead to sexual arousal, both positive and negative emotional reactions, and to participation in some form of sexual activity that the individual viewer tends to prefer.

Conflicts over the positive and negative potentials of sexually explicit material were once based in two major theoretical camps. **Modeling theory** held that when people were exposed to sexual acts through pornography, there was a greater likelihood that they would copy this behavior in their own lives. Another point of view, called the **catharsis theory,** maintained that pornography actually prevented violence or unconventional sexual behavior by releasing sexual tension in the viewer or reader. More recently, sexually explicit material has been examined from the perspective that it might result in attitudinal changes (Davis & Bauserman, 1993).

National Commissions on Pornography

Dozens of studies have attempted to examine the effects of sexually explicit materials on adults. Some of these studies have been part of national efforts to resolve questions about the regulation of pornography. In the United States, during the Nixon and Reagan administrations, groups were established to examine the effects of pornography and the regulation of pornography.

kiddie porn: the distribution and sale of photographs and films of children or younger teenagers engaging in some form of sexual activity.

modeling theory: suggests that people will copy behavior they view in pornography.

catharsis theory: suggests that viewing pornography provides a release for sexual tension, thus preventing antisocial behavior.

Presidential Commission on Obscenity and Pornography, 1970

This commission's majority report recommended the repeal of legislation prohibiting the sale, exhibition, or distribution of sexual materials to consenting adults. The report stated that the recommendation was based on the commission's having found "no evidence to date that exposure to explicit sexual materials plays a significant role in the causation of delinquent or criminal behavior among youth or adults." Additionally, the commission declared that pornography did not cause "social or individual harms such as . . . sexual or nonsexual deviancy or severe emotional disturbance" (pp. 32, 58). A minority of commission members did not concur with the report, however, and the U.S. Senate and President Richard Nixon rejected the commission's recommendations. Some critics maintained that the commission should have considered more thoroughly evidence about the connections of violence and sex and about how people sometimes imitate the behavior they observe in others. Neither did it use any studies done with young people. Instead, the conclusions about youth were drawn from retrospective reports by adult research subjects (Cline, 1974).

United States Attorney General's Commission on Pornography, 1986

In 1984, a new commission was established to hold hearings on the effects of pornography. From its inception, this commission was clearly charged with making recommendations on how "the spread of pornography could be contained." Its work was governed by a premise that pornography was a "serious national problem." Commission members were chosen for their recognized antipornography stances. The commission had neither the funds nor time to support new research studies, relying instead on the testimony of witnesses. This led to claims that the group's conclusions were simplistic and unjustified by scientific data (Mosher, 1986). The majority report concluded that violent pornography caused sexually aggressive behavior toward women and children and fostered accepting attitudes toward rape. There were mixed opinions on the potential effects of pornography that the commission deemed "nonviolent and nondegrading." The commission did make recommendations for the control and elimination of pornography, by enforcing stricter laws and stiffer penalties for offenders. Others opposed the recommendations as unconstitutional intrusions on various civil liberties.

It is clear that governmental commissions serve mainly to fulfill the political agendas of particular administrations. To a degree, however, they may also reflect the attitudes of a society. Comparing the conclusions of the 1986 commission report with the one that appeared in 1970 provides interesting speculation about how social attitudes and values regarding pornography and individual freedom may have shifted during that period.

Exposure to Sexually Explicit Materials

Thirty-five years of research have amassed a variety of findings concerning exposure to sexually explicit materials and the effects of that exposure. Writers of commentaries or opinions about pornography often begin with some ideological assumption and then cite research in a highly selective way to support their assertions (Stires, 1999). Researchers may have their own particular attitudes and points of view that they bring to their work (Robinson, Scheltema, Koznar, & Manthei, 1996). There have been a few surveys that have attempted to integrate the available findings, but they have lacked any overall theoretical context from which to understand the conclusions. Consequently, there has been a great deal of confusion about the results of research on sexually explicit materials and exactly what those results mean.

Davis and Bauserman (1993) have done the most comprehensive job to date of systematically analyzing and integrating research on sexually explicit materials, using contemporary psychological theory on attitude change as a basis of understanding. Their analysis has brought some fundamental principles about the effects of pornography into perspective. They see sexually explicit material as a form of *persuasive communication,* because it clearly has an impact on those who view it. The questions revolve around how much impact, and what kinds of impact, it actually has.

Arousal and Emotional Reactions

To be commercially successful, pornography must produce sexual arousal and positive emotional reactions as defined by the viewer. These also appear to be the primary motivations for people to seek out and view sexually explicit materials. Almost all such materials do produce arousal, as demonstrated by the self-reporting of research participants or by direct measurement of genital and other physiological changes. Emotional responses have been measured on scales of 5 to 50 points of variation, on which people rate their intensity of both pleasant and unpleasant reactions. Seventy to 90 percent of both men and women have measurable physiological arousal in response to sexually explicit material. Self-reporting scales have found that either there are no particular differences between men and women, or men experience somewhat more arousal than women when viewing pornography. There is no support in the research literature for the contention that women are not aroused by graphic depictions of sex that lack romantic aspects or that they are more aroused when romance is included in the depictions.

It is fairly consistent across various studies that men react with more positive emotions to sexually explicit material and that women react with higher levels of negative emotions. People who find material sexually arousing are more likely to react positively to it, but sometimes the arousal and emotional reactions are quite independent of one another. Depicted sexual behaviors that the individual considers bizarre or socially deviant are likely to produce a negative emotional response, even if the person has also been sexually aroused by seeing them (Robinson et al., 1996). Average adult males tend to have the highest levels of arousal in response to sexually explicit materials featuring adults of their preferred sex, but they may also have substantial levels of arousal when postpubescent children or adolescents of the preferred sex are shown. They have minimal levels of response, although often measurable levels, in response to children depicted in pornography. The research confirms that for every type of sexually explicit stimulus, there are at least some people who react with arousal and positive emotions. For those same stimuli, there are other people who are not aroused and/or have a negative emotional response (Davis & Bauserman, 1993).

Effects on Attitudes

There have been many claims about how viewing sexually explicit materials might change people's attitudes toward sexuality, relationships, or other people. Theories of attitude change postulate that there are two paths through which human beings process persuasive communication such as sexually explicit material. The *central* processing route involves careful, thoughtful, and systematic processing of the information, whereas the *peripheral* processing route is more automatic and involves a minimum of cognitive effort. It is theorized that for real attitudinal change to occur, material must be processed thoroughly through the central route and that clear motivation and ability must be present within the individual to pursue this path. For most people, sexually explicit material is viewed solely for its arousal value, and psychologists believe that as such it tends to distract viewers from processing it through any central path. It is not likely that it leads to substantial or long-term attitudinal changes in most people. However, the effects of such materials are the result of complex interactions of the viewer's predispositions, the nature of the pornography being viewed, and the amount of exposure. The research suggests that a single exposure to sexually explicit stories, pictures, or films produces minimal change in

sexuality-related attitudes. More exposure may result in somewhat more permissive attitudes, as viewers experience less anxiety and more positive feelings.

There has been a great deal of research focused on the effects of pornography on the attitudes of men toward women. The findings show that males who have a history of more exposure to sexually explicit materials do not hold more negative attitudes toward women, and in fact they may be more gender egalitarian in their attitudes. Research subjects tend to respond more negatively to scenes depicting sexual aggression, and more positively to egalitarian scenes, but attitudes seem unaffected (Bauserman, 1998). On the other hand, exposure to massive amounts of material that depicts callousness or adversarial relationships with women seems to strengthen such attitudes in men who have a predisposition toward them. For the most part, exposure to sexually explicit material appears to have little effect on attitudes (Bauserman, 1998; Davis & Bauserman, 1993; Pollard, 1995).

Effects on Behavior

The research on the possible behavioral effects of sexually explicit materials has focused primarily on sexual and aggressive behaviors. As might be anticipated, most research has found that at least some, and often the majority of, participants report an increase in sexual behavior within 24 hours following exposure. These tend to be behaviors in which the person would participate with some frequency anyway, including sexual thoughts and fantasies, daydreams, talking about sex, masturbation, and sexual intercourse. Sexual behaviors that occur with lower frequency for the individual do not seem to increase following exposure.

It is neither ethical nor practical for researchers to carry out "real-world" studies determining if people will behave in a sexually aggressive manner following exposure to pornography. Instead, researchers have created an artificial situation to measure aggression: After a subject has been exposed to pornography, a "confederate" will attempt to provoke aggressive behavior by insulting the subject. Males who are exposed to nonaggressive pornography are no more likely to aggress against females than controls who have been exposed to neutral, or nonexplicit, material. Exposure to aggressive depictions in pornography sometimes seems to increase nonsexual aggression somewhat, although usually only when provoked again by a confederate. These effects have been limited to laboratory settings and seem to be short term, disappearing rapidly (David & Bauserman, 1993). Intellectual ability of subjects has also been shown to be a variable in such research. Lower IQ men are more likely to be more sexually suggestive toward women and stand closer to them following the viewing of sexual violence, although no difference was noted in higher IQ men (Bogaert, Woodard, & Hafer, 1999). Other research has found that pornography produces no antiwoman aggression, fantasies, or attitudes in men (Fisher & Grenier, 1994).

Pornography, Aggression, and Violence

FOH Although researchers have difficulty designing studies to find if exposure to pornography will cause sexual aggression or violence, they have done studies to see if an association can be found between a history of exposure to pornography and later sexual behaviors. Early studies on longer-term effects of pornography were particularly concerned with how exposure to pornography might relate to antisocial or criminal sexual behavior in males. Institutionalized sex offenders and pornography users who frequented "adult" bookstores and cinemas were compared to a carefully matched sample of individuals in a control group. It was found that the controls—the average, nonoffender heterosexuals—had actually been exposed to more pornography during adolescence than other groups surveyed, and to more explicit forms of pornography as well. Some interesting findings emerged concerning sex-offender groups. Unlike the controls, they reported responses to pornography typical of people who had a great deal of emotional guilt about sexual thoughts and behaviors, and at the same time they had less frequent exposure to pornographic materials. It also seemed that the sex offenders' reactions to pornography during adulthood were more typical of what one might expect of adolescents—especially because arousal so often led to masturbation. The control groups tended to seek heterosexual outlets after being aroused by erotic materials.

Should pornography be available to the general public? Should there be any restrictions in terms of age of consumer or theme of material?

In studying the use of pornography among a population of child molesters and a control group, it was found that the child molesters had in fact been significantly older when first exposed to pornography than the controls. There were no significant differences found in how frequently the pornography was used when they were adults (Nutter & Kearns, 1993). Several researchers have concluded that there is no demonstrable evidence to support the contention that use of pornography might be associated with a greater likelihood of committing sexually violent acts such as rape (Gentry, 1991). In a survey of four countries where pornographic materials are widely available—Denmark, Sweden, Germany, and the United States—

there did not seem to be any correlation between that availability and the incidence of rape in the society (Kutchinsky, 1991). It has been proposed that motivation to rape may not be influenced by exposure to pornography, but rather that pornography could reinforce already existing beliefs and values about rape. The idea that pornography causes contempt for women and encourages the treatment of them as sexual objects is one that deserves much more concern and study, and yet such research should also include ways of briefing experimental subjects so that any negative effects of the materials may be mitigated (Allen, D'Alessio, Emmers, & Gebhardt, 1996; Diamond & Uchiyama, 1999).

There is a considerable amount of research that has focused on male responses to depictions of coercive sex or rape. There seems to be a distinct difference in how men respond to portrayals of realistic rape, in which the woman shows pain and revulsion, and what psychologists call "rape myth" portrayals, in which the woman eventually becomes aroused and participates willingly. The realistic depictions tend not to be as arousing as the rape myths and often produce negative emotional responses (Bauserman, 1998). It may also be that greater exposure to sexually explicit material that features violence may cause some men to believe more strongly in the rape myth (Davis & Bauserman, 1993; Perse, 1994). However, the research conditions themselves may play a significant role in these results, with real-life conditions producing no noticeable changes in acceptance of rape myths, whereas more direct experimental conditions did produce some such changes (Allen, Emmers, Gebhardt, & Liery, 1995).

Pornography, the Courts, and the Law

The pornography issue is intimately associated with the principles of freedom of speech and freedom of press and the role of the courts and the law in upholding those principles. Although some crusade against censorship and for the freedom to read or view whatever sexually oriented matter one wishes, others argue that "trash" can and should be distinguished from "art" and that censorship should be allowed even in a democracy. Two fundamental issues in the censorship argument are the assumptions that sexual images will lead to inappropriate behavior and that these images objectify human beings, in a sense dehumanizing them. There are those who do not feel that the evidence supports such assumptions, and that although censorship may offer the illusion of solving social problems, in reality it leads to the loss of freedoms (Pally, 1994). There is evidence that enforcement of antipornography laws does not significantly change

CASE STUDY

A T-Shirt Places a Male Residence Hall Under Fire

A freshman residence hall that had traditionally been all male had developed a reputation for its macho image on the campus. In fun, the dorm was nicknamed "The Cave," and its residents took pride in their special identity. Although college officials discouraged use of the building's nickname, the staff who lived there often boasted of the camaraderie that its residents seemed to share. They had intramural sports teams, parties, and a variety of annual special events. One of The Cave's traditions was to create a specially designed T-shirt for its residents each fall. One particular year, the T-shirt pictured a drawing of two cavemen figures dragging a cavewoman by the hair toward a door labeled "The Cave."

Soon after the T-shirt began to appear, there was an outcry from various campus constituencies condemning the shirt and what was perceived as its antiwoman message. Some faculty members banned the wearing of the T-shirts in the classroom, claiming that it constituted harassment of women. Many of the men wearing the shirt took offense at this reaction, saying that there had been no malicious intent in the shirt's design and claiming that the U.S. Constitution protected their right of freedom of expression. They received support from some women on the campus, who agreed that the shirt certainly did not reflect the attitudes of men in the dorm toward women.

They argued that opponents were going too far in their assumptions. College officials made certain that institutional funds had not been used to pay for the T-shirt, and they also issued a statement that they did not support the negative message it conveyed. However, officials also declined to prohibit the wearing of the shirt on a general basis. They reminded those individuals who felt that the shirt was in any way personally harassing that they could lodge complaints using the institution's grievance procedures.

The "Cave T-Shirt," as it came to be known, turned out to be a highly educational phenomenon. It generated many open debates and classroom discussions about individual rights of expression versus the rights of individuals to live and work in a nonhostile environment. It provided an excellent real-life situation that tested the complicated issues on all sides of the question. The controversy led men and women to talk more openly about their attitudes toward one another. As things turned out, no one ever brought formal complaints about the T-shirt, and the wearers of the shirt tried to be considerate of those faculty members who explained that they were personally offended by the picture. Although it rather quickly faded from popularity, the T-shirt's impact remained legendary on the campus.

the rate of arrests for rape, prostitution, or other sex offenses (Winick & Evans, 1996).

> *What is your response to the Cave T-shirt controversy as described in the case study entitled "A T-Shirt Places a Male Residence Hall under Fire"?*

Local governments, state courts, federal legislation, and courts have tended to be inconsistent in their treatment of cases related to sexually explicit materials. In 1868, obscenity was given a basic legal definition as any material whose tendency was to "deprave and corrupt those whose minds are open to such immoral influences, and into whose hands a publication of this sort may fall." It was illegal to purvey obscenity to the public. In the landmark 1957 Supreme Court case of *Roth v. United States,* obscenity was redefined as matter appealing to prurient interest ("a shameful or morbid interest in nudity, sex, or excretion, which goes beyond customary limits of candor"). The Court further ruled, however, that censorship of obscene material would not be allowed if the material had some "socially redeeming significance." In 1969, in the case of *Stanley v. Georgia,*

the Court ruled that a person is entitled to possess pornography in the privacy of his or her own home and to use that pornography to satisfy whatever intellectual or emotional needs he or she desires.

In 1973, the Supreme Court took a different position on pornography. It decided that a connection between pornography and antisocial behavior could be neither proved nor disproved. On this basis, the Court ruled that state legislatures themselves may adopt their own limits on commerce in pornography, placing more of the responsibility for judgments about pornography on local governments. The Court also dropped the obscenity standard of lack of "redeeming social value," in favor of a new standard specifying that the work, taken as a whole, must lack serious literary, artistic, political, or scientific merit. The Court limited the standard to works that depict or describe sexual conduct. The vagueness of these definitions, and the apparent reversals in Supreme Court positions, continue to create confusion in other court decisions, and to lead to widely disparate attitudes toward pornography in different communities around the country.

The controversy has continued in other arenas. There have been bills entertained by legislatures that would permit suits by people who felt they had been victims of crimes somehow associated with the use of pornography. Like similar legislative attempts, these are considered to be a radical departure from accepted constitutional principles relating to freedom of expression. The Supreme Court of Canada decided that pornographic materials by definition "subordinated or degraded" women and declared that it was therefore legitimate to suppress such materials. Deciding what constitutes undue sexual exploitation is still left to individual prosecutors and lower courts in Canada, and this has created a great deal of confusion and debate. Again, the problems seem to lie in the vague definition of what constitutes pornography, the assumption that it is harmful, and the provision that anyone harmed may bring suit (Katz, 1994). Clearly, pornography presents a very real challenge in defining freedom of expression and setting the boundaries that any society will use in regulating such materials.

What role, if any, should the government take in legislating sexual behavior or access to sexually explicit materials?

◼ Legal Aspects of Sexual Behavior

Lawmakers and law enforcers seem to fall into two major philosophical camps. Some believe that the law has a responsibility to enforce private morals publicly and to prohibit whatever the community or society deems to be morally wrong or offensive. The other philosophical camp holds that the purpose of the law is to protect rather than to prohibit. They are not concerned about laws against sexual activities that involve consenting adults, and they believe that government should stay out of the bedrooms of private citizens (Posner & Silbaugh, 1996).

It seems that in the area of sexual behavior, for every activity that some people find disturbing or worthy of moral disapproval, a law has appeared to prohibit the activity. There have been laws that have attempted to regulate the criteria of consent for sex, the nature of the sexual act, the object to which it may be directed, and where the act may take place. Although the laws concerning sexual behavior differ among the states, it is likely that a great many adults in the United States have performed sexual acts considered at least in some states to be criminal under the law. There are only two types of sexual behavior that are usually not potentially subject to criminal prosecution so long as they are practiced in private: solitary masturbation and intercourse between husband and wife.

Several states have statutes specifically prohibiting sexual activity between persons of the same gender. Some other states have laws that prohibit forms of behavior that fall into the category of "deviate sexual intercourse," without necessarily specifying the gender of the participants. This means that the behaviors could be considered criminal between heterosexual partners as well. These laws are often called **sodomy laws,** the term "sodomy" being applied rather freely to many behaviors that are legally defined as deviate sexual intercourse including oral-genital, genital-anal, oral-anal, and manual-genital contact (Portelli, 1998). More than half of the 50 states no longer have sodomy laws, essentially permitting consenting adults to share private sexual acts of their choosing (SIECUS Public Policy Dept., 1998). However, the U.S. Supreme Court has handed down several decisions affirming the right of individual states to pass legislation that could limit specific sexual rights, including certain sexual activities.

The debate continues over whether sex-related laws should be for prohibition or protection. The American Bar Association has joined the Group for the Advancement of Psychiatry in calling for sex offenders to be confined for appropriate treatment of their sexual disorders rather than just incarcerated for punishment. Those who are in favor of legal reforms argue that laws prohibiting sexual behavior between consenting adults are attempts to impose specific moral and religious standards on citizens.

Sex and the Constitution

The legal aspects of sexual behavior cannot be fairly considered without examining some of the constitutional implications. Since the U.S. Constitution was written, there has been a conflict over the extent to which it guarantees personal liberty in cases in which other people are not harmed. The debate has sometimes focused on the laws governing, or attempting to govern, sexual behavior. Some experts insist that laws prohibiting consensual sexual activity between adults—particularly gay men or lesbians—are indeed unconstitutional. When these laws have been vaguely worded, courts have sometimes declared them "void for vagueness."

Three other constitutional principles have been used to overturn laws regulating consensual adult sexual behavior. One is the "independent rights" doctrine, which holds that the Constitution imposes

sodomy laws: laws in some states that prohibit a variety of sexual behaviors, often described as deviate sexual intercourse. These laws are often enforced discriminatorily against particular groups, such as gay males.

certain restrictions on state laws that might interfere with personal liberty. Another is the "right of privacy" doctrine, which, in many courts, has been used to uphold the concept that what people do in private should not be the concern of prohibitive laws unless someone is being harmed. In addition, the "equal protection" clause of the Fourteenth Amendment has been interpreted to require that state laws be nondiscriminatory both in their statutory expression and in their enforcement. Colorado became the first state to pass a state constitutional amendment in the 1990s that denied gays and lesbians legal protection from discrimination. The amendment never went into effect because of an initial court ruling against it, and the U.S. Supreme Court struck down the measure on constitutional grounds as discriminatory and hostile toward a particular group of people.

The debates over laws concerning consensual sexual behavior and other seemingly "victimless" crimes will continue. These issues should be of concern to all citizens because they often have implications for our freedom in other areas. In recent years, it has become clear that the makeup of both the Congress and the Supreme Court—the primary branch of government that interprets the Constitution and sets precedents about legal interventions—plays a key role in determining whether decisions lean in more conservative or more liberal directions with regard to sex-related issues (Daley, 1997).

Special Issues and the Law

Sexuality Education

Though it has not been subject to much court action, sexuality education has met with controversy that has reached as far as the U.S. Congress. As far back as 1919, federal authorities decided that sexuality education was more properly a task of the school, and there are still two federal education laws that prohibit the federal government from dictating the content of sexuality education courses (Daley, 1997). A landmark court case was initiated in 1970 against the board of education of Topeka, Kansas, alleging that the school district's sexuality education program was unconstitutional because it violated the parents' personal liberty to determine what subjects are taught. It was further alleged that the authority to instruct children about sexuality is reserved for the parents. At the conclusion of the trial, the judge found for the schools, permitting them to continue their program.

Although the teaching of sexuality education topics has been left to the jurisdiction of state laws and local boards of education, there have been continuing waves of antisexuality education sentiment. Citizen groups, often with religious affiliations, have attacked sexuality education in public school settings, pressuring boards

of education into reversing previous decisions. Some precedents have already been set, suggesting that religiously based sexuality education values are not to be considered suitable for the public schools. The issues of HIV and AIDS have become a new focus of groups that maintain that sexuality education only encourages and condones sexual activity among the young. Nevertheless, studies consistently demonstrate that two-thirds or more of all adult Americans favor sexuality education in public schools, and nearly all states mandate teaching about HIV/AIDS at some level in the educational structure. They are far less likely to mandate comprehensive sexuality education or the provision of information about contraception.

The U.S. Congress built $75 million of annual aid into the Maternal and Child Health block grant to be used by states in abstinence-based sexuality education through the end of the 1990s. It was used specifically to discourage sexual activity outside of marriage. This is part of continuing congressional debate on the content of sexuality education programs, with a growing likelihood that comprehensive sexuality education will be discouraged in favor of abstinence-based recommendations and mandates from the federal level (Daley, 1997).

Sexual Assault and Rape

Historically, women were not regarded as equal to men under the law and were instead treated as their possessions. Therefore, forced sex was viewed not as a crime against the female victim but as a property crime against the man who "owned" her, either her father or her husband. In the United States, laws passed in 1868 required that rape be corroborated by evidence of actual penetration, the use of force, and identification of the rapist. In the 1970s, corroboration laws were generally repealed, so that the burden of proof was lessened for the victim. Nonetheless, conviction has still depended on the prosecution's being able to provide tangible evidence that sexual assault has occurred. A landmark decision emerged in 1979 when a Massachusetts court found a man guilty of raping his wife. During the previous year, there had been a trial in Oregon involving a case in which a husband was accused of raping his wife, but there was no conviction. In the Massachusetts case, the couple had been separated for several months when the man forced himself into his wife's apartment and threatened to kill her if she did not have intercourse with him. A jury of eight men and four women found him guilty, and he was sentenced to 3 to 5 years in prison, along with several years of probation.

Many states have been reevaluating their legislation that applies to the investigation and prosecution of rape cases. Legislative measures have now been adopted in most states that help rape victims and increase the chances of convicting the perpetrator. Symptoms of the rape trauma syndrome are sometimes admissible as evidence in rape trials (see chapter 15, "Sexual Coercion, Rape, and Abuse"). Members of police agencies have also been receiving training with respect to sexual assault, especially those who deal with rape victims. Some local agencies provide counselors who act as advocates and sources of support for the rape victim throughout the judicial process. Some agencies also recommend third-party reporting of rape in case a victim is reluctant to come forward. This at least informs authorities that a rape has occurred, which may be valuable if the victim later decides to proceed with a report. It would appear that after centuries of neglect and mistreatment by most judicial systems, rape victims are finding the prospects of having their attackers prosecuted and convicted more probable than ever before.

Sex Workers and Nude Dancing

Legal reforms are difficult in the area of sex workers. Prostitution has often been considered a "victimless" crime because the sexual activity is seemingly between two consenting adults. Two types of laws attempt to control overt prostitution: (1) those that prohibit loitering with the intent to commit an act of prostitution; and (2) those that prohibit either offering or agreeing to an act of prostitution. Again, the basic philosophy behind such laws is the regulation of private morality. However, many groups insist that it is a social necessity to attempt legal control of sex workers. Police claim that the street environment generated by sex workers breeds crime of other sorts. Public health officials say that prostitutes are responsible for much of the increase in rates of sexually transmitted infections. Moralists attack sex workers on religious grounds.

Some people favor the *decriminalization* of prostitution, which would lead to regulation of the trade. Under such a plan, there would be certain age requirements, taxation rules, and standards of hygiene. Sex workers would be required to obtain a license. Decriminalization would protect the civil rights of both prostitutes and their clients. It would free sex workers from the system of arrests, bail, and release to the street; the abuse of pimps; and the harassment of society.

The Supreme Court has also been called on to decide on the constitutionality of nude dancing and stripping in bars. The owners of the Kitty Kat Lounge in South Bend, Indiana, had been convicted of violating a state law prohibiting nude dancing. G-strings and "pasties" over the nipples were considered to be minimum attire for a dancer. A federal court of appeals first overturned the conviction, maintaining that nude dancing is "inherently expressive," and therefore con-

stitutionally protected. However, the Supreme Court ruled that states may ban nude dancing in the interest of "protecting order and morality." The requirement for G-strings and pasties was considered appropriate because it combated what the chief justice called the "evil" of public nudity without suppressing the "erotic message" of the expressive dancing.

Reproductive Rights

Among the controversial issues that have found their way into courts and laws are birth control, welfare benefits for teenage and unwed mothers, sterilization, and abortion (see also chapter 10, "Decision Making about Pregnancy and Parenthood"). The Supreme Court did not declare bans on the use of contraceptives to be unconstitutional until the mid-1960s. Sterilization has been a more complicated issue. There have been several cases in the past in which black women or people with mental retardation have been sterilized without their consent. Such actions seem to rest on the assumption that judges and physicians know best and have the right, and privilege, to decide whether or not an individual will be a fit parent and whether or not the individual's children are apt to be "suitable" for society. This notion has been met by challenges. The Supreme Court refused to hear a case concerning a state law that would have required a minor woman to notify a parent 48 hours prior to obtaining an abortion because the Court had previously required such laws to have provisions to bypass such notification when parents cannot be involved. There are states, however, that have parental notification laws regarding abortion for minors.

Several states have attempted to pass laws that would prohibit abortion altogether and even limit the use of certain kinds of contraceptives. On the other hand, a few states have also passed laws affirming the right of women to obtain legal abortions. The Supreme Court is expected to continue handing down decisions that will have an impact on reproductive rights, and the U.S. Congress is expected to continue proposing legislation to govern various aspects of reproduction, contraception, and abortion.

The Rights and Responsibilities of Sexual Partners

HIV and AIDS created a whole new awareness of the dangers of sexual activity shared with someone who is unwilling to be open and honest about his or her sexual history. It is possible to contract a fatal disease, or a nonfatal sexually transmitted infection, from a partner who does not reveal his or her physical condition or who fails to provide appropriate protection such as use of a condom.

Most states have passed, or are at least considering passing, statutes that would make the rights and responsibilities of sexual partners clear. The individual who is aware of carrying genital herpes, hepatitis-B, or HIV, but fails to inform a sexual partner and fails to use adequate protection to prevent transmission of the disease, will most probably be prosecuted for criminal behavior. These criminal penalties, as well as civil suits, are bound to become more common as the risks of contracting HIV and other sexually transmitted diseases become greater. The outcomes of these cases will set legal precedents by which future relationships may well be governed. State laws have not been as aggressive in passing laws that protect the confidentiality of persons who have positive HIV tests, not only compromising the

privacy of these individuals but creating a disincentive to get tested (SIECUS Public Policy Dept., 1998).

The legal aspects of human sexual behavior will probably always be in conflict with some of the personal, emotional aspects. The public has a right to protection from dangerous behavior, and the individual has a right to behave in any way she or he chooses as long as the behavior does not harm others. In some cases, it is not possible to separate public and private rights. Then a legal interpretation must be made of the situation and a judgment passed on whose right has priority. As historical cycles vacillate between progressivism and conservatism, the judgment will continue to waver between what courts and legislatures consider the public good and private freedom.

Chapter Summary

1. Graphic depictions of human nudity and sexual behavior have been a part of every society and historical period. Pornography, or sexually explicit material, is generally meant to sexually arouse. Erotica is a name given to sexually realistic art or fiction.

2. In many ancient cultures, erotic art was used for purposes of instructing people in sexual behaviors. There has been controversy over use of public funding for the creation of art with sexual themes.

3. Writing about sex can be traced back 4,000 years. There have been cycles of acceptance and repression about erotic writings over the centuries. Prior to 1800, pornographic literature may have been a form of political protest.

4. Even in nineteenth-century Victorian literature, there were frank accounts of sexual behavior. Contemporary literature has explored all sex-related themes. Illustrations are now often used to enhance the impact of erotic material.

5. Adult magazines and tabloids proliferated by the late 1960s, and new sex magazines appear each year.

6. Sexuality has become increasingly open in films, television, and other media. Almost all sex-related themes have appeared in movies. The film rating system categorizes films using sexuality issues as criteria. R- and PG-rated films are the most popular at the box office.

7. Portrayals of women in films were once often stereotypical or negative, but more positive female roles have been available in recent years. Romantic themes are making a comeback in the movies and other media.

8. Hard-core pornography is now almost exclusively found in video format or on the Internet. Sexually explicit material is widely available today in North American and European countries.

9. The computer-accessed Internet now provides up-to-date information on sexuality as well as sexually explicit materials. There are computer bulletin boards and chat rooms through which people anonymously communicate intimate sexual messages. Attempts are being made to regulate sexuality-related communications through computer networks.

10. Advertising frequently makes use of sexual themes to popularize and sell products, sometimes using subliminal embedding techniques.

11. Child pornography represents a lucrative market, and it is prohibited in the United States by federal laws.

12. The presumed effects of sexually explicit materials have often been founded in either modeling theory or catharsis theory. New research has begun to place information about effects in the context of psychological attitude change theory.

13. The presidential commission of 1970 found no particular evidence that pornography caused criminal behavior or contributed to emotional problems. The pornography commission established in the 1980s made sweeping recommendations

about limiting pornography on the basis of its presumed negative effects.

14. Sexually explicit materials are clearly a form of persuasive communication. Exposure usually results in sexual arousal for both men and women and some sort of emotional reaction. Emotional reaction is often governed by the viewer's attitudes toward particular sexual behaviors.

15. When analyzed with contemporary attitude change theory that assumes both central and peripheral paths for processing persuasive communication, it seems likely that pornography has minimal effects on people's attitudes, including men's attitudes toward women.

16. Exposure to sexually explicit material is likely to increase sexual behavior the individual considers acceptable very soon after exposure. There is some controversy over whether sexually violent depictions might lead to a slight increase in aggression.

17. Some research claims that pornography can increase already held negative attitudes toward women, especially if it depicts sexual aggression or violence.

18. Sex offenders do not seem to have had earlier or more frequent exposure to pornography than control populations.

19. Sexually explicit material has been subject to various laws throughout recent history. Since 1973, individual states have been allowed to develop their own legislation.

20. In the United States, sodomy laws have prohibited certain sexual behaviors considered to be deviant. Civil rights groups have argued that any sexual behavior between consenting adults should be considered legal.

21. In the United States, some states have laws that may be used to restrict same-gender sexual behaviors. About half of states consider such behavior to be a criminal offense.

22. There are sometimes constitutional issues raised by the regulation of sexual behavior, centered on vaguely stated laws, the independent rights doctrine, the right of privacy, and discriminatory enforcement of laws.

23. State legislatures are sometimes called upon to determine whether sexuality education or HIV/AIDS education should be recommended or mandated in public schools. Courts and boards of education sometimes must determine the appropriateness of educational materials for public school use.

24. Rape has been considered illegal in recent history, although victims were often subjected to humiliating and difficult treatment in order to prosecute the rapist. Newer laws have allowed for greater sensitivity toward the victim, increasing the chances of conviction. There are also laws making marital rape a crime.

25. In most states, prostitution is prohibited by law. Nude dancing may be regulated by state laws.

26. Birth control in some states was prohibited by laws until the mid-1960s. Sterilization of people without their consent has been challenged in the courts. States are increasingly placing restrictions on abortion.

27. Increasingly, statutes are appearing to clarify that sex partners have certain legal rights and responsibilities.

Focus on Health Questions

You will find in this section the kinds of questions that you may have concerning your own health and sexuality. The page references indicate where in the text the answer is located; the exact place is marked with the logo: FOH

1. What is the difference between what people call pornography and erotica? 424

2. Does pornography including violent scenes encourage sexual violence? 438

3. Are there laws that prohibit some kinds of sex? 440

Annotated Readings

Boone, J. A. (1998). *Libidinal currents: Sexuality and the shaping of modernism*. Chicago: Chicago University Press. An intellectual perspective on the evolution of sexual values through literature.

Chancer, L. S. (1998). *Reconcilable differences: Confronting beauty, pornography, and the future of feminism*. Berkeley: University of California Press. A reliable guide for people attempting to understand the complicated debates that have been waged between feminists and a variety of controversial topics.

Heins, M. (1993). *Sex, sin, and blasphemy: A guide to America's censorship wars*. New York: New Press. An advocate for a liberal view of First Amendment rights, this author surveys major debates and leading figures on both sides of the issues.

Horrocks, R. (1995). *Male myths and icons: Masculinity in popular culture*. New York: St. Martin's Press. An analysis of male images in films, music, and pornography, offering insights into the impact they have on gender roles in our culture.

Hunt, L. (Ed.). (1993). *The invention of pornography: Obscenity and the origins of modernity, 1500–1800*. New York: Zone Books. A collection of papers that traces the social significance of pornography through history in several different European societies. The book offers some creative new perspectives.

Levesque, R. (1999). *Adolescents, sex, and the law: Preparing adolescents for responsible citizenship*. Washington: American Psychological Association. This book argues that society can only expect to foster responsible behavior among adolescents to the extent that we give them greater control over their rights.

McCormick, D. (1994). *Erotic literature: A connoisseur's guide*. New York: Continuum. A guide to world classics in prose and poetry, both ancient and modern, that have erotic themes. The book provides reminders of how central eroticism has been in literature across cultures.

Posner, R. A., & Silbaugh, K. B. (1996). *A guide to America's sex laws*. Chicago: University of Chicago Press. An overview of trends in laws regarding sexuality in the United States.

Waugh, T. (1996). *Hard to imagine: Gay male eroticism in photography and film from their beginnings to Stonewall*. New York: Columbia University Press. A scholarly treatment of the treatment of gay male images.

West, D. J., & Green, R. (Eds.). (1997). *Sociolegal control of homosexuality: A multi-nation comparison*. New York: Plenum. A collection of articles that present a cross-cultural view of how legal systems have been used in attempts to regulate and sanction same-gender sexual behavior.

Whatling, C. (1997). *Screen dreams: Fantasizing lesbians in film*. New York: St. Martin's Press. An examination of the portrayals of lesbians and their lifestyles in films.

Wolfthal, D. (1999). *Images of rape: The "heroic" tradition and its alternatives*. New York: Cambridge University Press. An art historian's view of the rape themes that were so popular in the male-dominated European culture of the fifteenth to seventeenth centuries.

Part 5

Dealing with Sexual Problems

■

It is likely that most people face some sort of sex-related problem sometime during their lives. The individual who faces a sexual problem may be forced to cope with a wide range of emotions, including guilt, anxiety, depression, self-doubt, and feelings of inadequacy. In seeking professional help, it is important to find someone who is well equipped to deal with sex-related matters. The four chapters in this part explore a variety of sexual problems, the different perspectives from which these problems may be viewed, and the ways in which professionals approach them. Chapter 15 reminds us that there has been an increase in awareness in recent years about coercive and exploitative sexual behaviors, including sexual harassment, forced sex, and child sexual abuse. People are now more willing to report such incidents to appropriate authorities and talk about the problems they have experienced as victims.

Sexual interaction has always been associated with the transmission of certain diseases, and that is one of the reasons that many social and religious codes of conduct have been established to regulate sexual behavior. For a time, however, it seemed that antibiotics would save us from the disease threats that came with sex. First herpes, and then HIV, represented cruel reminders that there are still health risks associated with shared sex. Chapters 16 and 17 examine the range of diseases associated with human sexual behavior, and offer up-to-date information on the HIV/AIDS crisis currently facing our world.

People's bodies do not always function sexually the way people expect or want, or the way a partner might prefer. Sometimes, that can mean that the person is experiencing a sexual dysfunction. Disorders of sexual desire and functioning are discussed in chapter 18, along with some of the approaches to treating them that have been developed in the field of sex therapy. Most sexual problems do not have to remain problems forever. The chapters in this section of the text provide helpful suggestions for preventing and seeking help with problematic sex.

Chapter 15
SEXUAL COERCION, RAPE, AND ABUSE

Sexual attractions, attitudes, and behaviors can become problematic. There has been increasing awareness of the negative effects of sexual harassment.

Chapter 16
SEXUALLY TRANSMITTED DISEASES AND OTHER PHYSICAL PROBLEMS

Part of responsible sexual decision making is to take appropriate measures to prevent the transmission of sexually transmitted diseases (STDs).

Chapter 17
THE HIV/AIDS CRISIS AND SEXUAL DECISIONS

HIV destroys the body's immune system so that opportunistic infections eventually weaken the victim. The final stage of the disease, AIDS, is fatal.

Chapter 18
SEXUAL DYSFUNCTIONS AND THEIR TREATMENT

Sexual dysfunctions may be caused by physical problems or psychological stress.

Chapter 15
Sexual Coercion, Rape, and Abuse

Chapter Outline

Note: A selection of Focus on Health questions appears at the end of each chapter. Answers to these questions are indicated within the chapter by the symbol in the margin. **FoH**

> I was in total shock when the dean told me my date had accused me of raping her. I just couldn't believe it. We didn't exactly talk about what we were going to do, but she never said no or tried to get out of bed. She seems to really believe that I forced her into this. It's all like a bad dream.
>
> —From a counseling session

This chapter examines various forms of sexual coercion, abuse, and victimization. Within a wide range of human sexual behaviors, some are seen as problematic in particular social and cultural belief systems. Behavior and feelings that are troublesome for one person may be pleasurable and enjoyable for another. In one sense, any kind of sexual activity may become a problem if someone is feeling worried, guilty, fearful, or ashamed about it. However, are the negative feelings justified in terms of present knowledge and attitudes, or do they simply stem from ignorance and misinformation? The answer is often rooted in complex social issues. To a degree, sexual behaviors and feelings become problems or "offenses" because of the cultural values that surround them and the social judgments that are made about them. In this sense, sexual problems are socially constructed (Simon, 1994). *Clearly, any sexual activity that involves the coercion, assault, abuse, or exploitation of someone else is a serious problem.* This chapter focuses on those sex-related behaviors, and the reactions to them, that constitute contemporary social problems.

When and How Does Sex Become a Problem?

Consider the following case study of a 34-year-old attorney who consulted a professional sex therapist. She complained of her lack of interest in sex and expressed hope that the therapist could help her become a more sexually active partner for her husband. She explained that her husband, a 36-year-old accountant, had a stronger sex drive than she did. On the surface of things, this might seem to be a relatively straightforward problem of sexual incompatibility—one partner wanting sexual involvement more frequently than the other. Sex counselors and therapists encounter such discrepancies in relationships often and use various techniques that may help to resolve the difficulties.

However, as the therapist gathered a thorough history of the woman's situation, a much more complex picture emerged. The woman reported that her husband desired and expected to have sexual intercourse two or three times every day. He wanted sex at bedtime and frequently upon awakening in the morning. It was not unusual for him to rouse his wife out of sleep in the middle of the night for sex. If they both came home for lunch during their afternoon breaks, he often wanted to have intercourse. At times she had protested, only to have him coerce her emotionally or even physically into intercourse. The woman did not question her husband's high level of sexual desire, and she wanted only to find ways of becoming a more willing and interested partner for him.

The therapist was now in somewhat of a dilemma, finding serious concerns other than the woman's level of sexual interest in the relationship. The therapist thought that the client probably exhibited normal levels of sexual arousal and that the constant excessive sexual demands and pressures of the husband had quite predictably led to sexual boredom, depression, and burnout on her part. The therapist was also concerned about the continuing patterns of noncommunication and coercion evident in the couple's relationship.

What should the therapist have done? Should she have attempted to fulfill the woman's request and tried to help her become more interested in sex? Redefined the problem in different terms and tried to help the woman to see it that way? Told the woman that she did not have a problem but that her husband did? Encouraged marriage counseling for the couple?

This case study illustrates some fundamental difficulties in considering problematic sex. For example, who is to define whether a problem actually exists at all? And to what degree does a problem exist? What problems are worthy of professional treatment? What are the standards by which problematic and nonproblematic behaviors are to be distinguished from one another? The following represent several causes of sex-related problems.

Negative Self-Attitudes

People often grow up with little information about bodily development or with misconceptions about sexual attractiveness. The young man unprepared for his first ejaculation of semen and the young woman shocked by her first discharge of menstrual blood are bound to experience some fear and worry. Those who have been encouraged to have negative feelings about the sex organs and sexual activities are bound to experience guilt over masturbation and sexual fantasies.

Society and the media often perpetuate stereotypes about sexual attractiveness and sexual behaviors. List several of these stereotypes as they apply to women and as they apply to men.

Society has perpetuated some rather specific stereotypes of sexual attractiveness through popular myths and advertising (see Fig. 15.1). Some individuals even become obsessive about perceived inadequacies of their bodies (Thompson, Heinberg, Altabe, &

FIGURE 15.1   *Stereotypes of Attractiveness*

Both men and women pursue endless hours of aerobics and weight training to make their bodies live up to stereotyped ideals of sexual attractiveness, like that of the strong, young, muscular male. Those who perceive themselves as not living up to these ideals may experience self-conflict and self-doubt, affecting their ability to understand and fulfill their sexual needs.

Tantleff-Dunn, 1999). Negative body image is associated with lower levels of sexual experience, which probably results from aviodance of certain social experiences (Trapnell, Meston, & Gorzalka, 1997).

Boys and men are more prone to be concerned about their height, the muscularity of their bodies, and the size of their penises. Girls and women are more prone to be concerned about their weight, their breast size, and the curvaceousness of their bodies. In a survey of college students, 11 percent of the males believed their penises to be below average in size, and 12 percent would consider having the organ enlarged if possible. Twenty-three percent of the women believed their breasts to be below average, but only 11 percent would consider having them enlarged (Elliott & Brantley, 1997; Lee, 1996). Eating disorders are particularly common in women who have difficulties perceiving their feminine qualities in positive ways. Those who end up feeling inadequate, who do not perceive themselves as living up to the prevailing standards of sex appeal, often experience negative feelings, low self-esteem, and even social isolation (Wierderman & Hurst, 1998).

Personal conflict is a frequent result of the struggles to understand and fulfill our sexual needs. Most

people have experienced their share of remorse, guilt, and self-hatred over sexual mistakes, misconceptions, or intrusive thoughts (Byers et al., 1998). Twenty-one percent of college students in one study indicated that sex generally fell short of their expectations (Elliott & Brantley, 1997), and over one-third of college women in another study experienced at least some guilt over their first sexual intercourse. Guilt seems to be more common in those with lower self-esteem, general uncomfortableness with sexuality, and poor communication with parents. It also seems to set the stage for later dissatisfactions with sex (Moore & Davidson, 1997). At times, the negative self-attitudes and guilt feelings become troublesome enough to warrant counseling or other professional help.

Coercion, Abuse, or Assault of Others

When sex is forced on someone against her or his will, there are many negative consequences for the victim. Although there are elements of mutual seduction in most forms of shared sex, the issue of consent may be a confusing and complicated one at times. Individuals must have the knowledge base to understand fully what they are consenting to, and the consent must be given freely. There may at times be physical or emotional coercion in persuading a partner to become sexually involved, and in such cases people may be more likely to be acquiescing to sex than they are consenting (Hickman & Muehlenhard, 1999). In a relationship, one person may be interested in sex before the other and may begin using various forms of pressure to convince the reluctant partner to get involved. Emotional blackmail, such as saying, "You would have sex with me if you really loved me," or hinting that the relationship will end if sex does not improve, certainly constitutes sexual coercion and a relational problem.

There are many forms of sexual coercion and abuse that are discussed later in this chapter. Most often, they involve one individual using some imbalance in age, status, or power to take advantage of someone else. The offender often uses various forms of rationalization to justify his or her coercive or abusive behaviors. In its more extreme forms, coercive sexual behavior takes the form of sexual assault, in which the offender forces another person into some undesired sexual activity.

Results of Prejudice and Ignorance

The price of being openly different sexually in any society can be high. On the other hand, a narrowly restricted, inhibited pattern of sexual living is not without its costs either. Although we have made some inroads in alleviating various forms of prejudice in recent decades, prejudice about sexual differences remains deeply ingrained in our society's values. Keep in mind that prejudice consists of holding strong attitudes that are seen as truth, even though they have no basis in fact. Prejudice grows out of exaggerated stereotypes and lack of information.

As any sex counselor can confirm, prejudice takes its toll. People with unconventional sexual orientations or lifestyles often feel forced into secret relationships and deception. They may end up feeling as though they live double lives, struggling to exhibit a socially acceptable public image while quietly maintaining a very different lifestyle in private. The stresses of such an existence can have serious consequences in a person's life. There may be a deepening lack of self-respect and self-esteem. Some enter into socially acceptable relationships in hopes that they will be able to pass as acceptable, only to experience instead a period of interpersonal conflict and unhappiness (Tyler et al., 1997).

When the Body Does not Function as Expected or Desired

Most of us have some expectations and hopes about how our sexual encounters with others should go. We just expect that our sex organs will go along too, cooperatively and excitedly. It can be quite a shock when that does not happen. Men and women may find difficulty in becoming sexually aroused. A man may not achieve erection of his penis; a woman may not produce lubrication in her vagina. There may be difficulty in reaching orgasm. It may happen too quickly or not quickly enough. There may be pain, or tightness, or dryness. For a variety of reasons, our bodies simply may not function sexually the way we want or expect them to.

These are the sexual problems that fall into the category of sexual dysfunctions. Although they may have physical roots, most often sexual dysfunctions are caused by psychological blocks and stresses. These problems are discussed in detail in chapter 18, "Sexual Dysfunctions and Their Treatment."

Self-Destructive Behaviors and the Paraphilias

FOH People who find themselves participating in some sexual activity they view as unhealthy or immoral can certainly experience self-destructive reactions with time (Brown, 1995). This includes those who choose sexual acts that involve violence or that are viewed as sexual offenses, for which arrest and prosecution are possible. They may also enter into certain situations with a false sense of invulnerability, believing that harm "won't happen to me" (Cohen & Bruce, 1997). It has been hypothesized that violent and antisocial sexual behaviors could be rooted in a link between stress and

sexual arousal at a biological level, or to some of the chemical disturbances of the brain associated with other obsessive or compulsive tendencies (Kafka, 1997a). Whatever their cause, it is the violent and self-destructive sexual behaviors that we have come to view as personal and social problems.

The paraphilias are characterized by sexual arousal to objects or situations that are not considered part of normative patterns of arousal and activity, and they frequently have self-destructive or victimizing aspects. The American Psychiatric Association's *Diagnostic and Statistical Manual of Mental Disorders* (1994) categorizes many forms of behavior under the label of paraphilia, including exhibitionism, voyeurism, sexual attraction to children, sadomasochism, fetishism, frotteurism, obscene telephone calls, necrophilia, zoophilia, and several other behaviors. An actual diagnosis of pathology with regard to paraphilias is thought to be unnecessary unless the individual acts on the sexual urges, fantasies, and attractions, or unless he or she is troubled by them. As discussed in chapter 13, certain of these behaviors—fetishism, for example—may be relatively harmless so long as they do not involve any sort of victimization of others.

The paraphilias are often the types of behaviors **FOH** that become classified as sexual offenses depending on the culture in which they occur (Simon, 1994). One dimension of the sexual offense is the mental control mechanism of the offender that leads to the paraphilic behavior (Johnston, Ward, & Hudson, 1997). The other dimension is the way in which a particular culture categorizes a range of sexual behaviors. Much more research is needed to compare paraphilic behaviors across cultures in any meaningful way.

It was once assumed that **paraphiliacs,** or people who were attracted to some form of paraphilia, tended to repeat the same behavior compulsively over time. Research has also suggested that paraphiliacs lack general controls over their behaviors because of chemical brain disorders or social disadvantage, and they may be prone to a variety of sexually impulsive behaviors (Kafka & Hennen, 1999). There has been some success in treating paraphilias with medications that are used in the treatment of depression and obsessive-compulsive disorders (Abouesh & Clayton, 1999; Balon, 1998).

The Sexual Addiction Controversy

What has come to be called **sex addiction** provides **FOH** another example of the crucial role expert opinion plays in defining and labeling sexual behavior. It is

paraphiliac: person who is drawn to one or more of the paraphilias.

sex addiction: inability to regulate sexual behavior.

CROSS-CULTURAL PERSPECTIVE

Kids for Sale: The Sex Industry in Thailand

"Sometimes you just have to swallow hard and drink another gin," said the teen-aged prostitute in Bangkok, Thailand. "I couldn't get through some nights unless I was drunk."

It is possible but not easy to imagine lives more hideous than those of the generations of children who are fed like cheap fuel into Thailand's flourishing sex industry. In some Thai villages, girls are dragged out of school as early as the sixth grade and taken to the brothels of Bangkok and other centers of the sex trade.

"At 10, you are a woman," according to a popular saying in Bangkok's red-light district. "At 20, you are an old woman. At 30, you are dead."

The demand for the young girls seems limitless. Each year tens of thousands of sex tourists from Germany alone visit Thailand, according to the international children's advocacy group Terre des Hommes. About 10 percent of the German sex tourists engage in sex with minors, the group said.

The traffic in very young girls has been accelerated by the mistaken but widespread belief that they are less likely to be infected with the AIDS virus.

"How would you like to marry a 14-year-old Asian virgin?" asks a brochure put out by Peter Stanton of PVS Publications in Santa Monica, Calif. Mr. Stanton offers a travel guide to the sexual resorts of Southeast Asia and personalized "Sex Tours to Thailand." Mr. Stanton's brochure asks, "Did you know you can actually buy a virgin girl for as little as $200?"

Andrew Vachss is a lawyer and writer from New York whose career is devoted to fighting the exploitation of children. His latest novel is "Batman: The Ultimate Evil," in which the caped crusader goes to war against the child sex industry in the fictional country of Udon Khai. Udon Khai is Thailand.

Mr. Vachss, whose wife, Alice, is a former sex crimes prosecutor for the Queens District Attorney's office, believes that not enough voices have been raised against the enforced prostitution of hundreds of thousands of children in Southeast Asia.

"Certainly Thailand is not the only country," he said, "but it is the international symbol of this problem. It has been a pedophile's paradise at least since Vietnam. It's a place where children are disposable, like Kleenex."

Mr. Vachss has earned the enmity of the Thai Government by insisting that it has condoned the exploitation of its children and by co-founding an organization called Don't! Buy! Thai!, which is calling for a complete boycott of goods made in Thailand.

In a letter denouncing the boycott, Akrasid Amatayakul, the chargé d'affaires at the Thai Embassy in Washington, told Mr. Vachss that "a horrendous problem of this magnitude must take time to solve."

Mr. Stanton of PVS Publications indicated in a telephone conversation that increasing attention to the problem of child prostitution in Thailand was having an effect. "It used to be easy to get girls under 18," he said.

Now, he said, "You have got to be careful because the Thai police don't want any bad publicity, and they don't want any news media going out there and finding any tourists with young girls."

On the tours he arranges, Mr. Stanton said, the client is hooked up with a "private tour guide" in Bangkok. The tour guide introduces the client to girls, who will be over 18, he said. But if the client wants someone younger, he should tell the guide, he said, and she would likely "take you to some of the local Thai brothels."

As for AIDS, Mr. Stanton blithely insisted there is no need to worry. He said, "There are a lot of researchers now who say HIV is not the cause of AIDS, and HIV is not sexually transmitted."

—Source: Bob Herbert. *The New York Times*, January 22, 1996, p. A15. Reprinted by permission.

---

clear that sexual activity becomes compulsive for some people and that regulating sexual behavior is difficult or impossible for them. In *Out of the Shadows: Understanding Sexual Addiction*, Patrick Carnes (1992) compared compulsive sexual behavior to alcoholism or other chemical dependencies. He has maintained that sex addiction is characterized by the typical symptoms of other forms of addiction, such as an inability to stop the behavior even in the face of serious consequences. These could include physical consequences, such as self-mutilation, disease, or unwanted pregnancy; occupational consequences, such as losing one's job or being charged with sexual harassment; and/or relational consequences such as losing one's partner. As with all compulsions, sexual addiction has been thought to follow a cycle of negative feelings that leads to repetition of the behavior and other sexual problems, and treatment programs have been developed that are similar to the 12-step programs used for alcoholics and drug abusers (Wilson, 1999).

Many sexologists have taken exception to the sex addiction model, believing it to be misleading and even dangerous because it may prevent people from getting appropriate treatment. They charge that the addiction model does not lend itself well to sexually compulsive behaviors. There is concern too that it has encouraged people to diagnose themselves as "sex addicts" when they may actually just be ignorant or misinformed about normal sexual behavior and also that the treatment approaches have been developed and operated largely by people who are not trained in the field of human sexuality. Again we face the difficulty of defining what is problematic. The sexual addiction movement has been seen as having a missionary zeal with a program that might be dangerously oversimplified for some people (Walters, 1999).

Sexual Harassment

A form of sexual coercion and exploitation that can be very subtle—even confusing to identify—and yet be highly upsetting to the victim involves unwanted sexual advances, suggestiveness, sexually motivated physical contact, requests for sexual favors, or coercion of one person by another, particularly in academic settings or the workplace. The term used to describe such behavior is **sexual harassment.** Although the definitions of sexual harassment may vary among people, it would appear to be widespread (see Fig. 15.2). Conservative estimates suggest that about 30 percent of women are victims of sexual harassment, whereas other estimates set the number closer to 90 percent. Studies have suggested that during their college years 50 to 60 percent of women are subjected to some sort of treatment that would clearly be defined as sexual harassment. The number of sexual harassment complaints filed with the U.S. Equal Opportunity Employment Commission more than doubled during the 1990s, leveling off at about 15,500 new cases every year. People's ratings of how serious a problem sexual harassment is in the workplace have been decreasing (Cloud, 1998b).

Have you ever thought that you were being sexually harassed? Describe the circumstances. Be sure to include how you felt.

Although studies have tended to focus on harassment of women, it is certainly not rare for men to be victims of sexual harassment. However, when faced with situations that are potentially sexually harassing, men are somewhat more likely to perceive women's behavior as simply being sexy rather than harassing.

FIGURE 15.2 *World Conference on Women*
At the World Conference on Women in Beijing, China, in 1995 delegates agreed to include, for the first time in a United Nations document, the recognition of women as sexual beings with rights. Although not binding, the document is politically influential, particularly in countries where women can be forced to have sex even by their husbands who are infected with the virus that causes AIDS. It gave women the right to have control over their sexual and reproductive health and the right to say no to unwanted sex. These women, including Adelaide Moundele-Ngollo, a delegate from Congo (left), visited the Great Wall during a break in the conference.

The U.S. Supreme Court has ruled that men can take legal action against other men who make unwanted sexual advances (Solomon, 1998). Studies of college men and women demonstrate that the males tend to be more tolerant of sexual harassment and more likely to see heterosexual relationships in adversarial terms, to believe the myths about rape, and to admit that under certain circumstances they might be sexually aggressive. Men who see a close connection between sexuality and social dominance are more likely to sexually harass (Bordo, 1998; Pryor & Stoller, 1994).

Sexual harassment may affect people in many different ways, sometimes even indirectly. There are four main bases for complaints about sexual harassment (Roberts, 2000; Williams & Brake, 1997):

1. *Coercion and bribery.* This form of harassment is linked to the granting or denial of some benefit or privilege. Legally it is called **quid pro quo** harassment, meaning that something is gained

sexual harassment: unwanted sexual advances or coercion that can occur in the workplace or academic settings.

quid pro quo: something gained from something given.

from something else. Most typically it takes the form of an individual who has, or is perceived to have, more power using sex as a form of coercion or bribery. An example might be a college professor suggesting to a student that complying or not complying with her or his sexual overtures will affect the student's grade one way or the other.

2. *Hostile environment.* If a person's school or work environment is made uncomfortable because of sexual innuendos, suggestive remarks or pictures, and uninvited advances, it is considered a form of sexual harassment. Court cases continue to affirm that school authorities and work supervisors have a responsibility to prevent the development or perpetuation of such hostile environments.

3. *Aggressive acts.* Among the more overt forms of sexual harassment are actual physical behaviors, such as unwanted embraces, kissing, touching, fondling, or more assaultive forms of sexual behavior.

4. *Third-party effects.* Sometimes a third person will be affected by the sexual or romantic relationships of others. For example, if one student is getting better grades because he or she is involved in a sexual relationship with the professor, other students who are legitimately working for their grades are unfairly affected. Or if a supervisor is having an affair with a secretary, making it more likely that the secretary will get pay raises or other benefits, other workers are affected. These are forms of third-party sexual harassment.

There are certain risk factors that increase the likelihood that sexual harassment will take place, including an unprofessional environment in the workplace, a sexist atmosphere, and lack of knowledge about the organization's grievance policies (O'Hare & O'Donohue, 1998). Victims of sexual harassment often minimize the importance of the event in their own minds, or they may react with shock and disbelief. They may feel ambivalent toward the offender and sometimes even blame themselves for not having prevented the situation from developing. In this sense, the injuries of harassment may be subtle and emotional, calling the victim's own sense of self into question. Only too often, these reactions lead victims to ignore the incident and not report it to anyone in authority. This is particularly unfortunate in cases where the harasser is unaware of how his or her behavior is being perceived. Sometimes, a simple and clear statement to the harasser that the behavior is unwelcome and considered to be sexually harassing will be enough to end it.

However, there is usually an imbalance of power in sexual harassment cases through which the offender tries to take unfair advantage of the victim (Bordo,

1998). The result of such a trap for the individual being harassed is often a sense of helplessness that can lead to depression, other emotional upsets, and physical illness. Victims have often been known to quit their jobs or leave school as a result of continuing sexual harassment that they feel at a loss to cope with.

Sexual Harassment in Schools and Colleges

A survey of 2,002 readers of *Seventeen* magazine found that 89 percent of girls said they had been targets of unwanted sexual comments, gestures, or looks during their precollege school years. The American Association of University Women sponsored a Louis Harris survey of 1,632 students in grades 8 through 11 in 79 U.S. schools to determine the incidence of sexual harassment (AAUW, 1993). This study found that 85 percent of the girls and 76 percent of the boys said they had been subjected to unwelcome sexual behavior at least once in their school lives. Two-thirds of the girls and a considerably smaller proportion of boys said they were harassed "often" or "occasionally." Sixty-five percent of the girls and 42 percent of the boys indicated they had been touched, grabbed, or pinched in a sexual way. Nearly one-fourth of the girls had been forced to kiss someone, and 10 percent of both the boys and girls reported being forced against their wills to do something sexual other than kissing. Eighty percent of the unwelcome sexual behavior had come from other students, with the remainder coming from teachers, coaches, or other adults.

These statistics were similar to those found in a 1996 survey of teenagers conducted by *USA Weekend,* which found that 81 percent of the girls and 76 percent of the boys said they had been sexually harassed. These studies have focused attention on sexually harassing behavior in the adolescent years. Even though many students, especially girls, found the behavior at least somewhat upsetting, there had been pressure on students to dismiss these activities as being part of growing up or "no big deal." This may set the stage for misperceiving the significance of sexual harassment later on in life (Pera, 1996). Because college students are adults, there is more likelihood of sexual contact between them and their professors, accompanied by all of the potential complications of such relationships (Williams, 1999).

Do you believe that colleges and universities have the right to prohibit or regulate consensual relationships between faculty and students? Defend your position.

One of the issues being debated in academia is whether even consensual relationships between faculty and students should be prohibited, because of the power imbalance and all of the potential for harassment. On one side of the argument are the issues of personal privacy and freedom for legal adults to make choices about their relationships. On the other side of the debate lie concerns about how imbalances of power, even when unintended, may lead to exploitation, sexual coercion, hostile environments, or third-party harassment. Sensitive to the risks of lawsuits, some universities have tried to enact policies that would prohibit all romantic and sexual relationships between faculty and students, but most have opted for less pervasive policies, prohibiting relationships specifically between a professor and a student whom the professor supervises in some way (Dziech, 1998; Franke, 1998). There is always the risk that one party, usually the student, will become hurt in some way by the relationship and bring some sort of charges against the other party. It is for these reasons that educational institutions need to develop sexual harassment policies with great care and to educate both students and faculty about the dangers and concerns. Any such policy must provide for grievance procedures, so that an individual who feels unfairly charged will be offered an opportunity for defense (Reese & Lindenberg, 1999).

Sexual Harassment in the Military

Results of a Pentagon survey of armed forces personnel showed that 82 percent of the women and 74 percent of the men had felt sexually harassed by teasing, jokes, remarks, or questions. Sixty percent of women and 51 percent of men reported having been victims of physical forms of harassment, including being leaned over, touched, cornered, pinched, or brushed against in a deliberately sexual manner. Fifteen percent of armed forces women and 2 percent of the males indicated that they had actually been pressured for sexual favors. The General Accounting Office has also reported that well over 90 percent of female students at national military academies experience some form of sexual harassment. Much of this harassment has not been formally reported or investigated, although new educational guidelines concerning the problem have been issued, and some disciplinary action has been taken against offenders (Sciolino, 1997).

The armed forces represent a somewhat special social situation because for such a long time they were male-dominated. As women have been gradually integrated into military service, sexual harassment and abuse have become serious problems. They seem to represent one of the ways in which military males attempt to reassert their dominance (Francke, 1997). The military considers even consensual sex between persons of different rank to be inappropriate because it can lead to a breakdown of discipline and cohesiveness of units. It is sometimes deemed to be rape, es-

pecially when a recruit is clearly in a position of being afraid to say no to a superior. The seriousness of sexual harassment and the issue of consenting for sex in the military has come into focus with scandals and court-martials of high-ranking officers at several installations. Experts agree that the living situations and power imbalances in military life create unique problems for women and men. The recent publicity about sexual incidents on military bases have reminded everyone that even in places of traditional male domination, sexual harassment and abuse will no longer be ignored (Thompson, 1998).

Sexual Harassment in the Workplace

Scenarios in the civilian world are similar. They involve, for example, the worker who is subjected to intimate touching or sexual innuendos from a superior. The worker often feels trapped in an uncomfortable situation, resenting the uninvited attention, but fearful that reporting it will create embarrassing confrontations or even jeopardize further employment. A study of 64 cases of women who had been sexually assaulted in their jobs found that only 21 percent had complained through appropriate workplace channels, and another 19 percent had quit their jobs. Most of the other women were afraid of the economic consequences of reporting the incident or quitting and therefore chose to remain on the job, sometimes being subjected to further sexual harassment (Schneider, 1991). There is evidence that women have become more willing to report harassment on the job in recent years, and complaints have been on the increase (Roberts, 2000).

American companies have realized that they can be held accountable for their workers' actions and that it is their responsibility to prevent the development of hostile work environments. Court cases have continued to support these positions. Men have also become more concerned about behaviors that could be seen as sexually harassing, and many men have been modifying their actions to prevent misunderstanding or the possibility that they would be charged with sexual harassment. Experts continue to wrestle with the complex issue of how to affirm positive relationships between coworkers. Although there may be sexual components in such relationships, appropriate constraints must be established on the degree to which sexuality becomes a part of workplace interactions (Reese & Lindenberg, 1999).

Responding to Sexual Harassment

Public and private schools, colleges, military service branches, and corporations now generally have specific policies defining what sort of conduct constitutes

How Men Can Tell If Their Behavior Is Sexual Harassment

Some men (and women) are confused as to what behaviors constitute sexual harassment. The following questions may be especially helpful in assessing one's own behavior:

- Would I mind if someone treated my wife, partner, girlfriend, mother, sister, or daughter this way?

- Would I mind if this person told my wife, partner, girlfriend, mother, sister, or daughter about what I was saying or doing?

- Would I do this if my wife, partner, girlfriend, mother, sister, or daughter were present?

- Would I mind if a reporter wanted to write about what I was doing?

- If I ask someone for a date and the answer is "no," do I keep asking?

- If someone asks me to stop a particular behavior, do I get angry and do more of the same instead of apologizing and stopping?

- Do I tell jokes or make "funny" remarks involving women and/or sexuality? (Such jokes may offend many people.)

If the answer to any of these questions is yes, the chances of the behavior being considered sexual harassment are very high. Because such behavior is likely to be high risk, if you have to ask, it is probably better not to do it.

—Bernice R. Sandler, "How Men Can Tell If Their Behavior Is Sexual Harassment," *About Women on Campus*, Vol. 3 (3), Summer 1994

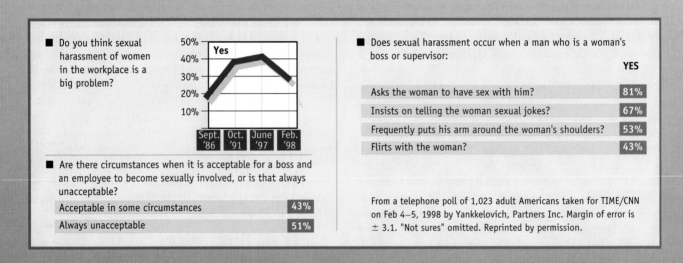

■ Do you think sexual harassment of women in the workplace is a big problem?

Yes — Sept. '86, Oct. '91, June '97, Feb. '98 (50%, 40%, 30%, 20%, 10%)

■ Are there circumstances when it is acceptable for a boss and an employee to become sexually involved, or is that always unacceptable?

Acceptable in some circumstances	43%
Always unacceptable	51%

■ Does sexual harassment occur when a man who is a woman's boss or supervisor:

	YES
Asks the woman to have sex with him?	81%
Insists on telling the woman sexual jokes?	67%
Frequently puts his arm around the woman's shoulders?	53%
Flirts with the woman?	43%

From a telephone poll of 1,023 adult Americans taken for TIME/CNN on Feb 4–5, 1998 by Yankkelovich, Partners Inc. Margin of error is ± 3.1. "Not sures" omitted. Reprinted by permission.

sexual harassment and outlining procedures for dealing with cases. Until recently, most legal cases related to harassment in the United States were decided under Title VII of the Civil Rights Act of 1964 and Title IX of the Education Amendments of 1972, both of which clearly prohibit sexual harassment of employees and students. After the U.S. Senate passed the Civil Rights Act of 1991, additional policies were implemented to deter harassment in the workplace. In 1993, the U.S. Supreme Court ruled unanimously that victims need not have suffered severe psychological damage in order to claim that they have been sexually harassed, a broader definition than was once accepted by the Court. However, even with such policies and precedents in place, sexual harassment can be a difficult issue to resolve. People in administrative positions may

not agree on how to define the problem, and they may have a stake in trying to protect the offender. It is also one of those offenses for which there is usually little tangible evidence to substantiate the victim's claims. It then becomes a situation of one person's word against another's.

Recommendations to those encountering sexual harassment emphasize the need to take as much control over the situation as possible. There are several specific suggestions for steps that can be taken:

1. *Seek sources of personal support.* Find an individual or small support group with whom you can share your fears and frustrations. This can provide support and encouragement through a difficult time, put the incident(s) and your

concerns in clearer perspective, and give you guidance in making decisions about how you want to proceed.

2. *Find out which authorities or administrators are designated for the reporting of sexual harassment.* Institutions usually have an affirmative action officer or other administrator who handles reports of sexual harassment. Even if these individuals feel that a lack of substantive evidence may make pursuit of a particular case difficult, they may have good suggestions for putting an end to the offensive behavior. Remember too that if a person in authority receives more than one complaint about a particular employee, he or she will have more evidence with which to act. In the case of a student who is being harassed by a professor, reporting the incident may be useful in rectifying a situation in which an unfair grade is eventually given by the teacher as retribution. Keeping careful records of classroom performance would, of course, be necessary in arguing such a point. Most forms of harassment can be considered violations of law, and you might consider reporting them to police authorities.

3. *Be clear about your needs.* One common reaction of many victims of sexual harassment is to feel guilty for having somehow precipitated the sexual advances. Regardless of any ambivalence you may have once felt about the offender, if you now feel certain that you do not appreciate the behavior, be firm in your resolve to end the harassment and be assertive about it.

4. *Write a letter to the offender.* This is considered one of the best approaches to ending sexual harassment. It is a clear and direct statement to the offender made without formal charges and public confrontation. It may also provide the harasser with a new perspective on the behavior. Not all offenders realize how negatively their actions affect others. A copy of the letter should be kept and used as supportive evidence later if the harassment does not cease. Such a letter should clearly and directly state the following: (a) specifically what actions have taken place, giving as many details, dates, and times as possible, but without evaluation; (b) the feelings and reactions that have been generated by the actions; and (c) a very short statement that you want the harassment to stop and also want your relationship to return to an appropriate professional, or student-teacher, level. Such letters are usually quite useful in placing a harasser on warning, and they typically lead to a quick cessation of the behavior.

5. *Consider making use of mediation services.* Even in those cases where an individual does not want to take formal action against a harasser, mediation may be helpful. It is a voluntary process in which an impartial mediator allows the two parties, the victim and the harasser, to explain their positions and feelings to one another, eventually developing a plan of resolution to which both parties can agree. This is an especially useful approach in more subtle harassment situations, where the offender could benefit from realizing how the actions have been affecting the victim.

Institutional policies and recent court decisions continue to confirm that everyone deserves to work or pursue an education in an environment that is free from inappropriate sexual overtures. If you find yourself subject to such behavior, take action promptly to avoid escalation in the tensions and consequences that may result.

◢ Sexual Abuse by Professionals

Closely related to the sexual harassment issue is a growing concern about professionals—physicians, therapists, clergy, lawyers, bodywork therapists, social workers—who take advantage of their patients or clients sexually. Although it is difficult to get accurate data on the frequency with which such behavior occurs, there is evidence that up to 10 percent of male therapists have engaged in intimate contact with patients either during or following the professional relationship and that smaller numbers of female professionals have done so (Thoreson, Shaughnessy, & Frazier, 1995). One study found that nearly 17 percent of male counselors had some form of sexual contact with a client or student following the end of the professional relationship. Research has shown that male counselors and educators who do not perceive this behavior as professional misconduct are more likely to have participated in such behavior (Thoreson, Shaughnessy, Heppner, & Cook, 1993). Most professions in which one individual is in a helping role for another have seen their share of reports about sexual abuse. Unfortunately, these professions have often been slow to acknowledge the scope of the problem, sort through the complex problems of who was responsible for the actions, and develop mechanisms for handling cases where sexual abuse is alleged (Finger, 2000; Friedman & Mobilia, 1995).

Dynamics behind Sexual Abuse of Female Clients

There seem to be particular dynamics behind the abuse of female clients by male professionals. Women come to these men in a highly vulnerable state. They may perceive the men as being warm, caring, and helpful. At the same time, men who have achieved professional status may sometimes see themselves as being above ordinary rules of ethical conduct. They may also see vulnerable women as potential sources of help for their own stresses, depressions, and relational problems. These perceptions conspire to create a situation where the patient is vulnerable to sexual abuse (Foster, 1995b; Rutter, 1990).

It has become increasingly clear that helper-client sexual exploitation often has disastrous consequences. The client may end up feeling used and angry, and whatever trust had been established for the professional is destroyed. The client may feel dehumanized by the actions. Again, there is a tendency for clients who have been sexually exploited to blame themselves and assume that they should have prevented the behavior. The professional, too, suffers serious consequences. His or her career can be jeopardized because of the abuse, and with good reason (Fones, Levine, Althof, & Risen, 1999). Experts agree that it is up to the professional worker to establish and maintain appropriate boundaries in the helping relationship (Finger, 2000). For these reasons, it is crucial that physicians, lawyers, therapists, and others in these professions pay attention to their feelings and reactions and that they work to prevent situations where unethical, exploitative actions might be likely (Plaut & Ginter, 1995). A number of states have enacted legislation providing civil and criminal penalties for professionals who violate ethical standards and participate in sexual or other inappropriate contact with their clients.

■ Sexual Coercion and Forced Sex

Forcing other people to have nonconsensual sexual activity is a behavior found in nearly every culture studied. Usually it is males who force women into sexual activities against their will. Social norms, and the types of sexual activities they regulate or prohibit, seem to play a major role in determining the types of forced sex that are allowed or condoned within a particular culture. These same norms determine how women are perceived within the contexts of sexuality and relationships and also the degree to which their perceptions of the experiences are used in determining what is consensual (Hickman & Muehlenhard, 1999).

It has been suggested that one way to conceptualize coercive sex is along a continuum of violence found in particular cultures. On one end of the continuum would be those sexual acts that tend to be *tolerated,* even though a level of coercion is involved. The degree of tolerance tends to be governed by social

norms relating to male dominance in the society, the general level of violence in the society, whether women are treated as possessions, who the perpetrator is, and what kind of sexual act is involved—that is, if it is penetrative or not. On the other end of the spectrum are those acts that would be considered *transgressive* in the society, meaning that they would clearly be considered wrong and subject to punishment. In any society, there may be sexual activities that fall into a transitional area between the tolerated and transgressive. In North America, for example, acts that once might have been tolerated as the girl's fault or bad manners on the part of a boy are now more clearly considered transgressions, such as date rape. In some other cultures, it would not be considered at all inappropriate for a man to force his wife to have sexual intercourse, whereas in North America this is now generally considered to be a crime (Heise, Moore, & Toubia, 1996).

In comparing the United States with Sweden, a country in which women tend to have more institutional power and where the levels of violent crime are generally lower, the rates of sexual coercion among university students seem directly related. They are far lower in Sweden than in the United States (Lottes & Weinberg, 1996). The United States now has one of the highest rates of sexual assault among developed countries. Fear of sexual victimization is prevalent among women, and it affects their lives profoundly. Studies have shown that the fear of sexual assault often makes women feel vulnerable. They grow up learning to limit and restrict their behavior in various ways, such as never walking alone in certain locations or at night, yet at the same time they also resent having to live with these fears and limitations (Schulhofer, 1998).

In general usage, the term "rape" refers to any form of sex in which one person forces another person to participate (see Fig. 15.3). When used as a verb, it means making an individual engage in a sexual act without that individual's consent or against that individual's will. In many states, rape is legally defined as forced vaginal sexual intercourse between a man and a woman. However, in about one-third of forced sexual encounters, penile-vaginal contact never occurs, but a variety of other forms of forced sex, including oral and anal penetration by the penis or vaginal penetration by fingers or objects, may occur. Recognizing that these acts may be just as physically and psychologically damaging to the victim as intercourse, the American Law Institute has recommended that violent and forced sexual acts all be prosecuted under the more general label of "rape and related offenses," and the term "sexual assault" is also often used. One of the most complicated issues in rape cases is the perception of consent (Lim & Roloff, 1999). Courts have often failed to find men guilty of

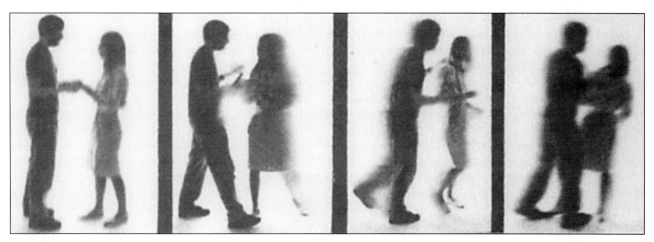

FIGURE 15.3 *Rape*

Rape is forced sexual participation, as depicted in this enactment using models. Although sexual assault is usually perpetrated against women, it is not limited to them; men and children are also potential rape victims.

rape when there has not been clear evidence of resistance on the woman's part, even though that may have been because she was very frightened or because her judgment may have been impaired by alcohol or other substances (Schulhofer, 1998).

Statutory rape is a legal term used in a situation where an adult or adolescent has sexual intercourse with a younger partner who is under the age of consent, even if that partner is willing to have sex. Age of consent varies in some states, but it is usually the age of 17 or 18. Men and children can be subjected to forced sex, as well as adult women.

Coercive and Abusive Relationships

There seem to be some common characteristics among people who tend toward sexually aggressive behavior. They are likely to have come from environments that yielded poor self-images and underdeveloped social skills. They may also have been subjected to violence or sexual abuse themselves and tend toward insecure and fearful attachment styles in their relationships (Julian, McKenry, Gavazzi, & Law, 1999). Abuse of alcohol often plays a role in sexually aggressive and coercive situations. Offenders may show serious personality disturbances, have difficulty maintaining social relationships, and have a propensity toward depression, loneliness, and personal rigidity. They may also have participated in prior paraphilic behaviors such as exhibitionism (Freund & Seto, 1998).

People who tend to resort to coercion and domination in order to solve conflicts are more likely to become aggressive in their behavior, and higher levels of traditionally masculine or macho traits are also associated with tendencies toward aggressiveness (Hammock & Richardson, 1992; Ray and Gold, 1996). Men

who are able to justify their sexual aggression through rationalization, who lack control of their emotions, and who seem to have other personality problems are apparently more likely to become sexually coercive or aggressive (Wryobeck & Wiederman, 1999).

Most commonly, sexual coercion takes the form of lies or false promises. In one study of 634 college males, 22 percent admitted to having lied an average of four times in order to have sex. Alcohol was often a factor in these situations. The most typical lies fell into the categories of indicating a higher level of caring or commitment than was actually the case or trying to deny that the relationship was a one-night stand. Men's attitudes toward women played at least some role in the likelihood of their telling such lies (Fischer, 1996).

Enough is known about the predictors of aggressive behavior to allow women to pay attention to certain warning signals in their relationships. These signals do not mean that a man will be sexually coercive or aggressive for certain, but they represent characteristics that can warn that a man has a greater likelihood of sexual aggression:

1. Lack of respect for women, as evidenced by his not listening well or ignoring what you say.
2. A tendency to become more physically involved and invasive than makes you feel comfortable, and yet he refuses to respect your discomfort.
3. Expression of generally hostile or angry reactions to women.
4. Disregarding your wishes and doing as he

statutory rape: a legal term used to indicate sexual activity when one partner is under the age of consent; in most states, that age is 18.

pleases; a tendency to make decisions about dating and other issues without consulting you.

5. A tendency to act jealous and possessive or to make you feel guilty if you resist sexual overtures.

6. Attitudes and values about women that are negative and domineering (such as "women are supposed to serve men").

7. A tendency to drink heavily and to get abusive when drunk.

Incidence of Forced Sex

Determining the incidence of forced sex is difficult because it is assumed that reported cases represent only the tip of the iceberg. The results of a 3-year study on forced sex in the United States, based on 40,000 interviews, indicated that 13 percent of women, or 12.1 million, had been raped, many of them during childhood or adolescence (National Victims Center, 1992). Several studies have shown that younger women are often subjected to unwanted sexual experiences. A survey of 1,149 teenage girls found that about 21 percent of them had experienced unwanted sexual contact within the previous year, with one-third of the cases involving forced sexual intercourse, and there was a higher proportion among older girls. The most likely perpetrators were boyfriends, other male friends, or first dates. Unwanted sex was more common among girls who had been subjected to earlier sexual abuse by an adult, who drank heavily, or whose parents failed to monitor their whereabouts and behaviors closely (Small & Kerns, 1993). In the *Details* magazine survey of college students, 29 percent of the women and 11 percent of the men reported that they had been physically forced into a sexual act by a date, sexual partner, or friend (Elliott & Brantley, 1997).

The National Health and Social Life Survey (NHSLS) interspersed questions about forced sex throughout the other questions. They asked about times when respondents had participated in sex against their will, because they were threatened or felt they had no choice. Twenty-two percent of the women had been forced to do something sexual at some time in their lives, almost always by males. Figure 15.4 summarizes the relationship these women had to the males who forced them into sex. Two percent of the men reported having been forced into some sexual activity, a third of the time by another male (Laumann, Gagnon et al., 1994).

NHSLS researchers were struck by the marked difference in the numbers of women who said they had been forced to do something sexual (22 percent) and by the small proportion of men who admitted ever having forced a woman to have sex (2.8 percent of the men surveyed). Even taking into consideration under-

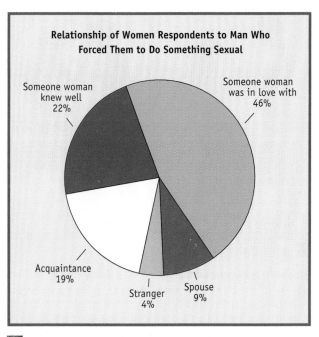

FIGURE 15.4 *Men Who Commit Rape*

NHSLS data suggest that, contrary to stereotypes, few of the men who force women to do something sexual are strangers. For more than three-quarters of the women who had experienced forced sexual contact, the victimizer was either a man whom the woman was in love with (46 percent) or knew well (22 percent) or her husband (9 percent).

Source: From *Sex in America,* by Robert Michael. Copyright © 1994 by C.S.G. Enterprises, Inc., Edward O. Laumann, Robert T. Michael, and Gina Kolata. By permission of Little, Brown and Company, Inc.

reporting and not telling the truth, the researchers felt that this result was reflective of some other phenomenon. In other questions, it was clear that almost no men found the idea of forced sex at all appealing. It was concluded that the most likely explanation was that most men who had forced women to have sex did not recognize how coercive the women had perceived their behavior to be (Michael et al., 1994). This is another reminder that sexual behavior has different meanings to different people, and the issue of consent is one that has often been muddled in our culture. Women and men seem, at least sometimes, to approach these issues from very different perceptual frameworks (Hickman & Muehlenhard, 1999; Lim & Roloff, 1999). See Table 15.1.

Acquaintance Rape

The NHSLS data showed that only 4 percent of the males who had forced women to have sex were strangers (Laumann, Gagnon et al., 1994). In a more limited sample of data, that of rapes reported to authorities, strangers were the perpetrators in only about 22 percent of the cases. The rest were committed by

Table 15.1   *What Constitutes Rape?*

Do you believe a woman who is raped is partly to blame if:

	Age	Yes	No
She is under the influence of drugs or alcohol	18–34	31%	66%
	35–49	35%	58%
	50+	57%	36%
She initially says yes to having sex and then changes her mind	18–34	34%	60%
	35–49	43%	53%
	50+	43%	46%
She dresses provocatively	18–34	28%	70%
	35–49	31%	67%
	50+	53%	42%
She agrees to go to the man's room or home	18–34	20%	76%
	35–49	29%	70%
	50+	53%	41%

		Yes	No
Have you ever been in a situation with a man in which you said no but ended up having sex anyway?	Asked of females	18%	80%

Would you classify the following as rape or not?

		Rape	Not Rape
A man has sex with a woman who has passed out after drinking too much	FEMALE	88%	9%
	MALE	77%	17%
A married man has sex with his wife even though she does not want him to	FEMALE	61%	30%
	MALE	56%	38%
A man argues with a woman who does not want to have sex until she agrees to have sex	FEMALE	42%	53%
	MALE	33%	59%
A man uses emotional pressure, but no physical force, to get a woman to have sex	FEMALE	39%	55%
	MALE	33%	59%

		Yes	No
Do you believe that some women like to be talked into having sex?	FEMALE	54%	33%
	MALE	69%	20%

Source: From Yankelovich Clancy Shulman, "What Constitutes Rape" in *Time,* June 3, 1991; from a telephone poll of 500 American adults taken for *Time/CNN* on May 8, 1991. Copyright © 1991 Time Inc. Reprinted by permission.

current or former husbands (9 percent), fathers or stepfathers (11 percent), other relatives (16 percent), boyfriends (10 percent), and other acquaintances, including friends, neighbors, and coworkers (29 percent) (Koss, 1992). When the rape is committed by a boyfriend or other acquaintance, it is called **acquaintance rape** or **date rape.**

Acquaintance rape happens on all college campuses and in many other nonacademic settings. Twenty percent of college women in another study indicated that they had been forced to have sexual intercourse, most often by someone known to them (Brener, McMahon, Warren, & Douglas, 1999). Other studies have suggested that as many as one-third of college women have been victims of nonconsensual sex by the time they are juniors or seniors and that about a third of college males report having been perpetrators of such encounters (Elliott & Brantley, 1997). Use of alcohol or other drugs on the part of both the victim and the perpetrator is very common in acquaintance rape situations (Bernat, Calhoun, & Stolp, 1998).

On college campuses, sexual victimization has often been associated with male athletes and fraternity members. It has been suggested that the elevated status of these campus constituencies and the sense of power they gain from being identified as a closely bonded group conspire to make them more likely to be sexually coercive toward women (Fromme & Wendel, 1995; Seto & Barbaree, 1995). There has been increasing alarm about the use of powerful drugs to spike drinks, causing women to become unconscious so that they may then be sexually assaulted. Rohypnol has received publicity in recent years as such a drug, but an even more dangerous and potentially fatal drug called gamma hydroxybutyrate, or GHB, has also received notoriety as a "date rape drug" (Gorman & Fowler, 1996).

acquaintance (date) rape: a sexual encounter forced by someone who is known to the victim.

Acquaintance Rape

Women

- Know your sexual desires and limits. Believe in your right to set those limits. If you are not sure, STOP and talk about it.
- Communicate your limits clearly. If someone starts to offend you, tell them firmly and early. Polite approaches may be misunderstood or ignored. Say "No" when you mean "No."
- Be assertive. Often men interpret passivity as permission. Be direct and firm with someone who is sexually pressuring you.
- Be aware that your nonverbal actions send a message. If you dress in a "sexy" manner and flirt, some men may assume you want to have sex. This does not make your dress or behavior wrong, but it is important to be aware of misunderstanding.
- Pay attention to what is happening around you. Watch the nonverbal clues. Do not put yourself in vulnerable situations.
- Trust your intuition. If you feel you are being pressured into unwanted sex, you probably are.
- Avoid excessive use of alcohol and drugs. Alcohol and drugs interfere with clear thinking and effective communication.

Men

- Know your sexual desires and limits. Communicate them clearly. Be aware of social pressures. It's OK not to "score."
- Being turned down when you ask for sex is not a rejection of you personally. Women who say "No" to sex are not rejecting the person; they are expressing their desire not to participate in a single act. Your desires may be beyond your control but your actions are within your control.
- Accept the woman's decision. "No" means "No." Don't read other meanings into the answer. Don't continue after "No!"
- Don't assume that just because a woman dresses in a "sexy" manner and flirts that she wants to have sexual intercourse.
- Don't assume that previous permission for sexual contact applies to the current situation.
- Avoid excessive use of alcohol and drugs. Alcohol and drugs interfere with clear thinking and effective communication.

—From a brochure published by the American College Health Association

Statistics aside, it is clear that acquaintance rape continues to affect the lives of many people and deserves careful attention from anyone involved in relationships where the possibility of such coercion exists. It is one of the most difficult sexual abuse situations to predict or avoid because most women have dated or befriended a man partly because they have assumed they could trust him. It is also of concern that up to one-third of college students indicate they have consented to unwanted sexual activity in order to satisfy a partner's needs, promote intimacy, or avoid tension in the relationship (O'Sullivan & Allgeier, 1998).

Misunderstandings and lack of communication between partners are crucial issues in acquaintance rape. Mixed signals can confuse both individuals. Research indicates that consent may involve both verbal and physical signals, but in fact it is most often given by making no particular response at all—simply going along with the activity (Hickman & Muehlenhard, 1999). Various studies have shown that some women admit to having said no to sex when they wanted their partners to persist longer and, in a sense, "talk them into it" (Schulhofer, 1998). Obviously, these confusing nuances of communication make the issue of acquaintance rape even more complicated (Rosenthal, 1997).

The "rape myth," often given credence by movie scenarios and other media, implies that even when women say no, they mean yes. Men sometimes think that it is their task to persuade women into sex until the woman finally realizes how good it is and ceases her protest. Research indicates, for example, that many college students, both male and female, do not consider a simple "no, I don't want to" sufficient reason to define subsequent sex as rape. How much physical force was used, how much the woman protested, and when in their interactions the woman's protest began seem to be important in making that determination (Hollway & Jefferson, 1998; Kalra, Wood, Desmarais, Verberg, & Senn, 1998).

Because of social pressures on women concerning their sexual expression, they may be truly confused about what they want and how far they should go. If a woman begins to place limits on a man in the midst of sex play, she may not be prepared to deal with his anger or expressed frustration. All of this can add up to an uncomfortable or even dangerous situation. Although most men are not potential rapists, this kind of setting can trigger violence and power issues in those men who are basically insecure, who need to prove their manhood to women, or who are simply used to getting and taking what they want (Belknap, Fisher, & Cullen, 1999; Sapp, Farrell, Johnson, & Hitchcock, 1999).

Do you believe that the focus on acquaintance rape on college campuses has been appropriate and necessary or overblown? Elaborate.

Acquaintance rape cannot always be prevented. In fact, research indicates the most frequent acquaintance rapists are men whose victims apparently know them well. However, there are several ways in which both women and men can reduce the risks. The most important steps involve developing the kind of relationship that is based on mutual trust, respect, and understanding. Training sessions for men, in which they are encouraged to have more empathy for women (see Fig. 15.5) may have some success, although it is also clear that clearer means of communication between partners are essential as well (Berg, Lonsway, & Fitzgerald, 1999). That takes work on many aspects of the relationship but especially on open and honest ways of communicating so that each other knows about needs and feelings.

If women are subjected to acquaintance rape or other forms of coercive sex, *it is important that they not blame themselves.* Many women feel that they should have been more forceful in their resistance or that they may have somehow encouraged the sexual abuse. This can be especially confusing if their body responded sexually during the assault. That does not automatically mean that they enjoyed the experience, nor does it mean that they really wanted it to happen.

Marital Rape

In former times, it was impossible in the eyes of the law for a woman to be raped by her husband. In many countries, this is still the case. It was once assumed

FIGURE 15.5 *Rape Prevention*

Antirape talks are an important part of educating the public about avoiding situations that might lead to rape. Here, male students at Hobart College in Geneva, New York, attend a rape-prevention workshop.

that it was a wife's duty to submit to her husband's sexual desires. In recent years, that assumption has been challenged, and the concept of **marital rape** has been accepted. Of women in the NHSLS who reported having been forced to have sex, 9 percent had been forced by their husbands (Michael et al., 1994). In the majority of marital cases that have gone to trial, the husbands have been convicted. The evidence suggests that marital rape is more likely to occur in relationships where there is continued disagreement, alcohol or drug abuse, and nonsexual violence (Nelson, 1997).

Because of increased awareness of marital rape, nearly all states have reassessed their rape laws and have eliminated any preferential treatment for husbands. A few states require extenuating circumstances—such as gross brutality—to be present before a husband can be so charged. Wives may be even less likely to report rape by their husbands to authorities because of potential consequences for themselves, their children, or

marital rape: a woman being forced by her husband to have sex.

the marriage. They sometimes still believe that it is their duty to submit to their husband's sexual demands. These beliefs often leave women feeling trapped, helpless, and fearful. Their feelings of self-worth and self-respect may plummet, with resulting depression and anxiety (DeMaris, 1997). In most cities and many rural areas, centers are springing up to help such victims of marital violence. They sometimes offer temporary housing for women and children who must leave a potentially violent home situation, along with counseling to help with decision making for the future.

In 1995, Muslim delegates to the United Nations mustered enough support to eliminate marital rape from a resolution on violence against women. They argued that marital rape is not considered a crime in many countries. Although not mentioning this act specifically, the final resolution urged nations to take measures "to prevent, prohibit, eliminate and impose effective sanctions against rape or sexual assault."

Men Forced to Have Sex

Rape of men was once considered by some to be a paradoxical concept, especially when rape was narrowly defined as penile-vaginal contact. However, there are increasing reports of men who have been subject to sexual abuse either by other men or by women, and sex forced on males is gradually becoming recognized as a real phenomenon. In a study of 204 college males, 34 percent reported having been pressured or forced into sexual activity since the age of 16, 24 percent by women, 4 percent by men, and 6 percent by both sexes. The most typical forms of coercion were employing tactics of persuasion, getting the man intoxicated, and threatening a withdrawal of love. In 12 percent of reported cases, physical intimidation or restraints were used (Struckman-Johnson & Struckman-Johnson, 1994). Men rarely report the crime (King & Woollett, 1997). Among male prison populations, sexual assault of men by men seems to be quite common. In one of the few studies available, of 486 male inmates, 101 had been targets of at least attempted sexual contact. Fifty percent of the victims had been subjected to anal intercourse (Struckman-Johnson, Struckman-Johnson, Rucker, Bumby, & Donaldson, 1996).

Women forcing men to have sex has received little attention in the sexological literature and has never been taken particularly seriously by the general public. The assumption is made that men would simply not be able to respond with erection unless they were willing to participate in sexual activity. In what has become a classic paper on sexual abuse of men by women, Sarrel and Masters (1982) cited evidence that males can be quite capable of erection and ejaculation in situations where they are afraid or anxious. In fact, anxiety may even heighten the potential for physical response,

even when the man is an unwilling victim. Sarrel and Masters cited 11 cases of sexual assault in which women threatened, restrained, and stimulated men until they responded sexually against their will. NHSLS data indicated that 1.5 percent of women admitted to having forced a male to have sex (Laumann, Gagnon et al., 1994). One study of sexually active college students found that 11 percent of men had been physically forced into sexual activity (Elliott & Brantley, 1997). At the very least, then, peer pressure and coercion lead many men into sexual experiences they later regret.

Males appear to react to sexual coercion and violence in the same essential ways as women, feeling a tremendous loss of control. Because it can be viewed as such a humiliating assault, males feel demasculinized, embarrassed, traumatized, and depressed. Males are taught that they should not be victims, and this probably often prevents them from ever reporting such abuse to authorities or fully coping with the reactions (Scarce, 1997; Struckman-Johnson et al., 1996). Yet males require the same sorts of support and counseling as do women to deal with the emotions, conflicts, and loss of self-esteem that follow a rape (King & Woollett, 1997).

The Aftermath of Forced Sex

Victims of forced sex experience a variety of negative reactions that can disrupt the physical, sexual, social, and psychological aspects of their lives. The majority of victims report feeling permanently changed by the experience. The psychological pain that follows a sexual assault may vary in its intensity, depending on a variety of circumstances, although the reactions are generally difficult and unpleasant (Lipschitz, Winegar, Hartnick, Foote, & Southwick, 1999; Shecter, 1996).

The typical reaction to forced sex, sometimes called the **rape trauma syndrome,** often occurs in two phases. The first (acute or disruptive) phase is characterized by what has been called posttraumatic stress disorder, involving stress and emotional reactions, such as anxiety, depression, lowered self-esteem, and social adjustment problems. The victims may be anxious to deny the experience, insisting they just want to put it all out of their minds. At the same time, they may be agitated, hyperalert, and filled with anxiety (Foa & Riggs, 1995; Morgan & Grillon, 1999). The second (recovery) phase may last many months and involves a long-term reorganization to regain a sense of personal security and control over one's environment. Relationships with a partner or family mem-

rape trauma syndrome: the predictable sequence of reactions that a victim experiences following a rape.

CASE STUDY

Rochelle Recovers from Acquaintance Rape

A friend of Rochelle's approached a residence hall advisor to report that Rochelle had been distressed by a nonconsensual sexual experience that had occurred over the past weekend. The RA dropped by to talk with Rochelle and subsequently went with her to the counseling center, where she proceeded to describe the incident to a counselor. She had been at a party with a male friend, and they both had been consuming large quantities of alcohol. When he had asked her to go back to his room, she had agreed. She told the counselor that she had been interested in some physical intimacy, but she did not want to have intercourse. In the room, they had gotten into bed together, but she left her clothes on. After kissing and touching for a few minutes, he had suggested they have intercourse. She said she was not interested, but he continued to press the issue. She remembered feeling dizzy and sleepy, and saying to him, "Maybe later." She had then apparently fallen asleep.

At some time later in the night, she awoke to find the man on top of her, having sex with her. Her clothing had been removed. She told him to stop, and after she pushed at him a couple of times, he had ceased the activity. Rochelle had then put on her clothes and returned to her own room. The next day, she felt angry and used, and she went to the man's room to tell him how upset she was with his behavior. He seemed surprised and defended himself by saying that she had told him it was all right to have sex. He said that she had even insisted he wear a condom, which he had done. She had no memory of doing so, and yet he continued to insist

that she had given her consent. She explained to the counselor that either he was lying, or she had been too intoxicated to remember saying yes. The counselor informed her that in that particular state, it was considered illegal to have sexual relations with someone who was too impaired by alcohol to give consent clearly and freely. They talked about the various options she had for taking action.

Over a period of a few days, Rochelle talked about her feelings and whether or not to pursue various options. The man also talked with the counselor, and he continued to insist that he had assumed she had been perfectly lucid when she had agreed to have sex. He explained that he was very frightened about being accused of rape and that he would fight such charges legally if necessary. He had told his parents about the incident, and they had already contacted an attorney. After deciding against pressing charges against him or pursuing campus disciplinary channels, Rochelle and the man agreed to try mediation as a route to resolving their differences. They met with a mediator for three sessions and came up with an agreement in which their differences in perception were recognized, and they agreed not to see each other further. The man admitted that he should have been more careful to make certain that her consent was legitimate and given without any confusion or reservation. Rochelle had been able to share her feelings of frustration and helplessness at having been taken advantage of. Both agreed that this had been a situation in which each of them should have been more careful.

bers may be seriously disrupted and need to be resolved over a period of time. Many victims feel a great deal of anger, which needs to be expressed outwardly rather than be allowed to turn into inner guilt, depression, or self-hatred (Layman, Gidycz, & Lynn, 1996; Stalker & Fry, 1999). Some women eventually feel the need to move residences, change jobs, and change their telephone listings.

Treatment following forced sex also proceeds in two phases. Early crisis intervention aims at helping the individual see herself or himself as a survivor rather than as a victim (see Fig. 15.6). She or he needs to accept the consequences of the rape and begin to reestablish a sense of personal competence and control. Often, it takes time to regain a sense of continuity and meaning in life. It is important for the victim to express feelings and to seek social support and counseling. Over the longer run, treatment focuses on sexual and relational problems that have resulted from the

trauma, as well as reactions such as depression or physical symptoms of coping with stress. With proper follow-up and treatment, survivors of forced sexual experiences can make a complete recovery and live their lives with a comfortable sense of security and self-respect (Stalker & Fry, 1999). Many women experience a loss of interest in sex and are subject to specific sexual dysfunctions following an experience with forced sex, and they may wish to abstain from sexual activity for months following the incident. Some are reluctant to talk about such issues, and it has been recommended that counselors who work with rape victims take the time to bring up these sensitive subjects during the counseling process (Shecter, 1996).

Professionals who help victims work through the aftermath of forced sex have begun to identify criteria that indicate a successful resolution of the problems (Baldo, O'Halloran, & Jacobs, 1997; Miller et al., 1998; Wuest & Merritt-Gray, 1999):

FIGURE 15.6 *Rape Intervention Program*

Victims of rape need help in seeing themselves as survivors and in reestablishing a sense of self-worth. Other problems, such as depression and physical or sexual dysfunctions as a result of the rape, need to be confronted and treated as well.

1. The victim can think about the events of the assault at will, without being troubled by intrusive memories, nightmares, or frightening flashbacks and associations.
2. Memories of the event are accompanied by appropriately intense emotions, rather than a false sense of detachment.
3. The feelings associated with the forced sex may be identified and endured without overwhelming the victim.
4. Symptoms of depression, anxiety, and sexual dysfunction either have passed or are at least reasonably tolerable and predictable.
5. The victim is not isolated from relationships and has reestablished the ability to feel a sense of affinity, trust, and attachment for others.
6. Feelings of self-blame have been replaced by self-esteem, and the victim has assigned some meaning to the trauma and sense of loss. Obsessive thoughts about the event have been replaced by a realistic evaluation of it.

Police agencies are becoming better equipped to deal with reports of sexual assault. Officers have been trained to interview victims in a sensitive way that minimizes their humiliation and discomfort. Most sexual assault counselors agree that people should report incidents of being forced to have sex, even if they are not yet certain they want to proceed with prosecution of the perpetrator. The victim should receive a medical examination prior to showering or douching, in order to gather important evidence such as semen samples. In an estimated 5 percent of female rapes, pregnancy results, and then decisions must be made about this unintended result. About 50 percent of such pregnancies end in abortion, and in about 32 percent of cases, the woman keeps the child (Holmes, 1996).

The courts have often had to wrestle with difficult issues relating to rape survivors' privacy. Many states have rape-shield laws that protect a victim from having any details of a former romantic relationship with the rapist, or other information about former sexual behaviors, admitted as evidence during the rapist's trial. There has been general agreement among the media that the names of victims will not be released. However, some accused offenders have declared this to be unfair to them because their names may be released before they have been tried. Decisions about these matters continue to be made in favor of protecting the victim.

Individual and group counseling are the most commonly used approaches for helping victims of sexual assault cope with their traumas. Most cities and larger communities have rape crisis centers that are equipped to help women deal with all aspects of the aftermath of forced sex. The partners of assault victims often become secondary survivors themselves, experiencing a whole range of emotional reactions and posttraumatic symptoms. They may also require support and counseling (Davis, Taylor, & Bench, 1995; Stalker & Fry, 1999).

There are a number of programs designed to help prevent sexual assault and help ward off potential attackers. There is evidence that women who convey attitudes of assertiveness and confidence are somewhat less likely to be sexually victimized. However, it may also be helpful to learn some specific physical self-defense skills because verbal resistance alone is not always sufficient to avoid physical injury. Studies of women who have either been raped or who have avoided rape suggest that screaming, fleeing, and forcefully resisting an attacker were more effective than nonresistance in reducing the severity of the sexual abuse (Zoucha-Jensen & Coyne, 1993).

■ Sexual Abuse of Children

A substantial percentage of children and adolescents are subjected to sexual abuse by adults or other adolescents, also known as **child molesting** or **pedophilia.** Analyses of various surveys, in which the incidence of child sexual abuse was reported over a wide range, have concluded that a reasonable summary statistic would be that about 20 percent of females and 5 to 10 percent of males are sexually abused as children. The abuse of members of both sexes is

child molesting: sexual abuse of a child by an adult.

pedophilia (pee-da-FIL-ee-a): another term for child sexual abuse.

almost always perpetrated by men. Girls were somewhat more likely to be abused by family members. Boys were more likely to be abused by strangers. There is generally a low rate of reporting of such incidents to authorities (Leventhal, 1998).

The NHSLS statistics, believed to be more representative of the U.S. population, indicated that 12 percent of the male respondents and 17 percent of the females reported having been sexually touched as children. The most typical forms of sexual activity reported included genital touching, kissing, oral sex, vaginal intercourse, and male-male anal intercourse. There were no differential statistics across race, ethnicity, or educational level. Girls were touched primarily by males. For 28 percent of these girls, the males had been aged 14 to 17 when the touching took place; for 63 percent, the males had been over 18. Only 4 percent of females indicated they had been touched by other females. Boys had been touched more frequently by females (for 45 percent, it was females aged 14 to 17, and for 9 percent, over 18), but they had also quite frequently been touched by other males (15 percent had been touched by males aged 14 to 17, and 23 percent by males over 18). Smaller groups of boys and girls had been touched by both males and females. One might generalize from these findings that girls are at greatest risk of sexual abuse from adult men, followed by adolescent males, whereas boys are at greatest risk from adolescent females, followed by adult men, and then by adolescent males (Laumann, Gagnon et al., 1994).

The stereotypes would have us believe that pedophiles are degenerate men who lurk in trench coats near schools and parks, waiting to accost youngsters. Actually, the majority of sexual abuse victims are molested by a family member or someone known to the child. As Table 15.2 shows, family friends and relatives are among the most common abusers of children. Files released by the Boy Scouts of America revealed that from 1971 to 1991, about 1,800 scoutmasters had been removed from duty because of suspected or actual sexual abuse of boys. The organization is producing videotapes and printed materials informing boys about how to protect themselves from sexual abuse.

There is evidence that abuse of boys is less likely to be reported than abuse of girls, but the phenomenon has been researched to a much lesser extent. Both of these facts need to be understood within the context of our culture's views of maleness and masculinity. Our society may at some level feel that boys really do not need or deserve the same protection from sexual abuse as do girls. It may also be that reporting an incident of sexual abuse would be viewed by the boy himself, or by someone close to him, as an admission of being a powerless victim, not a role that is respected for males (West, 1998).

Table 15.2	Relationship to Child Sexual Abuse Victims of Their Abusers (percentages)	
	Female Victims	Male Victims
Stranger	7%	4%
Teacher	3	4
Family friend	29	40
Mother's boyfriend	2	1
Older friend of respondent	1	4
Other relative	29	13
Older brother	9	4
Stepfather	7	1
Father	7	1
Other	19	17
Number of cases	289	166

Source: From *The Social Organization of Sexuality,* by E. Laumann et al. Reprinted with permission of The University of Chicago Press.

Note: The table adds to more than 100 percent because some respondents were touched by more than one adult.

Various models have been proposed that consider several different dimensions and levels of severity of a potentially abusive situation. First, the type of sexual behavior is considered, particularly whether physical contact has occurred (as in fondling, intercourse, or oral sex) or not (as in exhibitionism). The age of the subject of sexual contact is considered, as is the age of the perpetrator. Some social workers do not automatically assume the situation to have been abusive unless the perpetrator is at least 5 years older than the subject. Most agree that if the subject is under 12 and the perpetrator is older, then the situation may be assumed to be abusive. The relationship of the perpetrator to the subject is also considered, as well as the rather complex issue of the subject's degree of willingness to participate in the activity. When the victim is between the ages of 13 and 17, the issue becomes somewhat more complicated, and definitions of abuse will typically depend on the age of the perpetrator and whether the subject wanted the sexual contact (Feiring, Taska, & Lewis, 1999; Wyatt, 1990).

Because in our culture children are taught to respect and obey adults and at the same time are often given little direct information about sex and their own sex organs, they are easily manipulated, both physically and psychologically, and often easily frightened into silent sexual compliance. Child molestation is as much an act of power as it is a sexual act. The victims of abuse often blame themselves for what has happened, concluding that they have somehow been bad or deserving of punishment. This can result in persistent feelings of shame that pervade the individual's self-concept (Creamer, 1998).

Children are often reluctant to report sexual abuse, or they may lack the verbal development to explain clearly what happened. Unfortunately, even when children report sexual abuse, they sometimes are not taken seriously. In some instances, adults want to avoid confrontations with relatives or friends who might be accused of molesting their child. Those children who do report abuse sometimes communicate directly to a close adult or professional person, either in language or by demonstrating what happened on an anatomically correct doll (see Fig. 15.7). However, information gained from children's use of anatomically correct dolls has not been found all that reliable for deciding whether a child has been sexually abused (Hewitt, 1999).

Adult Sexual Abusers

We are just beginning to understand the psychological dynamics of adult perpetrators of child sexual abuse. Most professionals believe that such behavior may

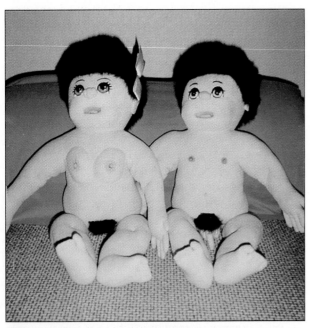

FIGURE 15.7 *Anatomically Correct Dolls*

These anatomically correct dolls called "Teach-A-Bodies" are used to educate young children about sex and to assist young victims in explaining what happened to them during an incidence of alleged sexual abuse. However, studies suggest that information gained from children's use of such dolls about incidents of alleged abuse may be unreliable.

well be rooted in the perpetrator's own treatment as a child, with at least some evidence suggesting that abusive adults were themselves sometimes sexually abused as children. However, preliminary research has also suggested that other factors are crucial in the development of sexually abusive behavior. For example, child abusers tend to have lacked confidants during their own childhoods and to have been emotionally isolated. They use sex as an escape from and solution to emotional pain (Haapasalo & Kankkonen, 1997). As adults, they tend to attribute sexual meanings to the normal behaviors of children and to view their victims as sexual objects. They may deny that they are sexually attracted to children. Although many of these same characteristics have also been noted in control groups of people who had not abused children, one significant difference is that control groups are not as likely to see sexual meanings in the behaviors of children (Proulx, Perrault, & Ouimet, 1999).

Adult male sexual abusers often come from families that have been rejecting and controlling but not necessarily harsh in discipline. They have often had disturbed relationships with their own fathers, are likely to have experienced some prior trauma in their lives, and may fantasize about children in sexual ways (Looman, 1995). Sexual abusers of children seem to have well-developed mechanisms for coping internally with what they have done. They may distort or rationalize their behaviors in their own minds, and they may also be very self-denigrating, making it even more likely that they will feel unable to control their paraphilic sexual urges. Some offenders blame their victims for the sexual abuse, or they blame third parties, such as a spouse, for not providing them sexual satisfaction (Blumenthal, Gudjonsson, & Burns, 1999; Wilson, 1999).

Little is known about women who sexually abuse children. Studies of convicted female child molesters have shown them generally to be of marginal intelligence, to have a history of sexual and physical abuse themselves, and to have dissatisfactions with their adult sexual lives (Kaplan & Green, 1995). They often act out of anger or to retaliate against a partner or spouse. Frequently, they commit the sexual abuse with another adult present, usually a male offender. It has been proposed that because we traditionally view women as nonviolent and nurturing, professionals and law enforcement personnel fail to ask victims questions that would help reveal the woman's role in abuse cases, and victims themselves may find it difficult to acknowledge or express the role a woman has played. Similarly, female offenders may be particularly reluctant to admit to the abuse because it is seen in our society as a particularly abhorrent and unexpected role for a woman. It may also be that the sexually abusive behavior of women is more covert than that of men, making it a less noticeable phenomenon to victims and authorities.

Recent attention has been focused on priests and other clergy who sexually abuse children. The Roman Catholic Church has come under fire for not acting more swiftly and proactively in some situations where priests have been accused of sexual abuse. As a result, the Church has recently adopted extensive new guidelines for dealing with such cases. Most churches are now realizing that it is crucial to take allegations of abuse seriously, remove the offender immediately if evidence is sufficient, comply with civil law and any civil investigations, and offer help to victims and their families. Formal procedures are now in place within most denominations for dealing with these cases (Sipe, 1995). Public agencies such as Big Brother/Big Sister programs are also using various psychological inventories to identify potentially abusive adult volunteers (Herman, 1995).

Child and Adolescent Sexual Abusers

There has been an increase in reported sex abuse perpetrated by both other children and adolescents. About one in every six sexual abuse incidents is committed by another child, often aged 6 to 9 years old. These children may have been victims of abuse themselves, and they tend to respond to counseling that helps them understand that the behavior is inappropriate (Hunter & Figueredo, 1999; Wendel, 1997). Adolescents typically abuse younger children or other adolescents. Teenage babysitters, or their friends, are common offenders. Adolescent sex abusers are usually males, although NHSLS data showed that boys are not infrequently abused by adolescent females (Laumann, Gagnon et al., 1994). Abusive adolescents often come from dysfunctional family backgrounds and have serious developmental and psychological difficulties (Carpenter, Peed, & Eastman, 1995). It is quite typical for juvenile sex abusers to have been subjected to physical abuse themselves, and sometimes sexual abuse. They are likely to have parents who have sexual pathologies, and they often show symptoms of depression (Rasmussen, 1999; Worling, 1995).

Parents who learn about a son's sexual abusiveness often experience difficulties in dealing with the situation. There may be tensions about communicating with the son about his actions and confusion over issues relating to punishment or treatment. Parents may feel overwhelmed by the situation and be troubled by a sense of helplessness. Gradually, they may begin to engage themselves in reevaulating their relationship with their offending son and become more actively involved in seeing the situation through to resolution. But these are not easy issues for families to face.

Effects of Child Sexual Abuse

Longitudinal studies about the effects of child sexual abuse suggest that symptoms of stress and trauma in the child gradually decline in the months following the abuse. Some studies have found that a substantial number of sexually abused children do not seem to show any measurable symptoms, nor do they necessarily define the experience in negative terms (Bauserman & Rind, 1997; Rind & Tromovitch, 1997). It may be that the degree of coercion and violence involved in sexual abuse is crucial in determining the amount of trauma experienced, but there seems to be general agreement that children cannot truly consent to sexual contact and that problems from being coerced into sexual activity by an adult may well create problems later in the individual's life (Campbell, 1995; Lange et al., 1999; Zweig, Crickett, Sayer, & Vicary, 1999).

Although it is difficult to generalize about the short-term or long-term effects of sexual abuse on children and adolescents, several categories of ill effects have been identified (Calam, Horne, Glasgow, & Cox, 1998; Feiring et al., 1999):

1. *Traumatic sexualization* means that the child's feelings, attitudes, and behaviors relating to sex may be exhibited in ways that are inappropriate to the child's age and stage of development. Sexually abused children may behave in inappropriate sexually aggressive ways (Meston, Heiman, & Trapnell, 1999).
2. *A sense of betrayal* may also result among children who find that someone they trusted and on whom they depended has caused them harm. This is particularly true when the perpetrator of the abuse is a family member. This sense of betrayal may be intensified if the child's report of sexual abuse is disbelieved or if the child is blamed for the event. Children often have negative reactions toward the abuser.
3. *Disempowerment* results when a child feels that his or her will or desires have been ignored and deliberately violated. The more physical force or coercion the perpetrator has used in the sexual activity, the greater the child's sense of powerlessness (Leventhal, 1999).
4. *Stigmatization* is particularly problematic when the child is expected to react with feelings of shame and guilt to the event. Such negative connotations may come directly from the abuser, who may want the victim to take the blame for the activity or be reinforced by others in the family or community who hear of the abuse.

We are just beginning to understand the effects that sexual abuse may have on later adult life. It has been found that it is a profound risk factor in depression, anxiety, sexual dysfunction, and suicidal feelings in women. Women who suffer from chronic pelvic pain, other gynecological problems, headaches, chronic gastrointestinal problems, phobias, and depression often have a history of sexual abuse, although the cause-and-effect relationship has not been firmly established (Bartoi & Kinder, 1998; Gladstone, Parker, Wilhelm, Mitchell, & Austin, 1999; Plichta & Abraham, 1996; Reilly, Baker, Rhodes, & Salmon, 1999). There is certainly evidence to indicate that among many adult psychiatric patients, substance abusers, and people with eating disorders, there is a history of sexual abuse at higher rates than in the general population (Deep, Lilenfeld, Plotnicov, Pollice, & Kaye, 1999; Schwartz & Cohn, 1996). In a study of about 1,600 women over the age of 17 in the Los Angeles area, nearly 20 percent reported having been sexually abused as children. In comparison to nonabused women, the abused women had more chronic diseases such as diabetes and arthritis, more general physical complaints, and poorer physical health overall (Plichta & Abraham, 1996).

Although most studies have assumed a cause-and-effect relationship between child sexual abuse and mental disturbance, it has also been proposed that certain mental disorders might also predispose some children to involve themselves in inappropriate sexual activities with adults. Researchers have often assumed that borderline personality disturbance could be caused by childhood sexual abuse. More recently, the alternate cause-and-effect pathway has been proposed (Bailey & Shriver, 1999). This points out the many subtleties that exist in interpreting causes and consequences of sexual abuse.

Although it has been widely accepted that adults who were abused as children are likely to become abusive to children themselves, recent reviews of the literature indicate that unqualified acceptance of that belief is unfounded. There are other factors associated with eventual sexually abusive behavior, including the social supports available while growing up, the extent of emotional isolation, and the effects of poverty and stress.

There is less empirical evidence about the effects of sexual abuse during a boy's childhood on his later development and adult sexual behavior. The studies that have been done suggest that these men may have confusion about their male identity, poor body image, or some difficulties in maintaining healthy, intimate relationships. Again, male socialization patterns appear to play a role in how men eventually perceive themselves in the aftermath of childhood sexual abuse (Bramblett & Darling, 1997; Meston et al., 1999). A study of boys who had been involved in sexual contacts with adults, but who had not been involved in any kind of clinical treatment, found a broad range of reactions ranging from the negative to the positive. The relationship to the adult, perceptions of consent,

and the presence of force were all factors that helped to determine boys' reactions to the behaviors (Bauserman & Rind, 1997).

It would appear that the effects of sexual abuse can be quite subtle but may also be long-lasting. For example, women with a history of forced sex in younger life are more likely to initiate voluntary sex earlier than others, have more sexual partners, and engage in more sexual risk-taking behaviors (Luster & Small, 1997; Stock, Bell, Boyer, & Connell, 1997). The most serious effects, such as severe mental disorders and behavioral problems, are usually the result of violence or severe coercion inflicted by the adult. Professionals agree that an important determinant of these effects is how the child is treated by authorities and then how much counseling help the child is given to deal with his or her own confusion and fear. Many victims of child sexual abuse do not confront their feelings and reactions until adulthood. There are now support groups that can help such adults deal with their experiences (Calam et al., 1999).

Treating Victims of Child Sexual Abuse

Crisis intervention may be the first line of action in treating child sexual abuse cases. A safe environment must be established for the child, and the offender must be removed from any contact with her or him. Legal authorities should be involved to handle any criminal charges and sanctions, and social service agencies should work with the child and family members. A variety of treatment programs have been developed to deal with sexually abused children, some of which involve family therapy because other family members may be deeply affected by the abuse as well. There is evidence that support from family members is extremely important for children who have been sexually abused. The level of support is sometimes compromised when another family member has been the abuser of the child (Jinich & Litrownik, 1999; Stroud, 1999).

The therapist treating an abused child must anticipate a variety of possible reactions in him or her. Many children express anger during the early stages of therapy, and they need to know that limits will be placed on expressing this anger. Later, feelings of guilt, shame, loss, neglect, and depression may emerge. In particularly violent sexual abuse cases, children may experience personality dissociation that can lead to disturbances involving multiple personalities. The therapist may also be called on to deal with the highly sexualized nature that has been stimulated in a young child and to help the child learn more age-appropriate responses.

CASE STUDY

Paul Revisits His Sexual Abuse as a Child

Paul had joined a support group for men who had recently been separated or divorced from their wives. During one of their meetings, he told the group that he felt some of his feelings of insecurity and his difficulties in communicating stemmed from the fact that he had been sexually abused during his childhood. He did not choose to elaborate, but the counselor who was facilitating the group invited Paul to pursue the matter further in private counseling. When he met with the counselor, he explained how difficult it had been to keep this secret for so long, and he still felt a sense of humiliation when he recalled the events.

The abuse had taken place several times and was perpetrated by the adult male leader of a church group to which Paul had belonged when he was 11 years old. The man had seemed to have a special liking for Paul, a fact that as a child he found flattering and appealing. He enjoyed the man's company and had accepted a few invitations to accompany him on camping trips just for the two of them. Paul's parents liked the man and seemed comfortable with their relationship. On one of the camping trips, the man had suggested they swim naked in a stream to clean up, and he had removed his clothes very freely. Although Paul had felt somewhat uncomfortable, he had done likewise, and they had gotten into the water.

The man started roughhousing in the water, and he eventually began to fondle Paul's genitals. Over several such camping trips, the sexual behavior had progressed to mutual masturbation and some oral sexual activity.

Finally, feeling overwhelmed by his conflicting feelings for the man, Paul had refused to go on any further trips with him. The man had expressed some hurt about Paul's decision, but he stopped inviting Paul to go. Soon, he seemed to have struck up a relationship with one of the other boys, a development that created both relief and resentment on Paul's part. Eventually, the man left the community, and Paul had never discussed the abuse with anyone until he had brought it up in the support group. As an adult, Paul still found himself conflicted by the fact that the sensations had been sexually enjoyable, even as the behaviors made him feel upset and used. He said to the counselor that he had hidden the incidents because he had not believed he had been forced into the activity. To him, his complicity had amounted to approval and consent. During several counseling sessions, Paul was helped to sort through the many complex feelings and reactions he had about his childhood sexual abuse. The counseling helped him to face various new facets of his sexuality and of his relationship with his ex-wife.

Many victims live with the secret of their sexual abuse well into adulthood. Therapy is most often initiated for other reasons at first because adult survivors of sexual abuse may experience a range of physical, psychological, and relational symptoms that interfere with their lives. They sometimes do not volunteer any information about childhood abuse unless directly questioned about it. It is important to work through all of the complicated feelings and reactions about the abuse and the offender. The therapist will help the individual express the range of emotions, which often includes anger diverted toward the abuser and others perceived as not having provided sufficient protection. Mental imagery techniques are used to help the survivor deal with anger and resentment. The ultimate goal is for adult survivors of child abuse to accept their feelings about the offender, develop a stronger and more positive sense of self, and work on developing a healthy and pleasure-oriented feeling about adult sexual interactions (McCarthy, 1997c; Nayak, Resnick, & Holmes, 1999). Group therapy approaches have proven to be particularly effective with some adults who were sexually abused as children (Morgan & Cummings, 1999).

Treating Offenders

Controversy has continued among professionals concerning the effectiveness of treatments for sex offenders. Although standard approaches to psychotherapy that do not focus specifically on the offending behavior tend to be of limited value, some treatment programs have been found to be quite successful with child sexual abusers (Alexander, 1999; Grossman, Martis, & Fichtner, 1999). They usually involve various combinations of group therapy, cognitive-behavioral techniques to help abusers gain better control over their sexual impulses, relapse prevention strategies to head off further occurrences of abuse, and education about sexuality. Abusers need to improve their self-concept, and they may be helped, through enhancement of their abilities, to empathize with the feelings of others (Craissati, 1999; Pithers, 1999). They may also be helped to redirect some of the skills they have used to abuse people into skills for preventing such abuse (Ward, 1999).

Treatment of sex offenders with drugs to reduce sexual drive has gained in popularity during recent years. Some of these drugs interfere with the production of male hormones or with the action of these

Knowing Consent When We See It

Intercourse often "happens" after voluntary hugging, kissing, and sexual touching, without coercive threats but also without either of the parties ever saying "Yes, let's agree to have sex now." In one of the most frequent scenarios the woman remains silent and relatively passive; she may even push the man's hands away several times or say "No, don't." Traditional rape laws permit a defense of "consent," but they don't say what consent is.

For many, the often-heard feminist view—that "no" means no—now seems obvious and uninteresting. In fact it is neither. By repeating the mantra " 'no' means no," anti-rape activists have sensitized many men and made some progress in changing assumptions about how women express interest in sex. But beneath the surface, in the messy, emotionally ambiguous real world of dating, petting, and sexual explorations, "no" doesn't always mean no.

A 1988 survey of undergraduates at Texas A & M University presents a detailed look at this problem. More than 600 women were asked whether they had ever engaged in acts of token resistance when they really wanted to have sex. Thirty-nine percent of the women reported that they sometimes said no even though they "had every intention to and were willing to engage in sexual intercourse." Of the sexually experienced women, 61 percent said that they had done so. Though these women were willing to engage in intercourse eventually, they didn't necessarily want the men to disregard their "no" and force them to submit right away; many women wanted their dates to wait or "talk me into it." But when a woman's "no" is equivocal, it means that her date, if he reads her intention correctly, should continue to press her for sex, perhaps in a physically assertive way. In fact, some of the women said that they told a date no because they "want[ed] him to be more physically aggressive."

An obvious concern regarding this study is that Texas A & M University may not be typical. The authors cautioned that the men tend to endorse gender roles that were prevalent in the 1950s. But subsequent studies elsewhere have reported strikingly similar findings, with no regional differences. A 1994 study at universities in Hawaii, Texas, and the Midwest found that 38 percent of the women sometimes said no when they meant yes. In a 1995 study at Penn State 37 percent of women reported having said no when they meant yes. For most women, most of the time, "no" does mean no. But sometimes it means "maybe" or "try harder." Sometimes, for some women, it means "get physical."

Some supporters of rape-law reform prefer to set aside these empirical findings. They probably fear that evidence of this sort will only reinforce society's willingness to tolerate male behavior that poses enormous risks for women. But sexual ambivalence and miscommunication, though they undoubtedly exist, do not automatically justify permissive legal standards. They need not dictate impunity for men who ignore women's verbal protests. Indeed, it is precisely because of these inconvenient realities that legal requirements such as "consent" and "reasonableness" solve so few of the difficulties.

Stephen Schulhofer, "Unwanted Sex," *The Atlantic Monthly,*
October 1998, pp.55–60. Reprinted by permission.

hormones (Rosler & Witztum, 1998). Antidepressant medications have also been used with offenders who seem to have depressive symptoms, and they may reduce the obsessive-compulsive tendencies that are sometimes part of the abusive behaviors. Although much remains to be done to clarify the effectiveness of medical treatment of child sexual abusers, the preliminary data available suggest that such treatments are of limited value unless they are part of a more comprehensive program of psychotherapy and behavior modification (Zonana & Norko, 1999).

Untreated sexual abusers tend to have a recidivism rate of between 35 and 50 percent. Cognitive-behavioral approaches that eliminate or reduce inappropriate sexual arousal seem to reduce recidivism rates somewhat over the short term, although long-term studies are lacking. The goal of all such treatment is to help the offender control future behavior so that sexual abuse is not repeated. Therefore, the operative word seems to be "control" rather than "cure" (Marshall, 1999).

Incestual Sex

Virtually every society has strong prohibitions against sexual relationships within families. This is often called the **incest taboo.** There are many theories about why the incest taboo exists, one of the most common involving the desire to avoid disruption of the family system. The biosocial theory holds that the intimacy

incest taboo: cultural prohibitions against incest, typical of most societies.

CASE STUDY

Sidney Deals with His Sexual Abuse of His Sister

Sidney was a junior in college when he consulted with a staff member in the counseling center. He had been feeling depressed and anxious, and he wanted to talk about a number of issues in his life. Foremost in his mind was the fact that his sister, who was 4 years younger than he, had confronted him recently about some sexual activity they had had when he had been 12 and she 8. On a few occasions when they had been alone at home, Sidney had masturbated in front of the younger sister, and one time he had coerced her into putting his penis into her mouth. After that incident, she had threatened to tell their parents, and he had ceased the activity.

Although Sidney reported to the counselor that he had originally experienced some guilt feelings about the abusive behavior, he had eventually put them behind him. He said he had only rarely thought about the incidents in recent years, and he had tended to dismiss them as childish exploration. He was shocked to have his younger sister confront him with her feelings of anger and resentment as she accused him of being a sex abuser. His first reaction was one of defensiveness, and he lied to the sister, saying that he did not recall the activities. Sidney later apologized to her, saying that he had not realized how much he had upset her, and he admitted that he

wished the events had never taken place. He explained that he could offer little excuse for what he had done and said that he would never think of being abusive to a child today. His sexual history and interests indicated no particular sexual affinity for children. The problem with his sister still seemed unresolved, and he asked the counselor for advice on how to deal with the situation even further.

During his next vacation home, he set aside time to have another talk with his sister. She told him that once she had been able to air her anger, she had begun to feel more forgiving. She had made a decision not to tell their parents because she felt that might be even more hurtful for everyone. Sidney assured her that if she wanted to tell them and it would be helpful to her, he was willing to deal with those consequences. He also encouraged her to seek counseling, as he had, to talk about the feelings involved. He offered to participate in the counseling process if she wanted him to do so. After a few weeks, Sidney reported to his counselor that his sister had seen a counselor several times, and she seemed to be much more comfortable. He was confident that their relationship as siblings could now grow more, and his own feelings of depression and anxiety seemed to have lessened.

among family members in early childhood development triggers innate sexual inhibitions about later sexual contact with family, but the theory remains unproven (Hendrix & Schneider, 1999).

There are exceptions to the taboo as well. In the Trobriand Islands, a girl who has intercourse with her mother's brother is committing incest. If she has intercourse with her father, she is not. Among the Kubeo Indians of South America, boys come of age only after having sexual intercourse with their mothers. Strictly defined, the term **incest** refers to sexual intercourse between close blood relatives. It tends to be used in a broader context these days, referring to any sort of sexual contact between close blood relatives, stepparents, or others who live together in a familylike system. Confusion concerning definitions of incest has created some difficulty in researching the extent of the problem. NHSLS researchers found that 9 percent of girls and 4 percent of boys had been involved with an older brother; 14 percent of girls and 2 percent of boys with their fathers or stepfathers; and 29 percent of girls and 13 percent of boys with another relative (Laumann, Gagnon et al., 1994).

Although there are few other reliable statistics to support contentions about the incidence of various forms of incest, it is believed that father-daughter sexual contact constitutes slightly less than 25 percent of incest cases. Stepfather-daughter incest accounts for about 25 percent of cases. The remaining 50 percent of cases involve brothers, uncles, in-laws, grandfathers, stepfamily members, and live-in boyfriends of mothers. It is generally believed that brother-sister incest is the most common among these cases. A study of sibling incest showed some dynamics that the families tended to have in common. The parents were often emotionally distant, inaccessible, and controlling. They tended to stimulate a sexual climate at home, and there were often family secrets, such as one parent having an affair. The incidence of mother-son incest is much less clear, and many researchers believe that although such behavior is not as common as incestual

> **incest** (IN-sest): sexual activity between closely related family members.

abuse of girls, it may also be reported with much less frequency (Lawson, 1993).

Incest often results from unhealthy family interactions, and its discovery causes reverberations throughout the family's entire structure. Families in which the relationship between the father and mother is weak, and in which a daughter takes on many household responsibilities, are susceptible to incestuous contact between father and daughter. Abuse of boys by their fathers is known to be more common in households where the father is very domineering, has alcohol and marital problems, and is physically abusive toward other family members. Abuse of boys by their mothers occurs more often when the mother is overreliant on the son for emotional support. Families in which there is a great deal of chaos, role confusion, and blurring of boundaries between generations are also frequently involved in incest (Maddock & Larson, 1995).

Like other forms of sexual abuse, incest is usually a confusing interaction for a child. Youngsters may be quite passive during the relationship and may even exhibit a kind of seductive behavior that encourages the sexual activity. As a result of the experiences, they may become highly erotic and more interested in sex than would be expected for their age, or they may exhibit self-destructive and aggressive forms of behavior because of their guilt, resentment, and low feelings of self-worth.

A primary goal in helping victims of incest has been to convince them that they are not to blame for the incestuous relationship. However, this approach may have its negative side as well. Even though such reassurances may be well intentioned, they may intensify the sense of powerlessness and lack of control the child has already felt because of the incident. While providing empathy and support through any traumatic responses they may have encountered, therapists can empower children to see future situations as at least potentially controllable. Treatment is an issue for the whole family and should be viewed as a healing opportunity for individual family members (Maddock & Larson, 1995). Women who have been victims of past incest must often work through barriers to the effective parenting of their own children (Armsworth & Stronck, 1999).

FOH It is not unusual for psychiatric patients, alcoholics, or perpetrators of sexual assault to admit during therapy that they were once victims of incest. Incest survivors are sometimes overachievers at work who tend to suffer from depression and suicide attempts (Haas, 1999). They may still be struggling to understand how and why the incest occurred. Research indicates that being able to deal with these unresolved feelings can help people gain a new sense of mastery over their lives. Group psychotherapy is one of the more common therapeutic approaches for incest vic-

tims, although one-to-one counseling is often used as well (Marotta & Asner, 1999). Therapists must often help adult survivors of incest deal with years of shame and anger that in many instances have caused difficulties in relationships. These adults need assurances that they are worthwhile and strong.

Recovered or False Memories: The Controversy

As awareness of the extent of childhood sexual abuse has grown in recent times, the controversial issue of remembering childhood sexual abuse through therapy has emerged. Some publications included lists of psychological and physical symptoms that were typical of adults who had been sexually abused as children. Some counselors and therapists began to explore in greater depth the histories of their adult clients with such symptoms, in hopes of finding out if these individuals had indeed been subjected to sexual abuse in their earlier lives. Articles based on case studies began to be written about clients' *recovered memories* of past sexual abuse, often by a family member. There were several highly publicized cases in which parents were sued by their adult daughters because of sexual or other abuse that had been remembered during therapy. Some of these parents insisted that they were being unjustly accused, and they claimed that unethical or incompetent therapists had, in effect, planted *false memories* about abuse in their clients (Pope & Brown, 1996).

What are your opinions regarding adult memories of childhood sexual abuse that are recovered in therapy?

This issue is still being debated. Although it has generally been accepted by those in the fields of psychology and psychiatry that traumatic events during childhood may be lost to conscious recall and later recalled, research has not been particularly supportive of that contention. There is a fair amount of evidence to indicate that adult victims of child sexual abuse remember the incidents in varying degrees of detail (Banyard & Williams, 1999; Gold, Hughes, & Swingle, 1999). There has also been controversy surrounding the reliability of the details of the memories that do exist. Studies demonstrate that fantasies may also be constructed out of events or emotions experienced during childhood or through suggestion by an outside person (Loftus, 1999), although questions have also been raised about the reliability of such research (Crook & Dean, 1999). Some observers have claimed that therapists who make assumptions about the truth of recovered memories go beyond the boundaries of good therapy when they insist that nonbelief in such memories is a "denial" of the truth. In this way, they actually construct a trap that is difficult for the client and others to escape. Yet, it is also true that therapists sometimes need to function as advocates for their clients (Courtois, 1999; Schooler, 1999).

As proponents of recovered memories call for understanding the victims of past sexual abuse, some family members who feel they have been falsely accused have rallied together within the False Memory Syndrome Foundation. This is a group that has dedicated its efforts to combating the possible effects of memories that are not accurate. The American Psychological Association appointed a task force to investigate this issue and bring some level of consensus to the debate, but instead it found that not much was known about the reliability of memory (Pope & Brown, 1996). There may be some people whose memories of sexual abuse during childhood have been repressed and may indeed be reconstructed. On the other hand, there is recognition that some individuals' memories may sometimes be incomplete, inaccurate, or invented out of other thought processes. Either way, the crucial issues revolve around how such memories should be treated in therapeutic situations and how reliable they should be considered when they are used in legal actions against actual or remembered offenders (Bremner, 1999).

◼ Preventing and Dealing with Problematic Sex

FOH Sexual problems and concerns need not be devastating or permanently disruptive. Before we move on to the following chapters, which deal with various types of sexual problems, it is important to discuss how each of us may work to prevent sexual problems in our own lives and to deal with them should they arise. Consider each of the following points with care, and think about how you might want to apply them in your own life.

Learning about Sex

It is a good idea to learn about your own body, its sexual parts, and what they are called. You should also understand the patterns of sexual response that are part of your body's repertoire. Gradually, with time and experience, you will begin to understand your own sexual orientations and preferences—the things that turn you on. However important sexual self-knowledge is, nonetheless, it is not enough. We also need to take time to understand the many individual sexual differences found in human beings. These range from different sizes of sex organs to different sexual orientations. Accepting the fact that we are all

different from one another can be an important step toward preventing sexual difficulties.

Children need to understand the concepts of appropriate and inappropriate touching, and they need to be alert to possible behaviors that could lead to sexual abuse. They should be taught to be alert to behaviors such as bribery and coercion that adults might use to entice them into sexual activity (Elliott, Browne, & Kilcoyne, 1995; Ward, 1999).

Knowing How to Communicate

Communication is fundamental to a continuing, healthy sexual relationship. Counselors who work with couples find that flaws in communication are one of the most common roots of sexual problems. There are many different things that must be communicated between people: thoughts, ideas, feelings, values, opinions, needs, and desires. Not only are they communicated verbally but also through eye contact, facial expressions, and body language. Communication is far more difficult than often believed, and most people are given very little help in learning how to communicate effectively. See chapter 8, "Sexuality, Communication, and Relationships," for a more complete discussion of communication and sexuality.

Having Realistic Expectations

People are prone to compare themselves to others sexually. "Am I normal?" is one of the most commonly asked questions when it comes to sex. The media provide models of sexual attractiveness and suggest standards of sexual prowess. All of this can create unrealistic expectations that people then struggle to live up to. Sexual problems often stem from setting expectations for one's attractiveness or level of sexual activity that simply cannot be met. It is important to know oneself sexually and to work toward sexual goals that are comfortable, attainable, and consistent with personal values. To live with unrealistic goals is to invite sexual problems.

Being Cautious and Responsible

Shared sex always has some consequences, potentially positive or negative. It is important to approach sexual decision making with an awareness of possible consequences, knowledge about sex, and open communication between the partners. Sexual problems such as guilt, unwanted pregnancy, contracting a sexually transmitted disease, and feelings of having been exploited can usually be prevented with a cautious attitude toward sexual choices.

Responsible sexual decisions are made by keeping the other person in mind as well as oneself. Only too often, people shirk their sexual responsibility with

Ten Reasons to Obtain Verbal Consent for Sex

Antioch College's policy requiring students to obtain verbal consent for each level of sexual behavior has been the subject of countless articles, many of them poking fun at it. Developed by students in the context of Antioch's "community governance," the policy was widely discussed before it was adopted.

One incoming student who learned of the policy at orientation was quoted as saying that if he had to ask, he wouldn't get what he wanted, a remark that unwittingly indicated the value of the policy.

The following may be helpful for those persons, like the incoming student, who need help in understanding *why it makes sense to ask.*

1. Because many partners find it sexy to be asked, as sex progresses, if it's okay.
2. Because sex is better when each partner enjoys what is happening and no one is being forced to do something he or she doesn't want to do.
3. Because if your partner is having a good time and is not forced to do something against her will, she may be more likely to want to see you again. Mutual respect is the best basis for friendship and intimacy.
4. Because forcing sexual activity on another person can violate state and federal laws and your school's policy. In most instances, unwanted touching and fondling is sexual assault.
5. Because it prevents misunderstandings (silence is not a "yes").
6. Because you won't be accused of rape.
7. Because you won't go to jail or be expelled.
8. Because it's better to be safe than sorry.
9. Because if you want to impose your sexual will on someone, your behavior has more to do with dominating that person than with enjoying sexuality and an intimate relationship.
10. Why would you want to have sex with someone who doesn't like what you are doing?

—"Ten Reasons to Obtain a Verbal Consent for Sex," *About Women on Campus,* Vol. 2, Winter 1994

excuses: "I didn't mean to go so far"; "It just happened"; or "I was so drunk I didn't know what I was doing." Responsibility means approaching relationships with an awareness of how powerful sexual emotions can be and how complicated the aftermath of sex can sometimes be, even if sex was desired at the time. Responsible sexual decision making can do more to prevent problematic sex than any other step.

Finding Sex Counseling and Therapy

FOH A part of being a healthy, sexually fulfilled person is knowing when you have exhausted your own resources. Sometimes we can cope with a problem ourselves, sometimes not. Often it helps just to talk things out with another person, pulling thoughts and feelings into a more manageable perspective, especially when we know that person will protect our confidentiality (Breslin, 1998). It can be important to have the objectivity that an outsider can bring to one's situation. Sometimes specific suggestions and strategies are in order that only someone with professional training can offer. Best friends seldom make the best counselors, regardless of how good their intentions may be.

Usually the best time to seek professional help is when you realize you need it and feel ready to seek it, even if you are nervous about it. Early intervention can prevent further complications. There is always one im-

portant point to keep in mind, however. No professional counselor or therapist can wave a magic wand and make the problem disappear. No treatment can be successful unless there is a sincere motivation to change. You will have to want to work on the problem and be willing to expend some energy doing so. If it is a problem shared between partners, then usually both people will have to be committed to working together on it.

Here are some specific guidelines to consider when trying to decide whether to seek professional help and then when looking for an appropriate counselor or therapist:

1. *Make a preliminary assessment of the seriousness of the problem.* This has implications for the type of help you may want to seek. Problems with disease or pain generally need to go to medical professionals. Concern over sexual orientation, decision making, and sexual behaviors may be handled by sex counselors. Sexual dysfunctions (see also chapter 18) are best dealt with by a specially trained sex therapist.
2. *Locate a qualified professional.* You may want to ask a trusted doctor, teacher, or religious leader to suggest a professional whom he or she would recommend for dealing with sexual problems. The yellow pages of telephone directories often list people who specialize in treating sex-related

concerns. Counseling centers or health centers in larger colleges and universities offer sex counseling and therapy services for students. Large medical centers usually offer a variety of sexual health services, and several organizations listed in the Appendix of this text can offer referrals.

3. *Investigate and ask questions.* It is always advisable to be an informed consumer. Do not be hesitant or embarrassed about checking out professionals' qualifications and inquiring about their background preparation. Asking questions during an initial visit, or even prior to a first visit, is a good way to find out what to expect. A true professional will not be offended or insulted by such questions. Here are some areas you might consider finding out more about:
   - What does the service cost, and how frequent are visits?
   - What sort of education, training, and other credentials does the person have?
   - What records are kept, and are they treated in a completely confidential manner? How long are records kept on file?
   - Is the professional appropriately licensed or certified by the state or by any professional society?

4. *Know what you are looking for.* You should be able to feel comfortable and relatively relaxed with a counselor or therapist. Look for the kind of atmosphere in which you are free to discuss sex openly and express your feelings without being judged, put down, or made to feel embarrassed. You should sense a degree of trust, caring, and respect between yourself and the therapist. Any counseling process has its ups and downs, but you should be able to feel eventual progress so long as you are working for it. If you feel discouraged, you should be able to discuss it with the counselor or therapist.

5. *Know what you are not looking for.* Be skeptical about anyone who promises quick and easy solutions. If the person seems to have personal values that might interfere with her or his objectivity

in assessing your situation, think about changing to another professional. Also watch out for any seductiveness or sexual aggression from the professional. This is considered unethical behavior and may be grounds for taking action against the offender. Be cautious, too, about people who seem overly anxious to persuade you to adopt their sexual values. And finally, unless the professional is a physician or other medical clinician who must conduct a legitimate physical examination, reject any suggestions that you should remove your clothing or submit to some sort of sexual touching. Codes of professional ethics consider such behavior inappropriate.

6. *Do not be afraid to seek help.* Professional help can often resolve sexual concerns and problems and help individuals and couples feel better about themselves. To seek such help is not a weakness but instead constitutes a sign of maturity, strength, and personal responsibility.

7. *Check with people who are familiar with the counselor's or therapist's work.* Word-of-mouth recommendations or criticisms are also worth taking into consideration. People who have had professional contacts with a counselor or therapist, either as a client or a colleague, may be able to offer especially valuable insights. However, such opinions cannot always represent the final word. Some people can be impressed by a professional who knows how to sound well-informed; some may gripe about the therapist who cannot perform miracles on demand.

Problematic sex need not be allowed to become a sexual catastrophe. Help is now available for any sexual problem, and it can be obtained confidentially from well-qualified professionals. Preventing and dealing with sexual problems is largely a matter of personal responsibility. We must be ready to accept that any sexual act has a variety of potential consequences, both positive and negative. Most of all, we must be responsible enough to recognize that anyone may experience a sexual problem, and then *do something about it.*

Self-Evaluation

Your Sexual Concerns and Problems

Most of us do not feel fully comfortable with or relaxed about all aspects of our sexuality all of the time. It is difficult to say when discomfort becomes a concern or when a concern becomes a problem. However, this questionnaire may help you to evaluate your particular sex-related worries and what you want to do about them. The chapters that follow may offer more information about your specific concerns. Before proceeding with the questionnaire, take the following two preliminary steps:

Step 1. Ask yourself if you really need to proceed with this questionnaire. If you have had or now have some area about sex about which you have experienced a continuing sense of unrest or worry, it probably will be worth your time to go ahead with the questions. If you feel fully comfortable with your sexual needs, feelings, orientations, and activities all the time, skip this questionnaire.

Step 2. If possible, make certain that you have all the facts about the sexual areas that are of special concern to you. Before going on with this questionnaire, read the earlier parts of this book pertaining to those areas. The table of contents and index can help you find appropriate information. You may even want to read some of the reference articles or books that are listed at the end of each chapter. Some worries and problems fade with appropriate, accurate sexuality education.

1. **Mentally, or on paper, list the sexual concern(s) or problem(s) that are presently most worrisome for you. Do not list more than three.**

2. **For each concern you have listed, answer the following questions:**
   a. For how long has this worried you?
   b. Can you identify the particular incident or time in your life when it started to become a real concern? If so, think it over in as much detail as you can recall:
      1) What were your feelings at the time?
      2) What are your feelings now as you think back?
      3) Is there anything that you wish you could change about the origins of your concern?
      4) If another person was involved in the origins of your concern, how do you feel about that person now?
   c. Is there another person directly involved in (or affected by) the problem now? If so, how would you summarize your present relationship with that person?

3. **Evaluate your concerns:**
   a. For each concern you have listed, read through the following categories and decide which category best

describes your concern. Note whether it is labeled with number I, II, III, or IV.

Category Number	Types of Concerns
I.	Body appearance Size or shape of genitals or breasts Sexual things you have done in the past, but no longer care about doing
II.	Sexually transmitted disease or other infection of sex organs Concern about having been infected with HIV Pregnancy or difficulty with birth control methods Fear of sexual exertion following a heart attack or other illness Other medical problems relating to sex organs
III.	Masturbation Sexual fantasies The things or people to whom you feel sexually attracted do not fit the typical socially acceptable male-female standard The sexual interests and/or activities of your partner or another important person in your life are upsetting to you in some way Lack of information about sex Lack of communication with a sexual partner
IV.	Deep, long-term guilt, dissatisfaction, or unhappiness with your sexuality You feel that you are being sexually harassed by another person A history of sexual abuse as a child that you have not dealt with completely or effectively Concern about rape or other forms of sexual assault or coercion You worry about your body image to the extent that you avoid eating, or binge on food and then vomit or take laxatives Sexual activities in which you now engage are unusual, illegal, or not generally accepted socially Problems with sexual functioning (e.g., impotence, premature ejaculation, lack of sexual arousal, difficulty reaching orgasm [in yourself *or* your partner])

   b. Do you feel discouraged, depressed, and hopeless about your sexual worries and problems? Do not give up on yourself, because for others to be able to help you, you must be willing to work on your problem. There may be many things that will help. Also, be careful of blaming someone else for your problem. Regardless of the type of problem or who has it, you are responsible for how it affects you and what you do about it—keep reading.

c. Now what are you going to do? First go back and note the category of your concern, chosen in part 3a. Regardless of the category, it might be worth considering talking with a professional counselor who has a good understanding of human sexuality. Here are some specific comments about each category; note the category you have chosen:

d. Category I for the most part includes problems that you cannot do very much about. One way or another, you are probably going to have to try to become more comfortable with what you have got or what you have done. Counseling could help you do that.

e. Category II consists of medical problems. If you have not already consulted a physician, do so. If you already have but are unsatisfied, try to find another physician who can help. Your city or county medical society might be able to help. Most cities also have STD and family planning clinics and HIV testing services.

f. Category III includes some of the most common types of sexual problems. Although many people learn to live with them, some form of counseling can often do wonders. See part d.

g. Category IV includes problems that might easily fit into category III but that also sometimes require more intensive kinds of sex therapy or psychotherapy. In seeking a professional to help you deal with such problems, choose carefully and check credentials.

h. Now, if you decide to seek professional help, consider the following:

1) Should your spouse or sexual partner be involved in the counseling? If you are having difficulty communicating, see chapter 7.

2) Try to gain a clear idea of what your goals are in dealing with your sexual concern(s), and express them to the person from whom you seek help.

Chapter Summary

1. The determination as to when some sexual orientation, preference, or behavior becomes a problem can be highly subjective. It often needs to be viewed within the contexts of an individual's reactions and lifestyle and the surrounding cultural and social belief systems.

2. Negative attitudes about the self, especially concern about one's body image, or lack of accurate information as related to sexuality can become a problem.

3. Sexual coercion, abuse, or assault of others represent serious sexual problems. The issue of what constitutes consensual sex, as opposed to acquiescence, can be a complicated one.

4. Ignorance about human sexuality can generate prejudice toward those who in some way are different sexually.

5. Some sexual behaviors, including some sado-masochistic activities, represent obvious physical dangers to individuals, sometimes reflective of self-destructive qualities. There may be a biological link between stress and sexual arousal.

6. There is a range of paraphilias, in which people respond sexually to objects or situations not usually considered to be sexually arousing. Paraphiliacs may be compulsive in their sexual behaviors.

7. There has been an ongoing controversy about whether people can become addicted to sex and whether sex "addiction" treatments are adequate.

8. Sexual harassment refers to unwanted sexual advances. There are four main types.

9. There is increasing awareness of sexual harassment in schools and colleges. There is controversy over the degree to which faculty-student relationships at colleges should be limited or prohibited.

10. The military has been facing serious difficulties with sexual harassment and the issue of consensual sexual relationships, and it has been developing educational programs.

11. Sexual harassment in the workplace has long been a problem, and laws require that workers be free from such pressures.

12. Most institutions have policies against sexual harassment, and several federal laws prohibit the behavior.

13. It is best to respond promptly to harassing situations by getting personal support, seeking out appropriate authorities, being clear about your needs, possibly writing a letter to the harasser, and making use of conflict resolution services.

14. Sexual abuse by professionals is prohibited by ethical standards, and it often represents coercion based on power imbalances in the relationship.

15. There are some predictors of aggression and violence in relationships. In female-male relationships, early warning signals suggest that a man has negative or disrespectful attitudes toward women and could potentially be abusive.

16. Forced sex is believed to be far more common than generally realized or reported. It often represents an attempt to humiliate someone and exercise power over her or him. Men and

women frequently perceive sexually coercive situations in different ways.

17. In many cases, the offender in forced sex is known by the victim, and so it is called acquaintance rape or date rape.

18. A small percentage of wives admit to having been raped by their present or former husbands. Husbands are now subject to the legal consequences of rape of their spouses.

19. Men can also be forced or coerced into having sex, sometimes by women, and sometimes by other men. They react with humiliation, depression, and posttraumatic stress, but they may be less likely than women to report such assaults.

20. Victims of forced sex go through various phases of the rape trauma syndrome, a type of posttraumatic stress disorder. They must adjust to the event, cope with a range of emotions, and attempt to reestablish a sense of control and safety in their lives. Counseling and support are necessary during these phases of adjustment.

21. Sexual abuse of children, called pedophilia or molestation, is a common and serious problem.

22. Adult sexual abusers may view children as sexually motivated, have a history of being abused themselves, and exhibit symptoms of denial and depression. More often than not, the adult abuser is known by his or her child victim.

23. When a child is sexually abused, he or she may have a sense of guilt, shame, and betrayal, and the abuse may lead to an unhealthy sexualization of the child's life. As adults, survivors of sexual abuse are likely to experience depres-

sion, anxiety, and other physical and psychological problems.

24. Victims of sexual abuse may be helped through immediate crisis intervention as well as longer-term supportive and counseling services.

25. Treatment programs are available for child sexual abuse offenders; the most effective of these programs emphasize ways of controlling their sexual impulses and reducing sexual desire for children. Some medications may have some effect in controlling sexual desire.

26. The term "incest" applies to sexual activity between closely related family members. It usually stems from unhealthy family patterns and creates serious confusion for the developing child or adolescent.

27. There is controversy over adult memories of childhood sexual abuse that are recovered in therapy. They have been used in lawsuits. Some accused parents have fought such cases, and some professionals argue that these phenomena may represent false memories.

28. The best ways to prevent and deal with sexual problems are to be knowledgeable about human sexuality, develop communication skills based on qualities that facilitate good relationships, keep realistic expectations about sex, and exercise caution and responsibility.

29. Sometimes it makes sense to seek professional help for dealing with sexual problems. Check out such professionals with great care and be suspicious about behavior that makes you uncomfortable or that seems to be unethical.

Focus on Health Questions

You will find in this section the kinds of questions that you may have concerning your own health and sexuality. The page references indicate where in the text the answer is located; the exact place is marked with the logo: **FoH**

1. Are there any types of sexual behavior that are in themselves dangerous? 451
2. What is a paraphilia? 451
3. Is it true that people can become addicted to sex? 451
4. What can I do if I am being sexually harassed? 456
5. What should I look out for in a partner that might warn of potential sexual abusiveness? 459
6. Can males be raped? 464

7. What are the typical psychological reactions to being a victim of forced sex? 464
8. How may victims of forced sex best be helped to recover? 465
9. How does sexual abuse affect children during childhood and then later on in adulthood? 469
10. What should be done for a child after it has been discovered that the child has been sexually abused? 470
11. Can child sexual abusers be treated? 471
12. What are the effects of incestual relationships on children? 474
13. Are there any ways to head off sexual problems before they occur? 475
14. If I have a sexual problem, how can I find a qualified professional to help me? 476

Annotated Readings

Biexedon, S. Y. (1995). *Lovers and survivors: A partner's guide to living with and loving a sexual partner*. San Francisco: Robert D. Reed. A recovery guide for survivors of child sexual abuse and their partners.

Craissati, J. (1999). *Child sexual abusers: A community treatment approach*. Philadelphia: Brunner/Mazel. Thorough coverage of the characteristics of child sexual abusers and various approaches to their treatment.

Ellis, L. (1998). *Theories of rape*. Bristol, PA: Taylor & Francis. A state-of-the-art look at research concerning forced sexual activity.

Eskenazi, M., & Gallen, D. (1992). *Sexual harassment: Know your rights*. New York: Carroll & Graf. Written by attorneys, this volume provides an overview of the law as it relates to sexual harassment and advice on how to pursue legal actions against various types of harassment.

Fontes, L. A. (Ed.). (1995). *Sexual abuse in nine North American cultures*. New York: Guilford. A fascinating cross-cultural view of the perceptions, prevention, and treatment of sexual abuse among diverse populations.

Francke, L. B. (1997). *Ground zero: The gender wars in the military*. New York: Simon & Schuster. Examines the many issues relating to sexuality, sexual harassment, and abuse in the U.S. military.

Friedman, J., & Boumil, M. M. (1995). *Betrayal of trust: Sex and power in professional relationships*. Westport, CT: Praeger. An overview of the problems and complexities associated with intimate and sexual relationships between professionals and their clients/patients.

Gartner, R. B. (1999). *Betrayed as boys: Psychodynamic treatment of sexually abused men*. New York: Guilford Press. Describes how men internalize the aftereffects of sexual abuse during their childhoods and explains various treatment approaches.

Gonsiorek, J. C. (Ed.). (1995). *Breach of trust: Sexual exploitation by health care professionals and clergy*. Thousand Oaks, CA: Sage. Based on conference papers, this book covers a wide range of topics relating to sexual abuse within professional relationships.

Hall, G. C. (1996). *Theory-based assessment, treatment, and prevention of sexual aggression*. New York: Oxford University Press. A scholarly and comprehensive overview of sexual offenses and their treatment.

Maddock, J. W., & Larson, N. R. (1995). *Incestuous families: An ecological approach to understanding and treatment*. New York: W. W. Norton. A comprehensive perspective that examines family dynamics relating to incest and focuses on treating entire families along with individual family members.

Marshall, W. L., Fernandez, Y. M., Hudson, S. M., & Ward, T. (Eds.). (1998). *Sourcebook of treatment programs for sexual offenders*. New York: Plenum. Describes model programs for offenders in a range of sexual categories.

Mendel, M. P. (1995). *The male survivor: The impact of sexual abuse*. New York: Guilford. An examination of the effects and needs of men who were subjected to sexual abuse as boys.

Nelson, N. (1997). *Dangerous relationships: How to stop domestic violence before it stops you*. New York: Plenum. Outlines the danger signals of coercive and violent relationships and offers suggestions for how to protect oneself and seek appropriate help.

Scarce, M. (1997). *Male on male rape*. New York: Plenum. A fascinating look at a complex subject, drawing on years of research, interviews with survivors, and case studies.

Sipe, A. W. R. (1995). *Sex, priests, and power: Anatomy of a crisis*. New York: Brunner/Mazel. Written by a former priest, this book includes honest and insightful coverage of the subtle and complex issues involved in sexual abuse and coercion by members of the clergy.

Chapter 16

Sexually Transmitted Diseases

Chapter Outline

History and Incidence of Sexually Transmitted Diseases

Nonviral Sexually Transmitted Infections

Gonorrhea

Syphilis

Chlamydia

Nonspecific Urethritis in Males

Vulvovaginal Infections

Viral Sexually Transmitted Infections

Genital Herpes

Genital Warts

Hepatitis B and Hepatitis C

Other Sexually Transmitted Infections

Pubic Lice

Sexually Transmitted Diseases of Tropical Climates

Sexually Transmitted Skin Infections

Preventing Sexually Transmitted Diseases

Legal Aspects of Sexually Transmitted Diseases

Sexual Effects of Debilitating Illnesses

Self-Evaluation

Examining Your Attitudes toward Sexually Transmitted Diseases

Chapter Summary

Note: A selection of Focus on Health questions appears at the end of each chapter. Answers to these questions are indicated within the chapter by the symbol in the margin. **FOH**

I couldn't understand why the nurse suggested that I have a test for a disease when I had no symptoms whatsoever. I was really shocked when the results showed that I had chlamydia. I never thought I would get one of those diseases. I'm pretty careful.

—Based on a counseling session

T he human body can experience a variety of diseases that either are transmitted by the intimate physical contact of sexual activity or have direct and indirect effects on sexual functioning. In recent years, medical science has been paying more attention to these sex-related conditions. Many sexually transmitted diseases (STDs) are continuing to spread rapidly among some populations. They are commonly called sexually transmitted *infections* (STIs), reflective of the fact that diseases are the symptoms of illness that may develop following an infection. Infections do not lead to noticeable disease symptoms in all cases. The two terms are used interchangeably in this chapter. Physicians and other health professionals also have a heightened awareness of the need to help patients understand and adapt to the sex-related effects of other illnesses. This chapter provides an overview of these topics. The findings about HIV and AIDS are somewhat different from those of other sexually transmitted diseases, and they are discussed separately in chapter 17, "The HIV/AIDS Crisis and Sexual Decisions."

History and Incidence of Sexually Transmitted Diseases

At various times in history, some sexually transmitted diseases, such as **syphilis,** have represented scourges that attacked societies. They were feared and often assumed to represent retribution from the gods. When soldiers of the French army were garrisoned in Naples in the winter of 1495, they suffered syphilitic sores on the genitals, followed by skin eruptions. The Italians called it the "French sickness," although the French blamed it on the Italians. The Turkish people would come to call it the Christian disease, and the Chinese dubbed it the Portuguese disease. Nearly every major nationality, ethnic group, and religion would eventually be blamed for the scourge of syphilis. Gonorrhea and syphilis were significant problems among U.S. troops during World War II, and extensive educational efforts were launched to prevent their spread. However, effective and rapid medical treatments for the venereal diseases (VD)—as they were once called—were generally lacking, and their incidence increased at alarming rates.

Which STDs do you believe are the most common in the United States?

When penicillin and other antibiotics began to appear in the late 1940s, it seemed as though VD had finally been conquered. By 1957, the number of cases of both gonorrhea and syphilis had dropped to an all-time low. However, as public concern began to fade and assurances of quick cure increased, the incidence of STIs began to rise again. It has been suggested that some health policymakers have always had mixed feelings about curing or eradicating STDs, because these diseases have been perceived as one factor that might discourage illicit sexual behavior. It seems likely that gonorrhea and syphilis might well have been completely eliminated if our culture had taken a less moralistic stance on STDs and had made more aggressive use of antibiotics (Michael et al., 1994). Instead, more antibiotic-resistant strains of these diseases have developed, and new disease-causing microbes, such as chlamydia and a variety of viral diseases, now have been added to the list of more than 25 infectious organisms that can be transmitted by intimate bodily contact. Several new STIs have been identified in recent years, and so the problem is an ever-evolving one (Donovan, 1997; Hsu, 1998).

A recent study called STDs the "hidden epidemic" **FOH** because they so often escape public attention. For one thing, many STDs lack clear symptoms and may go undetected. Partly for this reason, they may also have serious, longer-term health consequences including infertility, cancer, and other chronic illnesses. Another reason is that because of the stigma of STI, public discussion and education about STDs are often avoided, which may even inhibit health professionals from educating their patients about potential consequences (Donovan, 1997; Eng & Butler, 1996).

A survey conducted by the Kaiser Family Foundation found that U.S. teenagers often lack basic knowledge about STDs. Of those polled, 82 percent considered themselves at least fairly knowledgeable about STIs, but 23 percent of them could name no infection other than HIV. The majority of the respondents did not consider themselves at risk of infection, and yet about half of the sexually experienced teenagers did not use a condom every time they had sex. A similar proportion had never discussed STDs with their most recent sexual partner. A third of the teens surveyed assumed that they did not have an STI

syphilis (SIF-uh-lus): sexually transmitted disease (STD) characterized by four stages, beginning with the appearance of a chancre.

because they had no symptoms. When asked to name the most common STDs, only 13 percent named human papilloma virus (see p. 493) and only 3 percent named trichomonas (see p. 491), even though these two diseases are among the most common of the estimated 15.3 million new cases of STIs each year (Henry Kaiser Family Foundation, 1999).

The evidence indicates that two-thirds of the new STD cases each year are among those under the age of 25, but adults older than 25 do not seem to take the threat of infection any more seriously than do young people. It has even been suggested that young adult men be targeted for STD prevention education, because they seem to be at higher risk for exposure to STDs than are adolescents (Bradner, Ku, & Lindberg, 2000). Yet the consequences of these infections on human health continue to be staggering. There are over 100,000 women rendered infertile each year as the result of an STD. Half of the 88,000 annual ectopic pregnancies are due to a preexisting infection. Medical costs associated with STDs top $8 billion a year (Cates, 1998; Hsu, 1998).

What is your response to the suggestion that health policymakers have failed to use all of their resources to eradicate STDs?

The varying estimates concerning the incidence of STDs reflect the deficiencies in how the data are collected. Even though the Centers for Disease Control and Prevention (CDC) consider many STDs to be *reportable diseases* and gather statistics on them, many private physicians do not consistently report their occurrence. Public clinics are more likely to report those diseases that are easily diagnosed, such as the highly recognizable gonorrhea. They are less likely to be able to offer expensive diagnostic techniques necessary to

detect some of the viral STDs such as genital warts or hepatitis B. In addition, STDs are reported as "cases" rather than as patients, meaning that if the same individual were to report back to a clinic several times with a reinfection of the same disease, each new infection would be reported as a separate case. Patients with a bacterial infection are more likely to seek treatment than those with a viral STD (Brackbill, Sternberg, & Fishbein, 1999). It is now believed that 56 million people in the United States, or one out of every five, are infected with some form of viral STD (such as herpes or hepatitis B) that can be controlled but not cured (Committee on Prevention and Control of STDs, 1997). From a political perspective, it is worth noting that STDs are the only diseases that are categorized specifically by their mode of transmission.

The National Health and Social Life Survey (NHSLS) questioned its research participants about their own histories relating to several STDs. Eighteen percent of women and 16 percent of men, or about one person in six, had been diagnosed by a physician as having at least one of these diseases at some point in their lives (see Fig. 16.1). During the previous year, 1.5 percent had been diagnosed with an STD, 1 percent of which were bacterial infections, and 0.5 percent of which were viral. Women were more likely to have had an STD than men, reflecting the medical fact that it is about twice as easy for a male to transmit a sexual infection to a woman than it is for a female to transmit a disease to a male (Laumann, Gagnon et al., 1994; Panchaud, Singh, Feivelson, & Darroch, 2000).

Many people are mistakenly convinced that they could not contract an STD because of their care in choosing sexual partners or because they maintain high standards of personal hygiene. The NHSLS statistics confirm that STDs are not confined to the ignorant or uninformed or to those who have poor hygiene. Race,

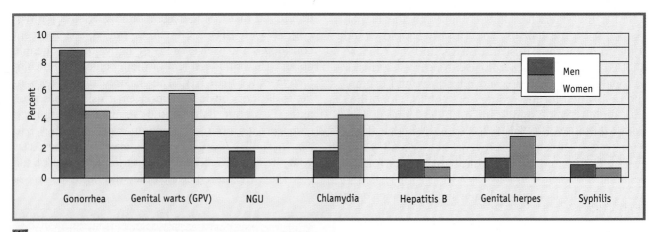

FIGURE 16.1   *Lifetime Rates of Sexually Transmitted Infections*

Statistics from the NHSLS indicate the percentages of respondents who had been diagnosed with various STDs during their lifetimes.

Source: From *Sex in America* by Robert Michael. Copyright © 1994 by C.S.G. Enterprises, Inc., Edward O. Laumann, Robert T. Michael, and Gina Kolata. By permission of Little, Brown and Company, Inc.

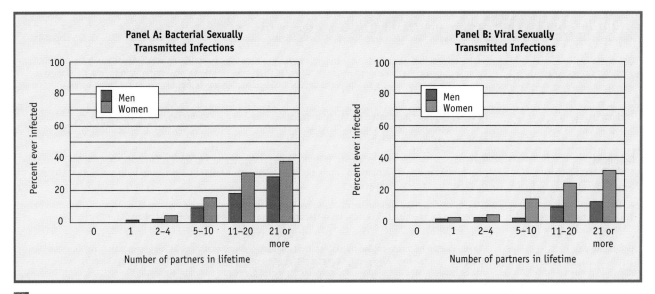

FIGURE 16.2   *Lifetime Rates of Sexually Transmitted Infections, by Number of Partners and Gender*

These two graphs, based on NHSLS data, show that the likelihood of contracting either bacterial or viral STDs increases proportionately with the number of sexual partners one has.

Source: From *Sex in America* by Robert Michael. Copyright © 1994 by C.S.G. Enterprises, Inc., Edward O. Laumann, Robert T. Michael, and Gina Kolata. By permission of Little, Brown and Company, Inc.

educational level, and socioeconomic group were all shown to be relatively insignificant factors in predicting risks of STDs. The high-risk profile that emerged from the research was, in fact, remarkably consistent and predictable. As Figure 16.2 shows, the risk of contracting STDs rises with the number of sexual partners a person has because, according to the data, those partners will have had many sexual partners themselves. People who have sex with multiple partners generally engage in casual sexual experiences with virtual strangers while under the influence of alcohol or other drugs. And even though they may have used condoms, they probably were not consistent enough to offset the risks (Michael et al., 1994). It takes only a single unprotected sexual encounter with an infected partner to become infected with the disease oneself.

Some people are embarrassed to seek treatment once they realize their symptoms are suggestive of STD. One of the difficulties with most STDs is that their symptoms may be relatively mild at first, especially in women. Gonorrhea, syphilis, and chlamydia are particularly known for the inconspicuousness of their symptoms in the early stages. They may progress into full-blown infections with potentially serious consequences before they have been recognized. Pelvic inflammatory disease (PID) in women often results from untreated STDs (see chapter 10, "Decision Making about Pregnancy and Parenthood").

The following sections outline basic information on STDs. See Table 16.1 for a summary of the information. For quick and accurate answers to personal questions you might have, or for referral to a local clinic for testing or treatment, call the STD National Hotline on weekdays at their toll-free number between 8:00 A.M. and 11:00 P.M. Eastern Time. The number is 1–800–227–8922 anywhere in the United States.

Nonviral Sexually Transmitted Infections

There are several STIs caused by bacteria or bacterialike organisms. When diagnosed and treated in the early stages, these diseases are the most likely to be cured.

Gonorrhea

With some 650,000 estimated cases of **gonorrhea** (in slang, called "clap" or "the drip") each year in the United States, it is also the second most commonly reported communicable disease. The CDC estimates that if unreported cases are included, there may be over a million cases of the disease annually (H.G. Miller, Cain, Rogers, Gribble, & Turner, 1999). There has been a gradual decline in the incidence of the disease in recent years, after an increase in the 1970s. However, the statistics on most STDs tend to show periodic fluctuations, the reasons for which are difficult to explain.

gonorrhea (gon-uh-REE-uh): bacterial STD causing urethral pain and discharge in males; often no initial symptoms in females.

Table 16.1   Common Sexually Transmitted Diseases

Chlamydia 3 million cases a year.	Bacterial infection acquired chiefly through vaginal or anal intercourse. Symptoms include genital discharge, burning during urination (nonspecific urethritis [NSU] in males); women may suffer pain in lower abdomen or pain during intercourse. Up to three-quarters of cases in women are without symptoms. Can be cured with antibiotics.
Trichomoniasis 5 million cases a year.	Parasitic infection most often occurring in female vagina and male urethra. Symptoms are often absent, especially in men. May include vaginal discharge, discomfort during intercourse, odor, painful urination. Can usually be cured with oral antibiotics.
Gonorrhea 650,000 cases a year.	Bacterial infection of cervix, urethra, rectum, or throat. Symptoms are often mild or absent, including discharge from penis, vagina, or rectum and burning or itching during urination. Can be cured with antibiotics, but penicillin-resistant cases are increasing.
H.P.V. 5.5 million cases a year.	Viral infection spread by anal, oral, or vaginal sex causes painless, fleshy warts in affected area. Warts can be suppressed by chemicals, freezing, laser therapy, and surgery. Some strains are associated with cervical and other cancers.
Genital herpes 1 million cases a year. About 45 million Americans carry the virus.	Usually caused by virus, spread by skin-to-skin contact. Symptoms include itching or burning and blisters, usually in genital area. May recur. Causes painful open genital lesions, sometimes accompanied by swollen, tender lymph nodes in the groin. No cure, but antiviral drugs can alleviate outbreaks.
Hepatitis B 100,000 to 200,000 cases a year. About 1.5 million Americans carry infection.	Virus found in semen, saliva, blood, and urine and passed through sexual contact, sharing drug needles, and piercing the skin with contaminated medical instruments. Infection attacks the liver. Most infections clear up by themselves within 8 weeks, but some individuals become chronically infected.
Syphilis 20,000 cases a year.	Bacterial infection usually acquired by vaginal, anal, or oral sex with someone who has an active infection. Produces painless sores which disappear within weeks, but without treatment disease may eventually damage heart, brain, eyes, nervous system, bones, and joints. Curable with penicillin.

Sources: American Social Health Association; Henry J. Kaiser Family Foundation.

Caused by the bacterium *Neisseria gonorrhoeae* (named after Dr. Albert Neisser, who discovered the bacterium in 1879), gonorrhea seems to be transmitted almost exclusively through sexual contact. Sexual activity—vaginal intercourse, oral sex, or anal sex—with an infected partner is riskier for women than for men. There is over a 50 percent chance of women contracting the disease on a single exposure during intercourse, whereas for men the risk is about 25 percent because bacteria migrate less easily into the male urethra than into the female vulva, where they have more moist locations in which to multiply. Of course, the risk increases for both men and women with each repeated exposure.

Babies may pick up the bacteria during the birth process if the mother is infected. Their eyes are particularly vulnerable to gonorrheal infection, and blindness can result. It is a routine precaution in most hospital obstetrical units to put a few drops of an antibacterial agent into the eyes of newborns in order to kill bacteria.

Symptoms

FOH Probably one of the major reasons that genital gonorrhea is the most commonly reported STD is that its symptoms tend to appear quite quickly and be decidedly unpleasant for men. However, it is also possible for the infection to be mild and relatively asymptomatic. In men, within 2 weeks after infection, burning and itching sensations develop in the urethra, especially during urination. There is also a thick, puslike discharge from the urethra, often showing up on underwear (see Fig. 16.3).

Although up to 80 percent of women do not detect gonorrhea in its earlier stages, its most typical early symptom is a green or yellow discharge from the cervical area, where the bacteria tend to strike first. There may then be some vaginal irritation or irregularities in menstruation. Gonorrheal infections in the throat tend to create soreness and some mucus in the throat. Rectal infection causes soreness, itching, rectal discharge, and bowel abnormalities.

If gonorrhea is not treated in its early stages, the initial symptoms usually disappear on their own, but the bacteria often move to other organs, causing more serious infections and complications. In men, it may affect the bladder, prostate, kidneys, or epididymis of the testes. Left untreated in either sex, the disease can cause sterility. In women, the infection often moves into the reproductive organs such as the uterus, fallopian tubes, and ovaries, and may eventually result in pelvic inflammatory disease (PID). Very occasionally, in either sex, the bacteria create systemic infections throughout the body, with generalized symptoms, arthritis, and complications in major organs such as the heart or brain.

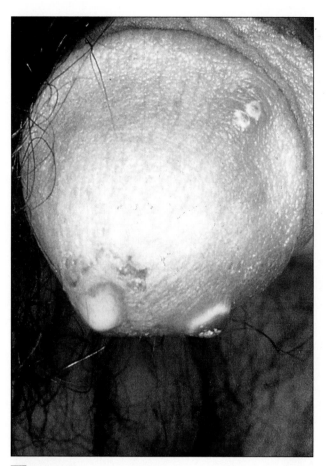

FIGURE 16.3 *Gonorrhea*

Symptoms of gonorrhea in men include a puslike discharge. About 80 percent of women, however, are asymptomatic.

Diagnosis

There are three main ways in which gonorrhea bacteria are identified. First, a smear is made of the discharge, taken from the penile urethra, cervix, throat, or rectum, depending on where infection most likely took place. The material is stained and examined microscopically for evidence of the bacteria. A culture may also be made, with bacteria grown on a nutrient medium and then examined for the gonorrhea bacterium. The culture method has been most widely used with women. More recently, a new enzyme-sensitive immunoassay test has been developed that can detect the bacteria with great accuracy.

Treatment

FOH Because there are many new strains of gonorrhea bacteria that are penicillin-resistant, the disease is now generally treated with oral dosages of the antibiotics ceftriaxone, ciprofloxacin, cefixime, or ofloxacin. Because some gonorrhea bacteria may not be completely eliminated by typical treatment, follow-up checks should be made about a week after treatment has ended. Treatment should include antibiotics that destroy **chlamydia** organisms as well, because that infection often coexists with gonorrhea. As with any STD, sexual partners of a patient with gonorrhea should be notified of their risk, so that they may seek appropriate diagnosis and treatment.

Syphilis

Intermittently throughout history, syphilis has been considered a scourge. Some historians have speculated that some of the "leprosy" present in biblical times may have actually been syphilis. An epidemic of the disease spread through Europe at the end of the fifteenth century, leading to further speculation that a virulent form of the disease was brought back to Europe by Christopher Columbus and his crew. In 1905, the spiral-shaped organism, or spirochete, that causes syphilis was identified and named *Treponema pallidum.*

The number of reported syphilis infections in the United States has traditionally been lower than reported cases of gonorrhea, and syphilis now averages slightly over 20,000 reported cases per year. The incidence of the disease has seen cyclic changes over the years, but it had dropped to its lowest rate on record by the end of the 1990s. Many states still require a blood test for syphilis as a prerequisite to obtaining a marriage license.

Symptoms

Syphilis can progress through four major stages, beginning 2 weeks to a month after infection. The first stage, or *primary syphilis,* is nearly always characterized by the appearance of a painless sore wherever the spirochete entered the body. The painless sore, called a **FOH** chancre, begins as a reddish bump that develops into a pimple. It then opens and ulcerates, often oozing pus until a scab develops. The chancre is sometimes surrounded by a pink border (see Fig. 16.4). This sore is infested with the treponema organism, and so the individual is highly infectious at this stage. Usually the chancre appears on the genitals, although it can appear on the mouth, anal area, and on fingers or breasts. In women it frequently occurs on the inner vaginal wall or cervix and sometimes in the rectum. Because it tends to be painless, it may not be noticed there. Within 4 to 6 weeks, the chancre heals even without treatment, and there may be no further symptoms for up to 6 months (Argasus Foundation, 1992).

chlamydia (kluh-MID-ee-uh): now known to be a common STD, this organism is a major cause of urethritis in males; in females it often presents no symptoms.

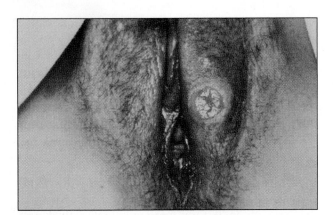

FIGURE 16.4(A)   *Primary Syphilis Chancre*
On female genitalia.

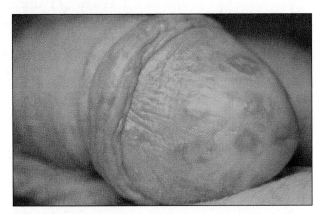

FIGURE 16.4(B)   *Primary Syphilis Chancre*
On the penis.

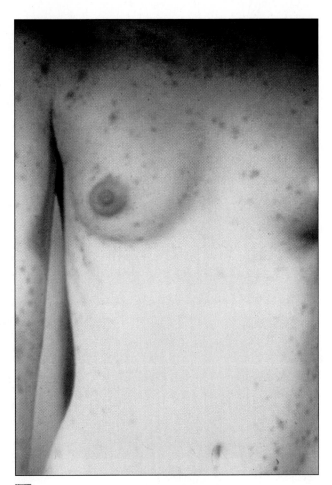

FIGURE 16.5   *Secondary Syphilis*

The next stage, *secondary syphilis,* usually begins with a bumpy skin rash (see Fig. 16.5), accompanied by general symptoms of illness such as fever, swollen lymph nodes of the neck, nausea, headache, sore throat, loss of scalp hair, and loss of appetite. More moist sores may appear around the genitals or anal region. Again, even without treatment, the symptoms eventually abate within a few weeks, and the disease enters its *latent stage.* It is estimated that slightly more than half of untreated syphilis victims remain in this latent stage for the rest of their lives.

FOH People who progress to the *tertiary syphilis* stage usually face serious complications resulting from the spirochete infecting inner tissues and organs. It may attack the heart, brain and spinal cord, eyes, joints, and numerous other areas, leading to life-threatening disease, blindness, psychosis, or paralysis. Although modern medical treatment has greatly reduced the number of syphilis cases progressing to the tertiary stage, they still occur. In later tertiary stages, the disease typically cannot be transmitted to others.

Congenital syphilis refers to an unborn fetus being infected by the disease from its mother's bloodstream while in the womb. It can result in significant birth defects, especially of the bones, blood, and kidneys. If a pregnant woman with syphilis is treated prior to the 16th week of pregnancy, congenital syphilis can be averted. It is important, therefore, that a pregnant woman have a blood test for syphilis before the fourth month of pregnancy.

Diagnosis and Treatment

The two main ways in which syphilis can be identified are through one of several blood tests or by microscopic examination of fluid from the chancre, in which the spirochete may be seen. Once diagnosed, it is usually treated in its primary and secondary stages by a single injection of penicillin. Tetracycline, erythromycin, or doxycycline may also be used. Latent and tertiary syphilis require larger doses of antibiotics over a period of several weeks. Because so many people who have been infected with syphilis are also infected with HIV, patients who have a positive test for syphilis should also be tested for HIV (Cates, 1998; Schofer et al., 1996).

Eradication of Syphilis

The U.S. Public Health Service has recently targeted syphilis for national elimination of the disease. It is believed that rates are now low enough, and treatment methods effective enough, that eradication of the disease is a very real possibility. Because syphilis infection is also associated with a higher risk of HIV infection, the 5-year effort is considered worth the investment of time and money that would be involved (St. Louis & Wasserheit, 1998). Because the genetic code of the *Treponema* organism has now been completely identified, there is also hope that treatments and vaccines could be developed that will aid in the eradication effort (Fraser et al., 1998).

Chlamydia

It has long been known that the organism *Chlamydia trachomatis* is a frequent cause of inflammation in the urinary and genital systems. Only in the mid-1980s, however, was chlamydia recognized as a widespread STD with a range of serious complications (see Fig. 16.6). The CDC estimate that there are close to 3 million chlamydial infections each year in the United States, although others believe the actual number to be much higher. It first became an officially reportable disease in 1995 and quickly took its place as one of the most common of the STDs and among the most commonly reported communicable diseases in the United States. The chlamydia organism invades the cells it attacks and multiplies within those cells. It therefore can create a variety of symptoms and can be resistant to some antibiotics. It is a particularly common infection on college campuses. Chlamydia prevention programs, involving education, screening, and aggressive treatment, have been found to lower the rate of this infection (H.G. Miller et al., 1999).

Like gonorrhea, chlamydia offers special risks to the eyes of newborns. *Conjunctivitis,* an inflammation of the eye, can be contracted at birth as the baby passes through the vagina, or birth canal. If it is not treated thoroughly and promptly, blindness can result. It may well be the most widespread preventable cause of blindness throughout the world. Babies may also develop chlamydial pneumonia during their first few months of life. Although the disease is spread primarily through sexual contact, once the infection is established it can be spread to other areas of the body or other people by hand contact, insects, or contact with human excretions. These modes of transmission are particularly prevalent in underdeveloped countries where there is overpopulation and inadequate sanitation.

CHLAMYDIA IS NOT A FLOWER

It's the nation's most prevalent sexually transmitted disease.

FIGURE 16.6   *Chlamydia*

Symptoms

The symptoms of chlamydial infection are often vague or nonexistent, and they can masquerade as symptoms of other diseases as well. This is one of the reasons that many such infections go unnoticed or are inaccurately diagnosed. In about 70 percent of all cases, there are no early symptoms, and it may take more serious later complications to alert the infected individual that something is wrong.

CASE STUDY

Carolyn Discovers A Sexually Transmitted Infection

Because her menstrual period was over a week late, Carolyn visited her college's health center for a pregnancy test. The test was negative, but the nurse practitioner thought she ought to have some other testing. Following the examination, the practitioner told Carolyn that she had a chlamydia infection. This surprised her because she had not experienced any symptoms that would have suggested that she had been infected by a STD. She was told that it would be important for both her and her sexual partner to be treated, or they would simply keep reinfecting one another. Carolyn expressed concern and embarrassment over telling her boyfriend, because when making a decision about having unprotected sexual intercourse, they had both declared that they had not had sex with previous partners. The nurse practitioner explained that if Carolyn had truly not had intercourse with other men, then her boyfriend must have contracted the disease from

another female partner. The nurse continued to press the importance of his being treated.

The next day, Carolyn returned to the clinic with her boyfriend. He had admitted that he had had a one-night stand with a woman just prior to the relationship with Carolyn, and he was anxious to receive treatment for the chlamydia. The nurse practitioner reminded both of them that if he had been exposed to one disease, there was at least a chance that he had been exposed to other diseases as well. She recommended further tests for the couple, including an HIV antibody test. This was alarming to both of them and escalated Carolyn's feelings of betrayal and mistrust. All of the other tests turned out to be negative, but the experience had created a significant strain in their relationship. The nurse practitioner recommended to Carolyn that the two of them seek some counseling help to examine their feelings more thoroughly.

In males who are symptomatic, there is often a burning sensation during urination and discharge of pus from the penis. If the organism moves farther into the body, swelling and discomfort in the testicles may result. Untreated, it can cause infertility in men. In females, the early symptoms are often mild but can involve itching or burning of the vulva, some discharge, and irritation during urination. In its later stages, the disease may cause PID, with fever, nausea, abdominal pain, and abnormal patterns of menstruation. It can also damage the fallopian tubes and is now known to be a common cause of infertility and ectopic pregnancy (Cates, 1998). There is mounting evidence that long-term infection with chlamydia may be linked to human heart disease (Bachmaier et al., 1999).

Diagnosis and Treatment

Until recently, tests for chlamydia were time consuming and expensive, requiring the growing of the organism in a laboratory culture for identification. There are now several tests available that can render a quick, inexpensive, and relatively accurate diagnosis. A new urine test for chlamydia is expected to become available very soon.

Once diagnosed, the disease can usually be cured with a week-long treatment of azithromycin, doxycycline, or erythromycin. Penicillin is not an effective treatment. As with any antibiotic treatment, it is crucial that the entire dosage of the prescribed medication be

taken. Otherwise the infection may continue in more persistent forms. Ointments containing tetracycline or erythromycin may also be applied to the eyes of newborns to prevent the development of chlamydial conjunctivitis.

Health workers continue to emphasize that chlamydia is a serious infection, now of epidemic proportions. Thus, people should pay attention to and seek appropriate medical checkups for any unusual sensations or discomforts in the genital or urinary tracts. It is a good idea to request a chlamydia culture test in routine pelvic exams.

Nonspecific Urethritis in Males

Sometimes called *nongonococcal urethritis (NGU)*, **nonspecific urethritis (NSU)** refers to any inflammation of the male urethra that is not caused by gonorrhea. NSU is a much more common infection than gonorrhea and has been on the increase. The most common cause of NSU is chlamydial infection, accounting for about half of the cases. Another 20 to 25 percent are caused by the mycoplasmic bacterium *Ureaplasma urealyticum*. The remainder of NSU cases are apparently caused by other microorganisms

nonspecific urethritis (NSU) (yur-i-THRYT-us): infection or irritation in the male urethra caused by bacteria or local irritants.

or by local irritation from soap, vaginal secretions, or spermicides, although the exact cause is sometimes impossible to isolate (Cates, 1998).

Although the symptoms are often less pronounced than those associated with gonorrhea, there is usually some degree of burning and itching during and after urination. There may also be some discharge of pus, often more evident in the morning.

Prompt treatment of NSU is crucial, even though the symptoms typically subside and disappear on their own within a few weeks, because the organism causing the inflammation will usually persist somewhere in the body. This can increase the likelihood of a repeat infection or of more serious complications at a later time. Again, antibiotics such as azithromycin, erythromycin, or doxycycline are most frequently used to treat NSU, although they are not always effective. Regardless of the cause, it is advisable for any sexual partner of a man with NSU to seek examination to determine the possible presence of infection as well.

Vulvovaginal Infections

FOH **Vulvovaginitis,** or infection within the vulval region and vagina, is extremely common and often not caused by a STD. Almost every woman will experience a vulvovaginal infection sometime. The lining of the vagina has a carefully balanced system for cleansing itself. Fluids from the tissues in the vaginal lining and the uterine cervix, along with discarded cells from the uterus, form a discharge that cleanses the vagina and protects it from infection by hostile bacteria. However, the balance of this cleansing mechanism may change during various stages of the menstrual cycle, during pregnancy, or with the use of birth control pills, antibiotics, or other medications. The pH of the vagina, usually slightly acidic, may become more alkaline. Any such upset can make the vagina more vulnerable to infection.

Symptoms

All types of vulvovaginitis are usually characterized by some discharge, the color, thickness, and odor of which varies with the type of infection. There are often sensations of burning and itching in the vulval region and outer vagina.

Types

There are four main types of vulvovaginitis. The first three may be transmitted by sexual activity, although their microorganisms are found naturally in the environment or in the body and may develop into an infection without sexual contact if the conditions present themselves.

1. *Bacterial vaginosis* is most often caused by the bacterium *Gardnerella vaginalis.* Men apparently can carry gardnerella, but they often do not experience any symptoms of disease. Occasionally, it causes urethritis, bladder infection, or infection of the penile foreskin in males. Vaginal gardnerella is treated with oral antibiotics such as penicillin, ampicillin, amoxicillin, or tetracycline, and with a drug called metronidazole, commonly known as Flagyl. Sexual partners are usually treated at the same time to reduce the risks of reinfecting one another. Bacterial vaginosis increases the risk of premature delivery for pregnant women, although this risk may be reduced with administration of the drug clindamycin (McGregor, 1995).

2. **Yeast infection*** in the vagina is sometimes called *monilial vaginitis.* It occurs when conditions within the vagina permit an overgrowth of a fungus *Candida albicans,* that normally is found there. Such infections can sometimes mask the presence of other STDs, and so it is important to check for other STDs whenever a yeast infection is found. This disease is treated with fungicides that are used within the vagina in cream or suppository form, such as miconazole or nystatin. Treatments for yeast infections are available without prescription, although studies indicate that women may not be using them appropriately because their self-diagnosis skills are not particularly accurate (Ferris, 1996).

3. **Trichomoniasis** is an infection caused by a one-celled protozoan organism, *Trichomonas,* that can take up residence within the vulva and vagina and in the male urethra as well. It is one of the most common causes of vaginal infection, causing some 3 million new infections each year. Frequently there are no noticeable symptoms. Again it is necessary to treat sexual partners as well as the woman infected, to prevent reinfection. The drug used is metronidazole (Flagyl),

Note: Yeast infections can also affect males, in the form of an itchy rash on the penis and scrotum.

---

vulvovaginitis (vaj-uh-NITE-us): general term for inflammation of the vulva and/or vagina.

yeast infection: a type of vaginitis caused by an overgrowth of a fungus normally found in an inactive state in the vagina.

trichomoniasis (trik-uh-ma-NEE-uh-sis): a vaginal infection caused by the *Trichomonas* organism.

which is not considered safe for use during pregnancy or when a woman is nursing a baby.

4. *Atrophic vaginitis* is caused by low estrogen levels and occurs almost exclusively after menopause. It is not a STD, although it can lower resistance to vulvovaginal infection by other microorganisms.

Prevention of Vulvovaginal Infections

One of the best ways to prevent sexually transmitted vaginosis is for the male to use a condom during sexual intercourse. There are several simple hygienic measures that can at least reduce the risk of vaginal infection through nonsexual contamination. These include daily washing of the vulva with mild soap and water, followed by thorough drying, because dampness heightens the risk of infection. For this reason too, underwear made of nonabsorbent synthetic fibers such as nylon is not recommended. Experts also recommend against the use of vaginal sprays and douches unless they have been specifically prescribed for some medical condition. They are often implicated in upsetting the balance of the vagina's natural cleansing mechanisms, increasing the likelihood of infection.

◾ Viral Sexually Transmitted Infections

The sexually transmitted viral infections are believed to have already infected at least 20 percent of the population. Although viral infections can often be kept under control, and their symptoms relieved, the virus typically continues to reside in the body's cells. This may lead to periodic outbreaks of symptoms or may be associated with cellular abnormalities that have been associated with certain types of cancer. In this sense, viral STIs are controllable but not yet curable.

Genital Herpes

Genital herpes is caused by the *Herpes simplex* virus. There are two strains of the virus, Herpes simplex virus type 1 *(HSV-1)* and type 2 *(HSV-2)*. Cold sores on the mouth are usually caused by HSV-1, whereas lesions in the genital area are caused most often by HSV-2. It is now known, however, that up to 20 percent of genital herpes is linked to the HSV-1 virus. Although it is not clearly understood why this is the case, it has been proposed that an increase in oral-genital sexual activities may play a role.

An estimated 45 million people in the United States have been infected with the virus, with up to another million contracting the disease each year. Research indicates that people tend to have unreasonable fears and misconceptions about herpes, leading to negative stereotypes regarding herpes sufferers. HSV-2 is transmitted almost exclusively by sexual contact, although the virus can survive externally for several hours in moist, warm conditions. Once the herpes simplex virus has been contracted, it may continue to live in the body, even if no symptoms of the disease are present.

There are no vaccines to prevent infection nor any medications to eradicate the virus from the body. The actual appearance of the painful herpes blisters seems to be associated with periods when disease resistance might be weakened by other illnesses, stress, exhaustion, or inadequate nutrition. It may also be triggered by irritation to the susceptible regions of the skin, such as by overexposure to the sun or irritation from clothing.

Symptoms

Genital herpes is characterized by the appearance of what may be painful or itchy clusters of blisters like cold sores on the sex organs. During the first outbreak, women usually have blisters on the cervix as well as externally on the vulva (see Fig. 16.7). Within a few days, the blisters open and ulcerate, leaving wet, open sores that are highly contagious. Care is especially crucial during these outbreaks to prevent transmission of the virus to other individuals or even to other parts of the infected person's own body. Exposure of the eyes to the virus is particularly dangerous because a severe eye infection called *herpes keratitis* may develop that can cause serious damage to the cornea. The sores should be touched as little as possible and only when followed by thorough washing of the hands. Sometimes outbreaks of the blisters are accompanied by other symptoms of illness, such as fever, achiness, or pain in the groin or thighs. It usually takes another 2 weeks for the sores to crust over and heal.

Up to 70 percent of people who have had a genital herpes infection will experience at least one recurrence of the disease. This usually begins with prickling or burning sensations in the skin where the blisters are about to appear. It is during such outbreaks that sexual contact, or any direct contact with the infected area, is particularly risky. It is advisable to avoid such contact until at least 10 days after the sores have healed completely. However, the risk of infection remains, even when the blisters are not present. Use of a condom reduces the chance of infection. Up to 30 percent of infected people never have a further outbreak of the herpes sores.

Most men do not experience any complications from a herpes infection, although herpes increases the

genital herpes (HER-peez): viral STD characterized by painful sores on the sex organs.

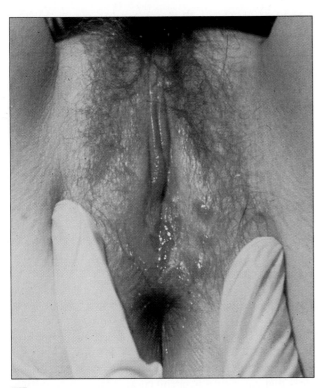

FIGURE 16.7   *Herpes Blisters in the Vulval Area*

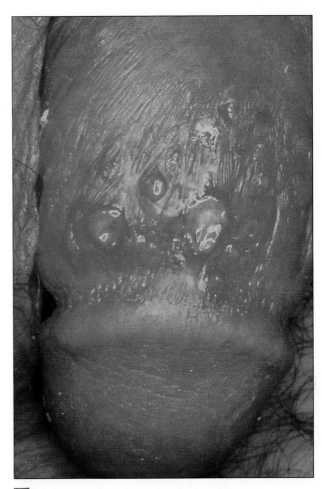

FIGURE 16.8   *Herpes Blisters on the Penis*

risks of being vulnerable to infection by HIV (see Fig. 16.8). Although relatively rare, there are possible complications for women and their babies. There is a higher incidence of cervical and vulval cancer among women who have had genital herpes, even though the cause-and-effect mechanism for this phenomenon is not understood. For this reason, women with HSV-2 are advised to have an annual pelvic examination and Pap smear to detect any abnormal cells in the cervix.

The second danger is to a baby during the birth process, in which the presence of HSV-2 can lead to seriously damaging infection or even death. This is called congenital herpes. In women with a history of genital herpes, cultures are taken from the cervix, vagina, and vulva several times during the final weeks of pregnancy to detect a possible recurrence of the disease. If there is a risk of infection to the baby during birth, the delivery may be accomplished by cesarean section.

Diagnosis and Treatment

Genital herpes is usually diagnosed by direct observation of the blisters, although a variety of tests are available that use cultures of the virus for positive identification. Although there is no cure for the disease, three antiviral drugs have been found to relieve some symptoms and may be used to suppress recurrences of the disease. They are acyclovir, famciclovir, and vala-cylclovir, and they can sometimes reduce relapse times

from a month to nearly a year. Acyclovir can be applied to the blisters in ointment form during the initial outbreak, although it proves less useful with recurrent outbreaks. Orally administered drugs have been shown to reduce recurrent infections in those who are susceptible to frequent outbreaks and also to reduce the duration and severity of the infection. The drugs have not been tested in pregnant or nursing women (Cates, 1998). Other antiviral drugs are presently being tested for possible use with herpes infections.

Health care professionals offer some suggestions for relieving the painful symptoms of a herpes outbreak, such as keeping the infected area as clean and dry as possible. Baby powder or cornstarch may be used to absorb moisture. Aspirin or other pain relievers can help, as well as direct application of an ice pack.

Genital Warts

Genital warts are caused by the *human papillomavirus (HPV)*, a virus similar to the one that causes warts in other bodily regions. There are over 50 known strains of the virus. The condition is also known as *condylomata acuminata* or *venereal warts*. This disease is now the most common sexually transmitted viral disease in the United States, with up to a million new cases occurring annually. **Genital warts** occur more frequently in people who began sexual activity comparatively early in their lives and have had multiple sexual partners and casual sexual relationships. Women with HPV are likely to have had male sexual partners with warts on the penis or partners who are carrying the virus (Kellogg-Spadt, 1998).

Symptoms

The warts, or condylomata, usually do not appear on the genitals for about 3 months after exposure to an infected partner. Their color and texture can vary with location, with soft, pinkish lesions occurring in moist areas and harder, greyish-white warts in dry areas. They have irregular surfaces (see Fig. 16.9). The warts usually grow on the penis, vulva, anal area, or urethra. If they grow inside the urethra, they can cause difficulty in urinating and lead to other infections. For the most part, they are not particularly painful or dangerous in themselves. However, some strains of HPV have been increasingly associated with a high incidence of cancerous or precancerous cells in the cervix, a condition called *cervical intraepithelial neoplasia (CIN)*. Well over 90 percent of cervical cancers are also infected with the virus. It is believed that these strains of the PMVs can cause abnormal cell division in cervical tissues (Tate, Resnick, Sheets, & Crum, 1996; Wheeler et al., 1996). More recent evidence indicates that these

viruses may also be implicated in a variety of other cancers, including those on the genitals or other bodily organs. It also appears that they can produce anal cancers; some cases have been identified in gay males.

Treatment

Genital warts can be removed by laser surgery, electrosurgery (using an electrical current), freezing with liquid nitrogen, or surgical excision. For external warts, chemicals such as podophyllin may be applied over a period of 3 or 4 weeks, often causing the lesions to heal. However, because the virus remains in the body, the warts can recur until immunity develops over several months or years (Cates, 1998; Ho et al., 1998).

Hepatitis B and Hepatitis C

There are five identified viruses that can cause the liver infection known as hepatitis. The *hepatitis A virus*, contracted through the mouth from food contaminated by fecal material, is generally not considered to be an STI. The **hepatitis B virus (HBV)** is a sexually transmitted virus that can cause liver infection. Although **hepatitis C virus (HCV)** is most often transmitted by direct contact with tainted blood, it is now believed that it can sometimes be transmitted sexually (Cohen, 1999b). HBV is more common than types A and C, with between 100,000 and 200,000 new cases occurring each year in the United States. An estimated 1.5 million people in the United States are chronic carriers of the virus, even though most are unaware that they have it. There is evidence that people who are infected with hepatitis C are more vulnerable to infection by hepatitis B and by HIV as well (Wong, 1996). Men and women who engage in high-risk sexual behavior are at greater risk of contracting hepatitis C (M.J. Alter, 1999). Both HBV and HCV may be transmitted by sharing intravenous needles for illicit drug use, but hepatitis B is more likely to be transmitted sexually because it is found in bodily fluids such as saliva, semen, vaginal secretions, and blood.

HBV has become such a major health problem in the United States, especially among young adults aged 15 to 25, that the American College Health Association has recommended that all college students be vaccinated against the disease (Gorman, 1998). The vacci-

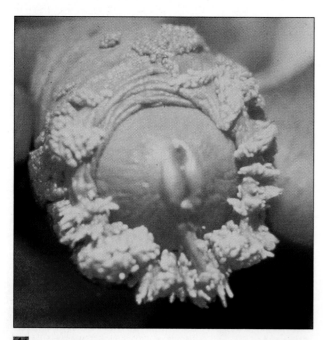

FIGURE 16.9 *Genital Warts around the Penile Glans*

> **genital warts:** small lesions on genital skin caused by papillomavirus; this STD increases later risks of certain malignancies.
>
> **hepatitis B virus (HBV):** liver infection that is frequently sexually transmitted.
>
> **hepatitis C virus (HCV):** liver infection that may occasionally be sexually transmitted.

Hepatitis B

Going back to school used to be a simple matter. Buy some shoes, grab a few pencils and head on out the door. But your academic survival kit isn't complete nowadays if you're missing the vaccination against hepatitis B, a virus that can destroy the liver.

Not only do more and more schools across the U.S. recommend the shots, but 22 states now require it for enrollment in kindergarten or first grade. Not to be outdone, the American College Health Association is launching a campaign this fall that features extreme-sports athletes like Olympic snowboarder Barrett Christy urging university students to roll up their sleeves.

The vaccination is a great idea, even if your memory of freshman English is receding as fast as your hairline. Hepatitis B strikes more than 200,000 Americans each year and kills 6,000, making it the third most deadly vaccine-preventable disease in the U.S., after the flu and pneumonia. There are, of course, other viruses that take a toll on the liver. But hepatitis A, which is transmitted via contaminated water and food (think raw oysters and salad bars), doesn't usually cause permanent damage. And there is no vaccine for hepatitis C, which is transmitted during sexual intercourse, among other ways.

Probably the biggest misconception about hepatitis B is that only drug users or prostitutes contract it. While it is true that most adults become infected through sex or exposure to contaminated needles, perhaps a third of all cases cannot clearly be linked to such causes. "Nature isn't tidy," says Dr. William Schaffner of the Vanderbilt University School of Medicine. "We had a case of two people who only worked together. One had hepatitis B, though he didn't know it, and the other didn't. On a single occasion, they drank from the same Coke. It happened at just the right time in the incubation cycle so that the second person became infected."

Timing is critical in other ways as well. About 90% of adults eventually shake off hepatitis-B infection, while the other 10% become chronic carriers and face a greater risk of liver damage, liver cancer, and death. Things get much worse when children are involved. About 90% of infected infants (who usually get the virus before birth) become chronic carriers.

It made a lot of sense back in 1991 for the Centers for Disease Control to target its vaccination efforts at children under the age of two. But researchers then found that 75% of new cases of hepatitis B in the U.S. occur in those between the ages of 15 and 39. So last year the CDC advised that all children up to the age of 18 get vaccinated. But remember: the disease can strike at any age. Thus most people will benefit from getting the shots. (One exception: those allergic to yeast, which is used to make the vaccine.)

The vaccine, given in three doses over six months, carries potential minor side effects, such as soreness and fever. And there have been reports of adults developing multiple sclerosis after vaccination, although most experts regard those outcomes as unfortunate coincidences. The vaccine is one of the safest inoculations available. Considering the often devastating consequences of hepatitis-B infection, particularly for young people, you and your children are better off getting the shots than taking your chances.

nation must be given in three doses, with a total cost averaging about $130. This creates a financial burden in many cases because colleges and universities cannot afford to provide the vaccine, and many individuals have difficulty paying for it. There is also a worldwide effort to make HBV vaccination more available to all populations that might be at risk.

Symptoms

Hepatitis B and C have several degrees of severity. They may have no symptoms at all or may cause complications serious enough to be fatal. About 5,000 people in the United States die each year from chronic liver disease caused by HBV or HCV. The typical early symptoms of both infections include loss of appetite, lethargy, headache, joint achiness, nausea, vomiting, diarrhea, yellowing of the skin (jaundice), darkening of the urine, and some enlargement of the liver. Usually hospitalization is unnecessary. Infection with hepatitis B or C increases later risks for developing liver cancer (Cates, 1998).

Treatment

As with all viral infections, there is no cure for hepatitis at present. Some medications can provide relief of symptoms, and a period of bed rest and heavy fluid intake is usually required. Gradually, the body's immune system conquers the disease, although in more severe cases this process can take several months. Sometimes, the virus develops into chronic conditions that can lead to destruction of the liver or other organs over a period of years.

Other Sexually Transmitted Infections

The list of disease agents that may be transmitted sexually continues to grow. This section contains information about several of those organisms.

Pubic Lice

FOH The STD commonly called "crabs" is caused by a tiny (1–4 mm) parasitic louse with the scientific name *Phthirus pubis.* Health workers often refer to an infestation of these lice as *pediculosis pubis.* The lice have claws that allow them to hold tightly to hairs, usually in the pubic, anal, and **perineal area.** Occasionally, they spread to the armpits or even the scalp. The lice found in head hair are usually of a different species, however, and are not spread by sexual contact.

Pubic lice bite into the skin to feed on blood from tiny blood vessels. This creates little papules on the skin that cause intense itching. They lay their eggs, or nits, on hairs to which they are tightly attached (see Fig. 16.10). These eggs can drop onto sheets or bedclothes and survive for several days. The lice can also live away from the body for about one day in clothing, sheets, towels, and even furniture, making their way to other people if the opportunity presents itself. Both the whitish nits and the adult lice themselves can be seen upon close examination.

Treatment

Any treatment must be thorough to ensure complete eradication of the lice. The best medication to use is a 1 percent lindane lotion or cream, which is applied to the infested area, then washed off after 8 hours. Lindane shampoo, applied for 4 minutes, is also available. The brand name of lindane is Kwell, and it is available only by prescription. Other shampoo treatments can be purchased without a prescription, including A-200 Pyrinate and Triple XXX. A repeat treatment is recommended after 7 days to take care of any eggs that may have been missed the first time. It is also crucial that all potentially exposed bedclothes, underwear, towels, or other materials be thoroughly washed or dry-cleaned. An insecticide spray is available to treat furniture as well. Close physical contact with others should be avoided until treatment is completed.

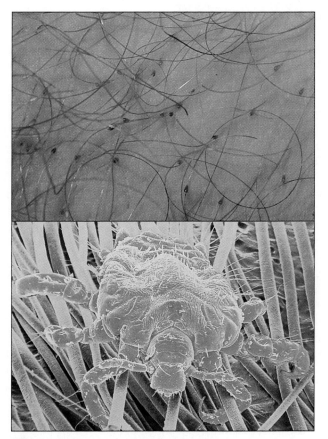

FIGURE 16.10 *Pubic Lice and Nits*
Pubic lice and nits on pubic hairs.

Sexually Transmitted Diseases of Tropical Climates

There are several other STDs that are more common in tropical climates but have recently been on the increase in temperate-zone countries such as the United States. **Lymphogranuloma venereum (LGV)** is caused by several strains of *Chlamydia* and produces painless, pimplelike ulcers on the genitals or rectum. There may be other symptoms, such as fever, hives, or swollen lymph nodes in the groin. If left untreated, it can cause blockage of lymph vessels, resulting in swollen limbs or bodily organs. In the tropics, this condition is called "ele-

perineal area (pair-a-NEE-al): the sensitive skin between the genitals and the anus.

pubic lice: small insects that can infect skin in the pubic area, causing a rash and severe itching.

lymphogranuloma venereum (LGV) (lim-foe-gran-yu-LOW-ma va-NEAR-ee-um): contagious STD caused by several strains of *Chlamydia* and marked by swelling and ulceration of lymph nodes in the groin.

phantiasis." LGV is treated with antibiotics such as doxycycline, tetracycline, or erythromycin, or sulfa drugs.

Chancroid is caused by the bacterium *Hemophilus ducreyi*. Within a week after infection, several small sores appear on the genitals. They are filled with pus and may rupture to form painful open sores that bleed easily. Antibiotics and sulfa drugs are effective in curing the disease; if it is left untreated, it can cause swelling, pain, and rupture of lymph tissue at the surface of the skin.

Granuloma inguinale is a rare infection caused by *Calymmatobacterium granulomatis*. It also involves the appearance of small blisters and swelling of lymph nodes. The sores often do not heal easily unless treated and can become infected, eventually causing permanent damage and scarring of tissue. It can be cured with antibiotics such as tetracycline, streptomycin, or erythromycin.

Because cases of LGV, chancroid, and granuloma inguinale number only in the thousands annually in the United States, they are diseases less commonly seen by physicians and STD clinics. This makes them harder to diagnose, which may result in dangerously delayed treatment.

Sexually Transmitted Skin Infections

There are two skin diseases in the United States that are transmitted by direct bodily contact, not necessarily sexual. One is **molluscum contagiosum,** a pox virus that causes small papules to appear on the skin. They often look similar to whiteheads and have a hard seedlike core. They usually do not create any discomfort or pain. Occasionally, they may become infected by other bacteria and ulcerate. Molluscum blisters often heal by themselves, although they may be removed by scraping, freezing, or treatment with chemicals. If all of the lesions are not removed, they will often recur.

Scabies is caused by a tiny mite that burrows under the skin to lay its eggs (see Fig. 16.11). It causes redness and itching and may lead to secondary infections. Epidemics of scabies often spread throughout schools, hospitals, or other institutions where people interact closely. Obviously, sexual contact also provides an easy mode of transmission for the disease. The same chemical lotions and creams used for pubic lice are effective with scabies as well.

■ Preventing Sexually Transmitted Diseases

The occurrence of many STDs in the population has reached epidemic proportions, and there is no particularly effective system in place for the prevention and

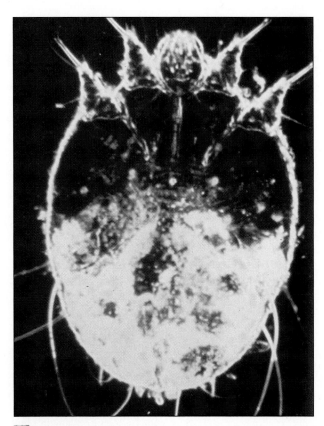

FIGURE 16.11 *Scabies Mite*

control of these infections (Eng & Butler, 1996). Some strains of STD-causing bacteria are showing signs of greater resistance to the antibiotics that have constituted standard treatments for years. It is estimated that over 20 million women in the United States would be interested in using some sort of STD-prevention chemical that

chancroid (SHAN-kroyd): an STD caused by the bacterium *Hemophilus ducreyi* and characterized by sores on the genitals, which, if left untreated, could result in pain and rupture of the sores.

granuloma inguinale (gran-ya-LOW-ma in-gwa-NAL-ee *or -NALE*): STD characterized by ulcerations and granulations beginning in the groin and spreading to the buttocks and genitals.

molluscum contagiosum (ma-LUS-kum kan-taje-ee-O-sum): a skin disease transmitted by direct bodily contact, not necessarily sexual, that is characterized by eruptions on the skin that appear similar to whiteheads, with a hard seedlike core.

scabies (SKAY-beez): a skin disease caused by a mite that burrows under the skin to lay its eggs, causing redness and itching; transmitted by bodily contact that may or may not be sexual.

CROSS-CULTURAL PERSPECTIVE
The Other Epidemic

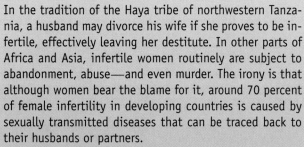

In the tradition of the Haya tribe of northwestern Tanzania, a husband may divorce his wife if she proves to be infertile, effectively leaving her destitute. In other parts of Africa and Asia, infertile women routinely are subject to abandonment, abuse—and even murder. The irony is that although women bear the blame for it, around 70 percent of female infertility in developing countries is caused by sexually transmitted diseases that can be traced back to their husbands or partners.

In Africa, infertility is epidemic among poor rural females whose husbands migrate to urban areas in search of work and return home with more than a paycheck to share. The vast majority of Africa's migrant workers live in cities where both the demand for prostitutes and the level of sexually transmitted disease are high. Women, especially female prostitutes, are often blamed for the spread of these infections. Studies by the World Bank and others confirm, though, that it is men seeking commercial sex who carry infection from one prostitute to another—and eventually even to their wives and girlfriends.

In a vicious cycle, these patterns of behavior reinforce the subordinate position of women in society. Men become infected through visits to prostitutes, who "choose" their profession from sheer lack of economic alternatives. Men transmit diseases to their wives, who are powerless either to prevent or treat them. Infection leads to infertility, which leads to divorce. In some cases, the ex-wife herself turns to prostitution to survive.

Yet infertility is just one of several conditions caused in women by a group of sexually transmitted diseases (STDs) that includes chancroid, chlamydia, gonorrhea, herpes, human papillomavirus, and syphilis. Cervical cancer, inflammation of the uterus, and ectopic pregnancy are some of the other life-threatening conditions that stem from these diseases.

These STDs take a disproportionate toll on women's lives. They cause far more death and illness in women than does AIDS—another STD—in men, women, and children combined. They also cause a large share of preventable infant deaths and disability each year. They reduce individual economic productivity, hamper efforts to slow population growth, and burden already poor health care systems. And worse yet, most STDs actually facilitate transmission of the AIDS virus. . . .

The use of condoms would markedly reduce the risk of infection, yet in many societies the prerogative of choosing what birth control method to use, and whether to use one at all, lies with the man. Examples from two regions illustrate starkly this imbalance of power.

In a survey of 144 Ugandan women, the overwhelming sentiment was that "because of their lack of decision-making power in matters of sex . . . women felt they were more at risk of becoming infected than men," states E. Maxine Ankrah, a lecturer at Makerere University in Kampala, Uganda. Faced with "philandering by their husbands [these women] say they prefer to abstain . . . or use condoms . . . but find their husbands won't cooperate." She concludes that with limited economic opportunities, there is no "clear path for these worried women to follow."

Women in Mexico face similar problems. As many as 60 percent of women there who seek state-sponsored birth control do so without the knowledge of their spouses, in large part because of the belief among men that contraceptive use will diminish their manhood or lead to infidelity. A wife found practicing birth control surreptitiously risks being physically abused. Under these constraints, it is clear that a woman's ability to negotiate protective measures is negligible.

Fear of violence or rejection by their partners also inhibits millions of women from acknowledging symptoms that might lead to prompt identification and treatment of STDs. Psychological deterrents, including strict mores proscribing even married women from discussing sexual problems, can create virtually insurmountable obstacles for women to disclose symptoms or complications.

—Jodi L. Jacobsen, "The Other Epidemic," *World Watch*, May/June 1992

could be placed in the vagina prior to sex. The pharmaceutical industry has been encouraged to work on the development of such vaginal microbicides that could reduce the risks of STIs (Darroch & Frost, 1999). Viral STDs, which may persist in the body as chronic or recurring infections, have been spreading at alarming rates. HIV disease has no cure at this time (see the following chapter). For these reasons, the possibility of contracting or transmitting disease should be weighed as part of everyone's responsibility regarding sexual behavior. Here are some specific suggestions for minimizing the chances of getting or transmitting a STD:

1. *Recognize that abstinence from sex represents a rational choice in the face of the evidence about STDs.* There are plenty of pressures to have sex. Our sexual feelings may be strong and difficult to resist. However, each individual must make his or her own decisions about how involved to get with others sexually. With the increase of persistent and dangerous STDs, abstinence or delaying sexual activity have become viable alternatives and rational choices.

2. *Remember that sexual sharing does not have to involve internal penetration.* Most of the serious STDs are transmitted by penetration involving mingling of bodily secretions (oral-genital, anal-genital, or penile-vaginal). The transmission of these diseases could be sharply reduced by emphasis on forms of sexual sharing that do not require such penetration. These include massage, most forms of mutual masturbation, and some degree of external mutual genital contact. Unfortunately, social values have often led us to believe that some form of penetration is necessary to legitimize a sexual experience. Given the prevalence of STDs, alternative values may well begin to filter into our social systems.

3. *Avoid multiple partners and partners who are not well known to you.* The more partners you have and the less well known they are to you, the greater the risks of contracting an STD. This is a fact that has been confirmed by research. Casual sex is simply riskier sex. There is less chance that partners' sexual histories will be known, that their suspicious symptoms will be noticed, and that you will be notified if a disease is eventually diagnosed (Finer, Darroch, & Singh, 1999).

4. *Take responsibility for yourself and your own protection.* There are several measures that you can take to protect yourself and reduce the risks of getting an STD. They may not always be easy steps to take and may require some degree of assertiveness, but they are part of sexual responsibility. First, it is important to talk with a partner about sex, and even to ask about possible infections, although there is evidence that such information exchange between partners is not always particularly accurate (Ellen, Vittinghoff, Bolan, Boyer, & Padian, 1998). You might want to ask if he or she has ever had a herpes infection or any recent symptoms of infections. Second, it can be important to observe your partner's genitals, checking for any sores, warts, discharge, lice, or rashes. It is also a good idea to take responsibility to wash your genital area with soap and water before and promptly after sex. Although these suggestions may not be conducive to sexual intimacy, they are worth considering as precautionary measures in preventing STDs. It is also important to avoid the use of alcohol and other drugs that may alter judgment. Indiscriminate use of such substances is associated with higher rates of STD (Shain et al., 1999).

5. *Use condoms, vaginal pouches, and spermicides.* Whenever there is a risk of an STD infection, male condoms or female condoms (vaginal pouches) can reduce the chances of transmission (see chapter 10, "Decision Making about Pregnancy and Parenthood," for more information, and chapter 17, "The HIV/AIDS Crisis and Sexual Decisions," for instructions on the proper use of condoms and vaginal pouches). They do not offer total protection but certainly reduce the risks substantially. Likewise, spermicidal foams and creams, especially nonoxynol-9, placed in the vagina kill some bacteria and offer a partial barrier against microorganisms. Studies have shown that the chemical reduces the risks of gonorrheal and chlamydial infection significantly.

6. *Get medical screening periodically, and seek medical treatment promptly if symptoms develop.* If you are sexually active, it is a good idea to seek screening tests occasionally that can determine if you might have one of the STDs that tends to have few symptoms in its beginning stages. STD clinics, family planning clinics, and college health centers are usually able to help with such screening. Whenever you have any suspicious or uncomfortable symptoms in the genital area or urinary tract, seek medical advice and treatment right away. Most cities have STD clinics, staffed by workers who have expertise in this area. Clinical workers are nonjudgmental, and the tests are nearly always painless (Linnehan & Groce, 1999).

7. *Inform sexual partners, and urge them to seek treatment.* Whenever an STD is diagnosed, it is crucial for sexual partners of the infected person to be notified and to have a physical examination. Remember, many STDs do not have obvious symptoms in the earlier stages but still require prompt treatment to prevent complications. Many STD clinics have found that it is best to provide a couple-friendly atmosphere in which both partners may be treated and counseled about their STI (Danielson et al., 1999).

How comfortable do you feel asking a potential sex partner about her or his history of STDs? Would you inform that partner of your history? Why or why not?

A Lover's Legal Checklist

Before engaging in sexual intimacy, consider these points to avoid both legal liability and the risk of infection. These questions may seem tough to handle in a romantic setting, but they are necessary to an exchange of genuine promises. They are the heart of your commitment to a healthy, meaningful relationship for you and your sexual partner.

Adapt this checklist to your own particular needs. Whether you use all of it or a part of it depends on you and your partner, your sexual history, and your personal concerns.

1. Share Your Medical History

Exchange with your lover:
- When you've each last had a medical checkup.
- What, if anything, that checkup showed.
- Whether either of you has had any recent STD symptoms.
- Whether previous lovers exhibited any of these symptoms.
- If either of you has a medical condition, whether it has been treated and cured. If it is recurrent or chronic, when were dates of occurrences?
- Information about blood transfusions received before 1985 (when effective blood screening for HIV began).

Consider a joint visit to the doctor.

2. Share Your Sexual History
- Discuss your recent sex life.
- Is either of you bisexual?
- Were any partners in a high-risk group?

3. Act with Integrity
- Make your promises genuine. Get all the secrets out.
- Don't let passion cloud your better judgment. Make sure that any risk you take is full and informed—not under the influence of drugs or alcohol.
- Be practical: Suggest a condom or spermicide.
- Be careful: Exchange letters with your partner, so that you have some written records of your communications.
- Make a physical examination part of your foreplay.
- If you have an STD, make sure that you have met your legal responsibility to your partner through full and complete disclosure. Your legal duty can be met with three simple words—for example, "I have herpes."
- Be trustworthy: Keep the information about your partner confidential.

4. Trust Your Feelings
- Don't underestimate your inner voice. If you feel insecure about your partner, practice caution.

When it comes to safe sex, selfishness is a virtue. Your partner should appreciate it as much as you do.

Lovers must ask questions *before* they engage in sexual intimacy. Use the Lover's Checklist as a resource for better communication. Don't be afraid to use it. It can preserve your good health and peace of mind.

—Margaret Davis and Robert Scott, *Lovers, Doctors, and the Law*, 1988, Perennial/Harper & Row, New York.

Legal Aspects of Sexually Transmitted Diseases

Most of us assume that a person would not knowingly or deliberately transmit a disease to another person. For the most part, such assumptions are probably correct. However, sexual behavior is an area of life about which people can be extremely private and secretive. They may feel uncomfortable with certain aspects of their past sexual activities and may worry that to discuss their sexual histories will jeopardize present relationships (Buysse & Ickes, 1999). People also tend to avoid protecting themselves against the riskier aspects of sexual behavior, especially when they are caught up in powerful romantic or sexual feelings.

In recent years, more attention has been focused on the legal responsibilities of sexual partners as they relate to STDs. Individuals who have contracted an STD after being assured that there was no danger of doing so, or without being informed of potential risks, have resorted to legal action. Multimillion-dollar lawsuits have been brought against celebrities, for example, for infecting sexual partners with diseases such as genital herpes. Legal experts warn that the law expects people to be responsible in their sexual behaviors and to protect others from potential harm that might come from sexual activity. As STDs have reached epidemic proportions, legal precedents are being established that demand even higher levels of responsibility during sexual encounters. Some legal guidelines are presented in the box on this page.

What is your reaction to "A Lover's Legal Checklist"? Does it seem to pit romance against responsibility? How would you suggest that the two be merged?

Describe what you foresee as some possible effects of medication and debilitating illness on sexual behavior.

◼ Sexual Effects of Debilitating Illnesses

There is a long list of other medical problems that can directly or indirectly affect one's sex organs and sexual functioning. The particular diseases and disorders of the female and male sexual organs were discussed briefly in chapters 2 and 3. Because sexuality is a part of the whole person, anything that affects physical or psychological health and well-being can have implications for sexual functioning as well. Unfortunately, health professionals often fail to assess the sexual implications of various illnesses and do not discuss these aspects with their patients. They may feel personally uncomfortable talking about sex with patients or be concerned about creating undue embarrassment in them. Especially in long-standing chronic illnesses, or in acute illnesses that create serious debilitation, careful sexual assessment should be an integral part of total health care. The partners of patients are often dealing with difficult emotional issues as well, which may affect their sexual attitudes and functioning. It has been recommended that partners be included in sexual assessment and counseling when a serious illness is being treated (Hollander, 1995; McCormick, 1996a).

Drawing by Peter Steiner from cartoonbank.com; © *The New Yorker Collection*, 1987. All rights reserved.

Treatments for some illnesses, such as medication for blood pressure or chemotherapy for cancer, can have direct effects on sexual functioning. Additionally, chronically ill people may begin to question their identities as women and men and the role that their sexual functioning now plays in their identities (Charmaz, 1994; McCormick, 1996a).

Among the diseases most frequently found to have adverse effects on sexual functioning are neurological disorders such as multiple sclerosis or stroke, diabetes, cardiovascular disease and heart attacks, chronic lung disease, cancer and its treatments, and arthritis. These illnesses and their treatments may weaken the body, interfere with the control of bodily functions, threaten self-esteem and body image, and interfere with interpersonal intimacy. Because of the potential sexual problems resulting from such diseases, patients should be given thorough information about what to expect and access to therapy designed to help them reestablish whatever degree of sexual functioning that may be realistically expected (Bergmark, Avall-Lundquist, Dickman, Henningsohn, & Stieneck, 1999; Meyerowitz, Desmond, Rowland, Wyatt, & Ganz, 1999).

Cardiac and stroke patients, for example, are often concerned about the amount of physical exertion that is safe for them during sexual activity. This can lead to psychological pressures that can in turn produce sexual dysfunctions. Erection problems are particularly common in men who have heart disease. Health workers can gradually encourage postheart-attack patients to get back in touch with their sexual feelings, even suggesting masturbation when the individual is physically ready for any exertion. Later, specific suggestions can be given for shared sexual activity, at first using positions requiring a lesser degree of physical strain and energy. With reassurance and education, most cardiac patients can reestablish full sexual lives (DeBusk, 1996).

Diabetes is known to cause some physical complications that can directly interfere with sexual activity. Two of the most commonly reported problems are difficulty having an erection in men and some degree of vaginal dryness and its associated discomfort in women. Physically based complaints of this sort then have their psychological spin-offs as well. People begin to feel sexually inadequate and fear failure during their sexual interactions. In turn, new pressures are created on communication within their relationships. Often, these difficulties can be alleviated by intervention from health professionals who are sensitive to the sex-related implications of diabetes (Weinhardt & Carey, 1996).

What did this chapter teach you about STDs that you did not know before reading it?

Mental illness may also adversely affect one's sexual activities. Its emotional disruption often leads to lack of interest in sex and loss of the ability to be sexually responsive. However, it has also been noted that many mentally ill people still have sexual needs and wish to pursue sexual activity. In institutional settings, it may be that mentally ill persons who seem especially preoccupied with sex are simply searching for human warmth and closeness. Activities such as masturbation may become ways for mental patients to control anxiety, affirm the existence of their bodies, or safely act out their sexual fantasies.

Increasingly, health professionals are realizing the importance of exploring sex-related issues with their patients. It is to be hoped that assessment of the potential sexual effects of various illnesses will soon become a standard and accepted part of medical evaluation and treatment.

Self-Evaluation

Examining Your Attitudes toward Sexually Transmitted Diseases

The following scale will give you an opportunity to explore some of your own beliefs, feelings, and intentions with regard to STDs. The scale was developed by Yarber, Torabi, and Veenker (1989) and has been tested with hundreds of college and secondary school students. The evaluation is for your own use only.

Directions: Please read each statement carefully. *STD* means sexually transmitted disease, once called venereal disease. Record your first reaction by marking an "X" through the letter that best describes how much you agree or disagree with the idea.

USE THIS KEY: SA = Strongly Agree
A = Agree
U = Undecided
D = Disagree
SD = Strongly Disagree

Example: Doing things to prevent getting an STD is the job of each person.   SA   A   U̶   D   SD

REMEMBER: STD means sexually transmitted disease, such as gonorrhea, syphilis, genital herpes, or HIV disease.

(Mark "X" through letter)

1. How one uses his/her sexuality has nothing to do with STD.	SA A U D SD
2. It is easy to use the prevention methods that reduce one's chances of getting an STD.	SA A U D SD
3. Responsible sex is one of the best ways of reducing the risk of STD.	SA A U D SD
4. Getting early medical care is the main key to preventing harmful effects of STD.	SA A U D SD
5. Choosing the right sex partner is important in reducing the risk of getting an STD.	SA A U D SD

6. A high rate of STD should be a concern for all people. SA   A   U   D   SD

7. People with an STD have a duty to get their sex partners to medical care. SA   A   U   D   SD

8. The best way to get a sex partner to STD treatment is to take him/her to the doctor with you. SA   A   U   D   SD

9. Changing one's sex habits is necessary once the presence of an STD is known. SA   A   U   D   SD

10. I would dislike having to follow the medical steps for treating an STD. SA   A   U   D   SD

11. If I were sexually active, I would feel uneasy doing things before and after sex to prevent getting an STD. SA   A   U   D   SD

12. If I were sexually active, it would be insulting if a sex partner suggested we use a condom to avoid STD. SA   A   U   D   SD

13. I dislike talking about STD with my peers. SA   A   U   D   SD

14. I would be uncertain about going to the doctor unless I were sure I really had an STD. SA   A   U   D   SD

15. I would feel that I should take my sex partner with me to a clinic if I thought I had an STD. SA   A   U   D   SD

16. It would be embarrassing to discuss STD with one's partner if one were sexually active. SA   A   U   D   SD

17. If I were to have sex, the chance of getting an STD would make me uneasy about having sex with more than one person. SA   A   U   D   SD

18. I like the idea of sexual abstinence (not having sex) as the best way of avoiding STD. SA   A   U   D   SD

19. If I had an STD, I would cooperate with public health persons to find the sources of STD. SA   A   U   D   SD

20. If I had an STD, I would avoid exposing others while I was being treated. SA   A   U   D   SD

21. I would have regular STD checkups if I were having sex with more than one partner. SA   A   U   D   SD

22. I intend to look for STD signs before deciding to have sex with anyone. SA   A   U   D   SD

23. I will limit my sex activity to just one partner because of the chances I might get an STD. SA   A   U   D   SD

24. I will avoid sex contact anytime I think there is even a slight chance of getting an STD. SA   A   U   D   SD

25. The chance of getting an STD would not stop me from having sex. SA   A   U   D   SD

26. If I had a chance, I would support community efforts toward controlling STD. SA   A   U   D   SD

27. I would be willing to work with others to make people aware of STD problems in my town. SA   A   U   D   SD

Scoring: Calculate total points for each subscale and total scale, using the point values below.

For items 1, 10–14, 16, 25

Strongly Agree = 5 points
Agree = 4 points
Undecided = 3 points
Disagree = 2 points
Strongly Disagree = 1 point

For items 2–9, 15, 17–24, 26, 27

Strongly Agree = 1 point
Agree = 2 points
Undecided = 3 points
Disagree = 4 points
Strongly Disagree = 5 points

Total Scale: items 1–27
Belief Subscale: items 1–9
Feeling Subscale: items 10–18
Intention to Act Subscale: items 19–27

Interpretation: The higher your score, the higher your risk of behavior that can spread sexually transmitted diseases.

Chapter Summary

1. Sexually transmitted diseases (STDs) have caused much human misery throughout the centuries and continue to represent serious health problems today. The development of penicillin was a major step in conquering some STDs.

2. It is estimated that there are 12 million new cases of STD in the United States each year, two-thirds in people under age 25. Fifty-six million people in the United States are infected with some viral STD.

3. The more sexual partners an individual has, and the less consistently condoms are used, the more likely infection with an STD becomes.

4. Gonorrhea can be spread through vaginal, anal, and oral sexual contact, and it infects over a half million people each year. The eyes of babies are vulnerable to infection during birth and are routinely treated to prevent gonorrheal blindness. Many strains of gonorrhea are now penicillin-resistant, and so other antibiotics are used for treatment.

5. Syphilis progresses through four major stages. About 20,000 people each year in the United States are infected with syphilis.

6. The large proportion of the population infected with the *Chlamydia* organism was not recognized until the mid-1980s. It is the cause of many different forms of genital and urinary tract infections in both men and women, and it can cause infertility. It is one of the most common STDs and of all reportable communicable disease.

7. Nonspecific urethritis (NSU) has been steadily increasing as an STD problem in males.

8. Vulvovaginal inflammation may be caused by bacteria, yeast organisms, or trichomonads. Taking proper hygienic measures and keeping the vulval area dry can reduce the risk of contracting vaginitis.

9. Genital herpes is caused by the herpes simplex virus. Once the virus has infected the body, it can cause recurrent outbreaks of the lesions. The disease has been associated with a higher incidence of cervical and vulval cancer in women and can be dangerous to newborn infants.

10. Genital warts (condylomata acuminata) are caused by the human papillomavirus (HPV) and is also associated with a higher incidence of cervical and anal cancers.

11. Hepatitis B virus (HBV) can cause serious liver infection, and it has now been recommended that college students be vaccinated against the virus. Hepatitis C virus (HCV) is also a serious disease, but it is less likely to be transmitted sexually.

12. Pubic lice must be thoroughly treated to ensure that all insects and their eggs have been eliminated from bodily hairs.

13. Lymphogranuloma venereum, chancroid, and granuloma inguinale are STDs that are more common in tropical climates.

14. Two skin diseases that may be transmitted by the intimate bodily contact of sex are molluscum contagiosum and scabies.

15. Part of responsible sexual decision making is to take appropriate measures to prevent the transmission of STDs. Considering abstinence, avoid-

ing penetration, avoiding multiple partners, avoiding abuse of alcohol or other drugs that impair judgment, knowing partners, getting screened for disease, and using condoms, vaginal pouches, and spermicides are among the

best preventative precautions. If infected, prompt medical treatment is essential, as is telling any potentially infected partners.

16. Any disease that affects general health or mental well-being can affect sexual functioning.

Focus on Health Questions

You will find in this section the kinds of questions that you may have concerning your own health and sexuality. The page references indicate where in the text the answer is located; the exact place is marked with the logo: FOH

1. Haven't most STDs been brought under control? 483

2. What are the symptoms of gonorrhea? 486

3. How is gonorrhea treated? 487

4. If one has syphilis, what does the sore that appears actually look like? 487

5. What are the other diseases that syphilis can cause? 488

6. Is it true that chlamydia is a common STD among college students? 489

7. Does chlamydia have any noticeable symptoms? 489

8. What are the other types of infection of the penis and vulva or vagina? 490, 491

9. How would I know if I have the virus for genital herpes? 492

10. Is there any cure or treatment for genital herpes? 493

11. Is it true that genital warts can cause cancer? 494

12. Can I be vaccinated against the type of hepatitis that is spread by sexual contact? 494

13. What are crabs? 496

14. How can I best protect myself from getting an STD? 497–499

15. Is it all right to have sex after one has recovered from a heart attack? 501

Annotated Readings

Donovan, P. (1993). *Testing positive: Sexually transmitted disease and the public health response.* New York: The Alan Guttmacher Institute. An overview of how society is responding to the increased incidence of STDs.

Ebel, C. (1996). *Managing herpes: How to live and love with a chronic STD.* Research Triangle Park, NC: American Social Health Association. A sensitive and complete guide to the disease and how to live with it, including suggestions for a satisfactory sexual life.

EDK Associates. (1995). *The ABCs of STDs.* New York: EDK Associates. A general, well-written, and understandable survey of the STDs.

Eng, T. R., & Butler, W. T. (Eds.). (1996). *The hidden epidemic: Confronting sexually transmitted diseases.* Washington, DC: Institute of Medicine. The alarming report of the Committee on Prevention and Control of STDs, bringing the extent of the problem into

perspective and offering specific guidelines for the future.

Monga, T. N. (Ed.). (1995). *Physical medicine and rehabilitation state of the arts review: Sexuality and disability.* Philadelphia: Hanley and Belfus. A survey of the various problems associated with helping people with chronic illness and disability establish satisfying sexual lives.

Muraskin, W. A. (1995). *The war against hepatitis B.* Philadelphia: University of Pennsylvania Press. Chronicles the history of this disease as an STD and describes efforts to develop treatments and vaccination initiatives worldwide.

Sipski, M. L., & Alexander, C. J. (1997). *Sexual function in people with disability and chronic illness.* Frederick, MD: Aspen. A thorough-going guide directed at health professionals who need to be aware of how to help people with chronic health problems adapt their sexual lives.

Chapter 17

The HIV/AIDS Crisis and Sexual Decisions

Chapter Outline

Note: A selection of Focus on Health questions appears at the end of each chapter. Answers to these questions are indicated within the chapter by the symbol in the margin. **FOH**

> Nobody here knows I have HIV except the health clinic, and I protect other people by not engaging in risky behavior. But what if I didn't care? What if the other HIV-positive people out there don't know or don't care? I got infected because I just didn't think it could happen to me. It did.

—From a written statement by a student

The epidemic of HIV disease and AIDS is now entering its third decade. It has garnered more attention than any new disease to appear in recent history, and it continues to spread. **Acquired immunodeficiency syndrome,** better known as **AIDS,** threatens significant portions of the human population. Although new disease epidemics come and go, HIV and AIDS have been directly associated with sexual activity, and such diseases tend to get people's attention. The prevalence of **human immunodeficiency virus (HIV),** the virus that can eventually produce AIDS when it infects humans, has raised political and economic issues. It has unleashed prejudice, especially homophobia, biphobia, and racism. HIV also seems to be changing how people approach their sexual activities, at least to some degree (Nathanson & Auerbach, 1999).

How do you feel the HIV/AIDS crisis will or will not impact your personal life now and/or in the future?

Research into this disease remains one of the most active areas in medical science today, although there are still methodological problems in getting accurate information about the relationship of human sexual behavior and the risks of HIV infection. New information is continually replacing old, and it is therefore crucial for you to inform yourself of any new findings. In recent years in North America, there has been a decline in the number of persons being diagnosed with HIV or dying of AIDS annually. This may well have created a false sense of security that the worst is over. Recent improvements in medical treatments have been delaying the onset of certain disease symptoms, but not curing the disease. Among some populations, the numbers of AIDS cases is actually on the rise. The realities of HIV/AIDS are still unsettling, and the epidemic is far from over. Taking into consideration the risks of HIV infection represents an essential component of being a sexually responsible individual (Haffner, 1998a). It may be your health and well-being, or your very life, that is at stake.

The Evolution of HIV and AIDS

In the early 1980s, articles began to appear in medical journals describing symptoms that had appeared in a number of gay men and users of intravenous drugs who shared needles. One of the things that all of these individuals seemed to have in common was an apparent weakness in their immune systems, the collection of mechanisms with which the body wards off disease. The patients experienced long periods of ill health while their bodies struggled to fight various bacteria, protozoa, and viruses. Eventually, the infections, often in rare forms, would become more tenacious, finally resulting in death. The Centers for Disease Control and Prevention (CDC) soon labeled the new and puzzling disorder acquired immunodeficiency syndrome. Before long, it became clear that the disease-causing germ, eventually identified as HIV, could be transmitted between people and that it was frighteningly lethal.

No one knows for certain how long HIV has been around. It may be that in earlier years, people who actually died of AIDS were diagnosed as having died of one of the many infections that the disease produces, or that medical personnel simply had no way of knowing what they were dealing with. In recent testing of blood human samples taken during 1959 in what was then the Belgian Congo of Africa, HIV has been identified (Balter, 1999). Although there have been some puzzling cases from earlier years leading to speculation about when and how HIV actually reached North America, it is generally believed that it arrived sometime during the mid-1970s.

The predominant theory, although it remains only a theory, about the origin of HIV is that a variant of the virus infected chimpanzees, perhaps for thousands of years. The virus eventually mutated into a form that could infect humans, and it may well have been transmitted to humans in central Africa during the butchering of chimps for food (Cohen, 1999a). The virus may have remained isolated in small, remote societies for decades until changing ways of African life brought it to urban centers, from which it was then transported to the rest of the world by infected persons. Changing lifestyles, such as increased international travel, have had profound effects on the spread of such epidemics. We will never completely understand the routes by which HIV has spread throughout the world. Once a

acquired immunodeficiency syndrome (AIDS): fatal disease caused by a virus that is transmitted through the exchange of bodily fluids, primarily in sexual activity and intravenous drug use.

human immunodeficiency virus (HIV): the virus that initially attacks the human immune system, causing HIV disease and eventually AIDS.

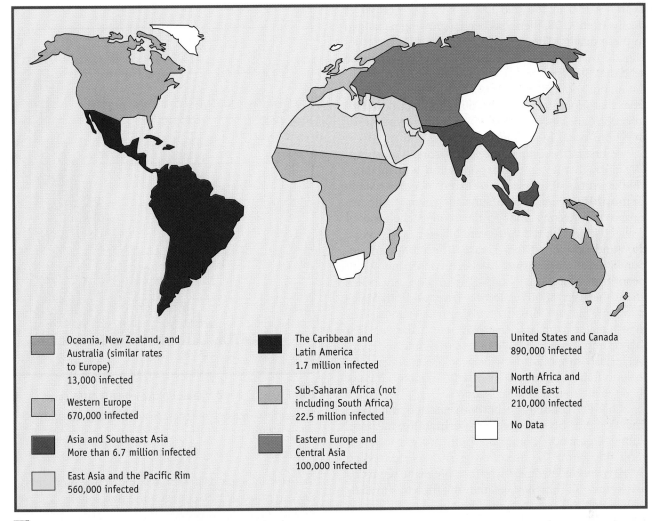

 **FIGURE 17.1**   *Global Rates of HIV Infection through 1998*

Although sub-Saharan Africa still has the most HIV infections, other regions of the world are seeing an increase as well. It is clear that expensive drugs have eased the problem somewhat in wealthier countries, but new infections and the death toll in poor countries keep growing.

Sources: Data from Science, UNAIDS, and World Health Organization.

pool of infected people was established in a population center that interacted with outside areas, it was only a matter of time before the virus would make its way into larger segments of the human population.

Statistics on the Prevalence of AIDS and HIV Infection

Epidemiological studies continue to survey the extent of HIV infection in North America and worldwide (see Fig. 17.1). One method used is surveillance data concerning the number of HIV-positive cases reported by hospitals, clinics, physicians, and medical record systems. It is believed that in the United States at least 90 percent of these cases are actually reported, a very high rate when compared with the reporting of other

diseases. Worldwide, by the end of the twentieth century, AIDS had become the fourth largest cause of human death. The rates of infection and death are much greater in the poorer nations of the world (Balter, 1999; Marby, 1999).

In the United States, because medical treatments are prolonging the life expectancies of HIV-infected persons, current estimates suggest that up to 900,000 people are living with HIV, with perhaps another 40,000 new infections occurring each year. Less than 20,000 people die each year, down from a peak of

epidemiology (e-pe-dee-mee-A-la-jee): the branch of medical science that deals with the incidence, distribution, and control of disease in a population.

nearly 50,000 in the mid-1990s. With the decline in deaths from AIDS, there has been a growing racial gap in these deaths. The more deaths from AIDS have declined, the more blacks become the majority of those who die. Blacks make up 13 percent of the U.S. population, but about 50 percent of AIDS deaths now come from that group, and close to 60 percent of new HIV infections are among blacks. Over 60 percent of new infections occur in people aged 13 to 24.

At first in the United States, HIV spread most rapidly through the gay male population and in intravenous drug abusers who shared needles. Many **hemophiliacs** and some surgical patients who received transfusions prior to the routine checking of donated blood for the virus were infected, and several thousand developed the disease. The number of reported cases among gays has been decreasing. It appears that educational campaigns to alert gay males about the risks of HIV infection have paid off. Males now transmit the virus to females much more often than females to males. That may reflect the fact that this country began with a larger pool of infected men, but it also supports the widely held contention that male-to-female transmission of HIV is more efficient than female-to-male transmission.

Children continue to be born infected with HIV. They seem to become infected **perinatally,** meaning during pregnancy, during the birth process itself, or soon after birth. The use of drugs such as zidovudine by HIV-infected women who are pregnant seems to lessen the risk that they will transmit the virus to their babies, and this has accounted for a marked decline in perinatal infections (Moore, 1999b). The drug has not been shown to produce ill effects for either the infant or the mother (Culnane, 1999).

HIV infection represents a serious global threat. The World Health Organization (WHO) estimates that there are currently about 33 million people infected with HIV worldwide, with over 3 million new infections each year (see Fig. 17.2). It is thought that about 75 percent of the global infections are through heterosexual contact. The predictions for the future from the WHO have been equally grim, as they estimate that by the year 2020, the disease could be responsible for the deaths of 121 million people. Southern and Southeast Asia and sub-Saharan African countries have been hardest hit by HIV infection and AIDS, where it is believed that 22.5 million people are living with HIV/AIDS.

Studies conducted on U.S. college campuses during the 1990s found that between 2 and 3 of every 1,000 blood samples of students showed evidence of being infected with HIV. Although this did not represent a random sample of the student population and simply used blood drawn at college health centers for other reasons, two studies have clearly demonstrated

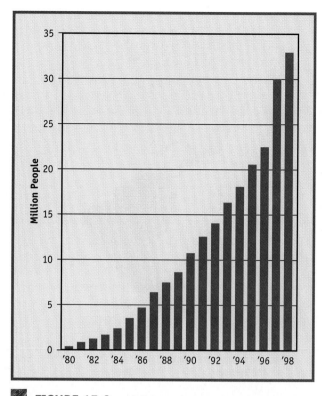

FIGURE 17.2   *Global Increase in HIV/AIDS Cases*

The startling increase in worldwide numbers of people living with HIV/AIDS, since 1980.

that HIV infection is a very real and active problem on the campuses of U.S. colleges and universities. The frequency of infection is even greater on some campuses in metropolitan areas, where as many as 1 percent of students have HIV (Keeling, 1995). However, these results also show that the infection is not yet rampant on college campuses and therefore may be prevented and controlled by careful choices of behavior.

Risks of Infection

Anyone may be potentially at risk of being exposed to bodily fluids in which HIV is present, if he or she chooses to engage in risky sexual behaviors. Semen, blood, and vaginal secretions are the fluids most often implicated in transmission of HIV.

For reasons that are not fully understood, HIV was first noticed in the United States among gay men who

hemophiliac (hee-mo-FIL-ee-ak): someone with the hereditary blood defect hemophilia, primarily affecting males and characterized by difficulty in clotting.

perinatal: things related to pregnancy, birth, or the period immediately following the birth.

had shared sex with large numbers of partners, which increased their risks of contracting and transmitting the disease (see Fig. 17.3). Sharing anal intercourse is especially risky behavior, although the number of males engaging in this behavior has been on the decline (Hewitt, 1998). The virus from the semen enters the bloodstream through the many small tears in the colon. Because a substantial number of women engage in anal intercourse with men, it should be recognized as a potentially risky sexual behavior for them as well (Elliott & Brantley, 1997).

The other group in which HIV spread rapidly was intravenous (IV) drug abusers, through sharing of needles. IV drug abusers represent the largest heterosexual population in the United States infected with HIV; they also represent a most significant vehicle for heterosexual transmission of the virus. Four themes have emerged in the research on bisexual men in the United States and Canada. In general, they tend to participate in less unsafe sexual behavior than exclusively gay

men. Some groups of bisexual men are at particularly high risk of HIV infection, and they also tend to use condoms less often with female partners than with their male partners. Bisexual men may also have high rates of injection drug use (Doll, Myers, Kennedy, & Allman, 1997; Hewitt, 1998). Figure 17.4 examines the various modes of transmission of HIV, proportionately, throughout the world.

Since the HIV epidemic began, the actual number of infections transmitted by heterosexual contact has been rising steadily. In studies that have been done on heterosexual couples in which one partner had already been infected with HIV, it is clear that the risk of women contracting HIV from men is 10 to 18 times greater than the risk of men getting the virus from women. The risks of transmission become even greater when there is another sexually transmitted disease (STD) already present. Inflammation of tissues from STDs may well make it easier for HIV to enter the body.

Several research studies have focused on particular characteristics of certain populations that might make them more vulnerable to HIV infection. There is evidence that people living in small towns and rural areas often assume that they do not need to worry about HIV or AIDS and that they are prone to engaging in high-risk sexual practices such as unprotected penetrative sex (Heckman, Kelly, Somlai, Kalichman, & Heckman, 1999). However, HIV continues to spread into rural areas, and it does not respect urban-rural barriers (McCoy, Metsch, McCoy, & Weatherby, 1999).

Among college students, there are a number of factors that can predispose individuals toward high-risk behaviors. Women who have been victims of childhood sexual abuse are more vulnerable (Whitmire, Harlow, Quina, & Morokoff, 1999). Alcohol consumption tends to reduce the likelihood of using condoms during sexual activity and increase the likelihood of other risky sexual behaviors among students (Koch, Palmer, Vicary, & Wood, 1999). However, these effects are somewhat moderated by both gender and levels of self-esteem. For students who do not drink much, high self-esteem is associated with greater condom use. Women are more likely to have sex after alcohol use, and men have higher intentions of using condoms (McNair, Carter, & Williams, 1998). Use of noninjectable drugs is usually correlated with higher levels of high-risk sexual behavior (Woody et al., 1999).

Although there are still unanswered questions about HIV infection in infants, some evidence suggests that HIV may be transmitted to the fetus from the mother's blood system or during the delivery process. Cesarean section birth seems to reduce the risks of HIV infection for infants, another indication that the

FIGURE 17.3 *AIDS Candlelight Memorial*

AIDS has devastated many gay communities in the United States, where HIV was first noticed. These women share a moment of grief during an AIDS candlelight memorial service in Union Square Park, New York City.

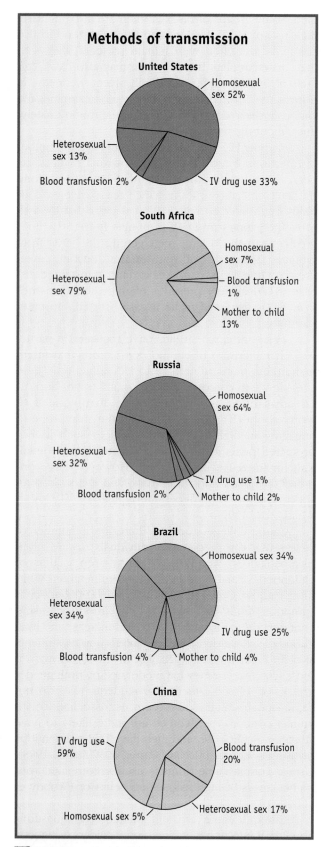

Methods of transmission

United States

Homosexual sex 52%
Heterosexual sex 13%
Blood transfusion 2%
IV drug use 33%

South Africa

Homosexual sex 7%
Blood transfusion 1%
Heterosexual sex 79%
Mother to child 13%

Russia

Homosexual sex 64%
Heterosexual sex 32%
IV drug use 1%
Blood transfusion 2%
Mother to child 2%

Brazil

Homosexual sex 34%
Heterosexual sex 34%
IV drug use 25%
Blood transfusion 4%
Mother to child 4%

China

IV drug use 59%
Blood transfusion 20%
Homosexual sex 5%
Heterosexual sex 17%

FIGURE 17.4   *Where the AIDS Epidemic Hit Hardest and Where It Is Growing the Fastest*

virus is transmitted during vaginal delivery. How quickly the disease develops in infants, and perhaps whether they contract HIV at all, seems to be related to the severity of the mother's infection. A mother's HIV infection probably has little effect on the fetus during most of pregnancy, and most fetal infections probably do not occur until late in pregnancy or during the birth process. There is also evidence that HIV may be transmitted in breast milk during nursing. Breast-fed babies are more than twice as likely as bottle-fed babies to contract the virus from an infected mother. Prenatal testing for HIV is recommended, so that if a pregnant woman is found to be HIV-positive, the baby can begin taking preventive medications soon after birth (Ahluwalia, DeVellis, & Thomas, 1998; Moore, 1999b).

Would you let an HIV-infected friend babysit for your children? Why or why not?

The CDC and other parts of the U.S. Public Health Service continue to promulgate regulations and recommendations for various occupational groups that would help them prevent the spread of HIV. The facts available at present, however, strongly suggest that IV drug abuse using shared needles and sexual activity represent the greatest threats for transmitting the virus today. Other forms of contact do not seem to represent major risks for infection.

The HIV Epidemic in Perspective

As we saw in the previous chapter, the spread of STDs is influenced primarily by the numbers of sexual partners a person has and how often he or she uses a condom. These factors, along with abuse of alcohol and other drugs, also constitute risk factors in contracting HIV. However, the researchers who conducted the National Health and Social Life Survey (NHSLS) found that the picture of the HIV epidemic and where it is heading is somewhat different from the pattern followed by other STDs (Laumann, Gagnon et al., 1994).

Urban areas continue to represent the epicenter of the epidemic, and it is beginning to concentrate more in poor neighborhoods where sale and use of IV drugs constitute an ongoing part of the culture. There continues to be controversy over whether the disease is likely to remain relatively confined to these groups and regions. There are many political and public policy issues that are impacted by this debate. There is a risk that if HIV is perceived as affecting groups that tend to be socially invisible or ostracized, momentum will be lost for the funding of research to cure and prevent the disease. There is also the concern that if education promulgates a "sex will kill you" message beyond what the data support, information about the very real risks of HIV infection will lose its impact.

NHSLS researchers proposed a social behavior model regarding the spread of HIV. In order for HIV to become an epidemic in the general population, two specific conditions need to be met: a sustained "bridge" from the infected population to the general population, and frequent sex or needle sharing among the members of the general population to perpetuate epidemic-level proportions of the disease. NHSLS data suggest that these conditions may not be being met currently (Michael et al., 1994). However, such findings should not be misconstrued to mean that anyone can afford to be complacent about the risks of HIV. Although epidemiologists and sociologists often view risk in terms of broad statistical generalizations, everyone must be concerned about the potential risks of individual behavioral choices.

At least in the United States, some experts believe that the challenge may well eventually become the need to sustain compassion, top-notch treatment, and research funds for those suffering from the disease, if they are not perceived as part of the privileged classes. For educators, it will be especially crucial to reach those in high-risk areas to educate them to make choices that will minimize the risks of spreading HIV. Another challenge will be to convince young people who are not as close to the population centers of HIV threat to take the risks of unprotected sexual activity or other behaviors as seriously as they must. The incidence of HIV infection has increased in rural areas (McCoy et al., 1999). Although some groups in some areas of the country may indeed be at less risk than others, it is also true that everyone should be fully knowledgeable about the possibility of HIV infection and assume that with any sexual partner there is at least some possibility of HIV transmission.

Do you think that people who have HIV should engage in shared sexual activity? Why or why not?

NHSLS data also demonstrated that many people do indeed seem to be taking the HIV/AIDS crisis seriously. Twenty-seven percent of the total number of respondents had been tested for HIV, a trend that was especially evident among those who were younger, more educated, and living in larger cities. Thirty percent of the total sample indicated they had changed their sexual behaviors because of AIDS, although there was no particular pattern by education or socioeconomic group. The most significant patterns relating to HIV testing and behavioral change were correlated with numbers of sexual partners. The more partners people have had, the more likely they are to have been tested and to have modified their sexual behaviors. Figure 17.5 summarizes the data (Michael et al., 1994).

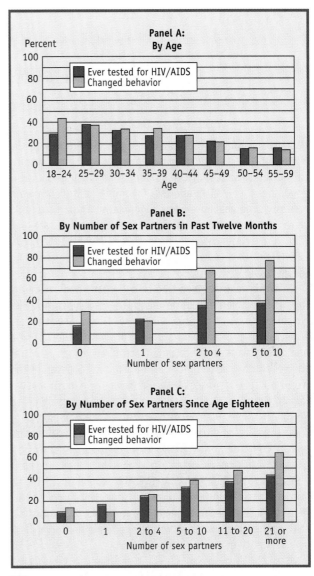

FIGURE 17.5 *Responses to HIV/AIDS: Percent Ever Tested for HIV/AIDS and Percent Reporting Change in Sexual Behavior in Response to AIDS*

Data from the NHSLS show the demographic groups that are most likely to be tested for HIV/AIDS. People in younger age groups, and those who have had more numerous sexual partners, are more likely to have been tested and to have modified their sexual behaviors.

Source: From *Sex in America* by Robert Michael. Copyright © 1994 by C.S.G. Enterprises, Inc., Edward O. Laumann, Robert T. Michael, and Gina Kolata. By permission of Little, Brown and Company, Inc.

◼ HIV: The Infection and the Virus

It is important to focus on the entire course of infection by the HIV and not just the late stage of that process that has become known as AIDS. This is crucial, because when HIV disease is diagnosed in its earlier

CROSS-CULTURAL PERSPECTIVE
The Global View of AIDS

Nations around the world are coming face-to-face with the HIV/AIDS crisis. Educational campaigns can have significant effects. South African students had much less knowledge about HIV/AIDS and less favorable attitudes toward safe sex, whereas more knowledgeable Australian students were far more likely to favor techniques of safe sex (Smith, de Visser, Akande, Rosenthal, & Moore, 1998). HIV is forcing some cultures to confront their long-standing values about sexuality.

In Latin America, men traditionally have had sexual affairs with women and other men rather freely. In not discussing the fact that they may carry HIV, many men are spreading the virus with its potential risks to their female and male partners and to unborn children. Brazil now has the second highest number of reported AIDS cases in the world outside of Africa. Bisexual behavior is quite prevalent in Brazil, a country where men are not considered to be gay if they have sex with women as well as men or if they take a "dominant" role in sexual acts with other males. Combined with the facts that condoms are often too costly for the poor majority and that available condoms are often of inferior quality, the behaviors of Brazilian men are making control of HIV infection highly challenging (Klein, 1998; Romero, Wyatt, Chin, & Rodriguez, 1999). The Brazilian government has implemented a massive sexuality education program (Suplicy, 1994).

Traditional values of Asian cultures have also interfered with realistic appraisal of the dimensions of the HIV problem. China and Japan have always avoided open discussion of sexual activities, and they have fostered a good deal of denial about the scope of HIV infection. Both countries are now seeing sharp increases in HIV infection within their populations, and they have been instituting HIV/AIDS education efforts. China has begun to admit the problem they are facing with what they sometimes call *the illness caused by love*. Thailand and Cambodia have already been hard hit by HIV, in part because these are nations where prostitutes are widely used by the male population. Large proportions of the female prostitutes have been infected with HIV for some time, and now it is spreading through their clients to other women in these countries. Massive educational efforts in Thailand have begun to change sexual behaviors and produce a decline in infection rates. Visitors from other Asian countries to Thailand, however, are often not as prepared for protecting themselves against the risks of contracting HIV (Sanitioso, 1999; Vorakitphokatorn, Pulerwitz, & Cash, 1999).

Many Asian governments have been reluctant to admit that serious problems exist in their countries, fearing that

they will discourage foreign tourists or investors who are essential to their economies. In India, it is clear that HIV infection rates continue to soar (see graph), and yet only recently has the government begun to institute the massive educational and medical efforts that will be needed to bring the situation under control (Bagla, 1998). In a country that has been reluctant to talk about sexual matters, the risks for HIV transmission because of ignorance loom even greater (Chandiramani, 1998).

In Russia and the other nations of the former Soviet Union, the situation is much like it was in the United States and Europe at the beginning of the epidemic. People know little about the disease and often participate in risky behaviors. Only small numbers of HIV cases have been reported, but it is assumed that there are many more.

HIV/AIDS continues to be a tremendous problem in Africa, where the rate of infection among women is higher than among men. Efforts are under way to help women gain greater freedom and control over their sexual lives, but this is a difficult task in view of cultural histories and imperatives. Sexual services are exchanged for material gain in some African cultures, placing women at even greater risk (Ankomah, 1999). Much less progress has been made in Africa toward educating adolescents about HIV sex-related risks and in encouraging safer sex practices (Stanton et al., 1999). Again, there is global evidence that politics, cultural values, and the HIV crisis are inseparably intertwined.

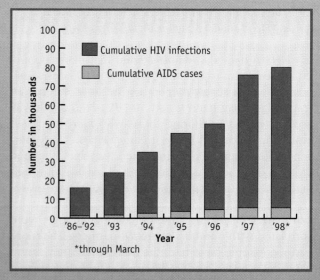

Number of Indian cases of HIV infection and AIDS is rising rapidly. Reprinted with permission of the National AIDS Control Organization.

stages, the patient may be able to get treatment that may delay certain aspects of the infection and prevent some complications. HIV infection passes through predictable stages, during which the body's immune system is gradually undermined. Although the duration of the infection varies, depending on the person's health and behavior, there is a gradual depletion of cells in the body that are crucial to its defense against disease-causing agents (Balter, 1998).

Soon after contracting HIV, some people develop a fever, swollen glands, fatigue, and perhaps a rash. This is called *primary HIV disease.* These early symptoms usually disappear within a few weeks as the body manages to ward off the infection with its immune defenses, and there may not yet be enough antibodies to show a positive HIV test. The second stage is called *chronic asymptomatic disease,* which is characterized by gradual decline in immune cells even though there are no particular disease symptoms. Eventually, most people infected with HIV begin to experience chronically swollen lymph nodes, although they may have few other symptoms. It is important to note that there are other diseases that can manifest these symptoms as well, most of which are not nearly as serious as HIV disease (Cowley, 1998; Schacker, Collier, Hughes, Shea, & Corey, 1996).

As the infection progresses, there is a continual drop in the number of immune cells in the body. The individual becomes increasingly vulnerable to **opportunistic infection,** in which disease-causing organisms normally present in the environment become able to attack the person by taking advantage of the weakened resistance. This is the third stage and is called *chronic symptomatic disease.* One of the most common infections in this stage of HIV disease is a yeast infection of the mouth called **thrush** (this disease in itself is not necessarily a sign of a serious disorder). There may also be infections of the skin and moist inner membranes of the body. There may be general feelings of discomfort and weakness, accompanied by sustained fevers, drenching night sweats, weight loss, and frequent diarrhea.

The actual incubation period for HIV is extremely variable. The diagnosis of full-blown AIDS is made after one or more of 26 diseases have been manifested in an HIV-infected individual. The term **syndrome** refers to a collection of disease symptoms that tend to cluster together. Unlike most syndromes, AIDS can have a spectrum of symptoms, and the disease can progress in many different ways (Lopez et al., 1999). Ultimately, there can be months of debilitating illness until the body can no longer prevail, and the victim dies.

Mechanism of HIV Action

Viruses are among the tiniest of microorganisms to infect human tissues. Typically, they attach themselves to the outside of a cell and inject their genetic material inside, where it takes over the DNA of its host cell to produce new viruses. These viruses then spread to other cells, disrupting or killing them as new viruses are produced. It is the destruction of tissue that causes the symptoms of the viral infection. HIV belongs to the class of viruses called **retroviruses.** In all living things, it is the hereditary code stored in the DNA of each cell's genes that determines the characteristics of the organism. The complex biochemical processes of life are governed by that code. The DNA passes its messages to another chemical found in all cells, RNA, which then plays many roles in helping the cell manufacture all of the products it requires to live and function. Retroviruses are unique in that their genetic code is instead carried in the form of RNA. When a retrovirus attacks a cell, a chemical orders the cell's RNA to translate the genetic blueprints of the virus into the cell's DNA, thus instructing it to make a whole new crop of virus particles. It is because this mechanism is the reverse of the usual order of things that these viruses are called retroviruses.

Usually, various elements of the body's immune system are able to develop antibodies to a particular virus, so immunity develops and the disease abates. Often this natural immunity remains and makes the host permanently immune to infection by the specific virus. Research is unraveling the complex chemical mechanisms by which HIV manages to make its way into the body's white blood cells, ultimately weakening and destroying the immune system. To reproduce itself and multiply in the body, HIV destroys the very cells that are essential in helping the body produce immunity to all disease. These cells are the T-lymphocytes known as CD4s, a type of white blood cell that plays a major role in bringing together the body's immune defenses (Balter, 1998; Cowley, 1998). HIV is capable of reproducing in staggering numbers, constantly needing to move on to new, uninfected cells in order to survive.

For reasons that are still not fully understood, the numbers of cells infected by HIV tend to remain relatively stable for a time, sometimes years, during which the person tends to be quite symptom-free. One theory

opportunistic infection: a disease resulting from lowered resistance of a weakened immune system.

thrush: a disease caused by a fungus and characterized by white patches in the oral cavity.

syndrome (SIN-drome): a group of signs or symptoms that occur together and characterize a given condition.

retrovirus (RET-ro-vi-rus): a class of viruses that reproduces with the aid of the enzyme reverse transcriptase, which allows the virus to integrate its genetic code into that of the host cell, thus establishing permanent infection.

CASE STUDY

Susan: An HIV—Infected Woman Plans Her Future

Invited to speak to a group of college student peer counselors, Susan described her discovery that she was infected with HIV: "I was not having any symptoms whatsoever, but the thought had been nagging at the back of my mind for a long time that I should get tested. I knew I had taken some risks in the past, and I was now with a new partner. We were using condoms. I finally decided it was time to get checked out. Even with these concerns, it honestly never occurred to me that I might actually have HIV. I figured I would get the test for my own peace of mind, and then make a fresh and more careful start in my sex life." She went on to talk about the testing process itself and then said, "You can imagine my shock at finding out that I was HIV positive. I went through all of the usual stages. At first, I just couldn't believe it, and yet this really dark and depressing feeling was always lingering around me. I got retested because I thought they might have made a mistake. When the truth finally sunk in, I spent months just feeling sorry for myself. My partner broke up with me soon after he found out, although he tried to be kind about it all."

Now, 2 years after learning of her HIV infection, Susan was focusing on the future. She was realistic about some of the limitations she faced, and she understood that the infection might well escalate to more troublesome symptoms and eventually full-blown AIDS. Yet she had finished her undergraduate degree and was pursuing a graduate program in social work. "I want to work with other HIV-infected persons, and with groups of noninfected people. In the next few years, we're going to have to struggle to understand all of the problems HIV is creating for our entire society. None of us knows how long we might live. I just want to make sure that I make the most of all the time I have, and try to stay as healthy as possible." She described the diet and regimen of exercise and rest she followed to keep her immune system as healthy as possible. As she concluded, Susan said, "So please be careful, and encourage your friends to be careful. HIV infection is something that is very real, and it can happen to anyone who is not careful. I'm living my life as fully as I can. I want you to do the same, and without HIV."

is that the immune system finally becomes exhausted by the infection and falters. At this point, the infected individual begins to become more vulnerable to opportunistic diseases. Antibiotics and other known medications are not effective against viral infections, although they may be extremely useful in combating bacterial opportunistic infections.

How HIV Is Transmitted

It is now clear that HIV is transmitted by the direct transfer of certain bodily fluids from one infected individual to another. The chronic asymptomatic phase of the disease may last for years before troublesome symptoms actually develop. However, the virus may still be transmitted by infected people who have not developed any symptoms. People with AIDS or who are experiencing other symptoms of HIV disease are even more likely to transmit the virus. HIV enters the body through internal linings of organs (such as the vagina, rectum, urethra within the penis, or mouth) or through openings in the skin, such as tiny cuts or open sores (Keeling, 1995).

Researchers have shown that the most typical fluids to be involved in transmission of the virus are blood, semen, and vaginal secretions. As discussed earlier, the virus can be transmitted perinatally, and

there is evidence that it can be transmitted to an infant through breast milk. Additionally, there is documentation of HIV being found in saliva, tears, urine, and feces, but little direct evidence exists that the virus has actually been transmitted by these secretions and excretions.

Several routes of HIV infection have been clearly documented:

1. Anal or vaginal intercourse.
2. Oral-genital sexual activity.
3. Contact with semen or vaginal fluids from an infected person.
4. Organs transplanted from infected persons.
5. Contact with infected blood, through use of contaminated needles and syringes shared by drug users, or used for tattooing, ear piercing, or injecting steroids.
6. Transfer from mother to child, the risks of which are increased when invasive procedures such as amniocentesis are used during pregnancy.

The risks associated with oral-genital sex have been difficult to quantify, partly because this behavior is usually practiced in conjunction with other sexual activities that may be highly risky. However, there are cases in which HIV was transmitted from a man's semen during fellatio (oral sex performed on a male).

There is less evidence of transmission during cunnilingus (oral sex performed on a female) (Schacker et al., 1996). There was also a study done with monkeys, in which a solution containing the HIV-like virus that can infect the animals was dribbled on their tongues. The researchers were surprised to find that it took a lower concentration of the virus in the solution to infect the monkeys orally than it did when applied rectally. Although there is no way to determine if such findings apply to humans, they have raised enough concern to cause experts to warn that oral-genital sex may be more risky than was once assumed (Baba et al., 1996).

Although ordinary kissing appears to pose only a minor threat, the CDC has reported a case of HIV transmission through kissing. Both parties had gum disease, confirming the earlier suspicion that viruses carried in saliva could enter the body through tiny breaks or sores within the mouth or enter the lymphatic cells in the tonsils. Experts therefore continue to caution against prolonged, wet deep kissing (French kissing).

Casual contacts with infected persons—even in crowded households, social settings, schools, or the workplace—are not dangerous. There are no documented cases of HIV being transmitted through food, water, toilets, swimming pools, or hot tubs, shared drinking or eating utensils, telephones, or used clothing. Several research studies have demonstrated that the virus is not transmitted by insects.

Can Immunity to HIV Develop?

So far, not all people who are infected with HIV have actually developed symptoms of disease or have progressed to AIDS. Five to 10 percent of individuals infected with HIV have remained asymptomatic even without any antiviral treatment, and researchers continue to study the reasons for this. It is not known as yet what proportion of infected persons will ultimately become ill with the disease, although one study suggested that 10 to 17 percent of HIV-infected people will remain AIDS-free 20 years after infection (Haynes, Pantaleo, & Fauci, 1996). There have also been suggestions that a small pecentage of the population may actually have some form of genetic immunity to HIV, and research has confirmed that certain genetic configurations might at least decrease or increase susceptibility to infection (Carrington et al., 1999).

Although it has been shown that a large enough concentration of HIV can cause AIDS on its own, there are a number of other factors that influence the progression of the disease, and in some individuals that progression is more rapid. For example, a person whose immune system is already impaired prior to HIV infection will tend to develop AIDS more rapidly than someone whose immune system is strong. Similarly, the more other infections an individual's immune system must fight, the more readily HIV can take hold and do its damage. Research is also indicating that HIV can interact with certain other viruses, such as one of the human herpes viruses, so that cellular infection by both virus particles becomes more efficient and rapid.

There have been a few cases in which adults and children who had originally tested HIV-positive have undergone *seroreversion,* meaning that they seem to have been able to clear HIV from their bodies. Some experts have expressed skepticism that these individuals were actually infected in the first place, and they believe that the original tests may have been contaminated. However, studies done in Europe on several hundred children who had been HIV-infected at birth indicate that at least a small percentage of them do seem to have cleared the virus from their bodies (Thompson, 1996).

Only further research will be able to tell us if some individuals have, or can develop, a natural immunity to HIV. In the meantime, it is important to remember that being infected with HIV does not constitute a death sentence. Some infected individuals remain free of disease symptoms for many years, and a few may never develop them. Health experts advise that changing health habits to keep the immune system strong is a wise idea for anyone who has been diagnosed with HIV infection.

■ HIV Testing, Treatment, and Vaccines

When HIV infects people, their bodies begin the natural process of combating the disease. Antibodies begin to form that will attempt to destroy the reproducing viruses. The tests that are most frequently used to confirm the presence of the virus can help detect the antibodies that a person's body is producing, although the antibodies may not be detectable for several months after the person has actually been infected. It has been generally accepted that such antibodies show up within 6 months following infection. However, continued testing at additional 6-month intervals following a potential exposure to HIV has sometimes been recommended.

The blood test currently in greatest use is an enzyme-linked immunosorbent assay **(ELISA)**. It is inexpensive, can be completed within 5 hours, and is not technically difficult to interpret. However, the ELISA test tends to give a high percentage of false positives, so the results may signal the presence of

ELISA: the primary test used to determine the presence of HIV in humans.

HIV antibodies when in fact none are present. A positive result is then further tested with the **Western blot** or immunoblot test. It is more accurate than ELISA, but because it is lengthy and expensive and must be interpreted by trained and experienced technicians, it is usually not utilized as a primary test in large-scale screenings. For people who fear needles, there are tests that can detect HIV in swabs taken from the mouth or in urine, but these tests are not widely used, and they are not thought to be as accurate as blood tests (Guest, 1998).

New generations of HIV tests are extremely sensitive and can distinguish between different strains of HIV. These tests are especially valuable to developing countries because they are only one-step procedures, require less sophisticated laboratory facilities, and can detect strains more common in those areas. There are also new tests being used to detect HIV in very young infants. This is especially positive, because early detection can lead to earlier treatment and a potentially longer period of survival.

Given the present state of HIV-testing technology, testing can have three possible outcomes: (1) clear confirmation of the presence of HIV antibodies; (2) clear confirmation that the antibodies are absent; or (3) an uncertain result that leaves patients frighteningly unsure (Crystal & Schlosser, 1999). When there has been a high risk of recent infection, physicians often recommend repeat testing after several weeks if testing has proved negative or uncertain. Increasing numbers of people under the age of 30 are planning to be tested for HIV. Because blood donated in clinics is automatically screened for HIV antibodies, some people are giving blood with the knowledge that they will be notified if they are HIV-positive. Health professionals have a responsibility to prepare patients through pretest counseling and offer follow-up counseling and support if the results are positive (Guest, 1998).

Depending on where one is tested, the results may be considered *confidential,* meaning that the individual's name would be connected to the test results, even though the results are not generally shared with others. This would be the case in most physicians' offices. Many clinics provide *anonymous* testing, in which the patient is assigned a number for obtaining the test results at a later time. In this way, the individual's name is never used, and privacy is assured.

Controversy over HIV Testing

FOH There has been a great deal of controversy over who should be tested for HIV and whether testing should be mandatory or voluntary. Most experts recommend that testing efforts should be expanded, but they are divided on whether testing should be mandatory. Some note that mandatory testing for the public welfare has been used with other STDs, such as syphilis, and that the seriousness of HIV infection certainly warrants similar intervention. They also advocate tracking down sexual partners of known infected people so they too may be tested. Mandatory testing for HIV has already been implemented among those applying for marriage licenses in more than half of the states, those seeking immigrant visas, and those wishing to enlist in the U.S. armed forces.

Some states have required parental consent before allowing minors to be tested, but that has been shown to reduce the likelihood that teenagers will be tested by at least 50 percent. When Connecticut eliminated its parental consent requirement, the number of youths aged 13 to 17 visiting public clinics increased dramatically (Meehan, Hansen, & Klein, 1997).

The policy of the Immigration and Naturalization Service prohibiting foreigners who are HIV-positive from entering the United States has angered many in the international community, but over two-thirds of American adults favor such a ban.

> *Do you think the government should continue mandatory testing of immigrants? Should the government continue to deny visas to HIV-infected foreigners? Why or why not?*

In rape cases, alleged rapists have been asked to submit to HIV testing, so that the victim may know if the risk of infection exists. Most states now have laws that can force convicted rapists to be tested. It has been suggested, however, that this information may not be as useful as it seems and that there can be a negative side. For example, there is always a chance that the rapist was infected after the rape actually occurred. In addition, there is a relatively small chance of becoming infected with HIV after one incident of intercourse, about 1 chance in 300 to 500. Therefore, the rape survivor may be left not knowing for sure if actual infection has taken place. No matter what the outcome of the testing, it will still be important for the victim to be tested immediately and also several months later.

Some states have already required their family planning and STD clinics to offer free, voluntary testing for HIV. The CDC has made the following recommendations concerning HIV testing:

1. Couples planning marriage should be provided "ready access" to testing and to information about HIV and AIDS.
2. People should have the "right to choose not to be tested" and be given appropriate counseling

Western blot: the test used to verify the presence of HIV antibodies already detected by the ELISA.

prior to testing. They should also give explicit consent, orally or in writing, before being tested.

3. Anyone seeking treatment for other sexually transmitted infections (STIs) should be encouraged to undergo HIV testing.

4. People with a history of IV drug use who have shared equipment with others should be encouraged to have tests, as should their sexual partners.

5. Pregnant women who are at high risk of infection or who "live in a geographic area or community with a high prevalence of infection" should be tested.

6. Women seeking family planning services should be routinely counseled about HIV infection and have testing made available to them.

It is crucial that people be helped through the early phase of making a decision about getting tested and also when sorting through their reactions to the possible results. The waiting period of several days before test results can be made available may create high levels of anxiety. Although some insurance companies do not want to require pretesting counseling because it adds to the expense, experts generally agree that such counseling should be a requirement.

Most state health departments also require that an individual come in person to find out the results, rather than be told over the telephone or by mail. Obviously, there is a degree of trauma and anguish connected with learning that the test results are positive. Counseling can provide not only support for the anxiety but also reassurance and advice about the future. The infected person must learn to make behavioral choices that will enhance the strength of his or her immune system and prevent the spread of the virus to others. Even if the test results are negative, counseling can be important in providing the person with information about avoiding infection in the future (Guest, 1998).

Although home testing has traditionally been discouraged by professionals in this field, because face-to-face counseling would not be available, it is also recognized that many potentially infected persons are avoiding testing because of embarrassment or the lack of anonymity (Oswalt, Welle-Grafe, Minter, & Glover, 1998). Home-testing kits in which one draws and tests one's own blood are not considered reliable, and they have not been approved by the Federal Trade Commission (FTC) (1999). The FTC has approved a variation on this theme, which requires that a blood sample taken at home be sent to a central laboratory. The person being tested calls a toll-free number after a few days to receive the result using a code number. If the test is positive, this is reported to the caller by a trained counselor, who discusses the implications of the test

with the person. There is still controversy over this approach because some professionals believe that face-to-face counseling should be required to help HIV-positive persons deal more effectively with their diagnoses.

Treatment for HIV Disease

As scientists increasingly understand the mechanisms by which HIV wreaks havoc with the immune system, progress has been made toward finding effective means of treatment and prevention. Even though the final stage of HIV disease, AIDS, is a fatal disease, appropriate medical treatment earlier in the course of the infection can prolong a patient's life and improve its quality. Experienced physicians can monitor progress of the virus and provide appropriate interventions because the strategy for treatment varies with the stage of the infection. As opportunistic diseases develop, carefully selected medications may be used to relieve symptoms or to help the body fight the infections.

If you contracted HIV, would you seek medical treatment to prolong your life, knowing that there is no cure for AIDS? Why or why not?

Since research with HIV treatments began, a remarkable number of new antiretroviral preparations have gone into testing. There are now so many, in fact, that the clinical testing system has been strained.

One of the most widely used drugs has been azidothymidine (AZT), although it can have severe side effects. Studies of the drug's longer-term effectiveness have been disappointing, and its modest benefits tend to fade within a year. The most hopeful treatment approach to emerge so far in treating HIV is the combination, or cocktail, therapy. It is based on the knowledge that HIV mutates rapidly to different forms and can therefore quickly become resistant to a particular drug (Kalb, 1998; Perrin & Telenti, 1998). Combination therapy makes use of two or more drugs at once, so that HIV is kept off balance and under control. One of the new drugs usually used as part of the therapy is a protease inhibitor, which attacks the virus in one of its reproductive steps. Unfortunately these combination therapies can be so complicated that many patients do not adhere to the treatment regimens faithfully (Gwadz et al., 1999).

So far, the combination therapies have shown promising results, often suppressing HIV replication considerably or nearly completely. However, these therapies have primarily been successful with patients who have not received earlier treatment. Therefore, there is still concern that HIV may eventually become resistant to the drugs, that the side effects

On the Campus, Testing for AIDS Grows Common

Elizabeth Rockett, a New York University senior, has gone to the health center on the bustling campus for the usual rites of passage for a modern female student, like getting birth control pills and gynecological care. Then, two weeks ago, she called there for something that reflects her generation's new approach to sex and mortality: a referral for an AIDS test.

"I had to work up my courage," Ms. Rockett said of her decision to have the blood test, which detects antibodies to H.I.V., the virus that causes AIDS. It was a relief but not a surprise to learn that her test was negative. Her fiancé had already tested negative.

"It seemed something you should know," said Ms. Rockett, 24, a politics major who plans to marry in December. "I would just hate for them two years later to say, 'You're pregnant and you have H.I.V.' Do you want to enter a marriage like that?" . . .

"It's a college thing," said Anissa Bone, 20, a dance and pre-med major at Columbia, who was tested in April (see Fig. 17.6). "Here's the first time people are having a sexual relationship. Most of my friends who are not in a monogamous relationship get tested regularly. Usually, it's after they switch partners." . . .

Many major schools now offer confidential testing in which the information is shared only by the doctor and the patient, said Paula Swinford, a member of the AIDS task force of the American College Health Association. About one-third of those schools offer anonymous tests, in which students do not give their names but are as-signed codes for their blood samples. Student demand for both has been steady, Ms. Swinford said.

"There are people who test pretty regularly, and many engage in condom use sporadically in between," said Ms. Swinford, who is also the director of health education at the University of Southern California. . . .

"Students were using the community testing service, but they were made for the community at large, not issues the college community is dealing with," Ms. Swinford said. "How do you tell your parents you are H.I.V. positive if your parents don't know you are sexually active or your sexual orientation?"

Like so many of the life-style changes emanating from the AIDS epidemic, much of the information about AIDS testing among college students is anecdotal, gathered by health care providers comparing notes on how best to help students. At most schools, the objective is to couple the test with counseling and information so students can make intelligent choices.

"I think testing should be a priority of the health service," said Alan Grumet, a first-year law student at N.Y.U. (see Fig. 17.6). "I assumed they would have that kind of service here, especially in these times now. Personally, if I were to be entering a serious relationship, I'd want to be tested and I'd want my partner to be tested."

—Felicia R. Lee, *New York Times,* October 4, 1993
Reprinted by permission.

FIGURE 17.6   *Testing for HIV on Campus*

Testing for HIV is commonplace on many campuses. Anissa Bone (left), a student at Columbia University, says, "Most of my friends who are not in a monogamous relationship get tested regularly. Usually it's after they switch partners." Alan Grumet (right), a student at New York University, says, "Personally, if I were to be entering a serious relationship, I'd want to be tested and I'd want my partner to be tested."

will eventually become toxic for the patients, or that the virus may be able to hide in various cells of the body only to reappear later on (Cohen, 1998). Research into new treatment approaches for HIV is continuing and will surely yield new and more effective therapies with time (Ho, 1998).

There has been some controversy over "morning-after" treatment for those cases in which a person realizes he or she has potentially been exposed to HIV. This involves a 6-week regimen of up to 20 pills a day, many of which can have unpleasant side effects. Many times, patients do not complete the treatment because of these effects. The complex issue is whether the risks of infection by one-time exposure justify the powerful medical treatment (Gorman, 1997).

Vaccines for HIV

Viral diseases can sometimes be prevented or brought under control by vaccination. Vaccines take advantage of the body's ability to "remember" a disease-causing agent. They involve introducing a harmless form of the germ into the body, so that the immune system is fooled into working as if it were being attacked by the actual germ and develops necessary antibodies to ward off later infections. This strategy has worked in controlling such diseases as smallpox and polio. One of the major problems in developing a vaccine to combat HIV is that the virus attacks the very mechanisms by which the human body develops immunity against disease (Baltimore, 1999).

The search for an HIV vaccine has been a top priority since 1984, and experts still rank such a vaccine as the most urgently needed in the world. There have been several major complications that make the search a difficult one. First, HIV seems to be able to "hide" in cells by installing its genes within the genes of the cell. Second, there is no particularly good animal model for the disease, and this is where testing would normally begin. Third, because HIV infection is so dangerous, experimental trials for a vaccine with humans have had to proceed with the utmost caution. In such trials, a substantial number of at-risk people are given the vaccine, and their rate of infection is compared to a control group of persons who have not received the vaccine. The earliest vaccine trials have yielded disappointing results, and the next results are not expected until 2003 (Wheeler, 1999b). Finally, there are concerns that there may be very real ethical problems in conducting vaccine trials with people in the less industrialized nations of the world who have not been given the benefit of other forms of medical treatment (Bloom, 1998).

CASE STUDY

Brent Worries about Potential HIV Infection

Brent came to a counselor he had been seeing about other issues to talk about a recent sexual experience. Brent was a gay man and had been active in a social group for gays. At one of the meetings of the group, he had met a gay male who was a few years younger than himself, and they had begun seeing each other. The younger man had been more sexually active than Brent, who had only had two previous same-gender sexual experiences. After an evening out, Brent and his new partner decided to have sex. One of the activities they had shared had been anal intercourse. While the other man had been having intercourse with Brent, the condom he had been wearing had broken without his knowledge, and he had ejaculated without the protection of the condom. He was apologetic and assured Brent that he did not have any diseases, but Brent was still worried. He admitted to the counselor that he did not fully trust the other man and was very aware that he had been active sexually with numerous partners.

This was the first time that Brent could potentially have been exposed to STDs, including HIV. He was, of course, most concerned about that possibility. The counselor reminded him that there were other diseases about which he should also be concerned. Brent reported that he had been vaccinated for hepatitis B before entering college. The counselor made contact with the health clinic and set up an appointment for Brent to be checked for various STDs. All tests proved to be negative. The other reality was that he would have to wait several months before a test for HIV could be considered reliable. This was highly uncomfortable for him, and he continued to talk with the counselor regularly about his worries. During the waiting period, he also had a flulike illness, and this frightened him even more. The health clinic assured him that his symptoms were exactly like those that were being experienced by many other people at that time of year. After 6 months, Brent had the blood tests for HIV, which involved another 2 weeks of tense waiting for the results. He was relieved to learn that the tests were negative, and he had them repeated after another 6 months for further reassurance. From then on, he explored ways of keeping his sex life as safe and protected as possible.

Because there are different strains of HIV, there is some concern over whether several vaccines will have to be developed to protect people from AIDS. Some virologists believe that enough weak spots can be found that are common to most of the strains, so that a single vaccine can produce immunity. Animal testing with vaccines demonstrated enough success that experimental trials with humans are now under way (Letvin, 1998). The first tests are being done with *therapeutic vaccines* that are used to expand the immune responses of people already infected with HIV in an effort to delay or prevent the onset of disease symptoms. It is not yet known if therapeutic vaccines could reduce the risks of an infected individual transmitting HIV to others. As these vaccines prove themselves to be safe, they may well be tested on uninfected people as *preventative vaccines* that would forestall infection with the virus in the first place.

International experts from all over the world are working on the development of a vaccine. The National Institutes of Health have nearly doubled the amount of research funding available for developing an AIDS vaccine. Scientists seem to be in general agreement that it will take several more years of painstaking research and clinical testing before reliable treatments or vaccines for HIV disease become available (Baltimore, 1999). The United Nations has established a global program to fight HIV infection and AIDS. In the meantime, society must continue to face the many issues that the disease has created.

HIV and Society

Whenever new diseases have swept through populations, crises of morality have accompanied the disease (see Fig. 17.7). Should victims of the disease be cared for or isolated so they cannot infect others? What can be done about the social stigma that may develop for those with the disease and those who live with them? How much energy and what resources should be diverted from finding cures and preventative measures toward caring for victims who seem surely doomed? These are ancient questions that still catch us off guard. We must examine the applicability of time-tested solutions today and sort through new ethical insights that may help with the HIV/AIDS dilemma.

Can you think of any jobs from which HIV-infected individuals should be excluded?

HIV has touched every aspect of society. It has led to courageous and generous actions, and, at the same time, it has led to irrational and mean-spirited behavior. Regardless, HIV will not be ignored. National and

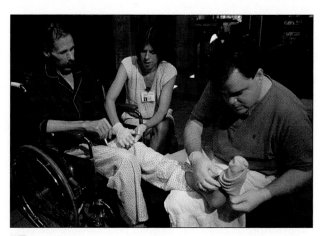

FIGURE 17.7   *Caring for People with HIV/AIDS*

Medical treatment is only one aspect of the overall care people need who are living with HIV/AIDS. Companionship, counseling, and attention to personal needs all contribute to enhancing the quality of life of HIV/AIDS patients.

international activist groups have called for increased governmental action on HIV/AIDS, even as once-promising national task forces and committees have gradually disbanded. They have reiterated that it is time to stop blaming any group of people for the disease and instead to mount a concerted effort to fight the virus. They charge that the greatest threats in the HIV/AIDS crisis at present are public complacency and governmental inaction.

Individual Freedom vs. Public Health Interests

During historical disease epidemics, individual rights have sometimes been subordinated—often to cruel dimensions—to protect the general population. Lepers were forced into exile; victims of bubonic plague were jailed or confined, often along with their healthy relatives. In the nineteenth century, legal systems began to develop more rational principles for protecting the public from infected individuals. Quarantines of various degrees of severity were imposed for certain infectious diseases. There have been some restrictions on people relating to HIV disease, but in contemporary society precedents of individual freedom, privacy, and confidentiality have generally prevailed.

However, in a number of cases, people have been stigmatized or denied certain rights because they were known to be HIV-positive or to have AIDS (Herek, 1999). HIV-infected children have been denied admittance to schools because of fear that their presence would place classmates at risk. Some office workers have threatened to quit rather than work with infected people. Some insurance companies have canceled health insurance coverage for people who have been identified as HIV-positive. The U.S. Supreme Court has now ruled that HIV-positive people, even if they have no symptoms, are protected from discrimination by the Americans with Disabilities Act.

A number of states require premarital HIV testing, and officials of the CDC fear that such moves may drive infected people underground to protect themselves from discrimination. Others insist that society has used mandatory quarantines, tests, and legal sanctions during epidemics before, and that indeed these represent legitimate approaches to protecting the public health. A Florida county court ruled that an HIV-positive man had to obtain written consent from any potential sexual partner before engaging in sexual contact.

It is crucial that we maintain a level of rationality and good sense with regard to this disease. No group should have to accept the blame for HIV or AIDS or be stigmatized because of the disease. It is important that we find ways of reducing the spread of the virus, developing effective treatments and preventions, and educating people thoroughly about the risks of sexual behavior. There is nothing to be gained by succumbing to a mentality that can only foster attitudes of mistrust and discrimination.

Other Ethical Issues and HIV/AIDS

There are a number of other ethical issues that have arisen concerning HIV and AIDS. There will be more in the years ahead. Here is a summary of some of the more pressing issues:

1. *The issue of confidentiality.* In the field of medicine, patient confidentiality has traditionally been afforded the utmost respect. Yet some information from health records has been subject to disclosure, with the patient's permission, for a variety of purposes. The question remains: Who should be allowed access to information about an individual's sexual lifestyle or infection with HIV? Such information can affect reputation, employment, and insurance coverage. Yet, if an individual who is known to be HIV-infected continues to behave in ways that are clearly endangering others, how and under what circumstances would it be legitimate for the infection to be revealed? Several states have passed legislation giving physicians the discretion to decide about releasing information about people with HIV.

   There is also a controversial push for states to maintain names of infected persons in order to assure they get proper medical treatment. Others insist that names are not necessary.

Do you believe doctors should have the right to reveal a patient's HIV status to anyone? For instance, should doctors inform school systems that a student is HIV-positive? Should coaches know an athlete's status? Explain your position.

Among nonmedical professionals, such as counselors, social workers, and psychotherapists, the confidentiality dilemmas have become more complex. Ethical guidelines require such professionals to violate confidentiality if a third party is facing some immediate threat of danger, but the guidelines about potential HIV infection are less clear. Everyone agrees that the first line of action would be to strongly encourage the client to inform others about the disease and cease any behaviors that could potentially endanger others. If that fails, there is less agreement as to how the professional should proceed. There are legal implications on both sides of the dilemma. On the one hand, the professional could be subject to charges for either violating client confidentiality or creating negative consequences for him or her. On the other hand, the professional could be charged with negligence in not notifying another person who might be at risk of serious medical consequences from HIV infection. Only further clarification of ethical guidelines and legal precedents will help professionals make their decisions.

2. *The costs of caring for HIV-infected patients and supporting research.* The costs of HIV and AIDS are proving to be staggering, and there is already a marked shortage of facilities to care for patients with these diseases. The U.S. government is now spending over $1.7 billion annually on HIV/AIDS research (see Fig. 17.8). However, there has been a developing controversy that certain other diseases that affect as many or more people as HIV are not getting their fair share of research dollars (Marshall, 1997b). Some states in which the rates of infection are particularly high are contributing millions each year to efforts to contain the infection. The increasing number of patients with HIV disease is raising the issue of where the money will come from to care for them. The direct cost of caring for patients, and indirect costs, including lost wages and earning power of patients, are costing the nation billions of dollars.

3. *Legal ramifications of HIV/AIDS.* As ethical problems multiply, the judicial system is increasingly being called upon to resolve disputes revolving around HIV and AIDS. Already several criminal and civil cases have reached the courts in which

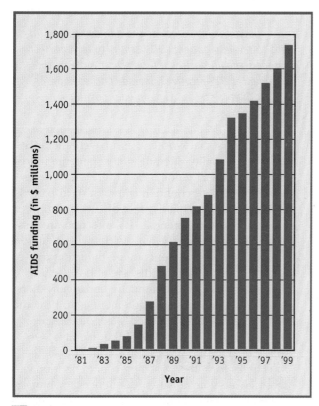

FIGURE 17.8 *U.S. Funding for HIV/AIDS Research*

In the United States, there has been controversy over the use of funding for researching particular diseases. Because HIV and AIDS are relatively new and still spreading, the amount of federal spending continues to rise, but in recent years it has been leveling off.

Source: Reprinted with permission from Jon Cohen, "AIDS: A Justifiable Share," *Science,* Vol. 276, p. 345 and Jon Cohen, "NIH Concocts a Booster Shot for HIV Vaccines," *Science,* Vol. 281, p. 1270. Copyright © 1997 and 1998 American Association for the Advancement of Science.

approach involving both the biomedical and behavioral sciences. The most successful strategies in changing behavior have included repeated media messages; person-to-person discussion with parents, trusted peers, or community members; increasing availability of condoms; and a political climate that enables open discussion of HIV and sexuality (Furstenberg, Geitz, Teitler, & Weiss, 1997). Where women are culturally and economically subordinate to men, empowerment of groups of women has been effective, because it allows them more power in controlling sexual interactions. In some societies, for example, female prostitutes have organized so that they can require that their customers wear condoms.

HIV Education

Everyone seems to agree that educational efforts regarding HIV and AIDS must receive a high priority, especially for young people (see Fig. 17.9). Most states already require their schools to offer HIV/AIDS education. However, there is controversy over at what age such education should begin and what its content should be. In many ways, these controversial factors are extensions of debates that have been raging in the field of sexuality education for years. Some experts recommend beginning HIV/AIDS education with 9-, 10-, and 11-year-olds; others oppose starting at such early ages. Some groups claim that it is unrealistic to expect all youth to abstain from shared sexual activity because of the HIV scare, and they advocate the teaching of safer sex practices that will at least minimize the risks of contracting HIV. Critics of this approach believe that teaching about preventative measures condones casual

people are accused of deliberately or carelessly exposing others to HIV. Charges have stemmed from situations in which people who knew they carried the virus continued to have unprotected sexual relations. More than half of the states have statutes that make it a criminal offense to knowingly transmit a STD, and HIV is increasingly being treated in the same manner. Litigation on issues regarding HIV and AIDS will be on the rise in years to come.

◼ HIV and Personal Decisions about Sex

The growing problem of HIV infection is beginning to change people's sexual behavior. The disease will be brought under control only through a multidisciplinary

FIGURE 17.9 *HIV/AIDS Awareness and Education*

Jeff Getty, an AIDS patient who received a baboon bone marrow transplant as an experimental treatment, holds a press conference with other AIDS activists to heighten consciousness about the need for new research on treating HIV-positive individuals.

Silence Equals Death

To anyone outside his special circle, the fate of a young Texan named James would have seemed as predictable as it was tragic. The Austin restaurant worker had developed the telltale red-and-purple lesions and had suffered night sweats, diarrhea and weight loss. Then came the inevitable coda; his doctor informed him that he had AIDS. In fact, his T-cell count was down from a normal range of 800 to 1,200 to a depressing 12.

But James, as he told his doctor, did not know what AIDS was. Nor did he know what HIV was, or for that matter a virus. He agreed to the recommended treatments, but aside from that, he lived as he had before—including his active and unprotected sex life. He was sure he would get better.

James' hospital called in Stephan Kennedy, an outreach worker who deals exclusively with HIV-infected and AIDS patients such as James. To Kennedy the young man's incomprehension was painfully familiar. "I used a lot of analogies," Kennedy recalls. "I said, 'The HIV is a worm, and the apple is your body. The worm gets into your body, eats a little and then goes to sleep. Then it wakes up again and starts eating some more and some more and some more, until the apple becomes rotten. And that is what is happening to you.'"

That chilling explanation helped, but it was many more such conversations before James truly understood, shortly before his death. It wasn't that he was dumb; it was that he was deaf. . . .

Today, 13 years into the epidemic, the average deaf person may—just recently—have learned AIDS exists. But, say activists in the field, most of America's deaf adults and teenagers still do not know what "HIV positive" means, that it can be contracted from someone who shows no symptoms, how to have safe sex or avoid infection through needles, or that women can catch it. . . .

The first language of more than half of America's deaf, whose number is variously estimated at between 250,000 and 2 million, is American Sign Language (ASL). That elegant mode of communication, a combination of signs and gestures, is not based on English. Thus the English reading level of the average deaf adult at the completion of formal education is usually placed somewhere between the third and the eighth grade. Says New York social-services counselor Donna Leshne: "The knowledge base is lacking. With all the ways we have of transmitting information, they're just not receiving it. . . ."

The language problem is only the first barrier to understanding. Many deaf people have only a rudimentary understanding of anatomy, disease and medicine. African-American deaf people, who employ their own dialect of ASL, are yet more isolated from mainstream information—and so more endangered. Residential schools for the deaf tend to be more puritanical than those for the hearing, and sex education is less comprehensive. Some social scientists also believe that needle drug use is higher because of alienation and loneliness. . . .

America has traditionally paid little attention to deaf people, so they are used to second-class treatment. It will take more than words to counter the fatalism expressed by Steven Collins, the current chairman of the National Coalition on HIV and the Deaf Community, as he surveys the current dilemma. "I'm sad but not shocked," he types on his TTY. "Deaf is a small community. Deaf is not important. Deaf people are dying because of that."

—David Van Biema, "AIDS," *Time,* April 4, 1994. Reprinted with permission.

sex. Among schools that have mandated HIV/AIDS education, some have also required that the emphasis be placed on sexual abstinence.

Most experts agree that, in the general population, older teenagers and young adults tend to be the most sexually active and therefore at higher risk than some other groups. They also tend to have attitudes of invulnerability and assume that the negative consequences will not happen to them, creating a false sense of security (Curtin, 1996). Reports from high schools and colleges have suggested that some students have been slow to accept the potential risks of HIV and AIDS around them. College students are still sometimes neglecting to use condoms in their sexual activities. There is evidence that as educational efforts increase, the incidence of

risky behavior is indeed declining, but not to the extent that professionals would prefer (Keeling, 1999).

Unfortunately, some people are still participating in risky sexual behaviors without the protection of condoms. In the *Details* magazine survey of American college students, less than half were able to say they always practiced safe sex, and over 10 percent indicated they did so only rarely or never (Elliott & Brantley, 1997). Lower levels of self-esteem, use of alcohol and other substances, and lack of skills in communicating with sexual partners can all play a role in reducing the likelihood that people will use condoms. Experts believe that HIV education must go beyond the presentation of information to help everyone develop the intentions and skills they need to successfully protect themselves from infection (Crosby, Yarber, & Meyerson,1999; Rosser, Gobby, & Carr, 1999).

Most magazines and television networks are now willing to accept advertisements encouraging the use of condoms, and the ads have been becoming increasingly frank (see Fig. 17.10). Numerous school systems, especially those in urban locations, now make condoms available to high school students, and occasionally to younger students as well. There has been a modest but steady demand for condoms in these schools. Condom vending machines have also been installed in some small-town high schools, sometimes despite strong opposition from parents and segments of the community. Close to 70 percent of adults favor the distribution of condoms in schools and the promotion of condom use in schools, by the government, and through television (Yarber & Torabi, 1999). The evidence also continues to show that availability of condoms does not increase teen sexual activity (Raab, 1998b). It does lead to an increase in the rate of protected sexual activity, although there are still significant numbers of teenagers who have sexual intercourse without such protection (Furstenberg et al., 1997).

The issue of HIV/AIDS education is taking sexuality education in new directions and encouraging further debates about curriculum content and philosophy. One thing is certain: No one grows up today without hearing a great deal about HIV, AIDS, and their connections to sex.

Can Sex Be Safe and Satisfying?

FOH Everyone has to make his or her own decision about sexual behavior considering the risks of HIV transmission. Although slightly more individuals than in the re-

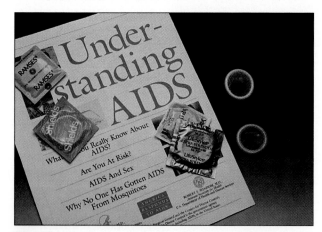

FIGURE 17.10   *Condom Advertisement*

The Centers for Disease Control and Prevention and other agencies hope to educate the public about safe sex and the use of condoms by advertisements like this.

cent past may be postponing penetrative sexual contact until they find lasting, monogamous relationships, others are clearly choosing to share sex now. How seriously they consider the risks of contracting HIV, or what sorts of practices they employ to decrease those risks, depends on a variety of psychological and social factors, including the following:

1. *Degree of willingness to be prepared for sex.* The fear of condemnation from parents, religious leaders, and society has often made it difficult for young people to plan ahead and prepare for sexual activity. Many therefore prefer to regard sex as accidental or spontaneous in order to bear less responsibility for a bad decision or immoral behavior. Such attitudes can only interfere with the kind of mutual questioning and preparation that can render a sexual encounter safe from disease (Britton, Crimini, & Rak, 1999).

2. *Self-esteem and assertiveness.* To protect oneself against HIV infection requires enough self-esteem and sense of self-worth to remember that one's health must be protected. It also means having enough self-confidence and assertiveness to make it clear that certain rules must govern a sexual encounter. This sort of behavior is often difficult for people who believe that their popularity, attractiveness, or even an entire relationship may be in question (Afifi, 1999; Kalichman & Nachimson, 1999).

3. *Willingness to overcome peer pressures about use of condoms.* As birth control devices, condoms have often been given a bad name. Some people claim they reduce sexual sensations. They may be embarrassing to purchase. For such a simple device, they are frequently not used completely correctly, and they occasionally break or slip off. The fact remains, however, that for now latex condoms represent one of the best protections against HIV transmission in sexual encounters. Those that are lubricated with nonoxynol-9 or other microbicides provide even more protection because spermicidal chemicals destroy HIV on contact. People are learning that sex with condoms is not only safer but can still be pleasurable and satisfying. Although use of condoms has been increasing, rates of consistent condom use still need to be increased (Anderson, Wilson, Doll, Jones, & Barker, 1999).

4. *Degree of understanding of personal vulnerability.* At various times in life, people are prone to feeling relatively invincible, or they may believe that any consequence, even a negative one, is reversible. It is crucial for everyone to realize that not only is HIV infection a very real threat, but for the time being it is irreversible. If you get the virus, there are complicated medical treatments

Table 17.1 — Degree of Safety in Types of Sexual Activity

Safest	Possibly Safe	Unsafe
Dry kissing	Vaginal or anal intercourse using a latex or synthetic condom	Fellatio or cunnilingus without a condom or rubber dam
Body-to-body contact and embracing	Wet kissing with no broken skin or damaged mouth tissue	Semen in the mouth
Massage	Cunnilingus using a dam	Vaginal intercourse without a condom
Mutual masturbation (with care in avoiding contact with semen)	Fellatio using a condom	Anal intercourse without a condom
Erotic books, movies, and conversation	Hand-to-genital stimulation without breaks in skin	Other anal contact, orally or manually
		Sharing sex toys

Sources: Hatcher et al., *Contraceptive Technology*, 17th edition, 1998, Ardent Media, New York, and Schacker et al., 1996.

that may delay the onset of diseases, but there is no way to get rid of it. At the present time, there is no cure.

5. *Willingness to accept the struggles of establishing a sexual identity.* Even people who consider themselves heterosexual sometimes have sexual encounters with members of their same gender. Because such choices may be personally difficult to accept psychologically, there may also be a tendency not to pay attention to proper protection during sex. For males who share sexual activity with other males, in particular, there must be careful consideration given to the risks involved, and both partners should take precautions to prevent transmission of HIV. Some young men who identify themselves primarily as gay are also having sex with women and thus need to take the same precautions (Myrick, 1999).

Despite the threat of HIV, couples can still regard sex in a positive way as an integral part of enhancing relationships. The threat should force potential sexual partners to think more carefully about their sexual decisions, open up channels of communication, and protect themselves more deliberately from the spread of disease. These new approaches to sex should prove of real value in reducing a spectrum of negative sexual and social consequences. See table 17.1.

Minimizing the Sexual Risks of Contracting HIV

FOH From the information now available about HIV, there are particular guidelines for having safer sex:

1. Know your sexual partners and their sexual histories. You risk contracting HIV if you have sex with someone who has had sex with someone else previously. The more sexual partners an individual has had, the greater the risk, although

it can sometimes take only one infected partner to get the virus. One rather disturbing study found that in a sample of 422 sexually active 18- to 25-year-olds, 34 percent of the males and 10 percent of the females admitted to having lied about their sexual histories in order to have sex with a new partner. When asked if they would lie to a partner about having a negative AIDS test when they actually had not had such a test, 20 percent of the men and 4 percent of the women said they would (Cochran & Mays, 1990). More recent research found that 40 percent of sexually active HIV-positive men and women did not disclose their status to sexual partners, and two-fifths of those who did not tell also did not use condoms consistently in their sexual contacts (Stein et al., 1998). You should be aware of this sinister type of risk.

2. If you are contemplating having sex with a new partner and there is no absolute guarantee that HIV is not present, it is crucial to make some agreements and live up to them:

    Agree not to share sex with any other partners for the duration of the relationship.

    Agree to be tested for HIV regularly after any sexual contact that could have transmitted it. It can take up to 6 months, or perhaps longer, for the antibodies to develop and show up on the blood test.

    Agree either to wait 6 months to share sex, after tests for HIV, or to use protection for that period of time.

3. The best form of protection is the use of a latex or polyurethane condom throughout a sexual encounter (Davis & Weller, 1999). The condom should be unrolled onto the erect penis before intercourse begins, leaving an empty (not air-filled) space at the tip for semen. This is best accomplished by pinching the tip of the condom while unrolling it onto the penis (see Fig. 17.11).

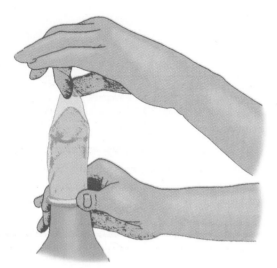

■ **FIGURE 17.11**   *How to Use the Condom*

Do not allow the penis to make sexual entry or contact before putting on the condom. Semen and sperm can escape from the penis at any time. The end of the condom should be pinched to exclude air before it is unrolled fully to cover the erect penis.

After ejaculation has occurred, the man or his partner should hold on to the base of the condom when removing the penis from the vagina so that the condom does not slip off or semen does not seep out of the open end of the condom. There are newly designed condoms that have adhesive around the shaft to prevent slippage and leakage. Condoms slip off or break between 2 and 3 percent of the times they are used. The "female condom" or vaginal pouch (see chapter 10, p. 324) also provides protection, but probably not quite as effectively as male condoms (Hatcher et al., 1998). More and more women seem to be receptive to using the female condom (Cabral et al., 1999).

4. During vaginal intercourse, a spermicidal foam containing nonoxynol-9 should be used in addition to the condom, because spermicides appear to help kill HIV on contact. There is increasing interest in the use of other microbicides during sexual activity and evidence that they may well reduce infection rates of HIV and other STDs.

5. Avoid direct contact with any bodily fluids or excretions from a partner.
6. Use a **rubber dam** during oral contact with the vulva or anus. Oral contact with sites where the virus could be harbored is considered risky. Some experts have recommended that small, square latex sheets of the sort dentists sometimes use in the mouth can be placed over the vulva, vagina, or anus. This would allow for some oral stimulation without direct contact from the tongue or lips. There is no research to date that can show how effective or necessary such a dam might be in preventing the transmission of HIV, but it represents the best precaution, given the present state of our knowledge. The latex dams are not widely available, but they could be obtained at medical/dental supply stores. Some dentists might be willing to provide them. Rubber dams may also be improvised by cutting a latex condom along its length, then spreading it out, or by cutting out a section of a surgical rubber glove. Rubber gloves or individual rubber fingercots that fit over a single finger might also be considered if a finger is to be inserted into the vagina or anus, to offer protection from the virus entering through a break in the skin from either partner.

These practices cannot provide a guarantee of safety against HIV transmission, but they can minimize your risks of contracting the virus. They also represent the most responsible ways of approaching sexual activity. HIV has mobilized the forces of science, medicine, and society in unprecedented ways. Never in history have people moved so quickly from recognition of a medical problem to comprehensive understanding of it. Never in recent history have people faced a disease of the proportions that HIV is now threatening. At the foundation of all the issues is the matter of personal decision making. It is through safe and sane approaches to sex that the spread of this disease can effectively be slowed.

rubber dam: small square sheet of latex used to cover the vulva, vagina, or anus to help prevent transmission of HIV during sexual activity.

Self-Evaluation

HIV/AIDS and Your Life

No disease in recent history has captured public interest and media attention in quite the same way as HIV infection and AIDS. They are diseases of controversy, most likely because HIV is frequently transmitted through behaviors that many people judge to be inappropriate or, at the least, find uncomfortable to discuss. Nevertheless, it is clear that the best ways to prevent the spread of HIV, and to protect oneself from infection, are to know the facts and make responsible and careful decisions. This self-evaluation will help you clarify your own knowledge base and personal attitudes relating to HIV and AIDS.

Assessing Your Knowledge, Attitudes, and Circumstances Relating to HIV/AIDS

The National Center for Health Statistics includes a group of questions about HIV and AIDS in its annual National Health Interview Survey (NHIS). Year-to-year, the survey has been demonstrating that in the United States, people's factual knowledge, attitudes, and level of awareness have been changing. This evaluation will help you note how your own knowledge, attitudes, and circumstances may have been changing over the years, and help you compare them to the findings of the 1992 NHIS.

HIV/AIDS Knowledge/Attitudes	Percent of 1992 NHIS Respondents Answering Affirmatively	How Would You Have Responded in 1992? (Yes/No)		How Do You Respond Today? (Yes/No)	
Do you recognize the term HIV?	95	Y	N	Y	N
Do you know that HIV can be transmitted via sexual intercourse?	96	Y	N	Y	N
Do you know that HIV can be transmitted via shared needles?	96	Y	N	Y	N
Do you know that HIV can be transmitted to infants by infected mothers?	94	Y	N	Y	N
Do you know there is no cure for AIDS?	93	Y	N	Y	N
Do you know that an HIV-infected person can look and feel healthy?	86	Y	N	Y	N
Do you know that a person can be infected but not yet have AIDS?	84	Y	N	Y	N
Do you know there is no vaccine against AIDS?	83	Y	N	Y	N
Do you know that transmission is very unlikely or impossible from eating in a restaurant where the cook is infected with HIV?	50	Y	N	Y	N
Do you know that transmission is very unlikely or impossible from coughs or sneezes?	47	Y	N	Y	N
Do you know that transmission is impossible from insect bites?	45	Y	N	Y	N
Do you believe it is possible to contract AIDS by donating blood? [It isn't possible.]	29	Y	N	Y	N
Do you have a lot of AIDS knowledge?	26	Y	N	Y	N
Do you have some AIDS knowledge?	45	Y	N	Y	N
Have you been tested for HIV?	32	Y	N	Y	N
Do you plan to be tested for HIV in the next 12 months?	11	Y	N	Y	N
Do you believe that condoms are very effective at preventing sexual transmission of HIV?	26	Y	N	Y	N
Do you believe that condoms are somewhat effective at preventing sexual transmission of HIV?	54	Y	N	Y	N
Do you know that latex and natural skin condoms differ in their ability to prevent sexual transmission of HIV?	27	Y	N	Y	N

HIV/AIDS Knowledge/Attitudes	Percent of 1992 NHIS Respondents Answering Affirmatively	How Would You Have Responded in 1992? (Yes/No)		How Do You Respond Today? (Yes/No)	
Do you know that oil-based lubricants can weaken latex condoms?	33	Y	N	Y	N
Have you had a friend or relative with AIDS or HIV infection?	12	Y	N	Y	N
Have you had a coworker with AIDS or HIV infection?	5	Y	N	Y	N
Do you have no chance of being currently infected with HIV?	73	Y	N	Y	N
Do you have no chance of becoming infected with HIV?	64	Y	N	Y	N
Have you ever engaged in behavior that would put you at risk of contracting HIV?	4	Y	N	Y	N

Source: National Health Interview Survey, 1992.

Considering Being Tested for HIV

The percentages of people being tested for HIV have been growing steadily. This reflects the likelihood that they have engaged in some sort of risky behavior at some point in their lives, whether they admit it or not. Although it may take up to 6 months, or more, for HIV antibodies to show up in the body, testing is one of the best ways of finding out your status and protecting your sexual partners. If you are involved in a relationship in which you may eventually wish to participate in unprotected, penetrative sex, and either one of you has had any possibility of HIV exposure, testing is the most sensible route to take. Unless you have participated in frequent high-risk behaviors, it is quite likely your test results will be negative. Nevertheless, it is best to find out for sure.

Here is a series of questions that can help you think through the process of being tested for HIV and also your reactions to that process. Consider your responses with care and then *get tested:*

Knowing the Mechanics.
Consult your local public health agency or student health center for more information, and try to secure answers to the following questions:

1. Where can you get tested for HIV?
2. Does your state or provincial government require reporting of test results to some central agency?
3. Will your name be associated with your test results as they are in *confidential* medical records? Or will the results be *anonymous,* identified only by a number you hold?
4. Who will be explaining the results of the test to you?
5. How long will it take to get the results?

6. Are you making the decision to be tested without coercion and with full and informed consent?

Knowing Your Motivations and Feelings.
7. Why are you considering being tested for HIV?
8. Is peace of mind important to you? Are you tired of wondering about the possibility you could have been infected?
9. Are you ready to cope with some anxiety while awaiting the results? Do you have sources of support and counseling in the meantime?
10. Are you ready to give honest answers to the health care provider who will interview you prior to testing?
11. Have you discussed HIV testing with your partner?

If the Results Are Positive . . .
12. How do you think you will feel, and whom will you tell first?
13. Who will be your sources of support and counseling?
14. Where will you seek further medical evaluation and treatment, and how will this be paid for?
15. What will be the implications for the various relationships in your life (relatives, friends, lovers)?
16. Do you know that you can still have a satisfying and productive life ahead?

If the Results Are Negative . . .
17. How do you think you will feel, and whom will you tell first?
18. Are you prepared to take appropriate precautions in the future to minimize the risks of HIV infection? What are your plans?

Chapter Summary

1. Human immunodeficiency virus (HIV) has created many medical, political, economic, and social issues. Acquired immunodeficiency syndrome (AIDS) was first identified in 1981. It is a disease that progressively destroys the body's immune system so that opportunistic infections weaken the victim. It is eventually fatal.

2. Although the origins of HIV are uncertain, it may have begun in Africa. HIV disease has infected millions of people throughout the world.

3. Epidemiological studies show that the incidence of HIV infection varies in different parts of the world. Although HIV spread first among gay males and intravenous (IV) drug abusers in the United States, HIV infection is now present among heterosexual adolescents, women, and children.

4. In sub-Saharan Africa and South and Southeast Asia, the rates of HIV infection and AIDS are particularly high.

5. HIV is transmitted from mother to infant, but not all infected children develop disease symptoms, and preventative treatments can reduce this risk.

6. HIV is more prevalent in urban neighborhoods, especially where there is a great deal of IV drug abuse. This could represent a challenge to keeping funding for seeking a cure for the disease.

7. HIV is a retrovirus, and several strains have been identified. The virus can probably attack several human tissues, but it particularly affects the T-lymphocytes known as CD4 cells that are crucial in the immune system.

8. The documented routes of HIV infection are anal or vaginal sexual intercourse; oral-genital sex; other contacts with semen, transplanted organs, or blood (as through contaminated needles); and transfer from mother to child perinatally or through breast milk.

9. It may be that some people can develop at least a temporary immunity to HIV. Research is continuing to determine if there are ways of enhancing immunity to HIV.

10. Tests to detect HIV antibodies in the blood may not show evidence of the virus for 6 months or more after actual infection. The ELISA test is usually confirmed with the Western blot test.

11. There is controversy over whether HIV testing should be required. In the United States, all potential immigrants and armed forces enlistees are required to be tested. Many states now require premarital testing. Home testing raises the problem of being notified of results without assurances of face-to-face counseling.

12. There is no cure for HIV infection. Treatment focuses on prevention and control of opportunistic infections. Research is focusing on the development of a vaccine to produce immunity to the virus, thus preventing infection.

13. Many drugs have been developed to treat HIV, and combination drug therapies involving protease inhibitors are proving to be the most effective. HIV can develop drug resistance because it mutates quickly and multiplies in great numbers. Many other drugs are being developed and tested.

14. Vaccines to fool the body into creating antibodies to help slow rates of HIV infection are being tested. Preventative vaccines are also being tested.

15. Caring and research for people living with HIV or AIDS raise issues of confidentiality and cost. Legal and ethical conflicts about HIV infection and confidentiality are becoming increasingly common.

16. HIV requires some new approaches to sexual decision making. Some sex should be avoided; use of condoms and other protective measures can reduce the risks of contracting HIV.

17. Sex can still be pleasurable and a safe part of relationships if approached responsibly and with appropriate precautions.

Focus on Health Questions

You will find in this section the kinds of questions that you may have concerning your own health and sexuality. The page references indicate where in the text the answer is located; the exact place is marked with the logo: **FOH**

1. What are the most common ways people are exposed to HIV? 510–511

2. Can a pregnant woman give HIV to her baby? 511

3. What sexual behaviors are the riskiest in terms of possible HIV exposure and infection? 516

4. What symptoms would I get if I have been infected with HIV? 515

5. Does everybody who is infected with HIV get AIDS and die? 517

6. What tests are used to determine if I am infected with HIV, and how reliable are they? 517

7. Should I get tested for HIV? 518

8. What medications are used to treat HIV disease? 519

9. Is there a vaccination I could take so that I won't have to worry about HIV? 521

10. What are the best ways of decreasing the risks of HIV infection during sexual activity? 526

Annotated Readings

A number of excellent books on HIV and AIDS are in various stages of preparation and publication. Watch your bookstores and consult with instructors who can keep you up-to-date on the latest references.

Aronstein, D. M., & Thompson, B. J. (Eds.). (1998). *HIV and social work: A practitioner's guide.* New York: Harrington Press. A practical guide for professionals who work with HIV-positive individuals and AIDS patients.

Cox, F. D. (1996). *The AIDS booklet.* Madison, WI: WCB/McGraw-Hill. A brief, up-to-date reference on HIV and AIDS, offered in readable, summary style.

Derlega, V. J., & Barbee, A. P. (Eds.). (1998). *HIV and social interaction.* Thousand Oaks, CA: Sage. A collection of articles that focus on the social consequences of HIV, which have for too long been ignored.

Elwood, W. N. (Ed.). (1999). *Power in the blood: A handbook on AIDS, politics, and communication.* Mahwah, NJ: Lawrence Erlbaum Associates. A comprehensive collection of chapters that puts many social implications of HIV into fresh political perspectives.

Johnson, M. (1997). *Working on a miracle.* New York: Bantam Books. A personal view of experimentation with combination drug therapies, written by a physician who was accidentally infected with HIV.

Levy, J. A. (1994). *HIV and the pathogenesis of AIDS.* Washington, DC: American Society for Microbiology. An excellent resource for understanding the virus and the mechanisms it employs during the disease process.

Martin, E. (1994). *Flexible bodies: Tracking immunity in American culture from the days of polio to the age of AIDS.* Boston: Beacon Press. From a very personal perspective of working with infected persons, this author examines the changing conceptions of the human immune system over several decades.

Masterton, G. (1994). *Single, wild, sexy, and safe.* New York: Signet Books. A guide for single women to finding sexual happiness, with partners or alone, in a safe way.

Myrick, R. (1996). *AIDS, communication, and empowerment.* Binghamton, NY: Harrington Park Press. A study of how public health communication about HIV/AIDS has factored into social attitudes and stigma about the disease.

Stein, T. J. (1998). *The social welfare of women and children with HIV and AIDS: Legal protections, policy, and programs.* New York: Oxford University Press. An excellent summary of the issues relating to HIV-positive women and children.

Chapter 18
Sexual Dysfunctions and Their Treatment

Chapter Outline

Note: A selection of Focus on Health questions appears at the end of each chapter. Answers to these questions are indicated within the chapter by the symbol in the margin. **FOH**

> When we first started having sex, he was far more interested in whether I had an orgasm than I was. The fact was, I almost never had an orgasm, but I still thought our sex life was great. As our relationship has grown, I now reach orgasm almost every time and would miss it more than I once did.
>
> —Statement written by a college student

Workers in the medical and helping professions—physicians, psychologists, counselors, and social workers, for example—have always been presented with the sexual concerns and complaints of their clients. Until the publication of *Human Sexual Inadequacy* by Masters and Johnson in 1970, these professionals rarely received any specialized training in dealing with sexual problems, and there were no clearly defined guidelines for treating such problems. People facing problems with sexual functioning were typically offered a vague blend of reassurance, moralizing, and poorly researched suggestions for living up to the performance standards of the culture.

Understanding Sexual Dysfunctions

The field of sex therapy has expanded rapidly, and the systematized treatment of sexual problems is commonplace. Dysfunctional symptoms have labels that can be used in both professional and popular communication. Sex therapy was originally backed by only rudimentary research studies, often flawed in their methodologies. Following this phase, more attention was given to the effectiveness of various treatment approaches, and debates emerged concerning which modalities worked the best. More recently, a number of new medical treatments have been developed. There is a growing gap between how physicians approach certain sexual problems and the therapeutic approaches that nonmedical sex therapists employ. Ironically, many of the newer medical treatments seem to be most effective when combined with some of the more traditional psychotherapeutic techniques. More definitive studies are still needed to answer some of the more pressing questions about sex therapy techniques and their comparative usefulness (Tiefer, 1997; Wiederman, 1998).

When Is a Dysfunction a Dysfunction?

Traditionally, men who experience difficulty controlling their ejaculations are said to suffer from premature ejaculation. Women who never experience orgasm are said to be experiencing orgasmic disorder. However, the situation may be more complex than these handy labels suggest. Who is to define whether or not some phenomenon of sexual response is a problem—a dysfunction or a disorder? If the woman enjoys her sexual encounters without feeling any need for orgasm, should she be treated for a dysfunction? If the rapidly ejaculating man and his partner are perfectly comfortable with his pattern of response, should they be made to feel they have a problem? It has been proposed that individual sexual responsiveness may in part be defined by people's gender roles or by rigid definitions of what constitutes a "normal" sexual response cycle. We must therefore allow for individual differences in actual response and in how that response is interpreted (Chalker, 1994; Tiefer, 1997).

There are some statistics available on the frequency of orgasm in women during shared sexual encounters. The most recent data in the United States from the National Health and Social Life Survey (NHSLS) found that among women aged 18 to 24, 8 percent never have orgasm. This number decreases among older age groups so that only 2 percent of women aged 40 to 59 report complete lack of orgasm (Laumann, Gagnon et al., 1994). Other studies confirm that there are some women who do not seem to experience orgasmic response in their sexual encounters. However, 20 to 33 percent of these women do not consider lack of orgasm to be a problem and indeed find their sexual interactions satisfying and happy (Heiman & Meston, 1998). There is less research on lack of orgasm in men, although the NHSLS data indicate that only about 1 percent of men say that they rarely or never reach orgasm (Laumann, Gagnon et al., 1994).

Sex therapy and sex research face many troublesome ethical issues. Effective sex therapy is based on several assumptions (discussed later in this chapter) concerning the removal of barriers to normal sexual functioning and the values of both therapists and patients. Treatment of sexual problems cannot be reduced to a series of mechanical steps, although there are specific skills that may help a great deal. Theory related to sex therapy continues to take shape. It has been suggested that helping people with sexual dysfunctions requires human sensitivity, creativity, openness to new directions, and well-honed skills. One cannot attempt to change sexual functioning without being prepared also to examine sexual values, the quality of relationships, and other highly subjective life issues (Tiefer, 1997; Wiederman, 1998).

Because we do not yet have reliable and valid norms for human sexual response patterns, we must use whatever statistical and clinical evidence is available, in order to establish ranges of sexual responsiveness that can then be used to make practical judgments about sexual dysfunctions. The individual's own sexual history and feelings are particularly important in arriving at any diagnosis. Sexual health seems to be intimately tied to other levels of physical and mental well-being. There is emerging evidence that for many women, sexual dysfunction is closely aligned with difficulties in their relationships, whereas male dysfunctions are often best studied from a medical point of view rather than a psychological or relational one (Leland, 1999a). It has also been found that the vast majority of people (94 percent) feel that enjoyable sexual relations add to a person's quality of life. More than half of the people in the same study reported that they at least sometimes experience sexual problems (National Institutes of Health, 1999).

Some professionals believe it is sufficient to assume that if some functional difficulty with sex prompts an individual or a couple to seek professional help, it is a dysfunction. However, this definition would leave out the many millions of others for whom sex is unsatisfactory but who are reluctant to seek treatment. A workable definition of dysfunction, above all, allows the therapist to exercise professional judgment in reassuring clients that they should not be fooled by unrealistically high sexual standards into believing they have a problem where none exists.

Most cultures through the ages have established certain mythical standards and expectations regarding sexual performance. The performance standards for men have been fairly rigid, whereas those for women have been more vague and mysterious. When people's bodies do not function sexually as expected and desired, they often feel frustrated, inadequate, and unhappy. In a society such as our own, which places a premium on being successful in sexual endeavors, to fail in a sexual encounter is perceived as tantamount to being a failure at manhood or womanhood. Whether or not these performance standards have some basis in the realities of human physiology or are simply the inventions of a sex-obsessed culture, many of them persist today and are perpetuated by the media.

Mythical Performance Standards for Men

Men have always been plagued by the standard that successful sex requires an erect penis. It is even assumed by most males that their partners cannot be expected to find sexual pleasure unless an erection is achieved and maintained. Closely allied to this standard is the standard of postponing ejaculation or orgasm. Because a penis tends to lose its erection following ejaculation, the longer a man can postpone ejaculation, the better a sexual performer he will be considered. A third standard might be best stated as the unquestioned assumption it has always been: that men reach orgasm without difficulty and find in this peak experience the ultimate pleasure of sex. It is now known that men do indeed have difficulties in reaching orgasm at times.

Mythical Performance Standards for Women

Historically, the sexual performance standards for women have focused on issues of sexual attractiveness and availability rather than desire. Women were once viewed by heterosexual men as passive, nonperforming sex partners. More recent attitudes have encouraged women to take a more active role in sex. However, women have also become more bound by new standards of sexual performance. Women are under pressure today to become intensely aroused and ready for sexual contact, to reach orgasm without difficulty, and to have more than one orgasm during a single sexual encounter.

These become the standards on which men and women pin their sexual hopes, play out their roles in bed, and judge their performances afterward. It is little wonder, then, that so many people end up feeling inadequate, dissatisfied, and disillusioned by what is actually happening in their sex lives. When individuals experience some functional problem during sex, or their bodies fail to perform as expected and desired with some consistency, they are said to be experiencing sexual dysfunction. Today, more than ever before, such problems need not signal a lifetime of unfulfilled sexual needs. As this chapter will demonstrate, most dysfunctions can be eased and corrected (Maurice, 1999).

What Labels Tell Us

Scientific communication demands that a terminology be available, and each of the sexual difficulties has been given a general label. The most commonly accepted source of diagnostic categories is the *Diagnostic and Statistical Manual of Mental Disorders,* now in its fourth edition and usually abbreviated as *DSM-IV* (American Psychiatric Association, 1994). However, it is important not to lose sight of the fact that such labels may have profound implications for the individual sufferer. Consider the term **impotence,** which conjures up images of failure and powerlessness, hardly reassuring concepts for the impotent man with erectile difficulties. A more positive term, **preorgasmic,** was once coined to describe women who had never been able to reach

---

impotence (IM-puh-tense): difficulty achieving or maintaining erection of the penis.

preorgasmic: women who have not yet been able to reach orgasm during sexual response.

Is Sex a Necessity?

The Viagra craze raises some tricky questions—about money. Should health insurance cover sexual satisfaction? If so, how much is enough?

Robert Pollyea just got a piece of his life back. Until a few years ago, the 66-year-old retired college professor had never complained much about his sex life. But a 1994 prostate operation left him largely impotent, and the penile injections his urologist prescribed were little help. "You have to go to the refrigerator with a syringe, fill it up and inject yourself," he recalls, "and while your wife is in there thinking, 'What the hell is going on?'" Everything changed when he started taking Viagra, Pfizer's new potency pill, a few weeks ago. "You use it and you have your foreplay," he says. "And when you're ready for intercourse you just do it. It's like when we were first married."

Thousands of older men are now realizing the same dream every day. Urologists are using rubber stamps to keep up with the demand for prescriptions, and Pfizer's stock has soared. But the erection pill's historic takeoff has caught the nation's health insurers off guard. Few of them have decided how to cover the new drug—and as demand explodes, that issue could get large and complicated. Should managed-care plans guarantee their subscribers some sexual pleasure? If so, how much is enough? How should they determine who needs treatment? And how should they pay the tab?

In clinical studies, 70 to 80 percent of impotent men have gotten good results. But a single pill costs $10—and demand for the drug has been breathtaking.

If even half of the estimated 30 million U.S. men with erectile difficulties start taking Viagra once a week, the cost would approach $8 billion a year. That's terrific news for Pfizer—even a $1 billion drug is considered a blockbuster—but a big burden for the health care system.

To control costs, health plans generally cover medical necessities, while eschewing treatment they deem experimental or purely cosmetic.

Viagra is not hard to classify one way or the other. Impotence is undeniably a medical disorder, but completely impotent men are not the only ones clamoring for Viagra.

Where should insurers draw the line? Not surprisingly, Pfizer and some patient advocates favor complete coverage. "Managed-care plans cover conditions like arthritis and allergies because they threaten people's quality of life," says Pfizer spokeswoman Mariann Caprino. "That's exactly what we're talking about here." Laurie Flynn, executive director of the National Alliance for the Mentally Ill, takes the same line, saying medical decisions shouldn't be "screened through the financial filter." But covering a drug like Viagra can have as many consequences as rejecting it. "Do you pay for Viagra or do you pay for prenatal care?" asks one managed-care executive. There's not an unlimited number of dollars here. We get a fixed premium, not one that adjusts because we have Viagra."

Insurers are likely to nix the drug altogether; dose for dose, it's actually cheaper than the injections and suppositories they already cover. The challenge is to deal with Viagra's overwhelming popularity. For the time being, Cigna Healthcare is limiting coverage to six pills each month, based on estimates of average couple's needs. And to qualify for that ration, you have to have a "pre-existing, documented condition of organic impotence, which is currently being treated by other medical means." Even if they're more expansive, other insurers will likely demand a diagnosis of "erectile dysfunction" before covering a prescription. But "dysfunction" is a relative term. "There's no blood test, no objective parameter," says Dr. Irwin Goldstein, a urologist at the Boston University Medical Center. "It's entirely subjective." In short, anyone who's dissatisfied could qualify as dysfunctional.

At the moment, some men are stretching the definition to absurd lengths. In New York, nightclub kids talk of using Viagra to trump the erection-quashing effects of disco drugs such as Ecstasy and crystal meth. Fortunately, the new pill won't fulfill such fantasies. Handy as it is for treating chronic impotence, there is not evidence that Viagra can boost a healthy man's sexual performance. As thrill seekers learn that lesson, demand may wane a bit. But for millions of men with erectile problems, Viagra seems sure to become a way of life—with or without insurance coverage. "Jack," a 28-year-old Brooklynite, has been partially impotent for six years due to a bike-seat injury. Viagra has restored his sexuality—and he hasn't taken a minute of flak from a health plan because he doesn't have one. "I have a friend who's a pharmacist," he says. "I pay $7 a pill and it's a steal."

By Geoffrey Cowley
With Theodore Gideonse and Ellyn E. Spragins
Newsweek, May 11, 1998. All rights reserved. Reprinted by permission.

Table 18.1	*The Sexual Response Cycle and Sexual Dysfunctions*	
Desire Phase Dysfunctions:	**Arousal (Vasocongestive) Phase Dysfunctions:**	**Orgasmic (Reversed Vasocongestive) Phase Dysfunctions:**
Normal asexuality: the individual who naturally has low levels of need for sexual gratification (not necessarily a dysfunction)	Problems in achieving a suitable level of sexual arousal	Problems in triggering orgasm, creating an inordinate orgasmic delay or a complete inability to reach orgasm
Hypoactive sexual desire disorder (HSDD)	Male erectile disorder	Male orgasmic disorder
Sexual aversion disorder: caused by anxiety and phobias relating to sexual activity	Female sexual arousal disorder: lack of vaginal lubrication, general sexual dysfunction	Female orgasmic disorder
	Involuntary spasm of outer vaginal musculature in women: vaginismus	Premature ejaculation: lack of ejaculatory control in men
		Postejaculatory pain

Source: Diagnostic and Statistical Manual for Mental Disorders, 4th ed. (DSM-IV), 1994, Washington, D.C.: American Psychiatric Association.

orgasm. This was a more upbeat, hopeful label because it implies that, although it has not yet been reached, a potential for orgasm still exists. However, the term never achieved wide acceptance among professionals.

There are certain modifying terms that are employed in diagnosing and describing sexual dysfunctions. The term **lifelong dysfunction** means that the problem has been present since the onset of the person's sexual functioning. The term **acquired dysfunction** is used in describing a dysfunction that has developed after a period of normal function. The terms "primary" and "secondary" were once used for lifelong and acquired, respectively. Thus, a woman with lifelong orgasmic disorder has never been able to reach orgasm, whereas the woman with acquired orgasmic disorder is no longer able to be orgasmic, but once was. Dysfunctions may also be *generalized* when the problem occurs in all of an individual's sexual encounters, or *situational,* meaning that it happens only under specific conditions, with certain types of stimulation, situations, or partners (American Psychiatric Association, 1994; Maurice, 1999).

What do you think is one of the most common complaints brought to sex therapists? Why do you think this?

The Sexual Response Cycle

In chapter 4, "Human Sexual Response," various models were described for understanding the predictable sequence of physiological events that constitute the human sexual response cycle. The Masters and Johnson (1966) model includes four phases: excitement, plateau, orgasm, and resolution. A three-phase model (discussed on page 94) is of greater value in understanding the relationship of sexual dysfunctions to sexual response (Kaplan, 1979). This model suggests that sexual response consists of three distinct components:

1. A desire phase, having to do with one's degree of interest in and desire for sexual gratification. Sexual desire is probably controlled by centers of the limbic system in the brain—centers that seem to activate as well as inhibit sexual desire. The desire phase precedes more profound physiological changes in the sex organs and throughout the body. This phase may be influenced by emotion, memory, and/or conditioning. Desire is usually an important component in the triggering of sexual arousal.

2. Sexual excitement, characterized by a buildup of blood in the genital areas that causes the typical signs of sexual arousal, such as penile and clitoral erection and lubrication of the vagina. This phase is accompanied by increased muscular tension and arousal throughout the body. It is controlled primarily by the parasympathetic division of the autonomic nervous system.

3. Orgasm, which triggers the reversal of the genital blood flow and muscular relaxation. This phase is mostly controlled by the sympathetic division of the autonomic nervous system.

Things can go wrong in any of these phases of sexual response. Table 18.1 summarizes the relationship of various sexual dysfunctions to the three-phase model. Each is described in more detail in the sections that follow. Many people seem to experience dysfunctions in more than one of the phases of sexual response.

lifelong dysfunction: a difficulty with sexual functioning that has always existed for a particular person.

acquired dysfunction: a difficulty with sexual functioning that develops after some period of normal sexual functioning.

Incidence of Sexual Dysfunction

Very little has been known about the incidence of sexual dysfunctions. It is assumed that many people who experience sexual disorders are reluctant to seek help because they would be uncomfortable discussing the details of their sexual functioning. The NHSLS researchers asked study participants if they had experienced particular sexual problems during the previous year for a period of several months or more. The findings are summarized in Figure 18.1. The findings are relatively consistent with those of studies done in other countries (Ventegodt, 1998).

The proportions of people reporting sexual disorders varied from about 5 to 25 percent, with the one exception that about one-third of women reported they had lacked interest in sex for several months or more. In general, women tended to report more sexual problems than men, except with regard to anxiety about performance and reaching orgasm too early. Ten percent of all the men reported having difficulty keeping an erection, and 19 percent of the women reported having trouble with vaginal lubrication. For both sexes, these problems occurred with higher incidence in the older age groups, although that trend was somewhat more marked for men than it was for women. This has been confirmed by other studies as well. Lack of pleasure during sex and inability to achieve orgasm were reported by women about three times more often than by men. In correlating these data with other findings, researchers found that people who reported themselves to be unhappy were more likely to report one or more sexual problems than people who reported being extremely or very happy. There was no way of determining a cause-and-effect relationship between these factors (Heiman & Meston, 1998; Laumann, Gagnon et al., 1994; Leland, 1999a).

Sexual Desire Disorders

Although most people can identify and describe inner feelings of needing or desiring sexual gratification, along with sexual fantasies, it is not yet well understood why the reported levels of interest in sex vary a great deal among individuals, as does the frequency with which they choose to have sexual activity. We do know, however, that these differences in sexual response, whatever their causes, can become an important concern. A discrepancy in level of sexual desire between two partners is a common complaint brought to sex therapists (Beck, 1995; McCarthy, 1999a).

It might be that low levels of sexual desire result from lack of activity in the brain centers that control sex drive, and this may in turn affect the levels of hormones that mitigate sexual desire. Surgery involving reproductive organs can also lower sexual desire (Galyer, Cona-

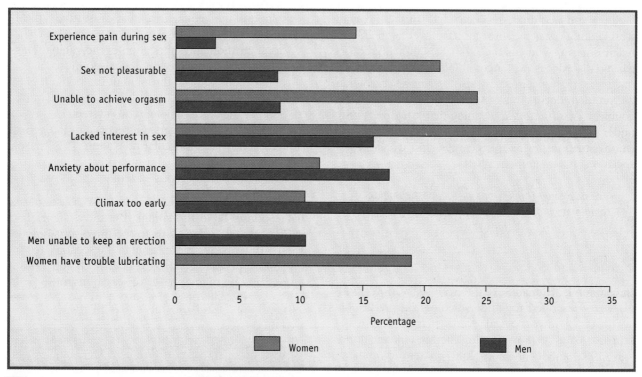

FIGURE 18.1   *Sexual Dysfunction, by Gender*

The percentage of people reporting sexual problems they experienced over several months or more during the previous year in the National Health and Social Life Survey.

Source: Laumann, Gagnon, et al., *The Social Organization of Sexuality* (p. 369), 1994, Chicago: University of Chicago Press. Reprinted with permission.

glen, Hare, & Conaglen, 1999; Warnock, Bundren, & Morris, 1999). Sexual boredom may play a role (Watt & Ewing, 1996). Sexual desire disorders seem to be more common in couples where there is less experimentation with sexual behaviors and a low level of pleasure associated with such experimentation. Diagnosing sexual desire disorders is somewhat difficult, because subjective judgments must be made about what is a "normal" human sexual appetite and how much distress the perceived lack of desire is creating. Although there may be no absolute scale of sexual desire, there are measurable discrepancies between people's sexual styles and interests (Kaplan, 1995; McCarthy, 1999a).

Some people seem to have very infrequent needs for sex and are not bothered by this. Even in a sex-saturated society, it is possible to maintain feelings of well-being and self-worth with minimal levels of sexual interest. It is also possible for some people to choose a celibate or sexually inactive lifestyle that represents a mature, responsible approach to life and is manifested by a suppressed sexual desire or at least a suppressed expression of the desire. This nonpathological way of life has been called **normal asexuality** and need not be considered a problem or dysfunction.

Sometimes, however, low sexual desire is viewed as a problem, and desire phase complaints are being brought to therapy clinics in increasing numbers. As a dysfunction, it is called **hypoactive sexual desire disorder (HSDD).** HSDD may be characterized by a loss of attraction to formerly exciting stimuli and a lack of pleasure even in direct stimulation of the sex organs. It may also result from a failure of sexual desire to develop during those years when it typically takes form. Dysfunctional individuals may not be particularly aroused by seeing attractive people, and they rarely seek sexual activity. They may still function normally when sexual stimulation is permitted, but the physical pleasure they derive from it is limited and fleeting (Kaplan, 1995).

There are some gender differences related to hypoactive sexual desire. Men with HSDD tend to be older than women, the average age for a male with HSDD being 50 and the average age for women being 33. Women with hypoactive sexual desire are more likely than men to report other forms of psychological distress, such as anxiety, depression, and hostility, and also to complain of higher levels of life stress. Women are more likely to have had another sexual dysfunction (such as arousal disorder) of long-standing duration, whereas men are more likely to have had another sexual dysfunction (such as erectile disorder) for just a short period before experiencing HSDD. For women, especially, HSDD is often rooted in other difficulties within a relationship that need to be resolved before sexual interactions can improve or become more frequent (MacPhee, Johnson, & Van der Veer, 1995; McCarthy, 1999b).

Sexual aversion disorder, characterized by fear or disgust about sex and avoidance of sexual activity is generated by anxieties and phobias about sexual contact (see Fig. 18.2). Some men and women develop fearful or avoidant reactions toward sex or its possible consequences and eventually become unreasonably aversive toward becoming sexually involved. These reactions can stem from psychological stress resulting from inhibiting or punitive upbringing, rigidly religious backgrounds, health concerns, or a history of physical and/or sexual abuse. Often such individuals become involved in close relationships and are successful in making themselves attractive to others. As the levels of intimacy and commitment deepen, however, there usually comes a point where they become fearful about sex. They may then find ways of sabotaging the relationship or finding fault with their partner, so they will not feel obligated to go any further with sex. They may, for example, become increasingly irritable or critical so that arguments are constantly developing. Research has shown that women are somewhat more likely to have aversive reactions to sexual activity than men, with more reports of sexual distress and avoidance, more fear of sexual intercourse, and greater concerns about HIV infection and unintended pregnancy (Kaplan, 1995).

It is often difficult for therapists to distinguish HSDD or sexual aversion from problems with arousal because individuals with HSDD and sexual aversions may also experience trouble in becoming sexually aroused. It will be up to the sex therapist to seek specific information about a particular person's level of sexual desire in order to make valid judgments about a proper course of treatment (Heiman & Meston, 1998).

Arousal Disorders

Whenever something interferes with blood flow into the sex organs, the human body fails to exhibit the preliminary signs of sexual arousal. In men, the penis fails to become erect or loses some of its erection. This has traditionally been called impotence but is now diagnosed as **male erectile disorder (ED).** In women, lack of arousal is characterized by the vagina remaining

normal asexuality: an absence or low level of sexual desire, considered normal for a particular person.

hypoactive sexual desire disorder (HSDD): loss of interest and pleasure in what were formerly arousing sexual stimuli.

sexual aversion disorder: avoidance of or exaggerated fears toward forms of sexual expression.

male erectile disorder (ED): difficulty achieving or maintaining penile erection (impotence).

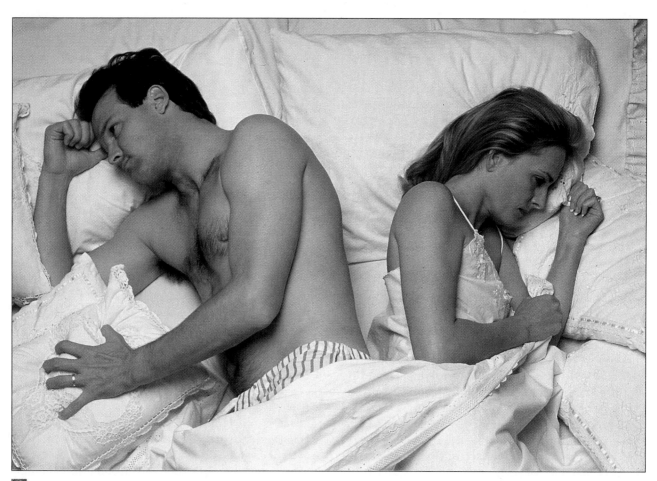

FIGURE 18.2 *Sexual Aversion Disorder*

An aversion to or fear of sexual intimacy is considered one form of sexual dysfunction. A real or imagined physical problem or psychological stress might cause someone to sabotage an otherwise satisfactory relationship in order to avoid sexual contact.

dry and tight. The term "frigidity" was once widely used to describe these symptoms, but it is no longer used by professionals because it is such a vague and negative label. The term **female sexual arousal disorder** is now the most widely accepted among professionals.

Because the control mechanisms in the brain and nervous system for the arousal phase of sexual response are different from those that control orgasm, it is possible—though unusual—for those who show few characteristics of arousal to be orgasmic. A man with erectile disorder may achieve orgasm, ejaculating with a flaccid (nonerect) penis. Likewise, some women who do not manifest the usual signs of sexual arousal such as vaginal lubrication and clitoral erection may still have an orgasmic response (Christ, 1998).

Although penile erection seems to be controlled primarily by spinal reflexes and can even occur in a male whose spinal cord has been severed above the erectile reflex center, the phenomenon is highly susceptible to input from the brain. Not only can thoughts, fantasies, and sensory stimuli trigger erection, but they can inhibit it as well. Most men will ex-

perience some instances of erectile difficulties during their lifetimes, typically as a result of fatigue, excessive consumption of alcohol, or simply not being in the mood for sex. A common pattern for the dysfunction is for erection to take place easily during masturbation, but to be lost during shared activities such as intercourse. Male erectile disorder can be caused by both physical and psychological problems or a combination of both (Heaton, 1998; Sbrocco, Weisberg, Barlow, & Carter, 1997). The older the man experiencing the difficulty, the more likely it is to be physically related. Because of potential organic problems, a thorough physical examination is crucial in evaluating erection disorder (Slob, Steyvers, Lottman, Van Der Werff Ten Bosch, & Hop, 1998).

There are several approaches used to determine whether erectile disorder may have physical causes. One simple and reliable method is measuring *nocturnal*

female sexual arousal disorder: difficulty for a woman in achieving sexual arousal.

CASE STUDY

Alan Tries a Medical Treatment for Erectile Disorder

When Alan first consulted a sex therapist, he was 42 years old and had been experiencing occasional erectile problems for about 5 years. For the previous year, the problem had become progressively worse, and he found it nearly impossible to achieve a full erection. After taking a full history of Alan's situation, the therapist concluded that there was ample evidence to suggest that his dysfunction might well be caused by some medical problems. He was referred to a urologist for further evaluation.

The urologist determined from a NPT test, and some further tests to examine circulatory patterns within the penis, that Alan did have some organic problems associated with his long-standing diabetic condition. They could interfere with erection. However, the physician also felt that at least part of the problem was psychological and that Alan had lost confidence in his ability to maintain erection during sexual activity. The urologist first recommended a combined approach involving both the injection treatment and further sex therapy. Alan learned how to administer injections of papverine di-

rectly into his penis, and this did sustain his erections for about an hour.

Alan was somewhat uncomfortable with self-injections, and when Viagra came on the market, he asked his physician to change to this method. When he took the medication about an hour before sexual activity, it worked well in giving him an erection that enabled sexual activity. As these treatments began to give him greater confidence in his sexual potency, he also continued to explore the sense of discouragement and anxiety he had felt for some time regarding sex. His partner also became involved in the therapy process, learning how to help reduce the performance pressures that had only increased the difficulties. After several months of the combined treatment, it became obvious that he was becoming more able to have occasional full erections without the medication. He knew that he had the medical treatment available as backup in case he had difficulty, giving him a greater sense of relaxation and confidence. This seemed to increase the likelihood of his achieving erection on his own.

penile tumescence (NPT), the number of times the man experiences erection while he is asleep. Normally, the penis becomes erect numerous times during a typical sleep cycle. If nocturnal erection is continuing normally, there is probably no organic cause for erectile difficulties. The man may be given a device that is attached to the penis at bedtime, which records spontaneous erections during the night (Montague, 1998). However, there are some indications that psychological stress may sometimes disrupt NPT, so there is a small chance that the cause of the erectile disorder might be misdiagnosed as physical when it is actually psychological (Maurice, 1999). Whenever potential organic conditions exist as a cause of erectile disorder, a thorough medical history should be taken, and some tests administered that, for example, may be used to determine whether blood flow to the penis has been hampered by damage to the blood vessels (Broderick, 1998).

Men in our culture place a great deal of importance on their penises and often consider erection to be one of the trappings of masculinity. They typically have adopted the unwarranted performance standard that good sex requires an erect penis. Therefore, experiencing erectile dysfunction can be devastatingly embarrassing and frightening for most men (see Fig. 18.3). They feel as if they are not whole men.

FIGURE 18.3 *Erectile Disorder*

Men in our society place great emphasis on their penises and a performance standard that may not be realistic for all people. Mental attitude, fatigue, alcohol, or organic problems can all affect a man's ability to have an erection. Failure to have an erection can lead to depression and further erectile problems.

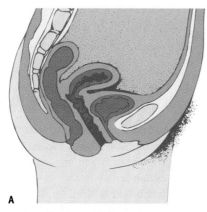
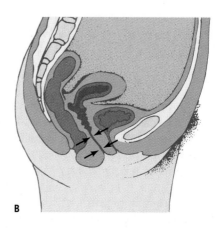

A   B

FIGURE 18.4   *Vaginismus*

Vaginismus is an involuntary constriction of the outer vaginal muscles, prohibiting intercourse. Vaginismus might be caused by ignorance of bodily functions or might be considered a physical manifestation of a psychological fear. The drawing on the left (A) illustrates the relaxed vagina, and the drawing on the right (B) illustrates vaginismus.

It is not unusual for men to experience trouble having an erection after having had some other sexual disorder for a period of time. If, for example, a man continually has trouble reaching orgasms or constantly believes he is disappointing a partner by ejaculating too rapidly, he may begin to feel frustrated and discouraged. He may eventually feel anxiety about any sexual involvement, and his body may fail to become aroused (DiBartolo & Barlow, 1996).

Women have traditionally experienced less pressure toward proving their womanhood by being able to become sexually aroused, primarily because they are at least physically capable of participating in sexual activity even without arousal. For the same reason, women are less likely than men to detect or report their own lack of arousal, and because they can conceive without ever becoming sexually excited or having enjoyed sex, little notice has been given to their arousal patterns. With increased attention given to female sexual response in recent times, however, some women have felt the need to fake arousal and orgasm to meet performance standards. Some women with sexual arousal disorder report that they still enjoy the physical intimacy of sexual contact. More often, unresponsive women eventually come to think of sex as something to be endured: They become trapped between their lack of physical arousal and their desire to live up to social standards of eroticism.

The partners of individuals with sexual arousal disorders vary in their reactions to the problem. Some are unconcerned because they care primarily about their own satisfaction. Others feel somehow responsible for the dysfunction and perceive it to be a function of their own unattractiveness or sexual inadequacy, and they may therefore feel hurt or disappointed. Oth-

ers recognize that such difficulties often do not signal any negative feelings toward them and simply accept incidents of this sort as temporary and transitory.

Vaginismus and Dyspareunia

The woman with **vaginismus** may occasionally enjoy sexual arousal and be capable of orgasms with clitoral stimulation. However, when an attempt is made to introduce a penis or other object into the vagina, the muscles surrounding its opening contract involuntarily (see Fig. 18.4). This holds the vaginal entrance closed and makes intromission impossible or painfully difficult. Some women with this dysfunction seem to be fearful about sexual intercourse or other forms of vaginal penetration, and they have misconceptions about the delicacy of the vaginal lining, believing that it can be easily injured. Some women with vaginismus are overly dependent on others or feel personally incompetent, although in general they do not seem to show unusually high levels of psychological distress (Heiman & Meston, 1998; Kennedy, Doherty, & Barnes, 1995).

Vaginismus is the major cause of unconsummated marriages (marriages in which sexual intercourse has not taken place). Because it interferes with sexual intercourse so blatantly, it is one of the sexual dysfunctions for which heterosexual couples are more likely to seek treatment. However, some heterosexual couples adopt alternative methods of sexual expression that are

---

vaginismus (vadg-ih-NISS-muss): involuntary contraction of the outer vaginal musculature when vaginal penetration is attempted.

CASE STUDY

Norman and Darlene Seek Help for Vaginismus

From the time they first attempted sexual intercourse, Norman and Darlene realized that something was wrong. Even during their foreplay, it was obvious that insertion into Darlene's vagina proved to be uncomfortable for her, and sometimes even painful. Intercourse proved to be impossible. For a time, they used other forms of sexual activity for mutual gratification, but when the problem persisted, they decided to seek help. Assuming that there was some physical problem, Darlene visited a gynecologist for the first time in her life. She had never had an internal examination before, and in fact had avoided them. During the examination, the gynecologist explained to Darlene that when insertion of fingers or a speculum had been attempted, there had clearly been an involuntary contraction of the outer vagina. She diagnosed the problem as vaginismus and referred Darlene and her partner to a sex therapist.

During the taking of her sex history, Darlene was asked to talk about any unpleasant or coercive sexual experiences she had encountered. For the first time, she was able to talk about an incident of sexual abuse when she had been a young teenager and also about an acquaintance rape in which she had been victimized during college. She had never talked about these incidents, except to briefly mention them to Norman. The therapist told the couple that such negative sexual experiences were quite common in women who were troubled by vaginismus.

The sex therapy consisted of talking together as a couple with the therapist and being assigned a graduated series of exercises designed to help Darlene become more comfortable with insertion into her vagina. Over a period of weeks, she began by inserting her own finger, and then allowing Norman to have control over the insertion. Eventually, she allowed him to use his fingers, and finally they were able to have intercourse. As the therapy process was nearing an end, Darlene reported that she had been enjoying a new sense of freedom and control during her sexual interactions with Norman, and she realized how much the tensions caused by her earlier traumas had affected her sexual well-being.

mutually pleasurable without intercourse. There are even documented cases of pregnancy resulting from semen being deposited near the vagina of women with vaginismus, without coitus actually having taken place. This should serve as a further warning to those who rely on withdrawal as a method of birth control.

It is quite typical for women who experience vaginismus to have had an unpleasant or forced early sexual experience. For example, those who have not been told that first intercourse may generate some pain and bleeding if a hymen is present may have a traumatic experience. There are other organic conditions that can result in **dyspareunia,** or painful sex, as well. There has been some research suggesting that women with dyspareunia may have some level of aversion and anxiety concerning intercourse (Wouda et al., 1998). These include dryness of the vagina caused by antihistamines or other drugs, infection of the clitoris or vulval area, injury or irritation in the vagina, and tumors of the internal reproductive organs. Such negative stimuli can easily establish fears of sex that are expressed through contractions of the vaginal musculature.

Gay men who participate in anal intercourse sometimes experience pain that inhibits their sexual enjoyment as well. Although this has not been widely studied, it appears that **anodyspareunia** is associated with the depth of anal penetration and rate of thrusting and with anxiety or embarrassment about the sexual activity. Lack of adequate lubrication often seems to play a role in generating the problem (Rosser, Short, Thurmes, & Coleman, 1998).

Orgasmic Disorders

Lifelong orgasmic disorder, in which an individual has never been able to achieve an orgasm, is far more common in females than in males. It has been estimated that from 5 to 20 percent of women are unable to reach orgasm through any form of stimulation (Heiman & Meston, 1998). There are very few documented cases of men who have never been able to reach orgasm, even through masturbation (Catalan, 1993). On the other hand, NHSLS data showed that between 5 and 14 percent of men reported some level of difficulty in reaching orgasm, at least in particular situations (Laumann, Gagnon et al., 1994).

There has been some speculation about why men experience this orgasmic disorder. One theory is that these men are so focused on their partners' pleasure, or have so many conflicting feelings about sexual pleasure,

dyspareunia: recurrent or persistent genital pain related to sexual activity.

anodyspareunia: pain associated with anal intercourse.

that they have what might be called a "numb" erection. In other words, even though they have no difficulty with erection, they do not experience many of the subjective sensations of sexual arousal and stimulation associated with orgasm.

Women, however, have not generally been given as much social permission as men for developing and enjoying their sexual responsiveness. As a result, more women experience orgasmic disorder, with a far greater range of variability than men. Orgasmic disorders are among the most common problems that women bring to therapists. It has been demonstrated that women with orgasmic disorder tend to have more negative attitudes toward sex, greater discomfort in communicating about sex, and higher levels of guilt over sexual matters (Heiman & Meston, 1998). In societies where there are fewer prohibitions on female sexual involvement and where sexual expression is permitted and even encouraged, women are less likely to experience orgasmic inhibition (Osman & Al-Sawaf, 1995).

Before reading on, can you think of some reasons that premature ejaculation might occur?

Premature Ejaculation: Lack of Ejaculatory Control

About 30 percent of men questioned in the NHSLS indicated they had a problem with reaching orgasm too early, although in other studies the incidence of this difficulty has been reported to be as high as 75 percent (Metz, Pryor, Nesvacil, Abuzzahab, & Koznar, 1997). Yet it would not be scientifically acceptable to assume that a substantial number of those men were dysfunctional and were experiencing what is termed rapid or **premature ejaculation.** As with much sexual behavior, the lines between normal function and dysfunction are not absolute. They may be largely culturally determined. For example, in East Bay, Melanesia, if men took more than 30 seconds to ejaculate after intromission, they would assume they had a problem. Clinical workers in the United States have variously defined premature ejaculation as orgasm occurring within 1 minute of intromission, or 2 minutes, and on up to 10 minutes, or prior to the man's accomplishing anywhere from 8 to 15 pelvic thrusts—arbitrary diagnoses, to be sure. Masters and Johnson (1970), acknowledging the arbitrary nature of their statement, chose to label a heterosexual man a premature ejaculator if he reaches orgasm prior to his partner in 50 percent or more of their coital experiences. This presumes that the partner is orgasmic within a reasonable length of time. More recently, a male has been considered dysfunctional if he persistently and recurrently ejaculates too rapidly for his own or his partner's sexual enjoyment, usually with minimal sexual stimulation, and is so consistently unable to exert ejaculatory control that one or both of them consider it a problem (Grenier & Byers, 1997; Metz et al., 1997).

There has been speculation that men who ejaculate rapidly might have a greater degree of penile sensitivity than other men, but research has not supported that conclusion. It has also been proposed that some men who ejaculate quickly may have a hypersensitivity of the sympathetic nervous system that renders it difficult for them to be aware of the sense of ejaculatory inevitability that typically alerts males that they are about to reach orgasm (Rowland & Slob, 1998). Under laboratory conditions, involving manual stimulation by a female laboratory worker or by vibrator affixed to the underside of the penis, most men seem to ejaculate within relatively brief periods of time. Under laboratory conditions, men who have previously self-reported premature ejaculation seem to take less time to ejaculate than males used as controls (Kameya, Deguchi, & Yokota, 1997; Rowland, Cooper, Slob, & Houtsmuller, 1997). The concept of a possible organic cause of premature ejaculation is relatively new and has met with opposition from some sexologists who believe it represents a continuing trend toward the medicalization of human sexuality. Nonetheless, studies have indicated some hormonal differences in men who ejaculate rapidly (Cohen, 1997). Other studies have failed to produce any consistent results that would help to explain why some men have difficulty controlling their ejaculatory response (Metz et al., 1997). However, some complaints about premature ejaculation seem to rest in exaggerated expectations about how long a sexual experience should actually last.

Premature ejaculation may not be related to timing so much as it is to a lack of voluntary control over the ejaculatory reflex. This is not surprising if we consider some typical ways in which males learn about their sexual responses. Most boys have begun masturbating with some regularity by the age of 15. Yet they usually have done so with little accurate sex information and with a measure of guilt. Therefore, they may develop a pattern of stimulating themselves relatively rapidly, reaching orgasm in a hurry. For some men, this rapid response might become habitual. Because of the intense arousal typical of their first shared sexual experiences, most males ejaculate quickly in these instances.

The end result of this conditioning can be a linear approach to their own sexual responsiveness. Men progress from the absence of arousal, through the stages of sexual excitement, and directly to orgasm,

> **premature ejaculation:** difficulty that some men experience in controlling the ejaculatory reflex, resulting in rapid ejaculation.

with little hesitation or modulation along the way. There is also evidence that anxiety plays a role in initiating rapid ejaculatory response, and physiological propensities may well be involved as well (Rowland & Slob, 1998). Men may feel disappointed and frustrated by their lack of control, but because they are still experiencing the pleasure of orgasm, they may not be urgently motivated to seek help with the problem (Metz et al., 1997). Often it is their partners, who are just building their own sexual arousal when these men ejaculate, who suffer the most. Continuing problems with premature ejaculation in a sexual partnership can generate conflicts and further sexual dysfunctions between the two people (Heiman & Meston, 1998). Partners who become angry and disillusioned by continuing patterns of premature ejaculation in the other partner may begin experiencing loss of interest and arousal for sex themselves.

Postejaculatory Pain

FOH This condition is a type of male dyspareunia, or recurrent painful sex, that results from a muscle spasm problem that can occur either during ejaculation or immediately after. This is a relatively rare difficulty, with one study finding the disorder in only 12 men out of 5,400 patients who reported sexual dysfunctions (Kaplan, 1993). The disorder is apparently caused by involuntary contraction of the ejaculatory musculature and some other associated muscles. Occasionally the cremasteric muscles that help control suspension of the testes in the scrotum are also involved. The result is intense pain following ejaculation. It usually subsides within a few minutes, but it can last longer.

Men who experience postejaculatory pain often develop a pattern of general sexual avoidance. Because their sexual activities end unpleasantly and uncomfortably, they may begin developing problems with erection or orgasm. Although the immediate cause of the pain is muscular spasm, there seem to be deeper psychological roots to the disorder. Many men who experience postejaculatory pain harbor guilt about sexual pleasure, are ambivalent about their relationships, and have repressed anger and resentment. Such inner conflict can add to concerns about experiencing pain and create a continuing cycle of pain associated with ejaculation (Heiman & Meston, 1998; Kaplan, 1993).

■ Causes of Sexual Dysfunctions

FOH The causes of any one person's sexual problems may be quite complex and involve overlapping physical, emotional, and relational components. Our understanding of the causes of functional sexual problems is based far more on clinical observations than it is on controlled research studies. Nevertheless, there are some generalizations that can be drawn from the information that has been accumulated over the years.

1. Sexual dysfunctions are most often caused by multiple factors. In deciding how to treat a sexual dysfunction, a sex therapist or physician must consider the range of factors that may be involved.

2. Some factors that cause sexual dysfunctions are of a *predisposing nature,* meaning that they are biological characteristics or prior life experiences that establish some fundamental vulnerabilities for eventual sexual disorders. A disease such as diabetes or a history of childhood sexual abuse may predispose an individual to sexual dysfunctions. It is then usually triggered by *precipitating factors,* such as alcoholism or job stress. Finally, there are *maintaining factors,* such as continuing relational problems, that perpetuate the sexual dysfunction over time.

3. Causes of sexual dysfunctions may also be classified into several human frames of reference. They may be inherently *biological* or *medical,* resulting from organic disturbances of the sexual response cycle. Dysfunctions are often *substance-induced,* either by the abuse of alcohol or drugs, or by the side-effects of prescription medications. They may be *psychological,* meaning that the processes of the mind, such as the stresses of performance pressure, are generating the disorder, or they may stem from a person's *social context,* growing out of relational tensions and poor communication.

Investigating Medical Causes

Prior to any treatment for a sexual dysfunction, any potential organic causes for the problem, such as an illness or anatomical defect, should be investigated. This may require an examination by a physician, including relevant laboratory testing. In most large clinics where sexual dysfunctions are treated, physical examinations are considered routine procedure. Many sex therapists, especially those working in private practice, require a physical examination by a physician only when a client's symptoms raise some suspicion of possible organic disorders. In such cases, referral would be made to a physician who possesses specialized knowledge.

Although dysfunctions such as premature ejaculation rarely seem to be rooted in illnesses per se, the possibility of organic causes exists. It is usually only if the onset of ejaculatory control problems is abrupt, following a long period of good functioning, that various potential neurological or urological disorders are investigated. The same may be said for vaginismus; it

CROSS-CULTURAL PERSPECTIVE
Sexual Dysfunctions in Other Cultures

Every culture has its own definitions for the meaning of sexuality, what constitutes a "normal" sexual relationship, the meanings of sexual dysfunctions, and how dysfunctions should be treated. Cultural beliefs have a strong impact on sexual functioning, and strongly held beliefs can make vulnerable individuals particularly susceptible to anxiety about sexual performance. The role of men and women in society and the expectations about sexuality play a crucial role in how sexual functioning is perceived (Osman & Al-Sawaf, 1995; Ventegodt, 1998). For example, in some Polynesian languages, there is no word for erection problems. It is simply assumed that when a male does not get an erection, he must not have wanted to have sex after all. Removal of performance pressures in such ways are exactly what Western modes of sex therapy have had to struggle to find ways of accomplishing. In some African cultures, it is preferred that women's vaginas be dry and tight for sexual intercourse, and many different herbal treatments and other techniques are used to achieve this dryness (Brown, Ayowa, & Brown, 1993). Although young women and men in these cultures have some ambivalence about the use of herbs and other agents for enhancing sexual enjoyment, and the techniques sometimes cause medical problems, people are also very knowledgeable about how to make use of the techniques (Pitts et al., 1994).

Most cultures have their folk remedies to allay men's concerns about sexual adequacy. Women's sexual dysfunctions are rarely addressed by these techniques, further evidence of the performance pressures felt by men in most parts of the world and of the lack of significance assigned to female sexual enjoyment. In some parts of Africa, for example, impotent men drink potions made of bark or resort to ritual ceremonies. Hashish is used in Morocco by dysfunctional males, and nonorgasmic women are encouraged to take a younger lover or have a lesbian relationship. In Thailand, men drink the bile of a cobra and the blood of a monkey, mixed in a local liquor. In India, men apply an herb to the penis that is a potent urinary irritant. However, workshops for people in India have been focusing on improvement of sexual functioning, and clinics have been emerging to treat Indian couples with dysfunc-

tions (McCarthy, 1998b; Verma, Khaitan, & Singh, 1998). Wives of impotent men in the West Indies may serve them the penis of a turtle marinated in wine or a soup made of ox penis and testes. European men usually treat their dysfunctions with various alterations in diet. In other parts of the world, seal testes and penises are consumed to cure erectile problems.

Traditional Chinese medicine has long made use of complicated herbal preparations and acupuncture, both of which are believed to bring the body's energies back into balance and restore normal sexual functioning. Even with the advent of newer treatment techniques in China, the traditional ways remain very popular. Some Chinese herbal plants, such as "ox-knee" root that is used for several sexual difficulties and milk vetch seeds that are used to treat premature ejaculation, have become endangered because of their widespread use (Zhigang, Xiaowei, & Shengbo, 1994). Traditional Western treatment methods are not always comfortable for Asian males, particularly those methods that suggest masturbatory activity (Gupta, 1999).

Although treatment approaches may differ significantly among various societies, they seem to be highly effective within the particular population for which they have been designed (Shokrollahi, Mirmohamadi, Mehrabi, & Babaei, 1999; Winston, Crane, & Ghosh, 1992). Lest we be too quick to dismiss the remedies of other cultures—or even those of our own—as superstitious and ineffective, it should be emphasized that modern sex therapy methods in Western cultures have yet to be fully tested by rigorous scientific standards.

As intercultural communication and mobility increase in our world, new problems are created by cultural differences between therapists and their clients when it comes to working on sexual concerns. If these differences are not resolved, they can interfere with the outcomes of treatment. Therapists must be sure to pay attention to processes of communication about sexuality, make their suggestions clearly, and be sensitive to issues that may be particularly uncomfortable for people from various cultures (Tafoya, 1995).

rarely has a direct organic cause. However, there are many diseases that can cause pain during sex, and pain is often the original stimulus that plays a part in the development of vaginismus. In treating vaginismus, it must be determined whether there are any painful conditions present that could further aggravate the spastic muscular contractions of the vagina (Maurice, 1999).

Sexual desire and arousal seem to be more susceptible to interference by physical problems. Any sort of illness characterized by general malaise, fever, or exhaustion can cause desire disorders, male erectile disorder, or female sexual arousal disorder. Because rather complex circulatory and neurological mechanisms are involved in arousal, any medical condition that interferes with these mechanisms will inhibit arousal. Spinal cord injury and blocked or diseased arteries leading to the genitals are common causes of arousal dysfunctions. It has been found that many men experiencing continuing erectile difficulty have leakage of penile veins, so that blood fails to be trapped in the erectile tissues. Diabetes often leads to the development of conditions that affect arousal, particularly erection of the penis (Hakim & Goldstein, 1996; Maurice, 1999).

Any painful condition in the body can interfere with the sexual response cycle, including heart conditions, lower back pain, sexually transmitted disease (STD) or other infection, and specific genital conditions such as cysts. Painful adhesions around the clitoris, for example, may make it difficult for a woman to reach orgasm. Male orgasmic disorder has few organic causes, although general systemic illness can interfere with orgasmic capacity.

In the past few decades, there has been some evidence that the pubococcygeus (PC) muscle, deep in the pelvis, must have good tone to permit a full orgasmic experience, particularly in women. Exercises have been developed to strengthen the PC muscle, often called Kegel exercises after the man who first suggested their use. He and subsequent researchers have claimed that women who strengthen this muscle are more able to build voluntarily the muscular tension that helps trigger orgasm. Some books on male sexuality have suggested that men's orgasmic responses can be heightened by strengthening the PC muscle as well.

Multiple sclerosis, brain disorders, endocrine gland diseases, lung disease, kidney disorders, and cancer are a few of the other illnesses that can be predisposing factors for sexual dysfunctions. Sometimes it is the individual's psychological reaction to a disease that actually precipitates the dysfunction. For example, those who have suffered a heart attack may be fearful of the exertion connected with sexual activity. Some research has gone into the determination of the limits of activity for various types of cardiac diseases, so that

patients may be given guidelines about exertion during sex. It has also been found that sexual dysfunction often occurs in men with kidney disease who have to undergo regular dialysis treatment. ED was traditionally thought to be rooted mostly in psychological causes. Recent work has shown, however, that many men who have problems with erection may have an underlying physical problem that can be compounded by psychological stress and worry (Montague, 1998). It is simplistic to view psychological and physical causes as mutually exclusive. Often, it is a combination of the two that leads to problems with erection. Table 18.2 summarizes some of the possible sexual consequences of various physical conditions that may produce sexual dysfunctions.

Alcohol, Drugs, and Medications

Many people experience their first sexual arousal problems after having drunk too much alcohol. As with other depressant drugs, such as barbiturates and narcotics, alcohol may at first lower inhibitions and cause people to feel an increased sexual desire. As concentration of the drug builds in the body, the physiological responses of sexual arousal are inhibited, leading to poor sexual performance. Some people believe that alcohol relieves sexual dysfunctions and even use it for self-treatment, when in fact it is actually more likely to cause the dysfunctions or make them worse. Although the research on cigarette smoking has not focused thoroughly enough on potential sexual problems, evidence is emerging that men who are heavy smokers are about 50 percent more likely to experience ED than nonsmokers (National Center for Environmental Health, 1995).

Many mood-altering or hallucinogenic drugs seem to have unpredictable effects on sexual functioning. Some—such as marijuana, LSD, and cocaine—are often reported to enhance sexual experiences when taken in highly erotic situations with positive expectations. However, the same drugs are capable of compounding negative moods as well and may even magnify preexisting sexual disorders (see Fig. 18.5). The placebo effect—the drug's perceived effect being generated by the consumer's expectations—undoubtedly plays a major role here. In addition, drugs such as marijuana and cocaine may enhance sexual satisfaction at first, but with chronic use begin to interfere with sexual responsiveness and pleasure. Use of anabolic steroids for muscle building has been found to be associated with increased erectile problems for males (Crenshaw & Goldberg, 1996).

Many chemical substances affect people's sex lives, by either producing changes in the level of interest in sex, diminishing general erotic pleasure, or altering the reactions of the genitals. Prescribed medications can

Table 18.2	*Organic Conditions That Can Cause Sexual Dysfunctions*
Sexual Dysfunction	**Potential Organic Causes**
Hypoactive sexual desire disorder	Diseases, abnormalities, or tumors of the pituitary gland Diseases of the immune system Infections, abnormalities, or tumors of the testes or ovaries Chronic kidney or liver disease, adrenal insufficiency, diabetes, hypothyroidism, Parkinson's disease, certain types of epilepsy, and strokes Diseases associated with chronic pain, debility, anxiety, or depression
Male erectile disorder	Congenital abnormality of or later injury to penis Multiple sclerosis or spinal cord injury Arteriosclerosis or blockage of blood vessels in penis Endocrine gland disease, especially if there is a testosterone deficiency Diabetes (probably impairs circulatory and neurological mechanisms of erection)
Female sexual arousal disorder	Estrogen deficiency, causing lack of vaginal lubrication Injury or disease of the central nervous system Multiple sclerosis, amyotrophic lateral sclerosis, alcoholic neuropathy Endocrine gland insufficiency, especially thyroid, adrenals, or pituitary Diabetes
Vaginismus	Factors that may cause pain or discomfort, such as previous surgery or vulvovaginal infection Endometriosis Rigid hymen or hymenal tags
Premature ejaculation	No documented organic causes, except the anxiety that may accompany various physical complaints
Female orgasmic disorder	Severe malnutrition, vitamin deficiencies Disease or injury of the spinal cord Diabetes Deficiency of thyroid, adrenals, or pituitary
Male orgasmic disorder	Injury to nervous system Parkinson's disease, multiple sclerosis, diabetes, alcoholism, uremia
Postejaculatory pain	Prostate infection or enlargement Infections of the epididymis or vas deferens Urethritis Other diseases of the penis

Sources: Data from H. S. Kaplan, *The Evaluation of Sexual Disorders,* 1983, Brunner/Mazel, New York; J. P. Wincze and M. P. Carey, *Sexual Dysfunction: A Guide for Assessment and Treatment,* 1991, Guilford Press, New York; N. McConaghy, *Sexual Behavior: Problems and Management,* 1993, Plenum Press, New York; and *Diagnostic and Statistical Manual (DSM-IV),* 1994, American Psychiatric Association, Washington, D.C.

exert profound influences over sexual desire and functioning and can be useful in treating serious dysfunctions. Antidepressant medications frequently cause a reduction in sexual desire or orgasmic capability (Ashton & Rosen, 1998; Labbate, Grimes, Hines, Oleshansky, & Arana, 1998). Some men who take phenothiazine tranquilizers are alarmed to find that they no longer experience ejaculation of semen at the time of orgasm. Other antipsychotic drugs may interfere with the triggering of orgasmic responses. The adverse sexual effects are usually reversed with a change in dosage or if the drug is discontinued. Some medications used to treat high blood pressure can cause arousal disorders. Stimulant drugs, such as amphetamines, sometimes enhance sexual awareness in small dosages but interfere with sexual responsiveness when consumed in larger quantities. Antiulcer medications and certain drugs for migraine headaches have been associated with disorders of hypoactive sexual desire and arousal (Crenshaw & Goldberg, 1996; Maurice, 1999).

Describe some emotional/psychological factors that you think might have an influence on sexual functioning. Be sure to include factors that influence male sexual functioning and factors that influence female sexual functioning.

Psychological Factors: The Pressure to Perform

Societally imposed standards of sexual performance reach almost mythological proportions for some people. The media add to the myths by suggesting that those who are physically attractive have sex all the time. People become convinced that all normal men get rock-hard erections on demand and have sexual intercourse for hours in every imaginable position without reaching orgasm, while their female partners writhe about in the throes of one orgasm after another.

FIGURE 18.5 *Marijuana and Sexual Functioning*

Sensations of touch and taste are generally enhanced by smoking marijuana, but increase in sexual desire may be as much a function of psychological expectation as of the drug. Testosterone and sperm levels may be reduced in some men by smoking marijuana, but the total effect on sexual functioning is not completely known. These youths in the Netherlands can easily buy and smoke marijuana in coffee shops.

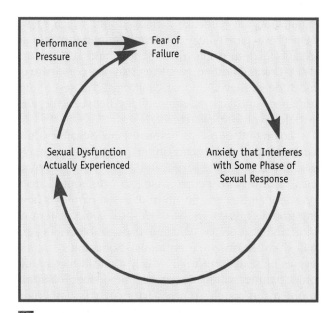

FIGURE 18.6 *Vicious Circle of Sexual Dysfunction*

Some people may be more prone than others to feel the pressure that society exerts to perform sexually. These real or imagined pressures may result in fear of performing adequately and ultimately produce sexual dysfunction.

They become convinced that all women must have size 5 bodies and flowing windblown hair. Both women and men may become so concerned about their body image that they are too preoccupied to experience the pleasure of sexual touch and intimacy, and they may actually avoid sexual encounters (Katz & Jardine, 1999; Werlinger, King, Clark, Pera, & Wincze, 1997). Even for those with less exaggerated sexual expectations, the pressures to perform can be enormous.

Stage fright is not an uncommon reaction to any situation in which a good performance is expected. It is just this kind of anxiety that can generate the typical vicious circle of sexual dysfunction that is shown in Figure 18.6. It is this pattern that can escalate what would have been an isolated sexual failure into a continuing cycle of sexual dysfunction (Adams et al., 1996). A term commonly used to describe the "stage fright" associated with sexual performance pressure is **spectatoring.** Instead of being able to relax and lose themselves in the sensual delights of the sexual experience, individuals may constantly seem outside themselves, wondering how they are doing and judging their sexual expertise, as if they were spectators at someone else's sexual event. They may also be especially conscious of their partner's degree of involvement and enjoyment in the sexual encounter. Performance anxieties may also revolve around poten-

tial negative consequences of sex, such as being caught while engaged in the act or fears of pregnancy or disease (Dove & Weiderman, 2000; Janssen & Bancroft, 1997).

Performance pressure is often rooted in an excessive need to please a partner. It is not unusual for a heterosexual man to assume that he is responsible for bringing pleasure to a woman, whereas heterosexual women are prone to believe they must serve a man's sexual desires and whims. One may also have a nagging insecurity generating continual worry that one's partner will become sexually bored or interested in someone else. All of these sources of anxiety are likely to interfere with sexual responsiveness at some level.

Relationships and Sexual Functioning

Many dysfunctions are rooted in problems that have developed in the partners' relationship. Lack of communication and intimacy is one of the most widespread of these problems (McCabe, 1997). Communication difficulties may be relatively uncomplicated at first, such as a failure to let one's partner know what types of

spectatoring: term used by Masters and Johnson to describe self-consciousness and self-observation during sex.

stimulation are particularly enjoyed and which might better be avoided. Left to fester, these minor relational irritants may turn into more serious and lasting conflicts. Communication problems may also originate at much deeper levels and be symptomatic of severe disturbances and lack of compatibility between the two people involved (Scharch, 1997).

Loving relationships have complex dynamics, and both the joys and discord in any relationship usually get played out in the sexual arena. When power struggles result in two people trying to gain control from one another, sex will be affected. If one partner is having trouble trusting in the other, or if some pattern of outright rejection has emerged, the possibilities of sexual dysfunction are enormous. Sometimes, subtle games of sexual sabotage, which result in turning off one's partner, will mask some of the deeper relational problems in couples. These factors may be important in determining the outcome of therapy for sexual problems as well. It is likely that the happier and more stable a couple's relationship is, the more positive and satisfactory the outcome of therapy (Lobitz & Lobitz, 1996; Schnarch, 1997).

▮ Treating Sexual Dysfunctions

Every individual troubled by a sexual dysfunction will have his or her own set of interacting causes (Heiman & Meston, 1998). Sometimes treatment can proceed without spending time elucidating all of these causes. Other times, an effective therapeutic outcome depends on the untangling of a complex web of medical, psychological, and relational causes. Because some people may be reluctant to seek help for such personal problems, home remedies and patent medicines are marketed that claim to cure various sexual dysfunctions. In the United States, males who are concerned about their lack of ejaculatory control sometimes purchase sprays or creams to be applied to the penis. These products primarily contain a mild anesthetic that dulls sensation in the head of the penis, but there is no evidence that they prolong sexual response. Men have also invented their own techniques for delaying ejaculation, such as wearing more than one condom or masturbating just prior to shared sex. They may try to distract themselves by thinking about other things, clenching their fists, or biting themselves to produce pain, or they may devise a number of other techniques. Unfortunately, such home remedies may only intensify the problem.

As they worked on developing a model for the effective treatment of sexual dysfunctions, Masters and Johnson (1970) realized that they needed techniques to help patients relax and restructure their behavior. Therefore, they were faced with the challenge of mod-

ifying psychological, relational, and cultural factors that were interfering with the physiological sexual responsiveness of the human body. They also believed that sexual dysfunctions could not be considered the problem of an individual but the problem of a couple, and so their treatment methods provided ample opportunity for sexually dysfunctional couples to learn more about their shared sexual feelings and responses.

Effective treatment for sexual dysfunction cannot be carried out solely in a step-by-step, mechanical way. Treatments must be designed and improvised for particular clients. The intricacies behind each individual and each relationship must be taken into consideration (Wiederman, 1998). It is, in a sense, an art to be practiced with skill and creativity.

Medical Treatments

Use of various medical regimens has been increasing in the treatment of dysfunctions. Because it is known that androgenic hormones such as testosterone have some influence on sexual arousal, there have been numerous studies on administering these hormones in order to increase both sexual desire and arousal capabilities. Although more research is needed, it does seem clear that the use of androgens can increase sexual desire in both men and women (Davis, 1998; Warnock et al., 1999) and that it can be successful in treating ED in men who have testosterone deficiencies (Heaton, 1998; Rakic et al., 1997). Some herbal preparations, although typically not subjected to rigorous scientific testing, have been used with some success in treating certain sexual dysfunctions, including ED (Cohen & Bartlik, 1998; Guirguis, 1998).

ED has also been treated successfully with muscle relaxants and a chemical called yohimbine (Rowland, Kallan, & Slob, 1997; Schiavi, White, Mandeli, & Levine, 1997). Certain antidepressant drugs have been found to slow down the ejaculatory reflex; thus, they have been used with some success in treating premature ejaculation (Rowland & Slob, 1998). Men who develop inhibited ejaculation because of such medications may be helped by changing to another drug (Assalian & Margolese, 1996). HSDD sometimes responds to treatment with medications, and, in cases of sexual aversion and phobia, antidepressant medications or anxiety-reducing drugs may prove effective (Perelman, 1998).

There are two medical treatments for ED that have received wide publicity. In one method, the man injects the muscle relaxant papaverine, or one of several similar chemicals that act locally within the penis to produce erection. A newer variation of this approach involved insertion of a tiny suppository of the chemical into the urethral opening, where it is absorbed into the spongy tissues. The erection may last for an hour or more, even after the man has ejaculated and feels finished with sexual activity (Christ, 1998; Heiman & Meston, 1998).

These treatments seem to work best when combined with appropriate sex therapy or psychotherapy. In cases where ED has psychological roots, the injection and suppository approaches can sometimes generate renewed levels of self-confidence that prove useful in overcoming the performance pressures that conspired to produce the problem in the first place.

One of the most significant medical advances to treat sexual dysfunctions in recent years has been the drug called sildenafil, popularly known as Viagra. When it was first approved for use in treating ED in 1998, it caused a media furor, and men rushed to their physicians for prescriptions. Viagra works by prolonging the effects of cyclic GMP, the substance that relaxes smooth muscles within the erectile tissues of the penis, allowing blood to flow in and cause erection (Padma-Nathan, 1998). Studies with Viagra demonstrate that it can be very effective in treating male ED, and that in most cases, side effects are minor and quite tolerable. It generally should not be used by men who have heart disease that necessitates taking medications such as nitroglycerin for chest pain (Balon, 1999; Rosenberg, 1999). Although the drug has not yet been extensively tested on women, or approved for the treatment of female sexual arousal disorders, some women have reported that it works for them as well (Mann, 1998). Yohimbine has also proven effective in the treatment of some women with HSDD (Piletz et al., 1998).

Although controversies abound about the dangers of medicalization of sex therapy (Tiefer, 1997), the evidence would suggest that medical treatments can indeed be effective, and their development will surely continue because the pharmaceutical companies are aware of the strong market available for drugs that will treat sexual dysfunctions (Segraves, 1998).

Biomedical Engineering Devices

Various sorts of vacuum and constriction devices and splintlike penile supports have been used to help men achieve and maintain erections, but their long-term usefulness has not been proven. They may also hold some potential risks for penile damage (Schuetz-Mueller, Tiefer, & Melman, 1995). Studies of the vacuum devices, in which the penis is "pumped up" within a vacuum tube and then a band is placed around the base, have shown the technique to be close to 90 percent successful, with a relatively low patient dropout rate (Heiman & Meston, 1998; Trapp, 1998).

In cases where some organic damage makes erection impossible, prosthetic devices have been developed that can simulate erection. They fall into two main categories: semirigid rods that are surgically inserted into the penis, leaving the organ in a somewhat permanently erect state that can be held in place by underwear, and inflatable tubular devices that can produce an artificial erection when surgically implanted into the penis (see Figure 18.7). Tens of thousands of these prosthetic devices are now being implanted annually, and they have a relatively high success rate. Repairs need to be made within the first five years in 5 to 10 percent of cases (Mulcahey, 1998). The ultimate success of the surgery, however, often seems to depend on the quality of the relationship between the man and his partner.

Psychotherapeutic Treatments

Although some dysfunctions are clearly rooted in negative emotional states such as anxiety, fear, guilt, or depression, others may be generated by unconscious psychological conflict. *Psychotherapy* is a term that applies to any one of a number of techniques that may help people resolve psychological problems. Psychodynamic therapy is usually a long-term form of therapy involving analysis of childhood factors and other psychodynamics that may ultimately result in unpleasant symptoms. In recent years, short-term forms of psychotherapy have gained in popularity, and they can be quite effective when they incorporate the specific treatment exercises developed in behavioral therapy.

Couples Therapy

A basic understanding of psychotherapeutic approaches to sex therapy is that a sexual dysfunction represents a shared problem, and therefore one to be worked on together. Sexual symptoms are often the outcome of a mixture of experiences that both partners have had during their lifetimes. Sometimes a dysfunction in one partner can actually act as a

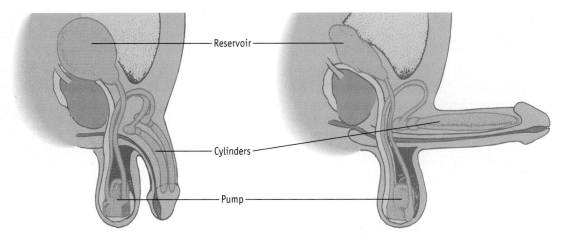

Reservoir

Cylinders

Pump

FIGURE 18.7   *Penile Implant*

If impotence cannot be cured, particularly if it is caused by an organic physical condition such as damage to the spine, intercourse can become possible by the implantation of a mechanical device. A reservoir filled with fluid is implanted in the abdomen. It is connected by tubes to a pump that is inserted into the scrotum, and this is connected to two cylinders that are slipped into the penis. To cause an erection, the man pumps the fluid into the cylinders; to reverse the procedure, he releases a valve in the pump, returning the fluid to the reservoir.

relationship or personal stabilizer for the other. For example, a man whose partner has vaginismus does not have to face any anxieties he himself may have about erectile function. Even liberal-minded and well-educated couples may be ignorant about one another's bodies and how best to pleasure them. Couples therapy provides a venue in which the couple may work together to improve their sexual life and focus on the relational dynamics that may play a role in the dysfunction and the therapy process (Hauch, 1998; Wylie, 1997). Couples sometimes decide not to remain together as a result of couples therapy, and this may even be viewed as a positive result of the therapy process (Vansteenwegen, 1998).

Hypnotherapy

There has always been some interest in hypnosis as a therapeutic approach for sexual problems. Hypnosis may be considered a form of psychotherapy that makes use of relaxation and suggestion in helping susceptible, or willing, individuals to change. Patients also need to be able to use mental imagery for mentally "rehearsing" situations that have formerly made them tense or anxious. There are case studies dealing with the successful use of hypnosis in treating a variety of sexual problems and dysfunctions. Hypnotherapeutic treatment is often used as an adjunct to other treatment techniques (Barham, 1998). Reports on the outcomes of hypnotherapy for sexual dysfunctions tend to be anecdotal in nature, and larger studies are needed. There are few generalized conclusions to be drawn at this time about the effectiveness of such methods.

Group Therapy

Group therapy has been successfully used with some sexual dysfunctions. Behavioral techniques are usually prescribed for individual patients within the course of treatment, and the group setting provides the support and information for the sharing of feelings necessary to a successful outcome. Barbach (1988) was one of the first sex therapists to employ group methods and developed a successful mode of treatment for women with orgasmic disorder, and group methods have been successful for men with ED or problems with ejaculatory control as well (Kanas, 1999). Even so, most people express a preference for individual treatment over group strategies, perhaps because the issues involved are often so deeply personal.

Behavior Therapy

Behavior therapy was the predominant mode of sex therapy for a number of years. Behavioral approaches typically involve the use of **systematic desensitization,** through which the patient gradually unlearns the tension-producing behaviors that are causing

behavior therapy: therapy that uses techniques to change patterns of behavior; often employed in sex therapy.

systematic desensitization: step-by-step approaches to unlearning tension-producing behaviors and developing new behavior patterns.

problems. Then more desirable behaviors are learned to replace the old dysfunctional patterns. Behavior therapy techniques still provide the basic structure for most psychotherapy-based sex therapy today. When used to treat sexual disorders, behavior therapy entails physical activities that are practiced at home by the couple, or in some cases as self-help approaches by single clients.

Most counselors and therapists are somewhat eclectic in their treatment of sexual dysfunctions, meaning that they combine therapy techniques in a variety of ways to meet the needs of individual patients as effectively as possible. Although they may draw methods from some primary school of thought, they recognize the need to be flexible and to keep pace with changing techniques and a growing body of research knowledge. Today, this increasingly means consideration of the medical treatments that are emerging for various dysfunctions (Althof, 1998; McCarthy, 1998a).

Surrogates

FOH Clients in behavioral sex therapy who do not have partners raise the additional issue of using **sexual surrogates,** or paid partners, for the purpose of practicing therapeutic exercises. In the early phases of their work to develop treatment strategies, Masters and Johnson used female surrogates to work with single men. These women were not prostitutes but instead were well-trained, sexually responsive women who were culturally matched with patients and who were able to cooperate in all of the behavioral exercises designed to improve sexual functioning. There have also been a few male surrogates who work with female partners. As might be anticipated, ethical difficulties arose with the use of paid surrogate partners because sex for pay is usually considered illegal and/or immoral. Masters and Johnson soon discontinued the use of surrogates, although some other clinics continue to believe they are the only viable option for single patients.

Combination Treatment Approaches

Given the growing consensus that sexual dysfunctions may have many different causes and that treatment strategies must be tailored to the specific needs of individual clients and couples, there is an increasing acceptance of combining treatment approaches in sex therapy. Psychotherapetic approaches have usually been eclectic in nature, meaning that they borrow from a variety of strategies in developing a treatment plan. With the emergence of apparently effective medical treatments, it is more crucial to consider these methods when working with sexually dysfunctional people. This requires closer communications among professionals from a variety of disciplines.

To simply prescribe a pill that will enhance sexual function may miss the relational dynamics that underlie a sexual problem. Focusing solely on psychological or relational problems may ignore legitimate medical conditions that are playing a primary role in generating sexual dysfunctions. Viagra, for example, can help a man regain his confidence in being able to achieve and maintain erection, while he and his partner work on the shared tensions that ED may have created in the relationship (McCarthy, 1998). Some individuals or couples may be resistant to using medications, seeing them as a failure of will and an unattractive "crutch" for solving the problem. Therapists can help overcome such resistance in patients (Althof, 1998).

Sex therapy is a rapidly changing field, and its future well-being may depend largely on the degree of flexibility everyone involved in sex therapy services can find in combining many different treatment approaches. There are many studies emerging that show the efficacy of combination treatment approaches (Bartlik, Legere, & Andersson, 1999; Gupta, 1999). For the good of clients seeking help with sexual dysfunctions, creative linking among the many disciplines that deal with sexual dysfunctions will be essential (Rowland & Slob, 1998).

What Is a Sex Therapist?

The term **sex therapist** entered popular usage in the early 1970s. Defined narrowly, the term refers to professionals who have been trained to treat male and female sexual dysfunctions. Counselors are now being trained to treat sexual problems as well. However, there is usually a broader context in which they work. Sex therapists and counselors attempt to restore sex to its natural context so that it can be a spontaneous human function and also to reestablish the positive pleasurable sensations and attitudes naturally present in childhood. They can help people enrich their sex lives, overcome lack of interest in sex, improve communication about sex between partners, and overcome specific sexual problems.

Because human sexuality is such a multidisciplinary field, professionals enter sex therapy from a variety of backgrounds. Some have had medical training as physicians or nurses. Some hold degrees in psychology, counseling, or social work. A few come from a background of pastoral counseling and hold degrees in religion. A national organization called the American

sexual surrogates: paid partners used during sex therapy with clients lacking their own partners; used only rarely today.

sex therapist: professional trained in the treatment of sexual dysfunctions.

Association of Sex Educators, Counselors and Therapists (AASECT) has taken the lead in establishing criteria with which to certify individuals who have met appropriate training standards as sex therapists. These criteria include not only degrees in one of the helping professions but specialized coursework in human sexuality and many hours of practical therapy work, under the supervision of an already certified sex therapist. AASECT was also the first organization to formulate specific ethics statements concerning how therapists were to conduct their work (see "Ethical Issues in Sex Therapy," p. 561).

Although the members of the sex therapy profession continue to call for strictly established guidelines to govern their work, state legislatures have been slow to enact regulations concerning licensing of sex therapists. This increases the risks for the consumer, because in many states anyone, regardless of training or other professional credentials, can lawfully call himself or herself a sex therapist and set up a private practice. Any new profession has its share of quacks and charlatans, and sex therapy has been no exception.

One way of finding a good sex therapist is to ask two or more trusted professionals whom they would recommend for help with a sexual problem. Sometimes an individual's name will come up more than once—probably a good sign. It is always appropriate to check out a sex therapist's qualifications directly as well. Consumers may wish to ask about degrees and training, the therapy model used, the kinds of records kept, the costs, and whether or not the therapist is certified to practice sex therapy by any professional group. More than half of patients do not seem to hold a particular preference for the gender of their sex therapists, but 30 percent prefer a female and 6 percent prefer a male. This may be one of the issues to be considered in making a choice of therapist (Kaplan, 1996). It is important to watch out for any sort of unethical behavior, such as a suggestion by a sex therapist that nudity or sexual relations with the therapist might be appropriate. It should be expected, however, that a therapist will ask rather specific and intimate questions about sexual functioning in evaluating the problem and deciding about a course of treatment.

One of the issues in treating sexual dysfunctions is the number of therapists to be involved. Some clinics still accept only couples for treatment and provide therapists of both sexes to work with those couples (see Fig. 18.8). Most sex counselors or therapists in private practice work alone and work effectively with couples. Lesbian or gay male couples may seek a therapist of the same gender. Some counselors and therapists will also agree to work with clients who do not have a partner available or whose partners are unwill-

FIGURE 18.8   *Co-therapist Counseling Session*

In the earlier days of sex therapy, couples were often seen by a co-therapy team consisting of a woman and a man as therapists. This model is still sometimes used today, since it may bring a more balanced approach to couples therapy. Even when there is only a single therapist, it is usually considered most beneficial to involve both partners in counseling sessions. This provides an opportunity for both to cooperate in finding solutions to their relational and sexual difficulties.

ing to participate in therapy. They use audiotapes, videotapes, online services, or other techniques designed specifically for clients without sexual partners. Certain types of problems are amenable to self-help approaches and do not necessarily require the cooperation of a partner.

The AASECT (P.O. Box 238, Mount Vernon, IA 52314–0238) and the Sexuality Information and Education Council of the U.S. (130 West 42nd Street, Suite 2500, New York, NY 10036–7802) can provide listings by mail, for a slight charge, of certified counselors and sex therapists, or of clinics that treat sexual dysfunctions. Anyone consulting a sex therapist should expect treatment that is conducted in a respectful, caring, and dignified manner. Potential medical problems should be investigated carefully. It is even appropriate to set some tentative deadlines by which certain goals are to have been met. If the results are not forthcoming, reevaluating the worth of the therapy process is certainly in order.

■ Behavioral Approaches to Sex Therapy

As discussed earlier in this chapter, behavior therapy techniques, involving the learning of tension-reduction techniques and more effective approaches to sharing sexual activity, are a mainstay of sex therapy. This section will provide an overview of how such techniques are employed in therapy.

Basic Goals of Behavioral Sex Therapy

Behavior therapy essentially involves unlearning ineffective, dysfunction-promoting sexual behavior and replacing it with more positive and healthy patterns. Sex therapists attempt to move their clients toward the following major goals:

Gaining a Sense of Permission to Value One's Sexuality

Those suffering from a sexual dysfunction often have long-standing problems in accepting and feeling good about their sexuality. Whether stemming from social pressures, religious training, parental attitudes, or previous negative experiences, sexually dysfunctional individuals may feel guilty and uncomfortable about their sexual feelings, attractions, and behaviors (McCarthy, 1997a). Therefore, a primary principle of therapy is to lend a sense of permission that it is all right to be sexual and that sexuality is a natural and healthy aspect of the human personality. Sex therapists encourage their clients to place a higher priority on sexual enjoyment, including saving time to work on sexual activities. Many sex therapy exercises are designed to help clients get in touch with their bodies, their sexual sensations, and their emotional reactions in more positive ways than ever before.

Taking More Time to Make Sexual Activity a Priority

We live in busy times, and in many relationships both partners have careers. Sexual activity may eventually take a backseat to other priorities in a couple's life together. In sex therapy, time is saved specifically for working on sexual problems. Therapists usually assign suggested activities and recommend a time frame for their completion. All of this helps the couple to develop a higher priority for improving sexual functioning.

Eliminating Elements That Are Blocking Full Sexual Response

The human sexual response cycle—starting with sexual desire and proceeding through sexual arousal, higher levels of excitement to orgasm, and then resolution—is a normal part of every human being. People seek therapy when some factor has interfered with all or a part of that cycle. Sex therapists, then, must work to eliminate whatever elements are necessary to restore full and satisfying sexual functioning. This means tracking down the causes of a dysfunction and then mapping out a realistic plan for correcting them (Maurice, 1999). This can be a simple matter of teaching

new relaxation and communication techniques (Hauch, 1998), or it may necessitate in-depth counseling for deep-seated personal or relational conflicts. If drugs or alcohol are part of the problem, they will have to be eliminated or reduced. Guilt reactions or other emotional blocks must also be overcome.

Reducing Performance Pressures

Sex therapy clients must learn how to stop focusing on their own sexual performance in order to relax and let sex happen. Behavior therapy provides techniques to distract people from this spectatoring and to keep their bodies as relaxed as possible. Partners are helped to change their emphasis from feeling responsible for giving one another pleasure toward working on their own sexual satisfaction.

Using Specific Sexual Exercises to Develop More Positive Ways of Functioning Sexually

Over the years, sex therapists have devised activities that can actually help a sexually dysfunctional person overcome the problem. These exercises are done at home in private and must be prescribed in a very systematic manner, with the opportunity available to talk about reactions after each stage. The sex therapist makes decisions about how quickly to move through increasingly intimate stages of therapy, depending on how both partners are progressing and feeling. These sexual exercises constitute the most significant route to behavioral change in this form of treatment.

Self-Help Approaches

Many sex therapists feel there is enough clinical data to justify prescribing self-help approaches to overcoming sexual dysfunctions, although there is little evidence to demonstrate the long-term effectiveness of such approaches. A few self-help guides are listed at the end of this chapter. Although the low cost and complete privacy of self-directed sex therapy are obvious advantages, it is also clear that many sexual dysfunctions can be effectively treated only by professional therapists. Self-help approaches cannot reach some of the more complex personal and relational factors that are at the root of many dysfunctions. The self-help guides may provide solid information, offer a positive beginning for many who want to improve their sexual functioning, and help people feel more relaxed in discussing sexual matters (Lankveld, Grotjohann, van Lokven, & Everaerd, 1999). Rarely can they effect a total cure.

Many therapists do suggest techniques for individuals to try at home on their own, not involving a partner. The two most common self-help themes make use of body exploration and masturbation. Many sexually dysfunctional men and women have never taken the time to become acquainted with their sex organs or even other parts of their bodies. Body exploration exercises involve viewing one's own body in a mirror and touching oneself to elicit emotions and physical sensitivities. Sometimes very specific directions are given to discover how various parts of the genitals respond to stimulation.

Masturbation exercises have proven especially useful in treating female orgasmic disorder and premature ejaculation. Once the orgasmic capability is well established through these self-help techniques, the woman gradually integrates her partner into the activities, teaching that partner the best approaches for bringing her to orgasm. Helping women learn how to have orgasm consistently has also proven valuable in the treatment of female HSDD.

As mentioned earlier, long-standing patterns of hurried masturbation may contribute to ejaculatory control difficulties in men. Self-help techniques that encourage men to slow down in masturbation have been effective in establishing more modulated forms of male sexual response that can carry over in the form of better orgasmic control with partners. Masturbatory self-help techniques may not be as suitable for individuals or cultural groups who have negative feelings or attitudes about masturbation.

There are other self-help techniques that can be used to reorient negative thought patterns about sex, rehearse fantasized situations with partners ahead of time, or learn patterns of distraction to prevent excessive focusing on one's own sexual functioning. There is general agreement among sex professionals that self-awareness, along with an ability to explain one's own sexual needs and idiosyncrasies to a partner, are important aspects of good sexual adjustment.

Partnership Approaches

FOH Most behavioral techniques used in treating sexual dysfunctions are prescribed for couples to use together. Therapists view the partnership therapeutic experience as being important in the couple's growing ability to communicate and function together sexually. Partnership approaches are used in graduated steps. Therapists usually need to be satisfied that each of the following stages of treatment has been mastered successfully before moving on to the next:

1. Learning how to enjoy and relax with one another's bodies while providing nonsexual touching and massage.
2. Providing each other with light genital stimulation, designed to be pleasurable, but without any pressure to respond with arousal or orgasm.

3. Learning how to communicate and physically guide one another toward the most effective forms of sexual stimulation.
4. Using specific exercises to reverse dysfunctional patterns and establish a pattern of sexual interaction that is pleasing and satisfying to both partners.

To accomplish the first three goals outlined, sex therapists prescribe various types of mutual body-pleasuring exercises, often called **sensate focus,** because they provide couples with an opportunity to develop and appreciate physical sensations generated by one another, bringing a physically pleasurable dimension into the relationship. An added positive outcome of sensate focus can be the reduction of power imbalances in the sexual relationship that may make one partner feel pressured, untrusting, coerced, or misunderstood (see Fig. 18.9).

The first phase of sensate focus activities involves nongenital touching. The partners are instructed by the therapist to be together nude, in as warm and relaxing a private setting as possible. They take turns giving and receiving gentle physical pleasuring that is not overtly sexual. With a minimum of talking, the giver provides caring touches to the partner in the form of massaging, tracing, and rubbing. The receiver has only to relax and enjoy the pleasant sensations, giving positive verbal suggestions for changing the form of touching if anything is in any way uncomfortable or irritating. After an agreed-upon length of time, the partners switch sensate focus roles. For many couples, these exercises represent the first time they have experienced physical intimacy and pleasure without the tensions and pressures of performing sexually. Obviously, such activities can be an important step in overcoming some dysfunctions.

In the second phase of sensate focus, light genital stimulation and teasing are encouraged, but without the goal of generating sexual arousal. The couple is in fact instructed not to allow sensate focus activities to lead to sexual overtures. Instead, they are told simply to enjoy and accept whatever sexual arousal may occur and then to let it dissipate. Again, sexual sensations are made a part of a relaxed, nonpressured context that is nonetheless pleasurable.

A final phase of mutual pleasuring typically involves some form of guiding procedure, in which one partner carefully shows the other how to give her or him optimum sexual stimulation. This will involve

> **sensate focus:** early phase of sex therapy treatment, in which the partners pleasure each other without employing direct stimulation of sex organs.

FIGURE 18.9 *Mutual Pleasuring or Sensate Focus*

some mutually comfortable position, in which the one partner can place a hand directly on top of the other's hand, carefully guiding it in genital stimulation. Figure 18.10 shows a position that is often used for women who are teaching their partners how to provide clitoral stimulation to produce orgasm.

The number of times that a couple participates in the various phases of sensate focus may depend on how well and how rapidly they seem to be proceeding. Therapists watch for potential resistance or other difficulties in the therapy process and try to ensure that positive results have been achieved at each stage before moving on (Sarwer & Durlak, 1997).

Sex therapists who employ behavioral therapy understand that it is crucial for couples to build a pattern of successful sexual experiences, reversing the series of failures they have been experiencing with the dysfunction. Therefore, during the early stages of treatment, therapists usually ask their clients to avoid sexual intercourse or other forms of sexual interaction that have been beset with problems. Gradually, as confidence and relaxation are achieved with each new goal, a couple will begin to attempt intercourse again.

It is also important to have a graduated and realistic strategy for bringing the couple back into sexual intercourse. Based on the assumption that most heterosexual couples in Western cultures use—and perhaps prefer—an intercourse position with the man on top and the woman on the bottom, the typical strategy usually begins with the woman in the top position. It seems to be effective in treating women's dysfunctions, because it affords them a greater sense of con-

trol over the sexual experience. On the other hand, it is useful in dealing with male dysfunctions, because they are more able to relax while their partner takes more of the responsibility for controlling the sexual action. This constitutes an interesting commentary on some typical causative factors behind female and male

FIGURE 18.10 *A Guiding Position for Clitoral Stimulation*

dysfunctions: Women often feel somewhat compromised by male-dominant intercourse positions, whereas men feel threatened by the weight of responsibility for sexual expertise usually assigned to them (McCarthy, 1997b).

An excellent intermediate step on the way to developing confidence with man-on-top intercourse is a face-to-face, side-by-side position that enables both partners to be more physically relaxed (see chapter 11, "Solitary Sex and Shared Sex"). Neither is called upon to support his or her full weight (see Fig. 18.11), resulting in a greater sense of shared responsibility. Sex therapists find that many heterosexual couples enjoy this position so much that they begin to use it on a more regular basis than their former man-on-top intercourse position.

The final therapeutic step, providing it is the desired goal of the couple, is to succeed in their usual intercourse position, with all sexual functioning proceeding as desired. Coital position may play a role in improving sexual functioning in other ways as well. One study showed that both women and men experienced more "complete and satisfying" orgasms when using a position in which the penis moves higher on the mons and clitoris and presses on this area (Hurlbert & Apt, 1995). Women who experience painful intercourse are often helped by positions where they are on top. Again, the process of overcoming a couple's sexually dysfunctional patterns involves a systematic process of desensitizing them to the tension-producing difficulties of the past, conditioning them instead to new, more mutually comfortable and enjoyable behaviors.

There are various technological advances that have been incorporated into sex therapy strategies. A number of erotic videos have been created to help demonstrate particular therapeutic methods to couples as well as to create sexual arousal. Other sex aids, including vibrators, body lotions, and other sex toys, are sometimes recommended to enhance couples' sexual

interactions (Striar & Bartlik, 1999). Computer CD-ROMs and online sexuality services have also been shown to have value in the treatment of sexual dysfunctions, and because of the possibility of using them in private, they have appeal to clients (Newman, 1997; Ochs & Binik, 1998). It may be anticipated that computer-accessed sex therapy tools will grow in popularity in the future.

Some Specific Behavioral Methods

Aside from the general techniques already described, there are specific behavioral exercises used in treating each of the sexual dysfunctions. An exhaustive survey of these techniques is not appropriate to this text, but some examples will be explored.

Vaginismus involves the involuntary contraction of vaginal muscles, making entry of the penis difficult or impossible for heterosexual intercourse. Because this dysfunction is almost always caused by fears and earlier negative experiences, it is crucial to help the woman learn how to develop a positive pattern of relaxation and pleasure with insertion into her vagina. The behavioral exercises used in therapy are therefore designed to reduce tension and permit this to happen. They might begin with the suggestion that the woman privately examine the opening of her vagina with a mirror, using some relaxation technique at the same time. Gradually, over a period of time, she will insert her little finger (or a small dilator made of plastic or rubber) into her vagina, also using relaxation. Eventually, the partner's fingers will be used in the same manner, but under the complete control and direction of the woman. In the final phases of treating vaginismus, the man's penis will be slowly and gently inserted, again with the woman having full control over how deeply and for how long this takes place. The ultimate goal is to achieve relaxed and pleasurable intercourse (Heiman & Meston, 1998; Vonk & Thyer, 1995).

FIGURE 18.11   *Side-by-Side Position for Relaxation*

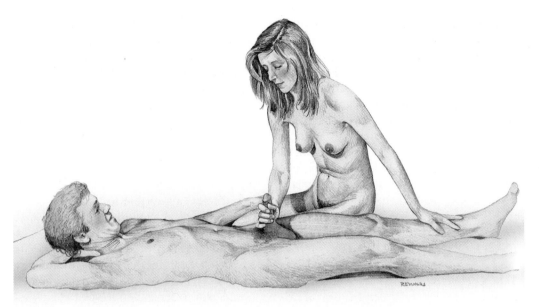

FIGURE 18.12 *Manual Stimulation of the Penis*

In the past, men tended to try to delay ejaculation by focusing on anything but their pleasurable sexual sensations. In treating premature ejaculation in males today, the emphasis is on helping the man to become aware of the inner subjective sensations that signal when his ejaculation is imminent. Men have pelvic sensations just prior to ejaculating that they need to identify, so that they may take some action to prevent orgasm before they have passed the "point of no return." There is a simple behavioral technique that many sex therapists suggest. Known as the stop-start method, it asks men to stop any stimulation when they feel the sensation of imminent orgasm. The sensations completely disappear quite rapidly, and stimulation may then be resumed. Most sex therapists recommend that the partner use slow manual stimulation on the man's penis at first, in a convenient position (see Fig. 18.12). The man gives a prearranged signal to halt the stimulation when he feels orgasm approaching. Some therapists recommend that the partner add the squeeze technique at this point, giving a firm squeeze to the head of the penis (see Fig. 18.13). This further diminishes the sensation of imminent orgasm (Rowland & Slob, 1998). Over a period of time, the man learns better control over his ejaculatory reflex and feels increased confidence in his sexual abilities. These behavioral exercises lead to the development of sexual patterns in which the man knows how to slow down and modulate his stimulation so that he takes longer to reach orgasm. In the intercourse sequence described earlier, he gradually integrates his control into sexual relations with his partner. During intercourse, the squeeze technique may also be applied at the base of

A

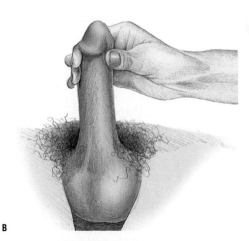

B

FIGURE 18.13 *The Squeeze Technique: Base of Penis (A) and Head of Penis (B)*

the penile shaft so that the penis need not be withdrawn from the vagina.

There are various specific behavioral methods used in the treatment of the other sexual dysfunctions. They help couples unlearn the conditions that have led to their sexual dissatisfaction and learn how to function normally and happily. Sometimes sex therapy aids people in saying no to sex when they are not in the mood or to particular sexual activities that they do not enjoy. Thus, sex therapists attempt to meet the specific objectives of their clients as realistically as possible.

■ A Critical Look at Sex Therapy

As a new field, sex therapy has only begun to be subjected to scientific studies of its effectiveness, and there have been few controlled studies to evaluate therapeutic outcomes. Progress and success in changing human behavior are difficult variables to quantify. Criteria for measurement are usually subjective, and researchers must rely on the self-reporting of clients, always subject to distortion and misunderstanding. Yet sex therapy is now considered a professional field that crosses several professional disciplines, and that attracts more practitioners and clients all the time.

Is Sex Therapy Effective?

The American Psychological Association has proposed two main categories of what they would consider validated treatments for various disorders, including sexual dysfunctions. One category, called *well-established treatments,* consists of those strategies that have been shown to work through carefully controlled group studies or large series of well-designed case studies. These treatments typically have manuals describing their use and clearly specify the types of clients with which they are most effective. The other category, termed *probably efficacious,* have—as the name implies—been subjected to less rigorous standards. This group consists of treatments shown to be effective in a very few studies or in studies less well-controlled than the other category. They usually do not have treatment manuals or clearly established guidelines for client identification (Heiman & Meston, 1998).

So far, the psychotherapeutic strategies for treating sexual dysfunctions tend to fall into the "probably efficacious" category. Valid scientific research must always be replicable. That is, the researcher must outline all of the experimental and control variables and analyze the results with statistical care, so that another researcher

could repeat the same procedures and expect similar results. Sex therapy has not been widely studied in this manner, and step-by-step treatment manuals tend not to be available. Many of the medical treatments for dysfunctions are new enough that data are continuing to emerge concerning their effectiveness, especially the various criteria of patients with which these treatments are most likely to lead to success. Because pharmaceutical companies have a greater financial stake in proving the effectiveness of medical treatments, they are providing funding for outcome studies that surpass any resources available for studying the effectiveness of psychological methods (Segraves, 1998).

Clinical results from practicing sex therapists would suggest that the outcomes of sex therapy tend to be relatively modest. Some dysfunctions, such as inhibited female orgasm and male premature ejaculation, seem to lend themselves better to standardized treatments than does HSDD. Those couples who continue their "homework" activities such as sensate focus into the late stages of therapy seem to have a better chance of positive outcomes (Sarwer & Durlak, 1997). Therapy may also be more effective with younger couples and those who have a higher level of positive regard for one another at the outset (Vansteenwegen, 1996). Some studies have suggested that sex therapy is not much more effective than less time-consuming medical approaches, such as administering a tranquilizer. Yet other research seems to support the contention that sex therapy can be highly effective when carried out over a full course of treatment by well-trained professional therapists, and when various methods of treatments are combined to meet the needs of particular clients (Althof, 1998; McCarthy, 1998b).

What are your opinions about sex therapy as one of the helping professions?

There is much to be done in determining the actual effectiveness of sex therapy. How is success in therapy to be judged: by the patient, by the therapist, or by an objective outsider? And by what criteria should it be judged? What methods are the most successful, and for what types of individuals? How are patients to be selected, and by whom? How long should sex therapy last, and how long should successful sexual functioning last before it is called a successful treatment? How expensive should therapy be? Most sexologists would agree that sex therapists should do more than restore desired sexual functioning. They should also provide a foundation for change within the individual and the relationship so that a relapse can be prevented, and they should assist in the correction of any medical conditions that may lie behind the problem. To this end, partners may also be helped to

FIGURE 18.14   *Mutual Understanding*

Sex therapists emphasize that communication and understanding are very important factors in solving sexual problems and developing a relationship that is complete and fulfilling for both partners.

establish more realistic sexual expectations of one another (see Fig. 18.14). Sex therapists can maximize the continuing value of treatment by encouraging occasional use of the behavioral techniques employed during therapy, continuing medical treatment as appropriate, and by suggesting follow-up visits if necessary (Maurice, 1999; McCarthy, 1998a).

Ethical Issues in Sex Therapy

Human sexual conduct is interwoven into our sociocultural values. Sex has become associated with a variety of moral issues. When professionals intervene in the sexual lives and decision making of their clients, there are also many ethical issues to be confronted. Work in sexology demands the highest standards of professionalism, confidentiality, and informed consent. Yet, professionals also bring their own sets of values to their work, and these values often influence the decisions they make about ethical behavior. Sex therapy has sometimes come under fire as being a white, middle-class, heterosexual phenomenon, lacking in multicultural awareness and technical expertise.

Sex therapists face their share of ethical dilemmas. For example, if, in the course of treating a married couple for some sexual dysfunction, one of the partners privately admits to having contracted an STD dur-

ing a recent extramarital affair, the therapist must make some decisions. Confidentiality has been promised, and yet the other partner may be at risk of catching the disease. The extramarital affair may have implications for the entire treatment process that cannot be explored so long as it is kept secret. The therapist may feel as though she or he has been drawn into a dishonest alliance with the partner who had the affair. Deciding how to proceed is an exercise in professional ethics for the therapist.

Ethical questions in sex therapy are raised daily. Who decides whether or not there is actually a problem at all? What methods will be used to treat the problem? Should masturbatory exercises be assigned to a client whose religion or culture sees masturbation as unacceptable? Should sexual intercourse be prescribed for an unmarried client?

AASECT has promulgated its own code of ethics. It deals with several basic issues, designed to protect clients from exploitation or incompetence. The main points of this code are as follows:

1. Sex therapists must receive adequate training and have a strong sense of integrity.
2. Strict standards of confidentiality must govern a sex therapist's work, and there should be no disclosure of information about a client without the individual's written consent.
3. Because clients are often in a vulnerable position, their welfare is to be protected and respected at all times by the therapist.

In making this final point, the AASECT Code of Ethics places strict limitations on nudity of clients and therapists and on the use of sexual surrogates as partners during therapy. Sexual contact between therapists and their clients has been a major concern in sex therapy ethics and has been the subject of some lawsuits.

All helping professions face their share of ethical dilemmas. Codes of ethics establish general guidelines but can never offer hard and fast advice to be used in a specific complicated case. It is crucial for sex therapists, as well as others in the helping professions, to understand their own value systems regarding sexuality and to sort through all of the moral and ethical issues involved.

It does seem clear that sex therapists must be cautious not to isolate the functioning of human sex organs too much from the psychology of each partner's personality or the more complex issues of a couple's relationship. Because human sexual response depends on an interaction of biological, psychological, relational, sociological, and cultural factors, the treatment of problems in responsiveness cannot proceed in a vacuum that focuses only on one factor (McCarthy, 1998b).

Sex therapy has often been restrictive, available only to heterosexual couples who could afford the luxury of full sexual enjoyment. Only recently have some therapists begun to treat other groups. There are individuals who desire treatment for sexual dysfunctions alone, either because the dysfunction has prevented them from finding partners or because their partners are unwilling to participate. There are same-gender couples who want to improve their sexual interactions, and sex therapy methods have proved to be successful with lesbian and gay male couples (MacDonald, 1998).

As professional organizations and state legislatures continue to examine these issues and to clarify standards for the training and licensing of sex therapists, the efficacy, methods, and ethical standards of the therapy process will also be clarified.

Chapter Summary

1. Individual differences in sexual responsiveness should be considered to determine whether a true dysfunction is present.

2. Every culture sets its own sexual performance standards—sometimes unrealistic ones. These may become debilitating pressures and unfair expectations for men and women.

3. The labels given sexual dysfunctions may carry negative or positive connotations.

4. Scientific terminology dictates that sexual dysfunctions may be lifelong or acquired, generalized or situational.

5. Sexual dysfunctions represent disruption with one or more of the three major phases of the human sexual response cycle: desire, arousal, or orgasm.

6. Individuals who have impaired desire for sexual gratification may be experiencing hypoactive sexual desire disorder (HSDD).

7. Sexual aversion disorder is characterized by fears about and avoidance of sexual activity.

8. Arousal problems are expressed as male erectile disorder (ED), involving interference with penile erection, or female sexual arousal disorder, characterized by an absence of vaginal lubrication and other signs of sexual excitement.

9. Vaginismus is caused by involuntary spasms of the outer vaginal musculature, resulting in difficulty with insertion into the vagina. Pain associated with sexual activity is called dyspareunia.

10. Both men and women can experience orgasmic disorder.

11. Premature ejaculation in males may well be a conditioned response and is the most common sexual dysfunction in men.

12. Postejaculatory pain is a relatively rare disorder involving involuntary muscular spasms that create pain associated with ejaculation in males.

13. Sexual dysfunctions may have causes at several different levels involving predisposing factors, precipitating factors, and/or maintaining factors. Causes may also be biological or medical (organic), substance-induced, psychological, or social/relational.

14. Performance pressures and difficulties in relationships (such as poor communication) are often at the root of sexual dysfunctions, although possible medical causes must first be investigated.

15. Alcohol, drugs, and medications can play a role in interfering with sexual response.

16. Behavioral techniques are widely used treatment by sex therapists, although medical treatments are becoming more common.

17. Oral medications such as Viagra or injection and suppository applications directly into the penis are sometimes used to treat ED. Medications are also used to treat premature ejaculation and HSDD.

18. Prosthetic and vacuum devices have also been used with some cases of male ED.

19. Psychotherapy, couples therapy, hypnosis, and group therapy have all been used to treat sexual dysfunctions.

20. The ethics, training standards, and certification standards for sex therapists are still being developed by national professional organizations.

21. For sex therapy clients without partners, sexual surrogates have sometimes been available, but this is not common practice today.

22. Behavioral sex therapy helps dysfunctional individuals to unlearn ineffective behaviors and replace them with positive, effective patterns of sexual interaction.

23. Specific homework exercises are assigned to those in therapy, using both self-help and partnership approaches.

24. There is debate about the actual effectiveness of sex therapy, and methods have been classified as well-established or probably efficacious in terms of their effectiveness.

25. Sex therapy raises certain ethical issues and dilemmas, and specific guidelines have been developed for the ethical conduct of therapists.

26. Sex therapy has gradually been made available to multicultural groups and to same-gender couples.

Focus on Health Questions

You will find in this section the kinds of questions that you may have concerning your own health and sexuality. The page references indicate where in the text the answer is located; the exact place is marked with the logo: **FoH**

1. I don't always have an orgasm when I have sex. My partner thinks this is a problem, but I feel perfectly satisfied with things the way they are. Do I have a problem? 534

2. My partner never seems to be interested in sex anymore. What is going on? 538

3. I have been having difficulty maintaining an erection. Is there any way to find out if this is a physical problem, or whether it is something going on in my mind? 539–542

4. What could cause sexual intercourse to be painful? 542–543

5. I think I ejaculate too soon, although my partner doesn't complain. Could I have a problem with premature ejaculation? 544

6. What could be going on if sometimes after I ejaculate, I get a pain inside my genitals? 545

7. What causes the body not to function sexually the way one would expect it to? 545

8. Will I perform better, sexually, if I have a few alcoholic drinks first? 547

9. If I'm taking prescribed medications, will they affect my sexual performance? 548

10. What is meant by "performance pressure"? 548

11. How does Viagra work, and is it always effective for men with erectile disorder? 551

12. If I go to a sex therapist, will I have to perform sexually with a stranger? 553

13. What is the best way to find a reliable and experienced sex therapist? 554

14. How can I practice being more relaxed sexually with my partner? 556

15. Does sex therapy always work? 560

16. Will a sex therapist need to examine my body or watch me do anything sexual? 561

Annotated Readings

Barbach, L. (1997). *Loving together: Sexual enrichment program*. Bristol, PA: Brunner/Mazel. A series of practical workbooks that may be used by individuals and couples for treating various sexual dysfunctions.

Bechtel, S., Stains, L. R., & Editors of Men's Health Books. (1998). *Sex: A man's guide*. New York: Berkley Books. Expert advice for men on well over 100 sexual topics.

Dunas, F., & Goldberg, P. (1998). *Passion play: Ancient secrets for a lifetime of health and happiness through sensational sex*. New York: Riverhead Books. A collection of healing techniques from Eastern traditions that can improve and enhance sexual function.

Haffner, D. W., & Schwartz, P. (1998). *What I've learned about sex: Wisdom from leading sex educators, therapists, and researchers*. New York: Perigee Books. These two highly respected sexologists have collected snippets of useful, easily applicable sexual information that could be helpful to any reader.

Heiman, J. R., & LoPiccolo, J. (1992). *Becoming orgasmic: A sexual and personal growth program for women*. New York: Fireside Books. Based on a wealth of experience from two highly respected sex therapists, this book presents a step-by-step approach to becoming orgasmic.

Kaplan, H. S. (1989). *How to overcome premature ejaculation*. Bristol, PA: Brunner/Mazel. Offers specific suggestions that men and their partners may use to slow down ejaculatory response. It sensitively discusses obstacles that may be encountered.

Klein, M. (1992). *Ask me anything: A sex therapist answers the most important questions for the 90s*. New York: Simon & Schuster. This comprehensive guide employs a question-and-answer format that presents sexual information in a down-to-earth style. Issues of sexual functioning are also addressed.

Maurice, W. L. (1999). *Sexual medicine in primary care.* St. Louis, MO: Mosby. A book designed as a guide for primary care physicians, it also has good information to share for intelligent lay readers.

Rosen, R. C., & Leiblum, S. R. (Eds.). (1995). *Case studies in sex therapy.* New York: Guilford. A fascinating collection of papers relating to the wide range of sexual dysfunctions and various approaches to treating them.

Schnarch, D. M. (1991). *Constructing the sexual crucible: An integration of sexual and marital therapy.* New York: W. W. Norton. This book offers an interesting perspective on the interconnectedness of the sexual relationship and the marital relationship. Not easy reading.

Sternberg, R. J., & Hojjat, M. (Eds.). (1997). *Satisfaction in close relationships.* New York: Guilford Press. A collection of 15 chapters that focus on various dimensions of maintaining happy and healthy sexual and loving relationships.

Zilbergeld, B. (1992). *The new male sexuality.* New York: Bantam Books. A very comprehensive book on male sexuality, with special emphasis on male sexual dysfunctions and how to deal with them.

Glossary

A

abnormal anything considered not to be normal, that is, not conforming to the subjective standards a social group has established as the norm. 198

abortifacients substances that cause termination of pregnancy. 329

acquaintance (date) rape a sexual encounter forced by someone who is known to the victim. 461

acquired dysfunction a difficulty with sexual functioning that develops after some period of normal sexual functioning. 537

acquired immunodeficiency syndrome fatal disease caused by a virus that is transmitted through the exchange of bodily fluids, primarily in sexual activity and intravenous drug use. 508

activating effect the direct influence some hormones can have on activating or deactivating sexual behavior. 109

acute urethral syndrome infection or irritation of the urethra. 50

adolescence period of emotional, social, and physical transition from childhood to adulthood. 166

affectional relating to feelings or emotions, such as romantic attachments. 203

afterbirth the tissues expelled after childbirth, including the placenta, the remains of the umbilical cord, and fetal membranes. 295

agenesis (absence) of the penis (ae-JEN-a-ses) a congenital condition in which the penis is undersized and nonfunctional. 81

AIDS acquired immunodeficiency syndrome. 508

amniocentesis a process whereby medical problems with a fetus can be determined while it is still in the womb; a needle is inserted into the amniotic sac, amniotic fluid is withdrawn, and fetal cells are examined. 289

amnion (AM-nee-on) a thin membrane that forms a closed sac around the embryo; the sac is filled with amniotic fluid, which protects and cushions the embryo. 272

anal intercourse insertion of the penis into the rectum of a partner. 356

androgen a male hormone, such as testosterone, that affects physical development, sexual desire, and behavior. Testosterone is produced by both male and female sex glands and influences each sex in varying degrees. 109

androgen insensitivity syndrome a developmental condition in which cells do not respond to fetal androgen, so that chromosomally male (XY) fetuses develop external female genitals. There also is a feminization of later behavioral patterns. 125

androgyny (an-DROJ-a-nee) the presence of high frequencies of both masculine and feminine behaviors and traits in the same individual. 130

anejaculation lack of ejaculation at the time of orgasm. 84

anodyspareunia pain associated with anal intercourse. 543

anorchism (a-NOR-kiz-um) rare birth defect in which both testes are lacking. 75

anti-Müllerian hormone secretion of the fetal testes that prevents further development of female structures from the Müllerian ducts. 120

aphrodisiacs (af-ro-DEE-zee-aks) foods or chemicals purported to foster sexual arousal; they are believed to be more myth than fact. 357

areola (a-REE-a-la) darkened, circular area of skin surrounding the nipple of the breast. 55

artificial embryonation a process in which the developing embryo is flushed from the uterus of the donor woman 5 days after fertilization and placed in another woman's uterus. 283

artificial insemination injection of the sperm cells of a male into a woman's vagina, with the intention of conceiving a child. 278

asceticism (a-SET-a-siz-um) usually characterized by celibacy, this philosophy emphasizes spiritual purity through self-denial and self-discipline. 212

asexuality a condition characterized by a low interest in sex. 401

autoerotic asphyxiation accidental death from pressure placed around the neck during masturbatory behavior. 418

autofellatio (fe-LAY-she-o) a male providing oral stimulation to his own penis, an act most males do not have the physical agility to perform. 348

B

Bartholin's glands (BAR-tha-lenz) small glands located in the opening through the minor lips that produce some secretion during sexual arousal. 45

behavior therapy therapy that uses techniques to change patterns of behavior; often employed in sex therapy. 552

benign prostatic hyperplasia (BPH) enlargement of the prostate gland that is not caused by malignancy. 82

bestiality (beest-ee-AL-i-tee) a human being's having sexual contact with an animal. 418

biological essentialism a theory that human traits and behaviors are primarily formed by inborn biological determinants such as genes and hormonal secretions, rather than by environmental influences. 14

biphobia prejudice, negative attitudes, and misconceptions relating to bisexual people and their lifestyles. 210

birth canal term applied to the vagina during the birth process. 294

birthing rooms special areas in the hospital, decorated and furnished in a nonhospital way, set aside for giving birth; the woman remains here to give birth rather than being taken to a separate delivery room. 297

bisexual refers to some degree of sexual activity with or attraction to members of both sexes. 204

blastocyst the ball of cells, after 5 days of cell division, that has developed a fluid-filled cavity in its interior; it has entered the uterine cavity. 272

bond the emotional link between parent and child created by cuddling, cooing, and physical and eye contact early in the newborn's life. 297

bondage tying, restraining, or applying pressure to body parts as part of sexual arousal. 417

brachioproctic activity a sexual activity, sometimes called "fisting" in slang, involving insertion of the hand into a partner's rectum. 358

brothels houses of prostitution. 413

bulbourethral glands another term for Cowper's glands. 82

C

call boys highly paid male prostitutes. 413

call girls highly paid female prostitutes who work by appointment with an exclusive clientele. 414

cantharides (kan-THAR-a-deez) a chemical extracted from a beetle that, when taken internally, creates irritation of blood vessels in the genital region; it can cause physical harm. 357

case study   an in-depth look at a particular individual and how he or she might be helped to solve a sexual or other problem. Case studies may offer new and useful ideas for counselors to use with other patients. 34

catharsis theory   suggests that viewing pornography provides a release for sexual tension, thus preventing antisocial behavior. 435

celibacy (SELL-a-ba-see)   choosing not to share sexual activity with others. 401

central arousal system   internal components of sexual arousal that come from the cognitive and emotional centers of the brain, forming the foundations for sexual response. 97

cervical cap   a device that is shaped like a large thimble and fits over the cervix; not a particularly effective contraceptive because it can dislodge easily during intercourse. 323

cervical intraepithelial neoplasia (CIN) (ep-a-THEE-lee-al nee-a-PLAY-zhee-a)   abnormal, precancerous cells sometimes identified in a Pap smear. 54

cervix (SERV-ix)   lower "neck" of the uterus that extends into the back part of the vagina. 51

cesarian section   a surgical method of childbirth in which delivery occurs through an incision in the abdominal wall and uterus. 294

chancroid (SHAN-kroyd)   an STD caused by the bacterium Hemophilus ducreyi and characterized by sores on the genitals, which, if left untreated, could result in pain and rupture of the sores. 497

child molesting   sexual abuse of a child by an adult. 466

chlamydia (kluh-MID-ee-uh)   now known to be a common STD, this organism is a major cause of urethritis in males; in females it often presents no symptoms. 487

chorion (KOR-ee-on)   the outermost extraembryonic membrane, essential in the formation of the placenta. 272

chorionic villi sampling (CVS)   a technique for diagnosing medical problems in the fetus as early as the 8th week of pregnancy; a sample of the chorionic membrane is removed through the cervix and studied. 289

cilia   microscopic, hairlike projections that help move the ovum through the fallopian tube. 53

circumcision   of clitoris—surgical procedure that cuts the prepuce, exposing the clitoral shaft; in the male, surgical removal of the foreskin from the penis. 46, 79

climax   another term for orgasm. 94

clinical research   the study of the cause, treatment, or prevention of a disease or condition by testing large numbers of people. 35

clitoridectomy   surgical removal of the clitoris; practiced routinely in some cultures. 46

clitoris (KLIT-a-rus)   sexually sensitive organ found in the female vulva; it becomes engorged with blood during arousal. 45

clone   the genetic-duplicate organism produced by the cloning process. 286

cloning   a process by which a genetic duplicate of an organism is made either by substituting the chromosomes of a body cell into a donated ovum or by separation of cells in early embryonic development. 286

cohabitation   living together and sharing sex without marrying. 181

coitus (KO-at-us *or* ko-EET-us)   heterosexual, penis-in-vagina intercourse. 200

coitus interruptus (KO-at-us *or* ko-EET-us)   a method of birth control in which the penis is withdrawn from the vagina prior to ejaculation. 319

coming out   to acknowledge to oneself and others that one is lesbian, gay, or bisexual. 387

comprehensive sexuality education   an approach to educating young people about human sexuality that includes information about sexuality, but also encourages clarifying values and developing decision-making skills. 217

computerized sperm selection   use of computer scanning to identify the most viable sperm, which are then extracted to be used for fertilization of an ovum in the laboratory. 281

Comstock Laws   enacted in the 1870s, this federal legislation prohibited the mailing of information about contraception. 315

conception   the process by which a sperm unites with an egg, normally joining 23 pairs of chromosomes to establish the genetic "blueprint" for a new individual. The sex chromosomes establish its sex   XX for female and XY for male. 118

congenital adrenal hyperplasia   a genetic disorder that masculinizes chromosomal females, and seems to lead to a masculinization of behavior as well. 124

consensual adultery   permission given to at least one partner within the marital relationship to participate in extramarital sexual activity. 184

contraceptive implants   contraceptive method in which hormone-releasing rubber cylinders are surgically inserted under the skin. 321

controlled experiment   research in which the investigator examines what is happening to one variable while all the other variables are kept constant. 36

coprophilia   sexual arousal connected with feces. 417

core gender identity   a child's early inner sense of its maleness, femaleness, or ambivalence, established prior to puberty. 127

corona   the ridge around the penile glans. 75

corpus luteum   cell cluster of the follicle that remains after the ovum is released, secreting hormones that help regulate the menstrual cycle. 61

Cowper's glands   two small glands in the male that secrete an alkaline fluid into the urethra during sexual arousal. 82

cryptorchidism (krip-TOR-ka-diz-um)   condition in which the testes have not descended into the scrotum prior to birth. 75

cunnilingus (kun-a-LEAN-gus)   oral stimulation of the clitoris, vaginal opening, or other parts of the vulva. 354

cyclic GMP   a secretion within the spongy erectile tissues of the penis that facilitates erection. 77

cystitis (sis-TITE-us)   a nonsexually transmitted infection of the urinary bladder. 50

DAX-1   the region on the X chromosome that seems to play a role in sexual differentiation. 119

deoxyribonucleic acid (DNA) (dee-AK -see-rye-bow-new-KLEE-ik)   the chemical in each cell that carries the genetic code. 270

Depo-Provera   an injectable form of progestin that can prevent pregnancy for 3 months. 322

desire phase   Kaplan's term for the psychological interest in sex that precedes physiological sexual arousal. 95

deviation   term applied to behaviors or orientations that do not conform to a society's accepted norms; it often has negative connotations. 199

DHT-deficiency syndrome   a condition in which chromosomally male fetuses have underdeveloped male genitals, and may be identified as girls at birth. However, at puberty they begin to develop masculine secondary sex characteristics, and seem to maintain masculine patterns of behavior. 125

diaphragm (DY-a-fram)   a latex rubber cup, filled with spermicide, that is fitted to the cervix by a clinician; the woman must learn to insert it properly for full contraceptive effectiveness. 323

diethylstilbestrol (DES) (dye-eth-a-stil -BES-trole)   synthetic estrogen compound once given to mothers whose pregnancies were at high risk of miscarrying. 54

differential socialization the process of treating boys and girls differently as they are growing up. 126

dihydrotestosterone (DHT) a chemical produced by the fetal testes that promotes further development of the testes, scrotum, and penis in the fetus. 121

dilation the gradual opening of the cervical opening of the uterus prior to and during labor. 293

dilation and curettage (D & C) a method of induced abortion in the second trimester of pregnancy that involves a scraping of the uterine wall. 334

dilation and evacuation (D & E) a method of induced abortion in the second trimester of pregnancy; it combines suction with a scraping of the inner wall of the uterus. 334

discrimination the process by which an individual extinguishes a response to one stimulus while preserving it for other stimuli. 159

dyadic withdrawal the tendency of two people involved in an intimate relationship to withdraw socially for a time from other significant people in their lives. 170

dysmenorrhea (dis-men-a-REE-a) painful menstruation. 63

dyspareunia recurrent or persistent genital pain related to sexual activity. 543

E

E. coli bacteria naturally living in the human colon, which often cause urinary tract infection. 50

ectopic pregnancy (ek-TOP-ik) the implantation of a blastocyst somewhere other than in the uterus, usually in the fallopian tube. 272

effacement the thinning of cervical tissue of the uterus prior to and during labor. 293

ejaculation muscular expulsion of semen from the penis. 84

ejaculatory inevitability the sensation in the male that ejaculation is imminent. 106

ELISA the primary test used to determine the presence of HIV in humans. 517

embryo (EM-bree-o) the term applied to the developing cells when, about a week after fertilization, the blastocyst implants itself in the uterine wall. 272

endometrial hyperplasia (hy-per-PLAY-zhee-a) excessive growth of the inner lining of the uterus (endometrium). 54

endometriosis (en-doe-mee-tree-O-sus) growth of the endometrium out of the uterus into surrounding organs. 54

endometrium interior lining of the uterus, innermost of three layers. 51

endorphins brain secretions that act as natural tranquilizers and pain relievers. 254

epidemiology (e-pe-dee-mee-A-la-jee) the branch of medical science that deals with the incidence, distribution, and control of disease in a population. 509

epididymis (ep-a-DID-a-mus) tubular structure on each testis in which sperm cells mature. 74

epididymitis (ep-a-did-a-MITE-us) inflammation of the epididymis of the testis. 75

episiotomy (ee-piz-ee-OTT-a-mee) a surgical incision in the vaginal opening made by the clinician or obstetrician to prevent the baby from tearing the opening in the process of being born. 294

epispadias (ep-a-SPADE-ee-as) birth defect in which the urinary bladder empties through an abdominal opening and the urethra is malformed. 81

erection enlargement and stiffening of the penis as internal muscles relax and blood engorges the columns of spongy tissue. 76

erogenous zone (a-RAJ-a-nus) any area of the body that is sensitive to sexual arousal. 163

erotica artistic representations of nudity or sexual activity. 424

erotocentricity (ee-ROT-oh-sen-TRIS-ih-tee) the application of ethnocentric-like judgments to sexual values and behaviors creating the assumption that our own ways of approaching sexuality are the only "right" ways. 201

erotomania a very rare form of mental illness characterized by a highly compulsive need for sex. 401

erotophilia consistent positive responding to sexual cues. 400

erotophobia consistent negative responding to sexual cues. 400

estrogen (ES-tro-jen) hormone produced abundantly by the ovaries; it plays an important role in the menstrual cycle. 59

ethnocentricity the tendency of the members of one culture to assume that their values and norms of behavior are the "right" ones in comparison to other cultures. 201

ethnography the anthropological study of other cultures. 35

ethnosexual referring to data concerning the sexual beliefs and customs of other cultures. 35

Eurocentric (ur-oh-SEN-trick) a cultural attitudinal framework typical of people with western European heritages. 6

excitement the arousal phase of Masters and Johnson's four-phase model of the sexual response cycle. 93

exhibitionism exposing the genitals to others for sexual pleasure. 415

exocytosis the release of genetic material by the sperm cell, permitting fertilization to occur. 269

F

fallopian tubes structures that are connected to the uterus and lead the ovum from an ovary to the inner cavity of the uterus. 53

fellatio oral stimulation of the penis. 353

female condom a lubricated polyurethane pouch that is inserted into the vagina for intercourse to collect semen and help prevent disease transmission. 325

female sexual arousal disorder difficulty for a woman in achieving sexual arousal. 540

fertilin (fer-TILL-in) a chemical in the outer membrane of a sperm that assists in attachment to the egg cell and penetration of the egg's outer membrane. 269

fetal alcohol syndrome (FAS) a condition in a fetus characterized by abnormal growth, neurological damage, and facial distortion caused by the mother's heavy alcohol consumption. 292

fetally androgenized females a condition in which hormones administered during pregnancy caused chromosomally female (XX) fetuses to have masculinization of genitals and perhaps of later behavioral patterns, even though they were raised as girls. 124

fetal surgery a surgical procedure performed on the fetus while it is still in the uterus or during a temporary period of removal from the uterus. 290

fetishism (FEH-tish-i-zum) sexual arousal triggered by objects or materials not usually considered to be sexual. 411

fetus the term given to the embryo after 2 months of development in the womb. 273

fibroid tumors non-malignant growths that commonly grow in uterine tissues, often interfering with uterine function. 54

fibrous hymen condition in which hymen is composed of unnaturally thick, tough tissue. 49

follicles capsules of cells in which an ovum matures. 53

follicle-stimulating hormone (FSH) pituitary hormone that stimulates the ovaries or testes. 59

foreplay sexual activities shared in early stages of sexual arousal, with the term implying that they are leading to a more intense, orgasm-oriented form of activity such as intercourse. 200

foreskin fold of skin covering the penile glans; also called the prepuce. 76

fraternal twins twins formed from two separate ova that were fertilized by two separate sperm. 270

frenulum (FREN-yu-lum) thin, tightly drawn fold of skin on the underside of the penile glans; it is highly sensitive. 75

frotteur one who practices frotteurism. 415

frotteurism gaining sexual gratification from anonymously pressing or rubbing one's genitals against others, usually in crowded settings. 415

fundus the broad top portion of the uterus. 51

G

gamete intrafallopian transfer (GIFT) direct placement of ovum and concentrated sperm cells into the woman's fallopian tube to increase the chances of fertilization. 281

gay refers to persons who have a predominantly same-gender sexual orientation and identity. More often applied to males. 203

gender dysphoria (dis-FOR-ee-a) another term sometimes used to describe a gender identity disorder. 132

gender identity a person's inner experience of gender feelings of maleness, femaleness, or some ambivalent position between the two. 118

gender identity disorder the expression of gender identity in a way that is socially inconsistent with one's anatomical sex. 132

gender role the outward expression and demonstration of gender identity, through behaviors, attire, and culturally determined characteristics of femininity and masculinity. 118

gender schema a complex cognitive network of associations and ideas through which the individual perceives and interprets information about gender. 139

generalization application of specific learned responses to other, similar situations or experiences. 159

gene therapy treatment of genetically caused disorders by substitution of healthy genes. 275

genetic engineering the modification of the gene structure of cells to change cellular functioning. 275

genital herpes (HER-peez) viral STD characterized by painful sores on the sex organs. 492

genital warts small lesions on genital skin caused by papillomavirus; this STD increases later risks of certain malignancies. 494

gestational surrogacy implantation of an embryo created by the sperm and ovum of one set of parents into the uterus of another woman who agrees to gestate the fetus and give birth to the child, which is then given to the original parents. 288

glans in the male, the sensitive head of the penis; sensitive head of the female clitoris, visible between the upper folds of the minor lips. 45, 75

gonadotropin-releasing hormone (GnRH) (go-nad-a-TRO-pen) hormone from the hypothalamus that stimulates the release of FSH and LH by the pituitary. 59

gonads sex and reproductive glands, either testes or ovaries, that produce hormones and, eventually, reproductive cells (sperm or eggs). 117

gonorrhea (gon-uh-REE-uh) bacterial STD causing urethral pain and discharge in males; often no initial symptoms in females. 485

granuloma inguinale (gran-ya-LOW-ma in-gwa-NAL-ee or -NALE) STD characterized by ulcerations and granulations beginning in the groin and spreading to the buttocks and genitals. 497

G spot a vaginal area that some researchers feel is particularly sensitive to sexual stimulation when its underlying spongy tissues are engorged with blood. 103

H

hard-core pornography pornography that makes use of highly explicit depictions of sexual activity or shows lengthy scenes of genitals. 431

hedonists people who believe that pleasure is the highest good. 212

hemophiliac (hee-mo-FIL-ee-ak) someone with the hereditary blood defect hemophilia, primarily affecting males and characterized by difficulty in clotting. 510

hepatitis B liver infection caused by a sexually transmitted virus (HBV). 494

hepatitis C virus (HCV) liver infection that may occasionally be sexually transmitted. 494

heterosexism the biased and discriminatory assumption that people are or should be attracted to members of the other gender. 210

heterosexual attractions or activities between males and females. 204

HIV human immunodeficiency virus. 508

homophobia (ho-mo-FO-bee-a) strongly held negative attitudes and irrational fears relating to gay men and/or lesbians and their lifestyles. 209

homosexual term traditionally applied to affectional and sexual attractions and activities between members of the same gender. 203

hookers street name for female prostitutes. 413

hormone replacement therapy (HRT) treatment of the physical changes of menopause by administering dosages of the hormones estrogen and progesterone. 67

hot flash a flushed, sweaty feeling in the skin caused by dilated blood vessels; often associated with menopause. 66

human chorionic gonadotropin (HCG) a hormone detectable in the urine of a pregnant woman. 292

human immunodeficiency virus the virus that initially attacks the human immune system, causing HIV disease and eventually AIDS. 508

hustlers male street prostitutes. 413

H-Y antigen a biochemical produced in an embryo when the Y chromosome is present; it plays a role in the development of fetal gonads into testes. 120

hymen membranous tissue that can cover part of the vaginal opening. 45

hyperfemininity a tendency to exaggerate characteristics typically associated with femininity. 130

hypermasculinity a tendency to exaggerate manly behaviors, sometimes called machismo. 130

hypersexuality unusually high level of interest in and drive for sex. 400

hypoactive sexual desire disorder (HSDD) loss of interest and pleasure in what were formerly arousing sexual stimuli. 539

hyposexuality an especially low level of sexual interest and drive. 400

hypospadias (hye-pa-SPADE-ee-as) birth defect caused by incomplete closure of the urethra during fetal development. 81

hypoxphilia creating pressure around the neck during sexual activity to enhance sexual pleasure. 418

hysterectomy surgical removal of all or part of the uterus. 54

I

identical twins twins formed by a single ovum that was fertilized by a single sperm before the cell divided in two. 270

immature oöcyte collection extraction of immature eggs from undeveloped follicles in an ovary, after which the oocytes are matured through cell culturing methods to be prepared for fertilization. 282

imperforate hymen lack of any openings in the hymen. 49

impotence difficulty achieving or maintaining erection of the penis. 535

incest (IN-sest) sexual activity between closely related family members. 473

incest taboo cultural prohibitions against incest, typical of most societies. 472

induced abortion a termination of pregnancy by artificial means. 332

infertility the inability to produce offspring. 290

infibulation surgical procedure, performed in some cultures, that seals the opening of the vagina. 46

informed consent   the consent given by research subjects, indicating their willingness to participate in a study, after they are informed about the purpose of the study and how they will be asked to participate. 36

in loco parentis   a Latin phrase meaning "in the place of the parent." 176

intersexuality   a combination of female and male anatomical structures, so that the individual cannot be clearly defined as male or female. 116

interstitial cells   cells between the seminiferous tubules that secrete testosterone and other male hormones. 73

interstitial-cell-stimulating hormone (ICSH)   pituitary hormone that stimulates the testes to secrete testosterone; known as luteinizing hormone (LH) in females. 83

interstitial cystitis (IC)   a chronic bladder inflammation that can cause debilitating discomfort and interfere with sexual enjoyment. 50

intracytoplasmic sperm injection (ICSI)   a technique involving the injection of a single sperm cell directly into an ovum. It is useful in cases where the male has a low sperm count. 281

intrauterine devices (IUDs)   birth control method involving the insertion of a small plastic device into the uterus. 326

introitus (in-TROID-us)   the outer opening of the vagina. 45

invasive cancer of the cervix (ICC)   advanced and dangerous malignancy requiring prompt treatment. 54

in vitro fertilization (IVF)   a process whereby the union of the sperm and egg occurs outside the mother's body. 279

isthmus   narrowed portion of the uterus just above the cervix. 51

K

kiddie porn   term used to describe the distribution and sale of photographs and films of children or younger teenagers engaging in some form of sexual activity. 435

kleptomania   extreme form of fetishism in which sexual arousal is generated by stealing. 412

L

labia majora   two outer folds of skin covering the minor lips, clitoris, urinary meatus, and vaginal opening. 44

labia minora   two inner folds of skin that join above the clitoris and extend along the sides of the vaginal and urethral openings. 45

labor   uterine contractions in a pregnant woman; an indication that the birth process is beginning. 293

lactation   production of milk by the milk glands of the breasts. 55

Lamaze method (la-MAHZ)   a birthing process based on relaxation techniques practiced by the expectant mother; her partner coaches her throughout the birth. 295

laminaria (lam-a-NER-ee-a)   a dried seaweed sometimes used in dilating the cervical opening prior to vacuum curettage. 333

laparoscopy   simpler procedure for tubal ligation, involving the insertion of a small fiber optic scope into the abdomen, through which the surgeon can see the fallopian tubes and close them off. 328

laparotomy   operation to perform a tubal ligation, or female sterilization, involving an abdominal incision. 328

latency period   a stage in human development characterized, in Freud's theory, by little interest in or awareness of sexual feelings. It was traditionally assumed to occur during middle childhood; recent research tends to suggest that latency does not exist. 26, 158

lesbian (LEZ-bee-un)   refers to females who have a predominantly same-gender sexual orientation and identity. 203

libido (la-BEED-o or LIB-a-do)   a term first used by Freud to define human sexual longing, or sex drive. 158

lifelong dysfunction   a difficulty with sexual functioning that has always existed for a particular person. 537

lumpectomy   surgical removal of a breast lump, along with a small amount of surrounding tissue. 59

luteinizing hormone (LH)   pituitary hormone that triggers ovulation in the ovaries and stimulates sperm production in the testes. 61

lymphogranuloma venereum (LGV) (lim-foe-gran-yu-LOW-ma va-NEAR-ee-um)   contagious STD caused by several strains of Chlamydia and marked by swelling and ulceration of lymph nodes in the groin. 496

M

male condom   a sheath worn over the penis during intercourse that collects semen and helps prevent disease transmission. 324

male erectile disorder   difficulty achieving or maintaining penile erection (impotence). 539

mammography   sensitive X-ray technique used to discover small breast tumors. 58

marital rape   a woman being forced by her husband to have sex. 463

masochist   the individual in a sado-masochistic sexual relationship who takes the submissive role. 417

massage parlors   places where women can be hired to perform sexual acts under the guise of giving a massage. 413

mastectomy   surgical removal of all or part of a breast. 59

ménage à trois (may-NAZH-ah-TRWAH)   troilism. 412

menarche (MEN-are-kee)   onset of menstruation at puberty. 59

menopause (MEN-a-poz)   time in midlife when menstruation ceases. 59

menstrual cycle   the hormonal interactions that prepare a woman's body for possible pregnancy at roughly monthly intervals. 59

menstruation (men-stru-AY-shun)   phase of menstrual cycle in which the inner uterine lining breaks down and sloughs off; the tissue, along with some blood, flows out through the vagina; also called the period. 62

microscopic epididymal sperm aspiration (MESA)   a procedure in which sperm are removed directly from the epididymis of the male testes. 282

midwives   medical professionals, both women and men, trained to assist with the birthing process. 297

mifepristone (RU 486)   a progesterone antagonist used as a postcoital contraceptive. 329

miscarriage   a natural termination of pregnancy. 332

modeling theory   suggests that people will copy behavior they view in pornography. 435

molluscum contagiosum (ma-LUS-kum kan-taje-ee-O-sum)   a skin disease transmitted by direct bodily contact, not necessarily sexual, that is characterized by eruptions on the skin that appear similar to whiteheads, with a hard seedlike core. 497

monogamous   sharing sexual relations with only one person. 184

monorchidism (ma-NOR-ka-dizm)   presence of only one testis in the scrotum. 75

mons   cushion of fatty tissue located over the female's pubic bone. 44

moral values   beliefs associated with ethical issues, or rights and wrongs; they are often a part of sexual decision making. 211

morula (MOR-yuh-la)   a spherical, solid mass of cells formed after 3 days of embryonic cell division. 272

Müllerian ducts   (myul-EAR-ee-an) embryonic structures that develop into female sexual and reproductive organs unless inhibited by male hormones. 120

multiplier effect   the combining of biological and socioenvironmental factors more and more with one another in the process of human development. 126

myometrium   middle, muscular layer of the uterine wall. 51

N

National Birth Control League an organization founded in 1914 by Margaret Sanger to promote use of contraceptives. 306

natural childbirth a birthing process that encourages the mother to take control, thus minimizing medical intervention. 295

natural family planning/fertility awareness a natural method of birth control that depends on an awareness of the woman's menstrual/fertility cycle. 326

necrophilia (nek-ro-FILL-ee-a) having sexual activity with a dead body. 419

nonspecific urethritis (NSU) (yur-i-THRYT-us) infection or irritation in the male urethra caused by bacteria or local irritants. 490

normal a highly subjective term used to describe sexual behaviors and orientations. Standards of normalcy are determined by social, cultural, and historical standards. 198

normal asexuality an absence or low level of sexual desire, considered normal for a particular person. 539

normalization integration of mentally retarded persons into the social mainstream as much as possible. 224

nymphomania (nim-fa-MAY-nee-a) a term sometimes used to describe erotomania in women. 401

O

obscenity depiction of sexual activity in a repulsive or disgusting manner. 424

onanism (O-na-niz-um) a term sometimes used to describe masturbation, it comes from the biblical story of Onan, who practiced coitus interruptus and "spilled his seed on the ground." 350

oocytes (OH-a-sites) cells that mature to become ova. 53

opportunistic infection a disease resulting from lowered resistance of a weakened immune system. 515

organizing effect manner in which hormones control patterns of early development in the body. 109

orgasm (OR-gaz-em) pleasurable sensations and series of contractions that release sexual tension, usually accompanied by ejaculation in men. 84, 94

orgasmic release reversal of the vasocongestion and muscular tension of sexual arousal, triggered by orgasm. 95

orgy (OR-jee) group sex. 412

os opening in the cervix that leads into the hollow interior of the uterus. 51

osteoporosis (ah-stee-o-po-ROW-sus) disease caused by loss of calcium from the bones in postmenopausal women, leading to brittle bones and stooped posture. 66

ova egg cells produced in the ovary. A single cell is called an ovum; in reproduction, it is fertilized by a sperm cell. 53

ovaries pair of female gonads, located in the abdominal cavity, that produce ova and female hormones. 52

ovulation release of a mature ovum through the wall of an ovary. 61

ovum donation use of an egg from another woman for conception, with the fertilized ovum then being implanted in the uterus of the woman wanting to become pregnant. 283

oxytocin pituitary hormone that plays a role in lactation, uterine contractions, response to physical intimacy and sexual satisfaction, and in initiating the birth process. 55, 254, 293

P

pansexual lacking highly specific sexual orientations or preferences; open to a range of sexual activities. 419

Pap smear medical test that examines a smear of cervical cells to detect any cellular abnormalities. 51

paraphilia (pair-a-FIL-ee-a) a newer term used to describe sexual orientations and behaviors that vary from the norm; it means "a love beside." 199

paraphiliac person who is drawn to one or more of the paraphilias. 451

paraplegic a person paralyzed in the legs, and sometimes pelvic areas, as the result of injury to the spinal cord. 225

pedophilia (pee-da-FIL-ee-a) another term for child sexual abuse. 466

pelvic inflammatory disease (PID) a chronic internal infection associated with certain types of IUDs. 326

penile strain gauge a device placed on the penis to measure even subtle changes in its size due to sexual arousal. 37

penis male sexual organ that can become erect when stimulated; it leads urine and sperm to the outside of the body. 75

perimenopause the time of a woman's life surrounding menopause, characterized by symptoms resulting from reduced estrogen levels. 65

perimetrium outer covering of the uterus. 51

perinatal a term used to describe things related to pregnancy, birth, or the period immediately following the birth. 510

perineal area (pair-a-NEE-al) the sensitive skin between the genitals and the anus. 496

peripheral arousal system external components of sexual arousal that reach the brain and spinal cord from the skin, genitals, and sense organs. 97

Peyronie's disease (pay-ra-NEEZ) development of fibrous tissue in spongy erectile columns within the penis. 81

pheromones human chemicals, the scent of which may cause an attraction or behavioral change in other individuals. 252

phimosis (fye-MOE-sus) abnormally long, tight foreskin on the penis, making it difficult to retract it easily. 80

pimps men who have female prostitutes working for them. 413

placenta (pla-SEN-ta) the organ that unites the fetus to the mother by bringing their blood vessels closer together; it provides nourishment and removes waste for the developing baby. 273

plateau phase the stable, leveled-off phase of Masters and Johnson's four-phase model of the sexual response cycle. 94

plethysmograph a laboratory measuring device that charts physiological changes over time. Attached to a penile strain gauge, it can chart changes in penis size. This is called penile plethysmography. 37

polyandry also referring to being married to more than one spouse, usually refers to a woman having more than one husband. Cross-culturally, it is less common than polygamy. 184

polycystic ovary syndrome (PCOS) (PAH-lee-SIS-tick) a disorder of the ovaries that can produce a variety of unpleasant physical symptoms, often because of elevated testosterone levels. 54

polygamy practice, in some cultures, of being married to more than one spouse, usually referring to a man having more than one wife. 184

pornography photographs, films, or literature intended to be sexually arousing through explicit depictions of sexual activity. 424

postpartum depression a period of low energy and discouragement that is common for mothers following child-bearing. Long-lasting or severe symptoms should receive medical treatment. 299

pregnancy-induced hypertension a disorder that can occur in the latter half of pregnancy, marked by a swelling in the ankles and other parts of the body, high blood pressure, and protein in the urine; can progress to coma and death if not treated. 298

preimplantation genetic diagnosis (PGD) examining the chromosomes of an embryo conceived by IVF, prior to implantation in the uterus. 279

premature birth a birth that takes place prior to the 36th week of pregnancy. 298

premature ejaculation difficulty that some men experience in controlling the ejaculatory reflex, resulting in rapid ejaculation. 544

premenstrual dysphoric disorder (PMDD) severe emotional symptoms such as anxiety or depression around the time of menstruation. 64

premenstrual syndrome (PMS) symptoms of physical discomfort, moodiness, and emotional tensions that occur in some women for a few days prior to menstruation. 63

preorgasmic a term that has been applied to women who have not yet been able to reach orgasm during sexual response. 535

prepuce (PREE-peus) in the female, tissue of the upper vulva that covers the clitoral shaft. 45

priapism (pry-AE-pizm) continual, undesired, and painful erection of the penis. 80

progesterone (pro-JES-ter-one) ovarian hormone that causes the uterine lining to thicken. 61

prolactin pituitary hormone that stimulates the process of lactation. 55

prolapse of the uterus weakening of the supportive ligaments of the uterus, causing it to protrude into the vagina. 54

promiscuity (prah-mis-KIU-i-tee) sharing casual sexual activity with many different partners. 400

prostaglandin hormonelike chemical whose concentrations increase in a woman's body just prior to menstruation. 335

prostaglandin- or saline-induced abortion used in the 16th to 24th weeks of pregnancy, prostaglandins, salt solutions, or urea are injected into the amniotic sac, administered intravenously, or inserted into the vagina in suppository form, to induce contractions and fetal delivery. 334

prostate gland located beneath the urinary bladder in the male; it produces some of the secretions in semen. 81

prostatitis (pras-tuh-TITE-us) inflammation of the prostate gland. 82

pseudohermaphrodite a person who possesses either testes or ovaries in combination with some external genitals of the other sex. 116

psychosexual development factors that form a person's sexual feelings, orientations, and patterns of behavior. 157

psychosocial development the cultural and social influences that help shape human sexual identity. 161

pubic lice small insects that can infect skin in the pubic area, causing a rash and severe itching. 496

pubococcygeus (PC) muscle (pyub-o-kox-a-JEE-us) part of the supporting musculature of the vagina that is in-

volved in orgasmic response and over which a woman can exert some control. 48

pyromania sexual arousal generated by setting fires. 412

Q

quadriplegic a person paralyzed in the upper body, including the arms, and lower body as the result of spinal cord injury. 225

quid pro quo something gained from something given. 453

R

random sample a representative group of the larger population that is the focus of a scientific poll or study in which care is taken to select participants without a pattern that might sway research results. 33

rape trauma syndrome the predictable sequence of reactions that a victim experiences following a rape. 464

refractory period time following orgasm during which a man cannot be restimulated to orgasm. 107

reinforcement in conditioning theory, any influence that helps shape future behavior as a punishment or reward stimulus. 159

resolution phase the term for the return of a body to its unexcited state following orgasm. 94

retrograde ejaculation abnormal passage of semen into the urinary bladder at the time of ejaculation. 84

retrovirus (RET-ro-vi-rus) a class of viruses that reproduces with the aid of the enzyme reverse transcriptase, which allows the virus to integrate its genetic code into that of the host cell, thus establishing permanent infection. 515

Rh incompatibility condition in which a blood protein of the infant is not the same as the mother's; antibodies formed in the mother can destroy red blood cells in the fetus. 299

RhoGAM medication administered to a mother to prevent formation of antibodies when the baby is Rh positive and its mother Rh negative. 299

rubber dam small square sheet of latex used to cover the vulva, vagina, or anus to help prevent transmission of HIV during sexual activity. 354, 528

S

sadist the individual in a sadomasochistic sexual relationship who takes the dominant role. 417

sadomasochism (sade-o-MASS-o-kiz-um) refers to sexual themes or activi-

ties involving bondage, pain, domination, or humiliation of one partner by the other. 417

sample a representative group of a population that is the focus of a scientific poll or study. 33

satyriasis (sate-a-RYE-a-sus) a term sometimes used to describe erotomania in men. 401

scabies (SKAY-beez) a skin disease caused by a mite that burrows under the skin to lay its eggs, causing redness and itching; transmitted by bodily contact that may or may not be sexual. 497

scrotum (SKROTE-um) pouch of skin in which the testes are contained. 73

secondary sex characteristics the physical characteristics of mature women and men that begin to develop at puberty. 128

selective reduction the use of abortion techniques to re-duce the number of fetuses when there are more than three in a pregnancy, thus increasing the chances of survival for the remaining fetuses. Also called selective termination. 271

self-gratification giving oneself pleasure, as in masturbation; a term typically used today instead of more negative descriptors. 199

self-pleasuring self-gratification; masturbation. 199

semen (SEE-men) mixture of fluids and sperm cells that is ejaculated through the penis. 81

seminal vesicle (SEM-un-al) gland at the end of each vas deferens that secretes a chemical that helps sperm to become motile. 81

seminiferous tubules (sem-a-NIF-a-rus) tightly coiled tubules in the testes in which sperm cells are formed. 73

sensate focus early phase of sex therapy treatment, in which the partners pleasure each other without employing direct stimulation of sex organs. 556

sex addiction inability to regulate sexual behavior. 451

sexology the scientific study of human sexuality. 32

sexosophy the philosophies and ideologies relating to human sexuality. 32

sex therapist professional trained in the treatment of sexual dysfunctions. 553

sexual aversion disorder avoidance of or exaggerated fears toward forms of sexual expression. 539

sexual differentiation the developmental processes—biological, social, and psychological—that lead to different sexes or genders. 118

sexual dysfunctions difficulties people have in achieving sexual arousal and in other stages of sexual response. 95

sexual harassment unwanted sexual advances or coercion that can occur in the workplace or academic settings. 453

sexual individuality the unique set of sexual needs, orientations, fantasies, feelings, and activities that develops in each human being. 204

sexual revolution the changes in thinking about sexuality and sexual behavior in society that occurred in the 1960s and 1970s. 11

sexual surrogates paid partners used during sex therapy with clients lacking their own partners; used only rarely today. 553

shaft in the female, the longer body of the clitoris, containing erectile tissue; in the male, cylindrical base of penis that contains three columns of spongy tissue two corpora cavernosa and a corpus spongiosum. 46, 76

shunga ancient scrolls used in Japan to instruct couples in sexual practices through the use of paintings. 424

Skene's glands secretory cells located inside the female urethra. 104

smegma thick, oily substance that may accumulate under the prepuce of the clitoris or penis. 46

social constructionism a theory that holds that human traits and behaviors are shaped more by environmental social forces than by innate biological factors. 14

social script a complex set of learned responses to a particular situation that is formed by social influences. 162

sodomy laws laws in some states that prohibit a variety of sexual behaviors, often described as deviate sexual intercourse. These laws are often enforced discriminatorily against particular groups, such as gay males. 440

sonograms ultrasonic rays used to project a picture of internal structures such as the fetus; often used in conjunction with amniocentesis or fetal surgery. 290

spectatoring term used by Masters and Johnson to describe self-consciousness and self-observation during sex. 549

sperm reproductive cells produced in the testes; in fertilization, one sperm unites with an ovum. 73

spermatocytes (sper-MAT-o-sites) cells lining the seminiferous tubules from which sperm cells are produced. 83

spermicidal jelly (cream) sperm-killing chemical in a gel-base or cream, used with other contraceptives such as diaphragms. 323

spermicides chemicals that kill sperm; available as foams, creams, jellies, or suppositories. 322

sponge a thick, polyurethane disk that holds a spermicide and fits over the cervix to prevent conception 322

spontaneous abortion another term for miscarriage. 332

SRY the sex-determining region of the Y chromosome. 119

statutory rape a legal term used to indicate sexual activity when one partner is under the age of consent; in most states that age is 18. 459

straight slang term for heterosexual. 204

streetwalkers female prostitutes who work on the streets. 413

suppositories contraceptive devices designed to distribute their spermicide by melting or foaming in the vagina. 322

syndrome (SIN-drome) a group of signs or symptoms that occur together and characterize a given condition. 515

syphilis (SIF-uh-lus) sexually transmitted disease (STD) characterized by four stages, beginning with the appearance of a chancre. 483

systematic desensitization step-by-step approaches to unlearning tension-producing behaviors and developing new behavior patterns. 552

T

testes (TEST-ees) pair of male gonads that produce sperm and male hormones. 73

testicular cancer malignancy on the testis that may be detected by testicular self-examination. 75

testicular failure lack of sperm and/or hormone production by the testes. 75

testosterone (tes-TAHS-ter-one) major male hormone produced by the testes; it helps to produce male secondary sex characteristics. 73

testosterone replacement therapy administering testosterone injections to increase sexual interest or potency in older men; not considered safe for routine use. 86

theoretical failure rate a measure of how often a birth control method can be expected to fail when used without error or technical problems, sometimes called perfect use failure rate. 314

thrush a disease caused by a fungus and characterized by white patches in the oral cavity. 515

toucherism gaining sexual gratification from the touching of an unknown person's body, such as on the buttocks or breasts. 415

toxic shock syndrome (TSS) an acute disease characterized by fever and sore throat, and caused by normal bacteria in the vagina that are activated if tampons or contraceptive devices such as diaphragms are left in for long periods of time. 323

transgenderism a crossing of traditional gender lines because of discomfort and nonconformity with gender roles generally accepted by the society. 132

transsexualism a strong degree of discomfort with one's identity as male or female, characterized by feelings of being in the wrongly sexed body. 132

transvestite an individual who dresses in clothing and adopts mannerisms considered appropriate for the opposite sex. 204

trichomoniasis (trik-uh-ma-NEE-uh-sis) a vaginal infection caused by the *Trichomonas* organism. 491

troilism (TROY-i-liz-um) sexual activity shared by three people. 412

true hermaphrodite a person who has one testis and one ovary. External appearance may vary. 116

tubal ligation a surgical cutting and tying of the fallopian tubes to induce permanent female sterilization. 328

typical use failure rate a measure of how often a birth control method can be expected to fail when human error and technical failure are considered. 314

U

umbilical cord the tubelike tissues and blood vessels originating at the embryo's navel that connect it to the placenta. 273

urethra (yu-REE-thrah) tube that passes from the urinary bladder to the outside of the body. 76

urinary meatus opening through which urine passes from the urethra to the outside of the body. 45

urophilia sexual arousal connected with urine or urination. 417

uterus (YUTE-a-rus) muscular organ of the female reproductive system; a fertilized egg implants itself within the uterus. 51

V

vacuum curettage (kyur-a-TAZH) a method of induced abortion performed with a suction pump. 333

vagina (vu-JI-na) muscular canal in the female that is responsive to sexual arousal; it receives semen for reproduction during heterosexual intercourse. 47

vaginal atresia (a-TREE-zha) birth defect in which the vagina is absent or closed. 51

vaginal atrophy shrinking and deterioration of vaginal lining, usually the result of low estrogen levels during aging. 50

vaginal fistulae (FISH-cha-lee *or* -lie) abnormal channels that can develop between the vagina and other internal organs. 51

vaginismus (vaj-uh-NIZ-mus) involuntary contraction of the outer vaginal musculature when vaginal penetration is attempted, making penetration difficult or impossible. 47, 542

values   system of beliefs with which people view life and make decisions, including their sexual decisions. 211

variable   an aspect of a scientific study that is subject to change. 36

variation   a less pejorative term to describe nonconformity to accepted norms. 199

varicose veins   overexpanded blood vessels; can occur in veins surrounding the vagina. 51

vas deferens   tube that leads sperm upward from each testis to the seminal vesicles. 74

vasa efferentia   larger tubes within the testes, into which sperm move after being produced in the seminiferous tubules. 73

vasectomy (va-SEK-ta-mee *or* vay-ZEK-ta-mee)   a surgical cutting and tying of the vas deferens to induce permanent male sterilization. 328

villi   fingerlike projections of the chorion; they form a major part of the placenta. 273

voluntary surgical contraception   sterilization; rendering a person incapable of conceiving with surgical procedures that interrupt the passage of the egg or sperm. 327

voyeurism (VOYE-yur-i-zum)   sexual gratification from viewing others who are nude or who are engaging in sexual activities. 9, 416

vulva   external sex organs of the female, including the mons, major and minor lips, clitoris, and opening of the vagina. 44

vulvovaginitis (vaj-uh-NITE-us)   general term for inflammation of the vulva and/or vagina. 491

W

Western blot   the test used to verify the presence of HIV antibodies already detected by the ELISA. 518

Wolffian ducts (WOOL-fee-an)   embryonic structures that develop into male sexual and reproductive organs if male hormones are present. 120

Y

yeast infection   a type of vaginitis caused by an overgrowth of a fungus normally found in an inactive state in the vagina. 491

Z

zero population growth   the point at which the world's population would stabilize, and there would be no further increase in the number of people on Earth. Birthrate and death rate become essentially equal. 306

zona pellucida (ZO-nah pe-LOO-sa-da)   the transparent, outer membrane of an ovum. 269

zoophilia (zoo-a-FILL-ee-a)   bestiality. 418

zygote   an ovum that has been fertilized by a sperm. 270

zygote intrafallopian transfer (ZIFT)   zygotes resulting from IVF are inserted directly into the fallopian tubes. 279

References

A

AAUW. (1992). *How schools shortchange girls: Executive summary*. Washington, DC: Author.

AAUW. (1993). *Hostile hallways*. Washington, DC: Author.

Abma, J., Driscoll, A., & Moore, K. (1998). Young women's degree of control over first intercourse: An exploratory analysis. *Family Planning Perspectives, 30*(1), 12–18.

Abouesh, A., & Clayton, A. (1999). Compulsive voyeurism and exhibitionism: A clinical response to paroxetine. *Archives of Sexual Behavior, 28*(1), 23–30.

Adam, B. D. (1998). Theorizing Homophobia. *Sexualities, 1*(4), 387–404.

Adams, S. G., Dubbert, P. M., Chupurdia, K. M., Jones, A., Lofland, K. R., & Leermakers, E. (1996). Assessment of sexual beliefs and information in aging couples with sexual dysfunction. *Archives of Sexual Behavior, 25*(3), 249–260.

Afifi W. A. (1999). Harming the ones we love: Relational attachment and perceived consequences as predictors of safe-sex behavior. *Journal of Sex Research, 36*(2), 198–206.

Ahluwalia I. B., DeVellis R. F., & Thomas, J. C. (1998). Reproductive decisions of women at risk for acquiring HIV infection. *AIDS Education and Prevention, 10*(1), 90–97.

Aitken, R. J. (1995). The complexities of contraception. *Science, 269*, 39–40.

Alan Guttmacher Institute. (1994). *Sex and American teenagers*. New York: Author.

Alexander, M. A. (1999). Sexual offender treatment efficacy revisited. *Sexual Abuse: Journal of Research and Treatment, 15*, 36–47.

Allen, M., D'Alessio, D., Emmers, T. M., & Gebhardt, L. (1996). The role of educational briefings in mitigating effects of experimental exposure to violent sexually explicit material: A meta-analysis. *Journal of Sex Research, 33*(2), 135–141.

Allen, M., Emmers, T., Gebhardt, L., & Liery, M. A. (1995). Exposure to pornography and acceptance of rape myths. *Journal of Communication, 45*(1) 5–26.

Alter, J. (1999, January 11). Shutting up about sex. *Newsweek*, 30.

Alter, M. J. (1999). The prevalence of hepatitis C virus infection in the United States, 1988 through 1994. *New England Journal of Medicine, 341* (8), 556–562.

Althaus, F. (1999). Teenage males increasingly use condoms, but half of those who have sex sometimes forgo protection. *Family Planning Perspectives, 31*(1), 50–51.

Althof, S. E. (1998). New roles for mental health clinicians in the treatment of erectile dysfunction. *Journal of Sex Education and Therapy, 23*(3), 229–230.

Altman, C. (1999). Gay and lesbian seniors: Unique challenges of coming out in later life. *SIECUS Report, 27*(3), 14–17.

Alvarez, W. A., & Freinhar, J. P. (1991). A prevalence study of bestiality zoophilia in psychiatric in-patients, medical in-patients, and psychiatric staff. *International Journal of Psychosomatics, 38*(1–4), 45–47.

Alzate, H. (1990). Vaginal erogeneity, the "G spot" and "female ejaculation." *Journal of Sex Education and Therapy, 16*(2), 137–140.

American College of Obstetrics and Gynecology. (1999, May 18). Pharmacists limit women's access to emergency contraception. News release.

American Psychiatric Association (1994). *Diagnostic and statistical manual of mental disorders* (4th ed.). Washington, DC: Author.

Analyse des Comportements Sexuels en France Investigators. (1992). AIDS and sexual behavior in France. *Nature, 360,* 407–409.

Anderson, J. E., Brackbill, R., & Mosher, W. D. (1996). Condom use for disease prevention among unmarried U.S. women. *Family Planning Perspectives, 28*(1), 25–28, 39.

Anderson, J. E., Wilson, R., Doll, D. T., Jones S., & Barker, P. (1999). Condom use and HIV risk behaviors among U.S. adults: Data from a national survey. *Family Planning Perspectives, 31*(1), 24–28.

Anderson, P. B., & Struckman-Johnson, C. (Eds.). (1998). *Sexually aggressive women: Current perspectives and controversies*. New York: Guilford Press.

Anderson, S. L., & Pollock, R. H. (1994). The making of an oral sex questionnaire. *Journal of Sex Education and Therapy, 20*(2), 123–133.

Anderson, W. F. (2000, January 1). A cure that may cost us ourselves. *Time*, 75–76.

Andrews, F. (1991). *The art and practice of loving*. New York: Jeremy P. Tarcher/Perigee.

Andrews, L. B. (1998, February 13). Human cloning: Assessing the ethical and legal quandaries. *Chronicle of Higher Education*, B4–5.

Angier, N. (1993, September 21). Radical new view of role of menstruation. *New York Times*, C1.

Angier, N. (1996, February 4). Intersexual healing: An anomaly finds a group. *New York Times*, E14.

Ankomah, A. (1999). Sex, love, money and AIDS: The dynamics of premarital sexual relationships in Ghana. *Sexualities, 2*(3) 291–308.

APHA (American Public Health Association). (1994). Resolution 6917: Sex education in school systems. *APHA public policy statements, 1948—present* (cumulative). Washington, DC: Author.

Appleby, P. R., Miller, L. C., & Rothspan, S. (1999). The paradox of trust for male couples: When risking is part of loving. *Personal Relationships, 6*(1) 81–93.

Aral, S. O. (1992). Dangerous hygiene. *Health, 6*(4), 13–14.

Arellano, C. M., & Markman, H. J. (1995). The managing affect and differences scale (MADS): A self-report measure assessing conflict management in couples. *Journal of Family Psychology, 9*(3), 319–334.

Argasus Foundation (1992). *The S.T.D. Handbook*. Burton, MI: Author.

Armstrong, K. A. (1995). The problem of using race to understand sexual behaviors. *SIECUS Report, 23*(3), 8–10.

Armsworth, M. W., & Stronck, K. (1999). Intergenerational effects of incest on parenting: Skills, abilities, and attitudes. *Journal of Counseling and Development, 77,* 303–314.

Ashton A. K., & Rosen, R. C. (1998). Accommodation to serotonin reuptake inhibitor-induced sexual dysfunction. *Journal of Sex and Marital Therapy, 24,* 191–192.

Assalian, P., & Margolese, H. C. (1996). Treatment of antidepressant-induced sexual side effects. *Journal of Sex and Marital Therapy, 22*(3), 218–224.

Atkins, D. (Ed.). (1998). *Looking queer: Body image and identity in lesbians, bisexual, gay, and transgender communities*. Binghamton, NY: Haworth Press.

Atkinson, M. (1998). Hot debates and difficult labors: Sexuality education in Queensland, Australia. *SIECUS Report, 26*(5) 11–13.

Atkisson, A. (1994). What makes love last? *New Age Journal, 11*(5), 74–79, 146–148.

Auger, J., Kunstmann, J. M., Czyglik, F., & Jouannet, P. (1995). Decline in semen quality among fertile men in Paris during the past 20 years. *New England Journal of Medicine, 332*(5), 281–285.

Axinn, W. G., & Thornton, A. (1992). The relationship between cohabitation and divorce: Selectivity or causal influence? *Demography, 29,* 357–374.

B

Baba, T. W., Trichel, A. M., An, L., Liska, V., Martin, L. N., Murphy-Corb, M., & Ruprecht, R. M. (1996). Infection and AIDS in adult macaques after nontraumatic oral exposure to cell-free SIV. *Science, 272,* 1486–1489.

Bachmaier, K., Neu, N., de la Maza, L., Pal, S., Hellel, A., & Penninger, J. M. (1999). Chlamydia infections and heart disease linked through antigenic mimicry. *Science, 283,* 1335–1338.

Bader, M. J. (1993). Adaptive sadomasochism and psychological growth. *Psychoanalytic Dialogs, 3*(2), 279–300.

Bagla, P. (1998). India prepares to join U.S., world teams. *Science, 282,* 1394.

Bailey, J. M., Nothnagel, J., & Wolfe, M. (1995). Retrospectively measured individual differences in childhood sex-typed behavior among gay men: Correspondence between self and maternal reports. *Archives of Sexual Behavior, 24*(6), 613–622.

Bailey, J. M., & Oberschneider, M. (1997). Sexual orientation and professional dance. *Archives of Sexual Behavior, 26*(4), 433–444.

Bailey, J. M., & Pillard, R. C. (1995). Genetics of human sexual orientation. *Annual Review of Sex Research, 4,* 126–150.

Bailey, J. M., & Shriver, A., (1999). Does childhood sexual abuse cause borderline personality disorder? *Journal of Sex and Marital Therapy, 25,* 45–57.

Baldo T. D., O'Halloran, M. S., & Jacobs, L. R. (1997). Sexual assaults and disordered eating in a nonclinical population of women. *Journal for the Professional Counselor, 12*(2), 75–85.

Baldwin, J. D., & Baldwin, J. I. (1997). Gender differences in sexual interest. *Archives of Sexual Behavior, 26*(2), 181–210.

Ballard, S. M., & Morris, M. L. (1998). Sources of sexuality information for university students. *Journal of Sex Education and Therapy, 23*(4) 278–287.

Balon, R. (1998). Pharmacological treatment of paraphilias with a focus on antidepressants. *Journal of Sex and Marital Therapy, 24* 241–254.

Balon, R. (1999). Sildenafil and sexual dysfunction associated with antidepressants. *Journal of Sex and Marital Therapy, 25,* 259–264.

Balter, M. (1998). HIV's early home and inner life. *Science, 282,* 1630–1631.

Balter, M. (1999). Virus from 1959 sample marks early years of HIV. *Science, 279,* 801.

Baltimore, D. (1999, May 28). Can we make an AIDS vaccine? *Chronicle of Higher Education,* A64.

Banaji, M. R. (1993). The psychology of gender: A perspective on perspectives. In A. E. Beall & R. J. Sternberg (Eds.), *The psychology of gender* (pp. 251–273). New York: Guilford Press.

Bancroft, J. (1989). *Human sexuality and its problems.* Edinburgh, Scotland: Churchill Livingstone.

Bancroft, J. (1990). The impact of sociocultural influences on adolescent sexual development: Further considerations. In J. Bancroft & J. M. Reinisch (Eds.), *Adolescence and puberty* (pp. 207–216). New York: Oxford University Press.

Bancroft, J. (1994). Homosexual orientation: The search for a biological basis. *British Journal of Psychiatry, 164,* 437–440.

Bancroft, J. (1999). Sexual science in the 21st century: Where are we going? *Journal of Sex Research, 36*(3), 226–229.

Bankole, A., Darroch, J. E., & Singh, S. (1999). Determinants of trends in condom use in the United States, 1988–1995. *Family Planning Perspectives, 31*(6), 264–271.

Banyard, V. L., & Williams, L. M. (1999). Memories for child sexual abuse and mental health functioning: Findings on a sample of women and implications for future research. In L. M. Williams & V. L. Banyard (Eds.), *Trauma and Memory* (pp. 115–125). Thousand Oaks, CA: Sage.

Barbach, L. G. (1988). *Becoming orgasmic.* Englewood Cliffs, NJ: Prentice-Hall.

Bardoni, B., et al. (1994). Dosage-sensitive sex reversal (DSS) gene on the human X chromosome. *Nature Genetics, 7,* 497–501.

Barham, M. (1998). Hypnotherapy and its uses and efficacy in sexual dysfunction. *CliniScope Monographs, 6,* 1–4.

Barinaga, M. (1994). Women in science '94: Surprises across the cultural divide. *Science, 263,* 1468–1472.

Barrett, D. C., Bolan, G., & Douglas, J. M. (1998). Redefining gay male anal intercourse behaviors: Implications for HIV prevention and research. *Journal of Sex Research, 35*(4), 381–389.

Barshay, J. J. (1993, February 9). Russian gay men step out of Soviet era shadows. *New York Times,* p. A1.

Bartley, N. (1994, February 13). The return of romance: Antidote to dreary reality of the 90's. *Watertown (NY) Daily Times,* p. 7. (Reprinted from *Seattle Times*)

Bartlik, B., Legere, R., Andersson, L. (1999). The combined use of sex therapy and testosterone replacement therapy for women. *Psychiatric Annals, 29*(1), 27–33.

Bartoi, M. G., & Kinder, B. N. (1998). Effects of child and adult sexual abuse on adult sexuality. *Journal of Sex and Marital Therapy, 24,* 75–90.

Basson, R. (2000). The female sexual response: A different model. *Journal of Sex and Marital Therapy, 26*(1), 51–65.

Bauserman, R. (1998). Egalitarian, sexist, and aggressive sexual materials: Attitude effects and viewer responses. *Journal of Sex Research, 35*(3), 244–253.

Bauserman, R., & Rind, B. (1997). Psychological correlates of male child and adolescent sexual experiences with adults: A review of the nonclinical literature. *Archives of Sexual Behavior, 26*(2), 105–141.

Baydar, N. (1995). Consequences for children of their birth planning status. *Family Planning Perspectives, 27*(6), 228–234, 245.

Beall, A. E. (1993). A social constructionist view of gender. In A. E. Beall & R. J. Sternberg (Eds.), *The psychology of gender* (pp. 127–147). New York: Guilford Press.

Bech, H. (1999). After the closet. *Sexualities, 2*(3), 343–346.

Beck, J. (1999). Should homosexuality be taught as an acceptable alternative lifestyle? A Muslim perspective: A response to Halstead and Lewicka. *Cambridge Journal of Education, 29*(1), 121–230.

Beck, J. G. (1995). Hypoactive sexual desire disorder: An overview. *Journal of Consulting and Clinical Psychology, 63*(6), 919–927.

Beecroft, C. (1992). Letter to the author [on behalf of the Society for the Second Self].

Begley, S. (1998a, April 20). New Hope for women at risk. *Newsweek,* 68–70.

Begley, S. (1998b, November 16). From human embryos, hope for "spare parts." *Newsweek,* 73.

Begley, S., & Glick, D. (1998, December 14). Eying the fetal future. *Newsweek,* 54–55.

Belknap, J., Fisher, B. S., & Cullen, F. T. (1999). The development of a comprehensive measure of the sexual victimization of college women. *Violence Against Women, 5*(2), 185–214.

Bell, A., Weinberg, M. S., & Hammersmith, S. K. (1981). *Sexual preference: Its development in men and women.* Bloomington: Indiana University Press.

Bellafante, G. (1998, June 29). Feminism: It's all about me! *Time,* 54–62.

Bem, D. J. (1996). Exotic becomes erotic: A developmental theory of sexual orientation. *Psychological Review, 103*(2), 320–335.

Bem, S. L. (1974). The measurement of psychological androgyny. *Journal of Consulting and Clinical Psychology, 42*(2), 155–162.

Bem, S. L. (1987). Masculinity and femininity exist only in the mind of the perceiver. In J. H. Reinisch, L. A. Rosenblum, & S. A. Sanders (Eds.), *Masculinity/femininity: Basic perspectives* (pp. 304–311). New York: Oxford University Press.

Bem, S. L. (1993). *The lenses of gender.* New Haven, CT: Yale University Press.

Bennett, N. G., Bloom, D. E., & Miller, C. K. (1995). The influence of nonmarital childbearing on the formation of first marriages. *Demography, 32,* 47–61.

Benson, P., et al. (1994). *Adopted adolescents.* Minneapolis, MN: Search Institute.

Beral, V. (1999). Mortality associated with oral contraceptive use. *British Medical Journal, 318*(7176), 96–100.

Berenbaum, S. A., & Hines, M. (1992). Early androgens are related to childhood sex-typed toy preferences. *Psychological Science, 3*(3), 203–206.

Berends, M. M., & Caron, S. L. (1994). Children's understanding and knowledge of conception and birth: A developmental approach. *Journal of Sex Education and Therapy, 20*(1), 18–29.

Berg, D. R., Lonsway, K. A., & Fitzgerald, L. F. (1999). Rape prevention education for men: The effectiveness of empathy-induction techniques. *Journal of College Student Development, 40*(3), 219–234.

Berg, P., & Singer, M. (1998). Regulating human cloning. *Science, 282,* 413.

Berger, D., Suematsu, H., & Ono, Y. (1994). Theories of sexual orientation: A reappraisal. *Archives of General Psychiatry, 51*(5), 432.

Bergman, S. J., & Surrey, J. (1992). *Work in progress: The woman-man relationship: Impasses and possibilities.* Wellesley, MA: Stone Center, Wellesley College.

Bergmark, K., Avall-Lundqvist, E., Dickman, P. W., Henningsohn, L., & Stieneck, G. (1999). Vaginal changes and sexuality in women with a history of cervical cancer. *New England Journal of Medicine, 340*(28), 1383–1389.

Bermant, G. (1995). To speak in chords about sexuality. *Neuroscience and Biobehavioral Reviews, 19*(2), 343–348.

Bernat, J. A., Calhoun, K. S., & Stolp, S. (1998). Sexual aggressive men's responses to a date rape analogue: Alcohol as a disinhibiting cue. *Journal of Sex Research, 35*(4). 341–348.

Bhugra, D. (1997). Coming out by South Asian gay men in the United Kingdom. *Archives of Sexual Behavior, 26*(5) 547–557.

Biale, D. (1997). *Eros and the Jews: From Biblical Israel to contemporary America.* Berkeley: University of California Press.

Bieschke, K. J., & Matthews, C. (1996). Career counselor attitudes and behaviors toward gay, lesbian, and bisexual clients. *Journal of Vocational Behavior, 48*(2), 243–255.

Billy, J., Tanfer, K., Grady, W. R., & Klepinger, D. H. (1993). The sexual behavior of men in the United States. *Family Planning Perspectives, 25*(2), 52–60.

Binik, Y. M, Mah, K., & Kiesler, S. (1999). Ethical issues in conducting sex research on the Internet. *The Journal of Sex Research, 36*(1), 82–90.

Blackman, S. (1996). Bumpy lifestyle led to external testes. *New Scientist, 151*(2043), 19.

Blake, J. (1994). Pediatric and adolescent gynecology. In L. J. Copeland (Ed.), *Textbook of gynecology* (pp. 592–618). Philadelphia: W. B. Saunders.

Blakeslee, S. (1991, November 14). Men's test scores linked to hormone. *New York Times,* p. A1.

Blanchard, R. (1997). Birth order and sibling sex ratio in homosexual versus heterosexual males and females. *Annual Review of Sex Research, 8,* 27–67.

Blanchard, R., & Bogaert, A. F. (1996). Homosexuality in men and number of older brothers. *American Journal of Psychiatry, 153*(1), 27–31.

Blau, M. (1994, November 28). Ordinary people. *New York,* 38–46.

Blinn-Pike, L. (1999). Why abstinent adolescents report they have not had sex: Understanding sexually resilient youth. *Family Relations, 48*(3), 295–301.

Bloom, B. R. (1998). The highest attainable standard: Ethical issues in AIDS vaccines. *Science, 279,* 186–188.

Blumenthal, S., Gudjonsson, G., & Burns, J. (1999). Cognitive distortions and blame attribution in sex offenders against adults and children. *Child Abuse and Neglect, 23*(2), 129–143.

Blumfield, C. G., Lin, S., Conner, W., Cosper, P., Davis, R.O., & Owen, J. (1996). Pregnancy outcome following genetic amniocentesis at 11–14 versus 16–19 weeks' gestation. *Obstetrics and Gynecology, 88*(1), 114–118.

Blumstein, P., & Schwartz, P. (1999). The creation of sexuality. In L. A. Peplau & S. Chapman. (Eds.), *Gender, culture, and ethnicity: Current research about women and men* (p. 363). Mountain View, CA: Mayfield.

Blumstein, P. W., & Schwartz, P. (1983). *American couples.* New York: William Morrow.

Bockting, W. O. (1999). From construction to contest: Gender through the eyes of the transgendered. *SIECUS Report, 28*(1), 3–7.

Bodlund, O., & Kullgren, G. (1996). Transsexualism—General outcome and prognostic factors: A five-year follow-up study of nineteen transsexuals in the process of changing sex. *Archives of Sexual Behavior, 25*(3), 303–316.

Bogaert, A. F. (1998). Birth order and sibling sex ratio in homosexual and heterosexual non-white men. *Archives of Sexual Behavior, 27*(5), 467–473.

Bogaert, A. F., Woodard, U., & Hafer, C. L. (1999). Intellectual ability and reactions to pornography. *Journal of Sex Research, 36*(3) 283–291.

Bolumar, F. (1996). Smoking reduces fecundity: A European multicenter study on infertility and subfecundity. *American Journal of Epidemiology, 143,* 578–587.

Boone, J. A. (1998). *Libidinal currents: Sexuality and the shaping of modernism*. Chicago: Chicago University Press.

Bordo, S. (1998, May 1). Sexual harassment is about bullying, not sex. *Chronicle of Higher Education*, B6.

Borneman, E. (1994). *Childhood phases of maturity: Sexual developmental psychology*. Amherst, NY: Prometheus Books.

Boswell, J. E. (1990). Sexual and ethical categories in premodern Europe. In D. P. McWhirter, S. A. Sanders, & J. M. Reinisch (Eds.), *Homosexuality/heterosexuality: Concepts of sexual orientation* (pp. 15–31). New York: Oxford University Press.

Botting, D., & Botting, K. (1996). *Sex appeal*. New York: St. Martin's Press.

Bouchard, T. J. (1994). Genes, environment, and personality. *Science, 264,* 1700–1701.

Boulet, M. J., & Oddens, B. J. (1996). Female voice changes around and after the menopause—an initial investigation. *Maturitas: Journal of the Climacteric, 23,* 15–21.

Bounds, W. (1995). The diaphragm with and without spermicide: A randomized, comparative efficacy trial. *Journal of Reproductive Medicine, 40,* 764–774.

Brackbill, R. M., Sternberg, M. R., & Fishbein, M. (1999). Where do people go for treatment of sexually transmitted diseases? *Family Planning Perspectives, 31*(1), 10–15.

Bradner, C. H., Ku, L., & Lindberg, L. D. (2000). Older, but not wiser: How men get information about AIDS and sexually transmitted diseases after high school. *Family Planning Perspectives, 32*(1), 33–38.

Braiterman, J. (1998). Sexual science: Whose cultural difference? *Sexualities, 1*(3), 313–325.

Bramblett, J. R., & Darling, C. A. (1997). Sexual contacts: Experiences, thoughts, and fantasies of Adult male survivors of child sexual abuse. *Journal of Sex and Marital Therapy, 23*(4), 305–316.

Brashear, D. B., & Munsick, R. A. (1991). Hymenal dyspareunia. *Journal of Sex Education and Therapy, 17*(1), 27–31.

Breakwell, G. M., & Fife-Schaw, C. R. (1992). Sexual activities and preferences in a United Kingdom sample of 16- to 20-year-olds. *Archives of Sexual Behavior, 21*(3), 271–293.

Bremner, J. D. (1999). Traumatic memories lost and found: Can lost memories of abuse be found in the brain? In L. M. Williams & V. L. Banyard (Eds.), *Trauma and memory* (p. 384). Thousand Oaks, CA: Sage.

Brener, N. D., McMahon, P. M., Warren, C. W., & Douglas, K. A. (1999). Forced sexual intercourse and associated health-risk behaviors among female college students in the United States. *Journal of Consulting and Clinical Psychology, 67*(2), 252–259.

Breslin, M. (1998). When physicians assure confidentiality, teenagers are willing to talk openly. *Family Planning Perspectives, 30*(1), 52.

Brick, P. (1999). Success stories: What statistics don't tell about sexuality education. *SIECUS Report, 27*(6), 15–21.

Brind, J. (1996). Induced abortion as an independent risk factor for breast cancer: A comprehensive review and meta-analysis. *Journal of Epidemiology and Community Health, 50,* 481–496.

Brinster, R., & Zimmerman, J. W. (1994). Spermatogenesis following male germ-cell transplantation. *Proceedings of the National Academy of Sciences, 91,* 11298–11302.

Britton, P. J., Crimini, K. T., & Rak, C. F. (1999). Techniques for teaching HIV counseling: An intensive experiential model. *Journal of Counseling and Development, 77,* 171–176.

Broderick, G. A. (1998). Impotence and penile vascualr testing: Who are these men and

how do we evaluate the etiology and severity of their complaints? *Journal of Sex Education and Therapy, 23*(3), 197–205.

Brody, J. E. (1998, January 30). Many women ignoring pesky, perimenopausal symptoms. *New York Times*, E1.

Brown, G. R. (1995, April). Cross-dressing men often lead double lives. *Menninger Letter,* 4–5.

Brown, J. E., Ayowa, O. B., & Brown, R. C. (1993). Dry and tight: Sexual practices and potential risks in Zaire. *Social Science and Medicine, 37*(8), 989–994.

Brown, L. S. (1995). Lesbian identities: Concepts and issues. In A. R. D'Augelli & C. J. Patterson (Eds.), *Lesbian, gay, and bisexual identities over the lifespan* (pp. 1–23). New York: Oxford University Press.

Brown, W. A. (1997). What are the best drug treatments for premenstrual syndrome? *Women's Health Digest, 3*(4), 235.

Bucar, L. (1999). *Caution: Catholic health restrictions may be hazardous to your health.* Washington, DC: Catholics for a Free Choice.

Buhle, M. J. (1998). *Feminism and its discontents: A century of struggle with psychoanalysis*. Cambridge, MA: Harvard University Press.

Buhle, M. J. (1999, February 5). Feminism, Freud, and popular culture. *Chronicle of Higher Education*, B4–5.

Bullough, B., & Bullough, V. (1997a). Are transvestites necessarily heterosexual? *Archives of Sexual Behavior, 26*(1), 1–12.

Bullough, B., & Bullough, V. (1997b). Female prostitution: Current research and changing interpretations. *Annual Review of Sex Research, 7,* 158–180.

Bullough, V. L. (1990). The Kinsey Scale in historical perspective. In D. P. McWhirter, S. A. Sanders, & J. M. Reinisch (Eds.), *Homosexuality/heterosexuality: Concepts of sexual orientation* (pp. 3–14). New York: Oxford University Press.

Bullough, V. L. (1994). *Science in the bedroom: A history of sex research*. New York: Basic Books.

Bullough, V. L. (1996). Our feminist foremothers. *Journal of Sex Research, 33*(2), 91–98.

Bullough, V. L. (1998). Alfred Kinsey and the Kisney Report: Historical overview and lasting contributions. *Journal of Sex Research, 35*(2), 127–131.

Bullough, V. L., & Bullough, B. (1995). *Sexual attitudes: Myths and realities*. Amherst, NY: Prometheus Books.

Burch, B. (1993). *On intimate terms: The psychology of difference in lesbian relationships*. Urbana: University of Illinois Press.

Burling, K., Tarvydas, V. M., & Maki, D. R. (1994). Human sexuality and disability: A holistic interpretation of rehabilitation counseling. *Journal of Applied Rehabilitation Counseling, 25*(1), 10–16.

Burnett, J. W., Anderson, W. P., & Heppner, P. P. (1995). Gender roles and self-esteem: A consideration of environmental factors. *Journal of Counseling and Development, 73*(3), 323–326.

Burns, L. H. (1999). Sexual counseling and infertility. In L. H. Burns & S. N. Covington. (Eds.), *Infertility counseling: A comprehensive handbook for clinicians* (p. 630). New York: Parthenon.

Burr, C. (1996). *A separate creation*. New York: Hyperion/Bantam Books.

Bursik, K. (1995). Gender-related personality traits and ego development: Differential patterns for men and women. *Sex Roles, 32*(9), 601–615.

Buss, D. M. (1994). The strategies of human mating. *American Scientist, 82*(3), 238–249.

Buss, D. M. (1998). Sexual strategies theory: Historical origins and current status. *Journal of Sex Research, 35*(1), 19–31.

Buss, D. M., Shackelford, T. K., Kirkpatrick, L. A., Choe, J. C., Lim, H. K., Hasegawa, M., Hasegawa, T., & Bennett, K. (1999). Jealousy and the nature of beliefs about infidelity: Tests of competing hypotheses about sex differences in the United States, Korea, and Japan. *Personal Relationships, 6*(1). 125–150.

Bussey, K., & Bandura, A. (1992). Self-regulatory mechanisms governing gender development. *Child Development, 63*(5), 1236–1250.

Butler, J. (1995). Melancholy gender-refused identification. *Psychoanalytic Dialogues, 5*(2), 165–180.

Butt, T., & Hearn, J. (1998). The sexualization of corporal punishment: The construction of sexual meaning. *Sexualities, 1*(2), 203–227.

Buttenschon, J. (1994). Sexuality and handicap. *Nordisk Sexologi, 12*(2), 137–145.

Buunk, B. P., & Bakker, A. B. (1997). Response to unprotected extradyadic sex by one's partner: Testing predictions from interdependence and equity theory. *Journal of Sex Research, 34*(4), 387–397.

Bux, D. A. (1996). The epidemiology of problem drinking in gay men and lesbians: A critical review. *Clinical Psychology Review, 16*(4), 277–298.

Buxton, A. P. (1999). The best interest of children of gay and lesbian parents. In R. M. Galatzer-Levy & L. Kraus. (Eds.), *The scientific basis of child custody decisions* (pp. 319–356). New York: John Wiley.

Buysse, A., & Ickes, W. (1999). Communication patterns in laboratory discussions of safer sex between dating versus nondating partners. *Journal of Sex Research, 36*(2), 121–134.

Byers, S., Purdon, C., & Clark, D. A. (1998). Sexual intrusive thoughts of college students. *Journal of Sex Research, 35*(4), 359–369.

Byers, S. E., & Demmons, S. (1999). Sexual satisfaction and sexual self-disclosure within dating relationships. *Journal of Sex Research, 36*(2), 180–189.

Byne, W. (1995). Science and belief: Psychobiological research on sexual orientation. *Journal of Homosexuality, 28*(3), 303–344.

C

Cabral, R. J., Pulley, L., Artz, L. M., Johnson, C., Stephens, R. L., & Macaluso, M. (1998). Women at risk of HIV and other STDs: Who is receptive to using the female condom: *Journal of Sex Education and Therapy, 24*(1&2) 89–98.

Cagampang, H. H., Barth, R. P., Korpi, M., & Kirby, D. (1997). Education now and babies later (ENABL): Life history of a campaign to postpone sexual involvement. *Family Planning Perspectives, 29*(3), 109–114.

Calam, R., Horne L., Glasgow, D., & Cox, A. (1998). Psychological disturbance and child sexual abuse: A follow-up study. *Child Abuse and Neglect, 22*(9). 901–913.

Calamidas, E. G. (1997). Promoting healthy sexuality among older adults: Educational challenges for health professionals. *Journal of Sex Education and Therapy, 22*(2), 45–49.

Campbell, J. C. (1995). *Assessing dangerousness: Violence by sexual offenders, batterers, and child abusers*. New York: Guilford.

Campbell, K. E., Kleim, D. M., & Olson, K. R. (1992). Conversational activity and interruptions among men and women. *Journal of Social Psychology, 132*(3), 419–421.

Caplan, P. J. (1991). How do they decide who is normal? The bizarre but true, tale of the DSM process. *Canadian Psychology, 32*(2), 162–170.

Carballo-Dieguez, A., Remien, R. H., Dolezal, C., & Wagner, G. (1999). Reliability of sexual behavior self-reports in male couples of discordant HIV status. *The Journal of Sex Research, 36*(2), 152–158.

Carlock, C. J. (1999). Gender and self-esteem. In C. J. Carlock (Ed.), *Enhancing self-esteem* (pp. 251–285). Philadelphia: Accelerated Development.

Carnes, P. (1992). *Out of the shadows: Understanding sexual addiction* (2nd ed.). Center City, MN: Hazelden.

Carpenter, D. R., Peed, S. F., & Eastman, B. (1995). Personality characteristics of adolescent sexual offenders: A pilot study. *Sexual Abuse: Journal of Research and Treatment, 7*(3), 195–203.

Carpenter, L. M. (1998). From girls into women: Scripts for sexuality and romance in *Seventeen* magazine. *The Journal of Sex Research, 35*(2), 158–168.

Carrier, J. (1995). *De los otros: Intimacy and homosexuality among Mexican men*. New York: Columbia University Press.

Carrington, M. et al. (1999). HLA and HIV-1: Heterozygote advantage and B*35-CW*04 disadvantage. *Science, 283*, 1748–1752.

Carter, J. A., McNair, L. D., Corbin, W. R., & Williams, M. (1999). Gender differences related to heterosexual condom use: The influence of negotiation styles. *Journal of Sex and Marital Therapy, 25*, 217–225.

Casper, L. M., Hawkins, M., & O'Connell, M. (1994). Who's minding the kids? Child care arrangements, Fall 1991. *Current Population Reports*, 70–76.

Casper, M. J. (1998). *The making of the unborn patient: A social anatomy of fetal surgery*. Patterson, NJ: Rutgers University Press.

Casper, M. J., & Moore, L. J. (1995). Inscribing bodies, inscribing the future: Gender, sex, and reproduction in outer space. *Sociological Perspectives, 38*(2), 311–333.

Cass, V. C. (1983–1984). Homosexual identity: A concept in need of definition. *Journal of Homosexuality, 9*, 105–126.

Cass, V. C. (1990). The implications of homosexual identity formation for the Kinsey model and scale of sexual preference. In D. P. McWhirter, S. A. Sanders, & J. M. Reinisch (Eds.), *Homosexuality/heterosexuality: Concepts of sexual orientation* (pp. 239–266). New York: Oxford University Press.

Catalan, J. (1993). Primary male anorgasmia and its treatment. *Sexual and Marital Therapy, 8*(3), 275–282.

Catania, J. (1997). 10% of sexually active U.S. adults use sex toys in part-ner sex. *Sexual Science, 38*(4), 1, 8.

Catania, J. A. (1999). A framework for conceptualizing reporting bias and its antecedents in interviews assessing human sexuality. *Journal of Sex Research, 36*(1), 25–38.

Catania, J. A., Binson, J. P., Peterson, J., & Canchola, J. (1997). The effects of question wording, interviewer gender, and control on item response by African American respondents. In J. Bancroft (Ed.), *Researching sexual behavior* (pp. 110–113). Bloomington: Indiana University Press.

Cates, W. (1998). Reproductive tract infections. In Hatcher, R. A., Trussell, J., Stewart, F., Cates, W., Stewart, G. K., Guest, F., & Kowal, D. *Contraceptive Technology* (pp. 179–210). New York: Ardent Media.

CDC Advisory Committee on the Prevention of HIV Infection (1995). External review of CDC's HIV prevention strategies: Summary of the final report. *SIECUS Report, 23*(2), 23–24.

Center for Reproductive Law and Policy. (1998). When given the facts, poll shows voters support the president's "partial birth abortion" veto. News Release. CLRP: New York.

Cerrone, G. H. (1991). Zoophilia in a rural population: Two case studies. *Journal of Rural Community Psychology, 12*(1), 29–39.

Chalker, R. (1994). Updating the model of female sexuality. *SIECUS Report, 22*(5), 1–6.

Chambers, V., & Chang, Y. (1999, March 1). High school confidential. *Time*, 62–64.

Chan, C. S. (1995). Issues of sexual identity in an ethnic minority: The case of Chinese American lesbians, gay men, and bisexual people. In A. R. D'Augelli & C. J. Patterson (Eds.), *Lesbian, gay, and bisexual identities over the lifespan* (pp. 87–101). New York: Oxford University Press.

Chan, J. M., Stampfer, M. J., Giovannucci, E., Gann, P. H., Ma, J., Wilkinson, P., Hennekens, C. H., & Pollak, M. (1998). Plasma insulin-like growth factor-I and prostate cancer risk: A prospective study. *Science, 279*, 563–566.

Chandiramani, R. (1998). A view from the field: Phone help line in India helps identify HIV risk behaviors. *SIECUS Report, 26*(5), 4–6.

Chandler, C. K. (1995). Contemporary Adlerian reflections on homosexuality and bisexuality. *Individual Psychology: Journal of Adlerian Theory, Research, and Practice, 51*(2), 82–89.

Chandra, A., & Stephen, E. H. (1998). Impaired fecundity in the United States: 1982–1995. *Family Planning Perspectives, 30*(1), 34–42.

Charmaz, K. (1994). Identity dilemmas of chronically ill men. *Sociological Quarterly, 35*(2), 269–288.

Chervyakov, V. (1997). Survey reports arguments to start sexuality education in Russia. *SIECUS Report, 25*(2), 8–9.

Cho, C., Bunch, D. O., Faure, J., Goulding, E. H., Eddy, E. M., Primakoff, P., & Myles, D. G. (1998). Fertilization defects in sperm from mice lacking in fertilin B. *Science, 281*, 1857–1859.

Christ, G. J. (1998). the control of corporal smooth muscle tone, the coordination of penile erection, and the etiology of erectile dysfunction: The devil is in the details. *Journal of Sex Education and Therapy, 23*(3), 187–192.

Christakis, D. A., Harvey, E., Zerr, D. M., Feudtner, C., Wright, J. A., & Connell, F. A. (2000). A trade-off analysis of routine newborn circumcision. *Pediatrics, 105*(1), 246–249.

Chua-Eoan, H. (1997, March 31). Fidelity = chastity. *Time*, 70.

Chung, Y. B., & Katayama, M. (1999). Ethnic and sexual identity development of Asian American lesbian and gay adolescents. In K. S. Ng (Ed.), *Counseling Asian families from a systems perspective* (pp. 159–169). Alexandria, VA: American Counseling Association.

Cibelli, J. B., Stice, S. L., Golueke, P. J., Kane, J. J., Jerry, J., Blackwell, C., Ponce de Leon, F. A., & Robi, J. M. (1998). Cloned transgenic calves produced from nonquiescent fetal fibroblasts. *Science, 280*, 1256–1258.

CLASP Collaborative Group. (1995). Low dose aspirin in pregnancy and early childhood development: Follow up of the collaborative low dose aspirin study in pregnancy. *British Journal of Obstetrics and Gynaecology, 102*, 861–868.

Claus, E. B., Schildkraut, J. M., Thompson, W. D., & Risch, N. J. (1996). The genetic attributable risk of breast and ovarian cancer. *Cancer, 77*(11), 2318–2324.

Clayton, A. H., Clavet, G. J., McGarvey, E. L., Warnock, J. K., & Weiss, K. (1999). Assessment of sexual functioning during the menstrual cycle. *Journal of Sex and Marital Therapy, 25*, 281–291.

Cleland, J., & Ferry, B. (Eds.). (1997). *Sexual behaviour and knowledge about AIDS in the developing world: Findings from a multisite study*. London: Taylor and Francis.

Clements-Schreiber, M. E., Rempel, J. K., & Desmarais, S. (1998). Women's sexual pressure tactics and adherence to related attitudes: A step toward prediction. *Journal of Sex Research, 35*(2), 197–205.

Cline, V. B. (1974). Another view: Pornography effects, the state of the art, and the pornography commission—A case study of scientists and social policy decision making. In V. B. Cline (Ed.), *Where do you draw the line?* (pp. 203–256). Provo, UT: Brigham Young University Press.

Cloud, J. (1998a, January 5). A different father's day. *Time*, 106.

Cloud, J. (1998b, March 23). Sex and the law. *Time*, 48–54.

Cloud, J. (1998c, July 20). Trans across America. *Time*, 48–49.

Cochran, S. D., & Mays, V. M. (1990). Sex, lies, and HIV. *New England Journal of Medicine, 322*(11), 774–775.

Cohen, A. J., & Bartlik, B. (1997). Ginkgo biloba for antidepressant-induced sexual dysfunction. *Journal of Sex and Marital Therapy, 24*, 139–143.

Cohen, D. (1999). Cost as a barrier to condom use: The evidence for condom subsidies in the United States. *American Journal of Public Health, 89*(4), 567–568.

Cohen, D. J., & Bruce, K. E. (1997). Sex and mortality: Real risk and perceived vulnerability. *Journal of Sex Research, 34*(3), 279–291.

Cohen, J. (1998). Exploring how to get at—and eradicate—hidden HIV. *Science, 279*, 1854–1855.

Cohen, J. (1999a). AIDS virus traced to chimp subspecies. *Science, 283*, 772–773.

Cohen, J. (1999b). The scientific challenge of hepatitis C. *Science, 285*, 26–30.

Cohen, J. E. (1996). *How many people can the earth support?* New York: W. W. Norton.

Cohen, P. G. (1997). The association of premature ejaculation and hypogonadotropic hypogonadism. *Journal of Sex and Marital Therapy, 23*(3), 208–210.

Colditz, G. A., et al. (1995). The use of estrogens and progestins and the risk of breast cancer in postmenopausal women. *New England Jour-nal of Medicine, 332*, 1589–1593.

Cole, C. M., O'Boyle, M., Emory, L. E., & Meyer, W. J. (1997). Comorbidity of gender dysphoria and other major psychiatric diagnoses. *Archives of Sexual Behavior, 26*(1), 13–26.

Collins, F. S., Patrinos, A., Jordan, E., Chakravarti, A., Gesteland, R., Walters, L., et al. (1998). New goals for the U.S. human genome project: 1998–2003. *Science, 282*, 682–689.

Commission on Obscenity and Pornography. (1970). *Report of the Commission on Obscenity and Pornography*. New York: Bantam Books.

Committee on Lesbian and Gay Concerns. (1991). Avoiding heterosexual bias in language. *American Psychologist, 46*(9), 973–974.

Committee on Prevention and Control of STDs. (1997). The hidden epidemic: Confronting sexually transmitted diseases (excerpt). *SIECUS Report, 25*(3), 4–14.

Coney, N. S., & Mackey, W. C. (1998). The woman as final arbiter: A case for the faculative character of the human sex ratio. *Journal of Sex Research, 35*(2), 169–175.

Conklin, S. C. (1997). Sexuality education in seminaries and theological schools. In J. W. Maddock (Ed.), *Sexuality education in postsecondary and professional settings* (pp. 143–174). New York: Haworth Press.

Conklin, S. C., & Goodson, P. (1998). Sexuality education for clergy: Empirical data, current efforts, future needs. *Journal of Sex Education and Therapy, 23*(1), 33–41.

Connell, R. W. (1999). Making gendered people: Bodies, identities, sexuality. In M. M. Ferree et al. (Eds.), *Revisioning gender* (pp. 449–471). Thousand Oaks, CA: Sage.

Cook, L. S., Koutsky, L. A., & Holmes, K. K. (1994). Circumcision and sexually transmitted diseases. *American Journal of Public Health, 84*, 197–201.

Cooper, A. (2000). Sexual pathology and the internet. *Professional Psychology: Research and Practice, 30*(2), in press.

Cooper, A., Scherer, C. R., Boies, S. C., & Gordon, B. L. (1999). Sexuality on the internet: From sexual exploration to pathological expression. *Professional Psychology: Research and Practice, 30*(2), 154–164.

Cooper, A., & Sportolari, L. (1997). Romance in cyberspace: Understanding online attraction. *Journal of Sex Education and Therapy, 22*(1), 7–14.

Cooper, A. J. (1996). Autoerotic asphyxiation: Three case reports. *Journal of Sex and Marital Therapy, 22*(1), 47–53.

Cooper, A. J. (1998). Sexually compulsive behavior. *Contemporary Sexuality, 32*(4), 1–3.

Cooperstock, M., & Campbell, J. (1996). Excess males in preterm birth. *Obstetrics and Gynecology, 88*(2), 189–193.

Courtois, C. A. (1999). Recollections of sexual abuse: Treatment principles and guidelines. *Private Practice* (p. 436). New York: W. W. Norton.

Couzin, J. (1998). RAC confronts in utero gene therapy proposals. *Science, 282,* 27.

Cowan, G., & Dunn, K. F. (1994). What themes in pornography lead to perceptions of the degradation of women? *Journal of Sex Research, 31*(1), 11–21.

Cowley, G. (1996, September 16). Attention: Aging men. *Newsweek,* 68–75.

Cowley, G. (1998, June 29). Sobering up about AIDS. *Time,* 60.

Cowley, G., & Springen, K. (1997, December 1). Multiplying the risks. *Newsweek,* 66.

Cowley, G., & Underwood, A. (1998, March 16). Is love the best drug? *Time,* 54–55.

Cox, D. J. (1988). Incidence and nature of male genital exposure behaviors as reported by college women. *Journal of Sex Research, 24*(1), 227–234.

Coxon, A. P. M. (1999). Parallel accounts? Discrepancies between self-report (diary) and recall (questionnaire) measures of the same sexual behavior. *AIDS Care, 11*(2), 221–124.

Craissati, J. (1999). *Child sexual abusers: A community treatment approach.* Philadelphia: Brunner/Mazel.

Crapo, R. H. (1996). *Cultural anthropology: Understanding ourselves and others* (4th ed.). Guilford, CT: Brown & Benchmark.

Creamer, D. A. (1998). Indicators of sexual abuse: A school-based perspective. *Journal for the Professional Counselor, 13*(1), 57–68.

Creamer, E. G. (1994). Gender and publications in core higher education journals. *Journal of College Student Development, 35,* 35–39.

Crenshaw, T. (1996). *The alchemy of love and lust.* New York: Putnam.

Crenshaw, T. L., & Goldberg, J. P. (1996). *Sexual pharmacology: Drugs that affect sexual function.* New York: W. W. Norton.

Crockett, L. J., Bingham, C. R., Chopak, J. S., & Vicary, J. R. (1996). Timing of first sexual intercourse: The role of social control, social learning, and problem behavior. *Journal of Youth and Adolescence, 25*(1), 89–111.

Crook, L. S., & Dean M. C. (1999). "Lost in a shopping mall"—A breach of professional ethics. *Ethics & Behavior, 9*(1), 39–50.

Crosby, R. A., Yarber, W. L., & Meyerson, B. (1999). Frequency and predictors of condom use and reasons for not using condoms among low-income women. *Journal of Sex Education and Therapy, 24*(1&2), 63–70.

Cross, J. C., Werb, Z., & Fisher, S. J. (1994). Implantation and the placenta: Key pieces of the development puzzle. *Science, 266,* 1508–1517.

Cross, S. E., & Markus, H. R. (1993). Gender in thought, belief, and action: A cognitive approach. In A. E. Beall & R. J. Sternberg (Eds.), *The psychology of gender* (pp. 55–98). New York: Guilford Press.

Crossette, B. (1996, July 11). New tally of world tragedy: Women who die giving life. *New York Times,* A1, A12.

Croteau, J. M. (1996). Research on the work experiences of lesbian, gay, and bisexual people: An integrative review of methodology and findings. *Journal of Vocational Behavior, 48*(2), 195–209.

Croteau, J. M., & Lark, J. S. (1995). A qualitative investigation of biased and exemplary student affairs practice concerning lesbian, gay, and bisexual issues. *Journal of College Student Development, 36*(5), 472–482.

Crowden, C. R., & Koch, P. B. (1995). Attitudes related to sexual concerns: Gender and orientation comparisons. *Journal of Sex Education and Therapy, 21*(2), 78–87.

Crystal, S., & Schlosser, L. R. (1999). The HIV-mental health challenge. In A. V. Horwitz & T. L. Scheid (Eds.), *A handbook for the study of mental health: Social contexts, theories, and systems* (pp. 526–549). New York: Cambridge University Press.

Culnane, M. (1999). Lack of long-term effects of in utero exposure to zidovudine among uninfected children born to HIV-infected women. *Journal of the American Medical Association, 281*(2), 151–157.

Cunningham, I. (1998). An innovative HIV/AIDS research and education program in Puerto Rico. *SIECUS Report, 26*(3), 18–20.

Curtin, K. A. (1996). Adolescent egocentrism and its relationship to HIV and AIDS. *Journal for the Professional Counselor, 11*(1), 31–39.

Cushman, L. F., Romero, D., Kalmuss, D., Dovidson, A. R., Heartwell S., & Rulin M. (1998). Condom use among women choosing long-term hormonal contraception. *Family Planning Perspectives, 30*(5), 240–243.

Cutler, W. B. (1999). Human sex-attractant hormones: Discovery, research, development, and application in therapy. *Psychiatric Annals, 29*(1), 54–59.

Cutler, W. B., Friedmann, E., & McCoy, N. L. (1998). Pheromonal influences on socio-sexual behavior in men. *Archives of Sexual Behavior, 27*(1), 1–13.

Cutter, R. (1994). *When opposites attract: Right brain/left brain relationships and how to make them work.* New York: Dutton.

Czuczka, D. (2000). The twentieth century: An American sexual history. *SIECUS Report, 28*(2), 15–18.

D

Dabbs, J. M., & Mohammed, S. (1992). Male and female salivary testosterone concentrations before and after sexual activity. *Physiology and Behavior, 52*(1), 195–197.

Dailard, C. (1999). State contraceptive coverage laws: Creative responses to questions of "conscience." *The Guttmacher Report, 2*(4), 1–2, 14.

Daley, D. (1997). The bridge to the 21st century: Where is it leading and what is the toll? *SIECUS Report, 25*(2), 22–23.

Danielson, R., Barbey, A., Cassidy D., Rosenzweig, J., & Chowdhury, D. (1999). Couple-friendly services in a metropolitan sexually transmitted disease clinic: Views of clients and providers. *Family Planning Perspectives, 31*(4), 195–199.

Darling, C. A., Davidson, J. K., & Conway-Welch, C. (1990). Female ejaculation: Perceived origins, the Grafenberg spot/area, and sexual responsiveness. *Archives of Sexual Behavior, 19*(1), 29–47.

Darling, C. A., Davidson, J. K., & Jennings, D. A. (1991). The female sexual response revisited: Understanding the multiorgasmic experience in women. *Archives of Sexual Behavior, 20*(6), 527–540.

Darroch J. E., & Frost, J. J. (1999). Women's interest in vaginal microbicides. *Family Planning Perspectives, 31*(1), 16–23.

Daskalos, C. T. (1998). Changes in the sexual orientation of six male-to-female transsexuals. *Archives of Sexual Behavior, 27*(6), 605–614.

D'Augelli, A. R., & Garnets, L. D. (1995). Lesbian, gay, and bisexual communities. In A. R. D'Augelli & C. J. Patterson (Eds.), *Lesbian, gay, and bisexual identities over the lifespan* (pp. 293–320). New York: Oxford University Press.

Davidson, J. K., & Darling, C. A. (1993). Mandatory guilt and sexual responsiveness among post-college age women: Sexual satisfaction revisited. *Journal of Sex and Marital Therapy, 19*(4), 289–300.

Davidson, J. K., & Moore, N. B. (1994). Guilt and lack of orgasm during sexual intercourse: Myth versus reality among college women. *Journal of Sex Education and Therapy, 20*(3), 153–174.

Davis, C. M., & Bauserman, R. (1993). Exposure to sexually explicit materials: An attitude change perspective. *Annual Review of Sex Research, 4,* 121–209.

Davis, C. M., Blank, J., Lin, H. Y., & Bonillas, C. (1996). Characteristics of vibrator use among women. *Journal of Sex Research, 33*(4), 313–320.

Davis, K. R., & Weller, S. C. (1999). The effectiveness of condoms in reducing heterosexual transmission of HIV. *Family Planning Perspectives, 31*(6), 272–279.

Davis, R., Taylor, B., & Bench, S. (1995). Impact of sexual and nonsexual assault on secondary victims. *Violence and Victims, 10*(1), 73–84.

Davis, S. R. (1998). The clinical use of androgens in female sexual disorders. *Journal of Sex and Marital Therapy, 24,* 153–163.

Davis, S. S., & Davis, D. A. (1995). The mosque and the satellite: Media and adolescence in a Moroccan town. *Journal of Youth and Adolescence, 24*(5), 577–593.

Day, S. M. (1995). American Indians: Reclaiming cultural and sexual identity. *SIECUS Report, 23*(3), 6–7.

Deacon, S., Minichiello, V., & Plummer, D. (1995). Sexuality and older people: Revisiting the assumptions. *Educational Gerontology, 21*(5), 497–513.

Dean, J. (1998). Sex spirit energy and power. *Contemporary Sexuality, 32*(3), 1–4.

DeBusk, R. F. (1996). Sexual activity triggering myocardial infarction: One less thing to worry about. *Journal of the American Medical Association, 275,* 1447–1448.

Deep, A. L., Lilenfeld, L. R., Plotnicov, K. H., Pollice, C., & Kaye, W. H. (1999). Sexual abuse in eating disorder subtypes and control women: The role of comorbid substance dependence in bulimia nervosa. *International Journal of Eating Disorders, 25*(1), 1–10.

Dekker, J., & Everaerd, W. (1993). Imagery and sexual arousal. *Sexual and Marital Therapy, 8*(3), 283–285.

DeLamater, J. (1995). The NORC sex survey. *Science, 270,* 501–503.

DeLamater, J. D., & Hyde, J. S. (1998). Essentialism vs. social constructionism in the study of human sexuality. *Journal of Sex Research, 35*(1), 10–18.

Delbanco, S., Lundy, J., Hoff, T., Parker, M., & Smith, M. (1997). Public knowledge and perceptions about unplanned pregnancy and contraception in three countries. *Family Planning Perspectives, 29*(2), 70–75.

Delbanco, S., Mauldon, J., & Smith, M. D. (1997). Little knowledge and limited practice: Emergency contraceptive pills, the public, and the obstetrician-gynecologist. *Obstetrics and Gynecology, 89,* 1006–1011.

DeMaris, A. (1997). Elevated sexual activity in violent marriages: Hyper-sexuality or sexual extortion? *Journal of Sex Research, 34*(4), 361–373.

Denny, D. (1999). Transgender in the United States: A brief discussion. *SIECUS Report, 28*(1), 8–13.

Denny, G., Young, M., & Spear, C. E. (1999). An evaluation of the Sex Can Wait abstinence education curriculum series. *American Journal of Health Behavior, 23*(2), 134–143.

Dessens, A. B., Cohen-Kettenis, P. T., Mellenbergh, G. J., Poll, N., Koppe, J. G., & Boer, K. (1999). Prenatal exposure to anticonvulsants and psychosexual development. *Archives of Sexual Behavior, 28*(1), 31–44.

DeVillers, L. (1997). *Love skills.* San Luis Obispo, CA: Impact.

Devor, H. (1993). Sexual orientation identities, attractions, and practices of female-to-male transsexuals. *Journal of Sex Research, 30*(4), 303–315.

Devor, H. (1997). Female gender dysphoria in context: Social problem or personal problem. *Annual Review of Sex Research, 7,* 44–89.

Diamond, M. (1998). Intersexuality: Recommendations for management. *Archives of Sexual Behavior, 27,* 634–641.

Diamond, M., & Sigmundson, H. K. (1997). Management of intersexuality: Guidelines for dealing with persons with ambiguous genitalia. *Archives of Pediatric and Adolescent Medicine, 151,* 1046–1050.

Diamond, M., & Uchiyama, A. (1999). Pornography, rape, and sex crimes in Japan. *International Journal of Law & Psychiatry, 22*(1), 1–22.

Diaz, R. M. (1999). Trips to fantasy island: Contests of risky sex for San Francisco gay men. *Sexualities, 2*(1), 89–112.

DiBartolo, P. M., & Barlow, D. H. (1996). Perfectionism, marital satisfaction, and contributing factors to sexual dysfunction in men with erectile disorder and their spouses. *Archives of Sexual Behavior, 25*(6), 581–589.

Dickinson, R. L. (1932). *A thousand marriages.* Baltimore: Williams & Wilkins.

Dittmann, R. W. (1998). Ambiguous genitalia, gender-identity problems, and sex reassignment. *Journal of Sex and Marital Therapy, 24,* 255–271.

Dittman, R. W., Kappes, M. H., & Kappes, M. E. (1993). Cognitive functioning in female patients with 21-hydroxylase deficiency. *European Child and Adolescent Psychiatry, 2*(1), 34–43.

Djerassi, C. (1999). Sex in an age of mechanical reproduction. *Science, 285,* 53–55.

Docter, R. F., & Prince, V. (1997). Transvestism: A survey of 1032 cross-dressers. *Archives of Sexual Behavior, 26*(6), 589–605.

Doell, R. G. (1995). Sexuality in the brain. *Journal of Homosexuality, 28*(3), 345–354.

Doll, L., Myers, T., Kennedy, M., & Allman, D. (1997). Bisexuality and HIV risk: Experiences in Canada and the United States. *Annual Review of Sex Research, 8,* 102–146.

Donald, M., Lucke, J., Dunne, M., & Raphael, B. (1995). Gender differences associated with young people's emotional reactions to sexual intercourse. *Journal of Youth and Adolescence, 24*(4), 453–464.

Donohue, J., & Gebhard, P. (1995). The Kinsey Institute/Indiana University report on sexuality and spinal cord injury. *Sexuality and Disability, 13*(1), 7–85.

Donovan, P. (1997). Confronting a hidden epidemic: The Institute of Medicine's report on sexually transmitted diseases. *Family Planning Perspectives, 29*(2), 87–89.

Donovan, P. (1998). School-based sexuality education: The issues and challenges. *Family Planning Perspectives, 30*(4), 188–193.

Dove, N. L., & Weiderman, M. W. (2000). Cognitive distraction and women's sexual functioning. *Journal of Sex and Marital Therapy, 26*(1), 67–78.

Driggs, J. H., & Finn, S. (1990). *Intimacy between men: How to find and keep gay love relationships.* New York: Penguin.

Drlica, K. A. (1996). *Double-edged sword: The promises and risks of the genetic revolution.* New York: Helix (Addison-Wesley).

Ducharme, S. H., & Gill, K. M. (1997). *Sexuality after spinal cord injury: Answers to your questions.* Baltimore: Paul H. Brookes.

Dugger, C. W. (1996, September 11). A refugee's body is intact but her family is torn. *New York Times,* A1, B6–7.

Dunn, M. E., & Alarie, P. (1997). Trends in sexuality education in United States and Canadian medical schools. In J. W. Maddock (Ed.), *Sexuality education in postsecondary and professional settings* (pp. 175–184). New York: Haworth Press.

Durrant, L., et al. (1996). New maternal blood test for fetal genetics. *British Journal of Obstetrics and Gynaecology, 103,* 219–221.

Dym, B., & Glenn, M. (1993). *Couples.* New York: HarperCollins.

Dziech, B. W. (1998, March 20). The abuse of power in intimate relationships. *Chronicle of Higher Education,* B4–5.

E

East, P. L. (1998). Racial and ethnic differences in girls; sexual, marital, and birth expectations. *Journal of Marriage and the Family, 60*(1), 150–162.

Eccles, J. S., Barber, B., & Jozefowicz, D. (1999). Linking gender to educational, occupational, and recreational choices: Applying the Eccles et al. model of achievement-related choices. In W. Swann & J. H. Langlois (Eds.), *Sexism and stereotyes in modern society: The gender science of Janet Taylor Spence* (pp. 153–192). Washington, DC: American Psychological Association.

Ecker, N. (1994). Culture and sexual scripts out of Africa: A North American trainer's view of taboos, tradition, trouble and truth. *SIECUS Report, 22*(2), 16–21.

Ecker, N. (1998). Where there is no village: Teaching about sexuality in crisis situations. *SIECUS Report, 26*(5), 7–10.

Edwards, M. (1996). We have a responsibility to dialogue with the media. *SIECUS Report, 24*(5), 5–9.

Edwards, M. (1998). Technology provides access to sexuality information and education worldwide. *SIECUS Report, 26*(5), 2.

Edwards, M. (1999). The age of cultural competency. *SIECUS Report, 27*(5), 2.

Edwards, T. M. (1998, July 13). The opposite of sex. *Time,* 39.

Egan, K. M., Newcomb, P. A., Longnecker, M. P., Trenthamdietz, A., Baron, J. A., Trichopoulos, D., Stampfer, M. J., & Willett, W. C. (1996). Jewish religion and risk of breast cancer. *Lancet, 347*(9016), 1645–1646.

Egypto, A. C., Pinto, M. C., & Bock, S. D. (1996). Brazilian organization develops sexual guidance programs defined by long-term communication. *SIECUS Report, 24*(3), 16–17.

Eisenman, R. (1994). Conservative sexual values: Effects of an abstinence program on student attitudes. *Journal of Sex Education and Therapy, 20*(2), 75–78.

Ekins, R. (1997). *Male femaling: A grounded theory approach to cross-dressing and sex-changing.* London: Routledge.

Elam-Evans, L. D. (1996). Trends in the percentage of women who received no prenatal care in the United States, 1980–1992: Contributions of the demographic and risk effects. *Obstetrics and Gynecology, 87,* 575–580.

Eliason, M. J. (1997). The prevalence and nature of biphobia in heterosexual undergraduate students. *Archives of Sexual Behavior, 26*(3), 317–326.

Ellen, J. M., Vittinghoff, E., Bolan, G., Boyer, C. B., & Padian, N. S. (1998). Individuals' perceptions about their sex partners' risk behaviors. *Journal of Sex Research, 35*(4), 328–332.

Ellin, A. (1994). Just friends: Can men and women do it—without doing it? In O. Pocs (Ed.), *Annual editions: Human Sexuality, 94/95* (19th ed., p. 227). Guilford, CT: Dushkin.

Ellingson, L. A., & Yarber, W. L. (1997). Breast self-examination, the health belief model, and sexual orientation in women. *Journal of Sex Education and Therapy, 22*(3), 19–24.

Elliot, A. N., & O'Donohue, W. T. (1997). The effects of anxiety and distraction on sexual arousal in a nonclinical sample of heterosexual women. *Archives of Sexual Behavior, 26*(6), 607–624.

Elliott, L., & Brantley, C. (1997). *Sex on campus.* New York: Random House.

Elliott, M., Browne, K., & Kilcoyne, J. (1995). Child sexual abuse prevention: What offenders tell us. *Child Abuse and Neglect, 19*(5), 579–594.

Ellis, H. H. (1936). *Studies in the psychology of sex* (7 vols. in 2). New York: Modern Library. (Original edition published 1896–1928)

Elomaa, K. (1998). Omitting the first oral contraceptive pills of the cycle does not automatically lead to ovulation. *American Journal of Obstetrics and Gynecology, 179*(1), 41–46.

Elwood, W. N., & Williams, M. L. (1999). The politics of silence: Communicative rules and HIV prevention issues in gay male bathhouses. In W. N. Elwood (Ed.), *Power in the blood: A handbook on AIDS, politics, and communication* (pp. 121–132). Mahwah, NJ: Lawrence Erlbaum Associates.

Eng, T. R., & Butler, W. T. (Eds.). (1996). *The hidden epidemic: Confronting sexually transmitted diseases.* Washington, DC: Institute of Medicine.

Engstrom, C. M., & Sedlacek, W. (1997). Attitudes of heterosexual students toward their gay male and lesbian peers. *Journal of College Student Development, 38*(6), 565–576.

Ericksen, J. A. (1998). With enough cases, why do you need statistics? Revisiting Kinsey's methodology. *Journal of Sex Research, 35*(2), 132–140.

Ericksen, J. A. (1999). *Kiss and tell: Surveying sex in the twentieth century.* Cambridge, MA: Harvard University Press.

Erickson, P. I. (1999). Cultural factors affecting the negotiation of first sexual intercourse among Latina adolescent mothers. *International Quarterly of Community Health Education, 18*(1), 121–137.

Erikson, E. (1968). *Identity: Youth and crisis.* New York: W. W. Norton.

Erwin, P. C. (1994). To use or not use combined hormonal oral contraceptives during lactation. *Family Planning Perspectives, 26*(1), 26–33.

Etaugh, C., & Liss, M. B. (1992). Home, school, and playroom: Training grounds for adult gender roles. *Sex Roles, 26*(3–4), 129–147.

Etzkowitz, H., Kemelgor, K., Neuschatz, M., Uzzi, B., & Alonzo, J. (1994). The paradox of critical mass for women in science. *Science, 266,* 51–54.

Everaerd, W., & Laan, E. (1995). Desire for passion: Energetics of sexual response. *Journal of Sex and Marital Therapy, 21*(4), 255–263.

Ewart, W. R., & Winikoff, B. (1998). Toward safe and effective medical abortion. *Science, 281,* 520–522.

Executive summary: Teens talk about adolescent sexuality in the 90s—A survey of high school students. (1994). *SIECUS Report, 22*(5), 16–17.

F

Farrer, J. (1999). Disco "super-culture": Consuming foreign sex in the Chinese disco. *Sexualities, 2*(2), 147–166.

Fast, I. (1993). Aspects of early gender development: A psychodynamic perspective. In A. E. Beall & R. J. Sternberg (Eds.), *The psychology of gender* (pp. 173–193). New York: Guilford Press.

Fausto-Sterling, A. (1993). The five sexes: Why male and female are not enough. *The Sciences, 33*(3), 20–24.

Federal Trade Commission. (1999, June). Home-use tests for HIV can be inaccurate. Washington, DC: FTC Consumer Alert.

Feeney, G. (1994). Fertility decline in East Asia. *Science, 266,* 1518–1523.

Feigenbaum, R., Weinstein, E., & Rosen, E. (1995). College students' sexual attitudes and behaviors: Implications for sexuality education. *Journal of American College Health, 44*(3), 112–118.

Fein, E., & Schneider, S. (1995). *The rules: Time-tested secrets for capturing the heart of Mr. Right.* New York: Warner Books.

Fein, S. B., & Roe, B. (1998). The effect of work status on initiation and duration of breast-feeding. *American Journal of Public Health, 88*(7), 1042–1046.

Feiring, C., Taska, L., & Lewis, M. (1999). Revisioning gender. In M. M. Ferree, J. Lorber, & B. B. Hess. (Eds.), *The gender lens* (p. xxxvi). Thousand Oaks, CA: Sage.

Ferree, M. M., Lorber, J., & Hess, B. B. (1999). Revisioning gender. In M. M. Ferree, J. Lorber, & B. B. Hess. (Eds.), The gender lens (p. xxxvi). Thousand Oaks, CA: Sage.

Ferris, D. G. (1996). Self-treatment for vaginal candidiasis misguided. *Jour-nal of Family Practice, 42,* 595–600.

Fihn, S. D. (1996). Association between use of spermicide-coated condoms and *E. coli* urinary tract infection in young women. *American Journal of Epidemiology, 144,* 512–520.

Finer, L. B., Darroch, J. E., & Singh, S. (1999). Sexual partnership patterns as a behavioral risk factor for sexually transmitted diseases. *Family Planning Perspectives, 31*(5), 228–236.

Finger, W. W. (2000). Avoiding sexual exploitation: Guidelines for therapists. *SIECUS Report, 28*(3), 12–13.

Fischer, G. J. (1989). Sex words used by partners in a relationship. *Journal of Sex Education and Therapy, 15*(1), 50–58.

Fischer, G. J. (1996). Deceptive, verbally coercive college males: Attitudinal predictors and lies told. *Archives of Sexual Behavior, 25*(5), 527–533.

Fischman, J., & Ray, L. B. (1994). Insights into reproduction. *Science, 266,* 1459.

Fisher, H. (1999). *The first sex: The natural talents of women and how they are changing the world.* New York: Random House.

Fisher, S., & Greenberg, R. P. (1996). *Freud scientifically reappraised: Testing the theories and therapy.* New York: John Wiley and Sons.

Fisher, W. A., Byrne, D., White, L. A., & Kelley, K. (1988). Erotophobia-erotophilia as a dimension of personality. *Journal of Sex Research, 25*(1), 123–151.

Fisher, W. A., & Grenier, G. (1994). Violent pornography, antiwoman thoughts, and antiwoman acts: In search of reliable effects. *Journal of Sex Research, 31*(1), 23–38.

Flowers, A. (1998). *The fantasy factory: An insider's view of the phone sex industry.* Philadelphia: University of Pennsylvania Press.

Foa, E. B., & Riggs, D. S. (1995). Posttraumatic stress disorder following assault: Theoretical considerations and empirical findings. *Current Directions in Psychological Science, 4*(2), 61–65.

Fones, C. S., Levine, S. B., Althof, S. E., & Risen, C. B. (1999). The sexual struggles of 23 clergymen: A follow-up study. *Journal of Sex and Marital Therapy, 25,* 183–195.

Foote, D. (1999, February 8). You could get raped. *Newsweek,* 64–65.

Forbes, A. (1998). Special Report: "Names" versus "unique identifiers": The how of HIV case reporting. *SIECUS Report, 26*(3), 3–10.

Ford, C. S., & Beach, F. A. (1951). *Patterns of sexual behavior.* New York: Harper.

Forste, R., & Morgan, J. (1998). How relationships of U.S. men affect contraceptive use and efforts to prevent sexually transmitted diseases. *Family Planning Perspectives, 30*(2), 56–62.

Forward, S., & Buck, C. (1992). *Obsessive love: When it hurts too much to let go.* New York: Bantam Books.

Foster, D. (1999, June 27). Six billion or so: Global population hitting a milestone. Associated Press as reported in *Watertown (NY) Daily Times Sunday Weekly,* 6–7.

Foster, R. A., & Keating, J. P. (1992). Measuring androcentrism in the Western God-concept. *Journal for the Scientific Study of Religion, 31*(3), 366–375.

Foster, S. (1995a, September). The myths behind male sexual abuse. *Counseling Today,* 35, 39.

Foster, S. (1995b, December). The sexual exploitation of women by men in power. *Counseling Today,* 1, 10–12.

Francke, L. B. (1997). *Ground zero: The gender wars in the military.* New York: Simon & Schuster.

Franke, A. H. (1998, July 17). The message from the Supreme Court: Clarify sexual-harassment policies. *Chronicle of Higher Education,* B6–7.

Fraser, C. M. et al. (1998). Complete genome sequences of *Treponema pallidum,* the syphilis spirochete. *Science, 281,* 375–388.

Frayser, S. G. (1995). Defining normal childhood sexuality: An anthropological approach. *Annual Review of Sex Research, 5,* 173–217.

Freund, K. (1990). Courtship disorder. In W. L. Marshall, D. R. Laws, & H. E. Barbaree (Eds.), *Handbook of sexual assault* (pp. 195–207). New York: Plenum Press.

Freund, K., & Seto, M. C. (1998). Preferential rape in the theory of courtship disorder. *Archives of Sexual Behavior, 27*(5), 433–443.

Frey, K., & Hojjat, M. (1998). Are love styles related to sexual styles? *Jour-nal of Sex Research, 35*(3), 265–271.

Frezieres, R. B., Walsh, T. L., Nelson, A. L., Clark, V. A., & Coulson, A. H. (1998). Breakage and acceptability of a polyurethane condom: A randomized, controlled study. *Family Planning Perspectives, 30*(2), 73–78.

Frezieres, R. B., Walsh, T. L., Nelson, A. L., Clark, V. A., & Coulson, A. H. (1999). Evaluation of the efficacy of a polyurethane condom: Results from a randomized controlled clinical trial. *Family Planning Perspectives, 31*(2), 81–87.

Friedman, E. B., et al. (1996). Reduced mortality associated with long-term postmenopausal estrogen therapy. *Obstetrics and Gynecology, 87,* 6–12.

Friedman, J., & Mobilia, M. B. (1995). *Betrayal of trust: Sex and power in professional relationships.* Westport, CT: Praeger.

Friedman, R. C. (1998). Internalized homophobia, pathological grief, and high-risk sexual behavior in a gay man with multiple psychiatric disorders. *Journal of Sex Education and Therapy, 23*(2), 115–120.

Friedrich, W. N., Fisher, J., Broughton, D., Houston, M., & Shafran, C. R. (1998). Normative sexual behavior in children: A contemporary sample. *Pediatrics, 101*(4), e9.

Fromme, K., & Wendel, J. (1995). Beliefs about the effects of alcohol on involvement in coercive and consenting sexual activities. *Journal of Applied Social Psychology, 25*(23), 2099–2117.

Frontain, R. J. (Ed.). (1997). *Reclaiming the sacred: The Bible in gay and lesbian culture.* Binghamton, NY.: Haworth Press.

Frost, J. J. (1998). Clinic provision of contraceptive services to managed care enrollees. *Family Planning Perspectives, 30*(4), 156–162.

Frost, J. J., & Forrest, J. D. (1995). Understanding the impact of effective teenage pregnancy prevention programs. *Family Planning Perspectives, 27*(5), 188–195.

Froster, U. G., & Jackson, L. (1996). Limb defects and chorionic villi sampling: Results from an international registry, 1992–1994. *Lancet, 347,* 489–494.

Fry, D. P., & Gabriel, A. H. (1994). The cultural construction of gender and aggression. *Sex Roles, 30,* 165–167.

Fu, H., Darroch, J. E., Haas, T., & Ranjit, N. (1999). Contraceptive failure rates: New estimates from the 1995 National Survey of Family Growth. *Family Planning Perspectives, 31*(2), 56–63.

Fu, H., Darroch, J. E., Henshaw, S. K., & Kolb, E. (1998). Measuring the extent of abortion underreporting in the 1995 National Survey of Family Growth. *Family Planning Perspectives, 30*(3), 128–133.

Furstenberg, F. F., Geitz, L. M., Teitler, J. O., & Weiss, C. C. (1997). Does condom availability make a difference? An evaluation of Philadelphia's health resource centers. *Family Planning Perspectives, 29*(3), 123–127.

Futterweit, W. (1998). Endrocrine therapy of transsexualism and potential complications of long-term treatment. *Archives of Sexual Behavior, 27*(2), 209–226.

G

Gabelnick, H. L. (1998). Future methods. In R. A. Hatcher et al., *Contraceptive Technology* (pp. 615–622). New York: Ardent Media.

Gagnon, J. H. (1999). Sexual conduct: As today's memory serves. *Sexualities, 2*(1), 115–126.

Gagnon, J. H., & Simon, W. (1973). *Sexual conduct.* Chicago: Aldine.

Gagnon, J. H., Simon, W., & Berger, A. J. (1970). Some aspects of sexual adjustment in early and late adolescence. In J. Zubin & A. N. Freedman, *Psychopathology of adolescence* (p. 278). New York: Grune & Stratton.

Gaither, G. A., & Plaud, J. J. (1997). The effects of secondary stimulus characteristics on men's sexual arousal. *Journal of Sex Research, 34*(3), 231–236.

Galyer, K. T., Conaglen, H. M., Hare, A., & Conaglen, J. V. (1999). The effect of gynecological surgery on sexual desire. *Journal of Sex and Marital Therapy, 25*(2), 81–88.

Gamson, J. (1998). *Freaks talk back: Tabloid talk shows and sexual nonconformity.* Chicago: University of Chicago Press.

Gamson, J. (1998). Publicity traps: Television talk shows and lesbian, gay, bisexual, and trans-gender visibility. *Sexualities, 1*(1), 11–41.

Garber, M. (1996). *Vice versa: Bisexuality and the eroticism of everyday life.* New York: Simon & Schuster.

Gardosi, J. (1996). The threadless copper intrauterine contraceptive device: Analysis of the first 150 women-years. *British Journal of Obstetrics and Gynaecology, 103,* 574–576.

Garos, S. (1994). Autoerotic asphyxiation: A challenge to death educators and counselors. *Omega: Journal of Death and Dying, 28*(2), 85–99.

Gauthier, D. K., & Forsyth, C. J. (1999). Bardback sex, bug chasers, and the gift of death. *Deviant Behavior, 20*(1), 85–100.

Gavey, N., McPhillips, K., & Braun, V. (1999). Interruptus coitus: Heterosexuals accounting for intercourse. *Sexualities, 2*(1), 35–68.

Gebhard, P. H. (1977). [Memorandum on the incidence of homosexuals in the United States.] Personal communication with National Gay Task Force.

Geer, J. H., & Manguno-Mire, G. M. (1997). Gender differences in cognitive processes in sexuality. *Annual Review of Sex Research, 7,* 90–124.

Geer, J. H., & Melton, J. S. (1997). Sexual content-induced delay with double-entendre words. *Archives of Sexual Behavior, 26*(3), 295–316.

Geis, F. L. (1993). Self-fulfilling prophecies: A social psychological view of gender. In A. E. Beall & R. J. Steinberg (Eds.), *The psychology of gender* (pp. 9–54). New York: Guilford Press.

Gentry, C. S. (1991). Pornography and rape: An empirical analysis. *Deviant Behavior, 12*(3), 277–288.

George, K. D. (1997). Male couples: The struggle with competition. *SIECUS Report, 25*(5), 11–12.

Gerall, A. A., Moltz, H., & Ward, I. L. (Eds.). (1992). *Handbook of behavioral neurobiology: Vol. 11. Sexual differentiation.* New York: Plenum Press.

Giami, A., & Schultz, M. (1997). Representations of sexuality and relations between partners: Sex research in France in the era of AIDS. *Annual Review of Sex Research, 7,* 125–157.

Gillis, A. M. (1995). Sex selection and demographics. *BioScience, 45*(6), 384–385.

Gilmore, S., DeLamater, J., & Wagstaff, D. (1996). Sexual decision making by inner city black adolescent males: A focus group study. *Journal of Sex Research, 33*(4), 363–371.

Gladstone, G., Parker, G., Wilhelm, K., Mitchell, P., & Austin, M. (1999). Characteristics of depressed patients who report childhood sexual abuse. *American Journal of Psychiatry, 156*(3), 431–437.

Glasier, A., & Baird, D. (1998). The effects of self-administering emergency contraception. *New England Journal of Medicine, 339*(1), 1–4.

Glass, L. (1992). *He says, she says.* New York: G. P. Putnam's Sons.

Glei, D. A. (1999). Measuring contraceptive use patterns among teenage and adult women. *Family Planning Perspectives, 31*(2), 73–80.

Glick, P., & Fiske, S. T. (1999). Gender, power dynamics, and social interaction. In M. M. Ferree (Ed.), *Revisioning gender* (pp. 365–398). Thousand Oaks, CA: Sage.

Godow, A. G. (1999). Playful language. *Contemporary Sexuality, 33*(2), 1–2.

Gold, J. H. (1997). Premenstrual dysphoric disorder. *Women's Health Digest, 3*(4), 232–234.

Gold, S. N., Hughes, D. M., & Swingle, J. M. (1999). Degrees of memory of childhood sexual abuse among women survivors in therapy. *Journal of Family Violence, 14*(1), 35–46.

Golden, F. (1998, September 21). Boy? Girl? Up to You. *Time,* 82–83.

Goldman, J. (1994). Some methodological problems in planning, executing and validating a cross-national study of children's sexual cognition. *International Journal of Intercultural Relations, 18*(1), 1–27.

Goldman, R., & Goldman, J. (1982). *Children's sexual thinking.* Boston: Routledge & Kegan Paul.

Goldstein-Lohman, H., & Aitken, M. J. (1995). Influence of education on knowledge and attitude toward older adult sexuality. *Physical and Occupational Therapy in Geriatrics, 13*(1), 51–62.

Goleman, D. (1994, March 22). The "wrong" sex: A new definition of childhood pain. *New York Times,* pp. C1, C9.

Golombok, S., & Tasker, F. (1995). Children in lesbian and gay families: Theories and evidence. *Annual Review of Sex Research, 5,* 73–100.

Gonsiorek, J. C. (1995). Gay male identities: Concepts and issues. In A. R. D'Augelli & C. J. Patterson (Eds.), *Lesbian, gay, and bisexual identities over the lifespan* (pp. 24–47). New York: Oxford University Press.

Good, G. E., Gilbert, L. A., & Scher, M. (1990). Gender aware therapy: A synthesis of feminist therapy and knowledge about gender. *Journal of Counseling and Development, 68*(4), 376–380.

Good, G. E., & Wood, P. K. (1995). Male gender role conflict, depression, and help seeking: Do college men face double jeopardy? *Journal of Counseling and Development, 74,* 70–75.

Goodkin, K., Blaney, N. T., Feaster, D. J., Baldewicz, T., Burkhalter, J. E., & Leeds, B. (1999). A randomized controlled clinical trial of bereavement support group intervention in human immunodeficiency virus type 1-seropositive and -seronegative homosexual men. *Archives of General Psychiatry, 56*(1), 52–59.

Goodman, D. D. (1998). Using the empowerment model to develop sex education for Native Americans. *Journal of Sex Education and Therapy, 23*(2), 135–144.

Gordon, P., & Benishek, L. A. (1998). Women with physical disabilities: How perceptions of attractiveness and sexuality may be impacted. *The Journal for the Professional Counselor, 13*(1), 19–30.

Gorman, C. (1997, June 23). If the condom breaks. *Time,* 48.

Gorman, C. (1998, September 28). It's worth a shot. *Time,* 98.

Gorman, C., & Fowler, D. (1996, September 30). Liquid X: A club drug called GHB may be a fatal aphrodisiac. *Time,* 64.

Gose, B. (1997, February 21). Gay students have their own floor in a U. of Massachusetts Dormitory. *Chronicle of Higher Education,* A37.

Gotlib, D. A., & Fagan, P. (1997). Mean streets of cyberspace: Sex education resources on the Internet's World Wide Web. *Journal of Sex Education and Therapy, 22*(1), 79–83.

Gottman, J. M. (1994). *Why marriages succeed or fail.* New York: Simon & Schuster.

Gottman, J. M. (1999). *Seven principles for making marriages work.* New York: Crown.

Grady, W. R., Klepinger, D. H., & Nelson-Wally, A. (1999). Contraceptive characteristics: The perceptions and priorities of men and women. *Family Planning Perspectives, 31*(4), 168–175.

Grady, W. R., Tanfer, K., Billy, J., & Lincoln-Hanson, J. (1996). Men's perceptions of their roles and responsibilities regarding sex, contraception and childbearing. *Family Planning Perspectives, 28*(5), 221–226.

Gräfenberg, E. (1950). The role of the urethra. *International Journal of Sexology, 3,* 145–148.

Grammer, K. (1996). Sex and olfaction. *Science, 273,* 313.

Greeley, A. (1992). *Faithful attraction.* New York: Tor Books/St. Martin's Press.

Greenberg, B. S., & Buselle, R. (1996). What's old, what's new: Sexuality on the soaps. *SIECUS Report, 24*(5), 14–16.

Greenberg, B. S., & Woods, M. G. (1999). The soaps: Their sex, gratifications, and outcomes. *Journal of Sex Research, 36*(3), 250–257.

Greer, R. A., Herkov, M. J., & Hill, L. L. (1994). Sexuality within a Russian geriatric sample: A pilot study. *Psychological Reports, 74*(2), 491–494.

Grenier, G., & Byers, E. S. (1997). The relationships among ejaculatory control, ejaculatory

latency, and attempts to prolong heterosexual intercourse. *Archives of Sexual Behavior, 26*(1), 27–47.

Gribble, J. N., Miller, H. G., Rogers, S. M., & Turner, C. F. (1999). Inter-view mode and measurement of sexual behaviors: Methodological issues. *Journal of Sex Research, 36*(1), 16–24.

Groneman, C. (1994). Nymphomania: The historical construction of female sexuality. *Signs, 19*(2), 337–367.

Groneman, C. (1995). Nymphomania and the Freudians. *Psychohistory Review, 23*(2), 125–141.

Grossman, L. S., Martis, B., & Fichtner, C. G. (1999). Are sex offenders treatable? A research overview. *Psychiatric Services, 50*(3), 349–361.

Guest, F. (1998). HIV/AIDS and reproductive health. In R. A. Hatcher, et al. *Contraceptive Technology* (pp. 141–178). New York: Ardent Media.

Guirguis, W. R. (1998). Oral treatment of erectile dysfunction: From herbal remedies to designer drugs. *Journal of Sex and Marital Therapy, 24,* 69–73.

Gupta, M. (1999). An alternative combined approach to the treatment of premature ejaculation in Asian men. *Sexual and Marital Therapy, 14*(1), 71–76.

Gur, R. C., et al. (1995). Sex differences in regional cerebral glucose metabolism during a resting state. *Science, 267,* 528–531.

Guzick, D. S., Carson, S. A., et al. (1999). Efficacy of superovulation and intrauterine insemination in the treatment of infertility. *New England Journal of Medicine, 340*(3), 177–183.

Gwadz, M., DeVogli, R., Rotheram-Borus, M. J., Diaz, M. M., Tri Cisek, James, N. B., & Tottenham, N. (1999). Behavioral practices regarding combination therapies for HIV/AIDS. *Journal of Sex Education and Therapy, 24*(1&2), 81–88.

H

Haapasalo, J., & Kankkonen, M. A. (1997). Self-reported childhood abuse among sex and violent offenders. *Archives of Sexual Behavior, 26*(4), 421–431.

Haas, C. (1999, April). The effect of incest on women's careers. *Counseling Today,* 14–16.

Haas-Wilson, D. (1997). Women's reproductive choices: The impact of Medicaid funding restrictions. *Family Planning Perspectives, 29*(5), 228–233.

Haffner, D. W. (1995). Facing facts: Sexual health for America's adoles-cents. *SIECUS Report, 23*(6), 2–8.

Haffner, D. W. (1996). Sex, lies, and political extremists. *SIECUS Report, 24*(5), 2–4.

Haffner, D. W. (1998a). The HIV pandemic still deserves the best from us. *SIECUS Report, 26*(2), 3–4.

Haffner, D. W. (1998b). Training for sexuality educators: Losing ground? *Journal of Sex Education and Therapy, 23*(1), 70–72.

Haffner, D. W., & Goldfarb, E. S. (1997). But does it work? Improving evaluations of sexuality education. *SIECUS Report, 25*(6), 3–12.

Haffner, D. W., & Portelli, C. J. (1998). On the brink of abolishing discrimination against lesbians and gays. *SIECUS Report, 26*(4), 3–4.

Haffner, D. W., & Wagoner, J. (1999). Vast majority of Americans support sexuality education. *SIECUS Report, 27*(6), 22–23.

Hakim, L. S., & Goldstein, I. (1996). Diabetic sexual dysfunction. *Endocrinology and Metabolism Clinics of North America, 25*(2), 379.

Hall, G. C., Hirschman, R., & Oliver, L. L. (1995). Sexual arousal and arousability to pedophilic stimuli in a community sample of normal men. *Behavior Therapy, 26*(4), 681–694.

Hall, J. (1999). An exploration of the sexual and relationship experiences of lesbian survivors of childhood sexual abuse. *Sexual and Marital Therapy, 14*(1), 61–70.

Halpern, C. T., Udry, J. R., & Suchindran, C. (1997). Testosterone predicts initiation of coitus in adolescent females. *Psychosomatic Medicine, 59* 161–171.

Halpern, C. T., Udry, J. R., & Suchindran, C. (1998). Monthly measures of salivary testosterone predict sexual activity in adolescent males. *Archives of Sexual Behavior, 27*(5) 445–465.

Hamer, D. (1999). Genetics and male sexual orientation. *Science, 285,* 803a.

Hamer, D. H., & Copeland, P. (1998). *Living with our genes: Why they matter more than you think.* New York: Doubleday.

Hamer, D. H., Hu, S., Magnuson, V. L., Hu, N., & Pattatucci, A. M. L. (1993). Linkage between DNA markers on the X chromosome and male sexual orientation. *Science, 261,* 321–327.

Hammer, J. C., Fisher, J. D., Fitzgerald, P., & Fisher, W. A. (1996). When two heads aren't better than one: AIDS risk behavior in college-age couples. *Journal of Applied Social Psychology, 26*(5), 375–397.

Hammock, G. S., & Richardson, D. R. (1992). Predictors of aggressive behavior. *Aggressive Behavior, 18*(3), 219–229.

Handy, B. (1998a, March 16). Beyond the pale. *Time,* 56.

Handy, B. (1998b, May 4). The Viagra craze. *Time,* 51–57.

Haqq, C. M., King, C., Ukiyama, E., Falsafi, S., Haqq, T. N., Donahoe, P. K., & Weiss, M. A. (1994). Molecular basis of mammalian sexual determination: Activation of Müllerian inhibiting substance gene expression by SRY. *Science, 266,* 1494–1500.

Harrison, P. F., & Rosenfield, A. (1996). *Contraceptive research and development: Looking to the future.* Washington, DC: National Academy of Sciences.

Hartman, K. (1996). *Congregations in conflict: The battle over homosexuality.* New Brunswick, NJ: Rutgers University Press.

Hartman, W., & Fithian, M. (1984). *Any man can.* New York: St. Martin's Press.

Harvey, S. M., Beckman, L. J., Sherman, C., & Petitti, D. (1999). Women's experience and satisfaction with emergency contraception. *Family Planning Perspectives, 31* (5), 237–240.

Hasenyager, C. (1999). Knowledge of cervical cancer screening among women attending a university health center. *Journal of American College Health, 47*(5), 221–224.

Hatcher, R. A., Trussell, J., Stewart, F., Cates, W., Stewart, G. K., Guest, F., & Kowal, D. (1998). *Contraceptive technology* (17th ed.). New York: Ardent Media.

Hatfield, E. (1999). Teaching human sexuality in U.S. universities. *Sexual Science, 40*(1), 2.

Hatfield, E., & Rapson, R. L. (1996). *Love and sex: Cross-cultural perspectives.* New York: Allyn & Bacon.

Hauch, M. (1998). The Hamburg model: Couples therapy at century's end. *Journal of Sex Education and Therapy, 23*(3), 237–244.

Haumann, G. (1995). Homosexuality, biology, and ideology. *Journal of Homosexuality, 28*(1), 57–77.

Haws, J. M., McKenzie, M., Mehta, M., & Pollack, A. E. (1997). Increasing the availability of vasectomy in public-sector clinics. *Family Planning Perspectives, 29*(4), 185–186.

Hayes, A. F. (1995). Age preferences for same- and opposite-sex partners. *Journal of Social Psychology, 135*(2), 125–133.

Haynes, B. F., Pantaleo, G., & Fauci, A. S. (1996). Toward an understanding of the correlates of protective immunity to HIV infection. *Science, 271,* 324–328.

Healy, B. (1995). Pepi in perspective: Good answers spawn pressing questions. *Journal of the American Medical Association, 273*(3), 240–241.

Heaphy, B., Weeks, J., & Donovan, C. (1998). "That's like my life": Researching stories on non-heterosexual relationships. *Sexualities, 1*(4), 453–470.

Heaton, J. P. W. (1998). Androgens, andropause, and erectile function. *Journal of Sex Education and Therapy, 23*(3), 232–236.

Heckman, T. G., Kelly, J. A., Somlai, A. M., Kalichman, S. C., & Heckman, B. D. (1999). High-risk sexual behavior among persons living with HIV disease in small towns and rural areas. *Journal of Sex Education and Therapy, 24*(1&2), 29–36.

Hedgepeth, E. (1996). Not all moral visions are created equal: Kohlberg's moral hierarchy applied to the politics of sexuality education. *SIECUS Report, 24*(6), 17–21.

Hedges, L. V., & Nowell, A. (1995). Sex differences in mental test scores, variability, and numbers of high-scoring individuals. *Science, 269,* 41–45.

Heiman, J. R., Meston, C. M. (1998). Empirically validated treatment for sexual dysfunction. *Annual Review of Sex Research, 8,* 148–194.

Heiman, J. R., Rowland, D. L., Hatch, J. P., & Gladue, B. A. (1991). Psychophysiological and endocrine responses to sexual arousal in women. *Archives of Sexual Behavior, 20*(2), 171–186.

Heinemann, L. A. J. (1998). Thromboembolic stroke in young women: A European case-control study on oral contraceptives. *Contraception, 57*(1), 29–37.

Heise, L., Moore, K., & Toubia, N. (1996). Defining coercion and consent cross-culturally. *SIECUS Report, 24*(2), 12–14.

Helminiak, D. A. (1999). Scripture, sexual ethics and the nature of Christianity. *Pastoral Psychology, 47*(4), 261–271.

Henderson, D. J., Boyd, C. J., & Whitmarsh, J. (1995). Women and illicit drugs: Sexuality and crack cocaine. *Health Care for Women International, 16*(2), 113–124.

Hendrick, C., & Hendrick, S. (1986). A theory and method of love. *Journal of Personality and Social Psychology, 50,* 392–402.

Hendrick, S. S., & Hendrick, C. (1999). Personality and human sexuality. In V. J. Derlega & B. A. Winstead (Eds.), *Personality: Contemporary theory and research* (pp. 432–457). Chicago: Nelson-Hall.

Hendrix, L., & Schneider, M. A. (1999). Assumptions on sex and society in the biosocial theory of incest. *Cross-Cultural Research: The Journal of Comparative Social Science, 33*(2), 193–218.

Henken, E. R., & Whatley, M. H. (1995). Folklore, legends, and sexuality education. *Journal of Sex Education and Therapy, 21*(1), 46–61.

Henry Kaiser Family Foundation. (1999, March 8). MTV and teen people: What teens don't know about STDs puts them at risk. News Release, KFF: Menlo Park, CA.

Henshaw, S. K. (1998a). Abortion incidence and services in the United States, 1995–1996. *Family Planning Perspectives, 30*(6), 263–270 & 287.

Henshaw, S. K. (1998b). Unintended pregnancy in the United States. *Family Planning Perspectives, 30*(1), 24–29, 46.

Herdt, G. (2000). Clinical ethnography and sexual culture. *Annual Review of Sex Research, 9,* 100–119.

Herdt, G. H., & Davidson, J. (1988). The Sambia "Turnim Man": Sociocultural and clinical aspects of gender formation in male pseudo-hermaphrodites with 5-alpha reductase-deficiency in Papua New Guinea. *Archives of Sexual Behavior, 17,* 33–56.

Herek, G. M. (1999). AIDS and stigma. *American Behavioral Scientist, 42*(7), 1106–1116.

Herek, G. M., Jobe, J. B., & Carney, R. M. (Eds.). (1997). *Out in force: Sexual orientation and the military.* Chicago: University of Chicago Press.

Herman, K. C. (1995). Appropriate use of The Child Abuse Potential Inventory in a Big Brothers/Big Sisters agency. *Journal of Social Service Research, 20* (3–4), 93–103.

Herold, E. S., & Milhausen, R. R. (1999). Dating preferences of university women: An analysis of the nice guy stereotype. *Journal of Sex and Marital Therapy, 25,* 333–343.

Herron, E. (1994). *Gender war/gender peace: The quest for love and justice between women and men.* New York: William Morrow.

Hershberger, S. L. (1997). A twin registry study of male and female sexual orientation. *Journal of Sex Research, 34*(2), 212–222.

Hershberger, S. L., & D'Augelli, A. R. (1995). The impact of victimization on the mental health of lesbian, gay, and bisexual youths. *Developmental Psychology, 31*(1), 65–74.

Hertzen, H. von, & VanLook, P. (1996). Research on new methods of emergency contraception. *Family Planning Perspectives, 28*(2), 52–57, 88.

Hessol, N. A., Fuentes-Afflick, E., & Bacchetti, P. (1998). Risk of low birth weight infants among black and white parents. *Obstetrics and Gynecology, 92*(5), 814–822.

Hewitt, C. (1988). Homosexual demography: Implications for the spread of AIDS. *Journal of Sex Research, 35*(5), 390–396.

Hewitt, S. K. (1999). *Assessing allegations of sexual abuse in preschool children: Understanding small voices.* Thousand Oaks, CA: Sage.

Heyman, B., & Huckle, S. (1995). Sexuality as a perceived hazard in the lives of adults with learning difficulties. *Disability and Society, 10*(2), 139–155.

Hickman, S. E., & Muehlenhard, C. L. (1999). "By the semi-mystical appearance of a condom": How young women and men communicate sexual consent in heterosexual situations. *Journal of Sex Research, 36*(3), 258–272.

Hill, C. A. (1997). The distinctiveness of sexual motives in relation to sexual desire and desirable partner attributes. *Journal of Sex Research, 34*(2), 139–153.

Hill, C. A., & Preston, L. K. (1996). Individual differences in the experience of sexual motivation: Theory and measurement of dispositional sexual motives. *Journal of Sex Research, 33*(1), 27–45.

Hillier, L., Harrison, L., & Bowditch, K. (1999). "Neverending love" and "blowing your load": The meanings of sex to rural youth. *Sexualities, 2*(1), 69–88.

Hillis, S. D. (1998). Higher hysterectomy risk for sterilized than nonsterilized women: Findings from the U.S. collaborative review of sterilization. *Obstetrics and Gynecology, 91*(2), 241–246.

Hillman, J. L., & Stricker, G. (1994). A linkage of knowledge and attitudes toward elderly sexuality: Not necessarily a uniform relationship. *Gerontologist, 34*(2), 256–260.

Hines, M., & Collaer, M. L. (1993). Gonadal hormones and sexual differentiation of human behavior: Developments from research on endocrine syndromes and studies of brain structure. *Annual Review of Sex Research, 4,* 1–48.

Hite, S. (1977). *The Hite report.* New York: Dell.

Hite, S. (1981). *The Hite report on male sexuality.* New York: Alfred P. Knopf.

Ho, D. D. (1998). Toward HIV eradication or remission: The tasks ahead. *Science, 280,* 1866–1868.

Ho, G. Y., et al. (1998). Natural history of cervicovaginal papillomavirus infection in young women. *New England Journal of Medicine, 338*(7), 423–428.

Hoffman, S. D. (1998). Teenage childbearing is not so bad after all . . . or is it? A review of the new literature. *Family Planning Perspectives, 30*(5), 236–243.

Hofstede, G. (1980). *Culture's consequences: International differences in work-related values*. Beverly Hills, CA: Sage.

Hogan, T. L., & Rentz, A. L. (1996). Homophobia in the academy. *Journal of College Development, 37*(3), 309–314.

Hogben, M., & Byrne, D. (1998). Using social learning theory to explain individual differences in human sexuality. *Journal of Sex Research, 35*(1), 58–71.

Holden, C. (1995). Winning with testosterone. *Science, 269,* 1341–1342.

Hollander, D. (1995). Sexuality and health care: An intimate relationship. *SIECUS Report, 23*(5), 2–3.

Hollander, D. (1997). Environmental effects on reproductive health: The endocrine disruption hypothesis. *Family Planning Perspectives, 29*(2), 82–86, 89.

Hollway, W., & Jefferson, T. (1998). "A kiss is just a kiss": Date rape, gender and subjectivity. *Sexualities, 1*(4), 405–423.

Holmes, M. M. (1996). Rape-related pregnancy: Estimates and descriptive characteristics from a national sample of women. *American Journal of Obstetrics and Gynecology, 175,* 320–325.

Hong, J. H., Fan, M. S., Ng, M. L., Lee, L. K., Lui, P. K., & Choy, Y. H. (1994). Sexual attitudes and behavior of Chinese university students in Shanghai. *Journal of Sex Education and Therapy, 20*(4), 277–286.

Honor, E. K., Williams, J. K., & Adams, M. R. (1996). Methyltestosterone does not diminish the beneficial effects of estrogen replacement therapy. *Menopause: The Journal of the North American Menopause Society, 3*(1), 23–26.

Hooker, E. (1993). Reflections of a 40-year exploration: A scientific view on homosexuality. *American Psychologist, 48*(4), 450–453.

Hooton, T. M., Scholes, D., Hughes, J. P., Winter, C., et al. (1996). A prospective study of risk factors for symptomatic urinary tract infection in young women. *New England Journal of Medicine, 335,* 468–474.

Hopkins, J. (1969). Lesbian personality. *British Journal of Psychiatry, 115,* 1433–1436.

Horowitz, D. (1998). *Betty Friedan and the making of "the feminine mystique."* Amherst: University of Massachusetts Press.

Horwood, L. J., & Fergusson, D. M. (1998). Breastfeeding and later cognitive and academic outcomes. *Pediatrics, 101*(1), e9.

Howes, R. J. (1995). A survey of plethysmographic assessment in North America. *Sexual Abuse: Journal of Research and Treatment, 7*(1), 9–24.

Hsu, G. S. (1998, June). America: Awash in STDs. *The World & I,* 55–61.

Humphrey, J. C. (1999). To queer or not to queer a lesbian and gay group? Sexual and gendered politics at the turn of the century. *Sexualities, 2*(2), 223–246.

Hunt, L. (Ed.). (1993). *The invention of pornography: Obscenity and the origins of modernity, 1500–1800.* New York: Zone Books.

Hunt, M. (1975). *Sexual behavior in the 1970s.* New York: Dell.

Hunter, D. J. (1997). Plasma organochlorine levels and the risk of breast cancer. *New England Journal of Medicine, 337*(18), 1253–1258.

Hunter, J. A., & Figueredo, A. J. (1999). Factors associated with treatment compliance in population of juvenile sexual offenders. *Sexual Abuse: Journal of Research and Treatment, 11*(1), 49–67.

Hunter, R. H. F. (1995). *Sex determination, differentiation and intersexuality in placental mammals.* New York: Cambridge University Press.

Hurlbert, D. F., & Apt, C. (1993). Female sexuality: A comparative study between women in homosexual and heterosexual relationships. *Journal of Sex and Marital Therapy, 19*(4), 315–327.

Hurlbert, D. F., & Apt, C. (1995). The coital alignment technique and directed masturbation: A comparative study on female orgasm. *Journal of Sex and Marital Therapy, 21*(1), 21–29.

Hurlbert, D. F., & Whittaker, K. E. (1991). The role of masturbation in marital and sexual satisfaction: A comparative study of female masturbators and nonmasturbators. *Journal of Sex Education and Therapy, 17*(4), 272–282.

Huyck, M. H. (1999). Gender roles and gender identity in midlife. In S. L. Willis & J. D. Reid (Eds.), *Life in the middle: Psychological and social development in middle age* (pp. 209–232). San Diego, CA: Academic Press.

Hyde, J. S., DeLamater, J. D., Plant, E. A., & Byrd, J. M. (1996). Sexuality during pregnancy and the year postpartum. *Journal of Sex Research, 33*(4), 143–151.

Hynie, M., & Lydon, J. E. (1995). Women's perceptions of female contraceptive behavior: Experimental evidence of the sexual double standard. *Psychology of Women Quarterly, 19*(4), 563–581.

Hynie, M., & Lydon, J. E. (1996). Sexual attitudes and contraceptive behavior revisited: Can there be too much of a good thing? *The Journal of Sex Research, 33*(2), 127–134.

I

Imperato-McGinley, J., Peterson, R. E., Gautier, T., Looper, G., Danner, R., Arthur, A., Morris, P. L., Sweeney, W. J., & Schackleton, C. (1982). Hormonal evaluation of a large kindred with complete androgen insensitivity: Evidence for secondary 5-alpha-reductase deficiency. *Journal of Clinical Endocrinology Metabolism, 54,* 15–22.

Innala, S. M., & Ernulf, K. E. (1992). Understanding male homosexual attraction. *Journal of Social Behavior and Personality, 7*(3), 503–510.

Irvine, J. M. (1995). *Sexuality education across cultures.* San Francisco: Jossey-Bass.

Isay, R. A. (1993). Dynamic psychotherapy with gay men: Developmental considerations. *American Psychiatric Press Review of Psychiatry, 12,* 85–100.

Isay, R. A. (1996). *Becoming gay: The journey to self-acceptance.* New York: Pantheon Books.

ISLAT Working Group. (1998). ART into science: Regulation of fertility techniques. *Science, 281,* 651–652.

J

Jaccard, J., Dittus, P. J., & Gordon, V. V. (1996). Maternal correlates of adolescent sexual and contraceptive behavior. *Family Planning Perspectives, 28*(4), 159–165, 185.

Jacklin, C. N., & Reynolds, C. (1993). Gender and childhood socialization. In A. E. Beall & R. J. Sternberg (Eds.), *The psychology of gender* (pp. 197–214). New York: Guilford Press.

Jacoby, S. (1999, September–October). Great sex: What's age got to do with it? *Modern Maturity,* 41–44.

James, C. (1993, October 10). You are what you wear. *New York Times,* pp. H13, H16.

Jamison, P. L., & Gebhard, P. H. (1988). Penis size increase between flaccid and erect states: An analysis of the Kinsey data. *Journal of Sex Research, 24*(1), 177–183.

Jankowiak, W. (Ed.). (1995). *Romantic passion: A universal experience?* New York: Columbia University Press.

Janssen, E., & Bancroft, J. (1997). Inhibition plays a role in new model of sexual arousal. *Kinsey Today, 1*(2), 3.

Janssen, E., & Everaerd, W. (1993). Determinants of male sexual arousal. *Annual Review of Sex Research, 4,* 211–245.

Janssen, E., Everaerd, W., van Lunsen, R. H. W., & Oerlemans, S. (1994). Visual stimulation facilitates penile responses to vibration in men with and without erectile disorder. *Journal of Consulting and Clinical Psychology, 62,* 1222–1228.

Janus, S. S., & Janus, C. L. (1993). *The Janus report on sexual behavior.* New York: John Wiley.

Jaroff, L. (1996, April 1). The man's cancer. *Time,* 58–65.

Jenks, R. J. (1998). Swinging: A review of the literature. *Archives of Sexual Behavior, 27*(5), 507–521.

Jenny, C., Huhns, M. L. D., & Arakawa, F. (1987). Hymens in newborn female infants. *Pediatrics, 80*(3), 399–400.

Jensen, L. C., Gaston, J. F., & Weed, S. E. (1994). Sexual behavior of nonurban students in grades 7 and 8: Implications for public policy and sex education. *Psychological Reports, 75,* 1504–1506.

Jensen, R. (1996). Advertising, sexuality, and sexism. *SIECUS Report, 24*(5), 10–12.

Jinich, S., & Litrownik, A. J. (1999). Coping with sexual abuse: Development and evaluation of a videotape intervention for nonoffending parents. *Child Abuse and Neglect, 23*(2), 175–190.

Joffe, C. (1999). Reactions to medical abortion among providers of surgical abortion: An early snapshot. *Family Planning Perspectives, 31*(1), 35–38.

Joffe, H., & Dockrell, J. E. (1995). *Journal of Community and Applied Social Psychology, 5*(5), 333–346.

Johnson, A., Wadsworth, J., Wellings, K., & Field, J. (1994). *Sexual attitudes and lifestyles.* Cambridge, MA: Blackwell Scientific.

Johnson, A. M., & Copas, A. (1997). Assessing participation bias. In J. Bancroft (Ed.), *Researching sexual behavior* (pp. 276–287). Bloomington: Indiana University Press.

Johnson, A. M., et al. (1992). Sexual lifestyles and HIV risk. *Nature, 360,* 410–412.

Johnson, J. H., & Turnbull, W. (1995). The women's conference: Where aspirations and realities meet. *Family Planning Perspectives, 27*(6), 254–258.

Johnson, P., & Nelson, M. D. (1998). Parental divorce, family functioning, and college student development: An intergenerational perspective. *Journal of College Student Development, 39*(40), 355–362.

Johnston, L., Ward, T., & Hudson, S. M. (1997). Deviant sexual thoughts: Mental control and the treatment of sexual offenders. *Journal of Sex Research, 34*(2), 121–130.

Johnston, M. W., & Bell, A. P. (1995). Romantic emotional attachment: Additional factors in the development of the sexual orientation of men. *Journal of Counseling and Development, 73,* 621–625.

Johnston, V. S., & Oliver-Rodriguez, J. C. (1997). Facial beauty and the late positive component of event-related potentials. *Journal of Sex Research, 34*(2), 188–198.

Johnstone, J., & Huws, R. (1997). Autoerotic asphyxia: A case report. *Journal of Sex and Marital Therapy, 23*(4), 326–332.

Jones, M. A., & Gabriel, M. A. (1999). Utilization of psychotherapy by lesbians, gay men, and bisexuals: Findings from a nationwide survey. *American Journal of Orthopsychiatry, 69*(2), 209–219.

Jones, W. K., et al., (1997). Female genital mutilation/female circumcision: Who is at

585

risk in the U.S.? *Public Health Reports, 112,* 368–377.

Julian, T. W., McKenry, P. C., Gavazzi, S. M., & Law, J. C. (1999). Test of family of origin structural models of male verbal and physical aggression. *Journal of Family Issues, 20*(3), 397–423.

Juzang, I. (1999). Reaching the hip-hop generation with "pro-social" behavior messages. *SIECUS Report, 27*(5), 3–5.

K

Kafka, M. P. (1997a). Hypersexual desire in males: An operational definition and clinical implications for males with paraphilias and paraphilia-related disorders. *Archives of Sexual Behavior, 26*(5), 505–526.

Kafka, M. P. (1997b). A monoamine hypothesis for the pathophysiology of paraphilic disorders. *Archives of Sexual Behavior, 26*(4), 343–358.

Kafka, M. P., & Hennen, J. (1999). The paraphilia-related disorders: An empirical investigation of nonparaphilic hypersexuality disorders in outpatient males. *Journal of Sex and Marital Therapy, 25,* 305–319.

Kalb, C. (1998, July 13). Now, a scary strain of drug-resistant HIV. *Newsweek,* 63.

Kalb, C. (1999, April 19). Hormones and the mind. *Newsweek,* 50.

Kalichman, S. C., & Nachimson, D. (1999). Self-efficacy and disclosure of HIV-positive serostatus to sex partners. *Health Psychology, 18*(3), 281–287.

Kalra, M., Wood, E., Desmarais, S., Verberg, N., & Senn, C. Y. (1998). Exploring negative dating experiences and beliefs about rape among younger and older women. *Archives of Sexual Behavior, 27*(2), 145–153.

Kameya, Y., Deguchi, A., & Yokota, Y. (1997). Analysis of measured values of ejaculation time in healthy males. *Journal of Sex and Marital Therapy, 23*(1), 25–28.

Kanas, N. (1999). Group therapy for sexually dysfunctional men—treatment without a pill! *International Journal of Group Psychotherapy, 49*(1), 147–149.

Kanouse, D. E., Berry, S. H., Daun, N., Lever, J., Carson, S., Perlman, J. F., & Levitan, B. (1999). Drawing a probability sample of female street prostitutes in Los Angeles county. *Journal of Sex Research, 36*(1), 45–51.

Kantrowitz, B. (1996, November 4). Gay families come out. *Time,* 50–59.

Kantrowitz, B., & Wingert, P. (1999, April 19). The science of a good marriage. *Newsweek,* 52–57.

Kaplan, H. S. (1974). *The new sex therapy.* New York: Brunner/Mazel.

Kaplan, H. S. (1979). *Disorders of sexual desire and other new concepts and techniques in sex therapy.* New York: Brunner/Mazel.

Kaplan, H. S. (1993). Post-ejaculatory pain syndrome. *Journal of Sex and Marital Therapy. 19*(2), 91–103.

Kaplan, H. S. (1995). *The sexual desire disorders: Dysfunctional regulation of sexual motivation.* New York: Brunner/Mazel.

Kaplan, M. (1996). Patients' preferences for sex of therapist. *American Journal of Psychiatry, 153*(1), 136–137.

Kaplan, M. S., & Green, A. (1995). Incarcerated female sexual offenders: A comparison of sexual histories with eleven female nonsexual offenders. *Sexual Abuse: Journal of Research and Treatment, 7*(4), 287–300.

Kasai, K. (1995). *External genitalia of Japanese females.* Tokyo: Free Press.

Kassindja, F. (1998). *Do they hear you when you cry?* New York: Delacorte Press.

Kassirer, A., & Griffiths, J. (1997). The effectiveness of "The responsible sexuality program": A brief high school sexual education intervention. *Journal of Sex Education and Therapy, 22*(2), 5–11.

Katz, A. (1995, November 14). New method aids infertile men. *New Haven Register,* A1, A13.

Katz, L. (1994). Censorship too close to home. *SIECUS Report, 23*(1), 15–18.

Katz, R. C., & Jardine, D. (1999). The relationship between worry, sexual aversion, and low sexual desire. *Journal of Sex and Marital Therapy, 25,* 293–296.

Kay, D. S. (1992). Masturbation and mental health: Uses and abuses. *Sexual and Marital Therapy, 7*(1), 97–107.

Keeling, R. P. (1995). Campuses confront AIDS: Tapping the vitality of caring and community. In S. J. Bunting (Ed.), *Annual editions: Human sexuality, 95/96* (20th ed., pp. 181–186). Guilford, CT: Dushkin.

Keeling, R. P. (1998). Mentoring: Preparing new professionals through significant relationships. *Journal of Sex Education and Therapy, 23*(1), 6–12.

Keeling, R. P. (1999). A synthesis of ways of knowing: New approaches to HIV prevention. *Journal of Sex Education and Therapy, 24*(1–2), 4–8.

Keil, J. E., Sutherland, S. E., Knapp. R. G., et al. (1992). Self-reported sexual functioning in elderly blacks and whites: The Charleston Heart Study experience. *Journal of Aging and Health, 4*(1), 112–125.

Keinplatz, P., McCarrey, M., & Kateb, C. (1992). The impact of gender-role identity on women's self-esteem, lifestyle satisfaction and conflict. *Canadian Journal of Behavioural Science, 24*(3), 333–347.

Kellogg-Spadt, S. (1998). Illuminating HPV: An experiential learning activity. *Journal of Sex Education and Therapy, 23*(3), 255–258.

Kelly, G. F. (1980). *Good sex: The healthy man's guide to sexual fulfillment.* New York: NAL/Signet.

Kelly, G. F. (1993). *Sex and sense.* Hauppauge, NY: Barron's Educational Series.

Kempner, M. (1998). 1997–98 Sexuality education controversies in the United States. *SIECUS Report, 26*(6), 16–26.

Kempner, M. E. (1999). Sexuality education controversies in the United States. *SIECUS Report, 27*(6), 4–14.

Kempton, W. (1993) *Socialization and sexuality: A comprehensive training guide for professionals helping people with disabilities that hinder learning.* Santa Barbara, CA: James Stanfield.

Kendrick, J. S. (1997). Vaginal douching and the risk of ectopic pregnancy among black women. *American Journal of Obstetrics and Gynecology, 176,* 991–997.

Kennedy, P., Doherty, N., & Barnes, J. (1995). Primary vaginismus: A psychometric study of both partners. *Sexual and Marital Therapy, 10*(1), 9–22.

Kennedy, P., & Whitlock, M. L. (1997). Therapeutic implications of conservative clergy views on sexuality: An empirical analysis. *Journal of Sex and Marital Therapy, 23*(2), 140–153.

Kenrick, D. T., & Trost, M. R. (1993). The evolutionary perspective. In A. E. Beall & R. J. Sternberg (Eds.), *The psychology of gender* (pp. 148–172). New York: Guilford Press.

Kerr, B. (1999, March 5). When dreams differ: Male-female relations on campuses. *Chronicle of Higher Education,* B7–8.

Kesteren, P. J., Gooren, L. J., & Megens, J. A. (1996). An epidemiological and demographic study of transsexuals in the Netherlands. *Archives of Sexual Behavior, 25*(6), 589–600.

Keye, W. R. (1999). Medical aspects of infertility for the counselor. In L. H. Burns & S. N. Covington (Eds.), *Infertility counseling: A comprehensive handbook for clinicians* (pp. 27–46). New York: Parthenon.

Khattak, S., K-Moghtader, G., McMartin, K., Barrera, M., Kennedy, D., & Koren, G. (1999). Pregnancy outcome following gestational exposure to organic solvents: A prospective controlled study. *Journal of the American Medical Association, 281*(12), 1106–1109.

Kieren, D. K., & Morse, J. M. (1992). Preparation factors and menstrual attitudes of pre- and postmenarcheal girls. *Journal of Sex Education and Therapy, 18*(3), 155–174.

Kiernan, K. E., & Hobcraft, J. (1997). Parental divorce during childhood: Age at first intercourse, partnership and parenthood. *Population Studies, 51,* 51–55.

Kiernan, V. (1998, February 27). Debate over cloning touches one of society's most sensitive nerves. *Chronicle of Higher Education,* A16–17.

Kiernan, V. (1999a, September 10). The growing conflict over producing stem cells. *Chronicle of Higher Education,* A21–22.

Kiernan, V. (1999b, December 10). Researchers decode a human chromosome. *Chronicle of Higher Education,* A22.

Kiersey, D., & Bates, M. (1984). *Please understand me: Character and temperament types.* DelMar, CA: Prometheus-Nemesis Book Co.

Kim, P. Y., & Bailey, J. M. (1997). Sidestreets on the information superhighway: Paraphilias and sexual variation on the Internet. *Journal of Sex Education and Therapy, 22*(1), 35–43.

Kimmel, D. C., & Sang, B. E. (1995). Lesbians and gay men in midlife. In A. R. D'Augelli & C. J. Patterson (Eds.), *Lesbian, gay, and bisexual identities over the lifespan* (pp. 190–214). New York: Oxford University Press.

Kimmel, M. (1997). *Manhood in America: A cultural history.* New York: Free Press.

Kimura, D. (1992). Sex differences in the brain. *Scientific American, 267*(3), 119–125.

King, M., & Woollett, E. (1997). Sexually assaulted males: 115 men consulting a counseling service. *Archives of Sexual Behavior, 26*(6), 579–588.

Kinsey, A. C., Pomeroy, W. B., & Martin, C. E. (1948). *Sexual behavior in the human male.* Philadelphia: W. B. Saunders Co.

Kinsey, A. C., Pomeroy, W. B., Martin, C. E., & Gebhard, P. H. (1953). *Sex-ual behavior in the human female.* Philadelphia: W. B. Saunders Co.

Kirby, D. (1993). Sexuality education: It can reduce unprotected intercourse. *SIECUS Report, 21*(2), 19–25.

Kirby, D. (1995). Douglas Kirby responds to the *Atlantic. SIECUS Report, 23*(3), 19.

Kirby, D., Korpi, M., Barth, R. P., & Cagampang, H. H. (1997). The impact of the postponing sexual involvement curriculum among youths in California. *Family Planning Perspectives, 29*(3), 100–108.

Kiselica, M. S. (1995, November). Understanding and helping teenage fathers. *Counseling Today,* 10.

Kitamura, K. (1996). *Survey on teenagers' unwanted pregnancy: Situation survey on sexual behavior, pregnancy, contraception and childbirth among teenage women in Japan.* Tokyo: Japanese Ministry of Health and Welfare.

Kitamura, K. (1999). The pill in Japan: Will approval ever come? *Family Planning Perspectives, 31*(1), 44–45.

Kittner, S. J. (1996). Pregnancy and the risk of stroke. *New England Journal of Medicine, 335,* 768–774.

Kitzinger, C. (1995). Social constructionism: Implications for lesbian and gay psychology. In A. R. D'Augelli & C. J. Patterson (Eds.), *Lesbian, gay, and bisexual identities over the lifespan* (pp. 136–161). New York: Oxford University Press.

Klaf, F. S., & Brown, W. (1958). Necrophilia, brief review and case report. *Psychiatric Quarterly, 32,* 645–652.

Klamen, D. L., Grossman, L. S., & Kopacz, D. R. (1999). Medical student homophobia. *Journal of Homosexuality, 37*(1), 53–63.

Klebanoff, M. A. (1999). The interval between pregnancies and the outcome of subsequent births: Editorial. *New England Journal of Medicine, 340*(8), 643–644.

Klein, C. H. (1998). From one "battle" to another: The making of a *travesi* political movement in a Brazilian city. *Sexualities, 1*(3), 327–342.

Klein, F. (1990). The need to view sexual orientation as a multivariable dynamic process: A theoretical perspective. In D. P. McWhirter, S. A. Sanders, & J. M. Reinisch (Eds.), *Homosexuality/heterosexuality: Concepts of sexual orientation* (pp. 277–282). New York: Oxford University Press.

Klein, M. (2000). Coming attractions: Sexual expression in the next decade. *SIECUS Report, 28*(2), 9–14.

Klepinger, D. H., Lundberg, S., & Plotnick, R. D. (1995). Adolescent fertility and the educational attainment of young women. *Family Planning Perspectives, 27*(1), 23–28.

Klitzman, R., Bodkin, J. A., & Pope, H. G. (1998). Sexual orientation and associated characteristics among North American academic psychiatrists. *Journal of Sex Research, 35*(3), 282–284.

Kluger, J. (1997a, January 27). Eggs on the rocks. *Time,* 105–106.

Kluger, J. (1997b, March 10). Will we follow the sheep? *Time,* 67–72.

Knodel, J., Low, B., Saengtienchai, C., & Lucas, R. (1997). An evolutionary perspective on Thai sexual attitudes and behavior. *Journal of Sex Research, 34*(3), 292–303.

Koch, P. B., Palmer, R. F., Vicary, J. R., & Wood, J. M. (1999). Mixing sex and alcohol in college: Female-male risk model. *Journal of Sex Education and Therapy, 24*(1, 2), 99–108.

Kohlberg, L. (1981). *Essays on moral development.* San Francisco: Harper & Row.

Koivula, N. (1995). Ratings of gender appropriateness of sports participation: Effects of gender-based schematic processing. *Sex Roles, 33*(7), 543–557.

Kolata, G. (1996, May 30). Study finds a way of freezing and reproducing sperm cells, grown in other species. *New York Times,* A24.

Komisaruk, B. R., & Whipple, B. (1995). The suppression of pain by genital stimulation in females. *Annual Review of Sex Research, 4,* 151–186.

Koonin, L. M., et al. (1997). Pregnancy-related mortality surveillance—United States, 1987–1990. *Morbidity and Mortality Weekly Report, 46*(4), 17–36.

Koonin, S. E. (1998). An independent perspective on the human genome project. *Science, 279,* 36–37.

Koss, M. P. (1992). Date rape: Victimization by acquaintances. *Harvard Mental Health Letter, 9*(3), 5–6.

Kost, K., & Forrest, J. D. (1995). Intention status of U.S. births in 1988: Differences by mothers' socioeconomic and demographic characteristics. *Family Planning Perspectives, 27*(1), 11–17.

Kost, K., Landry, D. J., & Darroch, J. E. (1998). The effects of pregnancy planning status on birth outcomes and infant care. *Family Planning Perspectives, 30*(5), 223–230.

Kowaleski-Jones, L., & Mott, F. L. (1998). Sex, contraception and childbearing among high-risk youth: Do different factors influence males and females? *Family Planning Perspectives, 30*(4), 163–169.

Krafft-Ebing, R. von (1965). (Trans.). *Psychopathia sexualis.* New York: Bell. (Original work published 1886)

Kristof, N. D. (1995, November 5). In Japan, brutal comics for women. *New York Times,* E1.

Krivacska, J., & Money, J. (Eds.) (1994). *The handbook of forensic sexology: Biomedical and criminological perspectives.* Amherst, NY: Prometheus Books.

Ku, L., Sonenstein, F. L., Lindberg, L. D., Bradner, C. H., Boggess, S., & Pleck, J. H. (1998). Understanding changes in sexual activity among young metropolitan men: 1979–1995. *Family Planning Perspectives, 30*(6), 256–262.

Ku, L., Sonenstein, F. L., & Pleck, J. H. (1994). The dynamics of young men's condom use during and across relationships. *Family Planning Perspectives, 26*(6), 246–251.

Kuczynski, A. (1999, May 2). Women's magazines' feminist edge lost to sex. *Watertown (NY) Daily Times Sunday Weekly,* 9.

Kulick, D. (1998). Transgender in Latin America: Persons, practices and meanings. *Sexualities, 1*(3), 259–260.

Kulin, N. A., Pastuszak, A., & Sage, S. R. (1998). Pregnancy outcome following maternal use of the new selective serotonin reuptake inhibitors: A prospective controlled multicenter study. *Journal of the American Medical Association, 279*(8), 609–610.

Kunkel, D., Cope, K. M., & Biely, E. (1999). Sexual messages on television: Comparing findings from three studies. *Journal of Sex Research, 36*(3), 230–236.

Kupper, L. (1995). Comprehensive sexuality education for children and youth with disabilities. *SIECUS Report, 23*(4), 3–8.

Kurdek, L. A. (1995). Lesbian and gay couples. In A. R. D'Augelli & C. J. Patterson (Eds.), *Lesbian, gay, and bisexual identities over the lifespan* (pp. 243–261). New York: Oxford University Press.

Kutchinsky, B. (1991). Pornography and rape: Theory and practice—Evidence from crime data in four countries where pornography is easily available. *International Journal of Law and Psychiatry, 14*(1–2), 47–64.

Kyman, W. (1995). The first step: Sexuality education for parents. *Journal of Sex Education and Therapy, 21*(3), 153–157.

Kyman, W. (1998). Into the 21st century: Renewing the campaign for school-based sexuality education. *Journal of Sex and Marital Therapy, 24,* 131–137.

L

Laan, E., & Everaerd, W. (1995). Determinants of female sexual arousal: Psychophysical theory and data. *Annual Review of Sex Research, 4,* 32–76.

Laan, E., Everaerd, W., Van der Velde, J., & Geer, J. H. (1995). Determinants of subjective experience of sexual arousal in women: Feedback from genital arousal and erotic stimulus content. *Psychophysiology, 32,* 444–451.

Labbate, L. A., Grimes, J., Hines, A., Oleshansky, M. A., & Arana, G. W. (1998). Sexual dysfunction induced by serotonin reuptake antidepressants. *Journal of Sex and Marital Therapy, 24,* 3–12.

Ladas, A. K. (1997). The G spot. *CliniScope, 3,* 1–4.

Ladas, A. K., Whipple, B., & Perry, J. (1983). *The G spot and other recent discoveries about human sexuality.* New York: Dell.

Lahn, B. T., & Page, D. C. (1997). Functional coherence of the human Y chromosome. *Science, 278,* 675–680.

Lamstein, E., & Haffner, D. W. (1998). Abstinence-only guidelines restrict postponing sexual involvement adaptation. *SIECUS Report, 26*(3), 23–25.

Landry, D. J., & Forrest, J. D. (1995). How old are U.S. fathers? *Family Planning Perspectives, 27*(4), 159–161, 165.

Lange, A., de Beurs, E., Dolan, C., Lachnit, T., Sjollema, S., & Hanewald, G. (1999). Long-term effects of childhood sexual abuse: Objective and subjective characteristics of the abuse and psychopathology in later life. *Journal of Nervous and Mental Disease, 187*(3), 150–158.

Langer, L. M., Zimmerman, R. S., & Katz, J. A. (1995). Virgins' expectations and nonvirgins' reports: How adolescents feel about themselves. *Journal of Adolescent Research, 10*(2), 291–306.

Lankveld, J. J., Grotjohann, Y., van Lokven, B. M. E., & Everaerd, W. (1999). Characteristics of couples applying for bibliotherapy via different recruitment strategies: A multivariate comparison. *Journal of Sex and Marital Therapy, 25,* 197–209.

Laqueur, T. (1992). *Making sex: Body and gender from the Greeks to Freud.* Cambridge, MA: Harvard University Press.

Laumann, E. O., Gagnon, J. H., Michael, R. T., & Michaels, S. (1994). *The social organization of sexuality.* Chicago: University of Chicago Press.

Laumann, E. O., Michael, R. T., & Gagnon, J. H. (1994). A political history of the national sex survey of adults. *Family Planning Perspectives, 26*(1), 34–38.

Launay, G. (1994). The phallometric assessment of sex offenders: Some professional and research issues. *Criminal Behavior and Mental Health, 4*(1), 48–70.

Laurent, B. (1995, November/December). Intersexuality: A plea for honesty and emotional support. *AHP Perspective,* 8–9, 28.

Lauritsen, J. L., & Swicegood, C. G. (1997). The consistency of self-reported initiation of sexual activity. *Family Planning Perspectives, 29*(5), 215–221.

Lawrance, L., Rubinson, L., & O'Rourke, T. (1984). Sexual attitudes and behaviors: Trends for a ten-year period, 1972–1982. *Journal of Sex Education and Therapy, 2*(2), 22–29.

Laws, D. R., & O'Donohue, W. (1997). *Sexual deviance: Theory, assessment and treatment.* New York: Guilford Press.

Lawson, C. (1993). Mother-son sexual abuse: Rare or underreported? A critique of the research. *Child Abuse and Neglect, 17,* 261–269.

Layman, M. J., Gidycz, C. A., & Lynn, S. J. (1996). Unacknowledged versus acknowledged rape victims: Situational factors and posttraumatic stress. *Journal of Abnormal Psychology, 105*(1), 124–131.

Layne, L. L. (1999) *Transformative motherhood: On giving and getting in a consumer culture.* New York: New York University Press.

Lee, P. A. (1996). Survey report: Concept of penis size. *Journal of Sex and Marital Therapy, 22*(2), 131–135.

Leibenluft, E. (1996). Sex is complex. *American Journal of Psychiatry, 153*(8), 969–972.

Leiblum, S. R. (1997). Sex and the Net: Clinical implications. *Journal of Sex Education and Therapy, 22*(1), 21–28.

Leiner, M. (1994). *Sexual politics in Cuba: Machismo, homosexuality, and AIDS.* Boulder, CO: Westview Press.

Leitenberg, H., Detzer, M. J., & Srebnik, D. (1993). Gender differences in masturbation and the relation of masturbation experience in preadolescence and/or early adolescence to sexual behavior and sexual adjustment in young adulthood. *Archives of Sexual Behavior, 22*(2), 87–98.

Leitenberg, H., & Henning, K. (1995). Sexual fantasy. *Psychological Bulletin, 117*(3), 469–496.

Leland, J. (1995, December 18). The trouble with Freud. *Newsweek,* 62.

Leland, J. (1999a, February 22). Bad news in the bedroom. *Newsweek,* 47.

Leland, J. (1999b, September 20). More buck for the bang. *Time*, 61.

Leland, J., & Miller, M. (1998, August 17). Can gays convert? *Newsweek*, 46–52.

Lemonick, M. D. (1996, March 18). What's wrong with our sperm? *Time*, 78–79.

Lemonick, M. D. (1997, December 1). The new revolution in making babies. *Time*, 41–46.

Lemonick, M. D. (1998, April 20). Doctors find a drug that can prevent breast cancer. *Time*, 62–63.

Lepine, L. A. (1997). Hysterectomy surveillance—United States, 1980–1993. *Morbidity and Mortality Weekly Report, 46*(SS-4), 1–16.

Lepowsky, M. (1994). *Fruit of the motherland: Gender in an egalitarian society.* New York: Columbia University Press.

Letvin, N. L. (1998). Progress in the development of an HIV-1 vaccine. *Science, 280*, 1875–1880.

Levant, R. F. (1996). The new psychology of men. *Professional Psychology: Research and Practice, 27*(3), 259–265.

LeVay, S. (1996). *Queer science: The use and abuse of research into homosexuality.* Cambridge, MA: MIT Press.

Leventhal, J. M. (1998). Epidemiology of sexual abuse of children: Old problems, new directions. *Child Abuse and Neglect, 22*(6), 481–491.

Levine, L. A. (1998). Peyronie's disease: A brief review of a difficult sexual dysfunction problem. *Journal of Sex Education and Therapy, 23*(3), 226–228.

Levine, S. (1998). Extramarital affairs. *Journal of Sex and Marital Therapy, 24*, 207–216.

Levine, S. B. (1995). On love. *Journal of Sex and Marital Therapy, 21*(3), 183–191.

Levine, S. B. (1996). "Love" and the mental health professions: Toward understanding adult love. *Journal of Sex and Marital Therapy, 22*(3), 191–202.

Levy, E. (1990). Stage, sex, and suffering: Images of women in American films. *Empirical Studies of the Arts, 8*(1), 53–76.

Levy, G. D. (1994). Aspects of preschoolers' comprehension of indoor and outdoor gender-typed toys. *Sex Roles, 30*(5–6), 391–405.

Levy, J., & Heller, W. (1992). Gender differences in human neuropsychological function. In A. A. Gerall, H. Moltz, & I. L. Ward (Eds.), *Handbook of behavioral neurobiology: Vol. 11. Sexual differentiation* (pp. 245–274). New York: Plenum Press.

Levy, S. (1997, March 31). U.S. v. the Internet. *Time*, 77–79.

Lichter, D. T., McLaughlin, D. K., & Ribar, D. C. (1998). State abortion policy, geographic access to abortion providers and changing family formation. *Family Planning Perspectives, 30*(6), 281–287.

Lief, H. I., & Hubschman, L. (1993). Orgasm in the postoperative transsexual. *Archives of Sexual Behavior, 22*(2), 145–155.

Lim, G. Y., & Roloff, M. E. (1999). Attributing sexual consent. *Journal of Applied Communication Research, 27*(1), 1–23.

Lindsay, J., Smith, A. M. A., & Rosenthal, D. A. (1999). Conflicting advice? Australian adolescents' use of condoms or the pill. *Family Planning Perspectives, 31*(4), 190–194.

Linnehan, M. J. E., & Groce, N. E. (1999). Psychosocial and educational services for female college students with genital human papillomavirus infection. *Family Planning Perspectives, 31*(3), 137–141.

Lippert, L. (1997). Women at midlife: Implications for theories of women's adult development. *Journal of Counseling and Development, 76*(1), 16–22.

Lips, H. M. (1999). *A new psychology of women: Gender, culture, and ethnicity.* Mountain View, CA: Mayfield.

Lipschitz, D. S., Winegar, R. K., Hartnick, E., Foote, B., & Southwick, S. M. (1999). Posttraumatic stress disorder in hospitalized adolescents: Psychiatric comorbidity and clinical correlates. *Journal of the American Academy of Child and Adolescent Psychiatry, 38*(4), 385–392.

Lish, J. D., Meyer-Bahlburg, H. F., Ehrhardt, A. A., & Travis, B. G., et al. (1992). Prenatal exposure to diethylstilbestrol (DES): Childhood play behavior and adult gender-role behavior in women. *Archives of Sexual Behavior, 21*(5), 423–441.

Litt, S. (1995). The origins of creativity: Sexuality, neurosis and the artist. *International Forum of Psychoanalysis, 4*(2), 97–103.

Lobitz, W. C., & Lobitz, G. K. (1996). Resolving the sexual intimacy paradox: A developmental model for the treatment of sexual desire disorders. *Journal of Sex and Marital Therapy, 22*(2), 71–84.

Lock, J., & Steiner, H. (1999). Gay, lesbian, and bisexual youth risks for emotional, physical, and social problems: Results from a community-based survey. *Journal of the American Academy of Child & Adolescent Psychiatry, 38*(3), 297–304.

Loftus, E. F. (1999). Lost in the mall: Misrepresentations and misunderstandings. *Ethics and Behavior, 9*(1), 51–60.

Logan, C. R. (1997, March). It takes a village to care for a lesbian. *Counseling Today*, 29, 35.

London International Group (1998). *The 1997 Durex global sex survey.* London: Durex Co.

Looman, J. (1995). Sexual fantasies of child molesters. *Canadian Journal of Behavioural Science, 27*(3), 321–332.

Looy, H. (1995). Born gay? A critical review of biological research on homosexuality. *Journal of Psychology and Christianity, 14*(3), 197–214.

Lopez, O. L., Wess, J., Sanchez, J., Dew, M. A., & Becker, J. T. (1999). Neurological characteristics of HIV-infected men and women seeking primary medical care. *European Journal of Neurology, 6*(2), 202–209.

Lott, B., & Maluso, D. (1993). The social learning of gender. In A. E. Beall & R. J. Sternberg (Eds.), *The psychology of gender* (pp. 99–123). New York: Guilford Press.

Lottes, I. L., & Weinberg, M. S. (1996). Sexual coercion among university students: A comparison of the United States and Sweden. *Journal of Sex Research, 34*(1), 67–76.

Louden, J. (1994). *The couple's comfort book: A creative guide for renewing passion, pleasure, and commitment.* San Francisco: HarperSanFrancisco.

Louderback, L., & Whitley, B. E. (1997). Perceived erotic value of homosexuality and sex-role attitudes as mediators of sex differences in heterosexual college students' attitudes toward lesbians and gays. *Journal of Sex Research, 34*(2), 175–182.

Love, P., & Robinson, J. (1994). *Hot monogamy: Essential steps to more passionate, intimate lovemaking.* New York: Dutton.

Ludwig, M. R., & Brownell, K. D. (1999). Lesbians, bisexual women, and body image: An investigation of gender roles and social group affiliation. *International Journal of Eating Disorders, 25*(1), 89–97.

Lueptow, L. B., Garovich, L., & Lueptow, M. B. (1995). The persistence of gender stereotypes in the face of changing sex roles: Evidence contrary to the sociocultural model. *Ethology and Sociobiology, 16*(6), 509–530.

Luster, T., & Small, S. A. (1997). Sexual abuse history and number of sex partners among female adolescents. *Family Planning Perspectives, 29*(5), 204–211.

Lytton, H., & Romney, D. M. (1991). Parents' differential socialization of boys and girls: A meta-analysis. *Psychological Bulletin, 109*(2), 267–296.

M

Maccoby, E. E. (1998). *The two sexes: Growing up apart, coming together.* Cambridge, MA: Harvard University Press.

MacDonald, B. J. (1998). Issues in therapy with gay and lesbian couples. *Journal of Sex and Marital Therapy, 24*, 165–190.

Macdonald, W. (1996). Effect of frequent prenatal ultrasound on birthweight. *Lancet, 348*, 482.

MacFarquhar, N. (1996, August 8). Mutilation of Egyptian girls: Despite ban, it goes on. *New York Times*, A3.

Macke, J. P., et al. (1993). Sequence variation in the androgen receptor gene is not a common determinant of male sexual orientation. *American Journal of Human Genetics, 53*, 844–852.

MacPhee, D. C., Johnson, S. M., & Van der Veer, M. M. (1995). Low sexual desire in women: The effects of marital therapy. *Journal of Sex and Marital Therapy, 21*(3), 159–182.

Maddock, J. W. (1997). Sexuality education: A history lesson. In J. W. Maddock (Ed.), *Sexuality education in postsecondary and professional settings* (pp. 1–22). New York: Haworth Press.

Maddock, J. W., & Larson, N. R. (1995). *Incestuous families: An ecological approach to understanding and treatment.* New York: W. W. Norton.

Mahoney, C. A. (1995). The role of cues, self-efficacy, level of worry, and high-risk behaviors in college student condom use. *Journal of Sex Education and Therapy, 21*(2), 103–116.

Major, B., Barr, L., Zubek, J., & Babey, S. H. (1999). Gender and self-esteem: A meta-analysis. In W. B. Swann & J. H. Langlois (Eds.), *Sexism and stereotypes in modern society: The gender science of Janet Taylor Spence* (pp. 223–253). Washington: American Psychological Association.

Malcolm, P. B., Andrews, D. A., & Quinsey, V. L. (1993). Discriminant and predictive validity of phallometrically measured sexual age and gender preference. *Journal of Interpersonal Violence, 8*(4), 486–501.

Malone, F. D., Craigo, S. D., Chelmow, D., & D'Alton, M. E. (1996). Outcome of twin gestations complicated by a single anomalous fetus. *Obstetrics and Gynecology, 88*(1), 1–5.

Manlove, J. (1997). Early motherhood in an intergenerational perspective: The experience of a British cohort. *Journal of Marriage and the Family, 59*, 263–279.

Mann, A. (1998, April 6). Cross-gender sex pill. *Time*, 62.

Manning, J. T., Anderton, R. H., & Shutt, M. (1997). Parental age skews child sex ratio. *Nature, 389*(6649), 344.

Manning, W. D., & Landale, N. S. (1996). Racial and ethnic differences in the role of cohabitation in premarital childbearing. *Journal of Marriage and the Family, 58*, 63–77.

Mansfield, P. K., Voda, A., & Koch, P. B. (1995). Predictors of sexual response changes in heterosexual midlife women. *Health Values: The Journal of Health Behavior, Education and Promotion, 19*(1), 10–20.

Marby, M. (1999, July 12). No money, no meds. *Newsweek*, 33–34.

Marin, B. V. (1997). Cross-cultural issues. In J. Bancroft (Ed.), *Researching sexual behavior* (pp. 363–366). Bloomington: Indiana University Press.

Marina, S. (1998). Human immunodeficiency virus type 1-serodiscordant couples can bear healthy children after undergoing intrauterine insemination. *Fertility and Sterility, 70*(1), 35–39.

Mark Clements Research. (1996). Sexual activity still flourishes after 65. *Contemporary Sexuality, 30*(4), 8.

Markman, H. J., Silvern, L., Clements, M., & Kraft-Hanak, S. (1993). Men and women dealing with conflict in heterosexual relationships. *Journal of Social Issues, 49*(3), 107–125.

Markowitz, L. (1997). The cultural context of intimacy. *Networker, 21*(5), 50–58.

Marotta, S. A., & Asner, K. K. (1999). Group psychotherapy for women with a history of incest: The research base. *Journal of Counseling and Development, 77,* 315–322.

Marsh, H. W., & Byrne, B. M. (1991). Differentiated additive androgyny model: Relations between masculinity, femininity, and multiple dimensions of self-concept. *Journal of Personality and Social Psychology, 61*(5), 811–828.

Marshall, D. S. (1971). Sexual behavior on Mangaia. In D. S. Marshall & R. C. Suggs (Eds.), *Human sexual behavior* (pp. 103–162). New York: Basic Books.

Marshall, E. (1997a). Embryologists dismayed by sanctions against geneticist. *Science, 275,* 472.

Marshall, E. (1997b). Lobbyists seek to reslice NIH's pie. *Science, 276,* 344–346.

Marshall, E. (1997). The battle over BRCA1 goes to court: BRCA2 may be next. *Science, 278,* 1874.

Marshall, W. L. (1999). Diagnosing and treating sexual offenders. In A. K. Hess & I. B. Weiner (Eds.), *The handbook of forensic psychology* (pp. 640–670). New York: John Wiley.

Marsiglio, W. (1998). *Procreative man.* New York: New York University Press.

Martin, J. A., & Park, M. M. (1999). Trends in twin and triplet births: 1980–97. *National Vital Statistics, 46,* 24.

Martin, P. Y., & Collinson, D. L. (1999). Gender and sexuality in organizations. In M. M. Ferree (Ed.), *Revisioning gender* (pp. 285–310) Thousand Oaks, CA: Sage.

Martinez, A. L. (1999). Cambios: A Spanish-language approach to youth development. *SIECUS Report, 27*(5), 9–10.

Martinson, F. M. (1994). *The sexual life of children.* Westport, CT: Bergin & Garvey.

Marx, J. (1995). Sharing the genes that divide the sexes for mammals. *Science, 269,* 1824–1825.

Marx, J. (1996). A second breast cancer suscepti-bility gene is found. *Science, 271,* 30–31.

Mason, M. (1994). *The making of Victorian sexuality.* New York: Oxford University Press.

Masters, W. H., & Johnson, V. E. (1966). *Human sexual response.* Boston: Little, Brown.

Masters, W. H., & Johnson, V. E. (1970). *Human sexual inadequacy.* Boston: Little, Brown.

Maticka-Tyndale, E., Herold, E. S., & Mewhinney, D. (1999). Casual sex on spring break: Intentions and behaviors of Canadian students. *Journal of Sex Research, 35*(3), 254–264.

Mauldon, J., & Delbanco, S. (1997). Public perceptions about unplanned pregnancy. *Family Planning Perspectives, 29*(1), 25–29, 40.

Maurice, W. L. (1999). *Sexual medicine in primary care.* St. Louis, MO: Mosby.

Mayden, B. (1995). Access to sexuality infor-mation for out-of-home youth. *SIECUS Report, 24*(1), 13–15.

McAninch, J., & Wessels, H. (1995, May 21). As quoted in: Penis study challenges need for risky surgery. *Watertown (NY) Daily Times,* G1, G7.

McCabe, M. P. (1997). Intimacy and quality of life among sexually dysfunctional men and women. *Journal of Sex and Marital Therapy, 23*(4), 276–290.

McCaffree, K. A. (1998a). A view from the field: The personal challenges and rewards of consulting worldwide on sexuality education. *SIECUS Report, 26*(5), 15–16.

McCaffree, K. A. (1998b). Who is a sexuality professional? *Journal of Sex Education and Therapy, 23*(1), 3–5.

McCarthy, B. W. (1997a). Chronic sexual dysfunction: Assessment, intervention, and realistic expectations. *Journal of Sex Education and Therapy, 22*(2), 51–56.

McCarthy, B. W. (1997b). Strategies and techniques for revitalizing a nonsexual marriage. *Journal of Sex and Marital Therapy, 23*(3), 231–240.

McCarthy, B. W. (1997c). Therapeutic and iatrogenic interventions with adults who were sexually abused as children. *Journal of Sex and Marital Therapy, 23*(2), 118–125.

McCarthy, B. W. (1998a). Integrating Viagra into cognitive-behavioral couples sex therapy. *Journal of Sex Education and Therapy, 23*(4), 302–308.

McCarthy, B. W. (1998b). Sex therapy workshops: The Indian experience. *Journal of Sex Education and Therapy, 23*(4), 309–311.

McCarthy, B. W. (1999a). The nonsexual marriage: Assessing viability and treatment options. *Journal of Sex and Marital Therapy, 25,* 227–236.

McCarthy, B. W. (1999b). Relapse prevention strategies and techniques for inhibited sexual desire. *Journal of Sex and Marital Therapy, 25,* 297–303.

McCollum, K. (1999, May14). Students find sex, drugs, and more than a little education on line, survey finds. *The Chronicle of Higher Education,* A31.

McConaghy, N. (1993). *Sexual behavior: Problems and management.* New York: Plenum.

McCormick, D. (1994). *Erotic literature.* New York: Continuum.

McCormick, N. B. (1996a). Introduction to special issue on chronic disease and sexuality. *Journal of Sex Research, 33*(3), 175–177.

McCormick, N. B. (1996b). Our feminist future: Women affirming sexuality research in the late twentieth century. *Journal of Sex Research, 33*(2), 99–102.

McCoy, C. B., Metsch, L. R., McCoy, H. V., & Weatherby, N. L. (1999). HIV seroprevalence across the rural/urban continuum. *Substance Use and Misuse, 34*(4–5), 595–615.

McCoy, N. L., & Matyas, J. R. (1996). Oral contra-ceptives and sexuality in university women. *Archives of Sexual Behavior, 25*(1), 73–90.

McDermid, S. A., Zucker, K. J., Bradley, S. J., & Maing, D. M. (1998). Effects of physical appearance on masculine trait ratings of boys and girls with gender identity disorder. *Archives of Sexual Behavior, 27*(3), 253–267.

McDermott, S., Martin, M., Weinrich, M., & Kelly, M. (1999, March–April). Program evaluation of a sex education curriculum for women with mental retardation. *Research in Developmental Disabilities, 20*(2), 93–106.

McDonald, K. A. (1998, February 6). Defining the nature of attraction. *Chronicle of Higher Education,* A14–15.

McDonald, K. A. (1999, June 25). Studies of women's health produce a wealth of knowledge on the biology of gender differ-ences. *The Chronicle of Higher Education,* A19–22.

McDougall, J. (1995). *The many faces of eros.* New York: W. W. Norton.

McFadden, D., & Pasanen, E. G. (1999). Spontaneous otoacoustic emissions in heterosexuals, homosexuals, and bisexuals. *Journal of the Acoustical Society of America, 105*(4), 2403–2413.

McGregor, J. A. (1995). Prevention of premature birth by screening and treatment for common genital tract infections. *American Journal of Obstetrics and Gynecology, 173,* 157–167.

McKenna, K. E. (2000). Central nervous system pathways involved in the control of penile erection. *Annual Review of Sex Research, 9,* 157–183.

McNair, L. D., Carter, J. A., & Williams, M. K. (1998). Self-esteem, gender, and alcohol use: Relationships with HIV risk perception and behaviors in college students. *Journal of Sex and Marital Therapy, 24,* 29–36.

Mead, M. (1930). *Growing up in New Guinea.* New York: New American Library.

Meadow-Orlans, K. P., & Wallace, R. A. (1994). *Gender and the academic experience.* Lincoln: University of Nebraska Press.

Medlar, T. M. (1993). Sexual counseling and traumatic brain injury. *Sexuality and Disability, 11*(1), 57–71.

Meehan, T. M., Hansen, H., & Klein, W. C. (1997). The impact of parental consent on the HIV testing of minors. *American Journal of Public Health, 87*(8), 1338–1341.

Melbye, M., Wohlfahrt, J., Olsen, J. H., Frisch, M., Westergaard, T., Helweg-Larson, K., & Andersen, P. K. (1997). Induced abortion and the risk of breast cancer. *New England Journal of Medicine, 336,* 81–85.

Mendelsohn, K. D., Nieman, L. Z., Isaacs, K, Lee, S., & Levinson, S. P. (1994). Sex and gender bias in anatomy and physical diagnosis text illustrations. *Journal of the American Medical Association, 272,* 1267–1270.

Mendes-Leite, R. (1993). A game of appearances: The "ambigusexuality" in Brazilian culture of sexuality. *Journal of Homosexuality, 25*(3), 271–282.

Mendez, Z. M. (1996). Columbia's national project for sex education. *SIECUS Report, 24*(3), 13.

Mervis, J. (1999). Efforts to boost diversity face persistent problems. *Science, 284,* 1757–1759.

Meston, C. M., Heiman, J. R., & Trapnell, P. D. (1999). The relation between early abuse and adult sexuality. *Journal of Sex Research, 36*(4), 385–395.

Meston, C. M., Trapnell, P. D., & Gorzalka, B. B. (1998). Ethnic, gender, and length-of-residency influences on sexual knowledge and attitudes. *Journal of Sex Research, 35*(2), 176–188.

Metz, M. E., Pryor, J. L., Nesvacil, L. J., Abuzzahab, F., & Koznar, J. (1997). Premature ejaculation: A psychophysiological review. *Journal of Sex and Marital Therapy, 23*(1), 3–23.

Meuwissen, I., & Over, R. (1991). Multidimensionality of the content of female sexual fantasy. *Behaviour Research and Therapy, 29*(2), 179–189.

Meyerowitz, B. E., Desmond, K. A., Rowland, J. H., Wyatt, G. E., & Ganz, P. A. (1999). Sexuality following breast cancer. *Journal of Sex and Marital Therapy, 25,* 237–250.

Michael, R. T., Gagnon, J. H., Laumann, E. O., & Kolata, G. (1994). *Sex in America: A defin-itive study.* Boston: Little, Brown.

Miki, Y., et al. (1994). A strong candidate for the breast and ovarian cancer susceptibility gene BRCA1. *Science, 266,* 66–71.

Milhausen, R. R., & Herold, E. S. (1999). Does the sexual double standard still exist? Perceptions of university women. *Journal of Sex Research, 36*(4), 361–368.

Miller, H. G., Cain, V. S., Rogers, S. M., Gribble, J. N., & Turner, C. F. (1999). Correlates of sexually transmitted bacterial infections among U.S. women in 1995. *Family Planning Perspectives, 31*(1), 4–8.

Miller, H. L., Miller, C. E., Kenney, L., & Clark, J. W. (1998). Issues in statutory rape law enforcement: The views of district attorneys in Kansas. *Family Planning Perspectives, 30*(4), 177–181.

Miller, K. S., Clark, L. F., & Moore, J. S. (1997). Sexual initiation with older male partners and subsequent HIV risk behavior among female adolescents. *Family Planning Perspectives, 29*(5), 212–214.

Miller, P. B., & Soules, M. R. (1996). The usefulness of a urinary LH kit for ovulation prediction during menstrual cycles of normal women. *Obstetrics and Gynecology, 87*(1), 13–17.

Miller, R. L. (1995). Assisting gay men to maintain safer sex: An evaluation of an AIDS service organization's safer sex maintenance program. *AIDS Education and Prevention, 7*(Suppl.), 48–63.

Miller, W. B. (1994). The relationship between childbearing motivations and attitude toward abortion among married men and women. *Family Planning Perspectives, 26*(4), 165–168.

Miller, W. B., Pasta, D. J., MacMurray, J., Chiu, C., Wu, H., & Comings, D. E. (1999). Dopamine receptor genes are associated with age at first sexual intercourse. *Journal of Biosocial Science, 31*(1), 43–54.

Milton, M., & Coyle, A. (1999). Lesbian and gay affirmative psychotherapy: Issues in theory and practice. *Sexual and Marital Therapy, 14*(1), 43–59.

Miracle-McMahill, H. L. (1997). Tubal ligation and female ovarian cancer in a large prospective cohort study. *American Journal of Epidemiology, 145,* 349–357.

Mitchell, W. B., DiBartolo, P. M., Brown, T. A., & Barlow, D. H. (1998). Effects of positive and negative mood on sexual arousal in sexually functional males. *Archives of Sexual Behavior, 27*(2), 197–207.

Monaghan, P. (1999a, February 26). Lessons from the "marriage lab." *Chronicle of Higher Education,* A9.

Monaghan, P. (1999b, July 30). Making babies with new technologies. *Chronicle of Higher Education,* A10–11.

Money, J. (1977). Determinants of human gender identity/role. In J. Money & H. Musaph (Eds.), *Handbook of sexology* (pp. 57–79). New York: Excerpta Medica.

Money, J. (1989). *Lovemaps.* Buffalo, NY: Prometheus Books.

Money, J. (1991). Semen-conservation theory vs. semen-investment theory, antisexualism, and the return of Freud's seduction theory. *Journal of Psychology and Human Sexuality, 4*(4), 31–45.

Money, J. (1994). *Sex errors of the body and related syndromes.* Baltimore: Paul H. Brookes.

Money, J., & Ehrhardt, A. A. (1972). *Man and woman, boy and girl.* Baltimore: Johns Hopkins University Press.

Montague, D. K. (1998). Erectile dysfunction: The rational utilization of diagnostic testing. *Journal of Sex Education and Therapy, 23*(3), 194–196.

Moore, K. A., Driscoll, A. K., & Lindberg, L. D. (1998). *A statistical portrait of adolescent sex, contraception, and childbearing.* Washington, DC: National Campaign to Prevent Teen Pregnancy.

Moore, M. (1999a). Most U.S. couples who seek surgical sterilization do so for contraception; fewer than 25% desire reversal. *Family Planning Perspectives, 31*(2), 102–103.

Moore, M. (1999b). Zidovudine given to infants soon after birth reduces perinatal HIV transmission. *Family Planning Perspectives, 31*(3), 103–104.

Moore, N. B., & Davidson, J. K. (1997). Guilt about first intercourse: An antecedent of sexual dissatisfaction among college women. *Journal of Sex and Marital Therapy, 23*(1), 29–46.

Moran, M. A. (1993). The effect of lovemaking on the progress of labor. *Pre- and Peri-Natal Psychology Journal, 7*(3), 231–241.

Morgan, C. A., & Grillon, C. (1999). Abnormal mismatch negativity in women with sexual assault-related posttraumatic stress disorder. *Biological Psychiatry, 45*(7), 827–832.

Morgan, T., & Cummings, A. L. (1999). Change experienced during group therapy by female survivors of childhood sexual abuse. *Journal of Consulting and Clinical Psychology, 67*(1), 28–36.

Morrison, D. M., Leigh, B. C., & Gillmore, M. R. (1999). Daily data collection: A comparison of three methods. *Journal of Sex Research, 36*(1), 76–81.

Mosher, D. L. (1986). Misinformation on pornography: A lobby disguised as an educational organization. *SIECUS Report, 14*(5), 7–10.

Mosher, S. W. (1998). Declining fertility (letter). *Science, 282,* 1419.

Mosher, W. D., & Bachrach, C. A. (1996). Understanding U.S. fertility: Continuity and change in the national survey of family growth, 1988–1995. *Family Planning Perspectives, 28*(1), 4–12.

Mulcahy, J. J. (1998). Review of penile implants. *Journal of Sex Education and Therapy, 23*(3), 220–225.

Murnen, S. K., & Byrne, D. (1991). Hyperfemininity: Measurement and initial validation of the construct. *Journal of Sex Research, 28*(3), 479–489.

Murphy, J. J., & Boggess, S. (1998). Increased condom use among teenage males, 1988–1995: The role of attitudes. *Family Planning Perspectives, 30*(6), 276–280, 303.

Murray, J. (1997). Men's bodies, men's minds: Seminal emissions and sexual anxiety in the Middle Ages. *Annual Review of Sex Research, 8,* 1–26.

Murray, S. O., & Roscoe, W. (1997). *Islamic homosexualities: Culture, history, and literature.* New York: New York University Press.

Myers, I. B., & McCaulley, M. H. (1985). *A guide to the development and use of the Myers-Briggs Type Indicator.* Palo Alto, CA: Consulting Psychologists Press.

Myrick, R. (1999). In the life: Culture-specific HIV communication programs designed for African American men who have sex with men. *Journal of Sex Research, 36*(2), 159–170.

N

Nardi, P. M. (1998). Interview with Igor Kon. *Sexualities, 1*(2), 229–238.

Nardi, P. M., & Schneider, B. E. (1998). Kinsey: A 50th anniversary symposium. *Sexualities, 1*(1), 83–106.

Narring, F., Michaud, P. A., & Sharma, V. (1996). Demographic and behavioral factors associated with adolescent pregnancy in Switzerland. *Family Planning Perspectives, 28*(5), 232–236.

Nash, J. M. (1997a, March 10). The age of cloning. *Time,* 62–65.

Nash, J. M. (1997b, June 30). Every woman's dilemma. *Time,* 60.

Nash, J. M. (1998, April 27). The personality genes. *Time,* 60–61.

Nathanson, N., & Auerbach, J. D. (1999). Confronting the HIV pandemic. *Science, 284,* 1619.

National Campaign to Prevent Teen Pregnancy. (1998). *Parents of teens and teens discuss sex, love and relationships: A summary of findings.* Washington, DC: Author.

National Center for Environmental Health. (1995). Smoking men at risk for erectile dysfunction. *Contemporary Sexuality, 29*(2), 8.

National Center for Health Statistics. (1991). *Advance report of final divorce statistics, 39*(12).

National Commission on Adolescent Sexual Health. (1995). *Facing facts: Sexual health for America's adolescents.* New York: Sex Information and Education Council of the United States.

National Council on Aging. (1998, September 29). Reporting on results of survey of senior citizens. Knight-Ridder Newspapers.

National Data Program for the Social Sciences. (1992). Trendlets: A change in sexual permissiveness. *GSS News, 6,* 4–6.

National Institutes of Health. (1999). Sexual satisfaction runs a respectable fourth. *Contemporary Sexuality, 33*(5), 9.

National Victims Center (1992). *Rape in America: A report to the nation.* Fort Worth, TX: National Victims Center.

Nayak, M. B., Resnick, H. S., & Holmes, M. M. (1999). Treating health concerns within the context of childhood sexual assault: A case study. *Journal of Traumatic Stress, 12*(1), 101–109.

Ndinya-Achola, J. O., Plummer, F. A., Piot, P., & Ronald, A. R. (1990). Acquired immune deficiency syndrome in Africa. In B. Voeller, J. M. Reinisch, & M. Gottlieb (Eds.), *AIDS and sex* (pp. 185–196). New York: Oxford University Press.

Nelson, J. A. (1994). Comment on special issue on adolescence. *American Psychologist, 49*(6), 523–524.

Nelson, J. B., & Longfellow, S. P. (Eds.). (1994). *Sexuality and the sacred: Sources for theological reflection.* Louisville, KY: Westminster Press/John Knox Press.

Nelson, K. L. (1996). The conflict over sexuality education: Interviews with participants on both sides of the debate. *SIECUS Report, 24*(6), 12–16.

Nelson, N. (1997). *Dangerous relationships.* New York: Plenum.

Nesca, M., Dalby, J. T., & Baskerville, S. (1999). Psychosocial profile of a female psychopath. *American Journal of Forensic Psychology, 17*(2), 63–77.

Nesmith, A. A., Burton, D. L., & Cosgrove, T. J. (1999). Gay, lesbian and bisexual youth and young adults: Social support in their own words. *Journal of Homosexuality, 37*(1), 95–108.

Neumann, P. J., Gharib, S. D., & Weinstein, M. C. (1994). The cost of a successful delivery with in vitro fertilization. *New England Journal of Medicine, 331,* 239–243.

New Adolescent Health Study (1995, June). New adolescent health study successfully completes first phase. *Health and Science Briefs from the National Institute of Child Health and Human Development.* Bethesda, MD.

Newman, B. (1997). The use of online services to encourage exploration of ego-dystonic sexual interests. *Journal of Sex Education and Therapy, 22*(1), 45–48.

Nichols, M. (1990). Lesbian relationships: Implications for the study of sexuality and gender. In D. P. McWhirter, S. A. Sanders, & J. M. Reinisch (Eds.), *Homosexuality/heterosexuality: Concepts of sexual orientation* (pp. 350–364). New York: Oxford University Press.

Nock, S. L. (1998). The consequences of premarital fatherhood. *American Sociological Review, 63*(2), 250–263.

Nordentoft, M. (1996). Intrauterine growth retardation and premature delivery: The influence of maternal smoking and psychosocial factors. *American Journal of Public Health, 86,* 347–354.

Norman, A. D. (1996). Lesbian and bisexual women in small cities: At risk for HIV? *Public Health Reports, 111,* 347–352.

Nottelmann, E. D., Inoff-Germain, G., Susman, E. J., & Chrousos, G. P. (1990). Hormones and behavior at puberty. In J. Bancroft & J. M. Reinisch (Eds.), *Adolescence and puberty* (pp. 88–123). New York: Oxford University Press.

Nutter, D. E., & Kearns, M. E. (1993). Patterns of exposure to sexually explicit material among sex offenders, child molesters, and controls. *Journal of Sex and Marital Therapy, 19*(1), 77–85.

O

Oakley, D., & Bogue, E. (1995). Quality of condom use as reported by female clients of a family planning clinic. *American Journal of Public Health, 85,* 1526–1530.

Ochs, E. P., & Binik, Y. M. (1998). A sex-expert computer system helps couples learn more about their sexual relationship. *Journal of Sex Education and Therapy, 23*(2), 145–155.

O'Connor, M. L. (1998). The number of abortions among U.S. women fell 5% in 1994, continuing a decline begun in the early 1990s. *Family Planning Perspectives, 30*(2), 101–102.

O'Donohue, W. T., & Plaud, J. J. (1994). The conditioning of human sexual arousal. *Archives of Sexual Behavior, 23*(3), 321–344.

Oh, M. K. (1996). Risk for gonococcal and chlamydial cervicitis in adolescent females: Incidence and recurrence in a prospective cohort. *Journal of Adolescent Health, 18,* 270–275.

O'Hare, E. A., & O'Donohue, W. (1998). Sexual harassment: Identifying risk factors. *Archives of Sexual Behavior, 27*(6), 561–580.

Okami, P., Olmstead, R., & Abramson, P. R. (1997). Sexual experiences in early childhood: 18-year longitudinal data from the UCLA family lifestyles project. *Journal of Sex Research, 34*(4), 339–347.

Okami, P., Olmstead, R., Abramson, P. R., & Pendleton, L. (1998). Early childhood exposure to parental nudity and scenes of parental sexuality ("primal scenes"): An 18-year longitudinal study of outcome. *Archives of Sexual Behavior, 27*(4), 361–384.

Okwumabua, T. M., Okwumabua, J. O., & Elliot V. (1998). "Let the circle be unbroken" helps African-Americans prevent teen pregnancy. *SIECUS Report, 26*(3), 12–16.

Oldham, J. D., & Kasser, T. (1999). Attitude change in response to information that male homosexuality has a biological basis. *Journal of Sex and Marital Therapy, 25*(2), 121–124.

Olenick, I. (1999). Levonorgestrol is a better emergency contraceptive than the combination pill. *Family Planning Perspectives, 31*(2), 104.

Olsen, K. L. (1992). Genetic influences on sexual behavior differentiation. In A. A. Gerall, H. Moltz, & I. L. Ward (Eds.), *Handbook of behavioral neurobiology: Vol. 11. Sexual differentiation* (pp. 1–40). New York: Plenum Press.

Osman, A. K., & Al-Sawaf, M. H. (1995). Cross-cultural aspects of sexual anxieties and the associated dysfunction. *Journal of Sex Education and Therapy, 21*(3), 174–181.

O'Sullivan, L. F., & Allegeier, E. R. (1998). Feigning sexual desire: Consenting to unwanted sexual activity in heterosexual dating relationships. *Journal of Sex Research, 35*(3), 234–243.

Oswalt, S., Welle-Grafe, H. M., Minter, L., & Glover, S. (1998). Need for HIV home testing kit option and education. *Journal of College Student Development, 39*(6), 627–628.

Over, R., & Koukounas, E. (1995). Habituation of sexual arousal: Product and process. *Annual Review of Sex Research, 4,* 187–223.

P

Padma-Nathan, H. (1998). The pharmacologic management of erectile dysfunction: Sildenafil citrate (Viagra). *Journal of Sex Education and Therapy, 23*(3), 207–216.

Pally, M. (1994). *Sex and sensibility.* Hopewell, NJ: Ecco Press.

Panchaud, C., Singh, S., Feivelson, D., & Darroch, J. E. (2000). Sexually transmitted diseases among adolescents in developed countries. *Family Planning Perspectives, 32*(1), 24–32, 45.

Paredes, R. G., & Baum, M. J. (1997). Role of the medial preoptic area/anterior hypothalamus in the control of masculine sexual behavior. *Annual Review of Sex Research, 8,* 68–100.

Pattatucci, A. M., & Hamer, D. H. (1995). Development and familiality of sexual orientation in females. *Behavior Genetics, 25*(5), 407–420.

Patterson, C. J. (1995). Lesbian mothers, gay fathers, and their children. In A. R. D'Augelli & C. J. Patterson (Eds.), *Lesbian, gay, and bisexual identities over the lifespan* (pp. 262–290). New York: Oxford University Press.

Patti, P. J. (1995). Sexuality and sexual expression in persons with mental retardation. *SIECUS Report, 23*(4), 17–20.

Paz, I. (1995). The cognitive outcome of full-term small for gestational age infants at late adolescence. *Obstetrics and Gynecology, 85,* 452–456.

Pennell, G. E., & Ogilvie, D. M. (1995). You and me as she and he: The meaning of gender-related concepts in other- and self-perception. *Sex Roles, 33*(1), 29–57.

Pennisi, E. (1995). Long-sought H-Y antigen found. *Science, 269,* 1515–1516.

Peplau, L. A., Spalding, L. R., Conley, T. D., & Veniegas, R. C. (2000). The development of sexual orientation in women. *Annual Review of Sex Research, 10,* 70–99.

Peplau, L. A., Veniegas, F. C., Taylor, P. L., & DeBro, S. C. (1999). Sociocultural perspectives on the lives of women and men. In L. A. Peplau & S. C. DeBro (Eds.), *Gender, culture, and ethnicity: Current research about women and men* (pp. 23–37). Mountain View, CA: Mayfield.

Pera, G. (1996, September 6). Agony of sexual harassment: Two sides. *USA Weekend,* 12–13.

Peraldi, F. (1992). Heterosexual presumption. *American Imago, 49*(3), 357–370.

Perelman, M. A. (1998). Commentary: Pharmacological agents for erectile dysfunction and the human sexual response cycle. *Journal of Sex and Marital Therapy, 24,* 309–312.

Perrin, L. & Telenti, A. (1998). HIV treatment failure: Testing for HIV resistance in clinical practice. *Science, 280,* 1871–1872.

Perse, E. M. (1994). Uses of erotica and acceptance of rape myths. *Communication Research, 21*(4), 488–515.

Person, E. S., Terestman, N., Myers, W. A., Goldberg, E. L., & Salvadori, C. (1989). Gender differences in sexual behaviors and fantasies in a college population. *Journal of Sex and Marital Therapy, 15,* 187–198.

Peters, D. K., & Cantrell, P. J. (1991). Factors distinguishing samples of lesbian and heterosexual women. *Journal of Homosexuality, 21*(4), 1–15.

Peterson, L. S., Oakley, D., Potter, L. S., & Darroch, J. E. (1998). Women's efforts to prevent pregnancy: Consistency of oral contraceptive use. *Family Planning Perspectives, 30*(1), 19–23.

Pettitt, D. J., et al. (1997). Breastfeeding and incidence of non-insulin-dependent diabetes mellitus in Pima Indians, *Lancet, 350,* 166–168.

Pfaus, J. G. (2000). Revisiting the concept of sexual motivation. *Annual Review of Sex Research, 9,* 120–156.

Phillips, K. A., & Knight, J. A. (1999). Putting the risk of breast cancer in perspective. *New England Journal of Medicine, 340*(2), 141–144.

Piaget, J. (1932). *The moral judgment of the child.* New York: Harcourt Brace.

Piccinino, L. J., & Mosher, W. D. (1998). Trends in contraceptive use in the United States: 1982–1995. *Family Planning Perspectives, 30*(1), 4–10 & 46.

Piletz, J. E., Segraves, K. B., Feng, Y., Maguire, E., Dunger, B., & Halaris, A. (1998). Plasma MHPG response to yohimbine treatment in women with hypoactive sexual desire. *Journal of Sex and Marital Therapy, 24,* 43–54.

Piper, J. M., Mitchel, E. F., & Ray, W. A. (1996). Evaluation of a program for prenatal care case management. *Family Planning Perspectives, 28*(2), 65–68.

Piper, J. M., Xenakis, E., McFarland, M., Elliott, B. D., Berkus, M. D., & Langer, O. (1996). Do growth-retarded premature infants have different rates of perinatal morbidity and mortality than appropriately grown premature infants? *Obstetrics and Gynecology, 87*(2), 169–174.

Pistole, M. C. (1995). College students' ended love relationships: Attachment style and emotion. *Journal of College Student Development, 36*(1), 53–60.

Pithers, W. D. (1999). Empathy: Definition, enhancement, and relevance to the treatment of sexual abusers. *Journal of Interpersonal Violence, 14*(3), 257–284.

Pitts, M., Magunje, N., & McMaster, J. (1994). Students' knowledge of the use of herbs and other agents as preparation for sexual intercourse. *Health Care for Women International, 15*(2), 91–99.

Plaud, J. J., & Bigwood, S. J. (1997). A multi-variate analysis of the sexual fantasy themes of college men. *Journal of Sex and Marital Therapy, 23*(3), 221–230.

Plaud, J. J., Gaither, G. A., & Weller, L. A. (1998). Gender differences in the sexual rating of words. *Journal of Sex and Marital Therapy, 24,* 13–19.

Plaud, J. J., Gaither, G. A., Hegstad, H. J., Rowan, L., & Devitt, M. K. (1999). Volunteer bias in human psychophysiological sexual arousal research: To whom do our research results apply? *Journal of Sex Research, 36*(2), 171–179.

Plaud, J. J., & Martini, J. R. (1999). The respondent conditioning of male sexual arousal. *Behavior Modification, 23*(2), 254–268.

Plaut, S. M. (1997). Online ethics: Social contracts in the virtual community. *Journal of Sex Education and Therapy, 22*(1), 84–91.

Plaut, S. M., & Ginter, H. B. (1995). Sexual boundaries between health professionals and clients: A blueprint for education. *SIECUS Report, 23*(5), 3–5.

Pleak, R. R., & Meyer-Bahlburg, H. F. L. (1990). Sexual behavior and AIDS knowledge of young male prostitutes in Manhattan. *Journal of Sex Research, 27,* 557–587.

Plichta, S. B., & Abraham, C. (1996). Violence and gynecologic health in women 50 years old. *American Journal of Obstetrics and Gynecology, 174,* 903–907.

Pluhar, E., Frongillo, E. A., Stycos, J. M., & Dempster-McClain, D. (1998). Understanding the relationship between religion and the sexual attitudes and behaviors of college students. *Journal of Sex Education and Therapy, 23*(4), 288–296.

Pollard, P. (1995). Pornography and sexual aggression. *Current Psychology: Developmental, Learning, Personality, Social, 14*(3), 200–221.

Pomeroy, W. B. (1997). Acceptance speech for the Alfred Kinsey Award. *Journal of Sex Research, 34*(3), 323–324.

Pope, E. (1999). When illness takes sex out of a relationship. *SIECUS Report, 27*(3), 8–11.

Pope, K. S., & Brown, L. S. (1996). *Recovered memories of abuse: Assessment, therapy, forensics*. Washington, DC: American Psychological Association.

Pope, R. L., & Reynolds, A. L. (1991). Including bisexuality: It's more than just a label. In N. J. Evans & V. A. Wall (Eds.), *Beyond tolerance: Gays, lesbians and bisexuals on campus* (pp. 205–212). Alexandria, VA: American College Personnel Association.

Popova, V. J. (1996). Sexuality education moves forward in Russia. *SIECUS Report, 24*(3), 14–15.

Population Reference Bureau. (1998). *United States Population data sheet*. Washington, DC: Author.

Portelli, C. J. (1998). Sexuality and the law. *SIECUS Report, 26*(6), 2–3.

Posner, R. A., & Silbaugh, K. B. (1996). *A guide to America's sex laws*. Chicago: University of Chicago Press.

Potter, J. (1989). Viewpoint: Circumcision should be stopped. *Contemporary Sexuality, 21*(10), 4.

Potter, L. S. (1999). Why must one "restart" a method that is still working? A case for redefining injectable discontinuation. *Family Planning Perspectives, 31*(2), 98–100.

Potterat, J. J., Rothenberg, R. B., Muth, S. Q., Darrow, W. W., & Phillips-Plummer, L. (1998). Pathways to prostitution: The chronology of sexual and drug abuse milestones. *Journal of Sex Research, 35*(4), 333–340.

Potts, A. (1998). The science/fiction of sex: John Gray's Mars and Venus in the bedroom. *Sexualities, 1*(2), 153–173.

Powis, B., Griffiths, P., Gossop, M., & Strang, J. (1995). Heterosexual anal intercourse, health risks and drug use: A review with special attention to drug users. *Drug and Alcohol Review, 14*(2), 223–229.

Prieur, A. (1998). *Mema's house, Mexico City*. Chicago: University of Chicago Press.

Proulx, J., Perreault, C., & Ouimet, M. (1999). Pathways in the offending process of extrafamilial sexual child molesters. *Sexual Abuse: Journal of Research and Treatment, 11*(2), 117–129.

Pryor, J. B., & Stoller, L. M. (1994). Sexual cognition processes in men high in the likelihood to sexually harass. *Personality and Social Psychology Bulletin, 20*(2), 163–169.

Pryor, J. L., Kent-First, M., Muallem, A., Bergen, A. H., Nolten, W. E., Meisner, L., & Roberts, K. P. (1997). Microdeletions in the Y chromosome of infertile men. *New England Journal of Medicine, 336*(8), 534–539.

Purifoy, F. E., Grodsky, A., & Giambra, L. M. (1992). The relationship of sexual daydreaming to sexual activity, sexual drive, and sexual attitudes for women across the life span. *Archives of Sexual Behavior, 21*(4), 369–385.

Purnine, D. M., & Carey, M. P. (1999). Dyadic coorientation: Reexamination of a method for studying interpersonal communication. *Archives of Sexual Behavior, 28*(1), 45–62.

Q

Quandagno, D., Sly, D. F., Harrison, D. F., Eberstein, I. W., & Soler, H. R. (1998). Ethnic differences in sexual decisions and sexual behavior. *Archives of Sexual Behavior, 27*(1), 57–75.

R

Raab, M. (1998a). Birth weight is lower among infants of U.S.-born than African-born Blacks. *Family Planning Perspectives, 30*(3), 150–151.

Raab, M. (1998b). Condom availability in high school does not increase teenage sexual activity but does increase condom use. *Family Planning Perspectives, 30*(1), 48–49.

Rakic, Z., Starcevic, V., Maric, J., & Kelin, K. (1996). The outcome of sex reassignment surgery in Belgrade: 32 patients of both sexes. *Archives of Sexual Behavior, 25*(5), 515–525.

Rakic, Z., Starcevic, V., Starcevic, V. P., & Marinkovic, J. (1997). Testosterone treatment in men with erectile disorder and low levels of total testosterone in serum. *Archives of Sexual Behavior, 26*(5), 495–504.

Rao, K. V., & Demaris, A. (1995). Coital frequency among married and cohabiting couples in the United States. *Journal of Biosocial Science, 27*(2), 135–150.

Rapp, R. (1999). *Testing women, testing the fetus: The social impact of amniocentesis in America*. New York: Routledge.

Rasmussen, L. A. (1999). Factors related to recidivism among juvenile sexual offenders. *Sexual Abuse: Journal of Research and Treatment, 11*(1), 69–86.

Ray, A. L., & Gold, S. R. (1996). Gender roles, aggression, and alcohol use in dating relationships. *Journal of Sex Research, 33*(1), 47–55.

Reese, L. A., & Lindberg, K. E. (1999). *Implementing sexual harassment policy: Challenges for the public sector workplace*. Thousand Oaks, CA: Sage.

Regan, P. C., & Berscheid, E. (1996). Belief about the state, goals, and objects of sexual desire. *Journal of Sex and Marital Therapy, 22*(2), 110–120.

Rehman, J., Lazer, S., Benet, A. E., Schaefer, L. C., & Melman, A. (1999). The reported sex surgery satisfactions of 28 postoperative male-to-female transsexual patients. *Archives of Sexual Behavior, 28*(1), 71–89.

Reichman, N. E., & Kenney, G. M. (1998). Prenatal care, birth outcomes, and newborn hospitalization costs: Patterns among Hispanics in New Jersey. *Family Planning Perspectives, 30*(4), 182–187.

Reid, J. D. (1995). Development in late life: Older lesbian and gay lives. In A. R. D'Augelli & C. J. Patterson (Eds.), *Lesbian, gay, and bisexual identities over the life span* (pp. 215–240). New York: Oxford University Press.

Reilly, J., Baker, G. A., Rhodes, J., & Salmon, P. (1999). The association of sexual and physical abuse with somatization: Characteristics of patients presenting with irritable bowel syndrome and non-epileptic attack disorder. *Psychological Medicine, 29*(2), 399–406.

Reinisch, J. M., & Beasley, M. L. S. (1990). *The Kinsey Institute new report on sex: What you must know to be sexually literate*. New York: St. Martin's Press.

Reinisch, J. M., & Sanders, S. A. (1992). Prenatal hormonal contributions to sex differences in human cognitive and personality development. In A. A. Gerall, H. Moltz, & I. L. Ward (Eds.), *Handbook of behavioral neurobiology: Vol. 11. Sexual differentiation* (pp. 221–243). New York: Plenum Press.

Reisberg, L. (1998, October 2). Seeking acceptance on fraternity row. *Chronicle of Higher Education*, A45–47.

Reiss, I. L. (1990). *An end to shame: Shaping our next sexual revolution*. Buffalo, NY: Prometheus Books.

Reiss, I. L. (1991). Sexual pluralism: Ending America's sexual crisis. *SIECUS Report, 19*(3), 5–9.

Reiss, I. L. (2000). Evaluating sexual science: Problems and prospects. *Annual Review of Sex Research, 9*, 236–271.

Reiss, M. J., & Straughan, R. (1996). *Improving nature? The science and ethics of genetic engineering*. New York: Cambridge University Press.

Remafedi, G. (Ed.). (1994). *Death by denial: Studies of suicide in gay and lesbian teenagers*. Boston: Alyson.

Remez, L. (1997a). Planned home birth can be as safe as hospital delivery for women with low-risk pregnancies. *Family Planning Perspectives, 29*(3), 141–142.

Remez, L. (1997b). Slightly increased risk of breast cancer among pill users disappears 10 years after discontinuation. *Family Planning Perspectives, 29*(3), 147–148.

Renaud, C., Byers, E. S., & Pan, S. (1997). Sexual and relational satisfaction in mainland China. *Journal of Sex Research, 34*(4), 399–410.

Resnick, M. D. (1997). Protecting adolescents from harm: Findings from the national longitudinal study of adolescent health. *Journal of the American Medical Association, 278*(10), 823–832.

Rhoads, R. A. (1995). Learning from the coming-out experiences of college males. *Journal of College Student Development, 36*(1), 67–74.

Rice, G., Anderson, C., Risch, N., & Ebers, G. (1999). Male homosexuality: Absence of linkage to microsatellite markers at Xq28. *Science, 284*, 665–667.

Rice, W. R. (1996). Evolution of the Y chromosome in animals. *BioScience, 46*(5), 331–343.

Rickard, W. (1998). A report on the International Conference on Prostitution—An Interface: Cultural, legal, and social issues. *Sexualities, 1*(1), 125–128.

Riddle, J. M., Estes, J. W., & Russell, J. C. (1994, March/April). Birth control in the ancient world. *Archaeology*, 29–35.

Ridley, A. J. (1999). Life-long absence of sexual drive in a woman associated with 5-dihydrotestosterone deficiency. *Journal of Sex and Marital Therapy, 25*(1), 73–78.

Ridley, J. (1993). Gender and couples: Do men and women seek different kinds of intimacy? *Sexual and Marital Therapy, 8*(3), 243–253.

Rind, B., Tromovitch, P. (1997). A meta-analytic review of findings from national samples on psychological correlates of child sexual abuse. *Journal of Sex Research, 34*(3), 237–255.

Ringheim, K. (1995) Evidence for the acceptability of an injectable hormonal method for men. *Family Planning Perspectives, 27*(3), 123–128.

Robbins, M., & Jensen, G. D. (1978). Multiple orgasm in males. *Journal of Sex Research, 14*, 21–26.

Roberts, D. (2000). Sexual harassment in the workplace: Considerations, concerns, and challenges. *SIECUS Report, 28*(3), 8–10.

Robinson, B. E., Scheltema, K., Koznar, J., & Manthei, R. (1996). Attitudes of U.S. and Czech/Slovak mental health and health professionals toward five types of sexually explicit materials. *Archives of Sexual Behavior, 25*(6), 601–628.

Rodgers, J. L., Rowem, D. C., & Buster, M. (1999). Fitting behavioral genetic models to NLSY kinship data. *Journal of Biosocial Science, 31*(1), 9–41.

Roffman, D. M., Shannon, D., & Dwyer, C. (1997). Adolescents, sexual health, and the Internet: Possibilities, prospects, and challenges for educators. *Journal of Sex Education and Therapy, 22*(1), 49–55.

Roldam, E. R., Murase, T., & Shi, Q. (1994). Exocytosis in spermatozoa in response to progesterone and zona pellucida. *Science, 266*, 1578–1581.

Romaine, S. (1999). *Communicating gender.* Mahwah, NJ: Lawrence Erlbaum Associates.

Romero, G., Wyatt, G. E., Chin, D., & Rodriguez, C. (1999). HIV-related behaviors among recently immigrated and undocumented Latinas. *International Quarterly of Community Health Education, 18*(1), 89–105.

Romieu, I. (1996). Breast cancer and lactation history in Mexican women. *American Journal of Epidemiology, 143,* 543–552.

Rosario, M., Mahler, K., Hunter, J., & Gwadz, M. (1999). Understanding the unprotected sexual behaviors of gay, lesbian, and bisexual youths: An empirical test of the cognitive-environmental model. *Health Psychology, 18*(3), 272–280.

Rosario, M., Meyer-Bahlburg, H., Hunter, J., Exner, T. M., Gwadz, M., & Keller, A. M. (1996). The psychosexual development of urban lesbian, gay, and bisexual youths. *Journal of Sex Research, 33*(2), 113–126.

Rosenberg, K. P. (1999). Sildenafil. *Journal of Sex and Marital Therapy, 25,* 271–279.

Rosenberg, M. J., Waugh, M. S., & Burnhill, M. S. (1998). Compliance, counseling and satisfaction with oral contraceptives: A prospective evaluation. *Family Planning Perspectives, 30*(2), 89–92, 104.

Rosenthal, A. M. (1996, June 2). U.S. should use influence to halt female mutilation. *Watertown (NY) Daily Times, Sunday Weekly,* 10.

Rosenthal, D. A. (1997). Understanding sexual coercion among young adolescents: Communicative clarity, pressure, and acceptance. *Archives of Sexual Behavior, 26*(5), 481–493.

Rosenthal, S. L., et al. (1997). Heterosexual romantic relationships and sexual behaviors of young adolescent girls. *Journal of Adolescent Health, 21,* 238–243.

Rosler, A., & Witztum, E. (1998). Treatment of men with paraphilia with a long-acting analogue of gonadotropin-releasing hormone. *New England Journal of Medicine, 338*(7), 416–422.

Ross, M., & Kantor, L. M. (1995). Trends in opposition to comprehensive sexuality education in public schools, 1994–95 school year. *SIECUS Report, 23*(6), 9–15.

Rosser, B. R. S., Gobby, J. M., & Carr, W. P. (1999). The unsafe sexual behavior of persons living with HIV/AIDS: An empirical approach to developing new HIV prevention interventions targeting HIV-positive persons. *Journal of Sex Education and Therapy, 24*(1&2), 18–28.

Rosser, S., Short, B. J., Thurmes, P. J., & Coleman, E. (1998). Anodyspareunia, the unacknowledged sexual dysfunction: A validation study of painful receptive anal intercourse and its psychosexual concomitants in homosexual men. *Journal of Sex and Marital Therapy, 24,* 281–292.

Rothman, B. K. (1999a). Now you can choose! Issues in parenting and procreation. In M. M. Feree & J. Lorber (Eds.), *Revisioning Gender* (pp. 399–415). Thousand Oaks, CA: Sage.

Rothman, B. K. (1999b, June 11). The potential cost of the best genes money can buy. *Chronicle of Higher Education,* A52.

Rowland, D. L. (1999). Issues in the laboratory study of human sexual response: A synthesis for the nontechnical sexologist. *Journal of Sex Research, 36*(1), 3–15.

Rowland, D. L., Cooper, S. E., Slob, A. K., & Houtsmuller, E. J. (1997). The study of ejaculatory response in men in the psychophysiological laboratory. *Journal of Sex Research, 34*(2), 161–166.

Rowland, D. L., Kallan, K., & Slob, A. K. (1997). Yohimbine, erectile capacity, and sexual response in men. *Archives of Sexual Behavior, 26*(1), 49–62.

Rowland, D. L., & Slob, A. K. (1992). Vibrotactile stimulation enhances sexual response in sexually functional men: A study using concomitant measures of erection. *Archives of Sexual Behavior, 21*(4), 387–400.

Rowland, D. L., & Slob, A. K. (1998). Premature ejaculation: Psychophysiological considerations in theory, research, and treatment. *Annual Review of Sex Research, 8,* 224–253.

Rowlands, P. (1995). Schizophrenia and sexuality. *Sexual and Marital Therapy, 10*(1), 47–61.

Rubinow, D. R., & Schmidt, P. J. (1996). Androgens, brain, and behavior. *American Journal of Psychiatry, 153*(8), 974–984.

Rubinson, L., & DeRubertis, L. (1991). Trends in sexual attitudes and behaviors of a college population over a 15-year period. *Journal of Sex Education and Therapy, 17*(1), 32–41.

Runganga, A. O., & Aggleton, P. (1998). Migration, the family and the transformation of sexual culture. *Sexualities, 1*(1), 63–81.

Runkel, G. (1998). Sexual morality of Christianity. *Journal of Sex and Marital Therapy, 24,* 103–122.

Russo, F. (1997, October). Can the government prevent divorce? *The Atlantic Monthly,* 28–42.

Russo, N. F., & Dabul, A. J. (1997). The relationship of abortion to well-being: Do race and religion make a difference? *Professional Psychology: Research and Practice, 28,* 23–31.

Rutter, P. (1990). *Sex in the forbidden zone: When men in power betray women's trust.* Los Angeles: Jeremy P. Tarcher.

Ryan, M. J. (1998). Sexual selection, receives biases, and the evolution of sex differences. *Science, 281,* 1999–2003.

Ryner, L. S., & Swain, A. (1995). Sex in the '90s. *Cell, 81,* 483.

S

Sable, M. R., Spencer, J. C., Stockbauer, J. W., Schramm, W. F., Howell, V., & Herman, A. A. (1997). Pregnancy wantedness and adverse pregnancy outcomes: Differences by race and medicaid status. *Family Planning Perspectives, 29*(2), 76–81.

Sabogal, F., Binson, D., & Catania, J. A. (1997). Researching sexual behavior: Methodological issues for Hispanics. In J. Bancroft (Ed.), *Researching sexual behavior* (pp. 114–133.). Bloomington: Indiana University Press.

Sachs, B. P., Kobelin, C., Castro, M. A., & Frigoletto, F. (1999). The risks of lowering the cesarian-delivery rate. *New England Journal of Medicine, 340*(1), 54–57.

Sadker, M. & Sadker, D. (1994). *Failing at fairness: How America's schools cheat girls.* New York: Charles Scribner's Sons.

Sanders, G., & Wright, M. (1997). Sexual orientation differences in cerebral asymmetry and in the performance of sexually dimorphic cognitive and motor tasks. *Archives of Sexual Behavior, 26*(5), 463–480.

Sanders, J. S. (1978). Male and female vocabularies for communicating with a sexual partner. *Journal of Sex Education and Therapy, 4,* 15–19.

Sanders, S. A. (1999). Midlife sexuality: The need to integrate biological, psychological, and social perspectives. *SIECUS Report, 27*(3), 3–7.

Sanders, S. A., & Reinisch, J. M. (1999). Would you say you "had sex" if . . . ? *Journal of the American Medical Association, 28*(3), 275–277.

Sanderson, C. A., & Cantor, N. (1995). Social dating goals in late adolescence: Implications for safer sexual activity. *Journal of Personality and Social Psychology, 68*(6), 1121–1134.

Sandnabba, N. K., Santtila, P., & Nordling, N. (1999). Sexual behavior and social adaptation among sadomasochistically-oriented males. *Journal of Sex Research, 36*(3), 273–282.

Sanford, K. (1994). Toward a masturbation ethic. *Journal of Psychology and Theology, 22*(1), 21–28.

Sangi-Haghpeykar, H., Poindexter, A. N., Bateman, L., & Ditmore, J. R. (1996). Experiences of injectable contraceptive users in an urban setting. *Obstetrics and Gynecology, 88*(2), 227–233.

Sank, L. I. (1998). Traumatic masturbatory syndrome. *Journal of Sex and Marital Therapy, 24,* 37–42.

Santelli, J. S., Brener, N. D., Lowry, R., Bhatt, A., & Zabin, L. S. (1998). Multiple sexual partners among U.S. adolescents and young adults. *Family Planning Perspectives, 30*(6), 271–275.

Santelli, J. S., Warren, C. W., Lowry, R., Sogolow, E., Collins, J., Kann, L., Kaufmann, R. B., & Celentano, D. D. (1997). The use of condoms with other contraceptive methods among young men and women. *Family Planning Perspectives, 29*(6), 261–267.

Santioso, R. (1999). A social psychological perspective on HIV/AIDS and gay or homosexually active Asian men. *Journal of Homosexuality, 36*(3–4), 69–85.

Sapp, M., Farrell, W. C., Johnson, J. H., & Hitchcock, K. (1999). Attitudes toward rape among African American male and female college students. *Journal of Counseling and Development, 77,* 204–208.

Sarrel, P., & Masters, W. (1982). Sexual molestation of men by women. *Archives of Sexual Behavior, 11,* 117–131.

Sarris, A. (1994, October, 31). As quoted in: Men, women and movie sex. *New York Times,* p. C1.

Sarwer, D. B., & Durlak, J. A. (1997). A field trial of the effectiveness of behavioral treatment for sexual dysfunctions. *Journal of Sex and Marital Therapy, 23*(2), 87–97.

Saul, R. (1999). Teen pregnancy: Progress meets politics. *The Guttmacher Report, 2*(3), 6–7.

Savage, O. M., & Tchombe, T. M. (1995). Anthropological perspectives on sexual behavior in Africa. *Annual Review of Sex Research, 5,* 50–72.

Savin-Williams, R. (1999). Ethnic-minority and sexual-minority youths. In L. A. Peplau & S. C. DeBro (Eds.), *Gender, culture, and ethnicity: Current research about women and men* (pp. 121–134). Mountain View, CA: Mayfield.

Savin-Williams, R. C. (1995). Lesbian, gay male, and bisexual adolescents. In A. R. D'Augelli & C. J. Patterson (Eds.), *Lesbian, gay, and bisexual identities over the lifespan* (pp. 165–189). New York: Oxford University Press.

Savin-Williams, R. C., & Diamond, L. M. (1999). Sexual orientation. In W. K. Silverman & T. H. Ollendick (Eds.), *Developmental issues in the clinical treatment of children* (pp. 241–258). Boston: Allyn & Bacon.

Sbrocco, T., Weisberg, R. B., & Barlow, D. H. (1995). Sexual dysfunction in the older adult: Assessment of psychosocial factors. *Sexuality and Disability, 13*(3), 201–218.

Sbrocco, T., Weisberg, R. B., Barlow, D. H., & Carter, M. M. (1997). The conceptual relationship between panic disorder and male erectile dysfunction. *Journal of Sex and Marital Therapy, 23*(3), 212–220.

Scarce, M. (1997). *Male on male rape: The hidden toll of stigma and shame.* New York: Plenum.

Schacker, T., Collier, A. C., Hughes, J., Shea, T., & Corey, L. (1996). Clinical and epidemiologic features of primary HIV infection. *Annals of Internal Medicine, 125*(4), 257–264.

Schafer, A. J. (1995). Sex determination and its pathology. *Advances in Genetics, 33*, 275.

Schaff, E. A. (1999). Low-dose mifepristone 200mg and vaginal mifepristol for abortion. *Contraception, 59*(1), 1–6.

Schairer, C., Lubin, J., Troisi, R., Sturgeon, S., Brinton, L., & Hoover, R. (2000). Menopausal estrogen and estrogen-progestin replacement therapy and breast cancer risk. *Journal of the American Medical Association, 283*(4), 485–491.

Schalin, L. (1995). On autoerotism and object relations in the psycho-sexual development: Some viewpoints on Freud's drive theories. *Scandinavian Psychoanalytic Review, 18*(1), 22–40.

Scharch, D. (1997). Sex, intimacy, and the Internet. *Journal of Sex Education and Therapy, 22*, 15–20.

Schellenberg, E. G., Hirt, J., & Sears, A. (1999). Attitudes toward homosexuals among students at a Canadian University. *Sex Roles, 40*(1–2), 139–152.

Schensul, J. J. (1999). Learning about sexual meaning and decision-making from urban adolescents. *International Quarterly of Community Health Education, 18*(1), 29–48.

Schiavi, R. C., Schreiner-Engle, P., Mandeli, J., & Schanzer, H. (1990). Healthy aging and male sexual function. *American Journal of Psychiatry, 147*(6), 766–771.

Schiavi, R. C., White, D., Mandeli, J., & Levine, A. C. (1997). Effect of testosterone administration on sexual behavior and mood in men with erectile dysfunction. *Archives of Sexual Behavior, 26*(3), 231–241.

Schissel, B., & Fedec, K. (1999). The selling of innocence: The gestalt of danger in the lives of youth prostitutes. *Canadian Journal of Criminology, 41*(1), 33–56.

Schlatterer, K., Yassouridis, A., von Werder, K., Poland, D., Kemper, J., & Stalla, G. K. (1998). A follow-up study for estimating the effectiveness of a cross-gender hormone substitution therapy on transsexual patients. *Archives of Sexual Behavior, 27*(5), 475–492.

Schlosser, E. (1997, February 10). The business of pornography. *Newsweek*, 42–52.

Schnarch, D. (1997). Passionate marriage. *Family Therapy Networker, 21*(5), 42–49.

Schnarch, D. (1998). Redefining foreplay. *Contemporary Sexuality, 32*(1), 1–3.

Schneider, B. E. (1991). Put up and shut up: Workplace sexual assaults. *Gender and Society, 5*(4), 533–548.

Schneider, M. (1993). Educating the public about homosexuality. *Annals of Sex Research, 6*(1), 57–66.

Schoen, C. et al., (1998). *The health of adolescent boys: Findings from a commonwealth fund survey*. New York: The Commonwealth Fund.

Schofer, H., et al. (1996). Active syphilis in HIV infection: A multicentre retrospective survey. *Genitourinary Medicine, 72*(3), 176–181.

Schooler, J. W. (1999). Seeking the core: The issues and evidence surrounding recovered accounts of sexual trauma. In L. M. Williams & V. L. Banyard (Eds.), *Trauma and memory* (pp. 203–216). Thousand Oaks, CA: Sage.

Schreurs, K. M. (1993). Sexuality in lesbian couples: The importance of gender. *Annual Review of Sex Research, 4*, 49–66.

Schuetz-Mueller, D., Tiefer, L., & Melman, A. (1995). Follow-up of vacuum and nonvacuum constriction devices as treatments for erectile dysfunction. *Journal of Sex and Marital Therapy, 21*(4), 229–238.

Schulhofer, S. (1998, October). Unwanted sex. *The Atlantic Monthly*, 55–66.

Schupack, D. (1994, August 7). Starter marriages: So early, so brief. *Watertown (NY) Daily Times*, p. 7.

Schuster, M. A., Bell, R. M., Berry, S. H., & Kanouse, D. E. (1998). Impact of a high school condom availability program on sexual attitudes and behaviors. *Family Planning Perspectives, 30*(2), 67–72, 88.

Schuster, M. A., Bell, R. M., & Kanouse, D. E. (1996). The sexual practices of adolescent virgins: Genital sexual activities of high school students who have never had vaginal intercourse. *American Journal of Public Health, 86*, 1570–1576.

Schwartz, D. (1999). Is a gay Oedipus a Trojan horse? Commentary on Lewes's "A special Oedipal mechanism in the development of male homosexuality." *Psychoanalytic Psychology, 16*(1), 88–93.

Schwartz, I. M. (1999). Sexual activity prior to coital initiation: A comparison between males and females. *Archives of Sexual Behavior, 28*(1), 63–69.

Schwartz, M. F., & Cohn, L. (1996). *Sexual abuse and eating disorders*. New York: Brunner/Mazel.

Sciolino, E. (1997, May 18). Army sorts through power, sex conflict. *New York Times*, A1.

Scott, P. M. (1996, August). Fitting a diaphragm. *Journal of the American Association of Physician Assistants*, 73–75.

Scully, R., Ganesan, S., Bown, M., DeCaprio, J. A., Cannistra, S. A., Feunteun, J., Schnitt, S., & Livingston, D. M. (1996). Location of BRCA1 in human breast and ovarian cancer cells. *Science, 272*, 123–125.

Seal, D. W., & Ehrhardt, A. A. (1999). Heterosexual men's attitudes toward the female condom. *AIDS Education and Prevention, 11*(2), 93–106.

Seem, S. R. (1997). Invisible youth: Counseling gay and lesbian adolescents. *The Journal for the Professional Counselor, 12*(2), 45–53.

Segraves, R. T. (1998). Editorial: Pharmacological era in the treatment of sexual disorders. *Journal of Sex and Marital Therapy, 24*, 67–68.

Seidman, S. (1991). *Romantic longings*. New York: Routledge, Chapman & Hall.

Seidman, S. (1992). *Embattled eros*. New York: Routledge, Chapman & Hall.

Seidman, S., Meeks, C., & Traschen, F. (1999). Beyond the closet? The changing social meaning of homosexuality in the United States. *Sexualities, 2*(1), 9–34.

Seidman, S. N., & Walsh, B. T. (1999). Testosterone and depression in aging men. *American Journal of Geriatric Psychiatry, 7*(1), 18–33.

Sell, R. L. (1997). Defining and measuring sexual orientation: A review. *Archives of Sexual Behavior, 26*(6), 643–658.

Sellers, N., Satcher, J., & Comas, R. (1999). Children's occupational aspirations: Comparisons by gender, gender role identity, and socioeconomic status. *Professional School Counseling, 2*(4), 314–317.

Seto, M. C., & Barbaree, H. E. (1995). The role of alcohol in sexual aggression. *Clinical Psychology Review, 15*(6), 545–566.

Seto, M. C., & Kuban, M. (1996). Criterion-related validity of a phallometric test for paraphilic rape and sadism. *Behaviour Research and Therapy, 34*(2), 175–183.

Sevely, J. L. (1987). *Eve's secrets: A new theory of female sexuality*. New York: Random House.

Shafik, A. (1996). Cervico-motor reflex: Description of the reflex and role in sexual acts. *Journal of Sex Research, 33*(2), 153–157.

Shahidian, H. (1999). Gender and sexuality among immigrant Iranians in Canada. *Sexualities, 2*(2), 189–222.

Shain, R. N., Piper, J. M., Newton, E. R., Perdue, S. T., Ramos, R., Champion, J. D., & Guerra, F. A. (1999). A randomized, controlled trial of a behavioral intervention to prevent sexually transmitted diseases among minority women. *New England Journal of Medicine, 340*(2), 93–100.

Shaver, P., & Hazen, C. (1993). Adult romantic attachment. In D. Perlman & W. Jones (Eds.), *Advances in personal relationships, Vol. 4* (pp. 29–70). London: Jessica Kingsley.

Shecter, J. (1996, April 19). Fighting for rape victims. *Chronicle of Higher Education*, A8.

Sheiman, J. A. (1999). Sexual abuse history with and without self-report of memory loss: Differences in psychopathology, personality, and dissociation. In L. M. Williams & V. L. Banyard (Eds.), *Trauma and memory* (pp. 139–148). Thousand Oaks, CA: Sage.

Shepperdson, B. (1995). The control of sexuality in young people with Down syndrome. *Child: Care, Health and Development, 21*(5), 333–349.

Sherins, R. J. (1995). Are semen quality and male fertility changing? *New England Journal of Medicine, 332*(5), 327.

Shimazaki, T. (1994). A closer look at sexuality education and Japanese youth. *SIECUS Report, 22*(2), 12–15.

Shokrollahi, P., Mirmohamadi, M., Mehrabi, F., & Babaei, G. (1999). Prevalence of sexual dysfunction in women seeking services at family planning centers in Tehran. *Journal of Sex and Marital Therapy, 25*, 211–215.

Shortridge, J. L. (1997). Nigerian guidelines for sexuality education introduced at ceremony in Lagos. *SIECUS Report, 25*(2), 4–7.

Shrieves, L. (1994, September 25). Nasty words: From no way to OK. *Watertown (NY) Daily Times Sunday Weekly*, p. 7. (Reprinted from *Orlando Sentinel*)

Shu, X. (1996). Parental alcohol consumption, cigarette smoking, and risk of infant leukemia: A children's cancer group study. *Journal of the National Cancer Institute, 88*, 24–31.

SIECUS Public Policy Department. (1998). SIECUS looks at states' sexuality laws and the sexual rights of their citizens. *SIECUS Report, 26*(6), 4–15.

Sieunarine, K. (1987). Non-venereal sclerosing lymphangitis of the penis associated with masturbation. *British Journal of Urology, 59*, 194–195.

Signorella, M. L. (1999). Multidimensionality of gender schemas: Implications for the development of gender-related characteristics. In W. B. Swann & J. H. Langlois (Eds.), *Sexism and stereotypes in modern society: The gender science of Janet Taylor Spence* (pp. 107–126). Washington, DC: American Psychological Association.

Sigusch, V. (1998). The neosexual revolution. *Archives of Sexual Behavior, 27*(4), 331–359.

Siker, J. S. (1994). *Homosexuality in the church: Both sides of the debate*. Louisville, KY: Westminster John Knox Press.

Silliman, B., & Schumm, W. R. (1999). Improving practice in marriage preparation. *Journal of Sex and Marital Therapy, 25*, 23–43.

Simon, R. J. (1998, October 2). Race and class drive most conflict now. *Chronicle of Higher Education*, B6.

Simon, W. (1994). Deviance as history: The future of perversion. *Archives of Sexual Behavior, 23*(1), 1–20.

Simon, W. (1999). Sexual conduct in retrospective perspective. *Sexualities, 2*(1), 126–133.

Simpson, J. A., Gangestad, S. W., Christensen, P. N., & Leck, K. (1999). Fluctuating asymmetry, sociosexuality, and intrasexual competitive tactics. *Journal of Personality and Social Psychology, 76*(2), 159–172.

Sinfield, A. (1998). *Gay and after*. London: Serpent's Tail.

Singh, S., & Darroch, J. E. (1999). Trends in sexual activity among adolescent American women: 1982–1995. *Family Planning Perspectives, 31*(5), 212–219.

Singh, S., & Darroch, J. E. (2000). Adolescent pregnancy and childbearing: Levels and trends in developing countries. *Family Planning Perspectives, 32*(1), 14–23.

Sipe, A. R. (1995). *Sex, priests, and power: Anatomy of a crisis.* New York: Brunner/Mazel.

Sipski, M. L., & Alexander, C. J. (1995). Spinal cord injury and female sexuality. *Annual Review of Sex Research, 4,* 224–244.

Sipski, M. L., & Alexander, C. J. (1997). *Sexual function in people with disability and chronic illness.* Frederick, MD: Aspen.

Sipski, M. L., Alexander, C. J., & Rosen, R. C. (1999). Sexual response in women with spinal cord injuries: Implications for our understanding of the able bodied. *Journal of Sex and Marital Therapy, 25,* 11–22.

Skakkebaek, N. E. (1992). Evidence for decreasing quality of semen during past 50 years. *British Medical Journal, 305,* 605–613.

Skeen, D. (1999). *Different sexual worlds: Contemporary case studies of sexuality.* Lanham, MD: Lexington Books.

Slijper, F. M. E., Drop, S. L. S., Molenaar, J. C., & Keizer-Schrama, S. M. P. F. (1998). Long-term psychological evaluation of intersex children. *Archives of Sexual Behavior, 27*(2), 125–144.

Slijper, F. M. E., Kamp, H. J., Brandenburg, H., Keizer-Schrama, S. M. P. F., Drop, S. L. S., & Molenaar, J. C. (1992). Evaluation of psychosexual development of young women with congenital adrenal hyperplasia: A pilot study. *Journal of Sex Education and Therapy, 18*(3), 200–206.

Slob, A. K., Steyvers, C. L., Lottman, P. E., Van Der Werff Ten Bosch, J. J., & Hop, W. C. (1998). Routine psychophysiological screening of 384 men with erectile dysfunction. *Journal of Sex and Marital Therapy, 24,* 272–279.

Small, S. A., & Kerns, D. (1993). Unwanted sexual activity among peers during early and middle adolescence: Incidence and risk factors. *Journal of Marriage and the Family, 55,* 941–952.

Smith, A. M., de Visser, R., Akande, A., Rosenthal, D., & Moore, S. (1998). Australian and South African undergraduates' HIV-related knowledge, attitudes, and behaviors. *Archives of Sexual Behavior, 27*(3), 279–294.

Smith, J. C., et al. (1994). Fatherhood without apparent spermatozoa after vasectomy. *Lancet, 344,* 30.

Smith, T. W. (1994). *American sexual behavior: Trends, socio-demographic differences, and risk behavior.* Chicago: GSS Topical Reports.

Smith-Warner, S. A. (1998). Alcohol and breast cancer in women: A pooled analysis of cohort studies. *Journal of the American Medical Association, 279*(7), 535–540.

Socarides, C. W. (1995). *Homosexuality: A freedom too far.* Phoenix: Adam Margrave Books.

Solomon, J. (1998, March 16). An insurance policy with sex appeal. *Newsweek,* 44.

Sonnet, E. (1999). "Erotic fiction by women for women": The pleasures of post-feminist heterosexuality. *Sexualities, 2*(2), 167–187.

Sorensen, R. C. (1973). *Adolescent sexuality in contemporary America.* New York: World.

Sparling, J. (1997). Penile erections: Shape, angle, and length. *Journal of Sex and Marital Therapy, 23*(3), 195–207.

Speas, R. R. (1990). Sex is sin. *Contemporary Sexuality, 22*(6), 4–5.

Spector, I. P., Carey, M. P., & Steinberg, L. (1996). The sexual desire inventory: Development, factor structure, and evidence of reliability. *Journal of Sex and Marital Therapy, 22*(3), 175–190.

Spector, I. P., & Fremeth, S. M. (1996). Sexual behaviors and attitudes of geriatric residents in long-term care facilities. *Journal of Sex and Marital Therapy, 22*(4), 235–246.

Spindel, B., & Duby, D. (1994). Attacks on the freedom to learn. *SIECUS Report, 23*(1), 19–21.

Sprecher, S. (1998). Social exchange theories and sexuality. *Journal of Sex Research, 35*(1), 32–43.

Sprecher, S., & Regan, P. C. (1996). College virgins: How men and women perceive their sexual status. *Journal of Sex Research, 33*(10), 3–15.

Sprecher, S., Regan, P. C., McKinney, K., Maxwell, K., & Wazienski, R. (1997). Preferred level of sexual experience in a date or mate: The merger of two methodologies. *Journal of Sex Research, 34*(4), 327–337.

Springen, K. (1999, April 12). Comeback of a contraceptive. *Newsweek,* 69.

Stackhouse, B. (1990). The impact of religion on sexuality education. *SIECUS Report, 18*(2), 21–24, 27.

Stalker, C. A., & Fry, R. (1999). A comparison of short-term group and individual therapy for sexually abused women. *Canadian Journal of Psychiatry, 44*(2), 168–174.

Stanton, B. F., Fitzgerald, A. M., Li, X., Shipena, H., Ricardo, I. B., Galbraith, J. S., Terreri, N., Strijdom, J., Hangula-Ndlovu, V., & Kahihuata, J. (1999). HIV risk behaviors, intentions, and perceptions among Namibian youth as assessed by a theory-based questionnaire. *AIDS Education and Prevention, 11*(2), 132–149.

Starr-Sered, S. (1999). "Woman" as symbol and women as agents: Gendered religious discources and practices. In M. M. Ferree (Ed.), *Revisioning gender* (pp. 193–221). Thousand Oaks, CA: Sage.

Steele, J. R. (1999). Teenage sexuality and media practice: Factoring in the influences of family, friends, and school. *Journal of Sex Research, 36*(4), 331–341.

Stein, A., Jackson, S., Murray, S. O., Stones, R., Shrage, L., & Hearn, J. (1999). A symposium on the Clinton-Lewinsky affair. *Sexualities, 2*(2), 247–266.

Stein, M. D., et al. (1998). Sexual ethics: Disclosure of HIV-positive status to partners. *Archives of Internal Medicine, 158*(3), 253–257.

Steinberg, L. (1994). *The sexuality of Christ in Renaissance art and in modern oblivion.* New York: Pantheon Books.

Steiner, M. (1997). Premenstrual syndromes. *Annual Review of Medicine, 48,* 447–455.

Stephan, C. W., & Bachman, G. F. (1999). What's sex got to do with it? Attachment, love schemas, and sexuality. *Personal Relationships, 6*(1), 111–123.

Sternberg, R. J. (1986). A triangular theory of love. *Psychological Review, 93,* 119–135.

Stevens-Simon, C., et al. (1998). Reasons for first teen pregnancies predict the rate of subsequent teen conceptions. *Pediatrics, 101*(1), e8.

Stevens-Simon, C., Kelly, L., & Singer, D. (1999). Preventing repeat adolescent pregnancies with early adoption of the contraceptive implant. *Family Planning Perspectives, 31*(2), 88–93.

Stewart, S. D. (1998). Economic and personal factors affecting women's use of nurse-midwives in Michigan. *Family Planning Perspectives, 30*(5), 231–235.

Stires, L. (1999). Two book reviews on pornography. *Archives of Sexual Behavior, 28*(1), 91–95.

St. Louis, M. E., & Wasserheit, J. N. (1998). Elimination of syphilis in the United States. *Science, 281,* 353–354.

Stock, J. L., Bell, M. A., Boyer, D. K., & Connell, F. A. (1997). Adolescent pregnancy and sexual risk-taking among sexually abused girls. *Family Planning Perspectives, 29*(5), 200–203 & 227.

Stockbridge, E. L. (1996). Power and the female condom (letter). *Family Planning Perspectives, 28*(2), 78.

Stokes, J. P., Damon, W., & McKirnan, D. J. (1997). Predictors of movement toward homosexuality: A longitudinal study of bisexual men. *Journal of Sex Research, 34*(3), 304–312.

Stoléru, S., Grégoire, M., Gérard, D., Decety, J., Lafarge, E., Cinotti, L., Lavenne, F., Bars, D. L., Vernet-Maury, E., Rada, H., Collet, C., Mazoyer, B., Forest, M. G., Magnin, F., Spira, A., & Comar, D. (1999). Neuroanatomical correlates of visually evoked sexual arousal in human males. *Archives of Sexual Behavior, 28*(1), 1–21.

Stone, R. (1994). Causes sought for sperm-count drop. *Science, 265,* 309.

Stone, V. E., Catania, J. A., & Binson, D. (1999). Measuring change in sexual behavior: Concordance between survey measures. *Journal of Sex Research, 36*(1), 102–108.

Storr, M. (1999). Postmodern bisexuality. *Sexualities, 2*(3), 309–325.

Stouthamer-Loeber, M., & Wei, E. H. (1998). The precursors of young fatherhood and its effect on delinquency of teenage males. *Journal of Adolescent Health, 22*(1), 56–65.

Strain, L., Dean, J. C. S., Hamilton, M. P., & Bonthron, D. T. (1998). Brief report: A true hermaphrodite chimera resulting from embryo amalgamation after in vitro fertilization. *New England Journal of Medicine, 338*(3), 166.

Strassberg, D. S., & Lockerd, L. K. (1998). Force in women's sexual fantasies. *Archives of Sexual Behavior, 27*(4), 403–414.

Striar, S., & Bartlik, B., (1999). Stimulation of the libido: The use of erotica in sex therapy. *Psychiatric Annals, 29*(1), 60–62.

Strider, W. (1997). Making sense of the Pap test. *Women's Health Digest, 3*(4), 250–251.

Stroud, D. D. (1999). Familial support as perceived by adult victims of childhood sexual abuse. *Sexual Abuse: Journal of Research and Treatment, 11*(2), 159–175.

Struckman-Johnson, C., & Struckman-Johnson, D. (1994). Men pressured and forced into sexual experience. *Archives of Sexual Behavior, 23*(1), 93–114.

Struckman-Johnson, C., Struckman-Johnson, D., Rucker, L., Bumby, K., & Donaldson, S. (1996). Sexual coercion reported by men and women in prison. *Journal of Sex Research, 33*(1), 67–76.

Suissa, S. (1997). First-time use of newer oral contraceptives, and the risk of venous thromboembolism. *Contraception, 56*(3), 141–146.

Suplicy, M. (1994). Sexuality education in Brazil (S. H. Ward, Trans.). *SIECUS Report, 22*(2), 1–6.

Swaab, D. F., & Gofman, M. A. (1995). Sexual differentiation of the human hypothalamus in relation to gender and sexual orientation. *Trends in Neuroscience, 18*(6), 264–270.

Swan, W. K. (Ed.) (1997). *Gay/lesbian/bisexual/transgender public policy issues: A citizen's and administrator's guide to the new cultural struggle.* Binghamton, NY: Harrington Park Press.

T

Tafoya, T. (1995). Cultural sensitivity: Room for the unexpected. *Contemporary Sexuality, 29*(9), 1–5.

Tang, C. S., Lai, F. D., Phil, M., & Chung, T. K. H. (1997). Assessment of sexual functioning for Chinese college students. *Archives of Sexual Behavior, 26*(1), 79–90.

Tannen, D. (1990). *You just don't understand: Women and men in conversation.* New York: William Morrow.

Tannen, D. (1994). *Talking from 9 to 5.* New York: William Morrow.

Taris, T. W., & Semin, G. R. (1997). Gender as a moderator of the effects of the love motive and relational context on sexual experience. *Archives of Sexual Behavior, 26*(2), 159–180.

Task Force on Postovulatory Methods of Fertility Regulation. (1999). Comparison of three single doses of mifepristone as emergency contraception: A randomized trial. *Lancet, 353*(9154), 697–702.

Tate, J. E., Resnick, M., Sheets, E. E., & Crum, C. P. (1996). Absence of papillomavirus DNA in normal tissue adjacent to most cervical intraepithelial neoplasms. *Obstetrics and Gynecology, 88*(2), 257–260.

Taubes, B. (1997). The breast-screening brawl. *Science, 275,* 1056–1059.

Tavris, C. (1994). Measuring up. In R. T. Francouer (Ed.), *Taking sides: Clashing views on controversial issues in human sexuality* (4th ed., pp. 14–22). Guilford, CT: Dushkin.

Tavris, C., & Sadd, S. (1977). *The Redbook report on female sexuality.* New York: Delacorte Press.

Tchernitchin, A. N., & Tchernitchin, N. (1992). Imprinting of paths of heterodifferentiation by prenatal or neonatal exposure to hormones, pharmaceuticals, pollutants and other agents and conditions. *Medical Science Research, 20*(11), 391–397.

Telljohann, S. K., & Price, J. H. (1993). A qualitative examination of adolescent homosexuals' life experiences: Ramifications for secondary school personnel. *Journal of Homosexuality, 26*(1), 41–56.

Tharaux-Deneux, C. (1998). Risk of ectopic pregnancy and previous induced abortion. *American Journal of Public Health, 88*(3), 401–405.

Thomas, D. B. (1995). Cervical carcinoma in situ and use of DMPA. *Contraception, 51,* 25–31.

Thompson, C. (1996). Can some infants beat HIV? *Science, 271,* 441.

Thompson, J. K., Heinberg, L. J., Altabe, M., & Tantleff-Dunn, S. (1999). *Exacting beauty: Theory, assessment, and treatment of body image disturbance.* Washington, DC: American Psychological Association.

Thompson, M. (1998, March 23). No go: Why the Army lost a high-profile sex case. *Time,* 52–53.

Thompson, S. C., Anderson, K., Freedman, D., & Swan, J. (1996). Illusions of safety in a risky world: A study of college students' condom use. *Journal of Applied Social Psychology, 26*(3), 189–210.

Thoreson, R. W., Shaughnessy, P., & Frazier, P. A. (1995). Sexual contact during and after professional relationships: Practices and attitudes of female counselors. *Journal of Counseling and Development, 74,* 84–89.

Thoreson, R. W., Shaughnessy, P., Heppner, P. P., & Cook, S. W. (1993). Sexual contact during and after the professional relationship: Attitudes and practices of male counselors. *Journal of Counseling and Development, 71,* 429–434.

Thrall, J. S., et al. (1998). Performance of Massachusetts HMOs in providing Pap smear and sexually transmitted disease screening to adolescent females. *Journal of Adolescent Health, 22*(3), 184–189.

Tiefer, L. (1997). The medicalization of sexuality: Conceptual, normative, and professional issues. *Annual Review of Sex Research, 7,* 252–282.

Tikoo, M. (1996). Sexual attitudes and behaviors of school students (grades 6–12) in India. *Journal of Sex Research, 34*(1), 77–84.

Tokatlidis, O., & Over, R. (1995). Imagery, fantasy, and female sexual arousal. *Australian Journal of Psychology, 47*(2), 81–85.

Townsend, J. M. (1993). Sexuality and partner selection: Sex differences among college students. *Ethology and Sociobiology, 14*(5), 305–329.

Traeen, B., & Kvalem, I. L. (1996). Sexual socialization and motives for intercourse among Norwegian adolescents. *Archives of Sexual Behavior, 25*(3), 289–302.

Trapnell, P. D., Meston, C. M., & Gorzalka, B. B. (1997). Spectatoring and the relationship between body image and sexual experience: Self-focus or self-valence? *Journal of Sex Research, 34*(3), 267–278.

Trapp, J. D. (1998) External vacuum therapy: A historical review. *Journal of Sex Education and Therapy, 23*(3), 217–219.

Trends in sexual risk behaviors among high school students—United States, 1991–1997. (1998). *Morbidity and Mortality Weekly Reports, 47*(36), 749–752.

Trivedi, N., & Sabini, J. (1998). Volunteer bias, sexuality, and personality. *Archives of Sexual Behavior, 27*(2), 181–195.

Trussell, J. (1998a). Contraceptive efficacy. In R. A. Hatcher et al., *Contraceptive Technology* (pp. 779–799). New York: Ardent Media.

Trussell, J. (1998b). Dynamics of reproductive behavior and population change. In R. A. Hatcher et al., *Contraceptive Technology* (pp. 745–777). New York: Ardent Media.

Trussell, J., Ellertson, C., & Rodriguez, G. (1996). The Yuzpe regimen of emergency contraception: How long after the morning after? *Obstetrics and Gynecology, 88*(1), 150–154.

Trussell, J., Koenig, J., Stewart, F., & Darroch, J. E. (1997). Medical care cost savings from adolescent contraceptive use. *Family Planning Perspectives, 29,* 248–255, 295.

Trussell, J., Sturgen, K., Strickler, J., & Dominik, R. (1994). Comparative contraceptive efficacy of the female condom and other barrier methods. *Family Planning Perspectives, 26*(2), 66–72.

Trussell, J., & Vaughan, B. (1999). Contraceptive failure, method-related discontinuation and resumption of use. *Family Planning Perspectives, 31*(2), 64–72, 93.

Trussell, J., & Vaughan, B. (1999). Are all contraceptive failures unintended pregnancies? Evidence from the 1995 national survey of family growth. *Family Planning Perspectives, 31*(5), 246–247 & 260.

Tuljapurkar, S., Li, N., & Feldman, M. W. (1995). High sex ratios in China's future. *Science, 267,* 874–876.

Turner, C. F., Miller, H. G., & Rogers, S. M. (1997). Survey measurement of sexual behavior: Problems and progress. In J. Bancroft (Ed.), *Researching sexual behavior* (pp. 37–60). Bloomington: Indiana University Press.

Turner, R. (1994). Perinatal and maternal outcomes not improved by routine ultrasound. *Family Planning Perspectives, 26*(1), 47–49.

Turner, R. (1999, February 1). Finding the inner swine. *Newsweek,* 52–53.

Turner, W. J. (1995). Homosexuality, Type 1: An Xq28 phenomenon. *Archives of Sexual Behavior, 24*(2), 109–134.

Tuzin, D. (1991). Sex, culture, and the anthropologist. *Social Science and Medicine, 33*(8), 867–874.

Tyler, J. M., Jackman-Wheitner, L. J., Strader, S., & Lenox, R. (1997). A change-model approach to raising awareness of gay, lesbian, and bisexual issues among graduate students in counseling. *Journal of Sex Education and Therapy, 22*(2), 37–43.

U

Udry, J. (1990). Hormonal and social determinants of adolescent sexual initiation. In J. Bancroft & J. M. Reinisch (Eds.), *Adolescence and puberty* (pp. 70–87). New York: Oxford University Press.

Udry, J. R., Morris, N. M., & Kovenock, J. (1995). Androgen effects on women's gendered behaviour. *Journal of Biosocial Science, 27*(3), 359–368.

Unger, J. B., & Molina, G. B. (1997). Desired family size and son preference among Hispanic women of low socioeconomic status. *Family Planning Perspectives, 29,* 284–287.

U.S. Attorney General's Commission on Pornography. (1986). *Final report of the Attorney General's Commission on Pornography.* Nashville, TN: Rutledge Hill Press.

Ussher, J. M. (1997). Premenstrual syndrome: Reconciling disciplinary divides through the adoption of a material-discursive epistemological standpoint. *Annual Review of Sex Research, 7,* 218–251.

V

Valente, T. W., & Saba, W. P. (1997). Reproductive health is in your hands: The national media campaign in Bolivia. *SIECUS Report, 25*(2), 10–13.

Valois, R. F., Kammermann, S. K., & Drane, J. W. (1997). Number of sexual intercourse partners and associated risk behaviors among public high school adolescents. *Journal of Sex Education and Therapy, 22*(2), 13–22.

Van den Bossche, F., & Rubinson, L. (1998). Contraceptive self-efficacy in adolescents: A comparative study of male and female contraceptive practices. *Journal of Sex Education and Therapy, 22*(2), 23–29.

Van de Ven, P., Rodden, P., Crawford, J., & Kippax, S. (1997). A comparative demographic and sexual profile of older homosexually active men. *Journal of Sex Research, 34*(4), 349–360.

Van Goozen, S. H. M., Wiegant, V. M., Endert, E., Helmond, F. A., & Dan de Poll, N. E. (1997). Psychoendocrinological assessment of the menstrual cycle: The relationship between hormones, sexuality, and mood. *Archives of Sexual Behavior, 26*(4), 359–382.

Van Leeuwen, M. S. (1998, October 2). Crucial steps needed to help bind families. *Chronicle of Higher Edcuation,* B8.

Vansteenwegen, A. (1996). Who benefits from couple therapy? A comparison of successful and failed couples. *Journal of Sex and Marital Therapy, 22*(1), 63–67.

Vansteenwegen, A. (1998). Divorce after couple therapy: An overlooked perspective of outcome research. *Journal of Sex and Marital Therapy, 24,* 123–130.

Varmus, H. (1994). NIH guidelines on the inclusion of women and minorities as subjects in clinical research. *Federal Register, 59,* 14508–14513.

Velde, E. R., & Cohlen, B. J. (1999). Management of infertility. *New England Journal of Medicine, 340*(3), 224–226.

Ventegodt, S. (1998). Sex and the quality of life in Denmark. *Archives of Sexual Behavior, 27*(3), 295–307.

Ventura, S. J., Curtin, S. C., & Mathews, T. J. (1998). *Teenage births in the United States: National and state trends, 1990–96.* Hyattsville, MD: National Center for Health Statistics.

Vercellini, P. (1996). Long-term treatment of pelvic pain associated with endometriosis. *American Journal of Obstetrics and Gynecology, 175,* 396–401.

Verma, K. K., Khaitan, B. K., & Singh, O. P. (1998). The frequency of sexual dysfunctions in patients attending a sex therapy clinic in North India. *Archives of Sexual Behavior, 27*(3), 309–314.

Vine, M. F. (1994). Cigarette smoking and sperm density: A meta-analysis. *Fertility and Sterility, 61,* 35–43.

Vonk, M. E., & Thyer, B. A. (1995). Exposure therapy in the treatment of vaginal penetration phobia: A single-case evaluation. *Journal of Behavior Therapy and Experimental Psychiatry, 26*(4), 359–363.

Vonk, R., & Ashmore, R. D. (1993). The multi-faceted self: Androgyny reassessed by open-ended self-descriptions. *Social Psychology Quarterly, 56*(4), 278–287.

Vorakitphokatorn, S., Pulerwitz, J., & Cash, R. A. (1999). HIV/AIDS risk to women travelers in Thailand: Comparison of Japanese and western populations. *International Quarterly of Community Health Education, 18*(1), 69–87.

Vyras, P. (1996). Neglected defender of homosexuality: A commemoration. *Journal of Sex and Marital Therapy, 22*(2), 121–129.

W

Waldo, C. R. (1999). Working in a majority context: A structural model of heterosexism as minority stress in the workplace. *Journal of Counseling Psychology, 46*(2), 218–232.

Wallen, K., & Parsons, W. A. (1997). Sexual behavior in same-sexed nonhuman primates: Is it relevant to understanding human homosexuality? *Annual Review of Sex Research, 8,* 195–222.

Walling, D. P., Goodwin, J. M., & Cole, C. M. (1998). Dissociation in a transsexual population. *Journal of Sex Education and Therapy, 23*(2), 121–123.

Walsh, A. (1993). Love styles, masculinity/femininity, physical attractiveness, and sexual behavior: A test of evolutionary theory. *Ethology and Sociobiology, 14*(1), 25–38.

Walsh, F. (1996). *Sin and censorship: The Catholic Church and the motion picture industry.* New Haven: Yale University Press.

Walters, G. D. (1999). *The addiction concept: Working hypothesis or self-fulfilling prophesy?* Boston: Allyn and Bacon.

Walters, S. D. (1999). Sex, text, and context: (In)between feminism and cultural studies. In M. M. Ferree (Ed.), *Revisioning gender* (pp. 222–257). Thousand Oaks, CA: Sage.

Ward, L. M. (1995). Talking about sex: Common themes about sexuality in the prime-time television programs children and adolescents view most. *Journal of Youth and Adolescence, 24*(5), 595–615.

Ward, L. M., & Rivadeneyra, R. (1999). Contributions of entertainment television to adolescents' sexual attitudes and expectations: The role of viewing amount versus viewer involvement. *Journal of Sex Research, 36*(3), 237–249.

Ward, T. (1999). Competency and deficit models in the understanding and treatment of sexual offenders. *Journal of Sex Research, 36*(3), 298–305.

Warnock, J. K., Bundren, J. C., & Morris, D. W. (1999). Female hypoactive sexual disorder: Case studies of physiologic androgen replacement. *Journal of Sex and Marital Therapy, 25,* 175–182.

Warren, C. W., Santelli, J. S., Everett, S. A., Kann, L., Collins, J. L., Cassell, C., Morris, L., & Kolbe, L. J. (1998). Sexual behavior among U.S. high school students, 1990–1995. *Family Planning Perspectives, 30*(4), 170–172, 200.

Watt, J. D., & Ewing, J. E. (1996). Toward the development and validation of a measure of sexual boredom. *Journal of Sex Research, 33*(1), 57–66.

Wattenberg, B. J. (1997, November 23). The population explosion is over. *New York Times Magazine,* 60–63.

Waugh, T. (1996). *Hard to imagine: Gay male eroticism in photography and film from their beginning to Stonewall.* New York: Columbia University Press.

Weed, S., & Jensen, L. (1993). A second year evaluation of three abstinence sex education programs. *Journal of Research and Development in Education, 26*(2), 92–96.

Weeks, J. (1998). The "homosexual role" after 30 years: An appreciation of the work of Mary McIntosh. *Sexualities, 1*(2), 131–152.

Weerakoon, P., & Stiernborg, M. (1997). Sexuality education for health care professionals: A critical review of the literature. *Annual Review of Sex Research, 7,* 181–217.

Wegesin, D. J. (1998). A neuropsychologic profile of homosexual and heterosexual men and women. *Archives of Sexual Behavior, 27*(1), 91–108.

Wehrfritz, G. (1996, April 1). Joining the party. *Time,* 46–49.

Weinberg, M. S., Lottes, I. I., & Gordon, L. E. (1997). Social class background, sexual attitudes, and sexual behavior in a heterosexual undergraduate sample. *Archives of Sexual Behavior, 26*(6), 625–642.

Weinberg, M. S., Williams, C. J., & Pryor, D. W. (1994). *Dual attraction: Understanding bisexuality.* New York: Oxford University Press.

Weinberg, T. S. (1995). Research in sadomasochism: A review of sociological and social psychological literature. *Annual Review of Sex Research, 5,* 257–279.

Weinhardt, L. S., & Carey, M. P. (1996). Prevalence of erectile disorder among men with diabetes mellitus: Comprehensive review, methodological critique, and suggestions for future research. *Journal of Sex Research, 33*(3), 205–214.

Weis, D. L. (1998). The state of sexual theory. *Journal of Sex Research, 35*(1), 100–114.

Weitz, C., & Osburg, S. (1996). Transsexualism in Germany: Empirical data on epidemiology and application of the German transsexuals' act during its first ten years. *Archives of Sexual Behavior, 25*(4), 409–425.

Welch, M. R., Leege, D. C., & Cavendish, J. C. (1995). Attitudes toward abortion among U.S. Catholics: Another case of symbolic politics? *Social Science Quarterly, 76*(1), 142–157.

Wendel, P. (1997, April). Counseling children who molest other children. *Counseling Today,* 1, 20.

Wennerholm, U. B. (1998). Postnatal growth and health in children born after cryopreservation as embryos. *Lancet, 351*(9109), 1085–1090.

Werlinger, K., King, T. K., Clark, M. M., Pera, V., & Wincze, J. P. (1997). Perceived changes in sexual functioning and body image following weight loss in an obese female population: A pilot study. *Journal of Sex and Marital Therapy, 23*(1), 74–78.

West, D. J. (1998). Boys and sexual abuse: An English opinion. *Archives of Sexual Behavior, 27*(6), 539–559.

Westfall, J. M., Main, D. S., & Barnard, L. (1996). Continuation rates among injectable contraceptive users. *Family Planning Perspectives, 28*(6), 275–277.

Weston, K. (1993). Lesbian/gay studies in the house of anthropology. *Annual Review of Anthropology, 22,* 339–367.

Whatley, M. H., & Trudell, B. K. (1993). Teen-Aid: Another problematic sexuality curriculum. *Journal of Sex Education and Therapy, 19*(4), 251–271.

Wheeler, C. M., Greer, C. E., Becker, T. M., Hunt, W. C., Anderson, S. M., & Manos, M. M. (1996). Short-term fluctations in the detection of cervical human papillomavirus DNA. *Obstetrics and Gynecology, 88*(2), 261–268.

Wheeler, D. L. (1999a, January 22). Prospect of fetal-gene therapy stimulates high hopes and deep fears. *Chronicle of Higher Education,* A13.

Wheeler, D. L. (1999b, March 26). As AIDS continues to spread, some scientists are pessimistic about developing a vaccine. *Chronicle of Higher Education,* A21.

Whipple, B. (1991). Female sexuality. In J. F. Leyson (Ed.), *Sexual rehabilitation of the spinal-cord-injured patient* (pp. 19–38). Clifton, NJ: Humana Press.

Whipple, B., Myers, B.T., & Komisaruk, B. R. (1998). Male multiple ejaculatory orgasms: A case study. *Journal of Sex Education and Therapy, 23*(2), 157–162.

Whitaker, D. J., Miller, K. S., May, D. C., & Levin, M. L. (1999). Teenage partners' communication about sexual risk and condom use: The importance of parent-teenager discussions. *Family Planning Perspectives, 31*(3), 117–121.

Whitam, F. L., Daskalos, C., Sobolewski, C. G., & Padilla, P. (1998). The emergence of lesbian sexuality and identity cross-culturally: Brazil, Peru, the Philippines, and the United States. *Archives of Sexual Behavior, 21*(1), 31–56.

Whitam, F. L., Diamond, M., & Martin, J. (1993). Homosexual orientation in twins: A report on 61 pairs and three triplet sets. *Archives of Sexual Behavior, 22*(3), 187–206.

White, S. M., & Franzini, L. R. (1999). Heteronegativism? The attitudes of gay men and lesbians toward heterosexuals. *Journal of Homosexuality, 37*(1), 65–79.

White, T. (1999). Homophobia: A misnomer. *Transactional Analysis Journal, 29*(1), 77–83.

Whitehead, B. D. (1994). The failure of sex education. *Atlantic, 274*(4), 55–80.

Whitley, B. E. Jr., (1998). False consensus on sexual behavior among college women: Comparison of four theoretical explanations. *The Journal of Sex Research, 35*(2), 206–214.

Whitmire, L. E., Harlow, L. L., Quina, K., & Morokoff, P. J. (1999). *Childhood trauma and HIV: Women at risk.* Philadelphia: Brunner/Mazel.

WHO Collaborative Study. (1997). Acute myocardial infarction and combined oral contraceptives: Results of an international multicentre case-control study. *Lancet, 349,* 1202–1209.

WHO Collaborative Study. (1998). Cardiovascular disease and use of oral and injectable progestogen-only contraceptives and combined injectable contraceptives: Results of an international, multicenter, case-control study. *Contraception, 57*(5), 315–324.

WHO Task Force on Methods for the Regulation of Male Fertility. (1996). Contraceptive efficacy of testosterone-induced azoospermia and oligozoospermia in normal men. *Fertility and Sterility, 65,* 821–829.

Wichstrom, L. (1999). The emergence of gender difference in depressed mood during adolescence: The role of intensified gender socialization. *Developmental Psychology, 35*(1), 232–245.

Widmer, E. D. (1997). Influence of older siblings on initiation of sexual intercourse. *Journal of Marriage and the Family, 59*(4), 928–938.

Widmer, E. D., Treas, J., & Newcomb, R. (1998). Attitudes toward nonmarital sex in 24 countries. *Journal of Sex Research, 35*(4), 349–358.

Wiederman, M. W. (1997a). Extramarital sex: Prevalence and correlates in a national survey. *Journal of Sex Research, 34*(2), 167–174.

Wiederman, M. W. (1997b). Pretending orgasm during sexual intercourse: Correlates in a sample of young adult women. *Journal of Sex and Marital Therapy, 23*(2), 131–139.

Wiederman, M. W. (1997c). The truth must be in here somewhere: Examining the gender discrepancy in self-reported lifetime number of sex partners. *Journal of Sex Research, 34*(4), 375–386.

Wiederman, M. W. (1998). The state of theory in sex therapy. *Journal of Sex Research, 35*(1), 88–99.

Wiederman, M. W. (1999). Volunteer bias in sexuality research using college student participants. *Journal of Sex Research, 36*(1), 59–66.

Wiederman, M. W., & Hurd, C. (1999). Extradyadic involvement during dating. *Journal of Social and Personal Relationships, 16*(2), 265–274.

Wiederman, M. W., & Hurst, S. R. (1998). Body size, physical attractiveness, and body image among young adult women: Relationships to sexual experience and sexual esteem. *Journal of Sex Research, 35*(3), 272–281.

Wilber, K. (1995). *Sex, ecology, spirituality: The spirit of evolution.* Boston: Shambhala.

Wilcox, A., Skjaerven, R., Buekens, P., & Kiely, J. (1995). Birth weight and perinatal mortality: A comparison of the United States and Norway. *Journal of the American Medical Association, 273*(9), 709–711.

Wilcox, A. J., Weinberg, C. R., & Baird, D. D. (1996). Timing of sexual intercourse in relation to ovulation. *New England Journal of Medicine, 333,* 1563–1565.

Williams, J. E., & Best, D. L. (1990). *Measuring sex stereotypes: A multination study.* Beverly Hills, CA: Sage.

Williams, N. (1995). How males and females achieve X equality. *Science, 269,* 1826–1827.

Williams, V., & Brake, D. L. (1997, April 18). Sexual harassment: Let the punishment fit the crime. *Chronicle of Higher Education,* A56.

Williams, V. L. (1999, June 18). A new harassment ruling: Implications for colleges. *Chronicle of Higher Education,* A56.

Wilson, E. O. (1998, April). The biological basis of morality. *The Atlantic Monthly,* 53–70.

Wilson, M. (1999). Art therapy with the invisible sex addict. *Art Therapy, 16*(1), 7–16.

Wilson, M. E. (1992). Factors determining the onset of puberty. In A. A. Gerall, H. Moltz, & I. L. Ward (Eds.), *Handbook of behavioral neurobiology: Vol. 11. Sexual differentiation* (pp. 275–312). New York: Plenum Press.

Wilson, R. (1999, February 12). For gay academics, benefits for partners have a financial and emotional impact. *Chronicle of Higher Education,* A10–12.

Wilson, R. A. (1964). *Feminine for life.* New York: Wilson Research Foundation.

Wilson, R. J. (1999). Emotional congruence in sexual offenders against children. *Sexual Abuse: Journal of Research and Treatment, 11*(1), 33–48.

Winick, C., & Evans, J. T. (1996) The relationship between nonenforcement of state pornography laws and rates of sex crime arrests. *Archives of Sexual Behavior, 25*(5), 439–453.

Winn, R. L., & Newton, N. (1982). Sexuality in aging: A study of 106 cultures. *Archives of Sexual Behavior, 11*(4), 283–298.

Winn, S., Roker, D., & Coleman, J. (1995). Knowledge about puberty and sexual development in 11–16-year-olds: Implications for health and sex education in schools. *Educational Studies, 21*(2), 187–201.

Winship, G. (1995). Condoms on the ward: Sexual health education in psychiatric treatment settings. *Therapeutic Communities: International Journal for Therapeutic and Supportive Organizations, 16*(3), 163–169.

Winston, C. M., Crane, T., & Ghosh, A. (1992). A psychosexual clinic in a rural district: Five years' experience in West Wales. *Sexual and Marital Therapy, 7*(1), 11–17.

Wisch, A. F., & Mahalik, J. R. (1999). Male therapists' clinical bias: Influence of client gender roles and therapist gender role conflict. *Journal of Counseling Psychology, 46*(1), 51–60.

Wise, P. M., Krajnak, K. M., & Kashon, M. L. (1996). Menopause: The aging of multiple pacemakers. *Science, 273,* 67–70.

Wise, T. N., & Goldberg, R. L. (1995). Escalation of a fetish. *Journal of Sex and Marital Therapy, 21*(4), 272–275.

Wiswell, T. E., Enzenauer, R. W., Holton, M. E., Cornish, J. D., & Hankins, C. T. (1987). Declining frequency of circumcision: Implications for changes in the absolute incidence and male to female sex ratio of urinary tract infections in early infancy. *Pediatrics, 79*(3), 338–342.

Wolfenden, J. (1963). *Reports of the committee on homosexual offenses and prostitution.* New York: Stein & Day.

Wolfthal, D. (1999). *Images of rape: The "heroic" tradition and its alternatives.* New York: Cambridge University Press.

Wong, V. (1996). Prospective study of hepatitis B vaccination in patients with chronic hepatitis C. *British Medical Journal, 312,* 1336–1337.

Woody, G. E., Donnel, D., Seage, G. R., Metzger, D., Marmor, M., Koblin, B. A., Buchbinder, S., Gross, M., Stone, B., & Judson, F. N. (1999). Non-injection substance use correlates with risky sex among men having sex with men: Data from HIVNET. *Drug and Alcohol Dependence, 53*(3), 197–205.

Wooster, R., Neuhausen, S. L., Mangion, J., Quirk, Y., Ford, D., et al. (1994). Localization of a breast cancer susceptibility gene, BRCA2, to chromosome 13q12–13. *Science, 265,* 2088–2090.

Worling, J. R. (1995). Adolescent sex offenders against females: Differences based on the age of their victims. *International Journal of Offender Therapy and Comparative Criminology, 39*(3), 276–293.

Wouda, J. C., Hartman, P. M., Bakker, R. M., et al. (1998). Vaginal plethysmography in women with dyspareunia. *Journal of Sex Research, 35*(2), 141–147.

Wright, L. W., & Adams, H. E. (1999). The effects of stimuli that vary in erotic content on cognitive processes. *Journal of Sex Research, 36*(2), 145–151.

Wright, W. (1999). *Born that way: Genes— behavior—personality.* New York: Alfred A. Knopf.

Wryobeck, J. M., & Wiederman, M. W. (1999). Sexual narcissism: Measurement and correlates among college men. *Journal of Sex and Marital Therapy, 25,* 321–331.

WuDunn, S. (1996, March 13). In single motherhood, Japan trails the world. *New York Times,* A1, 11.

Wuest, J., & Merritt-Gray, M. (1999). Not going back: Sustaining the separation in the process of leaving abusive relationships. *Violence Against Women, 5*(2), 110–133.

Wyatt, G. E. (1990). Changing influences on adolescent sexuality over the past forty years. In J. Bancroft & J. M. Reinisch (Eds.), *Adolescence and puberty* (pp. 182–206). New York: Oxford University Press.

Wylie, K. R. (1997). Treatment outcome of brief couple therapy in psychogenic male erectile disorder. *Archives of Sexual Behavior, 26*(5), 527–545.

Wysocki, D. K. (1993). Construction of masculinity: A look into the lives of heterosexual male transvestites. *Feminism and Psychology, 3*(3), 374–380.

Wysocki, D. K. (1998). Let your fingers do the talking: Sex on an adult chat line. *Sexualities, 1*(4), 425–452.

Y

Yamaguchi, K., & Ferguson, L. R. (1995). The stopping and spacing of childbirths and their birth-history predictors: Rational choice theory and event-history analysis. *American Sociological Review, 60,* 272–298.

Yang, N., & Linz, D. (1990). Movie ratings and the content of adult videos: The sex-violence ratio. *Journal of Communication, 40*(2), 28–42.

Yarber, W. L., & Torabi, M. R. (1999). Public opinion from a rural state about condoms for HIV prevention: 1993 and 1998. *Journal of Sex Education and Therapy, 24*(1&2), 56–62.

Yarber, W. L., Torabi, M. R., & Veenker, C. H. (1989). Development of a three-component sexually transmitted disease attitude scale. *Journal of Sex Education and Therapy, 15*(1), 36–49.

Yarhouse, M. A. (1999). Social cognition research on the formation and maintenance of stereotypes: Application to marriage and family therapists working with homosexual clients. *American Journal of Family Therapy, 27*(2), 149–161.

Yoder, J. D. (1999). *Women and gender: Transforming psychology.* Upper Saddle River, NJ: Prentice Hall.

Yohalem, L. (1995). Why do people with mental retardation need sexuality education? *SIECUS Report, 23*(4), 14–16.

Yonkers, K. A., Halbreich, U., Freeman, E., et al. (1997). Symptomatic improvement of premenstrual dysphoric disorder with sertraline treatment: A randomized controlled trial. *Journal of the American Medical Association, 278,* 983–988.

Youn, G. (1996). Sexual activities and attitudes of adolescent Koreans. *Archives of Sexual Behavior, 25*(6), 629–643.

Young, W. C. (1961). The hormones and mating behavior. In W. C. Young (Ed.), *Sex and internal secretions* (pp. 1173–1239). Baltimore: Williams & Wilkins.

Z

Zanjani, E. D., & Anderson, W. F. (1999). Prospects for in utero human gene therapy. *Science, 285,* 2084–2088.

Zelnik, M., & Kantner, J. F. (1980). Sexual activity, contraceptive use, and pregnancy among metropolitan-area teenagers, 1971–1979. *Family Planning Perspectives, 12,* 230–237.

Zhigang, L., Xiaowei, L., & Shengbo, L. (1994). Therapy for impotence with traditional Chinese medicine. *Journal of Sex Education and Therapy, 20*(2), 140–143.

Zhu, B. P., et al. (1999). Effect of the interval between pregnancy on perinatal outcomes. *New England Journal of Medicine, 340*(8), 589–594.

Zonana, H. V., & Norko, M. A. (1999). Sexual predators. *Psychiatric Clinics of North America, 22*(1), 109–127.

Zoucha-Jensen, J. M., & Coyne, A. (1993). The effects of resistance strategies on rape. *American Journal of Public Health, 83*(11), 1633–1634.

Zucker K. J. (2000). Intersexuality and gender identity differentiation. *Annual Review of Sex Research, 9,* 1–69.

Zucker, K. J., & Bailey, M. (1995). Untitled article. *Developmental Psychology,* in press. As reported in Goleman, 1994.

Zucker, K. J., Bradley, S. J., & Sullivan, C. B. L. (1993). Gender identity disorder in children. *Annual Review of Sex Research, 3,* 73–119.

Zweig, J. M., Crickett, L. J., Sayer, A., & Vicary, J. R. (1999). A longitudinal examination of the consequences of sexual victimization for rural young adult women. *Journal of Sex Research, 36*(4), 396–409.

Credits

Index

Note: Page numbers in italics indicate figures; page numbers followed by *t* indicate tables; bold-faced page numbers indicate defined terms.

Sex counseling/treatment. *See also* Sex
therapy
behavior therapy, **552**–553
for child sexual abuse offenders,
471–472
for child sexual abuse victims,
470–471
couples therapy, 551–552
finding therapist, 476–477
for gender identity disorder, 408
group therapy, 552
hypnotherapy, 552
for incest victims, 474
for rape trauma syndrome, 465–466
for sex addiction, 453
for transgenderism, 408–409
Sex fair, 5
Sex flush, 101, 105, 107
Sex offenders, treatment of, 471–472
Sex reassignment surgery, 132, 404–407
cost factors, 405
ethical issues, 405
female-to-male surgery, 406, *407*
hormonal therapy, 405
male-to-female surgery, 406, *406*
satisfaction factors, 407
Sex research. *See also* Sex surveys
Bloch, 21
Dickinson, 23
Ellis, 22
Freud, 21–22
future view, 31–32
Kinsey, 23–24
Krafft-Ebing, 21
Masters and Johnson, 24–25
timeline of, 28–29*t*
van de Velde, 22
Wright, 23
Sex research methods
case studies, **34**
clinical research, **35**
ethical issues, 36–37
ethnosexual field studies, **35**–36
experimental research, 36
limitations of, 26, 33, 34, 35, 37
observational research, 35
penile plethysmography, **37**
population samples, 33–34
surveys, 34
Sex surveys
on adolescent sexuality, 26, 31
on childhood sexuality, 26
on college students, 27
cross-cultural, 27
Hite reports, 25–26
Hunt Report, 25
Janus report, 27
limitations of, 26, 34
National Health and Social Life
Survey (NHSLS), 30–31
National Longitudinal Study of
Adolescent Health, 31
Redbook survey, 25
on same-sex couples, 26

on sexual knowledge, 27
on sexual preference, 26
Sex therapist, **553**–554
code of ethics, 561
finding therapist, 554
Sex therapy, 553–562
behavior therapy, **552**–553, 555
combination treatment approach, 553
effectiveness of, 560–561
ethical issues, 534, 561–562
Masters and Johnson, 25
partnership approaches, 556–558
for premature ejaculation, 559–560
self-help approaches, 555–556
sensate focus, **556**–557
sexual surrogates, **553**
for vaginismus, 559
Sex toys, types of, 410
Sex workers, 413–414
legal aspects, 442
Sexology, **32**
Sexosophy, **32**
Sexual arousal, 97–100
central arousal system, **97**, *98*
desire phase, **94**
dysfunction of, 537*t*, 539–543
and emotions, 98
and erotica, 410
excitement phase, **93**–94, 100–101
and fantasy experiences, 410–411
and fetishism, **411**–412
gender differences, 97–100
and group sex, 412
peripheral arousal system, **97**, *98*
and pornography, 410, 436–437
problem situations. *See* Atypical
sexual encounters
and sexual-enhancement toys, 410
Sexual attitudes
and aging and sex, 191
biphobia, **210**–211
and culture, 6–10, 17–18
demographic factors, 208*t*
double standard, 17
and exposure to pornography, 437
on gender identities, 18
on gender identity, 18
heterosexism, **210**
homophobia, **209**–210
on masturbation, 16–17
NHSLS statistics on, 206–209
on nonmarital sex, 17
on nudity and body, 18–19
procreational, 15
recreational, 15, 207, 207*t*, 208*t*
relational, 15, 207, 207*t*, 208*t*
and religion, 212–215
on same-gender sex, 18
on sex/romance, 19–20
and sexual individuality, 206–209
and sexual revolution, 11
on sexuality education, 20
social sexual standards, 199–201
traditional, 206–207, 207*t*, 208*t*
Victorian era, 10–11

Sexual aversion disorder, **539**
Sexual Behavior in the Human Female
(Kinsey), 23
Sexual Behavior in the Human Male
(Kinsey), 23
Sexual Behavior in the 1970s
(Hunt), 25
Sexual behaviors
anal intercourse, 356
and aphrodisiacs, **357**
erogenous zone stimulation, 352–353
fantasy experiences, 356–357
interfemoral intercourse, 356
masturbation, 345–350, 356
mutual manual stimulation, 355–356
oral stimulation, nongenital, 352
oral-anal sex, 355
oral-genital sex, 353–355
and pornography, 356
same-gender behaviors, 358–359
sexual intercourse, 359–367
sexual practices/appeal value,
352–353*t*
vibrators, use of, 356
Sexual coercion and abuse, 450,
458–475
abusive relationships, 459–460
child sexual abuse, 466–471
incest, 472–475
rape, 458–466
sex offenders, treatment of, 471–472
Sexual decision making, choice
theory, 162
Sexual desire
celibacy, **401**–402
erotomania, **401**
erotophobia-erotophilia, **400**
hypersexuality, **400**
hyposexuality, **400**, **539**
incentive motivation model, **94**
in Kaplan's model, 95
promiscuity, **400**–401
Sexual differentiation, **118**–126
biological sex, levels of, 117
and brain, 121–122
and chromosomes, 118–119,
120*t*, 270
gonadal development, 119–120
and hormones, 120–121
sex of fetus as choice, 284–286
sex organ development, 121, *122*
Sexual differentiation abnormalities, 121,
122–125
androgen insensitivity syndrome,
123*t*, 124–**125**
congenital adrenal hyperplasia
(CAH), 123*t*, **124**
DHT-deficiency syndrome, 123*t*, **125**
fetally androgenized females,
123–**124**, 123*t*
maternal anticonvulsant drug
use, 124
and prenatal synthetic hormones,
123*t*, 124